# ENCYCLOPEDIA OF WORLD BIOGRAPHY

## SUPPLEMENT

# 19

# ENCYCLOPEDIA OF
# WORLD BIOGRAPHY

## SUPPLEMENT

$\dfrac{A}{Z}$ **19**

**GALE GROUP**

*Detroit*
*San Francisco*
*London*
*Boston*
*Woodbridge, CT*

Staff

*Project Editor:* Jennifer Mossman
*Senior Editor:* Terrie M. Rooney

*Editorial Staff:* Frank V. Castronova, Leigh Ann DeRemer, Andrea Kovacs Henderson, Katherine H.Nemeh, Aaron J. Oppliger, Paul J. Podzikowski, Noah Schusterbauer

*Permissions Manager:* Maria L. Franklin
*Permissions Specialist:* Margaret A. Chamberlain
*Permissions Associate:* Shalice Shah-Caldwell

*Production Director:* Dorothy Maki
*Production Manager:* Evi Seoud
*Production Associate:* Wendy Blurton
*Product Design Manager:* Cynthia Baldwin
*Senior Art Director:* Mary Claire Krzewinski

*Research Manager:* Victoria B. Cariappa
*Research Specialist:* Barbara McNeil

*Graphic Services Supervisor:* Barbara Yarrow
*Image Database Supervisor:* Randy Bassett
*Imaging Specialist:* Mike Logusz

*Manager of Technology Support Services:* Theresa A. Rocklin
*Programmers/Analysts:* Mira Bossowska and Jeffrey Muhr

ISBN 0-7876-3183-3
ISSN 1099-7326

I(T)P™ Gale Group Inc., an International Thomson Publishing Company.
Gale Group and Design is a trademark used herein under license.

Printed in the United States of America
10 9 8 7 6 5 4 3 2

# CONTENTS

# INTRODUCTION

The study of biography has always held an important, if not explicitly stated, place in school curricula. The absence in schools of a class specifically devoted to studying the lives of the giants of human history belies the focus most courses have always had on people. From ancient times to the present, the world has been shaped by the decisions, philosophies, inventions, discoveries, artistic creations, medical breakthroughs, and written works of its myriad personalities. Librarians, teachers, and students alike recognize that our lives are immensely enriched when we learn about those individuals who have made their mark on the world we live in today.

*Encyclopedia of World Biography Supplement*, Volume 19, provides biographical information on 200 individuals not covered in the 17-volume second edition of *Encyclopedia of World Biography (EWB)* and its supplement, Volume 18. Like other volumes in the *EWB* series, this supplement represents a unique, comprehensive source for biographical information on those people who, for their contributions to human culture and society, have reputations that stand the test of time. Each original article ends with a bibliographic section. There is also an index to names and subjects, which cumulates all persons appearing as main entries in the *EWB* second edition, the Volume 18 supplement, and this supplement—nearly 7,400 people!

*Articles.* Arranged alphabetically following the letter-by-letter convention (spaces and hyphens have been ignored), articles begin with the full name of the person profiled in large, bold type. Next is a boldfaced, descriptive paragraph that includes birth and death years in parentheses and provides a capsule identification and a statement of the person's significance. The essay that follows is approximately 2000 words in length and offers a substantial treatment of the person's life. Some of the essays proceed chronologically while others confine biographical data to a paragraph or two and move on to a consideration and evaluation of the subject's work. Where very few biographical facts are known, the article is necessarily devoted to an analysis of the subject's contribution.

Following the essay is a Further Reading section. Bibliographic citations contain both books and periodicals as well as Internet addresses for World Wide Web pages, where current information can be found.

Portraits accompany many of the articles and provide either an authentic likeness, contemporaneous with the subject, or a later representation of artistic merit. For artists, occasionally self-portraits have been included. Of the ancient figures, there are depictions from coins, engravings, and sculptures; of the moderns, there are many portrait photographs.

*Index.* The *EWB Supplement* Index is a useful key to the encyclopedia. Persons, places, battles, treaties, institutions, buildings, inventions, books, works of art, ideas, philosophies, styles, movements—all are indexed for quick reference just as in a general encyclopedia. The Index entry for a person includes a brief identification with birth and death dates *and* is cumulative so that any person for whom an article was written who appears in volumes 1 through 18 (excluding the volume 17 index) as well as volume 19 can be located. The subject terms within the Index, however, apply only to volume 19. Every Index reference includes the title of the article to which the reader is being directed as well as the volume and page numbers.

Because *EWB Supplement*, Volume 19, is an encyclopedia of biography, its Index differs in important ways from the indexes to other encyclopedias. Basically, this is an Index of people, and that fact has several interesting consequences. First, the information to which the Index refers the reader on a particular topic is always about people associated with that topic. Thus the entry 'Quantum theory (physics)' lists articles on people associated with quantum theory. Each article may discuss a person's contribution to quantum theory, but no single article or group of articles is intended to provide a comprehensive treatment of quantum theory as such. Second, the Index is rich in classified entries. All persons who are subjects of articles in the encyclopedia, for example, are listed in one or more classifications in the index—abolitionists, astronomers, engineers, philosophers, zoologists, etc.

The Index, together with the biographical articles, make *EWB Supplement* an enduring and valuable source for biographical information. As the world moves forward and school course work changes to reflect advances in technology and further revelations about the universe, the life stories of the people who have risen above the ordinary and earned a place in the annals of human history will continue to fascinate students of all ages.

*We Welcome Your Suggestions.* Mail your comments and suggestions for enhancing and improving the *Encyclopedia of World Biography Supplement* to:

The Editors
*Encyclopedia of World Biography Supplement*
The Gale Group
27500 Drake Road
Farmington Hills, MI 48331-3535
Phone: (800) 347-4253

# ADVISORY BOARD

# ACKNOWLEDGMENTS

Photographs and illustrations appearing in the *Encyclopedia of World Biography Supplement,* Volume 19, have been used with the permission of the following sources:

**American Stock/Archive Photos:** Jimmy Dorsey, Sugar Ray Robinson, Lana Turner

**AP/Wide World Photos:** Eddie Bauer, L.L.Bean, John Berryman, Paul Bowles, James Cain, Ernesto Cardenal, Henri Cartier-Bresson, Joan Ganz Cooney, George Cukor, Imogen Cunningham, James Dickey, J.P. Donleavy, Michael Eisner, Jose Feliciano, Bill Ford, Lou Gerstner, Red Grange, Florence Griffith-Joyner, Jim Henson, Tommy Hilfiger, Whitney Houston, Ron Howard, Faisal Husseini, Mike Ilitch, Jackie Joyner-Kersee, Joseph Kennedy, William Kennedy, Norman Lear, Viola Liuzzo, Malcolm Lowry, George Lucas, Lucky Luciano, Shannon Lucid, Sean MacBride, Stanley Marcus, Wynton Marsalis, Marlee Matlin, Scott McNealy, James Michener, Glenn Miller, Robert Mondavi, Chuichi Nagumo, Patricia Neal, Paavo Nurmi, Gordon Parks, T. Boone Pickens, Ferdinand Porsche, Jr., Hal Prince, Richard Pryor, Ma Rainey, Pete Rozelle, Gerhard Schroeder, Wallis Simpson, Thomas Sowell, Wallace Stegner, George Steinbrenner, Casey Stengel, Helen Stephens, Martha Stewart, David Trimble, Matt Urban, Atal Behari Vajpayee, Jack Warner, Thomas John Watson, Jr., Steve Wozniak, Chien-Shiung Wu, Darryl F. Zanuck

**APA/Archive Photos:** Connie Mack

**Archive Photos:** Moshood Abiola, Harold Arlen, Max Beerbohm, Richard Branson, Lenny Bruce, Lepke Buchalter, Roy Campanella, Steve Case, Florence Chadwick, Chai Ling, Joan Crawford, E.L. Doctorow, Gertrude Ederle, Eileen Ford, Lou Gehrig, George Gipp, Bacharuddin Jusuf Habibie, Ben Hogan, Grace Kelly, Jack Kevorkian, Ernie Kovacs, Oscar Levant, William Levitt, Louis B. Mayer, Michael Milken, Billy Mills, Stan Musial, Richard Reynolds, Maurice Sendak, Nawaz Sharif,Eunice Kennedy Shriver, W. Eugene Smith, Preston Sturges, Arthur Tedder, Gloria Vanderbilt, Vercingetorix, Gianni Versace, Helmut Werner, Helen Wills,Aldolph Zukor

**Archive Photos/Reuters:** Helen Thomas, Alfred Eisenstaedt

**Jerry Baur:** Ngaio Marsh, Walker Percy, Jean Rhys

**Les Brown Enterprises, Inc.:** Les Brown

**Country Music Foundation, Inc.:** Jimmie Rodgers

**Steve Dipaola 1998/Nike, Inc.:** Phil Knight

**Fisk University Library:** Elijah McCoy

**General Electric:** Jack Welch

**The Granger Collection, New York:** Jan Matzeliger

**Henry Grossman:** Isaac Stern

**HarperCollins Publishers Inc.:** Shel Silverstein

**Hulton-Deutsch Collection/Corbis:** Derek Jacobi, Paul Poiret, Mary Quant

**International Portrait Gallery:** Richard Hughes

**The Kobal Collection:** Lon Chaney, Douglas Fairbanks, Jean-Luc Godard, Mae West

**Library of Congress:** Clarence Birdseye, Herman Hollerith, Belva Lockwood, Alice Paul, Mary Pickford

**Hugh Lofting, Literary Estate of:** Hugh Lofting

**Macmillan Children's Books Group:** Marguerite Henry

**Netscape Communications:** Marc Andreessen

**Penske Motorsports, Inc.:** Roger Penske

**Queens Library, Long Island Division:** Lewis Latimer

**Ken Settle:** Stevie Wonder

**Transcendental Graphics:** Ted Williams

**UPI/Corbis-Bettmann:** Robert Ballard, Rosa Bonheur, Adolphus Busch, Maureen Connolly, Alice Evans, Alfred Fuller, Barron Hilton, Maggie Kuhn, Suzanne Lenglen, Candy Lightner, Bill Pickett, Ethel Andrus, Vincent Bendix, William Bernbach, Harold Courlander, Charles Dow, H.J. Heinz, Konosuke Matsushita, Conde Nast, Maurice Richard, Walter Short, Cornelia Otis Skinner, Carl Spaatz, Ed Sullivan, Stella Walsh, Pat Weaver, Edward Weston, Ryan White

**USHMM Photo Archives:** Albert Speer

**Carl Van Vechten, the Estate of:** Mahalia Jackson

# OBITUARIES

The following people, appearing in volumes 1-18 of the *Encyclopedia of World Biography,* have died since the publication of the second edition and its volume 18 supplement. Each entry lists the volume where the full biography can be found.

**ABZUG, BELLA** (born 1920), liberal lawyer and unconventional politician, who worked energetically for civil and women's rights and served three terms as a member of the U.S. Congress, died of complications following heart surgery at Columbia Presbyterian Medical Center in New York, New York, March 31, 1998 (Vol. 1).

**BLACKMUN, HARRY** (born 1908), U.S. Supreme Court justice who became a passionate defender of the right to abortion, died of complications following hip replacement surgery in Arlington, Virginia, March 4, 1999 (Vol. 2).

**BRADLEY, TOM** (born 1917), first African American mayor of Los Angeles, who won election five times and served a record 20 years in office, died of a heart attack at Kaiser Permanente West Los Angeles Medical Center in Los Angeles, California, September 29, 1998 (Vol. 2).

**CARMICHAEL, STOKELY** (born 1941), American civil rights activist who stood at the forefront of the Black Power movement of the 1960s, died of cancer in Conakry, Guinea, November 15, 1998 (Vol. 3).

**DIMAGGIO, JOE** (born 1914), American baseball star whose 56-game hitting streak with the New York Yankees in 1941 made him an indelible American folk hero, died of lung cancer at his home in Hollywood, Florida, March 8, 1999 (Vol. 5).

**HUGHES, TED** (born 1930), eminent British poet who led a resurgence of English poetic innovation and was named poet laureate in 1985, died of cancer at his home in North Tawton, England, October 28, 1998 (Vol. 8).

**HUSSEIN IBN TALAL** (born 1935), third ruler of the Hashemite Kingdom of Jordan, was the longest-ruling monarch of his time and one of the most skillful politicians of the second half of the 20th century, died of cancer in Amman, Jordan, February 7, 1999 (Vol 8).

**KUBRICK, STANLEY** (born 1928), American film director who won acclaim for films he directed during the 1950s, but was best known for his later work including *Dr. Strangelove, 2001: A Space Odyssey,* and *A Clockwork Orange,* died at his home in Hertfordshire, England, March 7, 1999 (Vol 18).

**KUROSAWA, AKIRA** (born 1910), Japanese film director who was noted for his visually arresting and intellectually adventurous evocations of Japan's mythic past and agonized present, died of a stroke at his home in Tokyo, Japan, September 5, 1998 (Vol. 9).

**MARTIN, WILLIAM McCHESNEY, JR.** (born 1906), American business executive and federal government official, directed major financial institutions and played a prominent role in shaping national economic policy in the 1950s and 1960s, died of respiratory failure at his home in Washington, DC, July 27, 1998 (Vol. 10).

**MURDOCH, IRIS** (born 1919), British novelist and philosopher, whose works portrayed characters with warped and dreamlike perceptions of reality, died at a nursing home in Oxford, England, February 8, 1999 (Vol. 11).

**POWELL, LEWIS F., JR.** (born 1907), U.S. Supreme Court justice who led the moderate center faction during his 15-year tenure, died of pneumonia at his home in Richmond, Virginia, August 25, 1998 (Vol. 12).

**ROBBINS, JEROME** (born 1918), a major creative force on both the Broadway and ballet stages, who extended the possibilities of musical theater and brought a contemporary American perspective to classical dance, died of a stroke at his home in New York, New York, July 29, 1998 (Vol. 13).

**SHEPARD, ALAN** (born 1923), the first American in space, whose historic 1961 flight was immortalized in the book and movie, *The Right Stuff,* died of leuke-

mia at a hospital in Monterey, California, July 21, 1998 (Vol. 14).

**WALLACE, GEORGE CORLEY** (born 1919), governor of Alabama and presidential candidate who built his political career on segregation, died of respiratory failure and cardiac arrest at Jackson Hospital in Montgomery, Alabama, September 13, 1998 (Vol. 16).

**ZHIVKOV, TODOR** (born 1911), the Communist ruler of Bulgaria from 1954 until his ouster in 1989, died of complications following a respiratory infection at a hospital in Sofia, Bulgaria, August 5, 1998 (Vol. 16).

A

# Moshood Abiola

**The political turmoil endured by the citizens of Nigeria during the final decades of the twentieth century was led by a varied group of individuals. One of the most influential was Moshood Abiola (1937–1998), a Nigerian businessman educated in Scotland. He climbed to the top of several corporate ladders, building a political and financial empire.**

Moshood Kashimawa Olawale Abiola was born into a poor family in Abeokuta, Ogun State, Nigeria on August 24, 1937. Abiola received his primary education at Baptist Boys' High School and earned a scholarship to attend the University of Glasgow, Scotland, where he received a degree in economics. Abiola was raised in the Yoruba Muslim faith; the southern part of Nigeria where he was brought up is divided primarily between Christian and Muslim believers. Known for his outspoken political stances, Abiola lobbied the United States and several European nations in 1992, demanding reparations for their enslavement of African people and recompense for the fortunes made in harvesting Africa's raw materials.

## Muslim Marital Traditions

Following common tradition, Abiola took four wives; Simibiat Atinuke Shoaga in 1960, Kudirat Olayinki Adeyemi in 1973, Adebisi Olawunmi Oshin in 1974, and Doyinsola (Doyin) Abiola Aboaba in 1981. He is said to have fathered over 40 children from these four marriages. Abiola's second wife, Kudirat, was murdered in the capital

city of Lagos in 1996. There was speculation that her death was caused by the military, but no proof was ever found. His third wife, Doyin, ran a newspaper chain he owned until it was closed by the government. In 1992, Abiola was ordered to pay $20,000 a month in child support to a woman who claimed to be his wife. His lawyers argued in a New Jersey court that Abiola had only four wives; this woman was just one of his 19 concubines.

## A Businessman and Entrepreneur

Abiola was considered to be a genial businessman who amassed a fortune through his association with various enterprises, including publishing, communications, and oil. With his educational background in accounting, he easily assumed the position of deputy chief accountant at Lagos University Teaching Hospital from 1965 to 1967, and comptroller of Pfizer Products, Ltd. between 1967 and 1969. In 1969, he became the comptroller of International Telephone and Telegraph (ITT), Nigeria, Ltd., and rapidly rose to become vice president for ITT's Africa and Middle East branch. He was also chairman and chief executive officer of ITT Nigeria, Ltd. from 1972 through 1988. During this period Abiola founded and sat as chairman of Concord Press of Nigeria Ltd. and served as chief executive at Radio Communications Nigeria. While employed with ITT, he was frequently admonished by the general public due to the dreadful condition of the Nigerian telephone system. Abiola's detractors claim he profited financially at the expense of the citizens by using inferior materials and keeping extra profits for himself; charges he adamantly denied.

Much of Abiola's fortune, which was estimated at close to $2 billion, he freely distributed to others. He is said to have sent over 2,500 students through the university system as well as donating money to charities and championing

sporting events. His generosity earned Abiola the nickname "Father Christmas" among the citizens of Nigeria. In addition to his generosity, Abiola was considered an astute businessman. For over 20 years he carefully cultivated friends throughout the country. He considered himself well liked by the Nigerian military establishment, a miscalculation that would cost him dearly.

## Political Struggles

Nigeria, the most populous country on the African continent, obtained its freedom from Britain in 1960. During the four decades that followed, it endured several major political crises, including the collapse of civilian rule in the 1960s and the collapse of the civilian-headed "Second Republic" in the 1980s. Both of these crises were accelerated by civil violence in Yoruba, the southwestern district of the country. Historically, north-south conflicts have peppered Nigeria, as political power has been held by the north, the headquarters for the country's military. Abiola, who hailed from the southern district of Yoruba, brought a different perspective to the country's political makeup. His cultivation of people on both sides of the north-south divide ultimately proved to be beneficial.

## A Bid for Democracy

In 1993, the Nigerian government was undergoing another in a series of attempts at stabilization. Major General Ibrahim Babangida, together with Nigerian political leaders, inaugurated the Transitional Council and the National Defense and Security Council (NDSC). These governing bodies were designed to exist until democratic elections could be held to choose a president. On January 5, 1993, the process of screening over 250 presidential candidates was begun by the National Electoral Commission (NEC.) The NEC banned previous candidates and parties from campaigning, and so the long process began.

By the end of March, Abiola was chosen by the Social Democratic Party (SDP) as their candidate. The National Republican Convention (NRC) chose Bashir Othma Tofa and the elections were scheduled for June 12, 1993. The results clearly showed Abiola to be the winner. Babangida, wishing to continue military rule, petitioned the High Court to delay the elections, and on June 16 the announcement of the results was postponed. In defiance of the court order, a group called Campaign for Democracy released the election results, declaring Abiola to be the winner, with 19 of 30 states supporting him. Less than a week later the NDSC voided the election, supposedly to protect the legal system and the judiciary from being ridiculed both nationally and internationally. Both the U.S. and Great Britain reacted to this violation of democratic principles by restricting aid to Nigeria. Abiola, believing himself to have been given a mandate from the voters, joined the Campaign for Democracy in calling for voters to perform acts of civil disobedience in an attempt to force the election results to stand. In response, Major Babangida used the authority he still retained to ban both Abiola and Tofa from participating in any new elections.

On July 6, 1993, Nigerian leaders demanded that both parties agree to participate in an interim national government. They reluctantly agreed and, on July 16, plans were announced for a new election, but immediately abandoned. On July 31, Babangida, president of the NDSC, announced an interim government would take effect on August 27. He stepped down on the day before the new government took effect, handing power over to a preferred loyalist, Chief Shonekan.

Nigerians supporting Abiola demanded that power be turned over to him as the rightful winner of the original election. That election was considered by many to have been the cleanest in Nigeria's history and was praised as a concerted effort to overcome ethnic and religious divisions throughout the country. A. O. Olukoshi, a professor at the Nigerian Institute of International Affairs in Lagos, commented on the election and the majority win by Abiola, saying "Abiola allowed us to rise above ethnic and religious differences . . . this was the first time a Yoruba has been able to win votes both in the east and the north." By this point, Abiola had traveled to London where he denounced the entire process. Throughout August 1993, Nigeria was paralyzed by strikes and unrest, and came almost to a standstill. Abiola remained abroad for several months, finally returning to Nigeria at the end of the year. In November 1993, Chief Shoneken was overthrown by General Sani Abacha, as the military once again seized power in Nigeria.

## Continued Unrest

Resentment against the military grew during the first part of 1994. During the constitutional conference of May

23, the Campaign for Democracy called for a boycott of elections, demanding that the military return power to Abiola, the presumed winner of the prior year elections. On June 11, 1994, after declaring himself to be president before a group of 3,000, Abiola went into hiding. He called for an uprising to force the military to recognize the 1993 vote. The military, conducting a nationwide hunt, arrested him on June 23. The following day, 1,000 demonstrators marched on Lagos to demand Abiola's release. By July, a war of attrition by Nobel Prize winner, Wole Soyinka, was launched against the government. In response, the military charged Abiola with treason. Soyinka, one of the driving forces behind Abiola, was forced to flee the country after being charged with treason.

The oil workers went on a ten-day strike, crippling the nation's leading industry and bringing the country to an economic halt. Riots flared in Lagos and by the strike's third week, 20 people had been killed. By mid-August the strike had brought unrest to the northern and eastern part of the country as support for Abiola continued to increase. Abacha responded by firing any high ranking military he thought were not loyal, then fired the heads of the state companies and their boards. Abacha eventually crushed the strike after nine weeks. He arrested any pro-democracy leaders that could be found.

### Heart Attack or Poison?

Abiola remained under arrest for four years, and was not allowed visits by either his family or personal physician. He was denied proper medical care, even after being examined by state-authorized doctors. Abiola's daughter, Hofsad, said the family was allowed no contact during her father's four years in prison.

On July 7, 1998, only days before his scheduled release from prison, Abiola collapsed during a visit with a U.S. delegation and died in Abuja, Nigeria, of an alleged heart attack. His long-time friend and supporter, Wole Soyinka, expressed doubts that the death was the result of natural causes. "I'm convinced that some kind of slow poison was administered to Abiola," he told an interviewer after learning of his friend's death. Soyinka claimed that other Nigerian political prisoners had been injected with poison and indicated that he had received a note prior to Abiola's death stating that his friend would be killed within the next few days.

An autopsy found that Abiola's heart was seriously diseased and confirmed it as the cause of his death. The U.S. delegation visiting Abiola at the time of his attack saw no reason to presume foul play, indicating that the presiding doctors felt that the symptoms were consistent with a heart attack.

Abiola's death shocked and saddened a country that had come close to experiencing true democracy through valid elections for the first time in its history. The Roman Catholic Archbishop of Lagos, Anthony Okogie, commented on Abiola's passing by saying, "His death is the end of a chapter." Instead of celebrating his release and the possible resurgence of democracy, Nigeria stepped back to re-gather itself, and start the process again.

### Further Reading

*Atlanta Journal and Constitution,* July 16, 1998.
*Newsday,* June 9, 1995.
*Time,* August 9, 1993.
*AP Online,* July 7, 1998.
Encyclopedia Britannica Online, http://members.eb.com (February 16, 1999). □

# Marc Andreessen

**Marc Andreessen (born 1972) has been one of the key players in making the Internet and World Wide Web accessible to the masses, thanks to his development of Netscape Navigator, a browser that integrates text, graphics, and sound.**

The astronomical growth of the World Wide Web could not have occurred without a simple product that helped users find their way through the vast, and sometimes disorganized, material on the Web. The first such product, called a browser, was invented by a team including software developer and entrepreneur, Marc Andreessen. He developed the Mosaic program as a college student. It later became the Netscape Navigator when he co-founded his own company in 1994. This browser software had a profound impact on society. According to some estimates, Mosaic stimulated a 10,000 percent increase in the number of Web users within two years from its debut, and Netscape Navigator was even more popular.

### Young Computer Whiz

Andreessen was born in Iowa in 1972. He lived in the small town of New Lisbon, Wisconsin, with his parents, Lowell and Patricia. Marc Andreessen's father worked in the agricultural field and his mother worked for Lands' End, a catalogue retailer. Andreessen was not a typical New Lisbon boy. He spent his early years reading and learning about computers. In sixth grade, he wrote his first computer program—a virtual calculator for doing his math homework. But the program was on the school's PC, and when the custodian turned off the building's power, Andreessen's program was wiped out. The next year, his parents bought him his first computer, a TRS-80 that cost only a few hundred dollars. Marc taught himself BASIC programming from library books in order to develop video games for the new PC. Andreessen's teachers and classmates from New Lisbon remember him as a good student who excelled in computing, math, English, and history. Andreessen could even challenge teachers, and was known to question the relevance of their assignments. At the University of Illinois, Andreessen planned to major in electrical engineering, which he considered his most lucrative option, but then changed to computer science.

Andreessen became interested in the Internet while working at the University of Illinois National Center for Supercomputing Applications (NCSA) at Champaign-

Urbana. At the NCSA, he worked with a programmer, Eric Bina, to develop an interface that could navigate the World Wide Web by integrating text, graphics, and sound. The result was Mosaic, which the NCSA team completed in 1993 and posted for free over the Internet. Over two million copies of the browser were downloaded the first year. Mosaic was responsible for a 10,000-fold increase in Web users over a period of two years.

After graduating from the University of Illinois with a bachelor of science degree in 1993, Andreessen took a job with Enterprise Integration Technologies, a producer of Internet security-enhancement products, in California. He was contacted by Jim Clark, a former associate professor of computer science at Stanford University. Clark had founded Silicon Graphics Inc., a company which made computers that specialized in graphics processing. He was interested in starting a business with Andreessen. The two decided to combine Andreessen's technical knowledge with Clark's business expertise in order to launch their own company in 1994.

## Founded Netscape

The company was originally named Mosaic Communications Corp. When the NCSA, which owned the copyright to the Mosaic software, objected to the name, the partners changed it to Netscape. Andreessen, as head of technology, worked to make Mosaic faster and more interactive. He was assisted by several team members from the original Mosaic project at NCSA, whom he persuaded to join Netscape. Soon, the company released their new browser, which the

development team wanted to call "Mozilla"—short for Mosaic Killer. The marketing department, however, insisted on Netscape Navigator.

The program was distributed free on the Internet, and quickly became extremely popular. This established Netscape as a "brand" name, and prompted computer users to try other Netscape products. Soon, the company was profitable. On August 9, 1995, Netscape first offered shares in the company to the public. That day, shares were priced at $28 and opened at an unprecedented $71 a share. In one day, the 24-year-old Andreessen became worth more than $50 million. To celebrate, he bought his first suit. By December of that year, Netscape's stock reached an all-time high. The value of Andreessen's shares in the company skyrocketed to $171 million.

Andreessen was known for putting in long hours at Netscape, but his management style differed very much from that of his main competitor, Microsoft. Andreessen remained close to the programmers who worked for him, and maintained a collegial, team-like atmosphere. He did not insist that his employees work long hours—in fact, he encouraged them to limit office hours to 50 per week. Characteristic of this team-oriented approach was Andreessen's decision to offer Netscape's browser code over the Internet to anyone who wanted it. His reasoning was that the feedback he received from other software developers could lead to new ideas for Netscape. In July 1997, Andreessen became executive vice-president in charge of product development at Netscape. With a staff of 1,000, Andreessen hoped to stay ahead of the giant Microsoft. From the beginning, Andreessen had used innovative strategies to get his program out to the public. By allowing computer users to download Mosaic and Netscape Navigator for free, he took a chance. But the browsers became so popular that users quickly developed confidence in the Netscape brand, and purchased other Netscape goods and services.

## Competition from Microsoft

Microsoft Corporation, which had been focused primarily on its operating system and software for personal computers (PCs) until late 1995, began to realize the value of Internet browser software and announced that it intended to work in that area. In August 1995, Microsoft released the Internet Explorer 1.0 with its Windows 95 operating system. Later versions of Internet Explorer were given away for free and by December 1997, Netscape's lead in the browser market was down to 60%. In January 1998, Netscape decided to give its browser away for free. Andreessen's challenge was to get Netscape back to profitability. He no longer wrote software programs himself, but as the head of product development, envisioned new solutions for emerging technologies. With Netscape CEO Jim Barksdale, Andreessen shifted the company's focus away from the browser market and toward innovations for intranets (corporate networks) and electronic commerce. He also began developing Netscape's web site into an Internet gateway similar to that of America Online.

By late 1998, Netscape's share of the browser market had dipped to a little more than 50 percent. The United

State government, which had been investigating Microsoft's business practices since 1991, decided to prosecute Microsoft for unfair business practices. A lengthy court case ensued, in which the government proved that Microsoft used its clout in the marketplace to try to drive Netscape out of business. It did this, the government claimed, by tying its Explorer browser with its Windows operating system, which was installed on the vast majority of desktop computers. As the case stretched out, Andreessen and others in the computer industry were called to testify. Before the courts reached their decision, the leading Internet service provider, America Online (AOL), announced in late 1998 that it was acquiring Netscape. AOL then announced that Andreessen would be leaving Netscape in early 1999 to join their firm as chief technology officer. "His role is considered crucial to merging AOL's consumer-oriented focus with Netscape's technical expertise," wrote Jon Swartz in the *San Francisco Chronicle*.

Andreessen resides in Palo Alto, California, with his fiancé, Elizabeth Horn, and their pet bulldogs. After his job change, he began commuting between Netscape's Mountain View headquarters and America Online offices in Dulles, Virginia. Andreessen enjoys a range of interests, including science fiction, classical music, philosophy, and business strategy. As might be appropriate for a computer whiz, Andreessen claims to be a "Netizen" himself—he gets all his news from the World Wide Web, buys his books from the online site Amazon.com, and even uses the Internet to check theater times.

## Further Reading

*Newsmakers* Gale Research, 1996.
*Business Week,* April 13, 1998.
*CS Alumni News,* Winter 1994.
*Fortune,* December 9, 1996.
*Los Angeles Times,* October 28, 1996.
*Nation's Business,* January 1996.
*People Weekly,* September 11, 1995.
*San Francisco Chronicle,* January 26, 1999.
*Time,* February 19, 1996; December 7, 1998.
*USA Today* October 23, 1998.
*VeriSign, Digital ID Hall of Fame,* 1997.
*Washington Post,* March 25, 1997.
*E-Media* August 14, 1995. Available from http://www.e-media .com.
*Hoover's Online,* March 2, 1999. Available from http://www .hoovers.com. □

# Ethel Andrus

**The image of retirement as the end of a productive, contributory life has been considerably altered by the efforts of Ethel Andrus (1884–1967), founder of the National Retired Teachers Association (NRTA) and the American Association of Retired Persons (AARP). Although Andrus was dedicated to the improvement of living conditions and to the education of her students and their parents, her most signifi-**

**cant achievements occurred after her own retirement from teaching.**

Ethel Percy Andrus was born in San Francisco, California, on September 21, 1884. She was the younger of two daughters of George Wallace Andrus and Lucretia Frances Duke. The family moved to Chicago when Andrus was a baby so that her father could finish his legal education at the University of Chicago.

## Served the Community

Andrus spent most of her youth in Chicago, graduating from Austin High School. She taught English and German at the Lewis Institute (later, the Illinois Institute of Technology) while continuing her own education. She earned her B.S. from the Lewis Institute in 1908. Andrus was active in the community; she did volunteer work at Hull House and at the Chicago Commons, both settlement houses. Her urge to serve the community grew out of the example set by her father. She believed that we must do some good for which we receive no reward other than the satisfaction of knowing that we have provided an important service.

In 1910, Andrus returned to California with her family. She taught classes at Santa Paula High School for a year, then taught at Manual Arts High School and Abraham Lincoln High School in Los Angeles. Among her pupils were actors Robert Preston and Robert Young, and General James Doolittle. She became principal of Lincoln High School in

1917, the first woman in California history to hold such a post.

During her 28-year tenure at Lincoln High School, Andrus had many notable achievements. Her urban high school faced problems of juvenile delinquency as well as cultural, ethnic, and racial conflict. Andrus was determined to improve the quality of life for her students, their parents, and others in her community. She strove to instill in her students a sense of pride in their own cultural heritage and an appreciation of the cultural life and values in the United States. By encouraging her students to conduct themselves with self-respect, and by treating them with dignity, Andrus helped to lower the rate of juvenile crime. Her desire to achieve harmony in the neighborhood extended to the parents of her students as well as to the community at large. She established the Opportunity School for Adults, an evening program designed to assist immigrant parents of her pupils. The popularity of the program eventually led to its expansion into a full-time evening education institution through which people in the community could earn a high school diploma.

The contributions made by Andrus led to a substantial drop in juvenile crime and earned the school special citations from the juvenile court in East Los Angeles in 1940. Lincoln High School was selected by the National Education Association to be featured in its textbook *Learning Ways of Democracy.*

While working on behalf of her students and the community, Andrus continued her own education, earning her M.A. in 1928 and her Ph.D. in 1930 from the University of Southern California. Her doctoral dissertation promoted the establishment of a high school curriculum for girls that would be based on their nature and address their needs. She spent her summers teaching courses at the University of California at Los Angeles, the University of Southern California, and Stanford University.

### Retirement Led to Second Career

Andrus retired from teaching in 1944. It was then that her second career as an advocate for the retired and other older Americans evolved. Although she had her own income, the meagerness of her state pension, $60 per month, aroused her interest in the quality of life enjoyed by her fellow retired teachers. As welfare director of the southern section of the California Retired Teachers Association, Andrus began to examine pensions and other benefits provided to retired teachers across the country. Her research led her to believe that a national organization was needed to address the needs of her peers. She founded and became president of the National Retired Teachers Association (NRTA) in 1947.

### AARP Founded

As president and founder of the NRTA, Andrus devoted herself to improving the living conditions of her fellow retired teachers by lobbying for benefits such as affordable health insurance for persons over age 65, increased pensions, and tax benefits. She won a major victory in 1956, when she persuaded the Continental Casualty insurance company to underwrite a program for NRTA members—the first group health and accident insurance plan for retired persons over the age of 65. The popularity of the insurance coverage for retired teachers brought requests for Andrus to help other retired people to receive comparable benefits. In response, she established and became leader of the American Association of Retired Persons (AARP) in 1958.

Her continued concern for the costs of health care faced by retired people resulted in the creation of a nonprofit mail-order drug buying service in 1959. The service made it possible for members of AARP and NRTA to purchase prescription medicines at prices at least 25 percent below retail prices. Mail-order centers staffed by licensed pharmacists were established in California and in Washington, D.C. Prescription drugs were delivered directly to the doors of AARP and NRTA members. In announcing the establishment of the program, Andrus explained that the service was motivated by extensive research which revealed that "Americans over 65 years of age spend approximately ten percent of their average annual income for drugs and medications."

In July 1959, Andrus appeared before Congress to express her opposition to a health care bill based on an added payroll tax, as proposed by Representative Aime J. Forand, a Rhode Island Democrat. Instead, she proposed a nationwide system whereby the U.S. government would deduct from social security benefits the cost of premiums for those people who chose the plan. Administration of the plan would be handled by a private board of trustees. Andrus opposed the Forand bill because it denied freedom of choice. She appeared before Congress again—in December 1959—to protest the actions of Parke, Davis & Company of Detroit in cutting off sales to a distributor supplying discount drugs to retired members of the AARP and the NRTA.

### "Creative Energy is Ageless"

Andrus promoted the belief that retired people should remain actively engaged in life. She was opposed to mandatory retirement laws and advised people considering retirement to take up a second career. Andrus heeded her own advice: her second career evolved when she became an enthusiastic promoter of a wider range of opportunities for older people. She worked for the right of retired teachers to work as substitutes; encouraged older people to perform services such as tutoring children, working with the hearing-impaired, and becoming involved in church work and city planning; and organized a travel program through the AARP.

During a visit to New York in 1959, Andrus explained that both the NRTA and the AARP are based on the belief that "creative energy is ageless." In an interview with *Time,* in 1954, she said, "As it is, when you leave a job, they often just give you a gold watch and all you can do is look at it and count the hours until you die. Yet think of all the grand things we can do that youth can't. Think of all the things we already have done. Some day, the retired teachers in this country will have the dignity they deserve."

Andrus deplored the lack of wider job opportunities for older citizens. In 1963, she founded the Institute of Life Long

Learning to provide classes and seminars focused on the needs and interests of retired people and other older Americans. Additional branches of the Institute were established in California and Florida. Her efforts received national recognition and she was asked to serve as a member of the national advisory committee for the White House Conference on Aging in 1961. She also worked as executive secretary for the American School for Girls in Damascus, Syria; and as a member of the advisory board of the American Association of Homes for the Aged. Andrus edited four Association journals, including *Modern Maturity*, the monthly magazine of the AARP. She helped to establish Grey Gables, a retirement home for teachers, in Ojai, California, in 1954. She was named National Teacher of the Year in 1954.

## AARP Work Continued After Her Death

Andrus died in Ojai, California on July 13, 1967. She, and her work, were not forgotten. In 1968, the AARP Andrus Foundation was established. Its mission, as noted on the Andrus Foundation website, was "to enhance the lives of older adults through research on aging." In addition, the University of California, the AARP, and the NRTA established the Ethel Percy Andrus Gerontology Center in 1973. Another honor came 25 years later. In 1998, Andrus was inducted into the National Women's Hall of Fame.

Andrus's belief in and commitment to promoting the interests of older Americans continues through the work of the AARP and the NRTA, both of which have become powerful lobbying forces composed of more than 30 million members. Whenever there is an opportunity to improve the quality of life through education, employment, or advances in healthcare coverage, the AARP and the NRTA are there to continue her work. As noted on the AARP website "This remarkable American leader served as a role model at a time when women were not highly visible in public life." She "exemplified her legacy of service to others."

## Further Reading

Garraty, John A., and Mark C. Carnes, *Dictionary of American Biography, Supplement Eight, 1966-1970,* American Council of Learned Societies, 1988.

O'Neill, Lois Decker, *Women's Book of World Records and Achievements,* Anchor Press/Doubleday, 1979.

Sicherman, Barbara, Carol Hurd Green, Ilene Kantrov, and Harriette Walker, *Notable American Women—The Modern Period: A Biographical Dictionary,* The Belknap Press of Harvard University Press, 1980.

*New York Times,* April 12, 1959; July 17, 1959; August 23, 1959; November 5, 1959; December 12, 1959; July 15, 1967.

*Time,* May 10, 1954, p. 79.

"AARP Celebrates Women's History Month," *AARP Webplace,* http://www.aarp.org (April 13, 1999).

"About the AARP Andrus Foundation," *AARP Andrus Foundation Webplace,* http://www.andrus.org (April 7, 1999).

"What is AARP?" *AARP Webplace,* http://www.aarp.org (March 7, 1999). □

# Harold Arlen

**From the time of his birth until he wrote the music to his first popular hit, "Get Happy," the growth of Harold Arlen (1905–1986) from cantor's son to jazz pianist, composer, and arranger could not have been better orchestrated if he wrote it himself.**

Born in Buffalo, New York, on February 15, 1905, Harold Arlen (originally named Hyman Arluck) received his first introduction to music from his father, a cantor. As a youngster of seven, Arlen sang in his father's choir. Two years later, he began demonstrating his musical skill at the piano. He studied classical music and remained a student of classical piano etudes until 1917, when the jazz age introduced America to a new form of music. Arlen was immediately intrigued with this new style and was soon arranging songs and playing piano with his own group, the Snappy Trio. He assumed the leadership role, by arranging and performing numbers in a jazz format. He was also the vocalist.

The trio experienced immediate success and redefined themselves into a quintet, the Southbound Shufflers. The Shufflers entertained around the United States and across the border in Canada. Arlen's blossoming musical career quickly established him in the Buffalo music scene and, to his parents' dismay, he left school early to pursue a musical career. He was quickly absorbed into a popular local group, the Buffalodians, where his talents as pianist, vocalist, and arranger continued to define his future. It was not long before Arlen and his band were drawn to Broadway.

### New York Beckons

In New York City, Arlen landed a singing role in Vincent Yourman's Broadway musical *Great Day*. When Yourman discovered the young actor's many talents, Arlen was quickly moved to a role behind the scenes where he played piano for the performers and arranged music for the shows. His stage career ended, but his composing and arranging career flourished. It was during this time that Arlen teamed up with Ted Koehler, a young lyricist, for what would prove to be a long and successful relationship. Sometimes referred to as the "melody man," Arlen penned tunes to Koehler's words. He churned out a successive string of hits including "Get Happy," "Between the Devil and the Deep Blue Sea," "I Love a Parade," and "I've Got the World on a String." In 1931, Arlen took his talents to the stage with his first Broadway show *You Said It*.

### The Cotton Club Revues

The first Koehler/Arlen collaboration, *Get Happy*, was produced while working on Yourman's musical *Great Day.*. This tune was received with such enthusiasm by audiences that the duo quickly found new opportunities. In 1930, Arlen and Koehler joined Harlem's renowned Cotton Club. During the very productive years between 1930 and 1934 Koehler and Arlen produced many tunes for that club's revue that have become jazz and blues classics. One of the most popular performers at the Cotton Club, Cab Calloway, played and recorded such classics as "Trickeration," "Kickin' the Gong Around," "Without Rhythm," and "Minnie the Moocher's Wedding Day." The durability of these songs can be seen in the continued popularity of Calloway's recordings that are still sold today.

The years at the Cotton Club were among Arlen's most prolific. Noteworthy tunes emerging during this era included "Ill Wind," "Blues in the Night," and the seductive "Stormy Weather." "Stormy Weather" became a wildly popular song and eventually a trademark of singer, Lena Horne. It led the creative team to venture into movies, where they experienced their first film success, *Let's Fall in Love*. This film classic cemented Arlen and Koehler's reputations on the West Coast, and the pair continued their successful collaboration in Hollywood through many more film classics.

### Hollywood Success

While working in Hollywood, Arlen's style caught the attention of film producer, Arthur Freed. He signed Arlen to collaborate with lyricist E. Y. Harburg on a fantasy film. Both the movie—1939's *The Wizard of Oz* (1939)—and the musical score have remained popular for the greater part of a century. The best-known song from the score was "Over the Rainbow." It earned an Academy Award for the duo and became the hallmark song for the movie's star, Judy Garland. During his time in Hollywood, Arlen scored many other movies including *Cabin in the Sky* (1943) and *A Star Is Born* (1954).

The Hollywood of the 1930s and 1940s was ruled by a small group of businessmen best known for creating the "star system." They decided who would be a star, based in large part on an individual's ability to draw movie-goers to the theatre. Composers did not fall into that category. While Arlen remained in demand for the next two decades, because of the star system he remained behind the scenes and enjoyed a quiet life as a composer of songs that others made famous. However, his work was continuous and he maintained a good income during his years in Hollywood. A quiet man who preferred time with his wife Anya, son Sam, and the family dogs, he was content with his golf, tennis, and swimming. Although not a household name, his prolific songwriting was responsible for helping make others in Hollywood famous.

Arlen's productive career spanned the jazz age of the 1920s through Hollywood's bountiful years of the 1930s and 1940s. His talent for scoring both movies and Broadway musicals placed him among the finest composers and arrangers of the time. His works on Broadway continued even after his move to the West Coast. They include *Life Begins at 8:40* (1934), *Hooray for What?* (1937), *Bloomer Girl* (1944), *St. Louis Woman* (1946), *Saratoga* (1959), and *House of Flowers* (1954). During his long career, Arlen teamed with other well-known lyricists such as Johnny Mercer, writing such popular hits as "Ac-cent-tchu-ate the Positive," "That Old Black Magic," and "Blues in the Night." In 1954, he wrote the music for the Broadway hit *House of Flowers* with author Truman Capote and in that same year he worked in Hollywood with Ira Gershwin on the film *The Country Girl*.

Arlen continued to work into the 1960s, although there were few opportunities that enticed him. This was a time when he produced lesser-known orchestral compositions such as "Mood in Six Minutes," "Hero Ballet," and "Minuet,"—each of which was scattered throughout various films and shows, but did not achieve the acclaim of his earlier compositions. Arlen enjoyed shedding his reputation as a blues composer, and took advantage of this time to further expand his talents.

### High Praise from Peers

Arlen earned his place among such songwriting greats as George Gershwin, Cole Porter, Richard Rodgers, Irving Berlin, and Jerome Kern. Praise from such peers was high indeed. Gershwin referred to him as "the most original of composers." Rodgers took this a step further, saying "I caught on pretty soon to his unusual harmonic structure and form" which was "his own and completely original." Among Arlen's favorite pieces was a little-known song titled "Last Night When We Were Young," a favorite of performers like Frank Sinatra.

Although his career seems to have followed a direct path from local popularity to Broadway to Hollywood, Arlen did not become a household name. Even at the peak of his career he chose to remain behind the scenes, satisfied to compose and arrange music for others to perform. Arlen left a portfolio of over 300 tunes, many of which are still played every day throughout the world. After his death in New York City on April 23, 1986, Irving Berlin summed up the life of this brilliant composer at an ASCAP tribute, saying: "He wasn't as well known as some of us, but he was a better songwriter than most of us and he will be missed by all of us." Arlen's music remains fresh and continues to be performed throughout the world.

## Further Reading

Jablonski, Edward, *Rhythm, Rainbows, and Blues,* Northeastern University Press, 1997.

*Billboard,* April 27, 1996.

*Time,* September 4, 1995.

Harold Arlen Biography, http://www.mplcommunications.com/ mbr/harold_arlen/arlen_/featured_bio.html (February 23, 1999). □

# B

# Robert Ballard

**Robert D. Ballard (born 1942) has made some of the most important underwater discoveries in the late twentieth century in regards to science and exploration. Not only did he help advance the concept of plate tectonics and make important discoveries about ocean life, he also managed to find some of the most famous shipwrecks in history, including the German battleship *Bismarck,* the *U.S.S. Yorktown* from World War II, and the luxury liner *Titanic.***

Thanks to advances in technology, including night-vision cameras and fiber optics, scientists like Ballard can help bring information about the ships back up to the surface. "There's more history preserved in the deep sea than in all the museums of the world combined," Ballard suggested to Paul Karon in the *Los Angeles Times.* Despite all of his accomplishments in geology, oceanography, and archaeology, Ballard still gets most excited about his capability to scout new territories. "I think of myself as an explorer—that was always my career goal," he told Karon. "If I could go to Mars tomorrow, I'm gone."

Robert Duane Ballard was born June 30, 1942, in Wichita, Kansas, to Chester Patrick (an aerospace executive) and Harriet Nell (May) Ballard. However, Ballard and his three siblings were raised in southern California, where he developed a passion for the sea. The fair-haired teenager would spend much of his time at the beach near his home in San Diego, becoming an avid swimmer, surfer, fisherman, and scuba diver. Ballard's father was a flight engineer at a testing ground in the Mojave Desert, but was later appointed the U.S. Navy's representative to the famous Scripps Institute of Oceanography. When he was still in high school, Ballard wrote a letter to the Scripps Institute that asked, "I love the ocean—what can I do?" he recalled to Bayard Webster in the *New York Times.* Subsequently, the school invited him to attend a summer program.

Ballard went on to earn a bachelor of science degree in chemistry and geology in 1965 from the University of California at Santa Barbara, but he never lost interest in the sea. After graduating, he pursued post-graduate work at the University of Hawaii Institute of Geophysics in 1965-66, where he made money as the keeper of two trained porpoises at Sea Life Park. He went back to the University of Southern California in 1966-67, and meanwhile, in 1965, he signed up with the U.S. Army in its intelligence unit, where he eventually became second lieutenant. In 1967, he joined the U.S. Navy as a naval oceanographic liaison officer, making lieutenant junior grade. For this stint, he was sent to Woods Hole Oceanographic Institute, a private, not-for-profit research organization on Cape Cod, Massachusetts. After his naval assignment was completed, he decided to stay on the East Coast and work at Woods Hole, continuing his research in marine geology and ocean engineering.

## Studied Plate Tectonics

Joining Woods Hole as a research associate in ocean engineering in 1970, Ballard also pursued his doctorate degree at the University of Rhode Island. He began studying plate tectonics, which was a vanguard theory at the time, and earned his Ph.D. in 1974 with a dissertation on the subject. Plate tectonics suggests that the Earth's land masses are divided into sections, or plates, that move independently of the planet's mantle. This movement causes shifting of the land, which results in earthquakes at the boundaries

could help predict earthquakes, and they also found beds of natural resources such as petroleum and minerals.

In 1975 and 1976, Ballard and many of the Project FAMOUS team went to the Cayman Trough, a depression in the ocean floor just south of Cuba. They found that they had correctly predicted recent volcanic activity under the sea and picked up rock samples from the mantle of the Earth's crust. In 1976, Ballard was named an associate scientist at Woods Hole, and would later be promoted to associate scientist in ocean engineering in 1978 and senior scientist in 1983. In 1979, he embarked on what would yield one of his most exciting discoveries. Off the coast of Ecuador on the Galapagos Rift, where plates were moving more quickly and strange variances in water temperature were recorded, he discovered that hydrothermal vents were erupting from cracks in the Earth's crust and that marine life—crabs, clams, and tube worms—could survive there by chemosynthesis. The journey and the underwater footage was used in a 1980 National Geographic special called *Dive to the Edge of Creation.*

The amazing creatures and their means of survival led biologists to hypothesize that life may have begun by this chemical method, but in shallow water. On another trip near Baja California, Ballard took along some biologists and found even more proof. Tall geysers that he dubbed "black smokers" were found to sustain surrounding marine life, never before seen, that fed on the chemical-rich dark smoke gushing out of the 10- to 20-foot spews that threatened to melt the submarine's port holes. Marine biologists, up to that point, had assumed that no creature could survive so deep in the sea, where sunlight never penetrates. Though he is not a biologist and cannot authoritatively comment on whether life may have started by chemical methods, Ballard does believe that the smoky chimneys may be responsible for much of the world's mineral deposits.

## Unmanned Sea Exploration

In the early 1980s, Ballard went to work on developing technology for unmanned sea exploration. Sending teams of scientists is expensive and often fruitless, so Ballard decided that robotic means could lower costs and increase productivity for such projects. With funding from the U.S. Navy and the National Science Foundation, Ballard formed the Deep Submergence Laboratory at Woods Hole in 1981. He thus designed the *Argo-Jason* system, an automated submarine loaded with robotic equipment that could function as the scientists' eyes and ears underwater. *Argo,* about the size of a car, has three video cameras that can see in almost total darkness, and its smaller assistant, *Jason,* has a robotic lens and arms and can be sent out to retrieve items from the ocean. With it, Ballard told Webster in the *New York Times,* "We hope to get even clearer pictures of the sea floor and what goes on down there."

## Discovered *Titanic* in the North Atlantic

Some of Ballard's colleagues were dubious that his system would allow for unmanned exploration, but he did not waver. For its maiden run, Ballard sent *Argo-Jason* down to search for the British luxury liner *Titanic,* which had hit

(fault lines) and can also cause the shape of the land masses to change over time. Also in 1974, Ballard was promoted to assistant scientist in geology and geophysics at Woods Hole. Meanwhile, he was becoming interested in the research submarine *Alvin,* which was equipped with a remote arm for retrieving samples from the floor of the ocean. He was also intrigued by the idea of studying the Mid-Atlantic Ridge, a portion of a global underseas mountain range called the Mid-Ocean Ridge. When he suggested that the three-person *Alvin* be sent down, other scientists doubted the value of using a submarine for the project. "There were quite a few people . . . who felt that submarines were expensive toys that geologists played with, and that no real good science would come out of them," Ballard remarked to James Lardner in the *Washington Post.*

Nevertheless, by 1974, Ballard was named head of Project FAMOUS (French-American Mid-Ocean Underseas Study) and proved the naysayers wrong. The expedition began in the summer of 1974 with a fleet of four ships and three research submarines. During the project, Ballard designed a survey sled called *Angus* that carried a camera and could be controlled acoustically. It was sent down before *Alvin's* dives in order to take pictures so that the scientists could determine where they wanted to go. Ballard was on board the *Alvin* during most of its 17 dives to the ocean floor and thus was able to witness the rift formed at the juncture of the plates that form the eastern and western sides of the Atlantic seabed. In addition to the geological importance of the mission, Ballard and his team came back with data that an iceberg and sunk during its maiden voyage on the night of April 14-15, 1912, killing more than 1,500 of the 2,200 passengers. Ballard had long been intrigued by the legendary ship and its story, and eventually convinced the U.S. Navy to furnish a research ship, *Knorr,* and maps of the area where the ship was thought to have gone down. He assembled a group of French sonar researchers who set out for the North Atlantic in the summer of 1985. In late August, Ballard and his crew arrived on the *Knorr,* sending down the cameras and waiting for a sign. "The bottom was just going by and going by," Ballard told Karon in the *Los Angeles Times.* "And it's a boring bottom."

Less than a week later, on September 1, 1985, the *Argo* sent up an image of one of the *Titanic's* boilers as Ballard watched on a television monitor. He immediately knew it was the right ship, because he had studied it in detail. "It was a fluke," Ballard noted in *U.S. News and World Report.* "Any fishing boat could have done it." In a week and one day, the *Argo* videotape camera and the still camera on the *Angus* captured over 20,000 images of the shipwreck, including the damaged area and hundreds of artifacts such as bottles, china, a silver tray, and the barren lifeboat cranes. Ballard was strongly moved by the scenes and opposed anyone who wanted to profit from it, stating that instead, it should be declared an international memorial. The next summer, Ballard went down in the *Alvin* along with *Jason Jr.,* a remote "eyeball" that went inside the ship, and saw even more personal items, including a man's shoe and a porcelain doll's head. In 1997, a blockbuster film would be released based on the events of that tragic night, but fictionalized to provide an old-fashioned love story as well. Ballard remarked in *Newsday,* "The movie is excellent. It's a great Romeo and Juliet love story. I saw the ship I never saw, in all of its beauty and elegance."

After this notable discovery, Ballard also found the German battleship *Bismarck* in the Atlantic Ocean and in 1997 announced that he had found eight sailing ships, some dating back before the days of Jesus Christ, 2,500 feet below the surface off the coast of Tunisia in the Mediterranean. By then, Ballard was president of the Institute for Exploration based out of Mystic, Connecticut, and a senior scientist emeritus at Woods Hole. The finding of the Roman ships was especially important because it established that underwater archaeology could be performed in the deep seas of up to 20,000 feet. Previously, archaeologists limited their research to shipwrecks in coastal waters of less than 200 feet because they thought ancient mariners did not venture into deeper waters. In May 1998, Ballard made another major discovery when he photographed the aircraft carrier *U.S.S. Yorktown,* sunk in the Pacific Ocean by Japanese forces on June 7, 1942, during World War II's Battle of Midway. It was located in almost 17,000 feet of water, one mile deeper than the *Titanic,* about 1,200 miles northwest of Honolulu, Hawaii. The National Geographic Society helped sponsor the work.

Ballard has raised eyebrows among some fellow scientists due to what they consider his enthusiasm to seek publicity. He has appeared in television programs, given lectures, and written for *National Geographic Magazine,* in addition to writing in professional journals. He also established the Jason Foundation for Education and the Jason Project, which aims to increase students' interest in science. Like cosmologist Carl Sagan and underwater explorer Jacques Cousteau, Ballard has done much to bring science into the homes of laypeople, an accomplishment that he considers his public duty. "[Sagan and Cousteau] have probably sometimes lost some of the regard of their fellow scientists," Ballard admitted to Webster in the *New York Times.* "But look at the good they've done by making science exciting and making people aware of it! And don't forget that my science is paid for by some poor coal miner whose taxes go to support me while I'm having fun, so I feel it's responsible to go to him and the public and tell them what I'm doing."

In 1966, Ballard married Marjorie Constance Jacobsen, a medical receptionist. They have two sons, Todd Alan and Douglas Matthew, and live in Hatchville, Massachusetts. Ballard has won a number of awards, including the Science award from the Underwater Society of America in 1976 for exploration and research conducted in the Cayman Trough; the Compass Distinguished Achievement Award from the Marine Technology Society in 1977 for leadership in the area of deep submergence exploration; and the Newcomb Cleveland Prize from the American Association for the Advancement of Science in 1981 for the best scientific paper in a journal of science. He also received the Cutty Sark Science Award from *Science Digest,* 1982, for exploration conducted in Mid-Ocean Ridge, including the discovery of underwater hot springs and their unique animal communities. In 1985, he won a grant for $800,000 along with the Secretary of the Navy Research Chair in Oceanography, and in 1986, he was given the Washburn Award from the Boston Museum of Science. He was awarded the prestigious Hubbard Medal from the National Geographic Society in 1996. Ballard has written or cowritten 15 books and has published numerous articles in journals and magazines, including *National Geographic.*

## Further Reading

*Contemporary Authors,* volume 112, Gale Research, 1985.
*Contemporary Heroes and Heroines,* Book II, Gale Research, 1985.
*Atlanta Journal and Constitution,* May 20, 1998, p. A3; June 5, 1998, p. B4.
*Dallas Morning News,* July 31, 1997, p. 1A.
*Los Angeles Times,* January 6, 1997, p. D3.
*Newsday,* February 5, 1998, p. A8.
*New York Times,* December 28, 1982. p. C1; September 10, 1985, pp. A1, C3.
*Star Tribune* (Minneapolis, MN), July 31, 1997, p. 1A.
*U.S. News and World Report,* September 23, 1985, p. 9.
*Washington Post,* August 31, 1982, p. B1.
"Biography: Dr. Robert Ballard," National Geographic web site, http://www.nationageographic.com (July 12, 1998). □

# Eddie Bauer

**Eddie Bauer (1899–1986) was the founder of the retail stores and mail order company which bore his name. An avid outdoors man, Bauer parlayed his interests into a successful business based on quality products and serving consumer satisfaction.**

Eddie Bauer was born on October 19, 1899, on Orcas Island, located in Puget Sound off the coast of Washington state. His parents, Jacob and Mary Catherine Bauer, were Russian-German immigrants who operated an Italian plum farm. Eddie was the youngest child in the Bauer family. Orcas Island was a sportsman's paradise, with abundant supplies of fish and wildlife. As a child, Bauer was interested in the natural world that surrounded him. His father encouraged these interests. Young Eddie wanted to own his equipment for hunting and fishing. When he was eight years old, he received his first hunting rifle, an 1890 Winchester .22 Special Caliber. To make money, Bauer worked as a golf caddy and did odd jobs, beginning at the age of ten.

## Founded Sporting Goods Store

In 1913, Bauer's parents separated. He and his mother relocated to Seattle, where Bauer worked in a local sporting goods store, Piper & Taft. He continued to pursue his hunting and fishing hobbies, and began playing tennis as well.

Bauer hoped to have his own store and spent two years studying part time to achieve this goal. In 1920, he opened a sporting goods store in Seattle, with a $500 loan that his father co-signed. It was called Eddie Bauer's Tennis Shop. Bauer designed a special vice for stringing tennis rackets that was quite popular among his customers, and soon developed a reputation for his expert stringing. Eddie Bauer's Tennis Shop was only open during the tennis season. Bauer spent the rest of the year pursuing his own sportsman activities.

Eventually, the shop changed its name to Eddie Bauer's Sports Shop, and sold equipment for all kinds of outdoor activities, including golf. In 1922, Bauer attracted customers by giving them an unconditional guarantee, unheard of in that era. The creed for his business was, according the Eddie Bauer website: "To give you such outstanding quality, value, service and guarantee that we may be worthy of your high esteem." Customer satisfaction remained important to him throughout his career.

Bauer married the former Christine "Stine" Heltborg on February 21, 1929. Like her husband, the beauty shop owner was enthusiastic about hunting, fishing, skiing, and other outdoor activities. The couple had one son, Eddie Christian Bauer.

When Bauer could not find a product he wanted to sell, he designed, manufactured, and distributed it himself. One of the early examples of this practice was fly-fishing ties, which Bauer made by hand. In 1934, he took out a patent in the United States and Canada on what was called the "Bauer shuttlecock." This invention spread the game of badminton all over North America.

## Designed Insulated Jacket

Personal necessity led Bauer to design one of his best known products, the first quilted goose-down insulated jacket. He designed this jacket after contracting hypothermia while wearing wool in the rain on a winter fishing trip in 1936. Bauer remembered some of the light but warm goose down-filled clothing his uncle from Russia had told him about. That uncle served as a Cossack soldier in Manchuria during the Russo-Japanese War of 1904. Anthony and Diane Hallett quoted Bauer in the *Encyclopedia of Entrepreneurs:* "I remember my dad saying that if it hadn't been for those down-lined coats the Cossacks wore, my uncle would have froze to death." Bauer patented his design, after making jackets for his friends. The so-called "Skyliner jacket" became extremely popular with those who spent a significant amount of time outdoors, especially sportsmen and climbers. Soon, Bauer held 16 patented designs for quilted apparel, including a sleeping bag. Bauer continued to develop new and innovative products until his retirement.

Bauer's product line expanded to include women's wear (of which his wife was in charge), sleeping bags, tents, skis imported from Norway, hunting and fishing equipment, and boots.

## Supplied American Forces

During World War II, Bauer's parkas, backpacks, pants, and sleeping bags were standard issue for American troops. Bauer was able to solve several problems for the military. There had been a sleeping bag shortage until Bauer stepped in. He eventually sold the armed services over 100,000 sleeping bags. The U.S. Army commissioned Bauer to make what came to be known as the B-9 flight parka.

After the war, veterans who had worn one of the 50,000 jackets in combat, wanted to buy more. They knew exactly where to purchase these jackets because Bauer insisted that his company's label be included on all of his products. With this customer base, Bauer began a highly successful mail order business in 1945. His original mailing list included 14,000 names of soldiers who had worn his clothing, supplied by the American government.

Despite a thriving mail order business, Bauer's retail establishment was suffering, and the company almost went bankrupt several times. Bauer, whose health was affected by years of overwork and a serious back injury, was forced to take on William Niemi as a partner. This local businessman reorganized the store and soon improved the cash flow. Niemi and a revitalized Bauer decided to focus most of their efforts on mail order catalogs. By 1953, catalog sales totaled $50,000. Three years later, the total was $500,000.

Bauer continued to supply his equipment for significant events, including the American K-2 Himalayan Expedition and several journeys through Antarctica. In 1963, James W. Whittaker, the first American to climb Mount Everest, was wearing an Eddie Bauer parka. His whole expedition used and wore Bauer's products.

Bauer and Niemi included their sons, Eddie C. Bauer and William Niemi, Jr., as partners in 1960. The company continued to prosper throughout the 1960s, based mostly on mail order sales, though the original retail store remained open. In 1968, Bauer retired and sold his share of the business to the Niemi family for $1.5 million. That same year, the second Eddie Bauer store was established, the first of many retail stores that would open in the next three decades. By 1971, the company had become part of General Mills. The Eddie Bauer Company continued to build retail stores and expand its line of merchandise. By the time of Bauer's death, there were 39 retail stores and two million mail order customers. Bauer died of a heart attack in Bellevue, Washington on April 18, 1986, two weeks after his wife died of pancreatic cancer.

## Name Lived After Death

Eddie Bauer's name lived through the constant expansion of retail stores, merchandise lines, and mail order business. By 1988, there were 61 stores, all bearing Bauer's name. That year the company was bought by Spiegel from General Mills for $260 million. Bauer's name continued to appear on products for the home, many kinds of clothing, as well as specially designed automobiles and sports utility vehicles. By 1999, there were 530 Eddie Bauer stores throughout the world. The company continues to emphasize Bauer's 1922 customer satisfaction policy and unconditional guarantee.

## Further Reading

*Business Leader Profiles for Students.* edited by Sheila Dow, Gale, 1999.
*Contemporary Newsmakers* edited by Peter Gareffa, Gale, 1987.
Fucini, Joseph J. and Suzy. *Enterpreneurs: The Men and Women Behind Famous Brand Names and How They Made It,* G.K. Hall, 1985.
Hallett, Anthony and Diane. *Entrepreneur Magazine: Encyclopedia of Entrepreneurs,* John Wiley, 1997.
*Journal of Commerce,* November 13, 1996.
*New York Times,* April 26, 1986.
*About Eddie Bauer,* http://www.eddiebauer.com/about/frame_companyoverview.asp? (February 21,1999). □

# Leon Leonwood Bean

**Think of the mail-order business and several prominent names come to mind—Sears, Roebuck & Company, Montgomery Ward, and Spiegel's, to name just a few. But perhaps none has achieved the unique quality, charm, and character of L.L. Bean, Inc. Renowned for its dedication to customer service and satisfaction, the highly successful company can be said to truly to reflect the experience and ideals of its founder, L.L. Bean (1872–1967).**

Leon Leonwood Bean was born on November 13, 1872 in the small town of Greenwood, Maine. He was the son of Benjamin Warren Bean, a farmer and horse trader, and Sarah Swett. His parents died within four days of each other when Bean was 12 years old. He and his five siblings were sent to live with relatives in South Paris, Maine.

## Demonstrated Entrepreneurial Skills

Bean's first business transaction took place when he was nine years old. Given the choice of attending the local fair or selling steel traps to his father, Bean sold the traps and earned his first income. He developed a love of the outdoors when he was quite young, and earned money by engaging in occupations geared to the outdoors. He worked on farms, peddled soap, hunted, and trapped. At the age of 13, he killed and sold his first deer. Bean paid his own way through private school, but his formal schooling was limited. It included a commercial course at Kent's Hill Academy and a semester at Hebron Academy.

Bean's limited formal education apparently was compensated for by the extensive experience he acquired through participation in outdoor activities. As noted on the L.L. Bean, Inc. website, Bean grew tired of having wet, sore feet after hiking in the Maine woods, so he conceived of a way to keep his feet warm and dry. He designed a lightweight boot consisting of a rubber bottom and a leather top. Bean took his idea to a cobbler, and the first "Maine Hunting Shoe" was manufactured in 1912.

Bean then launched his first advertising campaign, designing a marketing brochure geared toward Maine hunters. In it, he fully guaranteed the quality of the Maine Hunting Shoe and promised a refund on any unsatisfactory product. Unfortunately, Bean had to refund money on 90 of the first 100 pairs when the shoes developed cracks. But as the L.L. Bean, Inc. website noted, this led to "Bean Boots" and the "legendary guarantee of 100% satisfaction" that the company still honors more than 85 years later.

Undaunted by this failure, Bean went to Boston. With a $400 loan, he persuaded the United States Rubber Company to help him improve the quality and usefulness of the shoe. Bean then began selling the product with confidence. He sold enough shoes that by 1917, he was able to move his business to the main street of Freeport, Maine. He employed people to cut and stitch the shoes. The following year, he applied for and received patents on his product from both the United States and Canada. In a happy coincidence, Bean began selling his product at the same time the United States Post Office launched it parcel post service. When Bean's brother became postmaster in Freeport, Maine, Bean opened his factory on the floor above the post office.

## Expanded Product Line

Bean's product line grew to include other items useful to people who lived, worked, and played in the outdoors. He designed and tested each product personally, believing that it takes a sportsman to design equipment for sportsmen. This practice resulted in products that were appreciated both for their practicality and price. His ideas included a duck hunter's coat that featured sewn-in mittens, all-wool socks, and the Maine Auto Sweater, designed for duck hunting and automobile riding. Bean also designed the Deer Toter. The Toter, consisting of a frame constructed on a bicycle wheel, made the task of transporting a dead deer much easier. It quickly became an extremely popular item for hunters. Over the years, Bean included even more equipment that was both practical and innovative, including items such as the Bean Sandwich Spreader, hunting knives, camping equipment, and an extensive line of clothing.

Bean did not believe in forcing unnecessary items on his customers. He frequently advised customers to return their Maine Hunting shoes for reworking or replacement—a practice that the company continues today. At the suggestion that he sell expensive eiderdown coats, Bean claimed that buying such a product would be a waste of the purchaser's money.

## Quality Customer Service

Treating customers well became a hallmark of Bean's business strategy. He kept his company open 24 hours a day, aware that hunters and fishermen frequently need equipment or a license in the middle of the night. He listened to and addressed every complaint about the quality of his merchandise. As noted on the L.L. Bean, Inc. website, his approach, often called "L.L. Bean's golden rule" to his dealings with customers was simple: "Sell good merchandise at a reasonable profit, treat your customers like human beings, and they will always come back for more." This formula met with obvious success: the Aga Khan, Bernard Baruch, Doris Day, Robert S. McNamara, Eleanor Roosevelt, Babe Ruth, Amy Vanderbilt, and Ted Williams bought their clothing and sports equipment from Bean.

Bean's initial three-page marketing brochure eventually expanded to become a 12-page catalog describing items such as the Maine Hunting Shoe, the Maine Cruising shoe, and the Maine Duck-Hunting Book. Over the years, the Bean Catalog (of which Bean was said to be particularly proud) was enlarged to include descriptions of 400 products, arranged in no apparent order. Its prose style was as clear, simple, straightforward, and unadorned as the manner of its originator. In one instance, Bean described a product as featuring a whistle "loud enough to be heard at a great distance." By 1967, the year of Bean's death, the L.L. Bean Catalog contained 100 pages.

The two books written by Bean, *Hunting, Fishing and Camping,* (published in 1942) and *My Story: the Autobiography of a Down-East Merchant,* (published in 1960), were also listed in the company catalog. The former sold 150,000 copies and included duplicate chapters, enabling the reader to tear out sections as needed (especially for use outdoors) while retaining a whole copy of the book. The book had run through twenty editions by 1963.

## A Successful Company

Reports of Bean's personal attention to customer service and the practicality, price, and quality of his company's products drew attention to the growing business. Bean and his company soon were featured in national magazines. People were attracted to the folksy image and charmed by the catalog, and soon both attention and sales began to increase.

The success of Bean's business strategy is reflected in the increase in profits between 1924 and the 1960s. In 1924, the company had been operating for 12 years, had twenty-four employees on its payroll, and posted $135,000 in sales for the year. In 1937, sales of $1 million were recorded. By 1950, the company had more than 100 employees and achieved sales of nearly $2 million. By 1964, sales reached $3 million and profits were $70,000. However, despite the considerable profits, Bean was opposed to expansion, fearing that his customers would dislike change and its implied loss of personal customer service.

Despite his increasing age, and frequent trips to Florida, Bean remained actively involved in the business. He continued to run the company with the assistance of his two sons and two grandsons. He continued to edit and proofread his catalog, checking galleys of the 100-page book the week before he died. The catalog was mailed to the public on the day following his funeral.

At the time of Bean's death in Popano Beach, Florida on February 5, 1967, L.L. Bean, Inc. was a $4,000,000 business. It remains family-owned and family-operated. The company retains its address on Main Street in Freeport, Maine, and is one of the most popular tourist attractions in the state, drawing several million people to its doors each year. In the late 1990s, the company was being run by Bean's grandson, Leon Gorman. Gorman has brought the company up-to-date in business practices, by computerizing the mailing lists, increasing the number of catalogs mailed, and modernizing the retail store.

Through its catalogs, Freeport-based retail store, and eight stores in Japan it sells more than 16,000 products to more than 3.5 million customers worldwide. The company upholds its 100% quality product guarantee, and continues to refund money or repair products—even those purchased many years ago. Perhaps most important, L.L. Bean, Inc. continues the dedication to high-quality products and customer satisfaction that personified its founder.

## Further Reading

Garaty, John A., and Mark C. Carnes, *Dictionary of American Biography,* Supplement Eight, 1966-1970, American Council of Learned Societies, 1988.
*Fortune,* April 5, 1993, p. 112.
*New York Times,* February 7, 1967, p. 39.
*Newsweek,* February 20, 1967.
*Time,* February 17, 1967, p. 90; February 20, 1967, p. 73.
*U.S. News and World Report,* March 25, 1985, p. 61.
"The Story of L.L. Bean," *Welcome to L.L. Bean,* http://www.llbean.org (March 8, 1999). □

# Max Beerbohm

**In the early decades of the twentieth century, Max Beerbohm (1872–1956) was a well-known carica-**

**turist, drama critic, and essayist, one of England's most popular—and at times, much pilloried—men of letters.**

Born in London on August 24, 1872, Henry Maximilian Beerbohm was the last of several children of a Lithuanian-born grain merchant, Julius Ewald Beerbohm. His mother was Eliza Draper Beerbohm, the sister of Julius's late first wife. It was a well-to-do London family, and Max grew up with the four sisters from his father's second marriage. He was also close to four half-siblings, one of whom, Herbert Beerbohm Tree, was already a renowned stage actor when Max was a child.

## An Undergraduate Prodigy

Beerbohm attended the Charterhouse School, a respected private academy for boys, and did reasonably well there. As a teen he became known for his wit and talent for sketching hilarious caricatures of his teachers and classmates. In 1890, he began at Merton, a college of Oxford University. Though he was an unenthusiastic student academically, Beerbohm became a well-known figure in campus social circles. He also began submitting articles and caricatures to London publications, which were met enthusiastically. By 1894, already a rising star in English letters, he left Oxford without a degree.

Through an acquaintanceship with an outstanding young illustrator and writer, Aubrey Beardsley, Beerbohm became involved with a controversial and acclaimed journal called the *Yellow Book,* upon its launch in 1894. For its first issue he penned "The Pervasion of Rouge," a satirical look at cosmetics, which were still considered somewhat disreputable for women. Beerbohm praised them for their ultimate good in terminating "the reign of terror of nature." This essay was singled out for vilification as "decadent," and subsequent issues of the *Yellow Book* containing his work, were roundly condemned by the establishment.

## First Book

In 1895, Beerbohm went to America for several months as secretary to Tree's theatrical company. He was fired when he spent far too many hours polishing the business correspondence. There he became engaged to an American actress of the troupe, Grace Conover, a relationship that lasted several years. Returning to England, Beerbohm found success with his first book, a collection of essays he had written while still at Oxford and published by Lane in 1896. *The Works of Max Beerbohm* launched his career spectacularly. "Replete with mock-scholarly footnotes and biographical information, *The Works* epitomizes Beerbohm's penchant for deflating pretentiousness with satiric imitation," opined Ann Adams Cleary in the *Dictionary of Literary Biography.* "Anything large—ideas, ideals, literary works, London crowds—caused him dismay."

In his first book, the 23-year-old Beerbohm announced gravely that he would now retire from letters, having said all there was to say. Of course, he did not. He penned his first piece of fiction, "The Happy Hypocrite," published in the *Yellow Book* in 1897. The following year, the esteemed playwright and essayist, George Bernard Shaw, gave up his drama critic's post at the *Saturday Review,* and Beerbohm assumed the duties. The *Saturday Review* was undergoing a resurgence of popularity under its new owner, the writer Frank Harris, who would later become a close friend of Beerbohm's. It was Shaw, in his final *Review* piece, who bestowed upon Beerbohm the lasting epithet, "the incomparable Max."

True to form, Beerbohm's first review was titled "Why I Ought Not To Have Become a Dramatic Critic." For the next twelve years, he wrote over 453 pieces of drama criticism. His own experiences and connections in the London theater world made him relatively immune from awe when it came to the writers, directors, or performers. "His impressionistic criticism, always entertaining, was often wittily contemptuous of the pretensions of players, playwrights, and playgoers alike," declared Cleary in her *Dictionary of Literary Biography* essay. Many of these articles were published in the 1924 volume *Around Theatres.* Later collections, brought forth several years after Beerbohm's death, include *More Theatres 1898-1903* from 1969 and *Last Theatres 1904-1910,* dating from 1970. Volumes of his essays—sequels to *The Works of Max Beerbohm*—appeared as 1899's *More* and *Yet Again,* issued in 1910.

## Distinguished by Prose and Pen

At Charterhouse, Beerbohm had learned Latin, and he would later say the classical language training was of great importance to him as a writer. A background in Latin, Beerbohm wrote in an essay titled "Lytton Strachey," published in *Mainly on the Air,* was "essential to the making of a decent style," he asserted, because "English is an immensely odd and irregular language." He expounded on that thought in a sentence that made clear his intent: "There are few who can so wield it as to make their meaning clear without prolixity—and among those few, none who has not been well-grounded in Latin."

Aside from his talents as a devastatingly adept and witty writer, Beerbohm also enjoyed a burgeoning career as a caricaturist. His subjects were the literary giants of English letters, British politicians, and the royal family. In these comical drawings, Beerbohm satirized the foibles of friends and dignitaries alike. A much-reproduced one of Oscar Wilde—a friend of Beerbohm's—helped launch this side of his career in 1894, just before Wilde was jailed on charges of sexual misconduct.

Beerbohm enjoyed numerous exhibitions of his drawings in private London galleries like the Leicester. Kenneth Baker, writing in the *Spectator* in 1997, asserted that Beerbohm's caricatures "single-handedly ... ended the long period of Victorian servility." The art of caricature, Baker went on to explain, had been extremely popular in eighteenth-century London, when print shops sold images of the royal family that went so far as to mock imagined sexual perversions. But during the Victorian era, English culture grew far more constricted and conservative, and political figures were depicted only as dignified personages. "As for the Queen, after 1870 any irreverent cartoons were tantamount to treason," Baker wrote in the *Spectator.* "Max Beerbohm helped to put an end to all this." Most of this artistic output was published in book form: *Rossetti and His Circle,* issued in 1922. It is considered representative of Beerbohm at the peak of his energies as a caricaturist.

## Beerbohm and the Duke of Windsor

Prime Minister Benjamin Disraeli and Edward VII were favorite targets of Beerbohm's pen. In 1923, another show of his work was held at the Leicester. Included was a caricature of the heir to England's throne, the man who later became the Duke of Windsor. The prince was still an enthusiastic bachelor as his brothers settled down into marriage, and Beerbohm's Leicester show exhibited "Long Choosing and Beginning Late," a drawing which presented an elderly prince marrying the daughter of his boardinghouse-keeper, complete with the *Times* of London newspaper announcement. It caused a great stir, and newspapers decried Beerbohm for his disrespect to the throne; one even portended this as "The End of Max Beerbohm."

In response, Beerbohm removed the drawing from the exhibition, and a few years later it was sold to a private party. Remarkably, in 1936 the actual Prince of Wales, by then King Edward VIII, abdicated his throne in order to marry an American divorcee, Wallis Simpson, whose mother had once run a boardinghouse in Baltimore, Maryland.

Beerbohm mocked the royal family in other ways. During the reign of the Duke of Windsor's father, George V, the court was known for its confining, and rather colorless atmosphere. For friends' eyes only, Beerbohm once penned a verbal duel between two courtiers that read, in part, "the King is duller than the Queen . . . Oh no, the Queen is duller than the King." Someone passed it to the royal family, and it was said that the jest kept Beerbohm from the honor of knighthood for twenty years. But Beerbohm also told one of his biographers, S. N. Behrman, that the Windsor family owned several of his caricatures of their ancestors for their own private amusement.

## Moved to Italy

Beerbohm had become a well-known figure in London literary circles. In 1908, he became engaged to Florence Kahn, an acclaimed actress from Memphis, Tennessee who was then touring England. They married in 1910, and Beerbohm gave up his post at the *Saturday Review.* He and his wife moved to a home called Villino Chiaro in Rapallo, Italy. At the time, Italy was a very inexpensive place to live, added to its bounteous geographic attributes. Beerbohm, however, never learned to speak Italian in his five decades as an expatriate.

In Rapallo he began writing fiction in earnest. His first and only novel, *Zuleika Dobson,* was published in 1911 and met with great success. Set at Oxford, it is a comic tale of a femme fatale visitor who lays waste to the entire male student population. The following year, a volume of Beerbohm's literary parodies, *A Christmas Garland, Woven by Max Beerbohm,* was published. It contained essays on the holiday season that mimicked the style of some of the greatest living writers of the day: Joseph Conrad, Thomas Hardy, Rudyard Kipling, George Bernard Shaw, and H. G. Wells. Another of Beerbohm's literary parodies was published in 1946 and mocked the style of Henry James. *The Mote in the Middle Distance* offers up "James's convoluted syntax within a trivial context," explained Cleary in the *Dictionary of Literary Biography,* as "Jamesian children lengthily consider the moral ramifications of peeking in Christmas stockings."

## An Eminent Retirement

The Beerbohms returned to England in 1915 on account of World War I, but were back in Rapallo by 1919. That same year, another book of fiction, *Seven Men,* was published. This work contained short-story profiles of six fictional characters; Beerbohm himself being the seventh. One of them, "Enoch Soames," followed the tragicomic tale of a failed writer, certain that history would correct the judgment of his peers. He struck a bargain with the devil in order to time-travel to the British Museum reading room in 1997, where he was appalled to find even more vicious negative assessments of his work.

Beerbohm more or less retired in the mid-1920s, and enjoyed the publication of a ten-volume series of his writings and caricatures. It bore the already-used, though now more appropriate title, *The Works of Max Beerbohm.* These were brought forth between 1922 and 1928 by Heinemann, his longtime publisher. By now Beerbohm was in his fifties. He returned to England around 1936 when his wife was cast

in a revival of *Peer Gynt* on the London stage. Beerbohm resumed writing essays when the British Broadcasting Corporation (BBC) invited him to give regular broadcasts. The success of these programs made Beerbohm a well-known emeritus of British humor. They were collected in the 1946 work, *Mainly on the Air.*

In 1939, Beerbohm finally received the title of "Sir" when he was knighted by King George VI. He and Florence remained in England throughout World War II. His humorous radio broadcasts helped to improve the morale of Britain's war-torn populace. In 1942, the Maximilian Society was created in his honor, upon the occasion of his seventieth birthday. Formed by a London drama critic, it boasted 70 distinguished members, and planned to add one more fan of Beerbohm's on each successive birthday. Their first get-together feted him with a banquet and the gift of seventy bottles of wine.

Beerbohm's wife died in 1951, and for the next few years a German woman named Elisabeth Jungmann looked after the ailing writer. They married in secret just a few weeks before he died on May 20, 1956 in Rapallo. His ashes lie in an urn at London's St. Paul's Cathedral. The most recent collection of his art, *Max Beerbohm's Caricatures,* was published in 1997.

## Further Reading

Behrman, S. N. *Portrait of Max: An Intimate Memoir of Sir Max Beerbohm,* Random House, 1960.
*Cyclopedia of World Authors,* edited by Frank N. Magill, Salem Press, 1997.
*Dictionary of Literary Biography, Volume 34: British Novelists, 1890-1929: Traditionalists,* edited by Thomas F. Staley, Gale Research, 1984.
*Dictionary of Literary Biography, Volume 100: Modern British Essayists,* edited by William Blissett, Gale Research, 1990.
*Spectator,* October 25, 1997. □

# Vincent Bendix

**Vincent Bendix (1881–1945) invented the starter drive first used in automobiles in 1914. He earned the name "The King of Stop and Go" as the result of his work on the starter drive and the four-wheel braking system. He was a leader in the aviation industry, and his innovations and business savvy helped to create a multi-faceted manufacturing company.**

Vincent Bendix was born August 12, 1881, in Moline, Illinois. His father, Jann, a Swedish Methodist Episcopal minister, changed the family name from Bengtson to Bendix when he moved with his wife, Alma Danielson, to the United States from Amaland, Sweden. Soon after Bendix's birth, the family moved to Chicago, which had such a thriving Swedish population that it was

## King of Go

Until Bendix's innovation, people had to start their cars by cranking them by hand, which was a nuisance in addition to being messy and often dangerous. A few other cars had mechanical starters, but Bendix's worked much better. However, to make his starters, Bendix needed a triple thread screw that was expensive and difficult to get because they had to be manufactured by hand. In 1913, Bendix located an outfit called the Eclipse Machine Company, in Elmira, New York, that used the exact triple thread screw that he needed. He contracted with the company to manufacture the parts, and started marketing his starter drive under the slogan: "The mechanical hand that cranks your car."

The starter revolutionized driving. About 5,500 were installed in the 1914 Chevrolet Baby Grand touring car. By 1919, 1.5 million—nearly every car on the market—had a Bendix starter drive.

## King of Stop

The years following the success of the starter drive were difficult for Bendix. He bought the Winkler-Grimm Wagon Company in South Bend, Indiana, planning to produce fire engines, but his plans were bungled when a big bid fell through and he had to sell the plant. A year later, he divorced his first wife. Then, in 1922, Bendix's father was killed when a car with unreliable brakes hit him on a Chicago street corner. "The accident caused Bendix to focus on the inadequacy of automobile brakes, and he vowed to devise a better braking system," wrote Rebecca Wolfe in the *St. Joseph Valley Record.* That same year, Bendix married Elizabeth Channon of Chicago. They were divorced ten years later and he reportedly had to pay her $2 million as a settlement.

In 1923, Bendix began to turn personal tragedy into another automotive innovation. He bought the shoe brake patents of French engineer Henri Perrot and took over Perrot's contract with General Motors. Thus Bendix Engineering Works introduced the first four-wheel brake system, which promised to provide cars with a reliable way to stop.

Business was brisk for Bendix, who immediately began trying to expand his company. In 1928, he tried to take over the Eclipse Machine Company, but found the management leery of his extravagant ways, so he enlisted the help of General Motors to negotiate the deal. In the next few years, more than 100 companies came under the umbrella of Bendix, including the Pioneer Instrument Company, Scintilla Magneto Company, Stromberg Carburetor Company, Jaeger Watch, and Hydraulic Brakes.

He was busy expanding his own personal empire as well. In 1928, Bendix paid $3 million for the Potter Palmer mansion on Chicago's Lake Shore Drive. He planned to construct a $25 million hotel, but instead was forced to sell the property, which he had filled with fine art, including Rembrandt paintings. Also in 1928, Bendix bought the former estate of automobile pioneer Clem Studebaker in South Bend, Indiana. He reportedly paid $30,000 simply to erect imported French gates at the entrance of what became known as Chateau Bendix. Despite the home's somewhat

dubbed the "Swedish capital." Even as a child, Bendix was interested in engineering and invented a chainless bicycle when he was just 13 years old.

At the age of 16, Bendix moved to New York City and found work running a hospital elevator. He helped out in the hospital's maintenance department as well, and gained a working knowledge of electricity. While in New York, he held a succession of jobs, including working in a lawyer's office, as a handyman in bicycle shops and garages, as an accountant for a brewery, and for the Lackawanna Railroad Company. In 1901, Bendix found a job working for Glenn Curtiss, who would later become a famous airplane builder. At the time, Curtiss was developing the Torpedo motorcycle. Bendix worked on motorcycles as well and developed his own experimental bike. He attended night school to study engineering, learning about internal combustion engines.

Bendix married in 1902 and moved back to Chicago five years later to take a job as a sales manager for the Holmsman Automobile Company, which at the time was a leader in the field of auto buggies. During this time, he designed his own car, the Bendix Motor Buggy, which he had built by the Triumph Motor Company in Cragin, Illinois. He sold around 7,000 cars, but Bendix was financially devastated when the company went into bankruptcy. Still, his limited success and experience gave him an idea for a mechanical starter for the motor car.

remote location, it drew huge crowds to lavish parties, which included golfing at a nine-hole course, and swimming in an electrically-lit pool.

The following year, Bendix spent $250,000 to buy yet another house—the Ocean Front Estate in Palm Beach, Florida. At the same time, he donated money to a Chinese and Swedish expedition to Inner Mongolia and China. He paid a Swedish man $65,000 to buy a Buddhist temple and bring it to the U.S. When that proved impossible, Bendix instead funded a team of Chinese architects from Peking to copy the Golden Pavilion of Jehol and rebuild it at Chicago's 1932-34 Century of Progress Exposition. The $250,000 pavilion was displayed once more at the New York World's Fair before being donated in 1943 to Oberlin College.

## Bendix Aviation Corporation

Despite his personal excesses, the Bendix Corporation continued to grow. Even though aviation sales were only eight percent of the company's revenue in 1929, Bendix renamed his company the Bendix Aviation Corporation. Although 1929 and the early 1930s marked the beginning of the Great Depression, Bendix managed to keep his company afloat by pioneering new inventions. During the Second World War he developed products to aid the war effort, like a radio direction finder for ships. The British and French were big Bendix customers during the war, and Bendix products like the pressure carburetor for airplane engines gave U.S. air troops an advantage as well.

Ironically, Bendix himself was fearful of airplanes and only flew about six times in his entire life. However, he saw huge potential in the field and, in 1931, agreed to bankroll the Bendix Transcontinental Air Races. The races, designed to foster development by airplane engineers, also helped to popularize flying. It drew such aviators as Amelia Earhart to compete for the $25,000 prize and Bendix Trophy. The first winner of the competition, Major James H. Doolittle, flew from Los Angeles to Cleveland with a record speed of 223 miles per hour. The flight took the pilot nine hours and ten minutes. In 1962, Captain John T. Walton won the competition's final race, flying from Los Angeles to New York in two hours, at an average speed of 1,215 miles per hour. The Bendix Trophy found a home at the National Air and Space Museum in Washington, D.C.

## Financial Decline

Bendix's extravagant lifestyle eventually caught up with him. In June 1939, he was forced to declare bankruptcy and sell off his personal things. At the time, he listed liabilities of $14 million and assets of only $1 million. He told *Time* magazine in 1939, "This is the biggest blow of my life." "His list of liabilities included unpaid bills and dues from some of the most exclusive and prestigious clubs, restaurants, and hotels across the country," Wolfe reported. "His personal life was scrutinized and the last of his belongings dragged out from under him. It was the complete demise of one of South Bend's greatest tycoons," said Rebecca Wolfe in the *St. Joseph Valley Record.*

For a long time, General Motors had been amassing Bendix Corporation stock. In 1937, it began taking over the company, changing its entire structure when word got out that a quarter of a million dollars a month was being lost with Bendix as plant manager. Bendix remained chairman of the board of Bendix Aviation until 1942, but then left to start yet another business.

The newest venture, Bendix Helicopter, Inc., was begun in 1944. Bendix hoped to produce a four-passenger helicopter when World War II ended. However, he died unexpectedly of a coronary thrombosis March 27, 1945 at his home in New York City. Bendix was 63. After his death, plans for the helicopter were abandoned.

## Bendix's Work Continues

The original Bendix Corporation continued to thrive without its founder. By 1976, it was named one of the five best-managed companies in America. According to Hope Lampert's *Till Death Do Us Part,* the company "owned an industrial winch-making company, a forest products company, and some timberland; Bendix made Fram filters, Autolite spark plugs, airplane wheels and steering gears. It made cutting tools for the Big Three car manufacturers. Bendix was strong and financially healthy."

A 1983 takeover was so controversial that two books, including Lampert's, were written about it. Bendix Corporation was bought for $1.8 billion by Allied Corporation, later known as AlliedSignal. This company produces chemicals and automotive safety equipment. By 1996, AlliedSignal had 36,000 employees around the world and annual sales of $2,377 million.

## Further Reading

Cunningham, Mary, with Fran Schumer, *Powerplay: What Really Happened at Bendix,* Linden Press/Simon and Schuster, 1984.

Garraty, John A., and Mark C. Carnes, *American National Biography,* Oxford University Press, 1999.

Lampert, Hope, *Till Death Do Us Part: Bendix Vs. Martin Marietta,* Harcourt Brace Jovanovich, 1983.

*Automotive News,* April 29, 1996.

*New York Times,* March 28, 1945.

*Scientific American,* May 1938.

*Time,* June 5, 1939.

AlliedSignal, http://www.alliedsignal.com:80 (March 19, 1999).

National Aviation Hall of Fame, http://www.nationalaviation.org (March 19, 1999). □

# William Bernbach

**William Bernbach (1911–1982) is responsible for creating many dramatic changes in the advertising industry after World War II. His gift for simple, yet memorable advertising came from his intense love of philosophy and literature. His campaigns were so successful that many are still cited today.**

ernbach was born in New York City on August 13, 1911 to Jacob and Rebecca Bernbach. As a child he enjoyed reading and writing verse and grew up with an appreciation of art. With the exception of a two-year tour of duty during World War II, Bernbach never strayed far from his roots in New York City. He attended New York University, receiving a bachelor's degree in literature in 1933. Bernbach also pursued studies in art, philosophy, and business administration that would serve him well during his career.

## Starting at the Bottom

After graduation, Bernbach learned quickly that job hunting during the Depression years would be a challenge. Although he had decided upon advertising as his preferred field, he was unable to obtain work in that line. Bernbach started at the bottom of the corporate ladder when he found work in the mailroom of Schenley Distillers Company. With his mind focused on an advertising career, the young man found himself whiling away his hours creating ads for his employer. He submitted one of his ads to Schenley's in-house advertising department but received no response. After a time, he saw his words appear exactly as he had written them, in the *New York Times*. In fact, so much time had passed since his ad's submission that Schenley's ad men had lost the identity of its creator. Fortunately, it did not take Bernbach long to make sure that Lewis Rosenthiel, the president of Schenley's, learned of the ad's true origin. Rosenthiel appreciated Bernbach's creative spirit, not to mention his brazenness in approaching him about his own

intellectual property. He gave Bernbach a raise and placed him in the advertising department.

During the 1939-40 New York World's Fair Bernbach worked as a ghostwriter for the promotion department. When the fair ended he joined the William H. Weintraub ad agency. With the onset of World War II, Bernbach put his career on hold and served for two years in the army. In 1943, he returned to New York and worked as the director of postwar planning for Coty, Inc until 1944. He left Coty to become vice president of advertising for Grey Advertising, Inc. From 1945 to 1949.

One of Bernbach's successes at Grey was his ad campaign for Ohrbach's Department Store. He took this budget-priced store, with its small advertising budget, and made it a household name through creative, humorous advertising. His ads were designed to be straightforward attention-getters—ones that would catch the consumer's eye while keeping the product name in front of the public. Bernbach believed that a successful advertising campaign was one in which the public remembered the product as well as the ad.

## Opens Own Agency

During his years at Grey, Bernbach's creative talents were challenged by customers who insisted on providing their own input on ad development. He was painfully aware that Madison Avenue, where ad-men were afraid to say no to their client, was hopelessly mired in conformity. Bernbach was beginning to realize that input from the client is vital, but the ad agency bears ultimate responsibility for the message. He fulfilled the dream of establishing his own agency when he found a kindred spirit in Ned Doyle, another vice president at Grey whose philosophy mirrored his own. On June 1, 1949, Doyle and Bernbach joined forces with advertising executive Maxwell Dane and formed Doyle, Dane & Bernbach (DDB). The mix was perfect: Dane was the organizer and administered the company; Doyle was the financial and marketing wizard; and Bernbach was given full control over the advertising that the agency produced. He acted in the role of president from 1949 until 1967 and oversaw all ads before they were presented to any client. In their endeavor, the founders of Doyle, Dane & Bernbach brought a new philosophy to the advertising world.

The agency was immediately successful. Bernbach brought Ohrbach's, his client from Grey, with him to DDB. He soon added other clients to their growing list. One of his popular New York clients was the Henry S. Levy bakery. Bernbach's "You don't have to be Jewish to love Levy's" ads raised product awareness throughout the entire New York City area, making Levy's the biggest seller of rye bread in the city. With the Levy ad, as with the ads for Ohrbach's before it, Bernbach gave advertising depth by making it three dimensional: raising awareness, using humor, and selling the product.

Bernbach's successes continued. One of his best-remembered efforts were Avis Rent a Car. Putting Avis second next to Hertz was a stroke of genius. The U.S. public loves an underdog and in 1963 when Avis began declaring openly, "When you're No. 2, you try harder," Hertz began looking over its shoulder. The Avis ad campaign was directly responsible for increasing Avis's market share by 28 percent, and closing the gap with frontrunner Hertz.

The other phenomenally successful ad campaign to spring from Bernbach's fertile mind was for the German automobile manufacturer, Volkswagen. In 1959, Bernbach designed an ad for the Volkswagen Beetle, placing the car in an upper corner of the ad surrounded by a sea of white space and placing just two words at the bottom of the ad: "Think Small." The ad was totally different from other automobile ads and sales of the VW Beetle soared up to 500,000 cars in a single season.

Clients flocked to DDB. Other successes included El Al Airlines; Polaroid, and Rheingold Beer. Volkswagen's ads were so successful, they remained a client for over 40 years. In 1968, Bernbach was elevated to chairman and chief executive officer, where he remained until 1974. He advanced to chairman of the executive committee and chief executive officer from 1974 until 1976. In 1976, Bernbach celebrated his 65th birthday and, according to the policies of the corporation, he retired. He was asked, however, to return as chairman of the executive committee, where he remained until 1982, overseeing the advertising activities of the firm. The success of DDB remains unparalleled in advertising history. Starting with $1 million in billing during its first year, by 1982 DDB billings has risen to approximately $1 billion.

## An Unconventional Philosophy

Bernbach's advertising philosophy went contrary to convention. His ads were always fresh, simple, and intelligent, yet exuded energy. Often self-deprecating, they were also frequently humorous, always tasteful, and artistic. He used shadows in photos to make a point, and especially liked working with dark shadows. He advocated a soft-sell technique to draw in the consumer that resulted in the product not getting lost in the advertising. If Bernbach believed a product could not live up to its advertising, he would not take on the client.

Bernbach's love of philosophy inevitably led to his study of human motivation. He realized that emotions such as love, hate, greed, hope, fear, etc., drove people to action and he tried to apply these emotions to his advertising in order to get the reader's attention. Bernbach was clear in his belief that his audience was intelligent and literate. He respected creativity in people and encouraged those in the advertising field to use their wits. He often said "Everything you write . . . everything on a page—every word, every graphic symbol, every shadow—should further the message you're trying to convey." Bernbach frequently addressed audiences of advertising executives to explain that advertising is not formulaic: a successful ad campaign is not run on mathematical equations where every ad follows the same steps. Creative advertising was, to Bernbach, composed more of intuition and a sense of artistry than of analytical prowess.

## The Personal Side

Bernbach married Evelyn Carbone on June 5, 1938. They had two sons, John Lincoln and Paul. Throughout his life, Bernbach developed an appreciation for art and literature. He was a quiet man who enjoyed reading poetry and listening to jazz and classical music with his wife. He appreciated creative people and helped open an industry to talented people from a variety of ethnic and religious backgrounds.

Bernbach's love for the arts and philosophy immersed him in an active social life outside of DDB. He was a Distinguished Adjunct Professor at New York University and vice chairman of Lincoln Center's film committee. Bernbach was on the board of directors and a member of the executive committee of the Legal Aid Society, the Salk Institute for Biological Studies, and the Harper's Magazine Foundation. He was on the board of directors of the International Eye Foundation, Mary Manning Walsh Home, Menninger Foundation, and Friend of American Art in Religion, Inc., and chairman of the board and executive committee member of the Municipal Arts Society.

During the last years of his long and prolific life, Bernbach struggled with leukemia. He lost the battle on October 2, 1982 and died in the Bronx, New York, at the age of 71. He is remembered as a driving force in the advertising field, one who was responsible for placing creative people in positions previously held by skilled but uncreative businessmen. By doing this, he changed the nature of U.S. advertising.

## Further Reading

*Advertising Age,* October 11, 1982, p. 80; August 11, 1986.
*Forbes,* June 20, 1983.
*Independent,* June 1, 1998.
Encyclopedia Britannica Online, http://members.eb.com (February 22, 1999).
William Bernbach, http://uts.cc.utexas.edu/~hyeong/adman .html (February 19, 1999). □

# John Berryman

**The life of John Berryman (1914–1972) is at the center of his poetry. Dealing with obsession, tragedy, desire, ironic comedy, and the deep pain of life itself, Berryman's poetry is both brilliant and tormented. With *The Dream Songs,* which took him 13 years to complete, Berryman claimed his place as one of the most innovative and important American poets of the twentieth century.**

John Berryman was born John Allyn Smith, Jr., in McAlester, Oklahoma, on October 25, 1914, the first child of John Allyn Smith and Martha Little Smith. Berryman's father had left his childhood home in Minnesota to relocate to Oklahoma, where he met and married Little, a schoolteacher. After ten years working as a banker in Okla-

homa, Smith moved his family, which by then included a second son, Robert Jefferson (born 1917), to Florida in order to benefit from an economic boom occurring at that time. Unfortunately, by the mid-1920s the boom was over, and Smith's business ventures in land speculation failed.

With his business career in shambles, Smith became depressed and withdrawn. His relationship with his wife, never a storybook romance, became even more unstable, and his wife began a relationship with John Berryman, the Smith's landlord. Depressed and intoxicated, Smith committed suicide by gunshot on June 26, 1926. Three months later, his widow married Berryman. Young John was soon officially adopted by Berryman, and he took his new step-father's name. The events surrounding his father's death, which occurred when Berryman was twelve, profoundly affected his life and his poetry.

The family moved to New York in late 1926, and in 1928 Berryman enrolled in South Kent School in Connecticut, a boarding school known for its competitive athletic programs rather than its academic excellence. Berryman, who had little ability and no interest in sports, did not fit in well at the school. His lack of coordination, along with a severe case of acne, made him an easy target for bullies. On March 7, 1931, he attempted suicide. Despite these troubles, Berryman excelled academically at South Kent, and became the first boy in the school's history to graduate early, not needing to complete his last term.

In 1932, Berryman entered Columbia College (later Columbia University) where he came under the influence of poet and scholar Mark Van Doren, who became both a father figure and a mentor. Berryman was a diligent student and began taking poetry very seriously; he had several poems and reviews published in the *Columbia Review* and *The Nation*. Upon graduating from Columbia College with a degree in English, Berryman earned the honor of being named a Kellett Fellow, which allowed him to study at Clare College, in Cambridge, England, for two years. During this time, he met such writers at W. B. Yeats, T. S. Eliot, W. H. Auden, and Dylan Thomas. During his second year, Berryman won the Oldham Shakespeare Scholarship, a prestigious award, and published several poems in the *Southern Review*.

## Early Poems

In 1939, Berryman found himself back in New York, working as a part-time poetry editor for *The Nation* and an instructor in English at Wayne University in Detroit (now Wayne State University). In December 1939, Berryman was hospitalized for exhaustion and symptoms diagnosed as epilepsy. Throughout his life, he would continue to battle for emotional and mental peace, a battle made more difficult by his increasing reliance on alcohol. In 1940, he accepted a teaching position at Harvard University, and his first poems were published, along with works by Mary Barnard, Randall Jarrell, W. R. Moses, and George Marion O'Donnell in the collection, *Five Young American Poets*. Berryman published these same poems separately in 1942. He received recognition for the technical preciseness of his verse, and some critics praised his impersonal style. Other reviewers felt that Berryman was too structured, that he cared too much about form and not enough about content, and that he lacked emotion, depth, and substance in his writing.

## Princeton Years

On October 24, 1942, while at Harvard, Berryman married Eileen Patricia Mulligan. The next year Berryman left Harvard but failed to immediately secure another desirable position. For part of 1943, he taught Latin and English at a prep school. However, before the year ended, Berryman was invited by poet Richard Blackmur to join the faculty at Princeton University as an instructor in English. He spent the next ten years at Princeton.

After teaching for a year, Berryman spent two and a half years in an independent study of Shakespearean textual criticism. He was appointed to teach again in 1946. Berryman's circle of friends widened considerably during his time at Princeton, and he taught such writers as W. S. Merwin, Frederick Buechner, and William Arrowsmith. In the classroom, he quickly became famous for his charismatic teaching style. By the mid-1940s, he had also earned a reputation for his heavy drinking, womanizing, and unpredictable temperament that could shift from endearing to intimidating. It was clear to his close friends and students that his eccentric behavior was the manifestation of deep inner angst. As the 1940s progressed, Berryman used alcohol more and more to deal with his insecurities, confusion, and self-loathing.

*The Dispossessed* was published in 1948. This volume of Berryman's poems was filled with hopelessness and chaos, often using the European holocaust to reflect his personal struggles. The syntax was labored and the poems were often difficult to comprehend. Although several critics acknowledged Berryman's potential, he was once again criticized for spending too much energy on the technical forms of his verse and somehow missing any depth of feeling and senses. Despite the mixed reviews, Berryman received the Sherry Memorial Award from the Poetry Society of America.

In 1947, Berryman's poetry found its emotional voice in the verse he wrote about an extramarital affair with the wife of a Princeton graduate student. Not published until 1967, *Berryman's Sonnets,* provides a running commentary on his conflicting feelings of exhilaration, guilt, anxiety, and hope. The sonnets use a Petrarchan form and are often choppy and distorted; the innovative form allows the reader to feel the inner conflict of the obsessed lover. Berryman used the name Lise for the woman, whose real name was Chris; some scholars suggest that he was using an Elizabethan-style anagram for "lies." The sonnets were reissued posthumously in 1988 in *Collected Poems, 1937-1972* under the title of *Sonnets to Chris.*

### Homage to Mistress Bradstreet

Berryman's next work, *Homage to Mistress Bradstreet,* which he began in 1948, was first published in 1953 in the *Partisan Review,* and then in book form in 1956. The poem is based on the life of the seventeenth-century American poet, Anne Bradstreet. The poet summons forth Bradstreet and then proceeds to fall in love with her. What follows is a mixture of historical facts and artistic embellishment in which Berryman encounters and responds to the dead poet. The reader experiences Bradstreet as a tragic yet creative character who rebels against her father, her husband, and God, paralleling Berryman's own tragic, creative existence. The long poem contains 57 stanzas of eight rhymed lines and is divided into five sections: Berryman's invocation of Bradstreet, a Bradstreet monologue, a dialogue between the two poets, another Bradstreet monologue, and finally a peroration by Berryman. *Homage to Mistress Bradstreet* received high praise from critics, who hailed it as Berryman's most mature work to date, a successful attempt at the poetic style of *The Dispossessed.* Critics acknowledged Berryman, along with his friend and fellow poet Robert Lowell, as the best American poet since T. S. Eliot.

In 1950, Berryman taught at the University of Washington and then was appointed Elliston Professor of Poetry at the University of Cincinnati for the following academic year. In the same year he published a critical biography, *Stephen Crane,* considered by some reviewers as tortured prose that relied too heavily on Berryman's psychological model for literary interpretation. Other critics, however, thought it to be an important and noteworthy work. In the early 1950s, Berryman also continued his Shakespearean research. He wrote on Christopher Marlowe, Monk Lewis, Walt Whitman, Theodore Dreiser, and Saul Bellow. In 1950, he won the American Academy award for poetry.

### Poetry and Indulgence

Although Berryman's poetry writing and his teaching career were flourishing, his obsession with self-examination, growing dependence on alcohol, and notorious womanizing were putting a strain on his personal life. Although he sought help from a psychiatrist and tried group therapy, he found little relief from his inner conflict or his dependence on alcohol. In the fall of 1953, after ten years of marriage, his first wife left him.

In the spring of 1954, he taught at the Writers' Workshop at the University of Iowa, then spent the following summer at Harvard. His reputation as an intense, passionate, and charismatic teacher followed him from classroom to classroom. He returned to the University of Iowa in the fall, but was forced to resign after spending a night in jail. Returning home intoxicated one night, he could not find his key and attempted to force his way into the house. The landlord's wife called the police and Berryman was charged with disorderly conduct. He resigned two days later.

### Two Decades at the University of Minnesota

In 1955, Allan Tate, a poet Berryman deeply admired, invited him to the University of Minnesota. Berryman was appointed lecturer in humanities. This would be Berryman's home for the rest of his life. At the University of Minnesota Berryman became extremely interested in dream analysis, which he studied in-depth and which subsequently led to his greatest work, *The Dream Songs* (1969).

In 1956, one week after finalizing his divorce from his first wife, Berryman married 24-year-old Anne Levine. The relationship did not fare well, and the couple argued often. In 1957, Berryman was promoted to associate professor and participated in a State Department sponsored lecture tour to India. By the next year, back in Minnesota, he was hospitalized for exhaustion and nerves. He would be hospitalized at least once a year for the rest of his life. In 1959, after a year of legal separation, he and his wife divorced. Their son, Paul, was two years old. In 1961, Berryman married 22-year-old Kate Donahue; they had two children, Martha and Sara.

### Dream Songs

*The Dream Songs* was first published in two parts. *77 Dream Songs* (1964) earned Berryman the Pulitzer Prize. *His Toy, His Dream, His Rest* (1968), the sequel to *77 Song Dreams,* completed *The Dream Songs,* series, which was released in 1969, and earned the National Book Award and the Bollingen Prize. There are 385 songs, with each song composed of three six-line stanzas. The songs are an account of a character, Henry, who speaks of himself in first, second, and third person, and sometimes encounters a nameless friend who gives him usually ineffectual and often humorous advice. Although Berryman maintained that Henry was not himself but a white, middle-aged American man, sometimes appearing in blackface, who had suffered a tremendous loss, the poem is clearly a reflection of Berryman's own thoughts, obsessions, pain, and often darkly comic understanding of life. The songs are Berryman's own self-destructive life in a verse style unique to Berryman. The syntax is awkward and demanding of the reader, yet intense and moving.

## The Final Years

In 1969, Berryman was appointed Regents' Professor of Humanities, and Drake University bestowed upon him an honorary degree. With *The Dream Songs* Berryman was widely recognized as a great American poet. Unfortunately, his subsequent work lack the brilliance of *The Dream Songs*. In *Love and Fame* (1970) his return to lyric form brought forth verse that was sometimes witty and ironic and sometimes vulgar and offensive. He continued to abuse alcohol, and sometimes during his lectures, his words were thick and his emotions extreme due to the effects of his drinking. He checked himself into an alcohol rehabilitation center once in 1969 and three times in 1970. He penned *Recovery,* (1973) an autobiographical novel of a recovering alcoholic, which reviewers agreed was more important as an account of Berryman's personal life than as a novel. His last book of poems, *Delusions, Etc.,* contained individual poems that revealed Berryman at his best, but as a whole did not satisfy the critics nor compare in importance to his earlier works, *Homage to Mistress Bradstreet* and *Dream Songs.*

In 1971, Berryman was awarded a Senior Fellowship from the National Endowment for the Humanities, enabling him to complete his critical biography on Shakespeare. Unfortunately, he could not find his way out of the same despair and indulgence that made his poetry so unique and powerful. On January 7, 1972, still haunted by his own father's suicide and with his youngest daughter just six months old, Berryman ended his life by jumping from the Washington Avenue Bridge in Minneapolis, Minnesota.

## Further Reading

*American National Biography,* edited by John A. Garraty and Mark C. Carnes. Oxford University Press, 1999.
*Benet's Reader's Encyclopedia,* fourth ed., edited by Bruce Murphy, HarperCollins, 1996.
*Contemporary Authors,* edited by James G. Lesniak. Gale Research, 1992.
*Contemporary Literary Criticism,* edited by Roger Matuz, Gale Research, 1991.
*Cyclopedia of World Authors,* revised third ed., edited by Frank N. Magill. Salem Press, 1997.
*Dictionary of Literary Biography,* edited by Peter Quartermain. Gale Research, 1986.
*Oxford Companion to American Literature,* sixth ed., edited by James D. Hart. Oxford University Press, 1995.
*New Republic,* April 9, 1990. □

# Clarence Birdseye

**There really was a Clarence Birdseye (1886–1956). If he hadn't visited the Arctic, there may never have**

**been frozen TV dinners. Now he is recognized as a major innovator in the food industry.**

As a young scientist working in the frozen North, it didn't surprise Birdseye to note that freshly caught fish, when placed on the Arctic ice and exposed to the wind, immediately froze solid. What did surprise Birdseye was that the fish, if thawed and eaten much later, retained all of its fresh characteristics. This discovery was to create a new food industry and make Birdseye a millionaire. The youthful Birdseye had the courage to thaw out the rock hard fish weeks later and cook them for dinner, as an experiment. At the time, this was a real risk. He could have become very ill by eating "rotten" fish; but he didn't. Instead, the young naturalist found that the fish tasted almost the same as if they had been fresh, and with the same texture.

Clarence Birdseye was born in Brooklyn, New York on December 9, 1886. He attended Amherst College, with the intention of becoming a biologist. But he didn't graduate. Instead, he went to work for the U.S. Biological Survey as a field naturalist. His supervisors sent him to the Arctic to do research on the ways of the native Americans who lived there, and even to trade some furs.

The combination of ice, wind, and low temperatures in the Arctic froze anything left exposed almost instantly. Birdseye soon realized that such quick freezing of certain foods kept large crystals from forming. Slow freezing attempts had resulted in the formation of large crystals, transforming the food so that it could never be eaten. But if the freezing was accomplished quickly enough, there was no damage to the cellular structure of the food.

As a young scientist, Birdseye was making notes on his fascinating discovery. He also realized that he had the germ of a new business that could be very profitable. Throughout his life, Birdseye was a skilled businessman. He did more than create the modern frozen food industry. He also obtained almost 300 patents for various inventions, many of them in the fields of incandescent lighting, wood pulping, and infrared heating.

### Birdseye Seafoods was Born

Birdseye knew that he had discovered something very important, but he wasn't certain what. All he knew for sure was that he had the beginnings of what could be a very profitable business. A careful man, he continued to work in various federal departments from 1917 to 1925, while perfecting his freezing methods. All the time he knew that the public would clamor to pay for all the various types of foods they could enjoy if they didn't have to be obtained fresh. He knew that frozen foods would be in demand if he could figure out exactly how to accomplish the freezing.

In September 1922, while still employed by the government, Birdseye returned to New York City and formed his own company, Birdseye Seafoods, Inc. The company was far from an immediate success, as Birdseye continued his experiments with fish filets. He would freeze them, then thaw them, at his plant headquarters near the Fulton Fish Market in New York. He didn't have to eat every experiment because he already knew that the food would be safe to eat. He was trying to perfect a way to ensure the flavor and texture of the food.

### The Final Secret

At last Birdseye discovered the secret to safely freezing food. After two years of experimentation, he tried wax-packing dressed fish and other foods in cartons then freezing them between two flat, refrigerated surfaces under pressure. The "double plate" freezer was the solution. This technique quickly froze the foods solid with almost no damage at all to their cellular structure. Foods packaged and frozen in this new way were almost exactly the same when thawed weeks or months later. Birdseye quickly applied for, and was granted, a patent on the exclusive method.

Birdseye knew he had found the answer to safely preserving foods for an indefinite time, an answer that could make him a fortune. With this new technique safely patented, he decided to form another company. On July 3, 1924, he formed the General Seafood Corporation with some rich partners who believed in his process.

General Seafood was the beginning of a food industry that has since become massive. A look in the refrigerated section of any local grocery store will reveal a stunning variety of delicious frozen foods. There will be many types of fish, the food item that started it all, and dozens of meat and poultry foods as well as French fried potatoes, milkshakes, and complete breakfasts and dinners. There are even pizza combinations and other specialty frozen foods

waiting for consumers. Recently, chain hamburger and hot dog companies began supplying their products in frozen form to supermarkets. This huge industry began with the discoveries of Clarence Birdseye.

Birdseye was a hard worker who was always thinking of new ideas. Even as he was perfecting his freezing techniques, he was also working on other food items. In the late 1930s, he perfected and patented a new food dehydrating process. However, he was so busy with his frozen food ideas that he didn't begin marketing the dehydrating idea until 1946.

### Birdseye Built a Successful Company

Company success didn't happen overnight. The first retail sale of frozen foods occurred on March 6, 1930, in Springfield, Massachusetts. Birdseye called it the "Springfield Experiment Test Market." In his frozen food cases he included 26 different types of fish, meat, fruit, and vegetables. He posted a number of rather questionable signs on the frozen food display with words like "50 Below Zero," but people bought the new items. They loved the idea that they could take home, thaw, and eat foods that were otherwise not available to them at a reasonable price.

Premature thawing continued, however, to be a problem. Birdseye contacted the American Radiator Corporation. This company agreed to manufacture low-temperature retail display units that would hold the frozen food in markets. Markets agreed to display only Birds Eye products. In return, they were able to lease the units for about eight dollars per month. The new units would keep the foods solidly frozen until customers bought them.

Always on the lookout for ways to expand his business, Birdseye began to lease insulated railroad cars in 1944. These cars were specially designed for the nationwide shipment of his frozen food products. This final move assured the success of Birdseye's company.

By the 1950s, frozen food sales exceeded one billion dollars every year. About 64 percent of all retail food markets had frozen food areas. Pre-cooked foods or prepared frozen foods began to account for a majority of the sales. There were even "boil-in" bags of frozen food items, derived from Birdseye's original experiments. The Association of Food and Drug Officials in the United States adopted a standard for the handling of frozen foods, to insure that foods were not allowed to thaw between manufacture and consumption. By then, most airlines were using frozen foods that could be prepared as needed on airliners.

### Birdseye's Company Today

Today, Birds Eye, Inc. targets the growing wave of health-conscious consumers. They were the first to introduce "Custom Cuisine," a line of six varieties of vegetables and sauces to which meat is then added. They also introduced foil wrapping on boxed vegetables, which holds moisture ten times better than waxed paper. The Food and Drug Administration has acknowledged that frozen foods, when correctly handled and cooked, are as healthy as the same foods would be if cooked fresh. Birdseye had come to the same conclusion decades before. There are now children's frozen foods, "family size" portions, appetizers, meal kits, and snacks. The fast-paced lifestyles of modern consumers have encouraged the continued growth of the frozen food industry.

The process invented by Birdseye is still in widespread use. It preserves not only the flavor and texture of the foods, but also their nutritional value. Clarence Birdseye indirectly improved the health of almost everyone in the industrialized world by providing fresh food in a convenient way. Before his death in Springfield, Massachusetts, on October 8, 1956, at the age of 70, Birdseye realized that his discovery on the cold tundra of the Arctic had grown into a highly successful business.

### Further Reading

*A Sudden Chill,* Time Life Books, 1991.
*Compton's Interactive Encyclopedia.*
*Encarta Encyclopedia.* □

# Emily Blackwell

**Emily Blackwell (1826–1910) was a pioneer in the field of medicine. She co-founded the New York Infirmary for Women and Children in 1857 and served for three decades as head of its medical school.**

Although she lived most of her life in the shadow of her older sister, Emily Blackwell made significant contributions of her own to the world of medicine and medical education. Those who knew and worked with her described her as a superb practitioner and an inspirational teacher. The high professional standards Blackwell set for herself and her students were in large part responsible for opening the medical field to women and convincing an often skeptical—and sometimes hostile—public to accept the idea of female physicians.

### An Unconventional Childhood

The sixth of nine surviving children born to Samuel and Hannah Lane Blackwell on October 8, 1826, Emily Blackwell spent her early years in the bustling commercial and industrial seaport of Bristol, England. There Samuel prospered as the owner of a sugar refinery. Its success provided a comfortable existence for his large, close-knit family, which also included several of his unmarried sisters.

Both Samuel and his wife were deeply religious and instilled a similar devotion in their children. They also held fairly liberal political and social views for their day, as evidenced in part by their attitude toward education. During an era when girls were expected to master only the subjects that prepared them to be good wives and mothers, the Blackwells saw to it that their daughters as well as their sons studied mathematics, science, literature, and foreign languages. The parents also whetted their children's natural curiosity about the world and encouraged them to express themselves freely. Emily especially liked to roam the fields

around Bristol, observing plant and animal life. These provided the foundation for her subsequent passion for botany and ornithology.

### Moved to the United States

In 1832, an economic downturn in England all but destroyed Samuel's business. He and Hannah decided to make a fresh start in the United States. The family at first lived in New York City, where Samuel opened a sugar refinery. Within a year or so they moved across the Hudson River to Jersey City, New Jersey. There they quickly became involved in the growing antislavery movement. Over the years family members developed close friendships with some of the country's most prominent abolitionists, including journalist and reformer William Lloyd Garrison, clergyman Lyman Beecher, his son Henry Ward Beecher, and Harriet Beecher Stowe, the author of *Uncle Tom's Cabin.*

Fire destroyed Samuel's sugar refinery in 1836, leaving the Blackwells deeply in debt. Two years later, depressed over his financial difficulties and physically ill with what was probably malaria, Samuel once again looked westward for a new beginning. This time, he moved his family to Cincinnati, Ohio, where he hoped to start a refinery operation that made use of sugar beets instead of cane sugar. But his health worsened, and he died in August 1838.

Once again, the Blackwells found themselves in dire straits. The three oldest daughters—Anna, Marian, and Elizabeth—opened a boarding school in the family home and operated it until 1842, when the two oldest boys, Henry and Samuel, obtained jobs that paid considerably more than their sisters were able to earn as teachers. By 1845, the Blackwells had paid off most of their debts, freeing Elizabeth to pursue her goal of becoming a doctor. After applying to and receiving rejections from 28 different medical schools, she was finally accepted by Geneva College (now Hobart College) in Geneva, New York, where she began her studies in 1847.

Meanwhile, Emily was struggling to find her own way in life. Bookish and painfully shy, she led a quiet, solitary existence of work and study that masked her growing sense of frustration and unhappiness. She desperately wanted to follow in her sister's footsteps and enter the medical field but was plagued by self-doubt about her suitability for such an undertaking. Instead, she tried teaching and found that she thoroughly detested it. As she confided to her diary around this time, according to writer Ishbel Ross in *Child of Destiny,* "I long with such an intense longing for freedom, action, for life and truth. I feel as though a mountain were on me, as though I were bound with invisible fetters. I am full of furious bitterness at the constraint and littleness of the life that I must lead. . . . "

### Admitted to Medical School

Elizabeth graduated from medical school at the head of her class in 1849, the first woman to earn a medical degree in the U.S. or Europe. After some additional study in Europe, she returned to the United States in 1851 and established a private clinic in New York City. Before long, she and Emily—who was now determined to become a doctor too—were discussing the idea of practicing medicine together. Emily applied to a number of medical colleges and was rejected by twelve of them (including her sister's alma mater) until Chicago's Rush College admitted her in 1852. During the summer before classes began, she lived with Elizabeth in Jersey City and obtained visiting privileges at Bellevue Hospital in New York City, where she was able to gain valuable experience just walking the wards.

Emily arrived at Rush College in October 1852. She did very well in her studies during her first year and returned to Bellevue Hospital as an observer during the summer of 1853. When it came time to go back to college in the fall, however, Emily had to make other arrangements; Rush officials had withdrawn permission for her to attend class in the face of intense pressure from the Illinois State Medical Society, whose members overwhelmingly opposed the idea of women practicing medicine. Transferring to Western Reserve University in Cleveland (now Case Western Reserve University), Emily continued her education and graduated with honors in the spring of 1854.

As Elizabeth had done before her, Emily then set off for Scotland, where she completed additional training in obstetrics and gynecology under the tutelage of a well-known Edinburgh physician, Sir James Young Simpson. She subsequently journeyed to London, Paris, Berlin, and Dresden, easily winning admittance to a number of clinics and hospitals, thanks to glowing recommendations from Sir James, to engage in further study and observation.

Emily returned to the United States in 1856 and found Elizabeth still fighting to gain acceptance among her fellow physicians and potential patients, most of whom looked upon female doctors with a great deal of suspicion, if not outright hostility. Instead of abandoning her dream, however, Elizabeth had come up with another plan: she would open a full-fledged hospital where women could consult a doctor of their own sex about uniquely female health problems and where training was available for women interested in becoming doctors. Emily agreed to help her achieve this ambitious goal, as did a third physician, Dr. Marie Zakrzewska, a young German-born woman of Polish ancestry whom Elizabeth had helped secure admission to medical school at Western Reserve University.

## Co-Founded Hospital for Women and Children

Together, the three doctors set out to raise the money they needed to buy a building and set up a hospital. Thanks to the financial backing of several sympathetic Quaker friends and others of a liberal bent whom they were able to persuade to support their cause, the Blackwell sisters and "Dr. Zak," as she was known, founded the New York Infirmary for Women and Children. It was the first hospital in the United States for women and the first one staffed entirely by women. Located in a poor neighborhood that was home to a large immigrant population of Germans, Italians, and Slavs, it officially opened its doors in May 1857. Elizabeth served as the director, Emily was the surgeon, and Dr. Zak was the resident physician. Patients were charged according to their ability to pay; four dollars a week if they could afford it, less

if they could not. The most destitute of those who came to see a doctor paid nothing at all.

Despite the revolutionary nature of a hospital staffed solely by women, its three founders carefully avoided giving the impression that they were activists of any sort. Most people at that time viewed the fledgling women's rights movement as eccentric, even dangerous; therefore, the Blackwells and Dr. Zak were concerned first and foremost with establishing themselves as competent physicians. To that end, they worked to maintain the highest medical standards while quietly overcoming the prejudices and fears of those they had vowed to serve as well as those who were keeping a close eye on their experiment. Before long, other women with an interest in medicine were coming to the infirmary to work as interns, nurses, and pharmacists.

While Elizabeth handled most of the administrative responsibilities associated with the infirmary and directed ongoing fundraising activities, and Dr. Zak tended to her rapidly expanding private practice (she left in 1862 to open her own hospital in Boston), Emily devoted herself entirely to patient care. By all accounts, she was an excellent physician and surgeon. Even her own sister—whose attention was increasingly focused on promoting good sanitation and social hygiene to prevent health problems—believed that Emily had a natural talent for practicing medicine that she herself lacked.

## Assumed Leadership Role

Emily also proved to be an able administrator and fundraiser. In mid-1858, Elizabeth left New York to spend a year in England, where she championed the cause of women physicians and advanced her views on social hygiene. During her absence, the number of patients at the infirmary increased to the point where the operation had to move to larger quarters in 1860. The sisters also expanded the scope of their efforts by launching the first in-home medical social work program in the United States, visiting the poor where they lived to offer basic health care and lessons in proper sanitation. And when the Civil War erupted in 1861, Elizabeth and Emily recruited and trained women who had volunteered to serve as nurses for the Union army.

After the war ended, the Blackwells set themselves yet another difficult task: convincing medical schools to admit women who had had some training at the infirmary. In 1868, when it became clear that their arguments had fallen on deaf ears, they initiated a full course of medical study at the infirmary that consisted of three years of training plus clinical experience. The following year, Elizabeth relocated permanently to England to continue the work she had begun there a decade earlier. Emily then took complete charge of both the infirmary and the school, serving not only as a physician but also as dean and professor of obstetrics and gynecology.

In 1871, after refusing the honor on several previous occasions because of her extreme shyness, Emily Blackwell finally accepted membership in the New York County Medical Society. Also during the 1870s, having finally gained confidence in her abilities as both a physician and a hospital administrator, she became more visibly active in the growing social reform movement. In that role, she tackled issues such as prostitution, sex education, and alcohol abuse.

## Spearheaded Period of Growth and Expansion

Under Emily's direction, the infirmary and medical school flourished and moved into more spacious quarters in the mid-1870s. In 1893, the study program for physicians expanded from three to four years. A year later, a comprehensive training course for nurses was established. In 1899, after Cornell University Medical College began accepting female students on an equal basis with men, Emily knew the day had come when there was no longer a need for a women-only medical school. So she arranged for the transfer of her students to Cornell, then retired from the practice of medicine and left the infirmary in the hands of its very capable staff. Some 150 years after its founding, the facility continues to operate as the NYU Downtown Hospital.

Following her retirement in 1900 at the age of 74, Blackwell traveled in Europe for about 18 months. She then divided her time between her winter home in Montclair, New Jersey, and a summer cottage in York Cliffs, Maine, both of which she shared with a former colleague at the infirmary, Dr. Elizabeth Cushier, and Dr. Cushier's niece, who was also a physician. She saw her sister one last time during the summer of 1906 when Elizabeth visited the United States. The following year, the elder Blackwell fell down a flight of stairs while vacationing in Scotland; she never fully recovered from the accident and suffered a stroke in May 1910. Emily lasted only a few months longer, succumbing to enterocolitis (inflammation of the small and large intestines) on September 7, 1910 at her summer home in York Cliffs, Maine.

By carrying on the work she and Elizabeth had begun together, Emily Blackwell helped pave the way for countless other women who were interested in pursuing professional careers in the field of medicine. In fact, more than 360 of them eventually graduated from the very college she established and ran with such skill. Thus, as both a physician and an educator, Emily Blackwell posted a number of accomplishments that easily rank alongside the more heralded ones of her sister.

## Further Reading

*American Reformers,* edited by Alden Whitman. H.W. Wilson, 1985.

Brown, Jordan, *Elizabeth Blackwell,* Chelsea House, 1989.

Chambers, Peggy, *A Doctor Alone: A Biography of Elizabeth Blackwell, the First Woman Doctor, 1821-1910,* Abelard-Schuman, 1958.

Hays, Elinor Rice, *Those Extraordinary Blackwells: The Story of a Journey to a Better World,* Harcourt, 1967.

Kline, Nancy, *Elizabeth Blackwell: A Doctor's Triumph,* Conari Press, 1997.

*Notable American Women, 1607-1950,* edited by Edward T. James. Belknap Press, 1971.

Ross, Ishbel, *Child of Destiny: The Life Story of the First Woman Doctor,* Harper, 1949.

"Blackwell, Elizabeth," *Infotrack Search Bank,* http://web2.searchbank.com/infotrac (February 7, 1999).

Chambers, Peggy, "Blackwell, Elizabeth," *Infotrac Search Bank,* http://web2.searchbank.com/infotrac (February 7, 1999).

"Emily Blackwell 1826-1910," *The National Women's Hall of Fame,* http://www.greatwomen.org (February 9, 1999).

Morantz-Sanchez, Regina, "Elizabeth Blackwell," *Infotrac Search Bank,* http://web2.searchbank.com/infotrac (February 2, 1999).

"NYU Downtown Hospital History," *NYU Downtown Hospital,* http://www.nyudh.med.nyu.edu (March 3, 1999). □

# Rosa Bonheur

**Rosa Bonheur (1822–1899) was a commercially successful painter in an era when few women were able to pursue a career in the arts. Her paintings fell squarely within the Realist school of the mid-nineteenth century, and her depictions of animals and rural scenes are still widely appreciated for their accuracy and artistic skill. Bonheur's belief in women's equality and her personal habits, which included dressing in men's clothing and smoking cigars, marked her as a precursor of early feminists.**

Rosa Bonheur was born in Bordeaux, France on March 16, 1822. A career in the arts seemed predetermined for Bonheur. Her father, Raymond, was a professional painter who specialized in portraits and realistic landscapes. He also supported his daughter's inclination toward artistic pursuits, teaching her to draw from an early age. Rosa Bonheur reveled in exploring the rural area surrounding her home in Bordeaux, and she exhibited an intense love of animals from her earliest years. Not surprisingly, her first drawings were of the farm and domestic animals she encountered near her home.

Raymond Bonheur moved his family to Paris in 1829 and established a studio which doubled as the family home. He joined the Saint-Simonian movement, a religious organization which advocated the equality of women in 1830, and lived apart from his family until 1832. Shortly after her father's return, Bonheur's mother Sophie died, and the family was left to survive without her income. The death of her mother changed Bonheur's prospects drastically, as her father was now obliged to enroll her in a trade school devoted to teaching young women marketable skills, such as sewing. Bonheur proved a rebellious pupil, however, and was expelled from the school after a very short time. Bonheur's father then enrolled her in a boarding school for wealthy young women but, once again, she was unwilling to submit to school discipline and routine, and was soon back with her family.

## Artistic Training

Following her second expulsion from school in 1835, her father decided to give Bonheur artistic training in his studio. The young girl proved an immediate success and applied herself vigorously to her studies. Bonheur's initial

artistic training was typical for her era. It included copying great works of art and making studies of landscapes and animals. Her father's approach to art, which stressed realistic depiction of scenes, was quickly adopted by the young pupil. She constantly strove to improve her drawing and painting skills to enhance the accuracy of her work. Her skill was apparent almost from the start, and she was able to sell some of her paintings to older art students, even in the early stages of her training. By 1836, Bonheur had emerged as one of her father's more promising pupils. She accompanied him while he painted a commissioned portrait of a wealthy young woman named Nathalie Micas. Rosa and Micas developed a friendship during the portrait sittings which would last throughout their lives. In addition to her training as a painter, Bonheur excelled at the creation of small bronzes of animals. Her approach to realism is shown in the 1840 work *Rabbits Nibbling Carrots,* in which she took pains to render the softness of the rabbits' fur by painting it using hundreds of fine lines. By her late teens, Bonheur's work had improved enough that she was ready to participate in her first public showing.

## Commercial Success

Bonheur submitted several paintings and small sculptures for inclusion in the prestigious Paris Salon art show of 1841. Her works met with the approval of both critics and the public. Shortly after the show, the Bonheur family moved to a new apartment in Paris, where they were able to keep a small menagerie including ducks, rabbits, quail, squirrels, and sheep. These pets provided Bonheur with

models for further artworks, and her skill continued to improve. She participated in shows throughout the 1840s. Her painting *Cows and Bulls of the Cantal* was awarded a gold medal at the 1848 show. She subsequently received a large commission from the French government to create a painting depicting plowing using animal power. The resulting *Plowing in the Nivernais,* which depicted two teams of oxen plowing a field, was again hailed as an artistic success. Bonheur's father died in 1849 and she was left on her own, a circumstance that prompted much personal and professional development.

## Personal Controversy

Unlike many artists, Bonheur's commercial success and public acceptance were assured from the early stages of her career. Her personal habits were quite controversial, however. Her desire to better understand the physiology of animals led her to visit the slaughterhouses of Paris, which forbade the presence of women on their premises. To circumvent this prohibition, Bonheur cut her hair very short and dressed in men's clothing, a mode of dress which quickly became her regular style. Eventually, Bonheur secured the official approval of the city of Paris to work and travel in men's clothing within the city limits. She also developed the traditionally male habit of smoking cigars. Although she never married, Bonheur's friendship with Micas continued to deepen and the two women lived together. Bonheur's personal habits aroused public curiosity, but she consistently maintained that her behavior was itself a form of performance art whereby she demonstrated that impersonating a man was the only means available to a woman wishing to secure social and professional equality. Similarly, Bonheur never discussed her sexual preferences and such questions were not asked of her given the prevailing mores of the era. As such, she has secured listing in some modern directories of gay and lesbian historical figures, although the true nature of her relationship with Micas was never made clear.

Bonheur's playful attitude regarding her public persona was exemplified by her reception of an 1857 portrait of herself by Louis Dubufe. In the painting, Dubufe portrayed Bonheur in a standing position, with her arm resting on a table. Bonheur was pleased with the portrait but painted over the table, replacing it with the forequarters and head of a large, red bull. The result was a whimsical painting which summarized Bonheur's art as well as her personality. In fact, when Dubufe sold the painting to a collector and explained Bonheur's changes, the collector, who paid 8000 francs for the painting, sent Bonheur a 7000 franc bonus for her input.

## Continued Acclaim

Bonheur succeeded her father as director of the School of Drawing for Young Girls, a position in which she was able to encourage young women to pursue artistic careers. She also began work on a painting depicting horses, which was destined to become her most famous work. To prepare sketches for the painting, Bonheur frequented the stables of the Paris Omnibus Company where she received ample opportunity to watch large draft horses at work and rest.

Finally, in 1853, her work was finished and *The Horse Fair* was the sensation of the Salon. The painting sold for the very high sum of 40,000 francs in 1855, and attracted the favorable attention of Queen Victoria of England, who invited Bonheur for a royal visit. The painting was eventually purchased by the Metropolitan Museum of Art in New York City, where it is currently housed. Bonheur's continuing commercial success enabled her to purchase a large chateau in the French town of By, to which she and Micas moved in 1860. The chateau included spacious grounds enclosed by a wall. Bonheur was able to maintain what amounted to a personal zoological garden, including dogs, Icelandic ponies, deer, gazelles, monkeys, cattle, yak, boar, and a lion. These animals became the subjects of many of Bonheur's works and provided her with great joy.

Bonheur painted animals and pastoral scenes throughout the remainder of her career, and continued to enjoy commercial and critical favor. She became the first female recipient of the French Legion of Honor in 1865. However, the award could only be presented to her when Emperor Louis-Napoleon was out of town, because he opposed the bestowal of this award on a woman. She later received a rosette denoting a second Legion of Honor and was very proud of this recognition, wearing her medals prominently when sitting for a portrait by Anna Klumpke in 1899. Bonheur continued to score artistic success until the time of her death. One of her more famous works depicted the American celebrity Buffalo Bill Cody, whose wild west show visited France in 1889. Bonheur delighted in painting the show's wildlife and cast, which included authentic Western cowboys, Mexican vaqueros, and Native Americans. She remained active following the death of Nathalie Micas later in 1889. At the time of her own death in By, France on May 25, 1899, Bonheur's studio contained more than 1800 studies and works, both finished and unfinished.

## A Place in History

Bonheur represented, in many ways, the epitome of the Realist school which dominated European painting in the mid-nineteenth century. She did not incorporate the more modern approach of the Impressionists, although she certainly must have been aware of their efforts. Indeed, while the Impressionists struggled to get their works admitted to the Salon in the 1870s, Bonheur's more representational works continued to find great favor. Her intention was never to interpret images in a new or innovative manner, but rather to render them as realistically as possible while bringing out their intrinsic visual qualities. Although her art is less "modern," and therefore less well remembered than that of her Impressionist contemporaries, Bonheur's attitude toward the role of women in society was quite modern indeed. Her brand of feminism stressed empowering women to occupy social and economic niches, such as that of being a professional artist. At the same time, her attitude reflected little of the Victorian moralism that characterized the women's movement during her era. Her career as a painter set her apart as a pioneer of women's empowerment but her activities as an art educator, and the example she set in her personal life, may in the final analysis have had a more lasting effect on European art than her paintings.

## Further Reading

Berger, Klaus, *Collier's Encyclopedia*, P.F. Collier, 1997.
*Columbia Encyclopedia*, Columbia University Press, 1993.
*The Continuum Dictionary of Women's Biography*, edited by Jennifer S. Uglow, Continuum, 1982.
*The Good Housekeeping Women's Almanac*, edited by Barbara McDowell and Hana Umlauf, Newspaper Enterprise Association, 1977.
*Larousse Dictionary of Women*, edited by Melanie Parry, Larousse, 1996.
Turner, Robyn Montana, *Rosa Bonheur*, Little, Brown and Company, 1991.
*School Arts,* December 1995. □

# Paul Bowles

**Even though Paul Bowles (born 1910) wrote stories, composed music, and lived in some of the world's most exotic places, he was not one who craved recognition. The general public, even those who considered themselves well-informed, might not have recognized his name. Yet, Bowles became the standard bearer for the "beat" generation, commonly referred to as "beatniks."**

Paul Frederick Bowles was born on December 30, 1910, in New York City. He was the only child of Claude Dietz Bowles and Rena Winnewisser Bowles. He was raised in Jamaica, Queens, on Long Island, one of America's first suburbs. Bowles' father was a dentist who had wanted to be a concert violinist. Despite the advantages of a middle class lifestyle, his childhood was not a pleasant one. As Bowles said of his father in a 1972 autobiography, *Without Stopping*, "I took for granted his constant and unalloyed criticism. His mere presence meant misery."

Bowles mentioned in a 1995 *Washington Post*, interview the story of how it seemed his father had tried to kill him. In February 1911, when Bowles was two months old, his mother's mother found him lying in a basket on the windowsill, window open and snow coming down. Had she not rescued the infant he would have been dead within an hour. That, at least, is what she told the boy [Bowles] a few years later. 'Your father's a devil,' she proclaimed." Bowles was much closer to his mother, a person of many cultural aspirations, herself a poet. Perhaps key to his later profession, Bowles spent much of his childhood alone. By his own admission, he had no other children in his life until he was five years old. His fantasies helped him to escape his unpleasant world, especially his father.

Bowles spent most of his summers in childhood and adolescence either at his paternal grandparents' home at Seneca Lake, in upstate New York, or his maternal grandparents' 165-acre farm in western Massachusetts. His elementary schooling was at the Model School, a teacher training school. There he studied music, learning piano,

music theory, and ear training. He was nine years old when he attempted to compose his first opera. Bowles relished the family phonograph and bought records on a regular basis. Because he was not allowed to play those records while his father was home, music became a forbidden pleasure.

Bowles attended public high schools in suburban New York, near his home in Jamaica. He was not at first fond of the time he was forced to spend there. When he went to Jamaica High School and joined the monthly literary magazine, his attitude began to change. He developed a passion for writing. Bowles began to collect books. He was particularly fond of those that were beautifully bound, and collected a number that were inscribed to him by the authors. This interest was sparked by an aunt who lived in Greenwich Village [New York] and introduced him to the head children's librarian of the New York Public Library.

In 1928, at the age of 18, Bowles had his first poem published in *Transition,* a prestigious avant garde literary publication. According to Streitfeld in the *Washington Post,* this was similar to the distinction of being published in the *New Yorker,* an unusual accomplishment for such a young writer. This was two months after he graduated from Jamaica High School. During that time, Bowles studied at the School of Design and Liberal Arts in Manhattan.

### Left College for Paris

Bowles entered the University of Virginia (UVA) in Charlottesville, and created quite a stir after only a few months. Without notifying his parents, or authorities at the school, he set off for Paris to work as a switchboard operator at the office of the *Herald Tribune,* a newspaper published primarily for Americans living in Europe. His parents eventually persuaded him to return to the United States, and to finish out his first year of college, which he did in the spring of 1930.

In the summer of 1931 he was introduced to composer Aaron Copland, who quickly became his teacher and mentor. In September of that year, he went to Yaddo, an artist retreat and colony outside Saratoga Springs, New York. Copland was scheduled to spend time there before he left for Berlin in November. Bowles thought it best to continue to study with him. He sailed for Paris and had plans to join Copland in Berlin three weeks later.

In December 1930, Bowles was asked by a friend to edit an issue of the University of Richmond's (Virginia) literary magazine, *The Messenger.* He was excited at the prospect of doing so, and decided to enlist contributions from several notable writers, including William Carlos Williams, Nancy Cunard, and Gertrude Stein. They all obliged. Bowles continued to correspond with Stein, and sent her a copy of the magazine when it was published. Thus began a friendship with Stein, and eventually with her companion Alice B. Toklas, that would continue for the rest of her life.

In his autobiography, *Without Stopping,* Bowles recalls his first meeting with the two women not long after his arrival in Paris. He stated, "One of the first things I did was to go around to 27 rue de Fleuras and find Gertrude Stein's door . . . Gertrude Stein appeared, looking just as she did in her photographs, except that the expression of her face was rather more pleasant. 'What is it? Who are you?' she said. I told her and heard for the first time her wonderfully hearty laugh. She opened the door so that I could go in. Then Alice Toklas came downstairs, and we sat in the big studio. We thought that you were an elderly gentleman, at least seventy-five,' Gertrude Stein told me. 'A highly eccentric elderly gentleman,' added Alice Toklas. 'We were certain of it.' They asked me to dinner for the following night."

Bowles said in his 1972 autobiography that, "I existed primarily for Gertrude Stein as a sociological exhibit; for her I was the first example of my kind. I provided her initial encounter with a species then rare, now the commonest of contemporary phenomena, the American suburban child with its unrelenting spleen." Stein pronounced an early dislike for Bowles' poetry, yet remained fascinated by his other work. At her suggestion, Bowles traveled to Tangier instead of spending his time on the French Riviera, as he had planned. When discussing their plans in her presence, Stein had said, "You don't want to go to Villefranche. Everybody's there. And St.-Jean-de-Luz is empty, and with an awful climate. The place you should go is Tangier." That travel suggestion proved to be an important one. In Tangier in the 1930s, Bowles found the intrigue on which he would thrive. In 1948, he moved there permanently.

From Paris, Bowles went to Berlin to continue his studies with Copland. There he met British writers Christopher Isherwood and Stephen Spender. Isherwood's story, *I Am a Camera,* that was taken to the Broadway stage in the late 1960s as the musical, *Cabaret,* patterned the lead character after a friend of his. For the story, Isherwood adopted Bowles' name. His character was called Sally Bowles.

Tangier would eventually become his home, both physically and spiritually. Bowles said to Streitfeld in a *Washington Post* interview that when he saw the desert, the Sahara, for the first time, "I had a big desire to keep going. That's the main thing—to continue and continue. I didn't ask what would happen. I didn't think anything would happen. I just thought I'd see more and more. I'd feel more and more. And, finally, of course, I'd have to return." That, too, might have been the beginning of the change of consciousness for the generation that would follow him out of another world war, a decade and a half later.

## Married to Soul Mate

Throughout the 1930s, Bowles worked with the Federal Theater Project in New York, part of the Works Progress Administration (WPA). During the Great Depression of the 1930s, President Franklin Roosevelt established various WPA programs across the Untied States—in everything from building bridges to painting murals on public buildings. It was a government-funded program to bring jobs to hundreds of thousands of unemployed Americans. The program was considered to be especially successful in the arts. Bowles began to write music for plays, in addition to his own compositions. He stayed with the project until 1937, when a spur-of-the-moment trip to Mexico with friends enticed him to resign in order to travel.

Shortly before his trip, Bowles met Jane Auer, a writer with whom he was immediately fascinated. She traveled to Mexico with them, only to depart early due to illness. When he returned to New York, he continued to see her. The two of them, as Bowles related, "used to spin fancies about how amusing it would be to get married and horrify everyone, above all, our respective families." On February 21, 1938, the day before Jane's 21st birthday, the two of them were married in Manhattan in a small Dutch Reformed Church. Gena Dagel Caponi, in her study, *Paul Bowles: Romantic Savage,* said that the "wedding gave his parents something to be unhappy about in the shape of an event they could not help but bless. It was a masterstroke of passive aggression."

The Bowles' marriage lasted until 1973 when Jane died in Malaga, Spain. She suffered years of ill health following a 1957 stroke that gravely affecting her eyesight. Both Bowles and his wife considered themselves homosexual, yet maintained a sexual relationship for at least some part of their marriage. More important to them was their companionship, and an unbreakable bond of love that did not stay bound to normal societal conventions. They were devoted to each other. But their wild lifestyle which included alcohol—Bowles himself noted that his wife was "overcome with a desire for alcohol"—as well as her mental and physical decline, created an aura of melancholy surrounding them. Bowles often set aside his own work to care for her.

## His Music, His Words

Bowles' life in New York throughout the 1930s and 1940s was at the center of the theatrical world. He was recognized as a key composer of what was known as

"incidental music," as the music that wove itself through many non-musical plays. Bowles worked with some of the best-known writers and playwrights, such as Orson Welles, John Houseman, William Saroyan. He teamed often with Tennessee Williams, for whom he composed the music for one of his most famous plays, *The Glass Menagerie.* K. Robert Schwarz in a *New York Times* article quoted composer Ned Rorem: "The melodies say what they have to say and then stop, without beating a dead horse. The accompaniments are exquisite, honed and pared like Faure. And he had a kind of monopoly on theater music in New York, since he was able to hit the nail on the head in illustrating what was going on." From 1942 until 1946, Bowles also served as music critic for the *New York Herald Tribune.* He wrote over 400 well-respected and sharp-witted reviews.

Bowles pursued other music, as well as his own. In 1959, he received a grant from the Rockefeller Foundation for a special project sponsored by the Library of Congress. His Moroccan music collection, housed in the Library of Congress, included recordings Bowles made during the four-month project. In addition to the recordings of music native to his beloved Morocco, he gathered photographs and other documentation of Moroccan folk, popular, and art music. Bowles captured the music and dance of various tribes and other groups of the area at 23 different locations. He added to the collection with further recordings made from 1960 to 1962.

Schwarz noted how Bowles' music contrasted with his novels, and other fiction. Bowles commented on that, too, having said, "The music and the fiction both come from the same mind but from different sections of it. It's like two separate symnasiums. I leave the room where I'm writing the words, shut the door, go in the other room and write music."

As prolific as his music had become, his writing was destined for a wider audience. The publication of his novel, *The Sheltering Sky,* in 1949 earned critical acclaim. The story focused on a married couple who seek life's deeper meanings throughout a spiritual journey through the desert. It was noted that the couple bore a striking resemblance, to Jane and Paul Bowles themselves. Bowles enjoyed a resurrection of interest in all of his writings, as well as his music, when famed Italian film director, Bernardo Bertolucci turned his most famous book into a movie, starring American actors Debra Winger and John Malkovich.

His other novels, which also dealt with Tangier and his journeys around the world, included: *Let It Come Down,* 1981; *The Spider's House,* 1982; *Points in Time;* 1984; *Too Far from Home: The Selected Writings of Paul Bowles,* 1995; and *Up Above the World,* (reprint edition) 1996. Among his numerous short stories were: *The Delicate Prey; A Hundred Camels in the Courtyard; Call at Corazon;* and *A Thousand Days for Mokhtar.* Bowles was known as a translator of many Moroccan folk tales.

Perhaps as fascinating as Bowles' fiction and poetry, were his own autobiographical journals and letters to friends. *In Touch, The Letters of Paul Bowles,* edited by Jeffrey Miller in 1994, revealed much of his personal life from 1928 through 1989. Bowles was a man who had led a life apart from the eye of the tabloid press. He did receive many visitors to his home in Tangier, although he had no telephone. Those who came, the famous and obscure, believed a visit to Bowles was essential if they were to be taken seriously by the literary world.

When Streitfeld interviewed Bowles during his 1996 visit to the United States, he had traveled to the States to receive medical treatment at Emory University in Atlanta. Bowles indicated the what kept him going during his stay in Atlanta was the thought that he would be returning to Morocco in a few days. Streitfeld asked him if he would ever come back to the States, especially for a planned festival of his music that spring. All Bowles said was, "I hope not."

In his late 80s, Bowles seemed ready for death. He had been the young man of the charmed Paris set before the war. He was the older man among the generation of the Beats, all of whom he outlasted—many by decades. His stamina, his self-proclaimed discipline imposed from his childhood, served him well. He survived all of the intoxicants the others did not. Bowles ended his autobiography with this contemplation in the very last paragraph: "Good-bye, says the dying man to the mirror they hold in front of him. We won't be seeing each other any more. When I quoted Valery's [French poet] epigram in *The Sheltering Sky,* it seemed a poignant bit of fantasy. Now, because I no longer imagine myself as an outlooker at the scene, but instead as the principal protagonist, it strikes me as repugnant. To make it right, the dying man would have to add two words to his little farewell, and they are: 'Thank God!'"

### Further Reading

Bowles, Paul, *In Touch, The Letters Paul Bowles,* edited by Jeffrey Miller, Farrar, Strauss and Giroux, 1994.
Bowles, Paul, *Without Stopping, An Autobiography,* G. P. Putnam's Sons, 1972.
*Contemporary Authors,* Gale, 1996, Volume 50.
Green, Michelle, *The Dream At the End of the World,* HarperCollins Publishers, 1991.
*New York Times,* September 17, 1995, p. 27; March 17, 1996, p. 32.
*Washington Post,* February 9, 1995, p. C1 □

# Richard Branson

**Charismatic entrepreneur Richard Branson (born 1950) became well known when his daredevil business tactics were upstaged by his death defying antics as a sportsman.**

Founder and mastermind of the Virgin business enterprise, Richard Branson hewed a reputation as one of the most popular personalities in all of England. The charismatic Branson attracted crowds and media attention everywhere, not only in the course of his business exploits but also for his adventurous lifestyle. At the height of his popularity, Branson's name was touted for prime minister, and even monarch, of his native Britain. Tongue-and-cheek

aside, Branson's financial escapades were serious business, and his adventurous personal nature projected an aura that seemed larger than life.

Richard Branson was born on July 18, 1950 into a middle class family in the English county of Surrey. Branson was the oldest of three siblings. His father, Edward (Ted) Branson was an attorney, in the tradition of the Branson family ancestry. Most agree that Branson inherited his Nordic looks as well as his adventurous spirit from his mother, Eve Branson, a one-time dancer and actress, and a former flight attendant. So energetic and spirited was Eve Branson, that she learned to fly gliders at a time when few women drove cars. She flew so well, in fact, that she trained with the Royal Air Force (RAF) cadets for duty during the Second World War. The Branson children were raised to be hearty, active, and brave.

Richard Branson was not adventurous by nature. Out of concern, his mother left him alone in the countryside one day, with instructions to find his own way home through the fields of Devon. Branson was only four at the time, and a neighboring farmer eventually discovered the boy and alerted the Bransons to retrieve their son. Young Richard, who spent that day chasing butterflies, was enamored by the exhilaration of freedom at such a young age. Years later, when his parents enrolled him at Stowe boarding school in Buckingham, he found the environment too restrictive. He dropped out of high school and moved to London, where he made his living as a publisher and later opened a retail record business.

## A Young Entrepreneur

After Branson arrived in London in 1967, at the age of 17, he undertook his first business venture. He published a magazine called *Student,* for young activists. The first issue was published in January 1968, and reached a printing of 100,000 copies at the peak of its popularity. *Student* was an excellent business vehicle, and resulted in a positive business experience for Branson.

Branson started his second business in 1970, a mail-order retail record company called Virgin Mail. The unfortunate occurrence of a British postal strike in 1971 forced Branson to realign his fledgling record company from a mail-order supplier into a successful discount record retailer in London. Branson's initial ventures into capitalism were encouraging, but generated "red ink" at the onset. As Branson saw his business debt swell to approximately $20,000 he devised an illicit pseudo-export scam that allowed him to evade the tax payments on his merchandise. For a time he eluded the authorities but was eventually brought to justice and to jail. It cost him (and his mother) $45,000 in bail to secure his freedom. In time and with perseverance he worked his way out of accrued business debts of $90,000, including fines and back taxes owed to the government.

## Virgin Records

In 1973, Branson expanded his business interests and established Virgin Records in part to provide a recording vehicle for a talented friend, Mike Oldfield. Through the new Virgin Records enterprise, Oldfield recorded an album featuring the tune "Tubular Bells," and the record became the soundtrack for the classic horror movie, *The Exorcist.*

In 1977, Branson signed the Sex Pistols to Virgin Records, a shrewd business move that plunged the small recording company into the mainstream of the punk rock era. Censors from radio and other media immediately banned one of the Sex Pistols earliest hits with Virgin Records, an irreverent tune called "God Save the Queen." The Sex Pistols, determined to make their music heard, retaliated with a "free concert" on the Thames River that resulted in 100,000 in record sales within one week. Following the scandalous success of the Sex Pistols, Virgin Records easily attracted a variety of the most popular artists of the times, including Boy George and the Culture Club, who sold 1.4 million records in the U.K. in 1983. Branson went on to sign contracts with singers and guitarists including Peter Gabriel, Phil Collins, Janet Jackson, and the Rolling Stones. By 1983, Branson's Virgin empire included 50 diverse companies.

In keeping with his radical business ethic, Branson established an international airline in June 1984, with a single leased airplane. The airline, Virgin Atlantic Airways Limited, survived the threat of foreclosure and in time grew into the world's third-largest transatlantic carrier.

## Secrets of Success

Virgin enterprises are a conglomeration of wholly owned subsidiaries and outside partnerships. Branson maintains a controlling interest in every company that he starts. Virgin interests include retail stores, a travel group, an entertainment group, a hotel enterprise, financial services, cinemas, radio stations, and Virgin European Airways. Branson runs the empire from the old villa where he lives with his family in London's Holland Park. Each business is a separate venture. He oversees each startup company, then delegates management and moves on. Branson relies on creative investment schemes and extremely private holdings. He retains control as CEO of his travel ventures, even as he acquires capital for his railway system venture. Branson strategically keeps each company small and controllable, despite the conglomerate structure, and operates each enterprise as an individual small business. His companies offer employees a pleasant work environment and the renegade Branson eschews computers; informal communication is the hallmark of the Virgin regime. The personal needs of employees take precedence, and even at times of dire financial straits, Branson humanely sidesteps layoffs.

## Virgin Travel Interests

In 1992, after 22 years at the helm, Branson reluctantly sold his Virgin Music Group to Thorn-EMI for a sum near one billion dollars. He made the sacrifice in the interests of Virgin Airlines which was in a state of financial disaster. Branson used the money in part to upgrade the airline with new amenities and services including seat-back videos, complimentary headsets, toiletries, stand-up bars, full-sized sleeper seats; luxury services such as masseuses, manicure, and free ground transportation by limousine were also introduced. British Airways, number one competitor to Virgin Atlantic, resorted to unduly aggressive competition against Branson's business savvy. In January 1993, Branson won a judgment of nearly one million dollars in a suit against British Airways for unfair competition.

Traditional investors fail to comprehend Branson's privately held Virgin resources that comprise an intricate web of trusts and holding companies which span the Atlantic Ocean into the British Virgin Isles. In 1998, Branson further unnerved financial pundits when he invested his own private interests into a series of rail lines including British Rail. As with many Branson business endeavors, the investments were in conflict with every traditional business tactic and mainstream corporate practice, yet Branson ably accomplished his ends. Branson's unique business style prompted David Sheff to comment in *Forbes* that Branson is, "One of the world's most fertile businessmen [with] highly unorthodox methods."

In 1999, and less than 30 years after the original conception of the Branson Virgin businesses, Branson boasted over 200 Virgin Megastores worldwide and a soft drink business—Virgin Cola—in direct competition with Coca-Cola. All told, Branson employed 24,000 employees in 150 companies, with revenues totaling an estimated five billion dollars each year from the entire Virgin Group—including the music stores and airline. The Virgin empire was last valued at an estimated $1.5 billion, and was the largest privately owned business in England.

## Adventure and Thrill Seeker

Branson is as well known for his death-defying "near-miss" accidents as for his business acumen. In 1987, he made his "virgin" parachute jump just weeks before embarking on a trans-Atlantic balloon voyage with co-pilot Per Lindstrand in the largest balloon ever made—replete with eight burners and twelve miles of fabric. In preparation for the balloon flight, Branson took a skydiving lesson and nearly killed himself when he inadvertently unhooked his own parachute. A courageous jump instructor rescued Branson in mid-air. Shortly afterward, Branson made the balloon trip from Sugarloaf Mountain in Maine, across the Atlantic to Ireland for the first trans-Atlantic crossing in a balloon. Branson attempted a landing upon arrival in Ireland, but encountered severe problems with the wind and narrowly escaped a harrowing death in the icy Atlantic Ocean.

In 1991, Branson became the first person to cross the Pacific Ocean in a balloon. He traveled nearly 7,000 miles between Japan and Canada, and clocked speeds as high as 240 miles per hour. The trip was fraught with tense moments, including the loss of two fuel tanks. The loss of balloon altitude control caused the crew to reach treacherous altitudes, well over 40,000 feet. Pilot and co-pilot later missed their landing goal by 2,000 miles. Originally headed for Los Angeles, they landed in a remote part of the North Canadian Rocky Mountains instead.

In January 1997, Branson made one of his first attempts to successfully circumnavigate the earth in a hot-air balloon. By December 1998, he was on his fourth attempt. Along with Lindstrand and Steve Fossett, Branson set out to be the first in history to accomplish the feat. Fossett and Branson—one-time adversaries in the race to circumnavigate—left Marrakech, crossed through Asia Minor and Asia and into the Pacific before a hurricane downed the crew off the coast of Hawaii.

For these and other exploits, Branson was cited by *Business Week,* as a new breed of "daredevil" CEO that needs to be curtailed by boards of directors in the interests of shareholders, in order to forestall pending doom that often accompanies such antics. Branson certainly fit the bill; he is an avid skier and speedboat racer, in addition to his skydiving and ballooning exploits.

In 1979, Branson purchased an island in the Caribbean. The land parcel, called Necker, consists of 74 acres. He purchased the land for $300,000, and since that time invested $20 million into customizing the island complete with a ten-bedroom house, two guest houses, a desalination plant, generator facilities, and imported foliage to intersperse with the indigenous neckerberry bushes that give the island its name. He rents the island for as much as $20,500 per night. His guests include many of the most prominent personalities in the world: the late Diana, Princess of Wales, director Steven Spielberg, actor Mel Gibson, and movie and television maven Oprah Winfrey.

A media phenomenon, Branson remains unaffected and dresses casually, in comfortable clothes. He was married to Kristen Tomassi in 1972; they divorced in 1976. In 1989, Branson wed Joan Templeman of Glasgow—He arrived at the wedding ceremony hanging from a helicopter. The couple has two children, Holly and Sam. Branson published his autobiography, *Losing My Virginity,* in 1998.

## Further Reading

*Business Week,* January 11, 1999, p. 50(1).
*Forbes* February 24, 1997, p. S94(7).
*Management Today,* April 1998, p. 38(5).
*People,* November 2, 1998 p. 141.
*Playboy,* February 1995, p. 114(5).
*Sports Illustrated,* February 12, 1999, p. 186.
*Time,* June 24, 1996, p. 50(4). □

# Les Brown

**Motivational speaker Les Brown (born 1945) made his name encouraging others to overcome any odds that might stand in their way.**

Les Brown has a dream, and he is living it. In 1986, broke and sleeping on the cold linoleum floor of his office, he began to pursue a career as a motivational speaker. By the early 1990s, he was one of the highest paid speakers in the nation. His company, Les Brown Unlimited, Inc., earned millions of dollars a year from his speaking tours and the sale of motivational tapes and materials. Brown's audience is wide: from Fortune 500 companies to automobile workers to prison inmates to special-education classes to ordinary individuals. His mission is to "get a message out that will help people become uncomfortable with their mediocrity," he explained to a reporter for *Ebony* magazine. "A lot of people are content with their discontent. I want to be a catalyst to enable them to see themselves having more and achieving more."

Brown's message works because "he kindles the warmth, humor, and well being in a society that's seen the gradual disintegration of families and mounting technology and alienation in industry," Maureen McDonald wrote in the *Detroiter.* Brown knows the function of the able individual in a worn community: he delivers not only nurturing words but money as well, donating 20 percent of his business revenues to fund drug prevention programs. His message also works, and for a stronger reason, because he is not an outsider, an academic who offers a theoretical prescription. "I can't lecture on something unless I am living it," Brown wrote in his 1992 bestseller *Live Your Dreams.* He connects with other people's lives—their misfortunes and missed opportunities—because he has been through it all and triumphed.

## Humble Beginnings

Leslie Calvin Brown and his twin brother, Wesley, were born on February 17, 1945, on the floor of an abandoned building in Liberty City, a low-income section of Miami, Florida. Their birth mother, married at the time to a soldier stationed overseas, had become pregnant by another man

and went to Miami secretly to give birth to her sons. Three weeks later, she gave them away. At six weeks of age, both boys were adopted by Mamie Brown, a 38-year-old unmarried cafeteria cook and domestic. The importance of her entrance into his life, Brown concludes, was immeasurable. "Everything I am and everything I have I owe to my mother," he told Rachel L. Jones of the *Detroit Free Press.* "Her strength and character are my greatest inspiration, always have been and always will be."

The confidence that Brown's adoptive mother had in him, the belief that he was capable of greatness, was not shared by his teachers. As a child he found excitement in typical boyhood misadventures. He liked to have fun, and he liked attention. Overactive and mischievous, Brown was a poor student because he was unable to concentrate, especially in reading. His restlessness and inattentiveness, coupled with his teachers' insufficient insight into his true capabilities, resulted in his being labeled "educably mentally retarded" in the fifth grade. It was a label he found hard to remove, in large part because he did not try. "They said I was slow so I held to that pace," he recounted in his book.

### Teacher Encouraged Him

A major lesson Brown imparts early in *Live Your Dreams* is that "there comes a time when you have to drop your burdens in order to fight for yourself and your dreams." It was another significant figure in Brown's early life who awakened his listless consciousness and brought about this awareness: LeRoy Washington, a speech and drama instructor at Booker T. Washington High School in Miami. While

in high school, Brown "used to fantasize being onstage speaking to thousands of people," he related to Jones, "and I used to write on pieces of paper, 'I am the world's greatest orator.'"

But it wasn't until he encountered Washington that he truly learned of the sound and power of eloquent speech to stir and motivate. Brown related in his book that when he once told Washington in class that he couldn't perform a task because he was educably mentally retarded, the instructor responded, "Do Not Ever Say That Again! Someone's opinion of you does Not have to become Your reality." Those words provided Brown's liberation from his debilitating label. "The limitations you have, and the negative things that you internalize are given to you by the world," he wrote of his realization. "The things that empower you—the possibilities—come from within."

Employed after high school as a city sanitation worker, but determined to achieve what he desired—perhaps for the first time in his life—Brown pursued a career in radio broadcasting. He had been enthralled throughout his life with the almost music-like patter of disc jockeys, so he repeatedly bothered the owner of a local radio station about a position until the owner relented. Having no experience, Brown was hired to perform odd jobs. Firmly intent on becoming a deejay, he learned all he could about the workings of a radio station. One day, when a disc jockey became drunk on the air and Brown was the only other person at the station, he filled in at the microphone. Impressed, the owner of the station promoted Brown to part-time and then full-time disc jockey.

In the late 1960s, Brown moved to Columbus, Ohio, where he had a top-rated radio program, and was eventually given added duties as broadcast manager. Here his world widened. He became more socially conscious and more of an activist, urging his listeners to political action. Part of the motivation behind this fervor came from Mike Williams, the station's news director and an activist who would eventually oversee Brown's motivational speaking tours and programs. "I thought he was a master communicator," Williams told Cheryl Lavin of the *Chicago Tribune.* "I knew it was a gift. I saw him as an international figure. I saw him in very large situations, moving audiences." But the owners of the radio station thought Brown was becoming too controversial of a figure. He was fired.

### Became Ohio Legislator

Urged on by Williams, Brown ran for the Ohio State Legislature, winning the seat of the 29th House District. In his first year, he passed more legislation than any other freshman representative in Ohio legislative history. In his third term, he served as chair of the Human Resources Committee. But he had to leave the state house in 1981 in order to care for his ailing mother in Florida. While in Miami, continuing his focus on social issues, Brown developed a youth career training program and held community meetings, speaking out on social injustice.

Again, controversies arose around him. The Dade County state's attorney general investigated his handling of the youth program. After a year, during which time Brown openly invited any inquiry, the case was dropped: no improprieties were found. The motivating factor behind the criticisms, Brown believed, was jealousy. "A lot of people felt threatened and offended because I came on very strong," he told Jones, "and I had an instant following they couldn't get." This effect was not lost on Brown. Encouraged again by Williams and by a chance encounter with motivational millionaire Zig Ziglar, who was earning $10,000 for one-hour talks, Brown decided to become a motivational speaker.

"Life takes on meaning when you become motivated, set goals, and charge after them in an unstoppable manner," Brown wrote in *Live Your Dreams*. It is a maxim he learned well. When he entered the motivational speaking arena in the mid-1980s, he had virtually nothing, having moved to Detroit with his clothes and just one tape of his motivational speeches. He rented an office that he shared with an attorney. He worked hard and always seemed to be the first one there in the morning and the last one there at night. Indeed, he never left the office, having to sleep on the cold floor because he could not afford an apartment. But he welcomed this ascetic lifestyle. "I didn't even want a blanket or a pallet on the floor," he explained to Jones. "I wanted it to be hard and cold so it would motivate me to keep striving. I didn't want to get soft."

## Became "The Motivator"

Brown read books on public speaking and studied the habits of established speakers. He first spoke to grade school students, then high school students. Clubs and organizations followed. Less than four years later, in 1989, he received the National Speakers Association's highest award—the Council of Peers Award of Excellence—becoming the first African American to receive such an honor. He was known in professional circles as "The Motivator."

"Victories can become obstacles to your development if you unconsciously pause too long to savor them," Brown wrote in his book. "Too many people interpret success as sainthood. Success does not make you a great person; how you deal with it decides that. You must not allow your victories to become ends unto themselves." His goal was not just to win awards, but to inspire people to pursue their own goals.

In 1990, Brown reached for a wider audience by recording the first in a series of motivational speech presentations for the Public Broadcasting Service (PBS-TV). He conducted motivational training sessions not only for executives of corporations such as American Telephone and Telegraph, General Electric, and Procter & Gamble, but also for prison inmates and—remembering his own background—for special education students in high schools. "We all have a responsibility to give something back," he told a reporter for *Upscale*. "I am who I am because of the relationships I have developed, because of the people who have enriched my life."

Brown details his life and the relationships that have helped shape it in his book *Live Your Dreams*. Much more than a simple autobiography, the book, which is divided into ten chapters followed by written exercises in a built-in workbook, focuses on areas of personal deficiency—such as fear, inattentiveness, and laziness—as well as on areas of personal value, such as self-knowledge, courage, and dreams. Brown makes vague, personal faults understandable and ambitious virtues attainable by elaborating on them through personal or historical narratives that are almost parable-like. He moves easily between the ordinary and the extraordinary to emphasize his point. For instance, a discussion about a boy who was scared of a bulldog that constantly chased him until he realized the dog lacked teeth might be followed on the next page by a discussion of how basketball superstar Michael Jordan handles the pressures of being a public persona.

To prove a maxim, Brown links the worldly with the mundane. In *Live Your Dreams*, he retells the stories of Terry Anderson, the Associated Press correspondent held hostage for seven years by Shiite Muslims, and that of an anonymous young boy who had to fight a neighborhood bully on a school bus. For further reinforcement, Brown sprinkles quotes throughout from historical figures such as former U.S. president Theodore Roosevelt, American nature writer Henry David Thoreau, and German poet Johann Wolfgang von Goethe, and from personal figures such as teacher LeRoy Washington and his own mother, Mamie.

The book's idealistic tone is tempered by an acceptance of life's realities. "You will be cruising along, knocking them dead, in full synchronization—and then you'll hit the speed bumps," Brown wrote. "You miss a bus. Your paycheck bounces. Your car won't start. That's life. Maybe it is set up that way so that we learn and grow." Brown knows this firsthand and that is his point: he has faced life's obstacles and has been inspired to overcome them in quest of his own dreams, so he tries to inspire those whose dreams are similarly thwarted by life's misadventures.

"I am intrigued by the concept of selling people on their own greatness with the same fervor that Madison Avenue sells them on the wondrous attributes of Nike athletic shoes, Chevy trucks, and Calvin Klein jeans," Brown wrote in *Live Your Dreams*. "What if our young people heard encouragement to dream and strive as many times a day as they are exhorted to drink Dr. Pepper or to go to the land of Mickey Mouse?" Brown got his chance to answer this question and share his philosophies with his widest audience ever when his own television talk show, the *Les Brown Show*, debuted in the fall of 1993. It was short-lived, despite receiving good ratings. The program, which was Brown's most ambitious project to date, was syndicated by King World, the same company that distributes the popular *Oprah* program. "I think people are ready to be entertained and inspired and I want to make them feel good about themselves," he explained to Jefferson Graham of *USA Today*. "I want to use TV in a way in which it's never been used before—to empower people."

## Books Became Best-Sellers

On August 29, 1995, Brown married Gladys Knight, the famous soul singer, in a private ceremony in Las Vegas, Nevada. They both had been married previously and between them had ten children and seven gradnchildren. The next year, Brown released his next book, *It's Not Over Until You Win!: How to Become the Person You Always Wanted to Be—No Matter What the Obstacle,* which covered a wide array of topics ranging from his marriage to the quality of television. A *Publishers Weekly* reviewer commented, "This volume successfully translates Brown's natural charisma from the podium to the page." His two books together sold more than half a million copies.

After the cancellation of his television show, Brown briefly went to work for radio station WRKS in New York then, in October of 1996, was hired on as morning host at WBLS, also in New York. However, in May of 1997 he announced that he would be leaving his job to spend more time on his speaking career and to undergo treatments for prostate cancer. He and Knight announced the next month that they were divorcing due to irreconcilable differences, though he claimed the two would remain friendly.

Into 1998, Brown's empire remained strong; he was reaping about $4.5 million per year from speaking engagements and television appearances. His Detroit-based firm continued to serve high-profile clients such as Chrysler, 3M, and Xerox Corporation. "Downsizing trends and the changing global market require people to reinvent themselves and think like entrepreneurs," Brown stated in *Black Enterprise.* In addition, Brown was branching out to train future public speakers, concentrating on promoting the field to more minorities.

## Further Reading

*Black Enterprise,* April 1998, p. 83.
*Booklist,* November 15, 1996, p. 546.
*Chicago Tribune,* December 10, 1991; April 13, 1992.
*Detroiter,* September 1991.
*Detroit Free Press,* November 5, 1992.
*Ebony,* October 1990.
*EM,* May 1992.
*Essence,* March 1993.
*Herald-News* (Joliet, IL), May 13, 1990.
*Jet,* November 27, 1995, p. 58; May 12, 1997, p. 35; June 23, 1997, p. 35.
*Publishers Weekly,* November 11, 1996, p. 65.
*Upscale,* August/September 1992.
*USA Today,* January 25, 1993. □

# Lenny Bruce

**American comedian Lenny Bruce (1925–1966) made fun of everything held sacred during the 1950s and early 1960s, from the Lone Ranger television character to the Pope and Jesus Christ. His irreverent "anything goes" style eventually caused him to be jailed for public obscenity.**

L enny Bruce shocked and entertained audiences during the politically conservative years following World War II. His irreverent and unabashed antics failed to amuse everyone, and on a number of occasions he was

charged with public obscenity. He was convicted in several states and spent his final years involved in court appeals, defending his right to free speech. Bruce's life and career ended tragically when he died of a narcotic drug overdose at age 40.

## First Comedic Influence

Bruce was born Leonard Alfred Schneider in Mineola, New York on October 13, 1925. As a child during the Great Depression, he lived with his mother and assorted relatives in a singularly Jewish environment. He saw his father infrequency, and life with Bruce's mother, comedian Sally Marr, was erratic at best. Bruce attended six elementary schools, sold pop bottles for spending cash, and stole lunches from other students. By his own admission, he sniffed aerosols as a youngster. Bruce's mother was completely uninhibited and supported herself in unconventional ways. For a time she operated a dance studio and furnished adult escorts. As Bruce grew to adulthood, his mother developed her own comedy act and performed in nightclubs. From his mother, Lenny learned to laugh at life's irregularities.

Bruce left home at the age of 16 and went to live with a couple named Dengler on their Long Island farm. He stayed on the farm until shortly after the beginning of World War II. In 1942, Bruce joined the U.S. Navy. After boot camp he served as an apprentice seaman on the *U.S.S. Brooklyn.* The ship was stationed in France and Italy, where Bruce experienced live combat conditions. He longed to return home. In order to secure a discharge, Bruce dressed like a female sailor until his superiors requested a dishonorable discharge. Through the intervention of the Red Cross, the Navy reversed the circumstance of the discharge and Bruce received an honorable release.

## Bruce Found an Audience

No longer able to live at the Dengler farm, Bruce returned to live with his mother. She was working as a stand-up comedian at various clubs around Brooklyn. Bruce accompanied her to work and watched her and the other performers present their routines. Bruce himself took the stage one evening at the Victory Club, as a stand-in master of ceremonies. He used the stage name "Lenny Marsalle" that evening but later settled on Lenny Bruce. Despite pre-show jitters, Bruce composed himself and delivered a string of ad libs. To his surprise, the audience laughed and found him marginally amusing. Bruce, who performed without pay that first evening, was instantly addicted to the world of entertainment. In time, he secured an agent and played amateur clubs and contest, sometimes for a $2 fee or for prizes. Bruce wrote an act for himself to perform on stage so that he would not get tongue tied. He did excellent impressions of famous movie stars including Humphrey Bogart, James Cagney, and Edward G. Robinson. In 1947, he used those impressions to win *Arthur Godfrey's Talent Scouts,* a radio show talent contest.

Bruce performed in vaudeville shows and in burlesque theaters during the late 1940s, but in time he joined the merchant marine, working on the Luckenback Line to the Middle East. As a merchant seaman, Bruce visited over two dozen countries. At every port of call he saw little of the terrain and the culture beyond the shore bars and brothels. Bruce adopted the promiscuous lifestyle of many soldiers and seamen among his peers. On board the merchant ships, he learned to smoke hashish.

## Return to Show Business

Shortly before he sailed with the merchant marine, Bruce met an exotic dancer named Harriet "Honey" Harlowe. Bruce was enamored with Harlowe after spending one evening with her at a party. The intense mutual attraction left a strong impression on Bruce, who eventually tracked her down by telephone while he was working on a merchant boat that was docked in Spain. The 25-year-old Bruce found Harlowe willing to wed and returned home as quickly as possible.

The newlywed couple re-entered show business in 1951. Bruce performed comedy while Harlowe sang and danced. They performed together in nightclubs. Bruce determined that he should raise money to pay for singing lessons for Harlowe, to enable her to resume her former career as an exotic dancer. Bruce, true to his outrageous comedic nature, concocted a false identity for himself. He assumed the identity of a priest and solicited donations for a leper colony in Guyana. Bruce collected $8,000 in three days before frustrated Miami law enforcement officials arrested him. He ceased his gigolo-like tactics and focused his efforts toward his stage career and his marriage.

The couple worked together until 1954 when both suffered severe injuries in a violent car crash in Pittsburgh.

Bruce was thrown from the car, fractured his skull, and suffered lacerations. Harlowe's injuries were much worse. She was unable to walk for four months. Eventually the couple recovered and moved to a chicken farm in Arcadia, California that was owned by Bruce's father and step-mother.

Bruce, who studied acting at the Geller Dramatic Workshop in Southern California, was acutely ahead of his time in his political sympathies. He had great concern for the poverty stricken, discounted anti-Communist propaganda, took issue with capital punishment and what he viewed as other social shortcomings. On stage, Bruce made fun of the established traditions of Middle America. He was a talented speaker, and although his act was meticulously prepared and rehearsed, he projected a spontaneity to his audience. His natural gift for weaving stories, combined with an unnatural ability to ramble into a stream of consciousness repartee, was fundamental to his genius.

## Obscenity Issues and Arrests

Kitty Bruce was born in 1955, the only child of Lenny Bruce and Harriet Harlowe. Soon Bruce became increasingly possessive of his wife, and developed a dependency on narcotic drugs. The couple divorced in 1957.

Within a year, Bruce established a following at several reputable nightclubs in San Francisco. His popularity soared as his reputation for using profanity and obscenity in his act grew. On stage, Bruce held nothing sacred. He clowned about perversion and sexual fantasies, taunted those who held the tenets of Judeo-Christian thought, and described the deep-seated racial tension in America. Lenny Bruce achieved high visibility. His antics were broadcast through the rapidly rising recording industry as well as through television. Many recognized the underlying truth in the Lenny Bruce message. This was true of the late San Francisco columnist Herb Caen, quoted in *Playboy*. "They call Lenny Bruce a sick comic—and sick he is. Sick of the pretentious phoneyness of a generation that makes his vicious humor meaningful." By the early 1960s, Lenny Bruce was invited to perform at Carnegie Hall. Despite the "adults only" nature of his act, he played to sellout audiences in 1960 and 1961.

In the midst of overwhelming popularity, Bruce was arrested for obscenity in San Francisco in October 1961. The case went to trial early in 1962 and ended in acquittal for Bruce. Later that year, he was arrested at the popular Gate of Horn Club in Chicago. In 1963, Bruce was refused admission to both England and Australia following a narcotics arrest and drug conviction earlier that year.

A conviction on obscenity charges in New York on November 4, 1964, caused another setback for Bruce, despite his earlier success in evading similar charges on the West Coast. The New York trial lasted six months. Despite petitions and testimony filed by prominent personalities including Gore Vidal and Norman Mailer, Bruce was convicted because he used "obscene, indecent, immoral, and impure" language and gestures in his performances. Bruce was sentenced to four months in jail, during which time his conviction in Chicago remained on appeal.

Bruce returned to San Francisco following his conviction in New York. Increasingly stressed and obsessed by his legal problems, he was determined to exonerate himself. Unfortunately, he was severely addicted to heroine at that time and lived mostly in seclusion after 1965. He stayed close to home and rarely worked. He gave his final comedic performance on June 25, 1966, at the Fillmore Auditorium in San Francisco. A few weeks later, on August 3, 1966, Bruce died of a drug overdose in Hollywood. His death was ruled accidental; he was 40 years old.

## The Legacy of Lenny Bruce

Shortly before his death, Lenny Bruce published his autobiography, *How To Talk Dirty and Influence People.* Another publication, *The Essential Lenny Bruce,* went to print in 1966 and featured his collected comedy routines. The 1971 Broadway play, *Lenny,* was based on his life, and a movie by the same name was filmed later. A retrospective biography, *Ladies and Gentlemen, Lenny Bruce!!* was written by Albert Goldman and published in 1974. Kitty Bruce compiled assorted memorabilia into a manuscript entitled *The Almost Unpublished Lenny Bruce: from the private collection of Kitty Bruce.* She published the book in 1984. In 1998, Bruce was the subject of a movie produced for the Home Box Office (HBO) cable network.

In the late 1950s, Lenny Bruce made a series of comedy recordings and selected albums including, *The Sick Humor of Lenny Bruce* and *Interview of Our Times,* later reissued on compact disc in 1992 as a two-volume release entitled *The Lenny Bruce Originals.*

## Further Reading

Bruce, Lenny, *How To Talk Dirty and Influence People,* Playboy Press, 1963, 1964, 1965.

Hamilton, Neil A., *ABC-CLIO Companion to the 1960s Counterculture in America,* 1997.

Thomas, William Karl, *Lenny Bruce: the Making of a Prophet,* Archon Books, 1989.

*Entertainment,* May 29, 1992; November 2, 1990.

*Playboy,* August 1991. □

# Jean de Brunhoff

**Often considered the father of the modern picture book, Jean de Brunhoff (1899–1937) is best known as the creator of Babar the elephant, one of the most beloved characters in twentieth-century juvenile literature. Lauded as an artist and writer of exceptional talent, Brunhoff is praised for creating classic works that have been popular with children and adults around the world.**

Brunhoff wrote and illustrated six stories about Babar and an alphabet book featuring the character. Throughout the series, the author depicts important events in Babar's life—his birth, the loss of his mother, his journey to the city, his education, his return home, his marriage, his coronation, the birth of his children, and the development of his kingdom—in what is considered a warm and believable manner. The Babar books are often noted for reflecting the personal life and philosophy of their creator. At the time of their publication in the 1930s, the stories were considered unique and even revolutionary. They were originally published as oversized volumes with the text printed in cursive writing and the watercolor and line paintings in spacious double-page spreads. This format led children to immerse themselves in the books. Brunhoff wrote his works in straightforward yet poetic prose and illustrated them in bright colors and economic line. He is often praised for the expressiveness and detail of his pictures as well as for his creative use of the double-page spread. Although some observers criticize Brunhoff for including death, war, nightmares, and other unpleasant facts of life in books for children, most view him as a writer and artist whose works have provided the world with one of its most memorable fictional characters.

## Early Life

In *Three Centuries of Children's Books in Europe,* Bettina Hurlimann called the author's life "inseparable from his books" and several critics believe that Babar is Brunhoff's characterization of himself. Born in Paris, on December 9, 1899, Brunhoff was the fourth and last child of Maurice de Brunhoff, a successful publisher, and his wife Marguerite. Jean attended Protestant schools, including the prestigious L'Ecole Alsacienne.

After graduation, Brunhoff joined the French army at the end of World War I and reached the front lines when the war was nearly over. Deciding to become a professional artist, he studied painting with Othon Friesz at the Acadamie de la Grand Chamiere in Montparnasse, producing landscapes, portraits, and still lifes that are thought to foreshadow his Babar books. In 1924, Brunhoff married Cecile Sabourand, a talented pianist from a Catholic family. The couple had three sons: Laurent, born in 1925; Mathieu, born in 1926; and Thierry, born in 1934.

## Creation of Babar

In 1930, Cecile de Brunhoff invented a bedtime story about a little elephant to amuse four-year-old Matthieu, who was ill. Matthieu and Laurent related the tale to their father, who named the elephant, illustrated the tale, and expanded it into a book. *Historie de Babar, le petit elephant* was published in 1931. It appeared in English as *The Story of Babar the Little Elephant* in 1933. The immediate success of the book prompted Brunhoff to create more stories about Babar and his family, as well as a concept book featuring the characters: *The Travels of Babar,* 1934; *Babar the King,* 1935; *ABC of Babar,* 1936; *Zephir's Holidays,* 1937; *Babar and His Family,* 1938; and *Babar and Father Christmas,* 1940. The popularity of his books prompted Brunhoff's commission to decorate the children's dining room of the ocean liner *Normandie* with paintings of Babar.

In the early 1930s, Brunhoff learned that he had tuberculosis. His illness forced the artist to spend long periods of time in a Swiss sanitorium. The Babar books are often considered a vehicle for the author to share himself with his family. Brunhoff died in Switzerland on October 16, 1937, at the age of 38. Ten years after Brunhoff's death, his eldest son Laurent revived the series with works of his own. Since that time, he has published more than 50 Babar books in several formats.

## Critical Reception

Reviewers are nearly unanimous in their assessment of Brunhoff as one of the most successful authors of children's literature. His contemporaries praised the freshness of his conception and the effectiveness of its execution. Writing in the *Spectator,* John Piper called him "Edward Lear's closest neighbour," adding that Brunhoff "had that power of careful observation that allowed him again and again to hit on ideas so simple and obvious that nobody has thought of them in that way before, although everybody wishes they had." Eleanor Graham of the *Junior Bookshelf* claimed, "Unquestionably, one man's whole genius went to the making of these books, his whole artistic skill, the full weight and strength of his personality, and all the wit and wisdom of his adult mind." In his introduction to *The Travels of Babar,* author A. A. Milne, himself the creator of another icon of childhood, Winnie-the-Pooh, noted, "If you love elephants, you will love Babar and Celeste. If you have never loved elephants, you will love them now. If you who are grown-up have never been fascinated by a picture book before, then this is the one which will fascinate you." Milne ended by saying, "I salute M. de Brunhoff. I am at his feet."

Contemporary reviewers comment on the cultural, political, and sociological characteristics of Babar's kingdom, while noting Brunhoff's artistry and the classic status of the series. Roger Sale, writing in his *Fairy Tales and After: From Snow White to E. B. White,* offered that the Babar stories "rightly rank with the Beatrix Potter books as the best ever made for very young children." In his introduction to *Babar's Anniversary Album,* a collection of three tales by Jean de Brunhoff and three by Laurent, author/illustrator Maurice Sendak wrote, "Babar is at the very heart of my conception of what turns a picture book into a work of art. . . . Beneath the pure fun, the originality of style, and the vivacity of imagination is a serious and touching theme: a father writing to his sons and voicing his natural concern for their welfare, for their lives . . . Jean's bequest to his family, and the world, shines from the books." In her biography of the Brunhoffs, *Jean and Laurent de Brunhoff: The Legacy of Babar,* Ann Meinzen Hildebrand concluded, "Whatever success and popularity Babar stories have today . . . is ultimately due to Jean de Brunhoff's creative genius and fatherly intelligence, bequeathed to a world of readers and, fortunately, to a son who could also make picture books."

## Further Reading

*Babar's Anniversary Album,* Random House, 1981.
*Children's Literature Review,* Volume 4, edited by Gerard J. Senick. Gale, 1982.
*Contemporary Authors,* Volume 137, edited by Susan M. Trosky and Donna Olendorf. Gale, 1992.
*Fairy Tales and After: From Snow White to E. B. White,* Harvard University Press, 1978.
Hildebrand, Ann Meinzen. *Jean and Laurent de Brunhoff: The Legacy of Babar,* Twayne Publishers, 1991.
*Junior Bookshelf,* January 1941.
*Something about the Author,* Volume 24, Gale, 1981.
*Three Centuries of Children's Books in Europe,* translated and edited by Brian W. Alderson. Oxford University Press, 1967.
*Writers for Children,* Scribner's, 1988.
*Spectator,* December 6, 1940, p. 611. □

# Lepke Buchalter

**At a time in U.S. history when gangsters were famous personalities, Louis ("Lepke") Buchalter (1897–1944) was one of the most famous of all. As head of Murder, Inc. he was also one of the most feared.**

Louis ("Lepke") Buchalter was born in New York City in 1897. The son of a Jewish hardware store owner on Manhattan's Lower East Side, his childhood was filled with street fighting and minor crimes. His only known occupation was as a criminal. Lepke (a childhood nickname by which he was universally known) graduated from simple pushcart robberies at the age of sixteen to organizing protection rackets the following year. Too short at five feet seven and one-half inches to intimidate those he sought to "protect," Lepke joined forces with Jacob ("Gurrah") Shapiro, a huge man whom he met when they both attempted to rob the same pushcart.

## Labor Activities

Being an intelligent young man, Lepke began to consider the potential of labor unions. He realized that if all the workers in an industry were members of a union, and if he could then control that union, he would be in control of the industry. By exerting pressure on both labor and management, he soon dominated entire industries by forcing employers to pay his organization in order to keep union workers in line. At the height of his power, Lepke controlled the entire garment trade and the bakery delivery truck union in New York City. He charged the bakers one cent per loaf for transporting their bread to market in a timely fashion.

## Organized Crime was a Business

From 1927 until 1936, Lepke and Shapiro had exported tens of millions of dollars from industries in New York City and across the United States. He always managed to cover his illegal activities. Although the authorities knew what he was doing, they didn't have enough evidence to prosecute him. Or, in some cases, they were paid off and merely looked the other way. The money rolled in. Lepke became one of the wealthiest of all the gangsters.

During the 1930's, Lepke was one of the most powerful figures in organized crime. For six years, he led Murder, Inc., the national crime syndicate's enforcement arm. If a crime boss wanted a murder committed, he would go

through Lepke to hire one of the killers. As many as 100 murders have been attributed to Lepke himself, since he sometimes enjoyed carrying out a contract on his own just to stay in practice. Those under his control probably killed hundreds more. He was considered by most law enforcement officials to be the number two mobster, behind Charles "Lucky" Luciano, the top crime syndicate leader. This was true even though Lepke was less well known. He tended to avoid the headlines and, unlike his colleagues, shunned publicity. Lepke didn't look the part of a hardened murderer and mobster. He generally wore a well-tailored suit and had the appearance of a businessman of some means. He had a wife and a son, and on the street or at a social occasion he didn't seem frightening at all.

## Political Influence

Lepke was also a powerful man in politics. He once offered a deal to United States Attorney for New York, Thomas Dewey. The deal might have assured Dewey of gaining the highest elected position in the United States, the presidency. Lepke offered to provide information on organized crime connections of top figures within President Franklin D. Roosevelt's cabinet. This included Sidney Hillman, president of the Amalgamated Clothing Workers and a top advisor to Roosevelt. Since Lepke had been involved in racketeering throughout the country, and was the "boss" of the garment district in New York, he was in a position to know of Hillman's connections.

Dewey turned him down. Although he was later nominated to run against Roosevelt, Dewey lost by a large margin. Political experts still speculate about what might have happened if Dewey had accepted Lepke's offer. That information would certainly have hurt Roosevelt in the election and might have changed the course of U.S. history.

## Final Capture

The capture and conviction of Lepke was almost like a motion picture script. He had gone into hiding in 1937, due to the intense pressure from lawmen like Tom Dewey. He was wanted for murder by the city of New York and a $25,000 reward was offered. The federal government, who matched the reward with another $25,000, wanted him for narcotics trafficking. This was a tremendous amount of money in the 1930's, but not a single person came forward to claim it. Most were simply frightened at what the still-powerful Lepke would have done to them. He still had his gang of thugs who would do anything to ensure his continued safety.

Finally, with persuasion from Lucky Luciano and thinking he had made a "deal" to serve only a short prison sentence, Lepke made an agreement with the noted radio and newspaper columnist, Walter Winchell, to turn himself in. J. Edgar Hoover, of the Federal Bureau of Investigation, approved the surrender arrangement. On August 24, 1939, Lepke reported to Winchell and Winchell handed him over to Hoover.

Unfortunately for Lepke, there was no deal. He had made a fatal mistake in coming out of hiding, or in believing what his friend Luciano and the authorities had promised. Nor did the syndicate come forward to help him, by pressuring those they were paying off to get him released. Gangland had turned against him. Lepke was promptly turned over to the Brooklyn District Attorney's office, and with the help of Tom Dewey, the United States Attorney of New York, he was vigorously prosecuted.

## Execution for Murder

Lepke was executed for the murder of Joseph Rosen, a candy store clerk. He could have saved his own life if he agreed to turn informant. Law enforcement officials, and especially FBI Director, Herbert Hoover, knew that Lepke could give them reams of information on other gangsters of the day. Despite pleas from his wife to save his life, he refused. Speaking of United States Attorney, James B. McNally, who had the power to stop the execution, Lepke's wife pleaded, "He'll listen to you, Lou. God knows you can tell him enough to save you." Even Lepke's 22-year-old son, Harold, begged his father to turn state's evidence.

Lepke refused. He knew that his time was limited whatever he decided to do and that, even if he gave in, they would execute him eventually. "I'll have six months or so, and that's all," he said. The six months, he knew, would be served in prison. Lepke said, "I'd rather go tonight." Witnesses present in the death house at Sing Sing Prison in Ossining, New York reported that he died with dignity in the electric chair on March 5, 1944.

The categories of organized crime at that time were listed by the Department of Police Studies of Eastern Kentucky University, and Lepke had a hand in each. Organized crime, said the University's Gary W. Potter, included the provision of illicit goods and services, conspiracy, the penetration of legitimate businesses, extortion, and corruption. This was the life of Louis "Lepke" Buchalter.

## Further Reading

*American Decades, 1940-1949.* edited by Victor Bondi, Gale Research, 1995.
Wetzel, Donald. *Pacifist, My War and Louis Lepke,* 1994.
*Time Magazine,* Time 100, Builders & Titans,
*Compton's Interactive Encyclopedia,* 1996.
*Microsoft Encarta,* 1994.
New York Daily News Online, www.nydailynews.com □

# David Buick

**David Buick (1854–1929) is remembered for his association with the automobile industry. The Buick name, which first appeared on an automobile in 1903, remains a vital part of the General Motors (GM) production line. Unfortunately, Buick the man never became as successful as Buick the automobile. Although he was a talented mechanic and inventor, Buick's poor business decisions and his inability to maintain financial stability finally led to his failure as an automaker.**

Buick was born on September 17, 1854, in Arbroath, Scotland, the son of Alexander Buick and Jane Roger. When he was two years old, the family immigrated to Detroit, Michigan. Alexander Buick died when his son was five years old, which placed an undue financial burden on the family. Buick attended elementary school, but he dropped out at the age of eleven to help his mother with the household bills. For the next few years, Buick found jobs delivering newspapers, working on a farm, and apprenticing as a machinist at the James Flower and Brothers Machine Shop, where Henry Ford also apprenticed in 1880.

When he was 15 years old, Buick got a job with the Alexander Manufacturing Company, a Detroit-based firm that made enameled iron toilet bowls and wooden closer tanks. Using the skills he had acquired as a machinist, Buick was eventually promoted to foreman of the shop. In 1878, he married Catherine Schwinck, with whom he had four children. His oldest son, Thomas D. Buick, would later work with his father in the automobile industry.

## Buick and Sherwood Plumbing and Supply Company

The Alexander Manufacturing Company failed in 1882 and Buick became partners with William S. Sherwood. The two assumed the company's assets to create the Buick and Sherwood Plumbing and Supply Company. Buick's later inept business deals suggest that Sherwood was the driving force behind the plumbing company's financial success,

while Buick contributed to that success with his mechanical skills and numerous inventions. In fact, by the end of the 1880s, Buick had received 13 patents—all but one related to plumbing. His most popular invention created a method of bonding porcelain onto metal. At a time when indoor plumbing was rapidly increasing in popularity, this patent contributed a great deal to the viability of his company. During the late 1890s, Buick became interested in gasoline-powered internal combustion engines. In December 1899, Buick and Sherwood sold the plumbing company for $100,000 to the Standard Sanitary Manufacturing Company. Drawn by his increasing infatuation with engines, Buick invested his share of the $100,000 in a new company that he named the Buick Auto-Vim and Power Company. Buick was completely disassociated from the plumbing business by 1902.

## A Move to Automobile Manufacturing

Buick Auto-Vim and Power Company sold marine and stationary engines that were commonly used to operate farm and lumbering equipment. Buick's first projects focused on attempting to increase the power of these standard engines. He also created a new "L-head" engine design with the help of Walter L. Marr and Eugene C. Richard. The L-head engine was an unsuccessful attempt to modify a marine engine to operate a carriage. Buick was not discouraged by the failure of his new engine, although he did find himself in some financial trouble. He then turned his attention to the development of a "valve-in-head" design, hoping to create a commercially viable automobile engine.

With the development of the valve-in-head design, Buick finally had an engine that would be successful in his early car models. Although he participated in the development of the engine, Marr and Richard did much of the design work. Marr, who designed an automobile engine as early as 1898, acted as Buick's general manager until the two had a disagreement and Marr left the company. Using the knowledge he had gained from his previous work for Olds Motor Works, Richard completed the job Marr had left unfinished.

## The Buick Manufacturing Company

Buick's financial problems continued to grow. In April 1891, he offered to sell Marr the Buick automobile for $300. He also offered Marr an assortment of engines, designs, and parts for $1,500. His attempt to sell these items for such a small amount suggests that he was interested in finding capital to continue his research and design in any manner possible. In 1902, he reorganized his company as the Buick Manufacturing Company, thus setting a path toward the development of a commercially successful automobile.

Buick eventually convinced Benjamin and Frank Briscoe, suppliers of metal parts to Detroit's young automobile industry, to forgive the debt he owed them and advance him $650 for the automobile on which he was working. The car was successfully road tested in early 1903. Although owned by the Briscoe brothers, the metal suppliers let Buick use the car to promote his business and raise money to support its production.

## The Buick Motor Company

Buick had little luck finding investors and, by spring of 1903, he returned to make another deal with the Briscoes. This agreement, however, would ultimately cost Buick his own business. The Briscoe brothers recapitalized Buick's company at $100,000, which now became the Buick Motor Company. As part of the deal, Buick received a loan of approximately $3,500 and became president of the company. In return, the Briscoes maintained $99,700 of the company's stock and Buick only held $300 in stock. Furthermore, Buick was given six months to repay his debt, at which time he would have the option of acquiring all the stock, but if he failed to meet this requirement, the Briscoes would assume complete control of the company.

Before the deadline of September 1903 was reached, the Briscoe brothers sold the Buick Motor Company to a group of business investors from Flint, Michigan, who were led by the president of the Flint Wagon Works, James H. Whiting. Construction of a Flint production plant began in September 1903, and the Buick Motor Company began production the following January. The once again reorganized company was incorporated on January 14, 1904, at a $75,000 capitalization. Buick became the company's secretary and also acted as general manager. As part of the reorganization, he and his son Thomas were given 1,500 shares of stock between them, but they was barred from actually owning the stock until Buick's debts, which were now owned by Whiting's group, were repaid.

## The Buick Model B

By the end of May 1904, Buick had joined with Marr to create the first valve-in-head double-opposed engine. The first Model B automobile was produced in July 1904. Marr and Buick's son, Thomas, test drove the prototype to Detroit on July 9 and returned on July 12. The trip home took only three hours and 37 minutes, averaging a speed of nearly 30 miles per hour. With the success of the test drive, which was reported favorably in the *Flint Journal,* commercial production of the Model B began in August 1904. On August 13, 1904, Buick Motor Company made its first sale, delivering a Model B to Dr. Herbert Hills of Flint. By mid-September, 16 more Buicks had been sold. Another 11 cars were delivered by the end of the year. In all, 37 Buicks were produced and sold in 1904.

Despite this successful start, Whiting was growing increasingly nervous about his investment. Buick had borrowed a significant sum of money from Flint banks to finance the commercial production of his automobiles, but he had not developed a marketing plan to insure that sales would increase. Whiting was also feeling pressure from the Association of Licensed Automobile Manufacturers, the holder of the patent for the Selden internal combustion "road engine," which was threatening to prohibit the production of the Buick automobiles on the issue of patent rights infringement.

## William Durant Takes Charge

Whiting looked to William C. Durant to solve his problems. Durant, the president of Durant-Dort Carriage Company of Flint, was known for his marketing savvy. When Whiting first approached Durant, he was reticent about entering the automobile industry. After personally testing the Buick, however, the idea of entering the business became more appealing. Finally, on November 1, 1904, Durant recapitalized the Buick Motor Company at $300,000. He became the newly reorganized company's president, and quickly moved David Buick out of any meaningful role in the company's business. Within a year, Buick had only 110 shares of stock and was working as an engineer in the "experimental room."

Durant proved his marketing skills over the next several years. In 1905, the Buick Motor Company produced 750 automobiles. The next year, production was doubled to 1,400 cars. A new design, the Model 10, hit the market in 1908 and proved to be extremely popular. Production boomed to 8,820, which was more than Ford and Cadillac production combined. Buick never profited from this commercial success; he still owed the company money, which he never repaid. Finally, he was forced to resign in 1908, forfeiting his stock shares and receiving at least $100,000 from Durant in severance pay.

In the same year, Durant formed General Motors with an initial capital stock of $2,000, which increased to $12.5 million 12 days after its inception. Durant hoped to use GM to buy control of car companies. On October 1, 1908, Buick Motor Company became his first purchase. Although it remained an independent company for another ten years, after 1908 the Buick Motor Company was essentially controlled by its holding company, GM.

## Left the Automobile Business

Buick used the money from his severance pay to finance an oil-company venture in California and land deals in Florida, all of which failed. Buick also failed in his attempts to create a carburetor company and an automobile company with his son Thomas. In the last years of his life, he taught mechanics classes at the Young Men's Christian Association in Detroit. He died in Detroit on March 6, 1929 at the age of 74.

## Further Reading

*American National Biography,* Vol. 3, edited by John A. Garraty and Mark C. Carnes, Oxford University Press, 1999.

Dammann, George H., *Seventy Years of Buick,* Crestline Publishing, 1973.

*Encyclopedia of American Business History and Biography: The Automobile Industry, 1896-1920,* edited by George S. May, Bruoccoli Clark Layman, Inc., 1990.

Weisberger, Bernard A., *The Dream Maker: William C. Durant, Founder of General Motors,* Little, Brown, 1979. □

# Leo Burnett

**Leo Burnett (1891–1971) founded the advertising agency that carried his name as well as the "Chicago School" of advertising. In Burnett's ads, visual,**

**meaningful images were emphasized over text-filled explanations of the product's features. Burnett and his agency were responsible for the creation of such famous product icons as the Pillsbury Dough Boy and the Marlboro Man.**

Burnett was born on October 21, 1891, in St. Johns, Michigan. He was the oldest child of Noble and Rose Clark Burnett, who ran a dry goods store. Burnett worked in the store as a youth, where he watched his father design ads to promote his business. He also lettered advertising signs for his father. But Burnett felt he was at a disadvantage. In *The Mirror Makers: A History of American Advertising and Its Creators,* author Stephen Fox quoted Burnett as saying "I always figured that I was less smart than some people, but that if I worked hard enough maybe I would average out all right." While attending high school, Burnett worked as a reporter for local, rural newspapers during the summer. After graduation, he taught school for a short while.

Burnett attended the University of Michigan, receiving a bachelor's degree in 1914. His dream at that point was to become publisher of *The New York Times.* To that end, he worked as a police reporter for a newspaper in Peoria, Illinois for one year. When he learned how much money could be made in advertising, Burnett decided to make a career change. He got a job editing an in-house publication for Cadillac dealers called *Cadillac Clearing House.* Burnett went on to become an advertising director for that company. He was mentored by Theodore F. MacManus, a leading figure in advertising at the time, known for his ethics.

On May 29, 1918, Burnett married Naomi Geddes, with whom he had three children, Peter, Joseph, and Phoebe. He then joined the Navy for six months. After the First World War ended, Burnett moved his family to Indianapolis, Indiana. He became the advertising manager for a new car company, LaFayette Motors, which was founded by former Cadillac employees. When the company left Indiana, Burnett stayed.

In 1919, he was hired by a local advertising agency, the Homer McGee Company. In this agency, Burnett handled automobile ads for several accounts. A rising star in the company, he was content to remain in this position for over a decade. Although he made half-hearted attempts to find jobs in New York City, the capital of advertising, nothing came of these efforts. When Burnett neared 40, he thought it was time to make a move and was hired by New York's Erwin, Wassey to work in their Chicago office as a vice president and the head of the creative department. Burnett worked at Erwin, Wassey for five years. There were some problems finding good creative personnel. Burnett brought in some people from the Homer McGee Company because many of his most creative people were being lured to New York City. One valued employee was Dewitt "Jack" O'Kieffe, who got an offer from a New York City agency. He gave Burnett an ultimatum: start his own agency or O'Kieffe would make the move.

## Founded Leo Burnett Company

On August 5, 1935, Burnett founded the Leo Burnett Company, Inc., in Chicago with $50,000 and several creative employees from Erwin, Wassey, including O'Kieffe. In *The Mirror Makers,* Fox quoted Burnett as saying "My associates and I saw the opportunity to offer a creative service badly needed in the Middle West. I sold my house, hocked all my insurance, and took a dive off the end of a springboard." What made Burnett's venture especially risky was the fact that advertising's big players were located on Madison Avenue in New York City.

The first years were hard. The Leo Burnett Company's first accounts were "women's products," including The Hoover Company, Minnesota Valley Canning Company, and Realsilk Hosiery Mills. The company billed less than $1 million in 1935-36. Yet Burnett persevered, and carved out his empire where he was most comfortable. Burnett was a modest man without the ego that dominated many advertising agency owners. In his obituary in *Time,* the unnamed author wrote, "He was, in brief, the antithesis of the popular conception of the sleek, cynical advertising man." Burnett named himself president and worked day and night, every day except Christmas. He had no real interests outside of advertising. While Burnett was unassuming and a horrible public speaker, his ads revolutionized the industry. Stuart Ewan of *Time* wrote, "Leo Burnett, the jowly genius of the heartland subconscious, is the man most responsible for the blizzard of visual imagery that assaults us today."

## Burnett's Revolutionary Ads

At the time, print ads focused on words, long explanations of why a consumer should buy the product. Burnett believed such advertising was misguided. As Fox wrote in *The Mirror Makers,* "Instead of the fashionable devices of contests, premiums, sex, tricks and cleverness, he urged, use the product itself, enhanced by good artwork, real information, recipes, and humor." Yet all visuals did not have to be direct in Burnett's opinion. They could also work subliminally. Ewan of *Time* wrote, "Visual eloquence, he was convinced, was far more persuasive, more poignant, than labored narratives, verbose logic, or empty promises. Visuals appealed to the 'basic emotions and primitive instincts' of consumers."

Burnett broke all the rules. For example, in the mid-1940s, it was basically taboo to depict raw meat in advertising. To send the message home in a campaign for the American Meat Institute, Burnett and his company put the raw, red meat against an even redder background. Such radical images caught the consumer's eye. Still, Burnett's agency only billed about $10 million a year for its first decade of existence. The world had yet to catch up to Burnett's ideas.

## Client List Grew

By the end of World War II, Burnett's billings began to increase, more than doubling to $22 million in 1950. By 1954, they doubled again to $55 million. Burnett's success increased for a number of reasons. He hired Richard Heath, who promoted the agency and brought in new, bigger clients, including Kellogg, Pillsbury, Procter & Gamble, and Campbell Soup. They were attracted by Burnett's creative ads. When television became a powerful advertising force in the 1950s, Burnett's company thrived because of its emphasis on the visual instead of market research. Ewan of *Time* wrote, "Burnett forged his reputation around the idea that 'share of market' could only be built on 'share of mind,' the capacity to stimulate consumers' basic desires and beliefs." Television did this best in Burnett's opinion, because the product's inherent drama could be presented via a series of memorable images.

In the 1950s, Burnett and his company developed a number of advertising icons that ended up lasting for decades. Among these were Charlie the Tuna for Starkist Tuna, Tony the Tiger for Kellogg's Frosted Flakes, the underemployed Maytag repairman, and the Jolly Green Giant. Like many of Burnett's icons, the Jolly Green Giant is an image based in folklore and therefore familiar to many consumers. The Jolly Green Giant was created for one of the company's first clients, the Minnesota Canning Company. Eventually, the company renamed itself Green Giant because of the power of this icon, and saw its sales dramatically increase from the $5 million figure in 1935.

### Developed the Marlboro Man

One of Burnett's most famous advertising icons was the Marlboro Man. When first introduced, in 1955, filter cigarettes were considered unmanly, intended for a female consumer. By using the manliest man—a tattooed cowboy astride a horse—filter Marlboros became viewed as a very masculine product by consumers. Burnett changed the way filter cigarettes were marketed and Marlboros became the best selling cigarettes on the market. By the end of the 1950s, the Leo Burnett Company was billing over $100 million annually.

Though the company and its clients had grown exponentially, Burnett remained very involved with his company. He headed the planning board, through which every ad had to pass. Burnett wanted to ensure consumers focused on the product, not the ad. Though he was in charge, the atmosphere at the agency was a true collaborative process. Burnett was a demanding boss, but one capable of self-deprecating humor. In the 1960s, Burnett received the recognition of his peers, as his ideas became more widespread and affected the industry as whole. In 1961, Burnett was one of the four original inductees into the Copywriters Hall of Fame. As Fox in *The Mirror Makers* wrote, "From Burnett came a tradition of gentle manners, humor, credibility, and a disdain of research." In the 1960s, the "Chicago school" of advertising became a common phrase to describe Burnett's ads. Some peers used it negatively, arguing that his ads were low brow and corny. Burnett shrugged off such views, in his company motto: "When you reach for the stars, you may not get one, but you won't come up with a handful of mud either."

### Recognized for His Accomplishments

The Leo Burnett Company continued to invent original icons and slogans. In 1965, Burnett and his team created the

Pillsbury Doughboy. In 1968, they created the Keebler Elves and Morris the Cat for 9-Lives cat food. Both the Pillsbury Doughboy and the Elves lived on for decades. Some of Burnett's slogans lived a similarly long life. Allstate Insurance Company still uses "You're in good hands with Allstate." In the mid-1960s, the Leo Burnett Company was hired by United Airlines to improve the company's image. Burnett and his creative team came up with "Fly the Friendly Skies of United," variations of which were used for over three decades. Because Burnett wanted his company to work closely with its clients, in the 1960s, they also assisted with product development. For example, they were involved in the creation of Glad sandwich bags for Union Carbide, the first plastic bags on the market.

Burnett died of a heart attack on June 7, 1971, at his home in Lake Zurich, Illinois. He was buried in the Rosehill Cemetery of Chicago. At the time of his death, the Burnett Company had over $400 million in billings that year, and was the fifth largest advertising agency in the world. His legacy lived on through his company which, in 1998, had achieved over $6 billion in billings, and retained many of his loyal clients and employees. Rita Koselka of *Forbes* wrote in 1990, "the Burnett agency has accomplished something that has eluded so many other businesses: It has managed to keep the spirit and drive of its founder alive and well almost two decades after the founder himself passed on." Burnett's legacy can also be found in the advertising industry at large. Ewan of *Time* wrote, "His celebration of nonlinear advertising strategies, characterized by visual entreaties to the optical unconscious, continues to inform contemporary advertising strategies."

### Further Reading

Fox, Stephan, *The Mirror Makers: A History of American Advertising and Its Creators,* University of Illinois Press, 1997.

Garraty, John A. and Mark C. Carnes, *American National Biography,* Oxford University Press, 1999.

Ingham, John N. and Lynne B. Feldman, *Contemporary American Business Leaders: A Biographical Dictionary,* Greenwood Press, 1990.

*Forbes,* September 17, 1990.

*Time,* June 21, 1971; December 7, 1998. □

# Adolphus Busch

**Adolphus Busch (1839–1913) had no idea he would become a wealthy beer baron by inventing the best-selling beer in the world. A German immigrant, he married the boss's daughter and turned her father's brewery into one of the major companies in the U.S.**

Adolphus Busch was born in Kastel, Germany on July 10, 1839. He was the second youngest in a family of 22 children (some were half brothers and sisters), born to Ulrich Busch and Barbara Pfeiffer Busch. As a young immigrant, Adolphus Busch may have had some concern

when he first arrived in the United States in 1857. He had no home, no family, and nowhere to go. But the young Busch had confidence in his abilities and was ready to accept the challenge presented by this huge, new country.

## Busch Traveled West

Young Busch traveled west from New York, and found employment as a clerk on the riverfront in St. Louis, Missouri. It was probably the luckiest thing that could have happened to him. The young German was enterprising, industrious, and determined. Not satisfied with the clerking job, he formed a brewery supply company in the city of many breweries. Soon, Busch's company was making a modest profit.

In 1860, and unknown to Busch, a man by the name of Eberhard Anheuser purchased one of the dozens of small, struggling breweries in St. Louis. The two men met when Anheuser came to Busch for supplies for his new business. His brewery, E. Anheuser and Co., was barely hanging on, making no profit. Anheuser and Busch became friends, and the older man introduced Busch to his daughter, Lilly. The two young people fell in love and married in 1864, beginning a long and successful union and also a new job for Busch. He dissolved his supply company and went to work for his new father-in-law as a beer salesman.

## A Hard-Working Businessman

Busch was never a timid man. He believed in evaluating a business honestly and working hard to improve it.

Busch eventually gained a reputation for being one of the most flamboyant industrialists of the nineteenth century. In place of the traditional calling card used by most businessmen of the day, Busch often presented business associates with a fancy brass pocketknife engraved with the name of his business. A peephole in the handle of the knife revealed a portrait of Busch. If you own one of those unique knives today, you own a valuable antique.

Busch advanced in his father-in-law's company through hard work and long hours, eventually becoming a full partner. As a result of his efforts, he gained a thorough understanding of the brewing business. Busch learned that beer first appeared in 8000 BC, as an accidental but very pleasant discovery. He knew that beer would be popular forever and hoped to develop the best possible product for his growing brewery. Busch traveled to Europe in order to study various brewing techniques. His goal was to create a beer that would sell beyond the limits of St. Louis, a beer that would appeal to tastes across the country.

In 1869, nearing his dream of a beer that would appeal to all, Busch bought half-ownership in the company. As part owner, he could further utilize the brewing secrets he learned in Europe. His best friend, Carl Conrad, agreed with Busch that such a universally popular beer could be created. The two master brewers experimented at the St. Louis brewery, coming closer to the taste they were seeking. Finally, in 1876, they combined traditional brewing methods with a careful blending of the finest barley malt, hops, yeast, rice, and water. When they tasted the latest of their experiments, Busch and Conrad knew that they had finally made a lager beer that would appeal to all. The new beer was beyond even their own expectations.

## Budweiser was Born

Busch named the new beer "Budweiser" after a small town in Germany. It soon became the best-selling beer in the world, outselling all other brands. The brewery was renamed "Anheuser-Busch," a name it still bears today. The company grew rapidly, eventually becoming a major international corporation with business and marketing activities throughout the world. Busch was named president of the company in 1880, upon the death of his father-in-law, Eberhard Anheuser. He continued in this position for 33 years, and is considered by most in the brewing industry to be the founder of the company.

Busch approved the eagle design of the brewery's logo in 1872, but why an eagle was used has been lost in history. Some say it is a mark showing respect for America. Others claim it merely means unlimited vision. The "A" in the logo stood for Anheuser, the original owner and father of Busch's wife.

Twenty years after he assumed the presidency of the company, Busch developed another beer brand he called "Michelob." This creation became the pre-eminent super-premium beer on the market. Busch also pioneered the use of pasteurization to ensure beer's freshness after bottling. He knew that beer does not "age" well and tastes best when it is consumed as soon after brewing as possible. Today, his brewery still marks all beer with the date of bottling, to ensure its freshness.

## A Lavish Lifestyle

Busch became one of the most resplendent and extravagant business leaders in the late 1800s. He developed a great zest for life, ostentatious habits, and a regal attitude toward the world. In addition to his lavish home in St. Louis, Busch maintained a great country estate, two homes in Pasadena, California, a property and hop farm at Cooperstown, New York, two villas at Langenschwalbach, Germany, and a private railroad car. All the estates were noted for their fabulous grounds, and Busch furnished his gardens and woods with carvings of the characters from Grimm's fairy tales. Forty to fifty gardeners were needed to maintain the spacious grounds.

When Adolphus and Lilly Busch celebrated their golden wedding anniversary in 1911, it was as though a king and a queen were being crowned. Busch crowned his wife with a $200,000 diadem. The president of the United States sent a $20 gold piece. Theodore Roosevelt sent a solid gold loving cup and the emperor of Germany sent a similar gift. Presidents, ex-presidents, and emperors paid tribute to the man who made beer.

## Anheuser-Busch Continued to Grow

According to brewery officials, Busch's company was ranked 29th among 40 breweries in St. Louis in 1860. Total beer production in 1870 was 18,000 barrels. By 1995, Anheuser-Busch had become the largest brewer in the world, holding more than 45% of the domestic beer market. Nearly one out of every two beers sold in the United States was an Anheuser-Busch product. In 1997, the company had worldwide beer sales of more than 96 million barrels.

Adolphus Busch died in St. Louis on October 10, 1913, but the brewery he created stands as a monument to his vision and hard work.

## Further Reading

A-B History, http://www.budweisertours.com/docs/stltourcenter.htm

Beer History, www.beerhistory.com

Anheuser-Busch History, http://www.anheuser-busch.com/history/abhist.htm

*Compton's Interactive Encyclopedia,* 1994

German American Corner, http://www.germanheritage.com/biographies/busch/busch.html □

# C

## James Cain

**Although he disliked the title, James M. Cain (1892–1977) is considered one of the preeminent "hard-boiled" crime writers of the 1930s and 1940s along with Dashiell Hammett, Horace McCoy, and Raymond Chandler. His explicit, stark style both startled and enthralled his readers, and his recurring themes of sex, violence, and greed brought controversy to his writing. Cain published his first and most popular novel, *The Postman Always Rings Twice,* in 1934.**

James Mallahan Cain was born on July 1, 1892, in Annapolis, Maryland. His father, James William Cain, was an English professor who taught at St. John's College in Annapolis and was president of Washington College in Chestertown, Maryland. His mother, Rose Mallahan, was a professional opera singer. Cain's parents, both of Irish descent, were Catholic, and Cain was baptized in the Catholic Church. At 13 years of age, he abandoned the church and never returned.

Cain attended Washington College and graduated in 1910 at the age of 17. His college experience was rather unremarkable. After college Cain worked at several different jobs, each rather unsuccessfully. He studied singing for a time in hopes of becoming an opera singer like his mother, but when he was told his voice was not good enough to make singing a career, he decided to become a writer. Cain returned to Washington College to teach English and math. In 1917, he earned a master's degree in drama from Johns Hopkins University.

## Career in Journalism

In 1917, Cain began his journalism career at the *Baltimore American* as a reporter. Here he met H. L. Mencken, who would become his mentor and lifelong friend. Mencken greatly admired Cain's writing, and later he would publish many of Cain's short stories and articles in the *American Mercury*. In 1918, Cain began working for the *Baltimore Sun,* but his career was put on hold when he enlisted in the United States Army during World War I. He served in France and edited his company's weekly paper, *The Lorraine Cross,* which became one of the most successful publications of the American Expeditionary Forces.

Cain returned to the *Baltimore Sun* in 1919, where he remained until 1923. In 1922, Cain made his first attempt at writing a novel. He spent one winter on sabbatical from the paper and wrote three novels. By his own acknowledgment, none of them were noteworthy, and none were ever published. In 1920, he married Mary Rebekah Clough, a teacher. The marriage was brief, however, and in 1923 they separated. In the same year, Cain left the *Baltimore Sun* to teach English and journalism at St. John's College in Annapolis, Maryland. From 1924 to 1931 Cain wrote editorials at the *New York World* under Walter Lippman. His editorials and other writings were also published in periodicals such as *The Nation, Atlantic Monthly, American Mercury,* and *Saturday Evening Post.* During this time, Cain established a reputation for his witty, sharp-edged satirical commentaries on politics and society. A collection of his essays was published in 1930 as *Our Government.*

In 1927, Cain was divorced from his first wife and married Elina Sjösted Tyszecka. One year later he sold his first piece of fiction, a short story entitled "Pastorale," to his friend Mencken at the *American Mercury.* It was a story about a grisly murder, told in the first person with a some-

what comic edge. In this first published fictional work, Cain had started to develop what would become his favorite theme: two people commit a murder but cannot live with the outcome of their crime. With the success of "Pastorale," Cain began to focus more of his attention on fiction writing.

## Hollywood Bound

Cain was working as managing editor of the *New Yorker* in 1931 when several Hollywood producers who had taken notice of his work invited him to California to write screenplays. However, he was unsuccessful as a screenwriter. Six months after moving to Hollywood, Cain was unemployed. Unwilling to leave California, he began free-lance writing articles, editorials, and short stories mostly political in theme. Cain also began writing the novels for which he is best known.

In 1933, still unsure that he could succeed as a novelist, he wrote a short story entitled "The Baby in the Icebox." The story was a turning point for Cain in several ways. It was the first story Cain had set in California, allowing him to write in the local idiom, a trend he would continue in his novels. The story, which was first published in the *American Mercury* by Mencken, found favor with well-known publisher Alfred A. Knopf, who encouraged Cain to attempt a novel. Paramount purchased the rights to "The Baby in the Icebox," and it was produced as a film under the title *She Made Her Bed.*

## *The Postman Always Rings Twice*

Cain's first novel, *The Postman Always Rings Twice,* was published in 1934 when Cain was 42 years old. The book was a popular success, but not without controversy. Told as a first-person confessional, his style was darker and more explicit than was customary at the time. His characters' weaknesses were their obsession for sex and money, and violence was their chosen tool to find both. Because of the controversy surrounding the novel, it was originally banned in Canada, and it was not made into a play until 1937. The movie based on the novel was released in 1946.

The story is told from death row by drifter Frank Chambers. He recounts the tale of wandering into a greasy roadside diner owned by a Greek named Nick Papadakis and his wife, Cora, and the tragic events that follow. Frank, who agrees to work at the diner, begins a passionate, sometimes violent, love affair with Cora. Cora convinces Frank to help her kill her husband to collect insurance money. Although they are unsuccessful in their first attempt, their second attempt is successful; Nick is dead and the insurance money is theirs. However, their crime becomes their undoing. As their relationship unravels, Cora is killed in a car accident and Frank is wrongly convicted of her murder.

*The Postman Always Rings Twice* was first named *Bar-B-Q* by Cain, but the publisher balked at the title. In searching for a new name, Cain was reminded by a friend of the Irish tradition that the postman always rang (or in the old days, knocked) twice to let the residents know it was the postman. Since everything in the novel seemed to happen twice, including the murder, Cain decided he had found his new title.

## The Productive Years: 1936-1947

Over the next several years, Cain wrote extensively. In 1936, he wrote a serial in *Liberty* entitled "Double Indemnity," a story about an insurance salesman who helps his lover kill her husband for insurance money. However, once the husband is dead, they discover that they no longer love each other. Cain once again stirred up controversy in 1937 with the publication of *Serenade,* which dealt with sex, violence, and homosexuality. It is based on the love affair between a Mexican prostitute and an opera singer. Cain found success again in 1941 with *Mildred Pierce.* Set in the context of the Great Depression, Cain dealt again with the discrepancy between the desirable and the attainable. The main character is a housewife who almost finds a way through her painful existence as the owner of a restaurant, but her efforts are ultimately undercut by her greedy daughter.

"Double Indemnity" was made into a movie in 1943, starring Fred MacMurray, Barbara Stanwyck, and Edward G. Robinson. *Mildred Pierce* reached the theaters in 1945, starring Joan Crawford, who won an Academy Award for her part. Due to the success of these two films, producers finally made the controversial *Postman Always Rings Twice* into a movie in 1946, starring Lana Turner and John Garfield. Although Cain never wrote any of his own screenplays, 13 films were made based on his fictional writing.

Cain divorced Tyszecka in 1942 and was remarried two years later to Aileen Pringle, an actress. Once again, the marriage was short lived and they divorced in 1947. In the same year, Cain married his fourth wife, Florence Macbeth Whitwell, an opera singer. Cain never had children from any of his marriages.

## American Authors' Authority

In 1946, Cain attempted to organize the American Authors' Authority to protect the rights and interests of writers. The organization would have acted as trustee of its members' copyrights and negotiated with publishers and producers on issues concerning copyrights, film adaptations, reprints, and translations. It would have also represented the member writers in litigation and lobbied Congress. Cain was most likely motivated by his own experience, since he earned some $100,000 for his writings compared to the $12 million that Hollywood collected for the films based on his novels and short stories. However, his idea failed for several reasons. First, producers and publishers lobbied against it. Second, it was a time of extreme anti-Communist sentiment. Although Cain vehemently denied it, some perceived that such an organization had Communist undertones. Third, many authors themselves were not interested in an endeavor with such commercial interests, thinking of themselves not as business people, but as artists and scholars.

## Returned to Maryland

By the mid-1940s, Cain had published his most important and most popular works. Although more of his novels were adapted into films, he never again achieved the success of his early works—*The Postman Always Rings Twice, Mildred Pierce,* and *Double Indemnity.* For reasons unknown, Cain and his wife left Hollywood and returned to Maryland in 1947. In the next 29 years, he wrote nine more novels; only three were published, and none were widely read. Cain died of a heart attack on October 27, 1977, in University Park, Maryland; he was 85 years old. His death sparked a renewed interest in his writing. *The Postman Always Rings Twice* was released as a remake of the original film in 1981. In 1982, a screen version of *Butterfly* (1947) was produced.

Cain was a master of the plot. Sex and violence, almost always intricately related, were the motivators that drove his characters to believe that the most absurd plan could succeed. The dramatic and the tragic are revealed in the event, which was much more important to Cain than characterization, narration, or social message. Cain's sparely worded style brought to life characters too weak to overlook what appeared to be an easy opportunity to gain love and money. Yet, the sense of desperation flows just below the surface, and the reader is quickly drawn into their all-consuming obsession for love and happiness.

Although a popular writer, Cain's place as a novelist in literary circles is often debated. To his credit, he attracted many readers who themselves were distinguished authors, including Albert Camus, who admitted modeling *The Stranger* after *The Postman Always Rings Twice.* To his detriment, Cain used variations of the same theme repetitively:

man and woman become lovers, woman convinces man to become involved in something sinister, usually criminal, and man is destroyed by his involvement with the woman. Besides *The Postman Always Rings Twice,* this is also the basic plot in numerous Cain novels including *Serenade, Double Indemnity, The Butterfly, The Magician's Wife,* and *The Institute.* Although not all of his novels are of equal value, there is little doubt that his controversial, stark, first-person narrative style had an impact on the twentieth century literary world.

## Further Reading

*American National Biography.* edited by John A. Garraty and Mark C. Carnes. Oxford University Press, 1999.
*Benet's Reader's Encyclopedia,* fourth ed., edited by Bruce Murphy. HarperCollins, 1996.
*Contemporary Authors,* edited by James G. Lesniak. Gale Research, 1991.
*Cyclopedia of World Authors,* revised third ed., edited by Frank N. Magill. Salem Press, 1997.
*Oxford Companion to American Literature,* sixth ed., edited by James D. Hart. Oxford University Press, 1995.
*Oxford Companion to Twentieth-Century Literature in English,* edited by Jenny Stringer. Oxford University Press, 1996.
Reilly, John M., *Twentieth-Century Crime and Mystery Writers,* second ed., St. Martin's Press, 1985. □

# Randolph Caldecott

**Often called the father of the picture book, Randolph Caldecott (1846–1886) is regarded as one of the greatest and most influential illustrators in the field of children's literature.**

An English artist who illustrated picture books, fiction, verse, and fables for children as well as novels, poetry, and nonfiction for adults, Randolph Caldecott is the creator of works that are often considered the first modern picture books. Recognized as an artistic genius who brought creativity, technical skill, and a new professional quality to the genre of juvenile literature, Caldecott is best known for creating sixteen picture books that feature traditional nursery rhymes and songs and eighteenth-century comic poems. They are illustrated with economical yet lively pictures in sepia line and watercolor. These books, which include texts by such authors as Oliver Goldsmith, William Cowper, and Edwin Waugh as well as those from familiar sources such as Mother Goose, depict classic rhymes such as "Hey Diddle Diddle," "The Queen of Hearts," "Sing a Song for Sixpence," and "The House that Jack Built"; songs such as "A Frog He Would A-Wooing Go" and "The Milkmaid"; and humorous verses such as *The Diverting History of John Gilpin* and *The Three Jovial Huntsmen.* In his illustrations, Caldecott introduced the technique of animation—the effect of continuous movement that takes the eye from page to page—to the picture

book. His illustrations are lauded for expressing Caldecott's insight into human nature as well as for including the humor, action, and detail that appeals to children.

Born in Chester, England, in the county of Cheshire, on March 22, 1846, Caldecott was interested in animals, sports, and drawing from an early age. By the age of six, he had become an avid sketcher. Caldecott attended the prestigious King Henry VIII School, where he became head boy. He also continued his artistic endeavors—drawing from nature, carving wooden animals, modeling from clay, and painting. Although he had a fairly idyllic childhood, Caldecott nearly died from rheumatic fever. After his illness, Caldecott's health was to remain precarious for the rest of his life. When he was fifteen, Caldecott's father—who did not encourage his son's interests—arranged for him to work in a bank in rural Shropshire. In his free time, Caldecott hunted and fished and attended markets and local fairs, sketchbook in hand. In 1867, he transferred to a bank in Manchester. Colleagues at the bank later recalled finding his drawings of dogs and horses on the backs of receipts and old envelopes. Caldecott joined the Brasenose Club—an exclusive gentlemen's club for literary, scientific, and artistic pursuits—and became an evening student at the Manchester School of Art. The next year, his first drawings were published in local newspapers and humorous periodicals. In 1870, Caldecott went to London, where his portfolio was received favorably. In 1872, he moved there permanently to become a freelance illustrator. That summer, he accompanied author Henry Blackburn, later to become his biographer, to the Harz Mountains in Germany. Caldecott's

drawings were gathered the next year and published in Blackburns's *The Harz Mountains: A Town in the Toy Country.*

In 1875, Caldecott provided the illustrations for his first children's book, Louisa Morgan's *Baron Bruno; or, The Unbelieving Philosopher, and Other Fairy Stories,* as well as for *Old Christmas,* a collection of Yuletide stories by American author Washington Irving. Two years later, his pictures graced another work by Irving, *Bracebridge Hall,* which is often thought to have cemented Caldecott's reputation as an illustrator. It also led to his association with Edmund Evans, a successful printer and engraver who had been publishing children's books illustrated by Walter Crane, one of England's best known artists, for twelve years. When Crane retired from the partnership, Evans invited Caldecott to continue in his place. Caldecott agreed to produce two picture books a year; these titles, published from 1878 to 1885, were to become his most acclaimed works. Through Evans, Caldecott became the first artist to be able to distribute his illustrations internationally. Since their initial publication, Caldecott's picture books have been issued in a variety of formats: in a single volume, in two collections of eight titles apiece, in four collections of two titles apiece, and in miniature editions.

In 1879, Caldecott moved to a country home in Kent and was elected a member of the Manchester Academy of Fine Arts. In 1880, he married Marion Brind. Although Caldecott loved children and often played with Walter Crane's, the couple remained childless. In 1882, Caldecott moved to Broomfield, Surrey, and entered into a successful collaboration with the children's writer Juliana Horatia Ewing, for whom he illustrated three books. He also continued to submit illustrations to periodicals, including *Punch,* the *Graphic,* and the *Illustrated London News.* In 1883, he illustrated *Aesop's Fables,* with text written by his brother Alfred. In 1885, he provided the pictures for a collection of fairy tales by the French fabulist, Jean de la Fontaine. Sent to the United States to draw sketches for the *Graphic,* Caldecott suffered an attack of acute gastritis in St. Augustine, Florida. He died on February 12, 1886, just before his 40th birthday. Prior to his death, Caldecott wrote, "Please say that my line is to make smile the lunatic who has shown no sign of mirth for many months."

## Caldecott's Illustrations

Caldecott is considered an exceptional artist whose illustrations reflect his originality and intelligence. Michael Scott Joseph of the *Dictionary of Literary Biography* has noted, "In Caldecott's work the illustrator becomes an equal with the author...," while William Feaver of the *Times Literary Supplement* commented, "A brilliant combination of free drawing . . . and tonal restraint . . . gave his work a spontaneous yet age-old character." Considered a quintessentially English artist, Caldecott characteristically illustrated his picture books with bucolic scenes of local country life. Generally setting his pictures in the England of a century before, Caldecott accurately depicted people, animals, and typography while investing his works with sly wit and a strong sense of the richness and color of everyday living.

The artist, who is often noted for the narrative quality of his pictures, created a style of pictorial storytelling by using subplots in his illustrations to enhance the meaning of the texts. Caldecott studied what he called the "art of leaving out as a science" and once wrote that "the fewer the lines, the less error committed." In his works, the artist uses a deceptively simple style to capture the essence of a subject with a minimum of lines, and he is often credited for his ability to illustrate a story completely while expanding its dimensions in just a few strokes. Caldecott's pictures, drawn with a brush used as a pen, appeared as both small line drawings and large double-page spreads. He is often acknowledged for the fluidity of his style, for the vitality of his renderings, for the beauty and accuracy of his backgrounds, and for his skill in depicting animals—especially dogs, horses, geese, and pigs—and facial expressions.

## Caldecott's Themes

Although Caldecott's books are filled with gaiety, they do not shy away from harsh realities. His illustrations depict sickness and death, both of humans and animals. In addition, Caldecott includes surprising, often shocking, revelations in his drawings and paintings. One of his most famous pictures accompanies the nursery rhyme "Baby Bunting." Caldecott shows a tiny child walking outdoors with its mother in a suit made of rabbit skins, including the ears. The artist captures the moment when Baby Bunting confronts a group of rabbits. As author/illustrator Maurice Sendak noted in his introduction to *The Randolph Caldecott Treasury,* "Baby is staring with the most perplexed look at those rabbits, as though with the dawning of knowledge that the lovely, cuddly, warm costume he's wrapped up in has come from those creatures." Sendak concluded that Baby Bunting's expression seems to query, "Does something have to die to dress me?" In the well known closing illustrations for *Hey Diddle Diddle,* Caldecott shows the anthropomorphized Dish happily running away with the Spoon; however, the final picture takes an unexpected turn: the Dish has been broken into ten pieces, and the Spoon is being taken away by her angry parents, a Fork and a Knife. However, most of Caldecott's illustrated tales and rhymes are filled with robust, rollicking activity and are underscored by the artist's celebratory approach to life.

## Critical Reception

A member, along with Walter Crane and Kate Greenaway, of the triumvirate of English artists known as the "Academicians of the Nursery," Caldecott is usually considered the greatest of the three. Admired by Van Gogh and Gaughin as well as by children's artists such as Beatrix Potter and Marcia Brown, he is praised for the variety and range of his talents. Caldecott's picture books are often thought to be a perfect blend of art, text, and design. Popular during his lifetime, his works became extremely influential after this death, and his style can be seen in the works of such artists as Hugh Thomson, L. Leslie Brooke, and Edward Ardizzone. In 1924, his drawing of "The Three Jovial Huntsmen"—taken from the book of the same name published in 1880—became the logo for the children's literature reviewing source the *Horn Book Magazine,* and in 1938 the American Library Association instituted the Caldecott Medal, an award presented to the artist of the most distinguished American picture book published each year. Although Caldecott's popularity is thought to have diminished in recent years due to changing tastes, his reputation is still stellar: most critics acknowledge that his books have timeless appeal and are among the best ever created for children.

Reviewers in both the nineteenth and twentieth centuries have been almost unanimously favorable in their assessment of Caldecott's work. In 1881, W. E. Henley of the *Art Journal* wrote that he "is a kind of Good Genius of the Nursery, and—in the way of pictures—the most beneficent and delightful it ever had. . . . Under his sway Art for the nursery has become Art indeed." The next year, artist Kate Greenaway, herself a popular and respected illustrator, wrote of Caldecott in a letter, "I wish I had such a mind." In 1930, Jacqueline Overton, writing in *Contemporary Illustrators of Children's Books,* commented, "There has never been any picture book like those of Caldecott's, before or since." Beatrix Potter, an artist whose stature is considered near or equal to Caldecott's, commented in a letter in 1942, "I have the greatest admiration for his work—a jealous appreciation. . . . He was one of the greatest illustrators of all." Four years later, Mary Gould Davis wrote a biography of Caldecott in which she concluded, "As long as books exist and there are children to enjoy them, boys and girls—and their elders—will turn the pages of the Caldecott picture books." Perhaps Caldecott's most vocal supporter is Maurice Sendak. In 1965, he wrote of Caldecott in *Book World,* "[N]o artist since has matched his accomplishments. . . . His picture books . . . should be among the first volumes given to every child." Thirteen years later, Sendak stated in his introduction to *The Randolph Caldecott Treasury,* "When I came to picture books, it was Randolph Caldecott who really put me where I wanted to be"; the artist concluded, "Caldecott did it best, much better than anyone who ever lived."

## Further Reading

*Beatrix Potter's Americans: Selected Letters,* edited by Jane Crowell Morse, Horn Book, 1982.

Blackburn, Henry, *Randolph Caldecott: A Personal Memoir of His Early Art Career,* Sampson Low, 1886; reprint by Singing Tree Press, 1969.

*Children's Books and Their Creators,* edited by Anita Silvey, Houghton, 1995, pp. 113-14.

*Children's Literature Review,* Volume 34, Gale, 1988.

*Contemporary Illustrators of Children's Books,* edited by Bertha E. Mahony and Elinor Whitney, 1930; reprint by Gale Research, 1978.

Davis, Mary Gould, *Randolph Caldecott, 1846-1886: An Appreciation,* Lippincott, 1946.

*Dictionary of Literary Biography: British Children's Writers, 1800-1880,* Volume 163, Gale, 1996, pp. 37-47.

*The Randolph Caldecott Treasury,* Warne, 1978.

*Something about the Author,* Volume 17, Gale, pp. 31-39.

Spielman, M.H. and G.S. Layard. *Kate Greenaway,* Putnam, 1905.

*The Art Journal,* 1881, pp. 208-12.

*Book World—The Sunday Herald Tribune,* October 31, 1965, pp. 5, 38.

*Times Literary Supplement,* January 21, 1977, p. 64. □

# Roy Campanella

**Hall of Fame catcher, Roy Campanella (1921–1993), was one of professional baseball's African American pioneers. Playing with Jackie Robinson on the Brooklyn Dodgers, Campanella won three Most Valuable Player awards in a 10-year career that was cut short by a crippling automobile accident.**

Campanella was one of many stars on the powerful Dodgers teams of the early 1950s, nicknamed "the Boys of Summer." Duke Snider, Gil Hodges, Jackie Robinson, and Pee Wee Reese got more attention. But Campanella was the heart and soul of the team, its most valuable player, and an astute handler of the Dodgers pitching staff. Something of an amateur psychologist, he knew when to coddle and when to needle his pitchers. "He was always doing something to help you win a game, whether it was digging out a low pitch, throwing out a baserunner, or hitting a home run," said Dodgers manager, Walt Alston. For his own part, Campanella professed an undying affection for baseball. "It's a man's game, but you have to have a lot of little boy in you to play it," he often said.

Roy Campanella was born on November 19, 1921 in a tough Philadelphia neighborhood known, ironically, as Nicetown. His father was Italian and his mother was African American. His parents worked hard and the five children pitched in to help. By the time he was nine, Roy was cutting grass, delivering newspapers, shining shoes, and delivering milk to earn money for family needs.

Despite his short, stocky stature, Campanella was powerfully built and a gifted athlete, especially at baseball. He played throughout his youth and showed tremendous promise, but his career was blocked by professional baseball's color bar. Though Campanella had an Italian surname, his skin was dark and his future seemed destined to be in the Negro Leagues, the home of so many great black players in the first half of the twentieth century.

At the age of fifteen, Campanella signed with the Baltimore Elite Giants, one of the Negro League's top teams. Teammate Othello Renfroe said he was the "biggest fifteen-year-old boy I ever saw in my life." The team's shortstop, Pee Wee Butts, would get mad because Campanella would throw the ball so hard to second base during infield practice. Campanella's parents, who were devout Baptists, wouldn't let him play on Sundays. Young Roy did not, at first, consider a career in baseball. "I remember I felt so lost," he told Dodgers biographer Peter Golenbock. "I had no idea in the world this would be my profession. Truthfully, I wanted to be an architect." But when the Giants asked Campanella's parents to let him leave school in the eleventh grade so that he could play full-time, they agreed.

For the next decade, Campanella excelled in the segregated world of black baseball, barnstorming on buses across the country and playing winter ball in Mexico, the Caribbean, and Latin America. He was such a natural leader and had such an astute baseball mind that he often managed clubs he played for in Latin America. Campanella figured he was destined to stay in the Negro League throughout his entire career. "I never thought about the big leagues, playing in it," he told Golenbock. "Never."

## Crashing the Color Bar

Jackie Robinson broke baseball's color bar when he signed a professional contract with Branch Rickey, president of the New York Dodgers, in October 1945. Robinson was groomed to be the first black player in the modern major leagues, but he spent the 1946 season with Montreal, then a Class AAA minor-league team. Rickey was determined to integrate all levels of baseball. He signed Campanella and another black player, pitcher Don Newcombe, to play with Nashua, New Hampshire, a Brooklyn farm team in the Class B New England League. The manager of Nashua was Alston, who would later manage the Dodgers.

Campanella was making about $500 a month in the Negro Leagues, but he accepted a pay cut and played for $150 a month at Nashua. "Roy of course was better than a Class B player," Alston said. "But he knew why he was there. He was part of Rickey's plan to begin integrating baseball. . . . he knew he was going to start something important." Campanella batted .290 and was voted the Eastern League's most valuable player. He even managed a game after Alston was thrown out by the umpire. In that game,

Campanella used Newcombe as a pinch-hitter and he slugged a game-winning home run. The next year, when Robinson was promoted to Brooklyn, Campanella stepped up to Montreal and had another strong season.

Campanella thought he would open the 1948 season as the Dodgers' catcher, but Rickey had other plans. He sent him to St. Paul, Minnesota, to be the first black player in the American Association, another minor league circuit. "I ain't no pioneer," Campanella grumbled. "I'm a ballplayer." At St. Paul, Campanella batted .325 and hit 13 homers in 35 games. At the end of June Rickey called him up to the Dodgers. In his first game, Campanella hit two home runs against the New York Giants, and got nine hits in his first twelve at-bats. At the age of 26, he was installed as the regular catcher and kept the job for ten seasons. Campanella at first relied on Rickey to help him win acceptance. "One of the main things he taught me: I had to get all of the white pitching staff to respect my judgment in accepting signs," Campanella recalled.

### Bulwark of the Dodgers

During Campanella's ten years with the Dodgers, they won five National League championships and finished second three times. Brooklyn was a powerhouse club filled with all-star caliber players. Most of them had more speed, more power, and more spectacular defensive opportunities than Campanella. But the solid, brainy catcher was such a mainstay of the team's success that he was voted the league's Most Valuable Player in each of the three seasons in which he batted over .300.

The muscular Campanella was a strong offensive force, even in the years when his batting average was low. He hit more than 30 home runs four times. In 1953, he hit 41 home runs and had a league-leading 142 runs batted in. During the eight-year stretch between 1949 and 1956, he averaged 28 home runs a season. His most important contributions were defensive ones. He had a strong and deadly arm. "Sometimes you won simply because he was there," Alston said. "They wouldn't try to steal on him. That keeps a guy on base and helps keep your pitcher's concentration on the batter."

Campanella was a genius when it came to keeping pitchers concentrated on their work—a catcher's most important role. He nurtured a great pitching staff that included Don Newcombe, Johnny Podres, Preacher Roe, Carl Erskine, and Clem Labine. "Just seeing him back there made you a better pitcher," Podres said. Campanella did not hesitate to criticize his pitchers if he felt that was needed to motivate them. "He knew that sometimes if he got me mad I'd pitch better," Newcombe said. "So he'd come out [to the mound] . . . and give me some needling. He knew when to do it and how." Golenbock said: "His most important attribute was that he had the respect of his pitchers, who trusted his judgment implicitly."

During his best years, Campanella was frequently compared to Yogi Berra, his counterpart as catcher with the perennial American League champion New York Yankees. Berra also won three MVP awards, in 1951, 1954, and 1955. Some believe Campanella might have won a fourth

MVP in 1954, if he hadn't suffered an injury to his left hand. He played even though it was partially paralyzed and eventually required surgery.

Campanella was behind the plate when the Dodgers played in the World Series in 1949, 1952, 1953, 1955, and 1956. They were losers each year except in 1955, when Brooklyn won its only world championship. Podres pitched a 2-0 shutout in the decisive seventh game and gave credit to his catcher. "That win was half Campy's," Podres said. "He never called a better game. He saw how my stuff was working and he seemed to know what the Yankee hitters were looking for."

Injuries plagued Campanella in 1956 as he batted only .219 and again in 1957 when he played in only 100 games and batted .242. "Campy's catching skills began to erode after a careless doctor cut a nerve in his right hand while performing an operation," Golenbock said. But Alston claimed that his career was far from over because "he was still the soundest defensive catcher in baseball."

### Career Cut Short

The 1957 season was the Dodgers' last in Brooklyn. The club was moving to Los Angeles the following year. It would do so without its star catcher. On the night of January 28, 1958, Campanella was driving to his home on Long Island when his car skidded on a slick road, struck a telephone poll, and turned over. Seat belts had not yet become standard safety equipment. The great catcher suffered multiple fractures and dislocations in the vertebrae in his neck and was permanently paralyzed from the shoulders down. He would never walk again.

Campanella ended his career with a .276 batting average, 242 home runs, and 865 runs batted in. If it hadn't been for the color bar that delayed his entrance to the leagues and the accident which ended his career prematurely, he likely would have posted home run and RBI totals to rival the best catchers of all time. In 1959, the Dodgers staged a benefit game at the Los Angeles Coliseum to honor Campanella and raise money for his medical expenses. The game attracted 93,103 fans, thought to be the largest crowd ever to see a baseball game. That year, Campanella published an autobiography, *It's Good to Be Alive*. When the book was re-released in 1995, *Publishers Weekly* said it "packs more uplift than any inspirational sports bio."

In some ways, Campanella became more famous in the wheelchair than he had been on the baseball diamond. He never complained about his injury, and became an inspiring figure. "Although he was a remarkable ballplayer, I think he'll be remembered more for his 35 years in a wheelchair," said Dodgers broadcaster, Vin Scully. The Dodgers hired him as a special instructor, and for 20 years he helped groom many young catchers during spring training. He also worked with disabled people through the Dodgers' community-service division. He was expert at cheering up people. Campanella once said: "People look at me and get the feeling that if a guy in a wheelchair can have such a good time, they can't be too bad off after all." Scully observed: "He looked upon life as a catcher. He was forever cheering up, pepping up, counseling people."

In fact, Campanella's life was not always easy. His first marriage dissolved and his house had to be sold in order to pay huge medical debts. In 1963, Campanella marrried a nurse named Roxie Doles. Throughout his ordeals, he remained extremely close to the five children from his first marriage: sons Roy Jr., Anthony, and John and daughters Joni and Ruth.

Campanella was voted into the National Baseball Hall of Fame in 1969. He died of a heart attack at his home in Woodland Hills, California, on June 26, 1993, at the age of 71. That evening, flags at Dodger Stadium flew at half-mast and the scoreboard showed highlights of Campanella's career. Alston, his mentor, remembered him this way: "I've never seen a more enthusiastic guy on a ball field, one who got more sheer joy out of playing."

## Further Reading

Campanella, Roy. *It's Good to Be Alive,* University of Nebraska, 1959.
Golenbock, Peter. *Bums: An Oral History of the Brooklyn Dodgers,* Putnam, 1984.
Honig, Donald, *The Greatest Catchers of All Time,* Brown, 1991.
*Jet,* November 19, 1984; July 17, 1989; July 12, 1993; November 15, 1996.
*People,* July 12, 1993.
*Time,* July 12, 1993. ☐

# Ernesto Cardenal

**Ernesto Cardenal (born 1925) a Roman Catholic priest, had become a poet of major standing by the end of the twentieth century. His epic works spoke to a proud people of its heritage. They spoke to people around the world, as well, with a human spirit that went beyond pure poetry.**

Cardenal's role as a priest and spiritual mentor was evident throughout his more than 35 books of poetry. He wrote poems, and translated the works of others—many speaking out against Anastasio Samoza, the dictator who ruled Nicaragua for decades. His support for the anti-government movement (Sandanistas), led to the overthrow of the Samoza dictatorship in 1979.

Ernesto Cardenal was born in Grenada, Nicaragua, on January 20, 1925. He was the son of Rodolfo and Esmerelda Martinez Cardenal. Ernesto was raised in a middle-class family of 19th century European immigrants. Legend had it that a family member was William Walker, one of many Southern Confederates who defected to Central and South America. Their intention had been to create a slave-holding state in Nicaragua in the way they had been unable to continue to do in the United States. His poem, *With Walker in Nicaragua,* is his own study of that expedition. Cardenal attended the University of Mexico from 1944 until 1948. He spent the following academic year (1948–1949) at Columbia University in New York City, studying American literature. Following his U.S. studies, Cardenal traveled in Europe, returning to Nicaragua in 1950.

Cardenal soon became involved in his country's political unrest. In 1954, he was one of the participants in what became known as the "April Rebellion," when anti-Samoza forces stormed the presidential palace. His political activities forced Cardenal to flee the country in 1957.

By the time of his return to Nicaragua, Cardenal had already begun publishing his poems, many with political themes. One poem in particular, his famous *Hora Zero* ("Zero Hour") that dealt with the assassination of Sandino, a revolutionary hero, was published underground. This and other poems had to be distributed clandestinely, evading the Samoza regime's watchful eye. Many of his early works were distributed along with other revolutionary literature.

Cardenal went to the Trappist monastery in Gethsemani, Kentucky as a novice and considered becoming a monk. He spent two years there with the noted author, Thomas Merton, known for his bestseller entitled *Seven Story Mountain.* In his introduction to Cardenal's spiritual writings published in *To Live Is to Love,* (1972), Merton talked about Cardenal's time with him at the abbey. "During the ten years that I was Master of Novices at Gethsemani Abbey in Kentucky, I never attempted to find out what the novices were writing down in the note-books they kept in their desks. If they wished to talk about it, they were free to do so. Ernesto Cardenal was a novice at Gethsemani for two years, and I knew about his notes and his poems. He spoke to me about his ideas and his meditations. I also knew about his simplicity, his loyalty to his vocation, and his dedication to love. But I never imagined that some day I was going to write an introduction to the simple meditations he was writing down in those days, nor that in reading them (almost ten years later) I would find so much clarity, profundity, and maturity."

Due to ill health, Cardenal left Gethsemani and returned to Nicaragua. His commitment vocation to the Roman Catholic priesthood did not waiver. He was ordained in 1965 in Madrid, Spain. Cardenal continued his work as a priest as well as his writing. A religious community Cardenal established on the island of Solentiname in Lake Nicaragua included writers, artists, other religious figures, and local peasants. From that commune he continued his work for the revolution. His philosophy and spirituality was an unusual mixture of Catholic Christianity and Marxist Socialism.

## Papal Reprimand

Cardenal was one of several key Central and South American priests who attempted to integrate their religious and political views into a new ideology that became known as "liberation theology." The focus of this movement was to join political with spiritual forces, and to preach liberation for all oppressed peoples. Advocates varied in the degree to which they strayed from traditional Roman church law. Some used it as a forum to call for the ordination of married men and women to the priesthood. Some were less radical in that regard, but courted political ideologies in equal standing with their religious function.

The success of the Sandanista revolution in 1979 brought a new role for Cardenal. He held the position of minister of culture until 1988. In 1983, when Pope John Paul II toured Central America, he expressed his concern for the discord in this region. As Richard N. Ostling reported in the March 7, 1983 issue of *Time* magazine, John Paul's flock in Latin America was "split into at least three factions: the traditionalist right wing, the reform-minded middle, and the radical revolutionary left." In direct defiance of the Roman Catholic code of canon law, (the group of law that exists to govern the operations of the Catholic church around the world) Cardenal and another priest, Miguel D'Escoto Brockmann held government positions. Canon law does not allow a priest to hold a government office without the permission of his local bishops. Even though the bishops withdrew that permission in 1981, Cardenal and Brockmann remained in office.

When John Paul visited Nicaragua in 1983, Cardenal attempted to greet the Pope in the traditional manner of dropping to one knee and kissing his ring. John Paul pulled his hand away from Cardenal and shook his finger at him. The world looked on uncomfortably.

Cardenal left the Sandanista movement in October 1994 when he became disillusioned with the government of President Daniel Ortega. "The truth is," Cardenal said at the time, "that a small group headed by Daniel Ortega has taken over the Sandinista Front. This is not the Sandanista Front we joined. Because of this I have considered it my duty to resign." As minister of culture, Cardenal had become increasingly subject to the control of government officials. He found he had less time to write. The major positive aspect of his work was setting up literacy and poetry workshops throughout the country.

## His Work in Words

Cardenal was a poet and writer who produced volumes of work. Much of it was translated into English and published for distribution around the world. Among his works in addition to *Zero Hour*, were: *Flights of Victory, Vida en el Amor*, (published in English as *To Live Is to Love*) in 1972; *Psalms of Struggle and Liberation*, for which he won the Christopher Book Award, and *With Walker*. His English translation poetry volumes included, *Marilyn Monroe and Other Poems*, 1965; *Apocalypse and Other Poems*, 1977; *Nicaraguan New Time*, 1988; *Cosmic Canticle*, 1993; and, *The Doubtful Strait*, 1995.

With *Walker in Nicaragua*, Cardenal seemed to be coming to terms with his own past, dealing with the purported familial connection he shared with Walker. As Elman further noted in his review in *The Nation*, the poem was "narrated by a survivor, in a voice still awed by the jungle, the deaths, the tropics, the wonder of a land, a people. It is a report on a time when the land was unsullied, the air clear, and imperialist either bloody-minded or awestruck." In a book review in *The Christian Century*, in May 1982, Cardenal's poetry found in *Psalms* was praised. "In the pages of *Psalms* can be found hymns of praise, strong paeans expressing exuberance and joy. Yet it is the harsh cry for justice and peace which makes these poems memorable," said the reviewer.

Cardenal brought the Nicaraguan struggle to every reader of his poetry. His vivid portrayals provided a critical glimpse into a society struggling against oppression. Cardenal traveled to Cuba in the early 1970s in order to seek out the history of other struggles. He spent four hours with Castro. Cardenal published notes from his trip, as well as the works of Cuban writers in a 1972 book entitled, *In Cuba. Choice*, magazine called Cardenal, "one of the world's major poets" who "struggled to convince himself that the underlying force in the universe was divine purpose rather than pure chance. For him, the politics of commitment was essential to the poetic discourse, just as love, the ultimate cohesive principle, was necessary to preserve the oneness of creation."

Cardenal left the government but continued his work for the literary consciousness of his country and the political consciousness that he needed to live a life of universal love. He served as vice president of *Casa de Las Tres Mundos*, a literary and cultural organization based in Managua, the capital city of Nicaragua. Cardenal also traveled to the U.S. to read and present his work to students and others. American poet, Robert Bly, said that Cardenal continued "the tradition of Pablo Neruda," who had said, "all the pure poets will fall on their face in the snow. Cardenal's poetry is impure, defiantly, in that it unites political ugliness and the beauty of imaginative vision."

## The Teacher

Cardenal's poetry was more than poetry alone. Thomas Merton concluded his introduction to *To Live Is to Love,* with these comments about Cardenal. "Ernesto Cardenal left Gethsemani because of ill health. However, today I can see that this is not the only reason: it did not make sense to continue at Gethsemani as a novice and as a student when actually he was already a teacher." Still Cardenal's own words at the end of that same book pointed to his own spirituality, his own sense of himself. He said, "God knows that what is not good for me today may be good for me tomorrow. And God may not wish something today that He may wish at some future time; or He may wish something to happen at a particular place which He does not wish to happen at another place, or He may wish something for me that He does not wish for others. When Joan of Arc was asked during her trial whether God loved the British, she answered: 'God does not love the British in France.' This hints at the mysterious vocation of us all. God may like a dictator who hails from Nicaragua, but He does not want him to be the dictator of Nicaragua."

Cardenal's life was continually evolving as he continued to answer what he believed to be his call from God. As a priest and poet he served an honest and generous piece of his own talents.

## Further Reading

*Contemporary Authors,* Gale, 1998, Volume 66.
*The Christian Century,* May 26, 1982, p. 638.
*The Nation,* January 28, 1984, pp. 96-99; March 30, 1985, pp.372-375.
*National Catholic Reporter,* February 6, 1981, p. 4; December 9, 1983, p. 3.
*Time,* March 7, 1983, pp. 52-54.
"Cardenal, Ernesto, biographical profile, New York State Writers Institute," *University at Albany—State University of New York website,* http://www.albany.edu/ (April 10, 1999). □

# Henri Cartier-Bresson

**A pioneer of photojournalism, Henri Cartier-Bresson (born 1908) is best known for his images of life in Europe during the 1930s through the 1950s. His work has long been honored with museum retrospectives, which have served to elevate his street-level imagery to the realm of artistic expression.**

Cartier-Bresson was born August 22, 1908 in Chanteloup, France, a rural village not far from Paris where the rivers Seine and Marne meet. In the 1990s it would become part of the parcel of land that comprised the Euro-Disney theme park. Henri was the first of three children in the prosperous Cartier-Bresson household, a home situated on Paris's rue de Lisbonne. His father's family had been in the thread manufacturing business since 1789, but both Cartier-Bresson's great-grandfather and a contemporary uncle were talented artists; even his business-minded father liked to sketch. The family of Cartier-Bresson's mother hailed from Normandy, and they, too, possessed a generations-old cotton-manufacturing firm. As the eldest son of the new generation, Cartier-Bresson was naturally expected to direct his education and training toward business in preparation for one day taking on a management role.

## A Subversive Student

As a teen, Cartier-Bresson grew into a disaffected bookworm and indifferent student, far more interested in banned literature than mathematics. He attended a Catholic academy in Paris, the Ecole Fenelon, and then went on to the Lycee Condorcet. Early on, he was deeply interested in intellectual currents that were, at the time, very much at odds with the standard Catholic-centered curriculum— psychoanalysis, Nietzschean philosophy, and even Hindu beliefs. One day, a teacher caught him reading the poet Arthur Rimbaud, but Cartier-Bresson was fortunate that the master had been friends with the Paris Symbolist poets in his student days; instead of punishing him, the teacher allowed Cartier-Bresson to read from his own collection of seditious titles in his office after school.

Cartier-Bresson was also very much lured by the visual arts, and visits to the studio of his painter uncle made lasting sensory impressions. He began painting himself around the age of 12. At first, he studied under a cohort of his uncle's named Jean Cottenet, and later studied privately with a "society" painter, Jacques-Emile Blanche, who had been the model for a character in one of Marcel Proust's novels. Expected to enter business school after finishing at the Lycee Condorcet, Cartier-Bresson instead failed the exam three times. By this point Blanche had introduced him to a number of notable names in Parisian artistic circles, and the teen was becoming deeply interested in Surrealism. Arising around 1924, with the writings of Andre Breton, this Paris-centered literary and artistic movement held that the subconscious, as explained by Sigmund Freud, could be unlocked. Surrealist artistic processes centered around "spontaneous" creative expression, such as automatic writing; its adherents also considered themselves willing outcasts from conventional society.

## Rejected Bourgeois Life

By 1925, Cartier-Bresson had finished the Lycee and won his parents' permission to study privately with Andre Lhote, a Cubist painter of admirable regard. After spending an extended period visiting a student cousin in England, he spent a compulsory year in the military around 1929, and was stationed at the airfield of Le Bourget, near Paris. His first experiences with a camera occurred with a Brownie he bought around this time. Later in 1930, deeply influenced by Joseph Conrad's novel *Heart of Darkness,* he boarded a ship headed for Africa. He disembarked at a French Ivory Coast village, and later moved inland to eke out a living by hunting with a rifle at night with a lamp mounted on his head. He fell into a coma after becoming ill with blackwater fever, and was forced to return to France.

The experience in Africa had erased from Cartier-Bresson any desire to earn his living by standing at an easel all day. In 1931, he embarked upon a long trip across Germany, Poland, Austria, Czechoslovakia, and Hungary with a writer friend. Back in France in 1932, he bought a Leica camera in Marseilles that he would use for the remainder of his career. From there he went on to other parts of France, and then Spain and Italy, and began photographing images that were revolutionary at the time for their portrayal of Europe's urban underclass and rural poor. It was at this point, wrote Peter Pollack in *The Picture History of Photography,* that Cartier-Bresson "took his first unforgettable picture: hilarious children chasing a wildly laughing, crippled child on crutches playing in the ruins of a stucco building in Seville."

Cartier-Bresson's work was revolutionary because he used a small, portable camera, which allowed him to record a "decisive moment" in time. That spontaneity—and the unrehearsed, unstaged glimpse into human nature that it captured—would become the distinctive element common to most of his images. The first exhibition of his photographs was held in 1933 at the Atheneo Club in Madrid. Later that same year his first American show took place at New York's Julien Levy Gallery. In 1934, he left for a long sojourn in Mexico, after an invitation from the government to participate in a photography project. Though the funding fell through, he stayed a year, living in a rather squalid area of Mexico City. He shared a flat with American poet, Langston Hughes, and several others.

## Traveled Extensively

Around 1935, Cartier-Bresson arrived in New York City for an extended stay. He exhibited with Walker Evans at Julien Levy, and found a vast trove of images for his lens across the city's crowded and colorful boroughs. Cartier-Bresson began dabbling in the cinematic arts with a fellow photographer, Paul Strand. He became further involved in film making in 1936, after returning to France. Cartier-Bresson served as second assistant director for a few films by the esteemed French director Jean Renoir. In 1937, he received a commission to make a documentary about a medical relief program providing aid to Loyalist fighters wounded in the Spanish Civil War.

Cartier-Bresson, now in his late 20s, was not an avowed communist, but had developed decidedly leftist sympathies nonetheless. When he married a dancer from Java, Ratna Mohini, in 1937, he needed a steady income, and thus found a job as a staff photographer for France's Communist daily, *Ce Soir.* In May of that year he was sent to cover the coronation of England's King George VI, and turned his camera toward the crowd instead, capturing many memorable images of working-class Britons gathered for the day's festivities. At *Ce Soir* he became friends with two other photojournalists, Robert Capa and David Seymour (known as "Chim"). The three often submitted their leftover work to an agency, Alliance Photo, and many of the images were published in *Vu,* the French version of the popular American photo-newsweekly, *Life.*

## Three Years as Prisoner

With the outbreak of World War II in 1939, Cartier-Bresson enlisted in the French army and was made a corporal in its film and photo unit. On the same June 1940 day that the French government capitulated to Nazi Germany and signed an armistice, the unit was captured in the Vosges Mountains and Cartier-Bresson was transported to a prisoner-of-war camp in Wuerttemberg. He made two unsuccessful attempts to escape in his thirty-five months of captivity, and finally succeeded on his third try. Sneaking back into a France still under German occupation, he obtained false identity papers and managed to find work as a commercial photographer, again in Paris. He was also active in an underground group that aided escaped POWs like himself, and organized secret photography units that documented the German occupation.

These resistance activities brought Cartier-Bresson to the attention of American military authorities and, in 1945, at the war's end, he was hired by the U.S. Office of War Information to make *La Retour,* a film about French citizens returning from prisoner-of-war and deportation camps. In 1947, he traveled to the U.S. when its American debut was planned as part of a Museum of Modern Art retrospective on his career. During this stay he was also able to fulfill a longtime ambition to travel across America.

## Pioneer of Photojournalism

Back in France in 1947, Cartier-Bresson, Capa, and Seymour founded Magnum Photo, a cooperative agency of photojournalists owned and run by the members themselves. "After the war, when Chim, Capa, and I met up again, someone pointed out that we should form an association," Cartier-Bresson recalled in an interview with Michel Nuridsany in the *New York Review of Books*. "... Chim and I would say to each other: 'That Capa's such a go-getter; he lives in fancy hotels, throws parties. We'll never be able to keep up.' It was very worrying. And then we realized that, while playing gin rummy with magazine owners, he would find us jobs. From that point on we shared all our money equally." Even the proceeds from Cartier-Bresson's first book, *Images a la Sauvette* (published in English as *The Decisive Moment*), which appeared in 1952, were shared.

Always modest about his achievements, Cartier-Bresson once said of his career as a photographer, "Not only am I an amateur; even worse, I am a dilettante," reported Roger Therond in *Contemporary Photographers*. Still, the English title of his first book reflects the essence of his greater contribution to photography: Cartier-Bresson merged the spontaneity provided by the miniature camera with the intuitive inspiration heralded by Surrealism. With his camera as a constant companion, he was able to capture the street scenes that exemplified the human-interest angle behind photojournalism itself. Surrealism, wrote Peter Galassi in *Cartier-Bresson: The Early Work*, considered "the street as an arena of adventure and fantasy only thinly disguised by the veneer of daily routine ... If Surrealism aimed to eliminate the distinction between art and life, no one achieved this goal more thoroughly than Cartier-Bresson in the early thirties. The tools of his art—a few rolls of film, the small camera held in the hand—required no distinction between living and working," Galassi wrote. "There was no studio, no need to separate art from the rest of experience."

### First Western Photographer in Soviet Russia

Cartier-Bresson's leftist sympathies helped secure a visa to enter and photograph China and the Soviet Union in the 1950s. At the time, both were totalitarian Communist nations more or less closed to Western visitors, and any images published in the West were heavily censored and aimed at depicting only the positive attributes of their ideology. Cartier-Bresson's book *China in Transition* was published in English translation in 1956, a year after *Moscow/The People*. The publication of other notable volumes of his work—*Les Europeens* (1955), *The World of Henri Cartier-Bresson* (1968), and *Henri Cartier-Bresson, Photographer* (1979) among many others—were tied to his conviction that his work should reach the widest possible number of viewers, instead of being restricted to the gallery-museum circuit of the "fine arts."

Cartier-Bresson has been feted with numerous international exhibitions of his work over the length of his career, including the Institute of Contemporary Arts in London in 1952 and Paris's Musee d'Art Moderne in 1981. In 1967, he became the first photographer in the history of the Louvre to have a second solo show. In 1999, Denmark's Louisiana Museum staged a retrospective featuring 185 of his photographs. The show, titled "Europeans," was divided—according to Cartier-Bresson's wishes—by country.

Surprisingly, in 1972 the famed photographer ceased working in this medium and began painting again. Famously reclusive, Cartier-Bresson lives in Paris in an apartment near the Louvre. He does return to photography for the occasional portrait, however. "That I enjoy quite a bit," Cartier-Bresson told Nuridsany in the *New York Review of Books*. "Or landscapes. But on the street, no. And I don't miss it, either. I tell myself simply, in passing, well, well, look at that, that would have made a photo. That's all."

### Further Reading

*Contemporary Photographers,* edited by Colin Naylor, St. James Press, 1988.

Galassi, Peter, *Cartier-Bresson: The Early Work,* Museum of Modern Art, 1987.

*Photography: Essays and Images,* edited by Beaumont Newhall, Museum of Modern Art, 1980.

Pollack, Peter, *The Picture History of Photography,* Abrams, 1969.

*New York Review of Books,* March 2, 1995. □

# Steve Case

**Steve Case (born 1958) is the co-founder of America Online, an Internet provider service that boasted its own unique content as well. It was instrumental in leading a vast number of people onto the "information superhighway." The company experienced rapid growth early on, and despite some stumbles, continues to be the most popular of its kind in the industry, capturing roughly 60 percent of the world market after its acquisition of CompuServe in 1998.**

Before the rise in online services, the Internet could be a confusing technological jumble to most users. Generally, only the savvy "computer geeks" were accessing its communicative powers, using modems to reach other users. However, companies soon began tapping into this unknown territory, and began offering computer users a logical, easier-to-use interface through which they could send e-mail and access information via the Internet. In 1985, Steve Case was one of the leaders of this drive to make the Internet understandable, founding a company that later became America Online. There were other firms in the same business, such as CompuServe (the oldest online service) and Prodigy, but Case's design was more successful in the long run. With his user-friendly graphics and innovative marketing strategies, he made the Internet easy and fun. The number of users who logged on to hear a clear, pleasant voice inform them, "You've got mail!" increased exponentially throughout the 1990s. "The geeks don't like us," Case told *Time* in 1997. "They want as much technology as possible, while AOL's entire objective is to simplify."

Case was born in Honolulu, Hawaii, on August 21, 1958. His father is a corporate lawyer and his mother a

teacher. Case has an older brother named Dan, an older sister, Carin, and a younger brother, Jeff. At the age of six, Case and his brother Dan opened a juice stand. They charged two cents a cup, but many of their customers gave them a nickel and let them keep the change. Several years later the two boys started a mail order company, selling a variety of products by mail and door-to-door. They then started an affiliated company which sold ad circulars. In addition, the two shared a newspaper route. So Case's hard-driving entrepreneurial spirit surfaced at an early age.

When Case attended Williams College, he majored in political science. "It was the closest thing to marketing," he told *Business Week.* While there he became the lead singer in two rock groups. One, The Vans, was an imitation of The Cars. The other, The The, was influenced by The Knack, whose one and only hit was "My Sharona." After graduating in 1980, Case landed a marketing position at Proctor & Gamble. One of the products he worked on was Lilt, the home hair permanent kit. He left the company after two years. Case then joined the Pizza Hut unit of PepsiCo. There he was manager of new pizza development. The job required much travel, looking for new ideas for toppings. His evenings out on the road provided the time to explore a new technological development, the personal computer (PC). He purchased a Kaypro portable computer and subscribed to an early online service called The Source. "I remember it being frustrating, but actually magical when you first got into the system and got access to information and were able to talk to people all over the world," Case recounted to Michael Dresser of the *Baltimore Sun.*

## Formed Prototype Online Service

In 1983, Case's brother Dan, who became the CEO of an investment firm, introduced him to the founders of Control Video Corporation. The company was starting an online gaming service for Atari computer-game machine users. Case was offered a job as a marketing assistant and he accepted. Unfortunately, as Case told Steve Lohr of the *New York Times,* "I arrived there just in time for the death of the video game business." The company went broke and the board fired the existing management team and brought in Jim Kimsey as chief executive officer. Kimsey and Case sought out venture capital and, in 1985, they co-founded Quantum Computer Services Inc. The company was an online service for users of Commodore computers, then a leading brand.

Quantum soon expanded to serve other computer users. Case made a deal with Apple Computer in 1987. Software packages were developed for the Apple II and Macintosh. Tandy Corporation quickly followed and a package was developed for the Tandy computer. Packages were also introduced for the DOS and Windows operating systems. By 1990, management decided to bring all of its segmented services together into one overall service and in 1991 the company was renamed America Online, or AOL for short. A year later AOL went public, raising money for further expansion. Case was named CEO shortly thereafter.

When he took over as CEO, Case saw his company lag behind CompuServe and Prodigy, the two major online services at the time. AOL had only 200,000 subscribers. Case developed a maximum growth strategy and put it in place. In early 1993, AOL cut its prices well below those of CompuServe and Prodigy. Massive numbers of diskettes were mailed out offering free trials. After this, membership grew at an accelerated rate. By the end of the year, AOL had trouble handling the huge influx of new subscribers. Users would get abruptly disconnected and in a real-time chat it would take minutes to post a message. Getting on the service during peak hours could actually take an hour. Numerous complaints led Case to send a letter of apology to subscribers, promising technical improvements.

## AOL Branched Out

Case signed deals to bring a number of content providers to AOL, including the *New York Times,* NBC, *Time,* Hachette magazines, and the financial services company Morningstar Inc. In August of 1994, AOL purchased Redgate Communications, bringing in multimedia expertise. In November of that year, it bought ANS, creator of the Internet network, gaining high-speed network capacity. In December, AOL acquired Booklink Technologies, which provided the service with a World Wide Web browser. Case also developed partnerships with cable companies such as General Instrument, Comcast, and Viacom. Cable provides the opportunity for a "high-bandwidth conduit, which will allow us to offer our customers much more engaging, multimedia-rich kinds of services," Case said to Kent Gibbons of *Multichannel News.*

Also in 1994, AOL announced a corporate reorganization, creating four new divisions. One aim was to pursue "a global strategy," the *Wall Street Journal* reported, seeking out business partners in Europe and Japan. John L. Davies, former senior vice president, was named president of AOL International. Case himself became head of the Internet Services division, in addition to his duties as president and CEO of the parent company. Michael Connors, another former senior vice president, was appointed president of AOL Technologies, to develop technology for the company. Ted Leonsis, president of recently-acquired Redgate Communications, was made president of the AOL Services division, overseeing the company's basic services and their development. Allyson Pooley, a securities analyst for Chicago Corporation, told the *Wall Street Journal* that the reorganization was a "positive move that will allow the company to better focus on areas where it sees growth." Commenting on the new structure to Jeffrey D. Zbar of *Advertising Age,* Case said, "We want to be the No. 1 consumer online service. We want to be the leader in the Internet. We want to be the leader internationally. We want to be the leading technology innovator."

A move by the giant Microsoft Corporation, headed by Bill Gates, caused some consternation for Case. The Microsoft Network, which was announced in 1994 and introduced the following year, bundled with Microsoft's Windows 95 operating system software. Integrating the network with the next generation of its widely used Windows software would be an "unfair advantage," competitors argued to the Justice Department. The government pursued a case against Microsoft, charging unfair business practices.

To strengthen its international presence, early in 1995 AOL formed a joint venture with Bertelsmann, a major German media company. In June of 1995, the Global Network Navigator (GNN) service was purchased. Originally an online magazine, AOL reworked it into an Internet access company and launched it in October 1995. Case told Robert Hertzberg of *Web Week* that the service was introduced "with more local dial-up numbers than any other national Internet access company." As to why AOL would want a second strictly-Internet service, Case remarked to Cathi Schuler of *CeePrompt! Computer Connection,* "People who are sophisticated users of the Internet and are seeking a full-featured Internet-only offering will likely opt for our new GNN brand. People who want a simple and affordable package that provides them with access to the widest possible range of content—included but not limited to Internet content—are likely to continue to opt for our flagship AOL brand."

By 1995, AOL had over three million subscribers and was still climbing fast. *Business Week* noted that, since 1993, "naysayers have predicted that Case would falter and AOL spin out of control," but both continued to forge ahead. Late in 1995, Case was elected chairman of AOL. In February of 1996, AOL bought Johnson-Grace, a data compression software maker, to help speed the transfer of text and image files. That same month Case brought in William Razzouk from FedEx as chief operating officer, a new position. Razzouk was to manage day-to-day operations. In March, Case put together several major deals to greatly expand AOL's reach. The company announced a deal with

Netscape; it would now offer the popular Netscape Navigator browser for use with GNN. It announced a pact with Microsoft; AOL would now integrate Microsoft's Internet Explorer into its online software. Microsoft, in turn, would include AOL in its Windows 95 operating system. A partnership with Apple Computer would put the AOL software on that system. Also, AT&T agreed to promote AOL and make it available on its WorldNet Internet access service.

## AOL Led Despite Troubles

AOL had five million subscribers by 1996 and had become "the nation's leading online service and single largest Internet access provider," reported John Simons of *U.S. News & World Report.* The company had kept up its momentum, Case told Simon, "because we embrace new technology, then mask its complexity." Not all was going smoothly for Case, though. In June of 1996, William Razzouk resigned after just four months with the company. Case was to resume the duties that had been assigned to Razzouk. The *Wall Street Journal* reported that Razzouk's departure came about because "insiders say he came across as a button-down, command-and-control executive in a company so casual it hosts on-site beer bashes."

Critics were also attacking AOL's accounting practices. Abraham Briloff, emeritus professor of accounting at City University of New York, called the company's methods "in-your-face arrogance." Briloff questioned AOL's accounting for the costs of acquisitions and also its deferral of marketing expenses for attracting new subscribers. With marketing expenses, for example, the typical company charges expenses against profits as it spends the dollars. AOL was spreading its costs over 24 months, increasing short-term profitability. Briloff argued that by applying more rigorous accounting principles, AOL would break even. "Push the pencil a little more," he added, "and it comes out negative." Allan Sloan in *Newsweek* noted that AOL has had to battle a rising turnover rate among subscribers. In the March 1996 quarter, "AOL added 2.2 million new customers, but lost 1.3 million old customers," Sloan related. The *Wall Street Journal* wrote that while some analysts think its turnover rate is "alarmingly high," others do not view it as excessive for the industry.

Case continued to make deals, establishing a Japanese joint venture with Mitsui and Nikkei. On July 1, 1996, AOL announced its new 3.0 software for Windows. A company press release said the new software would give its users "a faster and more convenient online experience, easier navigation, enhanced communication, and personalization of AOL to fit individual member's needs." In a July 19, 1996 statement, Case said that the company ended the June quarter with 6.2 million subscribers worldwide. He declared that the company was aiming for 10 million by the middle of 1997, a figure he reached by the fall of that year.

On August 1, 1996, the company announced that it was filing for a listing on the New York Stock Exchange. It had been traded on NASDAQ. A few days later AOL announced the purchase of the ImagiNation Network, a multiplayer games company, from AT&T. According to the press release, this would "dramatically expand AOL's online games offerings." August 7, 1996, however, was to become AOL's day of infamy. While conducting routine software maintenance early that morning, the company ran into problems and had a nationwide outage which lasted for 19 hours. The blackout was frustrating for users and embarrassing for the company. Newspapers across the country reported it. "All day long and long after AOL was A-OK, the press painted a grim portrait of Webbies all wired up with no place to go," remarked George Vernadakis of *Inter@ctive Week*. Case issued an apology to subscribers, Peter Coy of *Business Week* noted, but he added, "I would like to be able to tell you that this sort of thing will never happen again, but frankly, I can't make that commitment."

The next day, AOL announced that revenues for the fiscal year ending June 30, 1996 had passed the billion-dollar mark, almost triple that of fiscal 1995. Late in 1996, a huge number of new customers came on board when the company began offering a flat rate of $19.95 a month, as opposed to its previous practice of charging hourly rates. However, by 1997 some pundits again were predicting a decline because AOL was not providing enough access numbers for its ballooning customer base, causing a legion of frustrated users who could not connect due to busy signals. In addition to AOL having to wipe from the books every dime of profit, some individuals filed lawsuits against them for breach of contract, and 36 states threatened action over billing practices as well. In January of that year AOL began offering refunds to customers who could not enter the service due to user overload, and its stock took a tumble.

## CompuServe Folded into AOL

AOL experienced an upswing in 1997 when the announcement was made that it was purchasing rival Compu-Serve, which would operate separately but allow AOL to dominate the market, adequately fending off the Microsoft Network. Counting roughly 60 percent of all online users as customers, its stock rose 600 percent in 1998. By the end of that year, AOL had its best fiscal quarter ever and boasted about 17 million total customers worldwide, 15 million on AOL and the other 2 million on CompuServe. Its 1998 revenue was $2.6 billion, with a net profit of $92 million. Even though it raised its price in 1998, to $21.95 per month, subscribers did not flinch, because the service had established itself as more than just a gateway to the Internet: It was a "portal," with a distinct brand identity.

Late in 1998, AOL began an aggressive course of expansion and agreed to purchase a number of Internet-related businesses. First, it announced it was acquiring Netscape, the browser company that had seen its market share plummet from about 80 percent to roughly 40 percent due to competition from Microsoft's Internet Explorer. (This was also an issue in the U.S. Justice Department court case looking into Microsoft's business practices.) After this deal, Netscape cofounder Marc Andreesen joined the ranks at AOL, as chief technology officer. In early 1999, the company announced it was also buying Moviefone, the telephone service that provides local film listings and offers ticket sales. It also had plans for AOL TV, a service for accessing the Internet through a television instead of a com-

puter (other firms, such as some phone and cable companies, were simultaneously working on this as well). AOL projected that it would see $300 million in net profits by mid-year.

Throughout AOL's skyrocketing success, Case has received high praise.He is determined to make the online world of AOL an attractive, entertaining, and informative place for the masses.

## Further Reading

*Advertising Age,* September 12, 1994.
*Baltimore Sun,* March 6, 1994, p. 1D.
*Business Week,* January 11, 1999, p. 65.
*Capital Times* (Madison, WI), January 28, 1997, p. 6C.
*Computerworld,* November 4, 1996, p. 2.
*Dallas Morning News,* April 27, 1998, p. 1D.
*Detroit News,* November 15, 1994, p. 3E; January 1, 1996, p. B1; April 10, 1996, p. C1.
*Forbes,* January 11, 1999, p. 152.
*Fortune,* February 19, 1996, p. 58; February 15, 1999, p. 69.
*Internet Business Report,* May 1996, p. 3.
*Multichannel News,* June 13, 1994, pp. 3, 44.
*Newsweek,* May 27, 1996, p. 48.
*New York Times,* August 14, 1995, p. D1; February 2, 1999.
*PC World,* January 1997, p. 51; April 1998, p. 55.
*Red Herring,* April/May 1994.
*San Francisco Chronicle,* January 26, 1999.
*Time,* September 22, 1997, p. 46; December 7, 1998.
*United Press International,* January 27, 1999.
*U.S. News & World Report,* March 25, 1996, p. 53.
*Wall Street Journal,* September 8, 1994, p. B12; March 22, 1996, p. B1; August 8, 1996, p. B1; July 9, 1998, p. B4.
America Online press releases, July 19, 1996; August 1, 1996; August 6, 1996; August 8, 1996. Available at http://www.aol .com.
CeePrompt! Computer Connection, January 1, 1996. Available at http://www.ceeprompt.com.
Hoover's Online, March 2, 1999. Available at http://www .hoovers.com.
HotWired, June 19, 1996. Available at www. hotwired.com.
*Inter@ctive Week,* August 21, 1996. Available at http://www .zdnet.com.
Next Generation Online, March 14, 1996. Available at http://www.next-generation.com.
*Web Week,* December 1, 1995. Available at http://www .webweek.com. □

# Florence Chadwick

**Long-distance, open-water swimmer Florence Chadwick (1918–1995) was the first woman to swim 23 miles across the English Channel in both directions. She was known for her endurance swims in rough water.**

The daughter of a San Diego policeman, Florence Chadwick was born in San Diego, California on November 9, 1918. She grew up on the beach and began competing as a swimmer at the age of six, when her

uncle entered her in a race. An important win came at age ten after four years of defeat. In a two-and-a-half-mile "rough water" night swim, she finished fourth. When she was eleven, she won first place in a six-mile rough water race across the San Diego Bay Channel in her home town. For the next 19 years, she continued as a competitive swimmer. Chadwick's strengths were in distance and endurance—she never won a short-distance race in a pool. Although she tried out for the 1936 Olympic team, she failed to qualify because all of the events were swims of relatively short distance.

When she was 13, Chadwick came in second at the U.S. national championships. She later swam on her school teams in San Diego, graduating from high school in 1936. Chadwick went on to study at San Diego State College, Southwestern University of Law, and Balboa Law School. During World War II, she produced and directed aquatic shows for the U.S. military and, in 1945, she appeared with swimmer Esther Williams in the movie *Bathing Beauty.*

### Long-Distance Swimmer

Chadwick knew she excelled at endurance swimming, especially in open water. This kind of swimming demands special talents and a perseverance far beyond that expected of shorter-distance athletes. The English Channel was considered the greatest challenge by swimmers in Chadwick's time. (Since then, it has been surpassed by the crossing of the Cook Strait from the South Island of New Zealand to the North Island). As the *Encyclopedia of World Sport* notes, "Channel swimming is one of sport's most taxing chal-

lenges, with very high rates of failure. The fact that less than seven percent [of those] who attempt to swim across the English Channel complete the trip is a testament to the difficulty of the task. Only the very strong succeed."

Long-distance swimming, like marathon running and other endurance sports, requires athletes to keep good form, technique, and concentration for many hours. Most marathon swimmers swim between 60 and 70 strokes a minute. Therefore, a 10-hour swim would require 42,000 strokes, and a 14-hour swim would require 58,000 strokes—an incredible feat. There are also hazards unique to open-water, long-distance ocean swimming, as Pat Besford noted in the *Encyclopedia of World Sport*: "Long-distance swimming requires courage . . . to go through a pitch black night, fog, weed, flotsam, occasional oil fuel patches, swarms of jellyfish and maritime traffic." And as Kari Lydersen pointed out in *Just Sports for Women,* "Open-water swimmers have to constantly change their strategy as the race goes on, evaluating their position, the weather and water conditions while also dealing with obstacles such as stingrays and kelp beds. The result of countless hours of training can be ruined by a navigational error, and competitors usually come out of the water swollen and scarred from jellyfish stings, sunburn and swimsuit chafing." Although the distance across the Channel is only about 23 miles, the actual distance a swimmer will cover can be dramatically increased by currents, tides, wind, and waves.

Chadwick was inspired to make the crossing by the example of Gertrude Ederle, the first woman ever to swim across the Channel. Ederle made the crossing in 1926 and, although people believed that women were incapable of such an endurance feat, she not only completed the swim, but beat the record set by a man, by almost two hours. Chadwick wanted to surpass Ederle and become the first woman to swim the Channel both ways—from France to England as well as from England to France.

### Trained in the Persian Gulf

Chadwick got a job working for the Arabian-American Oil Company, moved to Saudi Arabia with the company, and began training in the rough waters of the Persian Gulf. Dedicated to her goal, she swam before and after work, and trained for up to ten hours a day on her days off.

In June 1950, Chadwick left her job and went to France to attempt her first Channel crossing. She heard that the London paper, *Daily Mail,* was holding a contest to sponsor applicants who wanted to swim across the Channel, but since no one at the paper had heard of Chadwick, they rejected her application. Despite this setback, she took a practice swim in the Channel in July, making the attempt at her own expense.

On August 8, 1950, after training for two years, Chadwick set a world record for the crossing, swimming from Cape Gris-Nez, France to Dover, England in 13 hours and 20 minutes. Her time broke the 24-year-old women's record, set by Gertrude Ederle; Ederle's time was 14 hours, 39 minutes, and 24 seconds. "I feel fine," Chadwick reported after finishing the swim. "I am quite prepared to swim back." She didn't swim back right away, but returned to Dover in 1951 and spent eleven weeks there, waiting for good weather and tides. On September 11, 1951, Chadwick finally decided to swim, despite dense fog and strong headwinds. Because of challenging winds and tides, this route across the Channel from Dover, England to Sangatte, France was considered more difficult than the France-to-England route. Previous swimmers had avoided it, and no woman had ever completed it. While swimming, Chadwick had to take anti-seasickness medication, but managed to finish in record time—16 hours and 22 minutes. The mayor of Sangatte waited to congratulate her as she emerged from the water.

When Chadwick returned to the United States, she had spent all her money on financing the Channel swim. Her home town of San Diego gave her a ticker tape parade. She regained some of the money by making television and radio appearances, as well as by providing endorsements and swimming exhibitions. She also traveled across the country lecturing on the value of sports and fitness, and teaching children to swim.

## Crossed the Catalina Channel

On July 4, 1952, at the age of 34, Chadwick attempted to become the first woman to swim 21 miles across the Catalina Channel, from Catalina Island to Palos Verde on the California coast. The weather that day was not auspicious—the ocean was ice cold, the fog was so thick that she could hardly see the support boats that followed her, and sharks prowled around her. Several times, her support crew used rifles to drive away the sharks. While Americans watched on television, she swam for hours. Her mother and her trainer, who were in one of the support boats, encouraged her to keep going. However, after 15 hours and 55 minutes, with only a half mile to go, she felt that she couldn't go on, and asked to be taken out of the water.

Brian Cavanaugh, in *A Fresh Packet of Sower's Seeds,* noted that she told a reporter, "Look, I'm not excusing myself, but if I could have seen land I know I could have made it." The fog had made her unable to see her goal, and it had felt to her like she was getting nowhere. Two months later, she tried again. The fog was just as dense, but this time she made it. After 13 hours, 47 minutes, and 55 seconds, she reached the California shore, breaking a 27-year-old record by more than two hours and becoming the first woman every to complete the swim.

On September 4, 1953, Chadwick swam the English Channel from England to France again, setting a new world record for both men and women of 14 hours and 42 minutes. In the same year, she swam the Straits of Gibraltar in 5 hours and 6 minutes—setting a new record for both men and women. She also crossed the Bosphorus between Europe and Asia both ways, and crossed the Turkish Dardanelles—all within a few weeks. On October 12, 1955, Chadwick set another record for crossing the Channel from England to France. This time, she made it in 13 hours and 55 minutes. In 1960, she made her last long-distance swim.

## Retired from Swimming

After retiring from swimming, Chadwick worked as a stockbroker in San Diego and continued to coach young people and promote long-distance swimming. She later served as vice president of First Wall Street Corporation. She was the only female member on the San Diego "Hall of Champions" board. She was inducted into the International Swimming Hall of Fame in 1970, and was inducted into the San Diego Hall of Champions in 1984. In the same year, she received the Living Legacy Award. Throughout the rest of her life, she worked with youth groups and encouraged young people to pursue their own dreams of excellence. Chadwick died at the age of 76 in San Diego, California, after a lengthy illness.

## Chadwick's Legacy

Chadwick easily broke many records set by men, shattering the notion that women were unfit for long-distance swimming. Today women hold many ultra long-distance records in swimming and other sports. Currently, the only person ever to have swum the English Channel three times consecutively is a woman. Chadwick was one of the pioneers. She helped to change attitudes toward women as endurance swimmers and cleared the way for others to follow.

## Further Reading

Hickok, Ralph. *A Who's Who of Sports Champions,* Houghton Mifflin, 1995.

Levinson, David, and Karen Christensen. *Encyclopedia of World Sport From Ancient Times to the Present,* ABC-CLIO, 1996.

Markell, Robert, Nancy Brooks, and Susan Markel. *For the Record: Women in Sports,* World Almanac Publications, 1985.

Sparhawk, Ruth M., Mary E. Leslie, Phyllis Y. Turbow, and Zina R. Rose. *American Women in Sport, 1887-1987: A 100-Year Chronology,* Scarecrow Press, 1989.

Vernoff, Edward, and Rima Shore. *The International Dictionary of 20th Century Biography,* New American Library, 1987.

*The Women's Sports Encyclopedia.* edited by Robert Markell. Henry Holt, 1997.

Woolum, Janet. *Outstanding Women Athletes: WhoThey Are and How They Influenced Sports in America,* Oryx Press, 1992.

Afterhours Inspirational Stories, http://www.inspirationalstories.com/07/3_07_019.html.

Electra, www.electra.com/ultraspo.html.

*Electronic Mail & Guardian,* http://www.mg.co.za/mg/news/98aug2/28aug-men_women.html (March 10, 1999).

*Encarta Online,* http://encarta.msn.com/index/conciseindex/65/065f4000.htm.

*A Fresh Packet of Sower's Seeds,* http://www.deaconsil.com/stories/goals.html

*Just Sports for Women,* http://www.justwomen.com/feat_distance.html.

*New York Post,* http://www.swimnyc.com/article071298i.htm (March 10, 1999).

*San Diego Online,* http://sandiego-online.com/retro/janretr4.stm

*WIC Biography,* http://www.wic.org/bio/chadwick.htm. □

# Chai Ling

**Chai Ling (born 1966) was commander in chief of a 1989 student-led protest in China's Tiananmen Square, which ended with the massacre of hundreds of demonstrators by army troops and riot police.**

Chai Ling was born in 1966 in the northeast Chinese province of Shandong. Both her parents were members of the Communist Party. As a young student Chai herself joined the Central Communist Youth League, which named her a "model student" during high school for her "good health, grades and moral character," reported Paula Chin of *People* magazine.

Chai began to question the politics she grew up with while studying child psychology as a graduate student at Beijing Normal University. She participated in demonstrations asking the government for democratic reforms in 1987, even though she realized that speaking out could have enormous implications. "I was afraid at first," she told the *Los Angeles Times* reporter Nikki Finke. "Because I know that in China the minimum jail sentence for counter revolutionaries is 17 years." Even though she knew the potential consequences, Chai and her classmates could not pretend to condone the inequality of the Chinese system, censoring of the Chinese people, and corruption among Chinese officials. "We saw all this," she told *Glamour* magazine, "and we felt a responsibility."

Instead of pursuing a career within a system she saw as wrong, Chai made a decision. "I knew I had two choices," Chai recounted in the *Los Angeles Times.* "One was to leave the country and do my graduate work at an American school, which was the secure route because I knew I'd have a safe personal future. The other choice was to stand up and fight and join the movement. And I knew that if I did that, my future would likely be imprisonment." Ultimately, Chai decided to risk the wrath of her country's government "because I really love my homeland," she told Finke.

In April of 1989, Chai joined fellow students who were staging a sit-in protest at Beijing's Tiananmen Square, objecting to the government's lack of response to their demands for more freedom. "We wanted to get the Chinese government to respect the constitution," she explained in a May 1994 discussion at the John Fairbank Center at Harvard University, as reported in *Current History* magazine.

## Massacre at Tiananmen Square

After several weeks in the square, Chai and several other protesters began a hunger strike, hoping to draw more attention to the cause and provoke international action. On May 12, she delivered a rousing speech that energized the movement. Her image was broadcast around the world and she was elected Commander-in-Chief of the Students' Democracy Movement. Cassette tapes of the speech were distributed all over China, inspiring thousands of Chinese students and workers to flock to the square to participate in the three-week protest. The crowd eventually swelled to the hundreds of thousands.

On the afternoon of June 3, soldiers gathered around the square, waiting for orders to clear out the protesters through force. Later that night, army troops in tanks rolled into the square, accompanied by riot police with guns. The lights were cut and shots began to ring out. Although the Chinese government has steadfastly maintained that it initiated no violence against the demonstrators, eyewitness accounts confirm that hundreds, if not thousands, of people were killed. "I could hear bullets flying and people screaming," she told *People* magazine's Paula Chin. "We climbed to the upper tiers of the People's Monument and could see the tanks lined up at the edge of the square."

The blood bath was not confined to the square, reported Liu Binyan in *Current History*. Dozens of people elsewhere in the country were executed for "rioting," he wrote, and "thousands more were arrested; many were sentenced to prison terms ranging from 3 to 15 years."

## Escape

Chai and her husband, Feng Congde, who was also active in the democracy movement, escaped the melee at the square. Still fearing for their lives, they immediately went into hiding. Knowing that they faced immediate execution if they were discovered, for ten months both Chai and Feng managed to avoid arrest as two of the Chinese government's most wanted criminals. Chai later credited ordinary Chinese citizens with saving their lives. "All this time, I had the support of lots of people," she told *New York Times* reporter Alan Riding. "People who had their own problems of family and work to worry about, but who helped and protected us with their own resources." Citizens quickly formed secret organizations to help dissidents hide and escape, even though they knew they, too, risked execution. Twenty other dissidents in China were executed while Chai and her husband sought sanctuary in the West.

At one point, Chai told the *New York Times,* she believed her husband had been captured. She learned he was safe within a week, but did not see or contact him for four more months. Sometimes she was hidden with others on the run, but she told Riding that "most of the time I was hidden alone and I had lots of time to reflect on what happened in Tiananmen Square." She concluded that the action didn't go far enough. "But I think that, after 40 years of repression, this was the most pacific and reasonable revolt imaginable."

Finally, Chai and Feng escaped to France and sought political asylum. Soon after leaving China, the couple traveled to the United States for a seven-city speaking tour. Chai led a memorial rally in front of the U.S. Capitol, urging supporters to keep fighting for the dream of a democratic China. Nominated for a Nobel Peace Prize in 1990, she was still not able to get a message through to her parents.

### Controversy over Role

History has somewhat weakened Chai's status as a folk hero. Some eyewitnesses, including Taiwanese pop singer Hou Dejian, have offered conflicting accounts of the night of June 3, when the melee on the square began. Hou wrote his version of the events, which were published in worldwide Chinese newspapers and reprinted in the book *Crisis at Tiananmen: Reform and Reality in Modern China.* He claimed that several hunger strikers decided that the best way to avoid slaughter would be to ask the students to withdraw peacefully from the square, requesting the troops to back down while the crowd dispersed. According to Hou, Chai opposed the plan, saying the students should stay in control of the square and citing a rumor that the government officials could bring the troops under control by daybreak so the students could peacefully retreat.

More questions were raised in *The Gate of Heavenly Peace,* a three-hour documentary film about the movement by Richard Gordon and Carma Hinton. The documentary's title is an English translation for "Tiananmen." The film, released in 1996, argues subtly but persuasively, reported Pauline Chen in *Cineaste,* "that the student protesters in their fight for democracy adopted the same extremism and repression of alternate views that they opposed in the government." Chai is included in Chen's assertion that "the students themselves, in favoring escalation of the movement over compromise with the government, in demanding further concessions after demands were met, and in allowing rhetorically powerful extremists to drown out more moderate views, both exemplify and perpetuate this political culture in China."

*The Gate of Heavenly Peace* features clips from a controversial interview with Chai filmed by American journalist, Philip Cunningham, on May 28, 1989, shortly before the demonstration turned deadly. "Unless we overthrow this inhumane government, our country will have no hope," Chai told Cunningham. "I feel very sad, because I cannot tell [the other students] that what we are actually hoping for is bloodshed, the moment that the government at last has no choice but to brazenly slaughter its own citizens." Later she asserts, "Only when the Square is awash with blood will China be awakened."

The film, Chen wrote, also questions the process by which Chai gained leadership of the movement, and asserts that the hunger striking leaders monopolized the loudspeakers, silencing any dissension. The Associated Press reported that Chai refused to appear in the film, and the Chinese government sought to stop showings of it in Hong Kong, New York, and Washington.

### Continuing to Fight

In 1990, Chai moved to the United States to earn a master's degree in international relations at Princeton University. She divorced Feng and found work as a computer consultant, continuing to speak on behalf of the struggle to liberate China.

### Further Reading

Mu, Yi, and Mark V. Thompson, *Crisis at Tiananmen: Reform and Reality in Modern China,* China Books & Periodicals, Inc., 1989.
*Christian Science Monitor,* May 1, 1996.
*Cineaste,* January 1996.
*Current History,* September 1994.
*Glamour,* December 1990.
*Los Angeles Times,* June 18, 1990.
*New York Times,* April 14, 1990.
*People Weekly,* June 18, 1990.
*Time,* June 17, 1996.
*World Press Review,* July 1990.
*Inside China Today,* http://www.insidechina.com (February 23, 1999). □

# Lon Chaney

**Lon Chaney (1993–1930), nicknamed "The Man of a Thousand Faces," appeared in 157 films between 1913 and 1930. He is remembered for his inventive use of makeup and his portrayal of grotesque characters. Chaney's most famous starring roles were in film productions of *The Hunchback of Notre Dame* and *The Phantom of the Opera.***

Alonzo "Lon" Chaney was born in Colorado Springs, Colorado, on April 1, 1883. He was one of four children born to speech and hearing impaired parents. Chaney's father worked as a barber. When young Lon was still a child, his mother became seriously ill and was bedridden for the rest of her life. He left school and spent much of his time caring for her and his siblings, and enter-

taining them with pantomimed stories. Chaney later recalled his childhood as a happy time, with a tightly knit family that spent much time together at home.

Chaney's older brother, John, was the manager of a theater. When Chaney was barely a teenager he started to work there, handling and then making props. He often watched the performances and became an apprentice stage hand. In later years, he still proudly displayed his membership card in the local stage hands' union. His father, however, thought that one member of the family in the theater was enough. Chaney moved to Denver where he worked during the next several years as a carpet layer, wallpaperer, interior decorator, and guide on trail rides to Pike's Peak.

When Chaney was in his late teens, he was invited to join his brother's production of a comic opera. Chaney immediately left his job as a decorator. The company was soon bought by Charles Holmes, who took it on a three-year tour across the West. The repertoire was mostly comic operas, and Chaney began to imagine a career as a comic actor. He also began to learn about stage design and choreography. Chaney did some work as a producer, and during these travels also started to develop the makeup skills that he would employ in his film career. In 1905, he married Cleva Creighton, a member of the company. Their son Creighton was born the following year.

## Headed to California and Film Career

After several years of traveling performances, Chaney joined a vaudeville team in San Francisco and began to

think about trying his luck at films. His wife was working as a nightclub singer and reportedly became an alcoholic. Although the reasons are not totally clear, she made an unsuccessful suicide attempt. The poison she drank destroyed her singing voice. Chaney divorced her and prevented her from having any contact with their son Creighton. He married Hazel Bennett Hastings, a union that lasted until his death. Chaney remained an intensely private person throughout his career. Rather than attend film openings, he preferred to go trout fishing. He rarely gave interviews. His own face without makeup was so seldom seen in photographs that Chaney was often unrecognized in public. Like his father, Chaney discouraged his son from becoming an actor.

In 1912, Chaney attempted to find work at Universal Studios in Hollywood. At that time, the studio was a converted corral with a single building where filming took place. Chaney was hired as an extra, which meant that he did everything from occasional bit parts to moving scenery. His first film appearance was in the 1913 film, *Poor Jake's Demise.* During the next few years he played small parts in about 70 short films and a few feature films at Universal Studios. Notable among these was 1919's *The Wicked Darling*—not for the quality of his performance, but because it marked his first recorded film appearance with director Tod Browning, with whom Chaney would make ten films.

Chaney remained with Universal Studios for six years, and recalled later how he fought to get his salary raised above one hundred dollars per week. He left that studio (although he later returned to it several times to star in feature films), and soon made his "breakthrough" in 1919's *The Miracle Man.* In this film he played a beggar who could dislocate his limbs at will. Although the director wanted to hire a contortionist, Chaney won the part at his audition. As he told *Movie Magazine* in 1925, "I flopped down, rolled my eyes up in my head like a blind man, and started dragging my body along the ground."

## Career Peaked in Two Famous Films

After *The Miracle Man,* Chaney was in demand for roles that highlighted both his talents as a character actor and his ability to endure sometimes extreme physical pain to portray a maimed or deformed character. Michael Blake, who has written a trio of biographies of Chaney, described just a handful of the roles played by Chaney: "a Russian peasant, a tough Marine sergeant, a century-old mandarin and his grandson, a tragic clown, a shrewd police detective, a crippled magician, a legless criminal, five different Chinese roles, a deformed bell ringer, a mysterious phantom, a Swedish farmer who becomes senile, a blind pirate, a deranged surgeon and his botched experiment (a half man/half ape), a scheming country lawyer, a veteran train engineer. . . ." To take on these roles, Chaney developed exceptional skills as a makeup artist, so much so that he was asked to write an entry on makeup for the 1923 edition of the *Encyclopedia Britannica.*

Chaney became one of Hollywood's most popular actors during the silent film era, eventually accumulating a total of 157 recorded film appearances between 1913 and 1930. In 1923, he starred in what would become one of his best-known films, a silent version of Victor Hugo's novel *The Hunchback of Notre Dame.* To play this role, Chaney endured incredible physical discomfort and often agonizing pain. He described the experience to *Movie Magazine:* "My body was strapped into a harness, which gave it the appearance of being stunted and deformed. I could work only a few hours a day, it hurt me so. I wore false teeth, which made it almost impossible for me to speak. Over one eye was a heavy lump of putty." The harness weighed 72 pounds; and the putty over his eye caused permanent blurring of his vision. In 1925, Chaney starred in a silent version of *The Phantom of the Opera,* once again playing a physically grotesque character at great cost to his own comfort. To play the title character (whose face was a "living death's-head," according to Michael Dempsey in *Film Comment*), Chaney reportedly inserted wires into his nostrils to make them point upward.

Even though he is best remembered for these portrayals of characters with a horrible physical appearance, Chaney did not see them as monsters. As he told reporter Louella Parsons in one of his few interviews (in the *New York Morning Telegraph,*), "I want always to create sympathy and in the end to win redemption. There would be no purpose in playing so hideous a character if in the end we could not feel the man had a soul and that he had been saved from utter degradation."

### Died at Dawn of "Talkies"

As the 1920s came to a close, a revolution occurred in filmmaking: the birth of the "talkie." Many silent film stars were unable to make the transition to the talking film, either because their voices were unsuitable or they could not adapt their acting styles to the new format. Chaney decided to take the chance and starred in a talking film, a remake of his popular 1925 silent film, *The Unholy Three.* In this film Chaney (playing a criminal ventriloquist, Professor Echo) showed his adaptability by using several different voices, including the voice of an old woman.

Chaney's career was suddenly cut short just as he was negotiating with his favorite director, Tod Browning, for the lead role in a sound version of *Dracula,* which could have been his greatest performance. On August 26, 1930, at the age of only 47, Chaney died in Los Angeles as the result of a throat hemorrhage from bronchial cancer, probably brought on by his heavy smoking habit. His final film, *The Unholy Three,* was released several weeks before his death. The role of Dracula went to the relatively unknown Bela Lugosi, who became a star. In future years Chaney's son Creighton (who changed his name to Lon Chaney, Jr.) also became an actor, appearing in almost 150 films. He often played monsters in horror films, including the Wolf Man, Frankenstein's Monster, the Mummy, and Dracula.

Many of Chaney's best film performances no longer can be seen. The nitrate film used in the early days of filmmaking deteriorated, and only about 25 hours of Chaney on film are known to exist, out of his 157 film appearances. Many of his roles are only captured now in publicity photographs and posters. Chaney's life story was told in the 1957 film, *Man of a Thousand Faces,* starring James Cagney.

### Further Reading

Blake, Michael F. *The Films of Lon Chaney,* Vestal Press, 1998
_____*Lon Chaney: The Man Behind the Thousand Faces,* Vestal Press, 1993.
_____, *A Thousand Faces: Lon Chaney's Unique Artistry in Motion Pictures,* Vestal Press, 1995.
*Entertainment Weekly,* Fall 1996 (Special Collector's Issue); September 12, 1997.
*Film Comment,* May-June 1995.
*Insight on the News,* February 19, 1996.
*Movie Magazine,* September 1925 [reproduced in *The Silents Majority: On-line Journal of Silent Film,* http://www.mdle .com/ClassicFilms/FeaturedStar/star8.htm (March 17, 1999)].
*New York Morning Telegraph,* September 2, 1923 [reproduced in *The Silents Majority: On-line Journal of Silent Film,* http://www.mdle.com/ClassicFilms/FeaturedStar/star8.htm (March 17, 1999)].
*The Silents Majority: On-line Journal of Silent Film,* http://www .mdle.com/ClassicFilms/FeaturedStar/star8.htm (March 17, 1999). □

# Roberto Clemente

**A dazzling baseball superstar of surpassing skills, Roberto Clemente (1934–1972) was the first great Latin American player to captivate the major leagues. His life was cut short when his plane, delivering relief supplies to earthquake-devastated Nicaragua, crashed on the last day of 1972.**

A Puerto Rican national hero, Hall of Fame outfielder Roberto Clemente spent his sparkling 18-year baseball career with the Pittsburgh Pirates. He enchanted fans with his powerful throwing arm, graceful outfield defense, and superb hitting. Clemente won Gold Glove Awards, symbolizing defensive supremacy, every year from their inception in 1961 until his death in 1972. He also was elected to the National League All-Star team 12 times. Clemente was an outspoken advocate for Hispanic rights and a humanitarian. His untimely death came while he was leading a mission of mercy.

Clemente's ancestors were Puerto Rican laborers who worked on the island's coffee and sugar plantations. His father, Melchor Clemente, was in his mid-50s when Roberto was born in the Puerto Rican town of Carolina on August 18, 1934. Roberto was the last of six children for him and his wife, Dona Luisa. Melchor Clemente was a foreman at a sugar cane mill and ran a small grocery. His wife rose early to do the family laundry for the owner of the mill. She was very religious, and often fed poor children who came to her house. Clemente's parents instilled in him the values of hard work, respect, dignity, and generosity. "I never heard any hate in my house," Clemente said. "Not for anybody. I never heard my mother say a bad word to my father, or my father to my mother." He revered his parents throughout his life.

Even in his childhood, Roberto was an organizer. He once led a group of boys in raising money to build a fence to protect his school, and another time rescued a driver from a burning car. Beginning at the age of nine, he got up daily at six o'clock to deliver milk for a penny a day, saving his earnings for three years in order to buy a bicycle. From an early age, Clemente developed a passion for baseball. "I wanted to be a ballplayer," he said. "I became convinced God wanted me to." He would hit bottle caps with a broomstick, throw tennis balls against walls, and practice his skills endlessly.

At the age of 18, Clemente attended a tryout camp conducted by Brooklyn Dodgers scout and future general manager Al Campanis. Among 70 players, Clemente stood out. "He was the best free-agent athlete I have ever seen," Campanis recalled. After playing with Santurce in the Puerto Rican winter league, Clemente signed with the Dodgers for a $10,000 bonus and a $5,000 salary. He played in 1954 with the Dodgers' Montreal farm club. But when Brooklyn didn't protect him on its roster, he was drafted by Pittsburgh. "I didn't even know where Pittsburgh was," Clemente later confessed. The Pirates installed him as their right fielder

## Pride of Puerto Rico

"Clemente was our Jackie Robinson," said Puerto Rican journalist Luis Mayoral. "He was on a crusade to show the American public what an Hispanic man, a black Hispanic man, was capable of." Robinson had broken baseball's color bar in 1947 with the Dodgers. Clemente was not baseball's first Hispanic player—others such as Minnie Minoso preceded him—but he was the first to make a major impact on the game.

When Clemente made his major league debut on April 17, 1955, he was listed as "Bob" on the Pirates roster because Roberto sounded too foreign. He made an immediate impression with his skills, his style, and his bearing. Though less than six feet tall and weighing only 175 pounds, Clemente swung an imposing 36-ounce bat. He stood far off the plate, legs spread wide, holding his bat high and leaning his powerful upper body over the plate. Using his quick hands and strong arms, he could handle pitches thrown in any location, often driving them to the opposite field.

Asked how to pitch to Clemente, Dodgers Hall of Famer Sandy Koufax replied jokingly: "Roll the ball." Clemente himself, not known for modesty, said: "Pitch me outside, I will hit .400. Pitch me inside, and you will not find the ball." Power was the only attribute separating Clemente from Willie Mays, to whom he was frequently compared as an all-around player. Clemente was a line-drive hitter who cleared the fences at the rate of about 15 home runs a season.

Whether in the field or on the basepaths, Clemente always hustled, often running out from under his helmet or hat "He played just about every game like his life depended on it," said his Pirates teammate, Willie Stargell. His acro-

batic fielding delighted fans. He covered an enormous amount of ground, caught fly balls no one else could reach, and made tremendous throws. Many experts considered his outfield arm the best ever seen in baseball. Few runners would try to take extra bases against him, yet he still led the National League in outfield assists in five seasons. One time, he threw out Lee May of Cincinnati trying to score from third base on a single.

Despite his skills, Clemente had a difficult transition to major league baseball. Sportswriters often misunderstood his broken English and misquoted him. Sometimes they even made his English look worse than it was. He also had frequent run-ins with quick-tempered Pirates manager, Danny Murtaugh. In his first five seasons, Clemente hit over .300 only once and never had more than seven home runs.

In 1960, he had a breakthrough season, leading Pittsburgh to the World Series. Against the vaunted New York Yankees, he had nine hits. After the Pirates won the Series on Bill Mazeroski's dramatic home run, Clemente skipped the team party and walked the streets of Pittsburgh to personally thank the fans. Yet the baseball writers elected Pirates shortstop Dick Groat, who had a .325 batting average with two homers and 50 runs batted in, as the league's Most Valuable Player in 1960. Clemente finished eighth in the voting with a .314 average, 16 home runs, and 94 runs batted in. Clemente publicly expressed his anger at the voting, saying it showed bias against Latin players.

In 1961, Clemente won the National League batting championship with a .351 average and hit 23 home runs. He hit above .300 in 12 of his final 13 seasons and led the league in batting three more times, in 1964, 1965 and 1967. In his homeland, he was a bona fide hero. Clemente became known as "the Pride of Puerto Rico."

## Speaking Out

Clemente was outspoken about his perceptions of prejudice toward Hispanic players. "Latin American Negro ballplayers are treated today much like all Negroes were treated in baseball in the early days of the broken color barrier," he told *Sport* magazine. "They are subjected to prejudices and stamped with generalizations." One example of such prejudice, Clemente thought, was writers' frequent portrayals of him as a hypochondriac. Clemente often complained of health problems, including backaches, headaches, stomachaches, insomnia, tonsillitis, malaria, sore shoulders, and pulled muscles. Often before stepping into the batter's box, he would roll his shoulders and neck, trying to align his spine. He insisted that his injuries were as real as the pains suffered by Mickey Mantle, a contemporary white superstar. He pointed out that nobody accused the great Mantle of being a malingerer.

Clemente grew increasingly annoyed that, unlike contemporary white stars, he never was asked to do commercial endorsements. "I would make a lot more money in baseball if I were a white American," he said in typically blunt fashion.

Intense and outspoken, Clemente often aroused controversy with his political views. He was a staunch advocate of Hispanic civil rights and a close associate of the Rev.

Martin Luther King Jr. Clemente was a frequent participant in the social issues and campaigns of the 1960s. "I am from the poor people; I represent the poor people," Clemente once said. "I like workers. I like people that suffer because these people have a different approach to life from the people that have everything and don't know what suffering is."

Clemente often took younger Latin players under his wing. In 1966, his young teammate, Matty Alou, wrested the batting championship from him. This was accomplished largely by following Clemente's constant admonitions to hit outside pitches to the opposite field.

## A Legacy of Hope

Clemente was more than a ballplayer. He was a remarkably sensitive and intelligent man. He wrote poetry and played the organ, worked in ceramic art, and studied chiropractic medicine. His strongest commitment was to the young people of Puerto Rico. During the off-season, he conducted baseball clinics all over the island, talking to children about the virtues of hard work, citizenship, and respect for their elders.

Clemente again led the Pirates to the World Series in 1971. With a show-stopping performance on national television, he finally achieved the recognition he had long deserved. Clemente hit a home run in the final game to help the Pirates win and was named Most Valuable Player of the Series. Asked by sportscasters how he felt, his first statement was to his parents, in Spanish. Translated, it was: "On the greatest day of my life, I ask for your blessing."

Toward the end of his career, Clemente felt he had made some headway against prejudice. "My greatest satisfaction comes from helping to erase the old opinion about Latin Americans and blacks," he said.

## A Fatal Plane Crash

In 1972, at the age of 37, he was still going strong. He played in only 102 games due to various injuries but still batted .312. On September 30, the last day of the season, Clemente got his 3,000th career hit, becoming the eleventh man to reach that famous mark. The hit, a ringing double, turned out to be his last. Moved by the plight of Nicaraguans devastated by a major earthquake, Clemente feared that the Puerto Rican military was intercepting relief shipments. He insisted on personally delivering supplies collected by the people of Puerto Rico. The prop-driven DC-7 that was carrying Clemente and the aid packages on December 31, 1972 crashed into the ocean soon after taking off from San Juan. The cause of the crash was never determined; a cargo overload may have been a factor. The island of Puerto Rico and the city of Pittsburgh were both overwhelmed by grief. A Catholic nun in Pittsburgh wrote a letter to Clemente's widow, Vera, saying: "He fell into the water so that his spirit could be carried by the ocean to more places." Three months after his death, the Baseball Writers Association voted Clemente into the Hall of Fame, the first Latin American player to be enshrined in Cooperstown.

Clemente long had dreamed about developing a youth camp in his native Puerto Rico. After his death, Vera Clem-

ente took the lead in developing the camp. Cuidad Deportiva Roberto Clemente was built on 304 acres of marshland donated by the Puerto Rican government. Over the years, its Raiders baseball academy developed a number of major league stars, including Juan Gonzalez, Roberto Alomar, Ivan Rodriguez, Sandy Alomar Jr., Benito Santiago, Carlos Baerga, Ruben Sierra, and Jose Guzman. Besides athletic facilities, it also has programs in drama, dance, music, folklore, and crafts. This camp is in keeping with Clemente's vision of a place where young people can follow their dreams.

Clemente's legacy of magnificent athleticism and an abiding belief in human potential proved a lasting one. At the 1994 All-Star Game in Pittsburgh, a bronze statue honoring Clemente was unveiled at Three Rivers Stadium. At a speech in Houston, a year before his death, Clemente had said: "If you have an opportunity to make things better, and you don't do that, you are wasting your time on this earth."

## Further Reading

Musick, Phil. *Who Was Roberto?: A Biography of Roberto Clemente,* Doubleday, 1974. [/reading
*Maclean's,* April 13, 1987.
*Smithsonian,* September 1993.
*Sporting News,* December 28, 1992; October 27, 1997; January 12, 1998.
*Sports Illustrated,* August 17, 1984; October 5, 1987; September 19, 1994. □

# Maureen Connolly

**Maureen Connolly (1934–1969) was one of the greatest singles players in the history of women's tennis. In 1953, she won four international tournaments known as the Grand Slam of Tennis, an accomplishment achieved by only two other female players since. She is rememberd as a pioneer of women's tennis, who made significant contributions to help popularize the sport.**

Maureen Catherine Connolly was born on September 17, 1934 in San Diego, California. She was the victim of a broken home. Her father, Marten Connolly, left the family when she was a toddler. Her mother, Jassamine Connolly, told the young girl that her biological father was deceased, an untruth that caused a rift between mother and daughter later, when Connolly achieved fame and Marten Connolly resurfaced.

Connolly was raised by her mother and a stepfather, August Berste, a musician by profession. Connolly's mother, an amateur pianist herself, urged her daughter to find a career in music, but Connolly had other plans. As a youngster she grew inspired by watching tennis players at a local park. By the time she was ten years old, she asked her parents persistently for a tennis racket. Connolly's parents indulged her wish and purchased a racket for $1.50.

Connolly was instantly obsessed with the sport of tennis. She practiced incessantly, even after dark and into the night. Initially she took lessons from Wilbur Folsom, but eventually she met Eleanor "Teach" Tennant, a distinguished and charismatic coach who agreed to work with the ten-year-old. Tennant instilled in Connolly a fierce sense of pride, confidence, and a desire to win. Connolly practiced with exceptional dedication.

Connolly was naturally left-handed, but with the help of her coach she developed a powerful right-hand swing. In her obsession to win she learned to generate hatred for her opponents on the court. At the same time, Connolly learned to conceal her emotion and remain expressionless during competition. The intimidating combination of Connolly's unflinching "court face" and powerful swing consistently overwhelmed her opponents. Retired tennis champion Ted Schroeder played partners with Connolly in mixed doubles at La Jolla in 1950, when she was only 14 years old. He recalled her unyielding determination to win. Schroeder's recollection of Connolly was quoted in 1998 by ESPN's Tom Farrey, "There's only one way to describe her—as an assassin . . . She was one of the nicest people you'd ever meet, but on the court, boy she went at it."

As Connolly grew into adolescence she remained unaffected by the rigorous regimen of her tennis practice. She was known to practice for three hours daily, seven days a week, yet she indulged her teen-age nature, despite the trappings of budding success. She sucked on sugar lumps, and loved to eat hamburgers. She was an average student at Cathedral High School in San Diego, and she crammed her studies into the precious few spare moments in her day. Her tennis wardrobe reflected the style of the times—She wore skirts made from cloth with a "sharkskin" finish that was popular in the 1950s; and she sometimes wore a tennis skirt with a poodle applique with rhinestone detail, also characteristic of the teen-age fashion of the times. Her "good-luck" jewelry consisted of a ring with double-dragons protecting a ball, and a heart-shaped locket given her by her mother. Connolly loved horses—perhaps more than she loved tennis—and enjoyed riding whenever time permitted. She practiced dancing, jumped rope, and performed calisthetics in an effort to maintain flexibility and to increase her stamina for tennis tournaments.

## Entered Competitive Tennis

Connolly entered her first tennis tournament shortly after she began to play at the age of ten and emerged as the runner up. In May 1947, shortly after she began working with Tennant, she won the 15-and-under title in the Southern California Invitational Tennis Championship. That early victory began on a winning streak that endured for 56 successive matches. By the age of 14 she was the youngest girl ever to win the national junior tennis championship. During an early match, Connolly lost control under the pressure of competition. She flew into a rage and threw her racket, but learned quickly to control her temper and to accept the decisions with grace. Off the court, she was a completely different person. Charming at all times, she endeared herself to every audience because of her youthful effervescence and extraordinary zest for the game of tennis. She won 50 championships by the age of 15 and was ranked 19th among women singles players in the U.S. Lawn Tennis standings in 1948. The personable, five-foot-three-inch teen-aged slammer became known affectionately as "Little Mo," after she won the national junior championship. The nickname, coined by a reporter, was derived from the "Big Mo," a term used in reference to the battleship U.S.S. Missouri.

Connolly graduated from junior competition to women's tennis after winning the USA Junior International Grass Courts Championships in 1949 and 1950. In 1950, her first year in the adult standings, she was ranked tenth among U.S. women singles players. In 1951 she successfully defended the Wightman Cup for the United States and was the youngest team member in the history of that competition. She went on to play for four consecutive years on the Wightman cup team, winning all of her matches in those tournaments. Connolly won eight successive tournaments in 1951, including the U.S. National Women's Title at Forest Hills—the competition that came to be known as the U.S. Open. Connolly, still a rookie at that time, was largely inexperienced in offensive playing techniques and was undeveloped in power serving, yet she was the youngest player in history to win the U.S. National Women's singles tournament, and she repeated the victory in 1952 and again in 1953. On July 5, 1952, at the age of 17, Connolly became the second youngest woman in history to win the women's singles tournament at Wimbledon, second only to Lottie Dod of England. Not since 1887 had the title gone to someone so young. Connolly retained the Wimbledon title through 1954.

## Won the Grand Slam

In 1953, after three successive U.S. National titles and two Wimbledon victories. Connolly attained the pinnacle of women's tennis with a series of wins known as the Grand Slam of Tennis. During that calendar year she won not only the U.S. Nationals and Wimbledon, but the Australian Championship and the French Open. The four competitions together comprise the Grand Slam. Not only was Connolly the first woman, she was also the youngest woman in history to win the four Grand Slam tournaments, all within the same year. Only two other women ever accomplished the feat after Connolly: Margaret Court in 1970, and Steffi Graf in 1988. Graf, who was also a child tennis star, was Connolly's senior by three months when she took the Grand Slam title, leaving Connolly as the youngest Grand Slammer in the history of women's tennis. Connolly won not only the Grand Slam, she won all but one game set of the competitions involved.

## Competitive Career Ended Tragically

In 1952, Connolly was the guest of honor at a parade organized by her home town of San Diego, following her unprecedented success at Forest Hills and Wimbledon. In recognition of her achievement, Connolly was given a horse named Colonel Merryboy. Two years later, on July 20, 1954, as Connolly rode Merryboy he became "spooked" and threw her from his back. In an instant Connolly was hurled into a cement truck and her leg was shattered by the impact. She spent some time in recuperation and returned to competitive tennis, but the extent of her leg injuries were ultimately too severe for the rigors of competition. On February 22, 1955, she announced that she would retire from professional tennis competition.

Connolly was not yet 21 when she announced her retirement. She had competed in women's professional tennis for less than five years. During her abbreviated career she amassed multiple wins in major tournaments around the world. In addition to her triumphs at the U.S. Nationals, Wimbledon, Australia, and France, Connolly won the Italian Championships in 1953 and again in 1954. She was honored by the Associated Press as the Female Athlete of the Year in 1951, 1952, and 1953. She was ranked the number one female tennis player in the world in 1952, 1953, and 1954.

## A New Life

On the day that Connolly retired from competitive tennis, she announced her engagement to Norman Eugene Brinker. Five months later, on June 11, the couple married in San Diego. The 23-year-old Brinker, a naval officer and Olympic equestrian athlete, was a student at San Diego State College at the time of their marriage.

After Connolly retired from competition she devoted her time to coaching. She contributed a sports column to the *San Diego Union,* and on February 6, 1956 she signed with Wilson Sporting Goods in Chicago as a sports ''pro'' (a

professional consultant) and public relations representative. Connolly by that time was just 21 years old. She devoted much of her energy to further the sport of tennis. She was deeply involved with tennis programs that encouraged women and children to play the game.

In time Connolly and Brinker set up housekeeping in Dallas, Texas where they raised two children. She was diagnosed with cancer and died in Dallas on June 21, 1969, at the age of 34. Before her death, Connolly was inducted into the International Tennis Hall of Fame in 1968. She was inducted posthumously into the Women's Sports Foundation Hall of Fame in 1987. The tennis world honors her memory with the Maureen Connolly Brinker Continental Players Cup for junior girls, an international competition that was dominated by Britain during the 1990s. In 1998, Farrey praised Connolly and held her as a standard for modern women's tennis contenders to emulate. ''Show me what Maureen Connolly showed us,'' he demanded, and went on, ''Her game demonstrated that she was No. 1.''

## Further Reading

Krull, Kathleen. *Lives of the Athletes,* Harcourt Brace, 1997.
Woolum, Janet. *Outstanding Women Athletes Who Influenced American Sports,* Oryx Press, 1992.
*Sports Illustrated,* August 29, 1988, p. 124.
ESPN SportsZone, July 1, 1998, available at http://espn.go.com/gen/columns/farrey (March 18, 1999). □

# Joan Ganz Cooney

**Although few know her name, parents and children all over the world love the work of Joan Ganz Cooney (born 1929), who founded the Children's Television Workshop and created some of the most famous educational programming in television history, including "Sesame Street," and "The Electric Company."**

Cooney, the youngest of three children, was born November 30, 1929, in Phoenix, Arizona, to Sylvan C. and Pauline Reardon Ganz. Her father killed himself when she was 26 years old, which, as Hilary Mills reported in *Vanity Fair,* sent Joan ''into a long period of anorexia, which today she considers a form of passive suicide.''

Early on, Cooney developed a strong sense of civic responsibility, which she credited to the influence of a priest named Father James Keller and his Christopher Movement, a 1950s Catholic group that encouraged Christians to work in communications. ''Father Keller said that if idealists don't go into the media, nonidealists would,'' Cooney told Michele Morris of *Working Woman.*

Heeding Father Keller's directive, Cooney in 1951 graduated from the University of Arizona in Tucson with a degree in English, then spent a year working as a writer for the *Arizona Republic* in Phoenix. Next, she moved to New

York City and found work as a soap opera publicist for NBC and then CBS television networks, where she promoted a variety show called the *U.S. Steel Hour* from 1955 to 1962.

Within a few years, Cooney had bluffed her way into a job producing documentaries at Channel 13, Manhattan's public television station. "I've never been qualified for any job I've been hired for," she later told Ray Robinson of *50 Plus.* Lack of experience notwithstanding, Cooney continually rose to the occasion. Within four years of her hire, she won her first Emmy in an award-studded television career, for "Poverty, Anti-Poverty, and the Poor," a three-hour documentary that traced a busload of poor people confronting officials of the government's War on poverty program.

Cooney's big break came when she received a grant from the Carnegie Corporation to do a study on educational programming aimed at disadvantaged children. She jumped at the opportunity to figure out a concrete way to help children. "I saw in a flash that that was where the power and influence of the medium was going to be," Cooney told *Working Woman.* "I could do a thousand documentaries on poverty and poor people that would be watched by a handful of the convinced, but I was never really going to have an influence on my times. I wanted to make a difference."

## A Legend was Launched

By 1967, reported Peter Hellman of *New York* magazine, Cooney and Carnegie Corporation Vice-President Lloyd Morrisett, who arranged funding for the study, "we're

convinced that a fast-paced, entertaining hour of educational TV each weekday, modeled after *Laugh-In,* [a comic variety show popular in the 1960s] could reach and teach pre-schoolers—especially the disadvantaged." They discovered that while middle-class children started school with a basic knowledge of letters and numbers, disadvantaged children didn't. Their study, *The Potential Uses of Television in Preschool Education* found that those same children watched an average of 27 hours of television per week. The duo figured that they could harness some of that viewing time into educational growth, like learning the alphabet.

Cooney and Morrisett managed to raise the show's first-year budget of $7 million through the U.S. government's Office of Education, the Corporation for Public Broadcasting, the Carnegie Corporation, and the Ford Foundation. "We had decided from the first that we wouldn't go around begging for pennies," Cooney told Peter Hellman of *New York* magazine. "Either we would get full funding to do the show right or we would drop it."

Children's Television Workshop has since branched out into a products division, which funds the show and others through its licenses of products ranging from books and toys to sheets, towels, and Big Bird toothpaste. The company in 1986 raised about $14 million a year from such deals.

Even after she conceptualized and raised money for the program's inauguration, the Children's Television Workshop board wasn't sure Cooney, with her relative lack of experience, was the right person to head the project. She has always given credit to her husband, Timothy Cooney, for encouraging her to hold firm for leadership of the Children's Television Workshop. "Without him," Cooney told *Vanity Fair's* Hilary Mills, "I don't know if I would have gone as far as I went." Joan Ganz Cooney has called Timothy Cooney, who once worked for New York City mayor Robert Wagner but quit to become a full-time activist, a "militant feminist." Married in 1964, the couple divorced 11 years later, and Joan Ganz Cooney continues to support him through alimony payments.

## Sunny Days

*Sesame Street* began many years of sunny days with its launch in November 1969. Filmed in Queens, New York, the show, with its urban tenement setting and multicultural cast of characters, reflects a world familiar to its target audience. Hispanic, black, and white actors share the stage with puppets like Bert and Ernie, Big Bird, Cookie Monster, Oscar the Grouch, Kermit the Frog, and loveable furry old Grover. The show frequently welcomes guests, as well, including Susan Sarandon, Robin Williams, Rosie O'Donnell, Jay Leno, James Taylor, and Lena Horne. Even the Count von Count would have trouble tabulating the show's estimated 11 million weekly U.S. viewers.

Broadcast in 141 countries, Sesame Street had won a record 71 Emmys by 1998. One secret to its success is its constant evolution. "The first Sesame Street shows were aimed at two- to five-year olds, the curriculum a narrow five or six subjects," noted Dan Moreau in *Changing Times.*

"Today the show examines more than 200, from geography to the color green." The show's writers particularly struggled over dealing with the death of Will Lee, who played Mr. Hooper, in 1982. Norman Stiles, then the head writer, remarked in *New York* magazine: "In any adult show, the choice would have been obvious—replace the actor or write him out of the script." Instead, the staff chose to dedicate a segment to Big Bird and others talking about his death and remembering him with fond memories. "We felt we owed something to a man we respected and loved," Stiles said.

Cooney is a constant advocate for innovation, noted Michele Morris in *Working Woman*. "Because she encourages the creative team to deal with current issues, such as changing male and female roles, sibling rivalry, child abuse, and death, the show stays fresh and contemporary." Led by Cooney, the Children's Television Workshop, which employs about 250 people, has gone on to produce a number of other educational shows, including *The Electric Company*, a reading program aimed at grade-school kids, *3-2-1 Contact*, a science show that Cooney especially hoped would lure girl viewers, and *Square One TV*, a program about math.

### No Dress Rehearsal

Cooney's career has included serving on the boards of corporations including Johnson & Johnson, Chase Manhattan Bank, and Xerox. Although she's still active in Children's Television Workshop projects, Cooney stepped down as CEO in 1990. With her husband second husband, Peter G. Peterson, a former U.S. secretary of commerce and investment banker whom she married in 1980, Cooney works with her own foundation, which focuses on children. Unable to have children of her own, she became a stepmother to Peterson's five children.

Cooney's zest for life was reinvigorated in 1975, after she was diagnosed with breast cancer and had a radical mastectomy, the surgical removal of both breasts. Her friend Stephen Schwarzman told Hilary Mills of *Vanity Fair* that "to understand Joan, you have to understand the cancer. Because of the cancer she has a policy of no bullshit. 'Life is too short, I could have checked out, I'm going to check out. There is no dress rehearsal.' That's one of her constant lines. Because of that she demands authenticity."

### Further Reading

*Who's Who of American Women*, Reed Reference Publishing Company, 1993.
*50 Plus*, December 1987.
*Changing Times*, July 1989.
*New York*, November 23, 1987.
*People*, November 2, 1998.
*Vanity Fair*, August 1993.
*Working Woman*, April 1981; May 1986. □

# Adolph Coors

**Adolph Coors (1847–1929) is a legend in the brewing business. He came to the United States as a penniless immigrant from Germany in 1868, with the dream of becoming a brewer of the finest beer in the world.**

Adolph Herrman Kohrs (who changed the spelling of his surname to Coors), was born on February 4, 1847 in Barmen, a Prussian city that would later be known as the German city of Wuppertal. His parents, Helena Hein and Johan Joseph Kohrs, were a working couple of modest means. To help the family, young Adolph was apprenticed to a stationer in the nearby town of Ruhfort, where he worked as a printer's assistant. When the family moved to Dortmund in 1862, Coors signed a three-year article of apprenticeship to the Henry Wenker Brewery. Although this job would lead to later fame and fortune, a tragic event also happened that year—both of his parents died, leaving Coors orphaned at a very young age.

Having to support himself financially, Coors completed his apprenticeship and went to work for Wenker Brewery, as a paid employee. He later worked for other breweries, learning the trade and dreaming of going to America and creating a perfect beer. Political unrest in Prussia forced Coors to make a decision. He knew that he would have to serve King William I or emigrate. Coors became one of the half million Germans who, between 1866 and 1870, left for America.

It wasn't an easy trip. Coors was 21 years old and penniless. He made his way to Hamburg and then stowed away on a ship bound for the United States. Coors was discovered long before the ship reached America's shores, but the captain was forgiving as long as Coors was willing to work in Baltimore to pay for his passage.

For the next year he earned his living as a bricklayer, stonecutter, fireman, and general laborer. Always restless, and not having forgotten his dream of a perfect beer, Coors left Baltimore 1869 for a job with the Stenger Brewery in Naperville, Illinois. He was hired as a foreman and, for two years, learned more about brewing. He saved his money and decided to head west. Even with some money in his pocket, he worked his way to Denver with a railroad job.

### Moved to Golden, Colorado

In Denver, Coors purchased a partnership in a bottling company and, by 1872, was the sole owner. He was described in a publication of the day as a dealer in, "bottled beer, ale, porter, cider, imported and domestic wines, and seltzer water." Although he was the owner of a successful business, Coors still dreamed of becoming a brewer. One day, during a walk around Golden, Colorado, he came across the rich Clear Creek valley, east of town. Bubbling up from the ground were many clear, cool springs of crystal pure water. He found an abandoned tannery on the bank of the river, at the base of Table Mountain. Coors knew that perfect water was the most basic ingredient of a perfect beer. He had found the right location for his brewery.

## A Modest Beginning

Jacob Schueler trusted Coors, and agreed to finance the young brewer with $18,000. Twenty-six-year-old Coors contributed his own fortune of $2,000. The partners bought land and spent all the rest of their money remodeling the old tannery and buying brewing equipment. In the very first year, the brewery showed a profit, with a premium beer that Coors had developed. His product used the finest ingredients available, and the profits were always reinvested in the business. By 1880, Coors was able to buy out Schueler and become the sole owner of his brewery.

In 1879, Coors married Louisa Weber of Denver and, by 1893, was the father of six children, three sons and three daughters. Coors stopped expanding his business for awhile and concentrated on marketing, a skill that seemed to come naturally to him. From 1880 to 1890, the brewery's output increased from 3,500 barrels a year to 17,600 barrels a year. During the next decade the firmly established brewery survived a national depression, a devastating flood, the growing threat of prohibition, and stiff competition from other brewers around the world. By 1900, the annual output had increased to 48,000 barrels.

In the late 1800s, Coors built a home on the grounds of the brewery. The home remained a family residence, surrounded by pine trees and lawns, much as it was when Coors built it. Most of the rooms retain their original design and décor. Books written by German authors fill the shelves in the library. Oriental rugs, handcrafted furniture, and a round table with a concealed radio near Coors' favorite easy chair are still in place. A large chandelier imported from Copenhagen hangs from a high ceiling, and a Steinway piano waits for players in the music room. There are 22 rooms in the grand Coors mansion. The entire house was moved several hundred feet to make room for additions at the brewery.

Two of Coors' sons, Grover and Adolph Jr., graduated from Cornell University in preparation for assuming a role in the family business. In 1912, when he was 65, Coors appointed his son, Adolph Jr., to be superintendent of the Coors Company. By then, all three sons were firmly involved with the company, which remained a family enterprise. By then it had also become a center for most community activities in Golden.

In 1914, the Volstead Act was passed, which prohibited the sale of alcoholic beverages in the U.S. This should have meant the end to a prominent brewery and to the fortunes of the family who owned it. The Act was devastating, but Coors and his family had planned ahead. They had devised ways to keep their brewery open as others around the country closed down. They could no longer brew their famous beer, but the vision of Coors led his company to other activities and the brewery survived.

During the 17 so-called "prohibition years," Coors turned his brewery into a cement manufacturing plant, and also a plant that fashioned scientific and chemical products made from porcelain. He made use of the brewing equip-

ment to produce several local products, including a near-beer called "Mannah." This recipe was produced like beer, but after fermentation the liquid flowed through a large still that condensed the alcohol out. The product could then be sold. The alcohol was pumped into government-bonded cellars for later sale to drug companies, hospitals, and other approved markets. During prohibition the Coors company also produced malted milk, which is made the same way as malted barley for beer. Coors eventually became the leading producer of malted milk, and would probably have continued selling to candy companies if the pressure of producing one of the most popular beers in the world hadn't forced cancellation of the malted milk division. Meanwhile, Coors Porcelain Company, created solely to get the company through prohibition, grew into one of the world's leading industrial and technical ceramic manufacturers.

## Prohibition Ends

During prohibition, Coors had to dump more than 17,000 barrels of beer into Clear Creek, but they remained in business. Of the 1568 breweries operating in 1810, only 750 reopened when the controversial Volstead Act was repealed in April, 1933. In the first year after prohibition ended, the Coors brewery produced more than 136,000 barrels of beer. By 1955, production had climbed to over one million barrels a year.

Because Coors worked hard and stayed out of the public spotlight, some people believed he was only interested in his business. Others felt he was a cold man. This was not true. Not only did Coors warmly support his employees and community, he was also a loving husband and proud father. It was said of Coors that his most enjoyable times were those spent with his family and friends. Coors had special lanes built so his boys could bowl, he played basketball and pool, and took great pleasure in eating dinner with his whole family every night in the spacious dining room. He did, however, insist upon dinner being served at precisely 6:30 p.m.

## New Products Introduced

During his lifetime, Coors consistently reinvested profits in the company, constantly expanding the brewery and improving the product. His overwhelming concern for the high quality of his beer never prevented his investigation of new ideas. It was his deep conviction that a good businessman needs to remain flexible enough to move with the times.

Adolph Coors Company, the holding company for its principal subsidiary, Coors Brewing Company, became a world leader in making and selling premium beers, always based upon Coors' demand that only the best products be used in the brewing. Eventually the brewery produced Original Coors Beer, Coors Light Beer, Coors Extra Gold Beer, Coors Non-Alcoholic brew, Keystone Beer, and other brews. It imported for sale George Killian's Irish Red Beer, George Killian's Irish Honey Ale, and Zima, a new type of alcoholic beverage.

Coors beer spread across the country by demand from beer lovers rather than by design of the company. It became almost traditional with traveling service men, salesmen, college students and others to take a six pack or a case of Coors on a trip to the east, to share with friends. Soon the friends began to demand that excellent beer from Golden, Colorado. As the fame of the product spread, distribution grew.

The company continued to introduce innovative products and practices, and to involve itself in new brewing technology. Tinplate cans, aluminum cans, a special malting process, the "sterile-fill" process and constant refrigeration are some of the practices introduced by the Adolph Coors Company.

Coors died in an accidental fall from a hotel window while visiting Virginia Beach, Virginia on June 5, 1929. He knew in retirement that his company had been built on solid foundations, and that it would survive and grow under the direction of his sons.

## Further Reading

Baker, Debbie. *Coors Brewing Company, Golden, Colorado*
Coors History, http://www.coorsandco.com/HI_index.html □

# Harold Courlander

**American folklorist Harold Courlander (1908–1996) was not a familiar name to most people during his lifetime. By preserving the history of Native Americans, as well as Asians, Indians, and countless African tribes, his work became crucial to an understanding of the paths traveled by world civilization.**

In 1967, Harold Courlander published a novel called, *The African.* Many people were more familiar with the author Alex Haley's book, *Roots,* published in 1978. It was developed into the most popular television mini-series of the 1970s. What connected the two stories, and the two men, was the court case that occurred when Courlander brought suit against Haley.

Courlander claimed that plots in Haley's *Roots* were directly lifted from *The African.* Haley argued that the story was exclusively that of his own family's rise from slavery in America. The lawsuit made headlines throughout the United States during the summer and fall of 1978. After six weeks of testimony, Haley offered to settle the case. He expressed his regret to Courlander, and made a financial settlement. Haley's reputation was damaged, while the integrity of Courlander was maintained. For a brief time, Courlander's name was noted outside the small circle who had always been familiar with his work.

## Boyhood Friendships Paved Career Path

Harold Courlander was born in Indianapolis, Indiana, on September 18, 1908. His parents were David Courlander and Tillie Oppenheim. Both families were of European Jewish origin. His father's family arrived in America by

1840. His mother had been born in England, where her Russian-born parents had lived briefly. Courlander was the youngest of three children, having two older sisters, Bertha and Adelaide. His father's hard work led to a successful tailoring business. But in 1913, he took on his brother-in-law as a partner, and his business began to fail. The family started over again, with a move to Detroit, Michigan when Courlander was five years old.

In her biography of Courlander targeted for the young adult audience, *A Voice for the People,* author Nina Jaffe noted that among Courlander's classmates in his Detroit neighborhood, there was not only the expected melting pot of European immigrants, but also "the children of black families who had migrated from the farms and small towns of the Deep South." They all came to Detroit in search of the American dream of a better life in the steel and auto factories. Courlander became fascinated by the stories his black friends knew and shared with him. A few years later, when his father became bedridden with a severe bout of rheumatoid arthritis, he would gather his children to his side and spin tales that kept them entertained for hours. The family struggled financially. Yet Courlander remained captivated by stories he heard.

When he was ten years old, Courlander was sent to an "open air school" in order to recover from a chronic illness. He spent much of the day outside in the fresh air in an attempt to regain strength. During that time, Courlander started writing stories and publishing his own newspaper, that he shared with his extended family. He knew that his future would be in writing.

Courlander was editor of his high school newspaper, an activity that often consumed his interest. After high school, he attended Wayne State University in Detroit for a couple of semesters. By 1927, he had transferred to the University of Michigan where he studied English literature and received a B.A. in 1931. A classmate of his, Betty Smith, would go on to write the best-selling novel, *A Tree Grows in Brooklyn,* which was made into a popular Hollywood movie in the 1940s. While at Michigan, Courlander's first play, *Swamp Mud,* won the prestigious Avery Hopwood award. Actor/director John Houseman produced the one-act play for performance in New York in 1941.

Courlander left New York City almost immediately following graduation. He intended to become a playwright, buoyed by his success in college. He also hoped to study with well-known Yale drama teacher, George Pierce Baker. Courlander took on whatever small jobs he could find, often writing book reviews. Jaffe reported that a book, *The Magic Island,* by William Seabrook caught his eye one day in a bookstore. His thoughts turned to the Caribbean and to the island of Haiti, as portrayed in the book. The exotic rituals of the Haitian people captured his imagination. When he discovered that Baker was out of the country and that his plans to study with him would be delayed, Courlander decided on another course. He bought a ticket on a steamer and sailed for Haiti.

## Explored Lives and Cultures

Courlander's trip to Haiti would be the beginning of a pursuit that would last his entire life. He had planned to write a novel. Instead, he spent six months talking to the people, getting to know them and their culture. He listened to their songs and their stories. He found the Creole language of the islanders a new experience to savor. As he would continue to do throughout his life, in many different countries and civilizations, Courlander began to understand the nuances of the language: "It crossed my mind to put down on paper some of the things I was hearing. I wasn't too clear why I was doing it, but that was all part of learning the language, too," noted Jaffe.

On October 2, 1937, the slaughter of thousands of innocent Haitian families—men, women, and children—living across the border in the Dominican Republic shocked the world. Rafael Trujillo, the army general who had taken control of the Dominican government in 1930, had ordered the brutality. Courlander responded to the news with the same horror. A friend had written and recounted his own experience in the aftermath of the killings. Courlander, who was living in New York City at the time, returned to Haiti. He traveled to the Dominican border where he received first-hand accounts from the survivors. He wrote an article in the *New Republic,* the following month. Courlander began to realize how important his writing could become, in telling stories no one else would tell.

In 1940, Courlander traveled to Cuba to continue his study of the indigenous people of the Caribbean islands. His work with the Office of War Information took him to Africa and India. According to *American Folklore, An Encyclopedia,* Courlander was a tireless worker in the "field," out

among the people he studied. He told the stories of the Haitians, the Cubans, and the Ethiopians through his novels, his poems, folklore collections, and nonfiction. From this initial work, he produced nine record albums, through the Folkways Ethnic Library Series, serving as collector, editor, and compiler. In 1947, he worked with Moe Asch to help establish Folkways Records in New York City.

What was most remarkable about Courlander during this time, and throughout much of his career, is that he usually held regular jobs, with nine to five schedules. Courlander spent many years as a commentator with the *Voice of America* and as an analyst with the United Nations. He served as editor of the *United Nations Review,* from 1956 to 1959. He had to his credit, either as author or editor, over 30 volumes of folk tales. His geographical areas of interest spanned the globe: Haiti, Nigeria, Ghana, Ethiopia, Indonesia, the Pacific Islands, and the American Southwest. Courlander was also well-known for his compendium of folk songs and tales from the African-American population. In 1956, some of that work was produced as a six-volume set for Folkways as *Negro Folk Music of Alabama.* A 1952 grant from the Wenner-Gren Foundation enabled him to travel to Alabama, where he collected his material.

In 1960, Courlander published what was likely to be his best-known book. *The Drum and the Hoe: Life and Lore of the Haitian People.* At the time, it was hailed by critic James G. Leyburn as a "fine example of bookmaking and a tribute to Courlander's perceptive respect for the culture." Other major books to his credit were *People of the Short Blue Corn: Tales and Legends of the Hopi Indians,* in 1970, and *The Fourth World of the Hopis,* in 1971.

A book he edited for Hopi elder, Albert Yava, *Big Falling Snow,* in 1978, related stories of Hopi religious beliefs and practices from the perspective of the natives themselves. His other books and stories included: *The Son of the Leopard,* in 1946; *The Fire on the Mountain and Other Ethiopian Stories,* in 1950; *The Tiger's Whisker and Other Tales from Asia and the Pacific,* in 1959; and his last novel, *The Bordeaux Narrative,* in 1990. For that novel, Courlander went back to his love of Haiti. In it, he examined the world of voodoo in the late 19th centruy. Folkore author, Stephen D. Glazier noted in 1992, that, "*The Bordeaux Narrative,* serves as an excellent vehicle for its author's vast knowledge of Haitian folklore as well as an opportunity to demonstrate his keen eye for ethnographic detail." Ironically, this was his first novel about Haiti. Courlander told Jaffe that he wrote it when he realized that he had never written a novel about Haiti, the place where he had begun his first and most life-changing years of fieldwork.

Jaffe wrote an article for the September 1996 issue of *School Library Journal,* which was published a few months after his death. She reflected on Courlander's work. He often had to argue with editors who continually classified much of his work as children's literature. Courlander had said that, "We think of folklore as children's literature, which it isn't, or wasn't, originally. It was for everybody. In African cultures especially, there is no distinction between young and old. Stories are . . . for older people and younger people. Everybody listens in. If the young people want an explanation, they get it from the tellers." Courlander did not believe that the important folk tales should be changed in order to make them more understandable to children. All folk tales were about the lessons and proverbs of life that involved the conversation between the storyteller and the audience who was listening.

Courlander often had to fight for the right simply to tell the stories of cultures different from his own, or different from what his editors thought should have been the moral. What was special about him is the way he walked into foreign worlds, observed but did not intrude. These cultures affected his life, to be sure. Yet he walked back into his own world, with its own stories. The respect for other cultures, the fascination and beauty Courlander found were the elements that made his work meaningful. He was a narrator, really, a mere writer, who saw the importance of making note of others' lives so different from his own.

Courlander was married twice. His first marriage was to Detroit social worker, Ella Schneiderman in 1939. The couple had one daughter, Erika, born in 1940; they divorced after World War II. His second wife, Emma Meltzer, was an artist he met during the war. They married in June of 1949 and had two children, a son, Michael, in 1951, and a daughter, Susan, in 1955. Emma Courlander and their children often accompanied him on his many field trips, especially throughout the American West.

Courlander died at his home in Bethesda, Maryland, on March 15, 1996, less than a year after his final trip to Haiti. His life spanned nearly the entire 20th century. He brought to his readers and other students of folklore, many centuries of civilizations—through his recounting of splendid oral traditions and music. The legacy he hoped to provide was a window into the sacred worlds of thousands of people, bringing them the notoriety he believed they deserved.

## Further Reading

*American Folklore, An Encyclopedia* Garland Publishing, 1996.
Jaffe, Nina *A Voice for the People,* Henry Holt and Company, 1997.
*American West,* November-December 1982, p. 70.
*Horn Book Magazine,* August, 1982, p. 419.
*National Review,* June 13, 1980, p. 743.
*School Library Journal,* September 1996, p. 132. □

# Joan Crawford

**Joan Crawford (1906–1977) was one of the most active and glamorous stars in Hollywood during the 1930s and 1940s. Her entire filmography spans a 45-year period from 1925 to 1970 and includes over 70 films, from silent pictures to talkies. Best known for her portrayals of ruthless women, Crawford counted Hollywood's most memorable actors among her co-stars.**

Joan Crawford was born Lucille LeSueur, on March 23, 1906 in San Antonio, Texas. Her parents, Thomas and Anna Bell Johnson LeSueur, had three children. The eldest of the three died in infancy. Their father, a laborer, deserted the family when Crawford was very young. She was raised along with her older brother, Hal LeSueur, in Lawton, Oklahoma and Kansas City. Her biological father appeared once, in 1934, when Crawford was 28. She spent a few days with him while making a film. Father and daughter were both intensely emotional over the reunion, but never saw each other again after that time.

After Thomas LeSueur left the family, Anna LeSueur moved with her two children to Lawton, Oklahoma where she married Henry Cassin. Cassin was the owner of a local opera house and an open-air theater. He gave his name to his new daughter, and from her earliest memories Crawford was known as Billie Cassin. As a young child, living as Henry Cassin's daughter, Crawford attended a tiny country school in rural Lawton. She was enamored by life at her stepfather's theater, and yearned to become a dancer and an entertainer. Her aspiration was seriously threatened at age six, when she jumped from a porch, onto a jagged piece of glass and seriously injured her foot. That same year, Crawford learned of her true identity when Henry Cassin, rumored to have connections with the underworld, was taken to trial for embezzlement. Cassin was not convicted, but he moved the family to Kansas City, to start a new life. Crawford attended Scarritt Elementary School, until her parents sent her to St. Agnes Convent School because they were unable to care for her. Henry Cassin became frustrated with the challenges of starting a new life and left the family when Crawford was ten. Rather than return to the public school, Crawford worked at the convent school in order to pay her own tuition and board.

After elementary school, her mother sent her to Rockingham Academy where she continued to support herself by working at the school. Crawford was dismayed to learn, first at St. Agnes and later at Rockingham, that she was not treated as an equal by the other girls at the school, because she worked for her own upkeep. She became depressed and tried to run away, but eventually returned to the school. After completing high school, she attended Stephens College in Columbia, Missouri, at the urging of Harvey Walter, her early grade school principal and secretary at Stephen's College. Crawford lasted only a few months at Stephen's College, before her desire to join the theater pulled her away. She joined a traveling dance troupe under her given name of Lucille LeSueur, but returned to Kansas City when the troupe disbanded. She worked as an operator for Bell Telephone Company, and then for various clothiers, before she succumbed once again to the lure of the chorus line. Crawford returned to Kansas City one final time before she embarked on her show business career once and for all.

## Early Career

Crawford left for Chicago where she met the renowned producer J. J. Shubert. He sent her to work in Detroit where she was discovered by talent agents. She took a screen test and signed a contract with Metro Goldwyn Mayer studios in Hollywood. Within the year, Lucille LeSueur became Joan Crawford. She played minor roles in movies with Jackie Coogan, Lon Chaney, ZaSu Pitts, and others. In 1928, she starred as a flapper in *Our Dancing Daughters,* the vehicle that brought the name of Joan Crawford to prominence. She emerged from the silent film era in 1929 when she starred in *Untamed,* her first ''talkie'' with co-star Robert Montgomery.

On June 3, 1929, Crawford eloped to New York with Douglas Fairbanks, Jr., son of Douglas Fairbanks, Sr. and stepson to Mary Pickford. Despite a concerted effort by Crawford, she never earned the acceptance of her in-laws. The rejection devastated Crawford and contributed in part to her divorce from Fairbanks Jr. Before and after the divorce, Crawford was enveloped by her stardom. Between 1930 and 1935 she made 17 movies, including *Grand Hotel* in 1932, in which she starred with Greta Garbo, Wallace Beery, and John and Lionel Barrymore. From 1930 to 1940 Crawford starred in eight pictures with Clark Gable including *Dance, Fools, Dance, Laughing Sinners,* and *Possessed.* Her relationship with Gable eventually overflowed beyond the movie set and erupted into a love affair that climaxed just prior to her divorce from Fairbanks in 1933.

After her breakup with Gable, Crawford embarked on what was perhaps her most brazen and scandalous love tryst. An affair with Franchot Tone, led to their marriage on October 11, 1935 in New Jersey. Initially, Crawford's involvement with Tone was fueled by a love triangle with screen legend, Bette Davis. Both Crawford and Davis each fancied herself as the sole object of Tone's affections, yet it was Crawford who emerged victorious and married Franchot Tone. The marriage lasted four years. During that time Crawford suffered two miscarriages and repeated beatings by her husband. The couple divorced in 1939, after Crawford discovered Tone in his dressing room with a young starlet, under compromising circumstances. After her divorce from Franchot Tone, Crawford adopted a ten-day-old infant and named the girl Christina Crawford.

## The 1940s

In 1940, Crawford starred with Clark Gable in *Strange Cargo,* and with Fredric March in *Susan and God.* In 1942, she made *Reunion in France* with John Wayne.

On July 21, 1942 Crawford married her third husband, Phil Terry. The couple adopted a boy whom they named Phillip Jr., but who was ultimately called Christopher. Their lives were impacted by World War II, and Terry, a would-be movie star, worked in a war plant. Crawford herself worked at a service canteen, where she served food to enlisted military personnel and assisted them in writing letters home. She also worked with the American Women's Voluntary Services, in providing day care to women who worked in the war effort.

In 1943, after 18 years with MGM studios, Crawford signed a contract with Warner Brothers. Two years later the war subsided and Crawford's career soared. In 1945, she completed her Oscar-winning performance in the film *Mildred Pierce.* At Christmastime that year, she received the Golden Apple from the Hollywood Women's Press Club. The following year, in the midst of mounting success in her career, she obtained her third divorce. Crawford testified during the divorce proceedings that Phil Terry was overbearing and inhibited her status as a movie star.

It was *Mildred Pierce,* co-starring Ann Blyth and Eve Arden, that brought Joan Crawford the recognition as a great talent. She won an Academy Award as best actress for her role in the movie. Due to a fear of live audiences Crawford developed a psychosomatically induced fever of 104 degrees and was bedridden on the day of the awards ceremony.

Crawford went on to make *Humoresque* with John Garfield and Oscar Levant in 1946, and *Possessed* in 1947. In 1949, she starred with Zachary Scott in Robert and Sally Wilder's *Flamingo Road.* Her career extended into the 1950s, with twelve new movies, including *Johnny Guitar* in 1954 and *Autumn Leaves* in 1956. She made five more movies during the 1960s, including the classic, *Whatever Happened to Baby Jane?* in 1962 with Bette Davis, and *Strait-Jacket* in 1964, with Diane Baker and Leif Erickson. Crawford's last film, in 1970, was Warner Brother's *Trog* with Michael Gough and Joe Cornelius.

## A Family and a New Husband

In 1947, after her divorce from Phil Terry, Joan Crawford adopted two baby girls, born one month apart. She called them her twins, although they were not related in any way. Crawford remained single until May 10, 1955, when she eloped with Pepsi-Cola executive, Alfred Steele. The couple lived an extremely lavish lifestyle in New York, where they spent an estimated $400,000, mostly in borrowed money, to renovate a townhouse. When Steele died unexpectedly of a heart attack on April 19, 1959, Crawford was left to pay the bills and to raise her four children. After Steele's death, Crawford inherited his spot on the Pepsi-Cola board of directors. She remained in that capacity, as the first woman ever to serve on that board, and went on to sign a publicity contract as a spokesperson for Pepsi-Cola.

In addition to her film career, Crawford made 13 television appearances during the last 25 years of her life. These included three appearances on *GE Theater* and one on *Zane Grey Theater* between 1954 and 1959. In 1961, she made a second appearance on *Zane Grey Theater,* and in 1968 she starred with comedienne Lucille Ball on the *Lucy Show.* In October 1969, Crawford substituted in four episodes of *Secret Storm,* in place of her eldest daughter, who was a regular member of that cast but who was ill.

With the help of Jane Kesner Ardmore, Crawford penned an autobiography in 1962, *A Portrait of Joan.* In 1971 she wrote a memoir called *My Way of Life.* Although conflicting reports surfaced over the years, Crawford professed devotion to her children repeatedly during her lifetime. She used her prominence and popularity to politicize in behalf of adoptive parents. She died of a heart attack at her home in New York on May 18, 1977. Sixteen years later, in 1993, her Oscar trophy sold at auction for $68,500.

### Further Reading

Thomas, Bob. *Joan Crawford, a Biography,* Simon and Schuster, 1978.
*Atlantic,* September 1991, p. 75.
*Ladies Home Journal,* April 1984, p. 60(7); October 1989, p. 142(5). □

# George Cukor

**Known for his ability to elicit great performances, American film director George Cukor (1899–1983) was a stylistic craftsman who made elegant comedies and dramas from the 1930s through the 1960s. He won an Academy Award in 1964 for directing the musical *My Fair Lady.***

Theatrically trained, Cukor liked to stage his movies with an emphasis on character, dialogue, and emotion, and a minimum of cinematic tricks or special effects. Rarely working with original material, Cukor preferred to interpret literary classics. His best films were smooth dramas and slick comedies with strong female leads and polished story lines, known in the trade as "women's pictures." He was nominated five times for Academy Awards for his directing.

### From Stage to Screen

Cukor was born in New York City on July 7, 1899. His parents were Hungarian Jewish immigrants who worked in the legal profession. As a teenager, Cukor started acting in plays. After undergoing military training, he became a stage assistant in Chicago in 1918, then returned to New York and was a stage manager on Broadway the following year. In the early 1920s, he directed a summer stock company in Rochester, New York, in which Bette Davis and Robert Montgomery began their careers. From 1926 to 1929, Cukor became a successful Broadway director of plays such as *The Great Gatsby.*

In a 1969 interview, Cukor said, "I was very lucky because, when I was young, I didn't know what the hell a director was and I wanted to be a director. I'm a great believer in work and character and all that, but unless you have the gift, it's a sad thing." Cukor possessed both the desire and the gift. In 1929, when the motion picture industry entered the sound age, Cukor relocated to Hollywood. There, he worked as a dialogue director on the World War I drama *All Quiet on the Western Front* in 1930.

Cukor co-directed three films for Paramount Pictures before making his solo debut in 1931 with *The Tarnished Lady,* a melodrama which featured British theatrical star Tallulah Bankhead. That was followed the same year by *Girls About Town,* a comedy about women looking for men with money who find true love instead.

In 1932, Cukor moved to the RKO studio and teamed with producer David O. Selznick. That year, Cukor did most of the actual directing, but was not so credited, on *One Hour with You.* The film's official director was Ernst

Lubitsch, whose sophisticated dramatic style had a profound influence on Cukor's film career.

Katharine Hepburn made her film debut in Cukor's 1932 film *A Bill of Divorcement.* It was the first of nine films Cukor would make with the legendary actress, including some of his most stylish social comedies. Cukor, Selznick, and Hepburn teamed up again in 1933 for the hit *Little Women,* based on Louisa May Alcott's literary classic. Audiences and critics loved the lavish, homespun drama. "The picture should go into the archives of Americana because it preserves something precious in our tradition that can never come back again," observed critic James Shelley Hamilton at the time. "Here the simple sturdy virtues live as we liked to think they lived in earlier times . . . intrinsic in a film that on the surface is above everything else entertaining, and appealing." Cukor was nominated for an Academy Award for his meticulous directing.

## Hollywood Heyday

Cukor and Selznick next moved to MGM Studios, where they collaborated on most of Cukor's films until 1950. Their first project was a Broadway theatrical adaptation, *Dinner at Eight,* starring Jean Harlow. The film earned Cukor another Oscar nomination but also garnered criticism from reviewers who felt he had merely filmed a play. "He set up his camera on a stage, and photographed *Dinner at Eight* just exactly as it appeared in the Music Box Theatre last year," wrote Pare Loretz of *Vanity Fair,* who charged that the picture moved "slower on the screen than it did on the stage." It was a criticism that would dog Cukor throughout his career. Other reviewers, however, appreciated the economy of his straight-ahead style. Henri Colip noted, "Cukor is static, he leans on dialogue and acting. But the admirable continuity of his films, their smoothness, makes for excellent cinema. His films are carefully done, consciously artistic, literary, poetic to the point of being effeminate."

Also in 1934, Cukor directed a film adaptation of the Charles Dickens novel *David Copperfield.* When Cukor wanted Maureen O'Sullivan to produce real tears for a deathbed scene, he twisted her feet to make her cry. *New York Times* critic Andre Sennwald called the film "a gorgeous photoplay which encompasses the rich and kindly humanity of the original so brilliantly that it becomes a screen masterpiece in its own right . . . the most profoundly satisfying screen manipulation of a great novel that the camera has ever given us."

In 1936, Cukor tackled Shakespeare with a new film version of *Romeo and Juliet.* It was not as well-received as his previous literary adaptations. Critic Alberto Cavalcanti said it was out-of-date: "It is impossible to realize how bad this film was unless you reflect upon how good it might have been." The novelist Graham Greene called it "unimaginative, coarse-grained, a little banal." Nonetheless, the film was nominated for an Academy Award.

## A Woman's Director

In 1937, Cukor directed the legendary Greta Garbo in a version of the Alexander Dumas drama, *Camille,* a nine-teenth-century French theatrical staple about a dying courtesan who falls for an innocent young man. It was a pairing of a screen goddess at the pinnacle of her popularity with a director who had a special gift for working with actresses. "Cukor had shown a sensitivity and particular aptitude for bringing out the best in women," noted film critic Bosley Crowther. "He was what Garbo required." The National Board of Review called Garbo's work "a performance hardly equaled, never exceeded in the history of the screen."

Cukor was the original director of the 1939 classic *Gone with the Wind,* but lead actor Clark Gable got him removed because he complained that Cukor paid too much attention to the female roles. Cukor, replaced by Victor Fleming, received no credit on the final cut of the box-office behemoth. Yet the film's stars, Vivian Leigh and Olivia DeHavilland, continued to get instruction from Cukor by visiting his home during filming. "He was my last hope of ever enjoying the picture," Leigh later said.

Cukor had established a reputation for being able to handle the most temperamental actresses. He was chosen to direct a cast of 135 actresses in MGM's all-female cast of *The Women* in 1939, including a trio of easily ruffled leading ladies, Norma Shearer, Joan Crawford, and Rosalind Russell. Cukor was careful never to call any of them to the set first, making sure they were treated equally, to the point that he would dispatch several assistants to knock on their trailer doors simultaneously.

In 1940, Cukor directed Hepburn with Cary Grant, in *The Philadelphia Story,* about a stuffy heiress who gets her comeuppance. *Halliwell's Film Guide* calls it "Hollywood's most wise and sparkling comedy, with a script which is even an improvement on the original play. Cukor's direction is so discreet you can hardly sense it, and all the performances are just perfect."

Cukor always allowed his actors to play to their strengths, giving them the freedom they needed to thrive. Film critic, Andrew Sarris, noted: "W.C. Fields is pure ham in *David Copperfield,* and Katherine Hepburn is pure ego in *The Philadelphia Story,* and Cukor is equally sympathetic to the absurdities of both . . . Cukor is committed to the dreamer, if not to the content of the dream. He is a genuine artist."

In a 1969 conversation, Hepburn told Cukor, "You are a very generous director because you let the actor put his mark on what he's doing and you don't have to have a big sign on your back saying 'This is a George Cukor Film.' At times I used to think, 'Gee, I wish George would put more of a "stamp" on things.' Well, your own stamp, of course, was the performances of your people. You never had to put a label on the bottle, it was unmistakable. Your interest was in character. You didn't get wedded to material, you got wedded to people."

## Hits and Misses

Throughout his career, Cukor had his share of flops. In 1941, a second matchup with Garbo on the disastrous *Two-Faced Woman* so infuriated Garbo that it prompted her to retire. But Cukor continued to coax amazing performances out of his leading ladies, including an Academy Award for Ingrid Bergman in the 1944 thriller, *Gaslight*. And Cukor flourished with his classic Hepburn-Spencer Tracy romantic comedies, such as *Adam's Rib* in 1949 and *Pat and Mike* in 1952. Of *Adam's Rib*, a courtroom comedy about husband-and-wife lawyers on opposite sides of a trial, the film review magazine *BFI Bulletin* noted, "Cukor has directed with a deliberate, polished theatricality which emphasizes the artificiality of the piece. The camera often remains anchored for quite an appreciable time so that the screen becomes simply a frame for the two stars."

Cukor displayed his suave mastery of domestic conflict in these and other films. Sarris noted, "when characters have to thrash out their illusions and problems across the kitchen table, Cukor glides through his interiors without self-conscious reservations about what is 'cinematic' and what is not."

Cukor continued to be the director who set actresses' careers into motion or put them in high gear. He first worked with Judy Holliday in *Adam's Rib*, then directed her in the 1950 classic *Born Yesterday*, for which she won an Oscar. In 1954, Cukor made his first film for Warner Brothers, directing Judy Garland in the musical *A Star is Born*. His next musical was *Let's Make Love*, a 1960 flop starring Marilyn Monroe. Cukor also worked with Italian superstar, Sophia Loren, directing her best Hollywood comedy, a Western spoof called *Heller in Pink Tights,* in 1959.

In 1964, Cukor directed the musical hit *My Fair Lady,* starring Audrey Hepburn. Though he won an Oscar, he also got his share of criticism. Sarris noted, "As a longtime admirer of George Cukor's directorial style, I had expected something more in the way of creative adaptation. With justice less poetic than prosaic, Cukor, long slandered as a 'woman's director,' will probably receive an overdue fistful of awards for one of his weakest jobs of direction." The film was a box-office winner, and garnered five Academy Awards, including best picture.

Though his string of hits eventually ended, Cukor continued working into his old age. At 77, he directed the first joint US-Soviet co-production, *The Blue Bird.* Cukor's last movie, directed at the age of 82, was *Rich and Famous,* starring Jacqueline Bisset and Candice Bergen. He died in Los Angeles on January 24, 1983.

Cukor's legacy continued to grow with retrospectives of his work and a renewed interest in the social comedies of the World War II era. "There is an honorable place in the cinema for both adaptations and the non-writer director," noted Sarris, "and Cukor, like Lubitsch, is one of the best examples of the non-writer auteur."

## Further Reading

*Brewer's Cinema,* edited by Jonathan Law, Market House Books, 1995.
Crowther, Bosley *The Great Films: Fifty Golden Years of Motion Pictures,* G.P. Putnam's Sons, 1967.
*Film Directors: A Guide to Their American Films,* edited by James R. Parish and Michael R. Pitts, Scarecrow Press, 1974.
*Halliwell's Film Guide,* edited by John Walker, Harper Collins, 1991.
*The International Encyclopedia of Film,* Crown Publishers, 1972.
*A Library of Film Criticism,* edited by Stanley Hochman. Frederick Ungar Publishing Co., 1974.
Sarris, Andrew, *The American Cinema: Directors and Directions 1929-1968,* E.P. Dutton & Co., 1968.
*The World Encyclopedia of the Film, edited by John M. Smith and Tim Cawkwell,* Galahad Books, 1972.
*Los Angeles Magazine,* March 1997. □

# Imogen Cunningham

**Imogen Cunningham (1883–1976) was an innovative American photographer. She was best known for her detailed, sharply focused photographs of plants as well as her revealing portraits. Cunningham took many well-known portraits of celebrities and artists, especially while working for *Vanity Fair* in the 1930s.**

Imogen Cunningham was born in Portland, Oregon, on April 12, 1883. She was the daughter of Isaac and Susan Elizabeth (nee Johnson) Cunningham. When she was a child, her family moved first to Port Angeles, Washington, then in 1889, to Seattle, where Cunningham's father ran a wood and coal retail business. One of ten children, Cunningham was named after a character in William Shakespeare's *Cymbeline.* The favorite child of Isaac Cunningham, she was educated at home by her father before enrolling in school at the age of eight. Cunningham was said to be interested in photography since childhood and was given art lessons, a luxury her family could barely afford.

## Aquired First Camera

Cunningham graduated from Broadway High School in Seattle, and entered the University of Washington in 1903. She paid for her own education by working as a secretary to a professor and making lantern slides for a botany class. Cunningham studied chemistry because a professor told her that this subject would be an excellent background for photography. Her interest in photography deepened when saw the work of Gertrude Kasebier, a professional photographer who Cunningham greatly admired. In 1906, Cunningham acquired her first camera, and took a portrait of herself in the nude. Her father built a darkroom in the family's woodshed.

In 1907, Cunningham graduated from the University of Washington. She wrote a senior thesis entitled "The Scientific Development of Photography," which examined the work of a local photographer, Edward Curtis. From 1907 until 1909, she worked as a professional photo-technician for his studio. Cunningham spent much of her time printing and retouching his negatives of Native Americans. She also learned the platinum printing process from A.F. Muhr, who worked at the Curtis studio.

## Studied in Germany

Cunningham studied printmaking and its technical aspects in Germany on a scholarship from her college sorority and a loan from the Washington Women's Club. She attended Dresden's Technische Hochschule under the tutelage of Robert Luther from 1909 until 1910. Her coursework included art history and life drawing, but she focused on platinum printing. Cunningham also wrote a thesis entitled "About Self-Production of Platinum Prints for Brown Tones." Important to her development as a photographer, was the International Photographic Exhibition. This exhibit featured both American and European photographers, and gave her an opportunity see the development of different styles.

After Cunningham's studies were completed, she traveled through Europe and returned to the United States at the end of 1910. On her way home, she met Gertrude Kasebier, the woman who inspired her to become a photographer. In New York she met another important photographer, Alfred Stieglitz. In *Imogen Cunningham: A Life in Photography*, Richard Lorenz quoted a letter of Cunningham's about that experience: "I was greatly impressed and rather afraid of him. I did not express myself in a way that anyone could possibly remember and I felt Stieglitz was very sharp but not very chummy. I also looked up Gertrude Kasebier, who was most cordial."

## Opened First Studio

Before 1910 was over, Cunningham had returned to Seattle and set up her own portrait studio. She also became active in the local art scene. Cunningham was a charter member and only photographer in the Seattle Fine Arts Society. Her most interesting work was not done in her commercial enterprise. For five years, from 1910 until 1915, Cunningham took romantic photos of several artist friends who maintained studios nearby. The photos were inspired by some favorite writings, especially William Morris and mythology. Most were taken in a soft focus. An early review, quoted by Lorenz in *Imogen Cunningham: A Life in Photography*, praised her work: "In addition to a thorough technical knowledge of her art, she has a fine imaginative feeling and a sense for the fitness of things which characterizes the true artist, whatever be the means of expression." Other critics found the pictures derivative. Still, in 1914, she was given her first solo exhibition at the Brooklyn Institute of Arts and Sciences.

On February 11, 1915, Cunningham married Roi Partridge, a Seattle etcher, photographer, and print specialist. They eventually had three children, Gryffyd (born in 1915), and Rondal and Padraic (twins born in 1917). Cunningham caused a local scandal in 1915 when she published nude photographs of her husband, taken on Mount Rainer. The couple had adjoining studios. They moved to San Francisco in 1917, at Cunningham's insistence. Partridge was often gone on sketching expeditions, leaving Cunningham in charge of their business affairs and children. In her first years in San Francisco, Cunningham did not often work professionally. She collaborated with Francis Bruguiere for a brief period in 1918, but devoted most of her attention to the three children. Her pictures were focused on herself and her family.

## Blossomed as an Artist

Cunningham's most creative period came in the 1920s and 1930s, when she was recognized as an innovator. She still had young children and her husband was teaching at Mills College, so she did not open a studio. Cunningham did not have many commissions, but she did take a portrait of the Adolph Bolm Ballet Intime, in 1921. Most of her work was done from home, where her style changed drastically. Her pictures became tightly focused, and her subjects were often found in nature. She took pictures of trees and tree trunks, studies of zebras on a trip to the zoo, snakes brought to her by her sons, and magnolia blossoms and calla lilies grown in her garden. One of the best know of this period is 1925's "Magnolia Blossom." Cunningham's photographs of flowers were not unlike the famous paintings of Georgia O'Keefe. Though the two artists worked at about the same time, Cunningham claimed that she was not aware of O'Keefe's work until many years later.

Cunningham continued to take portraits of those around her. In 1923, she began experimenting with double exposures. These pictures often featured meaningful settings and metaphors. Cunningham also experimented with pure light abstractions. As Lorenz writes in *Imogen Cunningham: A Life in Photography*: "By the end of the 1920s, Cunningham was undoubtedly the most sophisticated and experimental photographer at work on the West Coast." This position was cemented by Cunningham's involvement with the f./64 group and their realistic approach. This group (named for an extremely small lens opening) was founded in 1930. Members included Ansel Adams, Edward Weston, and other notable West Coast photographers. The group was known for its sharp focused photos and un-retouched images. These pictures featured more detail and a greater depth of field.

## Worked for *Vanity Fair*

Since the 1910s, Cunningham had been fond of the photographs featured in the magazine, *Vanity Fair.* By the late 1920s, Cunningham began submitting photographs for publication, but all were rejected. In late 1931, Cunningham's persistence paid off when she took portraits of the dancer, Martha Graham. This led to more work from the magazine. Cunningham was sent on assignment to take pictures of film stars in Los Angeles. Of this experience, Margery Mann in *Imogen Cunningham: Photographs* wrote, "Imogen turned the glamorous inhabitants of the higher world into human beings."

Much of Cunningham's works from this point forward were portraits, which used setting to enhance the textual definition. They were seen as being psychologically insightful. One of her most famous portraits was that taken of Morris Graves in 1950. This photograph is in many museum collections. Reviewing a book of Cunningham's portraits, Gretchen Garner of *Booklist* wrote, "The problem with Cunningham is her versatility. She is not easy to categorize as a portraitist, for she had no formulas and responded to each subject freshly. Consistent are her genuine interest in each person's uniqueness, her strong sense of design, and her ability to use light dramatically." Along similar lines, Raymond Bial of *Library Journal* wrote, "Cunninghams's refreshingly informal approach results in a collection of open, honest portraits of the notable people of her time. Along with the quiet dignity that pervades her work, there is an abiding sense of humanity and a touch of whimsy."

In 1934, Cunningham was offered a job in New York by *Vanity Fair.* Despite her husband's protests, she took the job. He filed for divorce soon after. Cunningham experimented with taking pictures on the street in New York, calling them "stolen pictures." She photographed many famous people, including the Mexican artist, Frieda Kahlo. Cunningham's work also appeared in other major American magazines. In 1937, she was included in her first big exhibition at the Museum of Modern Art, in "Photography, 1839-1937." Cunningham still regarded the Bay Area as her home and, in 1946, she bought a cottage in San Francisco.

In 1946-1947, Cunningham taught photography at the California School of Fine Arts in San Francisco. Though she believed in teaching photography to one's self, Cunningham taught at many institutions of higher learning in the Bay Area and was mentor to many student photographers. In 1947, she opened a home-based studio.

By the 1950s, Cunningham's work was reaching a wider audience and earning her more recognition. This began with a 1956 exhibition in the Limelight, a new gallery devoted to photography. From this point forward, Cunningham was regularly featured in prestigious exhibitions. She was also the subject of several documentary films. She frequently traveled to Europe. Cunningham still challenged herself as an artist. In the 1960s, she began experimenting with Polaroid cameras. She published her first monograph, in the 1964 issue of *Aperture,* which included Polaroid cameras. Cunningham published her first book in 1967, the same year she was elected to the American Academy of Arts and Sciences.

## Awarded Guggenheim Fellowship

In 1970, when she was 87 years old, Cunningham was granted a Guggenheim Fellowship. She used the money to print and organize her work. Three years later, at the age of 90, Cunningham had two major exhibitions in New York City. In a *New York Times* review, Hilton Kramer wrote, "Empathy rather than esthetic invention has been her forte, guiding her eye and her lens to her most powerful images." In 1975, Cunningham took the extraordinary step of creating a trust so that her work would be preserved, exhibited, and promoted. She did not need to worry. Throughout the 1970s and 1980s, Cunningham's work was exhibited in the United States and throughout the world. Her photographs appeared in prestigious museums and galleries across the U.S., including the Metropolitan Museum of Art in New York, the San Francisco Museum of Art, and the Art Institute of Chicago.

At the age of 92, Cunningham began what would be her last book, *After Ninety.* The book featured portraits of the elderly, many of whom were her friends. The project was cut short by her death in San Francisco on June 23, 1976. *After Ninety* was published posthumously in 1977, and from 1978 until 1981 an exhibit, based on the book, traveled throughout the United States. Of her career, Lorenz wrote in *Imogen Cunningham: Selected Texts and Bibliography,* "Very few photographers have encompassed the longevity, thematic diversity, and sublime vision manifested by Imogen Cunningham."

## Further Reading

*The Continuum Dictionary of Women's Biography.* edited by Jennifer S. Uglow, Continuum, 1989.

*The Dictionary of Art.* edited by Jane Turner, Grove, 1996.

*Imogen Cunningham: Selected Texts and Bibliography.* edited by Amy Rule. G.K. Hall & Co., 1992.

*International Center of Photography: Encyclopedia of Photography,* Pound Press, 1993.

Lorenz, Richard, *Imogen Cunningham: Ideas Without End,* Chronicle Books, 1993.

Lorenz, Richard, *Imogen Cunningham: Portraiture,* Bulfinch Press, 1997.

Mann, Margery, *Imogen Cunningham: Photographs,* University of Washington Press, 1970.

Slatkin, Wendy, *Women Artists in History: From Antiquity to the 20th Century,* Prentice-Hall, 1985.

*Booklist,* February 15, 1998.

*Library Journal,* August 1998.

*New York Times,* May 6, 1973. □

# D

## James Dickey

**James Dickey (1923–1997), with his unique vision, often violent imagery, and eccentric style, created for himself a place as an important American poet in the last half of the twentieth century. Although he drew much from his life experience, Dickey avoided the classification as a confessional poet because he wrote verse that touched at the heart of all human experience.**

Dickey was born on February 2, 1923, in Buckhead, Georgia, an affluent suburb of Atlanta. He was the second son of Eugene Dickey, a lawyer, and Maibelle Swift Dickey. The Dickeys' first-born son, Eugene Jr., had died of meningitis. Dickey attended North Fulton High School, where he was involved in football and track. After graduating in 1941, he attended Darlington School in Rome, Georgia, for one year. In the fall of 1942, he enrolled at Clemson A & M (now Clemson University) and played tailback on the freshmen football team. After just one semester, Dickey left college to enlist in the United States Army Air Corps. He saw action during World War II, flying approximately 100 combat missions in the South Pacific as a member of the 418th Night Fighter Squadron.

### The Making of a Poet

Dickey returned from active duty and entered Vanderbilt University when he was 23 years old. At college, he began to take his poetry seriously. Some of Dickey's poems appeared in *The Gadfly,* the Vanderbilt student literary magazine in 1947. *The Sewanee Review* was the first major periodical to publish his work. "The Shark at the Window" was accepted by the quarterly and eventually published in 1951. On November 4, 1948, Dickey married Maxine Syerson. They had two sons, Christopher and Kevin. The marriage ended with the death of Dickey's wife in late October 1976. Two months later, he married Deborah Dodson with whom he had one daughter, Bronwen. Dickey was awarded a bachelor of arts degree in English from Vanderbilt in 1949, graduating magna cum laude. He stayed at Vanderbilt one more year, and in 1950 earned a master of arts degree. His thesis was titled "Symbol and Image in the Short Poems of Herman Melville."

In 1950, Dickey became an instructor in English at Rice Institute (now Rice University). After only four months of teaching, he was recalled to active military duty due to the Korean War. After serving two years in the training command of the United States Air Force, he returned to Rice. In 1954, Dickey was awarded a fellowship from the *Sewanee Review,* which he used to travel in Europe and write poetry for a year.

Upon his return from Europe, novelist and historian Andrew Lytle helped Dickey secure a teaching position at the University of Florida. But two years later, in the spring of 1956, Dickey resigned due to a controversy surrounding a reading of his poem "The Father's Body," which was considered by some to be obscene. Frustrated with the university and gaining confidence in his ability to write, Dickey abandoned the academic life and moved to New York to enter the advertising business.

### A Successful Career in Advertising

Dickey landed a job as a copyeditor with McCann-Erickson, the largest advertising agency in New York at that time. He wrote jingles for its Coca-Cola account and be-

**87**

came an executive with the company before he left to work for Liller, Neal, Battle & Lindsey in Atlanta, Georgia, for twice the salary. He wrote on accounts for potato chips and fertilizer until he changed agencies once more, again receiving an increase in salary. As an executive at Burke Dowling Adams, also in Atlanta, Dickey's primary account was Delta Airlines. By the end of the 1950s, Dickey was earning a comfortable living.

While working in the advertising business, Dickey continued to write poetry. In 1958, he was awarded the Union League's Civic and Arts Foundation Prize for his poems that appeared in *Poetry: A Magazine of Verse.* In 1960, he published his first collection of poems as *Into the Stone, and Other Poems.* By 1961, he left advertising to devote more time to his writing. In the same year, he won a Guggenheim Fellowship. He used the money to travel in Italy, where he wrote *Drowning with Others,* published in 1962.

### Poet-in-Residence

When Dickey returned to the United States, he became the poet-in-residence at Reed College (1963–1964), San Fernando Valley State College (now California State University, Northridge, 1964-1965), University of Wisconsin at Madison (1966), University of Wisconsin at Milwaukee (1967), and Washington University (1968). From 1966 to 1968 he also served as consultant in poetry for the Library of Congress. During this time, he gained considerable recognition for his writing, especially for *Helmets* (1964) and *Buckdancer's Choice* (1965), for which he was awarded the 1966 National Book Award.

Both *Helmets* and *Buckdancer's Choice* deal with the modern suburbanite's attempt to maintain values and find meaning in a world so far removed from the natural that life becomes distorted and unreal. Death, war, the natural environment, and the self—common themes in much of Dickey's work—are represented in some of his most poignant and much-discussed poems. Throughout his career, Dickey would draw on his belief that civilization was alienated from nature, and any encounters between the two would be, by necessity, shocking and violent. For Dickey, encountering death enabled one to achieve a heightened sense of life.

"Firebombing," the first poem in *Buckdancer's Choice,* is told from the perspective of a pilot who momentarily flashes back 20 years to World War II and recollects dropping 300-gallon tanks filled with napalm and gasoline on neighborhoods not unlike his own: ". . . when those on earth/ Die there is not even sound; one is cool and enthralled in the cockpit/ Turned blue by the power of beauty/ . . . this detachment/ The honored aesthetic evil . . ." His inability to experience guilt during the moment of bombing is washed away by time, and the pilot, now safely home, re-encounters his actions, no longer protected from the feelings of horror and guilt.

*Poems, 1957-1967* (1968) is a collection of Dickey's early poems, some previously unpublished. First appearing in *Two Poems of the Air* (1964), "Reincarnation (II)" reappears in *Poems, 1957-1967* in a section titled "Falling." The poem is representative of Dickey's fascination with transformation and incarnation. An office worker, who sits at a clean desk every day, finds that death brings him new life when he is reincarnated as a migratory sea bird. "I always had/ These wings buried deep in my back:/ There is a wing-growing motion/ Half-alive in every creature." In many of his poems Dickey transforms his subjects into beings of the nonhuman world so that they can experience life from such a radically different view that the sense of self is renewed and restored, at least temporarily.

### Home for Life: The University of South Carolina

In 1968, Dickey became poet-in-residence at the University of South Carolina, and in 1970 he was named First Carolina Professor of English. Dickey remained at the University of South Carolina until his death in 1997. During the early 1970s, he wrote extensively, publishing his next collection of poems, *The Eye-Beaters, Blood, Victory, Madness, Buckhead, and Mercy* (1970); two books on creative writing, *Self-Interviews* (1971) and *Sorties* (1970); and the critically acclaimed and internationally best-selling novel *Deliverance* (1970). Dickey gained even more popularity after *Deliverance* was made into a successful film in 1972.

### Deliverance

*Deliverance* is a dark and violent story of four Georgia businessmen whose canoe trip down a rugged river turns into a terrifying experience of stalking, murder, and survival at all costs. Lewis Medlock, played by Burt Reynolds in the film version, is an avid bow hunter who convinces three friends to go on a weekend back-to-nature trip down a rugged stretch of the Cahulawassee River in Georgia. During the first day they overcome the obstacles and hazards of the harsh environment; they experience a sense of communion with each other and with nature around them. The next day their world is transformed by a series of horrible events that are set into motion when two members of the party, resting on the bank of the river, are overtaken by two malicious mountain men. One is being sexually assaulted at gunpoint when Medlock finds them and kills the assailant with his bow and arrow. The other runs away. Now the four are faced with decisions about justice, murder, and survival. The idyllic sense of nature is replaced by a nature where savagery and necessity are paramount.

The four men decide to bury the body, fearing how the locals would react to outsiders killing one of their own. The horror of the inescapable experience intensifies when Drew, the only one who wanted to tell the authorities, drowns and Medlock suffers a broken leg. Ultimately, Ed Gentry, the narrator of the story, is forced to kill the second assailant who continues to stalk them down the river. When the terrifying trip finally ends, each member is left to determine the line between meaning and meaninglessness.

After the success of the film *Deliverance,* (for which he had written the screenplay, suggested the theme song, and portrayed a minor on-screen character) Dickey achieved some popular fame. He traveled a circuit of college campuses, playing his guitar and reading his poetry.

## Later Works

Dickey also continued writing poems. *The Zodiac,* published in 1976, was a long poem based on Hendrik Marsman's poem of the same title. Presented in twelve parts, it is about an alcoholic who moves to Amsterdam to write and die. *The Strength of the Fields,* first written for President Jimmy Carter's inauguration in 1977, was published as a collection in 1979. *Puella,* published in 1982, is a long poem about a girl's journey into womanhood. Dickey also wrote several collections for children, including *Tucky the Hunter* (1978) and *Bronwen, the Traw, and the Shape Shifter* (1986). Collections of previous published works include *The Early Motion: "Drowning with Others" and "Helmets"* (1980), *The Central Motion* (1983), and *The Whole Motion: Collected Poems, 1945-1992. Deliverance* was Dickey's only successful attempt as a novelist. *Alnilam,* which was published in 1987, was a lengthy World War II novel about a recently blinded man looking for his son. The novel received mixed reviews and had little popular success. In 1994, his teacher, mentor, and fellow poet, Monroe K. Spears said in a profile of Dickey, which appeared in the *Southern Review:* "He has made poetry seem vital and important, not merely a superior form of amusement or a purely aesthetic activity, but related to the central activities and experiences of life."

Dickey died on January 19, 1997, in Columbia, South Carolina. He taught poetry at the University of South Carolina until the end, even having an oxygen tank wheeled into his classroom every day. Although best known for the novel, *Deliverance,* he was at heart a poet who captivated his readers with the intensity of his feeling and experience. Able to attract large audiences to his public readings in the late 1960s and 1970s, Dickey brought poetry to the masses and continues to enthrall the smaller audience of poetry readers today. In an interview with Frank Anthony that appeared in the *New England Review* in 1997, Dickey seemed to comment on his own place in literary history: "I remember talking to [poet] Robert Lowell about posterity—we differed on opinions of various writers—and I said I would leave that to posterity because after all it's the greatest critic of them all. He turned to me savagely and said, 'Posterity is a lousy critic!' Nevertheless, I would side with posterity, all things being equal."

## Further Reading

*Benet's Reader's Encyclopedia,* fourth ed., edited by Bruce Murphy. HarperCollins, 1996.
*Contemporary Authors,* edited by Pamela S. Dear. Gale Research, 1995.
*Cyclopedia of World Authors,* revised third ed., edited by Frank N. Magill. Salem Press, 1997.
*Dictionary of Literary Biography,* edited by Joseph Conte, Gale Research, 1998.
*Oxford Companion to American Literature,* sixth ed., edited by James D. Hart. Oxford University Press, 1995.
*Booklist,* July 1998.
*New England Review,* Fall 1997.
*New Yorker,* July 13, 1998.
*Southern Review,* Autumn 1994.
*Time,* February 3, 1997. □

# Edgar Laurence Doctorow

**E.L. Doctorow (born 1931) is widely regarded as one of America's pre-eminent novelists of the 20th Century. His work is philosophically probing, employing an adventurous prose style, and the use of historical and quasi-historical figures, situations, and settings. Politically active and outspoken, Doctorow urges other writers to follow his lead in expressing their opinions about issues outside the literary community.**

Edgar Laurence Doctorow was born on January 6, 1931 in the Bronx, New York. He was named after the great poet and short story writer Edgar Allen Poe, who had also lived in the Bronx. Doctorow's parents were both second-generation Americans who descended from Russian Jews. His mother, Rose (Levine) Doctorow, was an accomplished pianist. His father, David Richard Doctorow, owned a music shop. When his business was wiped out during the Depression, he sold home appliances to support the family.

Doctorow's household was rife with literary, intellectual, and political discussion. He would later characterize his childhood milieu as "a lower middle-class environment of generally enlightened socialist sensibility." Both Doctorow and his older brother had aspirations of being novel-

ists. "I always knew that writing was my calling," Doctorow told *Time* magazine. For a long time, however, he would resist this impulse, on the advice of friends and family. "People told me to look for physical labor and under no circumstances to get involved with the book business in Manhattan."

## Education

Upon finishing grade school, Doctorow attended the prestigious Bronx High School of Science. He then enrolled at Kenyon College in Gambier Ohio, a liberal arts school known to be a hub of literary study. One of Doctorow's professors at Kenyon was the renowned poet and critic, John Crowe Ransom. At this point, Doctorow was not focused on a literary career, however, preferring to major in philosophy. He also tried his hand at acting, appearing on stage in a number of campus productions.

After earning his undergraduate degree with honors in 1952, Doctorow moved on to graduate study in English drama at New York's Columbia University in the autumn of 1952. Here he was introduced to the work of the German Romantic playwright Heinrich Von Kleist, whose writing had a profound effect on the young student. Doctorow later modeled the protagonist of his most famous novel, *Ragtime* on the hero of one of Kleist's novels.

While studying at Columbia, Doctorow met and married Helen Setzer, a fellow graduate student. He was drafted into the Army in 1953 and was stationed in Frankfurt, Germany, where Helen gave birth to the couple's first child.

Upon leaving the service, Doctorow returned to New York, where he got a job at the reservations desk at La Guardia Airport. Tired of this, he moved on to a position as an "expert reader" for Columbia Pictures. His responsibilities included reading a novel a day and writing a 1200-word critique evaluating its cinematic potential. Doctorow acknowledged that the job gave him insights into the structure and pacing of genre novels that he would later use in his own writing.

## Early Novels

In 1959, Doctorow accepted a job as an editor for the New American Library. He remained there until 1964, using his free time to work on his own fiction. In 1960, Doctorow published his first novel, *Welcome to Hard Times*. A Western genre story, it was set in the newly settled Dakota Territory of the 1800s. The tale was told from the point of view of the mayor of the frontier town of Hard Times, in the form of a series of journal entries. Critics responded favorably, and the book was later turned into a motion picture starring Henry Fonda. Although Doctorow was now an established novelist, he was still unable to support his family entirely through his writing. He, therefore, accepted the post of editor-in-chief at Dial Press in 1964.

In 1966, Doctorow completed work on his second novel, *Big as Life*. This time he chose science fiction as his genre, spinning an outlandish tale about a group of people who band together to fight off two giant humanoids attacking Manhattan. The book was perplexing to some reviewers; others dismissed it as potboiler science fiction. Doctorow later withdrew the novel from print entirely, apparently disappointed at the critical reception it received.

## Acclaim for *Daniel*

As editor-in-chief at Dial Press, Doctorow spent the last few years of the 1960s working with some of the most talented authors of the time, including Norman Mailer, James Baldwin, and Richard Condon. But he quit his position in 1969 in order to devote more time to his own writing. The fruit of that effort was Doctorow's first non-genre novel, *The Book of Daniel* (1971).

The title character was based on Michael Meeropol, the son of executed Communist spies Julius and Ethel Rosenberg. Doctorow believed the execution was a major political crime of the 1950s and tried to express his confusion and outrage through the character of Daniel. He did extensive research into the lives of the Rosenbergs in preparation for writing his book. The hard work paid off, as critics almost universally praised the new work. *The Book of Daniel* was nominated for a National Book Award and made part of the required reading list at a number of colleges and universities.

## Awards and Riches

It took Doctorow four years to produce his next novel, but critics found it worth the wait. *Ragtime*, set in the decade prior to World War I, wove together a number of interconnected story lines, featuring both real-life and imaginary characters. Historical figures such as Harry Houdini,

William Howard Taft, and Sigmund Freud appear in its pages, though the major themes of the novel revolve around the fictional Coalhouse Walker, a black piano player persecuted for a crime he did not commit. The novel was an enormous critical and commercial success, fulfilling Doctorow's own vow that the book would reach vast new constituencies. *Ragtime* sold 200,000 copies in hardcover in its first year alone, and netted a lucrative $2 million for the paperback sale. It won Doctorow the National Book Critics Circle Award for fiction and was adapted as a feature film in 1982 and a Broadway musical in 1997.

With his first novel of the 1980's, *Loon Lake*, Doctorow returned once again to historical fiction. Set in and around the Adirondacks during the Great Depression, the book follows the wanderings of an ambitious drifter. Its experimental prose style and non-linear structure made it a difficult read for some, but critical response was mostly positive. For his next book, 1984's *Lives of the Poets*, Doctorow eschewed the novel form entirely, preferring to collect six short stories and a novella, all of which dealt with the relationship between art and politics.

## Artist and Advocate

During this same period, Doctorow himself was exploring that relationship through his actions and public pronouncements. Now an internationally famous and acclaimed author, he found time in his hectic schedule to publicly expound on his views about political and cultural matters. In 1980, Doctorow appeared before a Senate subcommittee to decry the encroachment of the entertainment industry into publishing. In 1983, the outspoken author delivered a scathing commencement address at Sarah Lawrence College in which he excoriated Ronald Reagan as "the most foolish and insufficient president in our history." Later that year he traveled to Beijing, China, where he lambasted American officials for encouraging the Chinese to translate and publish American books without duly compensating the American writers.

Doctorow became extremely active within the literary community. In 1982, he was appointed the Lewis and Loretta Gluckman Chair of American Literature at New York University. In 1984, he was elected to the American Academy and Institute of Arts and Letters. The following year he appeared at the Twentieth International PEN Conference to urge America's writers to speak out on political issues. Doctorow later had published a distillation of that argument in essay form entitled "The Passion of Our Calling."

## Bronx Novels

Doctorow's sixth novel, *World's Fair*, appeared in 1986. In it, Doctorow tackled a new literary form, the memoir, writing from the point of view of one Edgar Altschuler, a young man growing up in the Bronx during the Great Depression. Again, real historical personages and events like the Hindenburg disaster and the New York World's Fair of 1939, gave depth and verisimilitude to the narrative. Hailed as a triumph by literary critics, *World's Fair* was awarded the American Book Award for fiction.

The Bronx again provided the setting for Doctorow's next novel, *Billy Bathgate*, published in 1989. The book again explores the relationship between history and myth, as it follows the title character through his immersion in the gangster underworld of the 1930's. Young Bathgate's mentor throughout is the real-life gangster, Dutch Schultz. One of Doctorow's most accessible and accomplished novels, *Billy Bathgate* became an international bestseller and earned Doctorow the National Book Critics Circle Award for fiction.

## Doctorow in the 1990's

In the 1990's, Doctorow slowed his pace somewhat, publishing only one major new work of fiction. He purchased a summer home on Long Island and organized a three-day annual retreat weekend called "The Sag Harbor Initiative." There artists and politicians gathered to discuss major issues of the day.

Doctorow's eighth novel, *The Waterworks*, appeared in 1994. Set in New York City in the aftermath of the Civil War, the suspenseful narrative is told by an old, wry newspaper editor. Its real protagonist is Martin Pemberton, one of the paper's employees, who embarks on a quest to find the father he thought was long dead. Laced with historical and contemporary allusions, the book echoes earlier Doctorow works in its sweeping examination of the interaction among different social classes.

## Further Reading

Harter, Carol C. and James R. Thompson, *E.L. Doctorow* Twayne Publishers, 1990.
Levine, Paul, *E.L. Doctorow* Methuen, 1985.
Morris, Christopher D., *Conversations with E.L. Doctorow* University Press of Mississippi, 1999.
Parks, John G., *E.L. Doctorow* Continuum, 1991. □

# James Patrick Donleavy

**The literary career of J.P. Donleavy (born 1926) has spanned nearly 50 years, though he is most famous for his first novel, *The Ginger Man*.**

James Patrick Donleavy was born on April 23, 1926, in Brooklyn, New York. His parents were Irish immigrants who settled with their three children in the Bronx neighborhood of Woodlawn. Donleavy established a poor reputation in school when he was expelled from Fordham Preparatory, a New York Jesuit school. He served in the U.S. Naval Reserve during World War II, then used the GI bill to attend Trinity College in Dublin, Ireland. He lived in Ireland and England, eventually settling permanently in Ireland. Donleavy became an Irish citizen in 1967 as "a purely practical matter of tax," he told Thomas E. Kennedy of *Literary Review*. "Not actually to gain money so much as to simplify my life." He settled into a 25-room mansion, which once belonged to Julie Andrews, on 200 acres of land in Mullingar, about 60 miles from Dublin.

Donleavy married Valerie Heron, with whom he had a son, Philip; and a daughter, Karen. After his divorce from Heron, he married Mary Wilson Price in 1970 with whom he had a daughter, Rebecca; and son, Rory. Price and Donleavy were divorced in the 1980s.

Donleavy's life seemed to center around wild friends who provoked even wilder events, which he faithfully documented in his books. *J.P. Donleavy's Ireland* chronicles the years between Donleavy's move to Dublin in 1946 as a student and the publication of *The Ginger Man* in 1955. "More than just a string of drinking stories," wrote Kevin Scanlon in *Maclean's,* "the book documents Donleavy's metamorphosis from young American to Irish artist. And like the convert who embraces a religion more fervently than its priests, Donleavy frequently sounds more Irish than the Irish themselves. It is a joyous, passionate and resonant cry."

### The Ginger Man

Donleavy's first book was initially rejected by nearly 50 publishers. *The Ginger Man* is the story of Sebastian Dangerfield, "a solitary outsider in a hostile society who is motivated by greed, prurience, and envy," noted a reviewer for *Contemporary Literary Criticism.* Dangerfield "spends most of his time pursuing women and alcohol while neglecting his wife, child, and law studies, and he aspires to upper-class status but is unwilling to compromise his nonconformist nature to attain financial success." Donleavy wrote the book, noted Ginny Dougary of *The Times,* using "a style that was as arresting as his hero: a combination of whiplash narrative and stream of consciousness, punctu-

ated by the four-line haiku that were to become his trademark."

After several years of gathering rejections for the manuscript, the book finally found a publisher at Olympia Press in 1955. Without Donleavy's consent, the book was placed in the pornographic Travlers Companion series. This prompted the author to end his agreement with Olympia. Later Olympia sued an English publisher for breach of contract over the publication of a less offensive version of the book in 1956. The ensuing legal battle ended in 1979, when Donleavy bought the bankrupt company. The controversy disheartened and depressed Donleavy, who later told Thomas E. Kennedy of *Literary Review,* he had become something of a hermit. "As this litigation increased," Donleavy said, "my withdrawal from the world increased. Howard Hughes and his reclusive behavior in his life was no mystery to me."

A complete, uncut version of *The Ginger Man* was finally published in the United States in 1965. Since then, the book, which has never been out of print in the U.S., has sold several million copies and garnered a cult following. Fans like Robert Redford, Mike Nichols, Sam Spiegel, and John Huston vied for the rights to make film versions of the book, but Donleavy was reluctant to relinquish control of his story. His son Philip worked to produce the film in the early 1990s, but the project was never completed.

### Hard Act to Follow

Donleavy followed his bestseller with more than a dozen subsequent novels, plays, works of non-fiction and short stories, but none achieved the same level of success. Many, in fact, drew less-than-favorable comparisons to his first book. Dougary noted that other reviews "have been even more withering. The Observer's verdict on *Fairy Tales of New York,* for instance, is not untypical: 'An unstoppable flow of self-indulgent drivel.' "

Other critics defended Donleavy. Kennedy argued that critics pan the writer with complaints "that Donleavy merely repeats himself—in fact the theme and content of his books vary greatly, although they do share a vision of death's inevitability and man's dark-comically earnest wish to evade it. . . . " One book with Donleavy's brand of dark humor is *The Unexpurgated Code: A Complete Manual of Survival & Manners.* Published in 1975, the book mocks Victorian etiquette novels with a dose of bathroom humor.

Some of Donleavy's early writing explored genres other than the novel. He wrote short stories, publishing a collection called *Meet My Maker the Mad Molecule* in 1964. Other writings ended up on stage, including an adaptation of *The Ginger Man* that was produced in London and Dublin in 1959, and in New York in 1963. Later, he adapted several other novels for the stage, including *A Singular Man,* which was produced in Cambridge and London in 1964 and Westport, Connecticut, in 1967. *The Beastly Beatitudes of Balthazar B* made its way to the stage in London in 1981 and in Norfolk, Virginia, in 1985 productions.

## Inspired Controversy

Donleavy's writings continued to draw fire. His 1984 book, *De Alfonce Tennis: The Superlative Game of Eccentric Champions, Its History, Accoutrements, Rules, Conduct, and Regimen,* for example, led critic Andrew Brown, as stated in *Contemporary Literary Criticism* to comment, "it is pointless to speculate on the reasons this book was written as it was, or published at all. But why should anyone read it? . . . It is a deliberate attack on language with intent to maim, to remove even the possibility of meaning. It is the literary equivalent of heavy metal music. . . . "

As he entered his seventies, Donleavy steadily produced novels and attracted praise ranging from tepid to torrid. Donleavy's 1998 book *Wrong Information is Being Given Out at Princeton* introduced a man who marries into money but finds it isn't what he expected. A *Kirkus Reviews* writer noted of Donleavy, "the old dog is showing signs of age, but his friends will always be glad he's dropped in to say hello, even if their children find him a trifle unkempt and creepy."

Donleavy's career came full circle with the 1994 publication of *The History of The Ginger Man.* Seymour Lawrence, Donleavy's editor, told Wendy Smith of *Publishers Weekly,* "I had heard all these stories—he was living in a cottage without a toilet or heat, he was broke, his wife had just had a baby—and I urged him to write them down." The book, touted as an autobiography, focused on Donleavy's one real claim to fame. As Dougary pointed out, Donleavy's wife and child "seem hardly to exist," in the book, noting that "this lack of domestic detail and tenderness towards those who shared his life most intimately makes his own life seem as exaggerated and one-dimensional as a cartoon. It also gives the impression of a selfish man, forever swept up in his own obsessive quests."

## Further Reading

*Complete Marquis Who's Who,* Marquis Who's Who, 1997.
*Contemporary Authors,* New Revision Series, Vol. 24, edited by Deborah A. Straub, Gale, 1988.
*Contemporary Literary Criticism,* edited by Daniel G. Marowski and roger Matuz, Gale, 1987.
*Contemporary Novelists,* edited by Susan Windisch Brown, Gale, 1996.
*Booklist,* June 1, 1997.
*Kirkus Reviews,* February 1, 1994; April 15, 1997; October 1, 1998.
*Literary Review,* Summer 1997.
*Maclean's,* October 13, 1986.
*Newsweek,* September 15, 1975.
*Publishers Weekly,* December 13, 1993; February 28, 1994; April 7, 1997.
*Tennis Magazine,* July 1995.
*The Times,* May 28, 1994.
*Pure Fiction,* http://www.pcug.co.uk (March 19, 1999). □

# Jimmy Dorsey

**As the leader of one of the most popular swing-era bands and a skilled saxophone jazz soloist, Jimmy**

**Dorsey (1904–1957) became famous. With or without his equally well known brother Tommy, he was in demand in nightclubs and in the motion picture business.**

Jimmy Dorsey was born in Shenandoah, Pennsylvania on February 29, 1904. Along with his younger brother Tommy, Dorsey appeared destined to become a musician. Not that his father's brass band was all that successful, since he had to work on the side to support his family. But the elder Dorsey, a miner and music teacher, wanted a better life for his sons, and he felt music was the way. Both boys studied music with a real passion, each beginning with a cornet. Before long they were allowed to play in their father's band and by the time he was 17 years old, Jimmy Dorsey was playing clarinet in the well-known Jean Goldkette band. His fellow band members included, among other famous early-day jazz greats, Bix Beiderbecke and Frankie Trumbauer. Dorsey, a smooth and superbly skilled clarinet and saxophone soloist, honed his skills with the Red Nichols band in the later 1920s. He also played with the popular band of Ted Lewis.

## Feuding Brothers

The two brothers, Jimmy and Tommy, had a long-standing feud and each had a terrible temper. Their disagreements were legendary and created much gossip in the music business, explained trumpeter Max Kaminsky in his book *Jazz Band: My Life in Jazz,* "They had been brought up in a feisty Irish family where love was expressed with fists as much as kisses. Both Tommy and his brother Jimmy were natural born scrappers." But the brothers finally decided to join forces in 1933 by forming their own "Dorsey Brothers" band. They hired Ray McKinley to play drums, Glen Miller to play trombone, and singer Bob Crosby. The band was a solid success in the music business, and both Dorseys were doing well financially. But they couldn't get along with each other, and in 1935, after a terrible argument that caused Tommy to walk out, the Dorsey Brothers Band broke up.

Kaminsky said in his book, "When they had their own Dorsey Brothers orchestra they fought around the clock. Tommy would kick off the beat. Jimmy would growl, 'Always the same corny tempo!' Tommy would snarl, 'Oh yeah! And you always play those same corny notes!' Jimmy would leap up, snatch Tommy's trombone and bend it in two. Tommy would seize Jimmy's sax and smash it on the floor, and the fight was on."

Neither of the Dorsey brothers had a great influence on the jazz music of the day, and their influence on Swing was yet to come, but they were noted for their fine ensemble work and even more so for their outstanding musical arrangements. Together or apart, they were often at the top of the hit parade, and at one time or another they worked with all of the top soloists of the day. During the times when they played separately, with their own bands, one might be at the top of the biggest hit list on one month, then the other the next month. Each drew an enthusiastic crowd wherever they went.

Dorsey always favored the Selmer saxophone, and so the company produced a very special "Dorsey model." This saxophone was produced between the 26,000 and 27,500 serial number range, and became very valuable as a collector's item. The horn was elaborately engraved, and some collectors even had the Jimmy Dorsey name in the engraving. Jimmy was the brother most committed to jazz. He loved fast music and blaring brass while his younger brother, Tommy, preferred slow, easy music.

## Success in the 1940s

After the 1935 breakup of their popular band, Jimmy Dorsey took the remaining musicians and formed his own band. Though recognition took longer than he had hoped it would, Dorsey kept playing. In the 1940s he achieved success with his hit songs sung by Helen O'Connell ("Green Eyes" and "Tangerine") and Bob Eberle ("Amapola"). He continued to feature both popular singers, as his band traveled around the country, giving nightly performances.

## First Family of Music

The Dorsey brothers were the first family of music. Each brother continued a fascination with Dixieland music, and Jimmy incorporated the sound into his popular orchestra. Each Dorsey band had a famous singer, Bob Crosby with Jimmy and Frank Sinatra with Tommy. Jimmy Dorsey's band featured Ray McKinley on drums, while his brother had Buddy Rich.

Jimmy Dorsey was a natural leader, enabling him to unite a group of potentially volatile musicians into a smooth group. He was also a virtuoso performer on reed instruments. He specialized in speed on his clarinet or saxophone, in cramming many perfect notes into a very short span of time. Some examples of this type of music were "One O'clock Jump" and "John Silver." Fingers flying over the keys, rocking to the sound of the music, his orchestra backing him perfectly, Dorsey would play precisely, without a miss or a flaw. Big band followers always cheered his virtuosity.

His theme music was "Contrasts," and some of his greatest hits included "Amapola (My Pretty Little Poppy)," "In a Little Spanish Town," "Fools Rush In," "Tangerine," "I Got Rhythm," "Perfidia," and "Green Eyes." The Jimmy Dorsey band was immensely popular in the wartime film "Three Jills in a Jeep," made in 1944. The year before this film, Jimmy Dorsey and his orchestra appeared with Red Skelton and Eleanor Powell in a film called "I Dood It!" The film contained some of the best comedy routines in motion pictures. Dorsey's band introduced the modern jazz standard "Star Eyes," and the topical, "So Long, Sarah Jane" in the film. The picture also featured Dorsey in his famous "One O'clock Jump" signature song.

In 1944, Dorsey and his band appeared in a operetta with Marilyn Maxwell. Unfortunately, two Dorsey classics ("What Does It Take?" and "I Know It's Wrong") were cut from the final print of the film. Dorsey's band continued to flourish throughout the 1940s while other big bands faded into obscurity.

## The Dorseys are Reunited

In February 1953, with years of successful music behind them, the Dorsey brothers decided to reunite. This may have occurred because of the release of a somewhat fictionalized 1947 motion picture documentary called *The Fabulous Dorseys,* in which both musicians appeared as themselves. Their music received praise from the critics. Though each had made other films, it was their orchestras that attracted the most attention. The connection with Hollywood continued. They could even make march music swing, and often played "The National Emblem March" in swing-style. The combined Dorsey band continued the popularity of each musician. The brothers also seemed to be able to get along better than before.

The Tommy Dorsey Orchestra, featuring co-leader Jimmy Dorsey, was signed to do the band work for Jackie Gleason's "Stage Show" on television. Gleason's was the only bandstand show on TV in the mid-1950s. The Dorsey orchestra, therefore, received tremendous exposure and regained all of its old popularity among band lovers.

But the good times were drawing to a close. Tommy Dorsey died in November 1956, at the age of 51. Jimmy took over the leadership of the band and continued giving performances. The Dorsey band's memorable 1957 recording of "So Rare" became the last big hit from any major orchestra in the country. Ill health forced Dorsey to retire soon after the recording was made, although he lived to see the tremendous popularity of this great tune. Dorsey's own death came only six months after his brother, on June 12, 1957 in New York City.

Dorsey's music has retained its popularity long after the end of the big band era and his death. Remastered and digitized, it is available on tape or compact disk, and has remained in demand by music lovers throughout the world.

### Further Reading

*Compton's Interactive Encyclopedia*
Jimmy Dorsey, http://www.redhotjazz.com/jimmy.html
E! Online—Fact Sheet—Jimmy Dorsey. http://www.eonline
  .com/Facts/People/0,12,4603,00.html
Tommy and Jimmy Dorsey, http://rhino.com/features/liners/
  75283lin.html □

# Charles Dow

**Charles Dow (1851–1902), with his partner Edward Jones, founded Dow Jones & Company and *The Wall Street Journal*, in order to present business news in a simple, unbiased way. The paper became the most respected financial journal in the world. Dow also developed several stock averages and the Dow theory, based on his personal observations of the relationship between the stock market and general business activities.**

Charles Henry Dow, born in Sterling, Connecticut on November 5, 1851, was the son of a farmer who died when his son was six years old. The family lived in the hills of eastern Connecticut, not far from Rhode Island. Knowing that he did not want to be a farmer, the tall, stooped, bushy-bearded Dow decided to try journalism.

Dow did not have much education or training, but he managed to find work at the age of 21 with the *Springfield Daily Republican*, in Massachusetts. He worked there from 1872 until 1875 as a city reporter for Samuel Bowles, who taught his reporters to write crisp, detailed articles. Dow then moved on to Rhode Island, joining *The Providence Star*, where he worked for two years as a night editor. He also reported for the *Providence Evening Press*. In 1877, Dow joined the staff of the prominent *Providence Journal*. Charles Danielson, the editor there, had not wanted to hire the 26-year-old, but Dow would not take no for an answer. Upon learning that Dow had worked for Bowles for three years, Danielson reconsidered and gave Dow a job writing business stories.

Dow specialized in articles on regional history, some of which were later published in pamphlet form. Dow made history come alive in his writing by explaining the development of various industries and their future prospects. In 1877, he published a *History of Steam Navigation between New York and Providence*. Three years later, he published *Newport: The City by the Sea*. It was an account of Newport, Rhode Island's settlement, rise, decline, and rebirth as a summer vacation spot and the location of a naval academy, training station, and war college. Dow reported on Newport real estate investments, recording the money earned and lost during the city's history. He also wrote histories of public education and the prison system in the state.

Danielson was so impressed with Dow's careful research that he assigned him to accompany a group of bankers and reporters to Leadville, Colorado, to report on silver mining. The bankers wanted the publicity in order to gain investors in the mines. In 1879, Dow and various tycoons, geologists, lawmakers, and investors set out on a four-day train trip to reach Colorado. Dow learned a great deal about the world of money on that journey as the men smoked cigars, played cards, and swapped stories. He interviewed many highly successful financiers and heard what sort of information the investors on Wall Street needed to make money. The businessmen seemed to like and trust Dow, knowing that he would quote them accurately and keep a confidence. Dow wrote nine "Leadville Letters" based on his experiences there. He described the Rocky Mountains, the mining companies, and the boomtown's gambling, saloons, and dance halls. He also wrote of raw capitalism and the information that drove investments, turning people into millionaires in a moment. He described the disappearance of the individual mine-owners and the financiers who underwrote shares in large mining consortiums. In his last letter, Dow warned, "Mining securities are not the thing for widows and orphans or country clergymen, or unworldly people of any kind to own. But for a businessman, who must take risks in order to make money; who will buy nothing without careful, thorough investigation; and who will not risk more than he is able to lose, there is no other investment in the market today as tempting as mining stock."

## Working on Wall Street

In 1880, Dow left Providence for New York City, realizing that the ideal location for business and financial reporting was there. The 29-year-old found work at the Kiernan Wall Street Financial News Bureau, which delivered by messenger hand written financial news to banks and brokerages. When John Kiernan asked Dow to find another reporter for the Bureau, Dow invited Edward Davis Jones to work with him. Jones and Dow had met when they worked together at the *Providence Evening Press*. Jones, a Brown University dropout, could skillfully and quickly analyze a financial report. He, like Dow, was committed to reporting on Wall Street without bias. Other reporters could be bribed into reporting favorably on a company to drive up stock prices. Dow and Jones refused to manipulate the stock market.

The two young men believed that Wall Street needed another financial news bureau. In November 1882, they started their own agency, Dow, Jones & Company. The business' headquarters was located in the basement of a candy store. Dow, Jones, and their four employees could not handle all the work, so they brought in Charles M. Bergstresser, who became a partner. Bergstresser's strength lay in his interviewing skills. Jones once remarked that he could make a wooden Indian talk.

In the days before annual reports and press releases, getting information often took much patience and diplomacy. Dow and Jones' reporters visited the brokerages, banks, and company offices, looking for news. The reporters took messengers with them who would run back to the office with the stories. Someone would then dictate to a group of writers who, using styluses, would write on thin sheets of tissue paper that had carbon paper in between each sheet. In this way, each writer could produce 24 copies at a time. These copies were called "flimsies." Waiting messengers then raced down Wall Street delivering the "flimsies" to subscribers. This process was repeated several times a day. Eventually a late edition and a seven a.m. edition were added, based on private wires and stock prices in London.

In November 1883, the company started putting out an afternoon two-page summary of the day's financial news called the *Customers' Afternoon Letter*. It soon achieved a circulation of over 1,000 subscribers and was considered an important news source for investors. It included the Dow Jones stock average, an index that included nine railroad issues, one steamship line, and Western Union. Because the "flimsies" were inefficient to produce and difficult to read, the company started using a hand-operated press in 1885. However, their publications were still delivered by messenger until 1948.

## Birth of *The Wall Street Journal*

In 1889, the company had 50 employees. The partners realized that the time was right to transform their two-page news summary into a real newspaper. The first issue of *The Wall Street Journal* appeared on July 8, 1889. It cost two cents per issue or five dollars for a one-year subscription. Dow was the editor and Jones managed the deskwork. The paper gave its readers a policy statement: "Its object is to give fully and fairly the daily news attending the fluctuations in prices of stocks, bonds, and some classes of commodities. It will aim steadily at being a paper of news and not a paper of opinions." The paper's motto was "The truth in its proper use." Its editors promised to put out a paper that could not be controlled by advertisers. The paper had a private wire to Boston and telegraph connections to Washington, Philadelphia, and Chicago. It also had correspondents in several cities, including London.

Dow often warned his reporters about exchanging slanted stories for stock tips or free stock. Crusading for honesty in financial reporting, Dow would publish the names of companies that hesitated to give information about profit and loss. The paper soon had power and respect.

## Dow Jones Industrial Average

In the 1890s, Dow saw that the recession was ending. In 1893, many mergers began taking place, resulting in the formation of huge corporations. These corporations sought markets for their stock shares. The wildly speculative market meant investors needed information about stock activity. Dow took this opportunity to devise the Dow Jones industrial average in 1896. By tracking the closing stock prices of twelve companies, adding up their stock prices, and dividing by twelve, Dow came up with his average. The first such average appeared in *The Wall Street Journal* on May 26, 1896. The industrial index became a popular indicator of stock market activity. In 1897, the company created an average for railroad stocks.

Dow also developed the Dow theory, which stated that a relationship existed between stock market trends and other business activity. Dow felt that if the industrial average and the railroad average both moved in the same direction, it meant that a meaningful economic shift was occurring. He also concluded that if both indexes reached a new high, it signaled a bear market was underway. Dow did not believe that his ideas should be used as the only forecaster of market ups and downs. He thought they should be only one tool of many that investors used to make business decisions.

In 1898, *The Wall Street Journal* put out its first morning edition. The paper now covered more than just financial news. It also covered war, which it reported without rhetoric, unlike many of the other papers. Dow also added an editorial column called "Review and Outlook," and "Answers to Inquirers," in which readers sent investment questions to be answered.

## Endorsed a Presidential Candidate

Edward Jones retired in 1899, but Dow and Bergstresser continued working. Dow still wrote editorials, now focusing on the place that government held in American business. *The Wall Street Journal* started a precedent in reporting during the election of 1900 by endorsing a political candidate, the incumbent president William McKinley.

In 1902, Dow began to have health problems and Bergstresser wanted to retire. The two sold their shares of the company to Clarence Barron, their Boston correspondent. Dow wrote his last editorial in April 1902. A few months later, on December 4, 1902 he died in Brooklyn, New York, at the age of 52.

Vermont Royster, a later editor of the *The Wall Street Journal* said that Dow always believed that business information was not the "private province of brokers and tycoons. In writing about high finance, Dow used homely analogy and the language of everyday life. Neither as a writer nor as a person did he ever lose touch with Main Street."

## Further Reading

Rosenberg, Jerry M, *Inside the Wall Street Journal: The Power and the History of Dow Jones & Company and America's Most Influential Newspaper*, Macmillan, 1982.
*Providence Journal-Bulletin*, May 24, 1996.
*The Wall Street Journal*, July 3, 1984. □

# E

## Gertrude Ederle

**Gertrude Ederle (born 1906) was one of the most famous athletes in the world. On August 6, 1926, she became the first woman to swim across the English Channel from France to England, a feat she accomplished in 14 hours 34 minutes. Her time beat the previous men's world record by 1 hour and 59 minutes.**

The daughter of German immigrants to New York City, Gertrude Ederle was born on October 23, 1906. Her love of swimming began at an early age, when Ederle's family spent summers at a riverside cottage in Highlands, New Jersey. When they returned to the city for the winter, she swam in the 10th Avenue horse troughs, earning punishment from her father.

On August 1, 1922, when she was 15, Ederle grabbed world attention when she entered the Joseph P. Day Cup, a 3 1/2-mile race across New York Bay. As a long-distance swimmer, she was completely unknown; before that day, her longest race had been 220 yards. Amazingly, she beat 51 other contenders, including U.S. champion Helen Wainwright and British champion Hilda James. The experience made her realize that she had a talent for long-distance swimming. In the next few years, Ederle broke nine world records in distances from 100 to 500 meters, won six national outdoor swimming titles, and earned more than two dozen trophies. In the 1924 Summer Olympic Games in Paris, Ederle won a gold medal for the 400-meter freestyle relay, and won bronze medals in the 100-meter and 400-meter freestyle races.

In June 1925, Ederle swam 21 miles from the New York Battery to Sandy Hook, beating the men's record with her time of 7 hours, 11 minutes, and 30 seconds. She always enjoyed beating men's records, proving that women could succeed in reaching sports goals that most people thought were impossible.

### New Swimming Techniques

In the 1920s swimming in general, and endurance swimming in particular, underwent a boom in popularity. It became more socially acceptable for women to swim and to compete in sports. Certain technical advancements in swimming technique were incorporated into American training and Gertrude Ederle was among the first swimmers to benefit from these advancements. She used a style of crawl swimming that was adapted from one developed by her early coach, famed trainer and swimming advocate L. deB. Handley. He worked extensively with the New York Women's Swimming Association, where he volunteered his services because the organization was too new and poorly funded to pay him. Known as "the greatest swimming instructor in the world," Handley was devoted to advancing the cause of women's swimming and was also fascinated with different swimming strokes and their effect on a swimmer's efficiency and endurance. Until the early part of the century, the crawl stroke so common today was unknown. When Handley heard about the Australian crawl stroke, he experimented with it and adapted it. He discovered that women were better at the crawl than men because their bodies were naturally more buoyant and they could kick faster. "Obviously, then," Handley wrote, "these newer strokes will allow girls and women to utilize more adequately their natural resources and either cover a given course faster, or last longer in an unlimited swim, than earlier styles."

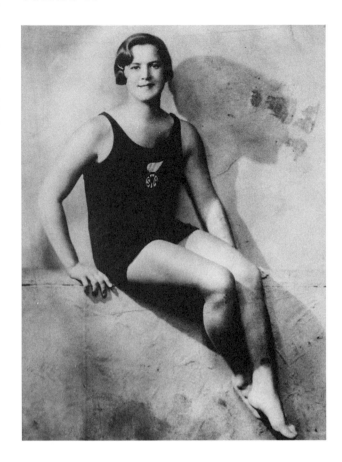

Ederle, who was one of his proteges in a long list of champions, swam an eight-beat crawl adapted from Handley's "six-beat-double-trudgeon crawl," which involved thrashing the legs four times for each arm swing, rolling the body heavily from one side to the other, and lifting the face toward the up arm on each stroke. Currently, most swimmers use a basic front crawl with a six-beat kick.

Handley wrote, "The extent of the progress may be gauged from the fact that American girls hold virtually all the world's swimming records for women today; while six years ago our national marks were so far behind the latter as to be a source of merriment to foreigners." Handley's earlier prophecy was correct; the new, efficient strokes, combined with natural talent, had led Ederle and many other women champions to victory.

## Swimming the English Channel

Having won so many honors, Ederle set her sights on "swimming's holy grail": to swim across the English Channel. If she succeeded, she would be the first woman ever to complete the arduous passage. The first authenticated swim of the English Channel was that of Captain Matthew Webb, in August of 1875. Only five people had ever succeeded in crossing it, all of them men: two American, two English, and one Argentine. One swimmer, William Burgess, had attempted the swim 32 times before completing it in 1911. Most people at that time believed that women were not capable of crossing the Channel because it was so difficult and dangerous. As the *Encyclopedia of World Sport* notes, "Channel swimming is one of sport's most taxing chal-

lenges, with very high rates of failure. The fact that less than seven percent [of those] who attempt to swim across the English Channel complete the trip is a testament to the difficulty of the task. Only the very strong succeed."

When Ederle made the crossing, Channel swimming was a relatively new challenge. As a result of the efforts of Handley and others, marathon swimming was in vogue. Judith Jenkins George, in an article on long-distance women's swimming in the *Canadian Journal of the History of Sport*, noted that "Thousands of spectators were drawn to the oceans, lakes, and pools to observe the swimming marathons of the 1920s and 1930s. The fad of endurance swimming lasted less than a decade yet, during this time, it captivated the public's interest and the athlete's imagination as a test of courage and stamina."

Gertrude Ederle captured the public's imagination more than most. The *Encyclopedia of World Sport* quoted the August 7, 1926 issue of *The New York Times,* that remarked, "The record of her 19 years shows her to be courageous, determined, modest, sportsmanlike, generous, unaffected and perfectly poised. She had, in addition, beauty of face and figure and abounding health."

Ederle first attempted to swim the Channel in August 1925. After swimming for nine hours, she got seasick and her trainer, Jabez Wolffe, forced her out of the water, despite the fact that she insisted that she wanted to go on. She fired Wolffe and replaced him with experienced Channel swimmer, William Burgess.

Ederle sailed for France for her second attempt to cross the Channel in June 1926. Her resolve was strengthened by the fact that competitors were trying to do the same thing. On August 3, Clarabelle Barrett began the swim but was lost in fog and officially declared missing. She gave up the swim only two miles from France. Lillian Cannon of Baltimore, Maryland was also preparing to make the crossing.

After she arrived in France, Ederle waited to start, anxiously watching the weather and hoping for good conditions. On August 6, she prepared to set out. As she stood on the beach on the Boulogne side of Cape Gris-Nez, Ederle's trainers coated her with a mixture of olive oil, lanolin, and Vaseline; the grease would help keep her warm in the frigid water and would also lubricate her skin as she swam. Ederle wore yellow goggles, a red diving cap, and a red two-piece suit, an unusual style at the time. She waded into the water at 7:05 am, shouted "Cheerio!" dove into the 60-degree water, and began swimming toward Dover, England. This route, from France to England, is considered more difficult and dangerous than the England-to France crossing because of prevailing winds and tides. Ederle planned to swim with a westering spring tide for two hours, then drift back to the middle of the channel on the north-northeast tide in the next three hours, and then swim hard for four hours.

Weather conditions rapidly deteriorated as the wind picked up and the waves grew higher. After she had been swimming for six hours, a line squall roiled the water into dangerous cross-currents. "After eight hours I knew I would either swim it or drown," she said later, according to Jay Maeder of the *Daily News.* After twelve hours she was exhausted, just swimming to survive. Her supporters, following in a boat, became worried about her safety. "Trudy, you must come out!" they shouted. "What for?" she yelled back, and kept swimming. Later, Ederle said she was most motivated by several encouraging telegrams that her mother had sent from New York, and which her supporters read to her during the swim. In addition, she said, her father had promised that if she made it, he would buy her any sports car she wanted.

At Kingsdown in Dover, screaming spectators, flares, and searchlights were waiting for her when she stumbled out of the water. She had beaten Enrique Tirabocci's record by almost two hours. Because of the storm, it was estimated that she had swum at least 35 miles. "No man or woman ever made such a swim," her trainer, Burgess, said, according to Maeder. "It is past human understanding." Ederle's father had bet Lloyd's of London that she would win; he received $175,000. To celebrate the victory, he handed out free frankfurters to his whole neighborhood.

Encyclopedia of World Sport quotes British swimming expert and sportswriter Alec Rutherford, who wrote, "The swim came to an end in what might be describes as a blaze of glory . . . huge bonfires were kept burning along the beach, lighting up the waters, so that those ashore could see the strong, steady strokes which Miss Ederle kept until she was able to touch bottom and walk ashore."

When Ederle returned to Manhattan, the city gave her a ticker-tape parade that attracted two million spectators. She was flooded with book, movie, and stage offers, as well as proposals for marriage. She embarked on tours of North America and New York that drained her health and led, in 1928, to a nervous breakdown. As Robert Markel remarked in Women's Sports Encyclopedia, "Her recovery was slow, and undoubtedly more difficult than any swim she ever made." Ederle later taught hearing-impaired children to swim. She developed a special understanding for children with this disability because the prolonged exposure to cold water during her English Channel swim had left her with a hearing loss.

## Further Reading

Encyclopedia of Swimming, edited by Pat Besford, St. Martin's Press, 1971.

Encyclopedia of World Sport, From Ancient Times to the Present, edited by David Levinson and Karen Christensen, ABC-CLIO, Inc, 1996.

Famous First Facts, edited by Joseph Nathan Kane, Steven Anzovin, and Janet Powell, H.W. Wilson, 1997.

The International Dictionary of 20th Century Biography, edited by Edward Vernoff and Rima Shore, New American Library, 1987.

The Women's Sports Encyclopedia, edited by Robert Markell, Henry Holt and Co., 1997.

Canadian Journal of the History of Sport, May, 1995, p.52.

"Amateur Coach Handley Was the World Authority on the Crawl Stroke," Swimnews Online, http://www.swimnews.com/Mag?1996/Janmag96/Handley2.shtml (February 22, 1999).

"A Century of Change," Swimnews Online, http://www.swimnews.com/Mag/1998/MayMag'98/centurychange.html (February 22, 1999).

"English Channel FAQs," NYC Swim, http://www.nycswim.org/ECQuestions.htm (February 22, 1999).

"Gertrude Caroline Ederle," Microsoft Encarta, http://www.netsrq.com/~dbois/ederle.html (February 22, 1999).

"Going the Distance," Just Sports for Women, http://www.justwomen.com/feat_distance.html (February 22, 1999).

"ISHOF Honorees," International Swimming Hall of Fame, http://www.ishof.org/HonorE.html (February 22, 1999).

"L. deB. Handley, the 'Gentleman Jim' of Swimming," Swimnews Online, http://www.swimnews.com/Mag/1995/Octmag95/handley.shtml (February 22, 1999).

"Swim it or Drown," New York Daily News, http://www.mostnewyork.com/manual/news/bigtown/chap55.htm (February 22, 1999).

"Tarzan's Scientific Stroke," Popular Science, http://www.popularscience.com/context/features/lookingback/july/tarzan.html (February 22, 1999). □

# Alfred Eisenstaedt

**Alfred Eisenstaedt (1898–1995) was an established photographer when he moved to the United States from Germany in 1935. But the photograph that won him the most fame was the won he took in Times Square on V-J (Victory over Japan) Day in 1945, ending World War II. The picture, that of a sailor in his blue uniform kissing a nurse in her white uniform, with a passion usually reserved for lovers, became synonymous with the mood of celebration the country felt at the war's end. Even those who did not know his name, knew his picture.**

Eisenstaedt was almost 47-years-old when he took that picture. He got it as he got many of his pictures—persistence rather than planning. He often noted that he had learned it was the reaction to an event that created the best picture, rather than the event itself. That day in August of 1945, Eisenstaedt was simply walking among the crowd that had gathered on the streets of New York. One of the people he noticed was a sailor who was kissing his way through the crowd. He followed him long enough to see him grab the woman whose outfit in white brought the contrast of the sailor's blue to his keen eye. At that moment, Eisenstaedt snapped the picture.

## Self-Taught Hobby Led to Career

Alfred Eisenstaedt was born on December 6, 1898, in Dirschau, West Prussia, then a territory of Germany, and later known as Tczew, Poland. His friends called him, "Eisie." He was the older son of Joseph and Regina Schoen Eisenstaedt. His father owned a department store and made an above-average living for his family. His uncle gave him a camera for his 14th birthday, but Eisenstaedt quickly lost interest in it.

Eisenstaedt graduated from the Hohenzollern Gymnasium in Berlin. He was drafted into the German army in 1916, in the midst of World War I. Eisenstaedt was sent to Flanders following his basic training. There he served as a field artillery cannoneer. His service came to an abrupt end

in December of 1917 when he was hit with shrapnel during British shelling in the second Allied western offensive. While Eisenstaedt nearly lost both his legs, the rest of his battalion was killed.

Eisenstaedt returned to Germany following the war and went back to the university. The economic decline of post-war Germany proved the undoing of the Eisenstaedt family business. They lost all of their money and Eisentaedt was forced to find work. For ten years he sold buttons and belts. In the 1920s, his interest in photography was revived. What caught his attention was a new camera called the Ermanox invented by fellow German, Erich Salomon. The camera was compact and worked with available light. This made it perfect for candid shots. What soon became commonplace, was then a groundbreaking development in the field of photography. In 1925, a friend demonstrated how to enlarge photographs. This was the turning point in his love for picture taking. Eisenstaedt set up his first darkroom in his family's bathroom.

Eisenstaedt was on vacation in Czechoslovakia in 1927 when he snapped a picture of a woman playing tennis. The story was told so many times in Eisenstaedt's lifetime that it became as well-known as the legendary photographer himself. This was the first photograph he sold. *Der Weltspiegel,* a German weekly, bought it for $3. He recalled later that, "I thought. You can get paid for this?" That payment encouraged him to spend more time taking pictures. An article in *American Photo,* magazine during the summer of 1991 did a feature on Eisenstaedt for their series entitled, *Legends: The Secrets of Their Success.* In it, Eisenstaedt offered this

anecdote about his deciding move. He said, "By this time [following his first sale] I was shooting local cultural events and personalities for the Associated Press [then known as the Pacific and Atlantic Photo agency] in my spare time. Finally, my boss approached me and said, 'Choose which you'd rather do—sell buttons and belts or take pictures.' When I said photography, he said, 'You're digging your own grave.'"

Less than a week later, and just three days after his 31st birthday, Eisenstaedt was on his way to Norway to capture shots of writer Thomas Mann as he accepted the Nobel Prize for Literature. It was his first assignment for the German magazine, *Funkstunde.* When he purchased a Leica camera, the first 35mm. still camera, in 1930 Eisenstaedt found the camera he would work with the rest of his life. The Leica was small. He could take many shots before he had to reload—making it the perfect instrument for this man who loved to take pictures.

It was Eisenstaedt's second free-lance assignment that revealed his true spirit. He was sent to cover a royal wedding in Italy. From Mussolini to the choirboys, Eisenstaedt took pictures of everything—everything except the bride and groom, that is. He later told *People* magazine that when he returned from the wedding, his "editor was very perplexed, but he couldn't fire me because I was working free-lance." His last major assignment from Germany took him to Ethiopia. When Italy invaded the country later that year, Eisenstaedt's photos were usually the ones that served as background for the news articles.

## Life In America

*Life* magazine featured a story on Eisenstaedt, *Little Big Man with a Camera,* by Richard Lacayo in September 1990. At five feet four inches, Eisenstaedt could squeeze into a room or a crowd unobserved, because of his size. In that article Eisenstaedt revealed his mood as he saw Germany changing around him and began to realize that the time had come to leave. He was snapping pictures of famed movie star Marlene Dietrich and happy, amusing pictures of waiters on ice, everything that brought him joy in his native surroundings. But then Adolf Hitler appeared, and life in Germany and all over Europe had begun to grow dim. "The old Europe was beautiful," Eisenstaedt said. "There were people interested in art and music. Then these horrible people came to power."

Eisenstaedt's arrival in America coincided with the arrival of a new magazine that was being published by Henry Luce. Eisenstaedt was hired as one his first four staff photographers. The new magazine had a simple title, *Life.* When Luce saw Eisenstaedt's photos with their casual ease, he liked them immediately. Eisenstaedt's picture of a "stiff-faced cadet at West Point," to use Lacayo's words, graced the cover of *Life's* second issue.

Eisenstaedt adapted to life in the United States. Like him, the country was simple, unceremonious, and full of unabashed vigor. By 1936, he was taking pictures of Hollywood celebrities. His editor at *Life,* told him before his first trip that, "The most important thing is not to be in awe of anyone. Remember, you are a king in your own profession." Eisenstaedt said that, "I never forgot those words." His small stature and his personality served him well with his many subjects. He told Vicki Goldberg of *New York* magazine that "they don't take me too seriously with my little camera. I don't come as a photographer. I come as a friend."

However, he was more than a friend to his subjects. "He was a fan, as well" Lacayo wrote in *Time* magazine on the occasion of the first Eisenstaedt retrospective exhibit at Manhattan's International Center of Photography. "In retrospect," Lacayo observed, "Eisenstaedt's exile to America starts to look like a stroke of luck. Amid the prevailing cheer of the postwar nation, his upbeat view of things probably found a more ready audience than it would have in the more somber precincts of Europe. His chief mode is celebration."

It was hard to find a celebrity whose picture Eisenstaedt did not take. He never took what might have been called a "critical" picture of anyone—anyone except the famed Nazi propaganda minister, Joseph Goebbels at the League of Nations in 1933, before he left Germany. Eisenstaedt recalled that as he clicked his shutter, the Nazi leader looked up with a terribly nasty look. "I had a photograph of him ten seconds before smiling," said Eisenstaedt. He had not been trying to make him look bad. Yet for the German photographer, who was also Jewish, the shot turned out to be an eerie premonition of the days to come.

As for the rest of his subjects, that list included Marilyn Monroe, the Kennedy family, Bob Hope, Bertrand Russell, Winston Churchill, Eleanor Roosevelt and countless others. Whether photographing a world leader or movie star he made them look no more distant than someone's next-door neighbor. Some had a difficult time taking him seriously for a reason other than his size. It was his simplicity, his fresh-faced sentiment as a photojournalist that often cast shadows on his art. In the April 1988 issue of *American Photographer*, John Loengard had his own story along those lines. That was the same month that the International Center of Photography in New York gave Eisenstaedt its annual master photographer award. Loengard said "I don't remember when I first saw Alfred Eisenstaedt's picture of the drum major practicing, but it was close to the time it was taken— 1950. I don't think I liked it. Too cute. I thought it was too perfect a realization of an expectation. My childhood was never that innocent. Was I too skeptical at too early an age because I lived in New York City? . . . this picture seemed like something that might illustrate a book about children. The kind bought by parents."

Eisenstaedt had seen a lot of discord and ugliness in his lifetime. If nothing else, he was only 19 when he nearly lost his life. Yet he saw that happiness was every bit the worthy subject that sadness might have been to another photographer. "Even when he returned to Germany in 1979," said Loengard, "Eisie did not use his camera to comment on the past. Instead, he marvelled at the sweet gaiety of a group of Lufthansa stewardesses, at the appearance of a Dalmatian dog in the back of a Porsche, at the rumpled clothes of film director Rainer Werner Fassbinder. 'I don't see Germany with political eyes,' he said. 'I see picture.'"

During his lifetime, Eisenstaedt published several books. His first, *Witness to our Time,* appeared in 1966. In the September 25, 1966 *New York Times Book Review,* P.G. Fredericks wrote, "Much has been made of Alfred Eisenstaedt as a photographer and rightly so, but what comes across in this book is his strength as a journalist. Over and over, he catches exactly the telling expression on a face or the revealing detail of a situation." Some of the other books that followed were: *The Eye of Eisenstaedt,* in 1969; *Martha's Vineyard,* in 1970; and *Witness to Nature,* in 1971. With John McPhee's text his photographs were published in 1972 in *Wimbledon: A Celebration.*

Eisenstaedt's personal life included his marriage to Kathy Kaye, a South African woman whom he met and married in 1949. She died in 1972. They had no children. When *New York Times,* writer Andy Grundberg interviewed for his feature in 1988, near the occasion of Eisenstaedt's ninetieth birthday, he was able to leaf through an entire box of prints and recall the the exact date the photo was taken—month, day, and year. His filing system was something only he could understand. To the observer, it was no system at all. It was then that he quoted George Burns. "He said something like, 'I keep getting older, but never old.' That's exactly how I feel."

Eisenstaedt died at his tiny cottage in Martha's Vineyard, Massachusetts on August 23, 1995 at the age of 96. The legacy he left behind was not a complicated one— simply stacks and stacks of pictures for people of the next generations to look at. His view of the world was a pretty view. And Eisenstaedt chronicled all of the decades of the 20th century in snapping its most cherished memories. He was just a guy who liked to take pictures.

### Further Reading

*Newsmakers,* edited by Louise Mooney Collins and Frank Castronova, Gale, 1996.
*American Photo,* July-August, 1991, p. 58.
*American Photographer,* December 1986, p. 44; April 1988, p. 20.
*Life,* May 1982, p. 115; December, 1986, p. 8; August 1988, p. 2; September, 1990, p. 84.
*New York Times,* September 15, 1986, p. 80.
*New York Times Book Review,* September 25, 1966.
*Time,* December 2, 1986, p. 7. □

# Michael Eisner

**As chairman and chief executive officer of the multi-billion dollar Walt Disney Productions, Michael Eisner (born 1942) is one of the most highly visible business leaders in the United States. With his impressive management skills, Eisner has become the leader of a vast communications and entertainment empire.**

Eisner was born in Mount Kisco, New York on March 7, 1942. His father, Lester Eisner, was a lawyer and administrator for the U.S. Department of Housing and Urban Development. His mother, Margaret Eisner, was a co-founder of the American Safety Razor Company. Young Michael grew up in the family's apartment on Fifth Avenue in New York City. Although his surroundings were luxurious, Eisner was required to read two hours for every hour of television he watched. His television viewing was strictly rationed and carefully controlled. His was not a pampered childhood. Eisner attended Denison University in Granville, Ohio. He began his college career with an interest in medicine but eventually switched to English literature and theater. During his summer vacation, Eisner worked as a page at the NBC television network in New York.

After graduation Eisner returned to NBC as a logging clerk, keeping track of television programs. Within a few weeks, he moved to the programming department at CBS, where he was responsible for placing commercials in the right places in children's programs. He didn't enjoy this work, so he mailed out hundreds of job resumes to various entertainment companies, including Walt Disney. He received one response.

### Diller was Impressed

ABC's Barry Diller was impressed with Eisner's resume. He knew his company needed bright young executives like Eisner, and he wanted to bring him on board. Diller convinced his board that Eisner should be the assistant to the national programming director at ABC, and Eisner jumped at the chance. He held the ABC job from 1966 to 1968.

During his time at ABC, Eisner married his wife, Jane, also known as "Tasty." Meanwhile, he began to show his real skills by producing a television special called "Feelin' Groovy at Marine World." The show was a success and in 1968 Eisner was promoted to manager of specials and talent, a job he held for less than a year before he was promoted to director of program development for the East Coast. This job made him responsible for Saturday morning children's programming, including animated programs based on the popular singing groups, the Jackson Five and the Osmond Brothers.

### Advancement at ABC

Eisner continued to climb in the entertainment business. In 1971, he became ABC's vice president for daytime programming. He promoted the vastly popular soap operas, *All My Children* and *One Life to Live.* Three years later, Eisner was promoted to vice president for program planning and development, and then became senior vice president for prime time production and development. It was Eisner who created such programs as *Happy Days, Welcome Back Kotter, Barney Miller,* and *Starsky and Hutch.* Thanks to the contribution of Eisner, ABC was able to move into first place in the network ratings, surpassing both CBS and NBC.

### Paramount Pictures

Eisner was on his way to the top. His old mentor from ABC, Barry Diller, had moved to Paramount Pictures as chairman of the board. In 1976, Diller offered Eisner the position of president and chief operating officer at Paramount. Eisner accepted and brought to his new job some of the cost-cutting lessons he had learned in network television. At that time, the average cost of making a motion picture was about twelve million dollars. Eisner's average cost at Paramount was only eight million. Despite reduced costs, Paramount moved from last to first place among the six major studios. Half of the top ten box office hits were Paramount pictures, including *Raiders of the Lost Ark, Saturday Night Fever, Grease, Heaven Can Wait, Ordinary People, Terms of Endearment, An Officer and a Gentleman, The Elephant Man, Reds, Flashdance, Footloose, Trading Places, Beverly Hills Cop, Airplane,* and three of the Star Trek motion pictures. It would be difficult to create a list of motion pictures with more power, entertainment value, and audience attraction.

### Walt Disney Company

In 1966, Walt Disney died. It was a loss of epic proportions for the entertainment world. An award-winning editorial cartoon that appeared in many newspapers was a drawing of the earth, with mouse ears and a tear running down. Audiences who had grown to love the work of Disney wondered what would happen to his pleasant, G-rated films and the theme parks he created. After the death of Walt, many in the industry felt that the Disney Company lacked leadership and direction.

Eisner left Paramount Pictures to become chairman and chief executive officer of the Walt Disney Company in September 1984. He replaced Hollywood super agent Michael Ovitz, who received a severance package worth about $90 million. Eisner signed a seven year contract extension worth about $250 million. Stockholders felt he was worth it. In only a few years, he was able to transform the company from an organization that lacked direction into an industry leader. Eisner also exercised stock options worth more than $229 million, with more options available to him. The studio quickly turned out several new animated features including *The Little Mermaid, Beauty and the Beast, Aladdin, The Lion King,* and *Pocahontas.* Every one of them was a huge success and earned millions of dollars for the Disney Company.

Eisner was considered to be the savior of Disney—the Prince who had awakened the Sleeping Beauty. Disney stock soared. Eisner had revived the Magic Kingdom. During that time, perhaps in part due to Eisner's love of hockey, Disney made the decision to join the National Hockey League by launching "The Mighty Ducks," named after a well known Disney motion picture. In May 1966, Disney acquired an interest in and became the general partner of major league baseball's "California Angels" later renamed the "Anaheim Angels." It was common to see Eisner wearing either a Mighty Ducks' or an Angels' baseball cap, and to be seen at the rink or the baseball stadium. Disney increased its participation in several other sports under Eisner's leadership. Golf, big time motor racing, soccer, marathon races and other sports were soon under the Disney umbrella, and in many cases were sponsored by Disney.

### Work in Progress

In his book *Work in Progress,* Eisner said, "At a certain level, what we do at Disney is very simple. We set our goals, we aim for perfection, inevitably fall short, try to learn from our mistakes, and hope that our successes will continue to outnumber our failures. Above all, we tell stories, in the hope that they will entertain, inform, and engage."

The Disney Company continued to market its various theme parks, including Disneyland in California and Disney World in Florida, and even built a massive new park near Paris called Euro Disney. But initial returns from the European park were disappointing. Low attendance brought a nearly one billion dollar loss in the first year. Plans to construct a huge historical park outside Washington, DC, were suddenly canceled. As if to counter these disappointments, he announced that Disney was acquiring his old company, Capital Cities, owners of the ABC television network. As CEO of Disney, Eisner had become the leader of a communications and entertainment empire without equal.

### Further Reading

Eisner, Michael. *Work in Progress.*
Michael Eisner Interview, http://www.achievement.org/autodoc/page/eis0int-1
Message from Michael Eisner, http://www.penguin.co.uk/readme/book_aut/Eisner/message.html □

# Alice Evans

**Alice Evans (1881–1975) was a pioneering scientist who established that humans contract the once-common, painful disease brucellosis from raw cow and goat milk. She lobbied successfully for the pasteurization of all milk and lived to see the disease fall into obscurity.**

For years, her findings were scorned and ignored because of her gender and because she did not have a doctorate degree. Evans contracted brucellosis while doing research, and suffered from the disease for 30 years. Brucellosis, a recurrent disease also known as Malta or undulant fever, causes shooting pain in the joints, fever, and depression.

### Science Prodigy

Alice Evans was born January 29, 1881, to William Howell and Anne B. Evans in rural Neath, a northern Pennsylvania town to which her grandparents had immigrated from Wales in 1831. She attended local elementary schools with her brother, Morgan, and graduated in a class of seven from the Susquehanna Collegiate Institute of Towanda, Pennsylvania, in 1901.

Lacking the money for college tuition, Evans reluctantly took a job teaching grade school, which was one of the few career options available to women at the time. She taught for four years until her brother told her about a free two-year nature study course for teachers at Cornell University's College of Agriculture. She attended the course, then stayed on to complete a Bachelor of Science degree in agriculture. Evans chose the relatively new field of bacteriology—the study of one-celled microorganisms—as her area of major emphasis. She was aided by a scholarship and by a tuition waiver underscoring the college's commitment to training leaders for the nation's agricultural industry.

Encouraged by her professor of dairy bacteriology at Cornell, Evans received a scholarship in bacteriology at the University of Wisconsin. This scholarship had never before been awarded to a woman. One of Evans' professors at the University of Wisconsin was Elmer V. McCollum, who later became famous for discovering Vitamin A. In 1910, Evans was awarded a Master of Science degree from the University of Wisconsin.

Her professors urged her to continue on for a doctoral degree, and Evans later continued her studies at George Washington University and the University of Chicago. However, she never completed her Ph.D., although she was awarded honorary degrees from the University of Wisconsin, the Woman's Medical College of Pennsylvania, and Wilson College. Eventually she became so respected in her field that most of her colleagues called her "doctor," even without the degree. In 1928, she was elected the first woman president of the Society of American Bacteriologists.

## Discovered Life's Work

By a stroke of luck, Evans was hired by Professor E.G. Hastings of the University of Wisconsin to work as a bacteriologist on a team developing an improved flavor for cheddar cheese, one of Wisconsin's primary industries. Technically the position was a Federal civil service post, working for the U.S. Department of Agriculture's Dairy Division of the Bureau of Animal Industry. Because space was limited while the bureau's main offices were being built in Washington, D. C., research was temporarily being carried out at several agricultural experiment stations at state universities. The USDA payed the salaries of the investigators and the state provided laboratory space and support.

After three years, Evans moved to Washington D.C. to work in the dairy division of the USDA's Bureau of Animal Industry (BAI). She found herself to be the only woman scientist employed in that particular department. Evans quickly gathered that the Washington staff was shocked that a state experiment station had hired a woman. Evans accidentally became the first woman scientist to hold a permanent appointment there. She would later recall in her memoirs, cited in John Parascandola's article in *Public Health Reports*, that "according to hearsay, when the bad news broke at a meeting of BAI officials that a woman scientist was coming to join their staff, they were filled with consternation. In the words of a stenographer who was present, they almost fell off their chairs."

Evans joined a team of scientists studying the sources from which bacteria entered dairy products. In addition, she took on the project that would become her life's work, studying the bacteria present in fresh cow's milk. She quickly identified a similarity between two bacteria: the organism that causes spontaneous abortion in cows (Bang's disease), and the organism that causes brucellosis in goats. Her discovery proved that humans could get sick from milk contaminated by bacteria living in cows. She announced her discovery in 1917 at the Society of American Bacteriologists. Her results were published in the *Journal of Infectious Diseases* the following year. The author of Evans' obituary in the *Washington Post* called the discovery "one of the most outstanding in the field of medical science in the first quarter of this century," but it was years before her findings were accepted by the scientific establishment and action taken. Paul De Kruif summed up the attitude of Evans' colleagues in his book *Men Against Death,* published in 1932. "If Evans were right," he imagined the scientists of the day as reasoning, "somebody much more outstanding than Evans would have run onto it long before. Such," De Kruif stated, "is the silliness of scientists."

As Evans herself pointed out in an early paper cited in *ASM News,* "Considering the close relationship between the two organisms, and the reported frequency of virulent strains of *Bacterium abortus* in cow's milk, it would seem remarkable that we do not have a disease closely resembling Malta fever in this country." Doctors eventually found brucellosis to be far more prevalent in the U.S. than they had realized. Mild forms of the disease had been misdiagnosed as influenza, while severe cases were confused with a number of diseases, including tuberculosis, typhoid fever, and malaria. Like many patients, Evans' own chronic case of brucellosis went undetected for months. She identified it entirely by accident, while comparing her own blood against that of a sick assistant.

Ironically, some of Evans' most vehement opposition came from bacteriologist Theobald Smith, who had been one of the first scientists to discover the bacteria in milk and warn about its possible health implications. Battling criticism from detractors in the scientific community, plus facing the resistance of a dairy industry that did not take kindly to the implication that their milk supply was dangerous or even deadly, Evans began to doubt her own facts. She largely abandoned her research for four years.

## Research Focus Shifted by War

During World War I, Evans took a job as a bacteriologist at the Hygienic Laboratory, which later became the National Institutes of Health. Wanting to be helpful in the war effort, she worked on improving the drug used to treat epidemic meningitis, a disease that was rampant in the military. Meningitis causes the tissues around the brain and spinal column to become swollen, and kills more than half of the people who contract it. Unfortunately, Evans wound up becoming ill herself, and so was incapacitated for much of the war.

Evans' theories about brucellosis and raw cow's milk were starting to become accepted internationally. Microbiologists from Holland, Austria, Italy, Germany, and Tunisia confirmed her findings. Evans expanded her research to include studying the blood of people ill with brucellosis. Helping Evans' case in the U.S. were Dr. Walter Simpson of Dayton, Ohio, who traced 70 cases of undulant fever to raw cow's milk, and Dr. Charles M. Carpenter, who identified dozens of cases in Ithaca, New York. Evans wrote a paper defending her work, which was presented at the World Dairy Congress in 1923. Ironically, she was too sick with undulant fever to attend the conference herself. Finally, Evans' assertions were accepted and pasteurization—heat treating milk to kill potential disease-harboring bacteria—became standard practice in the American dairy industry. Undulant fever lost its dangerous grip on milk drinkers.

Evans went from being ridiculed to being honored. In 1927, while suffering in the hospital from undulant fever, Evans learned she been had elected president of the American Bacteriologists Society. She was the first woman awarded that honor. Later, she served on the committee on infectious abortion of the National Research Council, and was a delegate to the International Microbiology Congresses in Paris and London.

Evans continued to be fascinated with diseases. Later in her career, she studied streptococcal infection, which causes strep throat and scarlet fever. She retired from the National Institutes of Health in 1945, but served for eleven years as president of the Inter-American Committee on Brucellosis. Throughout her career, Evans was active in a number of organizations. She was honored by the American Academy of Microbiology and the American Association for the Advancement of Science, and belonged to the Washington Academy of Sciences, the American Association of University Women, the American Association of the United Nations, and the United World Federalists.

## Made Headlines Once Again

Evans made headlines again in 1966, when she filed suit against the U.S. government. She was unwilling to sign an oath disavowing communist loyalty, as required on her Medicare application. At the time, the law prevented those with communist affiliations from receiving benefits. Represented by Lawrence Speiser of the American Civil Liberties Union, Evans charged that the disclaimer was unconstitutional, violating her right of free speech and association as guaranteed by the First Amendment. The suit was eventually dismissed by the U.S. District Court and Evans was awarded benefits without ever signing the oath.

Evans, who never married, lived in a retirement home from 1969 until her death in Alexandria, Virginia on September 5, 1975, following a stroke. She was 94 years old.

## Further Reading

The Biographical Dictionary of Scientists, edited by Roy Porter, Oxford University Press, 1994.
De Kruif, Paul, Men Against Death, Harcourt, Brace & Co., 1932.
Scientists: Their Lives and Works, edited by Marie C. Ellavich, UXL, 1997.
ASM News, September 1973.
Daily Review, (Towando, Pennsylvania), December 26, 1996.
Public Health Reports, September-October 1998.
Washington Post, December 31, 1927; September 8, 1975.
Washington Star, March 18, 1966; August 24, 1966; September 7, 1966; September 7, 1975. □

# F

## Douglas Fairbanks

**In the days of silent films, Douglas Fairbanks (1883–1939) was the king of dramatic actors. He surged across American motion picture screens performing dangerous stunts such as jumping from one high balcony to another or swinging by a rope from an old pirate ship. Fairbanks was an expert swordsman and handler of guns, a fine athlete, and managed to win the hand of the leading lady with perfect manners in almost every film he made.**

Douglas Fairbanks was born in Denver, Colorado on May 23, 1883. He was the son of an alcoholic father who left the family when Douglas was five years old. Born into the Jewish faith, he was taught at an early age to conceal this fact because his family considered it embarrassing. By the time he was just eleven years old, Fairbanks was acting in and around the Denver area. But New York City was where the major actors played. Since he knew already what he wanted to be, Fairbanks moved to New York when he was only seventeen years of age. He planned to sweep into the entertainment business, but instead was forced to take odd jobs to earn enough to eat.

Fairbanks worked as a cattle freighter and as a clerk on Wall Street. In his free time, he haunted the theaters trying to get an acting job. Finally, after two years, he made his Broadway debut as Florio in the Frederick Warde Company's production of *The Duke's Jester*. He was ambitious, hard working, and developing into an excellent actor, but was still unable to get the starring roles despite his hand-some appearance. Success continued to elude him, and he began to question his decision to become an actor.

In 1907, Fairbanks married Anna Beth Sully, owner of the Buchannan Soap Company, with offices in the Flatiron Building on Broadway. His father-in-law wanted Fairbanks to forget the acting business and work for the company. Fairbanks worked for the company for six months, then headed back to the theaters. His timing was good, for the Buchannan Soap Company went out of business shortly after he left.

Fairbanks got a string of minor parts, and was seen by important people, but the lead roles still didn't come. His wife Anna, a former socialite who was not accustomed to poverty, became pregnant. Although the marriage eventually collapsed, she gave birth to a son who was named after his father.

### An Offer from Hollywood

Fairbanks received an offer to move West and make "flickers," which is what Broadway actors called the silent films. At first he resisted, but when Hollywood offered over one hundred thousand dollars for a year of movie making, he reluctantly agreed. Fairbanks arrived at the Triangle Film Corporation in 1915, at the age of 31. At first, he failed to impress any of the film people. Director D.W. Griffith, who was assigned to work with Fairbanks, said of the new actor, "He's got a head like a cantaloupe and he can't act."

But Fairbanks proved that he could act, and very well. He made more than 25 films including comedies, romances, westerns, and drawing room satires. None of his early films were the type that made him famous, but they were still quite entertaining. Fairbanks became so popular that he was able to form his own production company, and began producing and writing his own films.

## United Artists was Formed

During a tour to sell war bonds in 1917, he met and fell desperately in love with actress Mary Pickford. However, he and Pickford were both married at the time, and having an affair was not acceptable in the early days of film—neither the fans nor the producers would understand. So the two hid their relationship for nearly three years, as both matured into solid actors and business people. In 1919, they formed United Artists with Charlie Chaplin and D.W. Griffith, in order to provide an independent distribution channel for artists who produced their own pictures. They hoped to break the practice of "block booking" films into theaters. Fairbanks and Pickford also took the bold step of divorcing their partners and getting married.

For the next few years, Fairbanks made a string of adventure films that have stood the test of time. He made *The Mark of Zorro* and *The Three Musketeers* in 1921, *Robin Hood* in 1922, *The Thief of Baghdad* in 1924 and *The Black Pirate* in 1926. These films were extremely expensive, beautiful, and smashing successes. Every detail of each film was handled by Fairbanks, and it was said that you could "feel his heart" in each scene. Pickford, meanwhile, was acting in her own films and becoming increasingly popular as well. The two were quite plainly the "King and Queen" of Hollywood during these years.

## The Academy of Motion Picture Arts and Sciences

By 1927, Fairbanks was 44 years old and knew he was nearing the end of his acting career. He remained active with the management of his business, forming the Academy of Motion Picture Arts and Sciences and overseeing the first award ceremony. He was also involved in the opening of Grauman's Chinese Theater on Hollywood Boulevard. The courtyard outside this famous tourist attraction featured the foot and handprints of movie stars, with his own and Pickford's being placed first. Finally, he helped open the Roosevelt Hotel, site of the first Academy Award presentation.

Fairbanks and Pickford lived in a mansion called "Pickfair" in the city of Beverly Hills. Crowds of people hovered around the gates of the estate day and night, each fan hoping to catch a glimpse of the two famous owners riding their horses on the grounds, or boating in the lake on their property. Fairbanks did make some good films at this time. He played the role of a real man with real problems in *The Gaucho, The Iron Mask, Reaching for the Moon,* and others.

In 1933, to the sadness of film fans, Fairbanks and Pickford announced their retirement from films, and soon after that the breakup of their marriage. They had decided to make a film together, *Taming of the Shrew,* and it was a disaster. Each blamed the other for the failure. Fairbanks' son, Douglas Jr., was becoming a big star, while his father was fading from the public eye.

After the divorce, Fairbanks married his mistress, Lady Sylvia Ashley. He had been suffering from heart trouble, but in early 1939 started writing a script for a new film in which he planned to star, along with his famous son. The script was never finished. Fairbanks died of a heart attack in his sleep in Santa Monica, California on December 12, 1939.

To show the depth of despair among fans when Fairbanks died, United Press published the following epitaph. "The body of Douglas Fairbanks Sr. lay tonight in an ornately carved bed before a window of his Santa Monica mansion which looked out on the vast Pacific. Through the night and day came a procession of Hollywood great and the forgotten who had worked with and known Fairbanks in his swashbuckling days. For hours Mr. Fairbanks' 150-pound mastiff named Marco Polo whined beside the death bed, refusing to move." The King of Hollywood was gone, and most agreed there would never be another like him.

## Further Reading

Carey, Gary. *Doug and Mary: A Biography of Douglas Fairbanks and Mary Pickford,* Dutton, 1977
Fairbanks, Douglas, Jr. *The Salad Days,* Doubleday, 1988.
Hearndon, Booton. *Mary Pickford & Douglas Fairbanks: The Most Popular Couple the World has Ever Known,* Norton, 1977.
Douglas Fairbanks Profile, http://www.mdle.com/ClassicFilms/ FeaturedStar/star1a.htm ed] □

# José Feliciano

**Singer and guitarist José Feliciano (born 1945) is one of the best known Hispanic entertainers in the United States and a major star in the Spanish-speaking world. His trademark is his furious guitar work and ability to re-invent rock classics with a Latin spin, as demonstrated in one of his biggest hits, "Light My Fire."**

José Feliciano was born on September 10, 1945, in Lares, Puerto Rico. His large family was barely supported by their father's work as a farmer. By 1950, Feliciano's parents had relocated to a Latino section of New York City's Harlem, where his father found work as a longshoreman. By this time, the young Feliciano was already beginning to develop his enormous talent for music. According to his press biography, "His love affair with music began at the age of three, when he first accompanied his uncle on a tin cracker can." By the age of six, Feliciano had taught himself to play the concertina simply by listening to records and practicing. Later in his career, Feliciano would master the bass, banjo, mandolin, and various keyboard instruments. These accomplishments were more remarkable because he was visually impaired since birth.

### Got Start in Coffee Houses

In his early teens, Feliciano discovered his instrument of choice: the acoustic guitar. Again, he taught himself to play simply by listening to records. The second of twelve children, Feliciano was blessed with a lucrative talent. By the age of 16, he was contributing to the family income by playing folk, flamenco, and pop guitar on the Greenwich Village coffeehouse circuit. At a time when his father was out of work, 17-year-old Feliciano quit school in order to perform full-time. He played his first professional show in 1963 at the Retort Coffee House in Detroit.

Back in New York, Feliciano was heard at Gerde's Folk City by an RCA Records executive, who quickly arranged a recording contract for the young singer. His first album, *The Voice and Guitar of Jose Feliciano,* and single, "Everybody Do the Click," were produced in English in 1964, but failed to make it onto the U.S. music charts. The album, however, was well received by disc jockeys; it was played regularly on their radio stations. In his first years with RCA, Feliciano's producers focused on his Puerto Rican background and marketed most of his albums to Latin American audiences; consequently, his name first became familiar to Spanish-speaking listeners. Indeed, as early as 1966, Feliciano played to an audience of 100,000 in Buenos Aires, Argentina.

### Sparked Career with "Light My Fire"

RCA began marketing Feliciano to the English-speaking audiences of England and the U.S. in 1968, when he released his version of the Doors' 1967 hit, "Light My Fire." His reworking of the now-classic tune peaked at number three on the U.S. pop music charts, selling over a million records and making the singer a celebrity overnight. Feliciano received two Grammy Awards for "Light My Fire," one for best new artist of 1968 and one for best contemporary pop vocal performance. *Feliciano!,* the 1968 album that featured "Light My Fire," was just as successful, earning the guitarist his first gold album.

Although that release was largely composed of songs written and previously recorded by other musicians, Feliciano was able to establish himself as an important artist by radically redefining the music that he recorded. Both the Latin influence in his style and his facility with the acoustic guitar greatly altered the quality of songs like "Light My Fire," that were originally recorded by rock bands using electric instruments. Of that song, *Rock Movers and Shakers* explained, "Its slowed-down, sparse acoustic-with-woodwind arrangement and soul-inflected vocal defines Feliciano's style." *Feliciano!* also garnered the unique honor, according to Thomas O'Neil, author of *The Grammys,* of becoming a favorite album among teenagers in the mood for romance.

Following the success of *Feliciano!,* its namesake went on tour in both the United States and England, displaying his talents as a guitarist and as a singer who could cover a variety of musical styles. At the time, he told *Melody Maker*'s Alan Walsh, "I'm just a musician. . . . not a pop musician or a jazz musician; just a musician. I play guitar but I also regard my voice as an instrument. I don't really like to be placed into a compartment and type-cast because I'd like to work on all levels of music."

Despite all the accolades, Feliciano's 1968 success was sometimes coupled with conflict. During a series of well-attended dates in England, the blind performer ran afoul of British quarantine laws about pets: Feliciano's seeing-eye dog could not enter the country. It was a problem for the musician not only because he needed the dog for navigation, but also because she had become something of his trademark onstage. The helpful canine led the singer to the center of the stage at the beginning of each performance and returned to bow with him at the end. Feliciano did not return to England for several years.

### Criticized for National Anthem Rendition

Invited to sing "The Star-Spangled Banner" at the fifth game of the 1968 World Series at Detroit's Tiger Stadium, Feliciano's disturbed many of his more conventional listeners with what the *Detroit Free Press* called his "tear-wrenching, soul-stirring and controversial" rendition. He was booed during the performance and received critical press for months to follow. The offending interpretation, according to the *New York Times,* was simply a matter of style: "His rendition was done in a slower beat, similar to a blend between soul and folk singing styles. He accompanied himself on the guitar." Though later artists would offer unique renditions of the anthem that were accepted as artistic variations, Feliciano had been the first to alter the song, which infuriated many. The *Times* quoted one listener as having responded, "I'm young enough to understand it, but I think it stunk. . . . It was non-patriotic." Another commented, "It was a disgrace, an insult. . . . I'm going to write to my senator about it."

Feliciano later recalled the incident with regret. "I did it with good intentions and I did it with soul and feeling," he told Michael Mehle in the Denver *Rocky Mountain News* in 1998. "When it happened, people wouldn't play me on the radio. They thought I was too controversial. After that, my life was not so good musically. . . . and I've been trying to dig my way back ever since." Feliciano continued to record and perform steadily since 1968, but never achieved the same level of popularity. The album *Souled* hit number 24 on the U.S. charts in 1969; also that year, *Feliciano/10 to 23* reached number 16 and earned the singer a second gold album. A little later, however, Feliciano's voice entered just about every American household when he recorded the theme song for the enormously popular television show *Chico and the Man,* in 1974, and "Feliz Navidad (I Wanna Wish You a Merry Christmas)," which became a holiday staple.

Numerous moves to different record labels and varying marketing strategies failed to re-ignite Feliciano's popularity with English-speaking audiences. In the mid-1970s, after about ten years of producing Spanish and English albums for RCA, Feliciano was signed briefly to the Private Stock label. When that company similarly failed to revive the interest of English-language audiences, Feliciano signed with Motown Latino, in 1980. He remained with Motown for several years but eventually made another switch, this time to EMI/Capitol, which by the early 1990s had developed a formidable Latin imprint.

### Still Acclaimed Despite Low Profile

Despite his relatively low profile in the U.S., Feliciano has enjoyed consistent international sales—more than enough to allow him and his family a comfortable life. He has earned 40 gold and platinum albums internationally. His series of recordings marketed for Spanish-speaking audiences in the 1980s garnered considerable acclaim, including Grammy awards for best Latin pop performance, in 1983, 1986, 1989, and 1990. In 1991, at the first annual Latin Music Expo, Feliciano was presented with the event's first-ever Lifetime Achievement Award. In 1998, he released the album *Senor Bolero* and completed a European tour.

In 1982, Feliciano married Susan Omillion, who had started a fan club for the singer in Detroit when she was 14 years old. This was a second marriage for Feliciano. His first wife was Hilda Perez, the manager of one of the cafes where he had performed in the 1960s. In 1988, the first of his children, Melissa Anne, was born; Jonathan José followed in 1991. The family purchased a renovated eighteenth-century inn and settled in the New York suburb of Weston, Connecticut. In his honor, the high school that Feliciano had attended in Harlem was renamed the Jose Feliciano Performing Arts School.

### Further Reading

*The Harmony Illustrated Encyclopedia of Rock,* edited by Mike Clifford, Harmony Books, 1988.
O'Neil, Thomas, *The Grammys: For the Record,* Penguin, 1993.
*Rock Movers and Shakers,* edited by Dafydd Rees and Luke Crampton, ABC/CLIO, 1991.
*The Rolling Stone Encyclopedia of Rock & Roll,* edited by Jon Pareles and Patricia Romanowski, Rolling Stone Press/ Summit Books, 1983.
*Billboard,* September 7, 1991.
*Detroit Free Press,* May 28, 1993.
*Down Beat,* February 5, 1970.
*Independent on Sunday,* June 21, 1998, p. 7.
*L.A. Clips press biography.*
*Los Angeles Times,* July 18, 1998, p. F1.
*Melody Maker,* October 19, 1968; October 26, 1968.
*Newsday,* August 9, 1995, p. A8.
*New York Times,* October 8, 1968.
*Rocky Mountain News* (Denver, CO), December 13, 1998, p. 3D. □

# Bill Ford

**For almost two decades, there was no Ford running Ford Motor Company. After Henry Ford II stepped down as chairman in 1979, only professional managers were allowed into the top position. Finally, in 1998, the company declared that chairman Alex Trotman would step down a year earlier than expected to let William Clay "Bill" Ford, Jr. (born 1957), assume control, with Jacques "Jac" Nasser functioning as president and chief executive officer.**

Speculation simmered for years that either Ford or his cousin, Edsel Ford II, were in line to become the next leader. However, it came to a full boil in 1996 when major business publications proclaimed that Ford would be the next chairman of the board, even if he would not be in charge of day-to-day operations per se.

Though his name was probably one reason that, at age 41, he was promoted to lead the world's second-largest industrial firm, Ford still had to work his way up from the bottom and prove his mettle. "I recognize that there are those who think this job was handed to me," Ford remarked to Keith Naughton in *Business Week*. "But I was under the microscope every step of the way. I had to have drive and ambition because people were looking for me to fail." Ford's immediate mission, in addition to making sure the company remained economically competitive, was to infuse environmental activism into the number two car corporation. He had made it no secret that he hoped to combine his personal devotion to environmental issues with his new position, thereby producing cleaner, more efficient vehicles. In addition to his career at the automaker, Ford in 1995 took charge of running the Detroit Lions football team for his father, who bought the team in 1964.

### A Normal Childhood

Bill Ford was born in Detroit, Michigan in 1957. He was the only son in a family of four children born to William Clay Ford, Sr. and Martha Park (Firestone) Ford. His father was the grandson of auto pioneer Henry Ford, and his mother was an heiress to the Firestone tire fortune. While other branches of the Ford clan were marred by unstable family relationships, Ford enjoyed a calm upbringing in a home that was as down-to-earth as possible, given the family's household name and incredible wealth. In fact, Ford was often shuttled to less affluent areas of town to play hockey. He excelled at sports, received good grades, and maintained a relatively normal existence without bodyguards or chauffeurs. Though he did have a nanny, his mother was around at all times. Later, Ford attended the Hotchkiss School in Lakeville, Connecticut, where he gained a reputation as a fierce soccer competitor. He became an avid football fan, no doubt because his father bought the Detroit Lions in 1963. After high school, Ford attended Princeton University, where he earned a bachelor of arts in political science and wrote his senior thesis on labor relations at Ford. Later, he went back to school to obtain a master of science in management at the Massachusetts Institute of Technology in 1984.

### Learned the Automobile Business

After college, Ford went to work at the family business, starting as a financial analyst and eventually rotating through eleven jobs in his first ten years with the firm. His father wanted him to have a well-rounded education about the business in case he would someday rise to the top. The senior Ford involved his son in labor negotiations when he was only 25 years old because he felt it was an important element in running the firm. Ford also worked in product planning and advanced vehicle development, helping to launch the first Ford Escort and Mercury Lynx, and also led the marketing efforts for Ford in the New York-New Jersey area. In 1986, he worked with Ford of Europe as director of commercial vehicle marketing. The following year, he ran Ford of Switzerland as managing director, succeeding in breathing life into what was previously a sagging enterprise. He was named vice president of Ford Truck Operations in 1988, and in 1990 he became director of business strategy for automotive operations. He has also served as general manager of the climate control division. In 1988, Ford joined the board of directors and eventually led two essential committees, finance and environment/public policy. By the mid-1990s, his name was being considered to take over from Alex Trotman, who had been with Ford since the mid-1950s and held the chairman and CEO positions since 1993.

### Managed a Football Team

Ford was also becoming involved with his father's enterprise, the Detroit Lions football team. He served as treasurer from 1980 to 1995, then became vice chairman and assumed responsibility for most of the operations. At his first NFL owners' meeting, he stood up to the threat of having the Lions' Thanksgiving game taken away and given to a better team (they have not won a championship since 1957). His emotional defense preserved the tradition and laid waste to his prior reputation as being somewhat meek. Furthermore, he took immediate steps to give the team a needed lift. First, he fired head coach Wayne Fontes and hired Bobby Ross, formerly of the San Diego Chargers. He then restructured an outdated ticket policy and stepped up marketing efforts. A new web site and weekly radio and television shows added to the facelift. Most importantly, he lobbied to bring the Detroit Lions back to Detroit. For two decades, the team played at the Silverdome, a sports arena located in suburban Pontiac. Crowds had dwindled throughout the years, and the franchise received one of the worst licensing deals in the league with stadium owners—the Lions obtained no revenue from concessions, suites, or parking. With a receptive mayor, Dennis Archer, in office in Detroit and a new baseball stadium being built for Detroit Tigers owner Mike Illitch, Ford seized the opportunity to contribute to civic pride and arrange a better deal. Ford negotiated to build a new 70,000-seat domed stadium in downtown Detroit next to the new ballpark, with the Ford family and corporate sponsors contributing about half the building costs and government agencies adding the rest.

Observers wondered if Ford's success with the football team would translate to running a gigantic corporation. When mulling over the possibility that Ford would be taking the reins of the automaker, some commentators predicted that it would be a boon for the company. Though Trotman was a respected leader, some thought Ford would soothe stock holders because he has a highly personal stake in the corporation. Not just a "company man," Ford is a part of the firm's history, as is his cousin, Edsel Ford II, who had maintained even closer ties. Edsel Ford II's father was head of Ford for three decades, and many suspected that he would be the successor once Trotman left. Edsel has had a long career at Ford and sits on the board as president of credit operations. However, Alex Taylor III reported in Fortune that insiders considered Bill Ford a superior choice, due to his diplomacy and previous involvement with the board. However, some directors were wary. Ford was still enmeshed in managing the Lions and raising four young children, and it was suggested that he would not have the time needed to devote to the job. Others were concerned that the appointment would further inflate the family's influence to the dismay of the rest of the stockholders. The family, though, had the ultimate say on the decision to elevate Ford to the top role. Even though Henry Ford II had stated firmly, "There are no crown princes in the Ford Motor Co.," according to Jolie Solomon and Daniel McGinn in *Newsweek,* the family does control 40 percent of the voting stock and holds three positions on the board, giving it enough clout to make certain things happen.

### A New Chairman

In the fall of 1998, Ford Motor Company announced that Bill Ford would become the new chairman, effective January 1, 1999, when Trotman retired a year earlier than expected. Although Ford would have the final word on company decisions, many were pleased that Jacques Nasser, former head of global auto operations, would be taking over the day-to-day management of the corporation as president and CEO. This dual management is common in Europe and Asia, but most American firms still rely on one person to hold the titles of chairman and CEO. Ford, however, welcomed the concept, explaining in a press conference, "I will lead the board and Jac will lead the company. This will be a partnership," according to Mary Connelly in

*Automotive News.* Nasser made his name as a "hard-charging Australian-bred task-master who expects results," as Connelly put it, with a history of slashing costs more than $4 billion in 1997 and the first half of 1998. Ford worked under Nasser in the 1980s, when he was a financial analyst in charge of Venezuela and Nasser was head of finance for Latin America and Asia. "We have a running start on this," Ford noted, according to Connelly. "We've known each other a long time. We find we are in sync more than we are not."

Ford's main goal in his new seat will be to maintain the company's solid financial record, continuing to cut costs and narrow the gap between it and the number one automaker, General Motors. Ford also needs to remain focused on increasing European sales, its largest market outside of the United States. The Asian-Pacific markets are also supposed to show strong growth as well, and it is essential that Ford Motor Company be competitive there. However, it appeared that Ford's other priorities included his longstanding commitment to environmental issues and vow to produce a high-selling environmentally-friendly vehicle. It is unusual to think of an automobile baron as an environmentalist, but Ford is just that. The proud owner of a Ford Ranger electric truck, he volunteered in Earth Day events and became involved with clean-water projects while a teenager. Later, he began reading about green issues and studied the works of nature authors Edward Abbey and Rachel Carson.

Of course, being responsible for keeping the company in business, Ford also sees economic opportunities in being an Earth-friendly company. He predicts an unprecedented ballooning of consumers seeking environmentally sound products in the twenty-first century, and said that companies that foresee this shift and address it will prosper, while laggards will fail. But his attention to marketing does not drive his activism. "There's no conflict between doing the right thing and the bottom line," Ford noted to Mary Connelly in *Automotive News.* "I don't see a conflict between shareholder value, customer value and social value." Ford also stated that his great-grandfather, Henry Ford, had always wanted to benefit the world and not adversely affect it, but that the company had gradually moved away from that. He remarked to Joseph R. Szczesny in *Time,* "I can remember when the board asked me to stop associating with the environmentalists. I said, 'Absolutely no.'" He believes his leadership will provoke the company to build cleaner-running vehicles.

### Family Life

Ford married a fellow Princeton student, Lisa Vanderzee, and they have two daughters and two sons. He says since he was not forced into working in the business, he will let his children make their own choices as well regarding their careers. The family lives in Grosse Pointe Farms, an upscale suburb of Detroit, where Ford can be spotted in-line skating through the quiet streets or getting ready for a fly fishing trip. As a nature lover, he likes camping, hiking, and skiing with his family, and also enjoys tae kwon do, hockey, tennis, coaching soccer, and collecting Civil War documents. He has pledged that his job will not detract from his personal life, and has no plans to cut down his involvement with his children. Ford is also a vegetarian who practices alternative healing methods such as acupuncture and herbal remedies, and he does not often drink alcohol. In addition to everything else, Ford is the chairman of the Henry Ford Museum and Greenfield Village in Dearborn, Michigan, and the vice-chairman and a member of the board of the Detroit Greater Downtown Partnership Inc. Though he seems to have as ideal a life as possible, balancing family, hobbies, a football team, and one of the world's largest corporations, Ford admits there are some drawbacks to carrying around his legendary surname. "Whenever I'm at a party," he told Naughton in *Business Week,* "people are always telling me either to get a new quarterback or make the Taurus back seat bigger."

### Further Reading

Automotive News, September 14, 1998, p. 1; September 28, 1998, p.

Business Week, September 28, 1998, p. 96.

Economist, September 19, 1998, pp. 9, 82.

Fortune, October 14, 1996, p. 26; October 12, 1998, p. 34.

Gannett News Service, September 21, 1998.

Los Angeles Times, September 12, 1998, p. D1; September 24, 1998, p. D1.

Newsday, December 12, 1997, p. A46.

Newsweek, October 7, 1996, p. 56.

Time, December 8, 1997, p. 74.

Time International, March 2, 1998, p. 42.

USA Today, December 2, 1997, 4B; September 14, 1998, p1B.

Ward's Auto World, October 1, 1994, p. 25.

"Lions' History," Detroit Lions web site, http://www.detroitlions .com (October 27, 1998). □

# Eileen Ford

**Eileen Ford (born 1922) was the founder and co-owner of the Ford Modeling Agency, one of the world's biggest, most prestigious, and successful modeling agencies. She was responsible for launching the careers of many famous models such as Brooke Shields, Candice Bergen, and Christie Brinkley.**

Eileen Ford was the daughter of Nathaniel and Loretta Marie (nee Laine) Otte, born on March 25, 1922, in New York City. Ford and her three brothers were raised in wealth in Great Neck, New York. The Ottes owned their own company, a firm that determined credit ratings of corporations. Ford told Judy Bachrach of *People Weekly,* "My family believed I could do no wrong. That's probably why I have utter confidence in myself—even when I shouldn't have. I got everything I wanted from my parents: Brooks Brothers sweaters, Spalding saddle shoes. None of the people I grew up with had identity problems. We all had perfectly marvelous lives." Ford was not motivated as a child to have a career or even attend a university. Loretta Otte eventually made her daughter attend Barnard College, from which she graduated in 1943 with a bachelor's degree in psychology. Ford wanted to go to law school, but the fashion industry lured her in a different direction.

Loretta Otte had been a model, and Ford also modeled during breaks from Barnard. Ford liked the allure of the industry. After graduation, she worked as a photographer's stylist at the Eliot Clarke studio for a year. Ford met Gerard "Jerry" W. Ford in August 1944 and eloped with him three months later, on November 20, 1944. Jerry Ford was a student and football player at Notre Dame University at the time of his marriage. The Fords eventually had four children: Jamie, Bill, Katie, and Lacey.

### Began Modeling Agency

In 1945, Ford continued to work as a stylist at the William Becker Studio. Her husband worked for Ford's father in the family company, while attending business school. Ford held several jobs, working as a copywriter for Arnold Constable from 1945 to 1946, then a reporter for Tobe Coburn in 1946. In order to earn extra money, she began doing bookings for two of her friends, who were models. The Ford Agency grew out of this experience.

The modeling industry was rather loosely organized at the time. Agencies found work for their models, but the models were expected to set their own rates and collect their own wages. Against the grain, Ford put the interests of the models and their careers first. She bargained with advertising agencies and photographers so that her models would have better deals. From 1946 to 1948, Ford's clientele grew from 2 to 34, and the agency took in $250,000 in 1948 alone. The demands of the agency grew and Ford's husband quit school and joined his wife at the agency. Long days became the norm as Ford found new talent while her husband dealt with the financial end. She developed a savvy reputation. James Mills in *Life* described her as "a tough businesswoman: demanding, untiring and persistent as gravity."

## Revolutionized Industry

Ford's business practices changed the industry, becoming standards of conduct. The Ford Agency would collect the models' fees and pay them on a weekly basis. They also set the standard of a 20% commission, 10% from the models' fee and the other 10% from the organization that hired the model. Ford was instrumental in setting fees for such things as cancellations, fittings, bad weather, and the type of modeling done. She was selective about what kind of advertisements her models would appear in. As Bachrach described in *People Weekly,* Ford, in the 1940s, said "no deodorant ads, no bra ads, no bathtub poses and no excessive display of bosom." This changed over time, though, reflecting changing social standards. By the 1990s, nudity and deodorant ads became acceptable.

## The Ford Family

Ford treated her models differently than other agencies on another level. She was a second mother to many of them. Ford gave them counsel on what to wear and how to handle hair and skin problems. She taught them proper etiquette. Many young models lived with the Ford family when they were first working in New York City and were expected to do household chores like a member of the family. Ford believed models needed the mothering. She told Mills of *Life,* "They're all just little kids. The one thing that makes a model the way she is her parents. Not her beauty. Each child wants desperately to prove himself to his parents. But today there are more adults willing to give less, or afraid to ask more, than there once were. And when children have no direction, and nothing is demanded of them, they're lost." In the same article, Ford said, "Most models are emotionally abandoned. They need me. I'm their mother."

Ford expected a certain moral standard for her models, which included a nightly curfew and a limit on the number of nights a model could go out. If Ford's standards were not met, they were released from the agency. A former Ford model, Cheryl Tiegs, told Bacharach of *People Weekly,* "Eileen is hard where her standards of discipline are concerned. There are too many beauties around to put up with girls acting up."

Ford and her agency developed so-called "Ford models," many becoming the superstars of the industry. She had an eye for finding new models. She told James Mills in *Life,* "There's a cockiness to them and there's just a way about them. It's their I don't know, they're just going to be good and you can just tell it. It's a way they have of moving, and it's a way of talking to you. I see girls that I know I absolutely know—will be star models within just a matter of weeks, and they always are." As Bachrach in *People*

*Weekly* wrote, "This preoccupation with what is proverbially only skin-deep is not second nature to Eileen Ford; it is her first and only nature." To discover new talent, she traveled four times each year in Europe, especially Paris and the Nordic countries, as well as other trips in the United States and Australia. Many also walked into her offices off the streets.

Ford favored a certain kind of female model. She preferred them to be blonde, with long necks, straight noses, and eyes that were wide-set, and a certain height and size cheekbones, hips, and breasts. Ford thought models with light-colored eyes photographed better. By favoring these characteristics, Ford determined the American standard of beauty for a generation, according to Bachrach in *People Weekly.* Ford told her, "There's no question I did that. I create a look and I create a style."

Ford did not take advantage of women who wanted to be models. Even those she did not take under wing, Ford tried to advise. *Life,*'s Mills quoted her as telling one such girl, "It's not the most important thing, you know, to be a model. It's just a job. And it's better to know the truth than because there are always people who want to take advantage, who will promise you things, and bad schools that will take your money." Ford told David Schonauer of *American Photo* that "It's the nicest thing I can do for a girl who isn't pretty enough to be a model. She has to get on with her life."

Ford's beliefs on this matter extended to her own family. She never let any of her three daughters model. She told Mills of *Life,* "I think that even if they could be I would rather they chose their own careers. Because when it's over, you have nothing. I don't mean financially, but inside. It's a temporary career and models are very young when it starts and their education suffers. And then in a few years you have nothing to do and you're just an old leftover model. And there's nothing in the world worse than that."

Ford's mentorship methods did not sit well with every model who worked for her. Some of her competitors do not think favorably of her either. John Casablancas had a positive working relationship with Ford when he worked exclusively in Paris representing models. But when he opened an agency, the Elite Agency, in New York City, Ford sued him. Casablancas told Bachrach in *People Weekly,* "Eileen is Mr. Hyde. And Jerry is Dr. Jeckyll. When I came to New York, my major problem wasn't lawsuits. It was personal attacks on how I directed my life as though I was some kind of fiend with Roman orgies. She's a sour, nasty old lady with a lot of enemies." Another rival told Bachrach in the same article, "Eileen is a very domineering lady. She is strong-willed and opinionated, and at Ford's there is fear and apprehension about anyone else making a decision. Eileen berates anyone who doesn't fall into line."

Despite what her detractors may have thought of her methods, by 1970, the Ford Agency was taking in $5 million per year, representing 180 models. Eventually the agency expanded to include divisions for male and children models (Brooke Shields was taken on as a client when she was eight). Jerry Ford took care of the male model division in the 1970s. Ford also formed a division that dealt with older models who still wanted to work in their 30s. By the 1990s, her female clientele numbered in the hundreds. Through all the years, Ford maintained a business-oriented perspective. She told David Schonauer of *American Photo,* "It's all about money. That might sound terrible in a magazine that's supposed to be about art and creativity, but it's the truth. Nobody gets in this business for the love of it. That's certainly true of models, and probably photographers as well."

Through the years, Ford put her experiences with models to use in a second career, as an author. She had a syndicated column about beauty for several years. She also wrote several nonfiction books such as *Eileen Ford's Model Beauty, Secrets of the Model's World, A More Beautiful You in 21 Days,* and *Beauty, Now and Forever.* In 1983, Ford received the Woman of the Year in Advertising Award.

## Retired from Agency

By the 1990s, the Ford Agency lost some of its luster. Ford was seen as living in the past, her standards of beauty slightly outdated in a multicultural-embracing United States. Schonauer wrote in *American Photo,* "the world had changed: The era of the megamodel, in which financial stakes were higher and personal loyalties more fragile, had dawned." In 1995, Ford named her daughter Katie CEO of the Ford Modeling Agency, but she remained co-chair (with her husband) of its board. As Ford told Roberta Bernstein of *Time,* "We were getting old. What were we going to do, let her be like Prince Charles and wait for us to die? It was her moment. You have to give people a chance." Ford was honored for her contributions to the industry, especially in photography, at the 1996 Festival of Fashion Photography. Ford's legacy remains clear. Roberta Bernstein of *Time* wrote "Eileen Ford, part pit bull, part den mother, and all business, helped shape what women looked like and how they dressed for nearly a half century."

## Further Reading

Jeffrey, Laura S., *Great American Businesswomen,* Enslow Publishers, 1996.
*American Photo,* May-June, 1993; July-August 1996.
*Life,* November 1970.
*New York,* July 24, 1995.
*People Weekly,* May 16, 1993.
*Time,* September 8, 1997. □

# Norman Foster

**Recognized as one of the world's great architects, Norman Foster (born 1935) is known for his complementary yet ultra-modern redesigns of classic buildings and for his simple, streamlined new structures. Called the "hero of high-tech," his architectural signature is a design that opens a building up to the public, is mindful of the environment, and saves money by using modern materials and advanced technology.**

Norman Foster was born on June 1, 1935 in Manchester, England. From 1956 to 1962 he studied architecture at Manchester University's School of Architecture and at Yale University in New Haven, Connecticut. In 1963, he founded the Team 4 architectural practice along with Richard and Sue Rogers and Wendy Cheeseman, whom he later married.

Foster and his wife founded Foster Associates in London in 1967. This innovative firm was noted for its dedication to architectural detail and craftsmanship. Use was often made of prefabricated off-site manufactured elements and special components were designed for particular projects. Foster Associates worked on transportation projects, large public structures, and modest houses. From 1968 to 1983, Foster collaborated with Richard Buckminster Fuller and others on the Climatroffice project. In 1969, he designed the administrative and leisure center for Fred Olsen, Ltd., in London.

In 1975, Foster designed the administrative headquarters for an insurance company, Willis, Faber and Dumas in Ipswich, England. For that building, Foster used modern materials and advanced technology to save money and energy. The curving building follows the irregular street patterns in the old market town. The exterior of the building is all glass. This creates the illusion that the open-plan offices extend out into the street. The roof is covered with grass, serving as insulation and creating a hanging garden. This building established Foster's reputation as an architect and won him the RIBA Trustees Medal in 1990. That same year he was knighted by Queen Elizabeth, giving him the title of Sir Norman Foster.

In the 1970s, Foster designed the Sainsbury Centre for the Visual Arts at the University of East Anglia in Norwich, England. Dennis Sharp, in *Twentieth Century Architecture: A Visual History* said: "The Sainsbury Art Centre . . . is described as a well-serviced metal-clad barn. . . . It is a highly tuned and well-engineered shed for art of considerable sophistication serving as a research institute with public access gallery. It was sponsored by private funds. The white walls and roofs take the form of continuous trusses and all services are housed within the 'outer wall zone'."

## International Recognition

From 1979 to 1986, Foster worked on the Hong Kong & Shanghai Bank. Michael Sandberg, the president of the Hong Kong & Shanghai Banking Corporation invited seven architects to design "the most beautiful bank in the world." The banker sought a building that would make a statement about the bank's wealth, power, and probity. Foster won the competition; no other architect received a vote. The building Foster designed, a steel and glass structure, was the most expensive in the world at that time. It cost five billion Hong Kong dollars to build and has 47 stories and is 590 feet high. It stands in the middle of other skyscrapers on Hong Kong Island, on the site of the first branch office of the bank.

Foster began the work—his first skyscraper—when he was 44 years old. He carefully studied the site and the urban environment. An advocate of technology, Foster found the densely packed urban context very challenging. He closely examined all previous high-rise buildings to learn from their design and to help him optimize the economic performance of the structure. He designed it with built-in flexibility, energy-saving ideas, and an improved work environment. Foster made the maximum use of natural light, included open work areas, and a lot of open spaces. No standard elements were used in the building. To develop the details, many models were made, some full sized. This added to the high cost of constructing the building.

Foster made the plan rectangular with service towers at either end. The bank has a steel load-bearing structure. Eight masts made of four linked cylindrical members are tied together in three places by enormous girders. Each story hangs from this structure. This building method allowed open facades with views north and south. Because the site was small and surrounded by other buildings, many elements had to be prefabricated off-site, including the steel frame and the mechanical service modules. The only part of the construction that took place on site was the final assembly and installation.

When visitors enter the building, they are greeted in the main hall by two escalators that lead through a curved, clear glass "belly." A ten-story atrium rises above. This area is flooded with sunlight from a "sunscoop" on the outside of the building. The only remaining parts of the original structure that once occupied the space are two bronze lions outside the bank. Visitors touch the lions for good luck before entering. This building, known simply as "the bank" in Hong Kong, became famous for its daring use of cellular interior spaces and won Foster international acclaim. The building's picture even appeared on Hong Kong's banknotes.

In 1983, Foster designed the sales center for Renault UK Ltd. in Swindon, England. In the mid 1980s, he worked on the furniture system for Tecno in Milan, Italy. He designed the office building for Stanhope Securities in Stockley Park near London in 1989 and the broadcasting building for the British television channel ITN in London in 1990.

In 1991, Foster designed London's third airport, Stansted. His goal was to return a feeling of excitement to air travel and to harken back to the days when terminals were simple buildings. Foster, who pilots his own helicopter, wanted to build the terminal around what air travelers actually need. Stansted, which was built to handle eight million passengers a year, has shortened walking distances and simplified circulation patterns. Passengers walk straight from the entrance to the check-in desk, to customs, to the waiting area, to the airplane. The terminal is built on two levels. The public concourse has arrivals and departures side by side. Tree-like tubular steel columns in clusters of four, set 35 yards apart, hold up the lattice domed roof, giving the concourse an airy feel. Sunlight filters through the roof to the interior, without making the building hot or clammy. The lower level, which is underground, contains a train station, baggage handling area, and storage facility.

## High-Tech Parliament Building

For five years, Foster worked on the redesign of the Reichstag, site of the German parliament in Berlin. He opened the interior space in order to fill the once gloomy structure with light. Foster's goal for the building was "to make democracy visible." This was achieved using huge expanses of glass. The roof is dome-like, with skylights inserted in it. The dome has an inverted conical core that sucks in light at the top and beams it out at the bottom, in order to light up the debating chamber. It contains a sunscreen that also helps regulate the building's temperature. The sunscreen moves to follow the path of the sun in the summer, preventing the chamber below from overheating. In the winter the screen is moved aside to allow the sun's warmth to penetrate. Fresh air enters the building through airshafts and is fed into the main chamber through the floor. As the air heats up and rises, it is drawn into a cone in the middle of the dome. An extractor finally expels it from the building.

Spiral walkways curve around the outside of the building from which visitors have an excellent view of the skyline and can see the Parliament at work. The debating chamber is enclosed in glass, allowing people to look in from the main lobby. Describing the building before its redesign Foster noted, "At the moment visitors are forced to sneak in guiltily through a side-entrance." The Reichstag gained back much of its nineteenth century grandeur in the redesign, but Foster added many high tech improvements. The dome structure saves electricity. Other energy savers include the use of underground water supplies, natural ventilation, and excess heat. In summer, cool water from a top reservoir underground circulates around the building through pipes in the floors and ceilings. This cools the building and warms the water. The water is then pumped into a lower reservoir that is very well insulated, thus retaining the heat. In winter the process is reversed. Hot water is pumped up to heat the building. The cooled water going into the top reservoir is ready to be used again the next summer. The Reichstag maintains its own power plant to drive the pumps. The plant is fueled by rapeseed oil, a totally renewable energy source with low carbon dioxide emissions.

## Greatest Achievement

Considered Foster's greatest achievement and the world's most ambitious engineering project, Hong Kong's Chek Lap Kok, the largest airport in the world, opened in July 1998. The airport cost $20 billion to construct. The eight-story terminal is one of the largest enclosed areas on earth. The 45 acres of lightweight steel roof cover six million square feet of glass-enclosed space. The terminal is so big, it can be seen from space.

The airport building was designed as a celebration of the modern age of air travel, providing a sense of adventure to passengers. Jonathan Glancey, architecture critic for the *Guardian* described what most people feel about flying and what Foster was trying to achieve. "They just see boring office-like interiors, boring people being bored, buying useless bits of duty free. What Foster says is: 'Hey look, flight really is a magical thing.' His building allows you to see the aircraft as soon as you walk in. It enables you to feel you're up in the air with the aircraft too, it's about excitement, it's about passion."

Foster has designed many other noteworthy public buildings including a 92-story tower in London; the American Air Museum in the United Kingdom; a rapid transit viaduct in Rennes, France; art galleries at London's Royal Academy; the Commerzbank Tower in Frankfurt, Germany; the Joslyn Memorial and Pavilion in Omaha, Nebraska; a Scottish housing project; and a cultural center in Nimes, France.

## Further Reading

Thiel-Siling, Sabine, *Icons of Architecture: The 20th Century*, Prestel, 1998.
*Economist,* March 23, 1991; February 11, 1995.
*World Press Review,* October 1994.
*BBC Online,* http://news.bbc.co.uk (March 14, 1999).
*Great Buildings Online,* http://www.greatbuildings.com (March 14, 1999). □

# Alfred Fuller

**The line of brushes sold by Alfred Fuller (1885–1973) took him from rags to riches. He felt that products should be made to work correctly and to last a long time. This idea was new at the beginning of the twentieth century, when cleaning tools were poorly constructed and needed to be replaced often.**

Alfred Carl Fuller was born on January 13, 1885, on a farm in the Canadian town of Grand Pre, Nova Scotia. His parents were Leander Joseph, a Mayflower descendant, and Phebe Jane (Collins) Fuller. Fuller was the eleventh of twelve children born to poor but hard working parents. He attended grammar school, but never went to high school and had no business experience. At the age of 18, in 1903, Fuller left Canada to seek his fortune in the U.S. He joined two brothers and two sisters in Somerville, Massachusetts, a suburb of Boston. Fuller lost three jobs—train conductor, handy man, and wagon driver—during his first two years of work. In 1905, he took a job as a brush and mop salesperson. During that year, Fuller learned a lot about brushes. He also managed to save $375 and used the money to start his own business.

## Designed to Work, Crafted to Last

Fuller set up a workshop in the basement of his sister's house. He spent $80 on equipment and materials. On a bench between the furnace and the coal bin, Fuller constructed twisted wire brushes by using a small, hand cranked device. He made his brushes at night and sold them during the day. The 21-year-old was determined to create the best products of their kind in the world. Fuller felt that brushes should be constructed to last, an unusual idea at the time. Cleaning tools at the turn of the century were not well

made and required frequent replacement. Fuller noted, "By the time I began to sell brushes in 1906, most of the cheaper brands on the market were of twisted-in wire. The fiber materials employed were as haphazard as the techniques of fabrication. For most processors, anything they could lay their hands on was good enough; they did not want their wares to endure too long, or there would be no repeat business. This philosophy has become known as calculated obsolescence. . . . " Fuller refused to accept this. He was determined to create products that were practical and long lasting. His simple philosophy was to design it to work, craft it to last, and guarantee it no matter what.

The brushes available at the turn of the century were very outdated and could not perform many of the tasks needed at that time. Fuller sold his first brush to a woman who used it to clean a radiator. Fuller noted "After that I studied a housewife's needs and we made a brush for every need." Fuller saw the need for brushes that would perform specific functions, such as cleaning silk hats, spittoons, Victorian furniture, and floors. Eventually the company produced over 700 types of brushes, including the "handy," a free vegetable brush that salespeople gave to each customer.

## Secret to Selling

In 1908, Fuller married Evelyn W. Ells, with whom he had two sons. When Fuller's sales amounted to $50 a week, he moved his company to Hartford, Connecticut—a city he had visited on his sales trips. He rented space in a shed for $11 a month and hired a shop assistant. At first he called his company the Capitol Brush Company, but after he found out that someone else was already using that name, he renamed his business the Fuller Brush Company in 1910.

Customer education was a hallmark of Fuller's business. Because his products were so different from others, customers had to be shown how to use them. Salespeople had to know all about the product and the specific household problems they were made to solve. Fuller's salespeople were experts in home care, could determine the needs of their customers and were willing to demonstrate what each product could do. The secret to selling, according to Fuller, was to be unfailingly polite and helpful. As Fuller went door-to-door selling his wares, he would say to each potential customer, "Good morning, madam. If there is anything wrong in your house that a good brush could fix, perhaps I can help you." Fuller's salespeople gained a reputation for being persistent but polite. One salesman even changed a customer's tire.

By 1910, the Fuller Brush Company employed 25 salespeople and six factory workers and had reached $30,000 in sales. The salesmen covered New England, New York, and Pennsylvania. Wanting to expand his operation, Fuller placed a small advertisement in a magazine. In a few months, he had over 100 salesmen who sold Fuller brushes across the United States. In 1913, Fuller incorporated the business, becoming its president, treasurer, and a director. By 1918, his sales had reached $500,000.

In 1923, sales reached $15 million and there were thousands of "Fuller Brush Men," as they were named by the *Saturday Evening Post*. Fuller Brush Men were well known sights in neighborhoods. Comic strips such as Dagwood and Blondie, Mutt and Jeff, Mickey Mouse, and Donald Duck featured Fuller Brush Men. Walt Disney's film *The Three Little Pigs,* showed the big bad wolf approaching the pigs' house dressed as a Fuller Brush Man. The 1948 movie, *The Fuller Brush Man,* starring the famous comedian Red Skelton, poked fun at the occupation. By 1947, sales reached $30 million. The salesmen were independent contractors who bought their products from the company, paying wholesale prices. They sold them at retail prices and kept the difference, making about 30 percent profit. Each salesman covered a territory of about 2,000 homes. In the first 50 years of the company's existence, Fuller salespeople reached an estimated nine out of ten American homes, selling over $800 million worth of products.

In 1948, women salespeople, called "Fullerettes" were added to the sales force, to help market cleaning supplies and cosmetics. A Fullerette was featured in the 1950 film, *The Fuller Brush Girl,* starring Lucille Ball as scatterbrained saleswoman who attempted to sell cosmetics door-to-door with disastrous results. Fuller did not mind the jokes about his company. He felt that all the free publicity kept his advertising budget low.

## Attempted to Build Morale

Selling door-to-door was a tough job. Salespeople received many rejections. Only two out of seven people who tried being Fuller Brush salespeople lasted at the job. Fuller knew how hard the work was, so he tried to build morale with company songs, pep talks, bonuses, commissions, and a 22-acre company park with a clubhouse. He tried to pass on his optimism and energy to his salespeople by telling them that "American ends with 'I can' and dough (meaning money) begins with 'do.'"

During World War II, the company made fewer products for civilians and instead produced brushes for cleaning guns. Fuller remained president of the Fuller Brush Company until 1943, when his son Alfred Howard took over. His second son, Avard Ells, was in charge of sales. Fuller served as chairman of the board until 1968, when the company was sold to Consolidated Foods. By the 1970s, the company was still going strong, with over 25,000 salespeople covering the United States, Canada, and Mexico.

In 1959, Fuller became a member of the Horatio Alger Association of Distinguished Americans, which values dedication, purpose, and perseverance. In 1960, he published his autobiography, *A Foot in the Door: The Life Appraisal of the Original Fuller Brush Man, as told to Hartzell Spence.* Fuller loved travel and golf, but his main interest outside of work was Christian Science. When Fuller died in West Hartford, Connecticut on December 4, 1973, the Fuller Brush Company's income was $130 million annually.

Fuller's second wife, Mary Primrose Fuller, whom he married in 1932, donated her family home in Yarmouth, Nova Scotia, Canada, to the Yarmouth County Historical Society in 1996. The home, built around 1895, was used as the family's summer residence. The house still contains furniture that belonged to the Fuller family, including a fine Persian carpet and a baby grand piano, one of three made for royalty. The music-loving Mary Fuller died in October of 1997 at the age of 94. Her estate donated $15 million to the Hartt School, the University of Hartford's renowned music and performing arts school. Mary Fuller was a life-long amateur pianist who lived in nearby Bloomfield, Connecticut, a residential suburb of Hartford. Her bequest was the biggest gift in the university's 40-year history, and among the largest by an individual donor to any college or university in Connecticut history.

## Further Reading

Fuller, Alfred, *A Foot in the Door: The Life Appraisal of the Original Fuller Brush Man, as told to Hartzell Spence,* McGraw-Hill, 1960.

Mayberry, Jodine, *Business Leaders who Built Financial Empires,* Raintree Steck-Vaughn Publishers, 1995.

*Horatio Alger Association of Distinguished Americans,* http://www.horatioalger.com/member/ful59.htm (March 15, 1999).

*YCM—Pelton-Fuller House,* http://ycn.library.ns.ca/museum/fuller.htm (March 15, 1999).

*Your Fuller Brush Man Online,* http://www.bevfitchett.com/history.htm (March 15, 1999). □

# G

## Lou Gehrig

**One of baseball's greatest hitters, Lou Gehrig (1903–1941) was a teammate of Babe Ruth on the New York Yankees and drove in more runs in his productive 17-year career than all but two other men in history. But Gehrig is known primarily for having played in 2,130 consecutive games and for the crippling disease named after him.**

Nicknamed the "Iron Horse," Gehrig never missed a single game as the Yankees first baseman from June 1925 through April 1939. During that time he was a fearsome hitter and prolific run-producer, with a combination of batting average and power that rivaled Ruth's. Struck down in his 30s by the crippling muscle disorder, amyotrophic lateral sclerosis (ALS), Gehrig was immortalized for his emotional farewell speech at Yankee Stadium on July 4, 1939, when he said he was "the luckiest man on the face of the earth."

### A Strapping Youth

Lou Gehrig was born in New York City on June 19, 1903. His parents, Christina Fack and Heinrich Gehrig, were German immigrants who lived in the lower-middle-class section of Manhattan's Yorkville neighborhood in the early 1900s. Henry Louis (Heinrich Ludwig), the second of four children, was the only one who survived infancy. He weighed an astounding 14 pounds at birth and grew quickly into a strong boy.

The Gehrig family was poor. Heinrich Gehrig was an art-metal mechanic who worked sporadically due to drink-ing and ill health. Christina Gehrig took jobs as a maid, launderer, cook, and baker. From a young age, Henry helped his mother deliver laundry. He developed a close, lifelong attachment to her. Gehrig's father took him to gymnasiums to work on building up his muscles. Henry Louis was a remarkable young athlete. At age 11, he swam across the Hudson River.

At his mother's insistence, Gehrig went to Manhattan's High School of Commerce. But he spent as much time working as studying. When he was 16, he got a summer job with the Otis Elevator Company in Yonkers, New York, and was the company team's left-handed pitcher. Soon after that, he earned his first money at baseball, $5 a game, pitching and catching for the semipro Minqua Baseball Club. Gehrig gained fame in 1920 when his Commerce High School team, representing New York, played in Wrigley Field against Chicago's best high school team. Gehrig hit a ninth-inning grand slam to ice a victory and garner headlines in New York.

Columbia University recruited Gehrig on a football scholarship. Before enrolling in 1921, Gehrig tried out for legendary New York Giants manager John McGraw, who reprimanded him for missing a ground ball at first base and sent him to the Class A Hartford team, where he played 12 games. Gehrig didn't know that the professional play violated collegiate rules. He was banned from Columbia sports for a year. Playing one season of baseball at scruffy South Field, he hit long home runs off the steps of the Low Library and the walls of the journalism building, while others landed on Broadway. He pitched, played first base and outfield, and hit .444. Paul Krichell, a New York Yankees scout, signed him to a contract.

Gehrig arrived at Yankee Stadium via subway, carrying his spikes and gloves in a newspaper. He made an immedi-

ate impact by clouting long homers during batting practice. But he was returned to Hartford and played there for most of 1923 and 1924, appearing in only 23 games with the Yankees in those two seasons.

## Pipp's Permanent Replacement

Gehrig stuck with the Yankees in 1925. On June 1, he pinch-hit for shortstop Pee Wee Wanninger. On May 6, Wanninger had replaced Everett Scott in the lineup, ending Scott's record streak of 1,307 consecutive games played. On June 2, a batting-practice pitcher from Princeton hit first baseman, Wally Pipp, before the game. Pipp went to the hospital with a concussion and Gehrig replaced him in the lineup. Pipp never returned to his first-base job, and Gehrig went on to shatter Scott's mark by 803 games.

Gehrig batted fourth in the lineup, behind Ruth, and had a great career that was overshadowed by Ruth's fame and achievements. By the time Gehrig broke in, Ruth was already the nation's biggest sports star. Ruth was a flamboyant character with a voracious appetite for publicity, food, drink, and women. Gehrig, in contrast, was quiet and called little attention to himself. He was a team player, dedicated to winning and unimpressed by personal achievements. Ruth's frequent holdouts for higher salaries bothered Gehrig, to whom "the game was almost holy, a religion," according to sportswriter Stanley Frank.

Sportswriter Marshall Hunt described Gehrig as being "unspoiled, without the remotest hint of ego, vanity or conceit." With his Boy Scout aura, Gehrig inspired writers

to describe him as a paragon of virtue in contrast to Ruth. In fact, Gehrig was not that pure. He loved practical jokes and slapstick and sometimes crushed straw boaters on people's heads. Once, in a wacky effort to "break a slump," he urinated over the terrace of a friend's West End apartment.

In the bulky uniforms of those days, the thick-thighed Gehrig looked unathletic and soon acquired the nickname "Biscuit Legs." His fielding around first base was clumsy at first, but he worked hard to improve it. Sportswriter Frank Graham dubbed him "The Quiet Hero." His consecutive game streak eventually earned him the nickname "Iron Horse."

Gehrig was a key member of the 1927 Yankees, considered by many to be the greatest team of all time. That year, Ruth hit 60 home runs, which stood as the record until 1961. Gehrig hit 47, added a league-leading 52 doubles and 18 triples and led baseball with 175 runs batted in. The two were the heart of a lineup so powerful it was nicknamed "Murderer's Row." They led the Yankees to three World Series appearances from 1926 through 1928. In the 1928 series, Gehrig hit four home runs in the Yanks' four-game sweep and hit .545.

The team failed to win the next three years, but not for lack of production from Gehrig and Ruth. From 1929 through 1931, the two sluggers combined for 263 homers. Gehrig led the league with 174 RBIs in 1930 and 184 RBIs in 1931, which set the American League single-season record.

The uncomplaining Gehrig never made more than a third of Ruth's salary. It seemed something was always eclipsing him. Even Gehrig's four-homer game at Shibe Park in Philadelphia in June 1932 was overshadowed by the retirement of legendary Giants manager McGraw that same day. Gehrig's two homers in a 1932 World Series game in Chicago were forgotten in the legend of Ruth's mythic "called shot" homer the same day.

Remarkably little attention was paid to Gehrig's consecutive-games streak as it progressed year after year. In 1933, Gehrig surpassed Scott's record. He continued to play despite broken fingers, back pain, and sore muscles. Nothing could keep him out of the lineup. On September 29, 1933, he married a Chicago woman named Eleanor Grace Twitchell in the morning, then was rushed by motorcade to Yankee Stadium for an afternoon game.

In 1934, Gehrig won the league's Triple Crown, a rare feat, with a .363 batting average, 49 homers and 165 RBIs. Even then, he was not named the league's Most Valuable Player; Mickey Cochrane of the Tigers took that honor, with far inferior statistics. That year was Ruth's last with the Yankees. One day that season, Gehrig was hit during an exhibition game and suffered a concussion. But he played one inning the following day to keep his streak intact. A few weeks later, he couldn't straighten up, said he had a "cold in his back," and left one game after the first inning. Gehrig would suffer similar bizarre attacks over the next few seasons, seemingly harbingers of his fatal disease.

Gehrig played one season without Ruth before a new superstar, Joe DiMaggio, joined the Yankees. Again, the dependable Gehrig was left in the shadows. The Yankees returned to the World Series in 1936, 1937, and 1938. Gehrig turned the tide in 1936 with a key home run against ace pitcher Carl Hubbell of the New York Giants. He finished with a lifetime .361 Series average in 34 games and ranked in the Top Ten all-time in almost every Series hitting category.

## Heading for Home

By 1938, Gehrig was in a noticeable decline. His average of .295 was the lowest since 1925. Over the winter, he fell several times while ice skating. During spring training in 1939, his swings were weak; sometimes he had trouble getting up from a sitting position. Yet when the season started, manager Joe McCarthy continued to play Gehrig, to keep the streak alive. A sportswriter observed that Gehrig looked "like a man trying to lift heavy trunks into a truck."

When the Yankees arrived in Detroit for a May 2 game, Gehrig was hitting .143. He took himself out of the lineup, telling McCarthy it was "for the good of the team." Gehrig took the lineup card to home plate with Babe Dahlgren's name at first base. The Detroit fans applauded for two minutes. Gehrig tipped his cap and disappeared into the dugout and the record books. He would never play another game. His streak of 2,130 games was a record that would stand for 56 years. He finished with 493 home runs, 535 doubles, 162 triples, a .340 batting average and 1,990 RBIs, third-highest among all major leaguers.

A month later, Gehrig entered the Mayo Clinic and was diagnosed with ALS, a degenerative muscle disorder first described in the late 1800s by a French physician. Gehrig remained with the team, sitting on the bench. He professed awe at having a fan's perspective on his beloved game. "I never appreciated some of the fellows I've been playing with for years," he said. "What I always thought were routine plays when I was in the lineup are really thrilling when you see 'em from off the field."

On July 4, 1939, the Yankees staged a Gehrig Appreciation Day at Yankee Stadium. Ruth and other members of Murderer's Row returned for the ceremony, along with Yankee officials and dignitaries. At first, Gehrig was too overwhelmed to speak, but the crowd chanted: "We want Gehrig!" He stepped to the microphone, blowing his nose and rubbing his eyes. Cap in hand, he spoke: "Fans, for the past two weeks you have been reading about a bad break I got. Yet today I consider myself the luckiest man on the face of the earth. I have been in ballparks for 17 years and have never received anything but kindness and encouragement from you fans. Look at these grand men. Which of you wouldn't consider it the highlight of his career just to associate with them for even one day? . . . "When you have a father and mother who work all their lives so that you can have an education and build your body, it's a blessing. When you have a wife who has been a tower of strength and shown more courage than you dreamed existed, that's the finest I know. So I close in saying that I might have had a bad break, but I have an awful lot to live for. Thank you."

In December 1939, the Baseball Writers Association waived their usual five-year waiting period and unani-mously elected Gehrig to the Baseball Hall of Fame. Gehrig then took a job with the New York City Parole Commission. He rarely visited Yankee Stadium because it was too painful to see the game he missed so much. Gehrig died on June 2, 1941 in New York City, exactly 16 years after he had permanently replaced Pipp in the Yankees lineup.

The following year, movie producer Samuel Goldwyn released "Pride of the Yankees," a Gehrig biography with Gary Cooper in the lead role and Babe Ruth appearing as himself. It became one of the most popular baseball movies ever made.

Little understood then, ALS became more well-known as Lou Gehrig's disease. Its high-profile victim brought it attention, research, and understanding. The incurable disease strikes about 5,000 Americans each year; most die within two to five years. It is the only major disease named after one of its victims. David Noonan of *Sports Illustrated* noted the irony that "one of the greatest baseball players who ever lived is best known for the way he died."

## Further Reading

Hubler, Richard, *Lou Gehrig: The Iron Horse of Baseball,* Houghton Mifflin, 1941.
Robinson, Ray, *Iron Horse: Lou Gehrig in His Time,* W.W. Norton & Company, 1990.
*Sports Illustrated,* April 4, 1988; October 8, 1990; September 11, 1995. □

# Lou Gerstner

**Lou Gerstner (born 1942) rescued IBM, the world's largest computer maker, when he became its CEO in 1993. His career has been a study in corporate strategy and how to turn ailing companies around.**

For most of its long history, IBM symbolized American ingenuity and corporate power. The company held a special place in the hearts and minds of the public and became more than a corporation—almost a national treasure—based on its development of the computer industry. In the mid-1980s, with the arrival of the personal computer, IBM was slow to realize the wholesale changes the new systems would bring to their business. After losing money for a decade, the decision was made to hire Louis Gerstner as chairman and CEO. He had gained an impressive reputation for rebuilding American Express and RJR Nabisco, and it was hoped that he could do the same for IBM. Gerstner was the first outsider to ever hold this position. In the past, top executives had all worked at IBM for many years and been promoted through the ranks. Within two years, Gerstner's strategic plans, combined with tough, cost-cutting measures, had transformed the ailing company and made it competitive once again. By 1997, IBM would post revenues exceeding $78 billion and its stock price had quadrupled. Gerstner had led IBM back to the top of the computer industry and initiated one of the world's greatest success stories.

## Humble Beginnings

Lou Gerstner was born in Mineola, New York on March 1, 1942. Louis Gerstner, Sr. and his wife, Marjorie, raised four boys. The elder Gerstner worked as a night superintendent at the local Schaefer brewery, while his wife worked in the registrars office at a community college. Neither had a college education. All four boys excelled at Chaminade High School, a local Catholic boys school. Louis served as class president.

Gerstner attended Dartmouth College, majoring in engineering. He continued his education at the Harvard Business School and graduated in 1965. After graduation, Gerstner joined McKinsey & Co., one of the world's premiere strategic management consultant firms. Gerstner's hard work paid off at McKinsey. He became one of the youngest directors in the history of the company, at the age of 28.

## Onward and Upward

In 1978, Gerstner joined American Express as president of the American Express Card Division. A year later, he was named president of the Travel Related Services Group, responsible for both travelers checks and travel service offices. When the group became a subsidiary of American Express in 1982, Gerstner became chairman and CEO. In 1985, he was named president of American Express.

American Express made significant strides under Gerstner's leadership. Card membership rose from 8.6 million to 30.7 million. The company also introduced two popular credit cards: the Platinum and Optima. Gerstner's strategic skills were essential in helping the company capitalize on the growing credit card market. He further impressed analysts with his administrative and marketing abilities.

In 1989, Gerstner became chairman and CEO of RJR Nabisco Inc., the food and tobacco conglomerate. His leadership skills and strategic thinking would be put to the test at RJR Nabisco. Only a year earlier, the company was the prize in an epic takeover battle that was later immortalized in the book, *Barbarians at the Gate*. RJR Nabisco agreed to a record $24.53 billion leveraged buyout by Kohlberg Kravis Roberts & Co. (KKR) after a very public battle against a group led by its flamboyant CEO, F. Ross Johnson. In the aftermath of the fight, the company was faced with billions of dollars in new debt. Gerstner had to confront the declining domestic tobacco market and revitalize its workforce after the takeover. Throughout his tenure at RJR, Gerstner had to contend with huge interest bills, which kept profits low or nonexistent. Adding to the company's problems, was a steady decline in market share of the Winston cigarette, its biggest moneymaker.

It did not take long for Gerstner to begin transforming the company's corporate culture. In his first year, Gerstner traveled to RJR facilities all over the world, logging 250,000 miles in an effort to learn as much as he could about the company. His mantra centered on cutting bureacracy, acting with a sense of urgency, quality, and teamwork. He even printed up cards emphasizing these points and sent them to all 64,000 employees. He took tough steps to repair RJR and replaced managers who did not share his strategic vision. The *Wall Street Journal* reporter, George Anders, described the new RJR as "A no-nonsense, impatient company where top-level strategy meetings are sometimes held on the linoleum aisles of supermarkets. Bureaucracy, flamboyant spending, and intra-company rivalries are out. Teamwork, urgency, and a Japanese-style fixation on quality are in. The Gerstner agenda," said Anders, "includes no big risks, no big innovations: It centers on running the current operations to maximum efficiency."

Within two years, the company's stock gained approximately 50 percent and operating profit rose 31 percent. One of Gerstner's greatest achievements was to get the company's two distinctly different operating units (tobacco and food) to work together. Instead of competing with one another for research and marketing money, the two units began sharing information under Gerstner's leadership. He also put a halt to needless factory upgrades, which had been the norm under earlier administrations.

## Big Lou Leads Big Blue

In the early 1990s, the giant computer company, International Business Machines (IBM), was struggling. Long a symbol of American corporate power, IBM lost $2.9 billion in 1991 and $5 billion in 1992. By 1993, the company's losses surpassed $8 billion and the value of its stock had dropped from $42.6 billion to $19.7 billion. Gerstner was one of 16 top business leaders to be considered as a possible successor to John Akers, who had resigned as CEO on

January 26, 1993. After twice declining the position, Gerstner finally accepted.

Although not IBMs first choice, Gerstner's record at American Express and RJR impressed the search committee. He had a history of fixing ailing companies by making tough decisions to cut costs, including massive layoffs and improving efficiencies. IBM needed a strategist who would shake up the organization. According to *USA Today*'s Leslie Cauley, Gerstner "demanded the twin titles of chairman and CEO and the authority to assemble his own management team. He wanted authority to do whatever he deemed necessary to make IBM healthy."

The decline of IBM was tied to its weakening hold on the computer industry, especially in big mainframe computers. It could not make up for that loss in the highly competitive personal computer and laptop business. Competitors were beating the company to the market with new products and cutting prices, in an effort to undersell the giant. Gerstner's challenges were twofold: he had to attend to the mainframe sector, then decide how the company's 13 divisions would be structured in the future. He also demanded that $1 billion be cut from the research and development budget, which flew in the face of IBM tradition.

By the time the new CEO celebrated his second anniversary, analysts were already touting IBMs comeback. Taking a tough step toward shrinking operations, Gerstner slashed the global workforce from a 1985 high of 406,000 down to 220,000. He focused on improving global ties in the more than 140 countries in which IBM maintained operations and made sure IBM computer products were getting to customers faster. He shook up IBMs fabled corporate culture that hinged on formality, and allowed employees to dress informally. In 1994, IBM posted a profit of over $3 billion, the first time in a decade that IBM was in the black.

Gerstner reduced costs by more than $6 billion. He also began an aggressive worldwide advertising campaign that emphasized IBMs global operations. He capitalized on IBMs worldwide brand name recognition in marketing the company. Gerstner realized that the company spent too much time arguing about technology and not enough determining what new products customers needed and finding ways to meet their needs. Within a couple of years, customers cited IBMs improved products and responsiveness. Gerstner himself made it his policy to talk with at least one customer per day. He also reorganized the company's sales force around specific industries, to provide more knowledgeable customer service.

Gerstner and his management team knew they needed to transition the company into fast-growing areas, like personal computers and consulting services, while rebuilding the mainframe division. In 1995, IBM purchased Lotus Development Corporation for $3.52 billion in order to expand its software products division. Lotus grew into one of the world's leading spreadsheet and business software companies. When IBM bought Lotus, there were only two million users. By 1998, the number jumped to over 22 million. IBM also acquired Tivoli Systems, a network management business, to compete in the network market. Several other purchases strengthened the company in other areas, such as purchasing systems, chip manufacturing, and global management support.

The rebirth of IBM was symbolized by its "Deep Blue" computer. Programmed to play chess against world champion Gary Kasparov, Deep Blue defeated the grand master in a highly publicized six-game match in 1997. Many observers thought Deep Blue was the first incarnation of computer systems that could actually think like human beings.

## The Future

In Gerstner's first four and a half years, IBM shares quadrupled in value. In a complete transformation, the services business (which employs nearly half of the company's employees) accounted for 25 percent of sales. Gerstner was even willing to enter into an occasional alliance with competitors. In early 1999, IBM announced a seven-year $16 billion technology sharing arrangement with Dell Computer Corporation. The two giants will share patents and some development. Dell has agreed to purchase $16 billion worth of chips, disk drives, networking equipment, and other computer components. Dell will gain access to IBMs huge research and development operation (which routinely leads the world in new patents), while IBM strengthens its components division.

IBM has become more nimble under Gerstner. Instead of debating issues endlessly, he charged ahead. Gerstner is a tough-minded leader who was willing to revamp IBMs corporate culture in order to move the company forward. As a result, IBM has been able to capitalize on cutting-edge technologies, like electronic commerce. At the 1998 annual shareholders meeting, Gerstner explained, "We see the total market for Internet commerce hitting $200 billion by the end of the century. IBM is seen as the company for e-business solutions—by a 2 to 1 margin over our closest rival."

Although an unlikely choice to lead IBM in 1993, with little high tech experience, Gerstner's keen strategic sense and understanding of customer needs has been credited with resuscitating the ailing giant. Under Gerstner, IBM attained revenues of $78 billion in 1997, while net income exceeded $6 billion. IBM remains an American institution, and one of the world's most important corporations.

## Further Reading

*Computer Reseller News,* March 8, 1999, p. 1.
*Gannett News Service,* April 23, 1995.
*Investor's Business Daily,* January 21, 1998.
*Milwaukee Journal Sentinel,* September 8, 1996.
*Minneapolis-St. Paul Star-Tribune,* March 14, 1989.
*New York Times,* March 5, 1999.
*Sacramento Bee,* April 2, 1995.
*Time,* October 5, 1998, p. 29.
*Times of London,* April 4, 1993.
*Toronto Globe and Mail,* March 25, 1997.
*USA Today,* April 26, 1993.
*Wall Street Journal,* March 21, 1991; March 26, 1993; August 2, 1993.
Lou Gerstner: Personal Biography, http://www.ibm.com (March 1, 1999).

Lou Gerstner: Speeches, http://www.ibm.com (March 1, 1999).
□

# George Gipp

**George Gipp (1895–1920) was one of the greatest collegiate football players in history. He played with serious injuries, he played with illness, and he could almost always be counted upon to give his beloved alma mater, Notre Dame Unive rsity, a victory.**

George Gipp was born in Laurium, Michigan, on the Keweenaw Peninsula, on February 19, 1895. He was the seventh of eight children born to Mathew Gipp, a hard-edged, hard-working Baptist preacher, and his wife Isabella. Although young George was considered very bright, his grades in school were so bad that he never earned a diploma or a letter in any sport. He loved to sleep and to play ball. Otherwise, he liked to drink, play cards, and shoot pool.

A phenomenal athlete from the beginning, Gipp was six feet tall and weighed a solid 180 pounds. He could run, he could throw one of the old oblong footballs 50 yards and hit a target, he could drop kick it 60 yards directly through the goal posts, and he was excellent at basketball and hockey. He was also a skilled ballroom dancer, and once won a gold watch in a dance contest. His best game, though, was baseball.

"I remember my dad telling me there wasn't anything Uncle George couldn't do, and do better than any other guy," said Lillian Gipp Pritty, the daughter of Gipp's oldest brother Alexander, in the book *The Gipper* by John U. Bacon. "Uncle George could throw a ball from his knees at home plate with just his wrist all the way to second base, and the second baseman would say, 'Hey, Gipp, not so hard!'"

In the early part of the 20th century, a student didn't need high grades, or even to have graduated from high school, to be accepted at major colleges. Gipp applied for a baseball scholarship at Notre Dame University, and was accepted in 1916. But it wasn't Notre Dame that caused Gipp's well-known "high life style" of drinking and gambling. He had established that before he left for college and he was, after all, not "moving to the big city." In those days Gipp left a booming copper mining area of 90,000 people for South Bend, Indiana—a much smaller town.

Gipp had been working at construction in the winter after dropping out of Laurium's Calumet High School in 1913. He drove a taxi in the summer while playing semipro baseball. When three of his pals enrolled at Notre Dame, he followed. His college baseball career, however, lasted only one game. According to a 1985 *Smithsonian* magazine article, Gipp disregarded his manager's signals to bunt and instead hit a towering home run. He said it was "too hot" to be running around the bases after a bunt. His manager ranted and raved and Gipp, always an individualist and

somewhat hard headed, quit the team. But that was certainly not the end of his marvelous athletic career.

## Rockne Meets "The Gipper"

The famous Notre Dame football coach, Knute Rockne, saw Gipp for the first time on the school's football field in 1916, practicing drop kicks. The kicks were so long and so accurate that an amazed Rockne asked Gipp to join the freshman football team. With a "why not?" attitude, Gipp agreed. Soon after, in a game against Western Michigan University, the freshmen were losing. The quarterback ordered Gipp to punt, but he decided to drop kick instead. He kicked the ball 62 yards and perfectly through the goal posts. Notre Dame won again because of Gipp.

By 1917, Gipp was playing for Rockne on the varsity team. During the day, he would play football, at night he would play pool, or cards, or gamble in some other way. He tended to ignore the curfews of the team. Rockne, an ordinarily strict coach, allowed his star player some leeway. Gipp was earning a good living as a pool player. He would take on the pool sharks from Chicago who would come to town to fleece the college kids. The high-stakes games kept Gipp in plenty of pocket money. In fact, he once said, "I'm the finest freelance gambler ever to attend Notre Dame."

Gipp also regularly gambled on the very games in which he played, a practice now forbidden in most sports. He would meet with players from the opposing team and bet as much as they had. He would always bet on Notre Dame, and always to win. Then he would go on the field and win. Since there was no television then, he was often not recognized. He would, therefore, make bets with others in the bar or pool hall that "that Gipp fellow" would outscore the entire opposition single-handedly.

## A National Hero

Although he considered himself invincible, and was known to play while very ill, or with a bad sprain or even dislocation, Gipp was very well liked by fellow students and coaches. Almost idolized by his teammates, he rarely read of his own exploits in the newspapers and he avoided reporters. He was even known to leave a game when Notre Dame was far ahead just so he could cheer on the second-stringers from the bench. He never sought publicity, and a writer once said that although he often ignored team rules, it was never out of contempt but rather out of indifference.

During his career at Notre Dame, Gipp set records that still stand. He led the Irish in rushing and passing each of his last three seasons (1918, 1919, and 1920). His career mark of 2,341 yards stood for over 50 years, until Jerome Heavens broke it in 1978. Gipp did not allow a pass completion in his territory throughout his entire career. He scored 83 touchdowns from 1917 to 1920.

Gipp never attempted to hide his weaknesses, but he always tried to conceal the good things he did. In secret he often used the money he made from gambling to buy meals for poor families, or pay the tuition of a student friend who couldn't afford it. By the end of his junior season, Gipp had become a national symbol of the perfect football player. Newspapers from around the country covered his exploits on the field. In spite of his gambling, his casual charm, his reluctance to attend classes, and his frequenting of bars and pool halls, Gipp became a national hero.

In 1919, Gipp met Iris Trippeer and fell desperately in love. Trippeer's parents disapproved, since athletes of the day—even athletes as good and famous as George Gipp—had a very uncertain future. At that time there were no professional football leagues, where a college player could go on to make millions. Gipp had no idea what he was going to do after college, if he got back into college, and this bothered Trippeer very much. She tried to get Gipp to think about his future, but with little success.

## Expulsion from Notre Dame

In his junior year, Gipp was expelled from Notre Dame for continuing rules violations and for failing to obey school policies. He was on a scholarship and the school felt they had to take some action. Gipp went back to semipro baseball (a move that eventually cost the famous Jim Thorpe his Olympic medals).

When Gipp left South Bend, after his expulsion from school, he and Trippeer were separated. Gipp worked in a Buick factory by day, and played for a Flint, Michigan baseball team by night. He desperately missed Trippeer and wrote love letters to her regularly.

The outcry from students and faculty finally brought Gipp back to the Notre Dame campus, although other schools were interested in recruiting him. He was unwilling to change his ways, often stumbling to a game after a wild night on the town. But even then, he would play inspirational football.

## The End Nears

Gipp dislocated his shoulder during a 1920 game against with Northwestern University, but insisted on leaving the bench to play again. His play helped the team win, but his teammates saw that he was in agony, and with a very pale complexion. After the game, and in spite of his illness and his injury, he insisted on going to Chicago for a previous engagement. The cold wind there didn't help. When he returned to South Bend, he went to bed in his hotel room at the Oliver Hotel. During a banquet for the team at the same hotel, a very ill Gipp's condition was obvious. He had a cough he could not control, and entered a hospital that night. Sadly, there was no such drug as penicillin available in 1920, which would quickly have cured his throat and lung infections and pneumonia.

Rockne telegraphed Trippeer, and she visited the critically ill Gipp. While he was in the hospital, he was elected to the All-American team of 1920, the first time ever for a Notre Dame player. The entire sports world knew that Gipp was on his deathbed. Headlines across the United States read, "George Gipp Fighting a Brave Battle" and "Gipp Gains in Battle for His Life" and finally "Little Hope for Gipp." Sports fans and the general public, familiar with the football heroics of Gipp, waited for what they knew was coming. Coach Rockne was the last to visit Gipp at the hospital. The twenty-five-year-old athlete died quietly in South Bend, Indiana on December 14, 1920.

## Rockne Waited Eight Years

Coach Rockne waited eight years to tell his team the story of this final visit with Gipp. It was during a football game with arch-rival and much superior Army, a team expected to easily beat the battered and injured Notre Dame team. Rockne knew that his team had the talent, but perhaps not the heart, to beat Army. He was also one of the best locker-room speakers in the history of the game. Rockne spoke softly of George Gipp, a player every man in the room held in the highest possible esteem. With many of the players, it was an esteem bordering on worship. A solemn Rockne related to his team what Gipp had said on his deathbed: "Sometime, Rock, when the team is up against it, when things are wrong and the breaks are beating the boys—tell them to go in there with all they've got and win one for the Gipper."

The Notre Dame team, many weeping, charged onto the field and, in the major upset of the season, beat Army by a score of 12 to 6. Sports experts who watched the game said it was the most inspired football ever played anywhere.

## Further Reading

Irish, www.fas.harvard.edu/~jycollin/irish.html

Knute Rockne Biography, http://www.cmgww.com/football/gipp/gipp.html

The Legends, George "The Gipper" Gipp, http://www.nd.edu/~bblackwe/Gipp.html

The Traditions, www.nd.edu/~ndsi/trad/gipp.html □

# Jean-Luc Godard

**Jean-Luc Godard (born 1930) may be one of cinema's greatest names, but his films remain consistently abstruse and unseen by mainstream audiences. This is a situation the French-Swiss screenwriter, director, and occasional performer most likely prefers. Critics have cited the years prior to 1967 as Godard's most masterful period, when he and other young French directors broke new ground in what came to be known as cinema's New Wave movement, hallmarked by fresh conceptualization and technical tricks that challenged viewers' perceptions.**

Though a true Hollywood outsider vociferously critical of directors like Steven Spielberg, Godard has always paid homage to American film's golden era by including fleeting references to its bygone works—a poster on the wall, or a bit of dialogue—in his own films. In turn, Godard has influenced a new generation of filmmakers. Elements of his style—the arch dialogue, the quirky camera work—can be seen in the films of Quentin Tarantino, Gregg Araki, and John Woo, among others.

## Early Years

Godard was born in Paris on March 12, 1930, but grew up in Switzerland. He attended school in Nyon and, as a young man, returned to Paris for his university education. He studied ethnology at the Sorbonne, but also experienced the heady intellectual and freewheeling spirit of the Latin Quarter, the Parisian neighborhood that is home to the Sorbonne and its students. His primary interests were in theater and the written word, but "little by little the cinema began to interest me more than the rest," Godard told Jean Collet for his biography, *Jean-Luc Godard.* He began frequenting the Cine-Club du Quartier Latin, where he became friends with Francois Truffaut, Eric Rohmer, and Jacques Rivette. Like Godard, the other three would also achieve fame as the most influential of France's postwar filmmakers. The group skipped their classes for visits to the Cinematheque Francaise, France's museum of film, with its steady program of classic works. "We systematically saw everything there was to see," Godard told Collet.

With Rohmer and Rivette, Godard co-founded *La Gazette du Cinema* in 1950, which published their criticism of mainstream French films and their directors. It survived only five issues. Godard had yet to make his own film."I had ideas, but they were absolutely ridiculous," he commented to Collet. Instead he acted in the short works his friends were making in order to observe and learn. In 1954, Godard made his first foray into directing with *Operation Beton,* a short film centered around the construction of a dam

("beton" means concrete); Godard had worked as a laborer on the very project in order to save the money to make the film.

With his next short, 1955's *Une Femme Coquette,* comes evidence of Godard's interest in experimentation—the hand-held camera, jump-cutting from one scene to another, and other quirks which would later become hallmarks of his style. By 1956, Godard was writing regularly for France's respected journal of film criticism, *Le Cahiers du Cinema,* and becoming well-known for his polemics on mainstream filmmakers. He directed a project from after a script by Rohmer, *Tous les Garcons s'appellent Patrick* (title means "All Boys Are Called Patrick"), in 1957; the following year's short *Charlotte et son Jules* was both written and directed by Godard. He also appeared briefly, but its real star was a young French actor with a swagger, Jean-Paul Belmondo.

## New Wave Cinema

The year 1959 marks the formal birth of France's Nouvelle Vague (New Wave) cinema, when Godard, Truffaut, Rohmer and the others obtained the means to make the quirky, unconventional films they desired. Perhaps Godard's most famous film, and considered his first full-length feature, was made that same year and realized New Wave's concepts memorably. *A Bout de Souffle* (also known as "Breathless") premiered in March 1960 and was an immediate sensation. It pioneered the use of hand-held cameras, filming at actual, recognizable locations. Most radically, it was shot with the barest of script. "Breathless" made stars of Belmondo and his co-star, American actress Jean Seberg. They each appear as entirely vacuous characters, seemingly roused only by images from pop culture.

In the famous opening shot of "Breathless," Seberg's character, an American student living in Paris, is walking down the Champs-Elysees selling the *New York Herald Tribune*. She encounters her intermittent boyfriend, Belmondo's handsome thug who has just arrived in Paris to hide out from the authorities after a shoot-out in the countryside with police. Though there is talk of the two fleeing to Italy, and a hint that she may be pregnant, she realizes that Belmondo is wanted for killing a cop. In the end she turns him in. When Godard began the film, it was almost a freeform experiment, as he said in a 1962 interview in *Le Cahiers du Cinema*. "I had written the first scene, and for the rest I had a pile of notes for each scene. I said to myself, this is terrible. I stopped everything. Then I thought: in a single day, if one knows how to go about it, one should be able to complete a dozen takes. Only instead of planning ahead, I shall invent at the last minute."

## Banned by Government

Godard's next film, 1960's *Le Petit Soldat* ("The Little Soldier") was banned by the French government. At the time, France had been fighting a nationalist uprising in its North African colony of Algeria for several years, and *Le Petit Soldat* is set amidst this political backdrop. It chronicles the dilemma plaguing a right-wing terrorist assigned to kill a journalist sympathetic to the Arab cause; instead he falls in love with an operative for the other side, the Algerian liberation movement. "The burning political issue in France at that moment, the Algerian war, *Le Petit Soldat* addressed with an implicative urgency summed up in the image of a hesitant assassin walking behind his victim with a large pointed pistol along a crowded street without attracting anybody's notice—a startling image of the daily unbelievability of political violence," wrote Gilberto Perez in *The Nation* of the film and its message.

In 1961, Godard married the female lead of *Le Petit Soldat*, Anna Karina. She went on to play several leading roles in his subsequent works: she was the exotic dancer who wants a child from her unwilling boyfriend In 1961's *Une Femme est une Femme* ("A Woman Is a Woman"). In 1962's *Vivre sa Vie* ("My Life to Live") she was a record-shop clerk who drifts into prostitution for extra money with predictably disastrous consequences. In these and subsequent films of the decade, Godard perfected the signature elements of his work. The theme of alienation is prevalent in his films: Godard's protagonist is nearly always an outsider of some sort or at odds with "normal" (i.e., bourgeois) society. The techniques Godard and his camera operators developed were similarly revolutionary: in some cases, the camera would follow a character walking down a street for minutes on end—virtually unheard-of experimentalism at the time. Godard also had no qualms about confounding viewers with nearly inaudible dialogue.

## Absence of Plot

*Une Femme Mariee* ("A Married Woman"), released in 1964, typified the absence-of-plot style that Godard came to favor. It chronicles a twenty-four hour period in the life of a bored French fashion editor, and serves as a commentary on the seductive power of advertising imagery. The alienation of bourgeois society was a theme continued in *Pierrot le Fou*, a 1965 release that starred Belmondo as a man who escapes his tedious life with his criminal minded mistress, played by Karina. *Alphaville*, released the same year, was Godard's foray into science fiction. The film's hero is Lemmy Caution, played by American actor Eddie Constantine. Caution is posing as a journalist for a paper comically titled "Figaro-Pravda"—in the 1960s, the leading papers of France and the Soviet Union, respectively. He arrives in bleak Alphaville in a Ford Galaxy to track down the scientist in charge of Alpha-60, the computer that controls Alphaville and robs its citizens of individuality. Called at times Godard's only optimistic film, in the end Caution falls in love with the scientist's daughter and the pair flee.

Increasing evidence of Godard's left-leaning politics came with the 1967 film, *La Chinoise*. His real politicization occurred with the 1968 student riots in France, a week of street and labor unrest that galvanized the entire country and brought it to a virtual standstill. The following year, Godard released *Un Film Comme les Autres*, parts of which—interviews with workers at a car factory, for instance—were shot during the days of protest. At this point Godard began to make short films in 16mm he called cine-tracts, which crystallized his radical political views and offered up a heavy dose of propaganda; they are almost like commercials for a revolution. He also became involved with the militant Dziga Vertov group, who would finance many of his works of this era.

Another famous Godard work from these days was 1970's *One Plus One*, described by some critics as one of his dullest cinematic experiments. To make it, he traveled to England immediately after the May 1968 demonstrations. In the middle of nearly three months of filming a movie that basically showed the behind-the-scenes genesis of the Rolling Stones song "Sympathy for the Devil," band member Brian Jones was arrested, and production was held up by both fire and rain. "The result was Godard's most disjointed film to date," noted *The Oxford Companion to Film*. Godard also journeyed to the Czech capital of Prague to shoot *Pravda* ("truth" in Russian), which depicted the nation in the year since invading Russian tanks had arrived to quell a democratic uprising.

Godard was involved in a serious car accident in 1971, and for a time ceased to make standard-format films. He was still a political rebel, however. In the 1972 short *Letter to Jane*, he lets loose a 45-minute invective against American actor and activist Jane Fonda, then known for her similarly leftist politics. In the film, Godard discusses a photograph of her published in a French newspaper. "The narration calls attention to her facial expression which, Godard claims, differs from that of a North Vietnamese soldier in the background because she is the product of a jaded, capitalist society," according to *The Oxford Companion to Film*.

Rather than full-length feature films, much of what Godard produced over the next few years were video collaborations with his partner, Anne-Marie Mieville. These include *Numero Deux,* filmed in a television studio and ostensibly intent on examining relationships within a traditional family. What instead occurs is that Godard "makes explicit the relationship between home video and pornography—the fetishization of the primal scene," wrote Amy Taubin in the *Village Voice.*

### Returned to Longer Films

By 1980, Godard returned to longer films with *Sauve qui Peut (la Vie)* (titled "Every Man for Himself" for its American debut). Over the next few years he made several acclaimed works, including *Prenom Carmen* (also known as "First Name: Carmen") and *Je Vous Salue, Marie* ("Hail Mary"). This latter work was a retelling of the story of the Virgin Mary and the immaculate conception that received a great deal of publicity from Roman Catholic groups objecting to its nudity and sexual content. In 1987, Godard released his modern-day urban version of the Shakespearean family drama, *King Lear.* In the film, Burgess Meredith plays the doomed monarch, and Molly Ringwald his daughter Cordelia; Woody Allen also shows up. *Time* magazine's Richard Corliss called it "Godard's most infuriating, entertaining pastiche in two decades."

Godard contributed a segment to *Aria,* a 1988 film conceived as a series of vignettes based on well-known opera works. The following year he released parts one and two of an ongoing video-essay project, *Histoire(s) du Cinema.* Typically Godard, the quintessential anti-film, *Histoire(s)* blends bits and pieces from hundreds of films into a critique on the art form itself and a look at its relation to society. Katherine Dieckmann, writing in *Art in America,* called it "an expansive, densely layered, elegiac treatise on the fate of cinema." The title, which can mean either "history" or "story" in French, also serves to point out how filmgoers are beguiled by the false (the story) rather than the real (actual history), "and Godard struggles to expose how cinema's capacity to seduce and lull implicates it in certain atrocities of this century," Dieckmann wrote. In *Histoire(s),* she noted, "gritty newsreel footage of war mingles with an image of the 20th Century Fox logo and its sweeping klieg lights, with the none-too-covert message that these forms of spectacle aren't completely separate."

Two Godard films were released in 1990: *Nouvelle Vague* ("New Wave"), a pastoral work filmed in the Swiss countryside, and *Allemagne Annee 90 Neuf Zero* (also known as "Germany Year 90 Nine Zero"). Here Godard offers a sequel of sorts to *Alphaville,* set in a newly reunited Germany. Critics had once compared the bleak urban future-world of the 1965 film to the real East Berlin; in the latter work, Lemmy Caution tours the actual Berlin. In 1992, New York's Museum of Modern Art feted Godard with a retrospective of his work; not surprisingly, he did not attend his scheduled appearance, ostensibly because he was in the midst of finishing his next work, *Helas pour Moi.* The 1993 film starred Gerard Depardieu in the tale of the Greek deity Zeus and his transformation into human shape. *JLG/JLG,*

released in 1995, shows Godard alone in a series of interviews. Some of it takes place in Switzerland, where the filmmaker has a home in Roulle with a large video studio and editing facilities.

Godard's 1963 film, *Le Mepris* ("Contempt"), was re-released in 1997. In this work, French actor Brigitte Bardot plays a woman married to a screenwriter, a man hired to adapt the Greek literary saga *The Odyssey.* Famed German moviemaker Fritz Lang plays the actual director of the fake film. Bardot hates her husband, a weak-willed man caught between Lang, who wants to remain faithful to the original story, and a crass American producer played by Jack Palance who wants nudity and mermaids. Godard's actual film had been partly bankrolled by a well-known Hollywood executive whom he hated, and Palance's character is an evident mockery of the real-life producer. The film was done in only 149 shots.

The year 1997 also marked the release of another work to American filmgoers, *For Ever Mozart.* Shot in 1995 in Sarajevo, Godard makes another film-within-a-film about a movie crew attempting to get their job done while battling the moral bankruptcy they feel all around, an after-effect of the former Yugoslavia's years-long civil war. "After 40 years, Godard can still astonish and amuse in the cinematic shorthand he virtually created," wrote *Time* magazine's Corliss in reviewing *For Ever Mozart.* The critic lauded Godard's "encyclopedic wit, the glamour of his imagery, the doggedness of a man who won't give up on modernism. His crabby films are, in truth, breathlessly romantic—because he keeps searching for first principles in the pettiest human affairs. Godard gazes at the intimate and finds the infinite."

### Further Reading

Collet, Jean. *Jean-Luc Godard,* Crown, 1970.
*The Films of Jean-Luc Godard,* Studio Vista, 1967.
Kreidl, John. *Jean-Luc Godard,* Twayne, 1980.
*The Oxford Companion to Film,* edited by Liz-Anne Bawden, Oxford University Press, 1976.
*Art in America,* October 1993, pp. 65-67.
*ARTnews,* February 1993, pp. 57-58.
*Le Cahiers du Cinema,* 1962.
*Film Comment,* March 1996, pp. 26-30, pp. 31-41.
*Nation,* February 18, 1991, pp. 209-212.
*Time,* February 1, 1988; August 4, 1997.
*Village Voice,* November 24, 1992, p. 45; July 1, 1997, p. 89. □

# Red Grange

**Red Grange (1903–1991) made football history as one of the most remarkable amateur and professional gridiron athletes of all. He was called "The Galloping Ghost," and it was his presence that brought pro football from the sandlots to the big time.**

Harold Edward "Red" Grange was born on June 13, 1903 in Forksville, a village of about 200 people in an area of Pennsylvania lumber camps. He was the third child of Sadie and Lyle Grange, a lumber camp foreman. Grange was only five years old when his mother died. A few months later the family moved to Wheaton, Illinois, the home of his father's family. Grange's father opened a moving business. For a number of years, the Grange family lived with relatives until they could finally afford a home of their own. The main recreation of Grange and his friends was playing football in vacant lots around town, and basketball in converted barns. Although his doctor warned that he had a heart murmur, sports became the major part of young Grange's life.

Grange was a star player during his high school days at Wheaton Community High School, where he became known as the "Wheaton Ice Man." By then his father had become the local policeman, and the family was well settled. In his final high school game for the DuPage County championship against Downers Grove, Grange scored forty-five points. It is a single player record that still stands in high school championship games.

## A High School Injury

In Grange's senior year of high school, his team finally lost a game 39-0 to the powerful Scott High School in Toledo, Ohio. Part of the reason may have been that Grange was knocked unconscious during the game, and he remained so for the next two days. He had difficulty speaking for a time after that injury. This was the only time that Grange was ever seriously injured in a high school football game, despite the many hard tackles he received during those years.

Grange attended college at the University of Illinois, but decided not to play football. A four-letter sports star in high school, he considered either baseball or basketball to be his best way to earn a varsity letter in college. In 1922, when the call went out for freshmen football candidates to report to the field for practice, Grange didn't even answer. He admitted to friends that the other players were simply too big. Grange was not a large man by football standards. He weighed around 180 pounds during his career, and stood about five feet, ten inches tall. It was his Zeta Psi fraternity brothers who convinced him to try out for the team. He was placed on the first team after his coach saw him play.

## Success at Illinois

Illinois was undefeated in its 1923 season, with Grange leading the team. Before the end of the year, he was named an All American and he was known across America. Grange is credited with the wave of interest Americans began to show in football. Until that time, the game had been generally ignored by all but students. Baseball was the national sport, and all other games were only important on the campuses where they were played. But when Grange began to play football, millions of Americans started following Illinois or their own area college teams. With his almost impossible runs on the field, Grange inspired people to take an interest in his game.

In 1922, the Illinois football program had been a disaster. The following year, with Grange on the team, it was undefeated. The team was named co-champion of the Big Ten. Grange continued this dominance of football through his entire college career.

The University of Michigan was the tough opponent for the University of Illinois in October 1924. The Michigan Wolverines were going for the National Championship. Illinois players knew they had a difficult job ahead of them if they expected to win. The team was playing their first game in the brand new University of Illinois Memorial Stadium. It was dedication day for the largest campus stadium in college sports, so local fans wanted a victory desperately. Illinois had lost its last game, and Michigan was undefeated, very skilled, and a big favorite to win.

When Michigan kicked off to start the game, Grange magically zigged and zagged and dodged, carrying the ball all the way back for a touchdown. The crowd in the huge stadium roared their approval. On the very next offensive play, Grange ran for a 67-yard touchdown. On his next carry, he ran 56 yards for yet another touchdown. He scored the three touchdowns in less than seven minutes against the powerful Michigan defense. Before the game was over, Grange ran back another kickoff for yet another touchdown. He scored five touchdowns in all. Illinois won the game by a lopsided score of 39 to 14.

## "The Galloping Ghost"

Grange was destined to become football's number one celebrity and to blaze his way into football history. Writing about the game that October day, famed sportswriter Grantland Rice called Grange a "whirling dervish runner," and named him "The Galloping Ghost." It was a nickname that remained with Grange for the rest of his life, and was eventually emblazoned in the Professional Football Hall of Fame.

Jerry Liska, an Associated Press reporter, wrote in his book *Sports Immortals,* "The autumn wind still whistles shrilly through cavernous Memorial Stadium at the University of Illinois, as if in perpetual tribute to college football's legendary Galloping Ghost."

## Professional Career

Professional football was a generally unpleasant sandlot game with few fans in 1925. The teams were part of what was called the National Football League, but the league was only four years old and barely drawing any fans to watch their games. Pro football was a game of ex-high school and college players, and a few walk-ons, men who either loved the game with a passion or who could do little else with their lives.

Grange signed a contract with the Chicago Bears the day after his last college game. The team was under the direction of player/manager George Halas, who knew a gold mine when he saw it. To the great disbelief of almost everyone in football, he agreed to pay Grange the staggering sum of one hundred thousand dollars a year and a share of the gate receipts. At this time, most professional football players were being paid 25 to 100 dollars a game, and the top stars were getting about five thousand dollars.

Halas quickly set up a tour, in order for the Bears to take advantage of Grange's name recognition. The tour made transformed professional football into a major sport. Everywhere the team played, they drew huge crowds. Grange drew an astounding sixty five thousand people to the Polo Grounds in New York with his amazing broken-field running. Later that same year, the Bears played to a record seventy five thousand people in the Los Angeles Coliseum. People came to see Grange, and he never disappointed them. He was best at running the ball, but he was also great at passing, kicking, and on defense.

Liska, in an Associated Press story, called Grange "a picture of grace, balance and speed, the epitome of gridiron greatness, a Golden Twenties" athletic peer of Babe Ruth's, Jack Dempsey's, Bobby Jones's and Bill Tildon's. Grange, whose magic name turned pro football from an ugly duckling to a present-day gilded and plush bird of paradise, will be remembered as long as football is played in America."

He played with the Chicago Bears most of his career, but also spent a brief time with the New York Yankees football team, after helping to form the American Football League. He was in the spotlight wherever he played, even as his career was winding down. One of the last times he carried the ball for the Chicago Bears, he reversed and headed for the weak side of the line. A New York Giant lineman yelled loudly back at his linebackers, "Look out! There goes the old man!"

He was right, for 32 year old Grange swivel-hipped around every younger player in the Giants backfield and ran 63 yards, all the way to the twenty-yard line before a faster runner finally stopped him. By then it was apparent, however, that age and recent injuries were taking their toll. Grange had missed the entire 1927 season due to an injury.

## Retirement

When Grange retired from professional football in 1934, he became a well-known radio and television sportscaster, generally for the Chicago Bears. Grange also earned a good income from vaudeville and movie appearances. He was enshrined as a charter member in the Professional Football Hall of Fame in 1963. Grange spent his retirement years with his wife in Lake Wales, Florida. He died on January 28, 1991 in Lake Wales, at the age of 87. Most considered him to be not only one of the greatest players in history, but the man who established professional football as a fan attraction.

Grantland Rice wrote a flowery poem of tribute to Grange: "A streak of fire, a breath of flame, a gray ghost thrown into the game. Eluding all who reach and clutch; That rival hands may never touch; A rubber bounding, blasting soul, whose destination is the goal. Red Grange of Illinois!"

Grange changed the face of American sports, especially the game of football. He carried the ball 4,013 times as a high school, college, and professional football player, gaining 33,820 yards or over nineteen miles. This is an amazing 8.4 yards per carry. He scored a total of 2,365 points in 247 games.

## Further Reading

About Harold "Red" Grange, http://www.wheaton.edu/learnres/ arcsc/collects/sc20/bio.htm
Encarta Encyclopedia, http://www.encarta.com/find/Concise .asp?z = 1&pg = 2&ti = 0594800 0&o = 1
Professional Football Hall of Fame, http://www.profootballhof .com/enshrinees/grange.html □

# Florence Griffith Joyner

**Known for her outstanding athletic accomplishments as well as her sense of personal style, Florence Griffith Joyner (1959–1998) overcame difficult odds with her tenacious determination to achieve Olympic fame.**

Born Florence Delorez Griffith on December 21, 1959 in Los Angeles. "Dee Dee," as she was nicknamed in her youth, was the seventh of eleven children. Her mother, also named Florence, had married Dee Dee's father, Robert Griffith, after moving to California in search of a modeling career. The large family was settled in the Mojave Desert when the elder Florence decided that she needed to improve the educational opportunities for her

children. She left Robert in 1964 and moved the eleven children back to Los Angeles, into a neighborhood known as Watts. A single mother raising such a large family was a tough challenge but Dee Dee's mother always kept her hopes up for her children. Dee Dee recalls her mother saying, "I just want to get you guys out of here. This is not home."

## Doing Things Her Own Way

Dee Dee's personal style for fashion developed early in her childhood. She became known in grade school for her unusual hairstyles. Taught by her grandmother, who worked as a beautician, Dee Dee used her creativity to show her independence through her personal style, which would later become as well known as her athletic abilities. Most children would be happy to blend in with their peers, but Dee Dee wanted to stand out and be noticed. Griffith recalled in an interview for *Sporting News:* "We learned something from how we grew up. It has never been easy, and we knew it wouldn't be handed to us, unless we went after it."

Dee Dee's tenacious attitude and goal-setting ability was demonstrated on a trip to visit her father in the Mojave Desert. She caught a jackrabbit that attempted to outrun the determined child. Dee Dee's mother noticed her daughter's talent for moving with a graceful athleticism. When Dee Dee expressed an interest in running, her mother wholly supported her. At the age of seven, Dee Dee entered the Sugar Ray Robinson Youth Foundation running competition and defeated her opponent soundly. At the age of fourteen,

she won the Jesse Owens National Youth Games competition. She continued her track career into high school where she not only found success in competition but also in her academics. This led her to apply for admission to California State University at Northridge (Cal State).

Griffith's freshman year was filled with business courses and competing in 200-meter and 400-meter events for the track team. Although she proved that she could compete athletically and academically at this level, money became an issue and she was forced to leave school. Her coach, Bob Kersee, talked her into returning after he helped her find monetary support through financial aid.

## A Difficult Decision

In 1980, Griffith had a tough choice to make. Kersee left Cal State to work at the University of California at Los Angeles (UCLA), a school that had won renown for its track teams. In an interview for *Sports Illustrated,* Griffith recalls the dilemma "I had a 3.25 grade point average in business, but UCLA didn't even offer my major. I had to switch to psychology. But my running was starting up, and I knew that Bobby was the best coach for me. So, it kind of hurts to say this, I chose athletics over academics."

Griffith's choice was confirmed when her success under Coach Kersee continued. She was invited to the Olympic trials in 1980 and just missed qualifying for the team by seconds. This defeat only increased her determination. In 1982, she won the 200-meter race at the National Collegiate Athletic Association (NCAA) championship. The following year she won the 400-meter event at the NCAA. Griffith's flair for fashion began to match her running ability. She was known for her long fingernails that were polished with brilliant colors. Griffith's running outfits also captured attention as she began to wear skin-tight ensembles.

At the 1984 Olympic trials, Griffith won a spot on the track team and competed in the Olympic Games held in Los Angeles. With friends and family attending the competition to cheer her on, Griffith won the silver medal in the 200-meter race. She also was in contention for a position on the sprint-relay team, but U.S. officials at the games would not allow her to participate because of the length of her nails, which they felt would interfere with the baton hand-off. Griffith was disappointed with her own performance at the Olympics and took time off from competitive running to work as a beautician and a customer representative for a bank.

In the mid-1980s, Griffith began dating fellow Olympic athlete Al Joyner, who won a gold medal at the 1984 Olympics in the triple-jump competition. Joyner had come to California to train with Kersee for the 1988 Olympic trials. Al's sister, Jackie, was also training at the time with Kersee, who she eventually married. With the influence of Joyner, her interest in running competitively was re-ignited and she began to train again. Her sights were set on the 1988 Olympics in Seoul, South Korea. A formidable partnership was established on October 10, 1987, when Griffith and Joyner married.

## The Stage Is Set for the Olympics

Griffith Joyner found success at the 1987 World Games held in Rome, Italy. She won the silver in the 200-meter race and the gold as a member of the 400-meter relay team.

Over the next few months, Griffith Joyner concentrated on conditioning her body and mind by following a demanding training schedule. Urged on by her husband and Kersee, Griffith arrived at the Olympic trials in 1988 poised to set a record. In the 100-meter dash she achieved a time of 10.49 seconds—.27 seconds faster than the former record set by Evelyn Asford. There was no doubt that Griffith Joyner was setting the stage for a memorable performance at the Seoul Olympics. While her record-setting time brought Griffith Joyner accolades, it was her brightly colored running outfits designed by herself that gained her media attention and the nickname "Flo Jo."

Running in the 100-meter sprint at the Olympic Games in 1988, Griffith Joyner won the gold medal in a time of 10.54. She won another gold medal in the 200-meter race and set a new world record with a time of 21.34. Griffith Joyner also participated as a member of the 1,600-meter relay team that captured the silver. She ran this race after only a half-hour rest from a previous heat and with a thigh injury. Greg Foster, a world champion hurdler, commented in an article for the *Los Angeles Times Sports Update* regarding Griffith Joyner's personality: "The strength was there. A lot of times in track and field it is just believing in yourself." Her participation in the relay event demonstrated that belief in herself.

After the Olympics, Griffith Joyner received numerous awards, such as the U.S. Olympic Committee's Sportswoman of the Year, Jesse Owens Outstanding Track and Field Athlete, Sports Personality of the Year by the Tass News Agency, UPI Sportswoman of the Year, Associated Press Sportswoman of the Year, and *Track and Field Magazine*'s Athlete of the Year. Griffith Joyner was also awarded the Sullivan Trophy for being the top amateur American athlete.

Griffith Joyner began to spread her creative talent off the track. She developed a clothing line, created nail products, dabbled in acting, and authored children's books. Along with her husband, Griffith Joyner established the Florence Griffith Joyner Youth Foundation in 1992 to aid disadvantaged youth. In 1993, President Bill Clinton appointed her to the position of co-chairperson for the President's Council on Physical Fitness along with U.S. congressman Tom McMillen. Griffith Joyner commented on her appointment in an interview for *The New York Times:* "I love working with kids, talking with them and listening to them. I always encourage kids to reach beyond their dreams. Don't try to be like me. Be better than me." In 1995, she was inducted into the U.S. Track and Field Hall of Fame. The most important post-Olympic event, however, was the birth of a daughter, Mary Ruth.

## Tragedy Struck

Griffith Joyner attempted a career comeback at the Atlanta Olympic Games in 1996, but an injury ended that

pursuit. Keeping busy with her various business endeavors, she was flying to St. Louis, Missouri in 1996 when she suffered an apparent seizure and was hospitalized. She recovered with no apparent health problems. The world was shocked when Griffith Joyner suffered an epileptic seizure while sleeping at her home in Mission Viejo, California on September 21, 1998. She died at the age of 38. Thousands paid their last respects to an inspirational woman who captured much attention, not only for her athletic talent, but also for her community-oriented endeavors.

Throughout most of her career, Griffith Joyner had to deal with ugly rumors of steroid use for peak performance. She always denied these rumors and never once failed a drug test. An autopsy found no trace of any suspicious substances, finally putting to rest any notion of drug use. Hybl commented on the findings, "We now hope that this great Olympic champion, wife, and mother can rest in peace, and that her millions of admirers around the world will celebrate her legacy to sport and children every day. It is time for the whispers and dark allegations to cease."

## A Tribute to a Legend

As a tribute to his late wife's determination, Al Joyner announced that the clothing line that Griffith Joyner had been working on would be continued. In addition, partial proceeds would go towards supporting the Florence Griffith Joyner Memorial Empowerment Foundation. In an interview with *Sports Illustrated,* Joyner recalled that "Florence had long dreamed of having her own signature line. As with everything in her life, she put a tremendous amount of time, energy, and passion into making this line a success. By continuing the work she started, we are adding to her legacy."

## Further Reading

Aaseng, Nathan, *Florence Griffith Joyner,* Lerner, 1989.
*Sports Illustrated,* July 25, 1988; special Summer Olympics preview issue, September, 1988; September 14, 1988; October 3, 1988; October 10, 1988; December 19, 1988; December 26, 1988.
"Commentary on the Death of Florence Griffith Joyner," *Just Sports For Women,* http://www.justwomen.com/archive_gogirl/gogirl_092698_flojo_quotes.html," (February 27, 1999).
Dillman, Lisa, "Determination Lay Inside Diva of Track," *Los Angeles Times Sports Update,* http://www.latimes.com/HOME/NEWS/SPORTS/UPDATES/lat_reax0922.html," (February 27, 1999).
"FloJo's Career in Review," *CBS SportsLine,* http://cbs.sportsline.com/u/women/,"more/sep98/flojofacts92198.html (February 27, 1999).
"Florence Griffith Joyner," http://www.knickerbocker.com/highpark/florencejoynerbio.html," (February 27, 1999).
"Florence Griffith Joyner Dies At 38," *Channel 2000,* http://www.channel2000.com/news/stories/news-980921-163942.html," (February 27, 1999).
"Friends, fans pay respects to one of their own," *CFRA News Talk Radio,* http://interactive.cfra.com/1998/09/25/63882.htnl," (February 27, 1999).
Gerber, Larry, "Autopsy reveals Griffith Joyner died from Epileptic seizre," *Detroit News* http://www.detnews.com/1998/sports/9810/23/10230067.html (February 27, 1999).

"One of Griffith Joyner's Dreams Lives On," *CNN Sports Illustrated,* http://www.cnnsi.com/athletics/news/1998/10/21/joyner_goal/," (February 27, 1999).

"Sprinter Griffith Joyner, 38, Dies in Her Sleep, *Washington Post,* http://lupus.northern.edu:90/hastingw/joyner.html," (February 27, 1999). □

# Bacharuddin Jusuf Habibie

**An aeronautical engineer who became Indonesia's minister of technical development and eventually its president, B.J. Habibie (born 1936) was a lifelong devotee of Indonesian dictator Suharto. When student riots and economic turmoil forced Suharto from office, he named Habibie as his successor.**

Known as a big-government free-spender and a proponent of bizarre economic theories, Habibie seemed an unlikely candidate to bail out Indonesia from its severe economic crisis of the late 1990s. He was closely identified with Suharto's corrupt policies and distrusted by students, the military, and foreign investors. Yet he instituted reforms and steered the country toward free elections, remaining in power longer than most observers expected.

### Father Figure

Bacharuddin Jusuf Habibie was born on June 25, 1936 in the sleepy seaside town of Pare Pare in the Indonesian state of South Sulawesi. The fourth of eight children, he was nicknamed "Rudy" at an early age. His father, Alwi Abdul Jalil Habibie, was a government agricultural official who promoted the cultivation of cloves and peanuts. His grandfather was a Muslim leader and an affluent landowner.

As a child Habibie liked swimming, reading, singing, riding his father's racehorses, and building model airplanes. In 1950, when Rudy was 13, his father suffered a heart attack and died. Suharto, then a young military officer billeted across the street, was present at his father's deathbed and became Habibie's protector and substitute father. Habibie later wrote of Suharto: "I regarded him as an idol, who could serve as an example for all people . . . a young, taciturn brigade commander, with great humane feelings, and a fierce fighting spirit." Suharto's autobiography said Habibie "regards me as his own parent. He always asks for my guidance and takes down notes on philosophy."

Habibie's interest in building model planes continued while he excelled in science and mathematics at the Bandung Institute of Technology. His mother, R.A. Tuti Marini Habibie, arranged for him to continue his studies in Germany. At the Technische Hochschule of Aachen, Habibie studied aircraft construction engineering.

In 1962, on a visit home to Indonesia, he married H. Hasri Ainun Besari, a doctor. They had two children, Ilham Akbar and Thareq Kemal, both born in Germany. While Habibie was abroad, Suharto, who had become a general, succeeded General Sukarno as Indonesia's ruler in 1966.

After graduating with a doctoral degree from the Aachen Institute in 1965, Habibie joined the aircraft manufacturing firm Messerschmitt-Boelkow-Bluhm, rising to the rank of vice-president. As a research scientist and aeronautical engineer, he helped design several planes, including the DO-31, an innovative vertical takeoff and landing craft. He specialized in solutions for aircraft cracking, gaining the nickname "Mr. Crack" as one of the first scientists to calculate the dynamics of random crack propagation. He also became involved in international aircraft marketing activities and NATO's defense and economic development.

### Indonesia's Technology Czar

In 1974, Suharto asked Habibie to return to Indonesia to help establish an industrial base. Habibie jump-started an aircraft construction industry and a state airline company.

Soon he became Suharto's chief advisor for high-technology development. Habibie exploited the relationships he had developed in Germany and NATO to engineer a myriad of controversial deals involving aircraft, ships, heavy industry, and economic development.

As minister of research and technology, Habibie promoted the importation of high-tech goods and services. He liked to "leapfrog" over low-skill industries and move straight into high-tech ventures, spurning the basic development which might have brought needed employment to Indonesia's low-skilled masses. Habibie spent billions in public money on his strategic companies. His pet project was a national airplane, the propeller-driven N-250. Its producer was IPTN, a state company whose vice-president was Habibie's son. The national airplane venture consumed $2 billion in public funds, diverted from a project to save Indonesian forests.

Habibie often used his influence with Suharto to broker favorable deals for his family companies. For example, he pressured Merpati Airlines to buy 16 of IPTN's CN-235 airplanes, which were so poorly built they could fly for only an hour with a full load. Never popular with the military, Habibie angered officials by buying 100 German naval vessels without consulting top brass; the ships needed $1 billion in repairs.

For two decades, Habibie was a top insider in Suharto's corrupt, nepotistic regime. Like Suharto, whose family controlled much of Indonesia's economy, Habibie's relatives had their own business monopolies, often in partnership with Suharto's children. According to *Philadelphia Inquirer* reporter Trudy Rubin, "The state set up Habibie's 'strategic industries' in fields such as steel, shipbuilding and, especially, aircraft manufacture. His relatives were all involved as middlemen, agents, and supp liers." Habibie's family came to control two conglomerates—the Timsco Group, named after his brother Timmy, and the Repindo Panca Group, headed by his second son, Tareq Kamal Habibie. The conglomerate's 66 companies benefited from lucrative government contracts awarded by minister Habibie.

Habibie was widely known as a free-spending eccentric and an advocate of expensive government programs. His high-tech ventures failed to strengthen Indonesia's economy. Many of his projects lost millions of dollars. A relentless self-promoter, Habibie was known for talking endlessly in shrill tones while gesturing wildly. When he visited Tokyo to talk to Japanese bankers about refinancing Indonesia's $80 billion debt, he lectured them for two hours about what was wrong with the Japanese economy and came home empty-handed.

A small, wiry man, Habibie enjoyed classical music, motorcycle riding and swimming in his pool at his home on Jalan Cibubur. A devout Muslim, he founded the Indonesian Association of Muslim Intellectuals in 1990.

## Suharto's Man

Throughout his long tenure as technology minister, Habibie remained slavishly loyal to Suharto, and Suharto considered him his most reliable supporter. Habibie told *Newsweek* that Suharto was his "close friend" who "treated me like his own brother." Habibie often called the dictator "SGS," for "Super-Genius Suharto."

Eventually, Suharto's policies brought Indonesia's economy to the brink of disaster. In March 1998, as student demonstrations and civil unrest increased in intensity, Suharto installed Habibie as vice-president. As the economy collapsed, bloody student riots led to increasing calls from international allies for Suharto's resignation. Hundreds died in the civil unrest that finally forced Suharto from office in May 1998. Before he left the presidential palace, Suharto installed Habibie as his hand-picked successor.

The appointment of Habibie to head the troubled country seemed to appease no one. Protesters saw him as firmly tied to Suharto's system. Even after Suharto stepped down, the general's family members still controlled commerce and industry in the country. Foreign investors worried that Habibie's free-spending policies would exacerbate Indonesia's problems. The military distrusted him because, unlike previous Indonesian presidents, Habibie did not rise through their ranks.

On taking power, Habibie tried to distance himself somewhat from his lifelong idol. He pledged to build "a clean government, free from inefficiency, corruption, collusion, and nepotism." Soon after, Habibie's brother resigned from his leadership of an industrial development authority. He also freed high-profile political prisoners; lifted controls on the press, political parties and labor unions, and pledged negotiations to end the long conflict in the Indonesian state of East Timor.

Most observers doubted he could retain his power for several reasons. His reputation for wild spending came at a time when the failing Indonesian economy needed a bailout. The bankrupt Indonesian currency, the *rupiah,* fell in value by 36 percent when Habibie took office. Most of the country identified him closely with Suharto's regime and its policies, which had brought unbearable hyper-inflation and food lines.

"Indonesia's problems are so difficult to solve that not even an extraordinarily clever politician bolstered by overwhelming public support would find it easy to take over," observed *Time* magazine. "And Habibie . . . seems the least likely candidate. He has no political base, nor can he necessarily count on the long-term backing of the powerful military. Economists and stock analysts around Asia question Habibie's ability to bring sensible change to Indonesia's choking economy . . ."

Many foreign investors found a Habibie presidency frightening. One reason was Habibie's advocacy of a strange "zig-zag theory" of economics. He believed that cutting interest rates, then doubling them, then slashing them again, would reduce inflation. Critics scoffed at his abilities. "He is a clown, a joker, an entertainer," said Jusuf Wanandi, director of the Centre for Strategic and International Studies in Jakarta. Yet Habibie managed to consolidate his control over the country, primarily because the opposition was fragmented and frequently squabbling. The military, involved in government at every level, was deeply divided. Never modest, Habibie told *Time*: "There are two ways of making history: from within the elite—or from the outside. Being inside doesn't mean you're a puppet."

As Habibie maintained a grip on power, the economic decline of his country worsened, with one-fifth of the work force unemployed by the end of 1998. Unrest continued, and there were reports of the torture of dissidents by the military and new assaults on rebel sympathizers in East Timor. During renewed demonstrations by student protesters against the government in November 1998, 16 people died. Habibie enraged students by arresting a small group of dissidents and blaming them for provoking soldiers. Protesters demanded that Habibie step down. The armed forces insisted only rubber bullets and blanks had been used against protesters, but it was discovered that at least one student had been killed by live ammunition, a "dum-dum" bullet outlawed under the Geneva Convention's international rules of warfare. The military then tried to appease the protesters by announcing prosecutions of 163 soldiers and police. Habibie tried to downplay the conflict. "Our society still has not had the chance to live under the rule of law," Habibie told *Newsweek*. "The police do not understand the limits, though they are learning."

Renewed hostilities by Islamic militants against Indonesia's ethnic Chinese Christian minority raised questions about Habibie's goals. His religious supporters dreamed of him instituting a fundamentalist Muslim state. But Habibie told *Newsweek*: "The burning of churches and mosques is a criminal act we all condemn. . . . As a religious and intellectual man, I will be among the first who will fight against any attempt to make this country a religious state." Asked about Chinese Indonesians who feared an Islamic wave of repression, Habibie replied: "I wish we could change that like turning off the light. But it's not that easy. . . . The Chinese, I love them as I love the others. I only hate criminals."

Against all odds, Habibie retained power. He vowed to continue investigating Suharto and his dealings. He also promised to hold parliamentary and presidential elections in the spring and summer of 1999. A popular Indonesian magazine, *Tempo,* showed only seven percent of those polled would vote for Habibie.

Displaying for the world his high self-regard, Habibie opened his own web site on the Internet, including an extensive list of awards and personal achievements. In a fawning account posted on the web site, *B.J. Habibie: His Life and Career,* biographer A. Makmur Makka wrote: "He is the idol and the dream of all parents, who wish their offspring to become another Habibie. . . . He is an intelligent person, even a genius, and out of the 190 million inhabitants, there is only one B.J. Habibie." Makka also wrote: "B.J. Habibie seemed to possess supernatural power, which made him succeed in everything he did."

## Further Reading

*The Economist,* November 21, 1998; November 28, 1998.
*Newsweek,* June 1, 1998; January 25, 1999.
*Philadelphia Inquirer,* May 29, 1998.
*Time,* June 1, 1998.
*Time International,* August 3, 1998.
Makka, A. Makmur, *B.J. Habibie: His Life and Career,* http://habibie.ristek.go.id/english/ (March 25, 1999). □

# Henry John Heinz

**Henry J. Heinz (1844–1919) went bankrupt due to an overabundance of one very pungent herb, but he came roaring back with his "57 Varieties" of food products and eventually built his new company into a multi-billion dollar corporation.**

Henry J. Heinz was born in Pittsburgh, Pennsylvania on October 11, 1844. As a child, he worked in the basement of his Pittsburgh home, helping his father grind spices for his mother's pickles. Everybody in town loved the pickles, and after they were canned, young Henry would take them around to buyers. He became particularly adept at grinding the horseradish, and his later fortune rose and fell with this powerful herb. To make a living, he worked in his father's brick-manufacturing firm, eventually becoming a partner in the business.

The call of pickles and other prepared foods was too great, and Heinz left brick making to return to grated horseradish, one of his mother's most popular products. Heinz packed the horseradish in clear glass bottles to reveal it's purity. This was the first of many brilliant ideas that would eventually lead to his success. He built a model factory complex along the Allegheny River in Pennsylvania and

transformed a 19th century garden into a multi-billion dollar global food service business.

## Early Struggles

Heinz joined with a friend named Clarence Noble to peddle vegetables from the family garden to neighbors in the area. He was 25 years of age when the two formed the Pittsburgh partnership of Heinz and Noble, to produce "pure and superior" grated horseradish and other bottled products. Heinz was an excellent salesman and within a year his company had been solidly established. Everybody loved his horseradish. The only thing that threatened his business was an oversupply of horseradish. That is exactly what happened. In 1875, the price of this powerful herb fell to almost nothing. Heinz and Noble were forced to declare bankruptcy. It was a blow to young Heinz. Nobody wanted to pay his price when they could get horseradish elsewhere for next to nothing.

Never one to give up, Heinz plunged back into the bottled food business. He led his company with such maxims as: "Heart power is less than horse power." Heinz motivated his people by treating them well. The working conditions at his plant surpassed what many employees had at home.

## The Heinz Hitch

Heinz and his employees delivered products to customers first with a hand basket and later by pushcart. By the turn of the century, as demand and product line increased, a huge horse drawn wagon called the "Heinz Hitch" was used.

Many years later, Heinz's original Studebaker rig was found in an old storage shed in central Pennsylvania. It had deteriorated with wood rot and rust, and a tree was growing through a huge hole in its floorboards. The wagon was completely refurbished and became a popular attraction at fairs, expositions, and parades throughout the country.

## A Growing Business

The bright red product seen on every store shelf, on almost every restaurant table, and in most homes, was created by Heinz to get his second business going in 1876. He introduced a new type of tomato ketchup that was extremely successful in the marketplace. With this ketchup and his other products, including celery sauce, pickled cucumbers, sauerkraut, and vinegar, the business continued to grow. All were made with the very finest ingredients, according to his personal orders.

Heinz was certain he knew what the public wanted, so he soon added pickles, jams, jellies, and other condiments to his line of food products. Every vegetable and herb was picked when it was at its absolute peak of freshness, carefully sorted for best quality, then packed in a very clean factory. Heinz, himself, invented the "factory tour" for people who were interested in watching the process. This brilliant publicity move spread to hundreds of other companies after executives saw the public reaction to Heinz' idea.

## World's Largest Tomato Processor

Heinz soon became the world's largest tomato processor, even going so far as calling itself "tomato-obsessed." The company eventually provided more than one half the ketchup in the world, all based on Heinz' original recipe. It carefully studied the "lycopene" chemical found in tomatoes, trying to determine how much this substance can help to prevent cancer.

Always the promoter and forever thinking of new ways to acquaint the public with his products, Heinz introduced his famous "pickle pin" at the Chicago World's Fair in 1893. The little pin became one of the most popular promotional pieces in the history of American business. It was all free advertising, except for the minor cost of the pin. Original pickle pins became valuable in later years as collector items.

## "57 Varieties"

As the number of his products grew, Heinz began to consider a slogan. According to the H.J. Heinz Company, "While most advertising slogans come from 'creatives' on Madison Avenue, the creation of the renowned Heinz advertising phrase is surrounded in great mystery. A visionary, Heinz was inspired by the number 57. In reality, when Henry Heinz created '57 Varieties' in 1896, the company already had over 60 varieties of products. For reasons no one will ever know, Henry Heinz' mind was stuck on the number 57, and his phrase has stuck ever since."

The number was wrong, and over the years it would become far too low, but Heinz liked it. The fact that the company had more than 57 products didn't seem to matter. The "magic" number became synonymous with the H.J. Heinz Company, and continued long after Heinz turned over leadership of his vast empire to his son. Heinz plastered his name all over billboards, in magazines, and in newspapers, in a further effort to gain recognition for his company's products.

Heinz had become known as the "pickle king" by 1896. He was a millionaire and a national celebrity. It was difficult to go anywhere without seeing his name, and that was exactly how Heinz planned it to be. In advertising, and on store shelves, the bright red products were obvious.

## International Operations

"Our field is the world," Heinz had declared in 1886, after making the first overseas sale. He sent his sales force around the world, to every inhabited continent including Africa, the Orient, Australia, Europe and South America. Eventually the company manufactured more than 6000 varieties in over 200 countries and territories. Nearly half of the company sales came from non-U.S. operations.

The H.J. Heinz Company eventually went public as it acquired StarKist, Ore-Ida frozen potatoes, Weight Watchers International, and other subsidiaries under the direction of Heinz and his sons and grandsons. Nearly 70% of all sales were from products without the Heinz brand name.

The company also expanded into pet foods, celebrating its 100th anniversary with "Morris," the cat with nine lives. To help preserve the environment, Heinz Italia introduced its farm-to-factory "ecological oasis" for its baby food products in 1986. Heinz USA introduced the first fully recyclable plastic ketchup bottle in 1990, and StarKist became the first "dolphin safe" tuna.

Heinz son, Howard, guided the company successfully through the critical years of 1919 to 1941. By refusing to burden the company with debt during the speculative 1920's, by exercising great care during the depression years, and by introducing baby food and ready-to-serve soup, he allowed H.J. Heinz & Co. to survive and prosper. Following in his entrepreneur father's footsteps, he also increased promotion while he cut costs (but not wages. During the Second World War, under the direction of Heinz' grandson Henry John "Jack" Heinz, the company continued to grow.

Henry John Heinz died in Pittsburgh on May 14, 1919, pleased with his own efforts and those of his son. He would certainly have been pleased with his grandson, as well.

## Further Reading

Food Industry, Grolier, 1997
Heinz, Henry John, http://www.germanheritage.com/
    biographies/heinz/heinz.html
Heinz, Relishing the Past, http://www.heinz.com/js/about_rel
    .html □

# Marguerite Henry

**Marguerite Henry (1902–1997) is one of the best-known writers of animal stories for children. Her books continue to be widely read, and her legacy of exciting, touching stories will long be remembered.**

Marguerite Henry was born Marguerite Breithaupt on April 13, 1902, in Milwaukee, Wisconsin. She was the youngest of five children of Louis Breithaupt and Anna (Kaurup) Breithaupt. Her father owned a publishing business. Although Henry grew up in a home without any pets, she developed an early love for animals. She also took a keen interest in books and writing. She sold her first magazine article at the age of eleven, and worked for a time repairing books at the local library.

## Early Works

After graduation from Riverside High School in Milwaukee, Henry attended the Milwaukee State Teachers College and the University of Wisconsin in Milwaukee. On May 5, 1923, at the age of 21, she married Sidney Crocker Henry, a sales manager (he died in 1987).

Henry's writing career started rather slowly. She sold a few articles to the *Saturday Evening Post* and wrote several minor stories and information books for children. Her first full-length book, published in 1940, was titled *Auno and Tauno: A Story of Finland*. It was inspired by two Finnish friends who recounted their childhood experiences to her. This was followed by several other children's books, including *Dilly Dally Sally* (1940), *Geraldine Belinda* (1942), and *Their First Igloo on Baffin Island* (with Barbara True, 1943). The 16-volume "Pictured Geographies" series, illustrated by Kurt Wiese, was published in 1941 and 1946. Some of the titles included *Alaska in Stories and Pictures* (1941), *Canada in Stories and Pictures* (1941), *Mexico in Stories and Pictures* (1941), and *Australia in Stories and Pictures* (1946).

## Breakthrough Book

Henry's first book to win critical acclaim was *Justin Morgan Had a Horse,* published in 1945. The story is set in the late eighteenth century and tells the history of the Morgan horse, beginning with its founding sire in rural Vermont. After finishing the story, Henry went to the local library and scanned children's books, looking for the right illustrator. When she happened upon *Flip,* a book written and illustrated by Wesley Dennis, she knew she had found the right person to draw for her stories. She sent a copy of *Justin Morgan* to Dennis. When they met, according to *Something About the Author,* Wesley said, "I'm dying to do the book and I don't care whether I get paid for it." Thus began a long and successful partnership between Henry and Dennis, during which time they produced more than 20 books.

## The Legacy of *Misty*

A second endeavor for Henry and Dennis, *Misty of Chincoteague* (1947), became one of their most popular

and enduring works. Like most of Henry's books, the story is based on fact. Every year the residents of Chincoteague Island, off the coast of Virginia, round up wild horses on nearby Assateague Island and auction them off. Henry's story is about two children who long to own one of these wild ponies. Their dream horse is a mare called the "Phantom," who has resisted capture during the past two round-ups. Because the mare has a newborn foal, she becomes slower than usual. As a result, one of the children is able to catch her in his first year as a "roundup man." The mare becomes tame enough to win a race, but later escapes to her home island, leaving the children with her foal, Misty.

Misty was a real filly whom Henry spotted during Pony Penning Day at Chincoteague. The pony lived with Henry for several years, while her book was being written. Eventually Misty was sent back to the Beebe Ranch for breeding. After publication of the book, the pony became an instant celebrity and was even invited to a conference of the American Library Association. Later, a movie was made about her life. When her first colt needed a name, thousands of children wrote to Henry with suggestions. The popularity of Misty seemed to be universal. *Misty of Chincoteague* was named a Newbery Honor Book and won the Lewis Carroll Shelf Award in 1961. Miriam E. Wilt, in *Elementary English,* called *Misty* "one of the finest horse stories ever written."

Other books based on Misty and the Chincoteague ponies followed, including *Sea Star: Orphan of Chincoteague* (1949), *Stormy, Misty's Foal* (1963), and *Misty's Twilight* (1992), all illustrated by Dennis. In 1990, the Misty of Chincoteague Foundation, Inc., was formed

with the help of Henry. This nonprofit organization is dedicated to preserving the legend of the Assateague ponies. The foundation's goals include purchasing parts of the land where the original Misty and Stormy were raised and establishing a museum on the Island of Chincoteague.

## Merging History and Imagination

A characteristic of Henry's writing that made her "one of the twentieth century's finest writers of horse stories," as she is called in *Children's Books and Their Creators,* is "the historical authenticity of her plots and the vigor of her writing." Henry spent months researching each of her books. She also made trips to each story's locale and used interviews and letters to gather details before starting to write. For example, when preparing to write *Justin Morgan Had a Horse,* Henry corresponded with a 98-year-old resident of Virginia named David Dana Hewitt. Henry said of him in *Newbery Medal Books,* "In his fine, steady handwriting he made me see Virginia. Not the Virginia that greets you from paved highways, but the Virginia that lies deep in the soul of its people."

In *Twentieth-Century Children's Writers,* the editor states that "it is the magical appeal of history—the merging of fact with imagination with legend—that gives the Henry books their trademark." In addition, Henry was able to give both the people and the animals in her stories "character." Even though the animals are not made to seem like humans, they are depicted as having qualities such as courage, loyalty, and determination.

The aspects of Henry's writing that made her distinctive were even more apparent in the book she published the year after *Misty.* The idea for *King of Wind* initially came from Dennis, who illustrated the book. A breeder of thoroughbreds, Walter Chrysler, had asked Dennis to draw a head of the Godolphin Arabian, the founding sire of the thoroughbred breed, which the breeder wanted to use on his stationery. While researching what this horse may have looked like, Dennis learned the story of the horse who had lived in the early eighteenth century and been abused and neglected for years before becoming one of the three founding sires of the thoroughbred breed. Dennis related his findings to Henry, who was fascinated. Despite being warned by family members about the amount of research required to write a story that went from Morocco to France to England, Henry took on the project. "With great excitement I began to probe and pry into the life of this famous stallion who had rubbed shoulders with sultans and kings, with cooks and carters," Henry said in *Children's Literature Review.* To put herself "into the long ago and far away," Henry tacked up in her study photocopies of pictures from the time and place of the stallion's life. Soon, she said, "It was the present that grew dim and the long ago that became real!"

*King of the Wind,* published in 1948, won the Newbery Medal in 1949 and the Young Readers Choice Award in 1951. In addition to being historically accurate, the book was an exciting adventure story. It described how a mute stable boy cared for the Moroccan colt, which was later presented to the young king of France. Rejected by royalty, the stallion was forced to endure years of hard labor and abuse before becoming the famous sire.

## Other Works

Henry wrote many other horse books, several of which won awards. Some of these include *Born to Trot* (1950), *Black Gold* (1957), *Guadenzia: Pride of the Palio* (1960), *White Stallion of Lipizza* (1964), *Mustang: Wild Spirit of the West* (1966), and *San Domingo: The Medicine Hat Stallion* (1972). Horses were not the only heroes in Henry's stories. In 1953, she published *Brighty of the Grand Canyon,* a book about a burro whose loyalty and perseverance in the face of many trials endeared him to young readers. *Brighty* won the William Allen White Award in 1956. Other animals featured in Henry's books include dogs (*A Boy and a Dog,* 1944; *Muley-Ears: Nobody's Dog,* 1959); birds (*Birds at Home,* 1942); foxes (*Cinnabar: The One O'Clock Fox,* 1956); and cats *Benjamin West and His Cat Grimalkin,* a fictional biography, 1947).

In addition to her fictional animal stories, Henry wrote nonfiction as well. *Robert Fulton: Boy Craftsman* (1946) is believed by some to be the best of the series called "The Childhood of Famous Americans." Another nonfiction book by Henry is *Album of Horses* (1951), which describes many different breeds of horses, their histories and characteristics. Henry also wrote an *Album of Dogs* (1955). *The Little Fellow* (1945), though fiction, is aimed toward younger children and uses animal characters to help children learn about growing up and getting along with others. In addition to her books, Henry contributed to several magazines, including *Delineator, Forum, Nations' Business, Reader's Digest,* and *Saturday Evening Post.* She also wrote for *World Book Encyclopedia.*

Some of Henry's most popular books were made into movies. These films include *Misty* (Twentieth-Century Fox, 1961); *Brighty of the Grand Canyon* (Feature Film Corporation, 1967); *Justin Morgan Had a Horse* (Walt Disney Productions, 1972); *Peter Lundy and the Medicine Hat Stallion* (National Broadcasting Company, 1977, based on the book *San Domingo: The Medicine Hat Stallion*); and *King of the Wind* (HTV, London, 1990).

Henry enjoyed her work. As she said in *Newbery Medal Books,* "The doing is always so much more fun than the getting through. The only really dismal days in my life are those when I turn in a manuscript. I am suddenly bereft. . . . And then, oh happy relief! In a little while the manuscript is back home, with blessed little question marks along the margin. Then once again, I'm happy, I've got work to do!"

## Last Book

In 1996, Henry completed her last book, *Brown Sunshine of Sawdust Valley.* The story is about a ten-year-old girl who longs to own a horse. She and her father purchase a broken-down old mare at an auction, and with love and care from the girl, Lady Sue begins to thrive. She gives birth to Brown Sunshine, a spirited mule, who is crowned king of the Mule Day Celebration.

Henry died at her home in Rancho Sante Fe, California, on November 26, 1997; she was 95 years old. By the time of her death she had published more than 60 books for children. Her books continue to be widely read, and her legacy of exciting, touching animal stories for children will long be remembered.

## Further Reading

*Children's Books and Their Creators,* edited by Anita Silvey, Houghton Mifflin, 1995.
*Something About the Author,* Vol. 69, edited by Donna Olendorf, Gale Research Inc., 1992.
*Twentieth-Century Children's Writers,* edited by Laura Standley Berger, St. James Press, 1995.
*Publishers Weekly,* December 15, 1997.
"Marguerite Henry," *Misty of Chincoteague Foundation, Inc.,* http://www.modelhorses.com/mcf (March 1, 1999). □

# Jim Henson

**Influential children's entertainer Jim Henson (1936–1990) is best known for inventing the Muppets, a softer versions of puppets. His characters were a key component of *Sesame Street,* the children's educational television program seen worldwide. Henson's creations also appeared in their own program, *The Muppet Show,* as well as a number of other television programs and films.**

Henson was born on September 24, 1936 in Greenville, Mississippi, and grew up in the nearby town of Leland. His father worked for the federal government as an agronomist. When Henson was about ten years old, his family moved to suburban Maryland when his father's job took him to Washington, D.C. While in high school, Henson became intrigued by television and its possibilities. He was a fan of early puppet television shows *Kukla, Fran and Ollie* and *Life with Snarky Parker,* and their creators Burr Tillstrom and Bil and Cora Baird, respectively. Henson became involved in a local puppetry club. During the summer of 1954, a local television station, WTOP in Washington, D.C., needed a puppeteer for one of their children's programs. Henson and a friend put together several puppets and worked there for a short time.

## Created the First Muppets

In 1955, Henson entered the University of Maryland where he studied theater arts. He also landed a job as a puppeteer for another television station, WRC-TV, an NBC affiliate in Washington, D.C. Within a few months, Henson had his own show called *Sam and Friends.* The five-minute long program aired twice daily before two of the network's most popular shows for six years. While working on the show Henson met his future wife, another University of Maryland student named Jane Nebel. They eventually had five children together, who often accompanied their parents

However, the success of *Sam and Friends* gave Henson the money to pay his way through college. On graduation day in 1960, Henson bought a Rolls Royce automobile to take himself to graduation. He then turned his attention to the Muppets full time. They were featured in commercials for Wilkins coffee, their first nation-wide exposure in the late 1950s and early 1960s. Throughout the 1960s, Henson and his Muppets appeared on television variety shows such as *The Ed Sullivan Show, The Steve Allen Show,* and *The Jimmy Dean Show* as well as NBC's *The Today Show.*

## Moved to *Sesame Street*

In 1969, Henson was approached by the Children's Television Workshop for a new show they were creating called *Sesame Street.* Henson hesitated at first, because he did not want to be just a children's entertainer. But he eventually signed on and developed some of his most memorable Muppets: Grover, Big Bird, the Count, and Bert and Ernie, among others. Older Muppets like Kermit the Frog also made appearances. Henson's Muppets contributed to the popularity of the show. *Sesame Street* appeared in 100 countries in 14 different languages. Its international success made Henson famous throughout the world. As Eleanor Blau wrote in the *New York Times,* "the Muppets helped youngsters learn about everything from numbers and the alphabet to birth and death. They were role models and they imparted values."

By the mid-1970s, Henson wanted his own television show, but had problems getting one on American network television. Henson created two pilots for ABC under the title of *The Muppet Show: Sex and Violence* in the mid-1970s, but all major networks eventually passed on the project. Brian Henson told David Owen of *The New Yorker,* "The show was so wacky, so out of left field, that the networks didn't want anything to do with it." Still Henson managed to expand his Muppet empire in other ways. Muppets appeared in the first seven episodes of NBC's *Saturday Night Live* during its first season in 1975.

Henson's pilot was viewed by a British producer named Lew Grade. He agreed to fund the first season of what became known as *The Muppet Show.* The first episodes aired in 1976, appearing in syndication in the United States. *The Muppet Show* used both Muppets and Hollywood stars in a parody of the backstage antics. *The Muppet Show* also introduced another popular Muppet, the femme fatale pig named Miss Piggy, who was perpetually in love with Kermit. At its peak, the show had 235 million viewers each week in over 100 countries, making it one of the most widely watched programs in history. After five years, Henson voluntarily ended the show in 1981, when he feared the quality might begin to diminish. As Henson Associates Vice President Michael Firth told Kristin McMurran of *People Weekly,* "every time he reaches a plateau, he rumbles around and comes up with something new."

Henson's horizons expanded in a number of ways after *The Muppet Show.* He created new television programs. In 1983, *Fraggle Rock* was introduced, featuring completely new Muppet characters. Airing on HBO in the United States, the program featured three species living below

to work. *Sam and Friends* also marked the beginning of the Muppets, Henson's own invention.

Unlike puppets, who have solid, unchanging heads, Muppets were softer, with mouths that moved and expressive eyes. The Muppets were more animated than puppets. As was written in *Broadcasting* magazine: "Jim Henson was the first and the best to create a new form of puppetry tailored to the technical constraints and newfound freedoms of television." One of Henson's most famous Muppets, Kermit the Frog, was introduced on *Sam and Friends* in 1955. The original Kermit was made from Henson's mother's old spring coat and a ping pong ball cut in half. Kermit did not begin as a frog but evolved into one. Similarly, Kermit's character gradually became more complex. As Stephen Harrigan wrote in *Life* magazine: "he [Henson] did not just perform Kermit, he was Kermit." Harrison Rainie in *U.S. News & World Report* quoted Henson as calling Kermit "literally my right hand."

In addition to Kermit, Henson created over 2000 Muppets in his lifetime. James Collins of *Time* wrote, "The beauty of the Muppets . . . was that they were cuddly but not too cuddly, and not only cuddly. There is satire as sly wit. . . . By adding just enough tartness to a sweet overall spirit, Henson purveyed a kind of innocence that was plausible for the modern imagination. His knowningness allowed us to accept his real gifts: wonder, delight, optimism."

Henson took six years to graduate from the University of Maryland because of the demands of his television show.

ground, the Fraggles, the Gords, and the Dozers. The show primarily followed five Fraggles, including Gobo and Mokey, and promoted harmony in living. *Fraggle Rock* aired for four season in the United States, Canada and several other countries. It was eventually syndicated in 96 countries. Of his experience on the show, producer Duncan Kenworthy told Kristin McMurran of *People Weekly*, "When Jim directs, there is an excitement and a delight. He draws the best from everyone. He keeps track of the small things that are so key to all puppet work on television." Henson also produced a successful cartoon based on *The Muppet Show* called *The Muppet Babies,* beginning in 1984, as well as numerous television specials.

Henson also produced television shows that were relatively unsuccessful, including *Jim Henson's The Storyteller,* a rather dark show which featured adapted folktales and stories from mythology. It was canceled after only a few episodes. In 1989, Henson produced a variety show called *The Jim Henson Hour.* It was canceled after ten episodes, though it eventually won an Emmy award. He also created a show for HBO called *The Ghost of Faffner Hall,* which featured music, Muppets, and special celebrity guests.

Henson had done some corporate work beginning in the late 1960s, when he produced short films and videos for IBM that touched on business topics. Beginning in 1985, Henson expanded his corporate work and produced more than two dozen short films and videos designed for business meetings, continually adding new titles. He also designed characters and creatures for other films via the Jim Henson Creature Shop, based in London, England. For example, he designed the face masks for the movie version of *The Teenage Mutant Ninja Turtles.*

Henson also dabbled in his own feature films. Characters from *The Muppet Show* were featured in a trio of films beginning in 1979 with *The Muppet Movie.* It was followed by 1981's *The Great Muppet Caper,* which was also Henson's directorial debut, and 1984's *The Muppets Take Manhattan.* All three movies did extremely well at the box office. His subsequent efforts, however, did not fare as well. *The Dark Crystal,* with all new Muppets, made a poor box office showing in 1982. The dark fantasy, *Labyrinth,* was also a box office failure. These failings affected Henson deeply, though he was wealthy and had had good business sense throughout his career. Though a quiet, kind man, Henson was also a strong leader who valued employees and let them have fun with their jobs. Harrigan of *Life* magazine described him as "a quiet, authoritative, beloved man without a trace of aggression but with a whim of steel."

In 1989, Henson began negotiating a merger with Disney Corporation to reduce the pressure of running his own business. Had the sale been completed, Henson's already large fortune would have increased by an estimated $100 to $180 million. Puppeteer Kevin Clash told Harrigan of *Life,* "He wanted those characters [the Muppets] to be around when he wasn't and the main company that could do that was Disney." Henson had doubts about the merger because Disney's corporate policies were quite the opposite of his. As Owen of *The New Yorker* explained, "To Henson and

his associates, the Muppets were not products; they were friends."

While the negotiations were still in progress, Henson became seriously ill. A kind and patient man, Henson did not alert a doctor or visit a hospital because he did not believe he was sick; nor did he want to bother anyone. He had been raised as a Christian Scientist, a religion that does not subscribe to conventional health care practices. By the time he sought medical attention, it was too late to treat him. Henson died an untimely death from an aggressive form of pneumonia called Group A streptococcus in New York City on May 16, 1990.

Henson left his company to his children, as he and his wife had separated in 1986. His son Brian continued the family tradition by becoming a puppeteer and president of Jim Henson Productions. The deal with Disney was never completed, but the companies did do some business together, most notably by including the Muppets in Walt Disney World and producing one of Henson's last ideas, the television show, *Dinosaurs.* At the time of Henson's death, James Collins in *Time* magazine wrote, "Through his work, he helped sustain the qualities of fancifulness, warmth and consideration that have been so threatened by our coarse, cynical age."

## Further Reading

Brownstone and Irene Franck, *People in the News,* Macmillan, 1991.
Curran, Daniel, *Guide to American Cinema, 1965-95,* Greenwood, 1998.
Monaco, James, *The Encyclopedia of Film,* Perigee, 1991.
*Broadcasting,* May 21, 1990.
*Forbes,* June 11, 1990; November 21, 1994.
*Fortune,* February 4, 1985.
*Life,* July 1990.
*Maclean's,* May 28, 1990.
*Newsweek,* May 28, 1990.
*The New York Times,* May 17, 1990.
*The New Yorker,* August 16, 1993.
*People Weekly,* July 17, 1983; Spring 1990; May 28, 1990; June 18, 1990; April 8, 1991.
*Time,* May 28, 1990; June 8, 1998.
*U.S. News & World Report,* May 28, 1990; July 2, 1990. □

# Milton Hershey

**After enduring years of failure, Milton Hershey (1857–1945) built a business empire as the world's first mass producer of chocolate bars. Through generous donations, he used his entire fortune to help those less fortunate than himself.**

Milton Snavely Hershey was born on a central Pennsylvania farm in Derry Township, on September 13, 1857, to Henry H. Hershey and Fannie B. Snavely. Hershey inherited the entrepreneurial spirit from his father who moved the family often, attempting a variety of business ventures, including farming and cough drop manufacturing. Because of all the moves, Hershey's early schooling was haphazard, ending after the fourth grade.

At the age of 14, Hershey went to work as an apprentice with the printer of a German-American newspaper in Lancaster, Pennsylvania. After dropping a tray of type, made up of the hundreds of tiny metal pieces once used to print newspaper pages, he was fired. His mother found him a second apprenticeship, this time with Joseph H. Royer, a confectioner in Lancaster, Pennsylvania. From 1872 to 1876, Hershey helped Royer with his candy-making business and ice cream parlor, learning skills that would later help him build his own candy empire.

## Tried and Tried Again

At the age of 19, Hershey parted company with Royer and started his own candy business in Philadelphia. He hoped to find an eager buying public in the thousands of people visiting the city for the Great Centennial Exposition celebrating the 100th anniversary of the Declaration of Independence. With money he borrowed from his uncle and the help of his mother and aunt, Hershey began making taffy and caramels, which were sold from a pushcart. The business scraped by for six years. In 1882, Hershey collapsed from the strain of working all day (selling the candy) and all night (manufacturing it). Forced to admit failure, Hershey closed up shop.

Hershey decided to seek his fortune in Denver, Colorado, along with his father, who had also moved west. He worked for a candy company in Denver, where he learned how to improve the quality of his chocolate by adding fresh milk. With his father, he moved to Chicago, and opened yet another candy business. Like the others, it also failed.

Moving to New York City in the spring of 1883, Hershey worked for a candy business called Huyler and Company, and started manufacturing Hershey's Fine Candies. Unfortunately, sugar prices increased and Hershey lost his candy-making machinery. In 1885, he returned to Lancaster, Pennsylvania.

After so many failures, his aunt and uncle refused to loan Hershey any more money. He became partners with William Henry Lebkicher, a man he had hired in Philadelphia. The two men scraped together enough money to start the Lancaster Caramel Company, where Hershey devised a formula using fresh milk to make "Hershey's Crystal A" caramels. Finally, he found success. An English importer ordered $2,500 worth of caramels to ship to England. The proceeds allowed Hershey to expand his business.

Borrowing $250,000 from the Importers and Traders Bank of New York City, Hershey expanded once again. The Jim Cracks, Roly Polies, Melbas, Empires, Icelets, and Cocoanut Ices sold very well. By 1893, the Lancaster Caramel Company had opened candy-making plants in Mount Joy, Pennsylvania, Chicago, and Geneva, Illinois, employing 1,400 people.

## Established Hershey Chocolate Company

Hershey used the World's Columbian Exposition in Chicago—celebrating the 400th anniversary of Christopher Columbus's arrival in the New World—as an opportunity to study chocolate making as it was practiced in Europe. He examined chocolate-rolling machinery from the J.M. Lehmann Company of Dresden, Germany, finally deciding to buy it for his own company. At that time, milk chocolate was regarded as a luxury imported item, made by hand in a secret Swiss process. Hershey was confident that he could mass-produce enough chocolate to satisfy the demand of the American public. In 1894, he opened the Hershey Chocolate Company, producing breakfast cocoa, baking chocolate, and sweet chocolate coatings for the caramels.

After perfecting his recipe, Hershey expanded the business to produce 114 kinds of chocolates, including novelty items like chocolate cigars and chocolate bicycles. In order to focus all his attention on the chocolate business, Hershey sold the Lancaster Caramel Company in 1900 for one million dollars to his competitor, the American Caramel Company. He kept exclusive rights to supply dipping chocolate to the company, however, and used the money from the sale to build a new chocolate factory.

In 1897, Hershey purchased the Derry Church homestead where he had been born, intending to give the farm to his parents. Instead, he decided to use the rural Dauphin County land to build his chocolate plant, since it was ideally situated in an area full of dairies, and had plenty of fresh water necessary for cooling the factory's output. He bought 1,500 acres of adjacent property and, in 1903, began construction on the chocolate plant. Hershey knew his workers would need a place to live and raise their families. In conjunction with the new factory he planned and built an entire utopian community, complete with houses, a post office, churches, shops, schools, and even a trolley car for transportation.

Hershey planned that his new factory would mass-produce only one product, making it affordable for everyone. Working with his recipe makers, he developed a formula for milk chocolate that allowed for mass production. In February 1900, he introduced the milk chocolate Hershey Bar, which sold for pennies and brought affordable chocolate to the masses. The bars were so popular that Hershey found he did not need to advertise. Although the company continued its no advertising policy until 1968, Hershey was fond of the occasional self-promotion. One of the first automobiles in Pennsylvania bore the Hershey name painted on its side, drawing attention and orders for the Hershey salesmen who zoomed around at the car's top speed of nine miles per hour. Despite its cost of $2,000, a huge sum at that time, the electric car generated crowds and headlines wherever it went.

The company and the town prospered. In 1908, the Hershey Chocolate Company incorporated. By 1915, the plant had expanded to cover 35 acres, with sales growing just as quickly. Within 20 years, sales had increased to $20 million. The community, with its chocolate-related street names, offered housing, sewerage, electricity, schools, stores, a hospital, and fire department, a park and zoo, as well as a trolley line to bring in workers from neighboring towns.

In the years following the collapse of the stock market in 1929, nearly one third of United States workers lost their jobs. Anxious to help his own employees—plus take advantage of the Depression's low construction costs—Hershey embarked on a building project in 1930 that included a hotel, a high school, community building, sports arena, and a new air-conditioned office building. The Hotel Hershey incorporated his favorite details from hotels worldwide. Hershey would later note proudly that none of his workers were ever laid off during the Depression; in fact, he hired 600 additional laborers. The company diversified and branched out, making different kinds of candy, including the foil-wrapped Hershey's Kisses (introduced in 1907), Mr. Goodbar, the Krackel Bar, and Hershey's Miniatures. After losing money on a sugar deal, Hershey bought land in Cuba, where he began growing and processing his own sugar cane.

Despite efforts to anticipate his workers' every need, some employees attempted to form a union in 1937, to protest working conditions that included a 60-hour work week. The Congress of Industrial Organizations (CIO) shut down the factory with a strike that only ended when local dairy farmers, whose livelihoods depended on selling milk to the company, physically attacked the workers. By 1940, the American Federation of Labor (AFL) had organized a union at the plant, creating an association to promote and protect the rights of the workers.

### Hershey's Living Legacy

In 1898, Milton Hershey married Catherine Elizabeth "Kitty" Sweeney, an Irish-Catholic from Jamestown, New York. Anxious to use their wealth to help those less fortunate than themselves, the Hersheys founded a school for orphaned boys in 1909. Originally called the Hershey Industrial School, it was designed to train boys in farming and industrial trades so they would become able to support themselves. After Kitty Hershey died in 1915, Hershey donated his entire fortune—$60 million—in a trust to the school. It was renamed the Milton Hershey School and expanded to serve children of both sexes from disrupted homes from kindergarten through high school. The 10,000-acre school, through its trust, owns 40 percent of the stock of Hershey Foods, and controls 75 percent of the corporation's voting shares. "I don't think I'd be alive today without that place," Hershey School graduate Randy Zerr told Eric Ries of *Techniques.* "If there's anything I can do for the school, I will." Zerr took advantage of the school's horticultural program and works as a groundskeeper at Franklin and Marshall College in Lancaster, Pennsylvania. Many Hershey graduates go on to college. Some have even graduated to executive positions within the Hershey Chocolate Company.

The Hershey Chocolate Company continued to create new products. During World War II, they developed an unmeltable, four-ounce bar with extra calories and vitamins, which could be used as emergency provisions for soldiers and sailors. The company made more than a billion of the "Field Ration D" bars. In 1942, the U.S. government gave Hershey the Army/Navy E award for his civilian contribution to the war effort. In 1995, he was honored once again by being pictured on a postage stamp commemorating him as part of the U.S. Postal Service's Great Americans series.

Hershey died in Hershey, Pennsylvania on October 13, 1945, one year after his retirement as chairman of the board. He was 88 years old. By the end of his life Hershey had donated most of his money to his town and the school he built. After his death, the sale of Hershey's personal possessions raised less than $20,000. The chocolate factory he built in Hershey, Pennsylvania, remains the largest in the world. In 1963, the Hershey Chocolate Corporation donated $50 million to build the Milton S. Hershey Medical Center of Pennsylvania State University, which houses a hospital, medical school, clinics, and research facilities.

The town of Hershey, Pennsylvania is still home to about 12,000 people and draws more than 30 million visitors each year. They come to see Hershey Park, which boasts a roller coaster, Ferris wheel, other rides, and a visitor's center. The center, built in 1973 to accommodate the massive crowds packing the factory tours, draws more visitors annually than the White House. Guests can take a tour through a mock chocolate factory that includes a ride through a simulated roasting oven, and culminates with samples of Hershey chocolate.

### Further Reading

*American National Biography,* edited by John A. Garraty and Mark C. Carnes, Oxford University Press, 1999.

Morton, Marcia and Frederic, *Chocolate: An Illustrated History,* Crown Publishers, Inc., 1986.

Simon, Charnan, *Milton Hershey: Chocolate King, Town Builder,* Children's Press, 1998.

*American History,* March/April 1997.

*American History Illustrated* March-April 1994.

*Business Week,* February 22, 1999.

*Candy Industry,* October 1995.

*Chicago Tribune,* 1999.

*Dallas Morning News,* 1997.

*Detroit Free Press,* 1999.

*Techniques,* April 1, 1998.

Hersheys Corp., www.hersheys.com, (February 24, 1999). □

# Tommy Hilfiger

**Tommy Hilfiger (born 1952) has brought the fashion industry to its knees with his enormous success in the retail clothing market. His all-American designs appeal simultaneously to everyone from 60-year-old golfers to gangsta rappers, a near-impossible feat in the demographics-oriented rag trade. But the key to Hilfiger's professional triumph isn't the clothes; it's the label.**

Tommy Hilfiger has been referred to as the Ralph Lauren of a new generation, but he has clearly come unto his own in the world of fashion. With successful lines of men's clothing, women's clothing, home furnishings, and a unisex fragrance, Hilfiger became the fashion guru of the 1990s and the biggest thing to hit the fashion industry in a decade. An enticement to a wide variety of consumers, his designs are casual while his prices remain moderate. Hilfiger's most praiseworthy achievement, however, is his precision of brand execution. Alan Millstein, editor of *The Fashion Network Report* trade magazine, described the method behind Hilfiger's success to *USA Today*: "It's a combination of great marketing, merchandising, and hype. He's packaged better than any designer since Ralph Lauren."

## Small-Time Start in Retail

Tommy Hilfiger was born in 1952. The second of nine children, he grew up in Elmira, New York where he devoted hours to studying the music and styles that were popular in the glamour centers of culture like New York and London. He idolized rock stars, especially Mick Jagger. But Hilfiger didn't possess any extraordinary talents or an academic background that would propel him to success. However, he did have a certain charm and style that he supposedly inherited from his father, Richard "Hippo" Hilfiger, a watchmaker by trade. Although, Hilfiger has described himself as a scrawny, dyslexic kid who became the class clown to mask his embarrassment over less-than-average grades.

Hilfiger was still a high school senior when he set out to provide the young people of Elmira with bellbottom jeans. In 1969, he drove to New York City where he spent his life savings of $150 on 20 pairs of Landlubber jeans. He brought them back to Elmira and opened a hippie clothing shop called The People's Place. By the time he was 26, this shop had expanded into a chain of seven stores, scattered throughout upstate New York and catering to the college campus crowds. Hilfiger ran the stores for ten years, until the retail market went into an economic slump and he went bankrupt. Hilfiger discussed his business' failure with Lisa Armstrong of the *London Times.* "I was hard on myself," he said. "I vowed never to fall into sloppy work habits again. Money, after a certain point, is not what drives me." He admitted that fear of failure is his impetus to succeed.

Hilfiger never went to design school, but he began to experiment with fashion design in the early 1970s, while he was running The People's Place. By 1979, he had sold his business and moved to Manhattan with his wife Susan Cirona, who had been a creative director of his People's Place boutiques. He began to work as a freelancer and befriended a number of people in the business, including the late designer Perry Ellis. Within five years Hilfiger was working under contract with Asian textile mogul Mohan Murjani, the man behind the trendy Gloria Vanderbilt jeans. In 1986, Murjani and Hilfiger placed a billboard on Times Square that announced Hilfiger would soon dominate men's clothing, although at the time he was hardly known. Under Murjani's management, the Tommy Hilfiger menswear collection grossed $5 million in the first year and $10 million in the second. However, these were modest sales by fashion industry standards. In 1988, Hilfiger bought out Murjani and joined Silas Chou, a Hong Kong clothing manufacturer. By that time, the company was bringing in around $25 million a year. They began their new endeavor cautiously, hiring experienced executives from well-known companies like Ralph Lauren and Liz Claiborne. Three years later they took the company public. By 1999 the company was grossing more than half a billion dollars and was the highest-valued clothing stock on the exchange.

## An All-American Look

Although he is not readily acknowledged as a true designer, Hilfiger is incessantly compared to fellow American designers Calvin Klein and Ralph Lauren. He has admitted to redesigning and updating clothes rather than creating brand new fashions, but that hardly matters to the throngs who adore the red, white, and blue rectangular Tommy label. Hilfiger threads inspire devotion from consumers who love his all-American chinos, chambray shirts, knit polo shirts, jeans, and other wardrobe essentials. Jodie L. Ahern summed up the allure in her *Minneapolis Star Tribune* report: "His clothes are classic, comfortable, high-quality garb that appeal to young and old and are priced in the upper-moderate range. It's really that simple." Hilfiger consciously eschews the virtuoso fashion-designer image, following the lead of mainstream retail stores like The Gap and Banana Republic, which provide stylish, well-made clothing at reasonable prices. Nonetheless, he was gratified to win Menswear Designer of the Year in 1995 after having been snubbed the year before when the Council of Fashion Designers of America left the category unawarded.

Though some disdain Hilfiger's designs, challenging his status as a true "designer," it is difficult to criticize the businessman behind the brand name. "Tommy will never be on the designer rack," Millstein admitted to *USA Today.* "But he's powerful enough to have become a brand name. That's what every designer really wants to be." Hilfiger understands the difference between designers and "brands." He admitted to the *Minneapolis Star Tribune,* "I treat my company the way the French designers treat their Saint-Laurent or House of Chanel. We do fashion shows, we use the best photographers, the best models, we hire the best people, we believe the show is very important. But beyond that facade we make sure that we're very tedious in building our brand. It's a designer brand. Calvin and Ralph and Donna (Karan) and Armani are designer brands, but some of the other designers are not designer brands. Once you become a recognized brand the licensing becomes incredibly profitable." Most designers take the traditional route to fashion fame, beginning with an expensive couture line, which few ordinary women buy. They generally cash in on their fame later by lending their name to mass market clothes. Hilfiger used music videos like a catwalk to reach the young, fashionable crowd. The aggressive construction of his empire and the advertising onslaught, which costs up to $20 million a year, are what has made Hilfiger a household name.

People are attracted the sense of fashion they get from the everyday clothes. The distinctive Tommy label gives them the recognition and acceptance they crave. Hilfiger, who built his company on a brand, is very particular about what the Tommy logo represents. "It is important that my logo communicates who I am to the consumer," he tells the *Minneapolis Star Tribune.* "It has to say, 'I am about movement, energy, fun, color, quality, detail, American spirit, status, style, and value.' The brand must relate to the consumers' sensibilities. Whether they are based upon sports, music, entertainment, politics, or pop culture—it must have the cool factor."

### Celebrity Chic

One of a designer's best marketing tools is dressing celebrities. Hilfiger established himself first with young rappers whose influence was glorified through music videos and television. In 1992, he dressed Snoop Doggy Dogg for a Saturday Night Live appearance. Other artists soon adopted his clothes, and the relationship between clothes and music became so tight that Hilfiger wound up in rap lyrics. Since then, Hilfiger's trendy status has attracted many more big names to his designs. He has dressed music stars like the Fugees, Bruce Springsteen, Mariah Carey, David Bowie, and TLC. Michael Jackson wore a Hilfiger sweater in promotions for his album *HIStory.* Some of his fans include celebrities like Leonardo DiCaprio, Sidney Poitier, and Quincy Jones. He's also used names to sell his merchandise in print ads. Errol Flynn's grandson, Luke, and Jackson Browne's son, Ethan, were used to sell Hilfiger's fragrance. Hilfiger originally set out to dress celebrities and has specifi-

cally targeted the young, up-and-coming, cool crowd. This has been an enormously successful strategy for the designer whose company experiences a surge in sales whenever a name like DiCaprio appears in Hilfiger clothes.

Celebrities lend their assets to Hilfiger's merchandise, but his real customer base is with real people, especially kids. Hilfiger may appeal to all ages, but what sets him apart from other designers is his lock on the youth market. Hilfiger is known to be a kid at heart, a favorable prerequisite to selling to kids. His love of all things fun is manifested in his office decor: a red leather jacket signed by Bruce Springsteen, photos of Mick Jagger and John Lennon, electric Gibson guitars, a Superbowl football signed by Floyd Little, and books on trains, vintage convertibles, and sports.

Hilfiger has also been anointed as fashion's nice guy by the national press. The image is supported by his philanthropic deeds. He has been involved in the raising of money for multiple sclerosis research (one of his sisters suffers from the disease), sponsoring T-shirt sales during one of Sheryl Crow's concert tours and then donating the money for breast cancer research, and raising money for a youth center serving lower-income families.

Hilfiger says he would like to be known as an important American designer. With a $600 million a year business, some would consider him pretty important. He owns a quarter of the company and is personally valued at around $100 million. However, Hilfiger's popularity with the masses may be a signal that his decline as an innovator for young style-setters is imminent. The Hilfiger name has saturated the market and is already becoming passe in the urban environments that often define what is up-and-coming. Nevertheless, Wall Street continues to show enthusiasm for Hilfiger stock. The company is hoping to stay on top of its brand development, which will include a broad expansion of the product line and more overseas sales. Hilfiger maintains to the *Albany Times Union,* "the key is to keep coming back, but coming back in different ways."

Hilfiger and his wife have four children and live in a 22-room estate on a converted farm in Greenwich, Connecticut. He also owns homes on Nantucket and the Caribbean island of Mustique.

### Further Reading

*Albany Times Union,* January 25, 1998.
*Daily News Record,* November 2, 1998.
*London Daily Telegraph,* August 22, 1998.
*London Independent,* August 4, 1996.
*London Times,* February 24, 1999.
*Minneapolis Star Tribune,* June 22, 1996.
*Portland Oregonian,* December 13, 1998.
*USA Today,* June 14, 1995. □

# Barron Hilton

**Barron Hilton (born 1927), son of the founder of Hilton Hotels, became head of the company in 1966. Disparaged by some as the lucky son of Conrad**

**Hilton, he led the company into the gaming industry and was one of the first in the hotel industry to use management leaseback deals.**

Conrad N. Hilton bought a small Texas inn in 1919. From that purchase grew the Hilton Hotels Corporation. Hilton's philosophy about the hotel business was that no hotel should be built unless there was a need for it. Once need was determined, the right location had to be chosen and construction had to be financed in a conservative manner. Conrad Hilton's sons, William Barron (known as Barron), born on October 23, 1927 in Dallas, Texas, and Eric, born in 1930, followed their father into business.

In 1959, Conrad Hilton started the Carte Blanche credit card business, with Barron Hilton in charge. The company lost $2 million in six years, before it was sold to Citibank. Barron Hilton was very interested in making gambling a part of the Hilton empire. This led him to move the company's focus away from hotels. In 1964, the company spun off its international hotels to shareholders because Barron argued that the parts were worth more than the whole, a move that some questioned. In 1967, Barron convinced his father, the biggest stockholder of Hilton International, to sell his shares to Trans World Airlines (TWA) in exchange for that company's stock. Barron, an aviation enthusiast, thought the TWA stock would go up in value, but instead it plummeted. Barron Hilton took over as president and chief executive officer of the Hilton Hotels Corporation in February 1966.

When Conrad died in 1979, at the age of 91, Barron became the new chairman of the board.

## Started Leasebacks

Hilton was one of the first businesspeople to use management leaseback deals. In 1975, the company sold half its equity in six major hotels, but continued to manage the properties in return for a percentage of room revenues and gross profits. This was one of the first management leaseback deals in the hotel industry. He received $83 million in the deal, which was used to buy back 20 percent of the company's stock. This turned out to be a smart purchase because the stock increased in value sevenfold.

In 1972, Hilton bought control of two Las Vegas casinos, paying $112 million for them. Growth in the hotel part of his empire came from expanding the number of hotels it franchised. His strategy of owning very few properties outright was later imitated by other hotel companies in the 1980s.

Seemingly a contrarian in the 1980s, Hilton sold many of his assets when others in the industry were building. Other hotel chains developed new formats such as suite hotels and vacation ownership resorts. He watched and waited. Some critics viewed him as being overly conservative, but his waiting paid off. When he saw which of the new formats were successful, he came up with similar products of his own. This watch and wait strategy caused the company's stock to increase in value.

When his father died in 1979, he left Hilton several hundred thousand dollars in cash. The bulk of his fortune, almost 13.5 million shares of Hilton Hotels stock, went to the Conrad Hilton Foundation to help Roman Catholic nuns worldwide. Hilton controlled another 3.4 percent of the 25 million shares. He claimed his father's will gave him the option to buy the stake from the foundation at the 1979 price of $24 a share, a total of $330 million less than the 1988 market price. A California superior court ruled against Hilton in 1986. The settlement, reached in November of 1989, gave four million shares to Hilton outright, 3.5 million shares to the foundation, and six million shares to a trust, with Hilton serving as executor. He was allowed to keep 60 percent of any dividends paid on the trust's shares for the next 20 years. After the year 2008, those payments and ownership of the shares revert to the foundation. The settlement meant that Hilton could vote the foundation's shares, giving him control of over 25 percent of the outstanding stock in the company. In April 1998, the Securities and Exchange Commission approved the sale of as many as 24 million Hilton shares from the charitable trust he controls.

## Took a Gamble

Hilton, an avid poker player, wanted to increase his company's involvement in the gaming industry. He was denied a gaming license in Atlantic City by the New Jersey Casino Control Commission in 1985, when alleged ties to organized crime were discovered. The commission stated that Hilton's 13-year relationship with Sidney Korshak, a Chicago labor attorney associated with organized crime figures, was the main reason the gaming license was denied. Hilton had already spent $320 million to build the casino, "the largest undertaking in the company's history," according to the 1984 annual report. Hilton sold his newly built property to Donald Trump, a real estate and casino czar. Hilton ended relations with Korshak in 1984, because the New Jersey authorities made it clear that Korshak was an obstacle to getting a license in Atlantic City. In 1991, Hilton finally received permission to operate a casino in Atlantic City.

Describing Hilton's caution in hotels and boldness in gaming, Amy Barrett wrote in *Financial World* in 1992, "Barron Hilton has been agonizingly prudent. During the past decade, while much of the hotel industry took part in a frenzy of overbuilding and outrageously priced buying . . . Hilton Hotels quietly passed. . . . Hilton actually sold assets in the second half of the Eighties. . . . But within the past year, Barron Hilton has undergone an awesome change in style, trading in his cautious stance for a gambler's studied swagger. His . . . company is leading the charge to build new casinos as a wave of legalized gaming rolls across the U.S. Readying a riverboat casino in New Orleans and joining two other gaming heavyweights . . . Hilton is no longer content to sit back and let others test the waters." In 1991, over half of the company's $185 million in operating income came from gaming.

### Bollenbach Took Helm

In the 1990s, the question of choosing a successor arose. Hilton's son David, born in 1952, and head of operations at the Flamingo Hilton in Las Vegas, was a possibility. His brother, Eric, who runs the company's international real estate development, was also under consideration. In 1996, Stephen Bollenbach, the former finance chief at Walt Disney Co., was named CEO of Hilton Hotels, becoming the first non-family CEO in the company's history. *Fortune* said of Bollenbach's new job, "Lazy and indecisive, Hilton has rested on its name in hotels and gaming while rivals such as Marriott and Promus rapidly expanded their franchises— and profits. Bollenbach will drive for growth in hotels, an industry that is reviving rapidly. Hilton carries a conservative amount of debt, seemingly odd for a company that owns casinos but catnip for Bollenbach, an apostle of leverage. He's going to roll the dice, pledging not only to buy big urban hotels but to challenge Marriott as well by building a slew of suburban inns. 'Now that the excess supply is gone,' he says, 'this is a wonderful time to grow in the hotel business.'"

In the late 1990s, Hilton Hotels was the third-largest lodging company in the world. It owned, managed, and franchised more than 250 hotels worldwide, including New York City's Waldorf-Astoria, Hilton Hawaiian Village, and Chicago's Palmer House Hilton. The company plans on expanding the Hilton Garden Inns, targeted at budget-conscious business travelers. In 1998, the company purchased the Mississippi gaming operations of Grand Casinos. Hilton then split into two companies so it could focus solely on hotels. The new company, Park Place Entertainment, now owns all of Hilton's gambling operations. Hilton had considered a split for years, hoping to boost his company's stock price by capitalizing on investors' willingness to pay much higher prices for lodging firms than for gaming companies.

### Recreational Activities

Hilton has been a private pilot since 1947 with multi-engine, helicopter, glider, and lighter-than-air ratings. He served on the Experimental Aircraft Association Museum Board. In 1956, Hilton formed the Air Finance Corporation for the purpose of leasing aircraft to commercial airlines. He and his wife, Marilyn, own a Nevada ranch. There they fly a hot-air balloon, a helicopter, and various airplanes. Hilton also enjoys shooting clay pigeons and fishing for trout and bass in his two private ponds.

Hilton is a director of The Conrad N. Hilton Foundation, The Southern California Visitors Council, and the Executive Council on Foreign Diplomats. He is an honorary director of the Boy Scouts of America and of the Great Western Council. Hilton is a Trustee of the City of Hope, Saint John's Hospital and Health Center Foundation in Santa Monica, California, the World Mercy Fund, the Eisenhower Medical Center, and the Criminal Justice Legal Foundation. He is a Chevalier of Confrerie de la Chaine Des Rotisseurs, a Magisterial Knight of the Sovereign Military Order of Malta, a member of Conquistadores del Cielo, the International Order of St. Hubert, the PEACE Foundation Council, and the National Honorary Advisory Committee of the Naval Aviation Museum Foundation. In 1986, the University of Houston conferred an honorary degree of Doctor of Humane Letters, and he was inducted into the Culinary Institute of America's Hall of Fame.

In 1998, Hilton received the honorary title of Knight Commander of St. Gregory the Great, a Catholic honor. He and his wife are generous donors to Catholic causes. Hilton has also received the Ellis Island Medal of Honor and the Freedom of Flight Award. On the list of the 400 Richest People in America, hotelier William Barron Hilton came in last, with a fortune of $500 million.

### Further Reading

*Financial World,* April 4, 1989; May 26, 1992.
*Forbes,* January 25, 1988.
*Fortune,* May 27, 1985; March 4, 1996.
*Nation's Restaurant News,* July 18, 1988; December 19, 1988.
*Travel Weekly,* February 23, 1987. □

# Ben Hogan

**Frequently revered, yet often misunderstood, Ben Hogan (1912–1997) carried a mystique and popularity in golfing circles experienced by few others. He became a phenomenon in the 1940s and 1950s, taking considerable numbers of Professional Golfers Association (PGA) events. Hogan gained a reputation for hard work and excellence both on the links and off.**

ogan was born in Dublin, Texas, on August 13, 1912, to Chester and Clara Hogan. Hogan's father, a blacksmith, took his own life when Ben was nine. His mother moved the family to Fort Worth shortly after her husband died. Hogan went to Fort Worth schools but never finished high school, opting for work instead. He sold newspapers at the train station and would caddy at Glen Gardens Country Club in Fort Worth whenever he could get the work. Jerry Potter, writing for *USA Today,* said that sometimes Hogan would save two newspapers and make a bed in the bunker near the 18th green. He would sleep there, so he would be first in the caddie line the next morning.

Potter quoted former PGA Tour player Gardner Dickinson, a Hogan student: "Ben was a little bitty fellow, so they'd throw him to the back of the line," Dickinson said. "That's how he got so mean." While some would call Hogan mean, others would say he just kept to himself. There is no question that, while polite on the course, Hogan was often brusque at other times, developing an enduring reputation as a tight-lipped competitor. It could be argued that his demeanor simply illustrated his penchant for action instead of words. Hogan was certainly not a natural when it came to golf. He would diligently work on his game, striving for perfection.

## Early Struggles

There could be only one reason for Hogan's perseverance: he loved the game. In 1929, 17-year-old Hogan turned pro and began playing in PGA tournaments full time

two years later with little more than pocket change. According to Potter, his early efforts were totally frustrating. "He had a long, loose swing that produced shots that were wild," explained Potter. "First he hit a big hook, then he hit a big slice." Hogan would not win a PGA tour event until 1938, seven years after turning pro.

In 1931 and again in 1937, Hogan attempted major tournaments without success. John Omicinski, writing for Gannett News Service, said that Hogan's game did not improve until he switched from a right-handed to a left-handed swing in the late 1930s and got "some rather simple grip tips from friend Henry Picard." He then "lost his duckhook and start smashing shots of such purity that people came from miles around just to watch them fly."

In 1937, Hogan and his wife, Valerie (whom he married in 1935), were down to their last $5 when he won $380 at the PGA tournament in Oakland, California. Although he only placed second, it was the incentive Hogan needed to keep at his game. Asked why he worked so hard, Hogan once explained to Potter: "I was trying to make a living. I'd failed twice to make the Tour. I had to learn to beat the people I was playing." Hogan claimed he never had a golf lesson, instead learning everything he could be watching experienced golfers at their game. "I watched the way they swung the club, the way they hit the ball," Hogan explained to Potter. Hard work on the practice green has become commonplace in a touring pro's regime, but it was unheard of in Hogan's day.

## Money Board Leader

Hogan was the leader on the money boards in 1940, winning the PGA's Harry Vardon trophy for his $10,656 income that year. Between 1939 and 1941 he finished in the money in 56 consecutive tournaments. In the PGA Oakland Open in 1941 Hogan tied the course record at the time with a 62. He was leader on the money board again in 1941 and in 1942, but had a two-year break from golf when he was inducted into the Army Air Force in 1943.

Hogan came on strong after his release from the Army. Some of his earliest wins after returning stateside were paid in war bonds. Hogan had a bout with influenza, however, that set him back, and he suffered through a serious putting slump. Jamie Diaz, writing in *Sports Illustrated,* said, "In 1946, Hogan suffered what some consider to be the most devastating back-to-back losses in major championship history. At the Masters, he had an 18-foot putt to win his first major PGA tournament. Hogan ran his first putt three feet past the hole, then missed coming back. Two months later at the U.S. Open at Canterbury in Cleveland, he was in an identical situation on the final green. Hogan three-putted again. Instead of ending his career, Hogan went on to the PGA Championship at Portland Golf Club and won, beginning his never-equaled hot streak in the majors."

Hogan was again the top money winner in 1946, and two years later became the first golfer to win three majors in the same year: the Western Open, the National Open, and the U.S. Open. He had finally hit his stride. Hogan would win nine of the 16 majors he entered from the 1946 PGA through the 1953 British Open. Still, Diaz claimed, "because of his inscrutable manner, there was always a sense that he carried something deep within that was even more interesting than his talent."

## A Devastating Accident

Perhaps it was Hogan's equanimity in defeat that so impressed the gallery. He possessed a grace and resilience that are emulated by many even today. Or perhaps it was his childhood poverty and his diligent effort to master his game that served to strengthen his character and his resolve. One of his most challenging bouts with adversity came early in 1949, a year that had started with Hogan winning two of the first four events of the season. On February 2, while he and his wife were driving his Cadillac back to Fort Worth, Hogan was hit head-on by a Greyhound bus. To protect his wife, Hogan threw his body over to the right, avoiding the steering column that could have easily crushed him. Instead, he suffered such severe injuries that doctors predicted he would never walk again. Hogan had another near brush with death before surgeons operated to stop blood clots from entering his heart.

Hogan not only taught himself to walk again, he also taught himself to play golf again. In rehabilitation treatment for ten months, some have claimed that Hogan practiced his swing until his hands bled. A mere 16 months after the head-on collision, Hogan walked through excruciating leg cramps to win the U.S. Open at Merion. As a testament to his dogged determination, Hogan was named Player of the Year in 1950. Sam Snead had earned the money title, won 11 events, and set a scoring-average record that clearly entitled him to the honor. But according to Diaz, "Snead was a golfer, and a great one. Hogan, because of his dedication and courage, was a hero."

## The Hogan Mystique

His fabulous on-the-course performances coupled with his silent, often aloof behavior created a mystique around Hogan that lives on today. He was often portrayed as stoic and severe, even downright rude by some. But Hogan actually preferred his actions to speak louder than his words. Often cutting young golfers off before they could complete a sentence, he would refer those seeking tips to one of his books. Hogan was always the consummate professional, never showing emotion on the course or suffering from distraction. His unwavering focus and ability to place the ball precisely where he intended contributed to the almost eerie presence he brought to the greens.

There are countless stories of his kindness to kids, his affability with some reporters, and his integrity and personal code of honor. Some say the harrowing experience of actually witnessing his father's suicide deeply impacted Hogan's ability to get close to people. Even players like Byron Nelson, who drove with Hogan to tournaments and grew up with him in Fort Worth, would say that they had a hard time keeping in touch. But his regard and admiration for his wife was widely known. Hogan's reputation as a superb athlete and the mystery of his subdued persona made him appealing to the masses. In 1951, Glenn Ford stared in *Follow the Sun,* a biographical film about Hogan and his wife.

## Won Three Major Tournaments

Hogan won six major championships after his car accident. In 1948, his book, *Power Golf,* a collection of golf do's and don'ts, was published; it was followed in 1957 by the best-selling *Five Lessons: The Modern Fundamentals of Golf,* co-authored with Herbert Warren Wind. In 1953, he won the Masters, U.S. Open, and British Open—returning to New York City for a ticker-tape parade. The same year, he started the Ben Hogan Co., a golf club manufacturing business.

Despite his success, the auto accident had made walking the courses particularly difficult for Hogan. Although he limited himself to seven tournaments a year since the accident, chronic pain would impede his future golf efforts. After his win in the 1953 British Open at Carnoustie, Diaz notes that Hogan "endured bitter disappointment in pursuit of a record fifth U.S. Open title."

Hogan's final PGA title victory came at the 1959 Colonial Open. In 1960, Hogan sold his golf-club company to AMF. According to Ron Sirak of the *Associated Press,* Hogan "tied for the lead in the 1960 U.S. Open until, gambling for the pin, he hit a ball that spun backward off the green and into the water on the next-to-last hole. Arnold Palmer won the tournament, with 20-year-old Jack Nicklaus finishing second. Hogan had passed the title of Greatest in the Game to a new generation."

Hogan became even more reclusive in his later years, and was rarely seen in public after his last PGA event in 1971. He retired to his hometown of Fort Worth, where the Colonial Country Club still bears a statue of his likeness at the entry plaza. Hospitalized for two months with pneumonia in 1987, Hogan dropped 30 of his scant 140 pounds. In 1995, he underwent emergency surgery for colon cancer and never really regained his previous vigor. His wife remained his constant companion and caregiver, even after Hogan was diagnosed with Alzheimer's disease. Hogan died on July 25, 1997 in Fort Worth, Texas, after suffering a major stroke. He was 84 years old.

With 63 victories, nine major championships, four U.S. Open titles, the career Grand Slam, and the winner of three professional Grand Slam events in a single season, Hogan enjoyed a stellar professional career that spanned five decades. Before Hogan there was little concept of the driving range. But Hogan's dedication to practice changed all that. He epitomized determination and courage. Although the game has moved on, Hogan's reputation for perfection and perseverance remains.

## Further Reading

*Dallas Morning News,* November 6, 1998.
*Detroit News,* July 30, 1997.
*Gannett News Service,* June 24, 1996.
*Shawnee News-Star,* July 26, 1997.
*Sports Illustrated,* August 4, 1997; June 27, 1955.
*USA Today,* July 28, 1997.
"About Ben Hogan," http://www.benhogangolf.com/about.html (February 27, 1999). □

# Herman Hollerith

**Herman Hollerith (1860–1929) was the inventor of the punched card tabulating machine—the precursor of the modern computer—and one of the founders of modern information processing. His machine was used to gather information for the 1890 census more efficiently. Hollerith's company later became part of International Business Machines (IBM).**

Herman Hollerith was born to German immigrants, George and Franciska (Brunn) Hollerith, on February 29, 1860 in Buffalo, New York. He began his university education at the City College of New York at the age of 15, and graduated from the Columbia School of Mines with distinction in 1879. While at Columbia, Hollerith took the standard course of study which required both classes and practical work. As an engineering student, he took chemistry, physics, and geometry, as well as courses in surveying and graphics, and surveying and assaying. Hollerith was also required to visit local industries, such as metallurgical and machine shops, in order to understand how they functioned.

Shortly after graduation, Hollerith got a job at the U.S. Census Bureau as an assistant to his former teacher, William Petit Trowbridge. He worked as a statistician, compiling information on manufacturers. His article, "Report on the Statistics of Steam and Water-Power Used in the Manufacture of Iron and Steel," was published in 1888 in the Census Bureau's *Report on Power and Machinery Employed in Manufacture.* His work revealed the problems of dealing with large amounts of data by hand. The 1880 census took seven and a half years to complete. Because of the large numbers of people immigrating to the U.S., the 1890 and 1900 censuses were expected to take much longer.

At the Census Bureau, Hollerith met Kate Sherman Billings, daughter of Dr. John Shaw Billings, head of the Department of Vital Statistics. In addition to his work at the Bureau, Billings designed seven medical institutions and the New York Public Library, was chair of the Carnegie Institution, member of the National Board of Health, and oversaw publication of the *Index Medicus,* which contained abstracts of medical publications. Because Billings liked to help talented young men, and because Hollerith was dating his daughter, Billings took an interest in him.

It was Billings who was thought to have provided Hollerith with the inspiration for the punched card tabulating machine. Hollerith acknowledged near the end of his life the help that Billings had given him. While Billings denied providing much assistance, it is clear that he relied heavily on Billing's design concept. Hollerith thought he could design the machine, and later offered to include Billings in the project.

In 1882, Hollerith became an instructor of mechanical engineering at the Massachusetts Institute of Technology (MIT). Because he disliked working with students, he left to go to St. Louis, Missouri, where he experimented with and designed an electrically activated brake system for railroads. The railroads, however, chose a steam-actuated brake system which had been designed by Westinghouse. In 1884, Hollerith got a job with the U.S. Patent Office in Washington, D.C., where he remained until 1890.

## Invented the Tabulating Machine

Hollerith continued to experiment with the elements for a punched card tabulating machine. Billings had recommended that he study a Jacquard loom, a mechanical loom or weaving machine, for inspiration. Jacquard had realized that weaving required a number of repetitive tasks which could be automated. "He conceived a system that relied on stiff pasteboard cards with various patterns of punched holes. At each throw of the shuttle, a card was placed in the path of the rods. The pattern of holes in the card determined which rods could pass through and thus acted as a program for the loom. This control system allowed for flexibility and various levels of complexity in the patterns," noted Mark Russo, in *The World's First Statistical Engineer.*

From the Jacquard loom, Hollerith deduced the pattern for his first attempt at constructing his tabulating machine. He used a single, continuous paper feed with holes punched in it, something like a player piano. The position of the hole on a line of the paper determined what it stood for. For example, a hole in one position indicated a male, in another a female; a hole in another position indicated that the person was born in the U.S., one in another, the person was a foreigner. As the roll of paper was fed through the tabulating machine, the holes would pass over a drum, completing an electrical circuit for each hole. Counters connected to the machine registered each electrical current caused by a hole as a hit for that statistic. Because it used electricity, Hollerith's tabulating machine anticipated the advent of computers. Also, the hole punching system is analogous to the binary system of zeros and ones, which is found in the digital data storage of computers. The continuous strip which Hollerith initially used was similar to the tapes used in early computers.

The problems with Hollerith's continuous paper strip were that it was easy to tear, it was difficult to find a specific piece of information on the strip, and it was almost impossible to re-sort information. For these reasons, Hollerith decided to use a card similar to the Jacquard cards used on the looms. The cards, which came to be called Hollerith cards, were small stiff-paper cards, the size of one dollar bills. The advantage of the cards was their relatively small size, and the fact that they could be sorted or re-sorted, and corrected. The drum was replaced by a press which sandwiched the cards. Pins over the holes would pass through the cards to be submerged in mercury, which created electrical circuits that yielded hits on counters.

In 1884, Hollerith was awarded his first patent and a contract to test the merits of his new machine. In spite of some problems, the test of mortality statistics at the Baltimore Office of Registration was successful enough that the machine was subsequently used in New Jersey and New York City for similar purposes. In 1885, Hollerith's machine was first used by the U.S. Navy. This military use gave Hollerith added prestige, increased sales, and the financial resources needed to make improvements.

The 1880 census was still not completed by 1885. Hollerith felt that his machine would speed the counting of the 1890 census. The Census Bureau was worried that they might have to count two censuses at the same time, because of the length of time it took to count them. The Bureau held a competition which proved Hollerith's machine much faster than any of its competitors. By the time of the 1890 census, Hollerith had made more improvements. He increased the categories which the machine could count, and adding a mechanical feeding device and a sorting box with a number of compartments. With Hollerith's machine, the counting for the 1890 census was completed in six weeks. The census was finished in two and a half years rather than the seven and a half years needed for the previous one. Hollerith had saved the U.S. five million dollars in expenses.

On September 15, 1890, Hollerith married Lucia Beverly Talcott. The couple subsequently had six children: Lucia, Nannie, Virginia, Herman, Richard, and Charles. Also in 1890, he was awarded the Elliott Cresson medal from the Franklin Institute of Philadelphia for the outstanding invention of the year.

### Expanded Uses of Machine

By 1891, Hollerith's machines were being used to gather census information in Canada, Austria, and Norway. Between 1890 and 1900, he expanded the commercial uses

of his machines to include railroad freight statistics and agricultural data. In 1896, Hollerith started the Tabulating Machine Company, to make his machines and sell the cards needed for them. Although business was good, Hollerith was suffering from emotional exhaustion. His employees never knew what he was going to do next. It was rumoured that he had extra strong doors installed in his home so that they would not fly off their hinges during his fits. His emotional state led to a falling out with the director of the census, which now handled much more statistical data for the government. After this incident, Hollerith devoted himself entirely to commercial work.

Never a man to leave things as they were, Hollerith immediately found new markets for his machines in the business world. Within 18 days after his machines were removed from the Census Bureau, he had placed them at the shops of the Atchison, Topeka, & Santa Fe Railroad and at the Denver Gas & Electric Co. Between 1905 and 1909, he substantially developed his business as he won over a number of large accounts and introduced an updated version of his machines.

In 1911, his company merged with two other companies, the Computing Scale Company of America and the International Time Recording Company, to become the Computing-Tabulating-Recording Company. Hollerith stayed at the merged company as a consulting engineer until he retired in 1921. In 1924, under the leadership of Thomas Watson, Sr., the merged company changed its name to International Business Machines (IBM). The machine that Hollerith developed was the initial reason for IBM's success. In his last years, Hollerith suffered from heart disease. He died at home in Washington, D.C. on November 17, 1929.

### Further Reading

Austrian, Geoffrey D., *Herman Hollerith: Forgotten Giant of Information Processing,* Columbia University Press, 1982.
Bruns, Leonard C., *Science & Technology Firsts,* Gale, 1997.
Debus, A.G., ed., *World's Who's Who in Science,* 1968.
*Dictionary of American Biography,* Volume XI, Supplement One.
*Datamation,* February 1982.
"The World's First Statistical Engineer," University of Rochester, Department of History, http://www.history.rochester.edu/steam/hollerith/first.htm (March 17, 1999). □

# Whitney Houston

**Award-winning singer Whitney Houston (born 1963) made her name with her powerful voice and emotional renditions of love songs, becoming one of rhythm and blues' most popular stars and selling hundreds of millions of albums. She later branched out into acting and eventually became a business mogul, setting up production and recording studios as she continued to deliver pop music performances.**

Though her style is characteristic of the vocal athleticism of rhythm and blues music in the post-hip-hop era, Whitney Houston has a star quality that recalls the entertainment dynamos of a previous generation: elegant, professional, and versatile. Despite criticism from some corners that she conveys more technique than feeling in her music, Houston has scored enough commercial victories in the mercurial pop world to gladden the heart of any music executive.

From the beginning of her career—with the highest-selling solo debut album in history—Houston went on to sell millions of copies of her subsequent releases and win numerous music awards. In 1992 she made her acting debut in a major motion picture, *The Bodyguard,* which became one of the most successful films in its company's history; her contributions to the film's soundtrack were also phenomenally popular. If there remained any show-business frontiers for Houston to conquer, none seemed beyond her reach. Yet, in the wake of a high-profile marriage and well-publicized motherhood, the entertainer has remained philosophical. "I almost wish I could be more exciting," she told *Entertainment Weekly,* "that I could match what is happening out there to me."

## Music Was In Her Roots

Houston was born in East Orange, New Jersey on August 9, 1963, the daughter of John R. Houston—who would one day manage her production company—and acclaimed gospel singer Cissy Houston. Music was very much a part of her childhood. Her cousin Dionne Warwick was another

successful chanteuse, and Houston grew up around such star vocalists as Aretha Franklin, Gladys Knight, and Roberta Flack. "When I used to watch my mother sing, which was usually in church, that feeling, that soul, that thing—it's like electricity rolling through you," she recalled to Anthony DeCurtis of *Rolling Stone.* "If you have ever been in a Baptist church or a Pentecostal church, when the Holy Spirit starts to roll and people start to really feel what they're doing, it's . . . it's incredible. That's what I wanted. When I watched Aretha sing, the way she sang and the way she closed her eyes, and that riveting thing just came out. People just . . . ooooh, it could stop you in your tracks."

Houston first sang publicly at the age of eight, performing "Guide Me, O Thou Great Jehovah" for a spellbound congregation at the New Hope Baptist Church. Four years later she was singing backups on recordings for such major stars as Chaka Khan and Lou Rawls. "I sound like my mother when my mother was my age," she told DeCurtis, "though I truly think my mother has a greater voice than me, because she's the master, I'm the student."

When she was 17, Whitney took a detour into modeling, appearing in magazines like *Glamour* and *Seventeen.* Her beauty and talent also got her acting jobs in episodes of two then-popular television programs, *Silver Spoons* and *Gimme a Break.* Houston ultimately found the fashion runway "degrading," as *Ebony* reported, and made her way back to music. She signed a management contract in 1981 and began seriously performing—both alone and with her mother. She was given the chance to sing the lead on the song "Life's a Party," which was recorded by the Michael Zager Band; Zager was so impressed by her voice that he offered her a record deal. Cissy declined the opportunity for her daughter, which turned out to be a wise decision. At a showcase performance in 1983, Arista Records president Clive Davis heard Houston perform and offered her a contract. This time Cissy's advise was to accept the offer, and Houston signed on.

## First Album Reaped Awards

Davis took the new singer under his wing. Though she sang a duet with soul superstar Teddy Pendergrass that hit the charts in 1984, Houston would spend much of the next two years working with her mentor. Davis gathered successful songwriters and producers and helped put together the "package" that would make Houston a star. He calculated correctly: her self-titled debut album, released in March 1985, began a gradual ascent to the top of the charts. The first single, "You Give Good Love," made its way to the number three position and the second, a cover of the late-'70s hit "Saving All My Love for You," hit number one later that year. Houston received the 1986 Grammy award for best pop vocal performance and came home with five trophies from the US music awards as well. Two more singles also topped the charts: "How Will I Know" and "The Greatest Love of All."

*Whitney Houston* finally hit the top of the U.S. album chart a year after its release; a number of singles also topped the U.K. charts. Accolades for the singer continued: Houston received an Emmy for work in a television variety program and commenced touring. Her concerts sold out throughout both the U.S. and Europe. Though Houston was suddenly showered in acclaim, she had her share of detractors. Her choice of material was generally safe, critics complained. Houston's voice, though a remarkable instrument, failed to convey much emotion. As music commentator Nelson George opined to *Newsweek*, "There's not a wisp of soul on those singles."

### Second Album Debuted at Number One

The simultaneously belittling and affectionate term "Prom Queen of Soul"—a parody of the royal sobriquet earned by fellow singer Aretha Franklin—was hard for Houston to shake. Yet the vocalist had only begun her meteoric rise. Her sophomore effort, *Whitney*, appeared in 1987 and debuted at the number one position on the *Billboard* chart—the first album by a female artist to do so. Its first single, "I Wanna Dance With Somebody (Who Loves Me)," rocketed to the top, followed by three other number-one hits: "Didn't We Almost Have It All," "So Emotional," and "Where Do Broken Hearts Go." The single "Love Will Save the Day" was a disappointment only when measured against Houston's other hits; it only made it to number nine. Meanwhile, "One Moment in Time," a ballad recorded by Houston for Arista's 1988 Olympics tribute album of the same name, topped the charts after *Whitney* ended its run. She continued to rack up awards, taking home the 1988 Grammy for "I Wanna Dance With Somebody" and, in January 1989, garnering both the female pop and soul/rhythm and blues vocal honors at the American Music Awards.

In addition to her activities in the musical arena, Houston has used her high public profile to aid causes she personally supports. She took time out of a busy schedule to headline at a birthday gala for South African leader Nelson Mandela at London's Wembley Arena.

### Married Bobby Brown

It was at the Soul Train Music Awards in 1989 that Houston crossed paths with someone who would have a lasting effect on her life. She made the acquaintance of singer Bobby Brown, a popular "New Jack Swing" performer in his own right. The two didn't hit it off immediately. Houston later recalled in the interview with DeCurtis: "I always get curious when somebody doesn't like me. I want to know why." She invited Brown to a party; he accepted. As they got to know each other better, they realized their feelings surpassed mere friendship. "After a year or so, I fell in love with Bobby," Houston explained after detailing her rebuff of his first proposal. "And when he asked to marry me the second time, I said yes." The couple was married in July 1992.

Prior to this, Houston recorded and released *I'm Your Baby Tonight*. The album was a slight disappointment; it didn't perform as well as its predecessors and stopped climbing when it reached the number three position. Even so, *I'm Your Baby*, which featured the chart-topping single "All the Man That I Need," achieved triple platinum status. She received the 1990 Hitmaker Award at the Songwriters

Hall of Fame and an invitation to the White House from President George Bush.

Around the same time, Houston was approached about a movie called *The Bodyguard*. Actor Kevin Costner, who planned to star in the film, was set on Houston for his female costar. He felt so certain that Houston was right for the role of imperiled singer Rachel Marron that he agreed to wait as long as she wanted—as long as she'd agree to do the film. "There are certain singers that occupy that territory that includes a world-class voice, real elegance, and a physical presence," Costner explained to *Ebony*. "Diana Ross and Barbra Streisand are two. Whitney Houston is another." But Houston would keep Costner waiting for quite some time.

Meanwhile, the singer was busy with other things. She sang the national anthem at the 1991 Super Bowl, a performance that crystallized strong patriotic sentiment during the period of U.S. involvement in the Persian Gulf War. There was a great demand for both a single and video of her rendition. She later sang the "Star Spangled Banner" again for returning troops at Norfolk Naval Air Station. However, Houston's prestige and success as an entertainer didn't protect her from rumors she found infuriating. These included speculation that she and Brown had a less-than-harmonious marriage. He had gained a reputation as "the bad boy of the business," and she was known as "the good girl."

### *Bodyguard* Combined Acting and Singing

After two years, Houston went ahead with plans to star in *The Bodyguard*. "I kind of waited too long for Kevin," she told DeCurtis, recalling her decision to appear in the film. "He called one day and said, 'Listen, are you going to do this movie with me or not?' I told him about my fears. I said: 'I don't want to go out there and fall.' His response was: 'I promise you I will not let you fall. I will help you.' And he did." In exchange for help with her acting, Houston gave her costar tips on singing.

*The Bodyguard* is about a singer (played by Houston) who requires the protection of a bodyguard (Costner) after being harassed by an obsessive fan; a romance then develops between the star and her protector. Although *Entertainment Weekly* included *The Bodyguard* in a list of films exploring "interracial romance," color mattered little to the audience and was not even addressed in the film. "Whitney, in a sense, is to music and now to film what [actor-comedian Bill] Cosby was to television," noted *Entertainment Weekly's* Sheldon Platt. "The American middle class looks upon her as a person, and they extinguish other ethnic or racial boundaries." Houston herself observed, "I don't think it's a milestone that a black person and a white person made a movie together. I think for people to look at this color-blind is a milestone."

Critical response to the film was mixed. "Houston, the Olympian pop-soul diva, has moments of quickness and humor; she shows more thespian flair than many musicians," stated Owen Gleiberman in *Entertainment Weekly*. "Her presence, though, is defined by the same glassy perfection that makes her singing, for all its virtuosity, seem fundamentally anonymous. Whitney Houston is a diamond without flaws: Her cat-faced Mayan beauty is like a mask, and beneath it one never senses a glimmer of vulnerability, pain, doubt." Houston rebuffed such evaluations in *Rolling Stone*: "People loved this movie—the critics dogged it, but people loved it." Houston was pregnant for most of the period of the film's media blitz, and becoming a mother overshadowed any negative reviews. "There's been nothing more incredible in my life than having her," she declared of her daughter, Bobbi Kristina.

Mixed reviews didn't affect *The Bodyguard*'s box-office success. It grossed $390 million worldwide by mid-1993. The soundtrack album, which featured six Houston performances, sold about 24 million copies. The biggest single generated from the soundtrack—and the longest-running number one single ever—was her rendition of Dolly Parton's "I Will Always Love You," which earned Houston two of her three Grammys in 1994.

In addition to her impressive showing at the Grammys, Houston took several other honors in 1994, including two Soul Train Awards, entertainer of the year honors at the National Association for the Advancement of Colored People's Image Awards, and seven American Music Awards. *Entertainment Weekly* had rated Houston number five among the top "Entertainers of the Year" for 1993. At the height of her professional game and happy with her new family, Houston was, in the magazine's phrase, "enjoying a success so relentless that nothing but sledge-hammered shards of conventional wisdom are left in its wake."

## Success Tainted by Rumors

Despite success, Houston's life was not pure bliss in 1994. *Redbook* declared it her "toughest year of all." She had experienced a miscarriage while engaged in a demanding 22-city tour, weathered a barrage of criticism about how she was raising her daughter, and had to deal with a persistent stalker. In addition, some media pieces questioned her relationship with her female assistant, wondering if the two were sexually involved. Reports highlighted some of her allegedly impatient and odd behavior, such as snapping at fans that sought autographs. Rumblings of marital difficulties continued into 1995, compounded by the fact that Brown had spent time at the Betty Ford Clinic for alcohol abuse.

In late 1995, Houston starred in *Waiting to Exhale*, an adaptation of a popular novel by Terry McMillan about four black women struggling to find harmony in their lives. The soundtrack featured three songs by Houston and was produced by Kenneth "Babyface" Edmonds. Both the movie and its soundtrack were popular, with Houston holding her own in an ensemble cast also featuring Angela Bassett, Lela Rochon, and Loretta Devine. The following year she starred in *The Preacher's Wife*, about a young woman who is having difficulty in her marriage to a minister as they try to build a new church together. Though it was not critically well-received, she earned an NAACP Image Award in 1997 as outstanding lead actress for this role.

Houston announced in November of 1996 that she was pregnant again, but suffered another miscarriage that December. The following year saw her play the Fairy Godmother in a pet project of hers, the highly-rated CBS television movie *Cinderella*, which won an Emmy Award. However, the scrutiny of her behavior continued, spotlighting the fact that she canceled an appearance on the *Rosie O'Donnell Show* in November of 1997. She blamed her absence on a bout of stomach flu, but was seen out and about with her husband later that day. Also that year, she and Brown separated for about a month, but were soon back together. The next year, rumors escalated about possible drug use on the part of both of them, which Houston denied.

Despite having to bear more than an average share of celebrity gossip, Houston kept her career sailing nicely into the late 1990s. In late 1998, she recorded a new album while managing to run a record label, Better Place Records, and a film production company, Whitney's BrownHouse Productions. In the meantime, she kept up with television appearances and charity events—she formed the Whitney Houston Foundation for Children in 1989 and also lent her support to the United Negro College Fund, the Children's Diabetes Foundation, St. Jude's Children's Research Hospital, and various AIDS-related causes. The performer reflected on the years she invested in her craft in an *Upscale* magazine piece: "I started out working in little night clubs—sometimes getting paid, sometimes not—sometimes performing for 200 people, other times working in front of ten. Today, it's like people just want to jump out there and immediately become stars, but it takes time and it takes not giving up. It takes believing in one's self in spite of negativity and what people say."

## Further Reading

*Contemporary Musicians,* edited by Julia Rubiner, Volume 8, Gale, 1993.
*Rock Movers and Shakers,* edited by Dafydd Rees and Luke Crampton, Billboard Books, 1991.
*Ebony,* January 1993, p. 118; December 1998, p. 156.
*Entertainment Weekly,* April 10, 1992, p. 8; December 4, 1992, pp. 42-43; December 25, 1992, p. 104; February 5, 1993, pp. 17-21; October 22, 1993, p. 40; December 31, 1993, p. 27; February 18, 1994, pp. 32-33; March 18, 1994, p. 103; January 10, 1997, p. 14; November 14, 1997, p. 6.
*Essence,* May 1997, p. 85.
*Good Housekeeping,* January 1997, p. 62.
*Los Angeles Times,* March 17, 1994, p. F10.
*Newsweek,* July 21, 1986, pp 60-61; November 23, 1998, p. 76.
*Redbook,* May 1995, p. 84.
*Rolling Stone,* June 10, 1993, pp. 46-49; January 27, 1994, p. 40.
*Time,* October 2, 1995, p. 89; December 4, 1995, p. 77.
*Upscale,* December 1993.
Internet Movie Database, March 3, 1999. http://us.imdb.com. □

# Ron Howard

**Former child actor Ron Howard (born 1954) may be remembered by some for his roles as Opie on *The Andy Griffith Show* and Richie Cunningham on *Happy Days*. He has also carved a niche for himself in Hollywood as a highly regarded director and producer.**

might be a good experience,'' Howard later told Peter Gethers in *Esquire*. ''If it wasn't, then I simply wouldn't have to do it again.'' Howard enjoyed the experience and continued acting in two CBS teleplays: ''Black December,'' on *Playhouse 90*, and ''Barnaby and Mr. O'Malley,'' on *General Electric Theatre*. Ronald Reagan hosted the production on *General Electric Theatre* and made special mention of Howard's contribution as Barnaby. Television producer Sheldon Leonard saw the production and wanted to cast him in *The Andy Griffith Show*.

### The Andy Griffith Show

On October 3, 1960, six-year-old Howard began a successful eight-year run as Opie Taylor on *The Andy Griffith Show*. Even when he would become a famous director, many still referred to Howard as ''Opie.'' His parents supported his career, but wanted him to have as normal a childhood as possible and, therefore, kept him enrolled in public schools. ''They didn't care how much money there was to be made,'' Howard told Darlene Arden in the *Saturday Evening Post*. ''They wanted me only to do the Griffith show and maybe one thing during the off-season, and that was that.''

Howard's off-season projects in the 1960s consisted mostly of films, including *Five Minutes to Live*, *The Music Man*, *The Courtship of Eddie's Father*, and *Village of the Giants*. By the time Howard was 15 years old, he had set his sights on becoming a director. He began shooting movies with a Super-8 camera and asking questions on the sets.

In January 1969, Howard played the son of a police detective in the television drama *The Smith Family*, starring Henry Fonda. Later in the year, he was featured, along with his younger brother Clint, in the film *The Wild Country*. Howard graduated from high school in 1972 and enrolled in the film program at the University of Southern California. During the same year, he starred in an episode of the comedy anthology *Love American Style*, called ''Love and the Happy Day.'' The episode became the pilot for the *Happy Days*. television series.

In 1973, Howard gained momentum as a teenage actor. He appeared in the horror film *Happy Mother's Day, Love George* with Patricia Neal and Cloris Leachman. Soon after, he starred in his first box-office smash, *American Graffiti*, directed by George Lucas. The movie received an Academy Award nomination for best picture, along with four other nominations.

### A Decade of *Happy Days*

The first episode of the hit television series, *Happy Days*, aired in January 1974. Howard played the starring role of Richie Cunningham and continuing with the series until 1982. He also appeared in two 1974 television movies, *The Migrants* and *Locusts*, and one major motion picture, *The Spikes Gang*. Around this time he left his studies at USC in order to learn the filmmaking business on the job.

In 1975, Howard began to steer his career toward directing. After an appearance in John Wayne's last film, *The Shootist*, Howard met Hollywood B-movie producer Roger Corman, who agreed to help him direct his first

R on Howard doesn't remember a time in his life when people didn't ask him for autographs. He appeared in his first movie at the age of 18 months, and remained in the entertainment industry throughout his life. He became well-known over the years for his role as freckle-faced Opie Taylor on *The Andy Griffith Show*, as redheaded Richie Cunningham on *Happy Days*, and later as a respected director of films, including *Splash*, *Parenthood*, the acclaimed *Apollo 13*, and *Ransom*. Despite living a life in the public eye, Howard has garnered a reputation as a ''nice guy'' and describes himself as reserved. ''I've always been a little shy, tended to keep to myself, was never sure what other people think of me, not real easy to get to know,'' Howard told Todd McCarthy in *Film Comment*.

Ron Howard was born in Duncan, Oklahoma on March 1, 1954, to parents with theatrical careers. His father, Rance Howard, worked as an actor and director of plays, and his mother, Jean Howard, was also an actress. Young Howard (then called Ronny) appeared in his first movie, *Frontier Woman*, when he was just 18 months old. He appeared on stage at the age of two in *The Seven Year Itch*. His father directed the summer stock performance at the Hilltop Theatre in Baltimore, Maryland. In 1956, Howard appeared on television in episodes of *Kraft Television Theatre* and *The Red Skelton Show*.

Three years later, Howard was cast in a feature film called *The Journey*, starring Yul Brynner and Deborah Kerr. In order to perform in the film, Howard was required to travel to Ireland. ''My parents talked it over and decided that since my dad would be there and since it was in Europe, it feature. In exchange, Howard would star in Corman's movie *Eat My Dust*. "I hated *Eat My Dust*, hated the script, but from my film-school days at USC, I knew that Roger Corman was like a ray of hope for student film makers," Howard told Todd McCarthy in *Film Comment*. "He was one guy who would take chances on directors." To Howard's surprise, *Eat My Dust* became a hit and Corman planned a sequel. He gave Howard the opportunity to develop a script with his father and direct the follow-up movie, *Grand Theft Auto*. Released in 1977, the film was shot in 22 days for $602,000. *Grand Theft Auto* ended up grossing $15 million, and opened the door to Howard's career as a director. He started his own company, Major H Productions, appointing his father as vice-president and his brother Clint as secretary. The following year, Howard directed the television movie *Cotton Candy*.

## Moved Behind the Camera

In 1979, Howard appeared in *More American Graffiti*, which became his last major acting credit. He signed a three-year exclusive contract with NBC to become a full-time executive producer-director in 1980. He directed *Through the Magic Pyramid* and *Skyward*, the latter starring Bette Davis, in 1981. The year became a landmark in Howard's life: he met his future partner, Brian Grazer. The two had met at Paramount Pictures while Howard was directing *Skyward*.

In 1982, Howard directed *Night Shift*, with Grazer producing. The film starred *Happy Days* co-star Henry Winkler, as well as the up-and-coming Michael Keaton. "Ron just sort of has this glow," Grazer told Christopher Connelly in *Premiere*. "When I hired him to do *Night Shift*, I'd never seen anything he'd directed. But I met him, and . . . you just don't imagine that anything bad could happen; If you're in an airplane with him, you just don't think if your going down." Two years later, Howard worked with Grazer again when he directed *Splash*, starring Daryl Hannah, Tom Hanks, and John Candy. The fantasy/romantic comedy became the hit that launched Howard's reputation as a director.

Howard further enhanced his reputation in 1983 when he directed *Cocoon* for Twentieth Century-Fox. The star-studded cast included Jessica Tandy, Maureen Stapleton, Hume Cronyn, Wilford Brimley, Don Ameche, and Jack Gilford. It is a fantasy about senior citizens that come into contact with extra-terrestrials. "I'd like *Cocoon* audiences to have the sense that something good can be right around the corner, and can happen to you if you're ready for it," Howard told Diana Maychick in *Mademoiselle*. "That's always been my attitude. I haven't changed much emotionally since I was 14. I talked to a lot of older people for this film, and they told me the same thing. You get your personality, whatever it is, early on. It doesn't alter that much over the years."

By the end of 1985, Howard had decided to move his family, which then included his wife Cheryl and three daughters, from Los Angeles to Connecticut. Though he had started out his life in show business, he didn't necessarily want his children to follow the same path. "I wouldn't allow them to be kid actors, knowing what I know," Howard told Sheryl Kahn in *McCalls*. "I am a rarity. I think my parents did a wonderful job, but I'm not sure that it's something you can guarantee."

## Formed Production Firm

Howard and Grazer cemented their business relationship officially in 1986, when they formed Imagine Entertainment. The film and television production company went public, initially selling 1.7 million shares at eight dollars each. By the end of its first day on the market, the price jumped to $18.25. "When I was 17, I wanted to go door-to-door in my neighborhood in Los Angeles to try and raise money to make a film," Howard told Peter Gethers in *Esquire*. "When Imagine came up, my mom reminded me of that."

Later that same year, Howard appeared in a made-for-television reunion of *The Andy Griffith Show* called *Return to Mayberry*. "Andy was like a wonderful uncle to me," Howard recalled to Jane Hall in *People*. "He created an atmosphere of hard work and fun that I try to bring to my movies." Howard also directed and produced the social comedy, *Gung Ho*, starring Michael Keaton. He went on to direct the $50 million fairy tale movie, *Willow*, in 1988. The following year, Howard co-wrote and directed the successful film *Parenthood*, which climbed to number one at the box office. The idea for the movie came from screenwriters Lowell Ganz and Babaloo Mandel on a trip to Argentina with Howard and Grazer for the filming of *Gung Ho*. The four men, along with their wives, devised lists of 20 experiences or feelings about their kids (which totaled 15 among the four couples), and the story went from there.

In 1991, Howard directed *Backdraft*, another high-budget film that featured a popular cast, including Kurt Russell, William Baldwin, Donald Sutherland, Scott Glenn, Jennifer Jason-Leigh, Rebecca De Mornay, Jason Gedrick, and Robert de Niro. The film became an immediate hit for its insights into the lives of firefighters and enjoys its own attraction at Universal Studios in Hollywood.

Howard's first box-office failure came in 1992. *Far and Away*, starring Tom Cruise and Nicole Kidman, barely broke even after it was released for worldwide distribution and Howard was stunned. "We always scored high at test screenings," he told Merideth Berkman in *Entertainment Weekly*. "Then we got some bad reviews I wasn't braced for. Because I wanted to make [the movie] for so long, it felt like a conclusion to the first phase of my career." However, the film didn't slow Howard's momentum. By 1994, his films had grossed a total of nearly $500 million. He and Grazer had worked out an arrangement to privatize Imagine Entertainment. Later that year, Howard released his third work with Michael Keaton, *The Paper*, which also featured Robert Duvall, Glenn Close, and Marisa Tomei.

## *Apollo 13* a Soaring Success

Howard's 1995 film, *Apollo 13*, starring Tom Hanks, Kevin Bacon, and Bill Paxton, returned him to the top ranks of Hollywood directors. "The bittersweet quality of Jim Lovell's experience definitely drew me in," Howard explained to Jeffrey Ressner in *Time.* "Here was a guy, arguably the best-equipped individual to walk on the moon, and the opportunity was pulled out from under him. It was devastating, and we can all relate to that kind of disappointment." *Apollo 13* received nine Academy Award nominations, including one for best picture.

Howard's November 1996 release, *Ransom,* starred Mel Gibson, Rene Russo, and Gary Sinise. Despite a strong cast, some critics felt that the film didn't realize its potential. Leah Rozen wrote in her review for *People:* "This is a confident piece of commercial filmmaking, but when the final credits roll, you'll wonder if director Ron Howard and the screenwriters couldn't have tried a wee bit harder to give the characters as much dimension as the chase scenes." Owen Gleiberman commented in an *Entertainment Weekly* review, "In *Ransom,* Howard is trying for a tone of tense malevolence he doesn't appear to be fully comfortable with."

Howard co-produced *From the Earth to the Moon,* which won an Emmy Award for outstanding miniseries. This was followed by the series *Sports Night* and *Felicity,* both of which first aired in 1998. In 1999, Howard produced the innovative Eddie Murphy animated program *The PJs.* He returned to directing with 1999's *EDtv,* which he also produced with Grazer. It featured a young man who agreed for his entire life to be televised around the clock. Though it bore an uncanny resemblance to the 1998 hit *The Truman Show, Edtv* was more of an upbeat comedy than a cynical commentary. As Howard described its theme to Jeannie Williams of *USA Today,* he might as well have been commenting on his own rich and longstanding fame. He explained that the film outlined how being a celebrity is "sometimes painful, sometimes kind of embarrassing, but it can also be thrilling and rewarding."

## Further Reading

*Entertainment Weekly,* April 1, 1994, p. 22; November 15, 1996, p. 47.
*Esquire,* December 1986, p. 256.
*Film Comment,* May-June 1984, p. 40.
*Library Journal,* October 15, 1995, p. 100.
*Mademoiselle,* July 1985, p. 44.
*McCall's,* August 1996, p. 39.
*Newsweek,* August 28, 1989, p. 56.
*New Yorker,* November 11, 1996, p. 124.
*People,* November 23, 1981, p. 46; April 14, 1986, p. 90; March 25, 1996, p. 122; November 18, 1996, p. 20.
*Premiere,* April 1991, pp. 97, 144; June 1992, p. 61.
*Saturday Evening Post,* December 1981, p. 36.
*Teen,* April 1986, p. 74.
*Time,* August 4, 1986, p. 56; July 3, 1995, p. 53.
*USA Today,* February 19, 1999, p. 3E.
Internet Movie Database, March 3, 1999. http://us.imdb.com. □

# Richard Hughes

**The British author Richard Hughes (1900–1976) rose to fame in the late 1920s and 1930s upon the publication of his best-selling and critically ac-**

**claimed first novel, *A High Wind in Jamaica.* By the end of his life he had completed four novels—along with a selection of plays, poems, and children's tales—and held a prominent place among his literary contemporaries.**

R ichard Hughes was born in the the English town of Caterham, Surrey on April 19, 1900. Although he wrote fondly of his childhood in England, Hughes became acquainted with mortality and loss at an early age. His birth preceded the death of a brother, Arthur Warren Collingwood Hughes, by only eight days. His older sister, Grace Margaret Lilias, died in 1902. When the boy was five years old he lost his father, Arthur Hughes, who had worked in the Public Record Office. The elder Hughes had undergone cauterization of his vocal cords as a treatment for cancer of the throat, but his end came suddenly as a result of pneumonia. This final and significant loss left Hughes and his mother, Louise Grace Warren Hughes, in a poor financial situation that the widow strove to rectify by writing fiction for magazines.

Louise Hughes amused her son with stories that captured his imagination. She told him about Jamaica, the wild and beautiful island where she had lived until she was a girl of ten. It wasn't long before young Hughes began to create his own compositions. In fact, he began to "write" before he learned how to read or to pen the words, reciting newly minted poems to his mother, who would then commit them to paper. By the age of seven he was composing rhymed quatrains that demonstrated a powerful knack for visualization and, it would seem, a wisdom beyond his years.

Educated traditionally, Hughes embarked on a study of Greek as a ten-year-old in preparatory school. He also learned Latin, to which he had been introduced at an even earlier age. The boy's godfather, Charles Johnson, was a scholar of Medieval Latin and, like Hughes' father, worked in the Public Record Office. He served as a model and mentor for Hughes, who excelled in academics. Awarded a scholarship, Hughes was invited to attend Charterhouse, a reputable secondary school, in 1913. Hughes was groomed at Charterhouse to become a military cadet; he attended an Army training camp upon graduation. Although Hughes expected to be posted in France and perhaps to die on the battlefield during World War I, an abrupt and welcome armistice saved the young man from such a fate.

## Published Stories, Poems, and Plays

Hughes was now free to resume his studies. Following his wishes, he matriculated at Oriel College, Oxford, in 1919. Here he kept company with many up-and-coming writers of his day, including Robert Graves, Aldous Huxley, and T. E. Lawrence. At Oxford Hughes published many of his own compositions, including essays, poems, short stories, and reviews. He gained considerable recognition as a playwright. Several of his plays were staged and he joined in an effort to create a Welsh National Theatre (Hughes considered himself to be, at heart, more Welsh than English). He served as co-editor (with Robert Graves and Alan Porter) of *Oxford Poetry* in 1921, and was credited with writing the first radio play, entitled *Danger,* which aired on the British Broadcasting Corporation (BBC) in 1924. The latter experience cemented an association with the BBC that Hughes would enjoy all his life. The radio network broadcast his stories and plays, as well as talks with the author.

While the 1920s was a time of growth and progress for Hughes as a writer, it was also a period in which he began to satisfy an appetite for world travel. He voyaged to America in a ship packed densely with European emigrants seeking a new life. After a three-week stay in New York and New Jersey, he returned to England to publish *The Diary of a Steerage Passenger,* a chronicle of his experiences both on board and off. He also traveled to Canada, Africa, and the Balkans, always preferring to see a rougher side of life and working to shed a British gentility that he found limiting.

Hughes' wanderlust, however, never exceeded his desire to write. The British publisher Chatto and Windus approached him when he finished his studies at Oxford, contracting him to produce a first novel, which he chose not to begin until reaching the age of 25. Prior to starting his novel, Hughes arranged for the publication of his early works, sending three manuscripts to the press: *Confessio Juvenis,* a collection of poetry; *The Sisters' Tragedy,* a selection of plays; and *A Moment of Time,* a book of short stories.

## Literary Fame

In his 25th year, as planned, he began writing what was to become *A High Wind in Jamaica,* a novel chronicling the 19th-century escapades of a group of children who are captured by pirates while sailing home to England. Here the extravagant tales recounted by his mother entered fully into Hughes' fictional work. The author had never visited Jamaica (though he would do so later in life), yet he insisted that lack of firsthand knowledge only enhanced his ability to write about the place. There was no disputing that *A High Wind in Jamaica,* originally published in 1929 as *The Innocent Voyage,* was an enchanted work—and one that catapulted Hughes to literary fame and widespread popularity.

The novel's readers, however, would remain largely unaware of a certain hardship that the author encountered while writing this celebrated work. Just as he was to begin the novel, Hughes suffered a nervous breakdown. Its onset was sudden and acute, though little else is known of his condition at the time, since Hughes declined to write or speak at length about his affliction. In his work *Richard Hughes: Novelist,* biographer and critic Richard Poole bases his understanding of Hughes' illness on the little writing that Hughes later devoted to the topic, commenting: ''[The nervous breakdown] appears to have been brought on in part by living with his mother, in part by the demands of writing. . . . '' The breakdown of 1925 was only the most prolonged manifestation of a psychic complaint which troubled him on and off during his twenties. He was fond of remarking that the illness acted on him like a stimulant, claiming that *The Sisters' Tragedy* was written during an attack of appendicitis. . . . The illness of 1925 was not to be trifled with, however. Hughes's infirmity marked an interruption—not a termination—of his work on the novel. When he was ready to begin writing again he did so very slowly. Ultimately, Hughes traveled to generate a jolt of energy. He restarted the novel in earnest during a six-month stay on an island in the Adriatic, and he concluded it in a frame house in New Milford, Connecticut. Thus, four years after his convalescence, Hughes produced the novel that created an instant sensation upon its appearance on the literary scene.

Hughes was not one to bask in the limelight of his widespread fame; rather, he almost immediately took the opportunity to travel again, preferring Morocco to the as yet unexplored terrain of celebrity. He did not turn away from the many new career possibilities that opened up to him after his success, however. Throughout the 1930s, he wrote regularly as a columnist and a reviewer for the *Spectator,* the *New Statesman,* and other renowned publications. His second novel, *In Hazard,* absorbed him during this time, as did his courtship and marriage, in 1932, to Frances Bazley, a painter from Gloucestershire.

The couple lived briefly in Tangier, then returned to England to start a family. A son, Robert, and two daughters, Penelope and Lleky Susannah, entered the world prior to their father's publication of *In Hazard,* another adventure at sea, which he completed in 1938. (The bulk of the novel was written atop an 18th-century watchtower in Laugharne Castle where the family lived.) Another daughter, Catherine Phyllida, and a son, Owain Gardener Collingwood, arrived in the early 1940s, during which time Hughes joined the Admiralty (the administrative department that governed

British naval affairs) as a civil servant. He was eventually named chief priority officer and carried out his duties until the end of the Second World War.

### The Human Predicament

Although Hughes had a chance to further explore his interest in maritime culture through his involvement with the Admiralty, the wartime climate was not conducive to writing, and the author's craft suffered from disuse during this period. He did, however, conceive the idea for a trilogy of novels, *The Human Predicament,* which he would not begin to write for several years. After the war he took part in the writing of an official history of the Admiralty, a dry work that, though useful to historians and war administrators, did little to exercise Hughes' imaginative powers as a writer.

Hughes had a chance to put his creative skills to use once again when, in 1950, a British filmmaking studio asked him to script a story that it had purchased. Although he refused to write love scenes (a woman was called in to do these), and although he disliked the offhand manner in which his script was later revised and altered, Hughes developed a penchant for the art of screenplay writing. He doctored a script that the studio had set aside, and he conceived and wrote *The Divided Heart,* a screenplay of his own. When the studio closed in 1954, however, Hughes' short-lived career in film came to an end. Eleven years later he was to see his own story, *A High Wind in Jamaica,* adapted for the screen.

It seemed that Hughes' writing pace slowed as the years went on. He delivered a series of lectures on the art of fiction and contemporary literary theory at Gresham College of the University of London in the mid-1950s, during which time he finally began to work on *The Human Predicament,* a trilogy that would absorb him for the next 20 years of his life. From 1955 to 1961 he wrote the first volume, *The Fox in the Attic,* which was received warmly by critics, some of whom compared him to epic novelist, Leo Tolstoy. But Hughes spent twice as many years writing his second volume, *The Wooden Shepherdess,* which finally appeared in 1973. The trilogy was to span the years between the two world wars, but Hughes never lived to complete it.

By December 1975 Hughes had become too ill to write any longer, and by March of the following year he was hospitalized for leukemia, the disease that would ultimately take his life. He died, surrounded by a family, in Moredrin, Wales on April 28, 1976, at the age of 76. In his obituary, the *New York Times* printed a 1962 quote in which the author described writing as "a race between the publisher and the undertaker." Although the undertaker won out before the final volume of *The Human Predicament* went to press, the publisher had triumphed enough previously to leave the world with a rich (albeit slim) legacy of Hughes' works.

### Further Reading

Graves, Richard Perceval, *Richard Hughes: A Biography,* Andre Deutsche, 1994.
Morgan, Paul, *The Art of Richard Hughes: A Study of the Novels,* University of Wales Press, 1993.
Poole, Richard, *Richard Hughes: Novelist,* Poetry Wales Press, 1986.
*New York Times,* April 30, 1976. □

# Faisal Husseini

**Palestinian political leader Faisal Husseini (born 1940) began his career in the 1960s with the Palestinian Liberation Organization when it was known for its terrorist activities. He managed to shed that image over the years to emerge as an advocate for peace in the region. After spending the turbulent 1980s in and out of jail and under house arrest for being a member of the PLO, Husseini has gained acceptance in the peace process as a moderate negotiator.**

As a senior official in the Palestinian National Authority headed by Yasir Arafat, Husseini champions compromises between Palestinians and Israel, hoping that one day Palestine can coexist as a state and hold Jerusalem as its capital. Extremists on both sides denounce his work and offer death threats, but he has persisted. He even visualizes that Israel and Palestine can someday join forces with other Middle Eastern nations to form a regional entity that works together for the good of all.

## Political Background

Husseini was born in 1940 in Baghdad, Iraq, and moved to Jerusalem as a child. His father, Abdul Kader Husseini, was a war hero who led Arab resistance forces against the creation of the Israeli state. He was killed in the 1948 Arab-Israeli conflict and was subsequently regarded as a martyr among Palestinians. Husseini's grandfather, Musa Kasim Pasha Husseini, was a prominent Palestinian nationalist leader during British rule. Another relative, Haj Amin Husseini, was the top political and Islamic religious leader—known as the Grand Mufti—of Palestine from 1921 until 1948. He vociferously opposed Jewish settlement in Palestine and the British occupation, and was eventually exiled. He settled in Germany and supported the Nazis.

Husseini and others in his family, waited in Egypt, like many wealthy citizens, while war ravaged their country. About 350 villages were wiped out and about half the population—perhaps 800,000 Palestinians—left the nation in 1948. Husseini attended college at the University of Baghdad and the University of Cairo, where he became friendly with Yasir Arafat, an engineering student who had started the liberation group "Fatah," in the mid-1950s. He would later become leader of the Palestinian Liberation Organization (PLO). Fatah supported the use of violent means in order to command attention for the Palestinian cause. Husseini became involved with Fatah and attended a military college in Syria. He graduated in 1967 and became an officer in the fledgling Palestine Liberation Army.

Husseini set up a training camp in Lebanon and assisted with other "military activities," according to an article in the *Christian Science Monitor,* which "included bombings and hijackings most of the world saw as terrorism." Husseini said later that although he did not approve of the tactics, they were effective in publicizing the situation.

## Returned to Jerusalem

On June 5, 1967, Israeli forces began what was later referred to as the "Six-Day War." Israel captured the Golan Heights from Syria; the West Bank and East Jerusalem from Jordan; and the Gaza Strip form Egypt. Since then, the ownership of those areas has been in dispute. Husseini moved back to Jerusalem and was soon arrested by Israeli soldiers for having two submachine guns in his home. He was jailed for a year. Throughout the 1970s, turmoil continued in the region, with another conflict breaking out in 1973. Husseini separated himself from terrorist activities and became more involved in politics. He held public forums with influential Israelis and helped with cooperative protests in conjunction with Israeli groups. Dedicating himself to peaceful solutions, he founded the Arab Studies Society in East Jerusalem in 1979, an institute for researching Palestinian history. In 1974, the Arab Summit named the PLO as the official representative body for Palestine. It was given observer status at the United Nations. Arafat, heading the PLO, signed the Camp David peace accords with Israel in 1978.

In 1982, Israel invaded Lebanon, where Arafat and other PLO officials held offices. Husseini was arrested and jailed numerous times from 1982 to 1987 for his PLO membership and was not allowed to travel outside of the country. In December 1987, a Palestinian uprising known as the *intifada* began on the West Bank and Gaza Strip. This revolt against the Israeli occupation was marked with violence and demonstrations. The Israeli army retaliated by striking back hard at the rioters and locking up Palestinian leaders, including Husseini, who was accused of inciting riots. The military also closed down his Arab Studies Society, though he later reopened it in his home. During Husseini's year-long prison term, he used his time to study Hebrew and English. His release was taken as a sign that Israeli defense minister, Yitzhak Rabin, was willing to compromise in order to defuse tensions in the area. Husseini, however, redirected Rabin to the PLO. That December, Husseini was placed under house arrest, purportedly because his public speeches fueled uprisings.

## Named Minister of Jerusalem Affairs

During the 1991 Gulf War, the PLO supported Saddam Hussein and Iraq. After the war, the United States worked to establish peace in the region and arranged a conference in Madrid, Spain, in late October 1991. Israeli prime minister Yitzhak Shamir, however, refused to negotiate with any known PLO members, so Husseini instead acted as a consultant to the Palestinian delegates. After Rabin took over as prime minister in 1992, he expressed willingness to discuss peace with the PLO, and Husseini was called to the table. However, Husseini and two other negotiators quit the talks in 1993 over differences with Arafat. He refused to accept their resignations. Subsequently, Israel officially recognized the PLO, and it was revealed that Rabin had begun secret discussions with the PLO in Oslo, Norway. In 1993, a peace agreement was signed in Washington, D.C., that allowed Palestinian autonomy in the Gaza Strip and Jericho, a town on the West Bank. It also set up a temporary authority, the Palestinian National Authority. Arafat returned to Gaza and named Husseini the minister of Jerusalem affairs for the Palestinian National Authority.

Rabin was assassinated in 1994 by a right-wing Israeli gunman. Benjamin Netanyahu, a right-of-center Likud Party member, was his replacement. This leadership change put new strains on the peace process. Netanyahu supported Jewish settlements in the region, including the construction of two Jewish housing projects in East Jerusalem. This point of contention sparked protests and violence. Husseini was injured in June 1998 when he was hit on the head by a rock. Other disputes involved residency permits and the plans for Israel to extend Jerusalem's boundaries. In addition, relations between Husseini and Arafat seemed to have soured, though Husseini continued to support the PLO publicly. As the fighting raged on into 1998, Husseini was doubtful that peace could be achieved as long as Netanyahu was prime minster. Husseini remained committed to the idea that Palestine should join with other Middle Eastern countries such as Israel, Jordan, Lebanon, Syria, and Egypt to form a larger, regional group, like the European Union.

Husseini is married and has two sons. Some observers feel he is being pushed out of the top ranks of the PLO due to his differences with Arafat, especially on human rights is-sues. Other argue that he could be in line as a successor, though Husseini denies the talk. He insists that if Jerusalem is not the capital of Palestine, then he will not become its leader.

## Further Reading

*Christian Science Monitor,* February 13, 1989, p. 4; April 30, 1998, p. 6.

*Jerusalem Post,* August 18, 1995; July 21, 1995; September 3, 1996, p. 2.

*Jewish Telegraphic Agency,* April 27, 1993.

*Los Angeles Times,* May 17, 1998, Opinion, p. 3.

*New York Times,* October 26, 1991, p. 4.

*Northern California Jewish Bulletin,* November 25, 1994.

*Reuters,* June 21, 1998.

*Time,* August 5, 1991, p. 30.

''A Brief History of Palestine,'' Palestinian National Authority web site, http://www.pna.com (September 1, 1998).

''Jewish Settlers' Move Sparks Palestinian Protest,'' June 8, 1998, CNN Interactive web site, http://cnn.com (September 1, 1998). □

# Mike Ilitch

**Michael "Mike" Ilitch (born 1929) began the Little Caesars Pizza empire in 1959 with one store in Garden City, Michigan. His business expanded to about 4000 stores by 1999. One of the 400 wealthiest people in the United States, Ilitch invested the fortune he made in his hometown of Detroit. He bought several major professional sports teams, including the Detroit Red Wings (professional hockey) and the Detroit Tigers (professional baseball), as well as other local enterprises in an effort to revitalize the city.**

Ilitch was born on July 20, 1929, in Detroit, Michigan, the son of Macedonian immigrants. Ilitch's father, Sotir, worked in the automobile industry as a tool-and-die maker for the Chrysler Corp. After graduation from Cooley High School, the Detroit Tigers professional baseball team offered Ilitch a $5000 bonus to sign. Ilitch requested double that amount, which the Tigers refused pay. Instead Ilitch spent four years in the U.S. Marine Corps, from 1948 until 1952, where he played baseball on base. When his tour of duty was over, Ilitch signed with the Tigers for $5000 and spent three years in the Detroit Tigers farm system, playing short-stop for the Tampa Smokers, among other teams. His family, however, did not support his career choice. According to Michael Oneal of *Business Week,* "Sotir Ilitch thought baseball was a bum sport."

In 1954, Sotir Ilitch arranged a blind date for his son with Ilitch's future wife Marian, then a Delta Airlines reservation clerk. They married the following year and eventually raised seven children: Denise, Ron, Michael Jr., Lisa, Atanas, Christopher, and Carole. Ilitch's career in baseball floundered. After breaking a leg, his career was over. To support the family, Ilitch worked for a cement company. He also worked as a door-to-door salesman for a dinnerware company and sold aluminum awnings. Ilitch thought his future was secure when he became a partner in an awning business. This, however, did not last long as his two partners insisted on buying him out.

## The Pizza Business

Ilitch founded Little Caesars Pizza in 1959 with $10,000 he had saved. Ilitch had previously made pizzas to support himself when he was playing in the minor leagues. Of his initial interest in the pizza business, Ilitch told Pat Jordan of the *New York Times Magazine,* "I was fascinated by water and flour. You knead it into dough, put it in the oven, and it comes out baked. Wow!" Originally, Ilitch wanted to call his restaurant Pizza Treat, but his wife thought the name should be snappier and suggested Little Caesars, based on her nickname for her husband. When their restaurant opened in a strip mall in Garden City, Michigan, Ilitch handled the pizza production, menu, and marketing, while his wife handled the cash flow. By 1962, they had their first franchise.

Little Caesars expanded throughout the Midwest. By not offering delivery and keeping staff to a minimum, Little Caesars had low overhead. In the mid-1970s, Ilitch came up with a marketing idea that changed the pizza industry and greatly increased his fortune: "Pizza! Pizza!" Little Caesars sold two pizzas for one relatively inexpensive price. In 1980, the company had over 200 franchises, still primarily in the Midwest. By 1983, the company had 300 restaurants and a year later, their sales totaled $290 million. The com-

**163**

pany exploded with their first national advertising campaigns in the mid-1980s.

Between 1987 and 1992, Little Caesars grew at a compounded annual rate of 42 percent. By the 1990s, Little Caesars was an international enterprise, with stores all over North America and parts of Europe. The chain had $2.15 billion in sales and 4000 stores in 1993, making it the third largest pizza chain behind Pizza Hut and Dominos. Little Caesars owns and operates one quarter of those restaurants. By 1994, the number of restaurants swelled to over 4500 in the United States and Europe. Ilitch's personal fortune stood at $300 million in 1993; by 1998, it was estimated at $630 million.

Ilitch retained private ownership of Little Caesars from the beginning, and was active in many aspects of the operation through early the 1990s. The entire Ilitch family was involved in the business. His wife, Marian, was the company's chief financial officer. Each of the seven children worked for the company at one time or another, and many important business decisions were made sitting around the kitchen table. Such family involvement was not always easy. Michael Oneal of *Business Week* wrote, "Arguments flare up, and boundaries between family and work break down. Mike Sr. says it's often a struggle to balance the roles of CEO and father. As Little Caesars has grown, consultants have sometimes raised red flags about the company's family structure."

Ilitch used the profits from his pizza empire to promote urban development in his hometown. Since 1982, Ilitch has invested over $200 million in revitalizing downtown Detroit. He bought and renovated the Fox Theater, a 1920s movie palace, in 1987. He turned the Fox Theater into one of the most profitable venues of that size and moved the headquarters of Little Caesars into buildings attached to the Fox. Ilitch told Keith Gave of the *Detroit Free Press,* "I was born in Detroit and raised here. I came from zero. This community helped make me. It's nice to give something back."

## Purchased Sports Teams

Ilitch's first venture into professional team ownership came in 1982, when he bought the Detroit Red Wings hockey club for $8 million. One of the National Hockey League's original six franchises, the Detroit Red Wings had not generated much interest, but Ilitch saw potential. Jack Falla in *Sports Illustrated* quoted Ilitch as saying, "This franchise is a sleeping giant waiting for someone to do something with it." He pumped money into the team and brought it back to life. By 1986, annual ticket sales surged from an anemic 1500 (less than 10% of the Joe Louis Arena's capacity) to near-sellouts. Within five years, the Red Wings regularly won their division championships and were contenders for hockey's ultimate prize, the Stanley Cup. In 1991, the National Hockey League awarded Ilitch the Lester Patrick trophy for his service to professional hockey. The value of his franchise was estimated at $200 million by the mid-1990s.

Ilitch and his family were enthusiastic about the sport, sponsoring youth hockey in the metro Detroit area. Falla in *Sports Illustrated* said Ilitch called himself "a fan with an owner's pocketbook." Ilitch was generous to his professional players, giving them unexpected bonuses. The only thing lacking in Ilitch's ownership experience was winning the Stanley Cup. He was ecstatic when the Red Wings finally captured the Cup in 1997 and 1998. Ilitch told Keith Gave of the *Detroit Free Press,* "This is the hardest job I've ever had in my life. Sometimes I wondered if we'd see it through to the end. But one of my strengths is perseverance and we hung in there." He would need these qualities when he bought the Detroit Tigers.

## Took on the Tigers

Ilitch bought the Detroit Tigers in 1993 for $85 million in cash from rival magnate Tom Monaghan, owner of Dominos Pizza. Monaghan had outbid Ilitch for the team in 1983. Baseball fans expected Ilitch to do great things for the team, reviving the dormant Tigers as he had the Red Wings. Unfortunately, this was not easily accomplished, due in part to the differences between the two professional leagues. Ilitch found that he had to fight those already in place within his own organization. Baseball also featured higher salaries than hockey and different revenue sharing arrangements. Some of the Tigers high-priced early signings did not work out. Ilitch lost money for several years.

After a few seasons, Ilitch regretted buying the team. As Pat Jordan wrote in the *New York Times Magazine,* "Ilitch's experience with the Tigers has so soured him on the game he has always loved that he admits, if he had to do it all over again, he wouldn't. 'I should have done more research,' he says. 'But I got excited.'"

Still, Ilitch remained determined. He gave up many of his duties at Little Caesars in 1993 to concentrate on his sports teams, especially the Tigers. One of his first orders of business was constructing a new stadium. This decision met with some resistance. Conservationists argued that Tiger Stadium, built in 1902, was one of the oldest and most beloved baseball parks in the league. Though Ilitch finally got the deal he wanted for his stadium in downtown Detroit, some locals believed he was greedy. They were critical of the manner in which the land was acquired, how the stadium would be financed, and the special treatment he received at the hands of the city government. Ilitch told Pat Jordan of the *New York Times Magazine,* "My problem is that I'm not politically astute. I have no chits to call in from politicians. I never needed anything from them. I just made my pizzas. I resent being tabbed as greedy. I could handle dumb."

Ilitch also invested in other local sports ventures. In 1988, he bought the Detroit Drive franchise in the Arena Football League. In 1993, he bought a professional soccer franchise in the Professional Soccer League, the Detroit Rockers. Ilitch also bought a farm team for his Detroit Red Wings, the Adirondack Red Wings as well as the management company, Olympia Arenas, Inc., that runs the Joe Louis Arena. He continued to expand his Detroit entertainment empire as well. Near his Fox Theater, he opened up a branch of the Second City Comedy Club. In 1996, Ilitch formed Olympia Development, Inc., a company that focused on developing real estate and entertainment in downtown Detroit. He also opened several upscale restaurants in the area.

After Ilitch turned his attentions away from his pizza business, Little Caesars began to suffer. Ilitch was forced to refocus his attention by 1997. When sales slumped and restaurants closed, he devised a new marketing plan and new products, closely analyzing the way Little Caesars did business to regain his share of the market.

Though Ilitch was very wealthy and successful, he was always seen as an average guy. Professor David J. Brophy told Oneal of *Business Week,* "Mike Ilitch is the kind of guy you'd like to have a beer with." Oneal went on to say, "Ilitch has never lost his Michigan twang or bar-stool wit." Another writer, Pat Jordan of the *New York Times Magazine* called him "timid," going on to say "Yet he acts less like a Caesar and more like a low-level employee who is terrified of his boss." Ilitch himself successfully lived by this philosophy, quoted by Oneal in *Business Week,* "Be humble and never toot your own horn. If you do something good, people will find out."

## Further Reading

*Business Leader Profiles for Students,* edited by Sheila Dow, Gale, 1999.

Hallett, Anthony and Diane Hallett, *Encyclopedia of Entrepreneurs,* John Wiley & Sons, 1997.

*Newsmakers: The People Behind Today's Headlines,* edited by Louise Mooney, Gale, 1993.

*Business Week,* August 17, 1992; September 14, 1992; Enterprise Special Issue, 1993.

*Detroit Free Press,* June 9, 1997; January 15, 1998; January 19, 1998; February 20, 1998; March 19, 1998; August 26, 1998.

*Detroit News,* June 11, 1997; August 13, 1998.

*New York Times Magazine,* September 18, 1994.

*Sports Illustrated,* October 14, 1985.

http://infoplease.com/ipsa/A019302.html (February 21, 1999).

□

# J

## Mahalia Jackson

**Throughout her celebrated career, gospel singer Mahalia Jackson (1911–1972) used her rich, forceful voice and inspiring interpretations of spirituals to move audiences around the world to tears of joy. In the early days, as a soloist and member of church choirs, she recognized the power of song as a means of gloriously reaffirming the faith of her flock. And later, as a world figure, her natural gift brought people of different religious and political convictions together to revel in the beauty of the gospels and to appreciate the warm spirit that underscored the way she lived her life.**

The woman who would become known as the "Gospel Queen" was born on October 26, 1911 into a poor family in New Orleans, Louisiana. The Jacksons' Water Street home, a shack between the railroad tracks and the levee of the Mississippi River, was served by a pump that delivered water so dirty that cornmeal had to be used as a filtering agent. Jackson's father, like many blacks in the segregated south, held several jobs; he was a longshoreman, a barber, and a preacher at a small church. Her mother, a devout Baptist who died when Mahalia was five, took care of the six Jackson children and the house, using washed-up driftwood and planks from old barges to fuel the stove.

### Sounds of New Orleans

As a child, Mahalia was taken in by the sounds of New Orleans. She listened to the rhythms of the woodpeckers, the rumblings of the trains, the whistles of the steamboats, the songs of sailors and street peddlers. When the annual festival of Mardi Gras arrived, the city erupted in music. In her bedroom at night, young Mahalia would quietly sing the songs of blues legend Bessie Smith.

But Jackson's close relatives disapproved of the blues, a music indigenous to southern black culture, saying it was decadent and claiming that the only acceptable songs for pious Christians were the gospels of the church. In gospel songs, they told her, music was the cherished vehicle of religious faith. As the writer Jesse Jackson (not related to the civil rights leader) said in his biography of Mahalia, *Make a Joyful Noise Unto the Lord!*, "It was like choosing between the devil and God. You couldn't have it both ways." Mahalia made up her mind. When Little Haley (the nickname by which she was known as a child) tried out for the Baptist choir, she silenced the crowd by singing "I'm so glad, I'm so glad, I'm so glad I've been in the grave an' rose again. . . . " She became known as "the little girl with the big voice."

At 16, with only an eighth grade education but a strong ambition to become a nurse, Jackson went to Chicago to live with her Aunt Hannah. In the northern city, to which thousands of southern blacks had migrated after the Civil War to escape segregation, she earned a living by washing white people's clothes for a dollar a day. After searching for the right church to join, a place whose music spoke to her, she ended up at the Greater Salem Baptist Church, to which her aunt belonged. At her audition for the choir, Jackson's thunderous voice rose above all the others. She was invited to be a soloist and started singing with a quintet that per-

formed at funerals and church services throughout the city. In 1934, she received $25 for her first recording, "God's Gonna Separate the Wheat from the Tares."

Though she sang traditional hymns and spirituals almost exclusively, Jackson continued to be fascinated by the blues. During the Great Depression, she knew she could earn more money singing the songs that her relatives considered profane and blasphemous. But when her beloved grandfather was struck down by a stroke and fell into a coma, Jackson vowed that if he recovered she would never even enter a theater again, much less sing songs of which he would disapprove. He did recover, and Mahalia never broke that vow. She wrote in her autobiography, *Movin' On Up:* "I feel God heard me and wanted me to devote my life to his songs and that is why he suffered my prayers to be answered—so that nothing would distract me from being a gospel singer."

Later in her career, Jackson continued to turn down lucrative requests to sing in nightclubs—she was offered as much as $25,000 a performance in Las Vegas—even when the club owners promised not to serve whisky while she performed. She never dismissed the blues as anti-religious, like her relatives had done: it was simply a matter of the vow she had made, as well as a matter of inspiration. "There's no sense in my singing the blues, because I just don't feel it," she was quoted as saying in *Harper's* magazine in 1956. "In the old, heart-felt songs, whether it's the blues or gospel music, there's the distressed cry of a human being. But in the blues, it's all despair; when you're done singing, you're still lonely and sorrowful. In the gospel songs, there's mourning

and sorrow, too, but there's always hope and consolation to lift you above it."

## Singing Career Blossomed

In 1939, Jackson started touring with renowned composer Thomas A. Dorsey. Together they visited churches and "gospel tents" around the country, and Jackson's reputation as a singer and interpreter of spirituals blossomed. She returned to Chicago after five years on the road and opened a beauty salon and a flower shop, both of which drew customers from the gospel and church communities. She continued to make records that brought her fairly little monetary reward. In 1946, while she was practicing in a recording studio, a representative from Decca Records overheard her sing an old spiritual she had learned as a child. He advised her to record it, and a few weeks later she did. "Move On Up a Little Higher" became her signature song. The recording sold 100,000 copies overnight and soon passed the two million dollar mark. "It sold like wildfire," Alex Haley wrote in *Reader's Digest.* "Negro disk jockeys played it; Negro ministers praised it from their pulpits. When sales passed one million, the Negro press hailed Mahalia Jackson as 'the only Negro whom Negroes have made famous.'"

Jackson began touring again, only this time she did it not as the hand-to-mouth singer who had toured with Dorsey years before. She bought a Cadillac big enough for her to sleep in when she was performing in areas with hotels that failed to provide accommodations for blacks. She also stored food in the car so that when she visited the segregated South she wouldn't have to sit in the backs of restaurants. Soon the emotional and resonant singing of the "Gospel Queen," as she had become known, began reaching the white community as well. She appeared regularly on Studs Terkel's radio show and was ultimately given her own radio and television programs.

On October 4, 1950, Jackson played to a packed house of blacks and whites at New York's Carnegie Hall. She recounted in her autobiography how she reacted to the jubilant audience. "I got carried away, too, and found myself singing on my knees for them. I had to straighten up and say, 'Now we'd best remember we're in Carnegie Hall and if we cut up too much, they might put us out.'" In her book, she also described a conversation with a reporter who asked her why she thought white people had taken to her traditionally black, church songs. She answered, "Well, honey, maybe they tried drink and they tried psychoanalysis and now they're going to try to rejoice with me a bit." Jackson ultimately became equally popular overseas and performed for royalty and adoring fans throughout France, England, Denmark, and Germany. One of her most rewarding concerts took place in Israel, where she sang before an audience of Jews, Muslims, and Christians.

## Participated in Civil Rights Struggles

In the late 1950s and early 1960s, Jackson's attention turned to the growing civil rights movement in the United States. Although she had grown up on Water Street, where black and white families lived together peacefully, she was well aware of the injustice engendered by the Jim Crow laws that enforced racial segregation in the South. At the request of the Reverend Martin Luther King, Jr., Jackson participated in the Montgomery bus boycott. This action had been prompted by Rosa Parks's refusal to move from a bus seat reserved for whites. During the famous March on Washington in 1963, seconds before Dr. King delivered his celebrated "I Have a Dream" speech, Jackson sang the old inspirational, "I Been 'Buked and I Been Scorned" to over 200,000 people.

Jackson died in Chicago on January 27, 1972, never having fulfilled her dream of building a nondenominational temple, where people could sing, celebrate life, and nurture the talents of children. *Christian Century* magazine reported that her funeral was attended by over six thousand fans. Singer Ella Fitzgerald described Jackson as "one of our greatest ambassadors of love . . . this wonderful woman who only comes once in a lifetime."

Jackson considered herself a simple woman: she enjoyed cooking for friends as much as marveling at landmarks around the world. But it was in her music that she found her spirit most eloquently expressed. She wrote in her autobiography: "Gospel music is nothing but singing of good tidings—spreading the good news. It will last as long as any music because it is sung straight from the human heart. Join with me sometime—whether you're white or colored—and you will feel it for yourself. Its future is brighter than a daisy."

## Further Reading

Goreau, L., *Just Mahalia, Baby,* Pelican, 1975.
Jackson, Jesse, *Make a Joyful Noise Unto the Lord!,* G.K. Hall, 1974.
Jackson, Mahalia, and Wylie, Evan McLeod, *Movin' On Up,* Hawthorne Books, 1966.
Schwerin, Jules, *Got to Tell It: Mahalia Jackson, Queen of Gospel,* Oxford, 1992.
*Christian Century,* March 1, 1972.
*Ebony,* March 1972, April 1972.
*Harper's,* August 1956.
*Reader's Digest,* November 1961.
*Saturday Review,* September 27, 1958. □

# Derek Jacobi

**Considered heir to a generation of British stage actors best known for their interpretations of Shakespearean heroes and villains, Derek Jacobi (born 1938) is also greatly respected for his film roles and television work.**

Jacobi was born on October 22, 1938, in the East London area of Leytonstone. His father, Alfred Jacobi, was a German immigrant to England and the manager of a department store. Derek was the only child of Alfred and Daisy Masters Jacobi, a secretary. When he was just four, his parents took him to a pantomime performance of *Cinderella*

at the London Palladium where Jacobi was one of several young audience members selected to come on stage. He was awed by the experience, and soon made his debut in the tough dual role of *The Prince and the Swineherd* at the age of six in a kindergarten-cast production staged at his local library. A few years later, Jacobi survived a childhood bout with rheumatic fever that left him unable to walk for a time; when he regained the use of his legs, he worked determinedly to recover his physical strength through vigorous exercise.

## Cambridge in the 1950s

Jacobi continued to act throughout his teens, and garnered favorable press for his debut as Hamlet in the 1955 National Youth Theatre production of the Shakespearean tragedy at the Edinburgh Festival. After graduating from Leyton County High School, Jacobi entered St. John's College at Cambridge University on a scholarship. He promptly enrolled in the university's venerable Amateur Dramatic Club as well as its Marlowe Society, the latter named in honor of the Elizabethan playwright and first English dramatist to write in blank verse.

Though Jacobi was officially a student in history, Cambridge was well-established as a training ground for the London stage. He recalled those spirited university days in a 1979 interview with Ruth Hamilton in the *New York Times.* "We acted all the time. It was like being in [repertory theater]. You fitted in your academic work between engagements," Jacobi reminisced. "What mistakes you made, you made in public—not the classroom." Both Ian McKellen and Trevor Nunn, later fellow luminaries in British drama as well, were friends of Jacobi's at Cambridge. The Marlowe Society's annual production was a much-anticipated event at the college, and Jacobi's senior year lead in *Edward II* landed him a job with the Birmingham Repertory Company in 1960.

## Talent Recognized by Olivier

In Birmingham, Jacobi moved from Jacobean and Elizabethan drama to roles in modern experimental theater. A stint in Birmingham was considered a stepping stone to the prestigious Royal Shakespeare Company. When Jacobi received what he believed was his RSC offer, he resigned from Birmingham and went to Stratford-upon-Avon. He was surprised to learn that he was simply being asked to audition; terrified at his blunder, he performed poorly and summarily received a rejection letter. Fortunately, he was able to return to the Birmingham company.

One of his idols, Laurence Olivier, had also achieved early fame in the Birmingham Company, and Olivier's attendance at a performance of Shakespeare's *Henry VIII* one day in 1963 propelled Jacobi to minor stardom when the veteran actor offered him roles in two productions that he was directing for the Chichester Festival Theater. Jacobi accepted, resigned again from the Birmingham Repertory, and later that year was also invited by Olivier to join the upstart National Theatre Company. He was just 24, and the only unknown member of the octet that had been hand-picked by Olivier.

Jacobi spent eight years with the National Theatre, which provided him with ample opportunity to take on an array of important roles from the annals of drama. These included the Shakespearean staples *Othello* and *Much Ado About Nothing*, as well as more contemporary works such as Chekhov's *Three Sisters* and plays by George Bernard Shaw and Noel Coward. *Othello* was even filmed by Warner Brothers and released for the screen in 1966. But over the decade, London's obstinate theater critics gave Jacobi mixed reviews for his work, and a poor reception at one 1971 production caused Jacobi to resign. He returned to the Birmingham Repertory and the following season won enthusiastic praise for his mad king in *Oedipus Rex*.

## Increasingly Diverse Roles

A serious film offer came for Jacobi in *The Day of the Jackal* in 1973; an assassination thriller set in France and based on the Frederick Forsyth novel of the same name. Jacobi also appeared in *The Odessa Files* and in an acclaimed film version of *Three Sisters* directed for the stage by Olivier. In addition to the forays into film, Jacobi also became involved with another respected and innovative drama group, the Prospect Theater Company. He appeared in several of its outstanding productions of classical, Elizabethan, and modern dramas both in London and in foreign locations.

Jacobi also began appearing in television projects, the first of which was a British production of a seven-part series for ABC-TV in 1973 on the Viennese waltz master, Johann Strauss and his family. But North American audiences came to know Jacobi through two series originally produced for British networks and then aired on public television. The first was *The Pallisers,* an adaptation of Anthony Trollope's work of fiction. Like other British imports on PBS during this era, it became surprisingly popular with American viewers. Jacobi was then cast as a doomed Roman emperor in the 13-part *I, Claudius,* based on the novels by Robert Graves. It debuted on PBS in 1977 to excellent reviews and very high ratings, and was periodically re-broadcast over the next few years.

## Jacobi as the Danish Prince

In November of 1979, the Prospect Theater Company became the first British troupe to perform in communist China, and Jacobi electrified Chinese audiences with his lead in *Hamlet.* It was also broadcast on live television, and 100 million Chinese reportedly tuned in as well. The following year, Jacobi finally made his Broadway debut in a play called *The Suicide* by Nikolai Erdman. Set in Moscow during the repressive Stalinist era, Jacobi's performance was widely reviewed and commended in the press. *The Suicide,* however, was an expensive production and box office receipts were less than expected; it closed less than two months later.

Also in 1980, Jacobi appeared as one of a notorious trio of elite Britons unmasked as Soviet spies in the Granada Television docu-drama *Philby, Burgess and MacLean.* The production won rave reviews on both sides of the Atlantic. But at mid-career as primarily a stage actor, Jacobi was most readily identified with his title role in *Hamlet,* which he reprised once more for a BBC-PBS production. Jacobi's interpretation of the inexperienced prince would become the definitive version of the popular Shakespearean tragedy for his generation; ironically, Olivier had gained fame himself decades before with his portrayal; a future colleague of Jacobi's, Kenneth Branagh, would inherit the crown later. Jacobi admitted it was difficult for a stage-trained actor to work in the electronic medium. "The main difficulty is the lack of an audience. The plays were intended for the theater," Jacobi said of *Hamlet* and other Shakespearean works to Hamilton. "They were written in such a way—certainly, with the great tragedies—that the actor reaches peaks and valleys and charts his way through the play in a series of rhythms. It's like a piece of music. In television, this, naturally, is cut up."

## "Absolute Stark Terror"

Jacobi finally received the long-awaited offer from the Royal Shakespeare Company in 1982. With the company, he returned to Broadway in 1984 for a dual tour of *Cyrano de Bergerac* and *Much Ado about Nothing.* The two roles were scheduled to run simultaneously, with Jacobi enacting the swashbuckler with the prominent nose during the matinee of *Cyrano de Bergerac,* and then readying for a hesitant Shakespearean lover for the evening's performance in *Much Ado about Nothing.* Initially, he was wary of accepting the roles, since he had been heavily involved in television work for the past few years. "I knew I had to get back to the theater, but I was afraid I was losing my nerve and never would," Jacobi told Leslie Bennetts of the *New York Times.* "I'll never forget opening night of *Much Ado* in Stratford— wearing high heels on a steeply raked glass stage. I knew the part backwards and forwards, but suddenly I thought I didn't know anything, and it was the worst moment of my life. My costume turned black with sweat. Stage fright is too mild a word for it; it is absolute stark terror."

Jacobi continued to work with the RSC and take the occasional film role. He was cast as Nicodemus in the 1982 film *The Secret of NIMH.* He won his first Antoinette Perry Award in 1988 for *Breaking the Code* as Alan Turing, the real-life English cryptographer who deciphered a vital enemy transmission code during World War II. That same year, he directed Branagh in the young actor's stage debut in *Hamlet,* and the following year appeared in Branagh's film version of *Henry V.* In 1996, Jacobi appeared as himself in the small independent film by Al Pacino, *Looking for Richard,* an exploration on the role of Shakespeare's *Richard II.*

### Unsure about Tonsure

Jacobi returned to PBS with great success in the mid-1990s as the lead in the *Mystery!* series *Brother Cadfael.* He played a twelfth-century crime-solving monk in Shrewsbury, England, an informally trained physician and veteran of one of the Crusades who solves local murder mysteries—at times against the orders of his religious superiors—using his extensive knowledge of botany. Based on the novels of Ellis Peters, the *Cadfael* series, which ran from 1994 to 1999, was filmed in Hungary and called for Jacobi to shave his head into the distinctive Benedictine tonsure. "They can get people on the moon but they can't create a state-of-the-art tonsured wig," Jacobi said in an interview with Patricia Brennan of the *Washington Post.* "I will only do three-and-a half inch diameter, no more—it's like being mutilated. I think one of the reasons [the monks] did it was self-mutilation, or the crown of thorns, or so that God can see your thoughts easier."

In 1998, Jacobi played the notoriously ill-tempered British painter Francis Bacon in the biopic *Love Is the Devil,* based on one of the artist's romantic involvements that ended in a suicide. "Jacobi projects Bacon's legendary charisma and cruelly cutting charm," said Robert Sklar in an *ARTnews* review. In 1999, the actor was scheduled to appear in *Joan of Arc: The Virgin Warrior.* Knighted by Queen Elizabeth in 1994, Jacobi also received several honors in 1997 in Washington, D.C. as part of an anniversary gala for the Folger Shakespeare Library. He attended a reception at the White House, was honored with a National Press Club luncheon forum, and was presented with the Sir John Gielgud Award for Excellence in the Dramatic Arts by the Shakespeare Theater.

Somewhat ironically, Jacobi is a firm believer that the part-time actor and corn merchant known as William Shakespeare did not actually write the plays credited to him. He and many scholars believe that the works were instead penned by the far more worldly and learned 17th Earl of Oxford, Edward Devere. Jacobi is far from a traditionalist regarding interpretations of the bard's plays, and has been showered throughout his career with critical affection for

bringing a modern feel to the centuries-old dramas. "Shakespeare is not easy, and the more accessible it can be made without ruining the ideas, the better," Jacobi told the *Washington Post.* "There is such a world of treasure to be found that the plays will never be exhausted. Each generation finds new truths, each actor finds new interpretations. There can't ever be a definitive production. [With each new production] you bring out another relevance, and make them understandable."

### Further Reading

*ARTnews,* September, 1998.
*Boston Globe,* November 8, 1998.
*New York,* September 22, 1980.
*New York Times,* June 10, 1979; October 24, 1984; January 20, 1985.
*Newsweek,* October 22, 1984.
*People,* November 10, 1980.
*Washington Post,* January 12, 1995; August 17, 1997. □

# Jackie Joyner-Kersee

**Multitalented athlete Jackie Joyner-Kersee (born 1962) was one of the top American track stars of the 1980s and 1990s, winning numerous Olympic medals and setting or tying records in several events.**

She was the first American ever to win a gold medal in the long jump and the first woman in history to earn more than 7,000 points in the grueling seven-event heptathlon. She won three Olympic gold medals, one silver, and two bronze, and she established a world record in the heptathlon. Her achievements are so astounding—and her personality so engaging—that she has become one of America's favorite track athletes. According to Kenny Moore in *Sports Illustrated,* Joyner-Kersee, "like her name, is a blend. Her years of hard, thoughtful training are the Kersee part, the expression of her husband-coach Bob Kersee's hatred of talent lying fallow. The Joyner half is Jackie in competition. She wants to win, but having won, wants to go on. She wants to impress, but having performed gloriously, still wants to go on. The Joyner gift is her open joy in practiced, powerful movement, in improvement for its own sake, and it causes observers to presume, in error, that what she does is without personal cost."

Indeed, Joyner-Kersee has often found herself in competition with only the clock and the yardstick, having left her competitors in the dust. Not satisfied just to win, she struggles for records, for solid recognition that she dominates her sport. She has won championships—Olympic and otherwise—with hamstring injuries, has broken world records in heat that would stagger a camel, and has managed through it all to maintain a stable relationship with her husband-coach Bob Kersee. As Ken Denlinger put it in the *Washington Post,* Joyner-Kersee "smokes the world's playgrounds as no other female athlete in history."

Before Joyner-Kersee set her sights on it, the heptathlon was a virtually unknown event in America. It has since become a track and field favorite, especially during the Olympics. For the heptathlon, athletes amass points by running a 200-meter dash, completing both high and long jumps, throwing a javelin and a shot put, running the 100-meter hurdles, and finishing an 800-meter run, all in the space of two days. The seven-event series demands skills in a variety of areas that most athletes choose as specialties.

Joyner-Kersee has been a star in the heptathlon since 1984, when she won a silver medal after losing the 800-meter run by a fraction of a second. In the 1988 and 1992 Olympics she won a gold in the event. Even more remarkable, she has managed to single out one specialty—the long jump—and win Olympic medals in that event as well. In 1988, she earned a gold medal for a jump; in both 1992 and 1996 she settled graciously for a bronze. A drug-free athlete sometimes faced with steroid-enhanced competitors, Joyner-Kersee is the first American woman ever to win an Olympic long jump competition.

## Aspired to Succeed

Born on March 3, 1962, Joyner-Kersee grew up in East St. Louis, Illinois, a poverty-stricken city on the Mississippi River. Her parents, Alfred and Mary Joyner, were barely in their teens when they got married. Mary was only 14 when her first child, Al, was born and just 16 when she gave birth to Jackie, in 1962. Both parents worked hard to provide for their growing family, Alfred in construction and on the railroads and Mary as a nurse's aid. The couple's salaries were

hardly adequate, and the Joyners knew real desperation. Moore in *Sports Illustrated* wrote: "Their house was little more than wallpaper and sticks, with four tiny bedrooms. During the winters, when the hot-water pipes would freeze, they had to heat water for baths in kettles on the kitchen stove. Their great-grandmother (on their father's side) lived with them until she died on the plastic-covered sofa in the living room while Jackie was at the store buying milk."

The Joyner family—especially Jackie—wished desperately for better circumstances. A grandmother had named her "Jacqueline," after Jacqueline Kennedy Onassis, the wife of former U.S. president John F. Kennedy, hoping that the youngster would someday be "first lady" of something. Joyner-Kersee's brother Al, himself an Olympic gold medalist, told *Sports Illustrated:* "I remember Jackie and me crying together in a back room in that house, swearing that someday we were going to make it. Make it out. Make things different." Their mother encouraged Joyner-Kersee and her brother to improve. Having been a teenaged parent herself, Mary Joyner told the children they could not date until the age of 18 and spurred their interest in other activities.

As a child, Joyner-Kersee began to study modern dance at the local community center. One day she saw a sign advertising a new track program and decided to give it a try. At first Joyner-Kersee lost every race, but soon she was winning. In 1976, she watched the Olympics on television and later recalled in the *Chicago Tribune*, "I decided I wanted to go. I wanted to be on TV, too." After that she tried harder and became a tremendously versatile athlete at a very tender age. The first competitor she beat regularly was her older brother, Al. The two siblings began to spur one another on to greater and greater achievements, growing very close in the process.

At the age of 14, Joyner-Kersee won the first of four straight national junior pentathlon championships. Track and field events were only part of the weapons in her arsenal, however. In high school she was a state champion in both track and basketball. Her Lincoln High School basketball team won games by an average of 52.8 points during her senior year. Joyner-Kersee also played volleyball and continued to encourage her brother in his sporting career. Her athletic achievements notwithstanding, she was an excellent student who finished in the top ten percent of her graduating class.

## Took to the Track

Joyner-Kersee was heavily recruited by high-ranking colleges and chose the University of California at Los Angeles. She began school there in 1980 on a basketball scholarship. Tragedy struck in her freshman year when her mother developed a rare form of meningitis and died at the age of 37. Stunned by the sudden and unexpected loss, both Jackie and Al Joyner dedicated themselves to athletics with new resolve. Having returned to UCLA, Joyner-Kersee became a starting forward for the Bruins and worked with the track team as a long jumper. She was rather surprised to find herself singled out by an assistant track coach named Bob Kersee, who detected untapped possibilities in the young collegian. "I saw this talent walking around the campus that everyone was blind to," he told *Sports Illustrated.* "No one was listening to her mild requests to do more. So I went to the athletic director and made him a proposition."

Kersee literally put his own job on the line, demanding to coach Jackie Joyner in multi-events, or he would quit. The university athletic department agreed to his plan. The coach remarked in *Sports Illustrated,* "By 1982, I could see she'd be the world record holder." Joyner-Kersee was already a powerhouse in the long jump and the 200-meter sprint. She was also a top scoring forward on the basketball team, so her endurance was excellent. Al Joyner taught her how to run the hurdles and to throw the javelin—a type of spear— and the shot put—a heavy palm-sized metal ball.

By 1983, Joyner-Kersee qualified for the world track and field championships in Helsinki, Finland. Her first chance to be a world champion ended in disaster, however, when she pulled a hamstring muscle and could not complete the heptathlon. Ironically, her brother Al was also present, and he too was injured. Al Joyner told *Sports Illustrated* that he consoled his sister by telling her, "It's just not our time yet." In 1984, both Jackie and Al Joyner qualified for the U.S. Olympic team. Having recovered from her injuries, Jackie was a favorite to win the heptathlon. Al, on the other hand, was not considered likely to win his event, the triple jump.

Confounding all predictions, Jackie won the silver medal in the heptathlon, missing the gold by only .06 seconds in her final event, the 800-meter run. Meanwhile, Al Joyner became the first American in 80 years to win the Olympic triple jump. The tears Jackie shed at the end of the day were not for her hair's-breadth loss, but rather for joy at her brother's victory. Both of them knew that Jackie would be back to compete another day.

## Set Records in Long Jump and Heptathlon

The depths of Joyner-Kersee's potential began to be apparent in 1985, when she set a U.S. record with a long jump measuring 23 feet 9 inches. By then she had quit playing basketball and was devoting herself exclusively to track, under the guidance of Bob Kersee. Their relationship became romantic after years spent working together as friends, and they were married on January 11, 1986. When Al Joyner was wed to a sprinter named Florence Griffith, the stage was set for the emergence of a track and field "family" of champions: Jackie Joyner-Kersee and Florence Griffith Joyner. The two women were among an elite cadre of track stars coached by Bob Kersee in preparation for the 1988 Olympic Games.

In 1985, Joyner-Kersee was ranked third in the world heptathlon. She changed that ranking forever at the 1986 Goodwill Games in Moscow. There she set a world record in the event with 7,148 points—more than 200 points higher than her nearest competitor in history. Just three weeks later she broke her own record with a score of 7,161 points in Houston, Texas, where temperatures reached 100 degrees during competition. Her devotion to the heptathlon was recognized by numerous awards, including the 1986

Sullivan Award for best amateur athlete and the coveted Jesse Owens Award.

Joyner-Kersee's performance at the 1988 Olympics was nothing short of phenomenal. Not only did she win a gold medal in the heptathlon, she also took the gold medal in the long jump, flying 24 feet, 3.5 inches. Her heptathlon score of 7,291 points was her fourth world record, and many predicted it would probably stand for several years. Joyner-Kersee's achievement in the 1988 Olympics was particularly exciting because multi-event track competitions and the long jump had been dominated by countries of the former Soviet Bloc, where steroid use among athletes was acceptable. Joyner-Kersee became not only the first American woman to win a gold medal in the Olympic long jump, she also became the first athlete in 64 years to win a gold in both a multi-event and a single event.

Much attention has been focused over the years on the relationship between Jackie Joyner-Kersee and her coach and husband, Bob. The pair have been spotted quarreling during competition. Kersee is an exacting man who makes his demands well known. The coach told the *Chicago Tribune* that he and his wife try not to take their disagreements home with them at night. "We want to make it in terms of the coach-athlete relationship, and we want to stay married for the rest of our lives," he said. "So we've got rules in terms of our coach-athlete relationship and our husband-wife relationship." He added: "I'm surprised it works as well as it does, and I'm happy it does for both of us. We enjoy sports so much, and we enjoy one another so much, it would be a shame if we let track and field get in the way of our personal life, or our personal life get in the way of track and field."

Joyner-Kersee has not been able to break her 1988 Olympic heptathlon record. Since then she has re-injured her hamstring and had moments when she lacked the resolve to continue. The incessant prodding of Kersee has kept her at the top of the world standings, however. In 1992, she sought to become the fourth woman in Olympic history to win four gold medals. Her performance in the heptathlon earned her another gold, but she could only turn in a bronze medal performance in the long jump. The 30-year-old Joyner-Kersee was gracious about her defeat in the long jump, because the winner was her close friend, Heike Drechsler, of Germany. Joyner-Kersee told the *Los Angeles Times* that she was thrilled for her rival. "With other athletes, even though you're fierce competitors, you get a sense of them as people, whether they're nice," she said. "You still want to beat them, but when the competition is over, you realize that there's more to life than athletics."

## Olympic Performance Slowed, but Career Flourished

Into the 1990s, Joyner-Kersee continued to compete in track and field, stating that she wanted to end her Olympic career on American soil. She entered the 1996 Olympics in Atlanta, Georgia, but was suffering from an injury to her right hamstring. She came away with another bronze in the long jump and withdrew from the heptathlon. Although she did not plan to compete in another set of Olympic games,

Joyner-Kersee had no plans to abandon the sport. For some time, Joyner-Kersee had indicated that she might look to other sports besides track and field. In 1996, she signed a one-year contract with the Richmond Rage, a professional team in the newly formed American Basketball League (ABL). She did not end up spending much time on the court, though, and left in mid-season due to concerns over possible injuries.

Joyner-Kersee continued to compete in track and field events once she gave up her basketball career while also keeping busy with other projects. She functioned as a spokesperson for Nike's PLAY (Participate in the Lives of America's Youth) program, helping to raise funds for youth activity centers and providing scholarship money to youth through the Joyner-Kersee Community Foundation. She also worked with children in her hometown of East St. Louis, Illinois. After many years of trying to rebuild the crumbling Mary E. Brown Community Center, she announced in 1997 that the Joyner-Kersee Community Foundation would provide funds to build a new recreational facility on 37 acres in the center of East St. Louis. In addition to basketball courts, ball fields, and indoor and outdoor tracks, the center was to be equipped with computers, a library, and other educational resources.

Joyner-Kersee published her autobiography, *A New Kind of Grace,* in 1997. She registered to become an agent with the National Football League Players Association in 1998 and founded a sports management company to represent athletes in a number of sports. By the end of the year she had signed three NFL players to her list. In addition, she won the heptathlon in the Goodwill Games in July of 1998, marking the end of her illustrious career. She officially retired at age 36 on August 1, 1998, with a long jump in her hometown that was mostly ceremonial. Up until and after her final event, she remained legendary not only for her extraordinary skill, but also for her charming personality. *Los Angeles Times* reporter Randy Harvey wrote of Joyner-Kersee: "She is one of the warmest, most even-tempered persons in athletics. The next bad word that anyone who knows her, including her competitors, says about her will be the first."

## Further Reading

*Chicago Tribune,* September 25, 1988.
*Ebony,* October 1986; April 1992; October 1992.
*Interview,* June 1997, p. 82.
*Jet,* October 7, 1996, p. 48; February 9, 1998, p. 46.
*Knight-Ridder/Tribune News Service,* August 2, 1996.
*Los Angeles Times,* September 14, 1988; September 29, 1988; February 17, 1990; June 22, 1992.
*Parade Magazine,* June 13, 1993, p. 14.
*Philadelphia Daily News,* August 7, 1992.
*Reuters,* January 8, 1997.
*Sports Illustrated,* April 27, 1987; September 14, 1987; October 10, 1988; August 3, 1998, p. 29.
*Time,* December 15, 1997, p. S16.
*Washington Post,* February 26, 1987; July 17, 1988; September 25, 1988.
*Women's Sports and Fitness,* January-February 1995, p. 21; November-December 1998, p. 42. □

# K

## Grace Kelly

**As a talented young film star, Grace Kelly (1929–1982) captured the imagination of the American public when she married Prince Ranier III of Monaco, to become Grace, Princess of Monaco. Her tragic and untimely death in 1982 touched the entire world.**

Grace, Princess of Monaco was born Grace Patricia Kelly on November 12, 1929 in Philadelphia, Pennsylvania. She aspired to an acting career in her teens, and was a major motion picture star by the age of 25. Kelly became acquainted with Prince Ranier Grimaldi III of the principality of Monaco during a photo session arranged by *Paris Match* in 1955. The couple was married in the spring of 1956, and they raised three children. Princess Grace brought a special aura of excitement and sophistication to Monaco that contributed to the growth of the principality into a major tourist haven and a playground for the rich and famous. She was noted for the manner in which she adapted her American ways to her lifestyle as a royal mother. It wasn't long before she won the love and respect of the entire world.

The fairy tale romance came to a tragic conclusion in 1982 when the princess suffered a debilitating stroke while driving her car on a twisting mountain road. The car, along with Princess Grace and her daughter, Stephanie, plunged 150 feet, causing fatal injuries to Princess Grace. Her daughter survived the ordeal, but the Grimaldi family, along with Monaco and the entire world, were left with only memories of the beloved Grace, Princess of Monaco.

The woman who would become the princess of Monaco was the granddaughter of the Kelly family patriarch, John Henry Kelly, who immigrated to America from Ireland in 1867. He fathered six sons, including George Kelly, a Pulitzer Prize winner; Walter C. Kelly, a vaudevillian personality; and John B. "Jack" Kelly, Sr., father of Grace Patricia Kelly. Jack Kelly was an Olympic sculler and a self-made millionaire. Her mother was Margaret Majer Kelly, a former model. Jack and Margaret Kelly had four children: Margaret "Peggy" (Baba) Kelly Conlan, born in 1925; John B. (Kell) Kelly, Jr., born in 1927; Grace Kelly, born in 1929; and Lizanne LeVine, born in 1933. All of the Kelly children were born and raised in Philadelphia.

The issue of religion was critical to the Irish-Catholic Kelly clan. Margaret Kelly converted from her Lutheran faith after her marriage, and the Kellys maintained a strict Catholic household. Jack Kelly held a reputation as an uncultured man who placed great emphasis on athletic prowess. Grace Kelly's brother took after his father and was an accomplished world class oarsman. Grace Kelly enjoyed playing hockey and swimming, but was not a passionate athlete. She preferred instead to practice ballet, to read, and to study theatrical arts.

Kelly attended the Catholic Ravenhill Academy in East Falls, Pennsylvania and eventually transferred to Stevens School, a secular academy. She was extremely reserved and quiet as a youngster, but was popular among her high school friends.

Kelly was always a stunning beauty, even as an infant. After graduating from high school in 1947, she attended the American Academy of Dramatic Arts in New York City. During her years at the Academy she lived at a hotel for women called the Barbizon. She supported herself through modeling and was in great demand as a cover girl.

After graduating in 1949, it was Kelly's desire to act on the live stage—not to make movies and television appearances. She worked in theaters in New York and Colorado, and, most notably, she performed with Raymond Massey in *The Father* before signing with agent Edith Van Cleve. To experts, including the great actress Helen Hayes, Kelly was unsuited to live stage acting because of her shallow voice. At Van Cleve's urging, Kelly studied privately under Sanford Meisner at the Neighborhood Playhouse in New York, and worked summer stock until Van Cleve—fully aware of Kelly's film potential—moved the young actress into television work. Kelly acted in 60 teleplays in New York, mostly between 1950 and 1951. Over the course of the next five years she made 11 movies. Some critics, including gossip columnist Hedda Hopper, accused Kelly of employing adulterous liaisons to further her film career. Others presumed that Jack Kelly's prominent position and political connections were in part responsible for his daughter's show business success. Jack Kelly, a Democratic Party boss in his native Philadelphia, was well acquainted with some of the most prominent figures of the times, including President Franklin Roosevelt. Powerful personalities such as Isaac Levy, founder of the Columbia Broadcasting System (CBS), were also counted among the Kelly associates. Regardless, Grace Kelly was determined to succeed without special considerations and did little if anything to "pull strings" of any nature in order to further her career.

## Film Career

In 1950, Grace Kelly made her feature film debut in a movie called *Fourteen Hours.* Her next film, *High Noon,* with Gary Cooper in 1952, marked the beginning of a string of motion pictures over the course of the next four years. To Kelly's displeasure, each of her films generated rumors of a love affair between Kelly and her co-star. Friends of the actress maintain that, in actuality, it was an actor named Gene Lyons who attracted Kelly's attention during those years. The two enjoyed a romance that matured during the filming of *High Noon* and later disintegrated while Kelly was on location in Africa for the filming of *Mogambo,* a 1953 release with Clark Gable. In 1954, Kelly starred in Alfred Hitchcock's *Dial M for Murder,* with Ray Milland. This was followed by a second Hitchcock thriller, *Rear Window* with Jimmy Stewart. *The Bridges at Toko-Ri,* with William Holden was completed in 1954. That same year, Kelly appeared with Bing Crosby in *Country Girl,* the film that earned her an Academy Award for Best Actress.

In 1955, Kelly starred in *Green Fire* with Stewart Granger, followed by *To Catch a Thief* with Cary Grant. In 1956, she starred in a musical adaptation of *Philadelphia Story* called *High Society,* with Bing Crosby and Frank Sinatra. The final film of her brief but intense career, *The Swan,* was released in 1956. She co-starred with Alec Guinness and received top billing for the first and only time in her career. During the years when Kelly was under contract with Metro-Goldwyn-Mayer, she shared her time between the incessant demands of Hollywood and her chosen home in New York City, where she aspired to find work on the Broadway stage.

## A Meeting in Monaco

In 1955, Kelly was in Monaco for the filming of Hitchcock's *To Catch a Thief* with Cary Grant. An introduction was arranged between the young American actress and the bachelor prince of Monaco as part of a publicity stunt by *Paris Match.* The pair met initially at the Cannes Film Festival in order to be photographed together for the magazine. The event was well publicized, down to the shimmering black cotton dress worn by Kelly. Later in 1955, the prince and the movie star spent Christmas together in Philadelphia with Kelly's family. Less than one week after the holidays, on January 5, 1956, Kelly and the prince announced their engagement from her parent's home. Kelly and the prince were wed in Monaco, where the ceremonies and festivities lasted for two days—April 18 and 19, 1956. A Catholic nuptial ceremony was celebrated at the Cathedral of St. Nicholas in Monaco. The prince and princess honeymooned aboard a royal yacht.

The royal couple's eldest child, Princess Caroline Louise Marguerite, was born in January of 1957. Their next child, Crown Prince Albert Alexandre Louis Pierre, was born in March of the following year. Their youngest child, Princess Stephanie Marie Elisabeth, was born in February of 1965. Princess Grace lived with her husband and children in a 200-room palace and maintained a private retreat in France at Roc Agel. Even as princess of Monaco, Kelly never shunned her American roots. She commuted regularly between Europe and Philadelphia, if for no other reason than to see her doctor, dentist, and bankers.

At home in Monaco, Princess Grace ran the palace to the best of her ability as a normal home. She expended great effort to stay intrinsically involved with her children and to personally tend to their needs. She cooked meals for her family, especially breakfast for her children. Despite her great wealth, she never succumbed to needless or excess extravagance. The populace of Monaco loved Princess Grace dearly, as did her film audiences in the United States. After she married, Princess Grace became involved in charitable pursuits and public service organizations. She served as president of the Garden Club of Monaco, president of the Red Cross of Monaco, and president of the organizing committee of the International Arts Foundation. Her fondest benevolent association was The Princess Grace Foundation, established to foster involvement among young people in the creative arts, especially to provide scholarships for eligible young students.

Princess Grace brought positive and long overdue changes to the social climate of Monaco. Her presence revitalized the mood of the principality, encouraged tourism, and endowed a dogged state with renewed hope and energy.

Not long after the birth of her youngest daughter, it was rumored that Princess Grace had grown increasingly unhappy and become homesick for the more casual atmosphere of the United States. She moved to an apartment in Paris, joined the board of directors of 20th Century Fox productions, and traveled frequently to the U.S. During the final years of her life, she involved herself in dramatic readings and pressing flower designs for linens, in addition to her royal responsibilities and her many charitable pursuits.

### Untimely Death

Princess Grace died unexpectedly from injuries incurred at the wheel of her own car, a Rover 3500, when it careened from a cliff and crashed 150 feet down the mountainside. The accident occurred at the Grimaldi's private retreat at Roc Agel. Princess Grace remained unconscious for two days before she died in Monte Carlo on September 14, 1982, following the removal of life-support apparatus. Later reports confirmed that she suffered a stroke at the time of the crash and would have been paralyzed on one side had she survived. Funeral services were held at the Cathedral of St. Nicholas in Monaco, the same church where she had been married in 1956.

The death of Princess Grace was felt around the world. The family of the princess acknowledged the receipt of tens of thousands of letters and cards of condolence. Mourners continued to leave flowers at the site of the auto crash for months afterward. Prince Ranier III admitted to "a heaviness of heart that I don't think will change in my lifetime," as quoted by writer Roger Bianchini in *Ladies Home Journal*. Ranier went forward with his wife's intended plan to build a house on Kelly ancestral lands in Ireland.

### Further Reading

*Collier's Encyclopedia,* 1997.

Englund, Steven, *Grace of Monaco: an interpretive biography,* Doubleday & Company, Inc., 1984.
*Cosmopolitan,* April 1991, p. 212.
*Entertainment Weekly,* September 11, 1992.
*Good Housekeeping,* September 1992.
*Ladies Home Journal,* April 1983.
*Life,* March 1983.
*People Weekly,* September 5, 1983; September 12, 1983. □

# Joseph Kennedy

**Considered by many to be America's version of the "royal family," the Kennedys of Boston, Massachusetts have enjoyed success and seen tragedy during the 20th century. The family patriarch, Joseph Patrick Kennedy (1888–1969) instilled values of dedication to public service, determination to succeed, and loyalty to family.**

Kennedy, a second-generation American of Irish descent, was born in Boston, Massachusetts, on September 6, 1888. His father, Patrick Joseph, was a well-to-do saloonkeeper. Patrick also was active in Boston politics, as Irish ward boss, state representative (five times), and state senator (one time).

Kennedy's parents were anxious for their son to succeed. But in the Boston social climate of the time, success was difficult to achieve for people of their background. It was Kennedy's mother, Mary Augusta, who decided that her son should be called Joseph Patrick rather than Patrick Joseph, after his father. She feared that "Patrick Kennedy" sounded "too Irish." Mary Augusta believed that in Brahmin Boston (a term used to describe Boston's social elite), being Irish and Catholic were impediments to entry into "better" society.

She arranged for her son to work for a millinery shop, delivering hats to well-to-do women. She instructed her son that, if asked his name, to reply simply "Joseph," so as to avoid drawing attention to his ethnic background. Both parents were aware that entry to the higher levels of Boston society dictated that Kennedy mix with those outside his Irish community. They sent their son to Catholic schools for his early education. When he was a bit older, however, he attended Boston Latin School and Harvard University, to be educated with Boston's elite Protestant families.

### Few Friends at Harvard

Although he made some friends at Harvard—especially among the few Irish students there—and was popular with young Irish women, Kennedy never was accepted by a majority of the students. Anti-Irish, anti-Catholic sentiment was strong. One friend warned Kennedy to be very careful in his behavior because Boston Brahmins were watching for any sign that would justify their prejudices. Kennedy's determination to ingratiate himself with the socially prominent Protestants was viewed by some as dis-

agreeable and pretentious. He was never invited to join any of Harvard's better clubs. Friends attested to what they felt was one of Kennedy's more admirable qualities: his adherence to the tenets of his religious upbringing. His Catholic faith was important to him and he attended mass regularly. On one occasion, he even hired a buggy so that all of his friends could ride with him to church.

## Business Success

Kennedy was a shrewd money maker. He showed an entrepreneurial spirit and an appreciation for money at an early age. Kennedy held a number of jobs as a youngster, including candy vendor, newspaper hawker, and play producer. He also performed jobs for Orthodox Jews, whose faith prohibited them from working on their holy days. During his student days at Harvard, he and a friend bought a bus and began operating sightseeing tours. Kennedy negotiated with another tour operator to share working hours. He was successful at this, earning $5,000 over the course of several summers.

## Marriage and Family

In 1914, two years after his graduation, Kennedy accepted a job as president of Columbia Trust Company Bank. At 25 years of age, he was the youngest bank president in the United States. During that same year, he married Rose Fitzgerald, daughter of Boston's mayor. Kennedy and Rose bought a small home in Brookline, Massachusetts, and started their family. In all, they had nine children: Joseph Jr., John (Jack), Rosemary, Kathleen, Eunice, Patricia, Robert

(Bobby), Jean, and Edward (Ted). Several of his children went on to develop distinguished political careers, including two U.S. senators and one president.

Kennedy supported his large family through numerous successful business ventures. He joined an investment banking firm, bought a chain of New England movie theaters, gained control of a film production company, bought and sold many properties in New York, invested in the stock market, and controlled a franchise on Scotch whiskey and British gin. All of these ventures proved lucrative. He may have earned as much as $5 million in three years from his motion picture work. He earned $8.5 million when he sold the alcohol franchise, which he had purchased for $118,000 13 years earlier. He always made a substantial profit on the properties he bought and sold.

## Movie Producer

Kennedy's career as a motion picture executive earned him kudos from some observers. He was wise enough not to tamper with a company that already was profitable. *Photoplay* magazine writer Terry Ramsaye said of him: "Now comes this banking person Kennedy and a very young person with freckles on his face and nonchalance in his manner. And he comes not as an angel hopefully backing a star-to-be nor by many of the other sidedoor entrances but bolting in the main gate, acting as though he knows just what he is doing. Apparently he does." In 1926, Kennedy's company FBO produced 50 films.

In Hollywood, Kennedy became friends with many well-known actors, Gloria Swanson among them. He became her adviser, consultant, and lover. Swanson named her adopted son after Kennedy. Their relationship lasted several years, but was broken off abruptly, according to Swanson, because she "questioned his judgment" and "he did not like to be questioned."

## Involved With His Children

Although his work as a motion picture executive meant that he frequently was away from his wife and children for long periods of time, Kennedy's interest in and concern for his children remained constant. The children lined up every Sunday to talk with him when he called—in part because their mother insisted on it. Kennedy apparently was happy to talk about his children with his friends in Hollywood; when Joe Jr. had measles, Kennedy told actor Tom Mix about it. Mix sent a telegram to Joe Jr., in which he described his own bout with measles.

Kennedy was concerned about the physical and emotional welfare of his children, too. When his son Jack became ill with scarlet fever, Kennedy spent several days in church praying for his son's recovery. When Robert was of school age, Kennedy complimented him on his efforts to distinguish himself from his two successful, older brothers.

## Political Ambitions

Kennedy's own political involvement began in 1932, when he supported the Democratic presidential nomination of Franklin Delano Roosevelt. He worked as campaign contributor, lender, and fundraiser. In return, President Roosevelt rewarded him with the position of first chairman of the Securities & Exchange Commission, a decision that was not popular in some circles. A *Newsweek* article asserted ''Mr. Kennedy, former speculator and pool operator, will now curb speculation and prohibit pools.'' The *New Republic* characterized him as ''the worst of all parasites, a Wall Street operator.'' Still, Kennedy did a thorough and honest job. Despite his wish to become secretary of the treasury, Roosevelt appointed him chairman of the Maritime Commission. Kennedy eventually resigned from the post, tired of dealing with unions and ship-owners. In 1938, Kennedy was appointed ambassador to England. During this sensitive period just prior to World War II, Kennedy made a number of unfortunate mistakes. He was an isolationist, and gave speeches that implied agreement with policies designed to appease Hitler. He announced plans to resettle 600,000 German Jews in other parts of the world—a strategy he had not discussed with President Roosevelt. There also was speculation in some newspapers that Kennedy was thinking of a run for the Presidency in 1940—speculation that irritated Roosevelt, although Roosevelt may have planted the story. Amidst mounting pressure, Kennedy was forced to resign his post in 1940.

Kennedy's life was fraught with tragedy during the 1940s. His eldest son, Joseph, Jr., was killed in action during World War II. His favorite daughter, Kathleen, was killed in a plane crash four years after the death of her husband. His son, Jack, was seriously wounded when his boat was attacked by the Japanese.

After World War II, Kennedy concentrated his efforts on getting his sons elected to political office. He began by working on Jack's campaign for representative in the 11th District of Massachusetts. Kennedy was a quiet but effective campaigner. He contacted every powerful person he knew to assist him—with votes and campaign contributions. The tactic—and his personal $50,000 contribution—proved successful. Kennedy employed the same successful strategy in 1952, when Jack ran for the state Senate.

## A Kennedy in the White House

Kennedy's next project—getting his son elected as the first Roman Catholic president of the United States—was launched in the late 1950s. His tactics caused considerable controversy during his son's run for the presidency. Kennedy was accused of influencing delegates at the National Democratic Convention and of buying the nomination for his son. Jack himself once observed ''Dad is a financial genius all right, but in politics, he is something else.'' Kennedy distanced himself from his son during the period prior to and during the nomination process, and did not return to Massachusetts until the election took place. His wife, Rose explained: ''He has been a controversial figure all of his life and he thinks it's easier for his sons if he doesn't appear on the scene.''

Jack Kennedy won the presidential election in 1960, fulfilling his father's dream. But Kennedy's reaction was modest: ''I have a strong idea that there is no other success for a father and a mother except to feel that they have made some contributions to the development of their children.''

## Tragic Years

Despite suffering a stroke in 1961, Kennedy remained active and interested in the lives of his grown children. However, tragedy continued to plague his last years. His son Jack was assassinated in 1963, before completing his first term as president. His son, Robert, was shot and killed in 1968, while campaigning for the Democratic presidential nomination. His youngest son, Ted, was involved in a scandal with a young woman who drowned while in his company.

Kennedy bore his sorrows with stoicism and courage until his death on November 19, 1969, at Hyannis Port, Massachusetts. The words of his longtime friend, Cardinal Cushing, best express Kennedy's importance in American life: ''His exceptional abilities were generously placed for many years in the service of his country. He instilled a sense of pride in his family so that all its members extended their increasing maturity into careers of unparalleled public service and achievement.''

## Further Reading

Collier, Peter, and David Horowitz, *The Kennedys: An American Drama,* Summit Books, 1984.
Whalen, Richard J., *The Founding Father,* New American Library, 1964.
*New York Times,* November 19, 1969, p.1; p. 50.
''The Kennedys,'' http://www.geocities.com/CapitolHill/Senate/ 1968 (March 29, 1999). □

# William Kennedy

**Author William Kennedy (born 1928) rose from literary obscurity to national renown following the publication of his 1983 novel *Ironweed*. Taken together, his gritty, downbeat novels form an intricate cycle spanning the history of his native Albany, New York. Kennedy has been awarded numerous literary honors and been hailed as one of America's most accomplished novelists.**

William Joseph Kennedy was born on January 16, 1928 in Albany, New York. His parents, William Joseph and Mary Elizabeth (McDonald) Kennedy, were descended from Irish immigrants who had settled in North Albany in the 19th century. Kennedy grew up in an Irish-Catholic neighborhood known locally as the North End or Limerick. As a child, he served as an altar boy at the Sacred Heart Church, and entertained dreams of one day becoming a Catholic priest.

Kennedy attended grade school at Public School 20. While in the seventh grade, he became fascinated by the world of print journalism. He began drawing cartoons and even started his own newspaper. Upon entering high school at the Christian Brothers Academy, he wrote articles for the school newspaper.

The allure of a career in journalism dovetailed nicely with one of Kennedy's other adolescent passions: politics. North Albany was a hotbed of Irish Democratic political activity. The area was dominated by a political machine organized by Daniel Peter O'Connell, whom Kennedy later used as the model for the character of Patsy McCall in his novel *Billy Phelan's Greatest Game.* Many of Kennedy's relatives held political jobs. His great-grandfather, "Big Jim" Carroll, served as a ward leader. His father worked the polls for the machine and occasionally took William Jr. to Democratic Party rallies. Two of his mother's brothers also served as political operatives.

## A Career in Journalism

Kennedy left Albany after high school to enroll at nearby Siena College in upstate New York. He was named executive editor of the *Siena News,* the college newspaper. Upon earning his degree, he took a job as sports editor and columnist for the Glens Falls *Post Star.* In 1950, he was drafted into the U.S. Army and assigned to the Fourth Division in Europe. But his journalistic skills did not go to waste here either. Kennedy worked on the division's newspaper until his discharge in 1952.

Kennedy returned to his home town in 1952, securing a job at the Albany *Times-Union.* He remained there for the next four years, at which time he accepted an offer to work for the *Puerto Rico World Journal.* However, that paper went out of business nine months later, leaving Kennedy temporarily out of work. He eventually landed a job at the *Miami Herald* and lived in that city for a time, but he

returned to Puerto Rico in 1957. There, two years later, Kennedy was named the first managing editor of a new paper, the *San Juan Star.*

## Changed Course

While in Puerto Rico, Kennedy met and married Ana Daisy (Dana) Segarra, a dancer, singer, and actress. Together they would have three children. During this period, Kennedy also began turning his attention to writing fiction. He enrolled in a creative writing class taught by the acclaimed novelist Saul Bellow at the University of Puerto Rico at Rio Piedras. Bellow was impressed with Kennedy's early attempts at fiction and encouraged him to continue developing his talent. For a time, Kennedy tried to write stories about Puerto Rico. However, he found it difficult to write authoritatively about an adopted land without sounding like a tourist. He soon found his muse urging him to the more familiar ground of his native Albany. After two years with the *San Juan Star,* Kennedy quit journalism altogether to concentrate on his creative writing.

Kennedy moved back to Albany in 1963. He was 35 and had climbed as high as he had ever aspired in the world of print journalism. His father's health was deteriorating, however, so Kennedy accepted a job as a part-time feature writer at the Albany *Times-Union* in order to pay the bills while he worked on his creative endeavors. He first earned public acclaim for a series of features he crafted about his home city, its history, politics, and colorful characters. These pieces later served as the genesis for Kennedy's 1983 collection *O Albany!.* In 1965, Kennedy was nominated for a Pulitzer Prize for a series of articles he wrote about Albany's poor neighborhoods.

Another lucrative avenue for Kennedy's writing talents was the world of book reviewing. From 1964 to 1972, he contributed 37 reviews to the *National Observer.* In the early 1970s, Kennedy also wrote for such prestigious national publications as *Life, The New Republic, Saturday Review,* and the *New York Times.* Despite all this success, however, Kennedy was becoming convinced that his real interest lay in writing novels.

## Early Novels

In 1969, Kennedy realized a dream when his first novel, *The Ink Truck,* was published. Inspired by a real-life labor dispute at the *Times-Union,* the book follows the exploits of Bailey, a columnist embroiled in a newspaper strike. Working in a sardonic prose style, Kennedy was able to weave into the narrative many of his observations about Irish Catholic life in Albany. Critics generally lauded *The Ink Truck* as a promising first novel, though they pointed to its somewhat sloppy construction and artistic debt to previous authors as shortcomings.

For his next work, Kennedy turned to Albany history for inspiration. *Legs* (1975) told the story of the final days of gangster Jack "Legs" Diamond, who died in a shootout with his enemies in an Albany boarding house in 1931. To bring the underworld milieu to life for his readers, Kennedy spent several years doing research on Diamond and the Prohibition era. It took eight drafts to get the level of verisimilitude he desired. This is a process he did not attempt again because, he admitted that too much research can overburden the imagination. Critics responded favorably to Kennedy's efforts, as *Legs* received mostly positive reviews.

Prohibition-era Albany provided the setting for Kennedy's next novel, *Billy Phelan's Greatest Game* (1978). This time, however, the milieu Kennedy chose to explore—Democratic machine politics—was closer to home and did not require such extensive research. The book is told from the point of view of a journalist, Martin Daugherty, and revolves around the unsuccessful attempt to kidnap the son of a prominent political boss. The title character, Billy Phelan, is a pool shark and ward operative who becomes entangled in a web of corruption. Once again, critics praised Kennedy, this time for his facility with the speech patterns and manners of Albany's political subculture.

## Greatest Work

Five years after *Billy Phelan's Greatest Game*, Kennedy completed *Ironweed*, the novel many critics believe is his masterpiece. Set in the Depression-ravaged Albany of 1938, the book traces the dissolute wanderings of Francis Phelan (father of Billy from Kennedy's previous novel). Relentlessly downbeat, the manuscript was originally rejected by Viking Press, Kennedy's publisher, on the grounds that it would not sell. Similar demurrals came from thirteen other publishing houses, prompting Kennedy's old friend and mentor, Saul Bellow, to intervene on his behalf. Bellow wrote a scathing letter to Viking executives urging them to publish *Ironweed* and assuring them it would be both a commercial and critical success.

After Viking acceded to Bellow's request, he was proved right on both counts. *Ironweed* was hailed as a masterwork and awarded both the Pulitzer Prize and the National Book Critics Circle Award for Fiction. Most gratifying for Kennedy, who had to struggle to make ends meet through the publication of his first three novels, was the fact that the novel sold 100,000 copies over the course of two years. Its artistic achievement earned Kennedy a MacArthur Foundation grant worth $264,000 over five years. The struggling novelist who had labored in relative obscurity was now a literary celebrity with the financial security he had long desired.

## Literary Celebrity

After the triumph of *Ironweed*, Kennedy did not rest on his laurels. He returned immediately to the life of letters, accepting appointment by New York governor, Mario Cuomo, to head a New York State Writers Institute. A collection of Kennedy's new and old essays about his home city, *O Albany!* was published later in 1983. In 1987, Kennedy wrote the screenplay for a film version of *Ironweed*, directed by Hector Babenco. The well-received adaptation was filmed on location in Albany and starred Jack Nicholson as Francis Phelan.

In interviews and addresses about his novels, Kennedy began openly referring to them as part of a cycle in which all the events and characters were somehow interconnected. His next two works fit into that pattern perfectly. The 1988

novel, *Quinn's Book*, was set in Civil War-era Albany and featured characters related to those in his previous novels. *Very Old Bones* (1992) expanded on the history of the Phelan family.

## Fruitful 1990s

In 1993, Kennedy was elected to the American Academy of Arts and Letters, a group of 250 prominent American artists, architects, writers, and composers. A non-fiction collection, *Riding the Yellow Trolley Car*, comprised of essays, memoirs, reviews, and reportage from his days as a reporter for the Albany *Times-Union*, appeared in 1993. Three years later, Kennedy diversified his artistic portfolio when his first play, *Grand View*, premiered at Capital Repertory Company in Albany. Although he adopted a different medium, Kennedy did not stray too far from his familiar turf. The play dramatizes the clash between the two major political parties vying for control of Albany's government.

In addition to his acclaimed novels and non-fiction collections, Kennedy has also co-authored two children's books with his son Brendan, *Charlie Malarkey and the Belly Button Machine* (1986) and *Charlie Malarkey and the Singing Moose* (1993). He returned to his familiar milieu for the next novel in the cycle, 1996's *The Flaming Corsage*. The book, which spans the period from the 1880s to 1912, concerns a tragic couple: Edward Daugherty, a brilliant playwright, and his equally headstrong wife, Katrina, whose lives are shaped by a 1908 murder-suicide in a Manhattan hotel room. Kirkus Reviews called it "the most impressive entry in the Albany Cycle since *Ironweed*."

## Further Reading

Lynch, Vivian, *The Novels of William Kennedy* International Scholars Publications, 1999.
Michener, Christian, *From Then into Now: William Kennedy's Albany Novels* University of Scranton Press, 1997.
Reilly, Edward C., *William Kennedy* Twayne Publishers, 1991.
Seshachari, Neila C., *Conversations with William Kennedy* University of Mississippi Press, 1997. □

# Jack Kevorkian

**Jack Kevorkian (born 1928) became known as "Dr. Death," in part, because he assisted many people in committing suicide. Kevorkian considered the right to die to be a basic personal right, having nothing to do with government laws. He felt there could be a time when a suffering person may choose death and that physicians should be allowed to assist.**

Jack Kevorkian originally wanted to be a baseball radio broadcaster, but his Armenian immigrant parents felt that he should have a more promising career. So he became a doctor, specializing in pathology. Kevorkian worked primarily with deceased people, performing autop-

sies in order to study the essential nature of diseases. His parents never imagined that he would be the one to design the first modern *Thanatron* (Greek for "death machine") nor that he would be the first to help people use this machine.

Kevorkian was born on May 28, 1928, in Pontiac, Michigan. He was raised in an Armenian, Greek, and Bulgarian neighborhood. Kevorkian attended the University of Michigan medical school and graduated in 1952. Kevorkian initially received his macabre nickname, "Dr. Death," for his pioneering medical experiments in the 1950's. He photographed the eyes of dying patients in order to determine the exact time of death. He believed that this precise knowledge would yield valuable information about diseases. Kevorkian served as associate pathologist in three Michigan hospitals: St. Joseph's, Pontiac General, and Wyandotte General. He also worked as a pathologist in some Los Angeles hospitals. Kevorkian was the founder and director of the Checkup Multi-Phase Medical Diagnostic Center in Southfield, Michigan and Chief of Pathology at the Saratoga General Hospital in Detroit. He published more than 30 professional journal articles and booklets, including *Prescription Medicine: The Goodness of Planned Death.*

As Kevorkian witnessed the suffering of terminally ill patients, he became convinced that they had a moral right to end their lives when the pain became unbearable, and that doctors should assist in this process. To that end, he designed and constructed a machine that started a harmless saline intravenous drip into the arm of a person wishing to die. When the patient was ready, he or she would press a button that would stop the flow of the harmless solution and begin a new drip of thiopental. This chemical would put the patient into a deep sleep, then a coma. After one minute, the timer in the machine would send a lethal dose of potassium chloride into the patient's arm, stopping the heart in minutes. The patient would die of a heart attack while in a deep sleep. The death, according to Kevorkian, would be quick, painless and easy. For a person suffering from the pain of terminal cancer or some other disease, the machine would provide what Kevorkian called a painless "assisted suicide."

## First Assisted Suicide

In June 1990, Kevorkian assisted in the first of many physician-assisted suicides. He used his machine to hasten the death of Janet Adkins, a 54-year-old woman from Portland, Oregon, who was suffering from Alzheimer's disease. The State of Michigan immediately charged him with murder, although the case was later dismissed, largely due to the unclear state of Michigan law on assisted suicide. By 1999, Kevorkian had been present at the death of nearly 130 people. In each case he made his assistance known to the public, as part of a determined campaign to change attitudes and laws on physician-assisted suicide.

## Public Reaction

Many agreed with what Kevorkian was doing. On June 21, 1996, during an interview with a Detroit radio station, famed broadcast journalist Mike Wallace said, "I am an old man. I'd be the first, if necessary, to go to Kevorkian." Wallace said he could imagine seeking Kevorkian's services if he were suffering from a painful and lingering disease. "You have the right as a human being to do what you want to do with yourself," said Wallace.

Others disagreed with this opinion. The National Spinal Cord Injury Association opposed assisted suicide because there were better ways around the problem. "Refusing medical treatment is your choice to die how you wish—in your own home with your family or in your hospital bed. Assisted suicide is you giving somebody the power to take your life away. A person is given the power to kill."

## Legal Issues

Despite constant legal problems, Kevorkian continued to assist with suicides. In 1994, he faced murder charges in the death of Thomas Hyde, who suffered from a terminal nerve illness known as Lou Gehrig's disease. Jurors agreed with the argument that there was no statute against assisted suicide in the state of Michigan, and thus Kevorkian could not be found guilty.

The Kevorkian team of defense lawyers won yet another acquittal. They successfully argued that a person may not be found guilty of criminally assisting a suicide if that person had administered medication with the "intent to relieve pain and suffering," even it if did hasten the risk of dying. Kevorkian was prosecuted four times in Michigan for assisted suicides, and he was acquitted in three of those cases; a mistrial was declared in the fourth.

In 1998, the Michigan legislature enacted a law making assisted suicide a felony punishable by a maximum five year prison sentence or a $10,000 fine. This law went into effect months before a ballot proposition legalizing assisted suicide was defeated by Michigan voters. It closed the loophole on relief of pain and suffering, which Kevorkian's lawyer's relied upon to obtain acquittals. The statute provides that a person who knows another intends to kill himself and provides the means, participates in the suicide, or helps to plan the suicide, is guilty of a felony.

Kevorkian proceeded with what he thought was right, and challenged authorities to arrest and prosecute him. On September 17, 1998 he took the ultimate step in the assisted suicide of Thomas Youk. Instead of asking the patient to press the button to inject the fatal dose of drugs, Kevorkian, after speaking gently to the man suffering from Lou Gehrig's disease, administered the drug himself. Furthermore, he videotaped the entire event so there would be no doubt of what he had done. He then gave the tape to the television show *60 Minutes*. The episode was aired for the whole world to see.

Shortly thereafter, Kevorkian was arrested in Michigan for first-degree murder. In this case, when he injected Thomas Youk with the lethal drugs, he committed euthansia, or mercy killing, not assisted suicide. Kevorkian was also charged under the felony law that bans assisted suicide, which went into effect approximately two weeks before Youk's death. Kevorkian decided to represent himself in the Youk murder trial. On March 26, 1999, he was convicted of the lesser offense of second degree murder by a Michigan jury.

In the maelstrom of opinion created by his beliefs, Kevorkian continued his campaign for legalized physician-assisted suicides. He expected to be arrested, and he often was. He felt he was doing his best for people who were terminally ill and suffering great discomfort. In so doing, Kevorkian raised national awareness of assisted suicide and forced the courts and legislatures to make decisions on this controversial issue.

## Further Reading

*Detroit Free Press,* March 7, 1997; December 10, 1998; November 21, 1998; March 23-28, 1999; April 12, 1999.
Euthanasia Research and Guidance Organization, www.FinalExit.org
Newsweek.com, Jack Kevorkian, Death Wish, http://newsweek .com/nw-srv/issue/14_99a/printed/us/na/na0714_1.htm □

# Mary-Claire King

**In 1990, after 17 years of painstaking work, geneticist Mary-Claire King (born 1946) announced that she was close to pinpointing the location of a gene that is responsible for some cases of inherited breast and ovarian cancer. Her work cleared the path for future research aimed at predicting who might be at higher risk for developing the disease and possibly devising better treatments.**

Mary-Claire King was born on February 27, 1946, in Evanston, Illinois, a suburb of Chicago, to Harvey W. and Clarice King. The family included a brother Paul, who later became a mathematician and business consultant, as well as a stepbrother and stepsister. King's father worked at Standard Oil of Indiana managing the personnel department. King studied mathematics at Carleton College in Northfield, Minnesota, graduating Phi Beta Kappa in 1966. Eager for a challenge, she enrolled in graduate school studying biostatistics at the University of California at Berkeley, where she planned to use her math background in the field of medicine. After a course with geneticist Curt Stern, King found she enjoyed the concrete applications of genetics and changed her major. She was granted a National Science Foundation fellowship from 1968 to 1972 for her graduate studies.

## Pursued Political and Social Causes

During the turbulent Vietnam War era, King organized a letter-writing campaign and petition drive at the University of California, protesting the American invasion of Cambodia. After then-governor Ronald Reagan sent the National Guard to the campus to remove students from the buildings, King became dismayed and dropped out. For a while, she worked with consumer watchdog, Ralph Nader, investigating the effects of pesticides on farm workers. He offered her a job in Washington, D.C., and she weighed the option heavily. She told her friend Allan Wilson, a professor of biochemistry and molecular biology at Berkeley, that she was disappointed with her academic research. "'I can never get my experiments to work,' I said," recalled King in *Omni*. "'I'm a complete disaster in the lab.' And Allan said, 'If everyone whose experiments failed stopped doing science, there wouldn't be any science.' So I went to work in his lab."

At the time, Wilson was looking into the genetic differences between chimpanzees and humans. King worked with him, despite doubts, and finished her dissertation outlining the fact that the DNA of humans and chimps is 99 percent identical. This indicated that the two species possibly had a common ancestor about five million years ago, a time estimate about ten million years sooner than previously thought, based on fossil evidence. The researchers were pictured on the cover of *Science* magazine in April 1975 for their discovery. Meanwhile, King received her doctorate from the University of California in 1973 and married Robert Colwell, a zoologist. They later had a daughter, Emily, but divorced when she was five. The couple went to the Universidad de Chile to teach. In September, after the assassination of Socialist government leader Salvador Allende, many left-wing supporters were killed, went into hiding, or left Chile. These included some of King's friends and students.

## Launched Breakthrough Cancer Research

Returning to the United States, King worked for a year in epidemiology at the University of California in San Francisco, then was hired as an assistant professor in that discipline at the Berkeley campus in 1976. She was promoted to associate professor in 1980 and professor in 1984. King spent her time studying 1,579 women, trying to prove that some breast cancer cases could be traced to a single gene. Aware of the fact that breast cancer sometimes runs in families, she studied chromosomes of related women who had the disease. After tedious work dating from 1974, a new technology breakthrough in the early 1980s made it possible to search for pieces of DNA from blood samples. In 1990, she presented her findings at the American Society of Human Genetics annual meeting in Cincinnati. King had narrowed the possibilities to a gene located on chromosome 17.

Following this remarkable news, a kind of "holy grail" search ensued in the scientific community, with about a dozen teams of researchers fervently trying to isolate the gene, dubbed BRCA1. In September 1994, Mark Skolnick and his colleagues at the University of Utah Medical Center won the race. King and her group, however, did not fail in their mission. Her original research, coupled with ongoing studies of BRCA1 and BRCA2 (another gene that was found a year later), had succeeded in raising awareness of breast cancer and the need for further study. King noted at a 1996 conference in Paris that immense achievements had been made in figuring out how the gene worked. She and some researchers at Vanderbilt University discovered that healthy genes may be able to halt, or even reverse, the effects of the mutant gene. This opened up the possibility of using gene therapy—correcting or replacing the gene—as a future method of treatment. Well into the 1990s, however, scientists still had few clues as to why breast cancer rates were increasing in developed nations such as the United States, Canada, and across Europe.

King's breast cancer research paved the way to determining whether other diseases could be inherited. "Before BRCA1, there was a widespread view that diseases like breast cancer were caused by multiple genes that interact with environmental factors. This didn't provide geneticists with a clear road ahead," noted Maynard Olson, a professor with the University of Washington, in Columns, the university's alumni magazine. "In the midst of that, Mary-Claire's initial report was a jolt. She told a different story: that in carefully selected families she could find a fairly simple genetic link for breast cancer. It provided us with a powerful path forward. We now know that many important diseases can be attacked in the same way."

## Crusaded for Argentina's "Disappeared"

King combined her activist zeal and her education in genetics to assist grandmothers in Argentina who had lost their grandchildren during the civil war of the 1970s. After a coup in 1975, the military began kidnapping huge numbers of people in order to instill terror. Many of the "disappeared," as they came to be known, were pregnant women or women with children. Older children were killed, and pregnant women were tortured. Their babies were sold or adopted by military members, after which the mothers were killed. The new parents would claim the children as their own, despite no sign of pregnancy by the military wives. Through subversive contacts, such as

midwives and obstetricians who were coerced to deliver the babies, family members tried to keep track of the relatives they had lost. By 1977, families began forming human rights groups to find the missing children.

In 1983, members of Abuelos de Plaza de Mayo asked the American Association for the Advancement of Science to provide a geneticist who could help determine if certain youngsters were their grandchildren. King went to Argentina in June 1984 to identify remains as well as perform HLA (human leukocyte antigens) typing on living children, a test that analyzes blood proteins. Thanks to King's help, dozens of children were reunited with their biological families. She also assisted with performing DNA tests on exhumed remains in order to initiate criminal cases against the murderers. In similar projects, King has helped the U.S. government and the United Nations identify the remains of soldiers who had been missing in action.

In the mid-1990s, King began doing AIDS research, trying to determine whether genetics plays a part in why some people quickly develop full-blown AIDS, while others live for years with the disease. At this time, she accepted a position at the University of Washington, where she teaches in the departments of medicine and genetics. King has worked with the Human Genome Project, a government-sponsored program to map and analyze all 100,000 human genes. In addition, she has served on the Special Commission on Breast Cancer of the President's Cancer Panel; the advisory board of the National Institutes of Health Office of Research on Women's Health; and on committees of the National Academy of Sciences and the National Institute of Medicine.

## Further Reading

Columns (University of Washington at Seattle), September 1996.
Currents (University of California at Santa Cruz), September 27-
    October 5, 1997.
Discover, January 1, 1995.
Lancet, June 29, 1996.
Newsday, September 29, 1992; May 14, 1996; December 8,
    1996; May 15, 1997.
New York Times, April 27, 1993.
Omni, July 1993.
U.S. News & World Report, September 26, 1994.
"Mary-Claire King: Geneticist and Political Activist," http://www
    .students.haverford.edu (May 19, 1998).
"Mary-Claire King biography," http://www.sjsu.edu (May 19,
    1998). □

# Phil Knight

**Phil Knight (born 1938) is the founder and head of Nike, Inc., the number one athletic shoe company in the world. Already a legend in the retail and marketing worlds, Knight has turned into something of a mainstream hero, the subject of admiring articles in popular magazines. It is a reputation Knight has**

**earned over the years as both a visionary businessman and a hard-nosed CEO.**

The man whom *The Sporting News* named the "most powerful" person of the year in sports for 1993 was no athlete, coach, or commissioner. Rather, it was the man who for nearly 30 years has shod the great sports stars as well as the Saturday-afternoon "jocks"—Nike founder and CEO Philip "Phil" Knight. The former college track runner refers to Nike's world headquarters as a campus and runs it that way. "His every move is now scrutinized as carefully as the glamorous superstars who wear his sneakers," reported Frank Deford in a *Vanity Fair* profile.

Knight was born in Portland, Oregon, on February 24, 1938, the son of William H. and Lola (Hatfield) Knight. Oregon's only billionaire "forged his go-it-alone philosophy while growing up in Portland, the son of a domineering but loving father who was publisher of the now defunct *Oregon Journal*," noted Susan Hauser in *People* magazine. Though too small to excel in contact sports, young Knight took refuge in track. When his father refused to give him a summer job at his newspaper, believing his son should find work on his own, Knight went to the rival *Oregonian,* where he worked the night shift tabulating sports scores and every morning ran home the full seven miles.

## New Running Shoe

That interest in sports—and especially track—gave Knight the impetus to study the way track shoes were being made and marketed in the late 1950s. For assistance he consulted his coach, the University of Oregon's famed Bill Bowerman, who himself would become a senior member of the Nike team. Together they determined that American shoes were inferior in style and quality, too heavy, and too easily damaged. The Japanese, on the other hand, were experimenting with new, trimmed-down styles fashioned in lightweight, hardy nylon. Knight wrote his Stanford business-school term paper on the subject, then a few years later got involved personally by visiting Japan and arranging to import new-design running shoes himself.

"Knight ran Blue Ribbon Sports [named for a beer label] out of a storefront hole-in-the-wall next to the Pink Bucket Tavern in a working-class section of Portland," noted *Sports Illustrated* writer Donald Katz. "From the beginning Knight's animating idea was to promote high-quality, low-cost Japanese shoes, at a time when high quality was rarely associated with Japanese products, and to eventually displace [rival brand] Adidas, the triple-striped German shoes worn by all serious track and field athletes at the time."

"In the early days, anybody with a glue pot and a pair of scissors could get into the shoe business," Knight told Geraldine Willigan in a *Harvard Business Review* interview. "So the way to stay ahead was through product innovation. We were also good at keeping our manufacturing costs down. The big, established players like Puma and Adidas were still manufacturing in high-wage European companies. But we knew that wages were lower in Asia." This fact has garnered criticism for Knight and Nike by those who point out the vast difference between the wages earned by a factory worker in Indonesia compared to the salary drawn by a Nike celebrity endorser. But Knight insisted in the *Sports Illustrated* article that "we're not gouging anybody. . . . A country like Indonesia is converting from farm labor to semiskilled—an industrial transition that has occurred throughout history. There's no question in my mind that we're giving these people hope."

Knight's reputation in the track and field world also helped him gain an early edge. "We just tried to get our shoes on the feet of runners," he said in Willigan's article. "And we were able to get a lot of great ones under contract—people like [distance stars] Steve Prefontaine and Alberto Salazar—because we spent a lot of time at track events and had relationships with the runners, but mostly because we were doing interesting things with our shoes."

## Unique Image and New Technology

From the start, Knight's shoes sported their own look (including the distinctive "swoosh" logo that still appears today) and their own attitude. An early effort to promote the newly dubbed "Nike"—pronounced NY-kee and named for the Greek goddess of victory—included a now-classic advertisement set at the 1972 Olympic track trials in Eugene, Oregon. The copy boasted that four of the top seven marathoners wore Nikes. As a *Time* writer pointed out, the ads conveniently "neglected to mention that runners wearing [Adidas] shoes placed first, second and third."

By the mid-1970s Nike was at the cutting edge of workout-shoe technology. For instance, it was Bowerman, the former track coach, who poured some liquid latex into his wife's waffle iron, thereby inventing the famous sole that made the earliest Nikes feel like bedroom slippers. Nike didn't exactly burst from the gate in profit, though. Major sports stars demanded major compensation for wearing Knight's brand. A turning point came in the 1980s, when tennis star Jimmy Connors won Wimbledon in a pair of Nikes and John McEnroe "hurt his ankle, [and] started wearing an obscure three-quarter [Nike] model that had sold all of 10,000 pairs that year. Because of McEnroe's strained ligaments," noted a *Vanity Fair* writer, "the model sold a million two the very next year. It was about that time when Knight woke up one morning worth $178 million."

There was one area in which Nike made a serious misstep. Knight acknowledged in a *Sports Illustrated* article that his company "lost its way" when it came to aerobics shoes. The longstanding boys-club atmosphere of the Nike boardroom saw little promise in a lightweight shoe for women to wear to their exercise classes. In fact, the notion of aerobics was laughed away as just the conceit of "a bunch of fat ladies dancing to music," as Hauser quoted in the *People* article. That lack of insight opened the door for an upstart company called Reebok, which then virtually cornered the market in this burgeoning subsection of the athletic shoe industry. That was the beginning of a long-standing rivalry between Nike and Reebok for market dominance.

Though sales slipped and profits fell during the mid-1980s, Nike regained its place at the top of the market in 1984, when Knight returned from a fact-finding trip to Asia. Knight is a firm believer in the Japanese way of doing business and conducting life: "He often greets his secretary with a courtly bow or 'moshi, moshi,' the Japanese equivalent of hello, and pads around behind sliding screen doors in a pair of cotton slippers," reported Hauser.

## Celebrity Athlete Endorsements

Known as a taskmaster CEO, Knight is also particular when it comes to matters of promotion. "Hi, I'm Phil Knight and I don't believe in advertising," was the way Nike's ad agency president remembered meeting his new client. Signing up perhaps the greatest basketball player of all time, the former Chicago Bulls' superstar Michael Jordan, was only one of the breakthrough strategies that made Nike-wearers the envy of schoolyard pickup games everywhere. Nike slogans—"Bo Knows," "It's Gotta Be the Shoes," and especially "Just Do It"—have entered the pop-culture lexicon. The Nike image has been linked closely with notable "bad boys"—names like McEnroe, Andre Agassi, and Charles Barkley—as well as icons like the Beatles (through Nike's controversial use of the song "Revolution") and Bugs Bunny.

But the world of sports endorsements is a brutal one, as the public learned at the 1992 summer Olympic games in Barcelona. America's basketball "dream team" swept the field to win the gold medal, but faced screaming headlines and heated debate when several members threatened not to appear in a medal ceremony unless they were wearing their Nike apparel—to the consternation of Reebok, the team's "official" sponsor. (Dream Team member Barkley ably summed up the controversy, said Katz in *Sports Illustrated,* when he told a reporter that he had "two million reasons not to wear Reebok.")

For all the controversy Knight has helped engender in his company, he points out that the tradeoff is an increased awareness by the media, whose stories about the shoes and those who endorse them are the kind of publicity that money can't buy. As he told Willigan, the athletic shoe industry, "and Nike in particular, gets a lot more press than many others because it's more fun to talk about us than about a company that makes widgets. On the one hand, we don't mind the attention; we like getting our name in the press. On the other hand, the company usually gets treated in a superficial, lighthearted way, which is not what we're all about. Nike is not about going to a ball game. It's a business."

A later addition to the business was sports management. Simply put, it ensured that Nike endorsers maintained consistency outside the company—most importantly, by not endorsing any other product that would interfere with the Nike image. Sports management was born after Knight caught Nike endorser Andre Agassi in a commercial for Canon cameras. While cameras themselves don't conflict with shoes, the message in the commercial certainly did. "When Agassi looked into the camera and said, 'Image is everything,' Knight flipped," says Katz. "It was 180 degrees from our imagery," Knight told the *Sport Illustrated* writer. "We work hard to convey that performance, not image, is everything."

Nike realized that image did count for something when it released a shoe displaying a logo that resembled the Arabic word for "Allah," or God. Many members of the Muslim faith were upset, and in June 1997 Nike recalled 38,000 pairs of the shoes and issued an apology. The company noted that the logo was an oversight and issued a statement saying they did not mean to offend anyone with it.

## Asian Labor Issues

The company came under increasing scrutiny for its wages and working conditions in Indonesia, China, and Vietnam. United Nations Ambassador, Andrew Young, released a report finding no issue with Nike's factories, noting that facilities were "clean, organized, adequately ventilated and well lit," according to a *Reuters Business Report* article. However, human rights groups charged that Indonesian workers were incessantly striking over low wages; Nike workers received $2.46 per day in a nation that counted $4 per day as the minimum subsistence wage.

Independent filmmaker Michael Moore, whose 1989 documentary *Roger and Me* depicted a heartless corporate mindset at General Motors, turned his cameras on Nike, among numerous other firms. Moore addressed the issue of how Nike treats its workers and requested jobs for people in his depressed hometown of Flint, Michigan. Knight countered that American workers do not want jobs in shoe factories, but Moore was able to find a crowd of jobless workers in Flint who would be happy to make Nikes. For his part, Knight was the only CEO to agree to appear in the Moore film.

The uproar over the Asian workers dragged on for Nike, and they eventually raised wages a small amount. Some American women's groups, protested that female employees—the bulk of Nike's Asian work force—were still working 100 to 200 hours overtime at Nike just to pay their bills. They issued statements accusing Nike of corporal punishment and sexual harassment in the shops as well. By mid-1998, Knight announced in a speech to the National Press Club that Nike was "dedicated to giving American consumers assurances that the products they buy are not manufactured under abusive circumstances," according to a *Gannett News Service* article. He added that he had been branded as a "corporate crook," and defended his business practices, citing "misinformation and misunderstanding" as reasons for the media assault on Nike. Knight noted that a number of policies were going to be implemented in their production facilities, including raising the working age to 16 at clothing factories and 18 at shoe factories; using safer, non-toxic glues when possible; adopting stricter, U.S.-dictated air quality standards; instituting on-site education programs, and more.

In addition to the Asian labor issues, many people remained outraged over Nike's escalating costs, especially since a large market for the products are poor, inner-city youth. One shoe endorsed by basketball player, Anfernee Hardaway, was tagged at $180, and the Air Jordans touted by superstar Michael Jordan had always been priced at over $100. Perhaps this combination of issues served to cause a slump. Sales and profits fell in 1998, and Nike laid off 1,900 employees. However, the company remained the world's largest shoemaker. It won a lawsuit in early 1999 that had accused the firm of lying to consumers about "sweatshop" conditions in Asian factories. Human rights groups remained unconvinced.

When not at the helm, Knight enjoys the fruits of his success. He and his wife Penelope "Penny" Parks have two grown sons and one foster daughter. They live in non-ostentatious comfort in Oregon, with a gaggle of pets and Knight's "only personal concession to flash: [a] black Lamborghini (vanity plates: NIKE MN) and red Ferrari," as Hauser noted in *People*. The workplace is also the scene of fun and comfort: Nike World Campus features three restaurants, plus fitness center, beauty salon, laundry service, jogging facilities, a day-care center, and other amenities.

Knight can't help but see success in Nike's future, as the company expands its product line to include a wide range of apparel and accessories. As a *Forbes* writer noted, the man who built an empire on a pair of shoes still cherishes the words of his track coach: "Play by the rules, but be ferocious."

## Further Reading

Strasser, Julie, *SWOOSH: The Unauthorized Story of Nike and the Men Who Played There,* HarperBusiness, 1993.
*Forbes,* August 2, 1993.
*Gannett News Service,* May 12, 1998.
*Harvard Business Review,* July-August 1992.
*Independent,* October 28, 1997, p. 15.
*People,* May 4, 1992.
*Philadelphia Inquirer,* October 10, 1998.
*Reuter's Business Report,* June 24, 1997.
*South China Morning Post,* February 8, 1999.
*Sports Illustrated,* August 19, 1993.
*Time,* June 30, 1980; February 15, 1982.
*U.S. News & World Report,* September 22, 1997, p. 48.
*Vanity Fair,* August 1993.
"Nike, Inc.," Hoover's Online, March 3, 1999. Available from http://www.hoovers.com. □

# Ernie Kovacs

**To many, Ernie Kovacs (1919–1962) was the most brilliant comedian in history. His zany, visual humor was unlike any other performer of his day. His motion pictures were a combination of slapstick and bits of humor that took intelligence to enjoy. Kovacs' television performances were even more unusual, and demanded greater concentration from the viewer.**

Ernie Kovacs was born in Trenton, New Jersey on January 23, 1919. As a youngster, he was drawn to the theater and the world of entertainment. Kovacs attended the New York School of Theatre and began acting in stock companies. He avoided military service during the Second World War because of a serious illness that hospitalized him for 18 months. Between 1945 and 1950, he earned a modest living as a columnist for the *Trentonian* newspaper and worked as a disc jockey for a local radio station.

During his performing life from 1951 until his death in 1962, Kovacs worked in over a dozen motion pictures and several very successful television series, including the immensely popular *Ernie Kovacs Show* and *It's Time for Ernie*. His television career began with a cooking program on station WPTZ in Philadelphia. The show was called *Deadline for Dinner,* but Kovacs generally referred to it as "Dead Lion for Breakfast." He also appeared as a guest performer on many other television programs.

## The Nairobi Trio

Those who knew, insisted that Kovacs was always one of the three silly and senseless entertainers known as the "Nairobi Trio." These performers were disguised as monkeys and appeared as a weekly segment on the Kovacs television program for many years. The remaining two Trio members were generally other famous entertainers of the day such as Sammy Davis, Jr., Dean Martin, or even Frank Sinatra. Unidentified and unacknowledged, top stars fought for the honor of being a Trio member.

Each monkey would elaborately play an instrument, with the "star" being the drummer. Throughout the heavy beats of the simple and basic music, the drummer would

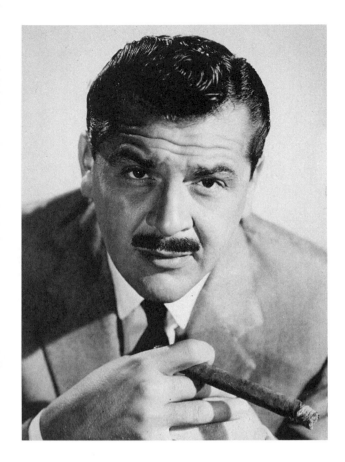

slowly turn and beat a quick measure on the piano player's head. The piano player, equally slow and also to the beat of the music, would turn and look up at the drummer. By then the drummer had turned away. That was the entire act. It never changed, week after week. Although it was done precisely the same way each time, with the same costumes and the same slow beat music, and although every viewer knew exactly what was going to happen, it was hilarious. Viewers couldn't seem to wait for the Nairobi Trio segment of the show. They would start laughing the moment the three monkeys appeared on the set. The Nairobi Trio continued to prove Kovacs' theory that repetition was funny.

## Successful Television Career

Because Kovacs' shows were full of antics such as the Nairobi Trio, they were a major success. It was not at all unusual to see a bent and broken file cabinet, or a shellacked chicken, or a variety of kitchen utensils dancing to weird and wacky music on a Kovacs show. A roasted turkey might wiggle across the set to some twisted melody.

Kovacs might come before the cameras as a cowboy readying for a "quick draw" against a "bad guy" in an old west town. Always in this type of very fast comedy sketch, and also in his famed Dutch Master's cigars commercials, the background music would be the lovely "Haydn's String Quartet, Opus 33, Number 5," the "Sarabande." But at the last instant Kovacs' gun would fall off or misfire, or his pants would fall down, or something else very visual would happen. He could draw laughter with a look, a gesture, or a flick

of his huge cigar. His performances were known for satire, zany originality, and visual gags.

"Percy Dovetonsils" was one of Kovacs' regular characters. With thick glasses and a silk smoking jacket, while sipping wine in a plush study, the lispy Percy would softly read poetry. Viewers had to listen to the words to get the humor Kovacs intended, but just seeing him every week was very funny to many. Some of his audience roared with laughter at the poetry, others invariably missed the point of the whole skit.

### Family Life

Kovacs was married to Bette Wilcox in 1945. They had two daughters, Bette Lee (Elisabeth) Andrea, born in 1947, and Kip "Kippy" Raleigh, born in 1949. The couple divorced in 1954 after an extended separation, with Kovacs retaining custody of his children. He married prominent entertainer Edie Adams in 1955, and lived with her and their daughter until his death in 1962.

Kovacs wrote two books. The first, *Zoomar,* was a witty but deeply felt autobiographical novel in his own inimitable style. It was published at the height of his popularity, in 1956. The other, published in 1962, was *How to Talk at Gin.* Kovacs was a compulsive "doodler" and some of the doodlings most admired by his daughter are reproduced in the latter book.

### A Tragic Accident

On January 12, 1962, Kovacs spent a long day working on one of his regular ABC television specials. Then he attended a party to celebrate the christening of fellow-comedian Milton Berle's son. He left around 1:30 in the morning, driving his new Corvair station wagon. While turning from Beverly Glen to Santa Monica Boulevard in Los Angeles, he lost control and spun into a utility pole. A passerby noted that the engine in the car was still running, so he reached in to shut it off. While doing that he discovered that the man slumped halfway out of the driver's seat was the famous comedian, Ernie Kovacs.

Kovacs died in the crash in Los Angeles on January 13, 1962—just ten days short of his 43rd birthday. Few of his saddened fans will forget the front-page newspaper photo of one of his cigars lying half-smoked along the curb at the scene of his death. For days following his accident, tributes appeared in newspapers around the world. New York Times columnist J. Gould wrote, "Sometimes Kovacs' point of view was wildly hilarious, sometimes thoroughly puzzling, but there was never a doubt about whose point of view it was. The loss of the man with the mustache, the cigar, and the smile not only deprives both the viewer and television of an artist who contributed the elusive and precious commodity of laughter, but also of a free and irreverent spirit who had many friends he never met."

Since the death of Kovacs, there has been one major biography, a television movie about his life, many tributes in the form of screenings and articles, and dozens of videotapes. When the videotapes are viewed, it is obvious that his comedic genius will perhaps never be matched. His use of video trickery was masterful, but it was always used as a means to the end he intended, and not merely for its own sake.

### Further Reading

The Boston Phoenix, http://weeklywire.com/filmvault/boston/e/erniekovacstv1.html
Compton's Interactive Encyclopedia, 1994
E!Online, http://www.eonline.net/Facts/People/0,12,8705,00.html □

# Maggie Kuhn

**Maggie Kuhn (1905–1995) became one of the most radical social activists of the last three decades of the 20th century. The Gray Panthers, an organization she helped to found, was instrumental in bringing about significant national reforms, including nursing home reform, the prohibition of forced retirement, and fighting health care fraud.**

Maggie Kuhn was born on August 3, 1905, in Buffalo, New York. Her family was conservative and middle class. They moved to Cleveland, Ohio, where Kuhn lived from 1916 until 1930. She attended the Western Reserve University's College for Women in Cleveland. Kuhn noted in a 1993 interview with Sandra Erlanger published in *CWRU Magazine,* that her activism had its beginnings in college. "I think it began with my sociology courses. . . . " said Kuhn. "Sociology, for me, related the community to the individual, and showed us a way to act responsibly in groups." With her sociology class, Kuhn visited jails, sweatshops, and slums. Kuhn described what she saw as "illuminating and shocking." She felt that her college career had a profound effect on who she became. "I'm eternally grateful for the education I got. . . . I was inspired by some very gifted women who were indeed part of the women's movement. And the memory lingers," Kuhn told Erlanger.

Kuhn majored in English with minors in sociology and French, graduating with honors. She accepted a job with the Young Women's Christian Association (YWCA), which was at the time, as Kuhn recalled, "the foremost advocate for working women. The women in the Y in those days were wonderfully radical. They were all socialists. They influenced me profoundly," Kuhn told Erlanger. Kuhn worked with the YWCA in Cleveland until 1930. When her father was transferred to Philadelphia, she continued working with the organization there. In 1941, she transferred to the New York City YWCA. This was the first time she lived away from her family.

### Forced Retirement Prompted Action

In New York, Kuhn studied social work and theology at Columbia University's Teachers' College and Union Theological Seminary. At the YWCA, Kuhn organized educational and social activities for young working-class women.

During World War II, women replaced men in factories. Kuhn worked with the YWCA's USO division to improve working conditions for those women. In 1948, the USO division was phased out, so Kuhn took a job with the General Alliance for Unitarian and Other Liberal Christian Women, in Boston. Eager to rejoin her ailing parents in Philadelphia, Kuhn took an executive position with the Presbyterian Church of the USA in 1950. She became assistant secretary of the Social Education and Action Department. During her years with the church, she edited the journal *Social Progress*. It encouraged Presbyterians to become involved with social issues, such as desegregation, urban housing, McCarthyism, the Cold War, nuclear arms, equality for women, and problems of the elderly.

In 1970, after 20 years on the job and seven months before her 65th birthday, Kuhn was asked to retire. "Truthfully, in those years I didn't think of myself as about to enter the ranks of the nation's old. . . . I was just me— neither young, old, nor middle-aged," she wrote in her autobiography, *No Stone Unturned: The Life and Times of Maggie Kuhn.* "I had never given retirement much thought." Kuhn tried to talk her supervisors out of the forced retirement, but they would not listen to her. "I felt dazed and suspended," she wrote. "I was hurt and then, as time passed, outraged. . . . Something clicked in my mind and I saw that my problem was not mine alone. . . . Instead of sinking into despair, I did what came most naturally to me: I telephoned some friends and called a meeting." Each of the six friends was also being forced into retirement. At the meeting, "we discovered we had new freedom as a result of retiring," Kuhn noted. "We had no responsibility to a corporation or organization. We could take risks, speak out. We said, 'With this new freedom we have, let's see what we can do to change the world.'"

## Founding of the Gray Panthers

Kuhn and her friends wondered how to participate actively with young people in protests against the Vietnam War and how to resist forced retirement. In dealing with the issues of political commitment and aging, Kuhn and her friends created a new movement, which fought against ageism, racism, sexism, and militarism. One hundred people attended the group's first public meeting. From its beginning, the group included members of all ages, brought together by their interest in liberal political and social causes. "We established ourselves firmly for justice and peace, and not as an isolated group by chronological age," said Kuhn in her interview with Erlanger. "This gave us an immediate intergenerational emphasis and point of view, which we've never lost."

At first called the Consultation of Older and Younger Adults for Social Change, the group was dubbed the Gray Panthers by a talk show host after the radical African American organization, the Black Panthers. The new name caught on. The group's motto was: "Age and Youth in Action." Kuhn held the title of national convener.

The Gray Panthers got its first national recognition in 1971, by organizing a "Black House Conference" to protest the lack of African American representatives at the first White House Conference on Aging. In 1972, Kuhn spoke at a press conference at the United Presbyterian Church general assembly. She caught the attention of reporters with her knowledgeable comments on retirement, nursing homes, sex at age 75, and social justice. Stories about her appeared in major newspapers and on television and radio stations across the United States. The popularity of the Gray Panthers rose rapidly as a result.

The organization under Kuhn's leadership peaked at 120 local networks in 38 states by 1979. Chapters, or networks as they are called, also exist in Tokyo, Dublin, Paris, Stuttgart, Sydney, and Basel. While most of the organization's work is done at the grassroots level, the Panthers have brought about national changes. They persuaded the National Association of Broadcasters to amend the Television Code of Ethics to include age, along with race and sex, to encourage media sensitivity. The Gray Panthers also helped found the National Citizens Coalition for Nursing Home Reform. Kuhn told Erlanger, "Our thrust has broadened over the years. It now recognizes our international impact and responsibility. We have not only observer status but also consultative status with the United Nations. We have direct access to all the specialized agencies of the Economic and Social Council." The group regularly advised the World Health Organization. In 1992, the International Year of Aging, the Panthers' UN representative chaired the 10th anniversary celebration of the UN Action Plan on Aging.

The Gray Panthers focused on three main issues in the 1990s: urban society, discrimination, and international pol-

icy. "We need to save the cities!" related Kuhn to Erlanger. "In urban policy we need to look at housing, including shared housing." In shared housing, older people, who often have homes that are too big for themselves and who need companionship, share their homes with younger people who need inexpensive housing. To bring about social change, the Gray Panthers first organized task forces to research issues. Kuhn noted, "You don't take to the streets until you've done your homework." Having adopted a position, the members tried to increase public awareness of the issue and influence public opinion and policy makers by writing letters and contacting elected officials. Because they are a nonprofit organization, the Panthers were not permitted to lobby.

The Panthers foresaw many of the issues regarding aging in America. Fifteen years before catastrophic health care became an issue in Congress, they demanded a decentralized national health service similar to the Canadian system. Before the public was aware of homelessness as a problem, the Gray Panthers advocated and practiced intergenerational home sharing, beginning with Kuhn's own house in Philadelphia. The Panthers have long fought for the abolition of forced retirement and to have older workers share their expertise with younger ones in radically restructured jobs. They differ from other advocacy groups for older people in that they do not pit the interests of the elderly against those of the younger generation. The Gray Panthers are one of the few radical social action groups from the Vietnam War era to survive.

The Panthers have demonstrated at meetings of the American Medical Association and the National Gerontological Society. They have monitored planning commissions, zoning boards, courts, banks, and insurance companies. They have physically "liberated" people from unsafe nursing homes. The group organized ongoing local and national "Media Watches" to eliminate all ageist programs and commercials from the air.

## Lived Her Beliefs

Kuhn practiced what she preached. She had housemates who were in their twenties and thirties. She provided them with low-cost housing and they shopped for her and took her to meetings. Kuhn engaged in almost nonstop public speaking, protesting, and testifying before Congress, state legislatures, and international bodies as the representative of seniors for social change. Although she sometimes used a wheelchair pushed by a travel companion, toward the end of her life Kuhn still traveled thousands of miles each year. Dressed in black athletic shoes, an elegant wool suit and a stylish hat, the petite, wispy-haired activist delivered lectures to motivate people to change American society. To make sure the audience listened, Kuhn sprinkled her lectures with shocking remarks. "One of the things I say in my speeches is there are three things I like about being old," said Kuhn. "I can speak my mind—and I do. I'm surprised with what I can get away with—that the audience doesn't boo and hiss! Second, that I've outlived much of my opposition; and third, I can reach out to the young. Many, many old people retire from their jobs and retire from life. They have no objective, no purpose. Every one of us needs to have a goal, a passionate purpose. . . . It's possible to have new roles and a new value system [in old age]. The five M's are what I talk about with old people: Taking on the role of the mentor; mediator; monitor of public bodies, watching city hall, the president and the statehouse; motivator; and mobilizer," Kuhn told Erlanger.

On her 80th birthday, Kuhn made a vow to do something outrageous at least once a week. In her late eighties she increased it to at least once a day. "You get people's attention that way. You get energized, you can make an impact, and it's just fun," she noted. A feminist from her youth, Kuhn devoted herself to work and social causes and helped change the way society views old age. Despite a variety of love affairs and two engagements, which she documented in her 1991 autobiography, Kuhn never married. She was the author of several books, including *You Can't Be Human Alone, Let's Get Out There and Do Something About Injustice,* and *Maggie Kuhn on Aging.* In 1979, Garson Kanin wrote about Kuhn in *Quest* magazine. "Those who fired her, fired her into the social atmosphere in the manner of a space missile, propelling her into fame and usefulness and glory." Kuhn died at her home in Philadelphia on April 22, 1995, at the age of 89.

## Further Reading

Kuhn, Maggie, *No Stone Unturned: The Life and Times of Maggie Kuhn,* Ballantine, 1991.
*CWRU Magazine,* February 1993.
*Nation,* May 28, 1990; May 29, 1995.
*New Age Journal,* January/February 1989.
*Witness,* May 1990.
"The Women of The Hall, 1998 Inductees," *National Women's Hall of Fame,* http://www.greatwomen.org/kuhn.htm (April 8, 1999). □

# L

# Lewis Latimer

**In the late 19th century, despite the seemingly insurmountable obstacles facing the son of a former slave, Lewis Latimer (1848–1928) contributed many technological advances in the field of electricity.**

Lewis H. Latimer was born on September 4, 1848, in Chelsea, Massachusetts. Latimer was the youngest of four children born to George and Rebecca Latimer. His father had obtained his freedom only six years earlier. George Latimer worked as a slave for various owners in Virginia until late 1842, a few months after marrying Rebecca Smith. The young couple decided that escaping to the free states north of the Mason-Dixon line to avoid slavery was the only way to ensure that their future children would have better opportunities.

## Escape to Freedom

The couple hid as stowaways aboard a ship headed for Maryland. Upon reaching the city of Baltimore, George and Rebecca began a perilous train journey to New York. Using his fair complexion to his advantage, George pretended to be a white slave owner with Rebecca posing as his slave. Reaching New York without incident, the couple then made their way to Boston, Massachusetts. Although at last residing in a free state, the couple was still concerned about slave catchers. Soon after the Latimers' escape from Virginia, James Gray, George's former owner, ran advertisements in various newspapers describing the young man to slave catchers. Consequently, after their arrival in Boston, George was identified as a runaway slave. He was arrested and Gray notified.

At the time, Boston was a center for the abolitionist movement, which opposed slavery on moral grounds. Taking up the cause of freedom for George were many famous abolitionists, including Frederick Douglass and William Lloyd Garrison. Even though there was a large public outcry in support of George, the Massachusetts Supreme Court ruled that he must be returned to his owner. After this tragic defeat, George's supporters met with Gray and offered to buy his slave. Gray agreed and George became a free man in late 1842.

## Fighting for an Education

After gaining his freedom, George and Rebecca settled in Chelsea, Massachusetts and started a family. Young Lewis Latimer attended Phillips Grammar School in Chelsea, where he showed much promise in the fields of mathematics and drafting. Because the family often needed money, Latimer sometimes left school to work with his father.

In 1858, Latimer's father left the family and his mother found work aboard a ship. With no parents at home, Latimer was sent to Farm School. His two older brothers attended the state-run school where students were taught vocational skills such as farming. Latimer quickly made plans with one of his older brothers, William, to escape to Boston, where they both hoped to find work. After reaching Boston, the two boys discovered that their mother had returned home.

Although he was reunited with his family, Latimer had to find work to help support himself, his mother, and his brother. Finding only opportunities in manual labor, Latimer searched for a job that would allow him to grow intellectually. He finally secured a job with a law firm and was quite happy. Unfortunately, the start of the American Civil War interrupted his career.

The Civil War began on April 16, 1861, and Latimer left his position with the law firm to join the Union effort. At the young age of 16, Latimer served onboard a gun-ship that protected Union shipping traffic on the eastern seaboard. Four years later, at the end of the war, Latimer was honorably discharged from the service.

## A Self-Made Man

Even with the passage of the Thirteenth Amendment to the U.S. Constitution, which prohibited slavery anywhere in the country, Latimer found it difficult to obtain a position that would offer him the opportunities and mental challenges that he sought. He applied for and received work in the office of Crosby and Gould, a patent law firm. While he did menial tasks at first, Latimer studied the technical patent drawings made by the men who worked as draftsmen. Drawings of inventions were needed before patent applications were submitted to the U.S. Patent Office. Upon confirmation of the invention, patents were issued to the inventor; the drawing protected his invention from counterfeiters who hoped to make money from someone else's hard work. While draftsmen usually obtained their skills from schooling, Latimer was never offered that opportunity. Instead, he created his own. With used drafting tools and books, Latimer studied at night and during the day he carefully watched as draftsmen created technical drawings. After much studying, Latimer presented his work to one of his bosses, who was impressed with his talent and offered him a job as a draftsman. Eventually, Latimer was promoted to the

chief draftsman position and remained with the firm for eleven years.

## Met Alexander Graham Bell

Latimer married Mary Wilson on December 10, 1873. It was a happy time for the young couple, as Latimer found success in his work and personal life. While still working for Crosby and Gould, he began to tinker with his own inventions. In 1874, Latimer received a patent for improving the mechanics of toilets, then known as water closets, on railway cars.

It was at this time that Latimer met and began working with the inventor, Alexander Graham Bell. Bell was trying to change human voices into electrical pulses that could be sent over wires. His work would eventually lead to the invention of the telephone. Because Bell's work was so intensive, he found it difficult to keep up his technical drawing submissions to the U.S. Patent Office. He went to Crosby and Gould and met Latimer, who completed the complicated drawing for Bell and sent them quickly to the Patent Office. Latimer's talent and speed paid off for Bell, who was granted a patent for the telephone on March 7, 1876.

In 1879, Crosby and Gould closed their offices and Latimer found himself without a job. On the advice of his sister, Latimer and his wife moved to Bridgeport, Connecticut, in search of employment opportunities. Latimer obtained a position as a draftsman at the Follandsbee Machine Shop. While working there he met Hiram Maxim, an inventor who developing an improved light bulb. Thomas Edison had just received the patent for the light bulb, but there was a flaw. It could only emit light for a few hours before it burned out. Maxim was interested in improving the life of the light bulb and recognized that, with Latimer's help, he would be in a better position to do just that.

After accepting a position with Maxim's company, U.S. Electric Lighting, Latimer immersed himself in the study of electrical technology. In 1881, Latimer and a co-worker, Joseph V. Nichols, developed an improved process for the manufacturing of the carbon filament that increases the life of the light bulb. This new procedure made the use of light bulbs more cost effective for the general public. Their patent on the new invention was granted in 1882 and paved the way for further development of the light bulb.

Latimer travelled to many major cities in North America, supervising the installation of electric street lights and electric light plants. At one point, Latimer was overseeing electrical installations in Montreal, where workers spoke only French. Typical of his dogged determination, Latimer taught himself French and was able to translate work orders for the laborers. Latimer became the chief electrical engineer for the U.S. Electric Lighting Company. He worked briefly in London, supervising the Maxim-Westin Electric Light Company, which later would be known as the Westinghouse Company.

After returning to the U.S. in 1882, Latimer was disappointed to find that the leadership of the U.S. Electric Lighting Company had changed, leaving him without a job. He found work at various electric companies, but devoted most of his talent and creativity towards developing an improved lamp. Meanwhile, on June 12, 1883, his daughter Emma Jeanette was born.

## Worked with Thomas Edison

In 1884, Latimer was offered an engineering position with the Edison Electric Light Company. The company's founder, Thomas Alva Edison, was devoting much time to improving electrical lighting systems. Latimer helped the legal department defend the company from outsiders who claimed Edison's inventions as their own. In 1890, Latimer revised an out-of-date technical manual entitled *Incandescent Electric Lighting: A Practical Description of the Edison System.* The book received enthusiastic reviews and became a standard in the field of electrical engineering. Latimer found success at work and great joy at home as his second daughter, Louise Rebecca, was born on April 19, 1890.

In 1896, Latimer served on the Board of Patent Control, which was formed by select individuals from the Westinghouse Company and General Electric Company. General Electric was created when Edison merged with one of its rivals, Thomson-Houston. The Board of Patent Control was formed to protect against costly lawsuits regarding inventions and patents, but was abolished in 1911. Edwin Hammer, a patent lawyer, offered Latimer a position as a patent consultant for the firm of Hammer and Schwarz. Hammer's brother, William, was collecting information on individuals who had pioneered in the field of electricity with the Edison Company. Latimer was selected as one of only twenty-eight men who were honored with membership to a group called the Edison Pioneers. Membership in this group represented the highest honor to individuals in the electrical field. On February 11, 1918, the Edison Pioneers met for the first time, on the seventy-first birthday of Thomas Edison.

While Latimer focused most of his attention on discoveries in the electric industry, he also found time for other activities. He developed an early version of a window air conditioner and a locking rack for hats, coats, umbrellas. Latimer won renown as a poet and many of his literary creations were published during his lifetime. He remained active in the cause of civil rights for African Americans. In a letter to fellow civil rights supporter Richard Greener, the first African American to graduate from Harvard University, Latimer said he was "heart and soul into the movement." Latimer was active in the Grand Army of the Republic (GAR), an organization which tried to keep alive the history of the Civil War veterans. Latimer died in Flushing, New York on December 11, 1928, at the age of 80.

## Further Reading

Ayer, Eleanor, *Lewis Latimer: Creating Bright Ideas,* Steck-Vaughn, 1997.
Haber, Louis, *Black Pioneers of Science and Invention,* Harcourt, Brace & World, 1970.
Low, W. Augustus, *Encyclopedia of Black America,* Da Capo Press, 1981.
McKissack, Patricia and Frederick, *African-American Inventors,* Millbrook Press, 1994.
Russell, Dick, *Black Genius and the American Experience,* Carroll & Graf, 1998. ☐

# Norman Lear

**While much of television's history is filled with banality, writer/producer Norman Lear (born 1922) is credited with enlarging the scope of the medium. With such groundbreaking television series as *All in the Family*, *Maude*, and *Sanford and Son* to his credit, Lear helped usher in an age of enlightenment in American entertainment, where sensitive social and political issues could be discussed without awkwardness.**

Norman Milton Lear was born in New Haven, Connecticut on July 27, 1922. His father Herman was a securities broker; mother Jeanette was a homemaker. Lear attended Boston's Emerson College, but dropped out in September 1942 to join the U.S. Air Force during World War II. Writing a war memoir for *People* magazine in 1995, Lear, an avowed pacifist, admitted he "just had to get into it. I was Jewish and I wanted to kill Germans." Lear received a Decorated Air Medal for his wartime accomplishments. Upon leaving the Air Force in 1945, Lear married and got a public relations job in New York City with George and Dorothy Ross, making $40 a week.

In 1949, Lear moved his family to Los Angeles, California where he entered the world of television, working as a writer for shows such as *The Colgate Comedy Hour*, and for such comedians as Martha Raye and George Gobel. Several years after arriving in Los Angeles, he divorced his first wife and, in 1956, married Frances Loeb. In 1959, Lear and partner Bud Yorkin created Tandem Productions, which produced motion pictures such as *Come Blow Your Horn* (1963), *Divorce American Style* (1967), *The Night They Raided Minsky's* (1968) and *Start the Revolution Without Me* (1969).

## Broke the TV Mold

In the early 1970s, Lear created a popular situation comedy series that would have a major impact upon television programming. Tandem Productions' new comedy was based on a British series called *Until Death do Us Part.* Lear and Yorkin secured the American rights to the show and, on January 12, 1971, *All in the Family* aired on CBS, breaking the taboos of television comedy with hilarious aplomb. Carroll O'Connor was cast as Archie Bunker, a cranky, self-assured working class bigot; Jean Stapleton played Edith Bunker, Archie's dim-witted, doting, and big-hearted wife; Sally Struthers was cast in the role of daughter Gloria; and Rob Reiner took the role of Mike Stivic, Gloria's liberal husband who was in constant conflict with Archie.

In a March 1999 interview on the news program *Dateline NBC*, Lear addressed the blandness permeating television at the time. "The biggest problem in comedy was Mom's dented the car, and how do we keep Dad from finding out, or the boss is coming to dinner and the lamb roast is ruined. We paid attention to our children. We paid attention to our marriages. We paid attention to the newspapers we read and the culture. And we chose our subjects from all these things that were influencing us." Lear received many professional and humanitarian awards, ranging from the William O. Douglas Award and a Man of the Year Award from the National Academy of Television Arts and Sciences.

Both critics and television historians agree that *All in the Family* had the most impact of any of Lear's productions. After living through the socially and politically charged climates of the 1960s, Lear pulled his stories out of the nation's newspapers and news broadcasts and made them relevant to viewers from all walks of life. The episodes caused controversy, but not at the expense of entertaining the nation. The show explored such charged issues as prejudice, rape, sexual dysfunction, menopause, homosexuality, and religion. As a result, it became a bastion of popular culture, spawning such consumer goods as soundtrack records, T-shirts, and board games. Carroll O'Connor's portrayal of Archie, the working-class bigot, struck a chord with viewers, who made his colorful vocabulary, "Meathead" (referring to his son-in-law) and "Dingbat" (his wife), part of the national lexicon. But while the Archie character was an icon for working class Americans, the show also raised the

public consciousness about women's issues through Stapleton and Struthers' characters. Although often overshadowed by her boorish husband, many of the show's strongest episodes revolved around the Edith Bunker character. The role of daughter Gloria closely paralleled the views of the women's movement in the United States at the time.

Despite the accolades and attention given to him in the wake of the show's success, Lear stressed that he did not intend to remedy societal ills. In a 1990 interview with the *Los Angeles Times,* he explained that the purpose of his show was to "lift up the apparent. They were saying far worse things than this in the schools and on the playgrounds. If I had any sense that this little half-hour situation comedy was going to reverse or change or even seriously affect 2000 or 2500 years of bigotry, I would have to be some kind of fool."

### Launched Spin-Off Shows

Lear and Yorkin created several successful spin-off shows based upon characters that originally debuted on *All in the Family. Maude* featured Bea Arthur as a thoroughly liberated modern woman. Lear's wife, Frances, took credit for the character. In a 1975 *People* magazine interview she explained that "a great deal of 'Maude' comes from my consciousness being raised by the women's movement; and from Norman's being raised by me." *The Jeffersons* dealt with African-American bigot, George Jefferson, (played by Sherman Helmsley) and his travails as a successful businessman in white America. Lear created other shows with varying degrees of success, including the Afro-centric comedy *Sanford and Son*, and its spin-off, *Grady*; the suburban, surrealist dark comedy *Mary Hartman, Mary Hartman*; *Good Times*; and *Hot L Baltimore*.

### Formed Political and Business Ventures

In addition to his television programs, Lear found other ways to express his political convictions. In 1981, he formed People for the American Way, a liberal coalition that promoted pluralism and raised public awareness about issues related to the First Amendment. Lear raised the ire of conservatives by creating a commercial featuring movie star Gregory Peck decrying the 1987 nomination of Judge Robert Bork to the U.S. Supreme Court. Lear scripted a 1982 TV special, *I Love Liberty*, which promoted liberal politics while acting as a salute to the Bill of Rights.

While Lear has creatively expressed his political viewpoints, his business acumen has made him a wealthy man. Residuals from his various shows have allowed him to amass a $225 million empire. When he dissolved his partnership with Yorkin, Lear started TAT Communications, which was later developed into Embassy Communications. In 1986, Lear and then-partner Jerry Perenchio sold Embassy to the Coca-Cola Company for $485 million. With the proceeds from his share of the sale, Lear financed a new company, Act III, which acquired trade magazines, television stations, and multiplex movie theater chains in secondary markets, in addition to bankrolling motion pictures. Two of the features that the company funded, *Stand By Me* and *The Princess Bride,* were directed by *All in the Family* star, Rob Reiner. When Lear divorced his wife of 29 years in 1986, she walked away with $112 million.

Despite a self-imposed retirement from the world of television in 1977, Lear returned in 1984 with ideas that tried to recapture the thought-provoking climate that made *All in the Family* and *Maude* such commercial successes. A situation comedy, *a.k.a. Pablo,* starring Hispanic comedian Paul Rodriguez stalled. Other Lear shows such as 1991's *Sunday Dinner* and 1994's *704 Hauser Street* failed to capture the success of his previous ventures. In a 1984 interview with the *Washington Post,* Lear decried the business trends prevalent in the television industry. "God forbid anything be an acquired taste. There's no chance for the public to acquire a taste because they yank it so quickly. As a result of America's fixation and obsession with short-term thinking, everything suffers. In every business, we innovate less and experiment less because of the need not to diminish a current profit statement but to have one that exceeds the last. Wherever we look."

Lear is still active in political and social groups such as People for the American Way and Common Cause. He married his third wife, psychologist Lyn Davis Lear, in 1987, and readily acknowledges that she is a conduit for his inner spiritual growth. In 1989, he founded the Business Enterprise Trust to promote social consciousness and vision in business. The following year, Lear showed support for the NAMES Project's AIDS memorial quilt by making a donation towards its maintenance. He has three daughters; Ellen, Kate and Maggie (from his first two marriages), and a stepson, Benjamin Davis (from Lyn Davis Lear's previous marriage). Lear resides in Mandeville Canyon, California. In late 1998, Lear told reporters he was working on a new show similar to *Sunday Dinner* that would explore human spirituality. "Every member of the species from the beginning of time has been seeking some understanding of why we're here and what [life is] all about," he told National Public Radio in 1994. "The varieties of religious experience are infinite."

When a reporter from the *Washington Post* asked Lear if he was worried that his reputation would diminish if each new project wasn't as successful as *All in the Family,* Lear gave a lucid response. "Of course it crosses my mind. But if you're sufficiently busy, you don't think about it. And I am sufficiently busy. I wake up every morning of my life hopeful, and I believe in the possible."

## Further Reading

McNeil, Alex., *Total Television: The Comprehensive Guide to Programming from 1948 to the Present,* 1996.
*Chicago Tribune,* May 31, 1991.
*Forbes,* January 25, 1988.
*Globe and Mail,* February 8, 1984.
*Los Angeles Times,* September 20, 1987; December 2, 1990.
*Newsday,* June 2, 1991
*People Weekly,* August 7, 1995; October 14, 1996.
*San Diego Union-Tribune,* May 23, 1995.
*Star-Tribune Newspaper of the Twin Cities Minneapolis.-St. Paul,* July 2, 1989.
*Toronto Star,* May 24, 1992.
*Wall Street Journal,* April 8, 1988.
*Washington Post,* March 4, 1984
*Weekend Edition* January 8, 1994.
"Norman Lear Helps Pave the Road to DC," http://www .aidsquilt.org/newsletter/archive/winter95/lear.html □

# Suzanne Lenglen

**Suzanne Lenglen (1899–1938) was a French national hero and became royalty to a generation of admirers in both Europe and America. She dominated women's tennis from 1919 to 1926, winning both Wimbledon and French singles titles six times.**

Through her parents' forceful persuasion, Langlen developed into one of the best female tennis players in the history of the game. She was a fragile woman, who lived for tennis and the good life. Lenglen expressed a joy for living that was infectious, but relied on her father's decisions when she was on the court. She had style and technique and a simplicity of form that made her tennis game seem effortless.

## Early Athletic Ability

Suzanne Rachel Flore Lenglen was born in Compiegne, France, on May 24, 1899. Her family was said to be of French and Flemish origins. Lenglen was raised in a comfortable, middle class family by her father, Charles, and her mother, Anais. By the age of eight, Lenglen showed early signs of athletic ability. She was an excellent runner, swimmer, and bicyclist. Her father believed that her ability at diabolo, a game played with a top balanced on a string between two sticks, contributed to her later poise under pressure at tennis tournaments.

On the French Riviera, Lenglen and her father admired the tennis players both for their skill and their social stature. Her father ardently studied the tactics and maneuvers of the players. However, when Lenglen requested a racket, he bought her an inexpensive one with the idea that hers was a passing fancy. Within a month, he purchased a more expensive racket, and had a special backboard constructed for her to practice against. Since there were not many tennis instructors around, her father decided to teach her himself. After observing the women of the time playing a patient, careful placement style of game, he decided it was not right for his energetic, enthusiastic daughter. After observing the men's style of more aggressive play, he decided to teach his daughter accordingly. The unintended result was that her father revolutionized women's tennis. Having no female role model for his daughter, he taught her to play with the strength and speed of a man, but with the grace of a woman.

By the fall of 1910, Charles Lenglen had enough confidence in his daughter to apply for a membership at the famous Nice Tennis Club. She was the first child to be given a provisional membership. Her father devised a training regimen, which included not only hitting the same shot over

and over again until it was perfected, but also such physical conditioning activities as jumping rope, running wind sprints, and swimming. He also found male players to hit with her. Frequently, his methods drove his daughter to exhaustion.

Both parents motivated Lenglen by means of psychological intimidation. When she performed well, they gave her love and rewards. When she did badly, they cursed at her and embarrassed her in public. The result was an emotionally battered tennis genius, dependent upon her parents for love and support. In spite of her outward portrayal of of assurance, she lacked self confidence and was desperately afraid of failure. Her only escape from her parents regimen was to get sick; so she did often.

### A French Hero

By 1912, Lenglen was winning regional championships. In 1913, she won the Nice Tennis Club championship, and then won an Italian championship as well. Stories of the young girl's prowess on the court were beginning to spread through the Mediterranean. In 1914, after she won the Carlton Club tournament in Nice against a seasoned Wimbledon player, she was known throughout Europe. The same year, she won the World Hard Court Championships in singles and doubles. Lenglen was becoming the most popular sports hero in France.

While many thought Lenglen was ready for Wimbledon, her father had seen the English champion play, and thought she was too strong for his daughter. Shortly

thereafter, World War I began and most tennis tournaments were suspended. Nevertheless, Lenglen was able to play with a number of male tennis stars who were recuperating from their wounds in Nice, and she was able to maintain her strict regimen of practice. After the war ended, the former combatants became sports fanatics. Lenglen became a national hero and an example for French women.

### Exciting Women's Final

When Lenglen and her father decided that she was ready for Wimbledon in 1919, she carried French national pride with her. Like other women players of the time, she wore a wide brimmed bonnet for sun protection, a short sleeved white blouse, and a mid-calf white cotton skirt, but she did not wear a corset or heavy underwear. Her attire was to change dramatically.

Before the final round at Wimbledon, her only real competition was Elizabeth Ryan, an American expatriate living in England, who would eventually win 19 doubles titles at Wimbledon. In a fiercely fought contest that seemed to go first for Lenglen and then for Ryan, rain halted the match for an hour. After Lenglen's father remonstrated her, she went back on the court and won quickly. In the final match, she faced the seven-time Wimbledon champion, Lambert Chambers, in what has been called "the greatest and most exciting women's final ever played." In a match that might have gone either way, Lenglen won the first set 10-8, while Chambers rallied to win the second 6-4. In the third set, Chambers had double match point, but Lenglen fought back each time, finally beating Chambers 8-6. Their match took 44 games to play, a record that held until 1970.

After the match, both players stated that they had played extremely well. But in later years, Chambers said the match was a tragedy for both of them. It was tragic for her because she was a point away from winning the match twice; tragic for Lenglen because it made her feel invincible. Chambers stated that this invincibility brought Lenglen "a subsequent compulsion for it, which brought endless sacrifices and unnatural unhappiness, out of all proportion to the rewards of her fame." After Lenglen's success, the British press loved her.

In the 1920 Wimbledon finals, Lenglen easily beat Chambers. But the big news was her change in appearance. She now wore full makeup, a full length coat of ermine or mink, and a scandalously short skirt with a tight-fitting top. The American tennis star Bill Tilden said of her in 1921, "her costume struck me as a cross between a prima donna's and a streetwalker."

### The Match of the Century

For the next three years, Lenglen won handily at Wimbledon. She had times of depression and illness, and times of being relentlessly upbeat. By the end of 1921, she was considered to be the dominant woman in tennis, although she had been beaten once in the United States by Molla Mallory. The match ended in a default because Lenglen claimed to be ill, possibly because her father had not accompanied her on the trip. In 1922, however, she demolished Mallory at Wimbledon, and gave similar treatment to an English champion at Wimbledon in 1923. Failure to recover from jaundice caused her to withdraw from Wimbledon in 1924. But by the following year, she recovered and completely dominated her games at Wimbledon.

In 1925, Lenglen beacame the first female athlete to transcend athletics and become a celebrity. She dropped her training regimen and acquired a retinue of camp followers. In 1926, she played the young American Helen Wills at Cannes in what has been described as "The Match of the Century." According to a contemporary journalist, Ferdinand Tuohy, the match was "a simple game of tennis, yet a game which made continents stand still and was the most important sporting event of modern times, exclusively in the hands of the fairer sex." While bookies had Lenglen as a 3-1 favorite, many people thought Wills would be lucky to win two games. Wills, who had previously won three singles titles at Forest Hills in the U.S., fought valiantly. While Lenglen won the first set 6-3, her game seemed somewhat off. Having ignored her father's advice not to play Wills, Lenglen struggled in the second set. Wills won three of the first four games, but Lenglen finally evened the score at 4-4 after a dubious call by a referee rattled Wills. Next it was Lenglen's turn to be rattled when a spectator announced that one of Will's shots was out at match point, causing Lenglen to mistakenly believe the game was over. Lenglen finally rallied to win the set at 8-6, and the match.

Because she had not decisively beat Wills, Lenglen's status diminished and she became increasingly depressed. She tried to play tennis, but her play was erratic at best. Lenglan never played Wills again. At Wimbledon in 1926, she withdrew after the crowds turned against her because of her inconsistency and an inadvertent snubbing of the Queen. This was to be her last Wimbledon appearance.

## Health Problems Took Over

Because of her father's failing health and his inability to protect her interests, Lenglen decided to give up her amateur states and become a professional player in 1926. However, she was not able to make the amount of money she needed or wanted. Her illnesses and nervousness worsened. The amateur clubs and associations tried to force her to remain an amateur, but she departed for a professional tennis tour of the U.S. and Canada. After the tour fell apart, she tried to tour with several others, but nothing came of them. Lenglen also tried to be reinstated as an amateur, but was denied this status.

Lenglen remained a celebrity, but looked increasingly unwell and unhappy. Her father's death in 1929 was a crushing blow. During her final years, she ran a tennis camp for the children of Paris which was financed by the French government. In 1934, she almost died of acute appendicitis. On July 4, 1938, at the age of 39, Lenglen died in Paris of pernicious anemia. In an obituary, the *London Times* called her the greatest woman tennis player of her time, and said that she made Wimbledon the greatest tournament in the world. The *New York Times* stated that she was the greatest female player who ever lived, "a flashing, tempestuous figure vibrant with life. . . . She never had a rival in accuracy and scientific placement."

## Further Reading

Engelmann, Larry, *The Goddess and the American Girl: The Story of Suzanne Lenglen and Helen Wills,* Oxford University Press, 1988.
*Sports Illustrated,* September 13, 1982; July 9, 1984; Fall 1991. □

# Oscar Levant

**If George Gershwin had an alter-ego, most people would agree that it was Oscar Levant (1906–1972), film composer and arranger. Levant, who was best known as a jazz pianist, was considered to have been the most accomplished interpreter of the vast songbook of U.S. composer George Gershwin, and was the first performer to record "Rhapsody in Blue" after Gershwin. He also scored numerous Broadway plays and Hollywood films, composed classical music, authored several books, and contributed numerous articles on musical topics.**

L evant was born in Pittsburgh, Pennsylvania on December 27, 1906 to Max and Annie Levant, Orthodox Russian Jews. His talent with music was recognized early in his life, but he was a troublesome child to his music teachers and his parents, displaying a constant aversion to people who represented authority. His father, a demanding parent, insisted that all of his sons receive musical training and perform at family recitals, exactly as he commanded. He was meticulous in his plans for these recitals, dictating what each boy would play and how each piece was to be performed. In one instance, Levant rebelled, performing a piece of his own choice as an encore. His father's anger resulted in a humiliating slap in the face, and the beginning of his life-long loathing of authority figures.

Levant's formal education concluded at the age of 15 when his father died and he moved to New York in order to find the freedom to pursue his music in his own way. He was quick to find work in the Prohibition nightclubs and speakeasies of New York. It was 1921, the Great Depression was still a song away, and Broadway was thriving. A talented young man with his musical skills was soon absorbed into the spirit of the theater district, where popular stars included Al Jolson and Fanny Brice, were themselves children of Jewish immigrant parents. Although trained in classical music, Levant quickly picked up on current musical trends and played them to his advantage. It was not long before Levant became a regular at Lindy's, one of the more popular city nightspots. His satiric wit and skills at the keyboard soon became fodder for gossip columnists such as Walter Winchell, who recognized the value of Levant's caustic remarks.

## Friendship with Gershwin

Levant first heard Gershwin's music when he was 12 years old, and was soon inspired to compose his own music.

It was not surprising that during his time in New York, Levant and Gershwin would strike up a friendship—a friendship that would prove to be both intense and distressing. This relationship would extend through many years of a love-hate dependence on both sides. Levant, while personally insecure about his own talents, seemed driven to surpass Gershwin. Were it not for his neurotic insecurity, he might have done just that. His association with Gershwin was a blend of envy and hero worship; they had a deep mutual regard for one another that thrived on competitiveness.

Levant and Gershwin came from similar backgrounds. Levant was born of immigrant Jewish parents and raised in Pittsburgh, while Gershwin was an immigrant boy raised on New York's Lower East Side. Gershwin astutely understood that he would have quicker success if he cast off his background, affecting an upper-class bearing. Levant, on the other hand, remained the rumpled sidekick with the European accent. Levant knew that Gershwin could never change what he was, but that was little comfort to a man who remained trapped in the insecurities of his own immigrant background. Throughout his life, Levant was incapable of moving out of Gershwin's shadow, a fact that caused him considerable frustration and fed his neuroses. It was after Gershwin's untimely death in 1937 that Levant became his foremost interpreter.

With Gershwin's death, Levant picked up his friend's music and soon became known as one of the best interpreter's of Gershwin's compositions in the business. It was as a result of his love for this music and his ability to

interpret it through subsequent recordings that Levant quickly became one of the highest paid musical artists in the United States. He would have enjoyed, and most likely commented on, the irony of having achieved this recognition not through his own compositions and arrangements, but through those of his friend and rival.

## A Man of Many Careers

Levant truly had five vocations: composer, pianist, actor, author, and arranger. He studied music under Sigismund Stojowski from 1935 to 1937 and studied composition under Arnold Schoenberg, where he composed several classical pieces, including his piano concerto. He received high praise for his talents from the likes of Vladimir Horowitz. Levant's composition skills extended through many forms of music, including classical, jazz, and Broadway musicals. Among his own compositions are "Blame It on My Youth," "Lady Play Your Mandolin," and his classical "Sonatina: First Movement: Con ritmo." He recorded numerous works by other composers and, in addition to his best-known recording of Gershwin's "Rhapsody in Blue," he recorded Gershwin's "Prelude I," "Prelude II," and "Prelude III." He did not stray too far from his classical background as a listen to his recordings of Ravel's "Menuet," Shostakovitch's "Prelude in A Minor," and Debussy's "Jardins Sous La Pluie" reveal. Levant's recording of Gershwin's serious concert piano pieces raised an awareness of Gershwin's many musical talents beyond the New York area.

Levant appeared as a soloist with the New York Philharmonic and the Cleveland, Pittsburgh, Philadelphia, Rochester, Los Angeles, and Montreal orchestras, among others. In Hollywood he applied his talents as a composer of motion-picture music and, for a time, was the "Music Expert" on the *Information Please* radio program.

Levant frequently served as a sidekick in movies, where his sardonic wit played well against the hero. He was always cast to type and audiences identified him with objects such as smoldering ashtrays and full coffee cups. He appeared in 13 movies, among them *Rhythm on the River, Kiss the Boys Goodbye, Humoresque, The Barkleys of Broadway,* and *An American in Paris,* the last a biography of his friend, George Gershwin. Levant stretched his talents to include authorship when he wrote *A Smattering of Ignorance* in 1940, *Memoirs of an Amnesiac* in 1965, and *The Unimportance of Being Oscar* in 1968. He contributed to such magazines as *Good Housekeeping, Harper's, Town & Country,* and *Vogue.* Regardless of his many talents and throughout his multi-faceted career, Levant never stayed with one thing long enough to build his reputation beyond that of second string.

## Personal Devils

Levant began to make the circuit of radio and television shows where his biting wit delighted listeners across America. In 1950, he suffered a heart attack and subsequently developed an addiction to the pain medication, Demerol. Despite his exceptional musical skills and quick wit, Levant was plagued with lifelong uncertainty and depression. As his bouts with depression progressed, he turned these sad episodes into biting commentary about himself, drawing out his lack of self-confidence for the world to see.

In the early 1950s, Levant hosted his own television talk show with guests of the stature of authors Aldous Huxley and Christopher Isherwood. He even brought his own psychiatrist, Dr. George Wayne, on the show from time to time. Television in its infancy was live. No one could be sure what Levant would do or say as the program progressed, and this show was often considered "must see TV" for everyone in Hollywood. His wit was notorious and, while he frequently used it against others, he more often used it against himself. Although Levant had the potential for becoming a success in this new medium, his increasing episodes of depression took their toll on his career. He recognized the affect his addictions had on his health and checked himself into Mt. Sinai Hospital each day after his show, but with little or no positive effects. He soon began to fade from the public's view.

In 1958, television host Jack Paar convinced Levant to appear on his program. For the next six years the composer appeared with regularity, amusing viewers with his neurotic satire. Levant both shocked and intrigued viewers with his open discussions about his neuroses and his addiction to painkillers. While his illnesses became more apparent with each appearance as his speech slowed, his wit remained as sharp as ever. His openness about his illnesses was unheard of during these early years of television and Paar was severely criticized for allowing Levant to appear when his deteriorating mental condition seemed at its worst. However, Levant's self-deprecating comments seemed to endear him to the public. He spoke at a time when others hid their problems or those of their families, and his frank approach to his addictions and illnesses was curious, amusing, and often sad. Fans could view their own problems through his eyes, a means of avoiding the essential confrontation at home.

In her biography *A Talent for Genius,* co-author Nancy Schoenberger described Levant as "the first public dysfunctional celebrity . . . that shocked and also amused because Oscar was funny when he talked about . . . group therapy." Schoenberger repeats Levant's satiric reference to a group trip to Disneyland: "To hell with Disneyland. I have my own hallucinations."

## A Troubled Personal Life

Levant married twice during his life. His first marriage to Barbara Smith, on January 5, 1932, lasted less than seven years. On December 1, 1939 Levant again dove into marital waters when he married June Gale. They had three daughters, Marcia Ann, Lorna, and Amanda. The marriage was often explosive and the couple frequently found their private lives the topic of newspaper articles. There were moments of physical abuse, once when Levant charged that June threatened him with scissors. Yet through all of the marital problems that racked their life together, Levant's wife of 33 years remained with him until his death.

On August 14, 1972, Levant, a man who spoke openly about the devils that plagued him, died peacefully. He was buried in Westwood Memorial Park, West Los Angeles, California. A man who never got beyond the shadow of his best friend during his lifetime, may well have taken that very step with the legacy of music he left behind. He would have enjoyed that irony.

## Further Reading

*Entertainment Weekly,* May 20, 1994.
*Forward,* June 24, 1994.
*Los Angeles Times,* August 23, 1997. □

# William Levitt

**William Levitt (1907–1994) gained national attention as the man who mass produced houses at a rate of one every 16 minutes. He was introduced to Americans on the July 3, 1950 cover of *Time* magazine as the "cocky rambunctious hustler" prone to exaggeration. Levitt touted his community as a new form of ideal American life.**

William Levitt's father, Abraham Levitt, was the son of a poor rabbi who immigrated from Eastern Europe. Abraham Levitt left school at age 10, but educated himself. At the age of 20 he entered law school, specializing in real estate law. He married Pauline Biederman in 1906. Their first son, William Jaird was born on February 11, 1907 in Brooklyn, New York. Five years later the couple had another son, Alfred Stuart. As a child, William Levitt would put on a suit, run into the living room and announce his plans to go to Manhattan to make money and live well. Levitt attended Public School 44 and Boys High School in Bedford-Stuyvesant. He played lacrosse and was on the swim team. Levitt majored in mathematics and English at New York University, but left in his junior year.

Abraham Levitt represented real estate clients and occasionally bought and sold properties. He used money that his wife made from sewing to buy vacant lots in Brooklyn. Around 1925, he received 100 plots in Rockville Centre from a bankrupt client and financed builders who bought the land and started to construct houses there. When the builders went out of business, he had to take control of the partially finished houses. Abraham encouraged his sons to finish the homes, with existing crews.

In 1929, Abraham founded Levitt and Sons, Inc. William Levitt became company president at the age of 22, handling the advertising, sales, and financing. Alfred Levitt, still a teenager, became vice president of design and drafted plans for the first Levitt house, a six bedroom, two bathroom Tudor style home that sold for over $14,000 in 1929. The Levitts sold 600 of these upper middle class homes, part of the Strathmore project, in four years, even though it was during the Great Depression.

In November 1929, William Levitt married Rhoda Kirshner. The couple had a son, William Jr., in 1933. Levitt

earned a reputation as the person to see for high-end, custom homes on Long Island, New York's North Shore, called the Gold Coast. The company built 200 homes in the North Strathmore development in Manhasset, which sold for $9,100 to $18,500. The Levitts built another 1,200 homes in Manhasset, Great Neck, and Westchester County. Radio stars, prominent journalists, surgeons, business people, and lawyers bought the upscale Levitt houses. Selling these homes made the Levitt family rich.

William Levitt, the grandson of a rabbi, did not sell these upscale homes to Jews. "Sure, he went along with the local practice of real-estate agents not selling to Jews. History should show that Levitt was part of the ugly gentlemen's agreement," noted Paul Townsend, Levitt's former public relations man. "Gentlemen's agreement" refers to the unspoken agreement among gentiles to discriminate against Jews. Levitt saw the policy as the unfortunate cost of doing business. Although Levitt opposed what he referred to as "institutionalized religion," those who knew him say he was not anti-Semitic. Levitt made large contributions to Israel. In 1947, he handed a $1 million check to Teddy Kollek (the future mayor of Jerusalem) as a loan for weapons. During his life, Levitt donated millions of dollars to Jewish charities.

## Mass Production of Houses

In 1941, the Levitts won a government contract to provide 2,350 housing units for defense workers in Norfolk, Virginia. While building these units, the brothers learned valuable lessons about the mass producing of houses. In 1944, William Levitt, then 36 years old and father of a 10-year-old son and a baby, James, was sent to Oahu, Hawaii as a lieutenant in the Navy Seabees. He was the personnel manager for 260 men in the Navy construction unit, but spent most of World War II gambling, drinking, and playing jazz piano. He also thought about what he would do after the war, knowing that his father and brother were making plans for him. Levitt felt that anyone who built a lot of low-cost housing after the war was going to be very wealthy. Wartime shortages had crippled the housing industry, but veterans were eager to buy homes and take advantage of government loans after the war.

While William Levitt was in Hawaii, his father took over as company president and planned to build a community of 6,000 low-priced homes in Nassau County, much larger than any other U.S. development. The company bought 1,000 acres of potato farms on Long Island. On July 1, 1947, Levitt broke ground on the $50 million development, Levittown, which ultimately included 17,000 homes on 7.3 square miles of land. Alfred Levitt created the mass production techniques and designed the homes and the layout of the development, with its curving streets. Abraham directed the landscaping, whose focus was two trees to each front yard, all planted exactly the same distance apart. William was the financier and promoter, who persuaded lawmakers to rewrite the laws that made Levittown possible. The houses, which were in the Cape Cod and ranch house styles, sat on a seventh-of-an-acre lot. They had 750 square feet with two bedrooms, a living room and a kitchen, an unfinished second floor and no garage.

To mass produce the houses, the company broke the construction process down into 27 operations. Specialized teams repeated each operation at each building site. Twenty acres formed an assembly point, where cement was mixed and lumber cut. Trucks delivered parts and material to homesites placed 60 feet apart. Then carpenters, tilers, painters and roofers arrived in sequence. One team used white paint, another red. One worker's only duty was to bolt washing machines to floors. The Levitts built up to 180 houses a week when most builders were constructing four or five homes a year.

Levitt revolutionized the home construction industry by sifting through outdated building codes and union rules and using new technologies to get quality building jobs completed quickly and cheaply. To save money on lumber, the Levitts bought forests and built a sawmill in Oregon. They purchased appliances directly from the manufacturer, cutting out the middleman. They even made their own nails.

The mass production methods kept costs so low that in the first years the houses sold for $7,990, a price that still allowed a profit of about $1,000. (In the late 1990s they sold for about $155,000.) When the Levitt homes went on the market in March 1949, eager buyers lined up to purchase them. On the first day, Levitt sold 1,400 homes. They could be bought for a $58 downpayment, and included a free washing machine and television. The success of Levittown depended on huge government assistance. The Federal Housing Administration guaranteed the loans that banks made to builders. The Veterans Administration provided buyers with low-interest mortgages to purchase those houses, thus the risk to the lenders was small.

Levittown later became racially mixed, but for years Levitt's sales contracts forbade resale to African Americans. He once offered to build a separate development for blacks but refused to integrate his white Levitt developments. "We can solve a housing problem, or we can try to solve a racial problem," Levitt said. "But we can't combine the two." In 1963, his all-white policies led to civil rights protests at another Levitt development, in Bowie, Maryland.

## Sold Business to ITT

Levitt and Sons built 15 other projects throughout Long Island. In 1952, they brought their mass production operation to Bucks County, Pennsylvania. After that development was completed in 1958, Levitt went to Delaware and constructed a 12,000-home Willingboro, New Jersey project.

Relations among the Levitt family fell apart in 1951 after Alfred divorced his wife, to marry a 19-year-old fashion model he met on a trip to Paris. The brothers split their business affairs in 1954. Alfred developed Queens apartment complexes and Suffolk housing developments. He died in 1966, at the age of 54.

William Levitt took his company public in 1960, but lost $1.4 million a year later as housing demand fell and huge tracts of land near metropolitan areas grew scarce. He quickly changed tactics, branching out to Chicago, Washington, D.C., and even France and Puerto Rico. Levitt reduced the scale of projects, dabbled in townhouses, and delegated authority and decentralized management. He posted a 20 percent average annual increase in sales into the late 1960s.

After he had built over 140,000 houses around the world, Levitt sold the company to the International Telephone & Telegraph Corp. for $92 million in July 1967. At the age of 60, he became incredibly wealthy, getting $62 million in the form of ITT stock. ITT changed the name of its new subsidiary to Levitt Corp. and Levitt agreed not to build in the United States for ten years. He entered the agreement thinking he would play a role in ITT affairs, but executives felt Levitt was too old to take on more responsibility.

## Lost Fortune

While he was married, Levitt had an ongoing love affair with his secretary, Alice Kenny. He married her in 1959, divorcing his wife after 29 years of marriage. In 1969, Levitt divorced his second wife and married Simone Korchin, an art dealer from France.

Levitt bought a 237-foot yacht, a 30-room mansion in Mill Neck, New York, $3 million in jewelry, paintings by Renoir, Monet, Degas, and Chagall, and a Rolls Royce. To avoid paying taxes, he had not converted his ITT stock to cash. Instead, he borrowed against it to build subdivisions in places like Iran, Venezuela, and Nigeria. When the ITT shares crashed, Levitt's holdings lost about 90 percent of their original value. Chase Manhattan Bank seized Levitt's stock as collateral. When the foreign projects floundered, he was millions of dollars in debt.

Regulators forbade Levitt from doing business in New York. They said he took homeowners' deposits for Florida homes and money that should have been used for repairs and maintenance. Investigators claimed that Levitt also looted at least $17 million from his family's charities to cover personal expenses. He was forced to sell his mansion.

Levitt died in Manhasset, New York on January 28, 1994, on the verge of bankruptcy and unable to pay his bills. In an interview shortly before his death, Levitt said he would like to be remembered as "a guy that, I suppose, gave value for low-cost housing. Not somebody that gave value for half-million-dollar houses. Anybody can do that." Levitt saw himself as more than a real estate developer. He sold people the American Dream, in its cold war guise. "No man who owns his own house and lot can be a communist," Levitt once said. "He has too much to do."

## Further Reading

Duncan, Susan Kirsch, *Levittown: The Way We Were,* Maple Hill Press, 1999.
Ferrer, Margaret Lundregan and Tova Navarra, *Levittown: The First 50 Years,* Arcadia Publishing, 1997.
"Levittown: Documents of an Ideal American Suburb," *Cultural History Projects,* http://www.uic.edu/~pbhales/Levittown/index.html (March 16, 1999).
"Suburban Legend, William Levitt: His answer to a postwar housing crisis created a new kind of home life and culture: suburbia," *Time.com,* http://cgi.pathfinder.com/time/time100/builder/profile/levitt.html (March 16, 1999).
"The Dream Builder," *LI History.Com,* http://www.lihistory.com/specsec/hslevpro.htm (March 16, 1999). □

# Candy Lightner

**Candy Lightner (born 1946) transformed a personal tragedy into a crusade against drunk driving. She founded Mothers Against Drunk Driving, a grassroots organization dedicated to curbing alcohol-related traffic deaths.**

Lightner was born May 30, 1946, to Dykes Charles Dodderidge and Katherine Dodderidge in Pasadena, California. She graduated from high school in 1964. After attending American River College in Sacramento, she married Steve Lightner, who was a U.S. Air Force serviceman like her father. Together they had three children. After her divorce from Steve, Candy Lightner supported herself by selling real estate in Fair Oaks, California. She had lived there for eight years when her life was turned upside down by tragedy on May 3, 1980.

Lightner's 13-year-old daughter Cari, while walking down a quiet street, was struck from behind by a car. The impact threw Cari 125 feet, knocking off her shoes and mutilating her body so badly that it was not possible to save her organs for donation. Clarence William Busch, the driver of the car, did not stop. At the time of the crash, Busch had four previous drunk driving convictions, for which he had

served, at most, 48 hours in jail. He had been arrested for another hit-and-run accident just two days before hitting Cari.

Cari's death was the most tragic event in Lightner's life, but not the first time an impaired driver had injured her children. Earlier, when Cari and her identical twin sister, Serena, were 18 months old, Lightner's mother's station wagon had been rear-ended by a drunk driver. In that wreck, Serena was bruised and covered with glass cuts. Six years later, Lightner's son, Travis, then four, had been run over while playing in front of the family's house. Travis was temporarily paralyzed on one side, and suffered a collapsed lung, broken ribs, a broken leg, and a fractured skull. He spent several days slipping in and out of a coma and required surgery multiple times to repair damage to his body. His head injury caused permanent brain damage. The driver, who was unlicensed, was impaired by tranquilizers at the time she hit Travis, but did not even receive a ticket.

Lightner was overwhelmed with anger when, several days after the catastrophe, she learned that the driver who had caused her daughter's death would likely serve little or no time in jail. "I was furious," Lightner recalled in her book *Giving Sorrow Words.* "I felt enraged and helpless." After learning the details of the accident from a highway patrolman, Lightner sat in a restaurant bar with friends, and watched her fury light the spark of action. "I'm going to start an organization because people need to know about this," Lightner angrily told her friends. One suggested a name for the group: MADD, Mothers Against Drunk Drivers.

One day she was a divorced mother of three selling real estate in California, not even registered to vote. Within months, Lightner was testifying before legislatures. "I had become a personality and a crusader with a cause," she recounted in *Giving Sorrow Words.* "The texture of my days changed enormously."

## Mothers Against Drunk Driving

By the time Clarence William Busch was sentenced to two years in prison, Lightner had breathed her passion into MADD. Scraping together seed money from sources including Cari's insurance policy and her own savings, Lightner quit her job and plunged into lobbying for tougher drunk driving laws. Her goal was to eliminate what she called "the only socially accepted form of homicide." Alcohol abuse resulted in an estimated 240,000 traffic deaths in the 1980s. "I had in mind twenty women marching on the Capitol in California," Lightner told *Vogue's* Lorraine Davis. "But within two months we were about one hundred people marching on the White House in Washington."

Fueled by her intense rage, Lightner turned over her life to MADD, to the exclusion of everything, including her surviving children. "I was unstoppable," she recalled in *Giving Sorrow Words.* "I was so obsessed that, in many ways, I did not permit life to go on outside of MADD." Lightner traveled the country giving speeches, rallying volunteers, and testifying in favor of tougher drunk driving legislation.

Lightner put her obsessive determination to work lobbying Governor Jerry Brown of California to create a state commission for studying drunk driving. After several months of daily visits to the governor's office, Brown formed the commission and made Lightner its first member. In 1982, President Ronald Reagan asked Lightner to serve on the National Commission on Drunk Driving. By 1984, MADD had successfully lobbied the U.S. Congress to raise the national legal drinking age to 21, a change said to save approximately 800 lives annually. Inspired by her mother's activism, Lightner's daughter, Serena, formed school-based SADD, Students Against Drunk Driving. Like MADD, the organization formed chapters across the country.

Over the next five years, as president and chairman of the board of MADD, Lightner appeared on radio and television shows including *Nightline* and *Good Morning America.* Her life was even the subject of a 1983 NBC made-for-television movie called *Mothers Against Drunk Drivers—The Candy Lightner Story.* During her career as an activist, she has served with many organizations, including the Sacramento County Task Force on Drunk Driving, Presidential Commission on Drunk and Drugged Driving, National Commission on Drunk Driving, National Partnership for Drug Free Use, and the National Highway Safety Commission. For her service, Lightner was awarded many honors, including honorary degrees in public service from Kutztown University in Johnstown, Pennsylvania, and Marymount College in Johnstown, Pennsylvania.

Even after Lightner moved on, MADD continued to grow as a national force. By 1999, the group had become the largest victim-advocate and anti-drunk driving activist organization in the world, with approximately three million members in more than 600 chapters throughout the United States, Canada, Australia, New Zealand, and Great Britain. Instead of trying to eliminate drinking entirely, the group focuses its attention on curbing drunk driving.

## Grieving Process Began

After leaving MADD, Lightner realized that by constantly being so busy, she had avoided experiencing the grieving process. She began to understand that she had never healed emotionally from her daughter's death, even though many years had passed. Lightner chronicled her grieving process in her 1990 book, *Giving Sorrow Words: How to Cope with Grief and Get on with Your Life,* which she co-wrote with Nancy Hathaway. "For five and a half years, instead of focusing on my grieving, I concentrated on the manner in which she died," Lightner wrote. "Practically everything I did was centered on the fact that she was killed by a drunk driver rather than the fact that she died." The book, which contains interviews with dozens of people who have coped with the death of a loved one, offers readers suggestions on how to deal with their own grief.

In addition to writing her book, Lightner continued to speak out against drunk driving in lectures across the country. In 1992, she founded a group called Victims in Action and its legislative arm, the Victims in Action Political Action Committee. In 1994, Lightner drew fire from MADD for lobbying on behalf of the American Beverage Institute, a trade group of restaurant and hotel executives. She took sides against her former allies over states wanting to pass laws lowering the blood alcohol level at which a driver is considered legally drunk from .10 to .08. Lowering the limit would not get the most dangerous drivers off the road, Lightner argued. Drivers with blood alcohol levels above .10, she asserted, cause more than 80 percent of drunk driving deaths. "The man who killed my daughter kept on driving drunk," Lightner told Katherine Griffin of *Health* magazine. "He has since been arrested several more times. In each case his blood alcohol content has been .20 or above. A small segment of our drinking/driving population causes the majority of the fatalities. So why aren't we going after them?"

Challenging rumors that she'd gone soft on drunk driving, Lightner maintained that she favored enforcement of existing laws that allow police to take away the cars of repeat drunk drivers. "I am still amazed that the man who killed my daughter is barred from ever owning a handgun," she told Griffin, "but he can own a car."

## Further Reading

Lightner, Candy and Nancy Hathaway, *Giving Sorrow Words: How to Cope with Grief and Get on with Your Life,* Warner Books, 1990.
*Prominent Women of the 20th Century,* edited by Peggy Saari, UXL, 1996.
*Who's Who of American Women,* Reed Reference, 1993-94.
*50 Plus,* May 1983.
*Health,* July/August 1994.
*Life,* fall 1989.
*North Country Times,* March 3, 1996.
*Vogue,* April 1986.
Mothers Against Drunk Driving, http://www.madd.org (March 8, 1999).
Women's International Center, http://wic.org (March 4, 1999). □

# Viola Liuzzo

**Viola Liuzzo (1925–1965) was the first white woman killed during the American civil rights movement. Inspired by the efforts of African Americans in the South to obtain the right to vote, she left her home in Detroit and participated in the Selma-to-Montgomery, Alabama march for black voting rights in 1965. While shuttling marchers in her car, she was shot and killed by members of the Ku Klux Klan, a white supremacist organization determined to keep segregation alive.**

Viola Gregg Liuzzo was born on April 11, 1925 in the small town of California, Pennsylvania. Her father, Heber Ernest Gregg, worked in a coal mine until his right hand was blown off in a mining explosion. He left school in the eighth grade, but taught himself to read. Her mother, Eva Wilson Gregg, had a teaching certificate from the University of Pittsburgh, but finding work was not always easy for her. Viola was the couple's first child. Her sister, Rose Mary, was born eleven years later. During the Great Depression, the family moved from Georgia to Tennessee, where Eva Gregg found a teaching position. The family was very poor and lived in one-room shacks with no running water. The schools Liuzzo attended did not have adequate supplies and the teachers were too busy to give extra attention to children in need. Because the family moved so often, Liuzzo never began and ended the school year in the same place. Although her parents argued against it, Liuzzo dropped out of school in the tenth grade. She and her father often argued about her social activities and, at the age of 16, Liuzzo ran away and married a much older man. The marriage lasted only one day.

## New Beginnings in Michigan

Liuzzo moved to Michigan with her family, where her mother found work in a bomb factory and then at a Ford Motor plant. Liuzzo worked as a waitress. She met and married George Argyris when she was 18. In 1946, their daughter Penellipi (Penny) was born and, in 1948, Mary Eva followed. After seven years of marriage, the couple divorced and Liuzzo received custody of the girls. Being a single mother proved difficult, and the girls were sent to live with their grandparents.

While working as a waitress in Detroit, Liuzzo met Anthony James (Jim) Liuzzo, a business agent for the Teamsters Union. Liuzzo converted to Catholicism and married him in 1950. The girls came to live with them and the couple soon had two sons, Thomas in 1951 and Anthony, Jr., in 1955. A daughter, Sally, was born in 1958 with severe

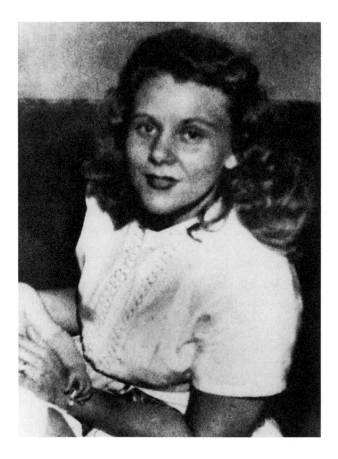

health problems, which she overcame with the help of her mother's care and attention. The family lived in a middle class, racially integrated neighborhood. Liuzzo had a reputation for helping others. She took particular pleasure in teaching her children about nature and would take them on walks and camping trips. Liuzzo loved to read philosophy and history. She read to her children from Henry David Thoreau's works and taught them the meaning of civil disobedience. Sarah Evans, the family's African American housekeeper and friend, taught Liuzzo how hard her life was because of racism and encouraged Liuzzo to join the National Association for the Advancement of Colored People (NAACP).

Liuzzo regretted dropping out of high school. In 1961, she enrolled in night classes at a career training school, the Carnegie Institute of Detroit. There she studied to become a medical laboratory assistant. She graduated in 1962, an honor student who received a gold trophy for her outstanding academic work. Using her new skills and knowledge, Liuzzo went to work for the Parkview Medical Center. She felt that labor practices at Parkview were unfair and tried to expose them to public scrutiny. Liuzzo claimed to have stolen a microscope and insisted on being taken to the police station. This action attracted media attention since her husband had become a local labor leader. Liuzzo next found part-time work at Sinai Hospital. In May 1962, she enrolled at Wayne State University, taking English and philosophy, among other courses. The university exposed Liuzzo to political ideas of the time, including debates about the Vietnam War and discussions on civil rights.

## Time for Action

In February 1965, a night demonstration for voting rights at the Marion, Alabama courthouse turned very ugly. State troopers clubbed marchers and beat and shot a 26-year-old African American named Jimmie Lee Jackson, who later died. His death spurred on the fight for civil rights in Selma, Alabama. The Southern Christian Leadership Conference (SCLC) scheduled a protest march for Sunday, March 7. Governor George Wallace banned the march, but the ban was ignored. Six hundred marchers headed for the arched Edmund Pettus Bridge that crossed the Alabama River. As the protesters reached the crest of the bridge, they saw a terrifying sight on the other side: state troopers armed with clubs, whips, and tear gas, and a sheriff's posse on horseback. When told to stop and disperse, the marchers refused. The troopers advanced on the marchers, clubbing and whipping them, fracturing bones and gashing heads. Seventeen people were hospitalized on the day later called "Bloody Sunday."

At Wayne State University, 250 students held a protest demonstration on March 12. They marched to the federal building in Detroit singing "We Shall Overcome," a civil rights song. Liuzzo participated in that march, becoming actively involved for the first time in the civil rights movement.

A march was scheduled for Sunday, March 21, beginning in Selma and ending at the state capital of Montgomery, 54 miles away. Marchers hoped to meet Governor Wallace to discuss the voting rights of black people. On the Tuesday before the event, Liuzzo packed a few things in a shopping bag and told Sarah Evans that she was going to Selma to help with the march. Evans begged her not to go, but Liuzzo was insistent. That night she called her husband and told him her plan. He tried to dissuade her, as did her daughter Penny, who told her, "Mom, I have a terrible feeling I'm not going to see you anymore." Liuzzo replied, "I need to be there . . . ." In Selma, Liuzzo greeted new arrivals for the march at the Brown Chapel reception desk. There she met Leroy Moton, a 19-year-old civil rights activist.

More than 3,000 people began the march on Sunday, March 21, including blacks, whites, doctors, nurses, working class people, priests, nuns, rabbis, homemakers, students, actors, and farmers. Many famous people participated including Dr. Martin Luther King, Ralph Bunche, Coretta Scott King, Ralph Abernathy, and Andrew Young. It took five days for the protesters to reach their goal. Liuzzo marched the first full day and returned to Selma for the night. On Wednesday she rejoined the march four miles from the end, where a festival was held with performances by many popular entertainers of the day, including Sammy Davis, Jr., Joan Baez, and Dick Gregory. Liuzzo helped at the first aid station. On Thursday, Liuzzo and other marchers reached the state capitol building, with a Confederate flag flying above it. Martin Luther King addressed the crowd of 25,000, calling the march, a "shining moment in American history."

## Violent End to Peaceful Protest

After the march, Liuzzo insisted on helping shuttle people from Montgomery back to Selma. After dropping passengers in Selma, she and Moton headed back to Montgomery. Liuzzo stopped at a red light, and a car with four white men pulled up alongside her. They saw a white woman and a black man in a car together. Because of segregation, blacks and whites in the South did not share public facilities and race mixing often led to violence. These men belonged to the Ku Klux Klan (KKK), a group that supported the continuation of segregation. They followed Liuzzo, who tried to outrun them. They caught up with her car and opened fire. She was shot in the head and died in Lowndesboro, Alabama on March 25, 1965.

The Liuzzo family was shattered to learn of her death. Adding to their grief were the phone calls and hate mail they received. The children were taunted in the streets with cries of "nigger lover." Yet many others called and wrote to express love and sympathy. President Lyndon Johnson appeared on television the next day to discuss the murder and arrest of the four Klansmen. Johnson told the American people, "Mrs. Liuzzo went to Alabama to serve the struggle for justice. She was murdered by the enemies of justice, who for decades have used the rope and the gun and the tar and feathers to terrorize their neighbors." Johnson announced that he planned to send an anti-KKK bill to Congress to demand an investigation into the "hooded society of bigots." Johnson used Liuzzo's murder to encourage Congress to pass the Voting Rights Act, which he signed into law in August of 1965.

## Justice on Trial

On May 3, 1965, the trial of Liuzzo's killers began. One of the men in the car, Gary Thomas Rowe, Jr., was an FBI informant and thus was protected by the FBI. The three others were indicted on a state charge of murder and a federal charge of civil rights violation. The all-white jury could not come to a decision and a mistrial was declared. The second trial began in October. The defense attorney attacked the credibility of the informant, Rowe, stating that he fabricated information. The men were found not guilty of murder. In the federal trial the defendants were found guilty of conspiracy to violate the civil rights of Liuzzo and were sentenced to ten years in prison, a landmark in Southern legal history.

In 1978, investigations revealed that Rowe, the FBI informant, may have been involved in the bombing of a church in 1963 where four black girls were killed. In November of 1978, a grand jury indicted Rowe for the murder of Liuzzo, but he fought the extradition proceedings against him. In 1980, an FBI file revealed that Rowe had clubbed Freedom Riders and that the FBI had paid his medical bills and given him a $125 bonus. The Liuzzo children sued the FBI for $2 million, blaming Rowe and the FBI for the murder. A federal judge blocked Rowe's extradition to Alabama. In Ann Arbor, Michigan, the Liuzzos got Rowe into court, but the judge threw out the case and ordered the family to pay back the government $80,000 in court costs. The family appealed and the fine was voided.

Difficulties in obtaining FBI files in the Liuzzo case led to a strengthening of the Freedom of Information Act. *Playboy* magazine sued the Department of Justice to gain access to the task force report on Gary Thomas Rowe, Jr. It took two and a half years of legal wrangling before Judge Norma Holloway Johnson ordered the report turned over to *Playboy*. The lengthy court battle ended in a landmark decision which endorsed the public's right to know.

## Further Reading

Mendelsohn, Jack, *The Martyrs: 16 Who Gave Their Lives for Racial Justice,* Harper & Row, 1966.
Siegel, Beatrice, *Murder on the Highway: The Viola Liuzzo Story,* Four Winds Press, 1993.
*Jet,* March 20, 1980.
*National Review,* July 10, 1995.
*Playboy,* October 1980; June 1983. □

# Belva Lockwood

**Belva Lockwood (1830–1917) was the first American female attorney and the first woman to run for president of the United States. She refused to accept discriminatory laws and asserted her right as a woman to plead cases before the U.S. Supreme Court. Lockwood waged a lifelong battle to attain equal rights for women, Native Americans, African Americans, and immigrants.**

Belva Lockwood was born Belva Ann Bennet on October 24, 1830 in Royalton, New York. She was the daughter of farmers, Lewis and Hannah Bennet, and was raised in the hills of western New York. As a child, she loved history and dreamed of becoming a teacher. At the age of 14, Lockwood graduated from the local public school and spent the summer teaching for $7 a week. She saved her money and used it to pay tuition at the Girls Academy in Royalton, New York. She graduated at 18 and married Uriah McNall. The couple had one child, a daughter named Lura.

Lockwood was 22 when McNall died. In order to support herself and her young daughter, she applied for a teaching position. When Lockwood discovered that she could earn only $8 a week while male teachers earned $16 to $20 a week for the same work, she refused to accept the discriminatory wage. She sold some of her late husband's property and used the proceeds to pay her tuition at Genesee Wesleyan Seminary, later called Syracuse University. Lura McNall went to live with her grandparents while Lockwood pursued a higher education. She studied science, mathematics, political economy, and the U.S. Constitution. She learned about the social causes of the day, including abolitionism, temperance, and equal rights for women. Lockwood graduated from the two-year program in 1857 and became head of the Lockport Union School District, where her progressive ideas shocked the other teachers and

school, and demanded her diploma. It arrived within a week. In September of that same year, she was admitted to the bar of the District of Columbia. She opened a law practice in her home and quickly established a clientele. Lura McNall assisted her mother by performing secretarial duties.

Lockwood discovered while working on a case of patent infringement, that women were not allowed to plead cases before the U.S. Court of Claims, without special permission. She requested permission, but was refused. She then petitioned Congress to grant women permission to practice before the Supreme Court. Congress passed the appropriate legislation five years later, in 1879. On March 3 of that year, Lockwood was granted permission to argue cases before the highest court in the United States. Three days later she was granted access to the U.S. Court of Claims, where she won some of her more memorable cases.

Among the significant litigation that Lockwood presented before the Court of Claims was a suit brought by Jim Taylor, a Native American from the Cherokee tribe. Taylor requested help to collect money owed to the Cherokee people by the U.S. government since the Treaty of New Echota of 1835. Lockwood fought for many years to help them collect the interest on that money. She pleaded the case before the U.S. Supreme Court and won an award of $5 million. At the time, It was considered to be the most important case, in terms of monetary compensation, ever brought before the U.S. Court of Claims and the Supreme Court.

Lockwood worked with the Universal Peace Union, in a struggle to attain equal rights for minorities. She contributed her talents to the cause of southerner, Samuel Lowery, who became the first African American to be admitted before the bar of the Supreme Court.

## Presidential Candidate and Diplomat

Lockwood was continually frustrated by the Republican Party and its apparent lack of interest in protecting the rights of women. She wrote to Marietta Stow, the editor of the *Women's Herald of Industry* in California. Lockwood stated, "Even if women in the United States are not permitted to vote, there is no law against their being voted for and, if elected, filling the highest office . . . Why not nominate women for important places?. . .The Republican Party . . . has little but insult for women when they appear before its conventions. It is time we had our own party, our own platform and our own nominees." Stow replied to Lockwood's letter with a startling proposition, "We have the honor to congratulate you [Lockwood] as the first woman ever nominated for the office of president of the United States." The Equal Rights Party had selected her as a presidential nominee to run in the election of 1884. The party awaited her reply.

Lockwood accepted the nomination and formulated her platform. She would seek to place women in public offices including the Supreme Court. Lockwood resolved to protect and foster American industries, to promote temperance laws, and to fight for full citizenship rights for Native Americans. Reporters and cartoonists poked fun at

parents. She insisted, for example, that girls be allowed to enroll in public speaking and physical education classes. After two years at the school district, she became head mistress at the Gainesville Female Seminary.

Resolute in her conviction to change the course of women's lives, Lockwood moved herself, her daughter, and her sister, Inverno, to Washington, D.C. in 1865. They established a school for young ladies as a means of support, and McNall involved herself in the administration of the school. Lockwood spent a portion of her time speaking out for women's rights and contacting legislators. She wrote letters to congressmen, observed the workings of the Congress, and attended meetings for social activism. Yet she felt increasingly abandoned by the elected officials in the federal government. It seemed to her that many had forgotten the words of the U.S. Constitution. She became outraged by the fact that female civil service employees made two to three times less than their male counterparts and drafted a bill to equalize the salaries of all civil service employees. The bill passed and became law. In order to further test the power of the courts, Lockwood decided to become a lawyer. She was refused admission at two law schools because off her sex. Finally she met William Wedgewood, vice chancellor of the National University Law School, who agreed to give her private instruction in law.

## Legal Career

In May 1873, at the age of 43, Lockwood completed her law studies, but was refused a diploma. She wrote to President Ulysses S. Grant, the titular head of the law her while the most ardent of feminists, Susan B. Anthony and Elizabeth Stanton, disapproved of Lockwood's presidential campaign, fearing that such a hapless endeavor might only serve to dilute the cause of women's rights. Lockwood herself took the campaign seriously; she visited many cities and states on a grueling campaign schedule. Her ideas reached many citizens through the newspapers.

Lockwood received at least 6,161 votes. There were more votes in her favor that the election judges refused to tabulate. In 1888, the Equal Rights Party of Iowa nominated her for the presidency once more, and again she campaigned in earnest.

During the 1880s and 1890s Lockwood realized a lifelong dream of traveling abroad. In 1885, the State Department appointed her as a delegate to the Congress of Charities, the first world pacifist gathering, in Geneva Switzerland. At the Congress Lockwood read a proposal for the formation of a world court, a suggestion that met with great approval. The following year, she became the official representative to the Second International Peace Conference in Budapest, Hungary. In 1889, Lockwood attended the Universal Peace Congress in Paris, and the following year she read a paper on disarmament at the International Peace Conference in London. In 1892, Lockwood was a member of the International Peace Bureau, which met in Bern, Switzerland.

## Personal Glimpse

Shortly after arriving in Washington, a toothache led to an acquaintance with Dr. Ezekiel Lockwood. She married the dentist in 1868 and gave birth to a daughter the following year. The couple named the little girl Jessie. Sadly, the child died of typhoid fever at a young age. When Lockwood opened her private law practice in the couple's home, her husband retired from dentistry to become a notary public and claims agent. He died in 1877. Lockwood's oldest daughter, Lura McNall, died during the years when Lockwood's life was absorbed by the North Carolina Cherokee claim recovery case. McNall left behind a young son, Forest, whom Lockwood continued to raise.

Lockwood assisted in the establishment of the Universal Franchise Association, and served as president to that organization. In 1869, she helped found the Equal Rights Association of Washington, an organization whose mission was to secure equal rights for all Americans regardless of race, color, or sex. Lockwood was often frustrated when hecklers disrupted the association meetings. Her words at one meeting were quoted in the *Washington Star:* "We cannot stop fighting until such legislation is passed, no matter what ridicule and humiliation we suffer doing so."

In 1912, at the age of 81, Lockwood retired from the practice of law, to devote her time to social causes. Three years later, she made her last trip to Europe, to send a message of peace to the women of the world. Lockwood died on May 19, 1917 in Washington, DC—three years before American women received the right to vote. In the 1980s, the U.S. Postal Service issued stamps to honor Lockwood. In the 1990s, a crater on the planet Venus was named in her honor. The perseverance and eloquence of Belva

Lockwood enabled her to accomplish many goals and to overturn a number of prejudicial barriers.

## Further Reading

Fox, Mary Virginia, *Lady for the Defense: A Biography of Belva Lockwood,* Harcourt Brace Jovanovich, 1975.
Kerr, Laura, *The Girl Who Ran for President,* Thomas Nelson, 1947.
*American History Illustrated,* March 1985.
*Ms.,* July/August 1998.
*Sky & Telescope,* May 1995.
*Smithsonian,* March 1981.
*Stamps,* June 23, 1984; June 7, 1986; July 5, 1986. □

# Hugh Lofting

**A childhood love of animals shaped the writing career of Hugh Lofting (1886–1947). His work was chiefly built around the creation of a fictional character, Doctor John Dolittle, who sought to help animals by learning their language. Lofting used this character to illustrate to his young readers that communication with others, even those who appear to be the most foreign, can go a long way toward creating a more harmonious world.**

Doctor John Dolittle was the protagonist in Hugh Lofting's long-running juvenile series. He promoted the idea that different entities (people and animals alike) could live compatibly and that this philosophy was most effectively passed on by reaching young children before biased attitudes were ingrained in them. If he could reach children with his message, he might point at least a portion of the population in the direction of world peace; this appeared to be his ultimate dream.

Hugh John Lofting was born at Maidenhead in Berkshire, England, on January 14, 1886. His parents were both Roman Catholic; but his mother, Elizabeth Agnes, was Irish, and his father, John Brien Lofting, was English. He had four brothers and one sister. By the age of eight Lofting had been sent to Mount Saint Mary, a Catholic boarding school, where he remained for the next ten years. Little is known either about his school days or about his childhood prior to that.

Although Lofting may have preferred to strike out on his own to pursue a writing career, he and his brothers were expected to seek professions that were more secure and dependable. Therefore, he decided to study civil engineering with a focus on architecture. In 1904, Lofting journeyed to the United States, where he enrolled at the Massachusetts Institute of Technology. By 1906, he had returned to England to complete coursework at London Polytechnic. During his college years he whetted his creative thirst by writing plays and short stories. After earning a degree in 1907, Lofting sought employment in the areas for which he had been trained.

## Changed Careers

Those early years saw Lofting changing jobs frequently. First he practiced architecture, then he prospected for gold and worked as a surveyor in Canada. During the next couple of years he traveled to West Africa and Cuba, where he served as a railway engineer. By 1912, he was back in the States, having firmly decided that engineering was not for him. He moved to New York and married Flora Small that year. He also began sending manuscripts of articles and short stories to magazines. Flora bore him, in quick succession, his first two children, Elizabeth and Colin. Despite taking up residence in the U.S., Lofting never became a naturalized American citizen. He remained a British subject throughout his entire life.

Due to the outbreak of the First World War, Lofting's writing career was temporarily put on hold. However, the events of the war were to have a considerable impact on him. Initially, he worked for the British Ministry of Information at its New York base. Two years later, in 1916, he joined the British army, becoming a member of the Irish Guards. Lofting saw combat in France and Flanders. It was his response to what he observed there that changed his life.

## Doctor Dolittle Created

Lofting's children looked forward to letters from their father. They wanted to know what things were like in the trenches. Lofting thought about what he could send them. Either his days were tediously spent and of no interest to a child or the events were so horrific they might inspire nightmares. He noticed in particular the cold, indifferent manner in which the war-employed animals were treated. Unlike wounded soldiers who were medically treated, any wounded animals were automatically killed and discarded as no longer useful. Out of Lofting's disgust over this apparent disrespect for the animals, Doctor Dolittle was born. Lofting created a doctor who decided to stop treating humans and to turn his attention to the medical treatment of animals. He determined that this was best achieved by learning their language. He sent the stories back home to entertain the children.

In 1917, Lofting was wounded in France. Two years later he was discharged and sent home to his family in the United States. They moved to Connecticut, and Lofting devoted his attention to his writing. His wife and children encouraged him to turn his stories into a book. His idea was well-received by the publisher, Frederick A. Stokes and a manuscript was completed in 1920. The public became enthralled with *The Story of Doctor Dolittle*. The exotic settings and fast-paced plotting, which included chases, captures, escapes, rescues, and a return-trip home, made for quick reading. The original idea of the doctor who talked to animals in order to help them generated much notice.

## Newbery Medal Award

In 1923, Lofting's second book, *The Voyages of Doctor Dolittle,* was published and received critical acclaim. It won a Newbery Medal that year. Reviewers found the story to be fuller and the writing to be more sophisticated, although still appealing for its intended audience. Doctor Dolittle grew as a protagonist who could perform fantastic feats. Lofting revealed some of the history of Dolittle's life, as well. He continued to focus on characters who might otherwise have been overlooked or dismissed. He turned a literary magnifying glass on the misfits and humanized them—even the animals. An important element was also added. The addition of the young character, Tommy Stubbins, provided the young readers with someone to whom they could relate more closely.

Encouraged by the enthusiastic reception of his first two books, Lofting put out four more. He also chose this time to contribute articles to the *Nation* magazine. Lofting tried to dispel the folk tales and legends of war heroes which "keep alive race hatreds," as related in *Something about the Author.*

## Tragic Losses

In 1927, Lofting's wife, Flora, died. The following year he married Katherine Harrower (also known as Katherine Harrower-Peters). Just a few months after their wedding she contracted influenza and died. Lofting's physical well-being began to decline, perhaps in response to his personal losses. He wrote some children's books outside the realm of his Dolittle series. After five years he produced *Doctor Dolittle's Return*. Although he had been ready to retire the doctor, his readers were clamoring for another installment in the series and Lofting decided to oblige them. This was considered by many to be his last quality work.

In 1935, he married his third and last wife, Josephine Fricker. They moved to Topanga, California. The following year their son, Christopher, was born. Lofting continued to write, but not with the fervor of his early days. The outbreak of the Second World War seemed to inject him with a growing pessimism about the state of the world, which was reflected in his writing. The first of three posthumous novels, *Doctor Dolittle and the Secret Lake,* depicted the biblical story of the flood from the animals' point of view. It included death and destruction, but ultimately friendship prevailed. Hugh Lofting died in Santa Monica, California on September 26, 1947, after a two-year illness.

### Blacklisted, Then Revised

His 12 Doctor Dolittle books went out of favor and out of print during the 1970s. They were blacklisted for almost two decades because some passages were construed as racist. It would seem probable that Lofting was unaware that his passages were both racist and condescending. In 1988, revised editions of the books were released. Some purists argue that the books should have remained intact. Lofting's son, Christopher, on the other hand, supported the revisions, even proclaiming that his father would have altered the objectionable passages himself.

Some of the books from the Dolittle series reflected an uneven quality of writing. The apparent intent of Lofting was that they should be taken as a whole, though. This was not a planned series. It evolved to reflect the growth of its creator as well as that of its main character. Consistent to the series, however, was the theme running through each book—that, by reaching out to one another through the offer of communication and friendship, anything was possible. Lofting fervently hoped that, with the right attitude and the right tools, living together in harmony was not such an outlandish idea.

### Further Reading

Blishen, Edward, *Hugh Lofting,* Bodley Head, 1968.
*Dictionary of Literary Biography,* Volume 160, Gale Research, 1996.
*Something about the Author,* Volume 100, Gale Research, 1999.
□

# Malcolm Lowry

**Malcolm Lowry (1909–1957) is best known for his one and only masterpiece, an autobiographical novel entitled *Under the Volcano.* It weaves together themes of alienation, love, political idealism, and myth. An uncontrolled alcoholic, Lowry's life was marked by self-destruction and desolation.**

Lowry was born on July 28, 1909, in New Brighton, near Liverpool, England, the fourth son of Arthur Osborne Lowry and Evelyn Boden Lowry. His father was a wealthy Liverpool cotton broker who provided Lowry with a conventional English upper-class childhood. He was

sent away to boarding school when he was eight years old and later briefly attended a public school where he wrote poems and stories for the *Leys Fortnightly,* the school magazine.

Later in his life, Lowry would lament frequently about his abysmal childhood. Most biographers attribute this to Lowry's tendency to embellish and fictionalize events to serve his own purposes. For example, he claimed that the noticeable scar on his knee, the outcome of a childhood bicycle accident, was the result of a gunfight during the Chinese civil war. Lowry did suffer from chronic constipation as a child and battled a bout of conjunctivitis as a preteen that affected the sight in both his eyes temporarily. He began abusing alcohol by the time he was 14 years old.

Although his father expected him to attend Cambridge and then take his place in the family business like his three older brothers, Lowry wanted some worldly experience to draw on for his writing. In May 1927, having finally secured his father's reluctant consent, Lowry set sail from Liverpool bound for Yokohama as a deckhand on the freighter *S. S. Pyrrhus.* He returned five months later with material for several stories that he would eventually expand into his first novel.

Lowry was particularly influenced by American writer Conrad Aiken and his 1927 novel, *Blue Voyage.* Precipitated by a fan letter, Lowry moved to Boston in the summer of 1929 in order to learn from Aiken. This apprenticeship financed by Lowry's father. Lowry was also very interested in the Norwegian writer, Nordahl Grieg, and his dark novel about a young man's adventures at sea entitled *The Ship Sails On.*

In the fall of 1929, Lowry attempted to placate his parents by enrolling at Cambridge University. His career as a student was unspectacular. He remained remote and aloof, spending most of his time working on drafts of his first novel *Ultramarine.* In his first term, he was deeply shaken by the suicide death of his roommate, Paul Fitte. Although the details of their relationship are unclear, Lowry was long haunted by the death. He later claimed responsibility for the tragedy and references to the incident appeared in his fiction. By the time he graduated from Cambridge in 1932, Lowry had earned a reputation as an excellent writer and a heavy drinker. Despite his unrelenting drinking, coupled with self-doubt, detachment, and despair, Lowry had a charm and a charisma that drew others to him, particularly in the barrooms.

### Ultramarine

*Ultramarine,* the first of two major works published in Lowry's lifetime, appeared in 1933. Lowry was 24 years old. It tells the story of an educated young man, Dad Hilliot, and his psychological and social development during his voyage to the Far East. Because of his upper-class background and sexual inexperience, Hilliot is rejected and ridiculed by the crew. Nonetheless, he is able to win their approval, after weeks of loneliness and internal anguish. The story is supposedly based on Lowry's experiences on the *S.S. Pyrrhus,* although he never achieved the level of acceptance his character did.

The reviews of *Ultramarine* were less than enthusiastic. According to critics, the main problem was a narrative line that could not sustain itself over the course of the novel. An additional problem was that Lowry attributed an undue significance to Hilliot's experiences. He also received criticism for his perfunctory treatment of the ports and countries encountered by Hilliot, preferring to focus on the inner psyche of his character. Although some critics saw evidence of Lowry's potential for extraordinary writing, *Ultramarine* was for all practical purposes a failure. Of the 1,500 copies printed, only half were sold. Later, Lowry would concur that the novel was not exceptional. He often spoke of rewriting it, but only a few minor revisions were ever made.

After leaving Cambridge, Lowry spent several months in London where he developed relationships with other writers, including Dylan Thomas. In April 1933, his restless spirit took hold and he began traveling through Europe with friend and mentor Aiken. While in Spain, Lowry met American writer Jan Gabrial and, after a brief romance, the two were married in Paris on January 6, 1934. However, the relationship was marked with conflict. Eventually Gabrial left Lowry in France and returned to New York. He published two stories about their tumultuous marriage as "Hotel Room in Chartres" and "In Le Havre." During this time Lowry also wrote a 1,000-page manuscript titled "In Ballast to the White Sea," a story with psychological overtones about a Cambridge student and his relationships with those around him. He never found a publisher for the novel, and years later the manuscript was destroyed in a fire.

In 1935, Lowry moved to New York. His out-of-control drinking precipitated a two-week stay in the psychiatric ward at Bellevue Hospital. The next year Lowry and his wife reconciled. They moved to Los Angeles, where they lived briefly before moving to Cuernavaca, Mexico. By 1937 Lowry's obsessive drinking had fractured his relationship with Gabrial for good; she left him and they never saw each other again. Already suffering from deep emotional and mental turmoil, Lowry sank deeper into despair. His drinking went unabated, and Lowry was jailed in Oaxaca. When he was ultimately deported in July 1938, he returned to Los Angeles.

Although his time in Mexico had been exceptionally painful and disturbed, it was also a time of inspiration and insight. His anguish became the subject matter for his one and only masterpiece, an autobiographical novel entitled *Under the Volcano,* which he began working on in 1936. After completing three drafts, Lowry was still unable to find a publisher. In the midst of his struggles, and shortly after arriving in California, Lowry met and fell in love with Margerie Bonner, an aspiring American writer and former child-star of silent films. When Lowry moved across the border into Canada after his American visa expired, Bonner went with him. They were married on December 2, 1940. For nearly 15 years, they lived in a squatter's cabin at Dollarton on the Burrard Inlet, near Vancouver. The shack burned down in 1944, and the manuscript of "In Ballast to the White Sea" was destroyed, but other works in progress were saved. After a time living with friends, they returned and rebuilt.

### Under the Volcano

On Christmas Eve in 1944, Lowry finished his final draft of *Under the Volcano.* It tells the tragic story of the last 12 hours in the life of Geoffrey Firmin. The entire novel takes place on November 2, 1938, with the exception of the first chapter, set in 1939. An alcoholic consumed by his vice, Firmin had been the British consul in Quauhnahuac, Mexico, but was removed after Britain severed diplomatic relations in 1938, over the oil crisis. His crumbling life served to reflect the political upheaval in Mexico at the time. Yvonne, Firmin's ex-wife, returns unexpectedly, but their attempts to reconcile are undercut by Firmin's continued drinking and abusiveness. The scene is further complicated by the arrival of two of Yvonne's ex-lovers, Firmin's half-brother and one of his friends, a French film director. Firmin spends the last hours of his life drinking and reflecting on his life. At the climax, Firmin is gunned down by a Mexican fascist who mistakes him for a criminal, and Yvonne is trampled to death by a runaway horse.

*Under the Volcano* weaves together themes of alienation, love, political idealism, and myth. In defense of his manuscript to London publisher Jonathan Cape, Lowry explained the significance of Firmin's doomed state: "The drunkenness of the consul is used, on one plane, to symbolize the universal drunkenness of mankind during the [Second World] War, or during the period immediately preceding it, . . . and what profundity and final meaning there is in his fate should be seen also in its universal relationship to the ultimate fate of mankind.'' The novel is a story of the pathetic deterioration of an alcoholic and the view of those who love him; it is also a study of Mexico, its politics, landscape, and place in history during the 1930s.

Lowry spent the next year drinking heavily while awaiting word from the publishers about *Under the Volcano.* He and Bonner took a trip to Mexico. Lowry wanted to show his wife the places he wrote about in the novel and he wanted to renew his friendship with a previous drinking companion. The trip did not go well. Lowry received unflattering comments from the publisher, and he discovered his old friend had been killed several years earlier in a barroom gunfight. Once again in the depths of despair, Lowry attempted suicide. Finally, the couple was deported from Mexico when Lowry refused to pay a small bribe to an immigration official.

*Under the Volcano* was finally published in 1947. The publicity he received from the book did not inspire Lowry to develop his talents. Although he continued to write and rewrite previous manuscripts, Lowry would not be published again during his lifetime. Still drinking heavily, he traveled with his wife extensively from 1946 to 1949. Finally returning to Canada, Lowry decided to try his hand at writing screenplays even though he had no experience. He completed a 455-page script based on Scott Fitzgerald's *Tender is the Night.* It was the first manuscript Lowry had actually finished in almost six years.

## The Last Years

By 1954, Lowry had been released by his publisher, Random House. One of his last unfinished works, *October Ferry to Gabriola,* takes place in the mind of unemployed lawyer, Ethan Llewelyn, as he journeys from Dollarton to Gabriola Island, just off the coast of British Columbia. The Random House editor complained about the book's lack of focus and clarity. Despondent over the termination of his contract, Lowry sought psychiatric treatment in 1955, but it seemed to do him little good. In February 1956, Lowry and his wife settled in Ripe, on the south coast of England. The couple argued. When Lowry threatened his wife with a broken gin bottle, she fled the house. She returned to their home in Ripe, England on the morning of June 27, 1957 to find Lowry dead from an overdose of sleeping pills.

Many of Lowry's unfinished and unpublished works were edited and published under the direction of his widow. *Hear Us O Lord From Heaven Thy Dwelling Place,* published in 1961, is a volume of seven short stories. Two of the stories drew attention: ''Through the Panama'' and ''The Forest Path to the Spring,'' a recounting of Lowry's time in Vancouver, were heralded as Lowry's best work since *Under the Volcano. Dark As the Grave Wherein My Friend is Laid,* (1968), is an autobiographical novel of Lowry's return to Mexico to look for his friend Marquez. *Lunar Caustic,* (1968), also autobiographical, is based on the time Lowry spent in Bellevue. Named for silver nitrate, the substance once used to treat syphilis, the novella is a shocking story of alcoholic Bill Plantegenet's time in Bellevue Hospital and his encounters with three other patients. His unfinished novel *October Ferry to Gabriola,* (1970), was considered thin and much more a remembrance of Lowry's time in Vancouver than a complete novel.

## Further Reading

*Benet's Reader's Encyclopedia,* 4th edition, edited by Bruce Murphy, HarperCollins, 1996.
*Contemporary Authors,* Vol. 131, edited by Susan M. Trosky, Gale, 1991.
*Dictionary of Literary Biography,* Vol. 15, edited by Bernard Oldsey, Gale, 1983.
*Encyclopedia of World Authors,* revised 3rd edition, edited by Frank N. Magill, Salem Press, 1997.
*The Nation,* December 11, 1995.
*New York Review of Books,* February 15, 1996.
*World Literature Today,* Autumn 1996. □

# George Lucas

**American filmmaker George Lucas (born 1944) was responsible for the creation of a number of the most profitable movies in history, including the *Star Wars* and *Indiana Jones* trilogies. Lucas is also responsible for many technical innovations in filmmaking, especially special effects.**

Lucas was born in Modesto, California on May 14, 1944, the only son among George and Dorothy Lucas's four children. His father sold office supplies and equipment and owned a walnut farm. George Lucas Sr. found his son difficult to understand and quite stubborn. Lucas enjoyed racing cars and was the proud owner of a souped-up Fiat in high school. He was not a good student, and barely made passing grades. Shortly before graduating from high school, Lucas was involved in a serious car accident and nearly died from his injuries. With broken ribs, Lucas spent three months in the hospital. This experience seriously affected his outlook on life. Lucas decided that he wanted to go to art school. His parents refused to support this decision, however, so Lucas instead studied social sciences at Modesto Junior College.

While at Modesto, Lucas developed an interest in photography and film. He began making films with an 8mm camera, though he knew little about the art and its history. Lucas combined his new interest with an old one when he began to photograph car races. He also became involved in the building of race cars. One was built for Haskell Wexler, a famous cinematographer, who befriended Lucas. With the cinematographer's help, Lucas entered the film program at the University of Southern California (USC). Lucas had a variety of interests in film school. He began in animation, then moved on to cinematography and editing. Lucas was determined to succeed as a filmmaker, and produced eight student films. One of these films, 1965's *THX-1138: 4EB* won several awards, including a first prize at the National Student Festival. In this short film, Lucas explored his version of the future.

Lucas graduated from USC in 1967 and worked on the fringes of the film industry for several years, holding odd jobs. He spent time as a cameraman for Saul Bass, filmed part of the infamous 1968 Rolling Stones concert in Altamonte, California, and worked as an editor for documentaries produced by the United States Information Agency. While working for the USIA he met Marcia Griffin, a film editor. They married in 1969, and adopted a child in 1981. The couple divorced in 1984 and Lucas later adopted two children on his own.

## Met Coppola

In 1969, Lucas won a scholarship from Warner Bros., which allowed him to watch a film being made. He was on the set of a film directed by Francis Ford Coppola entitled *Finian's Rainbow*. Lucas and Coppola developed a strong friendship. Lucas became an advisor on *Finian's Rainbow* and assisted in the editing room. This was the break he needed. Lucas worked on Coppola's next film, *The Rain People,* and made a documentary about the production called *Filmmaker*.

## First Feature Film

Through Coppola's newly founded film studio and independent production company, San Francisco's American Zoetrope, Lucas made his first feature, *THX-1138*. Based on the short film he made as a student, the full length movie took the futurism to an extreme. With an intelligent story, and no real special effects, Lucas's version of the future was not unlike George Orwell's *1984* with some elements of his

future hit, *Star Wars*. Though produced through Zoetrope, the financing for *THX-1138* were provided in part by Warner Bros. The studio did not like the film, and wanted their money back. Coppola convinced them to reconsider. After Warner Bros. edited five minutes off the film, *THX-1138* finally saw a limited release in 1971. It was never promoted by the studio. *THX-1138* was not a commercial success and received mixed reviews. Critics praised the technical aspects, but found the story to be derivative of other science fiction films. In 1978, *THX-1138* was re-released with the missing minutes restored, and it quickly became a cult classic.

## Success with *American Graffiti*

In 1973, Lucas experienced his first real success as a filmmaker with *American Graffiti*. The film was a nostalgic look at the early 1960s as Lucas remembered it, down to the most exacting details. The story focused on one summer night in 1962, and followed teenage boys and their cars. Lucas co-wrote the script and directed it, with Coppola serving as a co-producer. *American Graffiti* had a budget of a little more than $750,000 and was filmed in less than a month. Initially Universal, the studio which financed the production, was not happy with the finished product. Coppola offered to buy the film and release it himself. Although the studio did not believe it would make a profit, *American Graffiti* was released nonetheless. It took several months for the film to build a following, but *American Graffiti* became the sleeper hit of the year. By 1975, the film had grossed over $50 million; by 1998, $115 million. *American Graffiti* was one of the most profitable films of the 1970s, and received five Academy Award nominations and a Golden Globe for best comedy. Lucas was honored with several best screenplay awards.

## *Star Wars* Redefined Blockbuster

As soon as *American Graffiti* was completed, Lucas began working on the script for *Star Wars*. He planned his space fantasy as three sequential, interrelated trilogies, of which *Star Wars* was the first episode of the middle trilogy. This science fiction film included aspects of westerns, soap operas, serial swashbucklers, and other genres as well. Lucas told Gerald Clarke of *Time*, "I wanted *Star Wars* to have an epic quality, so I went back to the epics. Whether they are subconscious or unconscious, whatever needs they meet, they are stories that have pleased or provided comfort to people for thousands of years." The Lucas-directed *Star Wars* was released to near universal praise in May 1977. His very personal vision appealed to a mass audience. The film smashed all box-office records as audiences viewed it repeatedly.

One of the reasons for the success of *Star Wars* was its spectacular special effects and definitive production design. As with his earlier films, Lucas paid particular attention to details. *Star Wars* won Academy Awards for its special effects and technical aspects. Though *Star Wars* was made for about $10.5 million, the film grossed $400 million worldwide before its re-release in 1997. Despite this success, the experience of making the film left Lucas exhausted. A retiring man with simple pleasures, he found directing the massive set of *Star Wars* to be overwhelming at times. Lucas did not direct another film for twenty years.

Despite his experience directing *Star Wars,* Lucas proved to be a wise businessman. He declined to take a director's fee for his work on the film, in exchange for rights to merchandising. Lucas also retained the rights to the *Star Wars* sequels. It was the former, however, that made him immediately rich. Lucas merchandised *Star Wars* in every conceivable way, through books, toys, kits, and consumer items. Between 1977 and 1980, Lucas made $500 million off of *Star Wars* merchandise. He managed the merchandising through his company (LucasFilm Ltd.), established in 1979. Lucas set up other companies to deal with organizing his burgeoning film empire.

By 1980, the second installment in the trilogy was released. In the production of *The Empire Strikes Back,* Lucas was only the executive producer and wrote the story on which the script was based. There was some critical debate over the merits of the more complex story, but many noted that the special effects were technically better. *The Empire Strikes Back* earned $365 million at the box office. After his hands-off approach, Lucas returned to a more active role in 1983's *The Return of the Jedi.* He co-wrote the script with Lawrence Kasden, and again served as executive producer. Reviews were even more mixed than with *The Empire Strikes Back.* While special effects were excellent, critics thought they were overused and overwhelmed the characters and the story. As a whole, the trilogy grossed $1 billion. Their merchandising licenses, however, brought in over $3 billion.

## Created Indiana Jones

At the time Lucas began developing his concept for *Star Wars,* he had the idea that eventually led to another trilogy of films. The Indiana Jones series was developed as an homage to Saturday matinee serials and adventure films of the 1940s. Lucas conceived the story for the first Indiana Jones movie, entitled *Raiders of the Lost Ark,* and served as producer. His story again found mass appeal, both from critics and audiences. Lucas's involvement decreased in the next two Indiana Jones movies. He wrote the story for 1984's *Indiana Jones and the Temple of Doom* and produced *Indiana Jones and the Last Crusade.* Both of these films were not as popular as the first installment, with many critics finding the films to be derivative. Lucas used the Indiana Jones character in a 1992 series he produced for television. Entitled *The Young Indiana Jones Chronicles,* Lucas conceived of all the stories, but the show only lasted for one season.

Throughout the 1980s and most of the 1990s, Lucas primarily worked as a producer, with mixed success. Movies such as *Labyrinth* (1985), *Howard the Duck* (1986), and *Radioland Murders* (1994) were box office failures. Other films were more successful creatively and at the box office, such as *Tucker: The Man and His Dream* (1988) and *Willow.* (1988)

With profits from his film successes and LucasFilm, Ltd., Lucas founded Skywalker Ranch, a production facility near the Bay Area in California. Lucas based all of his

companies there, which covered every aspect of film. One in particular changed the face of the film industry. Originally founded to handle the special effects for *Star Wars,* Industrial Light and Magic (ILM) advanced film technology through research and development. ILM branched out to do innovative special effects for other movies, such as *Star Trek* and *E.T. the Extra Terrestrial.* ILM was responsible for THX, a digital sound system found in many theaters. Despite his contributions to the film industry, some critics believe that the emphasis on special effects overwhelmed the stories they were supposed to enhance. Lucas disagreed telling Richard Zoglin of *Time,* "Special effects are just a way of visualizing something on screen. They have expanded the limits of storytelling enormously."

## Returned to *Star Wars*

Though many doubted the other two *Star Wars* trilogies would ever be made, in 1994, Lucas began writing the scripts for the prequel trilogy. To prepare audiences, Lucas and Twentieth Century Fox reissued enhanced "special editions" versions of the original *Star Wars* trilogy in theaters beginning in 1997. Using the technology developed by his companies, Lucas fixed some of the errors in the first films and included scenes that technological limitations had previously prevented. In total, he added four and a half minutes to *Star Wars.*

In May 1999, Lucas released *The Phantom Menace,* the first installment of the prequel trilogy. Lucas directed this film and wrote the script. Because of the success of the *Star Wars* trilogy, a bidding war developed over the rights to release what would be guaranteed profit makers as well as the rights to make the toys. Because Lucas tapped into a childhood consciousness that was universal, his films have changed the world's standards for entertainment.

## Further Reading

Barson, Michael, *The Illustrated Who's Who of Hollywood Directors, Volume 1: The Sound Era,* Farrar, Straus and Giroux, 1995.

Curran, Daniel, *Guide to American Cinema, 1965-1995,* Greenwood Press, 1998.

*International Directory of Films and Filmmakers 2: Directors,* edited by Laurie Collier Hillstrom, St. James Press, 1997.

Monaco, James, *The Encyclopedia of Film,* Perigee, 1991.

Quinlan, David, *The Illustrated Guide to Film Directors,* Barnes & Noble Books, 1983.

*World Film Directors: Volume II,* edited by John Wakeman, 1945-85, H.W. Wilson, 1988.

*Advertising Age,* August 31, 1998.

*Esquire,* December 1996.

*Forbes,* March 11, 1996; October 14, 1996; September 22, 1997.

*Fortune,* October 6, 1980; August 5, 1985; August 18, 1997.

*Inc.,* June 15, 1995.

*Life,* June 30, 1983.

*Newsweek,* May 31, 1993; May 13, 1996; January 20, 1997.

*The Other Side,* March-April 1997.

*People Weekly,* June 23, 1983; March 26, 1984; February 26, 1996; November 30, 1998.

*Time,* May 19, 1980; May 23, 1983; June 27, 1983; June 16, 1986; September 22, 1986; March 2, 1992; September 30, 1996; February 10, 1997.

*Variety,* July 20, 1998; July 27, 1998. □

# Lucky Luciano

**Although he was once called "one of the 20 most influential builders and titans of the 20th century," Charles "Lucky" Luciano (1897–1962) was a mobster. His advice was sought after by world leaders, but he was still a kingpin of crime. He eventually died in Italy as a deported criminal.**

Luciano was born in Palermo, Italy on November 27, 1897. His parents, Antonio and Rosalia Cuania, brought their four children to New York City in 1907. His father, a sulphur pit worker in Italy, hoped to find a better life for his family. Luciano attended Public School 19, completing sixth grade. Arrested at the age of ten for shoplifting, he was released to the custody of his embarrassed parents. The arrest neither frightened him nor did it teach him a lesson. He was arrested several more times for minor theft. By 1915, Luciano had become a tough teenage hoodlum on the Lower East Side of New York.

## A Natural Leader

Luciano soon had a gang of tough Italian boys following him. He taught his gang the "protection" racket, and they spent their time collecting pennies from local Jewish boys who paid to keep from getting beat up. One young boy, Meyer Lansky, refused to be intimidated and instead laughed at the tough Italians. That bold defiance impressed Luciano. The unlikely pair became best friends and were able to merge the Italian and Jewish gangs on the Lower East Side. Their friendship resulted in a successful crime partnership that would last until their deaths. Lansky would eventually became the architect of Luciano's criminal empire in New York and around the world.

Luciano took a job delivering hats for a Jewish hat maker named Max Goodman. The relatively successful Goodman exposed Luciano to a middle-class lifestyle. But Luciano didn't plan to work as hard as Goodman. He soon realized that if he slipped some drugs into the hatbands, he could kill two birds with one stone. He also learned one of the most valuable lessons of his life, that of making money behind a legal "front." Soon he was making more money than he had ever seen before as a drug dealer. He even served a term at Hampton Farms for selling drugs. It was after his release from this state facility for youthful offenders that he changed his name. He felt that his given name of "Salvatore" or "Sal" was a girl's name, so he became known as "Charlie."

At first Luciano and Lansky, along with friends Frank Costello and Benny "Bugsy" Siegel, committed simple robberies to make ends meet. Eventually the ruthless natural leadership style of each man enabled them to rise to the top of their chosen profession. It was said of the Luciano organization that when they "downsized" some of their colleagues, the move was permanent.

## Prohibition Era

An action by the United States government gave Luciano the idea that propelled him to the top of the underworld. In 1919, the sale of alcoholic beverages was outlawed. It became clear that the demand for alcohol was still large and whoever could provide the drinks would become very rich. By 1920, he and Lansky were supplying alcoholic beverages to all the Manhattan "speakeasies" (bars).

As Luciano's fame grew, a war was being fought between major local gangs in New York. Luciano, at 23, aligned himself with the largest Mafia family, that of Guisseppe ("Joe the Boss") Masseria. He continued with his bootlegging empire, and controlled plants, distilleries, trucks, and warehouses for the sale of illegal alcohol. Some of his partners included Guisseppe ("Joe Adonis") Doto, "Waxey" Gordon, and Arnold Rothstein, who "fixed" the 1918 World Series.

## Boss of Bosses

Luciano began to reconsider his alliance with Guisseppe Masseria, who he realized wasn't the most powerful of the two major families. There are many different stories about the attempted murder of Luciano, who was becoming a problem for both bosses. Some reports indicate that gangsters in an Irish mob beat him nearly to death. Other reports claim it was police officers looking for a payoff, or federal officers who caught him with illegal alcohol, or the father of a girl Luciano had impregnated. Whoever was responsible,

Luciano was beaten severely, cut across the face with a knife, and dropped off as dead in a river on Staten Island. Having survived this vicious beating, he earned the nickname "Lucky."

Luciano realized that the war had to end, and that he should be in charge of all the gangs in New York City. He had to figure a way to get the two main bosses to kill each other, since Mafia "soldiers" on both sides of the continuing war were being killed every day. He realized that the continuing bloodshed between gangs was attracting more and more of the attention of authorities, and disrupting his lucrative businesses. He contacted the other boss, Salvatore Maranzano, and an arrangement was made to assassinate Masseria. Luciano met with his boss at a Coney Island restaurant to discuss plans to eliminate Maranzano. Masseria was delighted that his top lieutenant was forming such a plan against his old enemy. Luciano excused himself to use the rest room and four men entered the restaurant: Bugsy Siegel, Al Anastasia, Vito Genovese, and Joe Adonis. They shot Masseria to death. When Luciano emerged from the rest room the four men had disappeared and the police had no case against him.

Next on the list was Maranzana, who didn't know that most of his "underbosses" and "capos" had given their loyalty to Luciano. They saw that Luciano was a better businessman, who would bring them more profits. Maranzana invited Luciano to a meeting, where he planned to have him killed. Luciano didn't show up for the meeting, but four "tax men" did. Maranzana had been having tax problems, so the four were brought all the way to his inner offices. By the time his personal bodyguards realized what was happening, Maranzana was dead. They fled in fear, and the way was clear for Luciano to become the most powerful of all crime figures, the New York "boss of bosses."

Luciano adopted the efficient idea of "crime families," appointing faithful supporters to head each one. He wanted to establish order. With the help of his longtime friend, Meyer Lansky, he created "the commission" or "Unione Siciliano." A group of his Sicilian friends sat on the board, and all organized crime activities in the 1930s were decided by this commission.

Top crime bosses were also popular society figures. Luciano was often seen at restaurants and the theater with well known civic leaders, entertainers, and other notables. Although he had bodyguards with him, he didn't really need them. Luciano was clearly in charge of organized crime and nobody dared to challenge his authority.

## Prosecution

Law enforcement officials also knew who was the top crime figure in the U.S. In 1936, New York district attorney, Thomas E. Dewey, brought charges against Luciano for running a prostitution ring. Even though Luciano had once saved Dewey from an assassination plot, that did not stop Dewey from prosecuting him. Luciano insisted that he was not involved in prostitution. However, a series of witnesses testified against him and the district attorney won his case. Luciano received a 30 to 50-year prison sentence, the longest ever handed down for such a crime. He was incarcer-

ated in Dannemora, the so-called "Siberia" of organized crime.

## Deported to Italy

Efforts to secure his release proved futile until the Japanese attacked Pearl Harbor on December 7, 1941, and the U.S. declared war. The U.S. Navy feared submarine attacks and needed the cooperation of all waterfront workers to prevent this. Since Luciano still maintained complete control over the New York waterfront, even from prison, he was in a position to bargain for his freedom. In exchange for getting the dock workers to help the U.S. Navy and ordering the Italian Mafia to work against Benito Mussolini, back in Italy, Luciano was promised a parole. However, he had to agree to return to Italy and remain there for the rest of his life. When he left prison in 1946, Luciano was taken to Ellis Island and sent back to Italy. Although he promised to return to his adopted country, that never happened. Luciano died of a heart attack in Naples, Italy on July 26, 1962.

## Further Reading

Lucky's Dream, http://crimelibrary.com/gangsters/murder/murderlucky.htm
Murder, Inc., http://www.murderinc.com/fam/luciano.html
New York Daily News Online, www.newyorkdailynews.com
New York's Greatest Mobsters, www.laborers.org
Real Hoods, http://www.hoodlumonline.com/History/lucky.html □

# Shannon Lucid

**Astronaut Shannon Lucid (born 1943) set the U.S. record for spaceflight endurance by staying aboard the Mir station for 188 days in 1996. This also set the record for the longest time a woman remained in space.**

Lucid made aeronautic history after spending 188 days and 75.2 million miles in space, longer than any other American astronaut or any woman in the world. A Russian cosmonaut set the world's record for staying in space—439 days—but Lucid broke the female record, previously set by Russian Elena Kondakova, who was in orbit for just under 170 days. Lucid's stay on Mir was covered heavily in the American media, which played up her time away from her husband and three grown children, as well as her craving for the candy M&Ms. However, articles also pointed out that she was, at the time, the most experienced NASA member, holding a doctorate in biochemistry and having gone on four previous space flights. Her longest stint in space came at a high point in a life and career that, according to People's Richard Jerome, "reads like a collective work of Pearl S. Buck, Sinclair Lewis and Arthur C. Clarke."

Lucid was born in China in 1943. Her parents, J. Oscar and Mary Wells, were American missionaries in China. Lucid spent her early childhood in a Japanese internment

camp before the family was freed in a prisoner exchange and eventually settled near Oklahoma City. As a young girl she discovered a book on Robert Goddard, the father of rocketry, and it solidified her future. Lucid earned her pilot's license following high school. She then received her B.S. in chemistry from the University of Oklahoma, followed by a master's and doctoral degree in biochemistry, also from Oklahoma. Not even the birth of her second child, the day before an important exam, could stop Lucid from completing her requirements. She has three children—Kawai Dawn, Shandra Michelle, and Michael Kermit—with her husband, Michael F. Lucid.

### Became Astronaut in 1979

In 1973, "when NASA finally began recruiting women for the astronaut corps, Lucid scrambled to submit an application," wrote Sharon Begley in *Newsweek*. "NASA took her, one of the first American-born six women . . . ever selected for astronaut training." She was selected in January of 1978 and became an astronaut in August of the following year. Begley added that while undertaking the rigorous physical and psychological tests, Lucid and the other women recruits "proved that the Right Stuff does not reside in the Y chromosome."

While Lucid was not the first American woman astronaut in space—that distinction belongs to her fellow recruit, Sally Ride—she became America's most experienced astronaut, male or female. Lucid undertook her maiden voyage on the shuttle *Discovery* in 1985 and also logged three

flights prior to Mir, in 1989, 1991, and 1993, in addition to several orbital trips.

When Lucid was chosen for the Mir mission, she joined two male cosmonauts who became known in the American press as "the two Yuris"—Yuri Onufrienko and Yuri Usachev. She blasted off from the Kennedy Space Center in Florida on March 22, 1996. Living in the equipment-packed, 100-foot shuttle was an experience Lucid compared to "living in a camper in the back of your pickup with your kids . . . when it's raining and no one can get out." A biochemist, Lucid studied the effects of the space environment on living tissue. She also received an object lesson in international diplomacy when a Russian general remarked that with Lucid on board the shuttle should look tidier because "women love to clean." Lucid responded by saying that the three crew members worked as a team to maintain order on Mir. Similarly, when the two Yuris were perceived by the press to have insulted Lucid by placing tape over controls they hadn't wished her to touch, the astronaut replied that she would have done the same if she were the captain of the ship.

### Set Record on Mir

While Lucid had signed on for the long mission aboard Mir, the stint wasn't intentionally designed to be a record setter. Seven weeks were added to her flight time, first because of a mechanical glitch in the pickup shuttle, then because of Hurricane Fran's effect on the next shuttle launch. The shuttle *Atlantis* was originally scheduled to retrieve her on July 31, but it was pushed back to September. Lucid occupied her time by reading novels and histories of the American West sent up on supply ships, and by working on her experiments (including how protein crystals grow and how quail embryos develop in zero gravity).

Life on Mir was an adjustment. Lucid took only sponge baths the whole six months on board, and could only wash her hair every three days using a special no-rinse shampoo that NASA devised. She did manage to have privacy, because she had a separate module and toilet from the men. Lucid combated loneliness by excercising, sending frequent e-mail messages to her husband and children, and participating in press conferences and teleconferences. Though she eagerly awaited the next shipment of potato chips and M&Ms dropped off by the Russian robot supply ship *Progress,* she noted that the fruit and vegatable deliveries caused a bad odor in the ship. But she did enjoy the fresh tomatoes and onions, and their Sunday night Jell-O ritual was also a treat.

Finally, in late September 1996, Lucid left Mir for her pickup shuttle. After her craft touched down in Florida on September 26, Lucid was attended by doctors and assistants who meant to carry her to a medical transporter. But Lucid surprised the experts by standing and walking "wobbly and woozy," as she described it—to her vehicle. When Lucid reached the transporter, a *Newsweek* writer reported, "physicians began exhaustive tests to determine how weightlessness had affected her heart, muscles, bones, blood, urine, saliva, balance, strength, aerobic capacity—in short, anything that can be measured, observed, titrated, counted or otherwise quantified." In this way Lucid became "the most important body of data—literally—that NASA ever got its stethoscopes on." She would spend three years being monitored.

"A day after returning to Earth," Begley writes, "Lucid left [Cape] Canaveral aboard NASA 1 and landed at Ellington Field outside Houston. President Clinton met the entire Atlantis crew, where the commander in chief praised Lucid's achievement as 'a monument to the human spirit.' Lucid smiled on the podium behind him, a big Stars and Stripes fluttering in the stiff breeze behind her. To no one's surprise this time, either, she was still standing tall." Lucid was awarded a Space Medal of Honor in December 1996,

and in February of 1997, received a Free Spirit Award from the Freedom Forum.

## Further Reading

*Dallas Morning News,* September 27, 1996, p. 1A; September 28, 1996, p. 11F.
*Newsday,* July 16, 1996, p. A8.
*Newsweek,* September 30, 1996; October 7, 1996.
*People,* July 22, 1996.
*St. Louis Post-Dispatch,* September 1, 1996, p. 14A.
*Time,* September 30, 1996.
*USA Today,* September 26, 1996, p. 4A.
*U.S. News & World Report,* October 7, 1996.
*US Newswire,* February 13, 1997. □

# Sean MacBride

**Sean MacBride (1904–1988), who began his career with forerunners of the Irish Republican Army, later earned fame as a diplomat who worked 70 years for peace. His efforts focused on working toward a united Ireland, nuclear disarmament, and human rights.**

Sean MacBride was born in Paris to Irish exile parents on January 26, 1904. His father was Major John MacBride, who fought against the British in South Africa's Boer War of 1899-1902, struggling to free the country from British colonialism. MacBride grew up among his parents' intellectual friends until returning to Ireland in 1916, shortly after his father was executed by the British. Both were leaders of the 1916 Easter Uprising in Dublin, a week-long battle sparked on Easter Monday, in which Irish rebels hoped to defeat British troops to establish home rule for Ireland.

MacBride's mother was Maud Gonne, the daughter of a British army colonel. Gonne was a "beautiful Irish actress and revolutionary" wrote William G. Blair in the *New York Times*. "She was called the Joan of Arc of Ireland and was celebrated in the poetry of William Butler Yeats, who at one time was in love with her." Like her husband and later her son, Gonne fought for Irish nationalism, spending time in jail for her activities on behalf of Irish independence.

Shortly after returning to Ireland, MacBride began to follow in his parents' revolutionary footsteps. He lied about his age in order to join the Irish Volunteers, an underground army fighting to drive British colonizers out of the country.

In 1918, at the age of 13, MacBride was arrested by the British. Before the end of his career with the Volunteers, and later the Irish Republican Army, he would be sent to prison twice again, in 1922 and 1930.

Ireland has been a colony of Britain since being conquered in the 1600s. The Government of Ireland Act, passed in 1920, turned Ireland into two states, Northern Ireland and Southern Ireland. Southern Ireland, largely populated by Catholics, became a self-governing country but Northern Ireland remained a British colony. Many Irish citizens wanted to reunite the entire country and become independent from Britain, although some Irish citizens, especially Northern Ireland Protestants, prefer alliance with Britain.

Despite arrests and imprisonment, MacBride stayed with the IRA, and at 24 years of age became its chief of staff. He also worked as a journalist and studied law at the National University in Dublin. He was admitted to the Irish bar in 1937, at which point he left the IRA. Even though he denounced the group's increasingly violent tactics, he continued to defend IRA members in order to show the world how horrible and harsh Irish jails were. He became a successful trial lawyer in Dublin, becoming a senior counsel in only seven years.

## Stepped into Politics

From his vantage point as a lawyer, MacBride saw opportunities to further the notion of national independence from Britain by becoming a politician. He formed a radical nationalist party, called the Republican Party, or *Clann na Poblachta*, and challenged the party of Prime Minister Eamon de Valera, which was called *Fianna Fail*. Together with several other opposition parties, MacBride's Republican Party ousted *Fianna Fail*. He served in parliament from 1947 to 1958, and held an appointment to the Foreign

Ministry from 1948 to 1951. The Republican Party itself faded by 1965.

As part of the Marshall Plan, a U.S.-sponsored effort to help rebuild Europe after the destruction of World War II, MacBride served as vice president of the Organization for European Economic Cooperation, which later evolved into the European Economic Community. At the same time, he was tapped in 1950 as the president of the Council of Foreign Ministers of the Council of Europe.

## Path to Peace

MacBride's interests evolved to embrace the notion of peace in other countries and worldwide. He became assistant secretary general to the United Nations, and served as the United Nations commissioner for Namibia from 1973 to 1976. Experienced because of his work in Ireland, MacBride worked to help Namibia become free. As stated in *Sechaba*, at MacBride's funeral, President Tambo of the African National Congress called him "a great beacon, guiding and assisting oppressed people to the path of national liberation and self-determination." Tambo said, "Sean MacBride will also be remembered for the concrete leadership he provided to the liberation movements and peoples of Namibia and South Africa, driven by personal and political insight, arising out of the cause of national freedom in Ireland. We recall our debt to him in the brilliant way in which he focused the attention of the world on the grim process of colonialism and exploitation in Africa in particular. Our debt to him can never be repaid."

MacBride worked as president of the International Peace Bureau in Geneva, Switzerland from 1972 to 1985. The IPB works to attain worldwide nuclear disarmament. After MacBride died, the group established the Sean MacBride Peace Prize, to honor others who have "done outstanding work for peace, disarmament or human rights." Recipients have included The Committee of Soldiers' Mothers of Russia, a group opposed to the civil war in Chechnya; Selim Beslagic, a proponent of a multi-ethnic solution to the Bosnian crisis; and a British group that disarmed an aircraft going to Indonesia.

In 1961, MacBride helped found Amnesty International, a worldwide human rights monitoring organization. He served as the group's chairman until 1975. He was also secretary general of the International Commission of Jurists, another human rights group, from 1963 until 1970, and a member until he died.

MacBride's tireless work for human rights were recognized in 1974 when he was awarded the Nobel Peace Prize with Prime Minister Eisaku Sato of Japan. In 1977, MacBride became one of the few Westerners to win the International Lenin Prize for Peace Among Nations for his work in Namibia. He was only the second person to win both.

## Tireless Fighter for Justice

Still going strong at the age of 80, MacBride in 1984 helped draft and sponsor a code of behavior known as the MacBride Principles, aimed at forcing American companies who work in Northern Ireland to hire Roman Catholics and Protestants in equal numbers. The U.S. publication *National Catholic Reporter* noted that Catholics make up "about 42 percent of Northern Ireland's population but suffer unemployment at twice the rate of Protestants, according to the Washington-based Irish National Caucus."

The MacBride Principles were an effort to make American companies take responsibility for the employment practices of its factories in Northern Ireland. American companies such as American Brands, Du Pont, General Motors and Ford employ huge numbers of people in Northern Ireland. Companies that signed onto the principles would agree to make "every reasonable lawful effort to increase the representation of underrepresented religious groups at all levels of its operations in Northern Ireland," reported Steve Lohr of the *New York Times*. Tacked onto a budget bill, the MacBride Principles became part of U.S. policy when they were signed by President Bill Clinton on October 21, 1998. Clinton's budget also included $19.6 million in aid to the International Fund for Ireland.

MacBride died from pneumonia at the age of 83, January 15, 1988, at his home in Dublin, Ireland. His wife of 50 years, Catalina Bulfin, had died in 1976. MacBride is survived by his two children, Tiernan and Anna.

## Further Reading

*Contemporary Authors,* Volume 124, Gale, 1988.
*Facts on File World News Digest,* Facts on File, Inc., 1988.
*Boston Globe,* January 16, 1988.
*Irish Times,* July 9, 1994.
*National Catholic Reporter,* November 6, 1998.

*New York Times,* September 4, 1986; January 16, 1988.
*Peace & Change,* January 1999.
*Sechaba,* May 1988.
*Sewanee Review,* Summer 1994.
African National Congress, http://www.anc.org.za (March 19, 1999).
International Peace Bureau, http://www.ipb.org (March 28, 1999). □

# Connie Mack

**Connie Mack (1862–1956) was a patrician figure who managed more games than anyone else in baseball history. He led the Philadelphia Athletics to nine American League pennants and five World Series championships. Reserved and dignified, Mack left an indelible stamp on baseball.**

In his playing days, Connie Mack was a star catcher for Washington in the 1880s and the Pittsburgh Pirates in the 1890s. He managed the Pittsburgh team before taking over the Philadelphia Athletics in 1901. Mack eventually became sole owner of the Athletics and did not retire until 1950, at the age of 87.

## Early Years in Baseball

Cornelius McGillicuddy was born in East Brookfield, Massachusetts, on December 22, 1862, to Mary (McKillop) and Michael McGillicuddy. By the time he was nine, the tall, thin boy, nicknamed "Slats," was working at a cotton mill. His father died when Cornelius was a teenager, and he became the family breadwinner. At 16, he began work in a shoe factory and became a foreman by the time he was 20.

While working at the factory, McGillicuddy played semi-pro baseball for East Brookfield. When he was 21, the Meriden club in the Connecticut State League offered him $90 a month to play catcher. At that time it was a hefty salary. Meriden shortened his name to "Connie Mack" to fit on scorecards, and the nickname stuck. Mack went on to play for Hartford and then Newark, two other minor league teams. Then, along with four other players, he was sold for the then enormous sum of $3,500 to the Washington team in the National League.

In 1886, Mack played in ten games for Washington and hit .361. But after that season there was a key rule change: batters could no longer call for the pitcher to throw a high or low pitch. When pitchers learned that Mack couldn't hit low pitches, his batting average sunk to .201 in 1887 and to .187 in 1888. He was never a good hitter after that, but he was a good enough fielder that he hung on for eleven seasons as a big-league player. In 1890, he played for Buffalo (in the short-lived Players League), and from 1891 through 1896 he was a catcher for Pittsburgh.

At six foot one, Mack was a tall man for his era, commanding attention with his quiet, deliberate speech. He knew so much about baseball strategy that he quickly became a respected leader. At a time when baseball was a rowdy, disreputable sport, Mack always projected the aura of a gentleman. Devoutly religious, he never swore or drank. After Mack assumed the post of manager at Pittsburgh in 1894, he forbade his players from drinking alcohol during the season. In 1897, he played his last games while managing Milwaukee in the Western League. He managed four years for Milwaukee's owner, Ban Johnson, the pioneer organizer who soon turned the Western League into the American League.

## American League Stalwart

Mack was the major force behind the establishment of a Philadelphia club in the American League. The new league wanted to challenge the supremacy of the established National League, represented in Philadelphia by the Phillies. Mack recruited Benjamin Shibe, a manufacturer of baseball equipment, to become president and the club's chief financier. Shibe Park was built for a home field. Some critics derided the new club as the city's "white elephant," a useless acquisition, but Mack turned the insult into a logo, and for decades the team sported white elephants on its uniforms.

Under the leadership of Mack and Rube Waddell, a hard-throwing pitcher Mack had signed in 1900, the Athletics rose quickly to the top, winning the American League pennant in 1902. Mack led the team to a second pennant in 1905 and to its first appearance in the World Series, in which the Athletics lost to John McGraw's New York

Giants. In 1903, 1907 and 1909, Mack's club finished second in the league.

In 1910, Mack married Katherine Hallahan. From a previous marriage, he had three sons, Roy, Earle and Connie Jr., all of whom eventually became executives with the Athletics. The club would become virtually a Mack family business.

In 1910 and 1911, the Athletics returned to the World Series and became world champions, beating the Chicago Cubs and then the Giants. The team was anchored by its famous "$100,000 infield" of Hall of Famers Frank Baker, Eddie Collins, Jack Barry, and Stuffy McInnis. Mack said the 1912 team was one of his best, though it finished third. During that season the owners of the New York Highlanders (later renamed the Yankees) offered Mack the manager's job there, but he remained loyal to Shibe and Philadelphia. Again in 1913, the Athletics beat the Giants in the World Series. They repeated as league champions in 1914 but were upset by the Boston Braves in the Series.

Mack often was contrasted with McGraw, the fiery leader of the Giants, because their personalities and leadership styles were so opposite. "Mack, tall, thin as a beanpole, even-tempered, mild-mannered . . . was as much a father to his players as their manager," wrote baseball historians Lawrence Ritter and Donald Honig. According to historian Harold Seymour, Mack was "serene, mild-mannered, seldom ruffled . . . the stoically patient leader . . . inspiring affection and regard." Collins was among many who praised Mack for expressing strong confidence in his players' abilities. "You would have to comb the world to find a man possessed of such ability to make human beings extend themselves," Collins said.

## Peaks and Valleys

In his first 14 seasons at Philadelphia, Mack's Athletics finished in first place six times and in second place three times. They had only one losing season. But with the rival Federal League luring star players away and the club's finances dwindling due to indifferent attendance, Mack suddenly sold off all his aging stars. This move forever gained the cautious Mack the reputation in Philadelphia of being a skinflint who cared more about profits than pennants.

In 1914, Mack's team won 99 games and lost 53. The next year, the Athletics won 43 games and lost 109. Mack hunkered down to survive the lean years of World War I. Starting in 1916, his club finished in last place for seven consecutive years before making a slow climb back to contention in the mid-1920s.

Philadelphia became a baseball powerhouse again in the period from 1925 through 1933, led by such Hall of Famers as pitcher Lefty Grove, catcher Mickey Cochrane and slugging outfielder Jimmie Foxx, all players whom Mack had recruited and carefully nurtured. He worked hard to learn about promising young players and sign them, and always made a long-term commitment to their success. Mack prized intelligent, hard-working, self-motivated gentlemen, much like himself, and stocked his teams with former college players.

During the nine years of Mack's second dynasty, the Athletics finished in third place twice, in second four times, and won three pennants, from 1929 through 1931. In 1929, Mack stunned fans and baseball experts by passing up Grove to start journeyman Howard Ehmke in the World Series opener against the Cubs. Ehmke struck out thirteen batters and won the game, and Mack used Grove in the bullpen throughout the Series, which Philadelphia won. After the season, Mack was awarded Philadelphia's prestigious Bok Prize for service to the city; it had never before been given to a sports figure.

The Athletics repeated as world champions in 1930, then lost the World Series in 1931. Mack had what he called "the highest-priced ball club in the history of the game," but once again, Philadelphia fans seemed to tire quickly of all the winning. With the Great Depression deepening, attendance continued to fall. Mack again broke up his team, selling four of his stars to Boston in 1935. "It has hurt me worse to break up my great teams than it has the fans," Mack wrote in an article in 1936 for the *Saturday Evening Post*. But, as he explained in more hard-nosed terms in his autobiography: "Baseball is strictly a competitive business that must be conducted on sound business principles."

## A Symbol of Baseball

In 1937, Mack became the Athletics' president and treasurer. With his own finances tied even more closely to those of the club, he continued to spend little on acquiring established players. In Mack's final 16 seasons, his club became the laughingstock of baseball, never finishing higher than fourth place, and ending up in last place ten times.

Nonetheless, Mack's popularity grew. Fans would come to games just to see him standing in the dugout, waving his scorecard to signal his players on the field. He was named to the Baseball Hall of Fame at its inception as one of fifteen "Builders of Baseball." The Pennsylvania government set aside May 17 as Connie Mack Day. Philadelphia's George M. Cohan wrote a song, "Connie Mack Is the Grand Old Name." In 1941, against his wishes, the name of Shibe Park was changed to Connie Mack Stadium.

In a 1944 poll, Mack was voted the favorite manager of players and sportswriters. That year, a tribute to Mack was held before a home game. He was showered with accolades, and a baseball "dream team" as named by Mack appeared in their old uniforms. Still, Mack refused to retire from the game he loved.

In Mack's later years, he would not appear in the dugout until the game started, always dressed in his crisp blue suit with his high stiff collar. Decades before, most other managers had begun wearing team uniforms; Mack never did. He projected the formality and dignity of a bygone era, and was looked upon as a living baseball relic. Though he was still formally manager, his son Earle and others coaches actually ran the team in Mack's later years. Sometimes he could be heard ordering the names of bygone players into the game.

Historians argue that Mack's dismal final 16 seasons shouldn't diminish his credentials as one of baseball's greatest managers. "Like John McGraw, Mack had a staggering command of the details of the game," baseball researcher Bill James wrote.

Mack didn't retire until after the 1950 season, when he was almost 88. His 53 years as a major-league manager gave him career figures not approached by any other manager. He managed 7,755 big-league regular-season games and 43 World Series games, nearly 3,000 more than McGraw, who is second to Mack in games and victories. Mack's teams won 3,731 games and lost 3,948. He managed almost twice as many losses as anyone else in history; second was Bucky Harris with 2,218. With his refusal to give up despite losing season after losing season, Mack became the enduring, implacable symbol of baseball's resiliency and relentless optimism.

Mack remained president of the Athletics until 1954. After the season, Mack stepped down at the age of 92, and the Athletics moved to Kansas City, almost as if they could not bear to remain in Philadelphia without their founder and symbol. Mack died in Germantown, Pennsylvania on February 8, 1956.

### Further Reading

*The Baseball Encyclopedia*, Macmillan, 1990.

James, Bill, *The Bill James Guide to Baseball Managers from 1870 to Today*, Scribner, 1997.

McGillicuddy, Cornelius, *Connie Mack's Baseball Book*, Kingsport Press, 1950.

Ritter, Lawrence and Donald Honig, *The Image of their Greatness,* Crown, 1979.

Seymour, Harold, *Baseball: The Golden Age,* , Oxford University Press, 1971. □

# Stanley Marcus

**Retailing genius Stanley Marcus (born 1905) expanded his father's specialty shop into a full-service department store. Under his management, the Neiman-Marcus Department Store became one of the most renowned retail chains in the world, and developed a reputation for both the highest quality merchandise and unflagging customer service.**

Stanley Marcus was born in Dallas, Texas on April 20, 1905. He was one of four sons born to Herbert Marcus and his wife, the former Minnie Lichtenstein. Marcus's paternal grandparents were Jewish immigrants from Germany. His maternal grandparents, also immigrants, were Russian Jews. Herbert Marcus, along with his sister Carrie Neiman and her husband Al Neiman, founded the clothing store of Neiman-Marcus in 1907. It was a new innovation for customers to walk into a store and buy clothing, because most apparel was still sewn by dressmakers and tailors. Young Stanley spent a great deal of time at the family store, where his mother brought him frequently and left him to play. He was a bright and innovative boy who made toys from empty thread boxes and spools that he found in the alteration department of the store. At home, in the Marcus family, education was of primary importance. Marcus's parents supervised his homework, and his mother sent him to private elocution lessons where he became adept at public speaking. He had few friends as a child, and experienced bouts of anti-Semitism. The first such incident happened when he was still quite young. A gang of boys chased him home from school, and called him derisively "little Jew-boy."

Although Marcus failed the college entrance examination, his father sought an eastern prep school for him to attend. Many of the schools refused to accept the 16-year-old Marcus because of his Jewish heritage, a fact that shocked and stunned Marcus. When a friend offered to arrange for Marcus's admittance to Amherst, a small college in New England, Marcus accepted. However, his year at Amherst proved disappointing. The fraternities refused to admit him, again because of his religion, and he became alienated. He left for Harvard and joined an all-Jewish fraternity. At Harvard, Marcus enjoyed his English classes in particular. He was especially intrigued by the world of rare books when he enrolled in a class called, "The History of the Printed Book." At that time, Marcus decided to go into the book business, as a printer, publisher, or dealer. He even started his own mail order book service and acquired customers through letters of solicitation. As he explained in his memoir, "My moderate success through selling by letter proved to me that a letter was a very potent selling tool, if written interestingly and with a psychological understanding of its potential readers. Later, in my retail career, I used letters to sell millions of dollars of furs, jewels, books, golf balls, and antiquities through the mail." During summer vacations, Marcus worked at the family store, selling ladies' shoes.

As college graduation approached, Marcus discussed his publishing plans with his father. Although Herbert Marcus had no doubt that his son would follow him in the family business, Stanley Marcus feared that a career in retail sales would restrict his political self-expression. His father, a political conservative, assured his son that he would be free to express his liberal views and reminded him that the retail business would prove more lucrative than the book business. The extra income could be used to acquire a personal book collection. At his father's suggestion, Marcus went on to Harvard Business School to prepare for a career in retail. There he studied accounting, statistics, advertising, and finance.

### Learned the Ropes

In the summer of 1928, Herbert and Minnie Marcus went to Europe; they left their son in Texas to work at the store with his uncle, Al Neiman. Upon their return Neiman sold his interest in the family business back to his brother-in-law. Only Stanley Marcus and his father remained to manage the store. Marcus assumed control of merchandising and had financial control over two buyers, Carrie Neiman and Moira Cullen. Marcus' brother Edward joined the store in 1928, after leaving Harvard. That same year, the store introduced its personalized gift-wrapping service, which became a hallmark of the Neiman-Marcus retail chain. Marcus also introduced weekly in-store fashion shows, bridal fashion shows, and Man's Night. The two brothers came up with the idea of promoting the store through national advertising in *Vogue* and *Harper's Bazaar*. In one of his earliest promotions Marcus coordinated his effort with the State Fair of Texas. He developed a line of clothes and accessories based on the colors and motifs of the southwest. The store introduced the clothes at the first ever Neiman-Marcus evening fashion show, to which Marcus invited Edna Woolman Chase, editor of *Vogue*. Chase accepted the invitation and was very impressed.

In 1937, the store received major publicity in an article published in *Fortune*. Articles in *Collier's, Life,* and other magazines followed. Soon Marcus hired the store's first public relations director, Marihelen McDuff. In 1938, the store established the Neiman-Marcus Award for Distinguished Service in the Field of Fashion, a totally new sales promotion device. The following year, Marcus published his first article in *Fortune*. After the article appeared, he received solicitation for a number of speaking engagements and interviews. During World War II he worked for the federal government in Washington on a project to develop fabric conservation programs.

By 1944, all four Marcus brothers worked at the store. To distinguish the four siblings they were called Mr. Stanley, Mr. Herbert, Mr. Edward, and Mr. Lawrence. After the death of Herbert Marcus, Sr., the store board of directors elected Carrie Neiman to be chairman of the board. Stanley Marcus was named president and CEO, and his brother, Edward, was named executive vice-president. Marcus carried on the business philosophy he learned from his father. He encouraged his sales staff to be honest with customers and let them know if merchandise was not appropriate for their requirements.

### "Junk for Christmas"

Marcus was ever on the lookout for publicity opportunities for the store. He knew that if he listed unusual and exotic gifts in the Christmas catalogue, then radio, television, newspapers, and magazines would report the catalogue as news. With this in mind he devised such gifts as "his and her" airplanes, miniature submarines, parasols, camels, Chinese junks, and authentic Egyptian mummy cases. These "stunt" pages attracted significant publicity and generated increases in the store's mail order sales. Not every exotic item was a success. One memorable failure was an inventory of custom-designed watches with Chinese characters on the faces instead of numerals. As ordered, the Chinese characters on the watches would have referenced an ancient Chinese legend. Instead the characters on the watch read, "We shall take over America by force."

Marcus liked to be recognized for his progressive political viewpoints. In 1966, he defended three teenage boys who were expelled from a Dallas high school for wearing their hair too long. Marcus believed that the boys' constitutional rights were violated and offered them financial aid to fight the decision in court. Also in the 1960s, Marcus conscientiously retrained his staff to insure that African American customers would receive equal treatment alongside white customers.

### Life Outside the Store

Marcus and his wife, Mary "Billie" Cantrell had two daughters and a son. The couple entertained many celebrities, including the late Lyndon and Lady Bird Johnson, Prince Rainier and the late Princess Grace of Monaco, Christian Dior, Lord Mountbatten, and the late Coco Chanel, in their 12,000-square-foot-home filled with their collections of art, books, masks, pre-Columbian pottery, Middle Eastern ceramics, and architect-designed furniture.

In 1968, the 27 Neiman-Marcus stores were bought by a conglomerate called Carter Hawley Hale. Marcus remained actively involved in the business for another ten years, retiring at the age of 72. He kept active by consulting with local business and international clients, such as Harrod's Department Store in London—charging $200,000 for 24-hour access to his wisdom. He also kept occupied in speechmaking, and writing. He wrote several books and, for over a decade, contributed a weekly column for the *Dallas Morning News*. In celebration of his 80th birthday, Marcus fulfilled a lifelong dream—to perform in the circus as a clown. He celebrated his 90th birthday at a lavish party attended by 1,200 guests, who joined him from as far away as Italy, Denmark, and Japan.

## Further Reading

Marcus, Stanley, *Minding the Store: A Memoir,* Boston, Little
Brown, 1974.
Marcus, Stanley, *The Viewpoints of Stanley Marcus: A Ten-Year
Perspective,* University of North Texas, 1995.
*Advertising Age,* May 15, 1995.
*Boston,* February 1998.
*Fortune,* March 22, 1993.
*Inc.,* June 1987.
*Texas Monthly,* December 1992.
*People,* May 13, 1985. □

# Wynton Marsalis

**Successful jazz trumpeter Wynton Marsalis (born
1961) is America's top modern purist of the genre.
Influenced by the jazz artists from the early 1900s
through the 1960s and annoyed with the music labeled "jazz" in the 1970s, Marsalis took on the mission of not only creating "true" jazz, but teaching its
definition as well.**

A successful jazz and classical musician and composer, Marsalis had won more than eight Grammy
awards and released over 30 albums in both genres
by the late 1990s. In 1997, he received the first Pulitzer
Prize ever awarded for nonclassical music. He also co-
founded and directed the ground-breaking jazz program at
New York's Lincoln Center, and became an influential jazz
educator for America's youth.

Marsalis was born into a family of musicians on October 18, 1961, in New Orleans. His father, Ellis Marsalis,
played piano and worked as a jazz improvisation instructor
at the New Orleans Center for the Creative Arts. Before
dedicating her life to raising her six sons, Dolores Marsalis
sang in jazz bands. The second eldest child, Wynton's older
brother Branford set the stage as the family's first musical
prodigy. Branford Marsalis played both clarinet and piano
by the time he entered the second grade, and eventually
became a professional saxophonist.

Wynton Marsalis didn't follow his brother's lead quite
as diligently, however. When he was six years old, his father
played with Al Hirt, who gave the young Marsalis one of his
old trumpets. Wynton Marsalis made his performing debut
at the tender age of seven when he played "The Marine
Hymn" at the Xavier Junior School of Music. As a child,
Marsalis didn't take practicing the trumpet very seriously.
He spent more time with his school work, playing basketball, and participating in Boy Scout activities.

### Discovered Influences in Two Genres

When Marsalis was 12, his family moved from Kenner,
Louisiana, to New Orleans. When he listened to a recording
by jazz trumpeter Clifford Brown, he was moved to take his
trumpet seriously. "I didn't know someone could play a
trumpet like that," Marsalis later told Mitchell Seidel in

*Down Beat.* "It was unbelievable." Soon after, a college
student gave Marsalis an album by classical trumpet player
Maurice Andre, which also sparked his interest in classical
music.

Marsalis began taking lessons from John Longo in New
Orleans, who had an interest in both genres, as well. "I
hardly ever even paid him," Marsalis recalled to Howard
Mandell in *Down Beat,* "and he used to give me two- and
three-hour lessons, never looking at the clock."

Marsalis attended Benjamin Franklin High School in
New Orleans, where he graduated with a 3.98 grade point
average on a 4.0 scale. He became a National Merit Scholarship finalist and received scholarship offers from Yale
University, among other prestigious schools. He also attended the New Orleans Center for the Creative Arts. At the
age of 14, he won a Louisiana youth competition. This
award granted him the opportunity to perform with the New
Orleans Philharmonic Orchestra as a featured soloist.

During his high school years, he played a variety of
music with a number of groups, including first trumpet with
the New Orleans Civic Orchestra, the New Orleans Brass
Quintet, an a teenage funk group called the Creators, along
with his brother Branford. In 1977, Marsalis won the "Most
Outstanding Musician Award" at the Eastern Music Festival
in North Carolina.

### Started Spreading the News

He went on to study music at the Berkshire Music
Center at Tanglewood in Massachusetts, where he received

their Harvey Shapiro Award for the outstanding brass player. He turned down the scholarship offers from Ivy League schools to attend New York's Juilliard School of Music on full scholarship. While in school, he played with the Brooklyn Philharmonia and the Mexico City Symphony. He supported himself with a position in the pit band for *Sweeney Todd* on Broadway.

In 1980, Art Blakey asked Marsalis to spend the summer touring with his Jazz Messengers. His performances began to attract national attention, and he eventually became the band's musical director. While on the road with Blakey, Marsalis decided to change his image and began wearing suits to his performances. "For us, it was a statement of seriousness," Marsalis told Howard Reich in *Down Beat*. "We come out here, we try to entertain our audience and play, and we want to look good so they can feel good."

The following year, Marsalis decided to leave Juilliard to continue his education on the road. He played with Blakey and received an offer to tour with Herbie Hancock's V.S.O.P. quartet. Marsalis jumped at the chance, as the V.S.O.P. included bassist Ron Carter and drummer Tony Williams, who had both played with Miles Davis. "I knew he was only 19, just on the scene—it's a lot to put on somebody," Hancock told Steve Bloom in *Rolling Stone*. "But then I realized if we don't hand down some of this stuff that happened with Miles, it'll just die when we die."

### Warmed up Career

Marsalis performed throughout the United States and Japan with the V.S.O.P. and played on the double album *Quartet*. The increased attention led to an unprecedented recording contract with Columbia Records for both jazz and classical music. He released his self-titled debut album as a leader in 1981. Later that year, he formed his own jazz band with his brother Branford, Kenny Kirkland, Jeff Watts, and bassists Phil Bowler and Ray Drummond. His success didn't go unnoticed in his hometown, either. New Orleans Mayor Ernest Morial proclaimed a Wynton Marsalis Day in February of 1982.

Wynton Marsalis recorded one side of an album with his father Ellis and Branford Marsalis, called For Fathers and Sons. The other side was recorded by saxophonist Chico Freeman and his father Von Freeman. In 1983, Marsalis released jazz and classical LPS simultaneously. The jazz record, *Think of One*, marked the debut of his jazz quintet and sold nearly 200,000 copies, about ten times what was considered a successful jazz album. The recording and Marsalis received many comparisons to Miles Davis and other musicians of the 1960s. "We don't reclaim music from the 1960s; music is a continuous thing," Marsalis explained to Mandell in *Down Beat*. "We're just trying to play what we hear as the logical extension. . . . A tree's got to have roots."

He recorded his classical debut, *Trumpet Concertos*, in London with Raymond Leppard and the National Philharmonic Orchestra. In 1984, Marsalis set another precedent by becoming the first artist to be nominated or win two Grammy awards in two categories during the same year.

### Big Sounds in the Big Apple

He won another Grammy award in 1987 for his album *Marsalis Standard Time Vol. 1*. During the same year, he co-founded the Jazz at Lincoln Center program in New York City. When the program began, Marsalis became the artistic director for the eleven-month season. As part of his contract, he had to compose one piece of music for each year. Despite his new position, he continued to record and tour in both jazz and classical music.

He released *Majesty of the Blues* in 1989 and *The Resolution of Romance* in 1990. He dedicated the latter to his mother, and it included contributions from his father Ellis and his brother Delfeayo. "If you are really dealing with music, you are trying to elevate consciousness about romance," Marsalis explained to Dave Helland in *Down Beat*. "Music is so closely tied up with sex and sensuality that when you are dealing with music, you are trying to enter the world of that experience, trying to address the richness of the interaction between a man and a woman, not its lowest reduction."

Marsalis' study of New Orleans styles resulted in a trilogy called *Soul Gestures in Southern Blue* in 1990. Describing the set, Howard Reich wrote in *Down Beat*, "the crying blue notes of 'Levee Low Moan,' the church harmonies of 'Psalm 26,' the sultry ambiance of 'Thick in the South' all recalled different settings and epochs in New Orleans music. And yet the tautness of Marsalis' septet, the economy of the motifs, and the adventurousness of the harmonies proclaimed this as new music, as well."

Using history to create his present sound became Marsalis' goal, along with exploring the rich tapestry of the different eras and styles of jazz. His first commission for the jazz program at Lincoln Center, *In This House, On This Morning* was performed in 1993. In it, he used the music of the African-American church as his primary inspiration.

### Evolved into Jazz Spokesman

In the fall of 1994, Marsalis announced that his septet had disbanded. However, he continued composing, recording, and performing. The following year, he produced a four-part video series called *Marsalis on Music*, which aired on PBS. In May of 1995, his first string quartet, *(At the) Octoroon Balls* debuted at the Lincoln Center.

He continued to release classical works as well. He re-recorded the Haydn, Hummel, and Leopold Mozart concertos from *Trumpet Concertos* in 1994. Two years later, he released *In Gabriel's Garden*, which he recorded with the English Chamber Orchestra and Anthony Newman on harpsichord and organ.

"I want to keep developing myself as a complete musician," Marsalis told Ken Smith in *Stereo Review*," so I take on projects either to teach me something new or else to document some development. With this new Baroque album, I felt that I'd never really played that music before with the right authority or rhythmic fire." Marsalis produced the Olympic Jazz Summit at the 1996 Olympics in Atlanta, and won 1996 Peabody Awards for both *Marsalis on Music* and for his National Public Radio Show "Wynton Marsalis:

Making the Music." At the end of 1996, *Time* magazine named him one of America's 25 Most Influential People.

A major part of his influence went out to the country's youth. When he's not working on his own music, he traveled to schools across the country to talk about music in an effort to continue the tradition of jazz. "I'm always ready to put my own neck on the line for change," Marsalis told Lynn Norment in *Ebony*. "No school is too bad for me to go to. . . . I'll try to teach anybody. We are all striving for the same thing, to make our community stronger and richer. That's what the jazz musician has always been about."

## Won Pulitzer Prize

In April of 1994, his biggest piece, *Blood on the Fields*, had its debut performance at the Lincoln Center. Marsalis composed the oratorio for three singers and a 14-piece orchestra, and it described the story of two Africans, Leona and Jesse, who found love despite the difficulties of American slavery. "I wanted to orchestrate for the larger ensemble and write for voices—something I'd never done," Marsalis said to V.R. Peterson in a *People* magazine interview. "I wanted to make the music combine with the words, yet make the characters seem real."

With *Blood on the Fields*, Marsalis won the first non-classical Pulitzer Prize award in history. Because of his piece, the selection board changed the criteria from "for larger forms including chamber, orchestra, song, dance, or other forms of musical theater" to "for distinguished musical composition of significant dimension." Columbia Records released the oratorio on a three-CD set in June of 1997.

He followed the release with recordings of two other previously performed works on one album. His collaboration with New York City Ballet director, Peter Martins' *Jazz/Six Syncopated Movements* and *Jump Start* written for ballet director, Twyla Tharp, were both included on the record. Marsalis' work in jazz and classical music combined with his often outspoken attitude toward musical integrity surrounded him with controversy throughout his career. Despite the criticism, his talent was never questioned. As Eric Alterman described in *The Nation*, he's "a man universally acknowledged to be a master musician and perhaps the most ambitious composer alive."

## Further Reading

*Down Beat*, January 1982; July 1984; September 1990; December 1992; February 1994; May 1995.
*Ebony*, July 1994.
*Life*, August 1993.
*The Nation*, May 12, 1997.
*People*, May 12, 1997.
*Rolling Stone*, November 8, 1984.
*Stereo Review*, July 1996.
*Utne Reader*, March-April, 1996.
Sony music press materials, www.music.sony.com, 1997. □

# Ngaio Marsh

**Ngaio Marsh (1899–1982) was one of the most prolific mystery writers of her time. During her 50-year career, Marsh wrote 32 novels, several plays, and many short stories. She was also a noted theatrical producer and many of her mysteries involve theaters and actors.**

Edith Ngaio Marsh was born on April 23, 1899 (some sources say 1895), in Christchurch, New Zealand. She was the only child of parents who were avid readers, campers, and, most important for Marsh's future, amateur actors. The name Ngaio (pronounced "Nye-o"), by which she chose to be known, was reportedly suggested by her uncle, who was a missionary. In the native Maori language of New Zealand, "ngaio" was the name of a flowering tree, but also had many other meanings, including clever, light on the water, and a small insect.

Marsh developed an early interest in history and the theater, and also liked to paint. At 15, she entered art school at Canterbury University, and painted many New Zealand landscapes. Throughout her life, Marsh was very private about personal details, but around this time she is believed to have lost her fiance in World War I. Soon Marsh's love of the theater became the focus of her life. Inspired by a performance of *Hamlet,* she wrote a play called *The Medallion,* and by 1920, she was part of a theater company touring

New Zealand. She spent several years teaching speech and working on theater productions.

## First Mystery Published

In 1928, Marsh took her first trip to England, bringing the first chapters of a novel manuscript. Her mother came for a visit and became ill. While caring for her, Marsh read mystery stories and decided to convert her novel into a mystery. She worked on the manuscript until 1932, then returned to New Zealand where her mother soon died. Marsh spent the next few years writing, painting, producing plays, traveling in Europe, and caring for her elderly father.

The mystery she had begun in England, *A Man Lay Dead,* was published in 1934. It introduced the character who would reappear in her succeeding mystery novels and short stories, Scotland Yard Chief Inspector Roderick Alleyn. Marsh chose this name as a tribute to her father, who had attended Dulwich College, founded by Elizabethan actor Edward Alleyn. Roderick Alleyn, like the famous Lord Peter Wimsey character created by Dorothy Sayers, is a nobleman. But Alleyn was not quite as eccentric as Wimsey; although he was an Oxford graduate, Alleyn chose to join the police force as a constable and worked his way up through the ranks. Nevertheless, he retained his gentlemanly nature and was noted for his intellectual knowledge and charm as he investigated a murder. Alleyn, like Marsh, had a passion for Shakespeare, and often quoted his plays in the midst of an investigation. Marsh went on during her career to write 31 more full-length mysteries and numerous short stories. She was considered part of the "British Golden Age" of mystery writing, along with such authors as Agatha Christie, Dorothy L. Sayers, and Margery Allingham.

## Wrote Prolifically

After the publication of *A Man Lay Dead,* which received favorable reviews, Marsh quickly completed and published *Enter a Murderer* (1935), and co-authored *The Nursing-Home Murder* (1936). *Vintage Murder* (1937) was her first mystery to be set in New Zealand. Other works of the 1930s included *Death in Ecstasy* (1936), *Artists in Crime* (1938), *Death in a White Tie* (1938), and *Overture to Death* (1939).

Marsh worked at a slower pace during the 1940s because she served as a volunteer ambulance driver during World War II. However, she still had seven published mysteries during that decade: *Death of a Peer* (1940), *Death at the Bar* (1940), *Death and the Dancing Footman* (1941), *Colour Scheme* (1943), *Died in the Wool* (1945), *Final Curtain* (1947), and *A Wreath for Rivera* (1949).

During the 1950s and 1960s, Marsh remained extremely popular, and published many more murder mysteries: *Night at the Vulcan,* (1951), *Spinsters in Jeopardy* (1953), *Scales of Justice* (1955), *Death of a Fool* (1956), *Singing in the Shrouds* (1958), *False Scent* (1959), *Hand in Glove* (1962), *Dead Water* (1963), *Killer Dolphin* (1966), and *Clutch of Constables* (1968).

Marsh also continued to write and produce plays throughout her career as a mystery writer. One of the most unusual productions was a 1946 performance of *Macbeth,* set to bagpipe music. She also wrote and co-wrote plays based on several of her mysteries, including *The Nursing-Home Murder, Surfeit of Lampreys, False Scent,* and *Murder Sails at Midnight,* (based on *Singing in the Shrouds*).

Marsh remained active as a producer and writer into her final years. She produced Shakespeare's *Henry V* in 1972, and wrote and produced her last theatrical effort, *Sweet Mr. Shakespeare,* in 1976. During the 1970s and 1980s, she wrote several more mysteries, among them *When in Rome* (1970), *Tied Up In Tinsel* (1972), *Black As He's Painted* (1975), *Last Ditch* (1977), and *Grave Mistake* (1978). Her thirty-first mystery, *Photo Finish* was published in 1980 on the fiftieth anniversary of the Collins Crime Club.

## Mysteries Had Unique Qualities

Despite Marsh's roots in New Zealand, many of her mysteries were set in the English countryside. Most also have connections to the theater, some even having the murders committed during performances. Several critics have noted that Marsh's murderers often dispatch their victims in dramatic fashion befitting a play, using such methods as impaling, suffocation in a bale of wool, and spraying with weedkiller.

Marsh's mysteries also managed to combine a sense of elegance with a dose of social conscience. Although of upper class white origin herself, she was one of the first mystery writers to become an advocate of racial tolerance, perhaps because of her experiences in New Zealand, where the native Maori were an oppressed minority. Despite the often fiendish murderers in her books, Marsh was personally opposed to the death penalty. Occasionally she would have her character, Alleyn, express her opinions on this subject.

Added strengths of Marsh's writing were an attentiveness to the details of police procedures and a strong sense of humor. She kept a large library of reference works on law, pathology, and poisons. And, as she told *Australian Women's Weekly* in 1949, "I always make a point of keeping the most pleasant-sounding name for the murderer. As he or she is bound to come to an unpleasant end, it seems the very least the author can do."

Although some of her mysteries have been criticized for following a set formula and being a bit outdated, Marsh was quite happy to stick to her original style. Fans continued to support her efforts by responding enthusiastically to each new mystery. An example of her popularity was the "Marsh Million" day in 1949, when a million copies of her mysteries were published on a single day in London. As she was quoted in her *New York Times* obituary, she considered her work to be "in the line of the original detective story, where a crime is solved calmly." And even though she wrote so many books and stories in which Alleyn appeared, Marsh apparently continued to enjoy creating each new story. Marsh never married. She modelled Alleyn's eventual wife after herself; Troy, a painter, was a very independent woman who appeared in several of the Alleyn mysteries.

## Honored in Final Years

Marsh's autobiography, *Black Beech and Honeydew,* was published in 1965. She was made a dame of the British

Empire in 1966. But perhaps equally important to her was an honor she received the following year, when the Ngaio Marsh Playhouse was dedicated at Canterbury University in her hometown of Christchurch, New Zealand. She produced Shakespeare's *Twelfth Night* as the opening performance. In 1978, Marsh was honored with the Grand Master Award by the Mystery Writers of America.

Marsh died in Christchurch, New Zealand, on February 18, 1982. Her thirty-second and final mystery, *Light Thickens,* was completed only a few weeks before her death. It revolves around one of her greatest theatrical passions, Shakespeare's *Macbeth.* The Christchurch home in which she lived from the age of ten has been established as a historic site, and is filled with her collection of antiques. On her desk lies a fountain pen filled with green ink, her long-time writing tool.

## Further Reading

*Benet's Reader's Encyclopedia of American Literature,* Harper-Collins, 1987.
*Contemporary Authors* (New Revision Series), Vol. 58, Gale Research, 1997.
*Mystery and Suspense Writers,* Vol. 2, edited by Robin W. Winks and Maureen Corrigan, Scribner's, 1998.
*New York Times,* February 19, 1982.
"Ngaio Marsh," *British Golden Age Intuitionist Writers,* http://members.aol.com/MG4273/ngmarsh/htm#Marsh (February 24, 1999).
*Ngaio Marsh House,* http://canterbury.cyberspace.org.nz/public/histrust/ngaio.html (February 24, 1999). □

# Marlee Matlin

**Marlee Matlin (born 1965) won an Academy Award for her role as Sarah Norman in *Children of a Lesser God* in 1987. Just 21 years old, Matlin was the youngest performer ever to receive the "best actress" award, as well as the first hearing-impaired person to be given the honor. Since then, Matlin has performed regularly in films and television, and founded her own production company.**

Matlin was born on August 4, 1965 in Morton Grove, a suburb of Chicago. She had normal hearing at birth, but contracted roseola (measles) at the age of 18 months. The illness produced a high fever and serious complications, including the loss of most of her hearing. Today, Matlin wears a hearing aid and communicates by reading lips and using sign language. Unlike some hearing-impaired people, Matlin can speak, but relies on an interpreter for business meetings and interviews. "When I was young I knew I was deaf," she told *People* magazine in 1986. "I couldn't accept it. I was very angry until I did accept it, which wasn't until maybe two years ago."

Her parents, Libby and Donald Matlin, learned sign language, along with her two older brothers, Eric and Marc. "The children in the neighborhood didn't accept her," her mother told *Redbook.* To help her daughter find a supportive community, Matlin's mother encouraged her to spend free time at Chicago's Center of Deafness, where she began acting in the Children's Theater for the Deaf. At eight years of age, Matlin appeared in productions of *The Wizard of Oz* and *Peter Pan.*

Matlin attended John Hersey High School in Arlington Heights, also near Chicago. She was among the first generation of hearing-impaired children to attend public schools rather than institutions for the deaf. The school offered academic programs for the hearing-impaired and Matlin was soon participating in both the hearing and non-hearing worlds. In high school, her interest in acting waned. As she explained in an interview with the *Christian Science Monitor,* "I had no thought of becoming an actress, because I thought there were no opportunities." Instead, Matlin enrolled in Harper Junior College and began to pursue studies in criminal justice, but left feeling that "there wouldn't be enough deaf criminals out there to keep me working." Soon after, a friend encouraged her to audition for the Chicago revival of Mark Medoff's award winning play, *Children of a Lesser God.* Matlin went reluctantly, and was given the role of Lydia, a minor character. Her performance came to the attention of producers who were casting the film version of the play. When offered this opportunity, Matlin was initially hesitant, afraid of failing: "I said, 'The film version of *Children of a Lesser God*?' No-no-no-no-no. My mind wasn't open to it. I had no idea how many deaf actors were out there auditioning for the lead role."

## Sudden Success

Matlin's intense energy and her obvious chemistry with co-star William Hurt won her the role of Sarah Norman, an angry young deaf woman who refuses to speak because the hearing world refuses to sign. Medoff adapted the screenplay from his theater script, which he wrote for Phyllis Frelich, another hearing-impaired actress. The film tells the story of Sarah Norman's encounter with a teacher of the deaf, played by Hurt who, over the course of the film, falls in love with Sarah and learns to respect and appreciate her silent world. Matlin's performance, an entirely non-speaking role, earned her an Academy Award for best actress in 1987. "I think this film will open up the world to hearing-impaired people who are actors and actresses," Matlin said when the film opened. By 1997, Matlin was more realistic: "It's hard to find roles, period, regardless of whether I'm deaf or a woman," she told the New York Post. "My deafness is obviously an added difficulty, but you try to break whatever barriers you can."

The year after her Academy Award triumph, Matlin returned to present the 1988 Best Actor award. She began her presentation by signing with an interpreter, but stopped signing to read the list of nominations aloud; it was the first time Matlin had spoken on camera. She worked diligently with a speech therapist to perfect her presentation, but her effort proved controversial, angering many in the hearing-impaired community who thought Matlin was suggesting that speech was preferable to signing. Though Matlin has found it difficult to please some critics, her work on behalf of the hearing impaired has been a significant part of her professional life. "I'm trying to tell young people that you should give your time to others because there are people out there who really need it . . . particularly when the government is giving less," she told the Montreal Gazette in 1996. Matlin is spokesperson for the National Captioning Institute and has worked with a number of charitable organizations, including the Pediatric Aids Foundation and the Starlight Foundation.

During rehearsals for Children of a Lesser God, Matlin began a relationship with actor, William Hurt. Soon after filming ended, Matlin left her parents' home in Chicago to live with Hurt in Manhattan. The relationship lasted two years and, by all accounts, it was a volatile one. During this time she had little contact with her family or friends and became increasingly alienated from Hurt. Her self-esteem plummeted in the face of critics who argued that Matlin did not deserve the Academy Award because she was a deaf person playing a deaf person. Matlin's relationship with Hurt ended in 1987. She moved to California and lived, for a time, with Henry Winkler, best known for his role on the television situation comedy "Happy Days," and his wife, Stacey.

### Reasonable Doubts

Matlin's next few films, Walker in 1988, Bridge to Silence in 1989, Man in the Golden Mask in 1990, and The Linguini Incident in 1991, received little critical attention, though Bridge to Silence marked her debut in a speaking role. In 1991, Matlin turned to series television and landed the starring role of Tess Kaufman in the dramatic series Reasonable Doubts, which ran for two seasons before it was cancelled in 1993. Though she made a guest appearance in a 1990 episode of the popular situation comedy, Seinfeld, Reasonable Doubts offered Matlin the opportunity to develop a significant dramatic role as an assistant district attorney who happens to be hearing impaired. Executive producer Robert Singer had pitched the series to NBC with a hearing actress in mind, but then he met Matlin. "Right after meeting her I knew I wanted her to do it," he recalls. "She has a star quality that's unmistakable," he told the New York Times. In an interview with the Washington Post, Singer called Matlin "remarkable. She can do more saying nothing than most people can talking. . . . She really will take nuance and direction. You can make subtle adjustments with her and she just gets it. You tell her something and you see this light go on, and the next take, she has it. She has great instincts."

Matlin, the first hearing impaired actor to star in a dramatic television series, relished the new acting challenge. "At first, I could see that the writers were caught off guard," Matlin told the New York Times. "It takes time for people to assimilate ideas about deafness." For courtroom scenes, the writers provided her character with an interpreter; for other scenes Matlin used a combination of sign language and speech, conferring with the writers about what words were easier or more difficult for her to pronounce. She also coached co-star Mark Harmon, whose character needed to be fluent in sign language. Off camera, Matlin's bawdy sense of humor and irrepressible energy charmed the crew. Singer notes that "she has to look at you to know what you're saying. Because she can't inflect with her voice the way other actresses can, she compensates with body language and tremendous facial expression. And that comes across very strong, both on film and in life."

Reasonable Doubts was quite popular with the hearing-impaired community, although Matlin found herself once again caught up in controversy. Her signing wasn't clearly visible in all camera shots, a fact that angered some. Others had even more stringent requirements. "I even got a letter from a guy quite respected in the deaf community. He was worried about the image I present of deaf people. He told me I should stop swearing and I should stop using sexual connotations on my show because, hey, deaf people don't swear, deaf people don't have sex, deaf people don't get involved with violence. Well, there are plenty of deaf people who do, and why can't I represent that? You have to get real sometimes," Matlin told the New York Times.

After a cameo role in Robert Altman's The Player in 1992, Matlin went on to star in Hear No Evil in 1993 and Against Her Will: The Carrie Buck Story in 1994. In Against Her Will, Matlin played a hearing person for the first time in her career. The film was based on the true story of Carrie Buck, a developmentally challenged woman at the center of a landmark case that, in 1927, was heard by the Supreme Court. Their decision legalized the forced sterilization of such women. Matlin was drawn to Buck's story: "I was proud to portray her because I felt such an amazing instinct to protect her, to represent her in a positive way, while at the same time highlighting such a negative issue," she told the *Los Angeles Times* in 1994. Matlin was pleased with her work in the film, particularly because she was able to portray a hearing woman so convincingly.

Matlin returned to episodic television, with a guest appearance on *Picket Fences* as Laurie Bey, the "dancing bandit." The part earned her an Emmy nomination and Matlin counts it among her favorite roles. From 1992 to 1996, Matlin was a guest star on some of the most popular television shows, including *ER, The Larry Sanders Show, Spin City,* and *The Outer Limits.* From 1996 until 1999 she also appeared in a half dozen films: *It's My Party,* (1996), *Dead Silence,* (1997), *When Justice Fails,* (1998), *Two Shades of Blue,* (1998), and *In Her Defense,* (1998). A 1999 feature, *Freak City,* for the Showtime network, was "a cross between *One Flew Over the Cuckoo's Nest* and *Awakenings,* " Matlin told the Mining Co.'s Jamie Berke. In addition, Matlin, along with longtime interpreter Jack Jason, ran Solo One Productions. The company gave Matlin the control and autonomy she needed to pursue her career. Two television projects developed in 1999 were *Ninety Days at Hollyridge,* for the Lifetime cable network and *Isabel Crawford of Saddle Mountain* for CBS.

In the fall of 1993, Matlin married Kevin Grandalski, a police officer in Los Angeles. Grandalski learned to sign at Fresno State College, where he earned a bachelor's degree in criminal justice in 1988. The couple had a baby girl, Sarah Rose, on January 19, 1996. They plan to teach Sarah to speak with her hands as well as with her voice. In 1998, Matlin spoke to an audience about what she has learned from her disability: "The real handicap of deafness is not in the ear but in the mind," she said. "We all have challenges in life of one kind or another. We can achieve much more if we focus on our abilities rather than our perceived disabilities."

## Further Reading

*Associated Press,* January 13, 1997.
*Boston Globe,* March 22, 1996.
*Christian Science Monitor,* April 30, 1987.
*Gazette,* March 17, 1996.
*Ladies Home Journal,* April 1989.
*Los Angeles Times,* October 2, 1994; September 22, 1991.
*New York Times,* January 5, 1992; April 13, 1988.
*People,* March 15, 1993; November 22, 1993; April 2, 1993; April 10, 1989; October 20, 1986.
*Redbook,* April 1992.
*Star Tribune,* May 13, 1998.
*U.S. News & World Report,* November 10, 1986.
*Washington Post,* October 11, 1992.
"Marlee Matlin," *Miningco.com,* http://deafness.miningco.com/library/weekly (August 24, 1998).
"Marlee Matlin: Actress Filmography," Internet Movie Data Base, http://us.imdb.com (March 12, 1999). □

# Konosuke Matsushita

**Konosuke Matsushita (1894–1989) started with nothing but an idea for an electric plug, and created**

**a vast business empire that spread around the world. As the owner of Panasonic Corporation and other profitable business ventures, he amassed a personal fortune valued at more than three billion dollars.**

Since his name has never been prominently displayed, Konosuke Matsushita is not as well known as Sam Walton or Henry Ford or Honda or any of the other business giants who used their names on their products. But his company, Matsushita Electric Industrial Co. Ltd., generated more revenue during his lifetime than any of the others. Although he was generally unknown outside his native land of Japan, his company's sales eventually exceeded sixty three billion dollars every year.

## Humble Beginnings

Matsushita was born into humble circumstances in the Japanese village of Wasa, on November 27, 1894. He grew into a nervous, rather sickly young adult with an unpromising future. At a time when you had to be well educated, charismatic, even rich, to succeed, he seemed destined for a life of struggle. The youngest of eight children, Matsushita had a father who gambled away the family's money. At the age of nine, he took a job as an apprentice in a bicycle shop to help the family survive.

One of the traits that followed Matsushita throughout his career was a willingness to take risks. He did that when he quit his bicycle shop job to accept employment at Osaka

Light, an electric utility company. Matsushita was quickly promoted and eventually became an inspector, a respectable job at which many might have stayed until retirement. Perhaps Matsushita even considered that. However, while working at Osaka Light, he had managed to create a new type of light socket, one that was better than anything available at the time. Matsushita showed the invention to his boss, who was unimpressed.

Matsushita had no money and no real business experience, but he did have drive and ambition. So, in 1917, he decided to manufacture the device himself. With the help of his wife and three eager assistants, Matsushita began his business. The combined education of the five amounted to less than a high school education, and none had any experience in manufacturing an electric plug. But they had ambition. In a cramped two-room tenement house, they worked long hours, seven days a week. After several very lean months, they had completed a few samples of the new product.

Wholesalers generally rejected his new style electric plug. They told him it was acceptable, even innovative, but that he needed far more than one single item for the large wholesalers and retailers to be interested in his company. He persevered, and gradually people began to buy the plug, when they saw that it was better in quality and almost 50% lower in price. Matsushita kept his business afloat by taking on contracts for other items, such as insulator plates. By 1922, his firm was introducing new items every month. He was also developing business strategies that made him stand out from his competitors. He learned that a new product had to be 30% better and 30% less expensive, than one already on the market. By giving his products away, he could eventually sell many more of them. He also pioneered an effective after sale service program.

## Designed Bicycle Lamps

Bicycle lamps, a very necessary item in Japan, had bad reputations. They seemed to constantly fail. Matsushita realized that an efficient lamp for the millions of bicycles in his country could become a popular item. So he designed one. Although it wasn't an immediate success, his "bullet lamp" eventually became the standard by which the entire industry was judged. Matsushita's battery powered lamp became so successful that many people bought them for use in their homes to replace the traditional kerosene lamps. Matsushita Electric was on the way to becoming a giant in the industry.

The 1923 bullet-lamp was followed by an electric space heater, an electrically heated table, and a new type of thermostat. The first Matsushita radio, a 3 vacuum tube model, was introduced in 1931. It won first prize in the Tokyo Broadcasting Station radio contest. Other inventions followed, including electric motors and electric fans.

## Hard Times

Times were not entirely smooth along the way. Although refrigerators, washing machines, air conditioners, color television sets, and stereo equipment would eventually be produced, there were some setbacks. With the Great Depression of the 1930s, Matsushita saw sales fall dramati-

cally. But unlike other companies, he didn't lay off his growing number of employees, people he considered a part of his family. Instead, he shifted them about, moving factory workers to sales positions. At the same time he cut production schedules. Still, his warehouses were full of unsold merchandise.

Matsushita would not change his mind when managers insisted that the company must lay off employees and shut down facilities in order to survive. He cut work hours by half, but continued to pay his employees full wages. He also asked his workers to help sell the backlog of stock, and they responded. As other companies were failing, Matsushita Electric held on.

## World War Two

Matsushita's company was beginning to recover, when the Second World War brought devastation to his country. It is difficult to say how Matsushita felt about the war since he was a very private man, but his company did manufacture materials for the Japanese war machine. When Japan was defeated and the Allied powers took control, Matsushita was ordered to cease all production. Since his company had manufactured products to help Japan in the war effort, Matsushita Electric was burdened with severe restrictions. It appeared to be the end of his company, as it was with many other Japanese companies who never recovered after the war. Matsushita, himself, was nearly removed from the leadership of the company he created. His employees petitioned the military government to allow him to stay.

Matsushita convinced General Douglas MacArthur and other military governors that his company should be allowed to resume production of peacetime products. He promised that Japan would once again be a world power, but this time by peaceful means. He believed that his country could lead the world in electronics. The military governors, realizing that such a strategy would help Japan recover from the devastation of war, permitted Matsushita's company to reopen. Matsushita and his management team began to rebuild. Soon Matsushita Electric was back in production and making a profit. Morale among employees was strong.

Matsushita Electric continued to expand, acquiring many other companies. In 1952, it offered consumers the first black and white television sets. By 1959, Matsushita had established not only the Kyushu Matsushita Electric Company, the Osaka Precision Machinery Company (later renamed Matsushita Seiko), and the Matsushita Communication Industrial group (which manufactured the first tape recorder), but also Matsushita Electric Corporation of America. The company's first color television sets was marketed in 1960, as it continued to spread around the world with brand names like "National" and "Panasonic."

## Paternal Management Philosophy

When Matsushita began his company with a handful of nondescript electric plugs, few could have predicted the phenomenal success that lay ahead. He believed that a company should create wealth for society as well as for shareholders, and should always work to alleviate poverty.

Matsushita's business philosophy led to the Japanese "paternal management" tradition, whereby employees are viewed as being part of a "family" within the company, and are assured of lifetime employment, without fear of layoffs.

Outside the office of the Matsushita company, engraved in stone, is the creed and basic management objective of its creator and long-time president. The plaque says, "Recognizing our responsibilities as industrialists, we will devote ourselves to the progress and development of society and the well-being of people through our business activities, thereby enhancing the quality of life throughout the world."

One of the most lasting of Matsushita's business sayings was, "If we cannot make a profit, that means we are committing a sort of crime against society. We take society's capital, we take their people, we take their materials, yet without a good profit, we are using precious resources that could be better used elsewhere." His companies always made a profit. At one point, an American shopping for a video cassette recorder might look at GE, RCA, Sylvania, Magnavox, Montgomery Ward, Quasar and Panasonic without the knowledge that every one of these models was made by Matsushita.

Konosuke Matsushita was 94 years old when he died in Tokyo on April 27, 1989, leaving behind a vast manufacturing empire.

## Further Reading

*Fortune,* March 31, 1997
Matsushita Leadership, www.amazon.com □

# Jan Matzeliger

**Jan Matzeliger (1852–1889) revolutionized the shoemaking industry with his invention of the lasting machine. This invention reduced the cost of manufacturing shoes by one-half. He is remembered for his persistence and optimism in the face of prejudice and ill health.**

Jan Ernst Matzeliger was born on the northern coast of South America in Paramaribo, Dutch Guiana (now the Republic of Suriname) on September 15, 1852. He was the son of a Dutch engineer in charge of government machine shops and a Surinamese black woman, who was a slave. In 1855, Matzeliger went to live with his paternal aunt. At the age of ten, he was apprenticed in the machine shops run by his father, where Matzeliger developed an interest in machinery and mechanics. At 19, he went to sea on an East Indian merchant ship. When the ship docked in Philadelphia, Matzeliger decided to take up residence in the town. He worked at odd jobs including that of shoemaker's apprentice, and then moved to Boston in 1876. The following year, he settled in Lynn, Massachusetts, a manufacturing center on the north shore of Massachusetts Bay, ten miles northeast of Boston. Shoemaking began as a cottage industry in Lynn in 1635 and developed into factory production

by 1848, when the first shoe-sewing machine was introduced.

Matzeliger found work in the Harney Brothers' shoe factory where he operated a McKay sole-sewing machine. He also ran a heel-burnisher and a buttonhole machine, and cleaned the floors. Matzeliger took night classes and studied English on his own to improve his fluency. He held great respect for learning and collected a personal library of scientific and practical books with which he educated himself, studying physics and other subjects. In addition to his mechanical ability, Matzeliger was a talented artist. He painted pictures, which he gave to his friends, and he taught classes in oil painting.

## Persistence Paid Off

The methods of shoe production changed with the advent of the Industrial Revolution. Shoemakers used machines to attach inner and outer soles with pegs, and used devices to sew uppers to lowers. Cobblers cut, sewed, and tacked shoes with machines. One part of shoe manufacturing, the lasting, remained a manual operation. Many believed that it was impossible to design a machine to perform this final and important step. In 1880, Matzeliger became determined to devise a machine to perform this manual operation. The lasting process involved the mechanical shaping of the shoe upper leather over the last, which is a block or form shaped like a human foot, and attaching the shoe upper to the sole. He refused to believe that it was impossible to automate the task.

Matzeliger watched the hand lasters in the shoe factory during the day. At night, with scraps he salvaged from the factory, he tried to duplicate movements of the lasters. Secretly, Matzeliger made drawings. He experimented with a simple machine made of wire, wood, and cigar boxes, which took him six months to construct. Matzeliger's employer offered $50 for the machine, even before it was perfected. Matzeliger rejected the offer. He then tried making a lasting machine out of scrap iron, a project that took him four years. Matzeliger received an offer of $1,500 for his iron laster. Again he refused the offer and continued to perfect his lasting machine in a vacant corner of the factory where he was employed. He spent only five or six cents a day on food in order to conserve money for his experiments, and he sacrificed sleep. Matzeliger spent ten years in the development of his lasting machine and received little encouragement. When the secret of his project became known, in fact, the public laughed at him, but Matzeliger refused to be discouraged.

When the time was right, Matzeliger sought out investors to help finance a patent, and defray the cost of demonstrating and perfecting the machine. Charles H. Delnow and Melville S. Nichols agreed to provide capital for Matzeliger's invention in return for two-thirds ownership of the device. With sufficient financial backing, Matzeliger applied for a patent. The first diagrams of the machine that Matzeliger sent to the Patent Office in Washington, D.C. were so complex that officials could not decipher them. A representative from the patent office went to Lynn to observe the machine personally in order to comprehend how it worked. On March 20, 1883 Matzeliger received a patent for the lasting machine which could adjust a shoe, drive in the nails, and produce a finished product in one minute.

Matzeliger continued to improve his machine until it was ready for an initial factory test. The first public operation of the machine took place on May 29, 1885, when the machine broke a record by lasting 75 pairs of shoes.

Matzeliger, Delnow, and Nichols secured additional capital from George A. Brown and Sidney W. Winslow in order to finance the production of the lasting machine. Delnow, Nichols, Brown, and Winslow formed the Consolidated Lasting Machine Company. Matzeliger sold his patent rights to the investors in exchange for stock. The company grew rapidly. In the late 1890s, it merged with several small companies to form the United Shoe Machinery Corporation, which soon dominated the U.S. shoemaking industry. Sixty-five years later, the company was worth over one billion dollars.

Besides his lasting machine, Matzeliger patented several other inventions, including a mechanism for distributing tacks, nails, etc. in 1888. Additional patents were awarded after his death in 1889. In 1890, his nailing machine and a tack separating and distributing mechanism received a patent; in 1891 a patent was approved on another lasting machine.

## An Early Death

Matzeliger attempted to join the Episcopal, Unitarian, and Catholic churches in Lynn, but every congregation rejected him for reason of his skin color. Eventually, he joined the Christian Endeavor Society at the North Congregational Church, where he regularly attended services and took part in many church activities. At the church he made many friends with whom he spent time in outdoor excursions—exploring ponds, climbing rocks, and visiting a nearby island. There are no existing records to show that Matzeliger ever courted or married.

In the summer of 1886, Matzeliger fell ill with what he believed was a cold. He learned later that he suffered from tuberculosis. He remained active; even when confined to bed, he continued to paint and experiment. Matzeliger died on August 24, 1889 in Lynn, Massachusetts, one month shy of his 37th birthday. He was buried in the Pine Grove Cemetery in Lynn. Matzeliger left a large portion of his estate to the North Congregational Church. Years later, when the North Church suffered financial hardship, it was learned that the stock bequeathed by Matzeliger had increased greatly in value. The church was rescued from debt through the sale of that stock.

## Honored After Death

Matzeliger did not live long enough to see the true impact of his lasting machine on the shoe industry. The revolutionary invention enabled production of 150 to 700 pairs of shoes per day. In contrast, hand lasters could complete no more than 50 pairs in a day. The lasting machine cut the cost of shoe manufacturing by one half and thus reduced the price of shoes as well. Conditions in the shoe industry improved for workers and wages doubled. Lynn, Massachusetts, came to be known as "The Shoe Capital of the World." A school founded in Lynn to train young men to run the lasting machine graduates more than 200 students each year who in turn educated others in the United States and abroad in the use of the lasting machine.

Matzeliger was recognized for his efforts only after he died, when he was awarded the Gold Medal and Diploma at the Pan-American Exposition of 1901. In 1967, a series of radio dramas called "The Great Ones" was produced in recognition of the contributions of African Americans in science, art, and industry. The show broadcast a drama featuring the life of Jan Matzeliger. The U.S. Postal Service issued a stamp in his honor in 1991, as part of the Black Heritage Collection. A statue was erected in his honor in Lynn, and a life-size portrait of Matzeliger hangs on the wall of the North Congregational Church.

## Further Reading

Adams, Russell L., *Great Negroes Past and Present,* Afro-Am Publishing Company, 1969.

Altman, Susan, *Extraordinary Black Americans from Colonial to Contemporary Times,* Childrens Press, 1989.

Haber, Lois, *Black Pioneers,* Harcourt Brace, 1970.

*The Great Ones,* edited by William J. Kaland, Washington Square Press, 1970.

Kranz, Rachel, *The Biographical Dictionary of Black Americans,* Facts on File, 1992.

Logan, Rayford W. and Michael R. Winston, *Dictionary of American Negro Biography,* W.W. Norton, 1982.

Mitchell, Barbara, *Shoes for Everyone,* Carolrhoda Books, 1986.

Sullivan, Otha Richard, *African American Inventors,* John Wiley & Sons, Inc., 1998.

*Jet,* August 19, 1991; March 20, 1995; March 25, 1996.

*Stamps,* July 20, 1991.

"Jan E. Matzeliger," *Stamp on Black History,* http://library .advanced.org/10320/Stamps.htm#anchor305420 (March 10, 1999).

"Jan Earnst Matzeliger, Inventor," *The Knitting Circle,* http://www.sbu.ac.uk/stafflag/matzeliger.html (March 10, 1999).

"Jan Matzeliger 1852-1889," *Profiles of Significant African-Americans in Science, Medicine, and Technology,* http://sun3.lib.uci.edu/~afrexh/Matzeliger.html (March 10, 1999). □

# Louis Burt Mayer

**Louis B. Mayer (1885–1957) was one of Hollywood's original "moguls," a movie house pioneer who helped found one of the film industry's most prominent studios, Metro-Goldwyn-Mayer. From 1924 until 1951, Mayer ruled over a vast film empire, producing a string of classic hits and discovering countless stars. Mayer never strayed from a promise he made early in his career to create what he called "decent, wholesome pictures" the whole family could enjoy.**

L ouis Burt Mayer was born Eliezer Mayer in Minsk, Russia, on July 4, 1885. The product of a working-class Jewish family, he moved with his parents and two brothers in 1888, first to New York, then to St. John, New Brunswick, Canada. There, Mayer's mother peddled chickens door to door, while his father worked as a dealer in scrap metal. Upon completing grade school, Louis briefly joined his father's business before moving to Boston in 1904 to start his own junk enterprise. That same year he married Margaret Shenberg, the daughter of a kosher butcher.

## Entered Film Business

Mayer's arrival in Boston coincided with the nickelodeon craze that was sweeping the nation. Intrigued by the commercial potential of these "flickers," Mayer began a side business buying up and renovating rundown nickelodeon arcades, starting with The Gem in Haverhill, Massachusetts in 1907. The huge crowds that turned out that Christmas season to see Pathe's hand-tinted *Passion Play* convinced Mayer for all time of the mass appeal of wholesome family entertainment. Promising to show "only pictures that I won't be ashamed to have my children see" in his refurbished auditoriums, Mayer turned a tidy profit and was able to leave the junk business entirely. He formed a partnership with Nat Gordon, another theater owner, and began acquiring movie houses all over New England. Within seven years, the two men had assembled the region's largest theater chain.

Mayer's next goal was to acquire distribution rights to the films themselves. His first foray into this arena was an overwhelming success. Without having seen it, Mayer paid filmmaker D.W. Griffith $25,000 for exclusive northeast distribution rights for Griffith's Civil War epic *Birth of a Nation* (1915). At the time, it was the highest bid ever made for the exhibition of a single film. The arrangement eventually netted Mayer more than $100,000.

## Early Days in Hollywood

Having conquered exhibition and distribution, Mayer next moved into production. He joined the Alco Company (later Metro Pictures) in New York City, but was dissatisfied with the type of films the company was producing. He left Alco in 1917, moved to Los Angeles, and formed his own production house, The Mayer Company. The new company produced numerous romantic melodramas, many featuring starlet Anita Stewart. In 1923, Mayer hired Universal's Irving Thalberg as his production chief. The following year, at the instigation of Metro head Marcus Loew, Mayer merged his company with Metro Pictures and The Goldwyn Company and became West Coast head of the newly formed Metro-Goldwyn-Mayer (MGM). Thalberg was named production supervisor. *The Big Parade* (1926) and *Ben-hur* (1926) were among their early projects for the studio.

Mayer ran MGM with a ruthless efficiency. With wise use of resources and a strong promotional apparatus (including the slavish devotion of the Hearst newspapers), Mayer kept the studio profitable throughout the lean years of the 1930s. He discovered many of the era's top stars and got many others to swear an oath of fealty to the studio. Together with Thalberg, he helped launch the careers of such performers as Clark Gable, Jean Harlow, Spencer Tracy, Joan Crawford, Judy Garland, and Charles Laughton, along with numerous writers, directors, and producers. One of Mayer's personal "discoveries," Greta Garbo, went on to become a legendary Hollywood icon. The assemblage of talent paid off in the form of a string of classic features, including the first "talkie," 1927's *The Jazz Singer,* and such hits as *Grand Hotel* (1932), *Dinner at Eight* (1933), and *Camille* (1936).

## The MGM Style

While Mayer thought of himself primarily as a businessman, and professed not to have any interest in motion pictures as an art form, he did exert enormous influence over the style and content of MGM films. "He likes vast, glittering sets," wrote Henry F. Pringle in a profile of Mayer published in *The New Yorker.* "He approves of gorgeous gowns, pretty girls, lingerie sequences, and expensive assignations." Escapist musicals, sumptuous costume dramas, and screwball comedies accounted for the bulk of MGM's output under Mayer's aegis, a reflection of his earlier pledge to produce only those pictures his children could see. Mayer's creative influence reached its apex with the Andy Hardy series, a string of hits starring Mickey Rooney that were as successful as they were saccharine. To its critics, MGM's output during Mayer's reign was formulaic pap, but to Mayer it was just the kind of wholesome family entertainment Depression-era audiences wanted.

## Influential Figure

Few at MGM saw fit to argue with success, and for many of his 27 years there, Mayer was the highest-paid individual in the country. His annual salary, including bonuses, exceeded $1.25 million, a princely sum for the time. As his bankbook swelled, so did Mayer's influence—both inside and outside the film community. He took a leadership role within the movie industry, helping to found the Academy of Motion Picture Arts and Sciences in 1927. A staunch conservative, Mayer also became active in politics, at one point serving as state chairman of the California Republican Party. He formed a close personal friendship with President Herbert Hoover, who offered him the post of U.S. ambassador to Turkey in 1929. The mogul wisely declined. In 1934, Mayer threw the weight of his considerable influence behind California gubernatorial candidate Frank F. Merriam, in his campaign against muckraking author Upton Sinclair. Mayer produced a series of faux "newsreels" for Merriam (featuring paid actors) that were widely credited with swinging the election in favor of the Republican.

Though feared and respected, Mayer was little loved by his colleagues in Hollywood. Hot-tempered and imperious, Mayer made numerous enemies during his career. He was quick to punish those who did not accede to his wishes. When Clark Gable went to Mayer to ask for a raise, for example, Mayer threatened to tell Gable's wife about the actor's affair with Joan Crawford. Gable settled for a much lower figure than he originally requested. Others saw their careers cut off because of some perceived or actual slight to the great mogul. On at least one occasion, retribution was physical. Mayer reportedly struck one of MGM's biggest silent film stars, John Gilbert, for disparaging remarks Gilbert made about co-star Mae Murray.

Still other stars benefited from Mayer's largesse. Ann Rutherford, an MGM ingenue of the 1930s and 1940s, once successfully extracted a raise from the sentimental Mayer by lamenting her inability to buy a house for her aged mother. Perhaps Mayer recognized in her plea one of his own favorite tactics, using charm to gain his objective. Actor Robert Taylor fell victim to Mayer's charms when, upon asking for his raise, the weepy mogul hugged him and advised him to work hard and respect his elders and in due time he would get all that he deserved. Clark Gable had Mayer to thank for his freedom after the intoxicated star struck and killed a pedestrian with his car. Mayer reportedly convinced the district attorney to blame the homicide on a minor MGM executive (who was rewarded with a lucrative lifetime salary by the studio in exchange for his cooperation).

## Decline of Influence

Some may have questioned Mayer's methods, but not many dared complain too loudly while he was still at the top of the heap. Mayer reigned as the most powerful man in Hollywood throughout the 1930s and early 1940s. At that point, his influence began to wane. Inexorably, MGM began to lose its edge in the studio wars. Mayer's top lieutenant, Irving Thalberg, died in 1936, leaving MGM bereft of visionary leadership. Public taste began to turn against the wholesome escapist that Mayer favored. With few hits to back up Mayer's bluster, patience started running thin with the studio chief's despotic style.

In 1951, MGM's East Coast executives ousted Mayer after a brief power struggle. A defiant Mayer issued a statement denying he was through in Hollywood. But Mayer never returned to his former position of influence. He became an adviser for the Cinerama group, and spent his last years relentlessly lobbying stockholders of MGM's parent company, Loew's Inc., to overthrow the studio's management team. His efforts proved unsuccessful. He contracted leukemia and died in Los Angeles on October 29, 1957.

That Mayer was widely reviled in the Hollywood of his time as a crass, cruel vulgarian does not diminish one whit from his influence on the history of film. In fact, it was precisely his willingness to use his immense power in the pursuit of his vision of family entertainment that made him the prototypical Hollywood mogul.

## Further Reading

Altman, Diana, *Hollywood East: Louis B. Mayer and the Origins of the Studio System* Birch Lane Press, 1992.

Crowther, Bosley *Hollywood Rajah: The Life and Times of Louis B. Mayer* Holt, 1960.

Higham, Charles *Merchant of Dreams: Louis B. Mayer, M.G.M., and the Secret Hollywood* Dell, 1994.

Thomson, David *A Biographical Dictionary of Film* Knopf, 1994.

                    □

# Anthony McAuliffe

**Anthony McAuliffe (1898–1975) exhibited superior ability commanding airborne and regular army troops during the Normandy Invasion, Operation Market Garden, and the Battle of the Bulge, three of the most critical military engagements for the Western Allies against Nazi Germany during World War II. McAuliffe was also instrumental in the racial integration of the U.S. Army, for which he was particularly proud.**

B orn on July 2, 1898 in Washington, DC, to a father employed by the government, Anthony McAuliffe seemed destined for a career in the service of his country. He attended public schools in Washington, DC, and secured admittance to West Virginia University in 1916. McAuliffe embarked on his life's work following the U.S. entry into World War I, transferring to the War Emergency Course offered by the U.S. Military Academy in June 1917. He completed the course in November 1918, just days before the end of the war, and reentered the Academy as an officer cadet. McAuliffe graduated 29th in a class of 284 in June 1919.

## Peace Time Career

The years immediately following the war were a time of downsizing in the United States military. American participation in World War I, the "war to end all wars," was seen as an aberration. It appeared extremely unlikely that American military intervention would be required overseas in the foreseeable future. As such, the size of the American army was drastically decreased, and promotions for military personnel were few and far between. Against this backdrop, McAuliffe managed to advance his career, showing the promise that he was later able to fulfill under the pressure of battle.

Following his graduation from West Point, McAuliffe entered the Army Field Artillery School in Camp Zachary, Kentucky. He also married his high school sweetheart, Helen Willet Whitman, on August 23, 1920. The couple would eventually have two children. Upon finishing his artillery training, McAuliffe was transferred to the West Coast, serving from 1920 until 1922 at Fort Lewis, Washington, and the Presidios of San Francisco and Monterrey, California. He was promoted to first lieutenant and began a three-year stint at Schofield Barracks on the island of Oahu, Hawaii, in 1923. Upon his return to the mainland, McAuliffe was transferred to Fort Riley, Kansas, before settling at Fort Hoyle, Maryland from 1927 until 1932. McAuliffe returned to Hawaii from 1932 until 1936. He served as a general's aide until 1935, when he was promoted to captain.

Although his career path had led him to specialize in artillery operations and staff work, McAuliffe was determined to secure a position commanding combat troops. To this end, he enrolled in the Army Command and General Staff School at Fort Leavenworth, Kansas in 1936, completing the program the following year. He then served as an instructor at the Artillery School at Fort Still, Oklahoma, until 1939.

McAuliffe's career as a staff officer continued despite his desire for combat command. He was appointed to a study group examining race relations in the Army at the Army War College at Carlisle Barracks, Pennsylvania in 1940. This study group recommended that the Army become more fully integrated, an objective that McAuliffe remained committed to throughout his military career. His participation in the study group earned McAuliffe promotion to the rank of major and a transfer to the Army General Staff. He received a further promotion prior to the U.S. entry into World War II, becoming a lieutenant colonel in 1941.

## Field Command

The United States entered World War II on December 8, 1941, the day following the Japanese attack on Pearl Harbor. Officers with thorough training and experience quickly became a prized commodity. Overnight, the military embarked on an unprecedented expansion to meet the requirements of a global war. Given his success as a staff officer and desire to command troops, McAuliffe was promoted to colonel in 1942 and placed in command of the artillery elements of the newly formed 101st Airborne Division, which was slated to participate in the Allied liberation of France.

## D-Day

While U.S. forces battled the Axis powers in the Pacific and in North Africa and Italy during 1942 and 1943, the invasion of German-held France was forced to wait. The difficulties present in amphibious operations, and the anticipated strength of the German defense of the French, Belgian, and Dutch coasts, necessitated a large and meticulously planned buildup prior to invasion, which was not completed until spring of 1944.

Allied plans for the invasion of France, relied heavily on airborne troops in the initial stages of the operation. Allied airborne forces were to drop behind the invasion beaches of Normandy in the early morning hours of June 6, 1944, and secure vital roads and rail lines that the main body of the invasion force would require. The airborne forces would also delay the transfer of German reserve forces to the invasion area. This was to prove no simple task, given the technological limitations faced by airborne operations at the time. Without accurate navigation and positioning systems, most of the Allied airborne forces were dropped several miles from their planned landing zones. Many men and much equipment were lost during the risky night jump. In McAuliffe's case, his troops and equipment landed three miles from their intended landing zone and his immediate commander, Brigadier General D. F. Pratt, was killed during his parachute drop. Despite this disastrous beginning to the operation, McAuliffe quickly assumed Pratt's position and organized the capture and defense of a vital bridge over the Vire River and the key village of Pouppeville. His forces linked with invading troops, pressing inland on the morning of June 6, 1944.

In the days following the invasion, McAuliffe led a successful attack on the town of Carentan in support of the expansion of the Allied beachhead. McAuliffe's participation in the D-Day invasion and subsequent operations demonstrated his command abilities, as the 101st Airborne achieved most of its objectives despite encountering difficult and unforeseen obstacles. His confidence in his own abilities and those of his troops was evidenced in his behavior prior to the operation. As his men boarded their planes for the night parachute drop, McAuliffe had each of them exchange signed 100-franc notes so that they could all treat each other to a celebratory drink following their victory. Despite their bravery and determination, Allied airborne troops suffered heavier than expected casualties during the invasion of Normandy. The effectiveness of airborne operations, in general, came under some doubt. These doubts were to be confirmed by the failure of the next major Allied airborne operation.

## Market Garden

The 101st Airborne Division, and the rest of the Allied airborne forces, rested and replaced their losses in the months following the Normandy invasion. Other Allied forces pressed forward from the invasion area to liberate most of France and Belgium, and a portion of the Netherlands by the end of August 1944. Although the pace of the Allied advance had been swift after the invasion, it slowed to a standstill in the face of the natural obstacles presented by the Rhine River and its major tributaries. Many strategies for placing a large force on the eastern bank of the Rhine were debated by the Allied General Staff. A plan proposed by British Field Marshall, Bernard Montgomery, was approved by the overall commander of the Allied forces in the West, General Dwight D. Eisenhower. Montgomery, normally a very conservative general, had come up with a daring and innovative plan for using airborne forces to secure a series of critical bridges crossing the Rhine and Maas rivers, the Wilhelmina Canal, and several other large waterways crossing a 37-mile long area in the central Netherlands. In conjunction with this airborne operation, forces of the British XXXth Corps, comprising one armored and two infantry divisions, would drive along roadways linking the bridges secured by the airborne forces, thus breaking through the German lines on the lower Rhine.

Montgomery's plan, code-named Operation Market Garden, would employ the U.S. 101st and 82nd Airborne Divisions, the British 1st Airborne Division and 52nd (Airportable) Division, and the Polish 1st Parachute Brigade in its initial phase. McAuliffe, and the rest of the 101st Airborne Division, were scheduled to drop on the city of Eindhoven at the furthest point from the Allied lines, on September 17, 1944.

The 101st Airborne made its drop successfully and secured the town of Eindhoven. However, they were unable to prevent the Germans from destroying one of its key objectives, a large bridge over the Wilhelmina Canal. Other parts of Market Garden did not go even this smoothly. Allied intelligence failed to detect the presence of a German armored division in the operational area. Also, the Germans captured a complete draft of the plans for the operation. As such, the planned advance of the British XXXth Corps never materialized, leaving the Allied airborne forces trapped behind enemy lines. Under the leadership of General Maxwell Taylor, the 101st Airborne Division succeeded in making its way back to Allied territory, fighting a fierce battle at the town of Veghel at which McAuliffe provided distinguished service. His part in the battles led McAuliffe to be promoted to Brigadier General in the aftermath of Market Garden.

Market Garden ended in complete failure for the Allies, who suffered heavy casualties and wound up precisely where they started when the operation began. The operation also cooled any enthusiasm that might have still existed regarding the use of airborne troops. For the rest of the war, airborne troops were used in the same manner as normal infantry formations. Despite the eventual failure of Market Garden, the operation remains one of the more ambitious uses of airborne troops in military history, and was the subject of the film *A Bridge Too Far*.

## The Battle of the Bulge

In the wake of their heavy losses in Market Garden, the 101st Airborne Division was transferred to the Ardennes region, straddling southeastern Belgium, Luxembourg, and a portion of northeastern France. This region was believed to be a quiet region due to its geography, which was very hilly and heavily forested, and its road network, which was relatively undeveloped by western European standards. The region was viewed as unsuited to armored actions and was chosen as a good place for the 101st to rest and recuperate.

Despite its terrain and poor roads, the Ardennes was not impossible for armored units to cross, as the German army had proven in 1940 by using the region as a springboard for their surprisingly easy conquest of France. In fact, with the Allies now threatening to invade Germany itself, and the Russians preparing to enter East Prussia, the German high command had once again, at Hitler's insistence, identified the Ardennes as an ideal avenue for a surprise attack. The German Ardennes offensive was designed to catch the numerically superior Allied forces off guard, open a large hole in the Allied lines, and enable German armored formations to cross the Meuse River and capture the Allied supply nexus at Antwerp, Belgium. Although its chances for success were slim, the Germans committed the last of their reserves to the offensive, which was viewed as their last realistic chance to throw the Allies back and forestall the imminent invasion of Germany.

To have any chance of reaching its objectives, the German offensive had to be conducted in poor weather, which would negate the overwhelming aerial superiority of the Allies. As such, the German forces massed opposite the Ardennes waited in early December 1944 for a long-range forecast of several days of bad weather before launching their attack. Conditions were at last judged to be favorable on December 16, and the attack commenced that evening. German surprise was complete, and the Allied forces in the Ardennes were sent reeling for several days. The 101st Airborne Division, stationed just to the south of the German offensive, was ordered into battle in an attempt to patch some of the numerous holes that were developing in the Allied lines. Despite their initial successes, however, the Germans were met with heroic resistance all along their attack routes. Their armored columns were creating gigantic traffic jams on the Ardennes' overworked roads, leading them to fall dangerously behind their proposed timetable from the outset.

On the morning of December 18, 1944, elements of the 101st Airborne Division, the 10th Armored Division, the 705th Tank Destroyer Battalion, and the 755th Field Artillery Battalion, converged on the small town of Bastogne, Belgium, a critical road junction directly in the path of the German advance. Brigadier General McAuliffe assumed command of these forces and established a defense of the town. Although Bastogne was held during initial attacks, German forces encircled the town on December 20, leaving McAuliffe's troops isolated from reinforcement and supplies. By this point in the battle, because the Germans had fallen well behind their timetable, the capture of Bastogne had become the key to the battle. Try as they might, German forces could not dislodge McAuliffe and his scratch force over the next two days. Finally, on December 22, 1944, the commander of German forces encircling Bastogne offered McAuliffe the chance to surrender his forces. McAuliffe's one-word reply to this offer, a sarcastic "Nuts," was much celebrated in the Allied countries, summing up as it did their resolve to defeat the Germans regardless of cost.

The following day saw a break in the weather, allowing Allied aircraft to operate over the battlefield and provide air-dropped supplies to the hard-pressed defenders of Bastogne. Although the Germans attempted to reach the Meuse River for the next three days, the clear weather ensured that their offensive would fail. Elements of the 4th Armored Division, led by General George Patton, relieved the siege of Bastogne on December 26, 1944, and the Germans had retreated by December 29. His performance in what came to be known as the Battle of the Bulge secured McAuliffe's status as an international hero.

## War's End

McAuliffe was transferred to the 103rd Infantry Division in January 1945. He participated in the crossing of the Rhine River and the subsequent operations of the Allied forces in southern Germany and Austria. Troops under McAuliffe's command liberated the Brenner Pass linking Austria and Italy, and the Austrian city of Innsbruck. At the end of the war in Europe, in April 1945, McAuliffe was placed in command of the 79th Infantry Division for a short while, and then transferred to command the airborne center at Fort Bragg, North Carolina later the same year.

## The Atomic Age

In July 1946, McAuliffe was named the army ground forces advisor for Operation Crossroads, the experimental above-ground detonation of an atomic bomb on Bikini Atoll in the Pacific Ocean. His position regarding nuclear weapons was quite a conventional one for the time. He believed that the U.S. should stockpile atomic bombs as a deterrent to their use by any other power. His knowledge of artillery and familiarity with nuclear devices led McAuliffe to be appointed Army Secretary of the Joint Research and Development Board, in which capacity he served from August 1946 until December 1947. He then served as deputy director for research and development of the Army logistics division from 1947 until 1949, but yearned for another field command.

## Desegregation of the Army

McAuliffe was restored to field command in March 1949 as head of the 24th Infantry Division, stationed in occupied Japan. He was promoted to Major General in October of the same year and was transferred to become chief of the Army chemical corps. In this post he became an expert on chemical and biological weapons and the means to counter their use. By the outbreak of the Korean War, in the spring of 1951, McAuliffe was named assistant chief of staff for personnel of the Army and was promoted to lieutenant general. In this post, he was responsible for addressing the issue of race relations within the army, drafting recommendations for the inclusion of African-American troops in military formations.

During World War II, African-Americans had served with distinction, although most of them were placed in service and transportation units. African-American combat formations did exist, but were fully segregated from their white counterparts. This internal segregation of the army persisted into the Korean War, but was scheduled for review. In initial examinations of the racial composition of the Army, undertaken in 1950, McAuliffe recommended that African-Americans continue to be placed in segregated units, given the racial attitudes of American society as a whole. Existing African-American units were already overstaffed, however, so McAuliffe proposed creation of additional African-American formations. Manpower needs during the Korean War quickly dictated a review of these recommendations. The necessities of war had already led to the integration of several combat units operating in Korea. The performance of these units had been satisfactory and their integration had caused no serious morale problems, leading McAuliffe to revise his position and recommend full integration of the Army in the summer of 1951. By December of that year, he ordered all major commanders in the Far East to prepare and submit integration plans for their forces. These orders were extended to include European commands in 1952. Although desegregation would not proceed unhindered in the coming years, the Army would become one of the most integrated organizations in American society by the 1970s. Of all his accomplishments, McAuliffe was most proud of his role in eliminating racial segregation in the U.S. Army.

## Retirement

McAuliffe was transferred to Europe and placed in command of the 7th Armored Division in 1953, following a short stint as deputy chief for Army operations. He received a further promotion to four-star general in 1955, and was named commander in chief of the U.S. Army in Europe later that same year. McAuliffe retired from the Army in 1956.

As a civilian, McAuliffe drew on his military background in chemical warfare, taking a position on the board of directors of the American Cyanamid Company, a major manufacturer of chemicals. He also continued to apply his knowledge and skills to public service, acting as chairman of the New York State Civil Defense Commission from 1959 until 1963, at which time he retired to Chevy Chase, Maryland. McAuliffe spent his last years playing golf and bridge at the Army-Navy club. He died on August 11, 1975 in Washington, DC.

## Further Reading

*Dictionary of American Biography,* edited by Kenneth T. Jackson, Charles Scribner's Sons, 1994.

*Illustrated World War II Encyclopedia,* edited by Brigadier Peter Young, H. S. Stuttman Inc., 1978.

Koskimaki, George E., *D-Day with the Screaming Eagles,* House of Print, 1970.

Marshall, S. L. A. *Night Drop,* Little, Brown and Company, 1951.

McGregor, Morris J., Jr., *Integration of the Armed Forces 1940-1965,* Center of Military History, United States Army, 1981.

Toland, John, *Battle: The Story of the Bulge,* Signet, 1959.

*Webster's American Biographies,* edited by Charles Van Doren, G. & C. Merriam Company, 1974.

Weigley, Russell F., *Eisenhower's Lieutenants,* Indiana University Press, 1981. □

# Elijah McCoy

**Elijah McCoy (1843?-1929) made important contributions to the design of railroad locomotives after the Civil War. He kept pace with the progress of locomotive design, devising new lubricating systems that served the steam engines of the early twentieth century. These were demanding indeed, for they operated at high temperatures and pressures.**

The date of McCoy's birth is not known; various sources give it as March 27, 1843; May 2, 1843; and May 2, 1844. His parents, George McCoy and the former Mildred Goins, were fugitive slaves who had escaped to Canada from Kentucky. At the time, Canada was part of the British Empire, which had abolished slavery in 1833. When the Canadian leader, Louis Riel, launched a rebellion in 1837, the British government used troops to defeat the rebels. George McCoy enlisted with the British force. In return for his loyal service, he received 160 acres of farmland near Colchester, Ontario. Here, he raised a family of 12 children.

His father's ties to Britain proved useful as young McCoy pursued his education. As a boy, he was fascinated with tools and machines. At the age of 16, he traveled to Edinburgh, Scotland, to serve an apprenticeship in mechanical engineering. In Edinburgh, McCoy won the credentials of a master mechanic and engineer. Following the Civil War, the McCoys returned to the United States and settled near Ypsilanti, Michigan, outside of Detroit. Young Elijah sought work as an engineer, but met with defeat due to racial prejudice. Nevertheless, he obtained a job as a fireman and oiler on the Michigan Central Railroad in 1870. This was a responsible position, for service as a fireman was a customary prelude to promotion to the post of locomotive driver. Work as a fireman was a far cry from engineering, and it proved to be a physically demanding job. As a fireman, McCoy had to shovel coal into the firebox of his locomotive, at the rate of two tons per hour. He also had to walk around the locomotive and lubricate its moving parts using an oilcan during frequent stops, while it took on water.

## Pioneer in Automatic Lubrication

Locomotives were heavy, and subjected their moving parts to considerable wear. Lubrication was essential for these parts—many of which were applied to railroad axles. These axles carried the full weight of locomotives and railroad cars, and were particularly subject to wear. But engineers had arranged for them to rotate within oil-filled chambers. The rotation of the axle carried oil into its bearing, and the oiled bearing allowed the axle to turn freely while reducing wear to a minimum. However, the direct use of oil-filled chambers did not apply to a locomotive's steam engine, which provided its power. Many parts of this engine operated under the pressure of steam, which acted to push oil away from the moving parts. This made it necessary to stop the engine when oiling it. McCoy saw that he could

keep the engine running by using steam pressure to pump the oil where it was needed.

Working in a home-built machine shop in Ypsilanti, McCoy devised an invention that became known as the lubricating cup. It relied on a piston set within an oil-filled container. Steam pressure pushed on the piston and thereby drove the oil into channels that carried it to the engine's operating parts. McCoy received a United States patent for this device on June 23, 1872. He took his invention to officials of the Michigan Central Railroad and received their support. Installed on operating locomotives, it provided lubrication that was more regular and even than could be achieved by the old method of using an oilcan during intermittent stops. This proved to be quite useful, for locomotives lasted longer and needed less maintenance. McCoy's lubricating cup proved adaptable to other types of steam engines, which were used in factories and at sea. Versions of this cup became standard components on many types of heavy machinery, entering service on railways of the West, on Great Lakes steamships, and even on transatlantic liners.

### New Lubricators Served Powerful Engines

McCoy left the Michigan Central in 1882 and moved to Detroit, where he devoted a great deal of time to his inventions. He also worked as an industrial consultant, assisting the Detroit Lubricator Company and other firms. The technical demands of railroads soon provided him with further challenges.

With the increase of industry and passenger travel, railroad companies needed larger locomotives. James J. Hill, builder of the Great Northern Railroad, introduced monsters that were up to four times larger than their predecessors, along with large-capacity freight cars. Such locomotives burned coal in large amounts, and demanded high horsepower, while using less coal. The solution lay in the use of superheated steam, with high temperature and pressure. Superheating boosted the engines' efficiency, allowing a locomotive to get more miles per ton of coal. It also brought new problems in lubrication.

The author Robert C. Hayden, in his book *Eight Black American Inventors*, quoted an article in the *Engineer's Journal*: "There is no denying the fact that our present experience in lubricating the cylinders of engines using superheated steam is anything but satisfactory . . . If the oil feed was made regular so the steam would distribute it over the bearing surface of cylinder while the engine was working, these bearing surfaces would be better protected than is now otherwise possible."

Rather than use oil alone as a lubricant, designers preferred to mix the oil with powdered graphite, a form of carbon. Powdered graphite is soft and greasy, and easily withstands high temperatures. However, because it is a powder rather than a liquid, it can clog an engine. In April 1915, McCoy received a patent for what he called a "Locomotive Lubricator." Within his patent application, he claimed that this invention would permit the use of graphite "without danger of clogging."

Hayden cites a letter from a railroad superintendent: "We have found the McCoy Graphite Lubricator to be of considerable assistance in lubrication of locomotives equipped with superheaters. . . . There is a decided advantage in better lubrication and reduction of wear in valves and piston rings, and as a well lubricated engine is more economical in the use of fuel, there is unquestionably a saving in fuel."

### The Real McCoy

In reviewing the life of this inventor, writers and essayists often note that railroad purchasing agents commonly insisted on buying "the real McCoy." Other inventors were offering lubricators that competed with those of McCoy, but these agents would accept no substitutes. Many of these authors assert that the phrase "real McCoy" passed out of the specialized world of railroad engineering and entered general usage, where it came to mean "the genuine article."

While McCoy's inventions made millions of dollars, little of this money reached his pockets. Lacking the capital with which to build his lubricators in large numbers, he sold many of his patent rights to well-heeled investors. In return, he was given only the modest sums that allowed him to continue his work. McCoy received at least 72 patents during his lifetime, most of which dealt with lubricating devices, but retained ownership of only a few of them.

In 1868, McCoy married Ann Elizabeth Stewart; she died in 1872, at the age of 25. A year later, he married Mary Eleanora Delaney. This marriage lasted half a century, but did not produce children.

In 1920, at the age of 77, McCoy joined with investors and founded the Elijah McCoy Manufacturing Company in Detroit, serving as vice-president. The firm manufactured and sold his graphite lubricators, including an advanced version that also lubricated a railroad train's air brakes. Soon afterward, he and his wife, Mary, were involved in a traffic accident. Mary received injuries from which she never fully recovered, and which hastened her death. She died in 1923.

For McCoy, the end now approached as well. His health deteriorated and, in 1928, he entered an infirmary. Suffering from hypertension and senile dementia, McCoy died on October 10, 1929 in Eloise, Michigan.

McCoy was remembered in Detroit long after his death. In 1975, the city celebrated Elijah McCoy Day, as officials placed a historic marker at the site of his home. The city also named a street for him. These posthumous honors were modest, but they came a century after his invention of the lubricating cup, and demonstrated his enduring legacy.

## Further Reading

Haber, Louis. *Black Pioneers of Science and Invention*. Harcourt Brace Jovanovich, 1970.
Haskens, Jim. *Outward Dreams*. Walker, 1991.
Hayden, Robert C. *Eight Black American Inventors*. Addison-Wesley, 1972.
Klein, Aaron E. *The Hidden Contributors*. Doubleday, 1971.
Towle, Wendy. *The Real McCoy*. Scholastic, 1993. □

# Scott McNealy

**Scott McNealy (born 1954), co-founder, president, and CEO of Sun Microsystems, is an outspoken Silicon Valley maverick. He made his fortune by challenging the computer industry dominance of Bill Gates and Microsoft and championing a network-based computer system based on Sun's Java software, a universal programming language.**

McNealy is an unlikely Silicon Valley visionary. He is no technocrat. He didn't drop out of college to found Sun Microsystems. In fact, his background is in Midwestern manufacturing, where his father worked as a top executive in Detroit's automotive industry. Since a twist of fate brought him to California and the helm of Sun, McNealy has worked tirelessly to build the company into one of the world's leading corporations, based on the idea of network computing and a universal operating language. For more than a decade, he nearly single-handedly led the fight against Microsoft and Bill Gates and helped persuade the Justice Department to file historic antitrust charges against the software giant.

## Rustbelt Roots

McNealy is a product of the Rustbelt, but with an Ivy League twist. Born in Columbus, Indiana, on November 13, 1954, he was raised in the upper-class suburb of Bloomfield Hills, Michigan. McNealy attended Cranbrook Kingswood School, a prep school north of Detroit. A model student and athlete, McNealy captained the school's championship tennis team and excelled on the golf and hockey teams.

McNealy's early business education came at the hands of his father, William McNealy, a vice-chairman at American Motors Corporation. As a youngster, McNealy spent evenings at home discussing company strategy with his father. On weekends, while his dad caught up on paperwork, McNealy would walk around the factory floor. He picked up more lessons in corporate wisdom on the golf course, joining golf outings with famous automotive executives such as Lee Iacocca. Early on, McNealy recognized that AMCs troubles stemmed from an insufficient market share. The car manufacturer did not have the financial, marketing, or technological firepower to shape the direction of the industry.

Following in his father's footsteps, McNealy attended Harvard University and majored in economics, but he now jokes that he minored in beer and golf. In fact, he captained the Harvard golf team and missed the cut for the 1976 NCAA championship by one stroke. After a less than stellar undergraduate career, McNealy tried to get into business school, but was turned down by Harvard and declined twice by Stanford. Always deeply interested in manufacturing, he took a job as a foreman at the Rockwell International Corporation plant in Ashtabula, Ohio in 1976. The company, which built truck hoods, was preparing for an impending strike. The young manager worked 14-hour days for two months, landing in the hospital for six weeks with a case of hepatitis.

## Go West Young Man

McNealy's work record helped him get accepted at Stanford, although his study habits didn't really improve. Classmates remembered him preferring golf to attending classes. He even focused on manufacturing courses at a time when they were out of fashion. After graduating, his first job was with FMC Corporation, a defense contractor that made tanks. Later, he joined minicomputer maker Onyx Systems. McNealy had no desire to become a high-powered CEO after watching his parents' marriage dissolve as a result of the long hours that his father had to work. Instead, McNealy dreamed of running a small family machine shop that he could turn over to his children and take an early retirement.

In 1982, McNealy's life would change forever. He received a call from a former Stanford classmate, Vinod Khosla, who asked him to join with Bill Joy and Andreas Bechtolsheim to form a computer company called Sun (for Stanford University Network, where Bechtolsheim built the first workstation). The company focused on building high-performance computers based on readily available, inexpensive components and the UNIX operating system. McNealy and Sun leaders based their vision on the idea that computers reached their full potential only by working together in networks. Soon, Sun would become the largest company to build computers with its own design, own Sparc chip, and own operating system, called Solaris.

McNealy's manufacturing expertise helped the young company keep up with demand as sales jumped from $9 million in 1983 to $39 million in 1984. Sun grew so quickly, in fact, that expansion outpaced cash supply. McNealy found a benefactor in J. Philip Samper, then executive vice president at Eastman Kodak. On Samper's recommendation, Kodak pledged $20 million to Sun. In turn, they required that McNealy take over as president. In 1984, when Khosla left the company after a dispute with the board of directors, McNealy was named president. Considered too young for the job, the directors looked for a replacement, but McNealy's early success leading Sun secured his position as CEO.

Typical of many Silicon Valley success stories, Sun developed an irreverent corporate culture based on McNealy's own motto: "Kick butt and have fun." An admitted ice hockey junky, McNealy played on several teams near the Sun headquarters in Palo Alto, California. Dick Boyce, a Stanford classmate, told *Business Week* writer Robert D. Hof that McNealy "would be happy to be described as Joe Six-Pack working hard to get the job done."

Although Sun has a casual work environment and is noted for its laid back atmosphere, McNealy is an intense competitor. He explained to *Industry Week*'s Charles R. Day Jr., "There is nothing casual about Sun. We are intense, disciplined, driven, focused, at times even maniacal. Our culture is doing things that matter. And I'm an absolute believer in what we're doing. As the CEO you must be, or

you ought to be shot for not changing the company into what it ought to be doing."

## The Network is the Computer

Sun went public in 1986 and two years later had annual sales of $1 billion. However, like many successful young companies, Sun grew too fast. Recognizing the problems, McNealy revamped Sun's manufacturing systems and pared its product line. Attention was focused on workstations built around the high-powered processor, the Sparc chip. This reorganization helped Sun reach sales of $3 billion by 1992.

In the early 1990s, however, Sun's vision of the industry based on the UNIX system and networked computers lagged behind the Microsoft and Intel (Wintel) alliance. Microsoft already equipped more than ten million personal computers. McNealy realized his primary adversary was Bill Gates and Microsoft when Gates began touting Windows NT, a system that would match UNIX. He began a full-scale assault on Microsoft. McNealy unleashed numerous one-liners directed at Gates and the public perception of Microsoft's dominance. He ridiculed his competitors products as overly complex and unreliable. Sun's new slogan, "The network is the computer," was an effort to diminish the importance of the PC and establish the network-based system Sun favored.

McNealy didn't consider himself to be a visionary or intellectual. He claimed that Sun's strategies were borrowed from other industries. "Our whole concept of the computer as a network device," he told *Fortune*'s Brent Schlender, "is grounded in a business model that was stolen from every other large utility on the planet. You don't have a power-generating plant in your home; you're connected to a power grid."

McNealy's years of criticizing Bill Gates raised Sun's visibility and, in some sense, played on corporate America's fear of its reliance on Microsoft products. Some of these fears led to the Justice Department filing antitrust charges against Microsoft. McNealy claimed that opening competition in the software industry would lead to new innovations and choices for the consumer.

## Java Propels the Internet

The Internet has revolutionized the way the world conducts business. McNealy viewed the Internet as the third wave of computing, after the mainframe era and personal computer. Since its introduction in May 1995, Sun has been able to generate excitement over Java, a software language that can run on any hardware or operating system, thus bypassing Microsoft's Windows, which runs 90 percent of the world's personal computers. Sun formed an early alliance with Netscape. When Internet users downloaded Netscape Navigator, they were downloading Java as well.

The idea of Java was so original that few in the computer industry knew how to handle the concept. Soon, companies ranging from IBM to Netscape, and even rival Microsoft, licensed Java. Gates's browser war with Netscape forced him to match the Java feature Netscape used. Industry analyst, Jim Moore, explained to *Fortune* magazine, "Sun has suddenly become a thought leader for the whole industry."

Java allowed computer programmers to write a program once and run it without modification on any kind of computer. McNealy, understating the Java strategy, confessed to *Fortune*'s Schlender, "The concept that every computer should be able to speak and understand one universal language that nobody owned was stolen from cavemen who wrote on walls."

McNealy was quick to point out that the hottest Internet companies in the world, Amazon.com, eBay, and AOL, all ran on the network server and Java ideology that Sun had championed since its earliest days. Sun, however, is not willing to rest on its laurels. McNealy explained the company's competitiveness to *VAR Business* writer Lawrence Aragon, "We run scared, we run nervous, we run anxious, we run paranoid, we run at full speed. But we run for the long term. We don't have a strategy of the day. We have been giving our customers ongoing migration, ongoing enhancements and performance without blowing up their installed base."

Sun, with the Java programming language, has quickly grown into a formidable threat to Microsoft's operating system dominance. Sun has fortified itself for a long battle by forming alliances and partnerships with some of the world's strongest companies, such as IBM, AOL, Royal Philips Electronics, and Intel. Sun has also acquired more than a dozen companies since 1996, using the acquisitions to move into other technologies and consumer products.

## "Work Hard and Have Fun"

McNealy, clean cut with a toothy smile, is a self-professed workaholic. He routinely works 80-hour weeks and sets a frenetic pace, which insiders say often leads to "Sunburn." His work ethic is summed up by a favorite one-liner "have lunch or be lunch." McNealy describes the company as "very nervous inside" and he uses that anxiety to constantly reassess where Sun is headed. "The two pillars that we live on are open interfaces and the network computing model," McNealy explained to *Computer Reseller News,* "The rest of the time, its work hard and have fun."

McNealy's hard-charging leadership has paid off for Sun. The company's 1997 revenues reached almost $9 billion, while its net income jumped 60 percent over the previous year to $762 million. His personal value is estimated to reach $500 million.

## Further Reading

Cringely, Robert X., *Accidental Empires: How the Boys of Silicon Valley Make their Millions, Battle Foreign Competition, and Still Can't Get a Date,* HarperBusiness, 1992.
Wallace, James, *Overdrive: Bill Gates and the Race to Control Cyberspace,* John Wiley & Sons, 1997.
*Business Week,* July 24, 1989, p. 70; January 22, 1996, p. 66.
*Computer Reseller News,* November 17, 1997, p. 110.
*Fortune,* October 13, 1997, p. 70, 82; February 15, 1999, p. 84.
*Industry Week,* December 5, 1994, p. 12.
*New Republic,* May 9, 1994, p. 6.
*Orange County Register,* January 31, 1996.
*PC Week,* May 9, 1994, p. 1.
*USA Today,* January 19, 1988; April 1, 1996.
*VAR Business,* February 1, 1999, p. 47.
*Washington Post,* February 8, 1998.
"Sun Corporate Information," http://www.sun.com (March 1, 1999). □

# Chico Mendes

**Martyred activist Chico Mendes (1944–1988) devoted much of his life to bring literacy to the natives of the Amazon jungle, and was the guiding force behind the movement to organize the laborers of the rubber plantations in the South American rainforest. He alerted the world to the danger of ongoing deforestation in the Amazon jungle.**

Francisco "Chico" Mendes was a native of the Amazon rubber plantations and a rubber tapper by trade. As an adolescent he developed a keen awareness of the injustice imposed on his family and his community by wealthy rubber barons who owned the rainforest lands. Despite a stringent ban against education for the rubber workers, Mendes learned to read and spent much of his life in sharing that knowledge with other members of his community. He organized the plantation workers into labor unions, and brought their cause to the attention of the entire world when cattle ranchers—at the invitation of the Amazonian government—began a systematic deforestation of the precious rainforest lands that contribute a critical function in stabilizing the world climate.

## Tapped the Rubber Trees

Chico Mendes was born Francisco Alves Mendes on December 15, 1944, in the Brazilian village of Porto Rico. Mendes was the eldest of 17 siblings of whom only six survived into adulthood. The Mendes family lived in the state of Acre in Amazonia, the forest surrounding the Amazon River. They earned their living as rubber tappers, workers who extract latex from rubber trees and cure the substance for sale in the production of rubber. The Mendes family lived in extreme poverty; both parents and children worked to contribute to the support of the family. His father suffered from clubbed feet, a painful ailment that caused serious discomfort. By the age of eight Chico Mendes accompanied his father into the forest every day to assist in the latex tapping. The pair regularly left home before sunrise. During a typical day they walked 8 to 11 miles of trail. Along the path they made incisions in the bark of the rubber trees and attached cups to the trunks to collect the oozing latex (rubber sap). Deep in the forest the pair hunted tapir, peccary, armadillo, rat porcupine, and monkey to feed the family. In the afternoon they retraced their steps and collected the latex. In the rainforest there were no schools, and Mendes harvested latex full time by the time he was eleven years old. After the harvest they collected nuts to subsidize their income, and between the nut and rubber harvests they grew subsistence crops. Mendes was 17 when his mother

died in childbirth. In order to survive, his father tended the family crops, while Mendes cared for the children and harvested rubber six days a week.

Life in the rainforest was both difficult and dangerous. Health services were non-existent. Although the natives treated themselves with healing plants from the forest, the tappers habitually contracted lung diseases from the irritating fumes of the fires used to cure the latex. The wildlife and the terrain were equally treacherous—deadly plants and animals lurked in the foliage. The rubber barons who owned the plantations feared an uprising over the inhumane working conditions and prohibited the workers from learning to read, in order to perpetuate ignorance. Mendes's father was among the few tappers who could read, and he passed the knowledge on to his son. When Mendes was 12 years old he made the acquaintance of an escaped political prisoner, a communist revolutionary named Euclides Fernandes Tavora. Mendes frequented Tavora's residence for five years and learned about the teachings of Marx and Lenin, and the political history of Brazil. Before Tavora left the jungle he gave Mendes a radio, so that the boy could listen to Radio Moscow, and advised Mendes that the tappers should organize a labor union.

### Turned Activist

Initially, Mendes attempted to bring about change through a direct appeal. He sent a series of letters to the president of Brazil, describing the subhuman conditions imposed upon the rubber tappers. He denounced the bosses, who robbed the workers and charged inflated prices for goods—a practice that kept the workers in debt. Mendes complained that tappers were forbidden from attending school. Although his letters were largely ignored, Mendes was able to bring an end to the rent assessments paid by tappers for the use of forest trails among the rubber trees.

The 1970s and late 1980s were characterized by sporadic union violence in the regions of the rainforest, a situation that developed as the popularity of synthetic rubber surged and world demand for latex decreased. Consequently, the latex industry failed and the economy declined. In an effort to invigorate the economy the regional government offered incentives to cattle ranchers, to take over the rainforest lands previously allocated to the cultivation of rubber trees. Cattle ranchers responded and purchased the rainforest land from the rubber barons. The ranchers cleared the terrain for grazing. They cut and burned rainforest land and displaced rubber workers and other natives. Local priests responded by attempting to organize the displaced natives. They created "base communities" to provide education and political indoctrination. Mendes became involved in an effort to educate adults at a school near Xapuri in 1971. In his free time he harvested rubber for other tappers to earn extra money.

By the mid-1970s, the concepts of unionism began to take hold and an organized movement pervaded the area. Mendes abandoned his job as a teacher and moved to the city of Xapuri, where he worked as a clerk and devoted more of his time to organizing the unions. He also ran for and won a seat on the city council. In 1978, the unions of several towns in the state of Acre successfully formed an alliance and created an association of unions. In time the association's enrollment grew to 30,000 members.

As the unions gained strength, the workers sought to prevent the destruction of the rainforest. To accomplish this they embraced a tactic called *empate,* or blockade. *Empate* was a system devised by martyred union organizer Wilson Pinheiro, to prevent the destruction of the trees. It involved large bands of tappers who traveled to the forest areas that were scheduled for imminent destruction. They occupied the forest, wrecked the shacks of the cutting crews, and forced the crews out of the area. The ranchers retaliated and hired police to strong-arm the tappers. In one of his last interviews Mendes said: "We organized 45 *empates.* About 400 of us were arrested and about 40 tortured, and a few were killed, but we succeeded in keeping more than three million hectares of the forest from being destroyed. Thirty of our blockades failed and 15 worked, but it was worth it." Although few were killed during the *empates,* the ranchers singled out activist priests, lawyers, union presidents, and certain squatters, who were murdered by hired gunmen. In 1980, Mendes' lost his good friend and fellow union organizer, *empate* originator Wilson Pinheiro, who was slain in the turmoil. Mendes cautioned the protesters to remain nonviolent, but some tappers sought vengeance and murdered a rancher in retaliation for the death of Pinheiro. In response, the police rounded up and tortured over 100 tappers.

## Activist Horizons Expanded

In 1981, Mendes became president of the rural workers' union in Xapuri. He persuaded the tappers to form cooperative businesses, to sell the latex direct and eliminate the bosses and other middlemen who kept most of the profit. This system proved to be quite successful. Mendes established the Nazare School on a rubber plantation to train teachers who, in turn, started other schools. In 1984, at the national rural workers' organization convention in Brasilia, Mendes proposed a land system that would create rural land modules for the tappers, but the proposals were rejected. In 1985, Mendes and a colleague, Maria Allegretti, spent five months organizing a national meeting of the Rubber Tappers of Amazonia, which included seminars, cultural events, and strategy meetings. One hundred and twenty rubber tappers attended the affair in Brasilia, many of whom had never been more than a few miles from their homes. Mendes, Allegretti, and the tappers embraced a new approach that focused world attention on their plight. Mendes influenced the rubber workers to position themselves as defenders of the rainforest: to forego the issue of declining rubber production—to politicize instead for the preservation of the rainforest environment; and to stress to the world the value of other forest products including oils, nuts, and cocoa. At the Brasilia meeting the tappers established a national council and called for a system of land reform based on Mendes's earlier proposal of rural land modules. The system created extractive reserves, and allocated areas of the rainforest for rubber and nut harvesting.

## An Untimely Death

Mendes left Brasilia and returned to Acre to publicize the system of extractive reserves and to solicit support for the ecology measures discussed at the convention. He continued his work, built more schools, and supported the *empate* offensives until December 22, 1988, when he stepped from his house in the Brazilian town of Xapuri and into the path of a bullet.

The murder of Chico Mendes drew international attention, and over 1,000 mourners attended his funeral. The Brazilian government was compelled by the worldwide publicity to seek out the killer. After two years of stalling, the gunman, Darci Alves da Silva, went to trial. He was convicted of the murder along with his father, Darly, who was convicted for his role in plotting the murder.

Mendes died one week after his 44th birthday, leaving a wife and children. His first marriage to Maria Eunice Feitosa in 1969, ended in divorce. The couple had two daughters of whom only Angela, the eldest, survived past infancy. This marriage lasted a brief two years because his devotion to the cause of the tappers kept Mendes away from his family. In the 1980s, Mendes married a woman named Ilzamar, whom he had taught as a young girl on one of the rubber plantations. They had two children: Elenira, and Sandino.

## International Impact

Before his death, in 1987, Mendes traveled to the United States, where he spoke in Miami and in Washington, D.C. He explained that cattle ranchers systematically destroyed the rainforest and created hardship for the natives and rubber tappers. Mendes won two awards in 1987 for his efforts to preserve the environment: the Global 500 Award and Protection of the Environment Medal. His untimely death served to focus greater attention on the plight of the rainforest and, in 1989, a contingency of U.S. senators flew to Acre to discuss the issue. Brazil passed laws to protect the rainforest and approved a plan to replant 2.5 million acres of forest that had been destroyed. The government further agreed to create extractive reserves in the Amazon region. The first was named the Chico Mendes Extractive Reserve, and served as a home and refuge to 3,000 families of tappers and farmers.

## Further Reading

Burch, Joann J., *Chico Mendes, Defender of the Rainforest,* The Millbrook Press, 1994.

DeStefano, Susan, *Chico Mendes: Fight for the Forest,* Twenty-First Century, 1991.

Revkin, Andrew, *The Burning Season: The Murder of Chico Mendes and the Fight for the Amazon Rainforest,* Houghton Mifflin, 1990.

Shoumatoff, Alex, *The World is Burning: Murder in the Rainforest,* Avon Books, 1991.

*Audubon,* Jan-Feb 1992.

*Humanist,* March-April 1996. □

# James Michener

**James Michener (1907–1997) is best known for his many epic historical novels, which have sold an estimated 75 million copies worldwide. He was also a noted philanthropist, having contributed more than $100 million to universities, libraries, museums, and other charitable causes.**

James Michener could be said to represent the classic "rags-to-riches" story. He was born in Doylestown, Pennsylvania, on February 3, 1907, and abadoned by his parents. Mabel Michener, a poor widow, took him in. His foster mother made a scant living by taking in laundry and sewing. As Michener told Steve Wartenberg of the *Intelligencer-Record,* "We never had a sled, a baseball glove, or a bicycle." In the same article his boyhood friend Lester Trauch noted that "he was the poorest boy in school, but the brightest boy. He was the only boy who wore sneakers; the rest wore shoes. They were so worn his toes stuck out of the holes at the end, and the laces were so knotted you wondered how he ever got them on in the morning." At times, Michener was even sent to the local poorhouse to live temporarily while his foster mother struggled to make ends meet.

In 1921, Michener began what would become a lifelong inclination toward travel when he went on a hitchhiking tour that took him through 45 states. That fall he entered Doylestown High School, where his chief interest

book and began to spend his nights tapping it out with two fingers on an old typewriter, using the backs of letters from home, old envelopes, and official Navy correspondence. Ultimately the recording of his experiences became his first well-known book, *Tales of the South Pacific*, published in 1947. "I was hoping," Michener told Steve Wartenberg of the *Intelligencer-Record*, "I could write a series of stories that would tell men who were drafted into the military in those difficult years what life was like. I gambled that when they returned home and demobilized, they would remember their experiences as the most vital of their lives, and they would want to read about it, and my book would be there." Michener's gamble paid off—*Tales of the South Pacific* won a Pulitzer Prize in 1948 and was adapted by Rogers and Hammerstein into the popular musical comedy, *South Pacific* in 1949.

## The Epic Novels

In 1948, Michener and his first wife were divorced and he married Vange Nord, an aspiring writer. The couple bought some property and built a new house, and Michener proceeded to publish several more books, including *The Fires of Spring* (1949), *Return to Paradise* (1951), *The Bridges at Toko-Ri* (1953), and *Sayonara: The Floating World* (1954). In addition, Michener began working as a roving editor for *Readers Guide*, an endeavor he continued until 1970. In 1955, he and his second wife divorced and Michener married Mari Yoriko Sabusawa. Although they had no children of their own, throughout their 39-year marriage Michener and his third wife housed and cared for many underprivileged children.

With the publication of his first historical novel, *Hawaii*, in 1959, Michener's writing career took on greater challenges. Like many such novels that were to follow, *Hawaii* was based on extensive research into the social, cultural, economic, and political history of a particular region and spanned generations of a family. Others of this kind included *Caravans*, about a romantic American girl in Afghanistan (1963); *Centennial*, which presented the history of Colorado from prehistory through the twentieth century (1974); *Chesapeake*, a depiction of 400 years of history on Maryland's eastern shore (1978); and *The Covenant*, a full history of South Africa (1980). *Poland* (1983), *Texas* (1985), *Alaska* (1988), and *Caribbean* (1989) were others among the more than 40 books Michener published. *Space*, published in 1982, dealt with NASA and space exploration and was one of Michener's most popular books. His novels sold an estimated 75 million copies worldwide. Several were made into motion pictures, including *Tales of the South Pacific*, *Hawaii*, *Texas*, and *Space*.

Despite the popularity of his novels, Michener received mixed critical reviews. Some called him mediocre and long-winded, relying too much on trivial historical detail and not enough on imaginative language and subtlety. Others praised his ability to mold the vast amount of research into a story that taught about cultural diversity. Said Nelson De-Mille in *People Weekly*, "He's the grand old man of historical fiction" who "didn't play with the facts. He got them across in such a way that you actually learned something."

was sports, especially basketball. Upon graduation in 1925, he won a scholarship to Swarthmore College. He graduated from college *summa cum laude* in 1929 with a bachelor's degree in English and history. His first job was as an English teacher at Hill School in Pottstown, Pennsylvania, where he worked from 1929 to 1931. He then received a Lippincott Travel Fellowship and, for the next two years, traveled in Europe. His studied in Scotland, England, and Italy, worked on a Mediterranean cargo ship, and toured Spain with a troupe of bullfighters. Upon returning to the United States in 1933, Michener accepted a teaching position at George School in Doylestown. While there he met Patti Koon; they were married in 1935. The following year, Michener was offered an associate professorship at the Colorado State College of Education in Greeley, where he taught until 1939. He also obtained his master's degree in English in 1937. His next move was to Harvard University's School of Education, where he was a visiting professor from 1939 to 1940. In 1940, he began a nine-year stint as a social studies editor at Macmillan.

## Began a Prolific Writing Career

In 1943, an event occurred that would drastically change Michener's life, although perhaps not in the way he expected. He had enlisted as an apprentice seaman in the United States Naval Reserve when World War II broke out and, in 1943, was called to active duty. He was sent to the South Pacific in 1944, where he traveled from island to island, learning about local culture and history and hearing stories from the residents. Michener developed an idea for a

## Other Writings

Although Michener was best known for his novels, they were not his only products. His earliest work, which consisted of 15 articles on teaching social studies published between the years 1936 and 1942, provided examples of the way in which Michener used fiction as a teaching device. In his book *Return to Paradise* (1951), Michener alternated essays about Asia with stories designed to exemplify the essays. *The Novel* (1991), though fiction, taught about art and the craft of writing. Michener also wrote books about Japanese art: *Japanese Prints (From the Early Masters to the Modern,* 1959, and *Modern Japanese Prints,* 1962), the electoral college (*Presidential Lottery: The Reckless Gamble in Our Electoral System,* 1969), sports (*Sports in America,* 1976), and the 1970 shooting at Kent State (*Kent State: What Happened and Why,* 1971). He published his memoirs, titled appropriately *The World is My Home,* in 1992. In 1994, he wrote *Recessional,* about retirement life in Florida and gave readers insight into Michener's own thoughts and feelings at that point in his life.

## Political Activities

Michener first became active in politics when he was chairman of the Bucks County, Pennsylvania, campaign for John F. Kennedy in the 1960 presidential election. In 1962, he lost his run for Congress as a Democrat. He served as secretary of the Pennsylvania Constitutional Convention in 1967-1968, during which a new state constitution was written. Michener also served as a correspondent for President Richard Nixon during his 1972 trips to the Soviet Union and China.

## A Generous Philanthropist

Michener is known for his generous contributions to various organizations, estimated to be at least $100 million. Examples include $7.2 million to his alma mater, Swathmore College; $64.2 million to the University of Texas at Austin; and $9.5 million to the James A. Michener Art Museum in Doylestown, Pennsylvania. In addition, Michener designated the royalties from many of his books to various charitable organizations. In 1997, *Fortune* magazine listed Michener as the previous year's twenty-first most generous philanthropist. His response was characteristically humble. He said in the *Intelligencer-Record,* "I had been educated with free scholarships. I went to nine different universities, always at public expense, and when you have that experience, you are almost obligated to give it back. It's as simple as that." He phrased his position in another way in the Austin *American-Statesman* in 1996: "The decent thing to do," Michener stated, "is to get rid of some of this money."

## A Humble Recipient

Throughout his long career, Michener received numerous awards. Some of the most noteworthy include the Einstein Award from Einstein Medical College in 1967, the Medal of Freedom (the highest honor that can be bestowed on a civilian) from President Gerald Ford in 1977, the Pennsylvania Society Gold Medal in 1978, the Franklin Award

and Spanish Institute Gold Medal in 1980, and an award for Outstanding Philanthropist by the National Society of Fund Raising Executives in 1996. He has also received honorary degrees from more than 30 universities and has had libraries and museums named after him, even though Bruce Katsiff, director of the James A. Michener Art Museum, told the *Intelligencer-Recorder,* "He never wanted anything to be named after him." Another honor came in the form of a television series on PBS called *The World of James A. Michener,* a program that explored some of the regions in which his novels were set.

## The Last Years

In the midst of his professional achievements, Michener suffered a severe loss when his wife died of cancer in 1994. By this time Michener himself was in poor health; he had undergone hip surgery, major bypass surgery, and suffered from severe kidney problems which required dialysis treatments three times a week. Despite these ailments, Michener continued to write, publishing *This Noble Land: My Vision for America* in 1996 and *A Century of Sonnets* in 1997. In October 1997, Michener stated in a *Newsweek,* article that he had "accomplished what he wanted to accomplish" and had decided to unhook himself from the lifesaving dialysis machine. He died in his home in Austin, Texas, on October 16, 1997, at the age of 90.

Although Michener's generous donations undoubtedly helped many people, it may be the message he tried to convey in his books for which he should be most appreciated. That message was simple but clear: All people are the same, regardless of where they come from. As Michener stated in the *Intelligencer-Recorder,* "I really believe that every man on this Earth is my brother. He has a soul like mine, the ability to understand friendship, the capacity to create beauty. In all the continents of this world, I have met such men."

## Further Reading

*Cyclopedia of World Authors,* revised third ed., edited by Frank N. Magill, Salem Press, 1997.
*Oxford Companion to American Literature,* sixth ed., edited by James D. Hart, Oxford University Press, 1995.
*Newsweek,* October 27, 1997.
*People Weekly,* November 3, 1997.
*U.S. News & World Report,* October 27, 1997.
Groseclose, Karen and David A., "James A. Michener Chronology," http://www.jamesmichener.com (February 22, 1999).
Wartenberg, Steve, "The Author Became One of History's Great Philanthropists," *Intelligencer-Record,* http://www .jamesmichener.com (February 22, 1999).
Wartenberg, Steve, "James A. Michener," *Intelligencer-Record,* http://www.jamesmichener.com (February 22, 1999). □

# Michael Milken

**Michael Milken (born 1946) was nicknamed the "junk bond king," after he pled guilty to charges that he amassed hundreds of millions of dollars through**

**questionable financial dealings involving high-yield bonds. Milken served prison time then embarked on a life of legitimate business and philanthropic activity.**

Michael Milken acquired a dubious reputation during the 1980s, when he pled guilty to illegal financial dealings that reaped millions of dollars in profits. He emerged from prison as a legitimate entrepreneur. His probation officer, Michalah Bracken, praised Milken and wrote in a probation report that "[Milken] has contributed a significant portion of his earnings to charitable concerns, while retaining a modest lifestyle without obvious trappings of wealth. . . . Among Milken's strengths are his inability to accept defeat, his total commitment, . . . and his vision concerning business and society . . . despite his fall, Milken is an individual still able to contribute to society and to create positive changes in the future."

### Ideal Beginnings

Michael Robert Milken was born in Los Angeles on July 4, 1946 and grew up in Encino, California. Milken's paternal grandparents were Jewish immigrants from Poland. His mother, Ferne Milken, was energetic and ambitious. His father, Bernard Milken, worked for an accounting firm. At tax time, the entire Milken family helped Bernard Milken with his work. Michael Milken, an excellent math student, helped with the tax returns by the age of ten. School held

little challenge for young Milken, who was extremely bright as a child. His teenage ambition was to become a millionaire by the age of 30. Sports came easily to Milken as well, and he excelled at baseball.

Milken attended the University of California at Berkeley during the height of the Free Speech Movement. Initially he majored in mathematics, but changed to business in hopes of finding a challenge. Milken graduated from the University of California with highest honors.

Milken began his financial career at the university, informally as a fraternity member, when he invested money for his fraternity brothers in return for 50 percent of the profits. With no returns on losses to his clients, Milken had virtual assurance of profitability. He was also a student at Berkeley when he developed a theory about low-grade "junk" bonds—He believed that under a revised rating system junk bonds might pose a worthwhile risk. Conventional bond ratings ranked bonds on the basis of past performance—a company's respective ratio of debt to equity was used to determine whether its securities qualified as investment grade. Milken questioned this limited method of rating bonds. He believed that it was inaccurate and that other issues factored heavily into the potential for return on investments: cash flow, business plans, personnel, and corporate vision among others.

In August 1968, Milken married his high school sweetheart, Lori Hackel. The couple moved to Philadelphia, where Milken attended the Wharton School at the University of Pennsylvania. In 1970, he went to work for Drexel Corporation as assistant to the chairman and later became head of bond research. When Drexel merged with Burnham and Company in 1973, Milken headed the non-investment-grade bond-trading department, an operation that earned a remarkable 100 percent return on investment. By 1976, Milken's income was estimated at $5 million a year.

In 1977, Milken returned to his home state of California. He moved his High-Yield Bond Department to Los Angeles and purchased a house in Encino formerly owned by the movie star, Clark Gable. Milken's younger brother, Lowell, also worked at the Los Angeles office. In the early 1980s, Drexel-Burnham sponsored junk-bond-financed leveraged buyouts and hostile takeovers. Milken eventually made over $500 million by manipulating the junk bond and high-yield bond markets. In the mid-1980s, Drexel-Burnham began using a new technique, called the "highly confident" letter, a correspondence designed to convince commercial banks to finance corporate takeovers. The letters of confidence stated that Drexel was "highly confident" that the funds could be raised to finance the deal. During the company's first attempt at this scheme, Milken raised $1.5 billion in 48 hours.

### Shady Dealings with Boesky

In 1982, Drexel-Burnham took on a new client, financier Ivan Boesky. Milken's dealings with Boesky violated the securities laws, and Boesky later accused Milken of insider trading. In 1985, when the Securities and Exchange Commission (SEC) investigated hostile takeovers and "insider" trading (stock trading based on illegally obtained confidential information), the investigation focused on 12 transactions, eight of which involved Drexel-Burnham.

In June 1989, Milken resigned from Drexel to form his own company, International Capital Access Group. This new venture was supposed to help workers and companies in building businesses, but Milken's legal problems with the SEC prevented him from achieving his goal at that time. Milken initially decided to fight the SEC case but eventually pled guilty to six counts of violating federal securities and tax laws in the 98-count indictment. Milken was convicted and sentenced in 1990. At his trial he relied on a defense strategy that stressed his generous and philanthropic interests. He showed "deep remorse" for his crimes, and requested to perform community service rather than to serve prison time. He issued an apology and admitted that he cheated clients and plotted with Boesky to accomplish a corporate raid. Judge Kimba Wood sentenced Milken to probation on one count and two years of prison time for each of the five other counts (ten years total). Milken received a further sentence to perform 1800 hours of community service each year, for three consecutive years following his release from prison.

By March 1991, Milken was in prison at a minimum security work camp in Pleasanton, California. He served 22 months for securities fraud and other crimes and paid $600 million in fines to the government. The Federal Deposit Insurance Corporation (FDIC) sued Milken for $10 billion for crimes against the savings and loan industry. In a prison interview with Jesse Kornbluth, author of *Highly Confident: The Crime and Punishment of Michael Milken,* Milken justified his mistakes on a philosophical level. He explained that, "I believed in giving anonymously, praising others, and only speaking well of others. You can't live in this country today with those beliefs . . . When people find out, your philanthropy becomes tainted, you did it 'for some other purpose' . . . All those years, I thought the marketplace or the customer was the final judge. I was wrong. In the short run, it's the media."

## Back to Business

Milken completed his prison time in 1993 and resumed business dealings. He co-founded a company called Education Entertainment Network, that produces business videos and CD/ROMs. In 1996, he and Larry Ellison founded Knowledge Universe, a company dealing in a diverse variety of goods and services, including day care, executive education, corporate training, and toys. By March 1998, the SEC investigated Milken once again. He admitted to no wrongdoing and, instead, agreed to pay a fine of $47 million in response to SEC accusations that he served as a broker in violation of an SEC order that banned him from such activity. The SEC cited deals involving MCI, Rupert Murdoch's News Corp., and Ron Perelman's New World Entertainment.

## Cancer Threat

At the age of 46 Milken was diagnosed with advanced prostate cancer. He discussed his illness with *Time* journalist Leon Jaroff, "To say that the biopsy results were devasta-

ting would be an understatement. I remember lying in bed with my wife and talking about the 'Book of Job,' wondering how many more challenges were coming my way. I was in a state of depression." Milken took drugs to inhibit his body from producing testosterone and underwent supplementary radiation therapy that put the cancer into remission. The potentially fatal experience inspired Milken to focus on healthy living, and to alter his eating habits. He eliminated meat from his diet and, in 1998 along with co-author Beth Ginsberg, published a cancer-fighting cookbook that stressed low-fat, low-calorie recipes.

Public recollection of Milken's dubious business dealings often overshadowed the potential impact of his generous spirit. Although he tried to improve society through fund-raising and philanthropy, public suspicion lingered and hampered his efforts. In 1995, he donated $5 million to a large Jewish secondary school in Los Angeles. In gratitude the school was to be renamed Milken Community High School of Stephen Wise Temple until parents and students at the institution raised concerns about the name change. They questioned the sound judgment of naming a high school for Michael R. Milken, a federal felon of dubious character. Detractors of Milken speculated that his unethical business practices contributed to rampant corporate takeovers and may have slowed U.S. economic growth and contributed to recession. As Milken himself noted, far less media coverage focused on his legitimate activity, as in 1995 when he established a foundation to encourage the search for a cure for cancer. He pledged $25 million in support to the organization over a five-year period. The program, designated to increase public awareness of cancer and to support research on the disease, provides funds for basic and clinical research, recruits scientists, sponsors scientific meetings, and strives to increase public awareness of cancer.

## Further Reading

Bruck, Connie, *The Predators' Ball: the Junk-Bond Raiders and the Man Who Staked Them,* New York, Simon and Schuster, 1988.

Fischel, Daniel R., *Payback: the Conspiracy to Destroy Michael Milken and his Financial Revolution,* Harperbusiness, 1995.

Kornbluth, Jesse, *Highly Confident: The Crime and Punishment of Michael Milken,* William Morrow, 1992.

Stein, Benjamin, *A License to Steal: the Untold Story of Michael Milken and the Conspiracy to Bilk the Nation,* Simon & Schuster, 1992.

Stewart, James, *Den of Thieves,* Simon & Schuster, 1991.

*Forbes,* November 6, 1995.

*Fortune,* May 1, 1995.

*New York,* July 6, 1998.

*New York Review of Books,* May 26, 1994.

*New York Times,* September 25, 1998.

*Time,* April 1, 1996.

*U.S. News & World Report,* October 25, 1993; March 9, 1998.

*Wall Street Journal,* June 16, 1989; April 25, 1990; February 27, 1998.

"Down Payment On Justice," available at http://www.IntellectualActivist.com (February 23, 1998). □

# Glenn Miller

**With his orchestra, bandleader Glenn Miller (1904–1944) synthesized all the elements of big band jazz and gave a generation of young people the perfect example of smooth, sophisticated dance music. Miller's popularity as a music maker began in 1939 and continued with standards such as "Moonlight Serenade," "In the Mood," and "Tuxedo Junction."**

Miller was one of the most popular musicians of his time. Moreover, he was extremely patriotic and took his personal definition of "duty" very seriously. He used his power to create a successful military band on his terms. Then, just as he finally convinced the military to send his band to places where it could truly boost morale, he disappeared. Rumors circulated almost immediately, but Miller's fate remains a mystery.

## Music in his Blood

Alton Glenn Miller was born on March 1, 1904 in Clarinda, Iowa. His parents, Lewis Elmer and Mattie Lou (Cavender) Miller, raised four children. The family moved quite often during his youth, to places including North Platte, Nebraska and Grant City, Oklahoma. In the latter town, Miller milked cows at the age of thirteen in order to earn enough money to purchase a trombone. According to Geoffrey Butcher in *Next to a Letter from Home,* his mother was the "main strength of the family," and Miller inherited his strong character and love of music from her.

Miller did not, apparently, count on music to be his career, because he finished high school and attended classes at the University of Colorado. During his time in college, though, he continued playing the trombone and worked briefly with Boyd Senter's band in Denver during the mid-1920s. The lure of music proved too strong and Miller left the university after three terms to try his luck on the West Coast.

## A Promising Start

Miller played with a few small bands in Los Angeles until 1927, when he joined Ben Pollack's orchestra as trombonist and arranger. This was a wonderful opportunity for Miller since Pollack's band was well-known and respected. Pollack and his musicians moved to New York, and Miller was able to find so many opportunities to perform that he decided to strike out on his own. In addition to playing the trombone, he did arragements for Victor Young, Freddy Rich, and many others. Miller felt optimistic enough about his burgeoning career by 1928, that he decided to marry Helen Burger, a woman he had met in his student days at the University of Colorado.

For the next ten years Miller gained experience by organizing bands and arranging or playing for them. This included serving as the trombonist and arranger for the Dorsey Brothers, as well as organizing a band for the internationally famous Ray Noble, who had come to the United States from Great Britain. Miller not only organized a band for him, he also arranged and played for it. As Dave Dexter, Jr. related in *Down Beat* magazine, "it was with Ray Noble's band that he first earned national attention."

## The Glenn Miller Orchestra was Formed

Despite his success with Noble, Miller wanted to have a big band of his own, and turned down a lucrative job with the Metro-Goldwyn-Mayer film company to work on this project. In March 1937, Miller's dream became reality when he put together musicians such as Charlie Spivak, Toots Mondello, and Maurice Purtill to form the Glenn Miller Orchestra. Though Purtill soon left to play with Tommy Dorsey, the orchestra carried on for the rest of the year, playing one-night stands in various cities.

In 1938, Miller temporarily suspended the band. Purtill's absence brought about problems with the orchestra's rhythm section that continued to plague its leader. The members were not meshing with one another the way Miller had hoped. He wanted to achieve a full ensemble sound, rather than spotlighting a soloist. Miller decided to reorganize, using only a few of the band's original members. Later that year the Glenn Miller Orchestra added singer, Marion Hutton, to its roster. By 1939, the band was playing to standing-room-only crowds in New York City. They made radio broadcasts and recordings, which did much to spread the Glenn Miller sound across the country. Their most famous recordings included "Moonlight Serenade," "In the Mood," and "Chatanooga Choo Choo."

Miller's orchestra was famous for its well-blended balanced sound. Critics have noted that it was not a vehicle for star soloists, but rather that emphasis was placed on the output of the entire band. Miller was known to discourage musicians who stood out from the rest of the orchestra, and praise those who combined well with their fellows. The Glenn Miller Orchestra was acclaimed by a large variety of fans because it played many different types of big band music—everything from hot jazz to popular ballads. Miller and his band had appeared in two motion pictures for Twentieth Century Fox: *Sun Valley Serenade* and *Orchestra Wives*. They had achieved both fame and wealth.

## Wartime Activities

In 1942, during the Second World War, Miller decided to break up his orchestra in order to accept the rank of captain in the U.S. Army Air Corps. He was past the age when he might expect to be called to service. Nonetheless, Miller felt that he could and should do more to contribute to the war effort than play on the radio, safe from the action. He did not want to use his fame to excuse himself from what he felt was his patriotic duty. On October 7th, Miller enlisted in the army and invited members of his band to join him. They declined.

Upon his induction into the Army Air Forces (AAF), Miller was named director of bands training for the Technical Training Command. He was initially thwarted from implementing some his more creative plans. Several months later, though, after helping to organize almost 50 other bands, he was permitted to form a band of his own.

Miller wanted to incorporate string instruments into his band, in order to transcend the conventional sound of a dance band, which usually only included brass, reed, and rhythm sections. This was a highly innovative concept, and not all of the military bandleaders were open to his idea. In fact, he was reprimanded for an interview he gave to *Time* magazine in their September 6, 1943 issue, in which he criticized army band music of the time. He asserted that it should be up-to-date, so that the soldiers could enjoy it. He was also quoted as specifically criticizing the compositions of Sousa, which were standards for the army bands. Naturally bandleaders who were admirers of Sousa's works took offense. Miller later claimed he had been misquoted, but the magazine declined to print a retraction.

In November 1943, Miller was released from his other band responsibilities, leaving him free to concentrate on the growth and development of his own band. He wanted an ensemble sound, so improvisation by individual musicians was not tolerated. Miller also refused to give furloughs for band members. He felt that they were living the easy life, compared to soldiers out on the front lines. On the other hand, he was always willing to help musically talented servicemen find their way into a band, if he could manage it.

## Overseas Assignment

Miller was anxious to go overseas. After repreated requests, he received permission in June 1944 to take his band to England. They performed in conjunction with the British Broadcasting Corportaion (BBC). Wartime London was the site of air raid warnings, rations on most items, and demolished buildings. Appalled by the conditions and concerned for the safety of his band, Miller made arrangements to move to nearby Bedford. Besides their weekly BBC broadcasts, the band also visited military hospitals and airfields to perform. The applause they received gave Miller and his band immense satisfaction.

Miller again grew restless. His next mission was to have the band sent to France. Once more, he met with opposition from the AAF, not to mention the BBC, which was concerned about their weekly program featuring the band. By November 15, he finally received approval.

## A Mysterious Disappearance

Miller decided to fly to Paris to make arrangements before the arrival of his band. A Colonel Baessell was leaving for France and offered to let Miller ride along. They took off in a Norseman plane on the stormy afternoon of December 15, 1944. The plane, the pilot, and its passengers were never seen again. The plane never landed in France, according to flight records; nor was any wreckage found. The most-widely accepted theory asserted that the plane went down over the English Channel. Two months after his disappearance the Bronze Star was presented to Miller's wife, in recognition of his contribution to the war effort. On June 5, 1945, Glenn Miller Day was declared in the United States as a national tribute.

## Further Reading

*Baker's Biographical Dictionary of Musicians,* eighth edition, Schirmer Books, 1992.
Butcher, Geoffrey, *Next to a Letter from Home: Major Glenn Miller's Wartime Band,* Mainstream Publishing, 1986.
*Contemporary Musicians,* Volume 6, Gale, 1992.
Flower, John, *Moonlight Serenade: A Bio-discography of the Glenn Miller Civilian Band,* Arlington House, 1972.
*Down Beat,* October 1996, pp. 36, 38. □

# Billy Mills

**Billy Mills (born 1938) won what sports writers called the most sensational race ever run in Olympic history. A relative unknown, he came from behind to beat world champion runners in the 1964 Tokyo Olympic Games. Miller later became one of the most noted of motivational speakers.**

Mills was born on June 30, 1938 on the Pine Ridge Reservation in South Dakota. The young Native American ran like the wind over the prairies and hills near his Lakota Sioux Reservation home. His mother, who was one quarter Sioux, died when Mills was seven year old. His father, who was three quarters Sioux, died five years later. Native Americans considered him to be of mixed blood. The white world called him a Native American. Mills

claimed that running helped him to find his identity and to blunt the pain of rejection.

As a youngster, Mills admired the great war chief, Crazy Horse. This spiritual leader of the Lakota challenged him to follow his dreams, reach for goals, and succeed in life. Crazy Horse was a warrior, who led his life through responsibility, humility, the power of giving, and spirituality. Mills tried to live by the knowledge, the wisdom, and the integrity of Crazy Horse. After breaking many high school track records on the reservation, Mills received a scholarship to attend Kansas University. He then became an officer in United States Marine Corps.

As a young Marine lieutenant, Mills had been allowed to train for the 1964 Olympics, held in Tokyo, Japan. He qualified for the team in both the 10,000-meter race and the marathon, but was not expected to win either race. No American had ever won the 10,000-meter race in the Olympics. But Mills had always lived according to the teachings of his father, who had challenged him to live his life as a warrior and assume responsibility for himself.

Australia's Ron Clarke was world famous as a runner in the 10,000-meter event and was the odds-on favorite to win a gold medal. Mohamed Gammoudi, a Tunisian runner, was expected to finish in second place for the silver medal. Any of the other runners were capable of taking a third place bronze medal, according to the experts. It was thought that none of the other runners could win.

Mills, a believer in visualization or ''imagery,'' did not permit a negative thought to enter his head as he worked toward the biggest race of his life. He had for some time before been visualizing a young Native American boy winning the 10,000-meter event at the 1964 Olympics. He created that picture in his mind over and over again. If a thought about not winning came into his mind, he would spend hours erasing the negativity. There could be only one result!

As Mills lined up, there was only one thing on his mind, and that was to win. The gun cracked and the field broke away from the starting grid. As expected, Clarke and Gammoudi fell into first and second place. Mid-pack jostling and shoving allowed the leaders to pull away and Mills dropped back. It appeared he was out of contention and few paid any attention to the sleek Native American who was well back in the field. If they had looked, they would have seen him running as smoothly as the wind, without effort, in perfect control. Near the end of the race, Clarke and Gammoudi remained in the lead. The Japanese crowd cheered politely at what they had known all along was going to happen.

But suddenly the smooth running Mills stepped up his pace. He was closing on the leaders. The crowd fell silent. Mills increased his smooth, even pace, and drew closer to the leaders. With the three runners speeding down the last homestretch, Mills made a spectacular, totally unexpected move. He surged in front of Clarke, who was still running in second place, then Gammoudi, who was leading. At the tape, it was Mills, Gammoudi and Clarke. Mills had beaten Gammoudi by three yards and Clarke by a full second. He had completed the race in a new Olympic record time of 28:24.4, a full 46 seconds better than his best previous time.

The crowd went wild with cheering, for they had seen the impossible happen. They had seen an underdog, an unknown, a runner who wasn't given a chance to win, beat the favorite. They had witnessed one of the greatest upsets in Olympic history. After his great running victory at Tokyo, Mills was honored with the warrior name of 'Makata Taka Hela' by the Lakota Nation. It means ''love your country'' and ''respects the earth.''

Although he was never sent to Vietnam because of his rigorous training schedule in the Marines, Mills was deeply affected by the many combat deaths of men from his unit. He felt that he could not participate in a sport when people were being killed in Vietnam. Mills finished his Marine Corps tour of duty as a captain, then reentered civilian life as an official of the Department of the Interior. He followed this with a very successful career as an insurance salesman. Mills retired from his insurance business in 1994 and became a motivational speaker.

Mills, who was elected to the U.S. Olympic Hall of Fame in 1984, moved with his wife, Pat, and their three daughters, Christy, Lisa, and Billie JoAnne, to Fair Oaks, a Sacramento, California, suburb. He devoted all of his time to speaking to Native American youths and raising money for charities, such as Christian Relief Services.

## Further Reading

''Billy Mills, From Out of Nowhere,'' http://www.letsfindout .com/subjects/sports/bilymils.html

''Billy Mills,'' http://www.indianyouth.org/billy_mills.html
''Billy Mills,'' www.crazyhorse.org □

# Alan Alexander Milne

**A.A. Milne (1882–1956) worked as an essayist, a playwright, a poet, and an adult novelist, in addition to his important contribution as an author of juvenile books. Although he attempted to excel in all literary genres, he was master of Christopher Robin and Winnie-the-Pooh. His nature defied labels, such as "writer of children's literature," even though that was where he excelled.**

Modern-day readers might be surprised to learn that A.A. Milne did more than just write children's books, specifically the four books which remain popular today: *When We Were Very Young, Winnie-the-Pooh, Now We Are Six,* and *The House at Pooh Corner.* Milne jumped from one creative venture to another, reluctant to concentrate his attention in one field for any extended period of time.

## Educated in Style

Born Alan Alexander Milne on January 18, 1882, in London, England, he was the youngest child of Sarah Maria Heginbotham and John Vine Milne. His father was the headmaster at Henley House, a private school, where Milne received his early education. He shared a special kinship with his brother, Kenneth, and they remained close throughout their lives. At the age of nine, Milne and Kenneth, along with a childhood friend, dramatized a novel they had read. This exercise awakened his love of theater.

In 1893, Milne began his studies at Westminster School as a Queen's Scholar. Next he attended Cambridge University, following in his brother's footsteps. He was elected the editor of the literary magazine, *Granta.* Milne also wrote light verse for this publication. In 1903, he graduated with third honors in mathematics from Trinity College at Cambridge.

## Lucky Offers

After completing his college education, Milne began a career as a freelance writer. Within a short time, he was hired as an assistant editor for *Punch* magazine. His weekly essays were consistently light in tone, but tended to ramble. Milne had two goals: to please himself and then to entertain others. During this period he also published his first novel, *Lovers in London,* a collection of sketches. It was considered a critical failure and has since gone out of print.

Milne became active in London society. Although he was not born into the aristocracy, it fascinated him. At times he was known to have satirized the social elite, but he was also drawn to it. Considered to be an eligible bachelor, mothers of marriageable daughters sought him out. He was a frequent guest at weekend country estates.

## Loved to Make Them Laugh

On June 4, 1913, Milne married Dorothy de Selincourt. Later their son, Christopher, would write in *The Enchanted Places* that the couple had very few interests in common, but she laughed at his jokes. He seemed to have a need for her reassurance. The year following their wedding, Milne joined the army to offer his services at the beginning of the First World War.

Milne began as a signaling officer for the Fourth Royal Warwickshire Regiment and later served as an instructor on the Isle of Wight. Two years later he was stationed in France, where he wrote comical plays to lift the morale of the soldiers. His military service was interrupted when Milne contracted a serious fever and was sent home to recover.

## Critical Acclaim

In 1917, *Wurzel-Flummery,* Milne's first play was produced in London. He also published *Once on a Time,* which was originally written as an adult fairy tale for himself and his wife. Later, it was reclassified as a juvenile fairy tale. When Milne retired from the army in 1918, he decided to continue writing plays for a living and settled in London with his family. The following year, Milne achieved his greatest success as a playwright with *Mr. Pim Passes By.* It was produced in Manchester, London, and New York City. Both audiences and critics loved it.

Milne's only child, Christopher Robin, was born on August 21, 1920. He drew from his young son's life, in order to create the fictional character, Christopher Robin. It was meant as a tribute, but his son grew resentful of his fame-by-association later in life. The first book of the famous four, *When We Were Young,* was dedicated to his son. Shortly after the birth of Christopher, Milne purchased Cotchford Farm, which became the setting for subsequent Pooh stories. Most of the animals in the series were inspired by his son's stuffed animal collection. The teddy bear was originally named after their pet swan, Pooh. Only the characters of Rabbit and Owl sprang from Milne's imagination.

### Stale Drawing Rooms

Milne wanted to continue writing plays. However, after the success of the Pooh books, interest in his drawing room satires had waned. He sometimes ventured beyond the drawing room genre, but for the most part Milne seemed to fall back on what had worked for him in the past. Unfortunately, times were changing, and his lucky star was fading. No one was interested in the old-hat comedy of manners when fresh dramas from playwrights like Eugene O'Neill were being staged. Audiences turned their backs on his plays, which became increasingly mediocre. Publishers wanted more children's stories from Milne. The one exception was *The Red House Mystery,* which was well-received and remained a classic among mysteries.

By the 1940s, Milne shifted his energies toward writing novels, short stories, and war pamphlets. His financial situation was secure enough to permit the hiring of a cook and gardener. Milne spent his days writing from mid-morning until dinner, aside from breaks for lunch and tea. After dinner he enjoyed playing golf and completing crossword puzzles. Milne's life was pleasant, if not exciting or adventurous. Some critics have suggested that if he had not lived such a conventional life, his writing might have contained more passion.

### Milne's Private World

Milne was a very reserved person. His privacy affected not only his writing but also the relationship he had with his son. Since he was not an emotionally expressive man, it was difficult for Milne to reach out to his son. He may have made an attempt through the Pooh series, by basing the Christopher Robin character on traits that he observed in his son. While they did not interact a great deal, they did enjoy occasional activities together.

Throughout his life, Milne maintained a strong sense of loyalty to friends and family. As Charlotte F. Otten writes in *Dictionary of Literary Biography,* "Milne valued loyalty to one's friends and relations, displaying his own loyalty to, and love for, his brother Ken, by supporting him financially during his debilitating illness. Milne continued to support Ken's family after Ken's death." His high regard for friendship carried over as a strong theme in the Pooh books. One could not overlook the strong bond between Piglet and Pooh.

In 1952, Milne suffered a stroke, which rendered him partially paralyzed. He wrote little, if anything, after that. He died in the English town of Hartfield, Sussex on January 31, 1956.

Although Milne's first priority was to write for his own pleasure, he did enjoy the praise of an audience. He was determined to escape the limits of a label and did so by becoming prolific in many different genres. However, despite other moderate successes, Milne achieved greatness in one area alone. His Winnie-the-Pooh character has delighted children throughout the world. Even college students, considerably older than the target audience, responded with Pooh Societies. His legacy lived on in the form of animated movies, songs, and merchandise for infants and adults alike. Translations of his famous four books were produced almost immediately after *Winnie-the-Pooh* was first published. The little honey bear had firmly established itself as an enduring classic.

### Further Reading

*Dictionary of Literary Biography,* Volume 160, Gale, 1996.
Milne, Christopher, *The Enchanted Places,* E.P. Dutton & Co., 1975.
*Something about the Author,* Volume 100, Gale, 1999.
Swann, Thomas Burnett, *A. A. Milne,* Twayne Publishers, 1971.
□

# Lisette Model

**During the first half of the 20th century, the artistic life of America underwent a variety of profound changes. Lisette Model (1906–1983), with her stark realism and search for truth through photography, was at the forefront of these changes.**

L isette Model (nee Seyberg), was born into a wealthy family in Vienna, Austria on November 10, 1906. Her Jewish father and French Catholic mother raised her, her older brother, and her younger sister in the gentility of upper-class Austrian society. At the insistence of her mother, Model was raised in the Catholic faith. Fluent in three languages, she traveled extensively and received her formal education through private tutors.

As a child, Model was sexually molested by her father, a medical doctor and military man. While it was a situation Model did not dwell on, close acquaintances would verify her recollections of this experience. He father died of cancer in 1924. By this time much of the family fortune had disappeared.

Near the time of her father's death, Model studied music with composer, Arnold Schoenberg. She spent much of her time with the composer or traveling in his circle of acquaintances. Model regarded Schoenberg as one of her greatest friends.

### Moved to Paris

In 1926, Model moved to Paris, where she planned to transfer her musical studies from piano to voice. She referred to these studies as a concentration on audio senses. By the early 1930s, Model decided to give up music, but felt a need to continue artistic studies in some vein. While living in Paris, she met and married the Russian artist, Evsa Model. It was at this time that she began the photographic odyssey that would define the rest of her life.

By 1934, Model's mother and sister Olga, were living in Nice, France. Olga, an experienced photographer, taught her older sister the technical aspects of photography, including darkroom work. During her visit to France in 1934, Model took a series of portraits on the Promenade des Anglais that eventually became some of her most widely exhibited pieces and were referred to as the "Riviera" series. Although Model did not acknowledge having her work produced in Europe, this series of portraits was first published in the Communist magazine *Regards* in 1935.

Interested in art and married to a painter, Model's natural path was to explore her artistic side beyond music, and she entered into a career that would consume her for the remainder of her life. During her years as a teacher of her craft, Model shared her philosophy with her students. She believed that you should never take a picture of anything that you are not passionately interested in.

Moving to New York City in 1938 with her husband, Model was stunned by the city. There was a freshness to New York that overwhelmed her. During her first year and a half in America, she did not take any pictures. Instead she took in her surroundings, absorbing the many settings she encountered along the way.

## Success in America

Model attempted to support herself through her photography. She experienced her first success when *Cue* magazine published a series of her photographs in late 1940. The pictures were an artistic look at Fifth Avenue shops through plate-glass reflections. Her "Riviera" photos were printed some time later in *PM* magazine, and it was this exposure that introduced her style to the world. Although depending upon photography as her sole means of support was a difficult undertaking, Model was successful. Her success with *Cue* opened other doors, including that of Alexy Brodovitch, art director of *Harper's Bazaar*. Her work appeared with regularity in that periodical. Model became a premier photographer of New York City's dark underside, frequenting the Lower East Side and its small bistros. She was often compared with talented photographers like Berenice Abbott. In 1942, her photographs of an open-air patriotic rally, accompanied by blank verse written by Carl Sandburg, were published in *Look* magazine. As her reputation grew, her photos appeared in such magazines as *Ladies' Home Journal, Vogue, Saturday Evening Post,* and *Cosmopolitan* among others.

## Developed Unique Style

Model had a passionate relationship with her camera and her subjects. Edward Steichen, one-time director of photography at the Museum of Modern Art, considered her to be one of the foremost photographers of our time. Known for her stark, biting portraits of people on the street, Model

was capable of displaying a softer side through her work, as seen in her series' "Running Legs" and "Reflections."

Model had the ability to approach her subjects with a candor that many photographers never achieve. A physically large woman, she wanted to define the dignity of the stereotypical overweight immigrant woman. She found that the best way to achieve this was to compare women at different social levels—the social elite to the working class.

Model's attraction to the "common man," could be seen in her early pictures on the Promenade des Anglais and later in her pictures capturing the inhabitants of Manhattan's Lower East Side. Through these people she sought out life's extremes, exposing humanity in its baser forms yet touching on its heightened sensibilities. She was brilliant in her use of shadows, angles, grains, and other means available to expose the complexities of her subjects. Model was also willing to try new techniques. She experimented with cropped negatives, an approach many photographers would not think of taking, preferring to leave their negatives intact. By cropping her negatives, Model was able to manipulate the image in order to tell a story from her perspective, even if the original picture showed something different.

## Exhibited Worldwide

Model's photographs appeared on display in a number of shows, both individual and with others. She was a favorite at the Museum of Modern Art, where she had 13 one-woman shows between 1940 and 1962. Other sites where her work was displayed included New York City's Photo League, the Art Institute of Chicago, the California Palace of the Legion of Honor, New York's Limelight Gallery, the National Gallery of Canada in Ottawa, the Smithsonian Institution, Galerie Zabriskie in Paris, the San Francisco Museum of Art, Yale University's School of Art, Boston's Vision Gallery, Amsterdam's Galerie Fiolet, London's Photographers Gallery, and Austria's Tiroler Landesmuseum Ferdinandium.

## A Master Teacher

In 1950, Model became a master teacher of photography at the New School for Social Research in New York City and remained there until 1983. She developed close friendships with many of those she mentored and taught. Other well-known photographers that learned from her were David Bruce Cratlsey, who captured New York's gay and lesbian side; Leon Levenstein, a New York street photographer whose photographs marked the changing scene of the city; Joan Roth, best known for her sensitivity toward women and who credits Model with giving her the encouragement to see people she might not have noticed before; and Diane Arbus, who moved from the realm of fashion photography to chronicling the humanity that lives on the edge: the junkies, midgets, and giants of the world.

Model's relationship with Arbus was probably the deepest of all those she had with her students. By 1957, the year Arbus appeared at the New School, Model had already developed a reputation as both an inspiring teacher and a tough task-master. Although both women looked for the dark realities of the world around them, Model's work had been described as establishing generalizations as a means of creating a visually active image. Arbus, on the other hand, produced photographs grounded in intense, unsparing reality. While Arbus did not seek close friendships with other women photographers, she and Model shared an interest in exploring the extremes of humanity through the photograph.

### The Final Chapter

During the later years of her life, Model was a popular guest lecturer throughout Europe and the United States. She no longer actively sought work from publishers, preferring to remain in her teaching position. Model put aside many of her works, no longer cropping the negatives and manipulating the images that many considered to be excellent work, even in their untouched state. Reported to have recovered from a bout with uterine cancer in the mid-1960s, Model remained with the New School until her death in New York City on March 29, 1983.

### Further Reading

*Baltimore Jewish Times,* August 4, 1995.
*Independent,* October 18, 1997.
*Jerusalem Post,* June 30, 1995, p. 7.
*Jewish Week,* May 23, 1997.
*Newsday,* July 4, 1998, p. A2.
"Lisette Model," http://www.elsa.photo.net/lisette.html (March 1, 1999).
"Lisette Model," http://www.photo-seminars.com (February 16, 1999). □

# Tom Monaghan

**A strong work ethic and intense desire to make something of his life, led Tom Monaghan (born 1937) from the orphanages of Michigan to the creation of the second-largest pizza chain in the world. His business grew from a single $500 store in Ypsilanti, Michigan, to over 6,100 franchised and company-owned stores in 64 countries, with revenue of over one billion dollars.**

Until 1998, when he sold Domino's Pizza to Bain Capital for a billion dollars, Thomas S. Monaghan was known as the driving force that built the world's second-largest pizza company, behind Pizza Hut Inc. Monaghan was an innovator in the pizza industry and set the standards for other companies. He developed dough trays, the corrugated pizza box, insulated bags to transport pizzas, the pizza screen, a conveyor oven and a unique franchise system enabling managers and supervisors to become franchisees. He was also a flamboyant spender, who bought and sold the Detroit Tigers baseball team, Drummond Island, the biggest Frank Lloyd Wright collection in the world, a multi-million dollar collection of automobiles, a helicopter, and several airplanes. He devoted his vast

resources to helping Catholic causes. Monaghan donated $3.5 million to the rebuilding of the cathedral in Managua, Nicaragua, and supported a mission in the Honduran mountain town of San Pedro Sula. According to an interview in *The New York Times,* February, 14, 1999, Monaghan stated, "I don't want to take my money with me when I go, and I don't want to leave it for others. I want to die broke."

### Sent to Orphanage as Child

Tom Monaghan was born in the university town of Ann Arbor, Michigan on March 25, 1937, to Francis Monaghan, a truck driver, and Anna (Geddes) Monaghan. The family lived in a small farmhouse built by his father on land purchased from his grandmother. Water came from a near-by stream until they could afford a pump. When he was four years old, his father died of peritonitis on Christmas Eve, 1941.

Since his mother earned only $27.50 a week, she was forced to send Monaghan and his brother to a foster home and finally to the St. Joseph Home for Boys. He lived there for six and a half years, until his mother was able to reclaim him. From this experience, Monaghan developed his love for the Catholic church, an appreciation of architecture from taking care of the huge old mansion where he lived, and a sense that he could achieve anything from his beloved teacher, Sister Beranda. In other respects, the high spirited young man did not like the regimentation of life in an orphanage, which he equated to prison in his autobiography *Pizza Tiger.*

His mother completed nursing school when he was in the sixth grade. She began work at Munson Hospital in Traverse City, Michigan, and brought the boys to live with her. Monaghan helped financially by growing and selling vegetables from the backyard, catching and selling fish from Lake Michigan, and selling the Traverse City *Record Eagle* in front of Miliken's Department Store in the center of town. By this time he had become difficult to manage and was never able to live with his mother for long periods of time without disrupting the household.

Monaghan was sent to a foster home and attended St. Francis High School in Traverse City. As he stood knee deep in manure in his foster home's barnyard, he had a revelation that he wanted to be a priest. His parish priest arranged for him to enter St. Joseph's Seminary in Grand Rapids, Michigan, but he could not handle the discipline and was asked to leave in less than a year, for pillow fights and talking in chapel. In *Pizza Tiger* Monaghan admitted, "Never before or since have I felt so crushed. I am no stranger to failure, but no other setback devastated me as this one did, because it was so final."

### Struggled at School

After leaving the seminary, Monaghan returned to Traverse City and and attended St. Francis High School for a short time. His mother, becoming exasperated with his antics, placed him in a juvenile detention home. When his aunt and uncle found out, they were able to get him released into their custody. Monaghan finished forty-fourth in a class of forty-four at St. Thomas High School in Ann Arbor, Michigan. He hoped to go to college, but his grades were poor and he had no money. Monaghan enrolled in architectural trade school at Ferris State College in Big Rapids, Michigan, and worked at odd jobs to pay his tuition. He hoped to transfer to the University of Michigan, but lacked the funds. A poster advertised paid college tuition if he joined the army. This caught his attention and he filled out all the paperwork before realizing that he had joined the Marines.

After successfully completing his three year tour of duty in the Marines on July 2, 1959, Monaghan naively invested the $2,000 he had saved for tuition in a get-rich-quick oil scheme. He never saw his money again. Monaghan planned to attend the University of Michigan in the fall of 1959, but became ill with an infected eardrum and did not earn enough money to even afford the text books. He tried again in the spring of 1960, but dropped out after only three weeks.

## Pizza Business

From this inauspicious beginning one would not expect Monaghan to become a billion dollar businessman and philanthropist. In September 1960, his brother, Jim, heard that a pizza shop in Ypsilanti, Michigan, was up for sale. The owner was asking $500.00 plus about $400.00 in debts. The brothers bought the business, naming it Domino's Pizza. They had no intention of making this a life long career. Jim kept his post office job and Tom intended to return to the University of Michigan. Jim soon sold his half of the business to his brother for a 1959 Volkswagen Beetle that had been used as a delivery vehicle. Monaghan threw himself into the business of making the best pizza in the world. He created a very simple menu. He investigated what made the best sauce, purchased the highest quality toppings, made the freshest dough, used the most expensive flour and cheese, and guaranteed delivery as rapidly as possible. Business did well enough to open a second store in Mt. Pleasant, Michigan, catering to college studentds. Working 18-hour days and visiting more than 300 rival pizzerias, Monaghan utilized the best techniques and invented his own when none existed to stay in the forefront of the industry. In 1967, he sold his first franchise.

## All Did Not Go Smoothly

As the business continued to grow, Monaghan had to face a number of challenges. In 1967, a fire destroyed his anchor store in Ypsilanti, which supplied the other stores with food, as well as the company's offices. Most of the damage was not covered by insurance. By 1970, unrestrained expansion had put Domino's into $1.5 million dollars of debt. Monaghan turned the company over to Ken Heavlin, a local businessman on May 1, 1970, to avoid bankruptcy. Within a year he regained control and by 1973 Domino's had recovered. In September 1975, Amstar Corporation, the manufacturer of Domino Sugar, sued for infringement of trademark. That lawsuit continued until 1980 when a federal Court of Appeals judge ruled that the name

Domino's Pizza was unlikely to be confused with Domino Sugar.

As Monaghan became distracted by other interests, his company began a gradual decline. In 1990, he was forced to to sell some of his prized possessions and focus more attention on his business in order to return it to profitability. Domino's lost $78 million dollars in a court case to a woman injured by a company driver. As a result, the company decided to give up its guarantee of "delivery in thirty minutes or the pizza is free." Monaghan survived a boycott by the National Organization of Women because of his support of conservative candidates who were against abortion. He also faced opposition from various gay rights groups because of his support of the Catholic Church's position on homosexuality.

## Bought and Sold Detroit Tigers

Realizing a boyhood dream, Monaghan was able to purchase the Detroit Tigers baseball franchise in 1983 from John E. Fetzer for $53 million. He won a World Series in his first season as owner. According to Charlie Vincent, a columnist for the *Detroit Free Press*, February 14, 1992, "He reveled in the glory for a while, then said Detroit fans were the worst in the world." Vincent added, "Nothing was done to develop the people of Detroit as fans or the kids of Detroit as baseball players or baseball lovers." He fired Ernie Harwell, Detroit's favorite sportscaster and demanded that the taxpayers finance a new stadium, at a location of his choice. In 1992, Monaghan sold the team to his rival in the pizza business, Mike Ilitch, owner of Little Caesars Pizza.

## Frank Lloyd Wright Collection

As as a result of his lifelong love of architecture, Monaghan amassed one of the world's largest collections of furniture and artifacts created by Frank Lloyd Wright. At its peak, his collection had more than 300 items valued at $30 million. Monaghan established the National Center for the Study of Frank Lloyd Wright and built a 10,000 square-foot museum to hold the collection. In 1993, Monaghan closed and emptied the museum and began to sell the collection. He retained the "Prairie House" on the grounds of Domino Farms, which was built in the style of Wright's prairie houses.

At one point in his career, Monaghan owned over 250 antique automobiles, including an eight million dollar 1932 Bugatti Royale, housed in an museum especially built for them. He purchased Drummond Island, a resort on the Michigan-Ontario border with its own golf course called Pepperoni Links. Monaghan also owned five boats, three planes, and various other companies.

## Dedication to the Catholic Church

In 1998, Monaghan sold Domino's Pizza for a billion dollars, intending to devote the rest of his life and his money to spreading the Christian gospel, especially to the business elite. According to a February 14, 1999 article that appeared in the *New York Times*, a book changed the direction of his life. After reading *Mere Christianity* by C.S. Lewis,

Monaghan decided to give up his sin of pride and rededicate himself to God.

After meeting Pope John Paul in 1987, Monaghan founded *Legatus* (Latin for "ambassador"), to encourage Catholic executives to spread the Faith in their business and personal lives. *Legatus* now has 25 American chapters with more than 1,300 members, as well as groups in Canada, Mexico, and Honduras. The organization is funded through another of his charities, the Mater Christe Foundation. Monaghan also provided funding for the Ave Maria College; the conservative newspaper, *Credo*; a radio station; and the Thomas Moore Law Center. All are based in the Ann Arbor, Michigan area.

## Further Reading

Monaghan, Thomas and Robert Anderson, *Pizza Tiger,* Random House, 1986.
*Crain's Detroit Business,* September 28, 1998, p.1.
*Detroit Free Press,* November 5, 1990, p. 10F; February 14, 1992, p.1D.
*Detroit News,* February 7, 1993, C; December 22, 1993, p. A1; December 15, 1994, p. G3; September 27, 1998, p. C1; October 3, 1998, p. C3.
*New York Times,* February 14, 1999, Section 3, p. 1.
*U.S. News & World Report,* July 29. 1991, p. 43.
Media Kit, Domino Farms Headquarters, 1999 □

# Robert Mondavi

**Robert Mondavi (born 1913) has brought prestige to American wines and helped to popularize wine drinking across the nation. Since opening his own vineyard in 1966, he has seen California's Napa Valley develop into one of the finest wine-making regions in the world.**

Before Robert Mondavi, American wine was "understood . . . to be the stuff of skid-row jokes," wrote Paul Lukacs in the *Washington Times.* Most wines made in the country were low-priced table wine at best, not to be held in comparison with the excellent vintages from France. Frustrated, Mondavi set out to change that; he wanted to make Napa Valley wines competitive internationally. Most thought his aspirations were too lofty, but he broke away from his family's long-running business and founded his own firm in 1966 with his oldest son. At first, he simply hoped to produce world-class Napa wines, but eventually, his mission expanded to educating the American drinking public about the joys of wine consumption and promoting the industry as a whole. This gained him the reputation of being "the ambassador of wine" and earned him the nickname "The Patriarch." Mondavi's sales and marketing efforts have gone a long way to transforming the image of quality wine from being a bastion of the elite to being an unpretentious, regular part of a good meal.

Mondavi was born on June 18, 1913, in Virginia, Minnesota. His parents, Cesare and Rosa (Grassi) Mondavi, were Italian immigrants. His mother ran a boarding house for local Italian laborers and while his father was the proprietor of a grocery store and later, a saloon. However, Prohibition law was enacted in 1919, which outlawed the sale of beer and liquor, threatening Cesare Mondavi's business. The law allowed for individuals to produce up to 200 gallons of wine, though, so Mondavi's father decided to become a grape wholesaler for the many Italian families who wanted to continue enjoying their traditional wine with meals.

## Headed West

Cesare Mondavi's business often took him to the West Coast. So, in the early 1920s, the family relocated to Lodi, California, south of Sacramento. The clan included Mondavi; his older sisters, Mary and Helen; and his younger brother, Peter. Mondavi and his brother helped with the business, nailing together wooden crates for shipping wine. Early on, Mondavi showed a strong desire to succeed, playing on the Lodi High School football team even though he was a slight 140 pounds. When his team reached the regional championships, Mondavi was chosen "most valuable player." He also served as president of his class one year, and was on the swim team.

After high school, Mondavi was accepted at Stanford University and graduated in 1937. With guidance from his father, he began to study business, in anticipation of building a career in the wine industry. He also took chemistry classes to understand more about the technical side of wine making. In the fall of 1936, Mondavi got a job at the

Sunnyhill Winery, later called Sunny St. Helena. His father was a partner in the business. When Mondavi heard that the Charles Krug Winery, the oldest in Napa Valley, was up for sale in 1943, he convinced his father to buy it on the condition that he would work with his brother to build it up.

## Departed Family Business

For 23 years, Robert and Peter Mondavi ran Krug together. Throughout the years, Robert Mondavi remained dissatisfied with the quality of their output. He yearned to produce top-shelf products, such as those from the Beaulieu or Inglenook vineyards. More than that, he wanted his wines to be the best, striving for excellence in his work as he did in the rest of his life. Peter Mondavi, on the other hand, was content with churning out safe products and did not want to invest money on higher-quality production techniques or expensive promotion. In 1965, the brothers came to physical blows, and Robert Mondavi decided it was time to start his own winery.

The split from his family business resulted in litigation, literally pitting brother against brother. Mondavi sued Peter as well as his own mother for his share of the business. The case was settled in 1978, with Mondavi receiving an undisclosed sum and some parcels of vineyard. In 1966, Mondavi and some partners founded the Robert Mondavi winery, and set out to produce the kind of drink that would make him proud. In his first year, he produced an especially successful crop of sauvignon blanc grapes, and set a precedent by releasing it under the name Fume Blanc, a twist on the French name of "blanc fume."

Mondavi did not want to just imitate the European wines. He was sure that California could produce distinctive bottles that would compete against any from France, Italy, Germany, Spain, or Portugal. Mondavi was zealous in promoting his wares. He conversed regularly with wine writers in the United States and London, becoming a spokesman for the burgeoning fine wine industry in the Napa Valley. In addition to pushing his own products, Mondavi vocally supported efforts to change American attitudes about wine. For years, it had been thought of as either a very low-class beverage of derelicts or as a special occasion drink. He wanted people to imbibe as his Italian family did: regularly and in moderation, as part of daily life.

## American Wines Earned Respect

American wines, even good ones, still could not compete with the French. They were relegated to a lower caste and lacked the cachet of a French name. In 1976, this situation began to change. A British wine enthusiast named Steven Spurrier held a blind tasting in Paris featuring wines of California and France. All nine judges were respected French wine critics, sommeliers, and other oenophiles. The results were astounding. Though Mondavi did not attend the tasting, he was thrilled with the outcome. Of the whites, three out of four of the top-rated choices were from Napa; the top-ranked red was from Napa; many others ranked in the top ten. Mondavi wrote in his autobiography, *Harvests of Joy*, "Ten years before, I had made a bold claim and I had staked my future on it: that we in California could make

wines that would stand proudly alongside the very best in the world. Now here we were, proving just that, on French soil, no less." Even more amazing, some of the winning wines were undervalued in the United States, selling for $6 or $7 a bottle because the winemakers figured that Americans would refuse to pay any more than that. (A little later, good quality California wines would retail for about $50 a bottle, though most winemakers such as Mondavi would also produce decent products in the $10-$15 range as well.)

Following the Parisian tasting, the reputation of California wines received a deserved boost. In 1979, Mondavi purchased a facility in Woodbridge. The same year, he undertook a venture with the fabled Baron Philippe de Rothschild of Chateau Mouton Rothschild in France to produce Opus One. At the outset, this was designed to be a masterwork. The first case ever to be offered for sale was purchased at the 1981 Napa Valley Wine Auction for $24,000. It took some time for the new brand to catch on among wine lovers, but after some marketing efforts that allowed gourmet restaurant customers to sample the wine for about $10 a glass, Mondavi saw sales boom, and the Opus One label became the highest-priced wine in Napa.

## Mondavi Empire Boomed

The Mondavi Winery kept expanding, purchasing Vichon Winery in 1985 and Byron Vineyard & Winery in 1990. They introduced their Robert Mondavi Coastal wines, a moderately priced line, in 1994, and Italian varietals in 1995. Also in 1995, the Mondavis teamed up with Italy's Marchese de' Frescobaldi, and the next year, entered a joint venture with the Eduardo Chadwick family of Chile to produce and market the Caliterra brand. In 1996, the firm announced that they were moving the Vichon wines to France, introducing the Vichon Mediterranean line the following year. Mondavi stock went public in 1993, selling additional shares in 1995; but the family still controlled 92 percent of the voting power.

Mondavi married Marjorie Declusin in 1937. The marriage produced three children, Michael, Timothy, and Marcia. He and his wife divorced in 1979, and he married Margrit Biever the following year. Mondavi's children began running the winery in the 1980s, but Mondavi continued to make a lot of the decisions, much to their consternation. He transferred executive responsibilities to his two sons in 1990. Michael functions as the CEO, Timothy is managing director and wine grower, and Marcia is on the board of directors.

## Relished Role as Spokesperson

Into the late 1990s, Mondavi continued to function as a spokesperson for the firm and the wine industry as a whole. He raised the ire of Napa locals with his aggressive campaign to polish the area's tourism industry, backing a plan to build, using some public funds, a $50 million cultural complex in 2001 featuring upscale restaurants, art spaces, and an amphitheater. Mondavi has long promoted wine in conjunction with a love of the arts, hosting an annual summer music festival in Napa, literary readings in the tasting rooms, seminars on the details of wine making, and more. However, it is all part of his dedication to spreading the "gospel" of wine. "We have come a long way," Mondavi remarked to Lukacs in the *Washington Times* in 1998, "but we still have much more to do. But I'm optimistic. I believe that we will make more progress in the next few years than we have in the last ten."

Active in touting the benefits of wine while warning of the dangers of alcohol abuse, Mondavi started the Robert Mondavi Mission Program in 1988. Its educational programs focus on positive attributes of wine, featuring speakers ranging from sociologists and anthropologists to religious and governmental leaders, as well as scientific and medical researchers. This stemmed from Mondavi's dismay at the government's request to put warning labels on alcoholic beverages during the 1990s. As the decade progressed, he worked diligently to prove that moderate wine consumption was, in fact, a benefit to health. The popular media widely reported studies backing this claim. These messages helped to spur sales, especially of red wine. It was shown to have clear benefits, including a reduction in cholesterol levels.

Mondavi was instrumental in linking the consumption of wine with fine cuisine. In 1976, he started the Great Chefs of France program that brought chefs to his winery for cooking demonstrations and seminars. Mondavi was a founding co-chairman of the American Institute of Food & Wine, along with his good friend Julia Child. He also participates in a number of wine organizations.

### Innovative Production Methods

In addition to his public role as someone who has popularized wine drinking among Americans, Mondavi has been an innovator in production methods. He was one of the first to recognize the importance of using small oak barrels, as the Europeans did, in fermentation for high-quality bottles. However, his company also got the reputation of being a "test-tube" winery because of all the innovations they tried in order to improve their products. In the late 1960s, he borrowed an idea from the dairy industry and introduced the use of refrigerated stainless steel vats for fermenting large quantities of the drink. By 1993, Mondavi decided to consult with NASA to use data they collected by remote sensing. He was interested in photographs taken from a digital camera at an elevation of about 14,000 feet that would hopefully shed more light on which areas of the vineyards were infested with diseases, and which areas should be harvested at which times in order to prevent over-ripening of grapes. In addition, the Mondavi company created a capsule-free bottle design in 1994, as part of its environmental research.

### Further Reading

Mondavi, Robert, with Paul Chutkow, *Harvests of Joy: My Passion for Excellence,* Harcourt Brace, 1998.
*Newsmakers 1989,* Gale, 1989.
*Los Angeles Times,* June 24, 1998, p. H8.
*People,* October 12, 1998, p. 151.
*USA Today,* June 17, 1998, p. 1D.
*Washington Times,* September 2, 1998, p. E1.
*Wine Spectator,* September 30, 1998, p. 72.

Robert Mondavi web site, March 8, 1999. Available from http://www.robertmondavi.com. □

# Stan Musial

**Stan Musial (born 1920), one of baseball's greatest hitters, enjoyed an extraordinary career with the St. Louis Cardinals from 1941 through 1963. Called "Stan the Man" because of his intimidating presence at the plate, Musial won seven batting championships and three Most Valuable Player awards.**

Accommodating to fans and the media both during and after his playing career, Musial was considered one of the game's most gentlemanly and down-to-earth ambassadors. He came from rural Pennsylvania, never graduated from high school, and sometimes stammered in public. His love for baseball overcame all obstacles, however, and he became known nationwide as a symbol of batting excellence. "I was a poor boy who struck it rich in many ways through the wonders of baseball," Musial said in his autobiography.

### Meteoric Rise

The Cardinals' greatest player was born Stanislaus Musial in Donora, a mill town in southwestern Pennsylvania's Monongahela Valley on December 21, 1920. His father, Lukasz Musial, was a shy Polish immigrant who worked in the shipping department of a local mill. The parents of his mother, Mary Lancos, had migrated from Czechoslovakia, and her father was a coal miner. Mary and Lukasz Musial had four girls before their son, Stanislaus, was born in 1920. Stan also had a younger brother, who played minor league baseball after World War II.

Musial, a bashful boy, became interested in baseball because he had a neighbor who played semi-pro ball. "I could always hit," Musial told the *Sporting News.* "I learned to hit with a broomstick and a ball of tape and I could always get that bat on the ball." Musial, who batted and threw left-handed, acquired the habit of hitting to the opposite field while playing for the Donora Zinc Works team in 1937. At the hometown field, trolley tracks shortened the distance to the left-field fence, so Musial tried to aim that way. The ability to go the opposite way became one of his greatest weapons.

Musial was 16 and a flame-throwing but erratic pitcher when he signed his first professional contract. Pittsburgh never courted him. Instead, he signed with the St. Louis Cardinals, whose owner Branch Rickey was known for his scouting system. In the winter of 1937-1938, Musial starred on Donora High School's basketball team. The next two summers he pitched for Williamson, WV, in the Class D Mountain States League of the low minors. In 1939, the Williamson manager, Harrison Wickel, reported to the Cardinals that Musial, who had struck out 85 batters and walked 84 others in 91 innings, was the wildest pitcher he

"They horsed around more, cut up with hillbilly songs and musical instruments. . . . I never had the courage to try my harmonica outside my hotel room, but I could make my share of noise with that slide whistle and coat hanger. I always thought it helped to laugh it up before a game, not to become too tense."

Led by Musial's hot bat, the loose, inexperienced Cardinals surprised everyone by winning 106 games, including 43 of their last 52, to claim the National League pennant. Then St. Louis beat the favored Yankees in the World Series, and Musial was on a world championship team in his first full season.

Musial was disliked by Brooklyn Dodgers' fans, who bestowed his nickname. Groaning when he came up to bat in key situations, they would yell: "Oh no. Here comes that Man again." From then on, he was always "Stan the Man." Musial didn't find out till after he retired that Dodgers' shortstop, Pee Wee Reese, often used to steal his bat before games.

Musial had an unorthodox batting stance. He crouched down to make the strike zone smaller, held his hands back until the last possible instant, and punched many of his hits the opposite way. "A lot of guys saw my hitting style and said I'd never hit in the big leagues," Musial recalled. In fact, Musial feasted on all types of pitching. "I learned early to hit the curveball," Musial wrote in his autobiography. "From the beginning I was a natural fastball hitter, so they started throwing me curves, so many of them that I sharpened up against the breaking ball."

Musial contended that the most important aspects of hitting were relaxation and concentration. "It's necessary to have mental tenacity at the plate, but to avoid physical tension," he wrote. "If I freed my mind of all distracting thoughts, I could tell what a pitch was going to be when it got about halfway to the plate." In a later interview, Musial told the *Sporting News* he could always tell when a pitcher was going to throw him a fastball, his favorite pitch to hit: "I had a sixth sense. I don't know what else you call it, but it never deceived me."

The Cardinals had been a decent team, but with Musial batting third in the lineup they became a perennial powerhouse. Led by Musial's league-leading .357 average in 1943 and his .347 mark in 1944, the Cardinals won two more pennants during years when baseball's player ranks were being depleted by World War II. The Cardinals lost the World Series to the Yankees in 1943 and to their cross-town rivals, the St. Louis Browns, in 1944.

Musial was drafted in 1945, joined the Navy, and served on a ship repair unit in Pearl Harbor, Hawaii. He played baseball every afternoon on a base team to entertain service personnel. Without Musial, the Cardinals faltered in 1945. Musial returned in 1946 and resumed his incredible hitting, leading the league with a .365 mark and taking St. Louis to the World Series again. The Cardinals defeated Boston in a thrilling seven-game series billed as a showdown between Musial and Red Sox slugger, Ted Williams, to whom Musial was often compared. The Cardinals would never win another pennant during Musial's long tenure, though they came close several times.

had ever seen. He recommended Musial be released. But an injury to an outfielder forced Musial into the lineup, and he batted .352.

After the 1939 season, Musial married his high school sweetheart, Lillian Labash. They would have an enduring marriage and four children: son Dick and daughters Gerry, Janet and Jeanie.

In 1940, playing for Class D Daytona Beach in the Florida State League, Musial hit .311, playing the outfield between pitching assignments. During one game he injured his shoulder trying to make a diving catch in center field. It ruined his pitching arm, and his career seemed in jeopardy. But the Cardinals organization had recognized his remarkable hitting ability.

In 1941, Musial went from being an unknown, minor league player to a hitter who won a regular job in the major leagues. He was quickly promoted from Class C Springfield (Missouri), where he hit .379 with 24 home runs in 87 games, to Class B Rochester (New York). After Rochester finished its season, Musial was called up to St. Louis. He had six hits in a doubleheader and hit .426 in 12 games. No one ever asked him to pitch again.

## The Cardinals' Man

The next season, Musial was installed in left field for the Cardinals. At 21, he was the youngest player on a youthful, carefree squad. "There were more small-town and farm boys then and fewer college men," Musial recalled in his autobiography, *Stan Musial: "The Man's" Own Story.*

In 1948, Musial had his best year, batting .376 with 39 home runs and 131 runs batted in and a league-leading .702 slugging percentage. That year, he became the first National League player to win the Most Valuable Player award three times. Musial was a hitting machine—dependable and productive. He excelled at the two most important aspects of batting—getting on base and driving in runners. He liked light, thin-handled bats that he could whip around quickly. He would scrape the handles all season to thin the bats even more. Players around the league feared his screaming line drives.

Quiet and shy, Musial kept his opinions to himself. He generally stayed away from controversy. But when the Cardinals took advantage of his easygoing demeanor to hold down his salary, he staged several holdouts. Baseball experts agreed he and Williams were the best hitters of their era, and two of the best in baseball history. However, compared to later players like Mickey Mantle, who spent their careers in the New York limelight, Musial was relatively underpaid and under-recognized by the public.

### Enjoyed the Game

Playing outside a major media market throughout the 1950s and into the 1960s, Musial symbolized the workaday ballplayer who loved baseball and delighted loyal fans with his steady play. He became an institution in St. Louis, opening a restaurant in 1949 and remaining in the public eye throughout his career and after his retirement.

In May 1954, Musial hit five home runs in a double-header at Busch Stadium in St. Louis. About that time, Musial, never blessed with great speed, began playing more games at first base than in the outfield. He was never known as an outstanding fielder, but he worked hard to become an adequate one. His hitting, however, overshadowed all else. For 16 consecutive seasons, Musial batted over .300. Only Ty Cobb had more years in a row hitting .300. Musial led the National League in hitting seven times, and only Cobb and Honus Wagner won more batting titles.

After he failed to hit .300 in 1959, Musial considered retirement. However, to the surprise of many, he played four more seasons, getting frequent rests to nurse a myriad of injuries. He returned to the outfield to make room for first baseman Bill White. In 1962, at the age of 41, Musial played

left field and hit .330. "I was having too much fun hitting to want to quit," Musial recalled.

In 1963, his last season, Musial contributed as the Cardinals mounted a furious drive at the end of the season. He hit his last major league home run to tie the score in a key game against the Dodgers, but the Cardinals' pennant bid fell short. In his last day as a Cardinals player, Musial had two hits after being honored in pre-game ceremonies. "My heart is filled with thanks for so many who made these 22 years possible," he told the crowd.

Musial finished with 1,951 runs batted in, fourth on the all-time list, and with 6,134 total bases, second-highest in history. He also ranked in the Top Ten in career hits (3,630), runs scored (1,949), doubles (725), walks (1,599), and games (3,026). Though not a bona fide power hitter, he finished with 475 home runs. He led the league in hits six times, in doubles eight times, in triples five times, in runs five times, and in runs batted in twice.

### Retirement

After his retirement, "Stan the Man" remained a popular figure in St. Louis, running his restaurant and speaking frequently. When the Cardinals opened a new stadium, local baseball writers staged a testimonial dinner and raised $40,000 to erect a statue of Musial at the ballpark. In 1969, he was elected to the Hall of Fame in his first year of eligibility. His career had spanned the era from before World War II to the 1960s. "I believe I played in the most exciting era of baseball," Musial recalled in his autobiography. "I saw the game change from day to night, from regional to national, from long train trips to short plane flights, from cabbage leaves under the cap in hot weather to air-conditioned dugouts. . . .

"I say baseball was a great game, is a great game, and will be a great game. I'm extremely grateful for what it has given me—in recognition and records, thrills and satisfaction, money and memories. I hope I've given nearly as much as I've gotten from it."

### Further Reading

Broeg, Bob, and Stan Musial, Stan Musial: "The Man's" Own Story, as told to Bob Broeg, Doubleday, 1964.
American Heritage, October 1992.
Sporting News, July 28, 1997. □

# N

## Chuichi Nagumo

**Chuichi Nagumo (1887–1944) commanded the Japanese aircraft carrier striking force during the early stages of the Second World War. He lead this force in the raid on the U.S. Pacific Fleet at Pearl Harbor and the battles of Midway, Eastern Solomons, and Santa Cruz Islands.**

Chuichi Nagumo was born in Japan in 1887, during a crossroads period in Japanese history. The island nation had existed as an almost completely closed society for two hundred years, following the defeat of Shogun Hideoshi's invasion of Korea in 1596. By the early 19th century, small European settlements had been established in Japan, but trade with the outside world was nonexistent. All this changed overnight in 1854, when Commodore Perry sailed into Tokyo Bay and forced the Japanese to open their borders to international trade.

### Rush to Modernity

In the wake of Perry's exploits, Japanese authorities began a remarkable effort to develop a modern navy. They were assisted by European navies eager to sell their equipment and expertise. By 1873, the Imperial Japanese Navy operated its own dockyard, sent cadets for education at the U.S. Naval Academy, and established its own naval college in Tokyo. The Japanese naval college was operated with British assistance and the Imperial Japanese Navy would continue to maintain British seafaring traditions, including the playing of Western music on ceremonial occasions and the use of Western utensils during shipboard meals, throughout World War II. At the turn of the century the

Japanese naval college had moved to the island of Etajima, off Hiroshima. Japanese orders for warships exceeded those of all countries except England. The Japanese navy was also beginning to build its own modern warships. In less than 50 years, it had become a modern force, capable of competing with minor naval powers. For ambitious young men, the navy offered opportunity for advancement. Seeking a promising career, Nagumo entered the naval college at Etajima in 1904.

### Tsushima

Territorial disputes touched off the Russo-Japanese War the same year that Nagumo entered Etajima. The Japanese navy began the war with a devastating surprise attack on the Russian Pacific Fleet at Port Arthur. While the war on land quickly became a stalemate, the Russian Baltic and Black Sea fleets traveled to Asian waters to avenge Port Arthur. The Russian and Japanese fleets met in the Straits of Tsushima on May 27, 1904, and the new Japanese navy annihilated the Russians in one of the most decisive naval battles in history.

Nagumo completed his naval training in 1908, specializing in torpedo warfare, and rose steadily through the ranks during the next twenty years. He served as captain of the light cruiser *Naka,* the heavy cruiser *Takao,* and the battleship *Yamashiro,* before receiving a promotion to rear admiral and being transferred to the naval general staff for arms limitation negotiations with Britain and the United States in 1930.

### Empire

Japanese success in the Russo-Japanese War marked Japan as a naval competitor with the major European powers for the first time in its history. Japan's position was further

## Pacific War

Japan further distanced itself from Britain and the United States by signing the Tripartite Pact with fascist powers, Germany and Italy on September 27, 1940. Continued Japanese expansion in China eventually led the United States to stop exporting oil to Japan on July 26, 1941. Without oil, Japan would have been unable to continue military operations in China. Therefore, Japanese military leaders decided to conquer the Netherlands East Indies (now Indonesia), an oil-rich region, to supply its needs. The conquest of the Netherlands East Indies would entail operations near the shores of the U.S. territory of the Philippines and British Malaysia. It was, therefore, decided to attack U.S. and British forces, in conjunction with the with the move against the Dutch.

Japan's military leadership, aware that a war with the United States would be difficult to win, devised a daring strategy to knock the U.S. out of the war at its outset and secure U.S. acquiescence in Japan's conquest of the Netherlands East Indies. Their plan involved a massive air attack on the U.S. Pacific Fleet based at Pearl Harbor on the island of Oahu, Hawaii. Nagumo opposed the plan due to his doubts regarding the effectiveness of aircraft against warships. However, the head of the combined fleet, Isoroku Yamamoto, insisted that the operation go forward. Ironically, Nagumo was appointed to lead the attack due to his seniority.

## Pearl Harbor

Nagumo's fleet, comprising three battleships, six large aircraft carriers, and numerous smaller vessels, left Japanese waters to attack Hawaii in late November 1941. Despite rough seas north of Hawaii, Japanese carriers launched their planes without incident on the morning of December 7, and complete surprise was achieved in the initial attack. By the time the first raid was completed, the U.S. Pacific Fleet had suffered a staggering defeat, with four battleships sunk and nearly every aircraft on Oahu destroyed on the ground. Japanese losses amounted to 29 aircraft. Nagumo's unfamiliarity with naval aviation showed itself, however, when he opposed the launching of further raids, which could have destroyed millions of gallons of fuel stored at Pearl Harbor, Nagumo later summarized his reasons for the withdrawal by stating, ''1. The first attack had inflicted all the damage we had hoped for. Another attack could not be expected greatly to increase the extent of the damage. 2. Enemy fire had been surprisingly prompt even though we took them by surprise. Another attack would meet strong opposition. This would make our losses disproportionate to the additional destruction that might be inflicted. 3. Intercepted enemy messages indicated at least fifty large planes still operational. Also we did not know the whereabouts of the enemy carriers, cruisers, and submarines.'' On their return from Pearl Harbor, Nagumo's air forces also assisted in the Japanese conquest of Wake Island.

## Ceylon

Nagumo was hailed as a national hero following the Pearl Harbor raid, and he was granted an audience with the

enhanced by its conquest of German possessions during World War I, including the Mariana, Marshall, and Gilbert Islands, and Truk Atoll. By the late 1920s, Britain and the United States were becoming concerned about the growth of Japanese naval strength and convened the first London Conference in 1930, in an effort to avoid a naval arms race in the Pacific. Nagumo served on the Japanese delegation to the conference, where he helped secure the right of the Japanese navy to build as many submarines and light cruisers as any other country. He was promoted to the rank of admiral in 1935.

## The China Incident

Throughout the 1930s, Japanese involvement in China expanded steadily. Using the pretense of protecting Japanese nationals and their property, the Japanese army gradually occupied substantial territories within China, arousing a storm of international protest. What became known as the ''China Incident'' also created a division within the Japanese armed forces between those who favored expanding the war in China and those who urged withdrawal. Nagumo, who became the naval general staff chief of operations in 1936, was staunchly in favor of expanding the war. He also opposed the results of the second London Conference in 1934, at which Japan had agreed to limit its building of capital ships (battleships, battle cruisers, and aircraft carriers) to 60% of those built by the United States and Britain. By 1937, the China Incident had developed into a full-scale war, and diplomatic relations between Japan and the Western powers steadily worsened.

Emperor. After a brief stay ashore, Nagumo and his carrier striking force embarked for the Indian Ocean. There Nagumo's forces attacked merchant shipping, bombed the British naval bases at Trincomalee and Colombo on the island of Ceylon (now Sri Lanka), and won a naval air engagement with a British fleet, sinking the aircraft carrier *Hermes* on April 9, 1942. Nagumo's performance during this operation was effective, as his confidence had been boosted by the success of the Pearl Harbor venture. In fact, many Japanese leaders were infected with what was termed "victory disease," a form of overconfidence leading to carelessness, at this time.

## Midway

Despite the success of the Japanese during the Pearl Harbor raid, the United States showed no intention of giving up. American resistance led Admiral Yamamoto to devise another plan to draw the U.S. fleet into a decisive action, this time by attempting to occupy Midway Island in the central Pacific. Once again Nagumo opposed Yamamoto's plan, but was placed in command of the operation nonetheless. His striking force, this time comprising four fleet carriers and supporting ships, was assigned the dual mission of bombing the military facilities on Midway Island and destroying any U.S. fleets that appeared to oppose the invasion. In contrast with the Pearl Harbor raid, security was quite lax during preparations for the Midway operation and U.S. code-breakers were able to deduce when and where the Japanese would attack. Furthermore, in simulations of the Midway invasion plan, Nagumo and his staff foresaw a dilemma that could arise if American carriers should enter the battle while Japanese carrier aircraft were engaged in bombing the island, and this is exactly what came to pass on the morning of June 4, 1942.

Nagumo launched a raid on Midway Island at first light and had been attacked by planes from the island later in the morning. While his aircraft were preparing for a second attack on Midway, Japanese scout aircraft spotted an American carrier force. Nagumo was faced with the decision he dreaded: to rearm the planes already prepared to attack Midway, or to send them on their way and fail to respond to the challenge posed by the presence of the American carrier force. He chose to rearm his planes. While this process was underway, and his carriers' decks were loaded with aircraft, fuel lines, and armaments, he was attacked by American carrier-based planes. In a matter of minutes, three of Nagumo's four carriers, including his flagship, were in sinking condition. Nagumo at first refused to leave his stricken ship, but was physically dragged to safety by his staff. The battle continued throughout the day, resulting in the eventual loss of one U.S. fleet carrier, and the fourth and last of Nagumo's fleet carriers. Yamamoto called off the Midway operation, with Nagumo's agreement, in the early morning hours of June 5. The Japanese defeat was total, and the initiative in the Pacific War would soon turn to the Allies.

## Guadalcanal

Following the disaster at Midway, Yamamoto considered relieving Nagumo of his command. He feared, however, that Nagumo would commit suicide if removed from his post. The losses suffered at Midway forced the Japanese navy to abandon its quest for a decisive encounter with U.S. forces and concentrate instead on supporting land operations on Guadalcanal, in the Solomon Islands. In late August 1942, Nagumo's striking force, now comprising two fleet carriers and a smaller carrier, approached Guadalcanal while guarding troop transports sent to reinforce Japanese forces on the island. The American force was also comprised of two fleet carriers. In the ensuing battle, the Japanese lost their small aircraft carrier while heavily damaging one of the American fleet carriers. This battle at sea was inconclusive but Japanese land operations on Guadalcanal failed miserably. Nagumo was unable to avenge his defeat at Midway, but had performed competently and was to be given one last chance.

## Battle of the Santa Cruz Islands

The land battle on Guadalcanal continued into the fall, and the Japanese navy made one of its last attempts to support land operations on October 22, 1942. Although he was not in overall command of this mission, Nagumo did command its carrier forces, which comprised two fleet carriers and one smaller carrier. Once again, the Americans had two fleet carriers. The opponents made contact with each other on October 25 and launched attacks on the following morning. This battle ended in a marginal victory for the Japanese, who sank one American fleet carrier at the cost of suffering heavy damage to one of their fleet carriers and the loss of Nagumo's smaller carrier. This incomplete victory did not allow the Japanese to adequately reinforce their troops on Guadalcanal, and they evacuated the island in February 1943.

Admiral Yamamoto died when his plane was shot down in April 1943, and in the ensuing reorganization of the Japanese naval command structure, Nagumo was "promoted" to command the Central Pacific Area Fleet based on Saipan in the Northern Marianas Islands. This fleet existed only on paper, however, and Nagumo would not command any significant forces again in the war.

## Final Defeat

Nagumo remained on Saipan and assisted in the island's defense against the U.S. invasion, which commenced on June 15, 1944. Although Japanese forces offered suicidal resistance, their inferiority in numbers and firepower left the issue in no doubt, and American forces steadily overran the island. With nearly all of Saipan in U.S. hands and no escape possible, Nagumo committed suicide on the night of July 6, 1944.

## Further Reading

Agawa, Hiroyuki, *The Reluctant Admiral,* Kodansha International, 1979.

*The Japanese Navy in World War II,* edited by David C. Evans. Naval Institute Press, 1986.

Kemp, Peter, *The Oxford Companion to Ships and the Sea,* Oxford University Press, 1976.

MacIntyre, Captain Donald, *Aircraft Carrier,* Ballantine Books, 1972.

Prados, John, *Combined Fleet Decoded,* Random House, 1995.
Potter, John Deane, *Yamamoto,* Coronet Communications, 1971.
Toland, John, *The Rising Sun,* Bantam Books, 1981.
Ugaki, Admiral Matome, *Fading Victory,* University of Pittsburgh Press, 1991.
*Who Was Who in World War II,* edited by John Keegan, Thomas Y. Crowell Publishers, 1978.
*Who's Who in Military History,* edited by John Keegan and Andrew Wheatcroft, William Morrow & Co., 1976. □

# Condé Nast

**Condé Montrose Nast (1873–1942) was one of the world's most successful magazine publishers. Through his avant-garde periodicals, including *Vogue* and *Vanity Fair*, he set a new standard of fashion and home decorating for American women. He pioneered new techniques in marketing, printing, and magazine content, and nurtured the evolution of "cafe society," a blend of artists and elite society, that had never before come together.**

Condé Nast was born on March 26, 1873 in New York City, the son of William Nast and Esther Benoist. When Nast was three, his father left for Europe, where he spent the next 13 years. Esther Nast took her four children to live in St. Louis, Missouri, with her family. Although she was a descendant of French aristocracy, she raised her children on a dwindling personal fortune, with little financial contribution from her husband. The Nast children learned to play musical instruments and studied languages. They were raised in their mother's religion, Catholicism. Nast attended public school in St. Louis. A wealthy aunt paid for his college education at Georgetown University, where he excelled in rational philosophy and mathematics. There Nast met Robert J. Collier, whose father owned a weekly magazine called *Collier's.* Together the friends edited the school newspaper and performed at musical events. Nast went on to earn a law degree from Washington University.

In 1897, Collier offered Nast a job on the staff of his father's magazine in New York City, for a $12 weekly salary. Nast expanded the magazine's readership from a circulation of approximately 19,000 to over 568,000 over the course of ten years. Advertising revenues went from $5,600 to more than one million dollars in the same period. Nast introduced a number of innovations at *Collier's,* such as color pages, two-page spreads, and the "special number" (an issue devoted to one topic). Nast also divided the United States into marketing regions, noting that certain products sold more readily in certain areas of the country. When Nast resigned from *Collier's* his salary was $40,000 per year.

In 1902, Nast married Clarisse Couder, a society woman of French descent. Their son, Charles, was born in 1903 and a daughter, Natica, in 1905. In 1906, Clarisse took the children to live in France, where she socialized with artists, poets, and photographers, such as Rodin, Rilke, and Steichen. After a year, the children returned home, but Clarisse stayed in Europe for another year. Although his wife's background gave Nast an entrance into New York society, the marriage did not last. Clarisse moved out of their Park Avenue apartment in 1919, and the couple divorced in 1925. Nast gave her an annual income of $10,000, even after she remarried and divorced again.

## *Vogue* Set the Standard for Women's Fashions

Shortly after Nast married Couder, in 1905, he began negotiations for the purchase of *Vogue,* a magazine aimed at an elite stratum of society. He successfully acquired the magazine in 1909, with a circulation of 14,000 and advertising revenues of $100,000. His goal was to make it "the technical adviser—the consulting specialist—to the woman of fashion in the matter of her clothes and of her personal adornment."

Nast made many changes to *Vogue.* He converted the magazine from a weekly into a semi-monthly publication. He raised the price of an issue from 10 to 15 cents, added color covers, more advertising space, more clothing patterns, more society pages, and more fashion. The magazine reported news of an elite echelon of society—what they did and what they cared about: vacations, marriages, charity events, tennis tournaments, country clubs, horseback riding, summer homes, boarding schools, and garden clubs. Nast charged higher advertising rates in *Vogue* than did competing magazines. His justification for the high advertising rates were that, "*Vogue* is the elimination of waste circulation for the advertiser of quality goods. I determined to bait the editorial pages in such a way as to lift out of all the millions of Americans just the 100,000 cultivated people who can buy these quality goods."

In 1911, Nast bought interests in two other magazines, *House & Garden,* and *Travel.* Two years later, he wrote an article for the *Merchants' and Manufacturers' Journal,* wherein he described his own theory for creating a successful magazine—rather than appeal to the greatest number of people, a magazine should address the interests of a particular group of people. "A 'class publication' is nothing more nor less than a publication that looks for its circulation only to those having in common a certain characteristic marked enough to group them into a class. . . . The publisher, the editor, the advertising manager and circulation man must conspire not only to get all their readers from the one particular class to which the magazine is dedicated, but rigorously to exclude all others." By publishing a magazine that was aimed at the American upper class, Nast defined what it meant to be a member of that class. He also gave those who hoped to join that class lessons on what was needed to be a part of that select group.

## The Woman Who Was *Vogue*

Edna Chase began working in the circulation department at *Vogue* when she was 18 years old, in 1895. In 1914 she became the magazine's editor. Chase had high expectations of her staff. Women had to wear black silk stockings, white gloves, hats, and closed-toed shoes. On one occasion a *Vogue* editor tried to commit suicide by throwing herself in front of a subway train. Chase admonished the employee (who survived) and said, "We at *Vogue* don't throw ourselves under subway trains, my dear. If we must, we take sleeping pills."

Nast and Chase believed that the editorial and advertising areas of the magazine should be separated, and that advertised fashions should have no bearing on clothing styles featured in the articles. During the Great Depression this distinction grew more difficult to maintain. Advertisers expected to receive editorial coverage, in return for the exorbitant cost of advertisements. In 1934, Bergdorf Goodman spent over $16,000 for about 16 pages of advertising; the magazine gave the store over 60 pages of editorial space.

When World War I began, Chase worried that the fashion content of the magazine might dwindle, since most fashion originated in Paris at that time. She came up with the revolutionary idea of holding a charity fashion show featuring the work of New York designers. The idea of a fashion show "benefit" presentation was new, and Chase was uncertain as to whether or not society women might be attracted to such a venture. She managed to convince Mrs. Stuyvesant Fish to endorse the event, and thus many society women attended. There were no professional models in the United States, and so dressmakers' models were trained to walk down a runway. *Vogue* devoted 17 pages to coverage of the highly successful event. In so doing, *Vogue* opened

the market for American designers and ushered in a new era in fashion—one that was no longer dominated exclusively by Paris.

Nast was the first publisher to produce international editions of his magazine. Through British, French, Spanish, and German editions of *Vogue,* the magazine evolved, as one advertisement stated, ". . . [into] a living force in all of the civilized corners of the world."

## *Vanity Fair* Appealed to the Intellect

In 1913, Nast added two magazines to his publishing empire, *Dress,* and *Vanity Fair.* Around this time he met Frank Crowninshield and asked him to be editor of *Vanity Fair.* Crowninshield accepted on the condition that the magazine would contain nothing about women's fashion. Crowninshield intended that the mission of the magazine should be to cover the theater, art, literature, and sports. Of women readers he wrote, "For women, we intend to do . . . something which . . . has never before been done for them by an American magazine. We mean to make frequent appeals to their intellects. . . . " Crowninshield despised advertisements, and he intensely disliked a particular feature in his magazine called the "Well-Dressed Man." He believed that merchandising columns prostituted the magazine. When Crowninshield reduced space for the column to just four pages a year, Nast demanded the cut pages be replaced. Nast was well aware that editorial material focused on fashion greatly pleased his advertisers.

In 1921, Crowninshield moved into Nast's Park Avenue apartment. The two went to parties, openings, the theater, operas, and nightclubs. They entertained, traveled, golfed, and joined clubs together. They gave parties that brought together artists and society folk and initiated a concept called "cafe society." The relationship between the two men gave rise to gossip, although the two were never sexually involved. Crowninshield was not known to have had a physical relationship with anyone. Nast had two wives and several girlfriends. While Nast was still married to Clarisse Couder he became involved with Grace Moore, an opera singer. His other romantic interests were actresses, models, and debutantes. In 1928, Nast, then 55 years old, married a 20-year-old woman named Leslie Foster. In 1930, the couple had a daughter whom they also named Leslie. They divorced in the early 1930s. Nast was involved with Helen Brown Norden between 1932 and 1936.

## Financial Ruin

Nast changed the face of fashion photography forever. He hired well-respected photographers and urged them to take more realistic, relaxed, and informal photos. To ensure high quality publications, Nast purchased and renovated a printing plant in Connecticut. The Condé Nast Press earned a reputation for technical excellence, and Nast made several innovations in printing technology. When the stock market "crashed" in 1929, Nast no longer commanded the resources to indulge his perfectionist ideas of printing or anything else. He was ruined. On October 29, 1929, the stock value of Condé Nast Publications plummeted from $93 per share to $4.50. Nast owed two million dollars to a bank. He lost control of his publishing empire and within a few years was in debt for almost $5 million.

In 1930, Clare Boothe Brokaw (later Luce) went to work for Condé Nast Publications. By 1933, she was the managing editor of *Vanity Fair*. She suggested to Nast that he buy *Life,* a humorous magazine, and change the format to a pictorial magazine. Nast, who was devastated by his losses, rejected her advice. When Brokaw married Henry Luce, she persuaded him to follow her plan, and in 1936, Luce's new *Life* appeared on the scene. The publication became one of the world's most successful magazines.

In 1936, *Vanity Fair* merged with *Vogue.* Three years later, Nast started a new magazine called *Glamour.* Its objective was to recognize the Hollywood influence on fashion, beauty, and charm, and to bring those trends to the average woman. Nast used a new layout format for this magazine, the "crowded" page. Prior to this time, Nast publications presented stark, white pages with only one or two photos per page. The new *Glamour* magazine and its imaginative format were highly successful.

### A Sad End

In 1941, Nast developed health problems. His blood pressure soared, his heart began to fail, and he became dependent upon the use of an oxygen tank. He kept his failing health a secret from most people, until he suffered one heart attack in December of 1941 and another in September of 1942. He died in New York City on September 19, 1942. Eight hundred people attended his funeral. In January 1943, his possessions were auctioned off to pay his debts.

Nast believed that women should have the opportunity to have the prettiest clothes, the prettiest surroundings, and every known method to make themselves more attractive. His magazines still exist today. In 1998, the circulation of *Vogue* was 1,136,000. *Vanity Fair,* reestablished in 1983, had a circulation of 1,200,000 in 1998. Several other publications bear the famous name, such as *Condé Nast Bride's, Condé Nast Traveler,* and *Condé Nast Sports for Women.*

### Further Reading

Seebohm, Caroline, *The Man Who Was Vogue: The Life and Times of Condé Nast,* The Viking Press, 1982.
*Vogue,* May 1982. □

# Patricia Neal

**Patricia Neal (born 1926) is almost as well known for the events of her own life as she is for her career on stage and screen. In 1963, after winning her first Academy Award for Best Actress, Neal suffered three massive strokes. Her struggle to come back was both more dramatic and more triumphant than any of her roles on stage or screen.**

Patsy Louise ("Patricia") Neal was born in Packard, Kentucky on January 20, 1926. Her father, William Burdette Neal, was raised on a tobacco plantation in Virgina, and worked at the South Coal and Coke Company. Her mother, Eura Mildred Petrey Neal, was the daughter of Packard's town doctor, Pascal Gennings Petrey. She had an older sister, Margaret Ann, and a younger brother, William Petrey, whom they called "Pete." In 1929, the family moved to Knoxville, Tennessee where William Neal had gotten a new job.

### Drama Classes for Christmas

Although Neal was raised as a Baptist, she frequently attended the Methodist church with friends. On one of those occasions, during a Christmas program in 1936, she heard her grammar school teacher, Cornelia Avanti, present a monologue. She was so impressed that she wrote a letter to Santa explaining she wanted to study "dramatics" for her Christmas present. Her Aunt Maude's sister-in-law, Emily Mahan, had just returned from New York and opened her own drama school, so Neal's parents sent her to study with Mahan. Soon, Neal was organizing neighborhood productions, and presenting shows on the Neal family front porch. By high school, she was performing monologues in her Aunt Maude's sitting room. Word of mouth spread, and soon she was in demand for dramatic readings at local groups like the Knoxville Social Club. She won many awards for her readings, including the Tennessee State Award for dramatic reading. She also performed with the Tennessee Valley

Players. It was during this time that Neal decided that acting was the career path she would follow.

Neal enrolled in the drama school at Northwestern University in 1943. That following summer, she acted with a fledgling summer theater troupe in Eagles Mere, Pennsylvania. By the end of the summer, she had decided to quit school and went to New York with 300 dollars in her pocket. She moved to a West side apartment with three friends and began auditioning. She eventually landed the part of understudy for both lead roles in *The Voice of the Turtle,* and, at the suggestion of the show's producer, changed her name to "Patricia."

## From New York to Hollywood

The next year, Neal won the starring role in Lillian Hellman's *Another Part of the Forest.* The show opened at the Fulton Theater in New York on November 20, 1946. Neal was a critical success and won several awards including the Donaldson Award, the Drama Critics Award and the Antoinette Perry Award.

The silver screen was next. Neal accepted a contract from Warner Brothers, and later worked with MGM and 20th Century Fox. In her first role she played Mary in the 1949 movie version of *John Loves Mary.* This, as well as her next two films, *The Fountainhead* (1949) and *Bright Leaf* (1950), with Gary Cooper, were critical failures. The tide turned, however, in 1950 when she starred alongside Ronald Reagan in *The Hasty Heart.*

Shortly after arriving in Hollywood, Neal met and fell in love with Gary Cooper, who was married at the time. She and Cooper had an affair that began as the shooting of *The Fountainhead* ended. The low point of the affair came when Neal discovered she was pregnant. The two decided an abortion was the best solution to that problem. It was a decision she always regretted. The event hastened the end of their relationship in 1951.

Neal returned to New York, taking her own apartment on Park Avenue. She auditioned for Lillian Hellman and Kermit Bloomgarden in *The Children's Hour,* and was accepted for either of the two leading roles. She chose Martha. Just before rehearsals began for the play, she was introduced to Roald Dahl at a party at Hellman's home. The children's author, now famous for contributions like *Chitty Chitty, Bang Bang, Charley and the Chocolate Factory* and *James and the Giant Peach,* had come to the United States in 1942 to work in espionage for the British embassy in Washington. He soon after became a feature writer, contributing to several magazines including *The New Yorker.* Neal was not particularly interested in Dahl, but he persisted. "Deliberate is a good word for Roald Dahl. He knew exactly what he wanted and he quietly went about getting it. I did not yet realize, however, that he wanted me," Neal wrote in her autobiography, *As I Am.*

Neal wanted to settle down and start a family, so she married Dahl on July 2, 1953, though she would later admit that she didn't love him then. The couple eventually had five children. After the wedding, they purchased a home called Gipsy House, 30 miles from London, in Great Mis-

senden. They would live there in the spring and summer, and in New York the rest of the year while she was acting.

Neal continued to do stage work in both England and the United States throughout the 1950s, performing in *A Roomful of Roses, Suddenly Last Summer, Cat on a Hot Tin Roof,* and *The Miracle Worker.* She returned to the screen, too, performing in Elia Kazan's *A Face in the Crowd* in 1957. In 1961, she played the part of 2E in Truman Capote's *Breakfast At Tiffany's,* a supporting role to George Peppard and Audrey Hepburn's leads. In 1963, Neal co-starred with Paul Newman in the Elia Kazan film, *Hud.* She won an Academy Award, the New York Film Critics Award, and the British Motion Picture Award for "best foreign actress."

## Tragedy Came in Threes

All was not well in Neal's private life. A series of tragedies, beginning in the early 1960s, would put her career on hold for a few years. The first tragedy to hit the Dahl family was an accident. Five-month-old Theo suffered severe brain damage after being struck by a taxi while in his pram. Shortly thereafter, in 1962, the Dahl's oldest child, Olivia, came down with encephalitis and died. She was seven years old.

In 1965, during the filming of *Seven Women,* Neal suffered three strokes while pregnant with daughter, Lucy. She was 39. After surgery to remove blood clots on her brain, she fell into a 21-day coma. Newspapers prematurely published her obituary, but Neal was still fighting. The strokes left her paralyzed on her right side and greatly diminished her speech. The tragedy brought out Dahl's best and worst traits. As a stroke victim, he knew that Neal had a year or less to re-learn most of her basic skills. When she returned home from the hospital he forced her to ask for things by their proper names or go without them. They worked together for ten months. At the end of that time, the only remaining infirmity was a loss of vision in her right eye.

## A Triumphant Return

Neal returned to acting at Dahl's urging. In 1965, she won a British Film Academy Award for best foreign actress for *In Harm's Way.* In 1968, she was nominated for an Academy Award for her role in *The Subject was Roses.* In 1971, Neal was nominated for an Emmy Award for her performance in the film *The Homecoming: A Christmas Story.* It became the pilot for *The Waltons* television series.

Around this time, Neal met a young widow at the David Ogilvy advertising agency, Felicity Crosland. The two became friends and Crosland was invited to stay at Great Missenden. She eventually betrayed that friendship by becoming Dahl's mistress. When Neal learned of the affair, she was devastated and returned to New York, this time for good. She had come to depend on Dahl, and even love him. The couple divorced in 1983.

Neal eventually converted to Catholicism. On the advice of Gary Cooper's daughter, she entered the Regina Laudis Abbey, a New England Benedictine retreat. The nuns encouraged her to keep a journal of her memories and rediscover herself. The therapy was also intended to improve her memory, which had been affected by the strokes.

The journal became the basis for Neal's autobiography, *As I Am,* which was published in 1988. It helped her to come to terms with the divorce.

Never one to rest on her laurels, Neal has turned the knowledge she gained from being a stroke victim into a way to help others. The Patricia Neal Rehabilitation Center was opened in 1978 in Knoxville, Tennessee. The 72-bed facility is nationally recognized for its rehabilitation of patients with stroke, spinal cord, and traumatic brain injuries. Neal and Dahl had created a recovery system that is recognized worldwide. Thirty stroke centers in England now use those methods.

### Life On Her Own

In 1981, Anthony Harvey and Larry Schiller directed and produced *Gypsy House: The Patricia Neal Story,* staring Glenda Jackson and Dirk Bogarde for CBS television. Robert Anderson (*Tea and Sympathy*) wrote the script, which both Neal and Dahl reviewed and approved before shooting began. Jackson was nominated for an Emmy for her performance.

Neal continued to perform in several made-for-TV movies throughout the 1980s and co-starred with Shelley Winters in the ironically titled, *An Unremarkable Life,* in 1989. In 1999, Neal played the role of Cookie in the Robert Altman film, *Cookie's Fortune,* a murder-mystery involving two sisters in a small Mississippi town. Neal also took two cruises with the Theater Guild's Theater-at-Sea programs. She performed in one hour plays, read stories, and related incidents from her life.

### Further Reading

Neal, Patricia, *As I Am,* Simon and Schuster, 1988.
*Boston Globe,* May 1, 1988.
*Chicago Tribune,* April 3, 1988.
*Gannett News Service,* April 24, 1988.
*Globe and Mail,* March 30, 1981.
*Guardian,* July 27, 1996.
*Knoxville News-Sentinel,* November 24, 1998.
*Los Angeles Daily News,* October 26, 1989.
*San Francisco Chronicle, Sunday Review,* June 26, 1988.
*Tennessean,* November 15, 1998.
"All About Patricia Neal Rehabilitation Center," Patricia Neal Rehabilitation Center http://www.covenanthealth.com/aboutus/pnrc/pnrc-home.html. (March 9, 1999).
"Cookie's Fortune," IMDb http://us.imdb.com/Title?Cookie%27s+Fortune+(1999) (March 9, 1999).
"Patricia Neal: Greatness Through Understanding," WIC Biography http://www.wic.org/bio/pneal.htm March 9, 1999.
"Who Is Patricia Neal?" Patricia Neal Rehabilitation Center http://www.covenanthealth.com/aboutus/pnrc/patneal.html. (March 9, 1999). □

# John Nordstrom

**Nordstrom stores are known for outstanding customer service and product selection. The Seattle-based department store began as a small shoe store co-founded by Swedish immigrant John W. Nordstrom (1871–1963) in 1901.**

John W. Nordstrom endured many hardships before becoming a successful shoe retailer in the early 20th century. A difficult childhood, immigration to the United States, and a series of back-breaking jobs gave Nordstrom the drive he needed to succeed and taught him the value of hard work.

The founder of Nordstrom stores was born Johan W. Nordstrom on February 15, 1871, in Alvik Neder Lulea, Sweden, just 60 miles from the Arctic Circle. Nordstrom's father, a blacksmith, wagon maker, and part-time farmer, died when Nordstrom was eight. Three years later, Nordstrom's mother took him out of school to work on the family farm. Nordstrom, the third of five children, described his childhood as unhappy. His mother expected him to do as much work as his brother, who was ten years older.

Nordstrom left Sweden with two friends when he was 16. They traveled by boat to Hull, England, and then by train to Liverpool, where they began a ten-day voyage as steerage passengers to New York. From there, Nordstrom took a train to Stambaugh, Michigan, where a cousin helped him get a job loading iron ore onto railroad cars. This was the first of many manual jobs he held over the next five years. Nordstrom moved westward through Iowa, Colorado, California, and Washington, performing such back-breaking work as logging, coal mining, gold and silver mining, loading railroad ties, and carting bricks. In 1896, he settled in Arlington, Washington, about 50 miles north of Seattle. Nordstrom was one of many Swedish immigrants in the town. He started a potato farm on 50 acres of land and began courting a Swedish woman named Hilda Carlson.

A year later, the *Seattle Port-Intelligencer* reported that gold had been found in the Yukon territory. Like many West Coast residents, Nordstrom traveled north to seek his fortune. He took a coal freighter to Port Valdez, Alaska, and then traveled 1,000 miles on horse and on foot to Dawson in the heart of the gold fields. Accustomed to hard work, Nordstrom toiled in the gold fields for two years before striking pay dirt. When another miner challenged his claim, Nordstrom sold his share to the other miner rather than fight him in a corrupt arbitration process. He returned to Seattle with $13,000.

### Settled in Seattle

Nordstrom, who had changed his given name to John, married Hilda Carlson in 1900. The couple had five children: Everett, Elmer, Lloyd, Mabel, and Esther.

Nordstrom wanted to invest his earnings in a business. A Klondike friend, Carl F. Wallin, worked as a shoemaker and suggested that he and Nordstrom open a shoe store. Nordstrom invested $5,000 in the business; Wallin added $1,000. Their store, Wallin & Nordstrom, opened in 1901 in a 20-foot-wide Seattle storefront. The two Swedes, who barely spoke English, began their business with a $3,500 inventory of shoes, ranging in price from $1.95 to $4.95. Nordstrom knew nothing about selling shoes, as he recalled in his memoir, "Opening day, we had not had a customer by noon, so my partner went to lunch. He had not been gone but a few minutes when our first customer, a woman, came in for a pair of shoes she had seen in the window. I was nervous and could not find the style she had picked out in our stock. I was just about ready to give up when I decided to try on the pair from the window, the only pair we had of that style." The customer bought the shoes.

The partners relied on traveling salesmen to stock the store. At first, they bought only medium widths. But they soon realized that their Swedish customers required larger sizes, and they began keeping wider widths in stock. Little did they know at the time, the successor to their tiny store would one day have a national reputation for its extensive inventory.

Wallin & Nordstrom's first day sales totaled $12.50. Within a few months, Saturday sales reached $100. By 1905, the store's annual sales were $47,000. That year, the partners expanded for the first time. They bought a second shoe store and relocated their business. The business expanded several times, but it continued to carry conservative shoes, including many corrective "health" shoes, rather than fashion styles.

## Second Generation

Nordstrom's sons, Everett and Elmer, began working in the store as stock boys when they were young. By 1928, Nordstrom and Wallin's partnership was strained and Nordstrom sold his interest in the store to his sons. *The Nordstrom Way* describes the sons' ownership as "only on paper because their father had loaned them the money for the purchase and had co-signed a bank note to ensure them working capital." Although officially retired at age 57, John Nordstrom maintained an office at the store for the rest of his life. Wallin retired in 1929 and sold his share of the business to the Nordstrom sons, who renamed the store Nordstrom's. John Nordstrom's third son, Lloyd, joined the company in 1933.

Many years later, John Nordstrom was asked if he had taken a big risk when he turned his business over to his relatively inexperienced sons. He responded, "I only went through the sixth grade in grammar school in Sweden. My boys are college graduates. They must be a lot smarter than I ever was."

Nordstrom's survived the Depression, when retail prices dropped, forcing the business to sell twice as many shoes to maintain its sales volume. During World War II, shoes were strictly rationed. Because leather was reserved for Army boots, retailers were given quotas of shoes to sell and customers were issued ration stamps. They were allowed only three pairs per year. The Nordstroms traveled the country to maintain the inventory their customers were accustomed to, including odd sizes and women's work boots, which were in demand during the war.

Between the 1920s and the 1950s, Nordstrom developed the customer service philosophy for which the store is known today. Everett, Elmer, and Lloyd Nordstrom ran their business with a high level of personal service. According to *The Nordstrom Way*, they stocked high-quality merchandise and worked with suppliers to obtain the best values, unique items and a wide selection of styles and prices. Buyers were sticklers for quality and were known to examine merchandise scrupulously. Salespeople were taught to understand the products they sold.

Ironically, the company's customer service attitude could not change the owners' salesmanship abilities. In *The Nordstrom Way*, Lloyd Nordstrom said that he, his brothers, and his father were the store's worst salesmen, but they succeeded by providing good value and quality, and by hiring salespeople to move the merchandise out of the store. Today, everyone who works for Nordstrom's begins his or her career as a salesperson; managers are not hired from outside the company. Management believes the only way to learn how to care for customers is to grow up inside the company culture.

Under the management of Nordstrom's three sons, his business grew to be the largest independent shoe chain in the United States. By the early 1960s, the company had expanded to eight stores in Washington and Oregon and operated 13 leased shoe departments in other stores. Nordstrom's four-story Seattle store was the largest shoe store in the United States. The company's 1961 sales volume reached $12 million.

## Expanded into Apparel

Nordstrom's diversified into apparel when it bought Best's Apparel Inc., a fashionable Seattle women's clothing store in 1961. Six years later, annual sales were $40 million. Shoes accounted for half of sales.

During the 1960s, Nordstrom's became the first clothing retailer to pay its salespeople meaningful commissions. The Nordstrom family believed that cash incentives encouraged salespeople to work harder and to build customer loyalty.

Shortly after the purchase of Best's, on October 11, 1963, John Nordstrom died in Seattle, Washington of a cerebral hemorrhage, at the age of 92. He had visited his office at the company headquarters throughout his retirement to play cards or cribbage or just to walk around the store.

In 1968, Nordstrom's sons turned the business over to their sons. A plan was considered to sell the business to another retailer. Instead, the third generation took the company public in 1971. Nordstrom Inc. subsequently expanded into Alaska, California, and the East Coast. This expansion was considered risky because Nordstrom was not well known outside the Pacific Northwest. In 1995, six members of the fourth generation of Nordstrom's were named co-presidents of what had become a nationwide chain.

Today, the small shoe store founded by hard-working John Nordstrom in 1901 has grown into a nationwide fashion specialty chain known for its renowned services, generous size ranges, and a selection of fine apparel, shoes, and accessories for men, women, and children. Nordstrom has been called "America's Number One Customer Service Company" based on its policies of empowering salespeople to make decisions favoring the customer over the company. While the company's growth and expansion were largely orchestrated by the descendents of John W. Nordstrom, he founded the company on the principles that have fueled its success: exceptional quality, selection, service and value.

## Further Reading

Spector, Robert and Patrick D. McCarthy, *The Nordstrom Way,* John Wiley, 1995.
*Footwear News,* November 25, 1991.
*Nordstrom Inc. Annual Report,* 1987.
*Seattle Post-Intelligencer,* October 12, 1963.
"Nordstrom History," available at http://www.nordstrom.com (March 1, 1999). □

# Paavo Nurmi

**Paavo Nurmi (1897–1973) was one of the greatest distance runners of all time. Known as "The Flying Finn" and "The King of Runners," he dominated long-distance running throughout the early part of the twentieth century, setting 25 world records at distances from 1,500 meters to 20,000 meters and winning nine gold and three silver medals at three Olympic Games from 1920 through 1928.**

Born on July 13, 1897 in Turku, a port town on the southwest coast of Finland, Nurmi was the son of a carpenter and began running through the Finnish forests when he was nine. He later claimed that he grew up eating black bread and dried fish. If he did, this meager diet made him a champion. His father died in 1910 and Nurmi finished his schooling with an average of 9.38 out of a possible 10. He worked on docks and was a filer in an engineering shop for the next four years.

Nurmi was inspired to become a runner by the incredible performance of Finnish runner, Hannes Kolehmainen, at the 1912 Stockholm Olympics. Kolehmainen brought his small country to international attention by winning three gold medals in long-distance events. Nurmi was 15 years old at the time. He soon bought his first real pair of running shoes and started training.

## Disciplined Training

Nurmi was one of the first athletes ever to take a systematic approach to training. Although this approach is common today, in Nurmi's time no one had yet thought to train with a stopwatch to measure pace and time, or to cross-train by combining running, walking, and calisthenics. His major innovation in training was to run most of the race at an even pace. Because he ran with a watch, Nurmi, unlike other athletes, knew what his pace was while he was running and could plan his winning strategy. Before this, runners had run fairly slow laps around the track, conserving their strength until the last lap when they sprinted to the finish. The Sports Museum Foundation of Finland

quoted him as saying, "When you race against time, you don't have to sprint. Others can't hold the pace if it is steady and slow to the finish."

Nurmi's discipline took precedence over everything else in his life. "Success in sport as in almost anything comes from devotion," he said, according to Joe Brady in *Virtual Finland,* "The athlete must make a devotion of his specialty." Nurmi certainly did that, critically analyzing his daily training schedule, combining long, slow runs and long walks. Obsessed with running, he seemed to observers not to have any personality at all. Nurmi appeared to be a remote, cold, and inhuman running machine. He did not socialize with other athletes, never gave interviews, disliked publicity, and seemed never to let anyone get to know him, throughout a long career.

As Brady noted, "Nurmi was an introvert. To many observers he seemed bleak and remote, interested only in his running." Nurmi's inward intensity was a part of his personality, but also came from the fact that he was determined to leave records that would never be broken. According to the Sports Museum Foundation of Finland, Finnish journalist Martti Jukola wrote of him in 1935: "There was something inhumanly stern and cruel about him but he conquered the world by pure means: with a will that had supernatural power."

## Began to Race

In 1914, Nurmi joined Turun Urheiluliitto, a Turku sports club that he represented throughout his career. On

May 29 his training paid off—running at Turku, he set his first national record by running 3000 meters in 8 minutes, 36.2 seconds. There were no Olympic Games in 1916 because of World War I, but in 1920 Nurmi ran at the Olympic Games in Antwerp, Belgium. In the 5,000 meters, his first race, he lost to Joseph Guillemot of France. This would be the only defeat to a foreigner in an Olympic final during his entire career. He won gold medals in the 10,000 meters and the individual and team cross-country events, and a silver in the 5,000 meters.

After the Antwerp Olympics, Nurmi continued to win. He set his first world record on June 22, 1921, in Stockholm by running the 10,000 meters in 30 minutes, 40.2 seconds. After that, he set a new world record in distances ranging from 1,500 meters to 10,000 meters, racing with his stopwatch in hand, adhering to a rigid schedule he had planned beforehand. Instead of concerning himself with what his competitors were doing, Nurmi was more concerned with meeting his own high goals, set by his watch. By the end of 1923, Nurmi held world records in the mile, the 5,000 meter, and the 10,000 meter races, a feat that has never been done before or since.

At the 1924 Paris Olympics, the Flying Finn won five gold medals in six days. Nurmi won the 1,500 and the 5,000 meters within an hour of each other, won the cross-country race as an individual and as part of a team and won the 3,000-meter team race. In the 1,500-meter event, he ran 800 meters in 14:31:2, killing all opposition by effectively winning long before the race was over. He was so confident that he tossed his stopwatch onto the grass and cruised easily to the finish. In the 5,000 meters, he tried a different tactic. His rivals, Ville Ritola of Finland and Edvin Wide of Sweden, started with a fast pace. Nurmi ran steadily 40 meters behind them, waited for them to fade (meanwhile checking the pace with his watch), and then passed them. In the cross-country race, he stunned everyone with his seemingly superhuman performance—on a day so hot and humid that 24 of the 39 entrants collapsed along the way, Nurmi seemed untouched and won the race by two minutes.

In that same Olympiad, Finnish authorities barred Nurmi from competing in the 10,000 meters because they wanted to give Finnish runner Ville Ritola a chance to win a gold. This angered Nurmi, so he went to another track and ran alone, recording his time on his stopwatch. It was faster than the official time set by the gold medal winner.

## American Tours

In 1925, Nurmi embarked on a tour of the United States, running mostly on indoor tracks. In five months, he raced 55 times, won 53 of the races, lost once, and opted out of the race once.

Perhaps this tour tired him because Nurmi lost some of his edge. He began winning by shorter margins and he never bettered the three world records he had set in 1924 in the 1,500, 5,000, and 10,000-meter events. Despite the decline, Nurmi went to the 1928 Olympic Games in Amsterdam. If he performed well, it would open the door for him to enter the potentially lucrative American track circuit.

He won a gold medal in the 10,000 meters and took silver in the 5,000 meters and the 3,000 meters.

According to the Sports Museum Foundation of Finland, when he was 31, Nurmi told a Swedish newspaper reporter, "This is absolutely my last season on the track. I am beginning to get old. I have raced for fifteen years and have had enough of it." Nevertheless, he continued to run and, in 1929, went on his second American tour. By 1930, he had regained some of his old energy and form and set world records in six miles and in 20 kilometers.

## Barred from Olympic Competition

In 1932, Nurmi headed for the Olympic Games in Los Angeles, determined to defend his 10,000 meter record against rivals. He also hoped to win a gold medal in the marathon, just as his hero Hannes Kolehmainen had done in 1920. The IAAF barred him from Olympic competition because, they claimed, he was no longer an amateur: he had been paid travel expenses for a tour through Germany in 1925. At that time, athletes could only compete in the Olympics if they had not made money from their sport, so Nurmi was out.

Nurmi went to Los Angeles anyway, stayed in the Olympic village and kept training. Runners who saw him reported that he suffered from a foot injury and was barely able to walk. However, his determination was so great that Nurmi ran anyway. Other runners scheduled to compete in the marathon pleaded with IAAF officials to let Nurmi run, but their pleas were ignored. Barred from running, Nurmi could not bring himself to watch the 10,000 meters or the marathon. He later claimed that, if allowed to compete, he would have won the marathon by five minutes.

## Last Race

Because he had competed as a professional runner, Nurmi was no longer allowed to compete in international amateur events. In Konigsberg, Germany, on October 4, 1931, he won his last event outside Finland, a 5,000-meter race. He continued to run in Finland after that, and was known as the "national amateur." He ran his last race in Viipuri, Finland, on September 16, 1934, winning the 10,000 meters.

After retiring from running, Nurmi became a businessman and building contractor. He had saved and invested his money since the 1920s and now made a great deal more, mostly through house building; 40 townhouses that his company built are still standing in Helsinki today. In addition to business, Nurmi sometimes trained other Finnish runners. He hated publicity, but when World War II began and Finland was threatened by the Soviet Union, he went to the United States to gain support for the Finnish cause.

## Lighted the Olympic Flame

In 1952, the Olympic Games were held in Helsinki. As was the tradition, a relay of runners had carried a torch with the Olympic flame from Greece to Finland. No one new who the last runner would be, the one who would bring the torch into the stadium to light the Olympic flame for these Games. When the electric scoreboard flashed, "The Olympic torch will be brought into the stadium by Paavo Nurmi,'' the 70,000-person home crowd was stunned into silence. Then a huge roar filled the stadium and many Finns burst into tears.

Nurmi worked hard all his life and never retired, although an attack of coronary thrombosis slowed him down in the late 1950s. In 1967, he experienced another attack. The following year, he used his hard-earned money to set up a foundation to study that disease, providing buildings for the researchers to do their work and a large sum of money.

Nurmi died in Helsinki on October 2, 1973. On October 11, he was given a state funeral with full honors and was buried in his hometown of Turku. Since his death, statues of him have been erected all over Finland and at the International Olympic Committee headquarters in Switzerland. Medals and stamps have been issued in his honor and an asteroid was named after him. In 1987, Finland issued a ten-mark note with Nurmi on one side and the Olympic stadium on the other, making Nurmi the only Olympic athlete ever to be pictured on any nation's currency.

## Further Reading

''The Little Giant of the Olympics,'' Welcome to Finland, http://www.publiscan.fi/wtf7c.htm (February 23, 1999).

''Nurmi Breaks Two World Records,'' Media One Express, http://www.mediaone.net/fresno/explore/thisday/0106.html (February 23, 1999).

''Nurmi: The Original 'Flying Finn','' ESPNET SportsZone, http://espn.go.com/editors/atlanta96/features/nurmi.html (February 23, 1999).

''Paavo Nurmi,'' IAAF, http://www.iaaf.org/athletes/legends/ PaavoNurmi.html (February 23, 1999).

''Paavo Nurmi,'' Paavo Nurmi Background, http://paavonurmi .weppi.fi/background.htm (February 23, 1999).

''Paavo Nurmi,'' Virtual Finland, http://www.vn.fi/vn/um/finfo/ english/paavo.html (February 23, 1999).

''Paavo Nurmi 100 Years: Paavo Nurmi,'' Sports Museum Foundation of Finland, http://www.stadion.fi/ PAAVONURMIMI100/life.htm (February 23, 1999).

''Paavo Nurmi 100 Years: Paavo Nurmi as Seen by Others,'' Sports Museum Foundation of Finland, http://www.stadion.fi/ PAAVONURMIMI100/seenby.htm (February 23, 1999).

''1932—Los Angeles, California, USA, Timeblazers, http://www .timeblazers.com/Olym__1932.html (February 23, 1999). ☐

# P

## Gordon Parks

**Multi-faceted photojournalist, Gordon Parks (born 1912), documented many of the greatest images of the 20th century. He expanded his artistic pursuits from visual images to literature with his first novel, *The Learning Tree,* which he then adapted into an award-winning motion picture. Over the years, his works have included musical composition, orchestration, and poetry. The limit of Parks' talent remains to be discovered as he evolves with characteristic grace into the era of digital photography.**

Gordon Roger Alexander Buchanan Parks was born in Fort Scott, Kansas on November 30, 1912. He was the youngest of 15 siblings, the children of Andrew and Sarah (Ross) Jackson Parks. The rumor survives, more than eight decades later, that Parks was born dead. In what must have seemed a miracle, the attending physician was able to revive the infant. The physician, Dr. Gordon, acquired a namesake in the process.

The Parks family members were victims of extreme poverty. Andrew Parks was a dirt farmer whose wife passed away when Gordon was only 15. Following the death of Sarah Parks, members of the Parks family dispersed, and Gordon went to St. Paul, Minnesota to stay with an older sister. In St. Paul he attended Central High and Mechanical Arts High School, but the hardships of adult life set in before he received a diploma. Parks had failed to establish a congenial relationship with his brother-in-law. Thus, life became difficult. The relationship grew increasingly strained until Parks abruptly left his sister's household. Still in high school and jobless, he carried few belongings with him into the frigid Minnesota winter. He survived by taking odd jobs and tried to finish his education, but soon dropped out and drifted in search of work.

### Young Artist on His Own

Even as a very young child, Parks sensed his own gift of music. As a youngster, he played an old Kimball piano whenever he could find the time. He was, in fact, able to pick and play most instruments that crossed his path. That innate sense of music enabled Parks to secure work as a piano player, albeit in the setting of a brothel. In time Parks joined the Larry Funk Orchestra and went on tour until the band dissolved in New York, at which point he found himself in Harlem and jobless once again. Parks joined the Civilian Conservation Corps in 1933 and used that employment to return to Minnesota, where he married Sally Alvis. In 1935 Parks went to work for the railroad.

Parks was a porter on the Northern Pacific Railroad in the late 1930s when he purchased a 35mm camera, a Voightlander Brilliant, from a pawn shop in Seattle. He carried the $10 camera to Puget Sound and shot some pictures of seagulls. Those first pictures were impressive, and they were on display at the developer's shop within weeks. Soon Parks secured a professional "shoot" for a woman's apparel store in St. Paul. Eventually his work was seen by Marva Louis, wife of prize-fighter Joe Louis. In 1941, she convinced Parks to move to Chicago, where she used her influence to procure photography assignments for him. In his spare time, Parks photographed the urban ghettos, and again his work was impressive. Within the year, Parks received a fellowship from the Julius Rosenwald Foundation to study photography. He used the opportunity to apprentice with Roy Stryker at the Farm Services Admin-

istration (FSA) in Washington, D.C., beginning in January 1942. Parks documented images of the Great Depression. His first FSA picture, taken in 1942, was called "Washington, D.C. Government Charwoman." The classic photograph depicted a government employee, Ella Watson, who worked at one of the federal buildings in Washington, standing with a mop and broom against a backdrop of the American Flag. Parks found Watson to be an expressive subject, and he shot 85 pictures of her. The original photo of Watson, which is alternately titled "American Gothic, Washington, D.C." was one of over 200 works that Parks donated to Washington's Corcoran Art Gallery in 1998.

By 1943, Parks was a valued employee of Roy Stryker. When Stryker transferred to the Office of War Information, Parks went along. His assignment with the War Office was to document through photography the activities of the 332nd Fighter Group, the Tuskegee Airmen. He remained on that assignment until 1945 when he changed employers, again to work with Stryker. The pair went to work at Standard Oil in New Jersey where Parks photographed small towns and other urban views.

Parks was still employed by the federal government in 1944 when he accepted a freelance assignment from *Vogue* magazine to shoot some fashion sets. The *Vogue* assignments continued for several years. In 1947, Parks found the time to write a how-to book called *Flash Photography*. He followed with a second book called *Techniques and Principles of Documentary Portraiture* in 1948. Also in 1948, Parks embarked on what evolved into a 20-year career as a member of the photography staff of *Life* magazine. That

publication availed itself of his expressive artistry as well as his cultural background. As an African American, Parks received assignments few others would accept, including a moving and eloquent photographic documentary about the urban gangs in Harlem. Among the most expressive of the photographs in that work was a 1948 shot called "Red Jackson and Herbie Levy Study Wounds on Face of Slain Gang Member Maurice Gaines."

### Brings Color to *Life*

During his career with *Life,* Parks photographed some of the most beautiful scenery and people in the world. In 1950, he spent two years in Paris, as the European correspondent for *Life.* He worked in the exclusive areas that bordered the Mediterranean Sea—France, Italy, Spain, and Portugal. Parks was privileged to photograph world aristocracy and celebrities, including Duke Ellington, Ingrid Bergman and Roberto Rosselini, Gloria Vanderbilt, and Louis Armstrong. As *Life* opened new doors, Parks expanded his technical horizons. The growing popularity of film and television during the 1950s beckoned Parks to enlarge his creative arena. In 1958, he began his initial work with color photography, and the following year he added poetry to his repertoire. *Life* published a series of photographs by Parks, enhanced with verses of his own poems.

Parks went on to produce memorable photojournalism during the 1960s. In a 1961 essay on poverty in Brazil, his article centered on the family of Flavio Da Silva. Flavio, a twelve-year-old Brazilian boy at the time of the feature, was gravely ill, which put the welfare of his entire family into jeopardy. The Flavio Da Silva Story was hailed as a benchmark of journalism, partly because of the unanticipated outpouring of assistance provided to the Da Silva family in response to Parks' story.

Parks' work continued to profoundly influence the lives of his photographic subjects as well as his own family. In 1965, Parks documented the rift that occurred between civil rights leader Malcolm X and his church, the Nation of Islam. His work incensed the Nation of Islam, and *Life* was forced to provide security protection for Parks. His family left the country for a time, until the animosity subsided. In an earlier piece, in 1956, Parks described the plight of "Willy Causey and Family, Shady Grove, Alabama." The Causeys, too, were forced to flee their home under threats of retribution for Parks' honest yet disturbing journalism. The Causey essay, shot near Mobile, Alabama, was a documentary on the plight of segregated African Americans. In 1967, Parks documented a poverty-stricken family, the Fontenelles, from the tenements of Harlem. With intervention by Parks, the Fontenelles were assisted with $35,000 from *Life.* The money enabled the family to move to Long Island, although a series of tragedies continued to plague them.

Between 1968 and 1976, Parks worked in Hollywood as a screenwriter and film director. Beginning in 1968 and into 1969, he wrote the screenplay, produced the film, directed the filming, and composed the score for *Learning Tree.* The movie, which is autobiographical in nature, was filmed in Parks' hometown of Fort Scott, Kansas. Following the critical success of his first film, Parks made two films about the character Shaft, in the 1970s. In 1976 he filmed a movie, *Leadbelly,* about the life of the folk singer and guitarist, Huddie Ledbetter.

## Lengthy List of Credits

The resume of Gordon Parks reads impressively, with 14 books, eight films, 12 musical compositions, a ballet, exhibitions, photographs, and paintings to his credit. He donated a vast archive of his creative work to the U.S. Library of Congress in 1995, because he "wanted it all stored under one roof and a roof that I [Parks] could respect," he was quoted in *Jet.* James Billington, the librarian of Congress, graciously accepted Parks' offer.

September 17, 1997 marked the first ceremony of the Gordon Parks Independent Film Awards. Chris Williams won the directing award for *Asbury Park* and Sheldon Sampson won the screenwriting award for *Two Guns.* In 1988, Parks made a documentary for the Public Broadcasting System (PBS) entitled "Gordon Parks: Moments without Proper Names." In August of that same year, he received the National Medal of the Arts from President Ronald Reagan. At that ceremony the Washington Press Corps honored Parks with a standing ovation.

In 1989, at the age of 76, Parks penned a ballet entitled, "Martin," about Martin Luther King, Jr. The following year, Parks was inducted into the Journalism Hall of Fame by the National Association of Black Journalists. He also embarked on the exploration of a new artistic medium—digital ink-jet printing. Parks used the art form to create abstractions, many of which are based on photographs of landscapes; but other objects, even paintings, are used as well. With this new art form, Parks placed great emphasis on light and dark.

In addition to *The Learning Tree,* Parks penned three autobiographies: *A Choice of Weapons,* (1966); *To Smile in Autumn,* (1979); and *Voices in the Mirror,* (1990). His numerous poetry anthologies include *Gordon Parks: A Poet and His Camera, Arias of Silence,* and *Glimpses Toward Infinity.*

Among the many exhibitions of Parks' works were "Moments Without Proper Names," in 1996 at the Afro-American Historical and Cultural Museum in Philadelphia; and the retrospective "Half Past Autumn: The Art of Gordon Parks," which opened in September 1997 at the Corcoran Art Gallery in Washington, D.C. "Half Past Autumn" went on to St. Paul, New York City, Detroit, Memphis, West Palm Beach, Atlanta, New Orleans, Los Angeles, Cincinnati, and Chicago.

Parks has been the recipient of honorary degrees from a score of universities and art institutions. He was further honored by the Stockton School of East Orange, New Jersey—a communications media magnet, which was renamed the Gordon Parks Academy.

## First Black

The prairie country where Parks spent his childhood was replete with segregated public schools, racially motivated killings, and even segregated cemeteries. Parks himself, on one occasion, was left to drown in a river because of his race, but survived the attack. He learned from his parents to avoid the "decay" of racism. He was quoted in *Life,* "The anger and bitterness are there, but you use those emotions to help you do what you want to do." In adulthood, Parks was the first African American photographer at *Life* and earlier the first African American at FSA. He witnessed, during his early career in Washington, the segregation of lunch counters, theaters, and other public buildings. Parks' production of *The Learning Tree* was the first "studio-financed" Hollywood motion picture directed by an African American.

Parks presented his reflections on racism through selected works. *Born Black,* a collection of his photographic essays for *Life* on the topic of black activism, was published in 1971. Parks directed the movie, *Odyssey of Solomon Northrup* in 1988. It tells the story, based in fact, about a free black man from the North who was taken into slavery by Southerners in the 1800s.

## Close-Up

In contrast to his youth, Parks makes his home in a serene studio in Manhattan, overlooking the East River. He was quoted in *Life* concerning his latest creative outlet of painting, "I paint how I feel when I wake up. I may feel gentle, or very abrupt, like a dragon out of the sky."

Through nearly 50 years of married life, Parks maintained friendships with a trio of ex-wives. He and Sally Alvis Parks divorced in 1961 after 28 years of marriage. The following year, he married Elizabeth Campbell Rollins. They divorced in 1973. Later that year, on August 26, Parks married Genevieve Young. That final marriage lasted six years; the couple divorced in 1979.

Parks has three children from his first marriage: David, Leslie, and Toni Parks Parsons. An older son, Gordon Jr., was killed in a plane crash in 1979. Parks has two grandsons: Alain and Gordon III, and was honored to be named the godfather of Malcolm X's daughter, Qubilah Shabazz.

## Further Reading

*American Visions,* August/September 1997, p. 11.
*Jet,* April 30, 1990, p. 12; July 31, 1995, p. 21; June 17, 1996, p. 23; December 16, 1996, p. 34; October 6, 1997, p. 35; January 19, 1998, p. 21; October 19, 1998, p. 33; December 7, 1998, p. 22.
Knight-Ridder/Tribune News Service, February 2, 1994.
*Life,* October, 1994, p. 26; September 1997, p.94.
*New York Amsterdam News,* September 11, 1997, p. 29; September 25, 1997, p. 30.
*Modern Maturity,* June/July 1989, p. 56.
*PSA Journal,* November 1992, p. 26(8).
*Smithsonian,* April 1989, p. 66.
*USA Today,* September 1998, p. 46.
*World & I,* September 1993, p. 184(10). □

# Alice Paul

**Credited with revitalizing the movement for women's suffrage, Alice Paul (1885–1977) mobi-**

lized a generation of women who had grown impatient with the incremental measures being taken toward gaining the vote. Paul helped to found the Congressional Union (later the National Woman's Party) and led a movement dedicated to the passage of a constitutional amendment for women's suffrage. Her tactics led to the passage of the 19th Amendment to the U.S. Constitution in 1919.

Paul was born in Moorestown, New Jersey on January 11, 1885, just five years before the National American Woman Suffrage Association (NAWSA) was founded by Elizabeth Cady Stanton and Susan B. Anthony. Though her vision of women's rights was never as comprehensive as that of Stanton, Paul always remained committed to women's freedom. The oldest of four children, Paul grew up in a family committed to social justice. Her parents, William M. Paul, a businessman and president of the Burlington County Trust Company, and Tacie Parry, belonged to the Society of Friends and instilled in Paul the Quaker values of discipline, service, honesty, and equality between the sexes. Paul's forbears also included, on her mother's side, the Quaker leader William Penn, who advocated religious tolerance, and on her father's side, the Winthrops of Massachusetts. Her mother, one of the first women to attend Swarthmore College in Pennsylvania, took her daughter to her first suffrage meeting when she was just a child.

When Paul was 16, her father died suddenly of pneumonia. The family, though financially secure, accepted the guidance and authority of a male relative, whose conservative views created some tension in the household. Paul, who had attended a Quaker school in Moorestown, left home to attend Swarthmore College where she studied biology because, according to Christine A. Lunardini in *From Equal Suffrage to Equal Rights: Alice Paul and the National Woman's Party: 1910-1928,* "it was something about which she knew nothing." She discovered politics and economics in her senior year. Professor Robert Brooks recommended her for a College Settlement Association fellowship at the New York School of Philanthropy. When she graduated from Swarthmore in 1905, Paul spent a year there studying social work. She later earned a master's degree in sociology at the University of Pennsylvania and became interested in the problems raised by women's inferior legal status. She went on to earn a Ph.D. in 1912 from the University of Pennsylvania with a dissertation on the legal status of women, a law degree in 1922 from Washington College of Law, and a second Ph.D. in law in 1928 from American University.

## Seeds of Militancy

Paul's shift from social work to law reflected a more profound shift in her political sensibilities. In the fall of 1907, Paul interrupted her studies at the University of Pennsylvania to accept a fellowship in social work at the Quaker training school in Woodbridge, England. While she was studying at the University of Birmingham, Christabel Pankhurst, the daughter of the famous British suffragist Emmeline Pankhurst, was prevented from addressing a university audience there by a hostile crowd. Paul had never before witnessed outright opposition to the suffrage cause, and was shocked. The event radicalized her. On the invitation of the Charity Organization Society of London, she became a caseworker in Dalston and attended her first suffrage parade there in 1908. For the next two years, she worked closely with the Women's Social and Political Union, participating in the more militant strategies of British feminism: demonstrations, imprisonment, and hunger strikes.

## The National Association of Woman Suffrage Association

Paul left England after a brief incarceration at Halloway Prison for her suffrage activities and returned to the University of Pennsylvania in 1910. She resumed her studies, but with a new determination to change the legal status of women. At the NAWSA convention in 1910, Paul lectured on "The English Situation" in an attempt to bring the new militancy across the Atlantic. NAWSA resisted Paul's commitment to direct action, but a younger generation of activists found Paul's new optimism captivating. In 1913, she and Lucy Burns, a graduate of Vassar College whom she had first met in a police station in London, assumed leadership of NAWSA's Congressional Committee and began a campaign for a constitutional amendment that would enfranchise women across the nation.

For a federal campaign to succeed, Paul believed, it needed to have the support of the president. Paul selected March 3, 1913, the day before Woodrow Wilson's inauguration, for a massive suffrage parade on Pennsylvania Avenue, in Washington, D.C. Not only would the suffragists gain important publicity for their cause, they would also inform the president that they were willing to hold the party in power responsible for women's enfranchisement. Over 8,000 marchers participated; over a half million people gathered along the parade route. When President Wilson arrived at the train station that afternoon, few were there to greet him; instead they had gone to Pennsylvania Avenue to watch the suffrage parade. Though Paul had done her part to organize an ordered and peaceful march, an unruly crowd assaulted the suffragists while police stood by and did nothing. The near-riot resulted in a special Senate investigation that resulted in the removal of the superintendent of police. A few days after the parade, a Congressional committee sent a delegation to the White House to meet with the president, who politely asked for more time to consider the matter of women's suffrage. Nevertheless, Paul's first major organizing effort had met with some success.

## National Woman's Party

Despite the success of the suffrage parade, Paul encountered increasing resistance from NAWSA over the next several months. NAWSA members feared that Paul's political strategy of holding the Democratic Party responsible for enfranchisement would upset the tentative gains they had made at the state level. In addition, NAWSA had never really embraced Paul's vision of a constitutional amendment. By the summer of 1914, after a divisive struggle within NAWSA, Paul and Burns left to form a newly independent Congressional Union for Woman Suffrage, later renamed the National Woman's Party (NWP). By 1916, the struggle for women's suffrage had shifted to the federal level and Paul's militant tactics, which included picketing the White House, required a group of enthusiastic and dedicated suffragists. The members of NWP were mostly white, middle-class, enfranchised women who were willing to risk respectability, comfort, and even freedom to extend the franchise nationally. For the next two years, many members of NWP, including Paul, endured harassment, imprisonment, forced feedings, and threats, but continued to pursue the goal of a constitutional amendment with dogged determination.

## White House Pickets

In January 1917, the NWP stationed members in front of the White House in Washington, D.C. On the eve of America's involvement in the First World War, the tactic was confrontational and audacious; the NWP was the first group ever to picket the White House. Opponents would argue that it bordered on treason. For Paul, whose single-mindedness about women's equality had never wavered, America's involvement in a war for democracy had no moral ground if the nation refused to grant all of its citizens the right to vote. The NWP picketed the White House for 18 months. Thousands of local women, unaffiliated with the NWP, volunteered for the picket lines. While the public

initially supported the picketers, by April 1917 Wilson had declared war and support plummeted. The threat of arrest became imminent.

In June, NWP members Lucy Burns and Katherine Morey were arrested by district police, charged with obstruction of traffic, and released. Twenty-seven more women were arrested over the next several weeks. Soon, heavier sentences were handed down and 16 women were required to serve 60 days at Occoquan Workhouse, in Virginia. By September, the House voted to establish a House Committee on Woman Suffrage, and for the first time both branches of Congress had standing committees to consider the question of enfranchisement for women. Picketers were bolstered by the news and more women continued to risk arrest and imprisonment. Conditions at Occoquan differed little from conditions at most prisons in the early part of the twentieth century. Cells were small, dark, and unsanitary. Food was infested with mealworms. Prisoners were routinely harassed and intimidated. Soon, however, it became apparent that the suffragists, and especially their leaders, were being singled out by authorities frustrated by the picketers' tenacity.

In October, Paul was arrested on the picket line and sent to Occoquan. By the end of the month, she and fellow suffragist Rose Winslow began a hunger strike in order to secure their rights as political prisoners. Over the next three weeks, three times each day, Paul and Winslow were force fed; tubes were pushed into their noses and down their throats. In addition, Paul was moved to a psychiatric ward where she was monitored day and night by an attendant holding a flashlight up to her face. Lunardini notes that "prison psychiatrists interviewed her on several occasions and it was made clear to her that one signature on an admission form was all that was necessary to have her committed to an insane asylum."

By November 1917, the ordeal was over and the women were released from prison. President Wilson, who was wearied by the tactics of the NWP, announced his support for the suffrage amendment in January 1918. When the Senate refused to pass the bill, Paul once again resumed her picket campaign. When 48 suffragists were arrested, a public outcry prompted the women's release.

## Victory

By 1919, the amendment had passed both houses. Paul, however, continued to lobby until it was ratified in 1920. The passage of the 19th Amendment, for so long the focus of Paul's efforts, prompted the NWP to reconsider its political goals. Though she gave up leadership of the NWP after 1920, Paul's ideas still dominated. She drafted an Equal Rights Amendment (ERA), which was introduced in Congress in 1923. Her notion that "men and women shall have equal rights throughout the United States," was a controversial one. Many feminists worried that it would invalidate labor laws that protected women in the workplace, but Paul continued to insist on the simple principle of equality instilled in her by her Quaker upbringing.

Paul continued to struggle for women's equal rights throughout the middle decades of the 20th century. During

World War II, when the war effort required a temporary suspension of protective labor laws, the ERA was revived once again, endorsed by both parties, and debated in Congress. In the 1950s, Paul lobbied Congress to include sex discrimination among the equal protections advanced by the Civil Rights bill and succeeded in securing equal rights for women in employment in 1964.

Paul died on July 9, 1977 in Moorestown, New Jersey, convinced that organizers would be successful in securing the three states needed to ratify the ERA. The amendment, however, was defeated, ending the movement to provide women with a constitutional right to equal justice. Often rigid and conservative, Paul never embraced a broad social platform for women's rights. But her single-minded devotion to legal equality shaped the feminist movement over much of the twentieth century.

### Further Reading

*American National Biography,* edited by John A. Garraty and March C. Carnes, Oxford University Press, 1999.

*Encyclopedia of American Biography,* edited by John A. Garraty and Jerome L. Sternstein, Harper Collins, 1996.

Lunardini, Christine A., *From Equal Suffrage to Equal Rights: Alice Paul and the National Woman's Party, 1910-1928,* New York University Press, 1986.

*Reader's Companion to American History,* edited by Eric Foner and John A. Garraty, Houghton Mifflin, 1991. □

# Roger Penske

**Roger Penske (born 1937) became a rich man as the owner of Penske Corporation, a multi-billion dollar company involved in many things, including motor racing. Once a successful racecar driver himself, Penske seemed to have a sixth sense about race strategy. He became one of the most winning car owners of all time in the major forms of auto racing.**

The pit crew always called Roger Penske "Captain" during a race. Penske managed his racing teams with military precision, just as his pit crew serviced the car whenever it stopped. Penske was always cool, calm and collected, rarely becoming upset or agitated regardless of what was happening on the track. Considered to be a perfectionist, Penske was still easy to work for. If, that is, you planned to work hard toward a goal. For he was driven to perfection in business, in sports, and in his personal life, and he expected those around him to give the same dedication regardless of how much time or effort the job demanded.

### A Passion for Sports

Roger Penske was born in Red Bank, New Jersey on February 20, 1937. When he was young, the family moved to Ohio, and Penske attended Shaker Heights High School in suburban Cleveland. He was a member of the football team until a motorcycle accident shattered his ankle. Doc-

tors debated whether to amputate his foot, but finally decided to give the shattered bones time to recover.

After several months of rehabilitation, Penske taught himself to walk, then to run. He was finally well enough to return to football the next season. In his first game, he blocked two punts, falling on one for a touchdown, and Shaker Heights beat their rival, by a score of 23-14. Penske was the hero of the game.

Penske graduated from Lehigh University, with a degree in business administration. By then he had become very involved in automobile racing. He loved the sport with a passion. By checking into the university infirmary on Fridays to claim illness, he was excused so he could go to the track. Penske became a top Sports Car Club of America driver in his 1957 Corvette, but his father didn't like it.

"The worst thing that could happen to him would be to win a race," J.H. Penske told the *Cleveland Plain Dealer* sports editor, Hal Lebovitz, before Penske's amateur racing career really started. "Then," continued the father, "the worst thing happened."

### Named "Driver of the Year"

Penske went on to win *Sports Illustrated* magazine's "Driver of the Year" award, and to be named by Frank Blunk, the late motor sports writer for the *New York Times,* as "North American Driver of the Year" in 1962. Penske's victory in three races during Nassau Speed Week capped a near-perfect season, in which he also won the *Los Angeles Times'* Grand Prix at Riverside Raceway in California, against an international field. He had suddenly achieved worldwide recognition as a racecar driver.

Penske was a racecar driver who always studied the rules carefully. Once at Riverside, he arrived with a slim car that had much less resistance to air than the others. The rules said the cars in that series had to have two seats, even if the second seat wasn't usable. So most of the cars were built with seats side by side. Not in Penske's car. The rules only said "two seats," they didn't say where the seats had to be. Penske put his smaller seat behind him in the driver's compartment, not beside him. His car was sleeker and faster, and he won the race. That was how Penske operated, and how his so-called "unfair advantage" reputation began. He always seemed to be one step ahead of his competitors.

Penske was racing the legends. Only a year after his Riverside win, he overcame a bad start in his first stock car race (he was bumped off the track by another car) to duel wheel-to-wheel with top driving stars, Joe Weatherly and Darel Dieringer. He defeated them and won his first and only NASCAR (National Association of Stock Car Auto Racing) Grand National Race in the Riverside event. Soon after, he retired from driving. Penske had plans that would not allow racing. Typical of him, he gave up an activity he loved to begin one he felt would be just as successful.

## Managed Successful Racing Team

Penske teamed with a young engineer by the name of Mark Donohue, a relationship that would bring Penske some of his highest and lowest moments. Together, the two dominated American road racing with a series of 1960s championships in Trans-Am, the US Road Racing Circuit, and SCCA endurance racing. This was the beginning of a racing team that won a Trans-Am title for American Motors and led to SCCA professional racing, the thundering Can-Am series, Indianapolis-style open wheel racing, and world class Formula One. With Donohue in the cockpit and Penske managing the team, the two won in every series in which they raced. The pinnacle was reached when the Penske-Donohue team won the famous Indianapolis 500 mile Speedway Race in 1972.

## Created the Penske Corporation

While building his reputation as a meticulous and tireless racing team manager, Penske was also creating a dynamic, fast growing company known as the Penske Corporation. He started his business career after college by joining the Alcoa Company as a sales engineer. In 1964, he left that position to become general manager of McKean Chevrolet in Philadelphia, and then bought out the owner when he retired in 1965. This was the beginning of Penske's business empire, which grew to include many auto dealerships and other, much larger companies. The Penske Corporation became a multi-billion dollar industry, employed more than 28,000 people, and had more than 1,800 facilities throughout the world.

## Worst Day in Racing

Penske and Donohue took on Formula One racing in Europe. This is said by racing experts to be the type of racing that demands the most skill and dedication. They were doing well, and Donohue was becoming known as a world champion driver, when a 1975 practice accident before the Austrian Grand Prix ended the adventure. Donohue flipped off the track due to a deflating tire. His bouncing car killed one course marshal and injured another in the violent crash, but Donohue seemed to have escaped unharmed. Two days later he collapsed. The young driver died during brain surgery. Penske was devastated.

However, Penske's racing involvement continued. Working over the next few years in various racing series with top drivers, his cars won many races. His drivers included Gary Bettenhausen, Bobby Allison, Tom Sneva, John Watson, Rick Mears, Bobby and Al Unser, Sr., Danny Sullivan, Al Unser, Jr., Paul Tracy, and World Driving Champions Mario Andretti and Emerson Fittipaldi. Penske's cars won in NASCAR and in Formula One races. In the 25 Indianapolis 500 races that Penske entered, his cars won an amazing ten times. He set records for winning that will probably never be equaled. In Championship Auto Racing Teams (CART) racing, an organization Penske created and managed with a cooperative board of directors, his cars won almost 100 races. His cars won nine National Championships, and more than 30 races on the NASCAR circuit. Penske was far and away the most winning car owner of all.

Penske always insisted upon designing and building his own cars for each series, especially the open-wheel "Indy-type" racing cars. He often said he got far more pleasure out of winning with a car that he had designed than winning with cars everybody else was driving. This sometimes held his teams back, as they sorted out the problems in new designs and innovative construction. But eventually the Penske cars would begin winning. When others began imitating Penske, he would design new ones, with even more innovative features. Once he re-designed a Mercedes engine with very short push rods for the Indianapolis race, and his car dominated the event. The next year he came back with yet another design and, to the surprise of racing fans everywhere, Penske's cars didn't even qualify for the race considered to be one of the most important in the world.

## Acquired Race Tracks

As he continued to build his business empire, Penske acquired racetracks. He became the owner of Michigan Speedway, Nazareth (Pennsylvania) Speedway, North Carolina Motor Speedway and, in 1997, he built the state-of-the-art California Speedway, a few miles from Los Angeles. The holdings of the Penske Corporation came to include Detroit Diesel Corporation, Diesel Technology Company, Penske Truck Leasing Company, Penske Automotive Group, Penske Auto Centers (the automotive service centers in K-Mart stores throughout the United States) and Penske Motorsports, handling the motor racing activities. Penske also became the co-owner of cars belonging to other racing teams that he thought were innovative, or could win.

Penske always exuded a "star quality," standing calm and self-assured in his racing pits, but he tended to avoid crowds and publicity. He was recruited to succeed Lee Iacocca at Chrysler Corporation, a job he did not take. He sat on the board of directors of General Electric and Philip Morris. Unlike most other chief executive officers of billion dollar corporations, Penske continued to don a fire suit so that he could personally manage the racing teams he loved.

Penske settled in Bloomfield Hills, Michigan, with his wife. His two oldest sons from a previous marriage became executives in his corporation. Penske also had two daughters with his second wife, Kathryn. He continued to travel extensively in order to manage his many enterprises, but enjoyed returning home to relax. Penske has been consistently listed as one of the top "power players" in the world of motor sports, and is recognized throughout the world for his businesses and business connections.

## Further Reading

Olney, Ross R., *Drama on the Speedway,* Lothrop, Lee and Shepard, 1978

Olney, Ross R., *Modern Auto Racing Superstars* , Dodd Mead, 1978

Olney, Ross R., *Super Champions of Auto Racing,* Clarion Books, 1984 □

# Walker Percy

**Walker Percy (1916–1990) won the National Book Award for fiction in 1961 for his first published novel, *The Moviegoer.* In five subsequent novels and numerous essays, he explored his chosen theme of "the dislocation of man in the modern age." His work combined a distinctly southern sensibility with existential philosophy and a deeply-felt Catholicism.**

Walker Percy was born in Birmingham, Alabama, on May 28, 1916. He was a descendant of a distinguished Mississippi Protestant family that counted congressmen and Civil War heroes among its members. Before he was born, Percy's grandfather killed himself with a shotgun, setting a pattern of tragic death that would haunt the boy throughout his life.

## Early Influences

In 1929, Percy's father committed suicide with a shotgun. Percy, his mother, and his two brothers, Phin and Roy, then moved to Athens, Georgia. Two years later, Percy's mother was killed when she drove her car off a country bridge and into a bayou—an accident that Percy later came to consider a suicide. At the invitation of his bachelor uncle, Percy and his orphaned brothers moved to Greenville, Mississippi. There he finished his last three years of high school.

His uncle, William Alexander Percy, would exert a profound influence on his oldest nephew. Percy later called him "the most extraordinary man I have ever known." The urbane Uncle Will was a poet and writer, best known for his 1941 memoir, *Lanterns on the Levee.* An inveterate romantic, he once advised his nephew to set his poems "in some long-ago time" in order to keep them free of "irrelevant

photographic details." William Alexander Percy counted among his friends such "agrarian" poets as Allen Tate and John Crowe Ransom. He shared their resentment of the encroaching industrial and secular North, though he found the modernist technique of their verse unattractive.

## Friendship with Foote

When Percy was an adolescent, his uncle invited a local boy named Shelby Foote over to keep him company. Foote, a self-confident young man who had literary aspirations, became one of Percy's closest friends. Their lifelong friendship included voluminous correspondence, the literary record of which was later collected in book form. Foote later became a novelist and historian whose work greatly influenced Percy. His three-volume history of the Civil War is considered one of the definitive chronicles of that conflict.

Foote and Percy both attended the University of North Carolina at Chapel Hill. There the two undergraduates argued the merits of racial segregation. At the time, Percy favored the policy of separation of the races as true to the traditions of the South. The socially progressive Foote opposed the practice as backward and unfair. Percy was moved by Foote's argument and moderated his views over time. Percy also aspired to match Foote's literary prowess, with embarrassing results. He flunked his placement exam in English composition when he copied the style of William Faulkner.

## Life-Changing Illness

After graduating from college, Percy decided to embark on a medical career. He enrolled at Columbia University's medical school. Upon completing his education, he accepted an internship at New York's Bellevue Hospital. There Percy contracted tuberculosis. He spent most of the next four years recuperating at the Trudeau Sanitorium on Saranac Lake in the Adirondack Mountains of New York and in Wallingford, Connecticut. During this period of reflection, Percy began to question the ability of science to explain the basic mysteries of human existence. He read the works of Danish existentialist writer, Soren Kierkegaard, and the Russian novelist, Fyodor Dostoevsky. These works proved revelatory and inspired Percy to become a writer rather than a physician—a pathologist of the soul rather than the body.

Percy returned to his native South and lived, for a time, in Sewanee, Tennessee. In 1946, he married Mary Bernice ("Bunt") Townsend, a medical technician, and moved to New Orleans. Supported by a family trust fund, Percy spent the next seven years writing two novels that were never published. He studied semantics under the influence of Susanne Langer's *Philosophy in a New Key*. Percy converted to Catholicism, partly, he acknowledged, because of reading St. Augustine. He wrote scholarly articles for learned journals about existentialism and the philosophy of language, earning some notoriety in these fields. However, he realized that he could reach a wider audience and make more money by writing fiction.

## Emerged as Novelist

In 1961, Percy's first successful novel, *The Moviegoer*, was published by Knopf after long and creative editing and much rewriting in collaboration with editor, Stanley Kauffman. Percy later described the novel as the story of "a young man who had all the advantages of a cultivated old-line southern family: a feel for science and art, a liking for girls, sports cars, and the ordinary things of the culture, but who nevertheless feels himself quite alienated from both worlds, the old South and the new America." The book's protagonist, Binx Bolling, attempts to numb himself from this creeping alienation by attending movies and enjoying casual sex with his secretary, but he suffers an existential breakdown while attending the annual *Mardi Gras* celebration with his neurotic cousin, Kate. In its structure, the novel owed a debt to Albert Camus' *The Stranger,* a similar tale of a man confronting the emptiness of his life. But the dry, laconic voice was Percy's alone. He had found the style he would use for all subsequent works of fiction. *The Moviegoer* won the National Book Award and established Walker Percy as a major new talent in American fiction.

Percy's second novel, *The Last Gentleman,* explored similar philosophical terrain. It told the story of Williston "Bibb" Barrett, an old-fashioned southern gentleman living in New York. Barrett suffers from a recurring sense of *deja vu* and seems lost in the ultra-modern secular North. He returns to the South and takes a position as tutor to a terminally ill boy. Barrett's return to his roots is meant as an allegory of man's search for identity in an increasingly complicated world, stripped of the traditions and rituals that once gave life meaning. The book won high praise in literary circles and is generally considered Percy's most mature exploration of his core themes.

## Darker Visions

In 1971, Percy's work moved toward the surreal with the publication of *Love in the Ruins.* This was a satire about the descendant of a 16th century English saint living in the hyper-developed consumer society of the South in the near future. Inspired in equal parts by Aldous Huxley, George Orwell, and Kurt Vonnegut, the novel signaled a shift away from semi-autobiography toward a more socially critical fiction. The broad comic strokes of *Love in the Ruins* pleased some critics, but left others scratching their heads.

Percy continued on in this vein with his next novel, *Lancelot,* published in 1977. The story of a man fascinated by the courtly traditions of Arthurian romance and obsessed with discovering his wife's infidelity, it was Percy's darkest and most disturbing vision to date. The violent novel ended with a fire that destroyed the murderous narrator's gothic southern plantation house—a symbol, perhaps, of the consumption of the old value system of honor, chivalry, and social convention by the modern world. While this searing tale impressed many critics, it also left some wondering at the state of Percy's mental health.

## Last Works

Percy took five years off before producing his next novel, *The Second Coming,* in 1982. It saw the return of Will Barrett, the protagonist of *The Last Gentleman.* Now a retired widower, Barret lived in an exclusive North Carolina suburb where he had become "the world's most accomplished golf amateur." When his golf game turned sour, however, "hidden memories" popped up, including the truth about his father's suicide, previously thought to be a hunting accident. While Will is struggling with these revelations he meets Allison, a neurotic young woman who has escaped from a mental hospital and is living in an abandoned greenhouse. This semi-autobiographical novel returned Percy to the style of his earlier works. Its exploration of a father's suicide was perhaps the novelist's most direct attempt to confront his own tragic family history.

Percy's last novel, *The Thanataos Syndrome,* was published in 1987. It was a follow-up to *Love in the Ruins* that saw that book's hero, Dr. Tom More, investigating some mysterious personality changes in his wife and children. With the help of his scientist cousin, More discovers that a group of industrialists are releasing heavy sodium into the water supply to "improve" the social welfare. Perhaps Percy's most ambitious novel, *The Thanataos Syndrome* revisits old themes found in his previous works, while providing a forum for his biting commentary upon the postmodern predicament. The novel moves from existential themes found in his earlier novels to those subjects that most concerned him as a Catholic near the end of his life.

## Later Life

In his later years, Percy, his wife, and their two daughters lived in Covington, Louisiana, across Lake Ponchartrain from New Orleans. He once remarked, apropos of the suicide of his father and grandfather, that his longevity made him "the oldest male Percy in history . . . so what lies ahead is virgin territory; imagine a Percy with arthritis! senility! Parkinsonism, shuffling along, fingers rolling pills, head agoing! I don't know whether I'm looking forward to doing a great thing like Kant and Spinoza and Verdi in the 1980s or whether I'll jump in the Bogue Falaya next week with a sugar kettle on my head." He died at his home in Covington, Louisiana on May 10, 1990.

Over the course of 26 years, Percy published six novels and two collections of nonfiction. He enjoyed both critical and financial success and established himself as America's leading Catholic novelist. Percy's consistent themes were the decline of the old Southern order—with its paternalism, code of honor, and sentimentality—and its succession by the New South: a sterile Hollywood-like pursuit of the American Dream. His work influenced the efforts of novelists as diverse as John Hawkes and Richard Ford, and kept alive the rich tradition of southern fiction dating back through Welty, O'Connor, and Faulkner.

## Further Reading

Foote, Shelby et al., *The Correspondence of Shelby Foote and Walker Percy: A Life,* W.W. Norton & Company, 1996.
Samway, Patrick H., *Walker Percy: A Life,* Farrar Straus & Giroux, 1997.
Tolson, Jay, *Pilgrim in the Ruins: A Life of Walker Percy,* University of North Carolina Press, 1994. □

# Thomas Boone Pickens, Jr.

**T. Boone Pickens (born 1928) started the Mesa Petroleum Company with a $2,500 investment and built it into the largest independent oil and gas company in America. Then he shook corporate America with a series of hostile takeover attempts that earned him a reputation as a corporate raider. Pickens' ideas about corporate restructuring, and the tactics he used for achieving them, were controversial during the 1980s, but have become standard procedure in executive suites today.**

*F*ortune magazine called him the "most hated man in America" during the 1980s, but Pickens was a folk hero to many stockholders, who welcomed his criticism of large corporate executives whom he said were more concerned with their own salaries and perquisites than with shareholders.

Thomas Boone Pickens Jr. was born on May 22, 1928, in Holdenville, Oklahoma, the only child of Thomas Boone and Grace Pickens. Pickens' father was an oil company

lawyer who claimed a distant kinship to Daniel Boone. Pickens' mother ran the Office of Price Administration (OPA) for three Oklahoma counties during World War II. The OPA was responsible for rationing gas and other goods that were in short supply during the war.

Pickens' parents, along with a grandmother and aunt who lived next door, instilled the young boy with old-fashioned values. They encouraged him to work hard and use his time and money productively. Pickens, who was known as "Boone," filled his time with Boy Scout activities, clarinet practice, sports, and a newspaper route.

In 1944, the family moved to Amarillo, Texas, where Pickens' father took a job in the land acquisitions division of Phillips Petroleum Company. In his 1987 autobiography, *Boone,* Pickens described how overwhelmed he felt in the city. He had been well known in tiny Holdenville High School; he felt anonymous at Amarillo High. He begged his grandmother to allow him to move back to Holdenville and live with her, but she accused him of not wanting to "face the competition in Amarillo." Looking back on the experience, Pickens said, "Moving to Amarillo was probably the best thing that ever happened to me, for I discovered I could compete on an equal footing without feeling inadequate." Within a year, Pickens earned a starting position on the school's basketball team.

Pickens attended Texas A&M University for one year, then transferred to Oklahoma A&M at Stillwater, majoring in geology. In 1949, he married Lynn O'Brien, whom he had dated on and off since high school. Within a year, their first child, Deborah, was born. The couple had three more children, Pam, Mike, and Thomas Boone III.

Pickens graduated in 1951 and took a job as an on-site geologist with Phillips Petroleum in Bartlesville, Oklahoma. By 1954, Pickens was frustrated with work in the fields. He quit his job and worked for a while as an independent oilman. In 1956, he invested $2,500 and, with two partners, formed Petroleum Exploration, Inc. (PEI).

## Shrewd Financier

*Financial World* described PEI's early years as "a series of successful ventures in which [Pickens] demonstrated shrewd financial instincts and a creative approach to raising capital." The company went public in 1964 and was renamed Mesa Petroleum. During its first year, Mesa had revenues of $1.5 million and a net income of $435,310.

In 1969, Mesa merged with Hugoton Production Company, giving Mesa the leverage it needed to expand exploration and production operations. Pickens considered the acquisition the most important deal Mesa ever made. The next year, Mesa failed to take over Southland Royalty. Three years later, Mesa bought Pubco Petroleum. In 1976, he was outbid by Southland in his attempt to purchase Aztec, a gas company.

Pickens divorced in 1971 and a year later, he married Beatrice Carr Stuart, a divorcee with four daughters, whom he had first met in 1952. Bea was by Pickens' side throughout his subsequent career, serving as a confidante, adviser, and sounding board, according to his autobiography.

## Spotted Trends

Pickens' ability to spot trends helped Mesa grow. PEI began oil exploration in Canada in 1959. Twenty years later, according to *Financial World*, Mesa "got out of Canada . . . at a time when the country looked like fertile ground for American oil concerns. But it wasn't long before Canada took everyone else by surprise by implementing a new energy policy greatly favoring Canadian enterprises." Pickens left the country with more than $600 million. Also in 1979, Pickens withdrew from the North Sea, netting $65 million. When he left, he avoided a new British tax on North Sea oil production.

Pickens formed the first large, publicly traded oil royalty trust using Mesa properties in 1979. Stockholders were issued one trust unit per Mesa share. Under this arrangement, the cash flow of properties held in trust are distributed to stockholders. Management cannot spend the cash flow from those properties.

By 1981, Mesa was a major independent oil company with assets of more than $2 billion. Oversupplies of oil at this time caused prices to drop and Pickens looked for new ways to make money. According to William C. Wertz of *Financial World*, "He [Pickens] became a financier instead of an oilman and turned dealmaking on Wall Street into a highly lucrative enterprise that inspired many imitators."

Pickens launched a series of attempts to take over other, often larger, oil companies. Among his targets were Cities Service, Superior Oil, General American Oil of Texas,

and KN Energy. None of the acquisitions succeeded, but Pickens' overtures drove up the prices of his targets' stocks, netting him and other investors millions of dollars. Pickens became known as a greedy corporate raider and "greenmailer," an investor who threatens to take over a company by buying large blocks of stock, then selling the stock back for huge profits. Pickens preferred to describe himself as an advocate for stockholders. He targeted companies that he believed were mismanaged by executives who held little stock in their own companies.

His first large takeover attempt was Cities Service, a company 23 times as large as Mesa. In early 1981, Pickens owned four million shares of Cities Service stock, representing about five percent of the total. When Cities Service's management rebuffed his attempt at a merger, he sought partners for a hostile takeover. What followed was an 18-month struggle between the two oil companies. Mesa prepared a tender offer for 51 percent of Cities' stock. A tender offer was one of the takeover strategies of the 1980s in which a company offered stockholders of a target company a premium price for their stock. Before Mesa could make its offer, Cities Service made an offer for Mesa, putting Pickens in danger of losing his company. Pickens, who was a master at public relations, was now viewed in the media as an underdog. Eventually, both companies' offers fell through and Cities Service was acquired by Occidental Petroleum. Pickens made $30 million on his four million shares of Cities Service stock.

## Battled Gulf Oil

In 1983, Pickens embarked on the most highly publicized deal of his career when he began acquiring stock in Gulf Oil. Gulf was the sixth largest oil company in America, with annual revenues of $30 billion. But the company's oil reserves were low and its stock was undervalued. Like many other oil companies, Gulf was investing a lot of money in exploration with little results. High Organization of Petroleum Exporting Countries (OPEC) prices had maintained oil companies' cash flows in previous years, but by 1983, prices were down, leaving the oil companies in trouble. Peter Nulty reported in the December 26, 1983, issue of *Fortune*, that Pickens described oil companies as being in a "state of liquidation" and suggested that they liquidate efficiently by "pipelining more cash flow to shareholders as a return of capital, and less to exploration and diversification." This, Pickens said, would force the companies' undervalued stocks to go up. The large oil companies disagreed with Pickens, arguing that oil prices would eventually go back up and that there would be more large oil finds and alternative energy sources to develop.

Pickens believed the oil industry needed to restructure and he set about being a catalyst for change. In the biggest fight of his career, he targeted Gulf Oil for "restructuring." He formed the Gulf Investment Group (GIG), which acquired 11 percent of Gulf stock. As Gulf's largest stockholder, GIG asked management to place part of its domestic oil and gas-producing properties in a royalty trust. Since Mesa created the first royalty trust, other oil companies had done the same. Stock prices for oil companies whose properties were put in trusts were generally higher than those without. Pickens stood to gain $219 million in profit on the plan. Management refused GIG's request and initiated a proxy fight, in which stockholders were asked to vote for or against management's decision.

The battle between Pickens and Gulf Oil was one of the most publicized business stories of the year and made Pickens' name synonymous with "corporate takeover." Gulf management told stockholders that Pickens had "a history of hit-and-run tactics" and that a royalty trust was a "get rich quick scheme" that would "cripple the company and severely penalize the majority of the stockholders."

Pickens had positioned himself as a champion of oil company shareholders, many of whom were retirees and pension holders. *Texas Monthly's* Gregory Curtis said that Pickens claimed to be "warring on the lazy or ineffective corporate managers who seemed to think they owned the company themselves rather than the stockholders, managers who cared more about their own salary and perquisites than they did about the best interests of the stock-holders. . . . It was a message the country was ready to hear."

When the proxy votes were counted in December 1983, Gulf Oil management won by a narrow margin. Within six months, Gulf was bought by Standard Oil of California. Gulf's 400,000 shareholders reaped profits of $6.5 billion, including GIG's $760 million profit.

The federal government reacted to the merger-mania when Congress attempted to pass a bill that would curb oil company mergers. Pickens lobbied against the bill, saying it was not the government's responsibility to protect companies with weak management. He also believed that the oil industry should be allowed to restructure itself. The bill was defeated.

Pickens subsequently battled other oil companies, including Phillips and Unocal, reaping millions for Mesa Petroleum. He later failed in an attempt to gain a seat on the board of a Japanese auto parts manufacturer. In August 1986, Pickens launched the United Stockholders' Association (USA), a non-profit group dedicated to defending shareholders' rights. Within three months, USA had 3,000 members.

### Declining Popularity

Pickens' demonstrated his competitive spirit away from Wall Street as well. He has enjoyed tennis and racquetball throughout his life. He also plays golf and poker and hunts quail. He and his wife, Bea, were active in Amarillo. Bea worked on a project to build an ambulatory cancer center in the city. Pickens, a Republican, campaigned for Texas politicians and considered running for governor in 1990.

Pickens' popularity declined in the late 1980s. He became embroiled in political disputes and led a boycott of the Amarillo newspaper. He angered many people when he backed an unpopular president of West Texas State University, where he was chairman of the board of regents. Pickens moved Mesa from Amarillo to Dallas in 1989, disparaging the town he had lived in since he was a boy.

In 1996, after several years of debt, Pickens was forced to resign as Mesa's chairman. He and Bea divorced around the same time. Pickens retained two businesses, a natural gas trading company and a Southern California fueling firm, which he continues to operate. When Pickens left Mesa after 40 years, Joseph Nocera of *Fortune* noted that the once-controversial chairman, who dominated the front pages of newspapers ten years previously, had faded into obscurity. Nocera wrote, "more than any other raider . . . Boone changed the world." While corporate raiders have largely disappeared, takeovers are now even more common than in Boone's heyday, and they are largely driven by the CEOs who opposed Boone in the 1980s.

### Further Reading

Pickens, T. Boone Jr., *Boone,* Houghton Mifflin, 1987.
*Financial World,* December 31, 1983; May 5, 1987.
*Fortune* December 26, 1983; July 22, 1996.
*Texas Monthly,* July 1997.
"T. (Thomas) Boone Pickens Jr.," *A&E Network Biography,* http://www.biography.com (March 6, 1999). □

# Bill Pickett

**Known as the "Dusky Demon," Bill Pickett (1870–1932) was the best-known African American rodeo performer of all time. He invented the rodeo sport of bulldogging, now known as steer wrestling, and entertained millions of people around the world with his riding and roping skills.**

Western legend, Bill Pickett, was only five feet, seven inches tall and weighed only 145 pounds, but he was all muscle, a larger-than-life Western legend in his own time. His rodeo career spanned more than 40 years. He rode wild broncos and bulls, and was a professional cowboy and rodeo champion. Pickett performed all over the world in wild west shows, circuses. world's fairs, and worked for 25 years with the 101 Ranch's Wild West Show in Oklahoma.

### Invented Steer Wrestling

Steer wrestling, which is still a major event at all rodeos, was invented by Pickett. In this event, a 500- to 600-pound steer is released from a chute. One cowboy, called the "hazer," rides alongside it to force it to run straight, and the contestant is timed while he rides up along side the animal, which weighs twice as much as he does, grabs its horns and head, plants his feet on the ground to slow it down, and wrestles it to the ground. When the steer is on its side, with all four of its feet pointing in the same direction, the cowboy has won. A good cowboy can wrestle a steer to the ground in five to eight seconds, making the sport the fastest event in rodeo.

Pickett's signature move was to grab the steer by the horns, twist its neck, and bite the steer on one lip, then fall

backward and pull the shocked animal to the ground. This event has since been modified to lessen the danger and hurt to the animal. Pickett got the idea for "bulldogging," or steer wrestling, when he was ten years old and working as a cowboy in Texas. Frequently, the cowboys would have to catch a single animal, but there was so much brush nearby that ropes would snag and roping was impossible. In this situation, they had to wrestle the steer to the ground by brute strength or wrap its tail around their saddle horn before throwing it to the ground. Pickett, wrestling with a tough and determined longhorn cow, remembered a big dog he had seen, which brought down steers by gripping their noses in his teeth. Pickett bit the cow's lip as he had seen the dog do, and immediately brought her down. He used his biting trick to hold calves down while they were being branded, and to catch wild cattle in the brush. In the late 1880s, he began performing his stunts at county fairs and other public events.

## An African American Cowboy

Although there were thousands of African American cowboys who helped to shape the history of the American West, their stories have largely been left out of accounts of that time. Only recently have historians reclaimed this important part of American history. Pickett's great-grandson, Frank S. Phillips, Jr., has helped to fill in some of the missing information about Pickett. Phillips was raised by his grandmother, Bessie Pickett Phillips, Bill Pickett's second-oldest daughter. She told Phillips many stories about Pickett and other cowboys of Texas and Oklahoma. "As I grew older,"

Phillips recalled in his foreword to Cecil Johnson's book *Guts: Legendary Black Rodeo Cowboy Bill Pickett,* "I went to the movies and saw most of the cowboys she mentioned, but no Bill Pickett and no black cowboys at all, not even in disparaging roles. There was no mention of black cowboys, in the wild west magazines or in any of the western novels. I could not understand why."

Pickett was the second of 13 children born on December 5, 1870 in Travis County, Texas, to Thomas Jefferson Pickett, a former slave, and his wife Mary (Janie) Virginia Elizabeth Gilbert. He attended school until the fifth grade but then left to become a full-time ranch hand and improve his roping and riding abilities.

On December 2, 1890, Pickett married Maggie Turner. The couple eventually had nine children. To support his growing family, he began performing more widely, at bigger events, sometimes with his brothers. In 1905, a newspaper, *Leslie's Illustrated Weekly,* described him as "a man who outdoes the fiercest dog in utter brutality." This sensationalism surely drew the crowds of the time to see him.

### Joined the 101 Ranch

In 1907, Pickett went to Fort Worth, Texas, to wrestle some steers, make some money, buy a few presents for his wife and children and visit a cousin. He had no idea that Colonel Zack Miller of the Miller Brothers' 101 Ranch had come to town specifically to see his act.

The 101 Ranch was founded by seven men who realized that land in what was known as the "Cherokee Strip" was good for cattle. They leased 60,000 acres from the Cherokee Tribe and later added 100,000 acres leased from the Ponca Tribe. G. W. Miller, the founder, had created a ranching empire with over 200 cowboys by the time he died. When his three sons inherited the ranch most of their cowboys were not allowed to enter rodeos because they were too skilled and would be unfair competition. The Miller brothers decided to hold their own exhibition rodeos with their own cowboys—one of whom would soon be Bill Pickett.

Pickett began working for the 101 Ranch, and according to Cletus Johnson, was later described by Colonel Zack Miller as having "guts, bull strength, and the same peculiar sense of timing that makes art out of dancing." Pickett became the act's star attraction and appeared with the show for ten years. He traveled all over North America as well as in Argentina and England, where he performed for the British Royal Family. During this time, bulldogging, the sport he had invented, became a major rodeo event. It was modified because most cowboys did not want to take a big mouthful of a steer's lip or nostrils and because humane societies objected to the practice. Pickett often pretended to bite the animal while wrestling it down and was sometimes fined for cruelty to animals because of this convincing pretense.

### An Exciting Career

At a show at Madison Square Garden in New York City, a steer was frightened by the noise of the crowd, stampeded right out of the chute, jumped over the arena fence and thundered up into the stands. The steer climbed up the seats, as people scattered right and left in front of it. The legendary American humorist, Will Rogers, was Pickett's partner and the hazer for this event. He got the steer to turn around at the third balcony and Pickett rode his horse up into the stands, among the panicked people, and grabbed the steer by the lip. Rogers then roped the steer by the leg and dragged both steer and Pickett back down into the arena.

Some people claimed that Pickett had wrestled a buffalo bull and a bull elk with full horns to the ground. This may have been just publicity, but whether or not it's true, it is certain that none of the animals he threw ever tried to gore him after he got them on the ground.

In 1890, Pickett performed in a Mexican bullfighting ring after one of the Miller brothers bet 5,000 pesos that Pickett could ride a Mexican fighting bull for five minutes. He stayed on the animal for seven and a half minutes, winning the bet, but his horse was gored and Pickett broke three ribs and was severely gashed. Men from the 101 Ranch ran into the ring and roped the bull. The Mexican crowd, angered by what they saw as disrespect for their bullfighting tradition, threw bottles and trash at Pickett and the other cowboys until mounted police stopped them.

Richard E. Norman, a traveling filmmaker, made a feature film about African American cowboys called *The Bull Dogger,* starring Bill Pickett. Norman used extra footage from shooting this movie to make another film called *The Crimson Skull,* which also included scenes with Pickett. When the films were released, they were a big hit among African Americans who had heard of, but had never seen, African American cowboys.

### Retired from Performing

In 1916, Pickett retired from performing and lived on a small ranch he bought near Chandler, Oklahoma. When the 101 Ranch ran into financial troubles in 1931, he returned to help. In March 1932, Pickett tripped while roping a stallion and fell under the horse, which kicked him in the head. For the next 11 days he clung to life with a fractured skull. Finally, on April 2, 1932, he died in a hospital in Ponca City, Oklahoma.

Pickett's funeral was one of the largest ever held in Oklahoma. He was buried high on a hill at White Eagle Monument, where the Cherokee Strip Cowboy Association set up a limestone marker in his memory. According to Frank Billings, Colonel Zack Miller of the 101 Ranch called him "the greatest sweat-and-dirt cowhand that ever lived," and wrote a poem in his honor.

### A Legend of the West

The United States Post Office issued a stamp honoring Pickett as part of its "Legends of the West" series. After the stamps had been distributed, someone discovered that the image on the stamp was actually that of Pickett's brother Ben. The Postal Service recalled the incorrect stamps and then printed new ones with Pickett's photo. By that time a few sheets of the stamps had been sold and, because they were rare, were worth thousands of dollars. Other stamp collectors demanded that the Postal Service issue the incorrect sheets so that they could have a chance to own the rare

stamps, while the lucky few who already owned them sued the Post Office, hoping to prevent them from allowing other collectors to have the stamps. The lawsuits were a failure and the Postal Service finally organized a lottery to distribute 150,000 sheets of the "Ben Pickett" stamps to collectors.

Pickett was the first African American cowboy ever inducted into the National Rodeo Cowboy Hall of Fame. A statue of him wrestling a steer is on display at the Cowboy Coliseum in Fort Worth, Texas. A yearly event, the Bill Pickett Invitational Rodeo, is named after him. It has been running for more than 15 years in Los Angeles and is one that city's largest African American events. "My great-grandfather's principal memorial," wrote Frank S. Phillips, Jr. in his book *Guts* "is the rodeo event he created without which, although in a drastically modified form, no rodeo is complete."

### Further Reading

"Bill Pickett," Bill Pickett—MicroReference Entry, http://www.cs.uh.edu/~clifton/pickett.micro.html (February 26, 1999).

"Bill Pickett Invitational Rodeo Schedule for 1998," Bill Pickett Invitational Rodeo, http://home.earthlink.net/~bettypage/Opening.htm (February 26, 1999).

"Bulldogger Bill Pickett: Famous Black Cowboy," Bill Pickett: Champion Cowboy, http:camalott.com/~rssmith/pickett/htm (February 26, 1999).

"Coming to Cowtown to Catch Bill Pickett in Action," Virtual Texan, http://www.arlington.net/comm/virtual/pickett3.htm (February 26, 1999).

"A Great-Grandson Remembers Rodeo Star Bill Pickett," Virtual Texan, http://www.arlington.net/comm/virtual/pickett1.htm (February 26, 1999).

"Guts: Legendary Black Rodeo Cowboy Bill Pickett," Barnesandnoble.com, http://shop.barnesandnoble.com (February 26, 1999).

"The Legendary Bill Pickett," Virtual Texan, http://www.arlington.net/comm/virtual/pickett.htm (February 26, 1999).

"Legends of the West Stamps Recalled," Stamp on Black History, http://library.advanced.org/10320/Legends.htm (February 26, 1999).

"Steer Wrestling," Buffalo Bill Cody Stampede, http://www.westwyoming.com/cody-stampede/steerw.htm (February 26, 1999). □

# Mary Pickford

**Mary Pickford (1893–1979) was the first star of American cinema. Immensely popular in the silent era of motion pictures, Pickford was also a savvy businesswoman and the first female movie mogul. She and three other film legends (including one-time husband Douglas Fairbanks, Sr.) formed United Artists to produce and distribute their work.**

Pickford was born Gladys Louise Smith on April 8, 1893 in Toronto, Canada. Her father, John Charles Smith, was an alcoholic laborer who abandoned his

family. He died of a cerebral hemorrhage in 1898 after an accident at work. Her mother, Charlotte (maiden name, Hennessey) Smith, took in borders and sewing to support her family, which included Pickford's younger brother Jack and younger sister Lottie. One of Charlotte Smith's lodgers was the manager of a theater company in Toronto. Though her mother was initially leery of being involved with the theater, Pickford began acting at the age of six to support her family. She worked primarily in stock company melodramas in Toronto and tours across Canada. Pickford only attended school for three to six months, with Charlotte Smith educating her children at home. Pickford once quipped that road-side billboards taught her how to read. She had no real childhood.

In 1907, Pickford traveled to New York City by herself at the age of 14 to seek work, when the Canadian stock company production tours grew too demanding. She decided that if she could not be a Broadway actress, she would become a dress designer and quit show business. She managed an audition with a famous stage producer/mogul, David Belasco. Belasco and Pickford came up with the name Mary Pickford (Pickford being her paternal grandmother's name) and he cast her in his Broadway production of *The Warrens of Virginia*. The play was successful, and Pickford's acting improved. She later claimed that this experience taught her to act with heart and feeling.

## Turned to Film

By 1909, Pickford was lured by the movies. At the time, movies were still regarded as cheap entertainment, far infe-

rior to the stage. Her mother urged her to try movies because the family needed the money if they were to stay together. She was hired by D.W Griffiths at Biograph, appearing in her first film *The Lonely Villa* (or *Her First Biscuits* depending on the source) only after insisting on better terms than Griffiths originally offered. From the first, Pickford knew her worth as an actress and expected to be paid accordingly. Deborah G. Felder in *The 100 Most Influential Women of All Time* quoted producer Samuel Goldwyn as saying, "It took longer to make one of Mary's contracts than it did to make one of her pictures." This was a hallmark of her career, though it was considered unladylike and aggressive at the time. Pickford was still her family's primary source of income.

The public began to notice Pickford, dubbed "Little Mary" after some of the titles in the films. (There were no credits in films at this time.) She had a rare ability to silently express emotion. Pickford became known as the "Biograph Girl" and she appeared in over 100 Biograph films. Pickford was typecast as the moppet girl with hair full of curls (some of which were fakes bought from prostitutes for $50). As Felder wrote in *The 100 Most Influential Women,* "Her screen image—childlike, sweet, demure, with a touch of mischievousness, and a great deal of spunk—belongs to a completely different era. In an age which prided itself on its innocence, 'Little Mary,' was acclaimed as the feminine ideal." Many of Pickford's silent films paralleled her own life. She often played a girl who was trying to find her absent father and bring her family together.

In 1910, Pickford briefly defected from Biograph to a different film company, Independent Motion Picture Company. Here, she wrote a script (credited as Catherine Hennessey, her grandmother's name) entitled *The Dream* and appeared in the film. (Pickford wrote about 30 scripts over her career.) She also did five films for another company, Majestic, but returned to Biograph for a while. In 1911, Pickford secretly married an alcoholic Biograph actor named Owen Moore. They divorced after a shaky marriage in 1920.

## Returned to Stage

By 1913, Pickford severed ties completely with Biograph. She was back on the stage for one production (a Broadway play staged by Belasco entitled *A Good Little Devil*) before signing with Famous Players, owned by Adolph Zukor. He made her "America's Sweetheart." Pickford's salary was $500 per week, a princely sum at the time. In 1915, Pickford appeared in twelve films, including one, *The Foundling,* on which she served as producer. By 1916, Pickford was receiving $10,000 a week and a percentage of the profits as her salary. She invested much of the money wisely, especially in real estate. Though Zukor made a fortune off Pickford, her demands as an actress proved so exacting that he once offered her a quarter of a million dollars to retire. Still, Pickford later said these were the happiest years of her life. However, her childhood haunted her. She was always afraid of losing everything she had earned and did not enjoy the money.

## Career Reached New Heights

Between 1917 and 1919, Pickford appeared in higher quality films and was at the peak of her career and popularity. She made some of her best known movies and was in control of many aspects of production. She could pick and choose her scripts and directors, for example. Pickford also helped develop lighting techniques by insisting that Charles Rosher act as her cameraman for every movie. Pickford similarly furthered film narrative techniques. Despite this savvy, she was still cast as the little moppet girl. For example, in 1917, Pickford played a 12-year-old in *The Little Princess* though she was 24 years of age. Pickford continually challenged herself as an actress, playing more than one role in a film or roles that were physically demanding. In 1918, she and her mother formed the Mary Pickford Film Corporation, making her the first female film star to head her own film company.

In 1919, Pickford was lured away from Famous Players by First National, which offered her a $675,000 per year salary and 50% of the profits made by her movies. That year, Pickford also was one of the four principals who founded United Artists with famous actors Douglas Fairbanks (her fiancé) and Charlie Chaplin, as well as director D.W. Griffiths.

On March 28, 1920, Pickford and Fairbanks married, after a three-year affair. Their marriage was idealized by their adoring fans, and they were considered the first couple of Hollywood. Publicly, the couple encouraged this. Pickford and Fairbanks were the first stars to imprint their footprints in front of Grauman's Chinese Theater in Los Angeles. The private reality of their marriage was far from the myth. Fairbanks was jealous and had numerous extramarital affairs. Pickford also had affairs, as well as a problem with alcohol.

In the early 1920s, Pickford wanted to cultivate a more adult screen presence. To that end, she arranged for a European director, Ernst Lubitsch, to come to the United States. She appeared in his first American effort, *Rosita*, though she did not like working with him. Despite this and other efforts to be cast as an adult, Pickford was forced to do juvenile roles, like playing the son and the mother in *Little Lord Fauntleroy*, to please her audience. While Pickford wanted to take on more creative roles, she wanted to increase her box office receipts more.

The quality of her films began to decline as Pickford tried to escape her typecast moppet image. She appeared in her first, and most successful, sound picture in 1929. *Coquette* was the subject of controversy for fans because Pickford cut off her curls and bobbed her hair in the style of the flapper that she played. She won an Academy Award for best actress, although this decision was even more controversial. At the time, voting for the Oscars was done by the Academy's central board of judges. Pickford was a co-founder of the Academy and Fairbanks was its president. She used Fairbanks' position as leverage in her aggressive campaign to obtain the prize. As a result of this incident, voting for the awards was done by all Academy members from that year forward. Still, *Coquette* was one of the most successful films of Pickford's career, earning $1.3 million at the box office.

## Retired from Acting

Pickford's acting career faltered after her Academy Award victory, although she always tried to give the audience what it wanted. Pickford retired from acting in 1933, after an appearance in *Secrets,* her last film and a box office failure. Pickford believed her audience wanted her to always play the young girl and this was no longer possible at the age of 40.

In the 1930s, Pickford kept herself busy in a number of ways. She served as a vice president at United Artists from 1935 until 1937. She also produced films such as 1936's *The Gay Desperado.* Pickford continued to work as a film producer until 1948's *Sleep, My Love.* She was also active in charity work (especially the Motion Picture Relief Fund and Home), wrote books (an autobiography and a novel), and appeared on her own, short-lived radio show. Despite the end of her acting career, Pickford retained her popularity. Upon a visit to Toronto in 1934, more people came to see her than Prince Edward, the future king of England.

Pickford's personal life was not as rosy. Her drinking increased after her divorce from Fairbanks in 1936. The following year, she married her third and last husband, Charles "Buddy" Rogers, an actor and bandleader. They adopted two children, Ronald and Roxanne, in the mid-1940s. Her alcoholism grew more pronounced over the years, in part because she was still in love with Fairbanks.

Pickford had several offers to act in the 1950s, most notably in *Sunset Boulevard* and *Storm Center,* but she ultimately turned them down. In 1953, she and Chaplin, the only survivors of the four who founded United Artists, sold their shares for $3 million each. By 1972, Pickford had become quite reclusive. She was given an honorary Academy Award for her contributions to the cinema in 1975, but refused to appear in person at the ceremony. Pickford died of a cerebral hemorrhage on May 29, 1979, in Santa Monica, California. Her estate's net worth was estimated at $50 million. Richard Corliss in *Film Comment* wrote "Best to remember Mary Pickford as her fans did: part Eve, part angel, total evangelist for the blooming art of cinema."

## Further Reading

*The Continuum Dictionary of Women's Biography,* edited by Jennifer Uglow, Continuum, 1989.

Felder, Deborah, *The 100 Most Influential Women of All Time: A Ranking Past and Present,* Citadel Press, 1996.

Mordden, Ethan *Movie Star: A Look at the Women Who Made Hollywood,* St. Martin's Press, 1983.

Read, Phyllis J. & Bernard L. Witlieb, *The Book of Women's Firsts,* Random House, 1992.

Reynolds, Moira Davidson, *Immigrant American Women Role Models: Fifteen Inspiring Biographies, 1850-1950,* McFarland & Company, 1997.

*Film Comment,* March-April, 1998.

*Films in Review,* January-February 1997.

*Journal of Popular Film and Television,* Fall 1994.

*Maclean's,* November 3, 1997.

*New Yorker,* September 22, 1997.

*People Weekly,* May 21, 1990; Spring 1991.

http://web.lexis-nexis.com/universe (February 16, 1999). □

# Paul Poiret

**Paul Poiret (1879–1944) was an influential French fashion designer during the early twentieth century. He led a fashion renaissance that introduced free-flowing dresses, replaced tight corsets with brassieres, and added a new standard of artistic value to his fashion plates.**

Poiret was born on April 20, 1879 in Paris. His father was a cloth merchant, and Poiret lived with his parents and his three sisters in an apartment above the shop. Poiret's parents had an interest in the arts and embellished their home with whatever art works they could afford. The family also owned a country house outside of Paris, at Billancourt, where Poiret spent his spare time constructing fountains, pressing petals from the garden, and gathering odd bits of iron and junk into what he called his antique collection.

When Poiret was 12, he and his family moved to Rue des Halles in Paris, where Poiret attended Ecole Massillon. When his sisters contracted scarlet fever, he was sent away to boarding school in order to avoid the illness He was only an average student and was often homesick. Poiret was already interested in fashion and found pleasure in scanning magazines and catalogs; he also enjoyed going to the theater and art exhibits. After his graduation, at the age of 18, his father sent him to an umbrella maker to learn the trade. Poiret hated the business and continued to pursue his interest in fashion by drawing and sewing designs in his spare time, using a small wooden mannequin his sisters had given him.

## The Maison Doucet

Poiret's big break came when a friend encouraged him to take some of his designs to a woman named Mademoiselle Choruit, at the Maison Raundnizt Soeurs. Mme. Choruit was impressed with Poiret's work and bought 12 designs from him, encouraging him to return with more. From there, Poiret started to gain other clients and to visit other dress houses. In 1896, a designer named Doucet offered Poiret a full time job. Poiret had to take his disbelieving father to Doucet's studio in order to convince him that the offer was real.

Poiret thrived at the Maison Doucet, which was at the height of its prosperity. His first design was a red cloak; 400 copies sold and customers demanded the design in other colors. Thus Poiret's position in the designing business was secured. At Doucet's, Poiret created new designs every week, which were then exhibited by ladies at the horse races on Sundays. Poiret also designed costumes for various theatrical productions, which he enjoyed greatly.

Encouraged by Doucet, who expressed appreciation and admiration for his employee's designs, Poiret threw himself into his work. People began to recognize his name and his designs. He was encouraged to venture out into Parisian society a little more. Upon doing so, Poiret met Madame Potiphar, with whom he began a love affair. Relations with his father became tense, as Poiret developed a taste for independence. His relationship with Doucet suffered a similar strain because of some professional indiscretions. As a result, Poiret left the Maison Doucet, but was relieved to learn that his mentor did not bear a grudge. Poiret always respected Doucet and considered him to be a friend.

## Moved Up in the World of Design

Two months after leaving the Maison Doucet, Poiret was recruited into the army and spent the next year in military service. He did not enjoy this time, but did manage to gain a short leave of absence during which he returned to Paris and again engaged in, as Poiret explained in his autobiography, *King of Fashion: The Autobiography of Paul Poiret,* "the study of what pleased me: feminine elegance."

After fulfillment of his military obligations, Poiret returned to Paris and accepted a position at the dressmaking firm of Maison Worth, which was run by two brothers, Gaston and Jean Worth. Here, Poiret began to design dresses for the general public, rather than the high-society ladies of Paris. The result was a reformation in fashion that freed the body from constricting forms. Poiret's new dresses were simple in design, featuring a classical-style high waistline, tubular shape, and long skirt. The colors were plain and bold, often with very small designs, which were popular at the time.

Gaston Worth appreciated the profit Poiret's designs brought. His brother Jean, on the other hand, hated the lowering of standards he perceived Poiret was bringing upon their business. At one point Poiret presented some designs to a Russian princess, who was appalled with them. Discouraged at his inability to please such an audience, and becoming more interested in designing for the general market, Poiret left the Maison Worth and set out on his own.

With some financial help from his mother (his father had passed away by this time), Poiret set up shop at No. 5, Rue Auber, in Paris. His shop was modest, but Poiret gained the attention of passers-by with elaborate and colorful window displays. Within a month, his dress shop became popular. Poiret perfected the cloak that the Russian princess had scorned and that eventually became so popular that, as he said in his autobiography, "Every woman bought at least one." He called it "Confucius," and credited it with the beginning of the Asian influence in fashion.

This was the age of the corset, and Poiret waged war upon it. He popularized the brassiere, which gave women much more freedom and comfort. At the same time, however, he also created the innovative and popular tight skirt. Neither of these inventions were initially profitable because of his dishonest bookkeeper. The bookkeeper's response to Poiret's accusations of theft was to suggest that they visit a psychic, who promptly identified him as the man who was stealing money from Poiret. Thus the bookkeeper was dismissed, and Poiret was able to move on with his business in a more successful way. Eventually the shop at Rue Auber became too small to contain Poiret's growing business, and he moved into a house on Rue Pasquier. A dressmaker operating out of his home was not a common occurrence at that time, and Poiret raised many eyebrows and endured many slanderous comments because of his unusual business practices. None of the criticism, however, affected his growing reputation.

Poiret was becoming increasingly popular with the public, but was somewhat dissatisfied with his personal life. He had drifted in and out of love affairs and now longed for something more stable. He decided to begin a family and married a simple country girl whom he had known as a child. Poiret and his new wife traveled throughout Europe, learning more about the arts.

## A Strong Influence

In his autobiography, Poiret stated, "People have been good enough to say that I have exercised a powerful influence over my age, and that I have inspired the whole of my generation. I dare not make the pretension that this is true . . ."; however, he goes on to say that what influence he did have was not in the creation of new styles or restoring of color to a woman's wardrobe, both of which he did, but rather, he says, "It was in my inspiration of artists, in my dressing of theatrical pieces, in my assimilation of and response to new needs, that I served the public of my day." Fashion design had come under the influence of photography and the high standard of artistic influence, as revealed in the fashion plates of such publications as the *Journal des Dames et des Modes,* had disappeared. Poiret was re-freshingly innovative in his approach to design, restoring the artist as an important and creative force in fashion.

An important example of Poiret's artistic influence was in his work with Paul Iribe. With Iribe creating the drawings that pictured Poiret's dresses, they produced a publication for the elite society titled *Les Robes de Paul Poiret, racontees par Paul Iribe.* Poiret produced a similar album with artist Georges Lepape two years later titled *Les choses de Paul Poiret vues par Georges Lepape.* Both publications were tremendously successful. In these ways, Poiret helped artists gain exposure in the public eye and helped them develop their talents. Consequentially, fashion illustration and literature once again became very popular. New publications appeared, such as the monthly *Gazette du Bon Ton,* which featured many of Poiret's designs.

Poiret also promoted the careers of several actresses, who gained recognition partly because of the costumes he designed for them. Poiret was the first costume designer to consider the lighting and the background of each scene when creating dresses for a theatrical performance. For the first time, the costume creator and the scenic artists of the theater worked together to create a visual impression that was an experience in and of itself.

## Expanding Interests

Poiret continued to promote his own career. He said in his autobiography, "I did not wait for my success to grow by itself. I worked like a demon to increase it, and everything that could stimulate it seemed good to me." One of the ways he did this was by organizing a tour of the main capitals of Europe with nine models, showing his designs. The tour, taken in two automobiles, took Poiret and the women to such cities as Berlin, St. Petersburg, Moscow, and Bucharest.

Poiret's interests included painting, boating, and participating in the Mortigny Club, a group of artists and dignitaries. He also established a school of decorative art in 1912, which he named *Martine* and which later provided Poiret with the inspiration for his founding of the Maison Martine. His school provided young Parisian women the opportunity to learn about design. The curriculum was unstructured, and the women were allowed to create as they wished, without criticism. The school gained the attention of many artists, including Raoul Dufy. Dufy and Poiret struck up a friendship, and Poiret sponsored Dufy in his artistic endeavors. Poiret even ventured into the world of art exhibition in 1924, when he exhibited Dufy's work. The endeavor proved to be unsuccessful, and Poiret did not pursue it further.

## Perfumery and Parties

Poiret's career was temporarily halted when he was called into the military at the outbreak of World War I. He was released from service in 1917, after which he spent several months in Morocco, trying to recuperate from the experience of war. He then resumed his dressmaking business in Paris. By now he had established himself in the businesses of perfumery and interior decoration. Poiret also began conducting business with firms in America.

One of Poiret's favorite pastimes was giving parties, something that he had developed a passion for as a child. These huge *fetes* were elaborate and well attended and covered every gamut of entertainment, from dancers and orchestras to immense buffets and hundreds of carafes filled with exotic drinks. One party even featured a python, a monkey merchant, and a garden of wild animals. Some were based on themes, and others revolved around a performance in the "Oasis," a theater Poiret had created in his garden. Poiret also planned parties and balls for other people, events that were long remembered and talked about by those who attended.

Poiret spent his latter years indulging in his love of painting. He died on April 30, 1944 in Paris.

## Further Reading

*Choice,* February 1991.
Mackrell, Alice, *Paul Poiret,* Holmes and Meier, 1990.
Pile, John, *Dictionary of 20th-Century Design,* Roundtable Press, Inc., 1990.
Poiret, Paul, *King of Fashion: The Autobiography of Paul Poiret,* translated by Stephen Haden Guest, J. B. Lippincott, 1931. □

# Ferdinand Porsche

**Though he and his son founded the high-performance sports car firm that bears the family name, Ferdinand Porsche Sr. (1875–1951) is also remembered as the visionary who created the Volkswagen Beetle in the 1930s. Already a renowned automotive designer, Porsche's dream was to create a small, affordable car for the European mass market. The rise of the German Nazi Party made this "people's car" a government-subsidized reality.**

Ferdinand Porsche was born in the village of Maffersdorf on September 3, 1875. Later renamed Leberec when it reverted to Czechoslovakia, Maffersdorf was at the time part of Bohemia, an area heavily settled by German-speaking tradespeople and part of the Austro-Hungarian empire. Porsche's father, Anton, had a metalsmithing business in Maffersdorf. When his older brother was killed in an accident, it was expected that Ferdinand begin to train for the business. Metalwork did not wholly interest the young Porsche. One day, on a delivery errand to a neighboring town, he saw an electric light plant created to power a carpet factory, and was fascinated by it. The owner gave him a tour, explaining some basic principles of electricity. At home, Porsche began conducting his own rudimentary experiments with acids and batteries. His acumen increased to such a degree that, by 1893, his family home became the first in Maffersdorf to have electric light.

## The Horseless Carriage

Porsche was sent to the Imperial Technical School in nearby Reichenberg for a time and, at the age of sixteen, moved to Vienna. There he worked as a student employee at an electrical engineering company called Egger, while taking courses at Vienna's Technical High School. He also began dating a bookkeeper at the company, Louise Kaes, whom he would eventually marry.

Porsche was promoted to Egger's testing and experimental department, where he became interested in electric vehicles. In 1898, he was hired as chief designer for a coach builder's new automotive division. At Lohner he created two noteworthy cars, including the first front-wheel drive vehicle in history. Porsche was called for military duty in the Imperial Reserves around 1902, and served as a staff driver for the top-ranking officers of the Austro-Hungarian army. He even chauffeured the Archduke Franz Ferdinand, whose later assassination sparked World War I.

Back in civilian life, the gifted Porsche advanced rapidly. In 1905, he became technical director of a car company called Austro-Daimler. He continued to work on a more reliable gasoline engine, and often raced his prototypes in European track and endurance competitions. The company set up a division for the design of engines for the new airships and other early airborne conveyances, and he became involved in this as well. In 1909, Porsche set an altitude record for ballooning.

## Wealthy and Honored Innovator

By this point Porsche was married with two children—daughter Louise, and son Ferdinand Jr., nicknamed "Ferry." As a pioneer in automotive design, he earned quite a good salary. The family enjoyed a summer home called ''Louisenhuette'' in Austria's Rosalie Mountains, where Porsche drove a car he had built. He also plied the waters of nearby lakes in a boat, also self-built, named the *Argonaut.* Even his son was driving his own miniature vehicle by the age of ten. With the outbreak of World War I, Porsche concentrated on designing aircraft engines at Austro-Daimler. He also created the heavy artillery vehicles, known as *Motor-Moerser,* used by the German military to invade Belgium. For this and other innovations, he was promoted to managing director of Austro-Daimler in 1916 and awarded several government accolades. Porsche was most pleased, however, by the honorary doctorate in engineering given to him by Vienna University in 1917.

After the war's end, and the dissolution of both the Austro-Hungarian and German empires, Austro-Daimler fell into financial trouble. Porsche was hopeful that the company could emerge from this period with a small, affordable automobile that could be mass-produced in large numbers. He looked toward the very profitable success of the Ford Motor Company's Model T, assembled at vast and modern factories in Detroit, as a model. In 1921, Porsche had another hit with a car he designed for a wealthy Austrian count and film maker, Sascha Kolowrat. The ''Sascha'' was an open-air two-seater that reached speeds of 90 miles per hour, an extreme at the time. It also successfully made the 900-mile trip back from an Italian auto race, and received a great deal of press for this achievement. Porsche hoped to apply Sascha's technological innovations to the design of a mass-production vehicle for Austro-Daimler. Its board of directors said no, however, and so he resigned.

### Daimler-Benz Era

Porsche and his family moved to Stuttgart, Germany in the spring of 1923, where he took a job with Daimler Motor Works (no connection with Austro-Daimler) as its technical director. He was responsible for designing the famed Mercedes-Benz roadsters, the SS and SSK, both supercharged racing cars with very loud engines. In 1926, the company merged with another German automaker to become Daimler-Benz. Once more, Porsche encountered difficulties in convincing company executives of the feasibility of a small, mass-produced car.

Once again, Porsche decided to resign. He returned to Austria in early 1929, where he took a post with another automaker, Steyr—a comeback greatly heralded in the Vienna papers. During his brief stint at Steyr, Porsche developed an eight-cylinder engine for a model called the ''Austria,'' which featured an innovative rear suspension that yielded superlative handling. He would later copy this design for use in the forerunner to the Volkswagen Beetle. Porsche left Steyr when a merger made it part of Austro-Daimler, and returned to Stuttgart. There, in December 1930, he founded his own firm with his friend Karl Rabe, another engineer. His son Ferry, who had inherited his father's passion for car design, was also on staff.

The Porsche company's first design contract came for a large touring car for Wanderer, a German automaker in Chemnitz. They also did engine and suspension work for various European automakers. In 1932, Porsche visited the Soviet Union at the request of Josef Stalin, who offered him a post as chief construction director, complete with generous compensation, a villa, and the transfer of his entire Stuttgart staff. He was also promised unlimited development funds to build a small car. Porsche, who still loved to race his own cars on the track, declined the offer since the European Grand Prix circuit did not extend to Communist Russia.

### The ''People's Car''

Back in Stuttgart in the early 1930s, one of the projects that Porsche took on was a prototype for a sports car with a rear-mounted engine. A consortium of German automakers, including Audi and Wanderer, had formed the Auto-Union Company to build such a car to compete with Mercedes vehicles on the racetrack. Through this involvement, Porsche first met the new German chancellor, Adolf Hitler, at an Auto-Union meeting in March 1933.

A second connection to the Fuhrer came through a Daimler-Benz associate named Jakob Werlin. Hitler bought his first car from Werlin in 1923, when Nazi Party offices in Munich shared building space with a Mercedes dealership. In turn, Werlin later came to know Porsche when both were at Daimler-Benz. Despite his personal preference for the luxury sedan, Hitler was hoping that Germany could create a *Volks-wagen,* or ''People's Car,'' that fit in with his political and economic agenda. The fascist National Socialist Party had strong-armed its way to power in the early 1930s, and offered desperate Germans a plan to salvage their economy and national identity by various measures, including stripping German Jews of their citizenship and resurrecting an armaments sector banned by the 1919 treaty that concluded World War I. In the fall of 1933, Werlin invited Porsche to a meeting at Berlin's Hotel Kaiserhof, at which Hitler was also present. They discussed the creation of an affordable and reliable German car that might sell for under a thousand marks.

### Massive Factory Built

Porsche designed a prototype and submitted it to government offices in January 1934. A contract was drawn up between the RDA, the official association of German automakers, and Porsche's Stuttgart firm. To help reduce the cost of raw materials without direct government subsidies, a fund was created that eventually ballooned to $67 million. Marketed through the efficiently pervasive Nazi Party organization, the fund was essentially a state-sanctioned savings plan: thousands of German workers bought five-mark savings stamps weekly, which would later be redeemed for their own ''KdF-Wagen,'' as the vehicle would be called. The acronym stood for *Kraft durch Freude,* or ''Strength through Joy.'' Extensive testing of Porsche's prototypes began in 1936. Ground was broken by Hitler himself in May 1938 for the Volkswagen factory complex, ''KdF-City,'' situated near the town of Wolfsburg.

Very few KdF-Wagens (later rechristened as the *Kaefer,* German for ''beetle'') came off the assembly line before the outbreak of World War II in 1939. The huge Wolfsburg complex was easily converted over to the production of military vehicles and staffed with prisoners-of-war. During these years Porsche served as head of the German Tank Commission, for which he designed massive artillery vehicles so loud they shattered all nearby windows—and received numerous Nazi honors. He also traveled regularly to France to oversee production at the Peugeot autoworks, seized by the German occupation forces in 1940.

## Imprisoned in France

When Stuttgart was heavily bombed by Allied planes in 1944, Porsche and his family had already returned to their summer home in Austria's Zell am See. At the war's end he was placed under house arrest. French military authorities then invited the aged and distinguished designer back to Germany to discuss the possibility of manufacturing a Volkswagen-type car for France. It proved to be a ruse and Porsche was arrested as a war criminal for the Peugeot visits. He was 71 at the time, and imprisoned in Dijon. To secure his father's release, Ferry Porsche—also incarcerated for some months—spent a year working for the Italian racing consortium Cisitalia to build a Grand Prix Formula I car with Porsche technology. Cisitalia then secured, via various means, the exorbitant bond money—about $62,000—that France wanted in exchange for the elder Porsche's freedom. A year after his September 1947 release, the French warcrimes tribunal found him not guilty as charged, but the bond money was never refunded.

Porsche returned to his Austrian home, and was legally banned from traveling to Germany. Meanwhile, Allied occupation powers had taken over the Volkswagen plant, after first trying to sell it and then toying with the idea of demolishing it altogether. Because there was such a shortage of vehicles, permission was granted to begin producing the small, economical vehicle again. Several thousand were on the road in Germany by 1949, when their creator was allowed to return for a visit. He was reportedly surprised to see so many of them on the road, but saddened that his dream for a "people's car" had gone so awry. He died in Stuttgart, Germany on January 30, 1951 following a stroke. Porsche was buried in a chapel at Zell am See.

Ferry Porsche kept the Porsche firm going, having already launched a manufacturing company in 1948 with his father's help. From that point on Porsche would create a series of outstanding high-performance sports cars, including the 911 and the Boxster. The Wolfsburg autoworks—also VW's world headquarters—is still operational, and the Beetle would become the most successful and ubiquitous car in history. In 1998, the company introduced a re-designed Beetle that still featured many enduring—and endearing—features of Ferdinand Porsche's first prototype. At the time of Ferry Porsche's death in 1998, his nephew Ferdinand Piech was chair of Volkswagen.

## Further Reading

Nitske, W. Robert, *The Amazing Porsche and Volkswagen Story,* Comet Press, 1958.
*Detroit News,* March 28, 1998. □

# Hal Prince

**A director and producer whose long list of credits includes the musical blockbusters *West Side Story, Fiddler on the Roof, Cabaret, Evita,* and *The Phantom of the Opera,* as well as groundbreaking works with lyricist/composer Stephen Sondheim, Hal Prince (born 1928) is one of the towering figures in the American theater of the second half of the twentieth century.**

Proving that artistic and commercial success are not always mutually exclusive, Hal Prince has frequently managed to simultaneously please critics, audiences, and investors. "He's the best around by far. He has a sense of the function of music in a show. . . . He takes it seriously and is more daring, imaginative and endlessly creative. He likes to take chances. He has a sense of dignity of the musical theater and thinks it's the highest form of theater and I happen to agree with him," Sondheim said of Prince in an interview with Carol Ilson, author of *Harold Prince: From Pajama Game to Phantom of the Opera.*

## A Native New Yorker

Harold Smith Prince, known to his friends and colleagues as Hal, was born in New York City on January 30, 1928. He was the son of Milton Prince, a stockbroker, and Blanche Stern Prince. "We were privileged, upper-middle, lower-rich class, Jewish, both parents of German families which settled here soon after the Civil War," Prince wrote in his memoir *Contradictions.* His parents divorced when he was a small child and Prince was brought up in Manhattan by his mother and stepfather, also a stockbroker. He was taken to the theater often and saw many of the top stars and productions of the 1930s, such as Orson Welles in *Julius Caesar,* Tallulah Bankhead in *The Little Foxes,* and Burgess Meredith in *Winterset.*

As a teenager, Prince began attending the theater by himself. "I was weaned on the second balcony. Do you know how terrific it is to sit in the second balcony?" Prince was quoted in the *New Yorker* as telling a master class at the Manhattan School of Music. In 1944, after graduating from the Franklin School, a private school on the Upper West Side of Manhattan, Prince enrolled at the University of Pennsylvania in Philadelphia. Intending to become a playwright, he took a liberal arts course heavy on literature and history and wrote, acted, and directed plays for the student group, the Penn Players.

Receiving his bachelor's degree in 1948, Prince returned to New York where he attempted to sell his plays to theatrical producers. Though he found no takers for his plays, Prince did find a job through director George Abbott, a Broadway legend whose career began in the early twentieth century. "He was a young fella out of college and I put him to work. He was a very bright fellow, and he had a great deal of talent," Abbott said of Prince to a reporter from *Forbes.* While working days in Abbott's office running the

switchboard and delivering messages, Prince spent his nights as an assistant stage manager for the Abbott directed revue *Touch and Go.* He then was an assistant stage manager on the musical *Tickets, Please.*

In 1950, Prince was drafted into the U.S. Army and assigned to an anti-aircraft artillery battalion in West Germany. "I slept practically the whole two years, not just in bed but on my feet. . . . Actually it was not such a bad time. Being thwarted in 'progress' tranquilized me. I still think of those two years as real years. My life before and since hasn't been too heavy in the reality factor," Prince wrote of his military service in *Contradictions.*

### Broadway Producer at 26

Having been promised a job with Abbott when his army duty was up, he was immediately made an assistant stage manager in 1952 on the new musical Abbott was directing, *Wonderful Town,* starring Rosalind Russell. *Wonderful Town* opened on Broadway in the spring of 1953 and was a major success.

During the run of the show, Prince and Robert Griffith, *Wonderful Town's* principal stage manager and Abbott's chief assistant, decided to become producing partners and chose, as their first project, a musical version of *7 « Cents,* Richard Bissell's comic novel about a strike at a pajama factory. Building the show from scratch, Prince and Griffith hired the pop songwriting team of Richard Adler and Jerry Ross to compose the score, asked Bissell to write a libretto from his novel, and engaged an aspiring young choreogra-

pher, Bob Fosse, to work out dance routines. They also convinced Abbott to direct. Prince and Griffith raised money for the show, renamed *The Pajama Game,* from one hundred sixty-one backers, including several *Wonderful Town* chorus members who invested small sums.

Opening on Broadway with little fanfare in May 1954, at the end of the theatrical season, *The Pajama Game,* garnered rave reviews. "*The Pajama Game* wound up the season with as exuberant high spirits as New Year's Eve winds up the year. . . . There are the kind of peppy dance numbers that suggest a cheerleaders carnival, and there is a great deal of music with an infectious, elementary lilt," wrote a reviewer for *Time. The Pajama Game* won a Tony Award for best musical and ran for 1,063 performances.

Prince and Griffith re-teamed with Adler, Ross, Fosse, and Abbott on *Damn Yankees,* a musical about a middle aged baseball fan's magical transformation into a young slugger for his favorite team, the perennially losing Washington Senators. Opening in May 1955, *Damn Yankees* repeated the success of *The Pajama Game.* It ran for 1,019 performances and also won the Tony Award for best musical. "I had this absolutely charmed first couple of years. I really thought all you do is have hits; it never occurred to me that it could ever be another way," Prince said of his early producing career to Jeremy Gerard of the *New York Times* in 1987.

Although Prince and Griffith's production of *New Girl in Town,* a musical version of Eugene O'Neill's play *Anna Christie* starring Gwen Verdon, was only a minor success. In the spring of 1957, they were back on the hit-making track with *West Side Story,* a musical retelling of Shakespeare's *Romeo and Juliet* set in a New York City slum, and *Fiorello!,* a musical based on the early life of Fiorello LaGuardia, New York City's mayor in the 1930s and 1940s.

Opening in September 1957, and featuring music by Leonard Bernstein and lyrics by Stephen Sondheim, the now-classic *West Side Story* received mixed reviews at its premiere. Some critics celebrated its innovative blending of music and dance with a serious, contemporary storyline, while others were put off by its dark and gritty attitude. Coming to Broadway in November 1959, *Fiorello!*—with music by Jerry Bock and lyrics by Sheldon Harnick, received almost unanimous praise by critics and won the Tony Award for best musical. It also won the Pulitzer Prize for drama—an honor rarely bestowed upon a musical.

Prince and Griffith's style differed from that of many other producers in that they concentrated on one show at a time and personally involved themselves in all aspects of a production. "We're too involved with every detail to produce on an assembly line. We've noticed that other producers have people called 'production assistants,' but we can't comprehend what the job is. It doesn't exist here. We're our own 'production assistants,'" Prince told John S. Wilson of *Theatre Arts* in 1960.

### Became a Director

Prince's deep involvement with the creative side of his productions increased his interest in becoming a director. His move to direction was complicated by his older and more experienced partner, Griffith also having directorial aspirations. "Bobby had always wanted to direct himself and he'd never done it. So I couldn't either," Prince told *Forbes.* Prince's dilemma came to a sad resolution in 1961 when Griffith died suddenly of a heart attack. Almost immediately, Prince began accepting directing offers. With the exception of *She Loves Me,* a minor success in 1963, Prince's initial efforts at directing a Broadway musical were both critical and commercial failures.

Prince continued to produce shows directed by others, and his magic touch as a producer remained in evidence. Prince's production of *A Funny Thing Happened on the Way to the Forum,* Sondheim's musical take on Roman farce, opened in May 1962. *Fiddler on the Roof,* opened in September 1964, and told the story of Jewish villagers in turn of the century Russia, with music and lyrics by Fiorello's Bock and Harnick. Both were triumphs. *Fiddler,* which went on to a record-breaking run of 3,242 performances, was originally seen by many as too ethnic to please most audiences. Even Prince considered its potential limited. "There are at least three million Jews in New York, and I thought that should be enough to keep the show running for a couple of seasons. But I never foresaw that *Fiddler* would run the way it did," Prince told *Forbes.*

It was *Cabaret,* a tale of Berlin on the eve of the Nazi takeover of Germany with music by John Kander and lyrics by Fred Ebb, that established Prince as an important director. "Instead of telling a little story about the decadence of Berlin just before Hitler came to power into which casual musical numbers can be sandwiched whenever politeness permits, *Cabaret* lunges forward to insist on music as mediator between audience and characters. . . . We are inside music looking out, tapping our feet to establish a cocky rhythm and a satanically grinning style to which the transient people of the narrative must accommodate themselves," wrote Walter Kerr of the *New York Times.*

Prince also produced the show which opened in November 1966 and ran for 1,165 performances. *Cabaret* won the Tony Award for best musical and earned Prince his first best director award. His version of *Cabaret* was an ensemble piece and differed greatly from choreographer-turned-director Bob Fosse's 1972 film version of *Cabaret,* which was designed to show off the talents of its star, Liza Minnelli. Prince abhorred "star vehicles" and throughout his career has generally avoided working with big name performers. "Broadway doesn't need stars. They have a way of influencing material," Prince said to Hubert Saal of *Newsweek.*

Prince considered George Abbott, who died in 1995 at the age of 107, the primary influence on his directorial style and he emulated Abbott's cool, businesslike approach towards actors and other personnel. "George Abbott has no tolerance for histrionics or emotional bloodletting and neither have I. I demand punctuality and absolute quiet or I get growly. But that's as far as I go," Prince told Louis Botto of *Look.*

In other areas, Prince sees his directorial style as different from Abbott's, especially in regard to what constitutes a worthwhile evening at the theater. "I have a darker sensibility. . . . I'm political, he's not. I'm issue-oriented, he's not.

He really unabashedly wants people to have a good time, and sometimes I don't give a damn," Prince explained in an *A & E Biography* cable television documentary quoted by Ilson.

## Frequent Collaborations with Sondheim

Some of Prince's most influential work as a director has come in his collaborations with Stephen Sondheim. Beginning in 1970 with *Company,* a look at contemporary marriage seen through the eyes of a commitment-wary bachelor, Prince and Sondheim brought the musical to higher levels of subtlety and sophistication. Dubbed "concept musicals" by critics, Prince and Sondheim's shows were built around themes and ideas rather than a narrative plot, and were the biggest innovation in the musical theater since the early 1940s when Rodgers and Hammerstein pioneered the "book musical," which integrated music and dance with a relatively complicated storyline.

Among the grandest of Prince and Sondheim's collaborations is *Follies,* in which a reunion of former chorus girls serves as a device to examine the aging process and the vagaries brought about by the passage of time. In his review of *Follies,* Jack Kroll of *Newsweek* wrote—"How many theater people in this country have the talent, taste, inventiveness, resourcefulness and high professional standards of Prince?. . . . With *Cabaret, Company,* and *Follies,* Harold Prince has created a generation of musicals which capture much of our time in a form that, in his hands, refuses to die."

Opening in April 1971, *Follies* was a financial disaster that, despite a respectable run of 522 performances and a best director Tony Award for Prince, never came close to recouping its fabulous production costs. Though Prince is noted for his cost-consciousness as both a director and producer, he is not opposed to spending large sums when such spending seems called for artistically. "Everything can't be modest in size—some things just cry out to be musicals. Big musicals. And why shouldn't they be?" Prince told Gerard.

Prince's other collaborations with Sondheim produced *A Little Night Music* in 1973, a wistful look at romantic relationships that was their most commercially successful joint venture and *Pacific Overtures* in 1976, an exquisitely mounted production about Western contact with Japan in the nineteenth century. In 1979, *Sweeney Todd,* a bleak, melodramatic tale of the murdering "demon barber of Fleet Street," won several Tony Awards, including best musical.

Apart from Sondheim, Prince had other major successes during this period with *On the Twentieth Century* in 1978, a musical version of the 1932 comedy play *Twentieth Century,* with music by Cy Coleman, and lyrics by Adolph Green and Betty Comden, and *Evita* in 1979 (also in London in 1978), about the life of Eva Peron, the charismatic wife of Argentinian dictator, Juan Peron. *Evita* featured music by Andrew Lloyd Webber and lyrics by Tim Rice. Prince won yet another Tony Award for his direction of *Evita.*

## Brought the Phantom to Broadway

The critical and commercial failure of *Merrily We Roll Along* in 1981 caused Prince and Sondheim to go their separate ways. Though they have remained friends, they have not worked together since. After his break with Sondheim, Prince's career faltered with the expensive and well publicized flops *A Doll's Life* in 1982, and *Grind* in 1985. On the subject of failure, Prince told Sylviane Gold of the *New York Times*—"Does it matter? Yeah, it matters some. Then you move on. A certain amount of denial is very important to a life in the theater. And you can't play God. You can't always make things work out the way you want them to."

In the 1970s, Prince, who had never really enjoyed producing, generally limited his producing activities to shows he was also directing. In the 1980s, he eased out of producing entirely. Prince had always relied primarily on the backing of many small investors or "angels" genuinely interested in the theater. This method became obsolete as his group of long time backers began to pass away and Broadway finances became dominated by big spending corporate investors looking for large profits.

Prince's fortunes turned upward when reteamed with composer Lloyd Webber to direct *The Phantom of the Opera*, an extraordinarily popular musical version of a 1911 novel about a disfigured man who haunts a Paris opera house and makes a star out of the young singer he adores. Prince directed both the London production which opened in October 1986, and the New York production, which opened in January 1988. "*Phantom* powerfully delivers . . . a brilliantly manipulated journey," wrote William A. Henry III of *Time*. Many critics credited Prince with giving the melodramatic *Phantom* an intelligent edge and a genuinely romantic sensibility. "I wanted the show to have some depth. I wasn't looking to do Dracula with music," Prince explained to Patricia Morrisroe of *New York*. *The Phantom of the Opera* earned Prince another Tony Award for best director.

Prince scored yet another success when he joined forces with *Cabaret*'s Kander and Ebb on *Kiss of the Spider Woman*, a musical version of Manuel Puig's novel about the bond that forms between two men when they are thrown together in a prison cell. *Spider Woman* was initially developed by Prince and his collaborators in a 1990 production at the State University of New York at Purchase. It enjoyed a long run in Toronto before coming to Broadway under the aegis of Canadian impresario, Garth Drabinsky in 1993. "I love Broadway. I owe by life to Broadway. But there's no question that, because of the high costs, there are all sorts of pressures now—and there have been for at least the last ten years—that encumber the spirit with which you do your work . . . in the future there are going to be shows that have played all over the world and have never played on Broadway. That has rarely happened yet, but it's going to happen at lot," Prince told Mervyn Rothstein of the *New York Times* in 1990.

In 1993, Prince directed a Drabinsky-produced revival of the classic 1927 musical *Show Boat*. The highly praised production, which originated in Toronto, opened in New York in 1994. Undaunted by a troubled experience directing *Whistle Down the Wind*, an Andrew Lloyd Webber musical which had its New York premiere canceled after

poor reviews in Washington in early 1997, Prince immediately turned his attention to a revival of Leonard Bernstein's *Candide* that reached Broadway in the spring of 1997. "I never stop working," Prince told Gerard.

In 1998, Prince was back on Broadway yet again, this time with *Parade*, a work by young composer/lyricist Jason Robert Brown about the 1915 Georgia lynching of Leo Frank, a Jewish man whose death sentence for rape and murder had been commuted to life imprisonment by the governor.

Prince has been married since 1962 to Judith Chaplin with whom he has a son and a daughter. Prince remains a vital force in the theater. He is more interested in looking forward to new challenges than in looking back on past triumphs. As Prince told Jerry Tallmer of *Playbill*—"What I've learned over the years is that the impossibly difficult ideas are the best ideas. . . . It's the easy, can't-miss ideas that are always a problem for me."

## Further Reading

Hirsch, Foster. *Harold Prince and the American Musical Theatre.* Cambridge: Cambridge University Press, 1989.

Ilson, Carol. *Harold Prince: From Pajama Game to Phantom of the Opera.* Ann Arbor, MI: UMI Research Press, 1989.

Prince, Harold. *Contradictions: Notes on Twenty-Six Years in the Theatre.* New York: Dodd, Mead, and Co., 1974.

*Forbes*, February 1, 1972, pp. 20-25; January 18, 1982, pp. 55-56.

*Harper's*, August 1983, pp. 69-74.

Look, May 18, 1971, pp.34-38.

*New York*, January 18, 1988, p. 32.

*New Yorker*, July 17, 1995, pp. 23-24.

*New York Times*, December 4, 1966, sect. 2, p. 5; October 1, 1987, p. C21; April 26, 1990, p. C17; February 12, 1995, sect. 2, p. 8; March 23, 1997, sect. 2, p.5

*Newsweek*, December 2, 1968, pp. 105-106; April 12, 1971, p. 121; July 26, 1971, pp.68-70

*Playbill*, November 30, 1998, pp.10-12.

*Theatre Arts*, October 1960, pp. 20-21, 73-74.

*Time*, May 24, 1954, p. 66; March 5, 1973, p. 78; February 8, 1988, p. 83.

*Washington Post*, December 4, 1994, p. G6. ☐

# William Cooper Procter

**William Cooper Procter (1862–1934) rose to the chairmanship of the Procter & Gamble Corporation and never sacrificed his ideals of humane business management. He devoted a great deal of attention to devising systems that would reward employees for both loyalty and efficiency. Procter was remembered for his "radical" labor practices, including the five-day workweek and an employee profit-sharing plan.**

Procter came into the family business as a production laborer and worked his way up through the ranks. In 1907, he was named president and chief executive of Procter & Gamble, following the tragic suicide of his father, William Alexander Procter. As William Cooper Procter rose through the company ranks, he developed close emotional ties and concerns for the lowliest of the workers. He strove throughout his lifetime to ease their burden. It was his belief that such a business ethic would maximize profits for all concerned. Procter felt that financial benefits would naturally accrue to a company when the work force shared in the profits.

## Started At the Bottom

William Cooper Procter was born in Glendale, Ohio on August 25, 1862. He was the grandson of Procter & Gamble co-founder, William Procter, and was the only son of Procter & Gamble heirs, William Alexander and Charlotte Elizabeth (Jackson) Procter. He attended Princeton University before going to work at Procter & Gamble in 1883.

Despite his background and higher education, Procter started at the bottom of his family's business, as a production laborer. Despite his prestigious family ties, Procter mingled freely with his fellow workers. He sat on the factory floor and ate lunch from a paper sack, without pretense or pride. In time, he noted an overwhelming sense of despair among the employees of his grandfather's company, and was compelled to approach his family with concerns about the employees' grueling six-day work schedule (69 hours per week). At young Procter's suggestion, in 1885, the senior Procters agreed to roll back the work hours with no loss of pay to the workers, a radical innovation in labor policy, and one that set a precedent for American industry. Procter's goal was to foster loyalty among the workers and to create incentives for all, in order to improve efficiency and to maximize profits. He wrote in his business diary, "Any worthwhile change in the conduct of a business must first and last have the element of lessening the cost."

Despite the reduced work hours, union agitators at Procter & Gamble challenged management continually, for the loyalty of the factory workers. The employees staged walkouts on several occasions. This concerned Procter, who took it upon himself to devise a profit-sharing plan for the employees. Procter presented his profit-sharing plan to the company owners and, in April 1887, the company announced that every employee would receive a semi-annual dividend based on the ratio of personal wages earned to total company wages paid. The new and radical idea attracted attention from the press. Reporters visited the factory to interview Procter about his ideas. *Industrial Relations* reported that, "When William Cooper Procter suggested that it would benefit employer and employee alike to permit the employee to share in the company's profits, the family thought he had lost his senses. Such a thing was unheard of." Like the Procter family, the company workforce received news of the profit-sharing program with skepticism. They suspected Procter's motives, until he reminded them that, "The first job we have is to turn out quality merchandise that consumers will buy and keep on buying. If we

produce it efficiently and economically, we will earn a profit, in which you will share."

## Incorporation

Both the Procter and the Gamble families agreed that William Cooper Procter was the most promising candidate among the third generation of heirs to one day assume control of the company. In October 1887, they awarded him a five-percent partnership interest in Procter & Gamble. By 1889, he headed the entire Ivorydale factory in Cincinnati, Ohio. Procter prudently foresaw the need for additional plants, new equipment, and the development of new products, all of which required capital expenditures beyond the means of the company's resources. At Procter's suggestion, the company became a corporation and issued company stock valued at $4,500,000, in an effort to generate capital. At the first meeting of Procter & Gamble stockholders on July 17, 1890, Procter was named general manager.

Following the early retirement of Procter's uncle, Harley Thomas Procter, William Cooper Procter ran the corporation along with his father. One contemporary business publication dubbed the father-son team as the "architects of growth," because the Procters sought to bring more managers into the organization. They hired both from inside and outside the company and dispatched management recruiters to college campuses in search of the most qualified candidates.

## Increased Benefits to Workers

As Procter assumed greater power in the company, he continually addressed concerns over the employees' welfare. Although Procter and his father were known to help those employees in need, Procter was aware that the employees remained limited in their ability to set aside a portion of their wages toward retirement. He attempted to restructure the profit-sharing plan in such a way that every employee who contributed conscientiously toward maximizing profits would receive twice the normal profit-sharing dividend, while those with marginal enthusiasm would receive a standard share of profits. Ambivalent employees would receive only one-half of the standard share of profits, and disinterested workers would not share in the profits at all. Procter's plan, which was founded on a subjective appraisal at the discretion of company supervisors, failed to create the intended result because it lacked objectivity.

Undeterred, Procter went on to implement a revolutionary new stock-purchase plan for the employees, whereby workers could purchase one share of stock over a two-year period, with a $10 down payment. That plan failed to generate interest, because the workers feared the speculative risks of stock purchase. In 1896, Procter responded to the reticent employees with a precedent-setting policy—he guaranteed his employees against any loss, up to $1000, on any investment they made in the company through the stock purchase plan. In an announcement to the employees about the revised stock plan, Procter & Gamble issued a statement that, "[T]he plan forms a practical means of bringing the employer and employee nearer together, by inducing the employees to become part owners in the business. The plan furnishes you with an absolutely safe investment . . . and through your efforts you may increase both the dividends and the value of the stock you buy." In 1903, Procter further refined his plan by coordinating the profit-sharing plan with the Procter & Gamble stock purchase plan. For every dollar an employee might save, Procter & Gamble agreed to contribute four dollars towards the purchase of company stock. Procter & Gamble further guaranteed to buy back any employee stock at a minimum of the original purchase price, regardless of market value. Procter's combined profit-sharing/stock purchase incentives were well received by employees.

In 1917, workers at one Procter & Gamble plant organized a strike to demand a reduction of hours from a ten-hour workday to eight hours, with no cut in pay. Procter acquiesced to the strikers and established the Conference Plan in order to avert future strikes. He explained to a reporter, "The Plan is, I believe, the first move of its kind in business history. . . . We worked out the idea of having the employees elect by secret ballot a conference committee to meet monthly with management in order to bring to our attention matters that seemed to need correction. . . . The chief problem of big business today is to shape its policies so that each worker . . . will feel he is a vital part of his company with a personal responsibility for its success and a chance to share in that success."

A few years later the complex and inconsistent product demands of the wholesale grocery industry threatened to create a bottleneck in the Procter & Gamble workforce. Procter resolved the confusion by initiating direct commerce with the retail grocery industry. As a result of ceasing to do business with the wholesale grocers in 1923, Procter & Gamble was able to guarantee with confidence to its employees a minimum of 48 weeks of work each year.

### "A Life of Noble Simplicity"

Procter was a man of seemingly extraordinary energy; he spoke quickly and demanded attention. In 1930, an aging Procter—nearly 70 years old andsuffering from arthritis, backache, asthma, and other ailments—assumed the newly-created position of chairman of Procter & Gamble. Four years later, in the spring of 1934, his health worsened and he was confined to bed. His wife stayed at his bedside for days. He died on May 2, 1934 at the age of 71 and was buried in the Spring Grove Cemetery in Cincinnati, Ohio. Employees and former employees financed the creation of a life-sized marble statue to honor William Cooper Procter. It stands near the Ivorydale plant and bears the inscription, "He lived a life of noble simplicity, believing in God and the inherent worthiness of his fellow men." An editorial in the *Cincinnati Enquirer* read, "[T]he whole nation pays homage to his memory because his restless intellect and driving energy brought about, in our industrial fabric, startling innovations which set the pace for a growing nation."

### Further Reading

Schisgall, Oscar, *Eyes on Tomorrow: The Evolution of Procter & Gamble,* J. G. Ferguson, 1981.
*Advertising Age,* August 20, 1987. □

# Richard Pryor

**Richard Pryor (born 1940) was one of the most influential stand-up comedians of his generation, and starred in a number of hit films and comedy recordings. He created a new type of humor, one that blended self-effacing statements about being African American with sharp political insights.**

Richard Pryor was born on December 1, 1940 in Peoria, Illinois to LeRoy Pryor, Jr. (also known as Buck Carter) and Gertrude Thomas. A tough, streetwise kid, Pryor's father won a Golden Gloves tournament in Chicago at the age of 18. His mother worked as a prostitute and bookkeeper. Both parents were violent and alcoholic. Born out of wedlock, Richard suffered not only the stigma of illegitimacy, but also that of racism.

Pryor's youth was spent in a house of prostitution run by his grandmother, Marie Carter. His mother often disappeared for months at a time, and finally abandoned him when he was ten. His father rarely saw him. Therefore, Pryor's grandmother was his sole means of support as a child. She was strict and beat him when he misbehaved. Pryor frequented pool halls and was often in trouble. He was also the victim of physical and sexual abuse. When he was six, he was molested by a teenage pedophile named "Bubba," who, many years later, brought his own son to Pryor for an autograph. Rather than dwelling on his anger over the incident, Pryor worried that the pedophile's son was being subjected to abuse.

### Discovered His Talent

Around the age of ten, Pryor realized that he could make people laugh and pay attention to him. "I was a skinny little black kid with big eyes that took in the whole world and a wide smile that begged for more attention than anyone had time to give," Pryor wrote in his 1995 autobiography, *Pryor Convictions and Other Life Sentences.* In searching for love, he turned to comedy. By intentionally falling off a porch railing, he got people to laugh. On a rare outing with his father to a Jerry Lewis movie, Pryor saw his father break up with laughter. He decided to try to make his father and others laugh to win their approval and love.

One teacher in the several elementary schools he attended encouraged him. Marguerite Parker allowed him to stand in front of the class and entertain if he arrived on time. Another teacher, Juliette Whittaker at the Carver Community Center, gave him a chance to act. While at the Center, the 11 year old Pryor observed a rehearsal of *Rumpelstiltskin.* Telling Whittaker he would take any part, he proceeded to memorize all the parts. From Whittaker's plays, he received self esteem. She stated, "This child had a drive to be; he loved making people laugh, the spotlight, the attention you get. He needed that, the feeling of self-esteem he got. He was somebody." His comic abilities also created enemies who wanted to beat him up. He defused their envy with his jokes. Pryor was expelled from high school, but at

the Carver Community Center, he was the star of a number of Ms. Whittaker's plays.

## A Start in Stand-Up Comedy

By the age of 17, Pryor had fathered an illegitimate daughter, Renee. To escape from his responsibilities and his neighborhood, and to better his station in life, he joined the army the following year. Like the comedians Dick Gregory and Bill Cosby, Pryor saw the armed forces as an opportunity for advancement. His army career was undistinguished until he was discharged for slashing another soldier with a switchblade.

Shortly thereafter, he walked into Harold's Club in Peoria, and talked himself into a job. For the next several years, he acquired a reputation as a stand-up comedian in the black clubs of Chicago, Cleveland, and Buffalo. By 1963, he was a stand-up comedian in New York City. His hero and obsession was Bill Cosby. Pryor appeared on the Ed Sullivan and Merv Griffin television shows. He was one of the first black comedians to use the painful events from his own life for his comedy monologue. After his father's death, his memories of the hustlers, prostitutes, junkies, and winos of his youth took over his comedy routine. *People Weekly* noted, "Pryor had found his own stand-up persona, which grafted the profane edge of Lenny Bruce onto the pathos of Charlie Chaplin's Little Tramp." Pauline Kael portrayed him as "a master of lyrical obscenity; the only great poet-satirist among our comics." During the mid-1960s, Pryor's increased success brought more money and more stress, leading to a $200 a day cocaine habit.

Pryor moved to Los Angeles where he began to get small parts in movies. His big break came in 1972, when he played opposite Diana Ross in *Lady Sings the Blues,* for which he received an Academy Award nomination for best supporting actor. From 1974 until 1980 he starred in a number of hit movies, including *Uptown Saturday Night, Car Wash, Silver Streak, Richard Pryor: Live in Concert,* and *Stir Crazy.* During this time, Pryor also wrote comedy for the television shows, *Sanford and Son,* and *The Flip Wilson Show,* and aided Mel Brooks in writing *Blazing Saddles.*

## Drugs and Violence Out of Control

While his public persona was a success, his private life was a disaster. Although he was making millions of dollars, he was using large amounts of drugs and becoming self destructive. In 1977, he suffered a heart attack. Shortly after the death of his grandmother, in 1980, he attempted to commit suicide by dousing himself with cognac and igniting himself with a cigarette lighter. Although he initially claimed it was an accident caused when he was high on cocaine, he later admitted that he intended to kill himself. He spent six weeks in a burn unit, which he described as one of the worst experiences of his life.

Pryor had a history of violence going back to his youth. When he was high on cocaine, he frequently beat the women he was involved with. He almost beat to death his fourth wife, Jennifer Lee, in 1979, while both were under the influence of alcohol and drugs. In his autobiography, he stated, "Uninterested in relationships, I caught women as if they were taxis." In other words, he got in and out of relationships very quickly.

Pryor married six times, the last two marriages to the same woman. He has seven children: Renee, Richard, Jr., Elizabeth Anne, Rain, Steven, Franklin, and Kelsey, although he doesn't currently acknowledge Renee. He also has a grandchild, Randis.

## Cleaned Up His Act

In 1982, Pryor attempted to rehabilitate himself by joining a drug program to fight his addictions. The following year, after making the film *Superman III,* for which he received $4 million, he returned to abusing drugs and women. His daughter, Rain, recounted a turning point in his life "My dad was a very scared, closed person. Dad spent most of my childhood locked away in his room with his women and his drugs. He lived in his own reality. He trusted no one." In 1993, in Hawaii, Pryor had an epiphany and then a symbolic baptism. He threw his cocaine pipe in the garbage and allowed Rain to lead him into the ocean and immerse him in the water, although he was phobic about water. Rain stated, "For my dad, letting me lead him into the water was an expression of trust, almost unheard of for him. I think he was willing to trust me because I was a child. Why would I want to hurt him?"

## The Lowest Point

With his life starting to get on track, Pryor wrote, directed and starred in *Jo Jo Dancer, Your Life is Calling,* a semi-autobiographical movie. In 1986, he was stricken with multiple sclerosis (MS), a disease that destroys the protective sheath around the nerves. MS affects the ability to balance and walk; eventually an MS victim cannot even move. Pryor discovered that something was wrong while filming the movie *Critical Condition*. When the director, Michael Apted, asked Pryor to walk over to him. Pryor's body would not respond. When he was diagnosed with MS, Pryor was devastated. "I was depressed; it was the lowest point of my life. But I struggled with hope . . ." In 1990, he had a minor heart attack and his MS got worse. He could not get out of bed. Pryor stated, "We take so much for granted, but man, lose the movement of your legs and you begin to take a closer look at life." With the aid of a personal trainer, he was able to walk again. "Since the earthquakes . . . didn't kill me, the drugs didn't kill me, the fire didn't kill me (although it hurt like a bitch), and my ex-wives (God bless them all) didn't kill me, there is no way I'm going to let the MS kill me." In his last film, *Another You*, released in 1991, Pryor appeared clearly ailing, a fragile shell of his former manic self. In 1991, he suffered a massive heart attack, and needed quadruple bypass surgery.

Pryor received a star on the Hollywood Walk of Fame in 1993. In 1995, his autobiography *Pryor Convictions and Other Sentences*, was published. He was awarded the first Mark Twain Prize to celebrate American humor in 1998. Too weak to rise from his wheelchair, Pryor could barely whisper "thank you" when he accepted his award. The comedian wrote in a statement, "Two things people throughout history have had in common are hatred and humor. I am proud that, like Mark Twain, I have been able to use humor to lessen people's hatred."

## Further Reading

Parker, Janice, *Great African Americans in Film*, New York, Crabtree Publishing, 1997.
Pryor, Richard, *Pryor Convictions—and Other Life Sentences*, New York, Pantheon, 1995.
Williams, John A. and Dennis A. Williams, *If I Stop I'll Die: The Comedy and Tragedy of Richard Pryor*, New York, Thunder's Mouth Press, 1991.
*Entertainment Weekly*, April 30, 1993, p. 16; June 10, 1994, p. 76.
*Jet*, June 5, 1995, p.58; November 9, 1998, p. 16.
*The New York Times Magazine*, January 17, 1999, p. 28.
*People Weekly*, May 29, 1995, p. 76. □

# Q

# Mary Quant

**With her introduction of the miniskirt and new "mod" look, Mary Quant (born 1934) began a fashion revolution. Although her designs eventually faded in popularity, Quant's business expanded to include everything from carpet to swimsuits to toys.**

Mary Quant was born February 11, 1934 in London, England to Welsh teachers. Her childhood was disrupted and colored by World War II—for the better, she later recalled in her 1966 autobiography *Quant by Quant.* "Almost my first clear memory is the day we were evacuated from Blackheath to a village in Kent," she wrote. That village, on the east coast of England, placed the family directly beneath the path of enemy planes flying over the coast on their way to bomb London. "Because we had no understanding of the grim tragedies of war," she remembered, "this was tremendous fun." She would run with her brother, Tony, and friends to investigate and ransack crashed planes, taking everything they could carry. "Our prize possession was some poor pilot's thumb which had been shot off and which we carefully preserved in vinegar in an airtight bottle," she gleefully noted.

Quant's schooling was random as her parents moved the family around the countryside, seeking teaching jobs and safety. At one point, Quant's parents sent her away to a "very proper, very correct, absolutely heartless" boarding school near Tunbridge Wells. Normally, however, she was near her family, finding all manner of mischief with Tony. While living on the coast one summer, Quant and her brother formed a business teaching rich visitors to sail. When the weather didn't allow boating, Quant wrote in

*Quant by Quant,* she stayed home and sewed. "I think I always knew that what I wanted to do most of all was to make clothes ... clothes that would be fun to wear. As a very small child, I had idolized a little girl we knew who took tap dancing lessons and wore very skinny black sweaters, short black pleated skirts and long black tights, white ankle socks and black patent ankle strap shoes," Quant recalled. "How I envied her!" Her artistic expression was flavored with the same measure of mischief found in her other pursuits. "When I was about six and in bed with measles," she wrote, "I spent one night cutting up the bedspread with nail scissors. Even at that age I could see that the wild color of the bedspread would make a super dress."

After completing her primary education in 1951, Quant's parents encouraged her to begin pursuing a career. "It was made absolutely clear to both of us from the start that we would have to earn our own livings," she wrote. "My parents never even considered the possibility that marriage might be a way out for girls. I was made terribly aware that it was entirely my own responsibility to make a success of my life."

## Enrolled in Art School

Unfortunately, Quant's idea of a career path didn't quite match her parents' expectations. They wanted her to choose a sturdy, practical vocation. "It was only with the greatest difficulty that I ever persuaded them to allow me to go to art school," she related in *Quant by Quant.* "It was only when I managed to win a scholarship to Goldsmiths' that I was able to persuade them to agree to a compromise ... if they would allow me to go to Goldsmiths', I would take the Art Teachers' Diploma."

With her parents' qualified permission, Quant enrolled at Goldsmiths' College of Art in London. Almost immedi-

bright tights and bras called Booby Traps to young people. The shop capitalized on the buying power of baby boomers, those born during the sharp increase in birthrate following the end of World War II, who were beginning to grow into teenagers.

Naive about the mechanics of running a retail business, Quant and her partners sold their wares with a markup much smaller than any nearby store, without realizing they were actually taking a loss on many items. "It was no wonder we did such a roaring trade the moment we opened," she later wrote. "The shop was constantly stripped bare—sometimes we hardly had enough to dress the window—because we never bought enough of anything."

Quant quickly discovered that manufacturers weren't making the kinds of clothes she wanted to sell, so she set up her own manufacturing outfit in her apartment, hiring a dressmaker to come during the day and help. Quant herself sewed dresses at night to sell the next day in the shop. "I had to sell one day's output before I had the money to go out and buy more material," she recalled, noting that at first, "I didn't think of myself as a designer. I just knew that I wanted to concentrate on finding the right clothes for the young to wear and the right accessories to go with them."

Struggling to make ends meet and suffering ridicule from the press and some passers-by, Quant persevered. In less than ten years, her clothing designs was world famous, selling in 150 shops in Britain, 320 stores in the United States, and throughout the world: France, Italy, Switzerland, Kenya, South Africa, Australia, Canada, and more.

### Branched Out

In 1957, Quant and her business partner, Alexander Plunket Greene, were married. In 1970, they had a son, Orlando. "We had an awful wedding," she recounted in *Quant by Quant*. "The Registrar, or whoever it was, put on a sanctified Dearly Beloved voice; he treated us in an impossibly pompous manner and went purple in the face with the effort."

Shortly thereafter, they decided to take another plunge, and opened a second shop, this one in the more swank Knightsbridge neighborhood. Soon, their production shifted into even higher gear when, in 1963, Quant was approached to design a line for J.C. Penney, at that time the biggest retail chain in the United States. Quant was selected to give the stores a more up-to-date image, with her bright, geometric printed dresses. "It was the first time ever that the clothes of a named British designer had been promoted throughout a large chain of stores across the States," Quant recalled. "It was exciting but worrying too."

### Mod Look is Worldwide Phenomenon

She needen't have worried. Suddenly available on a mass scale, the "mod" look took the fashion world by storm. "I really believe that when the whole thing had first been planned, it had been looked upon purely as a promotional idea," she disclosed in *Quant by Quant*. The store's managers decided to stick with Quant as they watched sales soar.

ately she met Alexander Plunket Greene, who became her business partner and, later, husband. Her classmates, including Greene, were an education unto themselves, she wrote. "It was only when I went to Goldsmiths' that, for the first time in my life, I realized that there are people who give their lives to the pursuit of pleasure and indulgence of every kind in preference to work," Quant marveled. "At first it was a shock even to me; to my parents, such a thing was incomprehensible." Quant spent several years reveling in the atmosphere of Goldsmiths', but left after failing to earn her Art Teachers' Diploma. She took a job working for a Danish milliner, earning such a tiny salary she ate only occasionally.

### Opened Bazaar

Meanwhile, Greene and Quant had paired up with a friend named Archie McNair. When Greene inherited 5,000 pounds on his 21st birthday, the three decided to go into business together. They rented Markham House, a three-story building on King's Road in London's artist district, Chelsea. In Markham House, they opened a boutique on the first floor and a restaurant in the basement. They called the boutique *Bazaar*. Its owners knew little about the business beyond Quant's fashion philosophy: "I can't bear over-accessorization . . . a white hat worn with white gloves, white shoes and a white umbrella," she declared in *Quant by Quant*. "Rules are invented for lazy people who don't want to think for themselves."

True to her philosophy, Quant searched for the clothes she herself wanted to wear, selling miniskirts, funky dresses,

With the flood of Quant designs came a change in the way women dress. "Fashion had always been dictated from above, by Parisian couturiers and other authorities," wrote William L. O'Neill in *Coming Apart: An Informal History of America in the 1960s.* Fashion "was a monopoly of the rich. But in the sixties it was the young, and relatively unknown designers like Quant and Gernreich who catered to them, who set the pace. . . . Not since the 1920s had women's clothing changed so radically. No one could remember when the flow of fashion had been reversed on such a scale." Quant herself, in her autobiography, echoed the same sentiment. "There was a time when clothes were a sure sign of a woman's social position and income group. Not now," she wrote in 1966. "Snobbery has gone out of fashion, and in our shops you will find duchesses jostling with typists to buy the same dress."

Even as she was changing the look of women worldwide, Quant was getting a crash course in the fashion business. "We were not the first to find out it doesn't always pay to be first in the field," she wrote. "The pioneer is the one who makes the mistakes, discovers the snags and prepares the ground for those who more cautiously follow after." Case in point was Quant's foray into clothing made from PVC, a vinyl material. She designed a line in PVC and orders piled up, but Quant's manufacturers' machines couldn't sew the material.

Despite the setbacks, Quant won a prestigious Sunday *Times* Fashion Award, shocking an entire industry that had previously been ruled by couture houses selling expensive, made-to-order clothes by famous designers. Quant's place in fashion history was secured when the London Museum mounted its 1973 retrospective exhibit, "Mary Quant's London."

## Quant Empire Grew

Although Quant's designs eventually faded in popularity, the business continued to expand to include everything from carpet to swimsuits to toys. In 1983, she launched "Mary Quant at Home," a line of household furnishings featuring wall paper and china, based around a chosen color scheme. Color, in the form of cosmetics, was her lasting passion. In *Quant by Quant,* she explained her entrance into the field: "In the fifties, there was no makeup around that I wanted to wear," she told *Vogue's* Gully Wells. "So I started experimenting with crayons. The best were Caran d'Ache colored pencils. . . . Then the models started using theatrical makeup to get the look they wanted, so finally I decided to start producing my own line in 1966." Quant ultimately focused her energy almost entirely on her cosmetics line, which sold worldwide but was most popular in Japan, where, by the mid-1990s, Quant had more than 200 stores. Besides her autobiography, she had penned two additional books: *Colour by Quant,* published in 1984, and *Quant on Make-up,* in 1986.

## Further Reading

*Contemporary Designers, 2nd edition,* edited by Colin Naylor, St. James Press, 1990.

McDowell, Colin, *McDowell's Directory of Twentieth Century Fashion,* Prentice-Hall, Inc., 1985.

Quant, Mary, *Quant by Quant* G.P. Putnam's Sons, 1966.

Stegemeyer, Anne, *Who's Who in Fashion,* Fairchild Publications, 1988.

Vare, Ethlie Ann and Greg Ptacek, *Mothers of Invention: From the Bra to the Bomb: Forgotten Women & Their Unforgettable Ideas* William Morrow and Company, 1988.

*Management,* September 1997.

*Vogue,* July 1995; February 1999.

"Mary Quant," A&E Network Biography, http://www.biography .com (March 2, 1999). □

# R

## Ma Rainey

**The first popular stage entertainer to incorporate authentic blues in her song repertoire, Ma Rainey (1886–1939) performed during the first three decades of the twentieth century. Known as the "Mother of the Blues," she enjoyed mass popularity during the blues craze of the 1920s. Described by African American poet Sterling Brown in *Black Culture and Black Consciousness* as "a person of the folk," Rainey recorded in various musical settings and exhibited the influence of genuine rural blues.**

Ma Rainey was born Gertrude Pridgett in Columbus, Georgia, on April 26, 1886, to minstrel troupers—Thomas Pridgett, Sr. and Ella Allen-Pridgett. Rainey worked at the Springer Opera House in 1900, performing as a singer and dancer in the local talent show, "A Bunch of Blackberries." On February 2, 1904, Pridgett married comedy songster William "Pa" Rainey. Billed as "Ma" and "Pa" Rainey the couple toured Southern tent shows and cabarets. Though she did not hear blues in Columbus, Rainey's extensive travels had, by 1905, brought her into contact with authentic country blues, which she worked into her song repertoire. "Her ability to capture the mood and essence of black rural southern life of the 1920s," noted Daphane Harrison in *Black Pearls: Blues Queens* "quickly endeared her to throngs of followers throughout the South."

### Met Bessie Smith

While performing with the Moses Stokes troupe in 1912, the Raineys were introduced to the show's newly recruited dancer, Bessie Smith. Eight years Smith's senior, Rainey quickly befriended the young performer. Despite earlier historical accounts crediting Rainey as Smith's vocal coach, it has been generally agreed by modern scholars that Rainey played less of a role in the shaping of Smith's singing style. "Ma Rainey probably did pass some of her singing experience on to Bessie," explained Chris Albertson in the liner notes to *Giants of Jazz*, "but the instruction must have been rudimentary. Though they shared an extraordinary command of the idiom, the two women delivered their messages in styles and voices that were dissimilar and manifestly personal."

Around 1915, the Raineys toured with Fat Chappelle's Rabbit Foot Minstrels. Afterward, they were billed as the "Assassinators of the Blues" with Tolliver's Circus and Musical Extravaganza. Separated from her husband in 1916, Rainey subsequently toured with her own band, Madam Gertrude Ma Rainey and Her Georgia Smart Sets, featuring a chorus line and a Cotton Blossoms Show, and Donald McGregor's Carnival Show.

### Entered Recording Industry

With the help of Mayo "Ink" Williams, Rainey first recorded for the Paramount label in 1923 (three years after the first blues side recorded by Mamie Smith). Already a popular singer in the Southern theater circuit, Rainey entered the recording industry as an experienced and stylistically mature talent. Her first session, cut with Austin and Her Blue Serenaders, featured the traditional number "Bo-Weevil Blues". Fellow blues singer, Victoria Spivey, later said of the recording, as quoted in *The Devil's Music*, "Ain't

nobody in the world been able to holler 'Hey Boweevil' like her. Not like Ma. Nobody." 1923 also saw the release of Rainey's side "Moonshine Blues," with Lovie Austin, and "Yonder Comes the Blues" with Louis Armstrong. That same year, Rainey recorded "See See Rider," a number that, as Arnold Shaw observed in *Black Popular Music in America*, emerged as "one of the most famous and recorded of all blues songs. [Rainey's] was the first recording of that song, giving her a hold on the copyright, and one of the best of the more than 100 versions."

In August 1924, Rainey—along with the twelve string guitar of Miles Pruitt and an unknown second guitar accompanist—recorded the eight bar blues number "Shave 'Em Dry." In the liner notes to *The Blues*, folklorist W.K. McNeil observed that the number "is typical of Rainey's output, a driving, unornamated vocal propelled along by an accompanist who plays the number straight. Her artistry brings life to what in lesser hands would be a dull, elementary piece."

**A Shrewd Businesswoman**

Unlike many other blues musicians, Rainey earned a reputation as a professional on stage and in business. According to Mayo Williams, as quoted in the liner notes to *Ma Rainey's Black Bottom*, "Ma Rainey was a shrewd business woman. We never tried to put any swindles on her. During Rainey's five-year recording career at Paramount she cut nearly ninety sides, most of which dealt with the subjects of love and sexuality—bawdy themes that often earned her the billing of "Madam Rainey." As William Barlow explained, in *Looking Up at Down*, her songs were

also "diverse, yet deeply rooted in day-to-day experiences of black people from the South. Ma Rainey's blues were simple, straightforward stories about heart break, promiscuity, drinking binges, the odyssey of travel, the workplace and the prison road gang, magic and superstition—in short, the southern landscape of African Americans in the Post-Reconstruction era."

With the success of her early recordings, Rainey took part in a Paramount promotional tour which featured a newly assembled back-up band. In 1924, pianist and arranger Thomas A. Dorsey recruited members for Rainey's touring band, The Wild Cats Jazz Band. Serving as both director and manager, Dorsey assembled able musicians who could read arrangements as well as play in a down "home blues" style. Rainey's tour debut at Chicago's Grand Theater on State Street marked the first appearance of a "down home" blues artist at the famous southside venue. Draped in long gowns and covered in diamonds and a necklace of gold pieces, Rainey had a powerful command over her audiences. She often opened her stage show singing "Moonshine Blues" inside the cabinet of an over-sized victrola, from which she emerged to greet a near-frantic audience. As Dorsey recalled, in *The Rise of Gospel Blues*, "When she started singing, the gold in her teeth would sparkle. She was in the spotlight. She possessed listeners; they swayed, they rocked, they moaned and groaned, as they felt the blues with her."

Until 1926, Rainey performed with her Wild Jazz Cats on the Theater Owner's Booking Association circuit (TOBA). That year, after Dorsey left the band, she recorded with various musicians on the Paramount label—often under the name of Ma Rainey and her Georgia Jazz Band which, on various occasions, included musicians such as pianists Fletcher Henderson, Claude Hopkins, and Willie the Lion Smith, reed players Don Redman, Buster Bailey and Coleman Hawkins, and trumpeters Louis Armstrong and Tommy Ladnier. In 1927, Rainey cut sides such as "Black Cat, Hoot Owl Blues" with the Tub Jug Washboard Band. During her last sessions, held in 1928, she sang in the company of her former pianist Thomas "Georgia Tom" Dorsey and guitarist Hudson "Tampa Red" Whittaker, producing such numbers as "Black Eye Blues," "Runaway Blues" and "Sleep Talking Blues." As Bruce Cook noted in *Listen to the Blues*, these numbers "are as good as anything she ever recorded. Her voice is rich and full; she really sounds like the "Mother of the Blues.""

**Retirement**

Though the TOBA and vaudeville circuits had gone into decline by the early 1930s, Rainey still performed, often resorting to playing tent shows. Following the death of her mother and sister, Rainey retired from the music business in 1935 and settled in Columbus. For the next several years, she devoted her time to the ownership of two entertainment venues—the Lyric Theater and the Airdome—as well as activities in the Friendship Baptist Church. Rainey died in Rome, Georgia—some sources say Columbus—on December 22, 1939.

A great contributor to America's rich blues tradition, Rainey's music has served as inspiration for African American poets such as Langston Hughes and Sterling Brown, the latter of whom paid tribute to the majestic singer in the poem "Ma Rainey," which appeared in his 1932 collection *Southern Road*. More recently, Alice Walker looked to Ma Rainey's music as a cultural model of African American womanhood when she wrote the Pulitzer Prize-winning novel, *The Color Purple*. In *Black Pearls*, Daphane Harrison praised Rainey as the first great blues stage singer: "The good-humored, rollicking Rainey loved life, loved love, and most of all loved her people. Her voice bursts forth with a hearty declaration of courage and determination—a reaffirmation of black life."

## Further Reading

Barlow, William, *Looking Up at Down: The Emergence of Blues Culture*, Temple University Press.

Cook, Bruce, *Listen to the Blues*, Da Capo.

Harris, Michael W., *The Rise of Gospel Blues: The Music of Thomas Dorsey in the Urban Church*.

Harrison, Daphane Duval. *Black Pearls: Blues Queens of the 1920s*. Rutgers University Press.

Levine, Lawrence W., *Black Culture and Black Consciousness: Afro-American Thought From Slavery to Freedom*, Oxford University Press.

Oakley, Giles, *The Devil's Music: A History of the Blues*, Tappinger.

Shaw, Arnold, *Black Popular Music in America*, Schirmer Books.

□

# Richard Joshua Reynolds, Jr.

**Richard Joshua Reynolds, Jr. (1906–1964), son of the founder of R.J. Reynolds Tobacco Company, was a very successful businessman. He was involved with a variety of business ventures throughout his lifetime, and was also a generous philanthropist and active politician. Reynolds spent much of his fortune on a lavish personal lifestyle, but also founded several charitable organizations and contributed to many more.**

R ichard Joshua Reynolds, Jr., was born on April 4, 1906, in Winston-Salem, North Carolina, to Richard Joshua Reynolds and Mary Katherine (Smith) Reynolds. His father had started a tobacco company in the 1870s, which was formally established as the R.J. Reynolds Tobacco Company in 1890. This company, which is now a part of the RJR-Nabisco Corporation, produced the popular Prince Albert tobacco and Camel cigarettes. By the time Reynolds, Jr., was born, his father was a very wealthy man, and the Reynolds name was well known in Winston-Salem.

## Early Ventures

Reynolds attended public schools in Winston-Salem as well as Culver Military Academy in Indiana, the Tome School in Maryland, and Woodberry Forest in Virginia. After graduation from high school, he studied mechanical engineering and played football at North Carolina State College. His first business venture involved the establishment of a weekly local newspaper titled *The Three-Cent Pup,* which he started in 1917 with his friends Bill Sharpe and Bosley Crowther.

Reynolds had a strong interest in aviation and, at the age of 18, obtained his pilot's license. He was convinced that air passenger and freight transport held great economic opportunity and purchased Curtiss Field (later Roosevelt Field) on Long Island, New York. This was the airfield from which Charles Lindbergh took off for his famous transatlantic flight to Paris in 1927. Reynolds established the Ireland Amphibian Company of Mineola, New York, in 1926, and actively participated in the development of the first amphibian planes produced in the United States. He also served as president of Reynolds Aviation from 1927 to 1929.

At the age of 21, Reynolds gained access to a trust income of $100,000 and used it to live lavishly. He bought expensive cars, frequented fashionable cafes in New York, and showered women with extravagant gifts. In 1927, he mysteriously disappeared, generating rumors that something had happened to him. He was later found in St. Louis, where he had gone with a woman. He paid for his boisterous lifestyle when, in 1929, he killed a man while driving drunk. Reynolds was convicted of manslaughter and spent five months in jail. He bought an 1800-ton steam freighter and, from 1929 to 1932, captained the ship throughout the seas of North and South America and southern Europe.

## Business and Politics

Reynolds returned to Winston-Salem in 1932, and on January 1, 1933, married Elizabeth McGaw Dillard, daughter of another tobacco tycoon. Before divorcing in 1946, the couple had four sons: Richard Joshua, III, John Dillard, Zachary Taylor, and William Neil.

During the 1930s and early 1940s, Reynolds participated in a variety of business ventures. In 1935, he established Precision Films, Inc., a laboratory that developed color motion picture film, and served as president of the company for a time. In 1940, he purchased the bankrupt American Mail Line of Seattle, a shipping company, which he owned until 1951. Scrapping the old ships and building new ones, Reynolds was able to take advantage of the wartime shipping needs in the Pacific. He also saved Delta Airlines from financial troubles by buying a large share of its stock in 1940. Previously he had been a major stockholder in Eastern Airlines, but when Eastern refused to make Winston-Salem the hub of its Carolina operations, Reynolds sold some of his stock and invested instead in Delta, thus enabling Delta to remain competitive.

Reynolds began a public service career with his election as mayor of Winston-Salem in 1940. One of his goals was the clearing of the slums. Despite opposition from local slumlords, Reynolds was able to obtain a grant from the U.S. Housing Authority to finance this project. His political activity was extended beyond the local level in 1941, when Reynolds became chairman of the finance committee for the national Democratic Party.

His political activities were interrupted when Reynolds joined the U.S. Navy at the start of World War II. He served as chief navigator on the *USS Makin Island* and later was awarded the Bronze Star for the navigational skill he exhibited at Iwo Jima and in the Philippines. He was released to inactive duty in 1945 with the rank of lieutenant commander. After the war he took full financial responsibility for the production of a publication titled *The Escort Carriers in Action,* a volume of photographs and text that described the activities of warships in the Pacific. His contributions also included the donation of his own yacht to the Navy.

On August 7, 1946, Reynolds married Marianne O'Brien, an actress. He had two sons with O'Brien, Patrick Cleaveland and Michael Randolph. (Ironically, Patrick would later become known for his campaign against the tobacco industry and establishment of the anti-smoking group, Citizens for a Smoke-free America.) The couple divorced in 1952, and Reynolds remarried the same year to Muriel (Marston) Greenough in McIntosh County, Georgia. His third marriage lasted eight years, after which time Reynolds was divorced once again. His fourth and final marriage was to Annemarie Schmitt, whom he married in Muralto, Switzerland, on July 10, 1961 (some sources say 1963). She and Reynolds had a daughter, Irene Sabina, who was born two days after her father's death in 1964.

## Generous Donations in the South

As a philanthropist, Reynolds contributed to many causes. In 1936, he and his sisters founded the Z. Smith Reynolds Foundation (ZSRF), created from the estate of their brother, Zachary S. Reynolds. Reynolds' brother was shot to death in 1932, but the perpetrator was never identified. Reynolds served as president of this foundation, which contributed funds to many health-related and educational causes in the Carolinas and Georgia. The ZSRF's first major project was a program to combat syphilis, a common disease in the south. Later the federal government modeled a national campaign after the ZSRF program.

Reynolds also established the Sapelo Island Research Foundation (SIRF) at the University of Georgia in 1949. It was developed for the furthering of scientific research, specifically in the fields of marine biology, oceanography, and limnology. Other organizations that benefitted from Reynolds' generosity included the New York Maritime College in the Bronx and Wake Forest University, which was moved to a new campus in Winston-Salem (formerly part of the Reynolds' estate) in 1956. Reynolds also served as a trustee of the University of North Carolina. He helped fund several capital projects in Winston-Salem, including Tanglewood Park, Reynolds Park, Smith-Reynolds Airport, the Forsyth Country Club, the Young Women's Christian Association, the Wachovia Historical Society, and the City and Baptist hospitals. In 1948, Reynolds donated his family home to Winston-Salem for a library. In Darien, a town near his Georgia home, he contributed to the construction of an American Legion hall, a gymnasium for an African American public school, and a swimming pool.

## A Wide Range of Interests

Reynolds had a wide range of interests, including poetry, yacht racing, sailing, trotting horses, and skeet shooting. He was a member of the Reynolds Presbyterian Church and the New York Yacht Club. Reynolds was also a participant in many other groups and organizations, including the Quiet Birdmen of America and the Royal Ocean Racing Club of London, England. He maintained residences in North Carolina, New York, Florida, Georgia, and Europe, although he always considered his 44,000-acre estate on Sapelo Island, Georgia, to be his "real" home.

Reynolds' last years were characterized by some rather eccentric behavior. While living on Sapelo Island with his third wife, he constructed a pond that was to represent the world's oceans and the seven continents. It was rumored that Reynolds buried bags of gold in his backyard. Dissatisfied with his life in America and troubled by his turbulent family relationships, Reynolds settled in Lucerne, Switzerland in 1962. Before leaving, he called his four oldest sons together and reprimanded them for living off the family fortune rather than holding down jobs. Reynolds deeded most of his land at Sapelo to the SIRF, sold off his American assets, gave up his board membership with Delta Airlines, and dug up the bags of gold from his backyard in Georgia. Reynolds died on December 14, 1964, in Lucerne, Switzerland.

Although a major stockholder in R.J. Reynolds Tobacco Company, the only time Reynolds participated in the family business was when he served as director from 1942 to 1947. He was never employed by the company. However, he certainly made his mark in many other business ventures and helped many charitable causes, especially in his home states of North Carolina and Georgia.

## Further Reading

*American National Biography,* edited by John A. Garraty and Mark C. Carnes, Oxford University Press, 1999.
*Business Leader Profiles for Students,* edited by Sheila M. Dow, Gale, 1999.
*National Cyclopedia of American Biography,* James T. White, 1971. □

# Jean Rhys

**Jean Rhys (1890–1979) is best known for her novel, *Wide Sargasso Sea,* which was published in 1966 when she was 76. Rhys's life was profoundly marked by a sense of exile, loss, and alienation—dominant themes in her novels and short stories. Despite critical acclaim at the end of her life, Rhys died in 1979 still doubting the merit of her work.**

Rhys was born Ella Gwendolen Rhys (sometimes spelled Rees) Williams on August 24, 1890 in Roseau, on the Caribbean island of Dominica. Her father, Rhys Williams, was a Welshman who had been trained in London as a doctor and emigrated to the colonies. Her mother, Minna Lockhart, was a third-generation Dominican Creole. According to her biographer, Carole Angier, Rhys associated her mother with conformity and the "civilizing" mission of the English in the colonies at the end of the Victorian period. Her mother, Rhys claimed, was cold, disapproving, and distant. In one of the notebooks she kept during her life, Rhys recorded a time when her mother, after an attempt to discipline her daughter, gave her "a long, sad look," and said, "'I've done my best, it's no use. You'll never learn to be like other people.'" Rhys writes, "There you are, there it was. I had always suspected it, but now I knew. That went straight as an arrow to the heart, straight as the truth. I saw the long road of isolation and loneliness stretching in front of me as far as the eye could see, and further. I collapsed and cried as heartbrokenly as my worst enemy could wish."

As a child and adolescent, Rhys was, according to her own account, "alone except for books" and voices that "had nothing to do with me. I sometimes didn't even know the words. But they wanted to be written down, so I wrote them down." Finding little comfort at home, Rhys explored other worlds available to her. At a convent school that she attended, Rhys, an Anglican Protestant, was drawn to the ritual of Catholic worship. In addition to being fascinated by the sheer sensual component of the service, Rhys noted that "instead of the black people sitting in a different part of the church, they were all mixed up with the white and this pleased me very much." For Rhys, the black women who worked in her house as servants offered her access to a

secret world and a secret language, both far different from the disinterestedness of her mother. In her writing, Rhys would explore the tension between the ordered world of colonial life and the seductive world of island sensuality. But in her life, her sense of abandonment remained acute. "Gradually," she wrote, "I came to wonder about my mother less and less until at last she was almost a stranger and I stopped imagining what she felt or what she thought."

## A Life of Exile

In 1907, Rhys left Dominica for England, where she enrolled in the Perse School for Girls in Cambridge. The departure was typical for young colonial women of her station who were encouraged to finish their educations abroad. Although Rhys embraced the journey with a sense of adventure, the contrast between the cold and damp English climate and the lush surroundings of her island home would haunt Rhys throughout her life. At the Perse School, according to Angier, she was tormented by classmates who disapproved of her Creole background and her quick mind. Rhys spent two years at the Perse School before enrolling in the Academy of Dramatic Art in 1909, intending to become an actress. Her stay was brief, but before she left, Rhys signed a contract to become a chorus girl. When her father died and money became scarce, she began touring England with a theater troupe. Neither the life of the theater nor the drab towns in which she performed held much charm for Rhys, but she did find a sort of camaraderie among the chorus girls. According to Angier, "the girls spoke a secret language, like the ones at home—the servants' patois, or the Carib women's language, which the men didn't know.'' Rhys, writes Angier, ''shared their reliance on mascots, superstition, lucky charms. Above all she shared their simple division of the sexes. Men were either protectors or exploiters; women were either winners or losers, and what they won or lost was men.''

Rhys would be linked to a succession of men all of her life. Her emotional and financial dependence on them was exacerbated by her life-long alcoholism. ''When slightly tight,'' Rhys wrote later in her life, ''I can relax—also there are red letter days when I feel that after all I'm as much fun as the next woman really. However this doesn't happen often.'' Rhys's first love affair, her most traumatic and defining, began in 1910 when she met a distinguished and respectable Englishman named Lancelot Hugh Smith. Smith's power and charm captivated Rhys, but she was devastated when he ended the affair and arranged to pay Rhys a monthly allowance. Alone with her despair, Rhys began to write diaries and notebooks recording her emotional states; it was her first attempt since she was a girl in Dominica to order her experience through writing. In the voice of Julia, the protagonist of her second novel *After Leaving Mr. Mackenzie,* Rhys wrote, ''I knew that if I could get to the end of what I was feeling it would be the truth about myself and about the world and about everything that one puzzles and pains about all the time.'' Rhys packed these notebooks away in the bottom of an old suitcase and they remained hidden for years, but the idea of writing had taken hold.

Rhys continued to receive money from Smith and for the next few years lived a meager life in a London boarding house. In 1917, she met Jean Lenglet to whom she became engaged after a few short weeks. Her relationship to Lenglet reinforced a pattern of exile and rupture that would become a familiar one to Rhys. By 1919, they had married and moved to Holland, where Rhys worked in a office. Shortly after, they moved to Paris. Rhys, now pregnant, worked for a time as an English tutor. She gave birth to a son, William Owen, who died within a few weeks. Lenglet, who had by this time become involved in a number of clandestine and illegal activities, continued to travel across Europe, at times to elude authorities. From 1919 to 1922, Rhys followed Lenglet to Vienna, Budapest, Brussels, and Paris, all the while working at odd jobs in offices and dress shops or translating articles into English to help support her husband. In Brussels, Rhys had another child, Maryvonne.

## Early Literary Career

In 1923, Lenglet was finally arrested and extradited. Rhys, alone and desperate, turned for support to the writer Ford Madox Ford, who had published some of her short stories in the *Transatlantic Review.* Rhys became involved in a complicated and, by her own account, abusive relationship with Ford and his mistress, Stella Bowen. She wrote about this relationship in her first novel, *Quartet,* published in 1929. When the affair ended, she returned for a short time to her husband and daughter, who were now in Amsterdam, but Lenglet's suspicions about her relationship with Ford and Bowen brought the marriage to an end. When Lenglet

and Rhys separated, Rhys left Maryvonne in her father's care. Though her affair with Ford Madox Ford helped to end her marriage, and brought her much unhappiness and pain, the encounter nonetheless allowed Rhys entry into the contemporary literary world. Her career as a writer was finally launched.

During the next ten years, Rhys would write three more novels, *After Leaving Mr. Mackenzie,* (1930); *Voyage in the Dark,* (1935); and *Good Morning Midnight,* (1939). In 1992, Ann Hulbert, a reviewer for the *New Republic,* described Rhys's early work: ''The style of her novels is pristinely pared down in describing depravity and excess, perfectly balanced in evoking instability; she is a master of dialogue between characters for whom communication is mostly a lost cause.'' After the publication of *Quartet,* Rhys met Leslie Tilden Smith, a literary agent who helped her find publishers for her novels. They married in 1934, after living together for five years. During the time she wrote most of her early novels, Rhys depended on Smith to type her manuscripts, subsidize trips to Paris, and manage her writing life. The process of writing for Rhys was always a difficult one; over the course of these years she became severely depressed.

With the start of World War II in 1939, Smith was gone much of the time. The short stories Rhys produced during this period, none of which were published until later in her life, are marked by violence and paranoia. In 1945, Smith died suddenly, leaving Rhys completely alone and virtually helpless. Two years later, she married Smith's cousin and estate executor, a soliciter named Max Hamer. Like Rhys's first husband, he became involved in illegal financial dealings. By this time, Rhys had virtually disappeared from public view; her novels went out of print and she was presumed dead. By 1949, Rhys, as she put it, ''cracked'' and assaulted a neighbor who was rude to her. She spent a week on the hospital ward of Holloway prison before being released on probation. Shortly after this, Hamer was arrested for stealing checks. While he served his prison term, Rhys lived in poverty and continued to drink.

## A Brief Renaissance

By 1950, luck had changed for Rhys when she answered an advertisement placed by Selma Vaz Dias, an actress who had adapted *Good Morning, Midnight* for the radio and needed Rhys's permission to perform it. The BBC initially rejected the adaptation, and *Good Morning, Midnight* wasn't broadcast until 1957. At that time, Rhys once again caught the attention of literary agents, this time Francis Wyndham, an admirer of her work who would later become her most competent promoter. He was interested in gaining publishing rights to *Wide Sargasso Sea,* a novel Rhys had begun almost 20 years before, in 1939. They agreed that she would deliver the novel in nine months, but it took another eight years for her to finish the manuscript. *Wide Sargasso Sea,* a retelling of Charlotte Bronte's *Jane Eyre* from the perspective of Bertha Mason, Rochester's mad Creole wife whom he locks in the attic, was psychologically and structurally complicated for Rhys. In order to finish the novel, Rhys had to return to the scenes of her past, to the island she had left as a girl and to the abandonment she had suffered as a young woman. The novel was a critical success, winning the W. H. Smith literary award for excellence. She was 76 years old.

Despite this stunning achievement after a decade of obscurity and poverty, Rhys retreated further into the pain that had come to define her life. Though she produced two volumes of short stories, *Tigers Are Better-Looking* in 1968 and *Sleep It Off, Lady* in 1976, as well as a volume of autobiographical sketches in 1975 called *My Day*, Rhys regarded her later work as "no good, no good, magazine stories." She died on May 14, 1979 in Exeter, England. Though at times bitter and self-pitying, Rhys was also aware that her profound isolation intimately informed her work. "I have only ever written about myself," she once wrote, "people have always been shadows to me."

## Further Reading

Angier, Carole, *Jean Rhys*, Viking, 1985.
*Contemporary Authors,* Gale.
*Atlantic,* August, 1984.
*New Republic,* February 17, 1992; September 10, 1984.
*New York Times,* June 28, 1991. □

# Maurice Richard

**Maurice "Rocket" Richard (born 1921) was one of the greatest hockey players in the history of the game. For 18 seasons, he struck fear into the hearts of his opponents, terrorizing them with his hard hitting and goal scoring. His 50 goals in 50 games during the 1944-45 season, created a record that stood for 36 years. Richard led the Montreal Canadiens to eight Stanley Cup championships, including five consecutive victories from 1956 to 1960.**

Richard was born on August 4, 1921 in the Bordeaux section of Montreal. He began to play hockey soon after he learned to walk. As a child, he skated on a rink built by his father in the yard behind their house. Richard worked his way through the minor leagues, as many young hockey players who dream of playing in the National Hockey League (NHL) have done. He sometimes played for several teams at one time, while he also studied at Montreal Technical School to become a machinist. When he was 18 years old and playing for the Paquette junior team, he scored 133 of the team's 144 goals during the season.

In 1940, when Richard was 19 years old, he became a player on the farm club team of the Montreal Canadiens, in the Senior Hockey League of Quebec. He was on his way to the NHL and, to prove it, he scored two goals in his first game in the Senior League. However, in the third period of this game, he went down with a broken wrist and had to sit on the bench for the rest of the season. Despite that setback,

he earned a tryout with the parent club, and joined the Montreal Canadiens for the 1942-43 season.

As a "Hab," the nickname used by Canadien fans for the Montreal team members, Richard scored five goals and collected six assists in his first 16 games. Despite this impressive start, he suffered a broken ankle and many feared that Richard might be injury-prone. However, coach Dick Irvin had faith in Richard, and kept him on the disabled list.

## On the "Punch Line"

Returning for the 1943-44 season, Richard scored 32 goals in 46 games. He was naturally left-handed, but could shoot from either side. Therefore, he was put on the right wing of one of the most famous front lines in hockey history, the so-called "Punch Line." This line had Richard on the right, Elmer Lach at center, and "Toe" Blake on the left side. He won the title as the top scorer in the league, making 50 goals in the first 50 games and earning 73 points. With Blake's 67 points, the Canadiens had the highest scoring line in hockey that season.

Richard, who was known to have a quick temper on the ice, continued his scoring streak. By 1945 he was well known as "The Rocket." "From the blue line to the net, he was unequalled," said referee Bill Chadwick, a member of the Hockey Hall of Fame. "He possessed Herculean strength, and I once saw him score with a defenseman on his back," continued Chadwick. Many said he looked like "a small ox on skates." Richard was a small player in a big man's game, standing less than six feet tall and weighing only 180 pounds. Even at this size, many of the other teams in the NHL assigned two players to guard him.

Richard had a powerful drive to win. For 18 seasons, he struck fear into the hearts of his opponents, terrorizing them with his hard hitting and goal scoring. His 50 goals in 50 games during the 1944-45 season, created a record that stood for 36 years. He led his team to eight Stanley Cup championships, including five consecutive victories from 1956 to 1960. Richard led the NHL in scoring five times and had 544 regular-season goals. He finished his career with 82 playoff goals, scoring five goals in one playoff game.

In one game against the Boston Bruins, Richard was hit so hard that he lay motionless on the ice, blood pouring from his head. Fans thought he was dead, as the Canadiens' medical staff rushed him off the ice. The score was 1-1. Soon a dazed Richard was back on the bench, half-blind from blood running into his eyes. Suddenly he skated back into the game, grabbed the puck and raced up the ice. Bruin players tried to defend against the bloody, glassy-eyed Richard, but he closed in on Bruin goalie, Jim Henry, and managed to flip the puck into the goal.

## An Official is Struck

In a 1955 game between the Canadiens and the Boston Bruins, Richard was certain that Hal Laycoe had fouled him, so he hit Laycoe several times with his stick. Officials generally jump in and separate the players, one or both are sent to the penalty box, and the game goes on. When Cliff Thompson tried to stop the fight, Richard hit him, knocking him to the ice.

In hockey, players are allowed to hit each other, but never is a player allowed to hit an official. NHL president, Clarence Campbell, suspended Richard after an official hearing between all of those involved. However, this was not an ordinary one or two game suspension. Campbell removed Richard from the team for the rest of the season, including the Stanley Cup playoffs.

All of Canada was shocked. Montreal was especially upset, since hockey fans believed they needed "The Rocket" to win the coveted cup. Richard, himself, was stunned. He spoke to fans on a radio show, asking them to be calm. Hockey was a national passion, and Richard was one of the great heroes of the game. Many fans wondered how Campbell could do such a thing. His office was overwhelmed with calls, letters, and telegrams. Fans took up petitions and submitted them to the Canadian government in the hope that a politician could convince Campbell to change his mind and lift the suspension. Richard had been working on an all-time scoring title, and needed to be in the games to win it. Of even greater importance, the Stanley Cup finals were coming. None of the politicians wanted to get involved.

## A Full Scale Riot

After suspending Richard, Campbell attended the next game at Montreal and was attacked by a fan. It took a squad of police to restore order in the rink. The fans grew restless, then angry, and someone threw a smoke bomb onto the ice. Violence exploded in the grandstands, and soon debris was showered onto the ice. Tear gas bombs were exploded and the crowd turned into an angry mob. Campbell was rushed out of the arena. When officials decided to forfeit the game, pandemonium broke out. Fans poured out onto the streets in a violent mood. They started smashing windows in the Forum, the ice arena where the Canadiens played. Gunshots rang out, stores were looted, and a full scale riot was underway.

Eventually, fans calmed down and left the area. It was the worst riot in Montreal history, with more than $100,000 in damage to the main shopping area of the city. Campbell did not back down. The suspension was not lifted. Richard did not play for the rest of the season and failed to win the scoring title that year.

## Retirement

Richard ended his playing career in 1960, at the age of 39. He became a front office official for the Canadiens and continued his popular Sunday column in *Le Journal de Montreal* newspaper. Richard was inducted into the Hockey Hall of Fame in 1961. This is an honor usually granted to a player at least five years after he has retired. Richard was selected as an immortal of the game only nine months after he retired. In 1997, the city of Montreal unveiled a statue of Richard in front of the Maurice Richard Arena.

## Further Reading

Olney, Ross R., *This Game Called Hockey*, Dodd Mead, 1978
Olney, Ross R., *Superchampions of Ice Hockey*, Clarion Books, 1982
Classic Sports Legends, Rocket Richard, http://www.classicsports .com/cp/Hall_of_Fame/Rocket_Richard.htm, (May 10, 1999).
Richard's Biography, http://www.nhl.com/teampage/mon/r_bio .htm, (May 10,1999). □

# Sugar Ray Robinson

**Sugar Ray Robinson (1921–1989) was one of the first African American athletes who became well-known outside the boxing arena. He was the world welterweight champion from 1946 to 1951, won the middleweight title five times between 1951 and 1960, and has been universally acclaimed as one of the greatest boxers in the history of the sport.**

Born Walker Smith, Jr., in Detroit, Michigan on May 3, 1921, Robinson became interested in boxing as a teenager, when he moved to New York City with his parents. When he was 13, he fought in the Police Athletic League competition, and by the time he was 15 he was fighting unlicensed amateurs. At the beginning of his career, he used his real name and was known as "Smitty" to his friends. One night he showed up for an amateur fight, but did not have the official identity card he needed to fight. He

borrowed the boxing card from a friend named Ray Robinson. From then on, he used that name.

According to Ron Borges in *HBO World Championship Boxing* sportswriter Jack Case, who saw a young Robinson fight at the Salem Crescent Gym in New York in 1939, told Robinson's manager, George Gainford, "That's a sweet fighter you've got there." "Sweet as sugar," answered Gainford. The nickname "Sugar Ray," like manager Gainford, would be with Robinson for the rest of his career.

Robinson was married three times. His first marriage, when Robinson was still a teenager, produced one son, Ronnie Smith. The marriage was later annulled. He then married Edna Mae Holly and they had one son, Ray Jr., in 1949. Robinson married Millie Bruce in 1965, and the two would remain together for the rest of his life.

### Early Professional Career

Robinson became a professional boxer in 1940. His first fight, against Joe Echevarria, ended with Robinson's victory in the second round.

Robinson served in the U.S. Army during World War II, but his major battles during that time were with a boxing rival named Jake LaMotta. Robinson had been unbeaten in his first 40 fights. The 41st was against LaMotta. Robinson had easily beaten LaMotta in a 10-round match in New York City, but at a rematch in Detroit, LaMotta won. This was the first defeat of his career. Three weeks later, Robinson avenged himself by beating LaMotta again. This would be a pattern that repeated itself throughout his career; when an-

other boxer beat him (and it happened rarely), Robinson came back in a rematch and pounded the other boxer into defeat.

"That was the thing about Robinson," boxing trainer and historian Teddy Atlas told writer Borges. "He not only won his rematches, he stopped the guy. . . . He was magnificent after a loss. . . . He corrected his mistakes and took his opponent apart if they fought again." Atlas also told Borges, "If I had a guy who beat Ray Robinson I'd be sure to do one thing. Don't give him a rematch. Ray had more than talent. He had genius."

After defeating LaMotta in the rematch, Robinson would continue to win for the next eight years. In 1945, Robinson beat LaMotta twice more, prompting LaMotta to say, according to Ron Flatter of *ESPN.com,* "I fought Sugar Ray so often, I almost got diabetes." LaMotta also said, "No one else wanted to fight him. And no one else wanted to fight me, so thank God he was around so we fought each other."

### World Welterweight Champ

In December 1946, Robinson beat Tommy Bell after 15 rounds, earning the welterweight championship. In defending his title in 1947, Robinson knocked out Tommy Doyle in eight rounds. Doyle, who had sustained brain injuries in a previous match, never woke up. Ron Flatter, in *ESPN.com,* reported that when the police investigated the death and asked Robinson if he had meant to get Doyle "in trouble," Robinson replied, "Mister, it's my business to get him in trouble." Some people said that Robinson had dreamed, the night before this match, that he would kill his opponent, and that when Doyle did die, Robinson lost his "killer instinct." Even so, Robinson remained an incredible fighter.

### A Flamboyant Style

Robinson lived in larger-than-life style, with a pink Cadillac convertible, fur coat, and flashy diamond jewelry. He was the owner of a Harlem nightclub where jazz legends like Charlie Parker and Miles Davis played. Robinson was surrounded by an entourage of assistants, including a barber, secretary, voice coach, masseur, trainers, women, and his manager, George Gainford. He was an entrepreneur when that was an unheard-of thing for African Americans to do and at a time when many African Americans were not even allowed to vote. Robinson was a shrewd businessman and hard bargainer. Ron Flatter noted that he was "as much a part of the New York scene in the forties and fifties as the Copa and Sinatra." Fan Tallulah Dancier recalled in *Colored Reflections,* "I remember seeing pictures of him in *Ebony* magazine and *Jet* magazine with flashy diamonds, a huge fur coat, sitting on a Rolls Royce. But everybody liked him."

### "St. Valentine's Day Massacre"

In 1951, Robinson went up against Jake LaMotta again, in a match known as the "St. Valentine's Day Massacre." The referee stopped the fight in the 13th round, when LaMotta could barely stand and no longer had the strength to punch back.

Boxing had its shady side, and Robinson refused to give in to the Mob. He failed to obey the directives of what writer Ron Borges described as "a group of characters to whom legitimate business was only a figure of speech," and "carry" LaMotta through more rounds in that fight. As a result, Robinson was forced to leave the United States for a while because Jim Norris, a Mob-connected character who ran boxing in those days, froze him out of U.S. fighting. He headed to Europe, where his streak of 91 fights without a defeat ended when British boxer Randy Turpin took the welterweight title by winning a 15-round decision in London. Two months later, however, Robinson regained the title by beating Turpin in a 10-round technical knock out (TKO).

In 1952, Robinson went up for the light-heavyweight championship against Joey Maxim in Yankee Stadium. It was a hot night and the temperature in the ring was over 100 degrees. The heat, more than his opponent, wore Robinson down. By the 14th round, he couldn't get up to fight when the bell rang. Six months later, he announced that he was retiring from the sport.

## Returned to Boxing

For a short time, Robinson entertained audiences by tap dancing in a nightclub act and undertook various business ventures. But two years later, he was back in the ring, regaining the middleweight championship by beating Carl "Bobo" Olsen three times. He lost the title in 1957 in a bout against Gene Fullmer, but won it back four months later in a rematch. Robinson knocked Fullmer out in the fifth round with a left hook; it was the first time Fullmer had ever been knocked out.

Later that year, Robinson lost the title again, and won it back in a bloody battle against Carmen Basilio. Robinson gained an early advantage in the first fight, cutting open Basilio's eye and nose. An angered Basilio fought back furiously, leading to a split decision in Basilio's favor. Like many other boxers Robinson had beaten, Basilio hated Robinson and claimed that he wouldn never admit how hard he had been punched. "Robinson wouldn't tell the truth to God," Basilio said, according to Ron Flatter.

Robinson hated losing, and followed his classic pattern In a rematch six months later, even though he was sick with a virus, Robinson hit Basilio so hard he couldn't use his left eye and won a split decision, winning the middleweight championship for the fifth and last time.

## Career Declined

Robinson didn't fight for two more years. When he finally reentered the ring, he lost the title for good. On January 22, 1960, in a 15-round split decision against Paul Pender, the referee decided in favor of Pender. Ron Flatter reported that when Robinson's manager, George Gainford, complained, Robinson told him, "No beefs, George. Sometimes we got the best of it in the past."

Robinson made about $4 million during his career, but by the mid-1960s his lavish lifestyle had reduced his finances to nothing. In 1965, Robinson, broke and 44 years old—ancient in the grueling, youth-oriented sport of box-ing—had to fight five times in 35 days, receiving as little as $1,100 per fight. After losing ten rounds to Joey Archer, he announced his retirement and this time he meant it.

Robinson turned from boxing to show business, and recouped his financial losses, through acting and singing. He appeared on television and in movies and also started a youth foundation in 1969. Robinson moved to California with his third wife, Millie. In one of his last public appearances, Robinson was the best man at the 1986 wedding of his old rival, Jake LaMotta.

Robinson suffered from Alzheimer's disease and diabetes. He died in Culver City, California, on April 12, 1989, at the age of 67.

## An Enduring Legacy

Robinson's lifetime record was 175 wins, 19 losses, 6 draws, 2 no-contests, and 109 knockouts. That record has not been forgotten, nor has his incredible grace, speed, and flamboyant style, both in and out of the ring.

Ron Borges quoted trainer and historian Teddy Atlas, who said, "The great ones are pioneers in some way. That's what Ray was. He took speed and combination punching and a certain smoothness when it wasn't all connected and he connected it. Everything he did, he did with more meaning and more accuracy. He didn't just throw flurries, he threw tighter, harder combinations that were all meaningful." Trainer Eddie Futch told Borges, "He had marvelous balance and speed and superb reflexes. He was just as dangerous with either hand when going backwards and he knew almost everything there was to know about how to box."

*The Ring* magazine chose Robinson as the best boxer in its entire 75 years of publication, and said that "pound for pound" he was the best boxer in the history of the sport.

## Further Reading

"The Sugar in the Sweet Science," ESPN.com, http://204.202 .129.27/sportscentury/features/00947963.html (March 1, 1999).

"All-Time Greatest Fighters: Sugar Ray Robinson," HBO World Championship Boxing, http://hbo.com/boxing/ columnsfeatures/greats/cmp/greats-robinson.shtml (March 1, 1999).

"Sugar Ray Robinson," Colored Reflections, http://www.net4tv .com/color/50/Srobinson.htm (March 1, 1999).

"Sugar Ray Robinson," International Boxing Hall of Fame, http://www.ibhof.com/robinson.htm (March 1, 1999).

"Sugar Ray Robinson: God's Fighter," HBO World Championship Boxing, http://hbo.com/boxing/columnsfeatures/cmp/ robinsonarticle.shtml (March 1, 1999).

"Sugar Ray Robinson: Perspective," Colored Reflections, http://www.net4tv.com/color/50/SrobinsonPer.htm (March 1, 1999).

"Sugar Ray Robinson: The Bright Lights and Dark Shadows of a Champion," HBO World Championship Boxing, http://hbo .com/boxing/columnsfeatures/cmp/robinsondocu.shtml (March 1, 1999). □

# Arthur Rock

**Arthur Rock (born 1926) was the first venture capitalist. He invested in Fairchild Semiconductor, Intel, Apple Computer, and numerous other high-technology companies. His investments helped create many successful Silicon Valley companies.**

Arthur Rock was born in Rochester, New York, on August 19, 1926, the son of Hyman and Reva (Cohen) Rock. He earned a bachelors degree in business administration from Syracuse University in 1948 and a masters degree from Harvard in 1951.

## Invented the Term 'Venture Capital'

After graduating from Harvard, Rock joined the Wall Street firm of Hayden Stone & Co., where he worked as a securities analyst in the investment banking department, underwriting new stock issues. He was quite successful at picking applied science stocks in the late 1950s and early 1960s. In discussing that time, Rock said in *Charged Bodies: People, Power, and Paradox in Silicon Valley*, "It was a different era; there was really no one putting together money to go into high technology. Even the term 'venture capital' was unknown until 1965. I think I was the first one to use it. I can't remember anyone using it before that."

In 1956, engineers Robert Noyce and Gordon Moore helped William Shockley, the inventor of the transistor, set up Shockley Semiconductor Laboratories. One year later, eight engineers walked out on Shockley, fed up with his difficult temperament. The "traitorous eight," as they were called, wanted to set up their own transistor company, but needed investors. One of the eight young men had a father with an account at Hayden Stone. The man mentioned his son's predicament to someone at the investment banking firm. Soon after, a partner at the firm and Rock flew to California, met with the eight, and agreed to find the financing for their venture. It took Rock 35 tries before he found a company that would supply the money they needed. Fairchild Camera and Instrument, a company in Syosset, New York, put up $1.5 million in return for the right to buy the new company for $3 million if it succeeded. The company, called Fairchild Semiconductor, did succeed. Two years later Fairchild bought out the founders for $250,000 in Fairchild stock, worth $1.35 million in 1997.

Rock and Hayden Stone got involved with Teledyne soon after the company's founding in 1960 by Henry E. Singleton. Rock found the financing and became a member of the executive committee. Singleton found Rock to be "extremely brainy, perceptive, quick to grasp the essentials and reach a conclusion."

The San Francisco Bay Area was where all the high technology deals were taking place, so Rock moved to San Francisco in 1961. He set up a business with Thomas J. Davis, Jr. as his general partner. To fund the business, Rock assembled capital of $3.5 million from 25 limited partners, including Henry E. Singleton and Fayez Sarofim, a Harvard classmate. Davis & Rock existed from 1961 to 1968. This company was the first limited venture capital partnership.

Davis & Rock invested in 15 companies, including Anadex Instruments, Inc., General Capacitor, Astrodata, Teledyne, Benrus Watch Co., and Scientific Data Systems (SDS), founded by the mathematician Max Palevsky. Rock's company put $257,000 into SDS; the investment rose in value to $60 million and the company's sales went from $1 million to $100 million. The incredible success of SDS earned Rock a reputation as a great prognosticator of high-tech companies in which to invest. SDS was acquired by Xerox Corporation in 1969. Rock's share of Xerox stock was worth $4.6 million in 1970.

Rock, who does not have a technical background, chose SDS because he had confidence in Palevsky's drive to succeed. Rock recalled in *Business Week*, "I was convinced that he was going to make money. Very few people turn me on the way he did." Palevsky said that Rock's talent is "an ability to listen, not so much to what people say, because that may be technical, but to what people are expressing about themselves. He has a great deal of intuition."

## Funded Intel

By 1968, Noyce, Moore, and another Fairchild employee named Andy Grove, were ready to start a new company, Intel. They hoped to produce semiconductors used for computer memory. Noyce called his good friend Rock, with whom he used to hike and camp. Rock described how Intel began. "Bob (Noyce) just called me on the phone. We'd been friends for a long time.... Documents? There was practically nothing. Noyce's reputation was good enough. We put out a page-and-a-half little circular, but I'd raised the money even before people saw it." Rock made 15 phone calls in one afternoon and raised $2.5 million. C. Richard Kramlich, with whom Rock had founded Arthur Rock and Associates in 1969, recalled that it took Rock about two hours to raise the money. The raising of that much money in that short amount of time turned Rock into a legend. Rock was looking for more than investors. He also wanted people who could make a contribution to the company in the way of expertise. Rock himself invested $300,000 in the company and served as its first chairman.

In 1978, Mike Markulla of Apple Computer hooked up Steve Jobs and Steve Wozniak with Rock. Rock bought 640,000 shares of Apple Computer for nine cents a share, an investment of about $57,000, and he became a director of the company. Three years later, when Apple went public, his shares were worth $14 million, a return of 23,000 percent, further enhancing Rock's reputation.

In the late 1970s, Rock began working on his own under the name Arthur Rock & Co. His only employee was his secretary of many years, Marie Getchel. Rock helped launch Diasonics, a manufacturer of medical instruments. He was the company's founding chairman. When it went public in 1983, it was worth over $1 billion. Rock made $3.1 million when he sold 150,000 shares at the initial public offering. Rock also invested in ELXSi International, a computer company, and Rational Machines, a company that sells computer systems used to design software.

## "An Incredible Intuition"

Rock once described the role of a venture capitalist as someone who hunts for entrepreneurial dreamers possessed of "the potential to change the world." Rock analyzed the potential of a young company by focusing on the entrepreneur. "People, people, people," said Rock, in describing how he chooses companies to invest in.

Larry Mohr, a Silicon Valley venture capitalist, described what Rock looked for in an entrepreneur: "He wants to see fire in the belly and intellect. A lot of people would invest in just intellect. Not Arthur. He hates sloppiness and does not suffer fools gladly." Once Rock invests in a venture, he is very loyal. He often joins the board of directors and provides a steady stream of advice. "His individual contribution has been the difference between success and failure for us," said Paul Levy, co-founder of Rational.

Rock has few private investors as clients. He invests his own fortune and the money of a few friends, making three or four deals a year. The companies he finances are close to his office so he does not have to travel much. Rock searches for ideas, people, and products that together would create a new industry. He makes up his mind quickly, acts decisively, and moves silently. Palevsky said of him, "Arthur has an incredible intuition. His nose never ceases to amaze me."

## Concerned with Social Problems

Rock married lawyer Toni Rembe, his second wife, on July 19, 1975. They have a home overlooking San Francisco Bay. The couple has no children. Rock spends much of the winter in Aspen, Colorado, where he and his wife own a three-story condominium. He exercises for an hour every morning and skis most of the winter. Rock is a great fan of the San Francisco Giants baseball team. He also supports San Francisco's opera, ballet, and Museum of Modern Art. His personal art collection includes works by Robert Motherwell and Hans Hofmann. Rock enjoys hosting dinner parties with guests such as Opera Impresario Kurt Herbert Adler and *Rolling Stone* magazine editor Jann Wenner.

Rock has become very wealthy as a venture capitalist. In 1984, his personal fortune was estimated at $200 million, but he does not like discussing it. He told *Time*, "I don't like people to count my money. That isn't what turns me on." Rock does not like publicity and is so secretive "that he amounts to a sort of mysterious force in the financial world," according to journalist Michael Moritz.

Rock's main interest outside of work has been social problems. As far back as 1970 he spent time advising minority businesspeople. In 1998, he told *Forbes*, "Most successful men and women give generously to their universities, but it seems to me that those gifts increase the distance between the haves and the have-nots. We need to be doing something about inner-city education at early levels."

## Further Reading

Jackson, Tim, *Inside Intel: Andy Grove and the Rise of the World's Most Powerful Chip Company*, New York, Dutton, 1997.

Mahon, Thomas, *Charged Bodies: People, Power, and Paradox in Silicon Valley*, New York, New American Library, 1985.

Rogers, Everett M. and Judith K. Larsen, *Silicon Valley Fever: Growth of High-Technology Culture*, New York, Basic Books, 1984.

*Business Week*, May 30, 1970.

*Forbes*, November 1, 1968; February 27, 1984; June 1, 1998.

*Fortune*, July 7, 1997.

*Time*, January 23, 1984. □

# Jimmie Rodgers

**Jimmie Rodgers (1897–1933), known as "The Mississippi Blue Yodeler" and "The Singing Brakeman," was the first nationally-known country music star. He influenced many later performers from Hank Snow and Ernest Tubb to Lefty Frizzell and Merle Haggard. Rodgers was the first musician to be inducted into the Country Music Hall of Fame.**

Born in Meridian, Mississippi, on September 8, 1897, Rodgers grew up in hard times. He was the third son of Aaron Rodgers, a maintenance-of-way railroad foreman for the Mobile & Ohio Railroad. His mother died when he was four and Rodgers went to live with his mother's sister, a former teacher who had degrees in music and English. She introduced him to many kinds of music, including vaudeville, pop, and dance hall ditties. He was a wild boy and, when he returned to his father in 1912, he hung out in pool halls and seedy bars, though never got into serious trouble.

At the age of 12, he sang "Steamboat Bill" at a talent contest and won. It was his first taste of fame and he decided to start his own traveling show. His father tracked him down and brought him home, but Rodgers ran away again to join a medicine show—a traveling combination of entertainment and live commercials for mostly-useless and often dangerous medical remedies. By the time his father tracked him down again, Rodgers had had enough of life on the road. When his father gave him the choice of going to school or working on the railroad, Rodgers chose the railroad. He taught himself to play banjo, ukelele, and guitar and learned train songs, barroom ballads, slave songs, and blues tunes from the other railway men.

Rodgers worked as a brakeman for the New Orleans & Northeastern railroad for the next ten years, traveling along the south and west coasts. This was how he earned his nickname, "The Singing Brakeman."

## Two Marriages

In May, 1917, he married Sandra Kelly, whom he had known for only a few weeks. By the fall, they were already separated, even though she was pregnant. Two years later they officially were divorced and Rodgers met Carrie Williamson, a high-school student and preacher's daughter. They married in April, 1920, while she was still in school.

Soon after the marriage, Rodgers was laid off by the railroad and the couple entered some hard times. Rodgers took odd jobs and sang whenever he could. He was on the road performing when he received word that their second daughter, who was only six weeks old, had died of diphtheria.

In 1923, Rodgers contracted pneumonia and the following year was diagnosed with tuberculosis. Despite his doctor's advice, he left the hospital and formed a trio with fiddler Slim Rozell and his sister-in-law Elsie McWilliams. Rodgers had taught himself to play and sing, and was not able to read or write music; he relied on McWilliams for help. The two collaborated on writing the songs that Americans would be singing throughout the late 1920s and 1930s.

Rodgers sang with the trio, performed comedy skits in medicine shows, and continued to work for the railroad. Because he believed that a warm, dry climate would help his tuberculosis, he moved his family to Tucson, Arizona, and continued to sing there. The railroad, saying his performing interfered with his job, fired him.

Rodgers and his family then moved to Meridian, Mississippi, where they lived with Carrie's parents before moving again, this time to Asheville, North Carolina, in 1927. Although Rodgers planned to take another railroad job, his tuberculosis had advanced to the point where he was unable to do the work, and he took odd jobs as a janitor and cab driver, sang on a local radio station and took whatever other singing jobs he could find.

## Recorded with RCA Victor

Rodgers moved to Johnson City, Tennessee, where he joined a string band called the Tenneva Ramblers. This group was a trio before Rodgers arrived but he convinced them to let him be the lead performer because he already had a regular radio show back in Asheville. The group performed regularly on the radio and at local concerts.

Ralph Peer, a talent scout for RCA Victor records, came to Bristol, Tennessee, to record country and string bands. These recording sessions were the first time anyone had made an effort to record white rural music, known as "hillbilly music," for nationwide sale. The recordings, including those of Rodgers and the Carter Family, encouraged the beginnings of the country music industry.

Rodgers heard about the auditions and convinced the band to travel to Bristol. On the night before the audition, they had a heated argument about whose name should be billed first and the Tenneva Ramblers broke away from Rodgers, telling him to sing on his own. According to a biography on the *Jimmierodgers.com*, website, Rodgers said, "All right . . . I'll just sing one myself," and went to the audition anyway. He wanted to sing his signature song, "T for Texas," but Peer rejected that and instead recorded two songs, "The Soldier's Sweetheart" and "Sleep, Baby, Sleep." For these recordings, he was paid $100.

The record was released in October 1927. Although it wasn't a hit, Victor Records agreed to record more of Rodgers' songs. In November 1927, he recorded four songs, including "T for Texas," which was retitled "Blue Yodel," a song that gave Rodgers another nickname. "Blue Yodel," one of a very few early country records that sold over a million copies, led to success for Rodgers. He would eventually record 14 variations of "Blue Yodel," which Tom Piazza described in *www.sony.music* as "Loosely strung outlaw blues lyrics, sung in a sly, jaunty manner, alternated with Rodgers' trademark yodel in a unique overlay of the Southern rounder and the Western cowboy, literally and symbolically representing a blending of the streams of white and black rural music."

## Unique Style

Other singers of the Appalachian mountain music known as "Old Time Music" stayed within their traditional folk-music boundaries. But Rodgers blended country, gospel, jazz, blues, pop, cowboy, and folk and wrote most of his own best-loved songs. He also brought his distinctive yodeling style into his music. A biography in the Alabama Music Hall of Fame remarks, "Although Rodgers wasn't the first to yodel on records, his style was distinct from all the others. His yodel wasn't merely sugar-coating on the song, it was as important as the lyric, mournful and plaintive or happy and carefree, depending on a song's emotional content." He sometimes sang to his guitar only, but on other songs he had a full jazz band, including horns—very different from the traditional mountain string band.

Rodgers' songs spoke to Americans, many of whom had endured hard times. Fans responded to his humble background, honest singing and playing, and his drive to overcome poverty and illness. In addition, his songs were simple and easy to understand. As Tom Piazza wrote, "His career was a meeting point for images and folk material from the American South and West, from black and white traditions, and it offered clues to ways in which that material could be blended into the mainstream of popular music. . . . His songs. . .evoked both the expansive frontier spirit and the longing, backward glance toward home. Along with the Carter Family and others, he was both a preserver and a popularizer of a precious body of expression."

## First Country Music Star

Rodgers moved his family to Washington, D.C. He began singing on a weekly radio show as the "Singing Brakeman." Rodgers recorded more songs, including the four hits "Way Out on the Mountain," "Blue Yodel No. 4," "Waiting for a Train" and "In the Jailhouse Now." Ralph Peer and Rodgers experimented with the accompaniment, sometimes recording him with unlikely combinations such as a jazz band that included Louis Armstrong, jug bands, orchestras, and a Hawaiian combo.

By 1929, Rodgers was a star. He made a short film, titled *The Singing Brakeman,* recorded more songs, and made national tours. Although he was financially successful, all the money in the world couldn't stop the progress of his tuberculosis. He worked hard anyway, perhaps knowing that he would die young and wanting to make more money for his family's future. He recorded more songs, toured with Will Rogers on a Red Cross fund-raising mission to help farmers affected by a long drought in the southern states and built a home for his family in Kerrville, Texas.

Rodgers was deeply affected by the decline in the American economy. The Great Depression brought concert bookings and record sales to a virtual halt. Despite these difficulties, he continued to record new songs. In the six short years of his career, he recorded 127 songs.

## Health Declines

In 1932, Rodgers recorded with the original Carter Family, but was so ill by then that he could barely lift his guitar. Mother Maybelle Carter played and sang for him. "I had to play like him, you know, so everybody would think it was him. But it was me," she said, according to the *Jimmie Rodgers Home Page.*

Rodgers knew his health was rapidly declining and, according to the Alabama Music Hall of Fame, told his wife Carrie, "I want to die with my shoes on." He kept performing wherever he could, at vaudeville shows and radio programs. At one radio program in San Antonio, Texas, he collapsed from exhaustion and ended up in the hospital. Knowing death was near, he called Peer and told him to set up one more recording session in New York City in May of 1933. In this, his last recording session, tuberculosis had left him so weak and ill that a cot had to be set up in the studio so he could rest in between songs. In eight days, he recorded twelve songs.

Rodgers slipped into a coma and died of a massive lung hemorrhage in New York City on May 26, 1933. He was 35 years old. His body was taken to Meridian by train in a converted baggage car. The train's engineer blew its whistle throughout the journey. In Meridian, hundreds of country music fans were waiting. His body lay in state for several days to allow the fans to pay tribute to their beloved idol.

## Lasting Influence

A brass plaque dedicated to Rodgers in the Country Music Hall of Fame records that "Jimmie Rodgers' name stands foremost in the country music field as the man who started it all." His influence can still be heard in today's country singers, rock and rollers and blues greats like Blind Boy Fuller and Peetie Wheatstraw. Fans can visit the Jimmie Rodgers Memorial and Museum in Meridian, Mississippi, and attend the Jimmie Rodgers Festival, which is held in Kerrville, Texas, each year.

Bob Dylan wrote in the liner notes to a 1997 tribute album: "Jimmie Rodgers, of course, is one of the guiding lights of the twentieth century, whose way with song has always been an inspiration to those of us who have followed the path. . . . He was a performer of force without precedent with a sound as lonesome and mystical as it was dynamic. He gives hope to the vanquished and humility to the mighty."

## Further Reading

"Jimmie Rodgers," Rock and Roll Hall of Fame, http://www.rockhall.com/induct/rodgjimm.html (February 23, 1999).

"Jimmie Rodgers: 1993 Inductee, John Herbert Orr Pioneer Award," Alabama Music Hall of Fame, http://www.alamhof.org/rodgersj.htm (February 23, 1999).

"Jimmie Rodgers: Biography," http://jimmierodgers.com/Main/Biography/biography.html (February 23, 1999).

"Jimmie Rodgers: Biography," Sony Music, http://www.conymusic.com/artists/JimmieR . . . s/TheSongsOfJimmie Rodgers/biography.html (February 23, 1999).

"Jimmie Rodgers' Biography," http://www.ping.be/ml-cmb/jrbio.htm (February 23, 1999).

"Jimmie Rodgers: The Father of Country Music," Discover Texas, http://www.discover-texas.com/jimmie/ (February 23, 1999).

"Jimmie Rodgers—'The Singing Brakeman'," http://www.ils.unc.edu/dolma/rodgers.html (February 23, 1999).

"Songs of Jimmie Rodgers Resonate Still," *St. Louis Post-Dispatch,* http://www.stlnet.com/pdnews/jrodgers/ (February 23, 1999). □

# Pete Rozelle

**Pete Rozelle (1926–1996) served as commissioner of the National Football League (NFL) from 1960 until 1989, leading the League to unprecedented profitability and popularity.**

Born in the small California town of South Gate, outside of Los Angeles, on March 1, 1926, Alvin Ray "Pete" Rozelle took an early interest in sports. He played basketball and tennis for Compton High School, from which he graduated in 1944. Upon graduation, Rozelle enlisted in the U.S. Navy, serving until 1946. He

then enrolled in Compton Junior College and returned to the world of sports as the college's athletic news director. Rozelle also covered high school basketball for local newspapers. The same year that he entered Compton Junior College, the NFL's Cleveland Rams moved to Los Angeles and chose the college as the site of their training camp. Rozelle showed an interest in the team and became an assistant to Maxwell Stiles, the Rams' public relations director. Rozelle made a good impression on the Rams' administration, but his position was strictly temporary. In 1948, he left to finish his degree at the University of San Francisco (USF).

Rozelle graduated from USF in 1950 and became the University's athletic news director, a part-time position. He was able to attend major sporting events and made many contacts that would help him professionally in the years to come. One such contact was Tex Schramm, general manager of the Los Angeles Rams, who hired Rozelle to serve as the Rams' public relations director in 1952. Rozelle remained in that position until 1955, when he left to join the public relations firm of P.K. Macker in San Francisco. While in this capacity, Rozelle represented Australian athletes and sports firms during Australia's hosting of the 1956 Olympic Games.

While Rozelle advanced his career in public relations, the Los Angeles Rams were experiencing administrative difficulties. Fifty percent of the team was owned by Dan Reeves, and the other half was owned by two people who could not get along with him. To escape this strife, Schramm left the Rams in 1957, and the club was without a general manager. NFL commissioner Bert Bell offered the position

to Rozelle, who overcame initial misgivings and took the post before the end of the year. He proved an immediate success with the Rams, using his talents as a public relations professional to soothe the turmoil within the organization. In the process, he greatly impressed Reeves.

## State of the Game

The popularity of football had increased steadily throughout the 1950s. In 1958, the sport received a gigantic boost when one of its first nationally televised championship games (featuring the Baltimore Colts and the New York Giants) turned into one of the most well-played and exciting games of all time. Although interest in football had increased, a 1960 Gallup poll revealed that 34 percent of Americans named baseball as their favorite sport, with just 21 percent preferring football.

When the owners of NFL franchises met for their annual meeting in 1960, their league faced serious challenges. Bell, who had served as commissioner of the League since 1946, had died suddenly the previous year, and a rival professional league, the American Football League (AFL), had been established. The AFL promised to compete with NFL teams for both players and markets. Various factions among the 12 NFL owners advanced candidates to fill Bell's position as commissioner, but after ten days and 23 ballots, no candidate had secured a majority. Finally, Reeves put forward his employee, Pete Rozelle, as a compromise candidate. Rozelle was elected, but was opposed by some of the NFL's most established and influential owners.

## "League Think"

Upon becoming commissioner, Rozelle immediately set out to revolutionize the administration of professional football. Borrowing from the stated intention of the AFL owners, Rozelle proposed that all NFL teams pool revenues they received from television contracts and advertising, and then distribute them evenly. This approach to the distribution of media revenues was not popular with owners in large markets such as New York and Los Angeles, but Rozelle saw a collective approach as essential to the survival of teams operating in smaller markets, such as Green Bay, Wisconsin. Furthermore, by presenting a collective front, the NFL would be able to secure better national television contracts. Rozelle referred to his collective approach as "League Think." Although League owners soon saw the benefits of Rozelle's tactics, legal obstacles to his plan still existed. In order to pool their television revenues, the NFL would need a partial exemption from the Sherman Antitrust Act, which prohibits monopolistic business practices. Rozelle argued the NFL's case before the U.S. Congress and secured the required exemption in September 1961.

## Rise of the AFL

Under Rozelle's leadership, NFL television revenues tripled between 1962 and 1964 to $14 million per year, and the popularity of football began to increase rapidly. The AFL had also benefited from football's increased popularity and soon began to pose a serious threat to the NFL's prosperity. Competition between the leagues resulted in greatly increased salaries for players, which in turn began to effect the financial health of both leagues. The situation had become intolerable by 1966, and Rozelle was forced to act. First, he convinced the team owners in both leagues to allow the AFL to merge into an expanded NFL. Rozelle then convinced Congress to grant a further Sherman Antitrust Act exemption for the NFL to enable the merger to proceed. This merger also resulted in the creation of an end-of-season game between the champions of the NFL and the AFL, which soon became known as the Super Bowl. The first Super Bowl, matching the Green Bay Packers of the NFL and the Kansas City Chiefs of the AFL, was played in January 1967.

## Prosperity

The reconstituted NFL enjoyed unprecedented popularity throughout the 1960s and 1970s. Television revenues continued to rise and Monday Night Football, first shown on the ABC network in 1970, soon became a national institution. Gallup conducted another poll in 1972 that revealed football was the favorite sport of 36 percent of Americans while just 21 percent favored baseball. Despite the growth of the NFL during the 1970s, new challenges emerged. Players threatened to strike in 1974 for the right to become free agents when their contracts expired. Also, another rival league, the World Football League (WFL), came into existence the same year, but went defunct in 1975 due to insufficient financial backing. By 1980, the NFL comprised 28 teams, up from 12 in 1960, and had reached new heights in both profitability and popularity.

## Labor and Legal Challenges

Rozelle's ''League Think'' strategy had succeeded beyond the owners' wildest dreams, but the economic realities of sports were beginning to change again in the 1980s. Although the NFL's television revenues continued to rise, reaching an all-time high of $2.1 billion for the 1987 season, the importance of stadium leases, concessions, and the sale of ''luxury boxes'' became an increasingly important part of team revenues. Luxury boxes were private blocks of seats featuring amenities including televisions, bars, and buffets, which are normally sold to corporate clients for an entire season. Older stadiums, which lacked luxury boxes and were often owned by the home team's city, generated far less revenue than newer venues. Furthermore, cities desperate for a professional football franchise were willing to build stadiums at public expense and offer generous payments to teams willing to leave their traditional markets. Owners received offers they literally could not refuse. One of the League's most storied and profitable franchises, the Oakland Raiders, moved to Los Angeles after securing a favorable stadium lease in 1980. Rozelle opposed the move in the courts, as did the city of Oakland, but they were unable to prevent the Raiders from moving. The courts eventually ruled that the NFL would violate antitrust laws if it barred its owners from moving their franchises to secure more lucrative arrangements in new cities. Following the resolution of this case the Baltimore Colts, another of the NFL's most famous teams, moved to Indianapolis, Indiana, for the 1984 season.

The contractual rights of players continued to haunt the NFL during the 1980s. Throughout the League's history, players had, in effect, been the property of their teams. When a player's contract expired, he was forced to renegotiate only with his own team, rather than being able to market his skills to all NFL teams. This meant that players were forced to take whatever salary their teams were willing to pay, which had the effect of holding salaries down. In the heyday of the AFL, a sort of free agency had existed, since AFL teams felt free to offer contracts to NFL players, and salaries had risen dramatically. Following the incorporation of the AFL into the NFL, competition between franchises for players became almost nonexistent once again. Rozelle had done his best to secure this arrangement by instituting what became known as the Rozelle Rule, which required any team that signed a player previously belonging to another team to offer compensation for the lost player. The effect of the Rozelle Rule was to make signing a free agent a very risky prospect for a team, which would only find out after the fact what type of compensation they would be required to make to the player's original team. Under these circumstances, player salaries stagnated throughout the 1970s and the mood of the players became increasingly militant. Players struck in 1982 and 1987 to secure some form of free agency, or at least a modification of the Rozelle Rule. Eventually, a very controlled form of free agency was put into place, a salary cap installed, and the Rozelle Rule suspended. This compromise solution is still in effect today, although it had been made with some acrimony, alienating fans and hurting the League's popularity.

In addition to its labor and legal troubles, the NFL was increasingly confronted with the problem of substance abuse among its players. The use of steroids to enhance on-field performance, which had been condoned by many teams, became anathema due to public outrage and the discovery of the physical side-effects of steroid abuse. Additionally, off-the-field use of recreational drugs by players caused a seemingly unending series of embarrassing incidents. Rozelle was shocked by the pervasiveness of drug abuse in the League, as was the public, and by 1986, the NFL's television ratings were beginning to drop for the first time during his tenure.

## Another Rival

A new rival professional league, the United States Football League (USFL), came into existence in 1981. The USFL enjoyed far more secure financial backing than had the WFL, including among its owners multi-millionaire Donald Trump. Despite the fact that the USFL avoided direct competition with the NFL by playing its games in the spring, the very existence of the new league had the usual effect of creating a form of free agency and causing players' salaries to rise dramatically. The USFL enjoyed several years of prosperity before eventually moving its games to the fall in an attempt to compete directly with the NFL. It combined this move with the filing of an antitrust lawsuit against the NFL, seeking $1.5 billion in damages for what it alleged was the NFL's restraint of trade within the business of football. Under Rozelle's direction, the NFL successfully defended itself against the USFL's competitive and legal challenges.

The new league folded shortly after it lost the preliminary judgment in its court case against the NFL in 1987.

Rozelle guided the NFL through the troubled 1980s, with television revenues per team climbing from $69 million to $493.5 million between 1977 and 1986, but at a high personal cost. By the end of the decade, he was having difficulty sleeping and was smoking three packs of cigarettes per day. Rozelle's influence and effectiveness were officially recognized when he was elected to the NFL Hall of Fame in 1985. Despite this honor, the perception that the League's popularity and profitability were stagnating was beginning to undermine Rozelle's support among owners in the late 1980s. In 1989, with more than two years remaining on his contract, Rozelle decided that he had had enough and resigned as commissioner of the NFL.

Rozelle served briefly on the board of directors of NTN Communications, Inc. of Carlsbad, California, in 1994, before retiring due to his failing health. He died of cancer on December 6, 1996 in Rancho Mirage, California.

## Further Reading

*Columbia Reference Encyclopedia,* Columbia University Press, 1993.

Harris, David, *The League,* Bantam Books, 1987.

*Broadcasting and Cable,* April 18, 1994.

*Fortune,* August 4, 1986.

*Jet,* April 29, 1985.

*New York Times,* March 23, 1989.

*Newsweek,* September 20, 1982.

*Sporting News,* February 4, 1985; December 16, 1996.

*Sports Illustrated,* September 1, 1983; January 30, 1989; April 3, 1989.

*Time,* December 7, 1998.

*U.S. News and World Report,* January 26, 1987. □

# S

## Colonel Sanders

**Colonel Sanders (1890–1980) created the Kentucky Fried Chicken fast food chain at the age of 66. Pride in his product, high standards, and brilliant marketing help to establish him as an innovator in the fast food industry.**

Harland David Sanders was born on a farm in Henryville, Indiana on September 9, 1890. His parents, Wilbert Sanders, a butcher, and Margaret Ann Dunleavy, a homemaker, also had two younger children. Sanders' father died when he was five, so his mother took a job peeling tomatoes in a canning factory and earned extra money by sewing at night. Sanders had to take care of his siblings, learning how to cook so he could feed them. He held his first job at the age of ten, working on a nearby farm. Because the family was so poor, Sanders left school after sixth grade so he could work full time. His mother, desperate to improve the financial situation of her family, married a produce farmer and moved the family to suburban Indianapolis when Sanders was 12. Sanders fought often with his new stepfather. Within a year, his mother sent him back to Clark county, Indiana.

Sanders worked as a farmhand for $15 a month, plus room and board, until he was 15 years old. He was then able to get a job as a streetcar conductor in New Albany, Indiana. In 1906, while still under age, Sanders enlisted in the U.S. Army and spent a year as a soldier in Cuba. After completing his military service, Sanders married Josephine King in Jasper, Alabama. The couple had three children. During the early years of their marriage, Sanders and his family moved to Alabama, Tennessee, Arkansas, and finally back to Indiana. They divorced in 1947.

### Launched First Company

Sanders held a variety of jobs. He sold insurance in Jeffersonville, Indiana. Then he started a steamboat ferry company that operated on the Ohio River between Jeffersonville and Louisville, Kentucky. Eventually, Sanders took a job as secretary of the Columbus chamber of commerce. There he met an inventor who discovered how to operate natural gas lamps on a gas derived from carbide. Sanders bought the patent rights and launched a manufacturing company. Unfortunately, a rural electrification program made his company's product obsolete.

While working as a railroad man for the Illinois Central Railroad, Sanders took a correspondence course that allowed him to earn a law degree from Southern University. A local judge permitted him to use his law library and local lawyers helped his studies by explaining law terminology. When he lost his job with the railroad, Sanders began practicing law. He had some success in the legal field from about 1915 to the early 1920s, working in the Justice of the Peace courts in Little Rock, Arkansas. Sanders ruined his legal career, however, by getting into a brawl with a client in the courtroom. Although found innocent of assault and battery, Sanders' legal practice was through.

### Became an Honorary Colonel

In 1929, Sanders moved to Corbin, Kentucky, a small town at the edge of the Appalachian Mountains, and opened a gas station along U.S. Route 25. When tourists and traveling salespeople asked Sanders where they could get something to eat nearby, he got the idea of opening a small restaurant next to the gas station. The restaurant had one

**323**

table and six chairs and specialized in Southern cooking such as pan fried chicken, ham, vegetables, and biscuits. Sanders moved his establishment across the street to a bigger location, with room for 142 seats, a motel and a service station. He took an eight-week course in restaurant and hotel management from Cornell University to learn more about the business. Sanders' café had a homey atmosphere, with no menu, but good food. But when restaurant critic, Duncan Hines, listed Sanders' place in *Adventures in Good Eating* in the 1930s, its popularity increased.

In 1935, the popular café so impressed Governor Ruby Laffoon that he made Sanders an honorary Kentucky colonel for his contribution to state cuisine. In 1937, Sanders tried to start a restaurant chain in Kentucky, but his attempt failed. Two years later, he opened another motel and restaurant in Asheville, North Carolina, but this too failed.

Sanders continued to alter his chicken recipe to get the seasonings just right. In 1939, he devised a method to cook chicken quickly because customers would not wait 45 minutes for a batch to be fried up in an iron pan. Sanders used a pressure cooker, a new invention at the time, to cook chicken in nine minutes. He found that chicken cooked in this manner turned out to be moist and flavorful. Sanders' method is still being used today.

In 1949, Sanders was once again honored with the title of Kentucky colonel, this time by Lieutenant Governor Lawrence Weatherby. Sanders began using the title of "Colonel" and dressing in a white suit, white shirt, black string tie, black shoes, white mustache and goatee, and a cane—giving himself the appearance of a gentleman from the Old South. In 1949, Sanders married Claudia Ledington, an employee.

During World War II, gas rationing meant less travel, so Sanders had to shut down his motel. It reopened when the war ended. By 1953, his café was worth $165,000. In the early 1950s, Sanders signed up a few restaurant owners in an early form of franchise. He would ship them his seasoning, made from a secret recipe of eleven herbs and spices, if they agreed to pay him five cents for every chicken cooked with it. Pete Harman, a Utah restaurant owner who had met Sanders in Chicago at a seminar for restaurateurs, was his first franchisee. Harman, already a successful businessman, is credited with creating the marketing strategies that made Sanders' business a success. Harman is also responsible for inventing the name "Kentucky Fried Chicken," introducing the takeout bucket, and creating the slogan, "finger lickin' good."

In 1956, the federal government made plans to build a new highway, bypassing Corbin. The value of Sanders' site plummeted, and he auctioned off the property for $75,000 to pay his debts. At the age of 66 he was almost broke, living off a monthly Social Security check of $105 and some savings. Sanders then moved to Shelbyville, Kentucky.

## A Secret Recipe Spelled Success

With nothing to lose, Sanders took his spices and pressure cooker and traveled throughout the U.S. in his 1946 Ford. He visited restaurants, trying to convince the owners to use his recipe. Sanders had no luck with the better restau-

rants, said John Neal, a franchisee. "They all threw him out of their places. He found a lot of wonderful hard-working men and women who operated various and sundry restaurants who took his methods and paid him a nickel a head. The Colonel shipped them the seasoning. That's literally how he got started."

By 1960, Sanders had 400 franchisees, and his image was being used to sell chicken throughout the country. By 1963, he made $300,000 a year in profits, before taxes. In 1996, the number of franchises had grown to over 5,000 units in the U.S. and 4,500 overseas. Sanders carefully guarded his secret recipe of herbs and spices, hiring two different suppliers to mix up batches, which he would then combine himself and mail to franchisees.

Sanders was a perfectionist. He often burst into a restaurant's kitchen to scold an employee for not cooking his gravy correctly. Sanders would then show him how to cook it right. "The thing I remember about the Colonel is that he was very particular about doing things right," said Jackie Trujillo, chairman of Harman Management. "He used to visit us often," she said. "Service, quality and cleanliness was No. 1. He never backed down from that."

## Sold Company to Investors

In 1964, Sanders sold out to a group of investors, including John Y. Brown, Jr. and Jack Massey, for $2 million. He had been concerned about selling the business because he feared that the new owners might not maintain a high quality product. Friends and family finally persuaded the 74-year-old to part with his company. On January 6, 1964, he closed the deal. Besides the $2 million, he received a lifetime salary of $40,000 a year (later raised to $75,000). Sanders served as the company spokesman, making personal appearances and television commercials. He held on to his Canadian rights in the company and established a foundation in Canada, turning over his profits to charities, such as churches, hospitals, the Boy Scouts, and the Salvation Army. He also adopted 78 foreign orphans.

Kentucky Fried Chicken went public in 1969, and was acquired by Heublein Inc. two years later. In 1974, Sanders sued the company because he did not like changes they had made to the product. The suit was settled out of court for over a million dollars. R.J. Reynolds Industries acquired Kentucky Fried Chicken in 1982. It then passed to PepsiCo in 1986 for $840 million.

## Honored with Museum and Landmark

In 1974, Sanders published his autobiography, *Life As I Have Known It Has Been Finger Lickin' Good.* His daughter, Margaret Sanders, published *Eleven Herbs and a Spicy Daughter: Col. Sanders' Secret of Success,* in 1994.

Though he is said to have had a bad temper, Sanders inspired many in the restaurant industry by helping his franchisees, introducing a love for his product, and maintaining high standards. He has had a lasting impact on fast food, something he helped create. Industry leaders credit Sanders with being a stellar marketer. His innovations included selling busy people buckets of chicken to take home and using a character, himself, to sell a product.

Sanders died in Shelbyville, Kentucky on December 16, 1980, after a seven-month battle with leukemia. The Colonel Sanders Museum at Kentucky Fried Chicken headquarters in Louisville contains a life-sized statue of Sanders in a small theater, his office—exactly as he left it, his white linen suit, cane, shirt and tie, one of his wife's dresses, and his original pressure cooker. In 1972, his first restaurant was named a Kentucky historical landmark.

## Further Reading

*Dictionary of American Biography,* Supplement 10, 1976-1980.
Pearce, John, *The Colonel: The Captivating Biography of the Dynamic Founder of a Fast Food Empire,* Doubleday, 1982.
Sanders, Harland, *Life as I Have Known it Has Been Finger Linckin' Good,* Creation House, 1974.
Sanders, Margaret, *Eleven Herbs and a Spicy Daughter: Col. Sanders' Secret of Success,* Starr Publishing Co., 1994.
*Nation's Restaurant News,* December 15, 1986; February 1996.

☐

# Gerhard Schroder

**In 1998, Gerhard Schroder (born 1944) became the first challenger since World War II to unseat an incumbent chancellor in Germany. He defeated Helmut Kohl, who had been chancellor for 16 years. Schroder promised to continue social programs and reinstate mild cuts in worker benefits that Kohl had made, but he also pledged to modernize policy so that Germany could remain a global economic force.**

When Germans went to the polls in 1998, they were reluctant to make major changes. However, the Social Democratic candidate, Gerhard Schroder, convinced them that he was not an extremist. Although his party's leftist policies could offer benefits, he would not always tow the party line. He supported the working class, but also understood the importance of championing business. He patterned his image after that of American president Bill Clinton and British prime minister Tony Blair, both of whom claimed office after years of control by opposition parties.

While serving as a premier in the state of Lower Saxony from 1990 to 1998, Schroder emerged on the national scene as a charismatic, telegenic personality capable of stirring popular support for his party, which was eager to unseat Kohl's Christian Democrats. Despite a much-publicized divorce from his third wife in 1997, the charming Schroder, with his designer suits, cigars, and witty remarks, remained a favorite with the public. Many commentators professed skepticism about his leadership abilities, giving the opinion that Schroder was more interested in getting to the top than in effecting needed policy changes in the government. The country's generous social spending and rigid labor laws were making it difficult to compete in a world market, and critics wondered if Schroder would be willing to push

through the unpopular, but necessary, reforms that Kohl had begun. The majority of Germans, however, were willing to try a fresh face, and were anxious to see if he could follow through on his promise of balancing social programs and economic stability.

## Early Years

Schroder was born in the German town of Mossenburg on April 7, 1944, just a few days after his father was killed in Romania during World War II. His mother, Erika, remarried, but her second husband suffered from tuberculosis. In order to support her family of five children, she cleaned barracks for British occupation forces in the town of Lemgo, in northern Germany. Schroder began toiling in the fields at the age of 12 to bring in money. He quit school at 14 to take sales jobs in a china shop and then a hardware store. Schroder was an eager student, who paid for night courses in order to finish high school. Imre Karacs in the *Independent* reported that Schroder often told his mother, "One day I'll take you away from all this in a Mercedes." He went on to Gottingen University, where he studied law and joined the Young Socialists, a youth branch of the Social Democratic Party (SPD). Schroder became the group's leader in the district of Hannover, the state capital of Lower Saxony, in 1977. The following year he became the national chairman of the SPD Young Socialists. Meanwhile, Schroder pursued post-graduate work and obtained a law degree in 1976; he was a practicing attorney from 1976 to 1980.

Schroder combined his profession and his politics, becoming noted for defending Red Army Faction terrorist

Horst Mahler in a parole hearing, and also for his association with Willy Brandt, the former SPD chancellor. By 1978, he had completely embraced mainstream Marxism and was busy organizing protests against the United States and the deployment of NATO missiles in Germany. In 1980, Schroder won a seat in the *Bundestag*—the National Assembly branch of the legislature—as a member of the SPD from the district of Hannover. Shortly after that election, an incident occurred that became something of a folk legend in German politics. Schroder, according to Barry Came Wosnitza in *Maclean's*, was out drinking with friends one night and happened to walk past the government offices of Chancellor Helmut Schmidt. He climbed up the iron gates and shook them as he hung on, yelling, "I want to get in here," until police showed up and ordered him to get down.

## Premier of Lower Saxony

After six years in the Bundestag, Schroder returned to Lower Saxony in 1986, serving until 1990 as opposition leader in the parliament and chairman of the SPD Party Group. He made an unsuccessful bid to become premier of the state government of Lower Saxony in 1986. He ran again in 1990 and won the election. As he began his rise, Schroder's views became more moderate. This undoubtedly helped his success in 1990, as did the assistance of his third wife, Hiltrud, nicknamed "Hillu." As an environmentalist, vegetarian, and animal-rights proponent, she forged important relationships with members of the Green Party. According to Wosnitza in *Maclean's*, one of Schroder's associates noted, "She gave him the credibility he needed among the tree huggers and their friends." The pair became known as the German equivalent of the Clintons, a political power couple who were young, attractive, and on the move.

As the premier of Lower Saxony, Schroder formed what was dubbed a "red-green coalition," a combination of the socialist SPD party and the environmentalist Green party. He became nationally known through his popularity with the public, rather than his leadership abilities within his party. In fact, he built a reputation as a leader unafraid to cross party lines, rather than one bound to ideology. Though he held to socialist programs such as nationalizing some failing industries, he was viewed as being more pro free-market than most Social Democrats, thus earning him the tag of the "German Tony Blair." Media-savvy and good-looking, many felt Schroder could be the new face of Germany.

In 1996, his marriage dissolved after Schroder became involved with Doris Kopt, a journalist who had a daughter out of wedlock while she was living in New York. The German media, normally rather stoic on such matters, turned the event into a circus. Hillu Schroder subsequently wrote a scathing exposé of the relationship accusing her ex-husband of being mean, egotistical, cowardly, and opportunistic. Schroder countered in the media, claiming that she tried to force him to become a vegetarian, a serious offense in a nation that enjoys eating meat. He managed to emerge with his popularity intact. Schroder married Kopf three weeks after his divorce in 1997. "I'm a constant guy," Schroder once quipped, according to Wosnitza in

*Maclean's*. "I may swap wives every 12 years, but I'm faithful in between." His fourth wife quickly remarked, "Next time, you'll need somebody to push your wheelchair."

## Challenged Kohl

Schroder won reelection as premier of Lower Saxony in March of 1998 with a populist platform. "It makes sense that politicians think of people's feelings," he once announced to a cheering crowd, according to Lucian Kim in the *Christian Science Monitor*. By that time, he made it clear that he wanted to challenge longtime incumbent, Helmut Kohl, in a bid for the chancellorship. The SPD, long the underdog to the Christian Democratic Union, had managed to gain seats in 1994 and saw a chance to finally topple Kohl. Schroder lobbied to win his party's nomination against Oskar Lafontaine, the SPD chair. Lafontaine was more dedicated to the party's leftist politics, but Schroder was more popular among German voters. Though some criticized his state's fast-growing debt and high unemployment, Schroder pointed out that he suppressed the rise in unemployment by saving jobs. Again, critics observed that his methods included costly government bailouts. Schroder replied to a crowd, "It's always better to invest in jobs than to invest in unemployment," according to Mary Williams Walsh in the *Los Angeles Times*.

Schroder was ahead in the opinion polls and continued to win fans with his brief, ten-minute speeches. "People don't want to listen to hour-long oratory anymore," he commented, according to Jordan Bonfante of *Time* magazine. In fact, most of Schroder's campaign was marked by his willingness to give the people what they wanted. Observers noted that his reticence to discuss specific issues made it impossible to determine what he really stood for. He would appeal to the working classes, but he also held the title of the "Comrade of Business" due to his willingness to forge relationships with heads of industry. He promised to continue social programs and reinstate the mild cuts in worker benefits that Kohl had made, but he also pledged to modernize policy in order to remain a global economic force. Schroder also tapped into voters' reluctance to usher in an unproven leader after living with Kohl for 16 years. Not entirely happy with the way their country was heading, especially in terms of the double-digit unemployment, the conservative Germans were nonetheless concerned that a change could be for the worse. As a result, the SPD developed the slogan, "We won't change everything—we'll just do things better."

Schroder unseated Kohl in September 1998, making him the first candidate to oust an incumbent chancellor since the end of World War II. He won by a surprisingly wide margin of about six percentage points in an election that saw 81.5 percent voter turnout. The Christian Democrats suffered their worst numbers in over 40 years, taking just 35 percent of seats in the *Bundestag*, while the Social Democrats reaped about 41 percent. This was not enough to give the SPD a majority, so Schroder was expected to form another "red-green" coalition with the Green Party, who earned 6.7 percent of the seats. This put Schroder under some scrutiny, as the Green Party consisted of both prag-matic and extremist wings. It was possible that their radical elements could strain the partnership.

Schroder faced a number of challenges upon taking office, including participating in the unification of Europe with a common monetary system, balancing social justice and fiscal concerns, establishing ties with France, and pro-moting economic development in Russia. He also faced the task of establishing a policy on immigration (the SPD has generally taken a liberal stance in accepting non-Germans), as well as battling the high unemployment rate, especially in the former East Germany.

## Further Reading

*Current Leaders of Nations,* Gale Research, 1999.
*Christian Science Monitor,* February 25, 1998; September 10, 1998; September 29, 1998.
*Daily Telegraph,* September 28, 1998.
*Dallas Morning News,* October 1, 1998.
*Economist,* February 17, 1996; August 29, 1998; October 3, 1998.
*European,* January 19, 1998.
*Independent,* September 20, 1998; September 28, 1998.
*Los Angeles Times,* February 28, 1998; October 4, 1998.
*Maclean's,* October 12, 1998.
*Minneapolis Star Tribune,* September 28, 1998; September 29, 1998; October 1, 1998.
*New Republic,* October 19, 1998.
*Newsweek,* October 12, 1998.
*St. Louis Post-Dispatch,* September 28, 1998.
*Sunday Telegraph,* January 25, 1998; September 20, 1998.
*Time International,* September 7, 1998; October 12, 1998. □

# Delmore Schwartz

**Poet and critic Delmore Schwartz (1913–1966) stunned the literary world with the breathtaking achievement of his first published volume in 1938, earning him adulation as "the American Auden." His early success raised critical expectations that Schwartz could never fulfill. Depression and alco-holism marked his later years. Through both his art and his tragic death, Schwartz influenced such liter-ary legatees as John Berryman and Robert Lowell.**

Delmore Schwartz was born in Brooklyn, New York on December 8, 1913. His parents, Harry and Rose (Nathanson) Schwartz, were immigrants from Romania, part of the first great wave of Jewish emi-gration from Eastern Europe. Harry Schwartz grew prosper-ous in the real estate business, enabling the couple to move to an affluent Brooklyn neighborhood. When their first son was born, they gave him a traditional Jewish middle name, David, but a first name, Delmore, they intended to sound sophisticated and "American." Always sensitive about his first name, Schwartz would later deal with the issue in his poetry. Rose Schwartz gave birth to a second child,

Kenneth, in 1916. Marital problems, caused in part by Harry Schwartz's philandering, plagued their relationship. The couple separated for a time in 1923.

A precocious child with a flair for mimicry, Delmore Schwartz nonetheless had a difficult time in grade school. His only good subject was English, because it engaged his active imagination. His parents' tumultuous marriage, which ended in divorce in 1927, gave the boy plenty of material for morose reflection. He spent his time writing about his feelings in a series of journals. Early in childhood, Schwartz decided to become a poet.

Teachers who read Schwartz's early writing encour-aged him to develop his talents. As a teenager, he began to identify with the European avant-garde. His early verses were published for the first time in the *Poet's Pack of George Washington High School* in 1929. That same year, Schwartz's family lost much of its savings in the stock market crash. His father died in June 1930. An unscrupulous executor embezzled the small amount of money that re-mained in hie estate after the collapse. At the age of 16, Delmore Schwartz was left practically penniless and with-out an inheritance. His mother now provided his only means of support

## College Years

After graduating from high school, Schwartz enrolled in a college prep course at New York's Columbia Univer-sity. In 1931, he transferred to the University of Wisconsin, where he was exposed to Marxist philosophy and the bohe-mian ethic. Schwartz did not apply himself too diligently to his studies, however, and he left the university in June 1932, without completing his final exams.

Schwartz returned to New York City and enrolled at New York University. Schwartz took courses in classical, analytical, and contemporary philosophy. He graduated with a bachelor's degree in philosophy in 1935. While at NYU, Schwartz and a group of fellow students founded *Mosaic,* a literary magazine devoted to Marxist aesthetics. Norman Macleod, R.P. Blackmur, and William Carlos Wil-liams were a few of the prominent poets and critics who had their work published in *Mosaic.* As editor, Schwartz used the publication as a vehicle to air his own critical opinions. His essays earned the attention of the New York literary community.

## Working Writer

After completing his undergraduate degree, Schwartz began graduate study in philosophy at Harvard University. He remained there for the better part of two years, but left without receiving any kind of degree. During that time, Schwartz continued to write poems and critical essays, including some well-received translations of the French symbolist poet, Arthur Rimbaud. His work was published in *Poetry* magazine, and he was awarded the Bowdoin Prize for best essay by a graduate student in the humanities. In 1936, his poem *Choosing Company* was published in *American Caravan* magazine. Schwartz later explained that this poem illustrated the two difficulties he struggled with in his work: "trying to make a dramatic image of an idea" and "trying to make dramatic poetry out of American speech."

During his second year at Harvard, Schwartz's mother informed him that she could no longer support him financially. So, in March 1937, Schwartz returned once more to New York City. He was now devoted to working full-time as a writer and critic. Later that year, editor James Laughlin included some of Schwartz's poems in his annual anthology *New Directions in Prose and Poetry*. Schwartz's criticism, fiction, and poetry also appeared in the pages of such eminent literary magazines as *Poetry* and *Partisan Review*.

## Rising Star

Although Schwartz had yet to publish his first collection of poems, he was already being singled out as one of America's most promising young writers. Critics likened him to W.H. Auden and Hart Crane. In 1938, he attempted to meet those lofty expectations with his debut collection *In Dreams Begin Responsibilities*. The book, whose title was inspired by a line from William Butler Yeats, included a short story and a play, alongside numerous poems. It was widely praised as an audacious mix of styles and forms, proof positive of Schwartz's virtuoso mastery of the language. "[N]o first book of this decade in American poetry has been more authoritative or more significant than this one," wrote critic G.M. O'Donnell in the pages of *Poetry* magazine.

Still only 25, Schwartz was now recognized as one of America's pre-eminent poets. In June 1938 he married Gertrude Buckman, a high school friend. The couple divorced six years later. Schwartz's lofty reputation suffered the following year, when his translation of Rimbaud's *A Season in Hell* was criticized for its many verbal and grammatical errors. A shame-faced Schwartz was forced to revise the translation for publication the following year.

## Literary Fixture

In 1940, Schwartz was appointed Briggs-Copeland Instructor in English Composition at Harvard. He was granted a Guggenheim Fellowship, a cash grant which allowed him the freedom to complete the manuscript of a new verse play, *Shenandoah*. The new work, which was published in 1941, examined the naming rites of a Jewish child in the Bronx. Reviews were mostly negative, causing some to question whether Schwartz would ever live up to the promise of *In Dreams Begin Responsibilities*.

Schwartz was named the poetry editor for the *Partisan Review* in 1943. He remained with the magazine for the next four years, using the influential position to publish the works of other young poets. Schwartz also continued to write his own poetry. His semi-autobiographical piece *Genesis: Book One*, intended as the first book of a multi-volume epic, was his most ambitious work to date. Critics responded unfavorably, however, causing Schwartz to doubt his own creative abilities.

A better reception greeted *The World Is A Wedding*, a collection of Schwartz's short stories which appeared in 1948. "In so far as authenticity means truth, these short stories are the most authentic I have read in a long time,"

declared critic John Hay in the pages of *Commonwealth*. Shortly before the book's publication, Schwartz stepped down from his teaching post at Harvard and gave up the editorship at *Partisan Review*. He retained the post of associate editor and lectured on a visiting basis at such institutions as New York University, Princeton University, and the University of Chicago. Schwartz married for the second time, to Elizabeth Pollett, in June 1949.

## Later Works

In 1950, Schwartz published his next major volume of poetry, *Vaudeville for a Princess and Other Poems*. The 56 poems reflected a prevailing sense of failure and regret, which some critics attributed to Schwartz's inability to live up to the potential of his earlier work. Whether he was disappointed in the critical response to this volume or not, Schwartz spent most of the next decade writing only occasionally for magazines and anthologies. In 1955, he left the *Partisan Review* to take over as poetry editor of the *New Republic*, where he remained until 1957. His marriage to Elizabeth Pollett ended in divorce in 1955.

A retrospective collection of Schwartz's work *Summer Knowledge: New and Selected Poems, 1938-1958* was published in 1959. More than half the poems in the collection were drawn from *In Dreams Begin Responsibilities*, with only three coming from *Vaudeville for a Princess and Other Poems*. Schwartz personally re-ordered and re-titled some of the poems, and included a few of his more recent efforts. For the most part, critics dismissed these newer works as embarrassingly sentimental and labored, but praised the collection as a whole.

Long out of critical fashion, Schwartz enjoyed a brief revival of his reputation in the early 1960s. *Summer Knowledge: New and Selected Poems, 1938-1958* received the Shelley Memorial Prize, earning Schwartz a $1100 award. In 1960, the poet was awarded the Bollingen Prize for Poetry, and with it a stipend of $2500. A second volume of Schwartz's short fiction, *Successful Love and Other Stories* appeared in 1961.

## Final Years

Despite these accolades, Schwartz remained a troubled, unhappy man. He believed that critical recognition had come too late to save his tattered reputation as a poet who had showed early promise, but failed to live up to it. He wrote very little during the final six years of his life. In place of poetry, Schwartz filled his life with a diet of liquor, barbiturates, and amphetamines. His physical and mental condition deteriorated precipitously. Friends and supporters repeatedly tried to steer Schwartz away from his chemical dependencies, but their efforts proved fruitless. Novelist Saul Bellow, a friend of Schwartz's, based the title character of his classic *Humboldt's Gift* on the despondent, ruined poet.

Schwartz's condition became so grave that he was repeatedly committed for psychiatric treatment at New York's Bellevue Hospital. He resisted all treatment, however, and in January 1966 he left home to take up lodging in a succession of dilapidated hotels across the state of New York. On the morning of July 11, 1966 Schwartz suffered a massive heart attack while riding an elevator in New York City. His body lay in the morgue for two days before being identified. Coroners later determined that a lethal mixture of alcohol and drugs probably caused the poet's death.

## Further Reading

Atlas, James, *Delmore Schwartz: The Life of an American Poet* Farrar, Straus, and Guroux, 1997.
Bawer, Bruce, *The Middle Generation: The Lives and Poetry of Delmore Schwartz, Randall Jarrell, John Berryman, and Robert Lowell* Archon Books, 1986.
McDougall, Richard, *Delmore Schwartz* Twayne, 1974.
Phillips, Robert S., *Letters of Delmore Schwartz* Ontario Review Press, 1984. □

# Maurice Sendak

**Award winning illustrator and author, Maurice Sendak (born 1928), has been a major force in the evolution of children's literature since 1960. He is considered by many critics and scholars to be the first artist to deal openly with the emotions of children in his drawings both in books and on the stage, in his opera and ballet sets and costumes. This ability to accurately depict raw emotion is what makes him so appealing to children.**

Most people born in the last half of the twentieth century have read at least one of the more than 80 children's books written or illustrated by Sendak. Some critics contend that his drawings depict emotions too strongly for children to handle. In spite of this criticism, he has won almost every major American and international award for children's books and has been a major influence on several generations of children's writers.

## A Sickly Child

Sendak was born in Brooklyn, New York on June 10, 1928. He was the youngest son of Phillip and Sarah Schindler Sendak, Polish immigrants from small Jewish villages outside of Warsaw. Along with his sister Natalle, and brother, Jack, he grew up in a poor section of Brooklyn. His family moved to a new apartment every time one of their landlords decided to paint because his mother could not stand the smell of fresh paint. Suffering from measles, double pneumonia, and scarlet fever between the ages of two and four, Sendak was very rarely allowed outside to play. Between the frequent moves and the many illnesses, he did not make many friends and spent most of his time in bed, watching the other children play.

To pass the time, Sendak drew pictures and read comic books. His favorite was Walt Disney's Mickey Mouse. When he was well enough, he and his parents attended the local movie houses. Occasionally his older sister would take him to Manhattan to see movies at the Roxy or Radio

City Music Hall. Films of the 1930s, including the Busby Berkeley musicals and Laurel and Hardy comedies, had a profound influence on some of his illustrations.

The other great influence on his young life was his background as the son of Jewish immigrants from Poland. A portrait of his bearded maternal grandfather, who had died before Sendak's birth, was a prominent memory, as were his parents' stories of life in Poland. His mother told of hiding in the basement during attacks by the Cossacks on her village, while his father shared memories of a more comfortable middle class life. Sendak developed a rather pessimistic view of life from his parents' tales, which found its way into many of his own stories. Though his family was not particularly religious, they did attend services on High Holy Days and lived in an immigrant Jewish neighborhood. These were the people who populated his first illustrations, which some reviewers criticized as being too European. According to Sendak in Lane's *Down the Rabbit Hole: Adventures and Misadventures in the Realm of Children's Literature,* ''There is not a book I have written or picture I have drawn that does not, in some way, owe [those neighborhood children] its existence.''

School proved difficult for the young Sendak. He was obese and sometimes stammered. Creativity was not encouraged. Sendak was not a particularly good student and only excelled in his art classes. At home, he and his brother Jack made up their own storybooks by combining newspaper photographs or comic strip segments with drawings they made of family members. Sendak's father had the ability to create wonderful, imaginative tales that sometimes lasted for several nights. Both boys inherited this storytelling gift which they would later use to create books of their own.

World War II contributed to Sendak's view of the world as a dark and frightening place. All of his aunts and uncles in Poland died in the Holocaust; Natalie's fiancé was killed; and Jack was stationed in the Pacific. Sendak spent the war years in high school, working on the school yearbook, literary magazine, and newspaper. After school, he worked at All-American Comics, drawing background details for the *Mutt and Jeff* comic strip.

The summer of 1946 to the summer of 1948 were the happiest two years in Sendak's young life. He worked in the warehouse of a Manhattan window-display company called Timely Service and lived away from home for the first time. Sendak met the kinds of people he had not known in Brooklyn—real artists, who considered their work for Timely Service just a job that allowed them to paint seriously at night.

After leaving his first full time job in 1948, Sendak and his brother Jack created models for six wooden mechanical toys in the style of German eighteenth-century lever-operated toys. They were designed to portray parts in nursery rhymes and fairy tales. Jack engineered the toys, and Sendak did the painting and carving. Natalie sewed the costumes. The brothers took the models to the F.A.O. Schwartz toy store, where the prototypes were admired but considered too expensive to produce. Richard Nell, the window-display director, was impressed with Sendak's talent and hired him as an assistant in the window display department. This enabled Sendak to earn a living in the daytime and attend the Art Student's League at night. He took classes in oil painting, life drawing, and composition. He also spent time in the children's book department studying the great nineteenth-century illustrators (George Cruikshank, Walter Crane, and Randolph Caldecott) as well as the new postwar European illustrators (Hans Fischer, Felix Hoffmann, and Alois Carigiet).

### Illustrated First Book

While at Schwartz, Sendak met Ursula Nordstrom, the distinguished children's book editor at Harper and Brothers. She liked his work and offered him the chance to illustrate his first book, Marcel Ayme's *The Wonderful Farm*. They formed a close relationship, which would last for many years. According to Sendak in *The Art of Maurice Sendak*, "My happiest memories, in fact, are of my earliest career, when Ursula was my confidante and best friend. She really became my home and the person I trusted most." Sendak's first great success as the illustrator for Ruth Krauss's award winning *A Hole Is to Dig* was arranged by Nordstrom. Sendak was able to give up his full time job at Schwartz, move into an apartment in Greenwich Village, and become a free-lance illustrator.

The years between 1951 and 1962 are considered by Sendak to be his apprenticeship. He illustrated as many books as he could and learned to be flexible and adapt his drawings to the style of the text. According to Sendak, "I was going to learn how to draw in a variety of styles. I think my books are identifiable, but they all look different be-

cause illustrators are secondary to the text. If you insist on being primary to the text, then you're are bad illustrator." His own books during this period were not outstanding, with the exception of *The Sign on Rosie's Door* written in 1960. He based Rosie on a real girl he knew from his old neighborhood, and created a model for the typical Sendak character: strong-willed, honest, and imaginative.

### Where the Wild Things Are

With the publication of *Where the Wild Things Are* in 1963, Sendak felt that he had ended his apprenticeship. His childhood experiences, years of illustrations for other authors' books, and psychoanalysis came together in the fantasies of Max, the boy in the story who is sent to bed without his supper, and the monsters he encounters in the world of the wild things. The story is rooted in the very real fears that children have of being left alone or not cared for by their parents. Many critics and child psychologists, such as Bruno Bettelheim, felt that the book was too scary for sensitive children. Sendak was vindicated when the book won the Caldecott Medal in 1964. In his acceptance speech, he said, ". . .from their earliest years children live on familiar terms with disrupting emotions, fear and anxiety are an intrinsic part of their everyday lives, they continually cope with frustrations as best they can. And it is through fantasy that children achieve catharsis. It is the best means they have for taming Wild Things."

Just as Sendak's life appeared to finally be on track, disaster struck. In 1967, he learned that his mother had developed cancer, he suffered a major coronary attack, and his beloved dog Jenny died. In spite of his troubles, he completed *In the Night Kitchen* in 1972. This book generated more controversy because he showed a boy in full frontal nudity. Librarians drew diapers over the child. "It's as if my book contains secret information that kids would be better off not knowing. This whole idea, of course, is ridiculous." Sendak moved to Ridgefields, Connecticut, in 1972. There he worked ten-hour days on other authors' books as well as his own. *Outside Over There*, which he considers one of his more significant books, was written during this period.

### Opera Beckoned

By 1980, Sendak felt that he had done all that he could in children's literature and was ready to try something new. He was invited to design the sets and costumes for the Houston Grand Opera's production of Mozart's *The Magic Flute*. This was a wonderful opportunity, since Mozart was Sendak's favorite composer. He designed sets that he called "subterranean and bedeviled." This began a long collaboration which included fourteen works, the latest being *Hansel and Gretel* in 1998. Children, lost and alone, who are ultimately rescued and returned to their parents was a perfect Sendak theme. In *TCI* Sendak explains, "My main purpose in doing this opera, and doing it now, at this age [69], is that I'm overwhelmed by the abuse of children. *Hansel and Gretel* is a powerful analogy to modern day child abandonment and cruelty, an opera about pertinent forms of neglect. To mount it in a cutesy German forest is to limit it. Why is the fairy tale so famous? Because it's ter-rifying.''

Sendak also designed sets for ballets, most notably *The Nutcracker*, which he rewrote to suit his own vision of the story, and his own *Where the Wild Things Are*. A shy man who dislikes crowds, Sendak rarely attends the opera or ballet himself.

Sendak sanctioned the first museum exhibit of his art at the Please Touch Museum in Philadelphia in 1995. Over-size characters from four of his most popular books, includ-ing *Where the Wild Things Are* are included in the permanent exhibit. He has also collaborated on films and television projects involving his work. Sendak will never be mistaken for Walt Disney. Through the years he has re-mained true to his vision of life as seen through the eyes of a child.

## Further Reading

*Dictionary of Literary Biography,* Gale, 1987.
*Amusement Business*, Nov. 18, 1996, p34.
*Dance Magazine* February, 1997, p. 124.
*Detroit News,* January 10, 1997, p. A5; October 20, 1997, p. B5.
*TCI*, April, 1998, p. 24.
*Contemporary Authors.* Gale, http://www.galenet.com (February 15, 1999). □

# Nawaz Sharif

**Nawaz Sharif (born 1949) led his party to victory and became the prime minister of Pakistan in 1990. Supporters claim his political success lay in his busi-ness background. While most of Pakistan's political players were of the landed elite, Sharif's family built its fortune on a steel smelting factory. He took full advantage of his industrialist credentials, using a lib-eral reformist stance to attract votes from the busi-ness class.**

Niam Nawaz Sharif was born in Lahore, Pakistan on December 25, 1949, one year after the new na-tion's founding. He came from a family of indus-trialists who made their fortune in the politically significant province of Punjab. His father and six uncles controlled and operated an iron foundry in Amritsar. Sharif graduated from the Government College of Lahore, a recruiting source for the civil service. He received his bachelor of law degree from the Punjab University Law College, also in Lahore. Sharif helped establish the Ittefaq Islamic Academy in Lahore, where students receive religious instruction in addi-tion to their secular training. A practicing Moslem, Sharif comes from a religious family and has said he would make the teaching of the *Koran*, the Moslem holy book, a compul-sory subject up to the secondary level.

Sharif and his male cousins expanded his father's iron foundry only to lose it to a 1972 nationalization policy launched by the former prime minister, Zulfikar Ali Bhutto.

It was re-established in 1977 as Ittefaq Industries in Lahore. The business was returned after Sharif developed political links with then-president, Mohammad Zia ul-Haq. It was General Zia who brought down Bhutto in 1975, executing him two years later on charges of conspiracy. By 1990, Ittefaq Industries was one of Pakistan's most affluent con-glomerates, with more than $450 million in annual reve-nues, up from about $16 million in 1981. It included the country's largest private steel mill, a sugar mill, and four textile factories. With upwards of ten thousand employees, Ittefaq has played a significant role in the development and growth of industry in Pakistan. It has likely influenced Sharif's political career and pro-business stance as well.

## Began Political Career

Sharif began his political career in the early 1980s, while serving as director of the Ittefaq Group of Industries. In 1981, Sharif was appointed finance minister of Punjab Prov-ince by the Zia government. He used his newfound political authority to promote his pro-business stance and presented four successive development-oriented budgets targeting the improvement of socio-economic conditions in rural areas. Sharif raised the appropriation of funds for the development of these rural areas to nearly 70 percent of the province's annual development program. Four years later, Sharif be-came the Punjab's chief minister in a general election. He now had a great deal of influence over the province's industrial and agricultural power.

When Zia was killed in a 1985 plane crash, Benazir Bhutto, daughter of former prime minister Zulfikar Ali

Bhutto, assembled a coalition government. Sharif fiercely opposed this act. As a result, he became a leader of the newly formed Islami-Jahmoree-Itehad (IJI), a rightist coalition led by the Moslem League. He won both national and provincial assembly seats in 1988 general elections. Sharif eventually vacated the national assembly seat and returned to his role as chief minister of Punjab. A dispute with Bhutto over the distribution of government funds in Punjab vaulted him into the national spotlight.

## Became Prime Minister

Sharif's perseverance and political clout placed him in the vanguard of Bhutto adversaries. He proceeded to crush Bhutto's Pakistan People's Party (PPP) in the October 1988 election. Sharif was elected a Member of Parliament in the October 24, 1990 general elections, after leading a ten-party Islamic Democratic Alliance (IDA), an affiliation of liberal groups and rightist Islamic militants. On November 3, he was nominated by the IJI as its candidate for the premiership and was soon after sworn in as Pakistan's new prime minister. For three months prior to his victory Pakistan's top generals, bureaucrats and business leaders had been systematically stripping Bhutto's PPP of nearly all political power.

Pakistan's transition to democracy was a difficult undertaking, but Sharif's election proved a turning point. After having endured a long history of military dictatorship, Pakistan had elected a politician without roots among the country's traditional power brokers, the landed aristocracy. Sharif's election marked a major shift in Pakistan's geopolitical balance of power toward a new generation of entrepreneurial elites.

Most of Sharif's reforms were aimed at deregulating and liberalizing the economy. He quickly dismantled the socialist-style economy by selling off inefficient and bankrupt state enterprises, opening the stock market to foreign capital, and loosening foreign exchange restrictions. He took criticism for bold initiatives, such as providing unemployed youths easy installment loans to run duty-free imported taxis. Sharif also launched legislation that would make the Islamic code the supreme law of Pakistan. But it was his economic reforms, such as the lifting of control on foreign exchange and the start of privatization, that won accolades and support from the World Bank and the International Monetary Fund.

## Ousted from Parliament

Sharif became the target of many of the traditional landed interests, including Bhutto, because his policies deeply affected Pakistan's political and economic power structure. But his ouster came with an attempt to weaken the power of President Ghulam Ishaq Khan. Sharif had long been considered compliant, willing to quietly take orders from the president, but the two had clashed over reports of corruption in Sharif's government. The president dismissed Sharif in April 1993, after months of political turmoil. Army troops surrounded the state-controlled radio and television stations shortly after dark. An hour later, the president dissolved parliament, accusing Sharif of corruption and mis-

management. Sharif's family business had allegedly grown in value by about 20 billion rupees during his 30-month term as prime minister. He was dismissed under Pakistan's controversial Eight Amendment, that gives the president the power to discharge an elected government. The corruption charges against Sharif were later proven to have been false, and the Supreme Court restored him. But he and Khan were eventually manipulated into resigning due to their continuing hostility toward each other.

Bhutto was elected prime minister once again and Sharif served as opposition leader during her rule. But on November 5, 1996, President Farooq Leghari removed Bhutto from office on charges of corruption. This gave Sharif the opportunity to regain power. He engineered his political resurgence by converting himself into a populist leader. An electorate tired of corruption, inflation, and unemployment found his simple, straightforward approach in the election campaign appealing. He claimed his Pakistan Muslim League (PML) government was intent on taking drastic action to restore the national economy, root out corruption, afford easy justice and job opportunities on merit, set healthy democratic traditions, and restore Pakistan's sullied reputation. "Pakistan needs now to project a new image in the world," Sharif told Reuters in a pre-election interview. "We have become a laughing stock where every time the president and prime minister are fighting one another. This must now come to an end."

## Re-elected in Landslide Victory

On February 17, 1997, Sharif led the PML to a landslide victory (177–16), crushing Bhutto in the process. Sharif's Muslim League won a decisive parliamentary victory, winning 134 seats in the 217-seat parliament. Bhutto's PPP was second, winning 18 seats. The PML commanded around 165 seats when combined with its small-party allies, giving it a solid working majority. He stepped into office with the responsibility of reviving a crisis-laden economy. Domestically, Sharif was faced with boosting an economy plagued by budget deficits, 30 billion dollars of foreign debts, high inflation, and a nation with very high expectations for relief and a clean administration. On foreign affairs, he faced tensions with India and festering dissension in Afghanistan.

After retaking Parliament's highest seat, Sharif intended to focus on removing the obstacles blocking the economic development of Pakistan, namely corruption. But his endeavors were brought to a standstill by terrorist acts committed during the first six months of 1997. These acts forced Sharif to reevaluate his agenda, and he began to concentrate on establishing law and order. One of his first acts was to dismiss members of his own government, including a chief minister who belonged to Sharif's PML party.

Sharif has spent a great deal of his administration embroiled in a nuclear arms race with India. Estimates have placed Pakistan's nuclear arsenal of uranium at 200 kilograms, enough for 15 to 25 bombs. Sharif made an effort to allay Western fears of further expansion of its stockpile and possible nuclear weapons trading in a *U.S. News and World Report* article. "We have not and will not transfer sensitive technology to other states or entities," he was reported to have said. But it was feared that possible sanctions against the country would create an incentive. Pakistan was later condemned by the world for testing its nuclear weapons in an underground blast in June 1998.

Sharif has proven his ability to emerge as a strong leader. His first ousting marked the most important point in his career, by showing the skeptics that he wouldn't crumble under pressure. His stint as opposition leader and his eventual comeback affirmed that he could gain popular support on his own rather that with the backing of the army and bureaucracy. In his 1999 address to the nation cited in the *BBC Summary of World Broadcasts,* Sharif declared, ''I have neither hankered after power before nor is it my goal today. My goal is to make Pakistan a strong nation. My mission is to ensure our people's prosperity and to build a magnificent future for our youth.''

## Further Reading

*Agence France Presse,* February 17, 1997.
*BBC Summary of World Broadcasts,* February 22, 1999.
*Defense & Foreign Affairs' Strategic Policy,* February, 1999.
*Deutsche Presse-Agentur,* February 1, 1997.
*New Republic,* March 31, 1997, pp. 14-15.
*New York Times,* April 19, 1993.
*Reuters World Service,* February 2, 1997.
*U.S. News & World Report,* June 8, 1998, pp. 37-38.
*Xinhua General Overseas News Service,* November 6, 1990. □

# William Shawn

**During a career with the *New Yorker* magazine that spanned more than 50 years, William Shawn (1907–1992) shaped its distinctive content and style, influencing writers across the U.S. and helping to mold public opinion on important issues of the day.**

Described by a reporter for *Time* magazine as ''a quiet tyrant of talent and taste,'' William Shawn made his mark as the longtime editor of the *New Yorker,* a weekly publication known for witty cartoons, quality fiction, trend-setting nonfiction, and thoughtful social commentary. Nothing on its pages escaped Shawn's careful attention; his painstaking attention to detail and unwavering commitment to truth, logic, and clarity were legendary. So, too, was his gentle, courtly, and self-effacing demeanor, which endeared him to his staff. As an anonymous *New Yorker* staff member declared upon Shawn's death, ''No editor ever ruled a large and complex magazine as absolutely as he ruled this one; yet no editor, perhaps, ever imparted to so many writers and artists as powerful a sense of freedom and possibility.''

## A Comfortable Childhood

A native of Chicago, Illinois, William Shawn was the youngest of six children born on August 31, 1907 to Benjamin W. Chon, a salesman, and his wife, Anna Bransky Chon, both non-observant Jews of Eastern European origin.

(Early in his writing career, Shawn followed in the footsteps of one of his older brothers and changed the spelling of his surname.) Benjamin Chon was a self-made man who had started out as a street peddler and worked his way up to become the owner of a successful jewelry and cutlery store. He prospered along with the city's burgeoning meat packing industry during the early part of the twentieth century. As a result, he and his family enjoyed a comfortable life on the city's South Side.

The Chon household was a lively and happy one. All of the children took music lessons. William's instrument of choice was the piano; he subsequently developed into an above-average jazz pianist. He also liked sports, particularly baseball. Serious and shy, he was the quietest and most sensitive of his siblings and, as the youngest, he was smothered with attention. He was especially close to his mother, who was very protective of him, even more so after he survived a bout of scarlet fever during his teens.

## Left College to Become a Writer

In 1925, after completing his secondary education at a Chicago-area private school, Shawn headed off to the University of Michigan. Campus life was not to his liking, however, and he dropped out early in his junior year. On the recommendation of one of his English professors, he decided to do some writing. Seeking a bit of adventure and a more hospitable climate, Shawn moved to Las Vegas, New Mexico. There, he turned out a few pieces of fiction, none of which he was able to sell to the magazines he contacted. To earn a living, he began working as a reporter for the local newspaper, the *Optic.*

Shawn remained with the *Optic* for about six months before returning to Chicago. He soon found a job with the Hearst-owned *International Illustrated News,* writing captions and headlines for photographs and sending them out by wire to newspapers around the country. In September 1928, he married a fellow journalist named Cecille Lyon. Several months later they journeyed to Paris on a delayed honeymoon financed by Shawn's father. They remained in Europe for nearly a year, arriving back in the United States not long before the stock market crashed in October 1929.

During the early years of the Depression, Shawn worked as a free-lance writer, producing advertising copy and even some short stories that were published in the *Chicago Daily News* under a pseudonym. By 1932, however, there was no such work to be had in Chicago. He and his wife then moved to New York, where he hoped to try his luck as a songwriter. Unsuccessful at that, Shawn found a job writing publicity for J. C. Penney. That did not last long either. By the end of the year, he was once again unemployed.

## Joined the *New Yorker* Staff

Cecille Shawn had begun picking up some free-lance writing assignments from the *New Yorker,* which she promptly turned over to her husband to complete. This subterfuge continued until Shawn was officially hired in 1933 as a reporter for the publication's ''Talk of the Town'' section. Within two years, having demonstrated his conscientiousness and outstanding organizational skills, he was promoted to associate editor. In this role, Shawn was responsible for developing story and art ideas and writing captions.

In 1939, Shawn was named managing editor. Over the next dozen years, he worked in tandem with its founder and editor, Harold Ross. The legendary Ross was Shawn's opposite personality-wise but his spiritual soul mate in editorial matters. While Ross could be loud, melodramatic, and tactlessly blunt in his dealings with others, Shawn was mild-mannered, soft-spoken, exceedingly patient, and unfailingly courteous. He routinely addressed everyone—even people he had known for years—as "Mr.," "Miss," or "Mrs."; he in turn was always respectfully and affectionately known as "Mr. Shawn." This helped create a certain distance between him and his colleagues; indeed, as one who never shared a personal observation of any kind, he remained in many ways a rather mysterious figure. He was also mildly eccentric, with a phobic dislike of crowds, fast driving, self-service elevators, and air conditioning.

However, both Ross and Shawn shared an ardent enthusiasm for their work and spent long hours striving to make each issue of the *New Yorker* the absolute best it could be. As managing editor, Shawn presided over the fact-checking department for nonfiction pieces, establishing and maintaining rigorously high standards for accuracy and thoroughness that mirrored Ross's own passionate devotion to clarity and truth. "No 'fact' was ever taken for granted, if it could be independently verified," recalled William F. Buckley, Jr., in a *National Review* article in which he reminisced about his relationship with Shawn.

It was while serving as managing editor that Shawn began cultivating extremely close professional ties with a number of distinguished writers whose work appeared regularly in the pages of the *New Yorker*. After the Second World War, he greatly expanded this group and made some of them staff writers, paying each one a salary and providing office space as well.

### Named Editor of the *New Yorker*

In 1952, shortly after Ross's death, Shawn was named to succeed him as editor of the *New Yorker*. It was a post he held for the next 35 years, a remarkably long tenure in a business known for its frequent and sometimes turbulent comings and goings. Over time, his stature eclipsed that of his former boss, and the *New Yorker* reigned as the nation's preeminent magazine of literary and social commentary, particularly during the 1960s and 1970s.

Under Ross's direction, the *New Yorker* had provided its readers—mainly sophisticated, upper-middle-class residents of New York and its suburbs—with witty, occasionally caustic, observations on modern life through a mix of cartoons, straight reporting, and short fiction, most of it produced by a number of trend-setting writers. Shawn broadened and deepened this vision, ultimately changing the magazine "from a smarty-pants parish tip sheet into a journal that altered our experience instead of just posturing in front of it," according to *New York Times* book critic John

Leonard. While the humor remained, especially in the much-admired cartoons, serious fiction and reflective journalism assumed a more prominent role.

With Shawn at the helm, the *New Yorker* tackled a variety of controversial issues, including the environment, racial prejudice, poverty, war, and nuclear proliferation. As Philip Hamburger (himself a longtime contributor to the magazine) observed in a *New Leader* article, "He reached out to writers everywhere. No idea seemed alien to this man." In fact, many now-classic titles debuted in their entirety or were excerpted in the pages of the *New Yorker*.

### Attracted Stellar Contributors

Many important works appeared in the *New Yorker* during Shawn's tenure as editor. They include: *Eichmann in Jerusalem*, Hannah Arendt's report on the trial of the famous Nazi war criminal; *Silent Spring*, Rachel Carson's warning about the use of chemical pesticides and their impact on the environment; *In Cold Blood*, Truman Capote's ground-breaking blend of fact and fiction that chronicled the vicious killings of a Kansas family; and several essays on race by James Baldwin that were eventually collected in his book *The Fire Next Time*. Also appearing regularly in the *New Yorker* were film reviews by Pauline Kael, baseball articles by Roger Angell, and short fiction by John Updike, J. D. Salinger, and John Cheever, and many others.

For the most part, the writers Shawn collaborated with adored him and gave him credit for sharpening their focus and otherwise improving their skills. He was a meticulous editor with an intuitive understanding of writing and sympathy for the way writers were inclined to think and work. He reportedly read every single word that appeared in the *New Yorker* at least three times—in the manuscript stage, in galleys, and in page proofs. Ever so tactfully, he then led writers through a reading of their own texts, subtly emphasizing what he felt needed to be reworked or clarified in some way. "His style was to cause the author to acquiesce in the change, rather than to dictate the change," explained Buckley.

### *New Yorker* Sold to Media Empire

In 1985, the *New Yorker* was sold to Advance Publishing, part of a huge, family-owned media conglomerate headed by S. I. Newhouse. The literary world was soon abuzz with speculation about the fate of the magazine's 77-year-old editor and who might succeed him. Several names periodically surfaced as candidates for the post, but Shawn showed little inclination to retire, and Newhouse made no move to get rid of him.

The *New Yorker* continued along despite mounting criticism that it had grown stodgy and that its busy urban audience had neither the time nor the desire to read the extremely long and often demanding articles and stories that typically filled its pages. This was reflected in its declining circulation numbers and a drop in advertising revenues during the mid-1980s. But such business concerns held no interest for Shawn, who was totally absorbed in editorial matters. In fact, according to Joseph Nocera in the *New Republic*, Shawn pointed out shortly after Newhouse bought the *New Yorker* that he had "never published anything in order to sell magazines, to cause a sensation, to be controversial, to be popular or fashionable, to be 'successful.'"

## Forced Resignation

The end came in early 1987, when Newhouse forced a reluctant Shawn to quit and announced that his replacement would be Robert Gottlieb, the president and editor-in-chief at another Newhouse company, the New York-based book publisher Alfred A. Knopf. The news immediately sparked an angry revolt among more than 150 members of the *New Yorker* staff. They not only objected to what they regarded as Newhouse's shabby treatment of Shawn but also his refusal to appoint an insider to the job. (Gottlieb had never worked for the magazine.)

Their complaints fell on deaf ears, however, and Shawn quietly left his office for the last time on February 13, 1987. In a poignant farewell letter to his colleagues, he briefly reflected on his legacy, stating that out of love and a desire to discover and print the truth "we have built something quite wonderful together." He then resumed his own long-neglected writing and also accepted a position as an editor for the publisher Farrar, Strauss & Giroux, where he remained until his death from a heart attack on December 8, 1992 in New York City, at the age of 85.

Like his departure from the *New Yorker* several years earlier, Shawn's passing did not completely erase his presence from the magazine he had served so devotedly. He lives on in its pages and elsewhere, if only in the work of those writers he once nurtured. "Whatever we were when we came into his orbit, we became something more under his influence," asserted Gardner Botsford in a tribute piece to Shawn published in the *New Yorker*. "He sharpened our thinking, brought us sternly back from our vacant musings, oiled our transitions, and turned us into professionals of a greater competence than we would ever have achieved on our own." By fulfilling such an important role, declared an anonymous commentator in the pages of the same magazine, Shawn "became, while scarcely ever writing a word over his own name, one of the commanding figures of twentieth-century American letters."

## Further Reading

Mehta, Ved, *Remembering Mr. Shawn's New Yorker: The Invisible Art of Editing,* Overlook Press, 1998.
*Atlantic Monthly,* April 1998.
*National Review,* January 18, 1993.
*New Leader,* July 13, 1992.
*New Republic,* January 25, 1993.
*Newsweek,* March 14, 1983; January 26, 1987; December 21, 1992.
*New York,* January 26, 1987.
*New Yorker,* December 21, 1992; December 28, 1992/January 4, 1993; February 20, 1995.
*New York Times,* July 14, 1987; December 9, 1992.
*Time,* January 26, 1987; December 21, 1992. □

# Cindy Sherman

**Cindy Sherman (born 1954) used photography to challenge images in popular culture and the mass media. Her work concentrated on examining the way women are viewed by society. She used herself as a model in the 1977-1980 series of 69 black-and-white photographs called "Untitled Film Stills." Sherman's later series included themes of pornography, Old Master paintings, and fairy tales, as well as dismembered medical dummies in graphic poses.**

C ynthia Morris Sherman was born in Glen Ridge, New Jersey, on January 19, 1954 and was raised in suburban Long Island, New York. Her father's hobby was collecting cameras and taking family photos. As a child Sherman spent a lot of time playing dress-up, an activity that she later used in her work. In 1972, Sherman enrolled at the State University College at Buffalo, New York, as an art education major, where she began studying painting. Sherman painted self-portraits and realistic images she found in magazines and photographs. She failed her introductory photography course because of difficulty with the technological aspects of print-making.

## Introduced to Conceptual Art

In 1975, Sherman was introduced to conceptual art, which had a liberating effect on her. She returned to her childhood love of dress-up in her work, spending many hours trying to transform her appearance. She would then go out so that others could see her "work." Sherman now saw the potential of using photography to unleash her creativity. In 1975, she produced a series entitled "Cutouts" in which she was the character in her made up plot. She then took the photographs and cut them out and arranged them on paper panels. These works were included in an exhibit of New York artists. By the end of her second photography class, Sherman realized she would never paint again.

Upon graduation in 1977, at the age of 23, Sherman moved to New York City. She continued her role-playing and began photographing herself in her apartment, outdoors in New York City, on Long Island, and in the Southwest. Sherman shot most of the photographs, but family and friends took others. She posed in a repertoire of images familiar from popular culture. The prints were small black-and-whites. There were 69 photographs in the series, entitled "Untitled Film Stills," which Sherman created between 1977 and 1980.

Sherman's characters in the "Untitled Film Stills" were not specified, allowing viewers to construct their own narratives. She encouraged viewer participation by hinting, through the poses, that she was the object of someone's gaze. Her film stills looked and functioned just like real film stills, 8 x 10 inch glossies designed to lure the viewer into a drama, made all the more compelling because they were not real. "She's good enough to be a real actress," said pop artist Andy Warhol in comments included at the web site of the Museum of Modern Art in New York.

The entire series was first exhibited at the Hirshhorn Museum in Washington, DC, in 1995. It depicted the different identities that women have held since World War II. Similar characters appear in several photographs, forming mini-series within the larger group. The first six images depicted the same blond actress at different points in her career. In each shot, Sherman was alone, a familiar but unidentifiable film heroine in an appropriate setting. The portrayals included a floozy in a slip with a martini, a perky B-movie librarian, a secretary in the city, a voluptuous, a working class woman from an Italian neo-realist film, an innocent runaway, and a *film noir* victim. In some images, Sherman appears as a seductress. Amanda Cruz in *Cindy Sherman: Retrospective,* quotes Sherman as saying "to pick a character like that was about my own ambivalence about sexuality—growing up with the women role models that I had, and a lot of them in films, that were like that character, and yet you were supposed to be a good girl." Through her work, she asked viewers to question the way media images influence our ideas about gender roles.

At the *Masters of Photography* website, critic Lisa Philips is quoted as saying that Sherman's photographs "project a . . . mixture of desire, anticipation, victimization, and suffering," and as a photographer she deflected the gaze of the viewer away from her subject and "toward reproduction itself, forcing the viewers to recognize their own conditioning." Sherman's use of photography is predicated on the uses and functions of photography in the mass media, in advertising, fashion, movies, pinups, and magazines. Cruz said "Cindy Sherman began her now famous series "Untitled Film Stills" twenty years ago, at the end of 1977. Those small, black-and-white photographs of Sherman impersonating various female character types from old B movies and *film noir* spoke to a generation of baby boomer women who had grown up absorbing those glamorous images on television, taking such portrayals as cues for their future. With each subsequent series of photographs, Sherman imitated and confronted assorted representational tropes, exploring the myriad ways in which women and the body are depicted by effective contemporary image-makers, including the mass media and historical sources such as fairy tales, portraiture, and surrealist photography."

As early as 1979, articles about Sherman's work appeared in *Arts Magazine* and *October.* In nearly ten years she had over 30 one-person shows at prestigious museums and galleries in the U.S. and abroad. Over 100 articles in such publications as *Life,* the *Village Voice, Vogue, Art Forum* and the *Wall Street Journal* have featured Sherman and her work.

### Work Changed in Tone

In 1981, Sherman opened her first one-person show. As the 1980s progressed, her style began to change, becoming much darker. While Sherman worked for a clothing line, she produced photos that included very bizarre characters and poses. In the series "Fairy Tales," the typical images of fairy tales were replaced with death and decay. Monsters and beings with grotesque body parts exaggerated the male and female stereotypes in Western art. Sherman looked at the violence and horror in fairy tales and their sexual underpinnings.

"Sex Pictures" contained grotesque and surreal images created with mannequins and prosthetic devices. In Sherman's most graphic photos, she began to use body parts found at medical schools and incorporated them into her pictures. These body parts were intended to question the sexual tendencies of our culture.

Sherman turned to Old Master paintings for further inspiration, and created a series of photographs in which she was dressed as figures in famous works by Caravaggio, Raphael, and others. These photographs crossed the boundaries between postmodern playfulness and the exploration of self through portraiture. "Historical Portraits" is a photographic series devoted to reinventing classical high art using large color photographs. "Salome and the head of John the Baptist" was an important scene for the Symbolists of the late 1800s. Most artists painted this scene. Sherman also tried her hand at this subject. Her image "Untitled #228" shows Salome holding a knife and the severed head of a wrinkled old man.

"Untitled #204" is a photograph based on Jean Auguste Dominique Ingres' "Madame Moitessier." Ingres painted a middle-age woman reclining on a couch, dressed formally with elegant bracelets and a necklace. Sherman's interpretation is quite different. The face of Sherman's Madame is bruised and the clothes and jewelry are less elegant. Sherman juxtaposes how women were depicted in art with how women are actually treated. In one photo, Sherman exposes milk-swollen (plastic) breasts and holds a (false) pregnant belly under a shawl.

### "Untitled Film Stills" Bought for $1 Million

In 1978, Sherman received a National Endowment for the Arts fellowship. She also was given a MacArthur "genius grant" in 1995. The art market crash of the 1990s spared her, unlike many contemporaries. In December 1995, the Museum of Modern Art purchased the complete "Untitled Film Stills" for a reported $1 million, and exhibited the collection in 1997. The purchase insured that this landmark body of work would be preserved in its entirety in a single public collection.

Joining artist-directors like Robert Longo, Julian Schnabel, and David Salle, Sherman was signed in 1996 by Miramax to direct a low-budget film about an office worker turned serial killer.

Sherman's photographs can be found in a large number of museum collections and private galleries. Her work has been shown at the Ansel Adams Center of Photography in San Francisco and at A Gallery in New Orleans, but most of her showings are held in New York City. "Cindy Sherman: Retrospective" was exhibited at Chicago's Museum of Contemporary Art, in 1998. The show also traveled to Prague, London, Bordeaux, Sydney, and Toronto. Sherman lives in

New York and continues to produce personal work as well as commercial commissions.

## Further Reading

Schjeldahl, Peter, *Cindy Sherman,* Pantheon, 1984.
Smith, Elizabeth A. T., Amelia Jones, and Amanda Cruz, *Cindy Sherman: Retrospective,* Thames & Hudson, 1997.
"Cindy Sherman," *Elsa Dorfman Photography Reviews,* http://elsa.photo.net/cindy.htm (April 13, 1999).
"Cindy Sherman," *Masters of Photography,* http://www.masters-of-photography.com/S/sherman/sherman.html (April 13, 1999).
"Cindy Sherman," *The Eli Broad Family Foundation,* http://www.broadartfdn.org/bio-shermanb.html (April 13, 1999). □

# Walter Short

**Walter Short (1880–1949) commanded the Hawaiian Department of the United States Army when the Japanese launched a surprise attack at Pearl Harbor on December 7, 1941. The attack came as a complete surprise and inflicted perhaps the most decisive defeat ever suffered by U.S. forces. Short was held responsible and forced to retire from the military.**

Walter Campbell Short was born in the rural Illinois town of Fillmore on March 30, 1880. As the son of a physician, he enjoyed a comfortable upbringing. Short attended the University of Illinois, graduating in 1901. He then obtained a position as teacher of mathematics at the Western Military Academy for one year before accepting a commission in the U.S. Army in March 1902.

Short's progress through the military hierarchy was unremarkable but fairly impressive for a peacetime period. After a brief stint at the Presidio in San Francisco, California, he spent a five-year period with the 25th Infantry Division, based at Ft. Reno, Oklahoma. During this time, Short became acquainted with George Marshall, who would later become Army chief of staff during World War II. Short was posted overseas to the U.S. territory of the Philippines in 1907-1908 and then served with commands in Nebraska, California, and the territory of Alaska. He received promotions to the posts of secretary of the Army School of Musketry and commander in the 12th Infantry Division at Ft. Sill, Oklahoma, in the fall of 1914. He married in November of that year.

Short's first action assignment was with the 16th Infantry Division during the U.S. pursuit of Pancho Villa in Mexico in March 1916. Following this operation, he was assigned to train troops in the use of small arms and was subsequently transferred to Georgia. Upon the U.S. entry into World War I in 1917, Short went to France with the 1st Infantry Division, where he served with distinction as a staff officer and received the Distinguished Service Medal for his work in the development of machine gun tactics and the

training of machine gunners. Short saw combat in several of the largest battles involving U.S. forces during that war and was promoted to the temporary wartime rank of lieutenant colonel. In April 1918, Short was transferred to the training section of the Army General Staff, the position in which he served until war's end in November.

Immediately after the war, Short was named the assistant chief of staff for training in the Third Army. He was transferred to Ft. Leavenworth, Kansas in 1919 to become an instructor in the Army General Services School. Shortly thereafter, Short's temporary promotion expired, and he was reassigned with the rank of captain as the assistant chief of staff for operations and supply of the 6th Division, based in Illinois.

Short's slow but steady progress continued in the 1920s. He was promoted to major in July 1920, and completed the Army School of the Line the following year. In 1922, Short published a military textbook on machine gun use and tactics. He served in the Far Eastern Section of the Military Intelligence Division from 1920 until 1923. Following this service, Short was promoted to lieutenant colonel and attended the Army War College, from which he graduated in 1925. He served as an instructor at the Army Command and General Staff School at Ft. Leavenworth from 1928 until 1930. He was assistant chief of insular affairs and an officer in the Sixth Infantry Division at Jefferson Barracks, Missouri, before becoming assistant commandant of the Army Infantry School at Ft. Benning, Georgia. Short was promoted to brigadier general in December 1936. He took command of the Second Infantry Brigade at Ft. Ontario,

New York in February 1938. He was reassigned to command of the First Infantry Brigade at Ft. Wadsworth in June 1938, becoming commander of a larger force, the First Infantry Division, in 1939. Short received a further promotion, to major general, in 1940 and was reassigned to Columbia, South Carolina. He was selected to command a corps during army maneuvers later in the year.

In February 1941, Short's old acquaintance George Marshall, now Army chief of staff, appointed him to command the Army's Hawaiian Department and promoted him to the temporary rank of lieutenant general. In this position, Short was responsible for the ground defense of the Hawaiian Islands and jointly responsible with the U.S. Navy for the Islands' aerial defense.

On the eve of World War II, Short had enjoyed a successful military career. He had extensive experience as a staff and training officer, and some experience as a commander of troops. His rise through the ranks had been steady and somewhat rapid given the peacetime stagnation of the U.S. armed forces.

## Pearl Harbor

In the fall of 1941, tensions between the Japanese, the United States, and the European powers in the Pacific were reaching the breaking point. Code breakers in the United States were able to decode significant portions of Japanese diplomatic and naval communications, and were certain that an attack would be forthcoming. As such, war warnings were issued to all commanders in the Pacific, including Short and Admiral Kimmel on November 27, 1941. Short misinterpreted the message, which was vague in recommending a course of action to field commanders, as a warning to guard against sabotage of his forces by local Japanese sympathizers. The Japanese attacked Pearl Harbor on December 7, 1941, achieving complete surprise and inflicting perhaps the most decisive defeat ever suffered by U.S. forces.

The defeat at Pearl Harbor spurred the U.S. to enter World War II and fueled a national passion for revenge that would contribute to the eventual defeat of Japan. It also created feelings of shock and shame as armed forces personnel, government officials, and civilians wondered how American forces could have been surprised so completely, given the universally recognized tense political climate in the Pacific in the days prior to the raid. In such an atmosphere, the search for scapegoats was inevitable, and General Short and Admiral Kimmel were the most obvious targets for blame.

## Aftermath

On December 16, 1941, President Roosevelt appointed a commission to investigate the events leading up to the defeat at Pearl Harbor, and he relieved both Kimmel and Short of their commands on December 18. The commission's report, issued in January 1942, cited both Hawaiian commanders for errors in judgment and authorized Chief of Staff Marshall to retire them from active service. Marshall acted upon this recommendation. Short was demoted to the rank of major general and forced to retire on

February 28, 1942. He was not allowed to testify in his own behalf during these proceedings.

A military inquiry into the defeat also began early in 1942 and came to its conclusion in October 1944. This inquiry found Short responsible in part for the lack of preparation at Pearl Harbor, but also found fault with Chief of Staff Marshall for issuing vague and contradictory orders regarding preparations for war with Japan.

After his retirement from the military, Short took a position as a traffic manager for the Ford Motor Company in Dallas, Texas, where he remained until 1946. At that time he was able to testify before a congressional committee investigating the Pearl Harbor battle. In his testimony, Short argued that important information that could have averted the surprise had been withheld from him by both political and military agencies. He also freely admitted personal errors in judgment that had made the defeat more decisive than it otherwise would have been. Despite his testimony, the congressional committee concluded that Short and Kimmel were responsible for the defeat.

## Verdict of History

In the years since the disaster at Pearl Harbor, historians have found less fault with Short and Kimmel than did their peers. Preparedness orders issued by Marshall on November 27, 1941, were indeed vague. These orders led to Short's decision to bunch his aircraft on the ground making them easier to defend against sabotage by local Japanese sympathizers, but also easy targets for the military attackers. Revisionists have also postulated that President Roosevelt knew where and when the Japanese attack would occur and deliberately withheld this information from Short to ensure that they would attack and draw the U.S. into the war. Although code breakers in the U.S. knew that an attack was coming somewhere in the Pacific near the end of 1941, there is no hard evidence to verify that anyone knew that the attack would fall on Hawaii or any other U.S. territory. Furthermore, there is plentiful evidence that Marshall and Roosevelt were as shocked as everyone else when Pearl Harbor was attacked, although neither one may have regretted the subsequent U.S. entry into the war. Finally, it must be noted that the potential of naval aviation was grossly underrated by virtually all military establishments in 1941, and that many Japanese admirals opposed the Pearl Harbor raid on the basis that naval aircraft would not be able to decisively defeat a land or surface force.

As Gordon Prange so aptly stated in *Pearl Harbor: The Verdict of History,* "One may sympathize with Short, understand his motives, and agree that Washington (DC) did not give him all the facts in its possession. But these things cannot mitigate the fact that Short failed in the event for which his whole professional life had been a preparation. He was a good man and a competent general who meant all his actions for the best. However, according to the adage, the road to hell is paved with good intentions. And the private hell in which Short spent the rest of his life had at least some paving stones of his own quarrying." Short died in Dallas, Texas, on March 9, 1949.

**Further Reading**

*Dictionary of American Biography,* edited by John A. Garrity, Charles Scribners' Sons, 1974.
*Dictionary of American Military Biography,* edited by Roger J. Spiller, Greenwood Press, 1984.
*Illustrated World War II Encyclopedia,* edited by Peter Young, H. S. Stuttman, 1978.
Prange, Gordon W., *Pearl Harbor: The Verdict of History,* McGraw-Hill, 1986. □

# Eunice Kennedy Shriver

**Eunice Kennedy Shriver (born 1920) was one of the founders of the Special Olympics, which provided physical training and competition to mentally challenged athletes. She worked tirelessly to improve the quality of life for mentally challenged people and to provide them with opportunities to achieve, to become productive citizens, and to be respected members of their communities.**

S hriver was one of nine children born to Rose and Joseph Kennedy on July 10, 1920, in Brookline, Massachusetts. In her wealthy and politically powerful family, public service was an honored tradition. One of her brothers, John F. Kennedy, became president of the United States; two others, Robert F. and Edward M. Kennedy, were U.S. senators. All the Kennedy children were expected to compete and excel. Harrison Rainie and John Quinn, in their book *Growing Up Kennedy: The Third Wave Comes of Age,* quoted her as saying, "The important thing was win— don't come in second or third, that doesn't count—but win, win, win."

Most of the children followed this advice, entering public service or other competitive occupations. One child, however, did not. Shriver's sister, Rosemary, was born with mild mental retardation. As time went on and the children grew up, it became more and more apparent to the entire family, and perhaps to Rosemary herself, that she would never be able to keep up with her siblings. Gradually, Rosemary became more difficult to handle, hitting people and smashing things and, on one occasion, attacking her grandmother.

Rosemary underwent brain surgery in an effort to make her more calm. According to Peter Collier and David Horowitz in *The Kennedys: An American Drama,* the operation did reduce her rage, but it "made her go from being mildly retarded to very retarded." Rosemary, now unable to function except at a very childlike level, needed constant care. Joe and Rose Kennedy decided to commit their daughter to St. Coletta's, an institution in Wisconsin.

Everyone in the family was affected by Rosemary's condition; they all became more aware of the needs of mentally challenged people. Shriver, in particular, saw that mentally challenged people can often accomplish quite a lot. "Of all the family," Rainie and Quinn remarked, "Eunice is the one who has been the most attentive to seeing and occasionally caring for Rosemary."

## A Sense of Social Justice

Shriver was a devoted Catholic and had a strong sense of social justice. When she was 26, she ran a juvenile agency. Later she lived in a West Virginia prison so that she could understand the prisoners' lives. When prisoners were let out on work release, she welcomed them to her home, even after one of them robbed her. Shriver married R. Sargent Shriver, founder of the Peace Corps and U.S. ambassador to France. He shared her religious views as well as her sense of social responsibility and commitment to helping mentally challenged people.

Shriver's brother, President John F. Kennedy, also had a vision of helping mentally challenged people and their families. In 1961, Shriver helped to establish the Presidential Committee on Mental Retardation. In a news conference on October 11, 1961, Kennedy said, "This condition strikes those least able to protect themselves from it. . . . At one time, there was practically no effective program in the field of mental retardation. Whenever possible, the children were committed to institutions. They were segregated from normal society and forgotten, except by members of their family. . . . They suffered from lack of public understanding and they suffered from lack of funds."

## Camp Timberlawn

In June 1963, Shriver and her husband began a summer day camp at Timberlawn, the Rockville, Maryland home that they rented. The house was a huge Civil War-era mansion with over 200 acres of grounds. For five weeks every summer, 50 to 60 mentally challenged children and adults came to Camp Timberlawn. The camp had a song, a flag-raising ceremony, and many activities including swimming, baseball, soccer, volleyball, and an obstacle course. All campers had companions, usually teenagers, who helped them with activities and made sure they didn't get hurt.

The day camp was so successful in showing that mentally challenged people could benefit from sports and recreational programs, that Shriver, with the help of the Joseph P. Kennedy Jr. Foundation, decided to expand it throughout the United States. The Kennedy family had created the Joseph P. Kennedy Jr. Foundation in 1946 to honor the memory of Shriver's oldest brother, who was killed in a plane crash while serving in World War II. The foundation aimed to prevent mental retardation and to improve the lives of mentally challenged people.

In 1962, Shriver created the Joseph P. Kennedy Jr. Awards in Mental Retardation, and the National Institutes for Child Health and Human Development. Between 1963 and 1968, the Foundation provided grants to aid more than 80 public and private organizations in creating and administering similar day camps for mentally challenged people.

The Kennedy administration began testing the fitness of American school children, giving those who passed the Presidential Physical Fitness Award. Shriver was inspired to give similar tests to physically challenged children, providing silver, gold, and champ awards. This led to the idea of a physical training program and Olympic competition for physically challenged people.

Since 1964, the Chicago Park District had been an enthusiastic participant in the day camp programs. In January 1968, the District asked for a grant to fund an event to be held in a Chicago park. Shriver invited the District's representatives to Washington, where she told them that she approved their plan, but wanted to expand it to an international competition that would be called the "Special Olympics." The Foundation awarded the Chicago Park District a grant to develop and run the first Special Olympics Games.

## The Special Olympics

The first International Special Olympics Games were held on July 19 and 20, 1968, at Chicago's Soldier Field, with funding from the Joseph P. Kennedy Jr. Foundation and the Chicago Park District. One thousand athletes from 26 U.S. states and Canada competed in track and field events, hockey, and aquatic sports. Shriver, perhaps remembering her father's overemphasis on winning at all costs, modified the definition of "winning" for these games. All competitors in the Special Olympics were "winners," simply because they entered the competition. "Let me win. But if I cannot win, let me be brave in the attempt," is the oath taken by athletes in the Special Olympics. Shriver's son, Tim, told Rainie and Quinn, "The best way to describe it is that you

are expected to push, push, push, and do your best." As he told interviewer Oprah Winfrey, "Special Olympics is about . . . saying it's not what you're born with but what you bring to the table. If you run that race with everything God gave you, you've won."

Frank Gifford, in a foreword to the book *Skill, Courage, Sharing, Joy: The Stories of Special Olympics,* explained, "No person is too handicapped to take part in Special Olympics. Each competes to the extent of his or her abilities. And no achievement is too small, no time too slow. What these true Olympians may lack in speed or strength, they more than make up for with their effort and determination." He quoted Shriver, who said, "In a world where poverty, war, and oppression have dimmed people's hopes, Special Olympic athletes rekindle that hope with their spiritual strength, their excellence, and achievements. For as we hope for the best in them, hope is reborn in us."

Shriver wrote in her foreword to *Readings in Special Olympics,* "Special Olympians and their families are challenging the common wisdom that says only intellectual achievement is the measure of human life. They have proved that the common wisdom is wrong. Special Olympians and their families—more than one million of them—are proof that the value of human life should be measured in many ways."

The Games were so successful that in December 1968, Special Olympics International became an official nonprofit organization and a Special Olympics chapter was organized in every U.S. state, as well as in Canada and France. The program has grown phenomenally and is now known around the world. In the 1995 World Summer Games in New Haven, Connecticut, almost 7,000 athletes from 130 countries competed with the help of 2,000 coaches, 15,000 family members and friends, 450,000 volunteers, 500,000 spectators and 1,500 media members. Millions of people watched the games on television. As of 1999, more than one million athletes in 50 U.S. states and 150 countries competed in 26 sports; more than 15,000 games, meets, and tournaments were held during the year.

The Special Olympics movement embodies quality training and high levels of sportsmanship. Because of its commitment, it is the only sports organization that has received approval from the International Olympic Committee to use the word "Olympics" in its title. Its goals have expanded as society began to realize what mentally challenged people could accomplish. Currently, Special Olympics athletes also coach, officiate at events, give speeches, and hold regular jobs. As the Special Olympics *Quarterly Newsletter* from Spring/Summer of 1998 notes, "They surprise the world around them with their abilities! Today's Special Olympics movement does not exist for the athlete, but with the athlete—for they are the future, the leaders, the heroes as the movement reaches out to people with mental retardation all over the world."

## The Eunice Kennedy Shriver Center

In 1969, the Eunice Kennedy Shriver Center was founded. It was one of the first mental retardation and developmental disabilities research centers and university-affiliated programs in the United States. The Center conducts basic research to determine how biological and environmental factors influence human development, with a special influence on mental retardation and other developmental disabilities. In addition, the Center provides training and service programs for people with developmental disabilities and their families. President Ronald Reagan awarded Shriver the Presidential Medal of Freedom for her work "on behalf of America's least powerful people, the mentally retarded."

## Gratitude and Admiration

In 1995, Shriver was scheduled to speak to a gathering at Yale University as the 1995 Kiphuth Fellowship Speaker. The Kiphuth Foundation honors people who are distinguished in sports, literature, or the arts. Because she was ill at the time, her husband spoke for her. Mr. Shriver spoke about the beauty and purity of the Special Olympics, comparing them to professional sports. "The professional athlete doesn't really play the sport any more, but just goes out there to do his job and earn a living" he told Richard Seltenreich of the *Yale Daily News*. He praised his wife's dedication to expanding the lives of people with mental retardation through sports: "Through sports she brought out the best in others, giving them a friend and now a coach."

Quinn and Rainie quoted Shriver's nephew, Bobby Kennedy, who said, "She should have been president. She is the most impressive figure in the family. She has a carefully constructed set of values and she will not budge from them. She is highly principled in ways that are more sophisticated than anyone in the family. If you ask, most of my brothers, sisters, and cousins would say they'd like to be like her."

When a Toronto reporter asked Shriver how she felt about the athletes who take part in the games, she said, "I feel a sense of gratitude, a sense of admiration. I am very energized by them."

## Further Reading

Cipriano, Robert, *Readings in Special Olympics,* Special Learning Corporation, 1980.
Collier, Peter, and David Horowitz, *The Kennedys: An American Drama,* Summit Books, 1984.
Davis, John H., *The Kennedys: Dynasty and Disaster 1848-1983,* McGraw-Hill Book Company, 1984.
Rainie, Harrison, and John Quinn, *Growing Up Kennedy: The Third Wave Comes of Age,* G.P. Putnam's Sons, 1983.
Single, Doug, *Skill, Courage, Sharing, Joy: The Stories of Special Olympics,* Special Olympics International, 1992.
*Who's Who of American Women,* Marquis, 1998.
"Eunice Mary Kennedy Shriver," The National Women's Hall of Fame, http://www.greatwomen.org/shriver.htm (March 2, 1999).
"Founding of the National Mental Retardation Research Centers," National Mental Retardation Research Centers, http://129.59.193.102/~bednar/about/mrfounding.html (March 2, 1999).
"Mission Statement," Eunice Kennedy Shriver Center, http://www.shriver.org/mission.htm (March 2, 1999).
"Origins of Special Olympics," Special Olympics, http://www.paso.org/About/origins.htm (March 2, 1999).
"Shriver Lauds Special Olympics," Yale Daily News, http://www.cis.yale.edu/ydn/paper/4.6/4.6.95storyno.CE.html (March 2, 1999).
"Special Athletes," Oprah, http://www.oprah.com/scoop/archives/days/980722.html (March 2, 1999).
"Special Olympics History," Special Olympics, http://wpso.org/history.html (March 2, 1999).
"Welcome to Special Olympics," Special Olympics, http://www.specialolympics.org/welcome.html (March 2, 1999). □

# Shel Silverstein

**Although Shel Silverstein (1932–1999) did not intend to become a children's writer, he is best known for his poetry for children. *The Giving Tree, Where the Sidewalk Ends,* and *A Light in the Attic* are some of his most notable works.**

Shel Silverstein was born in 1932 in Chicago, Illinois. He started drawing and writing in his early teens because, according to him, he was not popular with the girls and was not good at sports. He did not have a lot of influences when he started to write and draw. But as he told Jean F. Mercier of *Publishers Weekly*, "I was also lucky that I didn't have anyone to copy, be impressed by. I had developed my own style." Indeed, that style is what has made him what some call a "literary cult figure."

Silverstein served with the U.S. armed forces in the 1950s, spending time in Korea and Japan. While in the service he drew cartoons for the *Pacific Stars and Stripes*. In 1952, he began his career as a writer and cartoonist for *Playboy* magazine. He was introduced to the distinguished book editor at Harper and Brothers, Ursula Nordstrom, who convinced him he could write for children.

## A Unique Style

Silverstein's poetry for children is often silly, humorous, and a little strange. The accompanying black-and-white illustrations, amusing and sometimes rather morbid, are an integral part of the poetry, often needed in order to interpret the poem itself. Silverstein has been compared to poets such as Edward Lear, A. A. Milne, and Dr. Seuss. Many of his poems are adapted from his song lyrics, and the influence of his song-writing background is apparent in the poems' meters and rhythms. Eric A. Kimmel, in *Twentieth-Century Children's Writers*, characterized Silverstein this way: "His poems read like those a fourth grader would write in the back of his notebook when the teacher's eye was turned." Kimmel goes on to say: "that may be precisely their appeal."

To say there is more than one interpretation of Silverstein's work is an understatement. Some believe it is simply amusing and fun; others contend that the silliness hides deeper symbolism. That symbolism has been classified by some as educational; by others as harmful to children. Regardless of the mixed critical reaction, Silverstein's books seem to be everywhere: libraries, classrooms, chil-

The story has been interpreted in many ways. Silverstein states in *Something About the Author* that it simply represents "a relationship between two people: one gives and the other takes." Barbara A. Schram classified it as "dangerous" due to its sexism and called it a "glorification of female selflessness and male selfishness," while William Cole called its message "a backup of 'more blessed to give than to receive.'" Christian ministers read it in terms of Christian self-sacrifice, and Alice Digilio assumed the tree represented the selfless love of parents and the boy the ingratitude of children (*Children's Literature Review*). Despite some negative reviews and some concerns that the book may be too advanced for children, it put Silverstein on the best-seller list for the first time.

### *Where the Sidewalk Ends* Brought Continued Popularity

Silverstein published three other children's books in 1964, in addition to *The Giving Tree.* They include *A Giraffe and a Half, Uncle Shelby's Zoo: Don't Bump the Glump,* and *Who Wants a Cheap Rhinoceros?* It was not until ten years later that he wrote his next children's book, but it became an instant success. *Where the Sidewalk Ends: The Poems and Drawings of Shel Silverstein* (1974) is considered a classic by many. Kimmel in *Twentieth-Century Children's Writers* asserts that, "No discussion of children's poetry can ignore *Where the Sidewalk Ends* and *A Light in the Attic.* [1981]. For better or worse, the monumental success of these two books has transformed the way poetry is taught in American schools." Myra Cohn Livingston in the *New York Times Book Review* compared one of Silverstein's poems in *Where the Sidewalk Ends,* part of which reads, "But the taste of a thumb / Is the sweetest taste yet," to Heinrich Hoffmann's 1846 piece "Little Suck-a-Thumb," in which children hear about "the scissors-man," who cuts off the offending thumbs of those who exercise this horrible habit. Unlike Hoffmann, Silverstein placed himself in the child's place much of the time, and his poetry, according to some, makes children feel like they have found a grown-up who understands them.

*Where the Sidewalk Ends* won the Michigan Young Readers' Award in 1981. The book was immensely popular, despite some content that was deemed "indelicate." For example, the collection includes poems about belching, nose picking, and smelly, disgusting garbage. Some critics continued to point out that Silverstein was "by no stretch of the imagination, a great poet" (Kimmel in *Twentieth-Century Children's Writers*). Still, Bernice E. Cullinan credited *Where the Sidewalk Ends* with making more children into poetry-lovers than any other book. Kimmel agreed that Silverstein's greatest contribution was in "convincing millions of children that poetry is neither difficult nor threatening."

### The "Missing Piece" Stories

Silverstein provided another challenge of interpretation to readers when he published the two books *The Missing Piece* (1976) and *The Missing Piece Meets the Big O* (1981). In the first, the "character" of the book is a circle with a wedge-shaped piece missing who is rolling along in search

dren's bookshelves, and they are being widely used in elementary schools to teach poetry.

Silverstein's first book for children, *Uncle Shelby's ABZ Book: A Primer for Tender Minds,* was published in 1961. This was followed by *Uncle Shelby's Story of Lafcadio, the Lion Who Shot Back* in 1963, about a lion who had kept a gun from an earlier encounter with a hunter and with practice became a good marksman. Zena Sutherland, in *Bulletin of the Center for Children's Books,* called the book "daft" and described it as "a nonsense story about utter success."

### *The Giving Tree*

One of Silverstein's most successful early books was *The Giving Tree* (1964). At first, publishers rejected the story. They thought that it fell between child and adult literature and would not sell. The story begins simply: "Once there was a tree . . ." and tells the story of a tree who gives everything to the boy she loves (the tree is characterized as female in the story). As a child the boy plays in the tree, gathers its leaves, swings on its branches, and eats its apples. Later he carves his and a girl's initials in its trunk, and as a young man he takes the tree's branches to build a house. As an old man, he needs a boat to take him away from it all, so the tree tells him to cut it down and make a boat, which the old man does. The tree, now just a stump, tells the man when he returns, now very old, to "Sit down and rest," and the tree is happy. But, as is common in Silverstein's work, it is not a happy ending. The tree has given up everything to the boy, who is now a bitter old man.

of its mate. When it does come across the missing piece, however, it is rolling too fast and goes right by it. Instead of ending the book there, Silverstein makes a point of telling the reader that the circle continues on, singing and still searching. Critics have approached the story from many angles, from accrediting it with a life-is-a-journey theme, to condemning it for suggesting that being alone is better than committing to another. In *The Missing Piece Meets the Big O*, the character is the wedge-shaped piece, first introduced in the previous book, who is looking for an object into which it can insert itself and thus gain a free ride in the world. Acting on the advice of the Big O, the wedge discovers that it can get around by itself after all and does not need someone to carry it. Most assume the message deals with the issue of independence, but not all agree whether such a message is more appropriate for children or divorced adults.

## Another Best-Seller

In 1981, Silverstein published another collection of poems and drawings, *A Light in the Attic.* This book was chosen by *School Library Journal* as one of the best books of 1981. Leigh Dean in *Children's Literature Review* credited it with making Silverstein the guru of elementary school teachers' poetry units. It remained on the *New York Times* best-seller list for more than three years. Containing 136 poems and 175 pages, *A Light in the Attic* again incorporates sometimes bizarre drawings with light, humorous rhymes about the fears and fantasies of children.

## Music and Film

Although Silverstein is best known for his children's poetry, he is also a folksong composer and has written dozens of songs. Some of these include "A Boy Named Sue," "One's on the Way," "Boa Constrictor," and "So Good to So Bad." Many artists have performed his work, including Johnny Cash, Lynn Anderson, and Jerry Lee Lewis. Silverstein also collaborated with the band Dr. Hook, producing a series of successful singles and albums. In 1980, he produced a folksong album titled *The Great Conch Train Robbery.* Albums of Silverstein's songs recorded by others include *Freakin' at the Freaker's Ball* (Columbia, 1972); *Sloppy Seconds* (Columbia, 1972); and *Bobby Bare Sings Lullabys, Legends, and Lies: The Songs of Shel Silverstein* (RCA Victor, 1972). In addition, Silverstein wrote the music for the films *Ned Kelly* (1970) and *Who is Harry Kellerman and Why is He Saying Those Terrible Things About Me?* (1971); and co-wrote the music for *Theives* (1977) and *Postcards from the Edge* (1990). A song from the latter film, "I'm Checkin' Out," written by Silverstein, received nominations for an Academy Award and a Golden Globe Award in 1991. Silverstein's other venture into the motion picture world came when he wrote the screenplay for *Things Change,* which was produced as a movie in 1988. Another achievement was the 1981 production of his one-act play "The Lady or the Tiger?" It was produced at the Ensemble Studio Theatre in New York City and starred Richard Dreyfus.

## Something for Everyone

Silverstein continued to work as a roving reporter and cartoonist. He was divorced and had one daughter. Because he kept a low profile and avoided publicity in general, little more is known about his personal life. He was a "free spirit," as is evidenced by his statement to Jean F. Merier in *Publishers Weekly:* "I'm free to leave . . . go wherever I please, do whatever I want; I believe everyone should live like that. Don't be dependent on anyone else—man, woman, child, or dog. I want to go everywhere, look at and listen to everything. You can go crazy with some of the wonderful stuff there is in life." As mentioned in *Something About the Author,* he did "hope that people, no matter what age, would find something to identify with in my books, pick one up and experience a personal sense of discovery." Silverstein died at his home in Key West, Florida on May 10, 1999.

## Further Reading

*Children's Literature Review,* edited by Gerard J. Senick, Gale Research, 1983.
*Something About the Author,* edited by Anne Commire, Gale Research, 1983.
*Twentieth-Century Children's Writers,* edited by Laura Standley Berger, St. James Press, 1995.
*New York Times Book Review,* March 9, 1986.
Friday, Sely, "Shel Silverstein," http://www.scep.nl.nasio/ Silverstein (March 3, 1999). □

# Wallis Simpson

**The romance between Wallis Simpson (1896–1986) and the Duke of Windsor caused one of the biggest scandals in the history of the British monarchy. She was a twice-divorced American, and "David," as she called the man who briefly reigned as King Edward VIII, was forced to abdicate his throne in order to marry her.**

Simpson was born Bessie-Wallis Warfield on June 19, 1896, in Blue Ridge Summit, Pennsylvania, a spa town where her parents had gone to help cure her father's tuberculosis. It was a futile attempt, for Teackle Wallis Warfield died just a few months later, leaving Alice Montague Warfield an impoverished widow. Both families hailed from the Old South, but the Montagues of Virginia had lost their fortune after the Civil War. Ironically, Wallis Warfield Simpson's genealogy gave her technically more English blood than members of the British royal family, who later shunned her. Until World War I, the House of Windsor had actually been called the House of Saxe-Coburg-Gotha, a line created by several intermarriages between English and German royal cousins.

## An Impoverished Childhood

Teackle Warfield had been an unsuccessful Baltimore businessman. After his death, Alice and Bessie-Wallis moved in with her mother-in-law in Baltimore. Hostilities between the women quickly escalated and they were forced to relocate to a dismal section of the city, where Alice Warfield was the proprietress of a boardinghouse for a time. In the end, however, the women were supported by the charity of Teackle's wealthy brother, Solomon Warfield. It was this uncle who paid the tuition for the private schools that Wallis attended.

By the time she was eighteen, Wallis had become an attractive young woman, known for her poised manners and vivacious personality. On a visit to Florida in 1916, she met a young naval lieutenant, Earl Winfield Spencer, and the two quickly fell in love. A native of Chicago, Spencer was one of the first twenty men in the U.S. Navy to earn pilot's wings. They married in November 1916. The brief courtship had not revealed Spencer's fondness for drink. The couple lived on the Pensacola naval base, which Wallis, as she was then known, detested. A deafening crash gong would sound whenever one of the base's planes had gone down. Once it tolled for her husband, who was fortunately unhurt when his aircraft dove into the bay. From these experiences she acquired a hatred of planes, and would suffer from a lifelong fear of flying.

## Lived in Asia

Wallis eventually separated from Spencer and settled in Washington near her mother. Her uncle forbade her to petition for divorce, which was a very scandalous legal act at the time. When Spencer was posted to the Far East, she conducted an affair with a dashing Argentinean diplomat. After he tired of her, she was brokenhearted, and joined Spencer in China in 1924. Though the marriage soon disintegrated once more, Wallis remained in China for over two years. She lived with some friends, American raconteurs by the name of Herman and Katherine Rogers, and supplemented her meager income as a naval officer's wife with poker-game winnings.

In 1926, Wallis defied her family and moved to Virginia for a year, in order to obtain a divorce. When her uncle died, she inherited a small trust fund that yielded $60 a month. She had probably counted on a more generous sum, since it was nearly impossible for a woman of her well-heeled, but unskilled and uneducated status to earn any income on her own in 1927. Instead, her disapproving uncle had directed that the bulk of his fortune be used to establish a home for "aged and indigent gentlewomen," where, according to the terms of his will, a room was to be reserved permanently for his niece, should she need it.

## Second Marriage

Before her divorce became final, in late 1927, Wallis had already met Anglo-American businessman, Ernest Simpson. This well-to-do, cultured Harvard alumnus had also extracted himself from an unhappy marriage. He moved to London to run his family's shipping business, while she stayed with friends in the south of France. Before long, she accepted Simpson's proposal of marriage, having few other alternatives. They married in July 1928.

In London, the Simpsons fell into a circle of well-connected American expatriates, and became friendly with Thelma, Viscountess Furness, who—though married—was also the mistress of the Prince of Wales, heir to the British throne. Simpson was known for her scathing wit and clever banter as a dinner guest. She and the prince probably met in January 1931. "David," as the prince was known, was a charming, affable man two years her senior, described as the world's most eligible bachelor. Though perhaps not in possession of a keen intelligence, the future king was a good soul who enjoyed gardening, bagpipe-playing, and charming women.

## Hand of Fate Forced Resolution

The prince soon became a frequent dinner guest at the Simpson home on Bryanston Square, and even bestowed upon Wallis a cairn puppy as a gift, after noticing her fondness for his own dogs. They began traveling together. Buckingham Palace courtiers were becoming distressed by the affair of the king's eldest son with a married, once-divorced American woman. The prince appeared to be deeply in love with Simpson. When she learned that her husband was having an affair in New York, Simpson hired a lawyer recommended by the prince.

Their blithe romance suddenly became a critical matter when King George V died on January 20, 1936. The Prince of Wales ascended to the British throne as Edward VIII, but the coronation would not take place until the spring of 1937, after an appropriate period of mourning. Despite his new duties as ruler of 486 million subjects, he and Simpson continued to be inseparable. In late 1936, the prime minister, Stanley Baldwin, confronted the new king over the affair. Edward firmly declared his intention to marry Simpson once her divorce was finalized. As rumors began trickling out in the British press, public and conservative clerical furor escalated. A constitutional crisis was feared. If the king disregarded parliamentary "advice" regarding suitable spouses for the royal family, there was the possibility of the entire government resigning in protest. Parliament would then have to be dissolved, and a general election called. The very end of the monarchy itself was predicted.

As word of her impending divorce leaked, Simpson began receiving abusive letters. Crowds gathered outside her London apartment. Her divorce would be final in April 1937, and the coronation was slated for May 12. The new king planned to boycott the ceremony unless he was allowed to marry Simpson, since no actual statute barred him from marrying anyone of his choosing, except a Roman Catholic. The king's surprising new sympathies toward millions of unemployed Welsh miners further alienated him from the ruling Tory government. Simpson departed England and tried to dissuade him from placing his throne in jeopardy.

## Abdication

A firm display of political opposition finally drove the exhausted and distraught king to abdicate his throne. On December 10, 1936, Edward announced his intentions in a radio broadcast to the nation. He declared: "I have found it impossible to carry out the heavy burden of responsibility and to discharge my duties as king as I would wish to do, without the help and support of the woman I love." This concluded one of the most heavily reported media stories of the decade. The former king was given the title Duke of Windsor, while his brother "Bertie," ascended to the throne. The new duke agreed to never return to England without permission of the reigning sovereign, in exchange for a generous annual income.

After a separation of several more months, before her divorce was final, Simpson and the Duke were wed at a chateau in France. The terrier that the duke had once given her, was sent to Simpson as their day of reconciliation neared. Shortly after the dog's arrival in France, he was bitten by a snake and died. Simpson considered it an ominous sign and wept profusely.

Simpson and the duke were married on June 3, 1937. The Anglican cleric who performed the ceremony was formally reprimanded. No member of the royal family attended the festivities. The duke received a letter from his brother, the new king, stating that any children resulting from his marriage to Simpson would not be royal and that his new bride would be denied the title of "Her Royal Highness (HRH)."

## Fear of Abduction

After their marriage, the Windsors toured Nazi Germany and were received by Adolf Hitler, a trip which further eroded popular support. When war erupted between England and Germany in 1939, the duke was immediately recalled to England and given a military commission in France. When the German army invaded France, they fled to neutral Spain and then Portugal. Winston Churchill, now prime minister, offered the duke a government post, but he dallied before accepting it in an attempt to win the "HRH" title for his wife. British leaders were concerned that the couple's previous display of Nazi sympathy made them vulnerable. The Germans, it was feared, could abduct the Windsors and re-install the duke on the British throne after a successful invasion of the British Isles.

The duke was safely ensconced as governor of the Bahamas in August 1940. He and the duchess lived there for five years and very much disliked the heat. Her only consolation was the occasional shopping trip to New York or Palm Beach. In 1941, it was reported that she and the duke visited a Canadian ranch with 146 pieces of luggage. This incident sparked a period of negative publicity about the Duchess of Windsor and her extravagant tastes in clothes and jewelry.

## A Life of Glamorous Leisure

Following the war's end, the Windsors lived primarily in France, eventually settling several miles outside of Paris at a home on the Bois de Boulogne. They each penned autobiographies in the 1950s (hers was titled *The Heart Has Its Reasons*) and she regularly appeared on lists of the world's best-dressed women. By the late 1960s, the duke had reconciled somewhat with his family. In 1967, he and the duchess returned to England for a formal visit. The duke had been a lifelong smoker, and was diagnosed with throat cancer in 1971. Queen Elizabeth visited the couple at their Paris home. The duke died on May 28, 1972 and his widow was invited to stay at Buckingham Palace for the funeral. A telephoto lens captured her watching the annual Trooping of the Colors, always held on the queen's birthday, from a window at the palace. She looked utterly bereft.

Back in Paris, the duchess rarely entertained after her husband's death. She began to suffer increasing health problems, including coronary artery disease. In the 1980s she lived in near-total seclusion, rarely seen in public. She died at home in Paris on April 24, 1986. The bulk of her estate was left to the Pasteur Institute, a leader in HIV/AIDS research. She is buried alongside the duke in the royal mausoleum at Frogmore.

## Further Reading

Birmingham, Stephen, *Duchess: The Story of Wallis Warfield Simpson*, Little, Brown, 1981.
*Dictionary of National Biography, 1986-1990*, edited by C. S. Nicholls, Oxford University Press, 1996.
Garrett, Richard, *Mrs. Simpson*, St. Martin's Press, 1979.
Martin, Ralph, *The Woman He Loved*, Simon & Schuster, 1973.
□

# Cornelia Otis Skinner

**During her lifetime Cornelia Otis Skinner (1901–1979) received recognition as a talented writer, actor, and monologuist. Her writing varied widely, and included comical essays about herself, in-depth studies of women from a wide range of social and economic backgrounds, memoirs, and biographies. Her intelligent style, combined with her wit, allowed her to succeed in many genres. She was also a gifted actress, performing one-woman monologues that were unique to her time.**

Cornelia Otis Skinner was born on May 30, 1901, in Chicago to Otis Skinner and Maud Durbin Skinner, both actors. In 1906, the family moved to Bryn Mawr, Pennsylvania, and Skinner's mother retired from the stage. Her father continued to tour, receiving widespread recognition and great fame, especially for his role in *Kismet*. As a child, Skinner was immersed in the theatre. She was continually surrounded by actors. Her father, often away on tour, wrote her long letters about his profession.

In 1918, Skinner attended Byrn Mawr College, where she became involved in theatre productions and played Lady Macbeth. During her sophomore year she left Byrn Mawr and moved to Paris. Skinner attended the Sorbonne and studied acting at the Jacques Copeau School and the Comedie Francaise, where she came under the influence of Emile Dehelly. Skinner, fluent in French, was very fond of Paris. This was reflected in her later writings.

## Early Roles in the Theatre

Skinner returned to the United States in 1921. She made her dramatic debut as Dona Sarasate in the stage adaptation of Blasco-Ibanez's *Blood and Sand* (1921). Over the next five years Skinner established a reputation for her stage acting with roles in *Will Shakespeare* (1923), *Tweedles* (1923), *The Wild Wescotts* (1923), *In His Arms* (1924), and *White Collars* (1925).

In 1925, Skinner wrote her first play for her father titled *Captain Fury,* which was produced off-Broadway. In the same year she wrote and performed her first one-woman show. Skinner used sharp wit and keen observation to create characters that fascinated audiences. Over the next several years she traveled the across the United States, performing her monologues. In 1928, she married Alden S. Blodget; the couple had one son. She made her debut in England at the St. James Theatre in 1929.

## The Monologues

During the early 1930s, Skinner focused on her interest in historical women. Researching her characters extensively, she wrote and portrayed a range of unique women in her monodramas, which included *The Wives of Henry VIII* (1931), *The Empress Eugenie* (1932), *The Loves of Charles II* (1933), and *The Mansion on the Hudson* (1935). Skinner

earned considerable recognition for her adaptation of Margaret Ayer Barne's novel *Edna, His Wife,* which toured London in 1937 and the United States in 1938. Skinner wrote the one-woman play *Paris '90* in 1952 along with Kay Swift, who provided the music and lyrics. The show, in which Skinner played fourteen different characters, was very successful. It also proved to be quite popular when released in a book adaptation as *Elegant Wits and Grand Horizontals* in 1962.

Skinner enthralled her audiences with her uncanny ability to switch characters with only a simple prop or a slight change in posture. Although many of her monodramas were set in places foreign to her audiences, Skinner enjoyed touring the United States, performing in small towns for people seldom exposed to the theatre. Her sharp wit and insightful humor into the everyday occurrences in life appealed to a wide audience. It was this insight that made Skinner a monologuist unmatched in her day.

## Traditional Theatre

In 1939, Skinner earned critical acclaim for her performance in the lead role of George Bernard Shaw's *Candida* during its 1937 London production and 1939 U.S. tour. When Shaw saw Skinner's performance, he cabled her the simple message "Excellent-greatest" to which Skinner replied, "Undeserving of such praise." The response from Shaw read, "Meant the play," and Skinner answered, "So did I." Skinner also played important roles in other classic theatre productions, including Angelica in *Love for Love* (1940), Emily Hazen in Lillian Hellman's *The Searching*

Wind (1944), and Mrs. Erlynne in *Lady Windermere's Fan* (1946). In 1952, Skinner won the Barter Theatre Award for outstanding acting on the Broadway stage.

## The Pleasure of His Company

*The Pleasure of His Company* (1958), co-written with Samuel Taylor, was a unique story for its time. In the story, Jessica Poole lives in San Francisco with her mother (played by Skinner) and stepfather, Kate and Jim Doughtery. She is about to be married to a handsome, wealthy rancher in a high-society wedding when her runabout, jet-setting father, Pogo Poole, appears on the scene, much to the dismay of Kate. Pogo, who wishes to be the father he never was, disapproves of the marriage. Jessica's grandfather agrees, believing that his intelligent granddaughter is being "cut down in the prime of her life by marriage." He adds to Kate's annoyance by questioning time-honored traditions, such as giving away the bride. "Why give her to somebody to use? She hasn't begun to use herself!" Although her husband-to-be is not a bad character, his obsession with ranching and bulls cannot compare to her father's exciting, adventurous life, and when Pogo and her grandfather suggest that she call off the wedding and go explore the world with her father, she can not resist. Kate, distraught over the upheaval in plans, reluctantly concedes, and the scene ends as Jessica and Pogo rush out the door.

Reviewers gave high praise to *The Pleasure of His Company*, particularly for its uncommon wit and intelligent dialogue. During a time when many theatre productions were deep psychological sketches of men, *The Pleasure of His Company* offered light comedy, filled with irony and satire. Interestingly, the play introduced a rather controversial idea in a manner that was not offensive to the audience. The idea that a young woman should aspire to a life filled with experiences and adventures and not look solely to marriage and motherhood as her source of identity was innovative for the late 1950s. The play was also critical of intelligent young women who married men of good looks and substantial wealth but without any interest in the arts or culture. Using satire, the authors challenged the role of women in society. When Kate defends her lifestyle by suggesting that she gives the best dinner parties in San Francisco, the audience hears its hollow ring, but they are never lectured or berated. Not only a critical success, *The Pleasure of His Company* was a popular success; it played on Broadway for a year and then toured the United States. The production was also made into a movie, starring Fred Astaire and Lilli Palmer.

## The Essays

After touring with *The Pleasure of His Company* in 1960, Skinner gave her last performance in 1964 in *The Irregular Verb to Love*. Although retired from the theatre, she continued to write. Over her lifetime she contributed numerous essays to publications such as *The New Yorker, Ladies' Home Journal, Vogue, Life, Harper's Bazaar,* and *Reader's Digest.* Many of her writings were a satirical look at her own life. In her essay "Where to Look" she discussed her acute sense of unease when she encountered a "where-to-look" situation, such as waiting for an elevator: "The act of waiting for an elevator brings out a suspicious streak in people. You arrive before the closed landing door and push a button. Another person comes along and, after a quick glance of mutual appraisal, you both look quickly away and continue to wait, thinking the while uncharitable thoughts of one another. The new arrival suspecting you of not having pushed the button and you wondering if the new arrival is going to be a mistrusting old meanie and go give the button a second shove; . . . an unspoken tension which is broken by one or the other of you walking over and doing just that. Then back to positions of waiting and the problem of where to look."

Compilations of Skinner's essays included: *Tiny Garments* (1932), *Excuse It, Please!* (1936), *Dithers and Jitters* (1938), and *Soap Behind the Ears* (1941). Selections from these publications appeared in *That's Me All Over* (1948), which contained drawings by Constantin Alajálov. In the 1950s, three more volumes appeared, also with Alajálov's drawings: *Nuts in May* (1950), *Bottoms Up!* (1955), and *The Ape in Me* (1959). These essays focused on Skinner's personal insights into the comic nature of life and employed a great deal of self-deprecating humor. In *The Ape in Me* she writes about her days in college: "I was known as the Tall Girl of my set and the few callow youths who 'dated' me would hardly have been able to let linger a kiss on any feature much above my chin . . . even if I thrust it forward in the manner of an amorous heifer."

## When Our Hearts Were Young and Gay

Skinner's highly celebrated autobiographical work, *When Our Hearts Were Young and Gay,* (1942) told the story of her experiences with her friend Emily Kimbrough, during their time together in Paris in the 1920s. Written with Kimbrough, *When Our Heart Were Young and Gay* takes a comical look at the two naive women and their encounters with such unexpected experiences as bed bugs and brothels. Once again told with Skinner's wit and talent for seeing the interesting in the ordinary, the book was a critical and popular success. It was a bestseller for eight weeks and sold over a million copies. In 1944, the book was made into a movie; in 1948, Jean Kerr developed it into a play.

Skinner completed her memoirs in 1948, focusing on her career and that of her father. The book was published in the United States as *Family Circle* and in England as *Happy Family*. In 1962, Skinner published *Elegant Wits and Grand Horizontals,* adapting and further developing material from her one-woman play *Paris '90*. Her next writing project once again earned praise from reviewers. *Madame Sarah* (1967), a biography of Sarah Bernhardt, was both a critical and popular success. *Life with Lindsay and Crouse,* a biography of Howard Lindsay and Russell Crouse, was Skinner's final book. It was published in 1976, when Skinner was 75 years old. She died on July 9, 1979 in New York City.

Throughout her career Skinner made significant inroads for women in the theatre. Her one-woman monodramas were innovative and demonstrated her extraordinary ability to bring the women she portrayed to life in front of her audience. As a playwright, actress, essayist, and author, she earned the admiration of her peers, the critics, and her fans.

## Further Reading

*American National Biography,* Vol. 20, edited by John A. Garraty and Mark C. Carnes, Oxford University Press, 1999.
*Benet's Reader's Encyclopedia,* fourth ed., edited by Bruce Murphy, HarperCollins, 1996.
*Cambridge Guide to Theatre,* revised ed., edited by Martin Banham, Cambridge University Press, 1995.
*Oxford Companion to American Literature,* sixth ed., edited by James D. Hart, Oxford University Press, 1995.
Shafer, Yvonne, *American Women Playwrights: 1900-1950,* Peter Lang Publishing, 1995.
*Something About the Author,* Vol. 2, edited by Anne Commire, Gale Research, 1971. □

# W. Eugene Smith

**W. Eugene Smith (1918–1978) is considered one of the masters of modern photojournalism. He created some of the most poignant images of war ever made. Smith's photo essays chronicling social injustice deeply moved the American public. His images of the devastating effects of mercury poisoning in Japan were some of his most evocative works.**

William Eugene Smith was born in Wichita, Kansas on December 30, 1918. He attended Catholic elementary and high schools there from 1924 to 1935. Smith took his first photographs between 1933 and 1935. Wichita press photographer, Frank Noel, encouraged him to contribute occasional photographs to local newspapers.

When Smith's father committed suicide, newspaper accounts of the incident greatly distorted the actual circumstances. This made him question the standards of American journalism. Smith vowed to become a photojournalist, applying the highest standards to his own career. He was determined to seek absolute personal honesty in his own documentary work.

Smith studied photography on a scholarship at the University of Notre Dame, in Indiana, from 1936 to 1937. After graduation, he worked for the *Wichita Eagle* and the *Wichita Beacon* and then became a *Newsweek* staff photographer in New York. He was fired because he used what was considered a miniature camera, a 2.5 inch format twin-lens reflex. From 1938 to 1939 Smith worked as a freelance photographer for the Black Star Agency, publishing photographs in *Life, Collier's, Harper's Bazaar,* and other periodicals, including the *New York Times.* He worked with miniature cameras, creating an innovative flash technique that allowed him to produce indoor photographs that had the appearance of natural or lamp light. Smith accepted a position as a staff photographer with *Life* and worked there from 1939 to 1941.

## Chronicled the Horrors of War

Smith visited Japan three times. His first visit was during World War II. From 1942 to 1944 Smith was a war correspondent in the Pacific theater for *Popular Photography* and other publications. In 1944, he returned to *Life* as a correspondent and photographer. Idealistic and emotional, Smith went to cover the battles of World War II filled with patriotism. He was so horrified by what he saw that he gave up determining who was right or wrong and dedicated himself to showing the horror and suffering he saw.

In 1944, from Saipan, an island in the western Pacific Ocean, Smith said in *W. Eugene Smith: Shadow and Substance: The Life and Work of an American Photographer,* "... each time I pressed the shutter release it was a shouted condemnation hurled with the hope that the pictures might survive through the years, with the hope that they might echo through the minds of men in the future—causing them caution and remembrance and realization." Later, he said, "I would that my photographs might be, not the coverage of a news event, but an indictment of war—the brutal corrupting viciousness of its doing to the minds and bodies of men; and that my photographs might be a powerful emotional catalyst to the reasoning which would help this vile and criminal stupidity from beginning again."

Smith was assigned to the U.S. aircraft carrier Bunker Hill in 1944 and photographed bombing raids on Tokyo, the invasion of Iwo Jima, and the battle of Okinawa. His dramatic photo essays produced a collection of timeless, evocative images, including that of a tiny, fly covered, half-dead baby held up by a soldier after being rescued from a cave in Saipan; a wounded soldier, hideously bandaged, stretched out in Leyte Cathedral; and a decaying Japanese body on an Iwo Jima beach. Smith's photographic record of the Pacific theater of World War II is considered among the grimmest and most powerful visual indictments of war. On a ridge along the coast of Okinawa in 1945, Smith was hit by a shell fragment that ripped through his left hand, his face, and his mouth. He was unable to work for two years.

## Set Standard for Photo Essays

After a long recuperation from his war wounds, Smith worked for *Life* between 1947 and 1954. His first photograph was one of his most famous. "A Walk to Paradise Garden" was an image of his two children walking toward a sunlit area on a wooded path. It was chosen as the final work in the *Family of Man* exhibition at the Museum of Modern Art in New York City in 1955. Working for *Life*, Smith published many important photo essays, including "Trial by Jury" in 1948, "The Country Doctor" in 1948, "Nurse Midwife" in 1951, "The Reign of Chemistry" in 1953, and "Spanish Village." These features set a new standard for evocative picture stories. They showed essential human experiences such as compassion, pride, daily labor, birth, and death, with strength, clarity, and beauty. His images were viewed as universal symbols. Smith's photo essay on the work of nurse-midwife, Maude Callen, touched American readers, who donated money to build her clinic in South Carolina. Photographers felt Smith represented the ideal of personal creative expression in the service of journalism. "A Man of Mercy," a profile of Dr. Albert Schweitzer as a medical missionary to lepers in Africa came out in 1954.

## Pittsburgh Project

Growing increasingly frustrated with the restrictions of working for *Life* magazine, Smith resigned at the end of 1954 and became a member of the Magnum Photo Agency in 1955. During the next three years he contributed photo essays to *Life, Sports Illustrated, Popular Photography,* and other periodicals.

Picture editor, Stefan Lorant, needed some photographs for a pictorial history of Pittsburgh. Proceeds from sales of the book would be used to support an urban renewal program. Smith was offered the assignment and received an advance of $500 with a final fee of $1,200. The job should have taken two to three weeks to complete. Instead Smith turned it into a three-year project that resulted in an essentially unfinished work, the "Pittsburgh" photo essay. He saw in this assignment the opportunity to expand the form of the photographic essay. Smith moved to Pittsburgh where he set up a darkroom in his apartment and hired an assistant and a local guide. Working intensely, he put a lot of his own money into the project. Smith created 11,000 negatives during five months in 1955 and a few weeks in 1957. This project faltered because of Smith's often self-destructive personality, his stubbornness, and legal complications. Lorant's book finally appeared in 1964 and included 64 of Smith's images.

Attempting to salvage the work, Magnum arranged for publishing agreements with *Look* and *Life*. The deals fell apart because Smith was dissatisfied with the page layouts and kept changing them. He tried to create a complex set of themes and metaphors with many meanings. The "Pittsburgh" essay has never been published in any form approaching Smith's book-length vision. The most complete version, in his own layout, includes 88 photographs covering 37 pages. It was published in *1959 Photography Annual*. Smith considered the work a failure, but the Pittsburgh project is regarded as a remarkable accomplishment that did much to push the photographic essay into a larger dimension.

During this time, Smith's marriage ended, his health deteriorated, and he was threatened with a lawsuit. He ran up huge debts with the Magnum Photo Agency and went bankrupt. This left his family in dire straits, despite the fact that Smith had received two successive Guggenheim Fellowships.

Other assignments followed. In 1956, Smith was commissioned by the American Institute of Architects to photograph contemporary American architecture in color. Smith's second trip to Japan was at the invitation of the Hitachi Corporation in 1961. He was asked to photograph the company and its employees and stayed for one year. In an essay written for the *Masters of Photography* website, Tony Hayden recalled seeing Smith at the Woodstock Festival in August 1969. Smith arrived at Woodstock after photographing singer Bob Dylan in New York City. Smith and Hayden spent the afternoon of the first day of the festival together walking around and taking photos. Hayden recalled that Smith seemed very sympathetic with the peace movement time and felt right at home at Woodstock. Hayden noted, "He was so humble that he could melt into the camera, be the camera and be a part, and subject, of whatever he chose to photograph."

## Mercury Poisoning in Minamata

In 1971, Smith returned to Japan for a third time and lived in the small fishing village of Minamata, with his wife Aileen. Although they planned to stay for only three months, the couple stayed for three years. Smith's photos on a mercury poisoning scandal in Minamata were published in *Asahi Camera, Camera 35,* and *Life* in an article called "Death-Flow from a Pipe," and in a book called *Minamata.* The photos brought world attention to the Minamata disease caused by mercury being released into the ocean by a company called Chisso. The most famous photo was that of Kamimura Tomoko in the bath, cradled by her mother. Born in 1956, Tomoko suffered from mercury poisoning. Mercury had entered her bloodstream through the placenta, leaving her blind, deaf, and with useless legs. Smith heard about Tomoko's daily afternoon bath and asked her mother if he could photograph them. He carefully checked the bath's lighting, which came through a dark window. Smith determined that three in the afternoon would be the best time, and took the famous photo in December 1971.

Smith and his wife were attacked and injured in January 1972 during a confrontation between mercury poisoning victims and Chisso employees at the factory in Goi. Victims were violently evicted from Chisso property. Smith had to seek medical treatment in the U.S. for his injuries. Ken Kobre described the attack in an essay at the *Masters Exhibition* website: "Smith almost lost his eyesight covering the story. He and his wife, armed with camera and tape-recorder, accompanied a group of patients to record a meeting the group expected to have with an official of the company. The official failed to show up. "But," Smith related, "suddenly, a group of about 100 men, on orders from the company, crowded into the room. They hit me first. They grabbed me and kicked me in the crotch and snatched the cameras, then hit me in the stomach. Then they dragged me out and picked me up and slammed my head on the concrete." Smith survived, but with limited vision in one eye.

This was Smith's last major story. It contained several of his most moving images. Smith said, "Photography is a small voice, at best, but sometimes—just sometimes—one photograph or a group of them can lure our senses to awareness. Much depends on the viewer; in some, photographs can summon enough emotion to be a catalyst to thought. Someone—or perhaps many—among us may be influenced to heed reason, to find a way to right that which is wrong, and may even search for a cure to an illness. The rest of us may perhaps feel a greater sense of understanding and compassion for those whose lives are alien to our own. Photography is a small voice. I believe in it. If it is well conceived, it sometimes works." Smith died in Tucson, Arizona on October 15, 1978.

### Further Reading

Frizot, Michel, *New History of Photography*, Konemann, 1999.

Hughes, Jim, *W. Eugene Smith: Shadow and Substance: The Life and Work of an American Photographer*, 1989.

Smith, W. Eugene and Ben Maddow, *Let Truth Be the Prejudice: W. Eugene Smith His Life and Photographs,* Aperture, 1998.

*W. Eugene Smith: Photographs 1934-1975*, edited by John T. Hill, Harry N. Abrams, 1998.

*Life,* Fall 1986.

*Modern Photography,* January 1984; October 1985.

Kobre, Ken, "A Last Interview With W. Eugene Smith (1918–1978)," The Master's Exhibition, http://www.nirvana.demon.co.uk/W.E.Smith.txt (April 17, 1999).

"PhotoReviews," *PhotoGuide Japan,* http://photojpn.org/DATA/review/docu1/smith.html (April 10, 1999).

"Smith, W. Eugene," *Masters of Photography,* http://www.masters-of-photography.com/S/smith/smith_articles1.html (April 10, 1999). □

# Thomas Sowell

**Thomas Sowell (born 1930) is noted for his conservative views on social and economic issues. An African American author and economist, Sowell opposes such programs as affirmative action, busing, racial quotas, minimum wage, and welfare. He has drawn fire from liberals and a number of African American leaders, while generating applause from fellow conservatives.**

S owell is an advocate of the "pull yourself up by the bootstraps" philosophy, which encourages people to improve their positions not by government intervention, but by personal ambition and hard work. He believes that government initiatives to ensure a fair playing field for African Americans have actually hurt their chances for equality. Regardless of whether or not one agrees with his views, Sowell is respected as a top economist, having published extensively in economic journals and general periodicals. He also spent the better part of three decades teaching in prestigious academic institutions. Into the 1990s, his name was commonly seen in a weekly column for *Forbes* magazine and on his syndicated column appearing in newspapers nationwide. Sowell is the author of over 20 books and has edited or contributed to others. "The word 'genius' is thrown around so much that it's becoming meaningless," remarked renowned economist Milton Friedman in *Forbes,* "but nevertheless I think Tom Sowell is close to being one."

Sowell was born June 30, 1930, in Gastonia, North Carolina, and spent much of his youth in Charlotte, North Carolina. Being a very private person, not much is known about his family or early years, except that he moved to Harlem in New York City with his parents at around the age of eight or nine. His father worked in the construction industry. Sowell attended classes for gifted students and was ranked at the top of his class at the prestigious Stuyvesant

High School. He left school in tenth grade and worked for the next four years in a factory, as a delivery person, and as a Western Union messenger. These lean early years would heavily influence his politics later in life and provide him with arguments during debates with liberal leaders.

## Higher Education

Sowell completed high school by attending night classes, then was drafted to serve in the U.S. Marine Corps in 1951. He spent two years at Camp Lejeune, North Carolina, where he worked as a photographer. Thanks to the G.I. Bill, he enrolled at Howard University in Washington, D.C., a majority African American institution, while working part-time as a photographer and a civil service clerk for the General Accounting Office. After three semesters, Sowell transferred to Harvard University. There, he wrote his senior thesis on the German political philosopher, Karl Marx. Sowell graduated *magna cum laude* with a bachelor's degree in economics in 1958. A Marxist sympathizer as an undergraduate, Sowell gradually became more conservative as he pursued his master's degree at Columbia University. He continued his education at the University of Chicago, where he studied under economist and Nobel laureate, Milton Friedman, and George Stigler. Sowell obtained his Ph.D. from the University of Chicago in 1968.

## Academic and Government Employment

Sowell began his illustrious professional career as a summer intern in 1960, then as an employee of the U.S. Department of Labor in 1960-61 as an economist. From there, he taught at Rutgers (1962–63) and Howard (1963–64) universities, later taking a post as an economic analyst with AT&T from 1964-65. Sowell taught from 1965-69 as an assistant professor of economics at Cornell and spent the summer of 1968 there as the director of the Summer Intensive Training Program in Economic Theory. After teaching from 1969-70 at Brandeis, Sowell went to the University of California, Los Angeles (UCLA) as an associate professor of economics, where he was promoted to full professor in 1974. He also served as project director of the Urban Institute from 1972-74. Sowell stayed at UCLA until 1980 and also taught there from 1984-89. In 1980, he was named a senior fellow at Stanford University's Hoover Institution.

In 1980, Ronald Reagan took control of the presidency and ushered in a conservative political era that would last most of the decade. It seemed that Sowell's time had come. He organized a Black Alternatives Conference in San Francisco to publicize the conservative voice of African Americans. About 100 Republican business professionals and educators attended, advocating right-wing policies such as lowering the minimum wage, doing away with rent control, and reorganizing federal programs. After that event, Edwin Meese III, then the director of Reagan's transition team, announced that the new president would appoint African Americans to his cabinet and other high-level positions. Sowell was offered a cabinet post, but did not even entertain the notion. According to a *Newsweek* piece from the time, "Such active participation in politics . . . would only damage his scholarly reputation." In February 1981, Sowell

agreed to serve on the White House Economic Advisory Board, but resigned after one meeting. The distance between Washington, D.C. and his home in Palo Alto, California, was "too much of a strain," as *People Weekly* reported.

## Wrote for Mass Media

Sowell continued working at the Hoover Institute, teaching at UCLA for part of the decade, and penning his controversial ideas. A prolific writer for much of his career, Sowell has churned out books nearly every year since 1971 and has contributed regularly to scholarly economic journals as well as periodicals, such as the *New York Times Magazine* and *Spectator*. His topics range from law to education in addition to economics and race relations. In 1984, Sowell began writing a newspaper column, believing that if George Will could make a point in 750 words, so could he. He was a regular columnist for the Scripps-Howard news service from 1984-90, then began writing a column for the weekly *Forbes* magazine as well as newspaper columns for the Creators Syndicate in 1991. He has been criticized by fellow economists who think his academic papers are not "formal" enough, but *Forbes* defended him by saying that his work was readable and not bogged down in algebraic formulas. A biography of Sowell on the web explained his desire to publish in the mass media: "Writing for the general public enables him to address the heart of issues without the smoke and mirrors that so often accompany academic writing."

## Controversial Views

Readers have also been taken aback by Sowell's authorship. His conservative opinions have been the cause of dissent. One of Sowell's often-targeted beliefs is that poverty among minority groups is less a result of racial and social discrimination than of a group's values, ethics, and attitudes. He contends that if discrimination is to blame for a group's lack of progress, then many of the Japanese, Chinese, and Jewish groups in America would never have reached the level of prosperity that they enjoy. As an example, he says that Chinese immigrants from a certain province have had more success in America than those from other areas. Those older immigrants from the Toishan district of the Kwantung Province are affluent, whereas newer immigrants from various other areas work in sweatshops and live in poverty. As he asserted in *U.S. News & World Report,* "The two have different cultures, and that accounts for the contrast in their situations. . . . The enormous difference between the groups cannot in any way be attributed to how the larger society treats Chinese people, because the average American employer cannot tell the two apart." He also cited statistics on West Indian blacks, who have higher incomes than whites in the United States, yet cannot be distinguished from other African Americans.

Sowell believes that government programs such as busing black children to white schools, welfare, affirmative action programs, and other social programs have hurt blacks by causing them to rely too heavily on government safety nets instead of using their own motivation to succeed. He also has said that government programs will harm African Americans by fueling racist sentiments of whites upset by busing, quotas, and other laws that Sowell feels discriminate against the majority. He claimed in *U.S. News and World Report* that the status of African Americans was rising prior to the Civil Rights Act of 1964 and that they were making strides in housing integration and career advancement. Thus the act did not really have the impact that people thought it did.

Sowell's 1990 book, *Preferential Policies: An International Perspective,* dealt specifically with the issue of affirmative action. In it, he vehemently opposed quotas in college admissions and jobs, using examples not just from American society, but from around the world. He argued that preferential treatment led to relaxed standards, which caused people to fail to reach their true potential. Quotas caused underprepared members of minority groups to suffer frustration and a higher drop-out rate, or may be a reason they were steered to "softer" fields of concentration instead of more practical pursuits at schools that fit their pace. Sowell also believed that quotas led to more interracial tension on campuses. Andrew Hacker in the *New York Times Book Review* related Sowell's claims that policies such as affirmative action make the "trendy middle classes" feel virtuous, as if they were somehow making up for slavery or for overrunning a native culture. Sowell disagreed with those who called for reparations to be paid by the government to African Americans for the slavery they endured, arguing that African Americans today should progress to thinking about the present, not the past.

Not surprisingly, many liberal African American leaders, including Jesse Jackson and Benjamin Hooks, as well as left-wing whites took offense with Sowell's arguments, saying, ironically, that he is the one promoting racism, and that his arguments are too simplistic. Economist Bernard Anderson of the University of Pennsylvania's Wharton School asserted in *Newsweek,* "We cannot separate the incredible gains that have been made [by blacks] from the strong role that the government has played." He added that the U.S. government is the largest single employer of middle-class African Americans in the nation. *People Weekly* reported that Carl T. Rowan charged that Sowell gave "aid and comfort to America's racists," but that "Sowell has dismissed Rowan as an 'idiot' whose 'dumb remarks' intimidate blacks holding differing views."

Sowell also expressed strong opinions in 1995, after publication of the controversial study, *The Bell Curve.* Emotions were highly charged when the book was released asserting that intelligence quotient (IQ) is genetic and that blacks scored lower on IQ tests than whites. Though it was derided by many as having a cultural bias, Sowell defended much of the study, detailing his arguments in a lengthy article in *American Spectator.* He did point out aspects that troubled him, but overall, he stated, "Contrary to much hysteria in the media, this is not a book about race, nor is it trying to prove that blacks are capable only of being hewers of wood and drawers of water."

With the repealing of affirmative action laws and the ensuing debates in the late 1990s, Sowell's works were more salient than ever. He continued to write a weekly column for Forbes, publish books, and make numerous appearances on the lecture circuit. Divorced from his first wife, Alma Jean Parr, he married again in the early 1980s, but remained secretive about his personal life; his name was not even posted on his office door at the Hoover Institute. He was reputed to be blunt and impatient, but humorous and outgoing among friends. Indeed, his wit often showed through in his writing. Known for his satire as well as his serious messages, Forbes once reprinted Sowell's "glossary of common political terms" as published in *National Review,* which included gems such as "Equal opportunity: Preferential treatment," "Stereotypes: Behavior patterns you don't want to think about," "Demonstration: A riot by people you agree with," "Mob violence: A riot by people you disagree with," "A proud people: Chauvinists you like," and "Bigots: Chauvinists you don't like."

Sowell's intent not to be swayed by voices of dissent among other African American leaders may be illustrated by one of his favorite quotations, as listed on his own home page and attributed to David Ricardo: "I wish that I may never think the smiles of the great and powerful a sufficient inducement to turn aside from the straight path of honesty and the convictions of my own mind."

## Further Reading

*American Spectator,* February 1, 1995, p. 32.
*Forbes,* August 24, 1987, p. 40; August 26, 1996.
*Newsweek,* March 9, 1981, p. 29.
*New York Times Book Review,* July 1, 1990.
*People Weekly,* December 28, 1981, p. 66.
*U.S. News & World Report,* October 12, 1981, p. 74.
*Washington Times,* September 18, 1995.
"Biography of Thomas Sowell," Conservative Current web site, http://www.townhall.com (April 28, 1998).
"Favorite Quotations," Thomas Sowell home page, http://www.tsowell.com (April 28, 1998).
"Online NewsHour: A Gergen Dialogue with Thomas Sowell—July 11, 1996," PBS web site, http://www.pbs.org (April 28, 1998). □

# Carl Spaatz

**Carl Spaatz (1891–1974) was an early advocate of the military applications of air power. He directed U.S. strategic bombing campaigns in both Europe and the Pacific during World War II.**

The career of Carl Spaatz paralleled the development of military air power during the twentieth century. He entered the military in the early days of aviation and ended his career in the era of jet engines, rocketry, and nuclear weapons. Spaatz played several roles in this development, first as a proponent of aircraft as a weapon, and finally in refining the techniques and objectives of strategic aerial operations.

Carl Andrew Spaatz was born into a German immigrant family in Boyerstown, Pennsylvania on June 28, 1891. His

father was a printer who also participated in local politics, once holding the position of state senator. Spaatz graduated from the U.S. Military Academy at West Point in 1914, where he acquired the nickname, "Tooey," which was to remain with him for the rest of his life. After leaving the Academy, Spaatz was assigned to Schofield Barracks in Hawaii. Spaatz's second posting was to San Diego, where he learned to fly.

### Birth of Military Aviation

During the U.S. pursuit of the forces of Pancho Villa in Mexico in 1916, Spaatz served as one of America's first military aviators. At the time, the Army did not view aircraft as a means for delivering weapons to a target, but instead used them strictly for reconnaissance purposes. In fact, the Army Air Service was a part of the Signal Corps prior to World War I.

Spaatz was transferred to France following the U.S. entry into World War I in 1917. He was assigned to a training program to learn about the more aggressive uses of military aviation being made by both Allied and German forces. Bored by his training, Spaatz flew unauthorized missions with a British combat air unit and managed to shoot down two German aircraft during one of his flights. Despite his insubordination, Spaatz was awarded the Distinguished Service Cross for this exploit. By war's end, he had been promoted to the rank of colonel.

In the years following World War I, military leaders debated the role of aircraft in future conflicts. Technological limitations restricted aircraft to relatively low speeds, altitudes, and payloads. It was extremely difficult to hit targets with bombs dropped from a plane. In such an atmosphere, many experts felt that aircraft would never be capable of playing a major military role, while others thought that technological advances would make aircraft the decisive factor in future conflicts.

The major early advocate of air power in the U.S. Army was the controversial Billy Mitchell, who staged a dramatic demonstration of offensive capabilities of aircraft by bombing captured German battleships in the early 1920s. Mitchell's activities angered the military establishment, and he was subjected to a court martial. Spaatz appeared as a witness on his behalf. Mitchell's eventual conviction represented a victory for opponents of expanded use of air power. Spaatz's identification with Mitchell ensured that promotions would be rare until the Army's overall attitude changed.

Throughout the 1920s and early 1930s, Army aviators staged a series of publicity flights to set aviation records and demonstrate to the public, and to their own superior officers, the expanding capabilities of aircraft. Spaatz participated in several such flights, including a 1929 endurance flight that featured 151 consecutive hours in the air and several in-flight refuelings. This sort of practical demonstration, combined with the continued development of military aircraft by other world powers, eventually led to the adoption of many of Mitchell's concepts and ensured the continuing development of U.S. military aviation.

As the U.S. military gradually accepted a broader role for aircraft, Spaatz was appointed to the Army Command and General Staff College in Leavenworth, Kansas, in 1935. This represented an opportunity to advance his career, but was considered a less desirable appointment than command of a field unit or a posting to the Tactical School at Maxwell Field. Spaatz completed his course and was recognized as one of the Army's leading experts on the uses of airpower on the eve of World War II.

### Strategic Bombing

Although the use of aircraft to bomb targets on the land and sea was generally accepted by military authorities in the 1930s, debate still raged on the question of the strategic uses of air power. Advocates of strategic bombing, which targets the enemy's economic infrastructure, argued that such bombing could win a war on its own. Opponents, however, doubted the ability of aircraft to create enough damage to appreciably affect the military capabilities of a large nation. The debate regarding the efficacy of strategic bombing continues to the present day.

### Battle of Britain

Advocates of strategic bombing had been successful enough to ensure that all belligerent nations possessed at least some strategic bombing capabilities at the outset of World War II. Furthermore, the Spanish Civil War and the Sino-Japanese conflict during the 1930s had shown yet another use for strategic aircraft: terror bombing against civilian targets to lessen a nation's will to resist. This form of bombing was also practiced in the early stages of World War II by the German *Luftwaffe*, which conducted terror operations against Rotterdam in the Netherlands and London, England. Given his interest in, and advocacy of, strategic bombing, Spaatz was assigned to London at the height of the Battle of Britain during the spring and summer of 1940. His assignment was to observe the tactics and affects of the German bombing campaign, and the countermeasures employed by the British to stop it.

The eventual German defeat in the Battle of Britain demonstrated the limitations of terror bombing as a means of defeating a belligerent nation. Furthermore, German attacks on British economic and military infrastructure, while somewhat more successful, also failed to produce a decisive result. Analysis of the battle by British military aviation expert Sir Solly Zuckerman revealed that increased use of aerial photography to both identify targets for strategic bombing and analyze the extent of damage caused by such bombing could have increased the effectiveness of the German aerial offensive. Spaatz became a proponent of systematic analysis as proposed by Zuckerman, and following his tenure in England, he was promoted to the position of chief of the Army Air Forces Materiel Division. He served in this capacity until the U.S. entry into the war in December 1941.

### World War II—Europe

Spaatz was promoted to the rank of major general in January 1942, and was placed in command of the Eighth U.S. Army Air Force, operating out of England, in July of that year. The Eighth Air Force commenced bombing raids on targets in continental Europe the following month. With his new command scarcely up-and-running, Spaatz was transferred to the position of Allied Air Forces Commander, to support the amphibious landing of U.S. troops in North Africa in November 1942. This command was reorganized in February 1943, and Spaatz became subordinate to British Air Marshall Tedder. However, he nonetheless received a promotion to the rank of lieutenant general in March 1943. In December of that year, Spaatz was transferred back to England and named commander-in-chief of the U.S. Strategic Air Forces in Europe.

Spaatz's experiences in the Mediterranean, which had included the suffering of heavier-than-expected losses in the attempt to bomb the German oil production facilities at Ploesti, Romania, had led him to demand the development of a long-range fighter aircraft capable of protecting bombers throughout their missions. Such an aircraft, the P-51 Mustang, became available in 1944, and the Allied strategic bombing program against Germany accelerated.

Zuckerman and Spaatz, drawing on their experiences early in the war, advocated precision daylight bombing of carefully selected targets designed to cripple Germany's fuel production and transportation capabilities. This approach was in direct contrast to that used by the British earlier in the war. The British had used nighttime bombing of entire areas of German cities, a method which combined elements of both strategic and terror bombing, while minimizing British losses. Furthermore, the British had focused on destroying military manufacturing facilities. The devel-

opment of long-range fighter aircraft greatly reduced the risk of daylight bombing and made Spaatz's approach more viable as the war progressed. Nevertheless, the British continued their night area bombing campaign throughout the war with Spaatz's approval, since this, in conjunction with the U.S. daylight campaign, made the bombing of Germany continuous. Unfortunate byproducts of strategic bombing, even the "precision" bombing done by Spaatz's command during the daylight hours, were the killing of civilians and the destruction of civilian properties.

To facilitate the amphibious invasion of France, all Allied air forces were placed under the direct command of Dwight Eisenhower from April to October 1944, thus putting Spaatz's strategic bombing campaign on hold for a time. During the Normandy battles, airpower scored one its most significant victories over ground troops during the reduction of the Falaise Pocket. Shortly after the D-Day landings on June 6, 1944, Allied air superiority over the battlefield was so complete that Spaatz's forces were authorized to continue their attacks on German fuel production facilities and transportation hubs. These attacks continued until the war's end in May 1945, with a level of success that is debated to this day. In June 1945, Spaatz was transferred to oversee U.S. strategic bombing operations in the Pacific.

### World War II—Pacific

Strategic bombing of Japan had proven a difficult prospect. Although Japanese defenses against U.S. bombers were nearly nonexistent, the fragmentation of Japanese industry into small facilities and the sheer size of Japanese cities made targeting nearly impossible. General Curtis Lemay, who commanded the strategic bombing effort in the Pacific until Spaatz's arrival, devised a macabre solution to the problem. By test bombing a replica of a Japanese village constructed in the Nevada desert, Lemay discovered that typical Japanese houses, which were constructed of wood and paper, were particularly vulnerable to a combination of fragmentation bombs followed by incendiaries. Lemay's methods took area bombing to its most devastating form, destroying Japanese industry by burning huge portions of Japanese cities. Civilian losses caused by this type of bombing were catastrophic, exceeding 80,000 killed in one raid on Tokyo alone. Spaatz approved Lemay's methods upon taking command. He also presided over the use of the atomic bomb on Hiroshima and Nagasaki in August 1945. Significantly, the Japanese did not surrender immediately upon realizing that Hiroshima had been attacked with a nuclear device, since fewer people had been killed than in many of the earlier, conventional firebombing raids.

### Postwar

In the years following World War II, Spaatz continued to advocate strategic bombing as a method of warfare. Although postwar analyses revealed that German and Japanese military production had continued to increase nearly until war's end, despite the visible destruction of their national infrastructures, the advent of nuclear weapons made strategic bombing a more potent weapon than ever before. Spaatz was made commander of the U.S. Army Air Force in

1946. He became the first chief of staff of the U.S. Air Force following its establishment as a separate service in 1947. Spaatz retired from the Air Force in 1948 and became a national security affairs correspondent for *Newsweek* magazine. He also served as chairman of the Civil Air Patrol and the International Reserve Committee following his retirement. Spaatz died in Washington, DC on July 13, 1974.

## Further Reading

*A Biographical Dictionary of World War II,* edited by Chrsitopher Tunney, St. Martin's Press, 1972.
Boyne, Walter J., *Clash of Wings,* Simon and Schuster, 1994.
*Dictionary of American Biography,* edited by Roger J. Spiller, Greenwood Press, 1984.
*Illustrated World War II Encyclopedia,* edited by Peter Young, H.S. Stuttman Inc., 1978.
*The Oxford Companion to World War II,* edited by I.C.B. Dear, Oxford University Press, 1995.
*Who Was Who in World War II,* edited by John Keegan, Thomas Y. Crowell Publishers, 1978. □

# Albert Speer

**Albert Speer (1905–1981) may have known of the atrocities committed in Germany during the Nazi era, but claimed he did not. He insisted that he was only "following orders" and had no knowledge of the details. Speer received a 20-year prison sentence at the Nuremberg war crimes trials at the end of World War II.**

Speer was born in Mannheim, Germany, on March 19, 1905, but grew up in the German city of Heidelberg. His father was an architect. Although Speer wanted to be a mathematician, he studied hard and became an architect in order to please his father. His girlfriend and eventual wife, Margarethe Weber, waited for him to complete his studies. Speer's family made it clear that Margarethe did not, in their opinion, measure up to the social standards of the Speer family, but the young couple ignored them and were eventually married.

Germany was in political and economic chaos following their defeat in World War I, and had not recovered years after the war's end. Adolf Hitler, who had been released from jail in 1925, after serving nine months of a five-year sentence, had reclaimed his leadership of the National Socialist German Workers' (Nazi) party. While in jail, Hitler wrote his political mandate, *Mein Kampf.* The party and Hitler's book appealed to young Speer. He joined the Nazi party in 1931 and was soon designing and building for the Nazis. Speer was pleased with the high level of responsibility given to such a young architect. In a Germany with high levels of unemployment, especially for architects, Speer was doing what he loved and being paid for it.

## A Budding Friendship

In 1933, the Nazi party was swept into power on a rising tide of German nationalism and economic discontent. Hitler was named chancellor and assumed the title of *fuhrer* (supreme leader). Speer was advancing rapidly in the party heirarchy. Hitler had a deep interest in architecture, and the two men became friends and collaborators on many projects. Hitler wanted buildings in Germany that would last one thousand years, and he felt Speer was the man who could design and build them. When Hitler wanted a balcony built so that he could appear before his people, he would draw a very skillful sketch. Then Speer would take the sketch, make up the blueprints, and oversee its construction. It was a comfortable partnership between two men who liked and respected each other.

By the age of 28, Speer was in the "inner circle" of power. Where Hitler went, he went. He designed the vast stadiums where Hitler held his great rallies and many other Nazi monuments.

No order for a building was too impossible for Hitler to give, and no challenge was too great for Speer to accept. Hitler wanted a new Reichs Chancellery in Berlin, and he ordered that it be one of the largest and most splendid office buildings of its day. Furthermore, he wanted it completed in only one year. With an army of laborers working in day and night shifts, and with Speer handling every detail of the planning and building, the architect finished the great building ahead of schedule. He proved to his *fuhrer* that he was an organizer as well as a builder, for the building was ready to be used when Hitler walked in on the first day. If there was any doubt of Speer's skill, it was gone.

The two men began to plan an entirely new Berlin. They had elaborate models constructed showing various buildings and street layouts. It was planned to be the most beautiful city in all of Europe. World War II stopped the plans, although both Hitler and Speer felt that the delay would be only temporary. Despite later claims to the contrary, Speer had become a dedicated party member who supported whatever Hitler wanted to do.

## Minister of Armaments and Munitions

When German troops moved into neighboring countries, Allied nations became increasingly disturbed. The invasion of Poland on September 1, 1939 led to a declaration of war. As battles against Allied troops were being fiercely fought, Hitler lost one of his most experienced munitions experts. Doctor Todt, the genius behind the *autobahns* and other projects in Germany, was killed in a plane crash. Hitler asked Speer, to take over as minister of armaments and munitions. It was a job that required the organization of industry. Although Speer didn't really want the assignment, he knew that his leader needed him. He accepted.

As the organizer of the German wartime economy, Speer held an extremely powerful position. Instead of ordering, commanding, and punishing, he approached industries in a friendly way. This led Speer to be accepted by the German workers, who labored twice as hard as before. His attempts to avoid bureaucracy worked well. He kept the wishes of working men and women in mind and, in the process, won many new friends. In spite of severe and constant Allied bombing of German factories, Speer did his job well and production continued until close to the end of the war.

## A Change of Heart

It was a disillusioned Speer, who violated Hitler's "scorched earth" orders near the end of the war. Hitler ordered the destruction of roads, factories, bridges, entire cities, in an effort to delay the end. Speer sided with the generals who refused to destroy Paris and other cities. Hitler would issue ruthless orders, then Speer, who had the power and the respect of those in charge of the army, would countermand them. Speer felt the German people would need the things that Hitler wanted to destroy. In his book, *Inside the Third Reich,* Speer explained that he could see no need to hurt the civilian population needlessly, since he knew the war was lost.

Hitler committed suicide in his bunker in 1945 as the Russian army approached Berlin. Admiral Karl Doenitz took over as the new leader in Berlin, but there was still an army-occupied area in northern Germany. Speer and others were in charge there. They attempted to negotiate a peace treaty with the Allies, but were unsuccessful and finally had to surrender.

## The Nuremberg War Crimes Trials

Soon after the war ended, the world was riveted by the war crimes trials held in the German city of Nuremberg between November 1945 and October 1946. Nazi leaders, including Speer, were put on trial for the crimes they had committed. He said later that he was certain he would be convicted and hanged, as was the fate of many of his Nazi high-command friends. He even confessed and pleaded guilty to what the Nazis had done, although he said he didn't really know all the details. Still, he was shown to have been one of the first to provide the labor needed to keep the war plants operating. He personally provided a labor force of 75,000 German Jews. Many experts believe that this group represented the first stage of the Holocaust, though Speer denied that he was aware of the killing of millions of Jews in concentration camps. He claimed that he was an "unwitting collaborator" in the horror.

Speer received a 20-year prison sentence and was sent to Germany's Spandau Prison. With the exception of three life sentences, Speer received the longest prison sentence of any Nazi leader. He was released in 1966, and began writing *Inside the Third Reich.* The book was published and quickly became a best seller. In 1976, he wrote another successful book, titled *Spandau: The Secret Diaries.* Speer died in London on September 1, 1981.

## Further Reading

*Nuremberg Trials,* Grolier, 1997
Speer, Albert, *Inside the Third Reich,* 1970
Van der Vat, Dan, *Good Nazi: The Life and Lies of Albert Speer,* 1997
Nazi Leader Biographies, www.nsdapmuseum.com □

# Wallace Stegner

**Although sometimes categorized as merely a "western writer," Wallace Stegner (1909–1993) was more than that: he wrote 30 books, both fiction and nonfiction, served as a mentor to many young writers, and worked in support of conservation issues throughout his lifetime.**

Wallace Stegner was born on February 18, 1909, in the rural community of Lake Mills, Iowa. Most of his childhood was spent moving from place to place as his father, George Stegner, a restless schemer, searched for a way to get rich quick. The family finally settled in Saskatchewan, Canada, although Stegner's father alternated between living with his wife and two sons to roaming the frontier, in search of his ultimate opportunity. George Stegner's life ended violently when he killed a woman he was with and then took his own life. Stegner purposely set out to be unlike his father by becoming bookish. Reading and writing gave him a hold on the world. As he said later, "What I most wanted was to belong to something" (*Audubon*). His father became, for Stegner, the

model for many characters in his books: characters who relentlessly and thoughtlessly sought personal gain without any consideration for who or what they destroyed in the process.

## Making His Own Way

As a young man Stegner worked his way through the University of Utah, graduating with a bachelor's degree in 1930. He went on to earn an master's degree in 1932 and a doctorate in 1935 from the State University of Iowa. In between his stints in graduate school and for the next several years after, he worked as an instructor at various institutions, including Augustana College in Rock Island, Illinois, the University of Utah at Salt Lake City, and the University of Wisconsin at Madison. In 1937, Stegner published his first novel, *Remembering Laughter,* which won first prize in a contest sponsored by the publishing company Little, Brown. He won $2500, which at that time was a fortune. The book became a literary and financial success and helped gain Stegner a position as an instructor at Harvard University, where he taught composition from 1939 to 1945. Stegner married Mary Stuart Page in 1934. The couple enjoyed a 59-year marriage and had one son, Stuart Page.

## Writer and Mentor

Stegner wrote several more books over the next few years, including the novels *On a Darkling Plain,* a story about a Canadian veteran who seeks peace on the prairie (1940), and *Fire and Ice,* about a college student who tem-

porarily joins the communist party (1941). *Mormon Country,* published in 1942, was a nonfiction account of the Mormon culture. None of the books achieved the success of his first novel until the publication of *The Big Rock Candy Mountain* in 1943. The novel is largely autobiographical, telling the story of a family's travels over the American and Canadian West as the father, Bo, relentlessly searches for the opportunity that will earn him his fortune. The character of Bo is obviously based on Stegner's own father, and the book, according to Mark Mardon of *Sierra* magazine, "expressed the dim view he [Stegner] held of those who exploit the West in their elusive dreams of grandeur."

At the end of World War II, Stegner returned to the West and became a professor of English at Stanford University in California, where he remained until 1969. At Stanford he set up what would become one of the most elite writing programs in the country and directed that program until 1971. Stegner established himself as what Peter Collier of *Audubon* magazine called "the leading teacher of writing of his generation." Some of the writers Stegner taught, who would eventually become well known, were Larry McMurty, Wendell Berry, Tillie Olsen, Edward Abbey, Ken Kesey, Robert Stone, and future U.S. poet laureate, Robert Haas. In addition to his teaching achievements, Stegner was named a Guggenheim Fellow twice, in 1949 and 1959; was awarded a Rockefeller fellowship to teach writers in the Far East in 1950-1951; gained a Wenner-Gren Foundation grant in 1953; received a Center for Advanced Studies in the Behavioral Sciences fellowship in 1956; and received several honorary degrees from various institutions. He also continued to write, publishing the novels *Second Growth,* which compared the lives of residents and visitors in New Hampshire (1947); *The Preacher and the Slave,* (1950); *A Shooting Star,* which told about the lives of wealthy northern Californians (1961); and *All the Little Live Things,* which contrasted the lives of an older cultured man and a young hippie (1967).

## The Pulitzer Prize

Stegner left Stanford in 1971 and devoted his time to writing. In 1972, he won the Pulitzer Prize for his novel *Angel of Repose,* a work that James D. Houston of the *Los Angeles Times Book Review* said is now "recognized as a masterpiece." It was also made into an opera by Oakley Hall and Andrew Imbrie in 1976. The book tells the story of a retired history professor in California who is editing the papers of his grandmother, a writer and illustrator of the nineteenth century. The professor has taken on the project to forget his own marital and health problems, and as he imagines the lives of his grandparents, he reflects on, and comes to an understanding of, his own life. This blending of past and present is vital to Stegner's major works and was apparent again in Stegner's 1976 novel *The Spectator Bird,* which won the National Book Award for Fiction in 1977. In *The Spectator Bird,* the older man first introduced in *All the Little Live Things* recounts a romantic event of his youth.

Stegner's concern with the past's influence on the present and a societal sense of identity is most apparent, though, in his nonfiction books. In discussing his love for the writing of history and his book *The Sound of Mountain Water: The Changing American West,* published in 1969, Stegner told David Dillon of the *Southwest Review,* "I think to become aware of your life, to examine your life in the best Socratic way, is to become aware of history and of how little history is written, formed, and shaped. I also think that writers in a new tradition, in a new country, invariably, by a kind of reverse twist of irony, become hooked on the past, which in effect doesn't exist and therefore has to be created even more than the present needs to be created." In his personal and public history of the "last plains frontier," where Montana and Saskatchewan meet and where Stegner grew up, titled *Wolf Willow: A History, a Story, and Memory of the Last Plains* (1962), Stegner searches for his own identity: "I may not know who I am," Stegner says in the book, "but I know where I came from."

Although Stegner is often classified as a regional writer, and many would agree with Daniel King of *World Literature Today* that Stegner is "the greatest writer of the West," others assert that he is much more than that. Richard H. Simpson of the *Dictionary of Literary Biography* maintains that his "main region is the human spirit" and "the central theme of all of his work is the quest for identity, personal and regional, artistic and cultural." James Hepworth in *The Quiet Revolutionary* points out that not all of Stegner's fiction is set in the West but that, certainly, "his impact, historically and environmentally, is Western."

## Environmental Concerns

Stegner's childhood experiences and the respect he developed for the wilderness while living in Saskatchewan undoubtedly had an influence on his future involvement in environmental and social issues. The first sign of what he might very reluctantly called activism came when he published the nonfiction work *One Nation* in 1945. The book criticized the racial and religious lines that were being drawn in the United States and was a foreshadowing of the social commentary Stegner would make in his later years. *One Nation* was recognized for its important message and won the Houghton-Mifflin Life-in-America Award and the Ainsfield-Wolfe Award, both in 1945. In 1953, he was convinced by a friend who was an editor at *Harper's Magazine* to write an article about the threats to the U.S. public lands. The following year Stegner published a biography about John Wesley Powell, a Colorado River explorer. The book gained the attention of David Bower, who was working to save the Dinosaur National Monument in Colorado and Utah, which was in danger of being flooded behind proposed dams on the Green River. *This is Dinosaur,* published in 1955, was Stegner's contribution to that cause, which helped keep the river flowing freely.

In 1960, Stegner wrote his famous *Wildnerness Letter,* which was originally delivered as a speech to David Pesonen of the University of California's Wildlands Research Center, who was conducting a national wilderness inventory for a presidential commission. In this speech Stegner said, "I want to speak for the wilderness idea as something that has helped form our character and that has certainly shaped our history as a people. Something will

have gone out of us as a people if we ever let the remaining wilderness be destroyed" (*Sierra*). Stegner did not think his message was extraordinary at the time, but it became a mission statement harked by conservationists around the world, despite its distinctly American references. It was also used to introduce the bill that established the National Wilderness Preservation System in 1964.

Stegner's involvement in environmental causes intensified when he was invited to be an assistant to the secretary of the interior, Stewart Udall, in 1961. Stegner spent three months in Washington, D.C. and, as a result of his research, published *The Quiet Crisis* (1963). In 1962, Udall appointed Stegner to the National Parks Advisory Board. This was followed by a three-year term on the Board of Directors of the Sierra Club, an organization on which Stegner had a profound effect and in which he participated for nearly 40 years. Vice-president of the Club, Edgar Wayburn, told *Sierra* magazine that Stegner "captured the possibilities and spirit of the American West. He understood what it could be."

## Stegner's Legacy

Despite great efforts in the conservation movement, Stegner considered himself first and foremost to be a writer. He continued to write both fiction and nonfiction until his death. Stegner published a *Collected Stories* edition in 1990, and his *Where the Bluebird Sings to the Lemonade Springs, Living and Writing in the West* (1992) consists of 16 essays on everything from family memories to environmental concerns. His last novel, *Crossing to Safety,* prompted Doris Grumbach of the *New York Times Book Review* to state that "Clearly Mr. Stegner has not gone unnoticed. But neither is he a household name, as he deserves to be."

Stegner died of injuries resulting from a car accident in Santa Fe, New Mexico, on April 13, 1993. He left a legacy as a teacher, an environmentalist, and, above all, a writer. Simply put by Daniel L. Dustin of the *Journal of Leisure Research,* he was "a highly gifted writer who practiced what he preached."

## Further Reading

*Benet's Reader's Encyclopedia,* fourth ed., edited by Bruce Murphy, HarperCollins, 1996.
*Oxford Companion to American Literature,* sixth ed., edited by James D. Hart, Oxford University Press, 1995.
*Audubon,* January 1997.
*Backpacker,* June 1998.
*Journal of Leisure Research,* Second Quarter 1998.
*Sierra,* July 1993.
*World Literature Today,* Winter 1998.
"Wallace Stegner," The Wallace Stegner Environmental Center, http://sfpl.lib.ca.us/stegner (March 1, 1999). □

# George Steinbrenner

**George Steinbrenner (born 1930), the Cleveland shipbuilding magnate who purchased the New York Yankees in 1973, has been one of professional sports**

**most controversial and quotable figures. Twice suspended by baseball for legal and ethical violations, Steinbrenner nevertheless earned the respect of his fellow owners for his record of success on the field. The Yankees won multiple championships under Steinbrenner's aggressive style of leadership.**

George Steinbrenner was born on July 4, 1930, in Rocky River, Ohio. His father, Henry Steinbrenner, owned a Great Lakes shipping company. His mother, Rita, managed their home in Bay Village, the suburb of Cleveland where Steinbrenner spent his formative years. As a child, Steinbrenner delivered eggs to earn spending money. His father, a former collegiate track and field star, instructed him to work hard and urged him to try competitive athletics.

At age twelve, Steinbrenner took up hurdling. Whenever he finished second in a track meet, his father appeared instantly at his side, demanding to know: "What the hell happened? How'd you let that guy beat you?" These scoldings instilled a perfectionist streak in the young Steinbrenner that he often cited as the key to his later success.

### Education and Early Career

Steinbrenner was educated at the Culver Military Academy in Indiana. He then went on to Williams College in Massachusetts where he continued to run track and edited the sports section of the campus newspaper. In the glee club, he stood directly behind future Broadway legend Stephen Sondheim and—by his own account—outsang him. After earning his bachelor's degree in 1952, Steinbrenner joined the United States Air Force. There he took charge of a succession of successful projects that showed his emerging leadership skills. He established a sports program and set up his own food service business on the base.

After three years in the military, Steinbrenner got a job coaching high school football in Columbus, Ohio. He later moved on to the college level, becoming an assistant at Northwestern and then at Purdue, but his Big Ten coaching career was to be short-lived. In 1957, at the request of his father, Steinbrenner returned to the shipyard, where he was put to work counting rivets in crawl spaces. He married the former Elizabeth Zweig on May 12, 1956, and seemed set to take over his father's business. The lure of big-time sports proved too powerful, however, and Steinbrenner invested a considerable sum of money into his first pro franchise, basketball's Cleveland Pipers. The team failed, and Steinbrenner lost all his savings.

### Builds Fortune

Urged to file for bankruptcy, Steinbrenner instead worked to pay off his debt. When his father retired in 1963, he took control of the family shipping business and helped turn around its sagging fortunes. With the money he made, he formed a partnership with a group of investors and bought into the American Ship Building Company. Elected to the company's presidency in 1967, Steinbrenner fetched his father out of retirement to help him run the operation. American Shipbuilding flourished under Steinbrenner's leadership and made him a multimillionaire.

In the late 1960s, Steinbrenner began to exert his newfound influence on the national level. He used his political connections to become the chief fundraiser for the Democratic Congressional Campaign Committee, raising nearly $2 million over a two-year period. The election of Republican Richard Nixon to the presidency in 1968 made Steinbrenner fear reprisals against himself or his business. In order to hedge his bets, the shipbuilder contributed to Nixon's 1972 re-election campaign. Unfortunately for Steinbrenner, his donations violated several campaign finance laws. He eventually pleaded guilty to all counts and was fined a total of $35,000.

### Yankee Owner

These charges came just as Steinbrenner was embarking on a new career as a major league baseball owner. In January 1973, Steinbrenner joined with a group of investors to purchase the New York Yankees for $10 million. Once baseball's hallmark franchise, the Yankees had slipped to second-division status in recent years under the ownership of CBS, and a management team headed by Mike Burke. Steinbrenner, who at first announced he would "stick to building ships" and let others run the team, promptly forced Burke out and hired Cleveland Indians' general manager Gabe Paul to supervise the rebuilding process.

In November 1974, baseball commissioner Bowie Kuhn did briefly return Steinbrenner to the shipyards when he issued him a two-year suspension for his campaign finance transgressions. In Steinbrenner's absence, Paul made a series of shrewd trades and personnel decisions that laid the groundwork for the Yankees return to prominence. By the time Steinbrenner returned from exile in 1976, the Yankees had a top-flight club poised to contend for a world title. The team won its division going away that season, then relied on a clutch ninth-inning, game-winning home run by Chris Chambliss to secure the American League pennant in a five-game playoff against the Kansas City Royals. Only a four-game sweep at the hands of the Cincinnati Reds in the World Series dampened the spirit of rejuvenation surrounding the Yankees.

## Championship Seasons

In 1977, Steinbrenner opened his checkbook to bring in free agent slugger Reggie Jackson, the former star of the Oakland Athletics. Jackson added considerable star power and clutch hitting to the team, but also heightened dissension in the clubhouse. He had a stormy relationship with manager Billy Martin and was considered selfish by his teammates. Nevertheless, the talented, if volatile, team survived these distractions to make it to the World Series for a second year in a row. This time they were victorious, ousting the Los Angeles Dodgers in six games. Steinbrenner had fulfilled his promise to bring a championship to New York.

He brought a second world title in 1978, though again at a high cost in terms of hostility. The simmering Martin-Jackson feud bubbled over in mid-season, prompting Steinbrenner to fire his manager. On his way out the door, Martin took a few parting shots at both Jackson and the team's owner. "One's a born liar, the other's convicted," Martin observed—an apparent reference to Steinbrenner's campaign finance activity. Relations between the two men would forever be colored by this ugly incident.

## Controversial Figure

Over the next few years, the Yankees continued to contend for the American League pennant. Steinbrenner's increasingly meddlesome management style was blamed for a lack of stability that doomed the team's best efforts. He hired Billy Martin back as manager again in 1979—only to fire him at season's end. It was the first of four instances in which the erratic Martin was invited back to take control of the club, only to be let go with assurances that he would never be hired again. In 1980, the Yankees won 103 games under manager Dick Howser, but Steinbrenner fired him after the team was beaten in the playoffs.

In 1981, the Yankees returned to the World Series. However, after beating the Los Angeles Dodgers in the first two games, the Yankees dropped the next three. Following Game Five, Steinbrenner called a late-night press conference to hold up a flimsily bandaged hand and announce that he had defended the Yankee honor by beating up two Dodger fans in an elevator. The Yankees failed to take a "get tough" cue from their owner and lost the sixth and deciding game. Before the game was even completed, Steinbrenner

ordered the Yankee publicity department to issue an apology to the people of New York City for the club's lackluster performance.

## Decline and Exile

The rest of the 1980s proved to be a bleak period for the Yankees and their fans. Steinbrenner signed many high-priced players, but with seemingly little regard for their adaptability to the pressures of playing in New York. Managers were put under intense pressure to succeed, subject to dismissal at any time according to the owner's whims. Three men were hired and fired during the 1982 season alone. Steinbrenner engaged in protracted contract squabbles with one star player, Don Mattingly, and publicly belittled another, Dave Winfield, by comparing him unfavorably to the departed Reggie Jackson. By 1990, the Yankees were one of the worst teams in baseball—thanks in large part to the instability wrought on the club by its owner.

By that time, Steinbrenner's relationship with Winfield had deteriorated to the point where he reportedly hired a known gambler to dig up information that would destroy the slugger's reputation. Acting on evidence of this plot, baseball commissioner Fay Vincent suspended Steinbrenner from baseball on July 30, 1990. Control of the Yankees was handed over to limited partner Robert Nederlander for an indefinite period. Yankee management used this period of "exile" to rebuild the team's shattered minor league system and make a few judicious trades. When Steinbrenner was allowed to regain control of the team in 1994, it was once again ready to contend for a world championship.

## Successful Return

Many observers expected Steinbrenner to return to his imperious ways and jeopardize the club's progress, but banishment seemed to have mellowed Steinbrenner. He changed his management style, showing a renewed willingness to let his "baseball people" run the team. Other than ousting manager Buck Showalter after the 1995 season, he made few personnel changes and largely avoided making the kind of public comments that had generated controversy in the past. Under new manager Joe Torre, the team capped a stellar 1996 season with a come-from-behind upset victory over the Atlanta Braves in the World Series. Two years later, the Yankees posted the best record in American League history, going 114-48. They then completed an impressive playoff run by sweeping the San Diego Padres in four games in the World Series.

During this period of success, Steinbrenner turned his attention more frequently toward the future of the Yankees. He lobbied city and state officials in New York for the construction of a new stadium, or at least the refurbishing of the old one. He engaged in negotiations to sell the team to a local cable company, but the talks broke down when the potential buyers would not agree to let him continue to run the team. In early 1999, Steinbrenner did reach a deal with the National Basketball Association's New Jersey Nets to merge business operations with the Yankees. The agreement would allow Steinbrenner to investigate the possibility of creating his own regional sports programming network, something that could generate the revenues necessary to keep meeting the Yankees' high payroll. Steinbrenner has repeatedly said that, no matter what ownership arrangement is struck, he will continue running baseball's premier franchise into the foreseeable future.

### Further Reading

Frommer, Harvey, *The New York Yankee Encyclopedia,* Macmillan, 1997.

Gallagher, Mark, *The Yankee Encyclopedia,* Sagamore Publishing, 1996.

Madden, Bill, *Damned Yankees,* Warner, 1991.

Schapp, Dick, *Steinbrenner!* Putnam, 1982. □

# Casey Stengel

**Baseball's clown genius, Casey Stengel (1890–1975) was known as much for his hilarious double-talk as he was for managing the New York Yankees and Mets. Nicknamed "The Old Perfessor," Stengel hid a fierce competitive drive behind his practical jokes and rambling monologues. His 14-year playing career was overshadowed by his 25-year career managing some of the best and worst teams in history.**

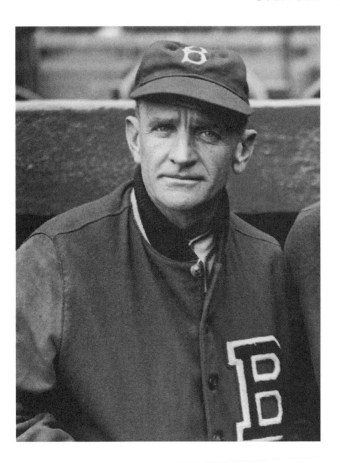

When Yankees owner George Weiss picked Casey Stengel to take over as manager in 1948, reporters ridiculed his choice. During Stengel's playing days, he was known more for his antics than his baseball acumen. In nine years managing the Brooklyn Dodgers and Boston Braves, his teams had nine losing seasons. But Weiss's choice proved inspired. Stengel became the most popular and influential manager in baseball, a star in New York City and a national celebrity. Along the way, he won more World Series games than any manager in history.

### Played the Clown

Charles Dillon Stengel was the last of three children born in Kansas City, Missouri on July 30, 1890, to Jennie Jordan, a cook, and Louis E. Stengel, an insurance agent. At Central High School, he played football, basketball and baseball. A left-handed thrower, Stengel pitched and also played third base and second base, positions rarely handled by lefties.

Stengel planned to be a dentist and went to dental college in the off-season, while playing ball in the summer. After playing for the semi-pro Kansas City Red Sox in 1908 and 1909, Stengel began his professional career in 1910 as a pitcher with Kankakee, Illinois, in the Northern Association. Soon he switched to the outfield, even though he had rarely played there before. Stengel spent five years in the minor leagues, playing for four teams. Even in those early days, he was a clown. During one game at Montgomery, Alabama, in 1912, he disappeared into a drainage hole in the outfield and popped up just in time to catch a fly ball.

Stengel debuted in the major leagues with the Brooklyn Dodgers near the end of the 1912 season. In his first game he had four hits and a walk, and in his first week he batted .478. *The Sporting News* exclaimed: "Charlie Stengel has come into the league with a tremendous crash, and appears to be the real thing."

Stengel soon acquired the nickname "KC" because he had grown up in Kansas City. Also at the time, the famous poem "Casey at the Bat" was a hit on the vaudeville circuit. When Stengel struck out a caustic fan might yell: "Hey, there's Casey at the bat!" From then on Stengel was Casey.

Stengel was a speedy, sometimes spectacular outfielder. He worked hard on his fielding, coming to Ebbets Field early and bouncing balls off the right field wall to learn the caroms. He was one of the first outfielder to wear sunglasses. As a hitter, he showed occasional power but was streaky, with long slumps. "I was very erratic," Stengel said in his 1961 autobiography *Casey at the Bat.* "Some days I was amazing, some days I wasn't."

During much of his career Stengel was a part-time player. Brooklyn manager Wilbert Robinson rarely let him play against left-handed pitchers, an early example of platooning, a system Stengel would later popularize as a manager. Stengel spent six seasons with Brooklyn, including an appearance in the World Series in 1916, then two with the Pittsburgh Pirates and two more with the Philadelphia Phillies.

Stengel's antics overshadowed his abilities. Sometimes he'd draw laughs by catching easy fly balls behind his back.

In 1919, Stengel was playing for Pittsburgh at Ebbets Field. He doffed his cap to the crowd and out flew a sparrow. He repeated the trick in 1920 in Philadelphia.

In 1921, Stengel was being traded to the powerhouse New York Giants. Legendary Giants manager John McGraw, a fiery, brilliant tactician, took Stengel under his wing. McGraw often used Stengel as a first-base coach and had him work with younger players. Stengel often visited McGraw's home and talked baseball.

In 1922 and 1923, Stengel hit .368 and .339 and appeared in two World Series with the Giants. He was a hero in the 1923 Series, winning the first game with a two-out, inside-the-park, ninth-inning home run and scoring the only run of the third game with a home run into the bleachers. Stengel's were the first World Series home runs ever hit in Yankee Stadium. In his three World Series games as a player, Stengel hit a robust .393.

Despite McGraw's affection for Stengel, he could see that leg injuries were slowing him. He traded his protégé to the Boston Braves. Stengel retired as a player in 1925, ending a career during which he batted .284 and averaged only 300 at-bats a season.

## Ups and Downs

In 1924, Stengel married Edna Lawson, an accountant he met at a ball game in 1923. They established a home in Glendale, California, where Lawson's father was a contractor. They had no children. Stengel poured his fatherly instincts into working with hundreds of young players.

In 1925, Stengel took his first managerial job, at Worcester in the Eastern League. In 1926, he took over at Toledo, an American Association club. He managed the Mud Hens for six years, bringing the franchise its first championship in 1927, and hitting a game-winning grand slam home run as a pinch-hitter in one game. But the club faltered after that. In Toledo, Stengel had frequent run-ins with umpires. And one day he forgot to put his pants on before going on the field for pre-game practice. From then on, fans yelled, "Casey, where are your pants?"

Stengel returned to New York in 1932 as a coach for Brooklyn. He took over as manager in 1934. During his three years there, the Dodgers were a losing team, but Stengel kept the fans entertained. In 1938, Stengel began a six-year stint with the Boston Braves, but the club finished seventh four years in a row.

In 1944, Stengel returned to the minor leagues to manage Milwaukee. He took over at Kansas City in 1945, and ran the Oakland team from 1946 through 1948. All were minor-league teams in cities that later would have major-league clubs. In his autobiography, *Casey at the Bat: The Story of My Life in Baseball,* Stengel admitted there were "half a dozen times . . . that I was going to quit baseball altogether."

## A Yankee Institution

Nothing in Stengel's career suggested what lay ahead when he took the helm of the Yankees in 1949. To baseball's premiere club, Stengel brought only a lackluster man-

agerial record and a reputation for silliness. But he soon made his mark. Despite an injury which sidelined Joe DiMaggio for 65 games, Stengel brought the Yankees a world championship in his first season.

During the 12 years Stengel managed the Yankees, they appeared in ten World Series, winning seven of them. Stengel holds the record for most World Series wins by a manager, 37, and most Series games managed, 63. He became a Yankee institution, as famous as his star players, Joe DiMaggio, Mickey Mantle, and Yogi Berra.

Stengel may not have invented platooning, but he popularized it. Until his Yankee days, most clubs stayed with a set lineup day in and day out. Stengel juggled lineups regularly, often playing a catcher in the outfield or an outfielder at first base, trying to get the most out of his 25-man roster and allowing slumping or injured players to rest.

Players had mixed feelings about Stengel. Clubhouse meetings might last an hour or more, with Stengel talking non-stop. "He confused a lot of players," complained star shortstop Phil Rizzuto. He also confused reporters, but they learned to love him. With his tortured syntax that became known as "Stengelese," the beak-nosed manager made great copy. He became a national celebrity, the subject of features in popular magazines, and a legend in his own time. Stengel was a clownish philosopher who proved winning and having fun were compatible.

Stengel anecdotes are abundant. One time, Stengel went to the mound to remove a pitcher. "I'm not tired," said the pitcher. Stengel replied: "I'm tired of you." Watching Jerry Lumpe in batting practice he told reporters: "He looks like the greatest hitter in the world until you play him." Another time he sat down next to Bob Cerv and told him: "Nobody knows this, but one of us has just been traded to Kansas City."

In vintage Stengelese, he once said of a speedy, weak-hitting player: "That feller runs splendid but he needs help at the plate, which coming from the country chasing rabbits all winter gives him strong legs, although he broke one falling out of a tree, which shows you can't tell, and when a curve ball comes he waves at it, and if pitchers don't throw curves you have no pitching staff, so how is a manager going to know whether to tell boys to fall out of trees and break legs so he can run fast even if he can't hit a curve ball?"

Stengel often performed clubhouse routines, practical jokes and pantomimes, one time sliding across a Detroit hotel lobby to illustrate his game-winning 1923 Series home run. Comedian George Gobel said: "If he turned pro, he'd put us all out of business." In *Casey: The Life and Legend of Charles Dillon Stengel,* biographer Joseph Durso summarized Stengel as "a national figure, an average player, a controversial coach . . . a mixture of Santa Claus and Jimmy Durante as he duck-walked out to home plate with his lineup card."

Rizzuto said Stengel "had two tempers, one for the public and writers, and one for the players under him. The players were frequently dressed down in the dugout and clubhouse. He could charm the shoes off you, if he wanted to, but he could also be rough." Stengel had plenty of other critics, too. A frequent charge was that he "over-managed" players. Some said anybody could have won with the great Yankee clubs of the 1950s.

In 1958, Stengel testified before a United States Senate committee which was investigating baseball's anti-trust exemption. His 45-minute, 7,000-word "Stengelese" monologue had senators and reporters scratching their heads and laughing uproariously. *Sports Illustrated* called the testimony "an amazingly frank, cheerful, shrewd, patriotic address that left the senators stunned, bewildered, and delighted."

After the 1960 season, Yankee officials announced they were letting Stengel go. Club executive Dan Topping explained later: "I'm just sorry Casey isn't fifty years old. . . . It's best for the future to make a change." Casey said: "I'll never make the mistake of being seventy again."

Casey turned down an offer to manage the Detroit Tigers. Then, at 74, he signed a contract to manage a new team, the New York Mets. Talking about his age and his health at a press conference, he noted: "Most people my age are dead at the present time." The Mets wanted Stengel as a distraction. "The idea was that the Mets would entertain the public with a kind of Circus Maximus," Durso wrote. "The ringleader: Casey Stengel."

On taking the reins, Stengel announced: "Come see my amazin' Mets, which in some cases have only played semi-pro ball." The name stuck, and the Mets became known as the "Amazin's," because of how frequently and ingeniously they lost. During Stengel's four years, the Mets won 194 games and lost 452. The zanier and more inept the club grew, the more attendance soared. Stengel often mocked his own players. "I been in this game a hundred years but I see new ways to lose I never knew existed before," he said.

After Stengel suffered a broken hip in 1965, he retired at the age of 75. His career as a baseball manager spanned 25 years and included three bad ball clubs and one great club. His teams won 1,905 games and lost 1,842. The baseball writers waived the standard five-year waiting rule and immediately elected Stengel unanimously to the Hall of Fame. Stengel died of lymphatic cancer in Glendale, California on September 29, 1975.

## Further Reading

Alexander, Charles, *John McGraw*, Penguin, 1988.

Creamer, Robert W., *Stengel: His Life and Times*, Dell, 1984.

Durso, Joseph, *Casey: The Life and Legend of Charles Dillon Stengel*, Prentice-Hall, 1967.

McLean, Norman, *Casey Stengel*, Drake, 1976.

Seymour, Harold, *Baseball: The Golden Age*, Oxford University Press, 1971.

Stengel, Casey, and Harry Paxton, *Casey at the Bat: The Story of My Life in Baseball*, Random House, 1961. □

# Helen Stephens

**Helen Stephens (1918–1994) was only a teenager when she became an track star, winning two gold medals in the 1936 Olympic Games. She set world, Olympic, American, and Canadian records in running, broad jump, and discus. Stephens later became the first female owner of a women's semiprofessional basketball team.**

Stephens was born on February 3, 1918 in Fulton, Missouri. She grew up on a 115-acre farm, the daughter of Frank E. Stephens and Bertie Mae Stephens. She was tall, slender and seemed born to run. As a child, she routinely raced boys on a mile-long run home from the schoolhouse, winning every time. Her cousin rode a horse and Stephens would trot along with them. "There were a couple of ditches on the way to school," Richard D. Mandell quotes her as saying in his 1971 book, *The Nazi Olympics,* "and the horse and I would take them together." Because she grew up on a farm and had a rugged, outdoor upbringing Stephens had been taught to use a rifle and was a good shot. But she thought it was more challenging and fun to hunt rabbits by running them down instead of shooting them.

When Stephens entered high school in Fulton, the athletic director discovered her running talent. In 1933, when she was 15 years old, all the students had to run the 50-yard dash in physical education class. The coach, Burton W. Moore, measured her time—an incredible 5.8 seconds. That time matched the current world record set by Elizabeth Robinson. An incredulous Moore went to town and had his watch checked for accuracy by a jeweler, who verified that it was keeping correct time. Moore was astounded but unsure how to handle this prodigy who was not even fully-grown and who seemed to run so easily. In gym class she matched the current women's world record for the standing broad jump, but she loved to run more than anything. Moore decided she would make a good sprinter and began training her for international competition. He coached her in the sprinter's technique of starting in a tight crouch and leaning forward as she ran, using her strong arms like pistons to drive herself forward.

## The Fastest Woman in the World

Stephens' first major competition took place in the summer of 1935 at an Amateur Athletic Union (AAU) Indoor Championship meet in St. Louis. The 17-year-old Stephens was so new to track and field competition that she had to borrow a sweatshirt and shoes for the meet. Although she was unknown, 4,000 fans showed up to see Stella Walsh, "the fastest woman in the world." Walsh set world records in almost every track event in which women ran. In the final heat Stephens ran against Walsh and set a U.S. record of 6.6 seconds for the 50-meter dash. When spectators congratulated her for beating Walsh, Stephens joked, "Who is Stella Walsh?"

During the rest of that meet, Stephens won the standing broad jump with a distance of 8 feet, 8 1/4 inches and won the women's shotput event with a distance of 39 feet, 7 1/4 inches. Fans began calling her the "Fulton Flash" and the "Missouri Express" and began talking about her potential for an Olympic career. Walsh, offended at the attention that was being given to Stephens, called her "that greenie from the sticks," igniting a career-long grudge between the two runners.

In that same year, at the Missouri Indoor Interscholastic Championships, Stephens set a new world record for the 50-meter dash with a time of 5.9 seconds, but the time was later disqualified because she had used starting blocks. At the 1935 Missouri Outdoor Interscholastic Championships, Stephens set a high school world record of 5.9 seconds for 50 yards and matched the world record for the 100-yard dash—10.8 seconds.

Stephens did a lot of running that year. She set a new U.S. women's record for the 100-meter race at the 1935 Ozark AAU district championships, with a time of 11.8 seconds. She also set a U.S. record in the 200-meter race with a time of 24.4 seconds and won the discus throw with a distance of 129 feet, 1 inch. At an exhibition 100 meters at another AAU event Stephens she set an unofficial world record with a time of 11.6 seconds.

Stephens entered William Woods College in Florissant, Missouri. In addition to track she competed in basketball, bowling, fencing and swimming. While still in college she won 12 national Amateur Athletic Union (AAU) titles and was the 1936 AAU champion in the shot put, 100 meters,

and discus. At the 1936 AAU Indoor Championships she kept her title in the 50 meters with a world record time of 6.4 seconds. Stephens also set a U.S. record in the shot put with 41 feet, 7 1/2 inches and set a record in the standing broad jump with a distance of 8 feet, 8 1/2 inches. She never lost a sprint event in her entire career.

## The 1936 Olympics

Stephens was viewed as one of the top women contenders at the 1936 Olympics. Women were not allowed to enter more than three Olympic events at the time. Stephens' best field events were the shot put and the standing broad jump. Women were not allowed to compete in these events at the Olympics so Stephens qualified for the discus, the 100-meter race, and as a team member on the 4 x 100 relay. She had not been seriously coached for the discus event and when she reached Berlin only threw it 112 feet, 7 1/2 inches. Her personal best for discus was 133 feet, 6 1/2 inches, nowhere near the record of 156 feet, 3 3/16 inches set by Gisela Mauermayer.

By this time, however, Stephens' fame as a runner had spread around the world and the spectators were waiting for her at the track. As she warmed up for the qualifying heat in the 100-meter race the spectators watched her. She was six feet tall, narrowly built and had a rangy, relaxed way of moving—until she started running. She finished ten meters ahead of everyone else in the race with a time of 11.4 seconds, half a second better than the time Stella Walsh had set at the 1932 Olympics. However, the judges decreed that she had been aided by a strong wind and disqualified her time. Her time in the final event was 11.5 seconds, which set a world record. This record would last for the next 24 years, until Wilma Rudolph broke it at the 1960 Olympics. Walsh, perhaps spurred on by the competition with Stephens, set her best time ever at 11.7 seconds. Now Stephens, not Walsh, held the title of "The World's Fastest Woman." Stephens also ran the anchor leg of the 400-meter relay at the Berlin Olympics, winning a gold medal in that event as well.

Stephens's incredible speed led Walsh to accusations that Stephens must really be a man—the logic being that no woman could run that fast. Stephens submitted to a physical exam by German officials who verified that she was female. Years later, Walsh was accidentally shot and killed as an innocent bystander in a Cleveland, Ohio robbery. An autopsy revealed that it was she, not Stephens, who was not what she seemed. Walsh had a genetic condition known as "mosaicism," which meant that she had a mostly male chromosome balance.

## After the Olympics

Stephens was named the Associated Press Athlete of the Year for 1936. The Associated Press polled sports editors across the United States in 1950 and asked them who they thought were the greatest athletes in the first 50 years of the 20th century. Stephens was named as one of the ten greatest female athletes of that period.

Stephens was never defeated in any running event. However, she retired from amateur sports after two and a half years, because she was bored by the lack of good competition. By that time she had won 14 AAU track and field titles, had never been defeated in any running event, and won top awards in the 50 meters, 200 meters, and the shot put.

Stephens toured with the House of David basketball team and gave exhibitions at half-time of her talents in running and heaving the shot put. Audiences were not always kind. When male spectators hooted at her, she stood still, tossed the heavy iron ball from hand to hand, and used the public address system to challenge any man present to compete with her in the shot put. Few men ever took her up on the offer and those who did always lost, silencing others who might have harassed her. She also challenged spectators to footraces, which she always won.

Stephens made her living playing basketball with the Professional (All-American) Redheads and founded her own semiprofessional women's basketball team, "The Helen Stephens Olympic Co-Eds" in 1938 when she was 20 years old. She was the first woman to create, own, and manage a semi-pro basketball team. The team played until 1952. Stephens also played semiprofessional softball and coached, managed, and owned some teams.

Stephens joined the Marines, serving during World War II. After the war she took a job with the Defense Mapping Agency Aerospace Center in St. Louis, Missouri, where she worked for 26 years.

## Still Undefeated

After retiring from the Aerospace Center, Stephens returned to William Woods College to be an advisor to the track and field program and to work as an assistant coach. From 1980 until her death she was a member of the board of the Senior Olympics Honorary Advisory Committee and was on the board of directors of the Senior Olympics Programs in 1980 and 1981. She was also active in Senior Olympics competition. David L. Porter reported in *Biographical Dictionary of American Sports,* "In seven years of Senior Olympic competition, Stephens has won over 50 medals in various sports and still has not lost a footrace. Clearly a pioneer in women's sport, the 1936 Olympic champion was the first woman inducted into the Missouri Sports and National Track and Field halls of fame." Stephens died on January 17, 1994 in St. Louis, Missouri.

## Further Reading

Guttmann, Allen, *Women's Sports: A History,* Columbia University Press, 1991.

Mandell, Richard D., *The Nazi Olympics,* Macmillan Company, 1971.

Markel, Robert, Nancy Brooks, and Susan Markel, *For the Record: Women in Sports,* World Almanac Publications, 1985.

Porter, David L., *Biographical Dictionary of American Sports,* Greenwood Press, 1988.

Wallechinsky, David, *The Complete Book of the Olympics,* Viking Press, 1984.

"AP Athlete of the Year," http://www.hickoksports.com/history//ssitest.shtml#women (March 3, 1999).

"The Finger: List-erine," *Thefinger.com,* http://www.thefinger.com/digits/fistfuls/ff27/pointer.html (March 8, 1999).

"Helen Stephens," *National Women's Hall of Fame,* http://www.greatwomen.org/stphens.htm (March 3, 1999).

"Helen Stephens Sprints," *USATF,* http://www.usatf.org/athletes/hof/stephens.shtml (March 8, 1999).

"Hickoksports.com Sports Calendar," *Arrivals February 3,* http://www.hickoksports.com/calendar/feb03.shtml (March 2, 1999). □

# Isaac Stern

**Isaac Stern (born 1920) is one of the foremost violinists in the world. He is renowned for his great musical talent, for his great energy, and for his enormous heart.**

Violinist Isaac Stern made his formal debut with the San Francisco Symphony as a teen-ager. Since that time he has played countless concerts around the globe. His world tours are an annual event. The crux of Stern's talent lies in his total mastery of each piece. Critics are amazed at his tone and his effortless style. Yet Stern is more than an accomplished musician, he is a great benefactor of the arts. He took it upon himself to spearhead the rescue of Carnegie Hall in New York City in 1960 when the building was slated for demolition. As founder and chairman of the Jerusalem Music Center, he travels regularly to Israel to sponsor master classes and workshops. Stern is well known for his efforts in mentoring young people and in sponsoring programs to encourage music for youth. Some noteworthy Isaac Stern students include violinist Itzhak Perlman, cellist Yo-Yo Ma, and Pinchas Zukerman.

Isaac Stern was born on July 21, 1920 to Solomon and Clara Stern, in the town of Kremenets in the Russian Ukraine. Stern's father was a contractor; his mother, a musician, attended the Imperial Conservatory in St. Petersburg. Fleeing the political upheaval in their native land, Stern's parents immigrated with their young son to the United States in 1921. Stern was ten months old at the time. The family made their home in San Francisco. In time Clara Stern began to share her love for music with her young son. She taught the boy to play the piano when he was six, and he started playing the violin at the age of eight. Stern was never labeled a prodigy, but his parents enrolled him at the San Francisco Conservatory of Music when he was ten years old. He studied there from 1930 until 1937 under Naoum Blinder, who was the concertmaster of the San Francisco Symphony. Blinder was very liberal in his teaching style; he never burdened Stern with tiresome hours of practicing scales. Instead, Stern learned to play as he listened to others perform; he learned to imitate the quality of the sounds he heard.

Accounts vary as to the progression of Stern's career as a virtuoso. He played his first recital in 1934 at the age of 13, and most likely it was two years later when he debuted with the San Francisco Symphony under Conductor Pierre Monteux. On October 11, 1937 he debuted in New York at Town Hall. Critics praised his performance, and he ac-

quired a manager, noted impresario Sol Hurok. Stern played seven concerts during his first year of tours; the following year that number doubled. On January 8, 1943 he debuted with a recital at Carnegie Hall. That concert earned critical acclaim and thereafter Stern was recognized worldwide as a master violinist. He was renowned for his style and flexibility, for his tone, and for the sure movement of his fingers and hands. So memorable was his first performance at Carnegie Hall, that 25 years later, in 1968, he performed a silver anniversary encore concert at Carnegie to mark the occasion.

Stern signed his first record contract in 1945 with a company that was then called CBS Masterworks, now Sony Classical Records. He remained with that record label throughout his career.

### New Horizons

In the 1940s, during the Second World War, Stern played for the Allied Armies in Greenland, Iceland, and the South Pacific. In 1944, he debuted with the New York Philharmonic under conductor Arthur Rodzinski. Stern's film debut was in 1946, in Warner Brothers' *Humoresque*, with Joan Crawford. Stern recorded the soundtrack for the film. His hands were superimposed in the stead of co-star John Garfield's when the script called for Garfield to play the violin. In 1952, Stern appeared in a film biography about his own manager, Sol Hurok, called *Tonight We Sing*.

Stern, began touring the globe in the late 1940s. He debuted in 1948 at the Lucerne Festival in Switzerland

under Charles Munch. He performed 120 concerts in 1949 alone, including a tour in South America. That same year he made his first visit to Israel. Stern played the Prades Festival with premiere cellist Pablo Casals from 1950 through 1952. In 1956, he became the first American musician since World War II to perform in the Soviet Union. That occasion also marked Stern's first return to Russian soil since he left with his family for the United States. After that initial trip, Stern visited and performed in the Soviet Union on various occasions during the 1960s. Eventually, he boycotted the Soviet regime and was grateful to return in 1997, after the Communist government collapsed. Quoted by ITAR-TASS news agency, he said, "I am glad to meet the Muscovites again."

Throughout his career Stern was the guest soloist with every major orchestra in the world. He performed his famous chamber music concerts at virtually all of the major festivals. The Istomen-Stern-Rose (chamber) Trio, co-founded by Stern in 1961, played through the early 1980s. It featured Stern, Leonard Rose on cello, and Eugene Istomen on piano. The group embarked on a world tour from 1970 to 1971, in commemoration of the 200th anniversary of the birth of composer, Ludwig Von Beethoven. Stern also collaborated with Emanuel Ax, Jaime Laredo, and cellist Yo-Yo Ma. Stern toured South America, Eastern Europe, the United Kingdom, Denmark, and France with the Franz Liszt Chamber Orchestra. He contributed to countless television specials during the 1970s and 1980s, including his work on the two series, *Tonight at Carnegie Hall,* and *Live from Lincoln Center.*

Stern celebrated his 60th birthday in 1980 by performing 60 concerts across four countries during the course of the year. Stern, who plays modern as well as classical music, was honored on multiple occasions to offer the premiere performances of compositions by William Schuman, Leonard Bernstein, Paul Hindemith, and other modern composers. Since his first visit to Israel, Stern maintained close ties with that nation. He returned frequently to perform, and to hold workshops and master classes.

In 1981, Stern filmed a documentary of his Chinese tour. The film, *From Mao to Mozart—Isaac Stern in China* won an Academy Award for best full-length documentary. The feature also received a special mention at the Cannes Film Festival. In 1987, Stern filmed *Carnegie Hall: The Grand Reopening,* a film which earned him an Emmy Award.

### Six Decades of Music

In 1993, the Arts & Entertainment Network (A&E) featured a biographical piece on Isaac Stern in a program called *Isaac Stern—A Life.* He made numerous television appearances, including *60 Minutes, Sesame Street, Live from Lincoln Center, Good Morning America,* and *Today.* Stern, along with Yefim Bronfman, toured the United States and the Far East during 1993 and 1994. The pair undertook a collaborative project to record the complete Mozart violin sonatas. They toured Russia in 1991, where they recorded a live performance of the Brahms Violin Sonata, the same piece that Stern performed during his debut with the San Francisco Symphony in the early 1930s.

In May 1993, Stern hosted a two-day chamber music workshop at Carnegie Hall, and another in Israel that same year. The Israeli workshop, called the Jerusalem International Music Encounter, attracted students from around the world. Stern reprised the event in 1995.

Stern celebrated his 75th birthday in 1995, and Sony marked the occasion with a set of 44 compact disks, entitled *Isaac Stern: A Life in Music (1946–82)*. After six decades of making music, Stern continues to perform in scores of concerts every year. His notable appearances in the 1990s included a performance with students at the San Francisco Conservatory and another at the Philadelphia Academy of Music. In 1994 and 1995 Stern toured with Yefim Bronfman and Robert McDonald.

Stern is devoted to humanity and finds that music is a natural form of expression for him. Quoted in the *Jerusalem Post*, he said, "We can sing, act, pray and do many things with music and all without one word. That is its real magic. Music can be violent because it grows in a violent world."

## Civic Duties

During the administration of President John F. Kennedy, Stern organized the National Council on the Arts, a program that evolved into the National Endowment for the Arts (NEA) under President Lyndon Johnson. In 1973, Stern founded the Jerusalem Music Centre where he held many master classes taught by international musicians. He also served as chairman of the American-Israel Cultural Foundation.

Stern voiced his political opinions in support of a boycott against a Greek military junta in 1967. He celebrated the end of the Six-Day War in Israel by performing a concert on Mount Scopus with Leonard Bernstein and the Israel Philharmonic. The concert was filmed as *A Journey to Jerusalem*.

Stern campaigned against Soviet opposition to the United Nations Educational Scientific and Cultural Organization (UNESCO) in 1974. He became a Commander of the French *Ordre de la Couronne* in 1974, and received the French *Légion d'honneur* in 1977 and Commander's Cross of the Danish Order of Dannebrog in 1985. Stern was named a fellow of Jerusalem in 1986. His biography, *Isaac Stern: A Life,* appeared in 1991. He was named the 1996 Honorary Fellow of the Diaspora Museum during a trip to Tel Aviv to perform for the 60th anniversary celebration of the Israel Philharmonic.

Three times married, Stern wed ballerina Nora Kaye on November 10, 1948 and divorced soon afterward. He then married Vera Lindenblit on August 17, 1951, following a truly whirlwind courtship—the couple met in Israel and married less than three weeks later. They divorced after 43 years, in 1994. They had three children: daughter Shira, and sons Michael and David; and three grandchildren. Stern married his third wife, Linda, shortly before the dedication of the Isaac Stern Auditorium at Carnegie Hall on January 28, 1997.

Renowned for his tireless energy, Stern loves to play tennis—with gloves to minimize blisters to his violin-playing hands. By his own admission he is not a disciplined individual; he accepts his spontaneous spirit, and concedes that the secret to the sensual character of his violin playing lies in the inability to limit his desires and wants. Stern plays his instrument, an Alard Guarnerius "del Gesu" violin, for hours on end, especially into the night.

### Further Reading

*Facts on File Encyclopedia of the 20th Century,* edited by John Drexel, Facts on File, 1991.
ITAR-TASS (news agency), September 15, 1997.
*Jerusalem Post,* December 25, 1996, p. 12; June 5, 1998, p. 10.
*Newsday,* August 16, 1994, p. A11; January 29, 1997, p. A13.
JMC Isaac Stern: Violinist, http://www.jmc.co.il/stern.html (March 12, 1999). □

# Martha Stewart

**Martha Stewart (born 1941) has become more than an author, entertainer, or businesswoman—she is an American icon. She has turned herself into one of the world's strongest brand names and sits atop a $200 million empire built around the ideas of domesticity, style, and elegance.**

Born Martha Kostyra on August 3, 1941 into a large Polish-American working class family in Nutley, New Jersey, Stewart's parents raised her to be self-sufficient. Both of her parents were teachers, and they were strict and disciplined at home. These values instilled a strong work ethic in the Kostyra children. At an early age, Stewart helped her three brothers and two sisters trap muskrats and sell the skins for extra money. Stewart's first thoughts about entertaining can be traced to the large Sunday dinners the Kostyras held each week with friends and family. Other chores performed under the watchful eyes of her parents, such as gardening, cooking, and sewing, were necessities to make ends meet in the lean years of her youth.

An excellent student, Stewart began modeling while in high school. In an interview with Morley Safer of *60 Minutes*, Stewart recalled those years: "Instead of going to the football games with my friends, I spent my time modeling clothes at Bonwit Teller on 57th Street. I was making, at first, $15 an hour, which was a lot better than the $1 an hour we were getting babysitting." Her girl-next-door appearance and photogenic face made her a favorite with photographers. The money she earned modeling helped Stewart make her way through Barnard College in New York, one of the nations top women's colleges.

While at Barnard, Stewart studied art history. Driven to succeed, she continued modeling, and eventually began appearing in major national and international magazines. Stewart was named one of the ten best-dressed college women in America by *Glamour* magazine, in 1961. Model-

ing helped pay her tuition, but she was constantly strapped for money, nonetheless. Stewart took a live-in maid position for two elderly widowed sisters on Fifth Avenue so she could move away from home.

## Marriage and Wall Street

Andy Stewart, a young Yale Law School student, entered Stewart's life early in her college years. Described as "love at first sight," the whirlwind courtship ended in marriage on July 1, 1961. They began life as penniless newlyweds living in New York City. Soon, Stewart interrupted her education at Barnard to help support her husband as he finished up at Yale.

By early 1965, Stewart was pregnant. She gave birth to a daughter, Alexis Gilbert, in September. A month later, the Stewarts bought a rundown 19th century schoolhouse in Middlefield, Massachusetts that had no running water or plumbing. Stewart would later recall planting gardens in front of the little house and in *Martha Stewart's New Old House,* she wrote about "lugging water in large pails from the stream to cook with, wash up with, and drink." It took the Stewarts five years to renovate the house. After her daughter's birth, Stewart's modeling career tapered off. She began looking for other moneymaking ventures.

One evening in 1968, Stewart brought up her career search with some friends and one suggested she call one of his stockbroker friends in New York. Stewart's mix of beauty and brains impressed Andy Monness, a partner in the firm. He hired her on the spot because she was bright, aggressive,

and hungry for success. Stewart passed the broker's exam easily and was registered with the New York Stock Exchange in 1968, right after her 27th birthday.

Stewart was successful and soon made a six-figure salary. She traveled to both coasts and led a celebrity lifestyle. Eventually tiring of the city life in New York, the Stewarts bought an old farmhouse in Westport, Connecticut that required more renovation. The house, dubbed Turkey Hill Farm by Stewart, would play a major role in her later career as a caterer and budding lifestyle expert.

Into the early 1970s, Stewart continued her string of successes on Wall Street, while her husband worked as a high-powered corporate attorney. However, the heightening Watergate scandal and uneasiness it caused on Wall Street led to problems for Stewart and the upstart firm where she worked. Unable to deal with the fluctuating market and unhappy that her accounts began losing money, Stewart resigned in 1973.

## Catering Queen

At age 32, Stewart once again found herself without a career. She retreated to Turkey Hill to decide what she should do next. Turkey Hill proved to be her inspiration. She threw herself into remodeling efforts and ways to improve the old farmhouse. Obsessive cleaning and home improvement projects served as a therapeutic escape for Stewart after the wild years spent on Wall Street.

No one had any idea at the time that Stewart's next move would launch her into the living rooms of millions of people and land her atop a $200 million multimedia empire. The accounts differ regarding Stewart's entry into the catering business: she has said that it grew out of cooking classes held for Alexis and her school friends, while others said it happened after long discussions with friends from Westport. Regardless, catering was an ideal choice for Stewart, ever the perfectionist and very concerned with details.

With partner Norma Collier, the catering company named "Uncatered Affair" was born. For several years, the two friends catered parties and taught cooking classes around Westport. The relationship soured, however, when Stewart's controlling instincts dominated the business. Her need to reign over everything around her proved the old adage about too many cooks in the kitchen.

Stewart's next effort was at the Westport Common Market, which combined an upscale mall and food court. Stewart approached the owners of the mall about running the area and serving freshly prepared food. After charming the owners over lunch at Turkey Hill, Stewart was given the job and a $250 a week salary. She renamed the food area the "Market Basket," and turned the store into a moneymaker. She hired women to cook the food at home and then resold it at the store. Stewart went too far, however, when she told a *New York Times* reporter that she was the "proprietor" of the shop. The owners fired her shortly after the story ran. Stewart kept this a secret and let people believe she left on her own to spend more time running her catering business.

Stewart got her first taste of national media exposure when *People* magazine ran a story on her and Andy, who had left legal work to become a publishing executive. The article mentioned how she catered parties for famous Westport residents like Robert Redford and Paul Newman. As her reputation spread, Stewart began getting further national press from *Mademoiselle, Bon Appetit, Good Housekeeping,* and *Country Living.* Stewart was hired to be the freelance food editor for *House Beautiful,* a national magazine that helped solidify her growing reputation.

### Best-Selling Author

Alan Mirken, president of Crown Publishing Group, attended several parties Stewart arranged and was taken by her style, good looks, and talent. After several attempts, Mirken convinced Stewart to write a book and paid her an advance of $35,000, a sum her husband negotiated using his knowledge of the book industry. The resulting book, *Entertaining,* became a bestseller and propelled Stewart to dizzying heights.

No longer just a successful caterer, she was on her way to becoming a national symbol of good taste and style. With the publication of her second book, *Quick Cook,* Jerry Oppenheimer wrote in his unauthorized biography *Just Desserts,* her publisher's goal "was to make her as recognizable as Betty Crocker." Putting out a book a year, Stewart's reputation spread across the nation.

Stewart's first national television appearances were with Willard Scott on the *Today* show. Scott visited Turkey Hill and viewers saw the Stewarts as they prepared for Thanksgiving. Stewart's true goal, however, was to have her own television show, like her idol, Julia Child. Her first television special and mail-order video appeared in 1986, called *Holiday Entertaining with Martha Stewart.* Several years later, Stewart would have her own television show, estimated to reach 97 percent of the country.

Stewart's seemingly perfect life has included some sour moments. In early 1987, Andy left her and began divorce proceedings. Years later, recalling the painful split on *60 Minutes,* Stewart said, "I know a lot of successful women who are not, at the present time, married. I hope that we could all find a balance, that you could balance a career, you can balance success, you can balance having a garden and having a husband at the same time."

Regardless of her personal situation, Stewart continued to build her business empire. She made a deal with media conglomerate Time Warner to produce her own magazine, *Martha Stewart Living,* which first appeared in late 1990. The company tied in appearances on the highly popular *Today* show. Stewart stayed with the program until January 1997 when she left to join CBS's *This Morning* as part of a package deal with CBS.

### Martha Stewart Omnimedia

Always demanding to take full control of her own destiny, Stewart left Time Warner in 1997 to form her own multimedia company. As a result, Stewart was Chairman and CEO of Martha Stewart Omnimedia, a $200 million dollar company. The cornerstone of the company was Stew-

art herself. Her television show, which appeared on 185 stations, and her radio show, which was carried on 260 stations, were both produced by Omnimedia.

Stewart achieved every goal she has set. Arguably, she was more recognizable than Betty Crocker. *Martha Stewart Living* magazine had a circulation of 2.1 million. She got 925,000 visitors to her web site every week. Revenues for her K-Mart-sponsored Martha Stewart Everyday collection reached $1 billion. In her free time, Stewart continued to write books (also released in several foreign languages) and had more than 25 bestsellers to her credit.

Like most popular culture icons, Stewart had her supporters and detractors. She was parodied relentlessly on *Saturday Night Live* and inspired the farcical magazine, *Is Martha Stewart Living?* However, the number of viewers, readers, and listeners do not lie. Stewart told MSNBC's Matt Lauer, "My whole business has been based on the pursuit of perfection and the pursuit of accuracy and good information and good inspiration. So if I am ever, you know, called difficult to work for, it's by people who really don't care about those qualities in work. But my whole life is based on those qualities."

Labeled "the world's No. 1 living mega-brand" by *Fortune* magazine, Stewart sits atop an empire built on the simple premise that domesticity is good and should play an important role in society. Perhaps Stewart's entire life can be summed up by the assertion she wrote in her high school yearbook, "I do what I please and I do it with ease."

### Further Reading

Oppenheimer, Jerry, *Just Desserts, The Unauthorized Biography, Martha Stewart,* Avon, 1997.
*Forbes,* March 22, 1999.
*Guardian,* April 15, 1996.
*Sacramento Bee,* June 27, 1997.
*San Diego Union-Tribune,* July 20, 1997.
*Tampa Tribune,* September 6, 1997.
*Washington Post,* March 17, 1996; January 23, 1997.
"She's Martha and You're Not," http://www.salon.com (March 1, 1999). □

# Paul Strand

**Paul Strand (1890–1976) was one of the most important figures in American twentieth-century photography. His work is characterized by great richness of surface detail. Strand photographed a variety of subject matter, including landscapes, portraits, architecture, and abstraction. In the 1950s and 1960s, he traveled throughout France, Italy, Egypt, and Ghana, producing a series of photography books.**

Paul Strand was born on October 16, 1890 in New York City. He was the only child born to parents of Bohemian-Jewish descent. Strand developed an early interest in photography and enrolled in the Ethical

Culture School in 1907. He attended the class taught by Lewis W. Hine, a pioneer in the field of photojournalism. Hine took Strand and other students to visit the Little Galleries of the Photo-Secession, better known as "291" after its address at 291 Fifth Avenue in New York. There he met Alfred Stieglitz, the leader of the Photo-Secession Group. On display were the atmospheric, soft-focus photographs, by the leading pictorialists of the day. These moody, richly-toned prints aspired to achieve the stature of painting.

Within a few years, Strand was "whistlering," as he called the technique of overlaying a fuzzy Romanticism onto views composed with flattened space, pattern, and high contrast. Other photographers using this style were Edward Steichen, Gertrude Kasebier, Clarence White, Alvin Langdon Coburn, and Karl Struss. When applied to the rhythms of city life, this "space-filling" approach created highly elegant images, such as "Winter, Central Park" in 1913-14. In this photograph, a tree's dark branches were shown against a snowy field while framing a single figure in the distance.

After graduation and a brief trip to Europe, Strand became a self-employed commercial photographer. He did his own photographic work on the side, experimenting with soft-focus lenses, and generally working in a pictorialist style. His work was exhibited at both the New York Camera Club and the London Salon. Strand brought his portfolio to Stieglitz in 1915 and was offered a show at the 291 gallery.

At the galleries Strand now saw the avant-garde paintings of Picasso, Cézanne, and Braque—which greatly influenced his work. In the next few years Strand was exposed to new abstract painting and sculpture exhibited by Stieglitz, as well as the photography of nineteenth-century masters such as David Octavius Hill and Julia Margaret Cameron. Strand also saw the works of such contemporary photographers as Edward Steichen. Although he was active for a brief period at the Camera Club, whose darkrooms he continued to use for two decades, Strand's ideas derived first from the people around Stieglitz and then from the group that evolved around the Modern Gallery in 1915, including Charles Sheeler.

## Stieglitz and Strand—A Common Influence

From 1915 to 1917, Stieglitz and Strand were in close contact and greatly influenced each other's work. At the end of this period Strand produced a body of sharp-focus work, including somewhat abstracted images of kitchen bowls and cityscapes. Steiglitz recognized the breakthrough this work represented. The last two issues of *Camera Work* were devoted to the most recent work of Strand. Stieglitz gave Strand a one-man show at the 291 gallery. Strand also exhibited at the Modem Gallery and the Camera Club, and won prizes at the Wanamaker Photography exhibitions.

Strand gradually rejected the soft-focus, manipulated, "painterly" pictorialism that was in vogue in the early 1920s. Instead, he viewed photography as a means for direct statements about life, nature, and the passing scene. In "Blind Woman, New York" (1916) Strand looks uncompromisingly at sightlessness, avoiding any attempt to reduce

the harsh impact of eyes that are open but cannot see. He favored the rich detail and subtle tonal range made possible by the use of large-format cameras. The purity and directness of Strand's images of natural forms and architecture foreshadowed the work of other American photographers seeking to express abstract formal values through the unadorned photographic image.

Strand became known as an advocate of the new realism called "straight" photography. He wrote *Photography and the New God* in 1917, and claimed that it was necessary for the photographer to "evolve an aesthetic based on the objective nature of reality and on the intrinsic capabilities of the large-format camera with sharp lens," as stated by Naomi Rosenblum in *A World History of Photography*. During this period, Strand took some of his best known photographs, such as "Shadow Pattern, New York" and "Wall Street" in 1915. Leah Ollman wrote in the *Los Angeles Times* that "Wall Street" remains the most startling of the group, not just un-romanticized but sinister; not just an image but an icon, a warning, a symbol as well as a document. In the photograph, a trickle of suited men and women, their long shadows dragging behind them, walks alongside the recently built J.P. Morgan Co. building, whose huge, dark recesses dwarf the passersby with the imposing powers of uniformity and anonymity. After more than 80 years, the image has stayed both tough and current." In one of the boldest photographs of the period, "White Fence" in 1916, Strand deliberately destroyed perspective to build a powerful composition from tonal planes and rhythmic pattern. Strand combined realism and abstraction in photographs of landscapes and close-ups of rocks and plants. By doing this he achieved a synthesis in a style he described as organic realism.

Strand was one of the first to use the candid-camera technique. Using a camera with a false lens mounted at a 90-degree angle to the real one, so that his subjects did not know they were being photographed, he experimented with human subjects. Strand extracted "a quality of being" from men and women with disabilities. During the 1920s, he photographed urban sites, continued with the machine forms begun earlier, and turned his attention to nature, using 5 x 7 and 8 x 10 inch view cameras and making contact prints on platinum paper. In these works, form and feeling were inseparable and intense.

## Motion Picture Work

Strand served in the Army Medical Corps during World War I, where he was introduced to X-ray and other medical camera procedures. On his return home, Strand worked as a freelance motion picture cameraman, photographing sports and medical films. He collaborated with Charles Sheeler on the short film *Mannahatta,* released as *New York the Magnificent* in 1921. He soon purchased an Akeley movie camera and worked as a freelance cinematographer until the early 1930s, when the industry for making news and short features moved from New York to California. While working as a motion picture cameraman, he spent his free time doing still photography, revealing the beauty of natural forms in Colorado in 1926 and Maine in 1927-28. In his photographs of Quebec's Gaspé Peninsula in 1929 and of New Mexico in 1930, he revealed a deep awareness of what he called "the spirit of place." In 1925, Strand was one of the photographers represented in the Seven Americans exhibition at the Anderson Galleries. Also in 1925, he began his famous series of close-ups of vegetation and other natural forms.

The 1930s was a time of political concern and activism for Strand. Aware of the revolutionary social ideas in Mexico through his visits to the Southwest, Strand was appointed chief photographer and cinematographer by the Mexican government in 1933. There he made still photographs and produced the government-sponsored documentary film *Redes,* (*The Wave,*) released in 1934. The film depicted the economic problems confronting a fishing village near Vera Cruz. Strand visited the Soviet Union where he met Russian director Sergei Eisenstein and other key Russian avant-garde artists. He futilely attempted to assist Eisenstein in 1935. Strand also worked with Pare Lorentz on the government-sponsored documentary film *The Plow that Broke the Plains* in the U.S.

A humanist with wide-ranging sympathies, Strand and other progressive filmmakers organized the nonprofit company, Frontier Films, to produce a series of pro-labor and anti-Fascist movies. He was active as a producer for Frontier Films on many projects. Of their seven films, Strand photographed the most ambitious production, *Native Land.* This film evolved from a congressional hearing into anti-labor activities, and was released in 1941. On the eve of World War II, its message was considered politically divisive. His newsreels became classics, exhibiting the same qualities that marked Strand's still photography: simple subjects, such as windows and doorways, machine forms, driftwood, cobwebs, rocks, the human face, presented with sharp precision and directness, but also with concern for abstract formal values.

During this time Strand also worked in Mexico, gathering images for *The Mexican Portfolio,* published with hand-pulled gravures in 1940. In 1943, he ended his film production and returned to still photography full-time.

### Combined Text with Images

The Museum of Modern Art in New York mounted its first full-scale retrospective of a contemporary photographer with the work of Strand in 1945. Unable to finance filmmaking after World War II, Strand turned to the printed publication for a format that might integrate image and text in a matter akin to the cinema. From 1946 to 1947 he collaborated with Nancy Newhall on the classic *Time in New England,* in which excerpts from various texts were joined with Strand's images of New England's artifacts, architecture, and regional attributes, seeking to evoke a sense of past and present.

Strand continued this type of work after he moved to Europe in 1950. His most famous later works were eloquent portraits of peasants and villagers he encountered while traveling in France, Italy, and the Outer Hebrides. Strand produced *La France de profil* (A Profile of France) with Claude Roy, 1952; *Un Paese* (A Village) with Cesare Zavat-

tini, 1954; *Tir a 'Mhurain: Outer Hebrides* with Basil Davidson, 1968; *Living Egypt,*1969; and *Ghana: An African Portrait,* 1976. He closely supervised the second printing of *The Mexican Portfolio* in 1967.

In 1971, the Philadelphia Museum of Art organized a major retrospective of Strand's work. A two-volume monograph from the years 1915-1968 was published by Aperture. Strand received many awards and honors in the last 20 years of his life: Honor Roll of the American Society of Magazine Photographers in 1963, David Octavius Hill Medal in 1967, Swedish Photographers Association and Swedish Film Archives Award in 1970. Major retrospectives were held at the New York Metropolitan Museum of Art and the Los Angeles County Museum in 1973. During his last years, Strand worked in close collaboration with his third wife, Hazel Kingsbury. He died after a long illness on March 31, 1976 at his home in Orgeval, France.

In 1990, the National Gallery of Art had a retrospective of Strand's work. His photographs from 1915 through the mid-1970s were exhibited at the Whitney Museum of American Art in New York in 1992. The Metropolitan Museum of Modern Art, New York, exhibited Strand's work in 1998, as did San Francisco's Museum of Modern Art.

### Further Reading

Duncan, Catherine, and Ute Eskildsen, *Paul Strand: The World on My Doorstep,* Aperture, 1994.
Hambourg, Maria Morris, and Paul Strand. *Paul Strand: Circa 1916,* Metropolitan Museum of Art/Abrams, 1998.
Peters, Gerald and Megan Fox, *Paul Strand: An Extraordinary Vision,* University of Washington Press, 1995.
Rosenblum, Naomi, *A World History of Photography,* Abbeville Press, 1997.
"Paul Strand," *Georgia O'Keeffe: Virtual Library,* http://scow .gslis.ucla.edu/students_a-l/aresnick/HTML/gok/strand.htm (April 16, 1999). □

# Preston Sturges

**Preston Sturges (1898–1959) was the first writer-turned-director in the history of talking movies, and one of the greatest film directors of any variety. He is best known for the comedies he made in the early 1940s. His films are distinguished by a zany wit and brilliant, madcap dialogue.**

P reston Sturges was born Edmund Preston Biden on August 29, 1898 in Chicago, Illinois. His was not a traditional upbringing. His mother, Mary, had several husbands and lovers. She was also a close friend of the dancer Isadora Duncan, sharing with her a lifestyle that might be described as "loose." In the autobiography, *Preston Sturges by Preston Sturges,* the director describes his mother as having a "vivid fantasy life . . . anything she said three times she believed fervently." In turn, his father, Edmund Biden, was an alcoholic.

By 1900, two years after Edmund Preston was born, his parents had divorced. Mary had earlier begun a relationship with Solomon Sturges, a wealthy Chicago stockbroker, whom she married in October 1901. In January 1902, Solomon formally adopted her son, who was thereafter known as Preston Sturges.

Sturges's mother soon found life as the wife of a Chicago stockbroker too restrictive. The couple agreed that Mary would spend half her time in Europe, half in Chicago. With her friend Isadora, she cavorted around the Continent, leaving Preston parked with various acquaintances, and, later, at various boarding schools. In 1911, Solomon Sturges filed for divorce. Even though he was not Preston's birth father, he still treated him as a son and the two remained extremely close—in contrast to Preston's relationship with his real dad, who only reappeared much later in his life to ask for money.

### The Young Continental

There were advantages to Sturges's bohemian childhood. As Donald Spoto wrote in *Madcap: The Life of Preston Sturges*, "[As a teenager], he had an easy poise and engaging charm, for his innate intelligence and quickness of wit had been naturally augmented by an exposure to the widest variety of cosmopolitan influences . . . he had become, in fact, a young Continental, with a keen appreciation of good food and wine, of wit, sensuality and sociability."

In his later teens, Sturges lived in New York, attending school on and off, and working in his mother's cosmetics business. In 1918, he reported as a cadet in the aviation section of the U.S. Signal Corps. He served for 14 months and received his commission as a second lieutenant. After completing his military service, he returned to New York and the cosmetics business. Sturges became interested in science and enjoyed playing with gadgets. For the next few years, he spent much of his time working for his mother and trying his hand at inventing.

Sturges was tall and handsome, and eventually stole 19-year-old Estelle Godfrey away from her rich husband. Godfrey, who was well-off financially, married Sturges in 1923. The two purchased a house in Westchester, New York. Between 1924 and 1926, they alternated between country life in the suburbs and an avid social life in the city; however, the marriage ended in 1927.

### A Late Bloomer

It was not until Sturges was about 30 that he began his writing career. An aspiring actress had ended an affair with Sturges, telling him that she had only dated him to find material for a play she wanted to write. Sturges told her that he could write a better play than she could. In three weeks, he produced a comedy based on the affair called *The Guinea Pig*.

While getting a play produced in the United States has never been easy, New York in the late 1920s offered many opportunities for a young playwright. Between Broadway and small theaters, about 250 plays were produced each year. Hoping to meet a prospective producer, Sturges entered the theater world as an assistant stage manager. Soon he met a lawyer, Charles Abramson, who told him that a playwright could produce a play himself for as little as $2,500, plus theater rental. A wealthy friend of his mother's lent him the money, and Sturges opened his play in early January 1929. Most of the New York papers gave it good reviews, and, for a small production, the show made a nice profit.

### First Big Success

Within a few months, Sturges had written his next play, *Strictly Dishonorable.* The plot revolved around an Italian opera star and ladies' man who seduces the innocent fiancee of an uptight prig. However, what begins as sexual conquest becomes love, and the play ends with the two set to travel the world and have 11 children. As Spoto writes in *Madcap,* the play ". . . had all the characteristics of Preston Sturges's best achievements of the stage and screen: the witty, pointed conversation; the acute sense of social satire; the deftly developed characters; and action as well as dialogue that typically derives from those characters—never from an imposed theme or labored thesis." The play was a big hit with audiences and made Sturges a wealthy man—at least temporarily.

With a successful show, Sturges was soon sought out by film studios to polish scripts. He was paid $10,000 to provide a few lines for the *The Big Pond,* which took him just a couple of days to complete. He also quickly wrote another play, *Rapture,* which opened in January 1930. The reviews were poor, and it closed after 24 performances. In November, his fourth play, *The Well of Romance,* lasted just eight days. After his fifth play, *Child of Manhattan,* was released, a *The New York Times* review stated, "The more young Mr. Preston Sturges continues to write follow-ups to *Strictly Dishonorable,* the more we wonder who wrote *Strictly Dishonorable.*"

Perhaps Sturges was distracted by his affair with Eleanor Post Hutton, a wealthy socialite. Her family was fiercely critical of the alliance, and the two eloped in April 1930. This marriage did not last either, and the couple parted in 1932.

## Go West, Young Writer

In December 1932, with a string of failed plays and in debt, Sturges headed West. He signed on for three months as a contract writer at Universal Studios for $1,000 a week. He was put to work on the film *The Invisible Man,* but the proposed director was unhappy with his work, and his option was dropped.

On his own, Sturges wrote *The Power and the Glory.* The film received mostly good reviews, but it did not do well at the box office. The unusual and powerful screenplay did, however, enhance Sturges's reputation significantly. In fact, it did much more. Not only did the film introduce Spencer Tracy to filmgoers, it was also sold on a royalty basis with the provision that it not be changed by the director—a first for Hollywood. Sturges was on the set throughout filming and had a major hand in the final product, acting much more like a playwright than screenwriter. Additionally, the experience made Sturges realize that it really was the director who held sway on the set, and it confirmed his ambition to direct his own films someday.

Over the next several years—while living with a fiery beauty, Bianca Gilchrist—Sturges worked as a screenwriter, spending a few months at one studio, then moving on to another. Columbia, Universal, and others all paid him handsomely to work on their pictures. Paramount was especially hospitable to writers, and it was there that Sturges perfected his skills as a writer of screwball comedies in films like *Easy Living.* By 1938, he was making $2,750 a week; he was one of the highest paid writers in Hollywood. That year, he married his third wife, Louise Sargent Tevis, who would give Sturges his first son in 1941, Solomon Sturges IV. The marriage was a relatively long one for Sturges, ending almost nine years later in 1947.

## Other Endeavors

With his improved financial situation, Sturges indulged his love for mechanical contraptions and established the Sturges Engineering Company in 1935. It sold an improved design of the internal combustion engine. Sturges was not a passive investor; he would stop by the factory to talk with the foreman and maintained a keen interest in technical developments. The company survived during World War II, but was liquidated soon afterwards.

Sturges also became involved in the restaurant business, financing Snyder's Restaurant in 1936. In 1940, he opened another, much bigger restaurant, The Players. It became a hangout for Hollywood celebrities, like Billy Wilder and Ernst Lubitsch. Both restaurants were money-losers. Snyder's closed in 1938; The Players lasted until 1953, but only with Sturges making up significant deficits.

## The Great Director

As the 1930s drew to a close, Sturges finally realized his dream of directing. He sold *The Great McGinty* to Paramount for $1 (eventually upped to $10 by the studio's legal department), with the condition that he would be allowed to direct it. While writer/directors, like Billy Wilder and John Huston, were to become common, in Sturges's day they were unheard-of. A political satire, *McGinty* was about, as Diane Jacobs wrote in *Christmas in July: The Life and Times of Preston Sturges,* "the American dream rebuked by American reality. About the inexorableness of character, the dire consequences of romantic love, the inadequacy of justice, and the quarrel between free will and destiny." Despite a bout with pneumonia, Sturges brought the film in ahead of schedule and under budget. *McGinty* was a resounding critical and financial success when it opened in 1940.

Over the next five years, Sturges would direct the string of comedy hits that movie watchers continue to adore: *Christmas in July, The Lady Eve, Sullivan's Travels, The Palm Beach Story, The Miracle of Morgan's Creek,* and *Hail the Conquering Hero.* These films, as David Everitt wrote in *The New York Times,* "were peopled with such characters as the man-crazy bobby-soxer Trudy Kockenblocker, the bemused millionaire John D. Hackensacker 3d, and a would-be war hero saddled with the moniker Woodrow Lafayette Pershing Truesmith." The movies are replete with brilliant, hilarious dialogue, like the repartee between gal-on-the-make Barbara Stanwyck and millionaire ophiologist (snake scientist) Henry Fonda in *The Lady Eve.* Geoffrey O'Brien wrote of Sturges in *The New York Review of Books,* "He breaks every rule of movies by putting language at the center and making the whole film swirl around it."

## Decline and Fall

*Hail the Conquering Hero,* released in 1944, marked the high point of Sturges's career. Soon afterwards, his *The Great Moment,* opened to mixed reviews and was a commercial failure. The following year, he joined with the tycoon Howard Hughes to form the California Pictures Corporation. Sturges was to make films; Hughes would make airplanes and supply the money for both. The venture soon went sour and Hughes ended the partnership.

The film that probably ended Sturges's career was *Unfaithfully Yours,* made for movie mogul Daryl Zanuck at Fox in 1948. It opened to only mildly positive reviews and was a commercial flop. Not only was the film expensive to make, but it was the victim of poor luck. Its plot includes a scene where the lead character, played by Rex Harrison, kills his wife. Just before the film was set for release, actress Carole Landis, apparently grief-stricken over a doomed, much-publicized affair with Harrison, committed suicide. There was no way Fox could show the picture under the circumstances, and its release was postponed for several months. Shortly afterward, another Sturges film, *The Beautiful Blonde from Bashful Bend,* also proved disappointing.

In 1951, Sturges married his fourth wife, Anne Margaret Nagle, known as "Sandy." They had two sons, Preston and Thomas Preston. Professionally, the 1950s were punctuated by failure. Sturges did manage to write and direct one movie for a French production company, which was released in America under the title *The French They Are a Funny Race.* The film did well in Europe and made a modest profit in the United States, but it did little to rehabilitate Sturges's reputation.

In February 1959, Sturges began work on his autobiography, commissioned by the publishers Henry Holt. In his *New York Review* article, Geoffrey O'Brien writes, "It was somehow in keeping with Sturges's destiny to have the rare privilege of scripting his own death scene." While working on his autobiography, Sturges wrote "[I have] a bad case of indigestion . . . I am well-versed in the remedy: ingest a little Maalox, lie down, stretch out, and hope to God I don't croak." As O'Brien reports, he died twenty minutes later, on August 6, 1959 in New York City.

## Further Reading

Jacobs, Diane, *Christmas in July: The Life and Art of Preston Sturges,* University of California Press, 1992.
Spoto, Donald, *Madcap: The Life of Preston Sturges,* Little, Brown 1990.
Sturges, Preston, *Preston Sturges by Preston Sturges,* Simon & Schuster, 1990.
*Atlantic Monthly,* February 1996.
*New York Review of Books,* December 20, 1990.
*New York Times,* July 19, 1998.
"Preston Sturges Index," http://www.geocities.com/Hollywood/ Set/7321/sturgesindex.html (March 9, 1999).
"The Official Preston Sturges Site," http://www.prestonsturges .com/biography.html (March 9, 1999). □

# Ed Sullivan

**Over the course of two decades, Ed Sullivan (1902– 1974) brought 10,000 performers into the homes of American viewers on his Sunday night television program. Some of America's favorite stars gained national exposure for the first time after appearing on his show, most notably The Beatles, but also Woody Allen, Jackie Mason, Phyllis Diller, the Singing Nun, Richard Pryor, and Rowan and Martin.**

Ed Sullivan was a stone-faced, awkward man who brought more talent and sparkle to television than perhaps anyone else, reigning as TV's "king of variety" for 23 years. He had a knack for picking the acts that America would enjoy. He could read an audience. If his test audience did not like the performer in question, the rest of the country would not see that performance on their televisions on Sunday night.

## Early Influences

Edward Vincent Sullivan was born in an Irish and Jewish section of Harlem in New York City on September 28, 1902. His father, Peter Sullivan, was the son of an Irish immigrant, the oldest of eight children, who never finished high school. He worked as a customs inspector. His mother, Elizabeth Smith Sullivan, was an amateur painter. Sullivan was a twin, but his brother, Danny, died before their first birthday. When Ed was five, the family moved to Port Chester, New York. There, his childhood was filled with the music his parents loved, and a blend of ethnic culture that included Gypsies and the Catholic Church. Growing up, he witnessed the disappearance of horses and carriages from the streets and their replacement by automobiles. This transformation would make our country seem smaller, much in the same way as Sullivan would later bring us a "consensus culture." He attended St. Mary's High School in Port Chester where he worked on the school newspaper and earned letters in four varsity sports. Sullivan turned down a chance to attend college, even though an uncle had offered to pay his tuition, and chose to go into the newspaper business instead.

The early years of his career saw him moving in rapid succession from job to job: from 1918-1919 he was a reporter for the *Port Chester Daily Item;* in 1919 he moved on to the *Hartford Post;* then, in 1920, he went to the *New York Evening Mail* where he stayed until the paper ceased publication. In 1924 and 1925, he wrote for the *New York World.* During the next two years he wrote for the *New York*

*Morning Telegraph* and the *Philadelphia Ledger,* following which he wrote for the *World and Bulletin* in New York. In 1927-1929, he served as sports editor at the *New York Evening Graphic,* the same paper at which Walter Winchell, developed his celebrated gossip column. Sullivan coveted Winchell's influence and wanted to move in the same circles. When Winchell left for the *Mirror* in 1931, Sullivan stepped in as the new columnist. A year later, the *Graphic* closed its doors. His journalism career stabilized when he began writing his "Little Old New York" column for the *New York Daily News* from 1932 until his death in 1974.

Sullivan took on radio interview shows on NBC and CBS to compensate for the pay cut of $175 a week that he took to work at the *Daily News.* Already wielding some influence, Sullivan introduced Jack Benny as the first radio entertainer on WABC, a CBS affiliate, in 1932. From 1936 to 1952, he had his own radio show on CBS called "Ed Sullivan Entertains." He also worked as a theater emcee at the Paramount and Loews' State Theaters. He also hosted dances and benefits like the 1947 Harvest Moon Ball, sponsored by the *New York Daily News* at Madison Square Garden. There, at the age of 46, Sullivan was discovered by an advertising man, Marlo Lewis.

## The Toast of the Town

On June 20, 1948, Sullivan hosted his first television show on CBS, *Toast of the Town,* sponsored by Emerson Radio. The show brought vaudeville to the small screen in living rooms across the country. It was an instant success. The sponsor was not convinced, however, and quickly dropped the show. The show continued when Lincoln-Mercury agreed to sponsor it. Sullivan is rumored to have been so grateful to the Ford Motor Company that he would send postcards to dealers when he was traveling. The show's name was changed to *The Ed Sullivan Show.* The formula remained the same for over twenty years: give America a pastiche of high, low, and middlebrow entertainment. It was a mix for the common man. Dean Martin and Jerry Lewis performed on that first show, along with dancer Kathryn Lee, pianist Eugene List, Rogers and Hammerstein, and a dance troupe, the Toastettes.

Part of Sullivan's success was that he never upstaged the talent he brought on the show. In fact, he was often criticized for having no personality. The *Celebrity Register* reported, "the secret of his success is that he has no style to go out of." Likewise, in 1955, *Time* magazine reported that Sullivan moved about the stage like a sleepwalker. "His smile is that of a man sucking a lemon; his speech is frequently lost in a thicket of syntax; his eyes pop from their sockets or sink so deep in their bags that they seem to be peering up at the camera from the bottom of twin wells. Yet, instead of frightening the children, Ed Sullivan charms the whole family." Much of Sullivan's strange demeanor owed to the fact that he had a stomach ulcer that he treated with belladonna, which also caused his eyes to dilate. He had also been in a car accident in 1956 that damaged his teeth and ribs. As he grew older, Sullivan developed coronary artery disease and a hearing loss.

## "Ladies and Gentleman, The Beatles!"

Sullivan had the most popular acts on his show, but the musical entertainers often generated the biggest audience response. Elvis Presley appeared on the show three times. Despite his somewhat scandalous reputation as "Elvis the pelvis," he was shown only from the waist up on his third appearance, aired on January 6, 1957, due to public outcry. Originally, Sullivan did not want Elvis on the show, deeming him too vulgar. But when Elvis had been a hit on Steve Allen's show, Sullivan decided to bring him on, working out a $50,000, three-performance deal with Presley's manager, Colonel Parker. Just as the appearances on *The Ed Sullivan Show* helped Presley's career, one appearance made the Beatles' career in America. Their debut on Sullivan's program (on February 9, 1964), gained the largest television audience in history at that time. The group sang "I Want To Hold Your Hand" and "She Loves You" to an audience of 73 million. America had just succumbed to the first wave of the "British Invasion."

The *Ed Sullivan Show* was also responsible for adding several "catch phrases" to the American vocabulary. Many comedians who appeared on the show, including Rich Little, Jackie Mason, and John Byner enjoyed impersonating Sullivan and would pick up on "Sullivanisms" like "a really big shew." Also, frequent character guests like puppeteer Maria Prego's Italian mouse Topo Gigo would say things like "Hey Eddie, kess-a-me goodnight!" And Pedro, a head-in-a-box hand puppet created by Senor Wences, who would say, "S'all right? S'all right!"

Sullivan's private life was as unconventional as his public life. He married Sylvia Weinstein on April 28, 1930. They were always on the go and lived in a world of convenience and artifice. The two lived in a suite of rooms at Manhattan's Delmonico Hotel. She never cooked. They always ate at restaurants or clubs. The hotel maid did the cleaning. Their daughter Elizabeth ("Betty") ate dinner with a paid companion at a restaurant until she was twelve. John Leonard wrote of the Sullivans in *Smoke and Mirrors: Violence, Television and Other American Cultures,* "Ed and Sylvia were children of the Roaring Jazz Age Twenties, that nervy postwar adrenaline-addicted Charleston state of mind confabulated in New York by admen, poets and promoters and then nationally syndicated by Broadway columnists like Damon Runyon, Walter Winchell, Louis Sobol, and Ed himself—men who had gone to newspapers instead of college."

Sullivan carried on some well-publicized feuds. First and perhaps most notably was his feud with Walter Winchell, but also with Steve Allen, Frank Sinatra, Jack Paar, Nat "King" Cole, and Arthur Godfrey. But he was generous to those he liked. For example, he paid for the funeral of dancer Bill "Bojangles" Robinson who was completely destitute at the time of his death.

Sullivan would use his name and influence for a good cause. Already the first "king of all media," with his own newspaper column, radio and television shows, Sullivan was also the first to organize and produce shows to benefit wounded servicemen. He put on 46 shows for Army Emergency Relief during World War II. Sullivan was also an active supporter of racial equality. He refused to drop African American acts from the show when his sponsors suggested he try doing so to get a larger Southern audience. In 1951, he wrote an article posing the question, "Can T.V. crack America's color line?" for *Ebony* magazine. In the 1960s, he also added an African American dancer to his chorus line—she was the first in television history.

Sullivan made television biographies of Rogers and Hammerstein, Helen Hayes, Beatrice Lilley, Walt Disney, Cole Porter, and specials like "The Story of A.S.C.A.P.," "The Story of Samuel Goldwyn," and "The Story of Robert E. Sherwood." He also took roles on screen in films including *Mr. Broadway* in 1933, *Big Town Czar* in 1939, *Bye Bye Birdie* in 1963 and *The Singing Nun* in 1965.

Sullivan was a complex character, who, whether you loved or hated him, could not be dismissed. He was very much a man of his time, yet his contributions to popular culture continue to resonate, even after he lost a battle against cancer and died on October 13, 1974 in New York City.

Sullivan left his legacy on America's popular culture. On August 30 1993, The Ed Sullivan Theater became the new home of *The David Letterman Show*. The theater, built in 1927 and christened the Oscar Hammerstein Theater, was the home of Sullivan's show from the night it debuted as *Toast of the Town* in 1948. Letterman often referenced Sullivan in his first monologues there. In March 1998, CBS presented "A Really Big Show: Ed Sullivan's 50th Anniversary," hosted by the Smothers Brothers. The show melded together reminiscences of the late, great, showman, as well as clips from the old shows. That same night, United Paramount Network (UPN) offered a pilot of it's computer-generated Ed hosting a new variety show produced by Andrew Solt, "The Virtual Ed Sullivan Show." If Sullivan had not been creepy before, he was now floating about the screen like Max Headroom, his computer-generated image floating over the movements of comedian John Byner. Also in 1998, the cable T.V. channel VH-1 presented 20 episodes of Ed Sullivan's Rock and Roll Classics, clipping together musical acts from the show in themed segments like Motown and The British Invasion.

Tom Smothers, of the Smothers Brothers comedy duo, said it well, "Ed Sullivan was almost like a non-host. He didn't have all the slick moves and stuff. But what he gave you was entertainment in its purest form. No ulterior motives, no hidden agenda. Just unadulterated presentations from the best performing artists of the time."

### Further Reading

*American Heritage,* March 15, 1997.
*Arizona Republic,* May 18, 1998.
*Business Wire,* January 31, 1992.
*Cincinnati Enquirer,* February 17, 1991.
*St. Petersburg Times,* May 17, 1998.
*San Antonio Express-News* May 19, 1998
*San Francisco Examiner,* February 17, 1991.
*Tampa Tribune,* May 12, 1998.
*Ed Sullivan Show Fun Facts* http://www.edsullivan.com/facts .html

*Who Was Ed Sullivan?* http://www.edsullivan.com/whowas .html □

# Arthur Sulzberger, Jr.

**The *New York Times* has been published for over 100 years, since Adolph Ochs purchased the newspaper in 1896. In 1992, his great-grandson, Arthur Sulzberger, Jr. (born 1951), became the fifth relative to act as its publisher and has since established himself as a strong yet personable manager and something of a pioneer at the old "Gray Lady."**

Sulzberger was born to Arthur Ochs and Barbara Winslow Grant Sulzberger in Mount Kisco, New York, on September 22, 1951. His parents divorced in 1956, but Sulzberger and his sister, Karen, still spent time with their father, often at their grandparents' estate near Stamford, Connecticut. The 262-acre property included a private lake taking up five acres, an Olympic-size swimming pool, and an indoor tennis court. As an adolescent, Sulzberger decided to go to Manhattan to live with his father and stepmother, Carol Fox Fuhrman, in their Fifth Avenue apartment. There he enrolled in a college preparatory academy, the Browning School, where he was on the debating club, played junior varsity football, and spent three years on the school newspaper. Though he went through a rebellious adolescence that lasted into his college years—growing his hair long, donning his father's old Marine Corps jacket, and getting arrested at peace rallies—he remained close to his supportive father.

Sulzberger completed high school in 1970 and attended college at Tufts University in Medford, Massachusetts. He graduated in 1974 with a bachelor's degree in political science. On breaks, he worked at the Boston *Globe* and Vineyard *Gazette* newspapers in Massachusetts, knowing that his future was in publishing. He told Alex S. Jones in the *New York Times,* "I was not pushed to do it either by myself or some strange sense of responsibility. It was something I wanted to do as long as I can recall." Sulzberger officially started his professional career at the Raleigh *Times* in North Carolina as a reporter in 1974.

### Married Girl Next Door

While visiting his mother in Topeka, Kansas, during a Thanksgiving holiday, Sulzberger met the girl next door, literally. She was Gail Gregg, also a journalist. They were married in 1975 and moved to London the following year, where they held wire service jobs. Although Gregg was adept as a journalist, often beating her husband to stories, she opted for a change when the couple moved back to America in 1978, and became an artist. Sulzberger knew, when he returned to the United States, that he was preparing for a permanent career at the *New York Times.* He did not fraternize with staff members, causing a rift between him and some who used to be friends. "When I moved back to

New York, I decided for my own mental health that my closest friends should be outside the *Times*," Sulzberger told Margaret Carlson in a *Time* magazine interview. "They can afford to be honest with me."

## Learned the Publishing Business

Sulzberger held a variety of increasingly responsible positions on the newspaper. From 1978 until 1992 he was Washington correspondent, city hall reporter, assistant metro editor, group manager of the advertising department, senior analyst in corporate planning, production coordinator, assistant publisher, and deputy publisher. Although he knew that a path would be cleared for his advancement, Sulzberger did not take this for granted. He quickly established a reputation for being a down-to-earth, hard-working journalist. *New York Times* columnist Anna Quindlen told Carlson, "From the moment he walked in the door, there were people desperately trying to dislike him. It proved to be impossible."

After working in the Washington, D.C., bureau from 1978 to 1981, Sulzberger returned to Manhattan as a general reporter on the metropolitan beat, where he covered the second term of Mayor Edward Koch, among other stories. He was promoted to assignment editor in 1982, which he called "the single most exhausting job I ever had," according to Carlson. As a rookie manager, he endeared himself to the reporters, operating a democratic newsroom and being available to his workers. He also learned that motivation was the key duty of a solid manager. After gaining exposure to the editorial operations of the newspaper, Sulzberger transferred to the business side. In 1983, he began selling advertising and overseeing a team of sales people. Around this time, he seriously began considering his future role in the paper's management and assessing his own style of supervision. As he told Alex S. Jones in the *New York Times*, "I don't think leadership demands yes or no answers; I think leadership is providing the forum for making the right decision, which doesn't demand unanimity."

In 1985, Sulzberger spent some time as a senior analyst in corporate planning before taking the job of production coordinator. In that capacity, he spent two nights a week supervising the printing of the paper. He was named assistant publisher in 1987, dealing with budget issues. His father promoted him to deputy publisher just over a year later. In that capacity, he was in charge of both the news and business sides. He had a hand in redesigning the metro and sports sections and also worked to infuse color into the "Gray Lady." Sulzberger was eager to bring more women and minorities on board. Female employees had filed a discrimination lawsuit against the *New York Times* in 1978. Into the 1990s, senior management positions were still held by white males. Sulzberger was committed to the concept of diversity in the workplace.

## Named Publisher

On January 16, 1992, Sulzberger was chosen to replace his father as publisher of the *New York Times*. He immediately pledged to continue the paper's outstanding quality, but also turned his attention to its financial health.

Sulzberger announced in early 1993 that the paper needed to trim ten percent of its workforce. Also in 1993, the *New York Times* bought the Boston *Globe* for well over one billion dollars. In late 1995, executives reported that another 190 jobs would be cut. Despite the job losses, Ken Auletta in the *New Yorker* remarked that Sulzberger eagerly worked to democratize the office climate. He hoped to wage a war "against an authoritarian decision-making process that exists on both the news and the business sides of the *Times*—a process that he believes breeds insularity and saps initiative." Auletta noted that Sulzberger and his executive editor, Max Frankel had introduced many improvements. They "have improved the writing in the *Times*, have provided readers with more analytical stories, have sharpened the Sunday magazine and the sports and metropolitan sections, have hired more women and minorities for the newsroom, and have given individual writers greater freedom in how they write." Auletta added, however, that employees thought Sulzberger still appeared to focus too much on how far the paper still had to go, rather than how far it had come.

Although in 1993, the *New York Times* only boasted about ten percent women executives on the news side of its masthead, some workers pointed out that Sulzberger's pace was not to blame. Auletta quoted Rebecca Sinkler, editor of the *New York Times Book Review,* as saying, "The *Times* is so big and powerful that changing it is like teaching a hippopotamus how to tango. Moving the hippopotamus around is frustratingly slow," confounding even the publisher, Auletta commented. To help effect change more quickly, Sulzberger has held numerous retreats in order to encourage greater communication. "He believes that self-discovery and candor flow from conflict and adversity and that improved teamwork will follow," Auletta explained, noting that Sulzberger's theories seemed to stem from his experiences with the group Outward Bound, of which he was chairman for the New York City center. Sulzberger also actively recruited minorities by holding dinners at National Association of Black Journalists conventions, and noticeably stepped up coverage of gay issues.

One of Sulzberger's boldest decision was to introduce color into the newspaper's main sections late in 1997. Other newspapers had been adding color to their pages for over 30 years, but the Times never followed suit. Worried that some traditionalists would protest, Sulzberger nevertheless saw the need to give the "Gray Lady" a makeover in order to keep the readers' interest and attract newer, younger subscribers. "We admit we're taking a risk," he told Lee Berton in the *Columbia Journalism Review.* "But we feel that not changing would be even riskier with our readers and advertisers." Sulzberger also assured shareholders, Berton reported, that "color design will reflect the taste and moderation that have always distinguished the Times's news judgment."

When Sulzberger's father turned 70 in 1996, many were anxious to see who would become the company's chairman and chief executive officer. Though he had certainly earned the title with the sweat he had poured into the paper, Sulzberger also had four male cousins and a female cousin in executive positions at the *New York Times.* The *New Yorker* reported at the time that although "Punch" Sulzberger would probably like to move his son up into the position, he shared with his three sisters 85 percent of the controlling stock, and they may have other ideas. The senior Sulzberger remained tight-lipped about it before finally stepping down on October 16, 1997 and announcing that his son would assume duties as chairman while company president, Russell T. Lewis, would become chief executive officer.

Despite Sulzberger's privileged background as heir apparent to the *New York Times,* Margaret Carlson in *Time* magazine characterized him as making a conscious effort to be an "average Joe." Carlson noted that Sulzberger used public transportation, toured Europe on a used motorcycle, helped at homeless shelters, and preferred inexpensive eateries. However, his veneer is not quite so humble. Known as a dapper dresser, a friend of Sulzberger's at the *New Yorker* mentioned that he looked like "an English gentleman." Sulzberger, in his free time, enjoyed rock climbing and *Star Trek: The Next Generation.* He and his wife have two children, Arthur Gregg and Ann Alden. The family lived on the Upper West Side of Manhattan in New York City since the early 1980s.

## Further Reading

*Columbia Journalism Review,* September-October 1997, p. 42.
*Editor & Publisher,* January 22, 1994, p. 17; January 11, 1997, p. 3.
*Fortune,* November 24, 1997, p. 46.
*HR Focus,* May 1994, p. 22.
*Mediaweek,* January 13, 1997, p. 6; October 20, 1997, p. 8.
*Newsweek,* September 15, 1997, p. 76.
*New Yorker,* June 28, 1993, p. 55; June 10, 1996, p. 44.
*New York Times,* January 17, 1992, p. A1; December 6, 1995, p. C4.
*Time,* August 17, 1992, p. 46.
*Wall Street Journal,* October 17, 1997, p. B5. □

# T

# Arthur Tedder

**Arthur William Tedder (1890–1967) may have been born into the elite of English society, but his was not a pampered life. He served his country as a hero, seeing action in two world wars and accepting the full responsibility of command over Allied air forces during World War II.**

Arthur Tedder was born on July 11, 1890 in the Scottish town of Glenguin. He began his military career in 1913 when he joined the British Army. In 1916, he transferred to the Royal Air Force (RAF), serving during World War I in France from 1915 until 1917 and Egypt from 1918 to 1919. He received his permanent commission in the RAF in 1919 and remained there after the war, serving as a director of training from 1934 to 1936. In 1936, Tedder was promoted to RAF commander in the Far East where he remained until 1938, when he became director general of research in the Air Ministry.

## The Middle East

Tedder's early experience with the RAF would prove invaluable during the war years. In his role as commander in the Far East, he would amass even more knowledge of military strategy. One of his first opportunities to apply his strong planning skills came in May 1941, when Tedder participated in the British evacuation of Crete. As German strength grew in the Middle East, British troops were forced back toward Canea and an evacuation of Crete was ordered. While the Royal Air Force at Egypt, under Tedder's command, promised fighter cover for the ships evacuating British ground troops, support was limited by the fact that few aircraft at his disposal had the necessary range to fly from Egypt to Crete. The operation suffered many casualties.

In November 1941, Tedder participated in Operation "Crusader," in Africa. The plans for attack on Tobruk were scheduled for November 23, 1941. On the 19th, Tedder reported to Prime Minister Winston Churchill that the initial air battle of November 18th had gone satisfactorily, although bad weather had adversely affected plans for neutralizing the enemy. He assured Churchill that the weather had also limited German action against the Allies during the first two days of the battle.

In the spring of 1942, when Germany's General Erwin Rommel launched an attack of Gazala west of Tobruk. Tedder communicated to Churchill that he had foreseen the attack and was ready for it. Rommel's attack on Tobruk failed and his troops were pummeled by Tedder's air forces. Unfortunately, the victory was short-lived, as Rommel turned the tide of battle from defeat to victory. With the loss of the tank battle, an immediate withdrawal of the 1st South African and 50th Division was ordered. The success of that withdrawal was due, in large measure, to the protection of Allied troops by the RAF.

In the summer of 1942, Churchill commended Tedder for his successful direction of the RAF. During August Tedder accompanied Churchill to Moscow where they met with Russian leader, Josef Stalin. Churchill proposed placing British and U.S. air troops at Russia's southern flank as a means of strengthening Russian air power and showing air superiority. Tedder's proposed plan received approval from Churchill with a recommendation that a similar proposal be drafted for presentation to U.S. President Franklin D. Roosevelt.

## The Battle of El Alamein

In October 1942, the battle against Rommel's forces for El Alamein [in North Africa] was launched. In contrast to battles fought earlier that same year, the British had the advantage of far superior forces. On the ground, Sherman tanks arrived from the United States, outnumbering the equipment of the enemy. In the air, Tedder, now air commander-in-chief in the Middle East, had air squadrons that included U.S., South African, Rhodesian, Australian, Greek, French, and Yugoslav forces assisting the RAF. The planes at his disposal numbered over 1,500, with 1,200 of those based in Egypt and Palestine in support of a ground attack on Alamein. By comparison, German and Italian serviceable aircraft numbered only 350.

Tedder applied this superior air capability to harassing the *Panzerarmee* supply flow, while also protecting the supplies of the Eighth Army. Working closely with the Royal Navy, he extended the harassment of the *Panzerarmee's* sea-artery supply and aided in the sinking of German supply ships. By September 1942, a third of Germany's supplies had failed to cross the Mediterranean, either sunk or returned to their source. The following month more than half of Germany's supplies failed to arrive. In a memo from Churchill to Tedder, the prime minister commended the commander for his leadership.

## The Casablanca Conference

During the Casablanca Conference at the beginning of 1943, Roosevelt and Churchill's combined chiefs of staff agreed that taking Tunis should be the next point of focus. It was at this conference that leadership of the Allied forces was conferred upon General Dwight D. Eisenhower. Naval command was placed under Admiral Cunningham and Tedder was named air marshal. Tedder assumed command of the front in February 1943, with the Battle of Tunisia at its height. Roosevelt suggested that it would be strategically advantageous for the Allies to stress these appointments and ensure that the leader's plans and duties be filtered to the enemy. Churchill agreed, but expressed concern that no favoritism be shown toward Eisenhower at the expense of commanders Alexander and Tedder, lest the general public be discouraged.

## The Italian Campaign

In May 1943, Tedder, Alexander, and Cunningham met and voiced agreement with Churchill and Brooke that Italy should be invaded. To convince Eisenhower, they met with Eisenhower, Marshall, and Bedell Smith to discuss the proposed taking of the island of Pantilleria as the southern assault on Sicily to begin this campaign.

By the summer Tedder's command had solidified in preparation for the invasion of Sicily. His forces included those of General Spaatz, U.S. Army Air Force; and Air Marshal Coningham. With a driving need to take ports and airfields early in the attack, Tedder argued to narrow the attack and seize the southeastern group of airfields. This was successfully employed through the use of amphibious load carriers.

As 1943 came to a close, Churchill proposed to Roosevelt a remodeling of leadership after discussion with Eisenhower, Alexander, and Tedder. For Operation "Overlord"—also known as "D-Day"—Churchill recommended Tedder as Eisenhower's deputy supreme commander because of the role planned for the air forces. Roosevelt gladly accepted this recommendation. As plans for D-Day began to solidify, Tedder's role became even more vital. Recent experiences had proven that success could best be achieved through a cooperative effort of all the military forces.

## D-Day Approached

The next step was implementing the "Transportation Plan." This operation was designed to use bombers to paralyze the French railway on the eve of Overlord. Eisenhower had worked closely with Tedder in the Mediterranean and he liked and admired the man enormously. Despite some opposition to the plan, he named Tedder to personally supervise the campaign. Tedder identified over 70 railroad targets in France and Belgium, intentionally directing traffic away from lower Normandy in order to maintain secrecy about the invasion site. Although opposition remained strong, Eisenhower was convinced that the Transportation Plan was necessary to the success of Overlord. The success of these attacks, in turn, convinced Tedder that they should be continued into Germany, where the collapse of the German rail system would result in the collapse of its economy.

With only hours left before the final decision had to be made on whether to begin Operation Overlord, bad weather raged across the English Channel and Eisenhower solicited his subordinates for their opinions. Tedder recommended postponement, concerned that poor visibility would have a devastating affect on the ability of his bombers to provide the cover needed. The decision, however, was to move ahead on June 6.

Historians generally agree that under the direction of Tedder, the Allied air forces commanded the skies. Their paralyzing effect on the enemy was a decisive factor in getting the Allied troops to shore on June 6. By destroying bridges over the Seine and Loire rivers, they effectively isolated Normandy, forcing the Germans into long detours and endless delays.

## The Aftermath

In the immediate aftermath of Overlord, additional operations were planned to keep the enemy off balance. One of these, which Montgomery had characterized as a major "break-out," resulted in the Allies' failure to take advantage of heavy enemy casualties. In an attempt to break through enemy lines and open the way to Paris, Eisenhower pushed Montgomery to take action and was assured that a "big show" would occur on July 9. Montgomery asked for and got air support from Tedder. However, Montgomery's attack failed and he called it off, angering both Eisenhower and Tedder. Two days later, Montgomery again promised an offensive he named Operation "Goodwood." Tedder arranged for a sensational show of support, bringing together 1,600 British and U.S. heavy bombers and 400 medium bombers, dropping a total of 7,800 tons of bombs on German defenses; 2,500 tons sited for the German fortifications at Caen; and 650 tons for Cagny. Tedder carefully coordinated the air attack with ground attacks in order to avoid any lulls that could give the enemy an opportunity to regroup.

The saturation bombing started the offensive, but it quickly failed. After sustaining heavy losses, Montgomery called it off. Tedder was furious at this second failure and demanded that Montgomery be fired, which did not come to pass.

## The Tide Turns

Throughout the last year of the war, the Allies achieved air superiority and the success of D-Day turned the tide of the war in Europe. In January 1945, Eisenhower sent Tedder to Moscow to seek assistance from the Russians, as a way of relieving pressure on Allied forces in the west. By May a total and unconditional surrender occurred with formal ratification by the German High Command in Berlin. Tedder signed on behalf of Eisenhower, Marshal Zhukov signed for Russia, and Field-Marshal Keitel signed for Germany.

## Peacetime Honors

In 1942, Tedder had been knighted. At the war's end, in 1946, he was elevated to the peerage and named a baron. Tedder served as Great Britain's first peacetime chief of air staff and as a senior member of the Air Council from 1946 until 1950. In 1950, he became chancellor of Cambridge University. Tedder published his memoirs, *With Prejudice:*

*The War Memoirs of Marshal of the Royal Air Force, Lord Tedder.* in 1966.

Tedder was married to Rosalinde Maclary, who died in 1943. At Rosalinde's request Tedder married again, to his young service driver, "Toppy" Seton. In his last years he became severely crippled with Parkinson's disease and died at Well Farm in Banstead, Surrey, England, on June 3, 1967.

## Further Reading

Ambrose, Stephen E., *Citizen Soldiers,* Simon & Schuster, 1997.
Ambrose, Stephen E., *June 6, 1944, D-Day: The Climactic Battle of World War II,* Simon & Schuster, 1994.
Blumenson, Martin, *Liberation,* Time-Life Books, 1978.
Churchill, Winston S., *The Grand Alliance,* Houghton, 1950.
Churchill, Winston S., *Hinge of Fate,* Houghton, 1950.
Churchill, Winston S., *Closing the Ring,* Houghton, 1950.
Churchill, Winston S., *Triumph and Tragedy,* Houghton, 1950.
Keegan, John, *Six Armies in Normandy,* Viking Press, 1982.
Liddell Hart, B. H., *History of the Second World War,* Putnam's, 1971.
Whipple, A. B. C., *The Mediterranean,* Time-Life Books, 1981.
*Independent,* February 24, 1994. □

# Helen Thomas

**Regarded as the dean of the Washington, D.C., press corps, reporter Helen Thomas (born 1920) has served as White House bureau chief for United Press International (UPI) since 1974.**

To those who regularly watch presidential press conferences, Helen Thomas is a familiar figure. Usually dressed in red (a tradition dating back to the administration of Ronald Reagan) and always seated in the front row, she is invariably the first or second reporter the president calls upon. It is an honor she has earned by virtue of her long and distinguished career in Washington, and it is one she relishes. Besides, it affords her the perfect opportunity to do what she does best—bluntly challenge the president (and other public officials) to tell the plain, unvarnished truth. "We (reporters) are not there to curry presidential favor, nor can we respond to efforts at presidential intimidation," she asserted in her memoir, *Dateline: White House.* "Our priority is the peoples' right to know—without fear or favor. We are the peoples' servants."

## Parents Valued Hard Work and Education

Helen Thomas was born in Winchester, Kentucky on August 4, 1920, the seventh of nine children. Her Lebanese immigrant parents, George and Mary Thomas, had arrived in the United States in 1903 with a mere $17 in their pockets. Living at first in Lexington, Kentucky, where several relatives had already settled, George Thomas supported his growing family as a door-to-door peddler of food and household items. Eventually, he was able to open his own

grocery store and move his family to the Kentucky town of Winchester. They later moved to Detroit, Michigan, where Helen Thomas was raised.

All of the Thomas children were brought up to value education, and all were expected to make something of themselves—"even us girls, as uncommon as that thinking was in those days," Thomas explained in an interview with Alan Ebert published in *Good Housekeeping*. She made up her mind while she was still in high school to become a reporter after a stint as a writer for the student newspaper. "A teacher praised my work," recalled Thomas in her memoir, "and I liked the bylines!" She pursued her dream of a career in journalism at Detroit's Wayne University (now Wayne State University), where she majored in English and once again worked on the school paper.

After receiving her bachelor's degree in 1942, Thomas headed straight for Washington, D.C., in search of a newspaper job. Before long, she landed one as a copy girl at the now-defunct *Washington Daily News,* where her duties in the male-dominated newsroom included fetching coffee and doughnuts for the paper's reporters and editors. The eager young woman nevertheless found the atmosphere exciting and stimulating and was convinced she had made the right career choice. Her mother kept asking her when she was coming home, but Thomas knew she had found what she has described as "a journalist's paradise" in Washington and that she was in the nation's capital to stay.

## Joined UPI Staff

Not long after she received a promotion to cub reporter, Thomas found herself without a job when a labor-management dispute at the *Daily News* resulted in massive staff cutbacks. Making the rounds once again, she was hired by United Press International in 1943. For the next dozen years, she wrote local news stories for UPI's radio wire service on subjects deemed to be of interest to women (the only topics female reporters were allowed to cover in those days). Beginning in the late 1940s, however, Thomas picked up some additional writing assignments, including the "Names in the News" column for UPI, which featured interviews with famous Washingtonians. From time to time, she also wrote about the comings and goings of President Harry S Truman's wife, Bess.

Thomas moved on to more serious reporting in 1955 when she was assigned to cover the U.S. Department of Justice. Her federal government beat later expanded to include the Federal Bureau of Investigation, the U.S. Department of Health, Education, and Welfare (now the Department of Health and Human Services), and Capitol Hill. She thrived professionally in other ways as well, serving as president of the Women's National Press Club in 1959-60.

## Covered Kennedy White House

Her big break came shortly after the 1960 presidential election when she was sent to Palm Beach, Florida, to report on the vacation of President-elect John F. Kennedy and his family. Determined to ferret out the details not only of their public moments but of their private ones as well, Thomas followed the Kennedys everywhere and talked to anyone she could find who had had some kind of contact with them. She focused in particular on the glamorous but aloof First-Lady-to-be, Jacqueline, a figure of endless fascination to the American public. Jackie did everything she could to thwart such intense scrutiny, but to no avail; Thomas interviewed caterers, hairdressers, and even employees of the diaper service company the family used to obtain the inside information she wanted. This relentless pursuit of the "story behind the story," combined with Thomas's bold tactics, her pointed questions, and sometimes biting sarcasm, have since become hallmarks of her reporting style and still occasionally annoy and exasperate the newsmakers she covers.

Once Kennedy took office, Thomas shifted her focus from the president's family to his policies. She began attending the daily press briefings at the White House as well as presidential press conferences, instituting the tradition of closing such sessions by saying, "Thank you, Mr. President" (a custom that endures to the present day). She enjoyed an especially friendly rapport with Kennedy, whom she had known since the early 1950s when he was a young, unmarried senator. "I liked JFK," Thomas told Ebert. "He had a marvelous wit, and I loved how he inspired young people. And he was a doting, loving father." As for his infidelities, she said, "in those years, that kind of inside information only circulated among the men. We women were excluded, almost as if the men had formed a protective shield against harm coming to a president because he proved to be 'human.'"

## Named UPI Bureau Chief

Before long, Thomas had expanded the scope of her coverage to include other U.S. government officials and world leaders, yet the White House remained her primary beat. During the early 1970s she posted a string of major accomplishments, both professional and personal. In 1970, she was named UPI's chief White House correspondent, and in 1974 she became chief of UPI's White House bureau, making her the first woman ever to hold that position for any of the wire services. The following year, she reached two more important milestones when she became the first woman admitted to the Gridiron Club (Washington's most exclusive press club) as well as the first woman elected president of the White House Correspondents Association. She also was the first female officer of the National Press Club, an all-male bastion that did not vote to accept women members until 1971. That same momentous year, Thomas married Douglas B. Cornell, a reporter for the rival Associated Press (AP) news organization.

Thomas has covered every president since Kennedy, noting in her memoir that "my sense of awe at the responsibility I have assumed has grown with the years. Presidents are human beings, and I have always tried to be conscious of that fact, trying not only to be accurate, but compassionate.... I have seen presidents in moments of glory, bursting with their own sense of being, caught up in public adulation. I have also seen presidents in despair, overburdened, brooding, emotional, seeking understanding."

Kennedy's successor, Lyndon Johnson, had a rocky, love-hate relationship with the Washington press corps. If Thomas wrote something he did not like, "he would walk right by me as though I wasn't there," she remarked to Ebert. At other times, he could be brimming with folksy friendliness and earthy candor. In his complexity, Thomas noted, he was "an incomparable combination of medicine man, evangelist, and statesman."

## Accompanied Nixon to China

Richard Nixon was among her least favorite presidents (although his wife, Pat, was one of her favorite first ladies). Their relationship started out as one of mutual respect, but as the Watergate scandal unfolded, Nixon became more and more hostile toward the press. Prior to that troubled time, however, Thomas was among those reporters handpicked by the White House to accompany the president on his historic visit to China in 1972. She was one of only three women out of 87 journalists granted permission by the Chinese government to make the trip.

Thomas characterized Nixon's successor, Gerald Ford, as a decent man who as president was approachable, accessible, and at ease with the office he held. She greatly admired his wife, Betty, whom she found to be "a no-nonsense, straightforward woman," as she told Ebert. "Many Republicans feared Betty's seeming liberalism and thought it might hurt the president and the party. But President Ford never panicked or interfered. He handled things

well. He matched his wife's courage. I thought he was a real man to her real woman."

Thomas always sensed Jimmy Carter felt out of place in Washington, "never quite connected, even to his own party," as she explained to Ebert. "But today, in terms of compassionate contribution to society, he certainly has proven to be our best past president." His wife, Rosalynn, "was never quite at ease with the press," reported Thomas. But the veteran White House correspondent described her as "a doer, very knowledgeable and intelligent."

## Critical of Reagan-Bush Years

As for Ronald Reagan and George Bush, Thomas found them both lacking in compassion. "All of us who covered the Reagans agreed that President Reagan was personable and charming. But I'm not so certain he was nice," she told Ebert. Nancy Reagan, Thomas opined, was "well-intentioned" but "insecure" and "the kind of woman who would never take credit but would want her husband to have it all." President Bush was a genuinely nice man, according to Thomas, but "he was not Ronald Reagan, and the ultra-right...never believed he was a true conservative.... I believe if he'd walked his own road, he would have been a very different president, and a better one." Thomas found his wife, Barbara, to be similar to Nancy Reagan in that "she often put her husband's views and feelings before her own because she believed her job was to support Mr. Bush in all things."

Thomas's initial impression of Bill and Hillary Clinton was a positive one, although the president at first seemed taken aback by this diminutive older woman with a habit of springing out from behind a bush to fire a question at him while he was on his early-morning run. "He's accomplished a lot more than people give him credit for," Thomas said to Kay Mills in a 1996 *Modern Maturity* article. Hillary she found to be much like Rosalynn Carter—dynamic, compassionate, well informed, and more than willing to speak her mind.

But in the wake of the impeachment battle that concluded in early 1999, Thomas described Bill Clinton in a UPI "Washington Window" news release as a man with "a big job ahead. He must repair his credibility, not just for his own sake, to be believed again, but for the United States." As for Hillary, Thomas noted in another UPI news release, she has "a lot of hang-ups about the press.... Not that she can't handle any question put to her, but she ignores even the simplest inquiry as if it was an intrusion.... The first lady is going to have to come to terms with the press if she really wants to make a run for a [political] post."

Over the years, Thomas found her job "exciting, demanding, inspiring—and sometimes depressing," but never boring. And she insisted that she still experienced a sense of wonder when she walked through the White House gates on her way to yet another briefing, press conference, or interview. With no plans to retire, she remained committed to seeking out answers to difficult questions and took very seriously her duty to "keep an eye on the president." Declared Thomas in her memoir: "As a reporter, I do not sit in judgment (although it may sometimes seem otherwise), but I do believe that our democracy can endure only if the American people are informed. The people decide, and therein lies the transcending greatness of the land we love."

## Further Reading

Thomas, Helen, *Dateline: White House,* Macmillan, 1975.
Thomas, Helen, *Front Row at the White House: My Life and Times,* Scribner, 1999.
*Good Housekeeping,* July 1993.
*Insight on the News,* April 27, 1998.
*Modern Maturity,* September-October 1996, pp. 46-47.
*New York Times,* December 8, 1991, p. 38.
"Backstairs at the White House," http://www2.vny.com/upiwire/backst.htm (March 4, 1999).
"Helen Thomas: First Lady of the White House Press," http://www.upi.com/corp/bio/helen_thomas.html (February 17, 1999).
"Washington Window," http://www2.vny.com/upiwire/window.htm (March 4, 1999).
"White House Correspondent to Receive 1998 Thomas Paine Journalism Award," http://www.mediapro.net/cdadesign/paine/award.html (February 13, 1999). □

# Jackie Torrence

**With animated language and facial expressions, hisses, shrieks, and other homespun vocal effects, Jackie Torrence (born 1944) has breathed new life into the age-old art of storytelling. Her retelling of African-American folktales and classic ghost stories, as well as her delivery of modern tales, has established Torrence as a strong presence among contemporary storytellers worldwide.**

Hailing from an extended family of tale spinners, Torrence learned everything she needed to develop her craft from her grandparents, aunts, and uncles. She was born on February 12, 1944, in Chicago, Illinois, but raised in the South. Torrence spent her early childhood on Second Creek in the North Carolina countryside, where she lived on a farming settlement with her grandparents. Jim Carson, Torrence's grandfather, regaled the family with traditional tales told to him by his own father, a former slave. It was from Carson that Torrence first heard many of the narratives her audiences enjoyed—the "Br'er Rabbit" parables (which recount the adventures of a furry friend) and other African-American tales that have been passed along from generation to generation by descendants of slaves in America's rural South.

## Overcame Childhood Speech Impediment

Torrence left her grandparents' farming settlement when she was ready to attend school in nearby Salisbury, where she lived with an unmarried aunt. As a schoolgirl, she discovered that she had a speech impediment and had to withstand the taunting and laughter of her classmates. She was a lonely child, and the speech impediment might have

destroyed her self-confidence were it not for the nurturing attention and coaching given to her by two extraordinary teachers. One of these, grammar school English teacher Pauline Pharr, invited Torrence to write stories and offered to read them out loud to the class, giving the shy child a "voice"—and a creative presence—in the schoolroom.

Just before she entered high school, Torrence discovered that she had impacted teeth, an uncommon condition in which a second set of teeth develops, cramping space in the mouth and obstructing speech. With corrective dental work, she was able to overcome her speech difficulties, though progress was slow and came only with persistent effort. A high school teacher, Abna Aggrey Lancaster, stepped in to offer the support and encouragement that Torrence needed, coaching her during and after school, and even on weekends. Soon Torrence was reading the Scriptures to audiences that gathered during school assemblies, gaining valuable experience for a future career that she would never have anticipated for herself.

After high school, she attended Livingstone College and joined the drama club, taking her newly found flair for public speaking to another level. But Torrence did not remain a coed for long. Before graduating, she met and married a ministerial student. The young couple began a life on the road, traveling from state to state and visiting church communities in the rural South. When Torrence told Bible stories to church members, she did not realize she was honing skills that would later come in handy.

Torrence gave birth to a child, whom she named Lori, but her marriage to the little girl's father did not last. Needing to find a job to support herself and her child, she left Lori with her mother in Granite Quarry, North Carolina. An opportunity for employment presented itself in the town of High Point, where the director of the public library hired her as an uncertified reference librarian. With her $99 paychecks, which she received every two weeks, she had barely enough money to make ends meet. But it was at the library where Torrence was to discover that her talent for storytelling could be put to professional—and even lucrative—use.

## Dubbed "The Story Lady"

It all started one winter day in 1972 when the children's librarian called in sick and the library director begged Torrence to put aside her other tasks and read a few of Richard Chase's *Grandfather Tales* to the rambunctious crowd of three- and four- year-olds that had gathered for story time. Torrence reluctantly agreed and was virtually thrown into what was to become her new role, as a teller of tales. With her irresistible manner and engaging expressions and gestures, she soon had the youngsters transfixed. In fact, the children were so taken with Torrence that she was named the library's regularly featured storyteller, with a reputation that was quick to grow. Soon larger-than-ever audiences filled the library's children's department, eager to hear tales from the one they called "The Story Lady."

Torrence's gift for tale telling was a boon not only for the library but also for Torrence herself, who discovered that demand for her services could relieve her from the burden of poverty. Off-hours, parents sought her out to entertain at their children's birthday parties. "When I found storytelling and realized that I could make that extra money, and pay my bills, and feed and clothe my child—I went after that job with a passion," she told Mary Whited in an interview for *Storytelling Magazine* in January 1999. "Storytelling meant that I didn't have to go on welfare or food stamps. In the beginning, I worked for anything. If someone had $5 to pay, I'd go. If they had $500 to pay, I'd go. If they had $2 to pay or even a box of canned food . . . I'd go."

When invitations poured in from people who wanted The Story Lady to work her magic at events in local and neighboring communities, it came time for Torrence to choose between her job at the library and a freelance profession that seemed promising, yet risky. She chose the latter, seizing every opportunity to build her career, which led once again to a life on the road. After an article about her appeared in the *Charlotte Observer,* word of The Story Lady spread to the National Storytelling Association, which invited her to attend a convention in Memphis. There, Torrence booked 50 engagements in one day, setting the fast pace of her career. Appearances at festivals and schools, as well as performances on radio and television, kept her moving from state to state, and eventually from country to country. Audiences welcomed her in Canada, England, and Mexico, and record companies released recordings of her storytelling.

After these dynamic days of her early fame, which grew steadily throughout the 1970s, 1980s, and 1990s, Torrence found the time to translate her highly visual, performance-based artistry to the page. In 1992, she wrote *Bluestory,* a play about blues music, legends, and poetry (she performed in the staged version, which opened to good reviews in London). In 1994, she published *The Importance of Pot Liquor,* a book that showcases the stories told to her by her grandparents. In 1998, she came out with *Jackie Tales: The Magic of Creating Stories and the Art of Telling Them,* which features 16 tales of all kinds, with storytelling tips and close-up photographs of Torrence that show how facial expressions and other tricks can make a story come alive.

But Torrence's stories do more than just entertain. Her "Br'er Rabbit" tales—and other African-American "animal tales" passed down to her from descendants of slaves—are rich with history and illuminating evocations of a lost age. They also document the antique dialect of the slaves, a mixture of African mother tongues and white English learned on southern plantations ("Br'er," for example, means "brother" or "mister"). On one level the tales serve as moral parables, in which wisdom is prized and greed is penalized, and on another they're instruments of insurrection, rife with seemingly nonsensical code words and phrases that signaled secret places where slaves would meet to escape north via the Underground Railroad. "Now people are realizing that the heritage of Br'er Rabbit is more than little kiddie stories," Torrence told *Seattle Times* reporter Mary Elizabeth Cronin in May 1998. "[T]hese stories were important to the making of history."

## Supported by the Storytelling Community

Torrence could keep up the hectic pace of her career for only so long before it began to take a toll on her health. A case of arthritis worsened in 1993, leaving her dependent on a wheelchair. Nevertheless, she kept going, scheduling six or eight appearances each month. But over the next five years, a series of disparate health problems escalated. In June 1998, she was hospitalized for Pickwickian Syndrome, a relatively rare, serious condition involving congestive heart failure, high blood pressure, diabetes, respiratory and pulmonary complications, weight control problems, and distressed or nonfunctional muscles and bones. Her condition left her immobile, and she had to learn once again how to walk and feed herself. A therapeutic regimen, which included oxygen treatment, physical therapy, and weight reduction, put her on the road to recovery. After losing 150 pounds and making strides in her rehabilitation, she was able to leave the hospital in October.

While she was hospitalized her medical bills piled up, depleting her health insurance coverage as well as her personal funds. She sank deep into debt—until the storytelling community rallied on her behalf, establishing the Jackie Torrence Medical Fund and raising thousands of dollars from supporters. At the 1998 National Storytelling Festival, where Torrence had been scheduled to perform, the storytellers who appeared in her stead donated their stipends to the fund. Other participants and attendees made contributions as well, yielding more than $5,700 at the festival alone. Though a gifted speaker, Torrence struggled to find the words to express her deep-felt gratitude in the pages of *Storytelling Magazine*: "I haven't worked since June, so I haven't made a cent. But my bills have been paid. I'm not eloquent enough to find the words to thank people for what they've done for me."

To Torrence's fans, however, her eloquence remains undisputed. Preserved on audio and video tape as well as in print, her vast repertoire of stories—which runs the gamut from hair-raising scary to knee-slapping silly—continues to delight audiences. She has taken her responsibility as a storyteller seriously, choosing her heroes and villains very carefully (in Torrence's world, stepmothers, who are far more plentiful in these days of broken families, no longer come across as evil). And her influence is far-reaching: Both Disney and Steven Speilberg's DreamWorks team have approached her for advice on telling stories better, while corporations like IBM and AT & T have learned from her how to sharpen their communications skills.

Although Torrence has benefited greatly from the support of others, particularly in recent times, she does not forget the years of struggle in which she relied solely upon herself. These are the realities that so many classic fairy tales neglect to impart—which is why you'll be hard-pressed to find a story like "Snow White" among Torrence's cache of tales. Relating a childhood anecdote in which an aunt told her, "Snow White, baby, you ain't never gonna be," Torrence explained to the *Seattle Times*: "It wasn't meant that because I'm black I'm never going to be white. It meant . . . whatever I get, there isn't going to be a prince getting it for me. I've got to make my own way."

## Further Reading

*Notable Black American Women,* edited by Jessie Carney Smith, Gale Research, 1992.

*Storytelling Magazine,* January, 1999, pp. 4-5.

"Jackie Torrence Updates," *Storynet,* http://www.storynet.org/resources/jackie.htm (February 21, 1999).

"Storyteller's Hisses and Howls Will Grab You," *Seattletime.com* http://seattletimes.com/news/entertainment/htm198/alttale_052198.html (February 21, 1999).

"Storytelling, African-American Style," *Northwest Family Magazine,* http://family.go.com/Features/family_1999_01/nwfm/nwfm19storytell (February 23, 1999).

"What's Hidden in Br'er Rabbit Story?" *Seattletimes.com,* http://www.seattletimes.com/news/entertainment/htm198/altbrer_052198.html (February 21, 1999). □

# David Trimble

**David Trimble (born 1944) was a member of the British parliament and a key figure in the historic Northern Ireland peace agreement of 1998. He was honored for this accomplishment with the Nobel Peace Prize.**

David Trimble began his career as a hard-line Protestant Unionist. To the surprise of most involved, he became a key figure in an historic peace agreement in violence-plagued Northern Ireland. After a long career as a law professor, he was elected in 1990 as a member of Britain's parliament. Trimble became leader of the pro-British Ulster Unionist Party in 1995. His tough stance against the Irish Republican Army (IRA), which struggled for the independence of Northern Ireland, aligned him well with the ideals of his party. His election was seen as a blow to the peace process in the region. No one expected that the temperamental member of the Orange Order would take center stage in forging a deal with his longtime enemies, setting aside personal skepticism to reach an agreement that would end three decades of conflict. In April 1998, Trimble was instrumental in hammering out the Good Friday compromise that was approved by a democratic vote on May 22, 1998. It established an independent legislative council for Northern Ireland and bridged a relationship with the Irish Republic, but allowed the region to remain part of Britain. Trimble was elected first minister of Northern Ireland in the new assembly. That December, Trimble and John Hume, of the Social Democratic and Labour Party (SDLP), were awarded the Nobel Peace Prize "for their efforts to find a peaceful solution to the conflict in Northern Ireland," according to the official Nobel Prize web site.

Trimble was born William David Trimble on October 15, 1944, in Belfast, Northern Ireland, to William and Ivy Trimble, whose roots were English Protestant. He grew up in a comfortable middle-class home and attended Bangor Grammar School, then studied law at Queen's University Belfast (QUB) in the late 1960s. A quiet and serious student, he completed his law degree and took a position at QUB as a lecturer in 1968. Though called to the Bar of Northern Ireland in 1969, he did not practice, preferring to stay on at QUB for much of his career. He was promoted to senior lecturer in 1977, and held that post until 1990. He also served as assistant dean of the law school.

## Political Beginnings

Trimble first entered politics in the early 1970s by joining a group called Vanguard. This organization sought to merge a number of splinter factions into one political party. It was created out of the philosophy of Northern Ireland's largest and most important Protestant party, the Ulster Unionist Party (UUP). Vanguard's leader, William Craig, became a controversial figure at the time for his statements opposing civil rights and promoting the use of deadly force—particularly against Catholics—in establishing a pro-British semi-independent Irish state. The paramilitary group's massive motorcycle rallies were a trademark, and Trimble is remembered for his support of a 1974 loyalist strike during which Protestants protested a power-sharing agreement. Trimble, however, often did not seem to agree with the group's inflammatory stance. In 1975, Trimble was elected to the Northern Ireland Convention from South Belfast, representing Vanguard. At one point, Craig reversed course and came out in support of a voluntary coalition with a major party, causing a rift in the ranks of Vanguard. Trimble stayed aligned with Craig and was named the party's deputy leader. Eventually, though, he drifted toward the mainstream and joined the UUP in 1978.

## Elected to Parliament

Although he spent many more years in academia, Trimble began serving as the UUP's honorary secretary. He was also chairman of the Lagan Valley Unionist Association and chairman of the Ulster Society from 1985 to 1990. These right-wing groups organized protests against the Anglo-Irish Agreement of 1985, which gave the Catholic Irish Republic a consultative voice in Northern Ireland politics. Trimble was then elected to the British Parliament from Upper Bann in a 1990 by-election. He established himself as an active politician, holding frequent meetings with other lawmakers in Ireland, England, and the United States. However, he was not known for his charm or compromising ways. Instead, he was viewed as a outspoken and rather undiplomatic personality, who was prone to rises in temper.

Peace talks ensued between Britain, Protestant and Catholic parties in Ireland, and Sinn Fein, the political arm of the IRA. Britain announced that, unless a majority wanted to keep the status quo, it was not interested in maintaining Ireland as a part of Great Britain. In 1993, the Downing Street Declaration was signed, which entitled Sinn Fein to participate in deciding the fate of Northern Ireland if the IRA agreed to renounce violence. Specific points came under debate for many months, but the IRA declared a cease-fire, and there seemed to be some progress toward a peaceful future for Ireland.

## Led Ulster Unionist Party

In 1995, much to the surprise of observers, Trimble was elected leader of the UUP over the more moderate, John Taylor. Several months prior to the 1995 election, an event occurred which cemented Trimble's reputation as a militant and increased his popularity within the ranks of the UUP. He was instrumental in opposing a police ban that tried to prevent a march of the Orange Order (a coalition of Protestant groups) in a Catholic district in Portadown, Armagh County. This event became known as "the siege of Drumcree." The following year, Trimble again attended the march in his Orange sash and bowler, and again the police were ordered to halt the march, but eventually relented. Trimble was seen on television walking down Garvaghy Road while throngs of Catholic protestors were beaten back by police. To the UUP, Trimble was a solid representative of Protestant loyalties and strength under duress. But to others, Trimble was seen as an extremist. His election was considered a blow to any hope of reaching an agreement.

After a temporary halt, talks with Sinn Fein commenced in Belfast in June 1996. Former U.S. senator, George Mitchell, was dispatched to Ireland to chair the peace talks, despite grumblings that he was pro-Catholic. After another pause, the talks geared up in September, despite the fact that a bombing by a splinter faction of the IRA killed 29 and injured more than 200 in Omagh. Also playing a large part in the talks was John Hume, leader of the Social Democratic and Labour Party (SDLP), the moderate Catholic party. He had been heavily involved with the peace talks for many years. Trimble remained firmly in favor of Ireland continuing to be part of Britain, but recognized a duty to sit at the table and discuss peace for the violence-weary region, both for moral and political reasons. For years, he refused to sit in the same room as Sinn Fein representatives. "We could have stayed back and waited for the talks to collapse without us," Trimble remarked, according to Barry Hillenbrand in *Time* magazine. "But then we would have been accused of blocking peace."

## Peace Agreement Reached

As the talks dragged on into 1998, Mitchell became concerned, as violence appeared to be increasing in the region. He worried that one of the leaders in the talks might be assassinated. Therefore, he and British prime minister, Tony Blair, set a deadline of May to either finalize an agreement or give up the effort. The parties set a new deadline of Thursday, April 9, 1998, at midnight (the day before the Christian holiday of Good Friday), although negotiations stretched out for 17 hours past that time. A landmark settlement that was reached on April 10, outlined a compromise. Northern Ireland would have its own assembly, thus governing itself, while remaining a province of Great Britain. A representative number of Catholics and Protestants would serve in this new legislature. In addition, the Republic of Ireland agreed not to claim the area as part of its own territory, although it would provide some guidance with issues such as tourism, transportation, and the environment. With this compromise, Catholics could forge a closer relationship with Ireland, while Protestants would be pleased that the region remained part of Britain. Subsequently, a majority vote from both sides was required for the treaty to become official. On May 22, 1998, the plan was approved by 94 percent of voters in the Irish Republic. In Northern Ireland, the vote was 71 percent approval.

Trimble took a considerable risk, both personally and politically, with his role in the peace talks. A large portion of Ulster Unionists and other Orange Order groups felt that he had betrayed their interests. After the vote, the region experienced some violent uprisings by disgruntled opponents of the plan from both sides. In some parts of his Portadown district, people were so angered that it was not safe for Trimble to visit. Despite these reactions, he was elected first minister of Northern Ireland at the new assembly's first meeting. Perhaps to allay the concerns of Protestants, he announced that the IRA would have to start decommissioning weapons before they would be allowed to participate in the provincial assembly. Sinn Fein was perturbed, countering that the stipulation of disarmament was not part of the original treaty, but Trimble disagreed. He offered to meet directly with Sinn Fein leaders, along with other party leaders, for discussion on moving forward. This was a major step in relations between the groups.

In September 1998, Trimble met and spoke with Sinn Fein leader, Gerry Adams, to discuss the future of the nation and the possibility of sharing power. Trimble labeled the meeting "civilized and workmanlike," according to Marjorie Miller in the *Los Angeles Times*. It marked the first time since 1922 that Irish Protestant leaders from Northern Ireland had met fact-to-face with Catholic leaders from the Irish Republic. Throughout prior peace talks, Trimble refused to make eye contact with Adams, and the two communicated entirely through intermediaries. Earlier in the week they had spoken to each other directly for the first time with others in the room. However, Trimble refused to shake hands with Adams until the IRA agreed to disarmament. Adams reportedly told Trimble that Sinn Fein has distanced itself from the IRA and is not even able to give such orders.

For their roles in the peace talks, Trimble and Hume were awarded the Nobel Peace Prize in a December 1998 ceremony. The winners split the cash, worth roughly $950,000. Adams was noticeably left out; but expressed support for the winners. Some commentators, and Trimble himself, worried that the honor was premature. Violence had persisted in the region and the IRA steadfastly refused to give up its weapons. If Trimble adopted a hard-line approach, the fragile arrangement could be threatened. On the other hand, a conciliatory attitude would surely serve to further divide his party. After the Nobel Prize winners were announced in the fall of 1998, Trimble, noted to the BBC, "We know that while we have got the makings of a peace, it is not wholly secure yet."

Though Trimble holds an extremely public place in world affairs, he is an intensely private man. He was married once and divorced. In 1978, he married Daphne Orr, one of his former law students. They have two sons and two daughters. Trimble enjoys reading and listening to opera; his favorites include Verdi, Strauss, and Wagner.

## Further Reading

*Modern Irish Lives,* edited by Louis McRedmond, St. Martin's Press, 1996.
*Arizona Republic,* October 17, 1998.
*Business Week,* June 29, 1998.
*Daily Telegraph,* October 17, 1998.
*Economist,* November 4, 1995; January 6, 1996; July 4, 1998; September 5, 1998.
*Independent,* January 27, 1996; November 7, 1996; December 24, 1996; July 22, 1997.
*Los Angeles Times,* September 11, 1998; October 17, 1998.
*Newsday,* October 17, 1998.
*New Statesman,* November 1, 1996; July 25, 1997; August 28, 1998.
*New Statesman & Society,* September 15, 1995.
*New York Times,* September 11, 1998.
*Reuters,* October 1, 1998
*Sunday Telegraph,* January 18, 1998.
*Time,* September 29, 1997.
*Time International,* June 1, 1998; October 26, 1998.
"Nobel Peace Prize 1998," Nobel Prize Internet Archive web site, http://www.nobel.se (December 8, 1998).
"Mr. David Trimble," Ulster Unionist Party web site, http://www.uup.org (December 8, 1998). □

# Lana Turner

**The rise of Lana Turner (1920–1995) from humble origins to Hollywood stardom made her an inspiration to a generation of young American women. She achieved great popular acclaim during her acting**

**career, but her personal life was marred by a series of failed marriages and scandals.**

Lana Turner was born on February 8, 1920 into a financially strained family that lived in the rural area of Wallace, Idaho. Her father, Virgil, held a variety of jobs, including miner, insurance salesman, and bootlegger. As the family struggled to make ends meet, they moved often and Turner's education suffered. In 1928, her parents separated, and she moved with her mother to stay with friends in Modesto, California. Turner's mother took a job in San Francisco and was reunited with her daughter after discovering that friends in Modesto had physically abused the child. In 1930, while Turner and her mother were in California, Virgil was killed after winning a high-stakes craps game. Turner and her mother remained in San Francisco for three years before moving to Los Angeles in 1933.

## Miraculous Discovery

The Turners did not have an easy life in Los Angeles. It was difficult for a single parent to make a living during the Great Depression, but Turner's mother made her daughter attend high school instead of taking a job to supplement the family income. Turner did not apply herself fully as a student, but that cavalier attitude had a totally unexpected consequence. One afternoon in 1936, she decided to have lunch at a nearby restaurant instead of attending classes. Accounts differ as to where she was eating, but it is thought that she was either at Schwab's drugstore (as Hollywood publicists later insisted), the Top Hat Cafe, or Currie's Ice Cream Parlor. As she ate her meal, Turner was noticed by Billy Wilkerson, publisher of the *Hollywood Reporter.* Wilkerson was so taken by her wholesome good looks that he introduced Turner to Zeppo Marx, a member of the Marx Brothers comedy team, who also ran a casting agency for the film industry. Marx immediately recognized what Wilkerson had seen in Turner and introduced her to Warner Brothers' film director Mervyn LeRoy, who in turn decided to cast her in his upcoming film *They Won't Forget.* LeRoy suggested that Turner adopt the first name of "Lana," advice which she readily accepted. In a matter of days Turner had gone from being a poor high school student to a film actress earning $50 per week, a handsome sum at the time.

Turner's first film appearance was as a little-noticed extra in the classic, *A Star is Born,* but her second performance in *They Won't Forget* had an electrifying effect. As Turner herself recounted years later, she and her mother attended the first screening of the film and were mortified by the whistles from men in the audience when Turner appeared onscreen wearing a tight fitting sweater. In fact, Turner would come to be known as the original "Sweater Girl." Although the enthusiastic male response may have embarrassed Turner, to Hollywood filmmakers, such reaction meant only one thing—box office success.

## Professional Success and Personal Strife

During the next two years, Turner continued to make films while completing her high school education at studio schools. LeRoy transferred to Metro-Goldwyn-Mayer Studios (MGM) in 1938, and was followed by Turner. She completed her high school studies in 1939, and began spending more time making movies. Turner was given her first starring role later the same year in *The Dancing Coed.* As Turner's career progressed, she began making a name for herself among Hollywood's party set. In 1940, she married bandleader, Artie Shaw, on a whim in Las Vegas. Shortly thereafter turner became pregnant. MGM officials did not wish to see their sexy starlet assume a more maternal look and convinced Turner to obtain an abortion, an illegal medical procedure at the time. Her marriage to Shaw ended after only four months.

Turner's loyalty to MGM was rewarded, as she received increasingly important roles in the early 1940s. Her social life was also very active. She was reported to have dated such notable figures as actors Clark Gable and Robert Stack, bandleader Tommy Dorsey, and movie producer, aviation pioneer, and oilman Howard Hughes. Despite having had these highly publicized relationships, Turner's second marriage was to the relatively unknown Stephen Crane, a restaurateur from Indiana. Once again Turner became pregnant, only to discover that Crane was still legally married to his first wife. She was inclined to leave Crane, but at the studio's insistence, and after suicide attempts by Crane, she agreed to marry him again after his divorce was finalized in 1943. Their daughter, Cheryl, was born later in the year. Turner sued Crane for divorce in 1944. Despite personal turmoil, Turner continued to receive good parts, including the role of Cora Smith in *The Postman Always*

*Rings Twice* in 1945. She also became a favorite "pin-up" of servicemen during World War II.

Turner's personal life made bigger headlines than her movies during the late 1940s. Her involvement with actor Tyrone Power, who was married at the time, was widely followed by the popular press, as was her association with legendary singer Frank Sinatra. After Power divorced his wife in 1948, only to marry someone else, Turner immediately married Henry J. Topping, a businessman. Their marriage did not prove to be a happy one. Turner suffered a miscarriage, sued Topping for divorce, and made an attempt on her own life in 1951. Her fourth husband, actor Lex Barker, sexually abused Turner's ten-year-old daughter, Cheryl Crane. When Turner discovered Barker's crime in 1957, she immediately divorced him. According to Cheryl, Turner held a loaded gun to his head as he slept, before deciding that his life was not worth her incarceration.

## Indignity and Rejuvenation

Despite the turmoil of her personal life, Turner's career continued to thrive throughout the 1950s. Her performance as an abused starlet in *The Bad and the Beautiful* brought her first critical recognition. She also received an Academy Award nomination for her 1957 portrayal of Constance MacKenzie in *Peyton Place.* Her professional success was once again eclipsed by her life off screen, however. Turner confided to her daughter in 1958 that she feared that her current lover, small-time mobster Johnny Stompanato, would become violent with her. Shortly after this discussion, Stompanato threatened to cut Turner's face with a coat hanger. Upon hearing this threat from an adjoining room Cheryl found a large knife and went to her mother's defense. In the ensuing struggle, Cheryl fatally stabbed Stompanato in the chest. The stabbing was eventually ruled a justifiable homicide but the entire affair, including Turner's testimony at the coroner's inquest, was highly publicized. This negative publicity threatened to make Turner too controversial for any studio to hire. Under these circumstances Turner's next contract for *Imitation of Life* in 1959 called for her to be paid almost exclusively in royalties rather than the more customary salary. In this way the studio would not have to pay her much if the film proved a commercial failure. The strategy backfired however when *Imitation of Life* proved a tremendous success and eventually netted Turner $1 million. The success of the film demonstrated that Turner was still a popular actress. She continued to work steadily until the late 1960s.

## Denouement

By the end of the 1960s, Turner's age made her unsuitable for the type of role that she had played throughout her career. She still maintained an active and turbulent social life, marrying rancher Fred May in 1960. The marriage lasted for two years. Her sixth marriage, to producer Robert Eaton ended in 1969. Turner attempted to broaden her acting horizons by appearing on television but her series, *The Survivors,* lasted only 15 weeks in 1969. Shortly prior to the series' cancellation Turner entered her seventh and final marriage, to nightclub hypnotist, Ronald Dante. The marriage ended after just a few months, when Dante walked out on Turner and allegedly defrauded her of $35,000. For the rest of her life, Turner would remain single. In the wake of the failure of her marriage and *The Survivors,* Turner attempted to perform on stage. She was so painfully shy in front of a live audience, however, that she found it difficult to talk, much less perform. Her last feature film appearance was in *Bittersweet Love* in 1974. Turner enjoyed a final acting stint on the prime-time television drama *Falcon Crest* in the early 1980s. She retired from acting in 1983 and moved into a two-bedroom condominium in Los Angeles.

Turner's personal life improved during her later years. In 1985, her daughter Cheryl wrote an autobiography, *Detour: A Hollywood Story,* detailing the travails of her childhood. Although the book was highly critical of Turner as a mother, talking about its contents brought mother and daughter closer. Turner lived a quiet life, out of the public eye, during the 1980s. A heavy smoker throughout her life, Turner was diagnosed with throat cancer in the early 1990s. The cancer spread to her jaw and lungs by 1992, and she died at her home in Los Angeles on June 29, 1995.

Lana Turner exemplified Hollywood stardom during the 1940s and 1950s. Her improbable discovery and ongoing popularity made her a major public figure throughout her life. The notoriety of her off-screen activities did nothing to lessen her fame.

## Further Reading

*American National Biography,* edited by John A. Garraty and Mark C. Carnes, Oxford University Press, 1999.

Turner, Lana, *Lana,* E.P. Dutton, 1982.

*Entertainment,* April 10, 1992.

*Life,* October 1986.

*People,* February 15 1988; 17 July 1995. ☐

# U

## Matt Urban

**Matt Urban (1919–1995) was the most decorated soldier in U.S. military history, receiving 29 medals and awards for bravery during his 20 months of service in Europe during World War II.**

Matt Urban was born in Buffalo, New York, on August 25, 1919, just after the end of World War I. He excelled at sports, particularly boxing, and dreamed of a career as an athletic coach. Urban graduated from Cornell University with a degree in history and government. His career plans were interrupted by the entry of the U.S. into World War II in December 1941.

### Glory

While in college, Urban joined the Reserve Officer Training Corps and was an early draftee. His first assignment was as Morale and Special Services Officer with the 9th Infantry Division, which was to participate in the invasion of North Africa in November 1942. During the unit's first action, Urban exhibited the courage and willingness to take independent actions that were to make him an outstanding soldier.

While the 9th Division boarded landing craft to invade North Africa, Urban was ordered to remain aboard ship to prepare entertainment for troops returning from the battle. Upon hearing that heavy resistance was being met on the beach, Urban defied his orders and rowed himself to shore in a rubber raft to participate in the battle. While he was preparing to leave the ship, his colonel threatened him with a court martial for disobeying orders. Urban insisted that his rightful place was at the side of his friends who were in

danger, and defied a direct order. Upon reaching the beach, Urban replaced a wounded platoon leader and was promoted to executive officer of the F Company of the 2nd Battalion for his exploits.

By March 1943, U.S. forces had advanced to Tunisia, where they and the British Eighth Army had trapped the remnants of the Afrika Corps. In an attempt to break out of their entrapment, German troops attacked U.S. positions in the vicinity of the Kasserine Pass, in the first major action involving American ground forces in World War II. Urban distinguished himself in these engagements, knocking out a German observation post single-handedly and then leading F Company in a successful frontal assault on a strong enemy position. He suffered injuries to his hand and arm during these operations. Urban's unit also repelled numerous German attacks on their positions. For his efforts in the Battle of Kasserine Pass, Urban received two Silver Stars, a Bronze Star, and two Purple Hearts.

Following the Allied victory in North Africa, the 9th Division was shifted to Britain and participated in the invasion of Normandy. On June 14, 1944, Urban's unit became involved in an engagement near the town of Renouf, France, just inland from Utah Beach. During this fight, Urban used a bazooka to destroy a German tank and suffered a severe injury to his left leg. On the following day, he was shot through the right forearm, and was evacuated to England to recuperate.

While confined to a hospital in southern England, Urban read a newspaper account of his unit's exploits near the town of St. Lo, France. When he heard that the 2nd Battalion had suffered heavy casualties, Urban discharged himself from the hospital and made his way to the front, still limping from his leg wound. Upon his arrival at the front, Urban was immediately engaged in a furious firefight. With the 2nd

Battalion pinned down by heavy artillery fire and threatened with encirclement, Urban led his force forward, helped man a tank that had suffered crew losses, and eventually brought the battalion to safety. Shortly after this battle, the commander of the 2nd Battalion was killed, and Urban was promoted to become his replacement. When subsequently wounded by shrapnel in the lower back and chest, Urban refused hospitalization to remain in action with his unit. Marveling at his ability to return to action after being wounded, Urban's fellow soldiers nicknamed him "The Ghost."

Soldiers who were not familiar with Urban could find his motivation and initiative in combat baffling. In after-action reports of Urban's conduct in the battles near St. Lo, one soldier referred to him as "one of the craziest officers" who was "probably a replacement" given his seemingly foolhardy lack of fear during fierce combat. The same soldier went on to report that Urban's heroics, despite their apparent craziness, inspired his unit to move forward and fight their way to safety.

Allied forces broke out of the Normandy Peninsula during the summer of 1944 and raced across France and into Belgium, Luxembourg, and the Netherlands. By September, Urban and his unit were involved in fighting in the vicinity of Philippeville, Belgium. As the 2nd Battalion attacked German defensive positions, Urban was hit in the neck by a machine gun bullet. His injuries appeared so severe that he was administered last rites by a priest on the scene. Urban managed to survive his injuries; however, he suffered permanent damage to his vocal chords. By the time he had recovered from this injury, in February 1946, World War II had ended. At the end of the war, Urban had accumulated 11 medals for participation and valor, but there were many more to come.

A colonel and a staff sergeant who had witnessed the limping Urban returning to the front to lead his men near St. Lo had filled out paperwork recommending that Urban be awarded the Congressional Medal of Honor. Unfortunately, the colonel was killed in action shortly thereafter, and the paperwork was lost in the Army bureaucracy where it would remain, unseen, for more than 35 years.

A reporter conducting research on Urban's military service in the late 1970s discovered the lost Medal of Honor recommendations. The Army began conducting investigations of his conduct to determine his worthiness for the Medal. Upon locating several eyewitnesses to Urban's exploits, the recommendation was upheld. On July 19, 1980, President Jimmy Carter presented Urban with the Congressional Medal of Honor. With receipt of this medal, Urban became the most decorated soldier in the history of the U.S. armed forces.

Urban's Medal of Honor citation was unusual for a reason other than its tardiness: it cited him not for one act of bravery alone, but for consistent bravery exhibited over several actions. As reprinted in the *Congressional Record* it reads: "Captain Urban's personal leadership, limitless bravery and repeated extraordinary exposure to enemy fire served as an inspiration to his entire battalion. His valorous and intrepid actions reflect the utmost credit on him and uphold the noble traditions of the United States Army."

After leaving the army, Urban secured a position as a writer on veterans' affairs for *Liberty Magazine*. After three years as a writer, Urban returned to the field of athletics and recreation as the city recreation director for Port Huron, Michigan, a position he held from 1949 until 1956. He then served as the director of the Monroe, Michigan community center for 16 years before becoming director of the Holland, Michigan civic center and recreation department in 1972. Urban became a devoted softball player and enthusiast, and was known around Holland as "Mr. Softball." He retired in 1989, stating that he might well have become a lawyer or public speaker had his vocal chords not been damaged in combat. Urban remained active in veteran's affairs and provided assistance to young people embarking on military careers. Urban died on March 4, 1995, in Holland, Michigan. The city of Holland named a public park and a recreation complex in his honor later that year.

## Further Reading

*Holland Sentinel,* February 27, 1995; March 5, 1995; March 7, 1995; March 10, 1995; May 2, 1995; May 24, 1995; November 14, 1995.
*People Weekly,* June 11, 1984.
*Reader's Digest,* December 1981. □

# V

## Atal Behari Vajpayee

**Indian prime minister, Atal Behari Vajpayee (born 1926), served briefly as India's head of state in 1996. Two year later he reclaimed that leadership role when the Bharatiya Janata Party (BJP) mustered enough support in parliament to lead a coalition government. Vajpayee was a popular leader who spent his entire career in service to his country. He was known to distance himself from Hindu extremists within his party.**

Vajpayee was born December 25, 1926, in the central Indian city of Gwalior, Madahya Pradesh. He was one of seven children of Shri Krishna Behari, a secondary school teacher and Hindu scholar. The family belonged to the Brahmin caste, the highest social level in Indian society. As a teenager, Vajpayee joined *Rashtriya Swayamsevak Sangh* (RSS), a secret right-wing Hindu youth organization whose name means "National Voluntary Service." He participated in the movement to liberate India from British colonial rule. As a result, he was imprisoned in 1942 and jailed for 24 days. Vajpayee graduated from Victoria College (now called Laximbai College) in Gwalior and went on to earn a master's degree in political science from Dayanand Anglo-Vedic (D.A.V.) College in Kanpur.

Vajpayee started taking courses for a law degree in Lucknow, the capital of Uttar Pradesh, but left school to take a job as the editor of a magazine published by the RSS. According to John F. Burns in the *New York Times,* the RSS "is considered the fountainhead of Hindu nationalism." On its own party's web site, the group reveals that the "RSS has always been dubbed 'communal,' 'reactionary,' and what not by its detractors." It was founded in 1925 and was nurtured in the 1940s by M.S. Golwalkar, who opposed Mahatma Gandhi's position of "Muslim appeasement." Although the RSS had "the greatest respect for the Mahatma," according to the BJP web site, 17,000 members of the group, including the leader, were accused of conspiracy in his murder. One Hindu nationalist, Naturam Vinayak Godse, was found guilty of the 1948 assassination, just a few months after Gandhi helped free India from British control.

### Elected to Parliament

In 1951, Vajpayee, who always wanted to become a journalist, "came into politics by mistake," as he told Hari Ramachandran in the Reuters news service. He joined an early conservative political party, *Jana Sangh*, which was heavily influenced by Hindu nationalism, and served as private secretary to its founder and president, Shyama Prasad Mukherjee. When Mukherjee died in 1953, Vajpayee stood out as a top name in the party, especially since he had also kept busy editing and writing for party publications, in addition to spending some time as a social worker. He became leader of the *Jana Sangh* party (which was the predecessor to the BJP) in 1957 and was elected to the lower house of parliament, *Lok Sabha* (House of the People) that same year. During this time, the country's leader was Jawaharlal Nehru, who led India from its independence in 1947 until his death in 1964.

In 1962, Vajpayee was elected to the other house of parliament, *Rajya Sabha*, or Council of States, where he served until 1967, and again from 1986 to 1991. The legislator served as president of his party, *Jana Sangh*, until 1977, spending the whole time as leader of the opposition in par-

**393**

liament. On June 26, 1975, he was arrested during Prime Minister Indira Gandhi's "emergency," a point at which she outlawed the RSS and arrested thousands. In 1977, Vajpayee became minister of external affairs, or foreign minister. He held that post until 1980, when he helped found the BJP, serving as its president from 1980 to 1986. Vajpayee was elected to the *Rajya Sabha* again in 1986, serving until 1991. In 1992, Vajpayee's party suffered a serious blow when Hindu extremists destroyed a sixteenth-century mosque in the northen town of Ayodhya, spurring nationwide riots that ended in more than 3,000 deaths.

Vajpayee had cultivated a moderate position within the staunchly pro-Hindu BJP and built an impressive resume of government activity. He served on the Indian Delegation to Commonwealth Parliamentary Association meetings held in Canada in 1966, Zambia in 1980, and the Isle of Man (Britain) in 1984. He held positions on the Committee on Government Assurances from 1966 to 1967 and the Committee on Public Accounts from 1969 to 1970. An avid traveler, he attended a parliamentary goodwill mission to East Africa in 1965, a parliamentary delegation to Australia in 1967, and an Indian delegation to an Inter-Parliamentary Union Conference held in Japan in 1974, Sri Lanka in 1975, and Switzerland in 1984. In addition, he was part of a parliamentary delegation to the European Parliament in 1983 and went along on a delegation to the United Nations General Assembly in 1988, 1989, 1990, and 1991. He also served on the National Integration Council in 1958-62, 1967-73, 1986, and again beginning in 1991.

## Became Prime Minister

Vajpayee briefly held the seat of prime minister in 1996, when the BJP took the most number of seats in parliament. Since no party held a majority, BJP was given the first shot at establishing a new government. In order to gain control, the BJP would have to form a coalition with other parties. However, a rift developed with the two other mainstream parties, the Congress Party and United Front, who feared that the BJP would be too divisive, given its strong pro-Hindu stance. Though Vajpayee had cultivated a reputation as a moderate, who put great distance between himself and the nationalistic elements within his party, the BJP could not garner enough support. After just 13 days in office, Vajpayee was forced to step down. The United Front, a loose coalition of left-wing and regional parties, was sworn in. In November 1997, the Congress party withdrew its support and Prime Minister I.K. Gujral's government fell. The president subsequently dissolved the *Lok Sabha*.

Early in 1998, India held elections once again. No party emerged with a clear majority, but the BJP roused enough support to lead a coalition government and, once again, Vajpayee was named prime minister. This time, after taking the oath, he won a vote of confidence from parliament and maintained his position.

## Nuclear Testing

In May 1998, the world was stunned to discover that India had detonated three nuclear devices in a series of underground tests. Shortly thereafter, neighboring Pakistan, India's major rival, responded with tests of their own. Many nations around the globe condemned the tests. The United States was embarrassed that it had not been able to anticipate the impending detonations, citing a massive failure on the part of American intelligence.

In the face of economic sanctions from America and other nations, Vajpayee defended the action, stating in *India Today,* "The decision to carry out these tests was guided by the paramount importance we attach to national security." He later added in the interview, "I would like to assure the people of the world, especially in our part of the world, that there is no cause for worry at all, much less any alarm, on account of India's action." He insisted that hundreds of nuclear tests have been performed by various countries, with no violent repercussions, and admitted that no further tests were scheduled. Vajpayee remarked, "Millions of Indians have viewed this occasion as the beginning of the rise of a strong and self-confident India," and brushed off threats of political and economic effects, saying, "Yes, our action has entailed a price. But we should not worry about it. India has an immense reservoir of resources and inner strength. . . . Sanctions cannot and will not hurt us."

Vajpayee has never married. Since the late 1950s, he has lived with the daughter of a close friend, Namita Bhattachariya; her husband, Ranjan; and their daughter, Neharika; first on the campus of Delhi University and later in a white colonial in central Delhi. He has adopted her family as his own and is secretive about his private life. Vajpayee is a noted poet and has published several volumes of verse. He is also revered as a colorful orator who never prepares a speech, preferring to speak extemporaneously. Collections of some of his addresses have been published. The statesman and poet's favorite activities are reading and writing. He also enjoys travel, the arts, film, gardening, and fine cuisine. Vajpayee is opposed to the caste system and promotes women's liberation efforts.

### Further Reading

*Current Leaders of Nations,* Gale Research, 1998.
*Arizona Republic,* May 13, 1998, p. A6.
*Dallas Morning News,* March 16, 1998, p. 7A; March 20, 1998. p. 15A.
*Independent,* May 2, 1996, p. 11.
*India Today,* May 25, 1998.
*Los Angeles Times,* May 19, 1996, p. A4; May 29, 1996, p. A4.
*Maclean's,* May 27, 1996, p. 28.
*New York Times,* March 28, 1977; May 16, 1996.
*Reuters,* May 15, 1996; May 28, 1996; February 16, 1998; June 8, 1998.
"Atal Behari Vajpayee: A Profile," Bharatiya Janata Party web site, http://www.bjp.org (July 12, 1998).
"BJP History: Its Birth, Growth & Onward March," Bharatiya Janata Party web site, http://www.bjp.org (July 12, 1998).
"Vajpayee to Become India's Prime Minister," May 15, 1996, CNN web site, http://www.cnn.com (July 12, 1998). □

# Gloria Vanderbilt

**"Little Gloria" Vanderbilt (born 1924) was the center of the most sensational custody battle in U.S. history. The girl who stuttered and could hardly put her feelings into words grew into a woman who discovered herself through acting, writing, drawing, painting, and designing. Her efforts led to the creation of a world-famous line of goods, all bearing her highly recognizable name.**

Gloria Vanderbilt, the great-great-great granddaughter of shipping magnate, Cornelius Vanderbilt, has been in the limelight since childhood, when her mother and aunt fought a very public custody battle over the "poor little rich girl." Vanderbilt first published a book of poetry in 1955 and has since published her memoirs and fiction. She married four times, only the last time happily. Vanderbilt made a name for herself as a very successful designer of jeans, perfume, shoes, linens, accessories, and even a frozen dessert. Then, tragedy struck when her 23-year-old son committed suicide before his mother's eyes.

### Confusing Beginnings

Gloria Laura Vanderbilt, born February 20, 1924, in New York City, came from a long line of wealthy and famous people. She was a descendant of shipping baron Cornelius Vanderbilt. In her mother's family were diplomats and judges. Vanderbilt's father, Reginald Vanderbilt, a rail-road heir, horse breeder, playboy, and alcoholic gambler, died when his daughter was 17 months old. Vanderbilt's mother, Gloria Morgan Vanderbilt, was a renowned beauty who took her daughter to live in Europe after her husband died. Her mother loved the cities and beaches of Europe and moved around quite a bit, living in Paris, Monte Carlo, Biarritz, and London. She socialized with many men, including a married businessman and a German prince, a member of the Mountbatten family, to whom she became engaged. Young Gloria spent much of this time with her grandmother, Laura Kilpatrick Morgan, and nurse, Emma Keislich, whom she called "Dodo."

Morgan became determined that her granddaughter would not live in Germany and plotted to have the girl live in America with her aunt, Gertrude Vanderbilt Whitney. At the age of ten, Vanderbilt became the subject of a bitter and public custody battle between her mother and her aunt. The battle captured the imagination of the American people, who read avidly about the proceedings in the daily newspapers. A newspaper article in the *Daily News* described Dodo's testimony: "For five hours Mrs. Gloria Morgan Vanderbilt . . . listened to a tight-lipped nurse denounce her with virtuous relish as a cocktail-crazed dancing mother, a devotee of sex erotica, and the mistress of a German prince." Custody of "Little Gloria" was given to Vanderbilt's aunt, but she could see her mother on weekends and for the month of July. Gloria spent the next seven years living on the east coast with her aunt.

## A Series of Husbands

Vanderbilt's aunt was aloof and old-fashioned, insisting that her niece be constantly chaperoned. In June 1941, at the age of 17, Vanderbilt went to California to visit her mother in Beverly Hills, where she felt like a bird released from a cage. There she dated movie stars and the rich and famous, including Howard Hughes. Not wanting to return to her life back east, and not wanting to remain with her mother, Vanderbilt decided to marry Pasquale ("Pat") De Cicco, a 32-year-old Hollywood agent. De Cicco spent his wedding night drinking and gambling. For the next three years he verbally and physically abused his wife. The couple eventually divorced.

Soon after Vanderbilt married the conductor, Leopold Stokowski. Stokowski had the reputation of being a ladies' man and had been involved with the actress Greta Garbo. He had been married twice. He and Vanderbilt lived quietly, in a small flat, for the first few years of their marriage. They had two sons, Stanislaus and Christopher. After five years of marriage, Vanderbilt began to see an analyst who advised her to express herself. She rented a studio where she wrote poetry and painted. She also began taking acting lessons and performing professionally for a short while. The Stokowskis divorced after ten years of marriage and fought a custody battle over their sons. Vanderbilt won. Vanderbilt later married Sidney Lumet, a television director. They remained married for seven years; when she ended the union, Lumet attempted suicide. Vanderbilt's fourth marriage to Mississippi writer, Wyatt Cooper, lasted 14 years, until Cooper's death in 1978, after a series of heart attacks. The couple had two sons, Carter and Anderson.

## A Commercial Success

Vanderbilt began her career as a commercial designer in 1971 when Don Hall of the Hallmark company saw Vanderbilt's drawings in an art gallery. The drawings were used in a line of paper goods. A collection of scarves was adapted from her paintings. Vanderbilt went on to design a line of blouses and a highly successful line of jeans. In 1980, she earned $10 million. Her name was seen on such products as perfume, sheets, shoes, leather goods, liqueurs, and accessories. In the mid-1980s, she launched a tofu-based frozen dessert. Vanderbilt was one of the first designers to make public appearances, a difficult thing for her because of her shyness.

Friends of Vanderbilt, who wished to remain anonymous, told *People* magazine in 1985, "There has always been a vulnerable, childlike quality about her. She has had despair and aloneness, and maybe as a result she has terminal narcissism. A whole slice of her is a dreamy child. . . . Sometimes she can hardly speak, she is so shy. But when something interests her she may get on a run and bore you to death about a great piece of lace or something."

In the 1980s, Vanderbilt began publishing her memoirs, *Once Upon a Time.* Vanderbilt said in an interview with *People,* that she did not write it as a form of therapy to resolve the pain she felt at her mother's indifference. "I did it because I'm a natural-born writer. I consider it a piece of work, not therapy. I always knew I would do the book, and

it fell onto the page." Her second book, *Black Knight, White Knight,* tells of her marriages to De Cicco and Stokowski. In it she wrote of Stokowski, "With time, bitterness and pain gently slipped away, and a mysterious loving light shines strongly through the crystal of memory. Because as I have come to understand myself—I have also come to understand him. My mother, too, I have come to understand . . . And although I still search for her, and part of me probably always will, it is an ache I have learned to live with, and we have found, she and I, a place of peace where we rest together: closer perhaps in death than we ever were in life."

## A Mother's Tragedy

In July 1988, Vanderbilt experienced the worst nightmare of her life. Her son Carter Cooper, age 23, plummeted from the terrace of her 14th-floor penthouse to his death as she watched powerlessly. Vanderbilt contended that her son was not depressed or suicidal, but was disoriented from asthma medication he had taken. At first she was unable to accept his death. Six weeks later she joined a suicide support group, which she credits with saving her life. "The Waspy background I came from, if you cried, you went into the bathroom and shut the door. Rich people do it differently. They don't communicate. The group met once a week. I wish it had met every day. You walk in, and it's a roomful of strangers—all rock bottom. There was someone who'd had it happen two days before; another to whom it had happened ten years ago. You could look at him and say, "It's been ten years, and he's alive and okay." It took three years for Vanderbilt to believe that she would survive her grief. In 1996, Vanderbilt published *A Mother's Story,* about her son's suicide. She is very close to her youngest son, Anderson Cooper, and delights in her two granddaughters Abra and Aurora Stokowski, the children of Stan Stokowski.

## A Stab at Fiction

In 1989, Vanderbilt published her first work of fiction, *Never Say Good-Bye: A Novel.* Book reviewer Joanne Kaufman called the work "an exercise in self-indulgence. . . . .There is an effortful quality to Vanderbilt's writing, that of someone trying far too hard for a literary patina." Her 1994 novel, *The Memory Book of Starr Faithfull,* received better reviews. Kathleen Hughes noted in *Booklist* that "Vanderbilt has persuasively re-created the life of an introspective child and the tormented woman she later became. The novel works both as an absorbing portrait of the sumptuous lifestyle of the privileged classes in the 1920s and 1930s and as the sad chronicle of an anguished life that slowly spiraled into madness."

## New Problems

In the 1990s, Vanderbilt sued her former lawyer and business manager, claiming that he and her psychiatrist formed an illegal company that defrauded her of $2 million. Because the lawyer failed to pay her taxes, when he should have, Vanderbilt was forced to sell her Southampton, New York, summer home and her Manhattan townhouse to pay the money she owed the Internal Revenue Service.

### "I Am Determined to Survive"

Vanderbilt has experienced more triumph, tragedy, and public exposure than most people can ever imagine. She sees herself as a role model for others who have suffered loss. I remember a visit from a friend whose daughter had taken her own life about three years before. She said to me, "You will laugh, and you will live again." Her words meant nothing to me. It was inconceivable. But of course she was right. It's almost nine years later now, and I've laughed and lived. But I'll never be the same. I am determined to survive because it will help others to know that if I can survive the worst thing that can happen, they can too."

### Further Reading

Goldsmith, Barbara, *Little Gloria. . .Happy at Last,* Alfred A. Knopf, 1980.

Vanderbilt, Gloria, *Black Knight, White Knight,* Alfred A. Knopf, 1987.

*Booklist,* November 1, 1994.

*Entertainment Weekly,* December 2, 1994.

*People Weekly,* June 10, 1985; May 6, 1996; March 31, 1997; April 9, 1990. □

# Vercingetorix

**Celtic chieftain Vercingetorix (c. 75 BC-c. 46 BC) battled valiantly to keep the Roman army from overrunning the territory of Gaul, as France was then called. His troops were defeated at Alesia and Vercingetorix was forced to surrender.**

Revered in France as its first national hero, Vercingetorix managed to unite several sovereign Celtic tribes to do battle against the aggressive Romans. Vercingetorix was an Arverni, one of the many Celtic tribes who ruled over what is France today, northern Germany, the Benelux countries, and the British Isles. Originally a migratory race, scholars theorize that the Celts hailed from what is now southern Germany. During the Iron Age, they settled across much of the western European continent, and were known to be skilled on horseback and fierce in battle; they were also excellent goldsmiths. By the fifth and fourth centuries BC, Celtic iron tool culture was firmly established across much of the European continent from Spain to parts of Asia minor.

### Developed but Disunited

The Celts conducted a system of trade with one another, and launched the viticulture industry in the Bordeaux area of France, still famous two millennia later for its wines. Culturally, Celtic Europe spoke similar dialects and shared a common faith in Druidism. This religion held that spirits lived in the natural world, in its forests and streams. A powerful caste of priests conducted Druidic rites and rituals, which in some cases involved human sacrifice. Despite their numbers, the Celts were not politically united, and this was to prove their fatal flaw. Instead, tribes such as the Arverni were ruled by chiefs with absolute sovereignty over their peoples.

The Celtic world into which Vercingetorix was born in about 75 BC had evolved into a complex society which made military success and economic stability dependent on peasant agricultural labor, and vice versa. This system was the precursor of feudalism, a noble-peasant economic dependency that would dominate Europe for much of the Middle Ages. Vercingetorix hailed from a noble ruling family likely situated in what is now the town of Auvergny—a name reflecting its Celtic Arverni origins—in south-central Gaul, as France was then called. He inherited the chieftainship of the Arverni from his father, Celtillus, who had attempted to ascend to a kingship over several other Celtic tribes during a time of political uncertainty in central France. As a result, Celtillus was likely slain by a conspiracy of nobles and chiefs in opposition to him. Ironically, his son would advance to the position of leader of several Celtic tribes, but only when the necessity of an alliance became apparent, when a determined Roman army threatened.

### Trained to Lead

As befitting the son of a Celtic noble and member of the warrior class, Vercingetorix was likely provided with military training from an early age. He was probably schooled in Druid beliefs and rites as well. During his lifetime, the Druids had become a powerful force in Celtic civilization, and were an adamantly conservative element very much opposed to Roman encroachment. Other Celtic tribes, such as the Boii, were more receptive to the economic promise and infrastructure development that Roman conquest offered.

In southern Italy, the Roman republic was evolving, through a series of wars, conquests, and personal betrayals, into an empire. Julius Caesar was a popular democratic leader, one of the men of the first Triumvirate who ruled around 60 BC, but departed from the comforts of the urbanized and highly developed capital to conquer Gaul. This decade-long military campaign is chronicled in his *De Bello Gallico* ("The Gallic Wars"), from which the story survives as an account of Vercingetorix and his times.

Caesar grouped all the Celts who lived in France as the "Gauls," though he recognized there were separate kingdoms such as Belgae, Alemanni, Boii, and Arverni, among many others. In 59 BC, Caesar named himself governor of Cisalpine Gaul, the section of northwest Italy that lies below the Alps. From here he and Roman soldiers began making incursions into the rest of Gaul on the other side of the mountains. He conquered the Suevi, a Germanic tribe of southwestern Germany, whose name lends itself to the modern term for this region, Swabia. Caesar and the armies then overran the Helvetii—the Celtic tribe who inhabited present-day Switzerland—then battled the Belgae, another powerful group of Celts centered in what is today northern France and Germany. The Romans also gained an important foothold after vanquishing the Veneti of northwest France, whose lands lay along the coast of the Atlantic. This allowed Caesar an opportunity for successful incursions to the British Isles in 55 and 54 BC.

## Roman Advances Increased

Varying tribes of Celts had been long threatened by the menace of Germanic peoples like the Suevi. The Germans periodically emerged from what was a vast and, to the Romans, mysterious forest that spread across Central Europe. At first Caesar helped the Celts of central Gaul repel German encroachments, and also acted as arbitrator between Celtic tribes and their enemy, but began attacking central Gaul's tribes such as the Arverni. Because of the harsh treatment Romans sometimes unleashed on those they conquered, Celtic uprisings in northern Gaul began in 54 BC and continued through the following year. During the winter of 53-52 BC, Caesar returned to Rome, but left a garrison of soldiers stationed in central Gaul.

An uprising of Celts, led by the Carnutes, slaughtered several Roman officials and traders at Cenabum (now Orleans, France) that winter. According to Caesar's chronicle, the news of the victory was shouted from Celtic settlement to settlement, and reached the borders of Vercingetorix's Arverni lands by the morning light. In his early twenties at that time, Vercingetorix wished to command a legion of Arverni and join with the Celts of central Gaul; his uncle, Gobannito, and several other elders thought this unwise, and so Vercingetorix was cast out of his capital, Gergovia, near what is today Clermont, France.

## A New Military Alliance

Caesar wrote respectfully of his Celtic foe in *The Gallic Wars*, noting that the exiled but determined Vercingetorix then gathered a militia of beggars and outcasts, and began convincing Arverni nobles to listen to his plan. Eventually he staged a coup in Gergovia and cast out those leaders who had rejected an offensive attack on the well-equipped, well-organized Romans.

Vercingetorix then sent out emissaries to secure an allegiance, via the enforced handover of hostages, with several other Celtic tribes who ruled over sections of Gaul. These included the Senones, Parisii, Pictones, Cadurci, Turoni, Aulerci, Lemovice, and Andi, among others. He was named commander-in-chief. That winter, with Caesar still in Rome, Vercingetorix and Celtic armies began battling Roman garrisons in northern France. Caesar returned immediately upon learning of the attacks, though crossing over the Alps with an army, horses, and supplies was no easy task during the winter months. Roman legions began attacking Celtic settlements in vulnerable southern Gaul, many of whose men and arms had been sent north with Vercingetorix. Meanwhile, Vercingetorix had launched an assault on Gorgorbina, a town of Celtic Boii already loyal to Rome.

Vercingetorix and his army were defeated at Vallaunodunum (modern Montargis), and then Caesar retook Cenabum from the Celts, and burnt it to the ground. Caesar was in the process of taking the town of Noviodunum, whose Celtic Bituriges were handing over tribute and men, when the army of Vercingetorix was spotted in the distance. The Bituriges quickly shut their gates on the Romans, and a battle with Roman cavalry followed. Noviodunum then fell to the Romans, who planned to take the city of Avaricum (Bourges) next.

## United with Aedui

As a result of these setbacks, Vercingetorix called a summit at Bibracte, the stronghold of the Aedui, another great Celtic tribe who ruled over the lands to the north and east of the Arverni. The Aedui, according to the classical historian Plutarch in *Lives of the Noble Grecians and Romans*, "had styled themselves brethren to the Romans, and had been much honoured by them." This last great alliance in effect made Vercingetorix the first—and last—leader of a unified Celtic nation.

Vercingetorix and his followers decided to burn their own settlements along the way, making it impossible for the Romans to obtain food in hostile territory. Twenty cities across the land of the Bituriges were set afire, and some in other areas as well. They decided not to burn Avaricum and defend it instead. But the Romans laid siege to Avaricum for several months, and eventually defeated the Celts in a bloody battle.

Next on the Roman agenda was Gergovia. Vercingetorix recovered sufficiently from the setback of Avaricum to defend his hometown with renewed troops and determination. When the situation degenerated into a stalemate, Caesar's armies began marching toward Lutetia

(Paris), burning everything Celtic they encountered along the way. Vercingetorix was forced to move against this, suffered an attack by the Roman cavalry, and had to retreat to Alesia. The walled center of the Celtic Mandubi tribe, Alesia was set on a hill and was theoretically easy to defend. The Romans built a massive fortification around it, however, with their usual marvels of defensive engineering constructed—towers, battering rams, screens on wheels—on the side facing the hill. They also constructed walls at the rear to protect it from Celts arriving as reinforcements, for Vercingetorix had sent out emissaries in the middle of the night back to their own home states for additional men, arms, and horses. Caesar wrote that a quarter-million Celts arrived to do battle at Alesia. Plutarch places this number at 300,000, and notes that inside Alesia's walls was already a Celtic force of about 170,000.

## Vercingetorix Surrendered

But the Romans, who also had dug deep trenches, simply waited for Vercingetorix and the Celtic army to run out of provisions. Vercingetorix sent out sorties to battle the Roman soldiers, but poor communication and coordination of efforts plagued the poorly-organized Celts, and they suffered numerous reverses. Vercingetorix's cousin, Vercassivellaunus, battled from the rear in one coordinated attack, but failed to break the Roman line. The Celtic troops facing the Romans from outside saw the futility of the effort, and abandoned Alesia.

When Alesia surrendered, Caesar demanded not just all arms of the Celts but their leader as well. Vercingetorix told his colleagues that they could either deliver him dead or alive to the Romans, according to their wishes. Alive, it was decreed. According to Plutarch, Vercingetorix prepared by "putting his best armour on, and adorning his horse, [then] rode out of the gates, and made a turn about Caesar as he was sitting, then quitting his horse, threw off his armour, and remained quietly sitting at Caesar's feet until he was led away to be reserved for the triumph." It was his last act as a free man as he was then taken into custody and returned with Caesar to Rome, where a 20-day public thanksgiving was called for the not-insignificant conquest of Gaul. Vercingetorix was allegedly dragged behind Caesar's chariot in the official victory parade. He died in Rome about 46 BC.

Caesar's conquest of Gaul resulted in the geographical boundaries of modern France. Moreover, the establishment of Roman government in the vast lands of the Celts would have other significant repercussions. Cities grew in size, connected by sturdy Roman roads initially built for military purposes, and the new Roman Gauls began to prosper from access to pan-European trade. Latin was imposed as a language, but a slang version (Vulgar Latin) was spoken by the soldiers and people. Its mixture with existing Celtic words developed into the French language.

Alesia is today the town of Alesia-St. Reine, and a large statue of Vercingetorix sits at Mont Auxois there. It was dedicated in the nineteenth century at a time when France rediscovered this long-forgotten Celt and declared him a figure of French resistance to the aggression of other European powers.

## Further Reading

Caesar, Julius, *The Gallic War,* English translation by H. J. Edwards, Harvard University Press, 1917.

Cole, Robert, *A Traveller's History of France,* Interlink Books, 1997.

*Dictionary of World Biography,* edited by Frank N. Magill, Salem Press/Fitzroy Dearborn Publishers, 1998.

Plutarch, *The Lives of the Noble Grecians and Romans,* The Dryden Translation, Encyclopedia Britannica, 1990. □

# Gianni Versace

**One of the most innovative fashion designers of the 20th century, Gianni Versace (1946–1997) startled the world with his clothes made from metal, plastic, and leather, and delighted ballet and opera lovers with his stunning theatrical costumes. Versace socialized with celebrities, who loved and wore his expensive clothing. The world was shocked when the designer was murdered outside his Florida mansion in 1997.**

Gianni Versace was born on December 2, 1946 in the industrial town of Reggio di Calabria, in southern Italy. His parents, Antonio, an appliance salesperson, and Francesca, a dressmaker and clothing store owner, had three children—Santo, Gianni, and Donatella. Gianni Versace spent much time in his mother's shop as a child. He watched her make clothes and admired the chic women who came into the shop. He knew at a young age that he would become a fashion designer. Versace also drew inspiration from the area where he lived. He often wandered among the ancient Greek and Roman ruins, which would later provide him with themes for his clothing. Although he loved clothes, art, and music, Versace studied architectural drafting. At the age of 18, while he was in school, he also worked for his mother as a buyer, going to fashion shows throughout Europe.

## Made a Name for Himself

Versace started designing clothes when he was 22. A local garment maker hired him to design a collection that was sold in Francesca Versace's store. Fashion models from Rome and Milan came to southern Italy to perform in runway shows. Soon Versace's name was heard in Milan, the center of Italian fashion.

On February 5, 1972, Versace flew north to Milan. Salvatore Chiodini and Ezio Nicosia of the Florentine Flowers clothing mill had asked Versace to hurry there to design a collection that had to be rushed. Versace designed some "instant" summer wear, which was so successful that he earned not only his four million lira wage, but also a Volks-

wagen convertible. He then designed Florentine Flowers' fall and winter collections.

During the early 1970s, "Made in Italy" clothing was just beginning to surface. Milan had just become the fashion capital and was the logical place for the emerging ready-to-wear industry. Chiodini and Ezio Nicosia's hiring of Versace marked a turning point in the fashion industry. They realized that clothes could not continue to be anonymous. Increasingly sophisticated buyers demanded a personal touch.

The work for Florentine Flowers was Versace's first independent assignment. Shortly thereafter he designed for De Parisini of Santa Margherita. In 1973, Versace designed women's ready-to-wear clothing for Callaghan, known for its knitwear and Genny, which featured leather and suede. In 1974, Versace created and developed his own line—Complice. Although he wasn't yet working under his own name, Versace already had his own label. Under the Complice name, Versace designed an all-leather collection. He was one of the few designers to feature leather at this time.

## A Family Business

In 1976, Santo Versace, Gianni's older brother, left his management consultant's practice in Reggio di Calabria and moved to Milan. Santo had earned a degree in business administration from the University of Messina in 1968. He and his designer brother set out to create the Gianni Versace label. In 1977, Donatella Versace Beck joined the business. Her husband, Paul Beck, also worked for the company,

overseeing the menswear line. At the beginning of 1978, the company opened its first Versace shop in Via Spiga, Milan, but it sold only Genny, Callaghan, and Complice lines as Versace's first fall women's collection had not yet been released. Versace's first signature collection was presented in March 1978. His first menswear collection followed in September. The collection was characterized by a stylish nonchalance and the use of pastel colors.

Versace decided to remain independent, becoming one of the few big labels in control of the entire product cycle, from design to retailing. Creative and marketing operations were handled through the company. On the manufacturing side, the company had a controlling interest in its production facility. Control of manufacturing was necessary in order to monitor quality and image. Eighty percent of the styles that reached the runway were produced by Alias. Retailing through boutiques was handled directly for image purposes in Paris, London, New York, Madrid, and Milan or through exclusive franchising and multi-label boutiques. To smooth distribution, buyers viewed the collections and placed their wholesale orders out of the company's Milan showroom. Retail operations were franchised.

## Awards and Artistry

In 1979, Versace, who was always greatly concerned with his image, began a collaboration with the American photographer Richard Avedon. In 1982, Versace won the first of a series of awards, "L'Occhio d'Oro," (Golden Eye) for the best fashion designer of the 1982-83 fall/winter collection for women. In this collection he displayed his famous metal garments, now a classic feature of his fashion. His metal mesh dress was inspired by the punk fashions he saw in London in 1980. To develop the mesh material, Versace worked with German engineers. In later collections, metal dresses were made in bright colors. In the 1980s, Versace introduced another technological innovation, the bonding of leather to rubber using lasers.

That same year, Versace began collaborating with the Teatro alla Scala and designing costumes for the Richard Strauss' ballet "Josephlegende." Versace felt that his involvement with costume design gave his clothing a new attitude. In his ready-to-wear line, many of his clothes reflected those needed for dance, allowing unrestricted movement. In 1983, at the show "E' Design," Versace displayed the synthesis of his technological research. The following year, Versace designed the costumes for Donizetti's opera *Don Pasquale* and for the ballet *Dyonisos* choreographed by the Belgian, Maurice Bejart. Bejart created a triptych dance in honor of the launch of the fragrance for men, "Versace l'Homme."

The National Field Museum in Chicago presented a major retrospective show of Versace's work in 1986. Versace designed the costumes for Richard Strauss' opera, *Salome* in 1987. On April 7, the book *Versace Teatro* was published. Two months later, Versace went to Russia with Bejart, for whom he designed the costumes of the *Ballet du XX Siecle*. In September 1988, Versace opened a 600-square-meter showroom in Madrid, his first boutique in Spain.

In 1989, the film *The Fortune of Friendship* was shown. It recounted the relationship between Versace and Maurice Bejart. In Milan, Versace presented "Versus," a new line for young people, which explored informal themes and served as an alternative to so-called conventional ways of dressing.

On October 21, 1990, the San Francisco opera season opened with Richard Strauss' *Capriccio,* with costumes designed by Versace. The following year the fragrance "Versus" was debuted and "Signature," Versace's classic line, was launched. Elton John, an ardent admirer of Versace, began his world tour for which Versace designed the costumes. In New York, for the Italian Trade Commission, Versace inaugurated the charity Gala "Rock'N Rule," with profits given to the Amfar anti-AIDS Association. A retrospective show at the Fashion Institute of Technology featured Versace's work.

The "Home Signature" line was launched in 1993, which included dinnerware, carpets, quilts, and cushions. Versace's spring collection for 1993 shocked many with its sadomasochistic styles. In 1994, the book *The Man Without Tie* came out. In 1995, Versace and Elton John held a party for the Elton John Aids Foundation. Versace opened his world flagship store in a 28,000-square-foot restored Vanderbilt townhouse on Fifth Avenue in Manhattan in 1996.

## A Violent End

Versace owned four homes around the world, including a mansion on Ocean Drive in Miami Beach, a villa on Lake Como in Italy, and a 15th-century palazzo in downtown Milan. He enjoyed listening to music and reading, especially biographies of musicians.

On July 15, 1997, Versace was shot in front of his Miami Beach, Florida home by Andrew Cunanan, who had crossed the U.S. on a killing spree. It is thought that Versace and Cunanan met in San Francisco when Versace was there designing costumes for the opera. After a private service in Miami, Versace's remains were cremated and brought back to Italy by his siblings. In Milan, 2,000 mourners attended a memorial mass held in the city's gothic cathedral. Many celebrities attended the funeral including Princess Diana, Elton John, Versace's favorite supermodel, Naomi Campbell, and Maurice Bejart. Versace's fashion colleagues paid their respects, including his archrival Giorgio Armani. Versace's companion Antonio D'Amico also attended.

The three Versace siblings controlled the company, with Gianni owning 45 percent, Santo 35 percent, and Donatella 20 percent. She had taken over more of the designing in the last five years of her brother's life because of his bout with cancer of the ear. Four days before his murder, Versace signed a contract to take his company public. Versace left his shares in the company, worth a reported $800 million, to his 11-year-old niece, Allegra, and a $28,500 monthly allowance to his companion.

In her book *Vulgar Favors: Andrew Cunanan, Gianni Versace and the Largest Failed Manhunt in U.S. History,* journalist Maureen Orth claimed that Versace had the AIDS virus when he was murdered. The Versace family won a legal battle in 1998 to exclude the designer's medical history from the police report on the crime. The family called

the allegation in Orth's book an invasion of privacy and a "scurrilous attack on the reputation of someone who was a victim of a horrible crime and is not here to defend himself."

## Versace Remembered

Robin Givhan wrote of Versace in the *Washington Post,* "Designer Gianni Versace is being mourned by the fashion industry as a fallen titan. Before Versace, there were no supermodels, no celebrities at shows and in advertising, no screaming fans. Fashion was not entertainment, it was merely clothes. . . . Over time, his work was celebrated not only in fashion annals for its brashness but also in museums because of the ways it reflected the culture and re-energized the Old World artistry of the . . . seamstress of the couture. . . . Versace understood the importance of marketing. He loved celebrities and knew that they not only attracted the attention of the press, but they also helped to set trends."

An exhibition celebrating the major themes of Gianni Versace's career in high fashion took place at The Costume Institute of the Metropolitan Museum of Art from December 11, 1997 to March 22, 1998. The exhibition began with "Versace: The Landmarks," a mini-retrospective of the designer's major themes, including the prints, the white suit on the cover of *Time* magazine on April 17, 1995, and Elizabeth Hurley's safety-pin dress. In the second gallery, the theme "Versace and Art" traced his inspirations from Warhol and modern abstract art. The third and largest gallery, "Versace and History" revealed his appreciation of ancient Greece and Rome, Byzantine crosses, madonnas, 18th-century court-style silhouettes, and 1920s and 1930s themes of the Vienna Secession, Vionnet, and Madame Grès. "Versace and Experiment" in the fourth gallery presented new materials, including plastic dresses, leather, including the 1992 "bondage" collection, and the metalmesh dresses. The final gallery, "Versace: The Dream," featured clothing for the theater. Richard Martin, curator of The Costume Institute called the exhibit an "extraordinary reckoning, a moment of assessment and farewell."

## Further Reading

Martin, Richard and Grace Mirabella, *Versace (Universe of Fashion),* Vendome Press, 1997.

Mason, Christopher, *Undressed: The Life and Times of Gianni Versace,* Little Brown, 1999.

Orth, Maureen, *Vulgar Favors: Andrew Cunanan, Gianni Versace and the Largest Failed Manhunt in U.S. History,* Delacorte Press, 1999.

Turner, Lowri, *Gianni Versace: Fashion's Last Emperor,* Trans-Atlantic, 1998.

*People,* July 21, 1997.

*Time,* July 28, 1997; October 20, 1997.

"Gianni Versace (1946–1997)," *The Costume Institute,* http://costumeinstitute.org/versace.htm (March 17, 1997).

"The Versace Story," *Modaonline,* http://www.moda.italynet .com/www.modaonline.it/STILISTI/VERSACE/story.htm (March 17, 1997). □

# Elisabeth Vigee LeBrun

**A favorite of the French queen, Marie Antoinette, Elisabeth Vigee LeBrun (1755–1842) began to support her mother and brother by painting portraits when she was only 15. She was one of the few women admitted to the Academie Royale in France. Perhaps best known for her portraits of members of Europe's royal families, many critics have called her "a woman before her time."**

Vigee LeBrun's most famous client was Marie Antoinette, France's much maligned queen. When the two met in 1778, Vigee LeBrun's art-dealer husband had gambled away his wife's earnings. Still, she was dauntless and set out to establish her own salon where she would court royal clients. In a November 1982 article for *Art in America,* Brooks Adams noted that in her memoirs, Vigee LeBrun said that her much sought-after salon was, "a place where art and society mixed, where noblemen and ministers were content to sit on the floor, to avoid the stiff, formal court entertainments at Versailles." In time, her portraits and memoirs alike painted a portrait of Vigee LeBrun as a woman born to contend with anyone.

## Unfortunate Circumstances

Marie Louise Elisabeth Vigee LeBrun was born in 1755 in Paris. Her father was Louis Vigee, a little-known portrait artist who worked in pastels. From the time she was small, he taught his daughter the skills of the trade. She proved to be somewhat of a prodigy. Her parents placed Vigee LeBrun in the convent of La Trinite, directly behind the Bastille. Her earliest memories were of drawing so frantically on the walls of her dormitory that the sisters regularly punished her.

When her father died, Vigee LeBrun was only 12. He had been her biggest supporter. For an article in *Antiques,* magazine in November 1967, Ilse Bischoff quoted Vigee LeBrun's father after he saw a drawing she had done as a small child. It was the head of a bearded man with the light of a lamp falling on his face. She took care to observe light and shade, and showed skill beyond her years. Her father had exclaimed, "You will be a painter if I ever saw one."

By the time she was 15, Vigee LeBrun had established a business as a painter that provided major financial support for her family. Her mother was a hairdresser from Luxembourg, who remarried not long after her first husband's death. Her stepfather soon began to squander her earnings. When she was only 21, she married an art dealer named Pierre LeBrun. It was clearly a marriage more of convenience, than of love. They had one daughter, Julie, born in 1780.

Vigee LeBrun's marriage helped her gain access to a world normally restricted to men. Although she was denied access to a male apprentice system, and was unable to participate in classes at the major art academies around the city, she gained admission to the lesser salon of the Academie de Saint Luc. However, the Academie Royale was closed to her without proper connections. In those days, being shown in lesser salons kept a painter away from the financial benefits to be gained from wealthier clients who frequented the prestigious Academie Royale.

When Vigee LeBrun was finally admitted to the Royale in 1783, her critics were not kind. She was accused of using her husband and the palace, most particularly her friendship with Queen Marie Antoinette. Another unfortunate rumor was that she had a long-standing sexual affair with the finance minister, Calonne. Her accusers contended that he aided her in squandering much of the Royal Treasury. That was never proven. Still, it was clear that she capitalized on her associations with the queen and the rest of the royal family. The aristocracy longed to be seen as simple, especially as unrest grew among the people outside of the palace confines. One portrait of Marie Antoinette was considered so scandalously informal, that it was withdrawn from the salon in the midst of her debut at the Academie Royale.

Vigee LeBrun's arch-rival was a woman painter named Madame Labille Guiard. They were admitted to the Academie Royale on the same day. For the rest of the decade, before the French Revolution erupted in 1789, the two women maintained their rivalry. At the time of the academy's biennial exhibitions, the bitterness they felt toward each other had reached the height of its intensity.

Vigee LeBrun painted one of her most acclaimed works in 1784. It was the portrait of Marie-Gabrielle de Gramont, Duchess of Caderousse. That was the same year she suffered a miscarriage, and painted only five portraits. Her usual output far exceeded that. The portrait was shown at the Salon of 1785 to much acclaim and became one of the artist's most celebrated works. In her memoirs, written fifty years later, Vigee LeBrun recalled the painting. "As I detested the female style of dress then in fashion, I bent all my efforts upon rendering it a little more picturesque, and was delighted when, after getting the confidence of my models, I was able to drape them according to my fancy. Shawls were not yet worn, but I made an arrangement with broad scarfs lightly intertwined around the body and on the arms, which was an attempt to imitate the beautiful drapings of Raphael and Domenichino . . . I could not endure powder . . . persuaded the Duchess to put none on for her sittings."

## Thrived in Exile

Vigee LeBrun was not immune to the anxious rumbling that became the French Revolution. What had begun on that fateful night of July 14, 1789, erupted further when mobs stormed the palace at Versailles on the following October 6. Vigee LeBrun had been in disfavor for her association with Marie Antoinette for some time and was considered to be a royal sympathizer. In her article in *Antiques,* Bischoff described the dramatic escape the artist made that night. "Vigee LeBrun escaped with her daughter, Julie, and a governess by public coach from Paris to Lyons and over the Alps to Italy. She left Paris disguised as a working woman, terrified of being recognized, since her self-portrait had been exhibited at the Academie Royale salon only two months earlier." During the next twelve years in exile, Vigee LeBrun traveled to Italy, Austria, and then to St. Petersburg, Russia, where she stayed six years, before going to England. The fame that came to her during the previous decade had preceded her. She was best-known as a painter of French women, one who had even managed to make Marie Antoinette look stunningly beautiful and loving.

Her reputation during her years abroad enabled Vigee LeBrun to amass a second fortune. Her husband divorced her in order to protect his own French citizenship. Yet, Vigee LeBrun managed to retain control of her money. In Rome she reacquainted herself with members of the French nobility who had fled into exile. In Naples she met and painted a portrait of Countess Skarvonsky, the beautiful niece and mistress of the Russian prince, Potemkin. In Russia, Vigee LeBrun was a favorite of Empress Catherine II. However, when a portrait of the Empress' granddaughters did not please her, royal patronage was withdrawn. Still, Vigee LeBrun managed to charm the rest of St. Petersburg society.

Vigee LeBrun's French citizenship was restored in 1802. She was then able to return for a brief visit to Paris, but soon moved to London. There she painted such noteworthy figures as Lord Byron and the Prince of Wales. Vigee LeBrun reportedly disliked London, yet found such support there she decided to stay. Among the circle of French exiles, Vigee LeBrun continued to enjoy the exclusive privileges of a wealthy lifestyle. In 1805, at the age of 50, she returned permanently to France.

## Memoirs were Published

Vigee LeBrun lived to the age of 87—remarkable for a woman of her era. In 1835, at the age of 80, she published her memoirs. She continued painting portraits into her later years, although none received the acclaim of her earlier work. Instead, it was her memoirs that would bring her greater notoriety. Vigee LeBrun revealed herself in her memoirs in a way her paintings never could.

When describing her exile, she was quick to comment of her displeasure at the noise and cooking smells that emerged from the households and markets of Naples. Her visit to Venice illustrated the vast differences between 18th and 19th century Europe. She presented an account of her pleasure in meeting Denon, a stylish character around town. Vigee LeBrun wrote, too, about his charming mistress, a woman named Isabella Marini, who later married Count Albrizzi. Vigee LeBrun painted her portrait, as well. Marini

permitted Denon to serve as her escort, since she would have been unable to go to any cafe without one. In her memoirs, Vigee LeBrun recounted a conversation with Marini. "People will think," Marini said to her, "I have broken up with him and this will go on the whole time you are here, because you cannot go about without an escort." Even for an independent woman such as Vigee LeBrun, restrictions of behavior were often severe.

Heralded as a heroine of the modern-day women's movement, Vigee LeBrun enjoyed renewed interest at the end of the 20th century. Some argued that it was her skill as a major portrait artist that deservedly brought her fame, not her gender. French writer and feminist, Simone de Beauvoir, complained as early as 1949 that women artists and writers "very often continued to be torn between their narcissism and an inferiority complex . . . Vigee LeBrun never wearied of putting her smiling maternity on her canvases." Endless critiques of her work continued to argue her true merit as an artist. As with any popular artist, painting such familiar subjects, many suggested that her work did not merit such applause. Had she not been a woman of such intrigue, at such odds with her place in time, perhaps Vigee LeBrun would have been destined for obscurity. Nancy Heller wrote in *Women Artists: An Illustrated History*, that "Vigee LeBrun's best portraits are vibrant evocations of individual personalities and vividly preserve a way of life that was fading even as she painted it."

What Vigee LeBrun offered to the generations that followed her was an intimate glimpse into a way of life that departed soon after she painted it. Her pictures bring pleasant punctuation to the memory of an era of indulgence and luxury among the upper classes. The vigor with which she lived, and how well she was able to support herself, might have been testimony enough to her place in history. Vigee LeBrun was not a woman who dared to let anyone forget her.

## Further Reading

Heller, Nancy G., *Women Artists: An Illustrated History*, Abbeville Press, Inc., 1997.
Vigee LeBrun, Elisabeth, *Memoirs of Madame Vigee LeBrun*, translated by Lionel Strachey, Braziller, 1989.
*Antiques*, November 1967, pp. 706-712 and January 1968, pp. 109-113.
*Art in America*, November 1982, pp. 75-80.
*Art News*, January, 1983, pp. 106-108.
*Burlington Magazine*, December 1981, pp. 739-740.
*Library Journal*, May 1, 1989, p. 86. □

# W

## Stella Walsh

**Stella Walsh (1911–1980) lived in the United States, but ran for her native country of Poland in track events ranging from the U.S. National Championships to the Olympics. Walsh set 20 world records and won 41 U.S. national titles between 1930 and 1954. She won the gold medal in the 100 meter race in the 1932 Olympics and took silver for the same event in the 1936 Olympics.**

Born Stanislawa Walasiewiczowna on April 3, 1911 in the Polish town of Wierchowina, Walsh came to the United States with her parents when she was two years old. The family settled in Cleveland, Ohio, and Walsh changed her name when she began school. Her career was long for a track athlete, lasting 24 years, from 1930, when she won her first AAU event, until 1954. Walsh won the 100 meters, 200 meters, and long jump events at three U.S. national championships—the first time in 1930 and the last time in 1948. Since her three-time sweep of the event, only one athlete, Marion Jones, has swept the events even once.

Walsh ran 100 yards in 10.8 seconds in 1930, becoming the first woman to run the distance in under 11 seconds. All eyes were on her at the Olympic trials at Chicago's Soldier Field in early July of 1932. Walsh was the main runner on the New York Central Railroad's Cleveland team. She wore sweatshirts with "Twentieth Century Limited"—the name of a fast train between New York and Chicago—printed on the back.

### Runs for Poland

Just before the Olympic trials, Walsh announced that she intended to become a U.S. citizen. At the same time, she lost her file clerk job with the railroad. Her main focus was finding a way to make a living. The city of Cleveland offered her a job in its Recreation Department, but she turned it down. At that time, athletes could only compete in the Olympics if they were amateurs and had not made money from their sport. If Walsh accepted the job, she would be disqualified from the Olympics. And the job did not pay well.

On July 12, one day before she planned to take out naturalization papers, Walsh took a job in the Polish Consulate in New York City and decided to run for Poland in the Olympics. She received heavy criticism in the press for this decision. One athlete benefited from Walsh's decision not to run for the United States. Babe Didrickson, an all-around athlete from Dallas, planned to qualify for several Olympic events. Because Walsh was no longer aiming for the U.S. team, this eliminated competition and cleared the way for Didrickson to become a star.

Walsh was accepted on the Polish Olympic team and competed in the 100 meters in the 1932 Olympics in Los Angeles. She had set a world record of 11.9 for this event in the trials the day before and was expected to win. Canada's Hilda Strike took her by surprise, taking the lead at the start and keeping it for 40 meters. Walsh caught her there, and the two were tied until the 80-meter mark, when Walsh swung into an intense finishing kick and won the race, matching her previous day's record time of 11.9.

After winning the gold, Walsh left immediately. This was a habit of hers; other athletes remarked on it, and did not understand why she was such a private person. She came to meets with her running clothes on, never changed

in the dressing room and left as soon as the meet was over. In her book *Their Day in the Sun: Women of the 1932 Olympics,* Doris H. Pieroth quotes reporter Muriel Babcock, who remarked, "She sneaked off from the stadium before her [Polish] team-mates did." Some athletes felt sorry for her because she was always alone but others were unsympathetic, angered by the fact that she lived in the United States and ran for another country.

## Rivalry with Helen Stephens

In a broadcast on National Radio on July 17, 1998, author Pat Shiel discussed his book, *Olympic Babylon,* with interviewer Amanda Smith. "One of the truly most bizarre stories from the Olympic annals," he said, "is that of the rivalry between the sprinters Helen Stephens and Stella Walsh." Walsh and Stephens had been rivals throughout their track-and-field careers. Walsh first encountered the American sprinter in 1935, where the farm girl and running prodigy was making her first major public appearance. No one had heard of Stephens and most of the spectators were on hand to see Walsh, who was known as "the fastest woman in the world." She would not keep the title for long. In the 50-meter event Stephens not only beat Walsh but also tied the record time for the event. Stephens also set a new world record for the 200 meters, a new world record in the standing broad jump, and won the shot put event. When spectators congratulated her on being the new "fastest woman in the world" and on beating Stella Walsh, she asked, "Who is Stella Walsh?" which angered Walsh. After this meet, Stephens was never defeated in a footrace and

regularly beat Walsh. According to Shiel, "Stella was not impressed by this and made it generally known that she thought the reason that Helen Stephens was beating her all the time was that Helen was a boy."

Walsh set a world record of 11.7 seconds in the 100 meters in 1934. In 1935, she set a world record of 24.3 seconds for 220 yards and in 1938 set a another world record of 19 feet, 9 3/4 inches for the long jump. In the 1936 Olympic Games in Berlin, Walsh ran for Poland again, setting a time of 11.7 seconds. But American runner Helen Stephens beat Walsh with her world-record time of 11.5 seconds. Walsh was angry at the loss. She protested to officials and the Polish press supported her. She claimed that Stephens was really a man, falsely running as a woman because no woman could run that fast. German officials performed a physical examination of Stephens and confirmed that she was a woman.

Walsh became a U.S. citizen in 1947, after her peak running career was over. She remained active, playing semiprofessional basketball and softball and running exhibition races. Apart from her Social Security check, these sporting events were her only source of income. In the late 1970s she became the editor of the sports section of a Polish newspaper in Chicago, and finally took a job with the Cleveland Recreation Department, where she organized track and field events and women's sports events.

## An Unexpected End

Walsh's life ended tragically on December 4, 1980, when she was 69 years old. On a shopping trip in Cleveland, Ohio she was in the wrong place at the wrong time—in the parking lot of a discount store, unloading her shopping cart during a robbery attempt. An innocent bystander, she was shot and killed by a stray bullet. The results of her autopsy by the Cuyahoga County Coroner's Office were startling and confusing. According to the autopsy, Walsh had a condition known as mosaicism, which meant that, chromosomally, she was mostly, but not all, male. Ironically, she suffered from the very condition she had accused Stephens of having. This condition, which is still not fully understood, has been the source of much confusion about Walsh. Some sources report that Walsh had both ovaries and testicles, while others say that she was "really" a man. It seems clear that she did have some level of physical androgyny but lived as a woman.

The confusion regarding Walsh has not abated. She is still widely regarded as an Olympic "cheater" and a man posing as a woman. Although her androgyny was the result of a medical condition and not a deliberate attempt to "cheat," Walsh was not inducted into the Ohio Hall of Fame. (Although she was admitted into the National Track and Field Hall of Fame, the Ohio Senior Citizens Hall of Fame, the Ohio Women's Hall of Fame, and the Cleveland Sports Hall of Fame). Some of the members on the induction committee felt that her genetic androgyny gave her an "unfair advantage" over other female athletes.

## Further Reading

Mandell, Richard D., *The Nazi Olympics,* Macmillan, 1971.

Pieroth, Doris H. *Their Day in the Sun: Women of the 1932 Olympics,* University of Washington Press, 1996.

Porter, David L., *Biographical Dictionary of American Sports,* Greenwood Press, 1988.

Wallechinsky, David, *The Complete Book of the Olympics,* Viking Press, 1984.

"Cathy's Forlorn Chase," *Sydney Morning Herald,* http://www.smh.com.au/news/9811/30/sport/sprts17.html (February 26, 1999).

"Gold Rush," *Time,* http://cgi.pathfinder.com/time/magazine/archive/1996/dom/960722/gold.html (February 26, 1999).

"History's Greatest Olympic Cheats," http://www.smh.com.au/atlanta/articles/2470.html (February 26, 1999).

"Jones Completes Triple at Track Championships," *ESPN SportsZone,* http://espn.go.com/other/news/980621/00746346.html (March 5, 1999).

"1997 Inductees," Ohio Women's Hall of Fame, http://www.state.oh.us/obes/hof/members.htm (February 26, 1999).

"Ohio Senior Citizens Hall of Fame," *Ohio Front Page,* http://www.webtest.state.oh.us/age/ (February 26, 1999).

"The Sports Factor," *Radio National Transcripts,* http://www.abc.net.au/rn/talks/8.30/sportsf/sstories/sf980717.htm (February 26, 1999.)

"Stella Walsh," *Ohio's Greatest Runners,* http://www.nd.edu/~pworland/ogr/walsh.htm (February 26, 1999).

"Stella Walsh Sprints," USATF, http://www.usatf.org/athletes/hof/walsh/html (February 26, 1999).

"This Week in Track and Field," USATF, http://www.usatf.org/news/6-12-98.htm (February 26, 1999). ☐

# Jack Warner

**With his three brothers, Jack Warner (1892–1978) founded Warner Brothers movie studio, one of Hollywood's premiere forces during the studio era. Warner was also an influential movie producer, responsible for 5,000 films over the course of his career.**

Born on August 2, 1892, in London, Ontario, Canada, Warner was the ninth of twelve children born to Benjamin and Pearl Leah Eichelbaum, and the youngest son of the seven children to survive into adulthood. Warner's parents were Jewish immigrants from Poland. Warner's father worked as a butcher, cobbler, and peddler to support his family. When Warner was two years old, the family moved to Youngstown, Ohio. In 1907, the family name was changed to "Warner." Jack Warner only had a fourth grade education and was a poor student while in school. This left him with life-long feelings of inferiority. His son Jack Warner, Jr., later told Jean Stein of *The New Yorker,* "I always felt, what the hell, he's a cum laude in his field, he doesn't have to feel negative about it. But he did have a great inferiority complex."

As a child, Warner wanted to be an entertainer, singing and telling jokes. When he was a teenager, he performed in vaudeville and at a local opera house under the name Leon Zuardo. Over his lifetime, he developed a reputation for telling bad jokes. Warner's niece, Betty Warner Sheinbaum,

told Jean Stein of *The New Yorker* that "He was cute and funny and he wanted to be in show business; he was a pest from the day he was born."

Warner's elder brothers, including the eldest Harry as well as Sam and Albert, entered the movie exhibition business while Warner was a teenager. In 1906, these four Warner brothers and their sister Rose, moved to New Castle, Pennsylvania where they ran a movie theater. Jack continued to exercise his desire to entertain by singing between movies as a "chaser" to rid the theater of its audience between films. In 1907, the Warner clan moved into distribution with its Duquesne Amusement Supply Company, which rented films to theaters. They were forced to sell the business in 1910 because Thomas Edison, the inventor of many technical aspects of film production, held many patents through which he tried to control the burgeoning film industry. The Warners temporarily turned to movie making. Warner and his brother Sam went to St. Louis to make a film, *The Perils of the Plains* which was of poor quality and did not do well at the box office. After Edison's trust was legally broken, the Warners returned to distribution temporarily and then, in 1912, tried to get production started again. Warner represented the family's interests in San Francisco at the time.

## First Warner Studio

World War I broke out and Warner and his brother Sam served in the Air Corps. During this time, Warner appeared in his only lead role in a military training film on the dangers of sexually transmitted diseases. By 1917, their efforts were concentrated on production, away from distribution. Warner moved to Los Angeles to start up a studio and worked as head of production for the new studio. The Warners' first hit was 1918's *My Four Years in Germany.* In 1920, Warner produced a 15-episode serial. Between 1920 and 1922, Warner produced about six feature-length films.

## Warner Bros. Studio is Born

In 1922, the Warners moved into a bigger studio, and the company officially became known as Warner Bros. in 1923, with Warner serving as head of production. The studio's earliest star was a dog named Rin Tin Tin. Warner Bros. slowly built up their stock of actors and the number of features the company released each year. By 1925, Warner was at the head of 30 features. Warner's importance in the studio grew throughout the 1920s as his responsibilities increased and he was making day-to-day decisions about who would work on what pictures. The studio however was not making much of a profit, though they had the theaters to show their pictures. In fact, Warner Bros. was deeply in the red.

## Gambled on Sound

To salvage the company, Warner Bros. became the first studio to take a chance on a new technology: sound. This was a risky proposition in 1925, when they first announced their intentions. First, Warner Bros. tried Vitaphone, which allowed for a synchronized soundtrack and special effects, but no dialogue. In 1926, the company released *Don Juan* in this format, but it did not do well. Audiences were already used to orchestras accompanying silent films. In 1927, the Warners made a bigger gamble by putting out *The Jazz Singer,* the first movie to feature sound which included dialogue. *The Jazz Singer* was the most expensive movie Warner Bros. made up until that time, but the risk paid off because their innovation changed the industry. Warner Bros. became a major studio, and had a huge jump on their competition. Unfortunately for the family, Sam Warner died the night before the premiere. Sam was Warner's favorite brother, the buffer between Jack and his eldest brother, Harry.

With the success of *The Jazz Singer,* Warner Bros. was able to acquire a better studio and bigger stars. In the 1930s, Warner oversaw plant operations and the studio. As the Warner representative on the lot, he was officially the vice president and chief of production. He made most of the artistic and financial decisions, and was highly concerned with keeping the movies under budget. One way he accomplished this was by focusing on one star (usually male) in each picture. Richard Schikel of *Fortune* wrote, "Efficiency was an obsession with crude, shrewd Jack Warner, who supervised production while his brother attended to more boring matters, like distribution and finance. Jack was known to prowl the lot looking for lights that had been left on unnecessarily."

Warner's penchant for thrift aside, Warner Bros. was amazingly successful in the 1930s. The company had a reputation for being intelligent, making socially aware films that have transcended time. Their film stars included James Cagney, Humphrey Bogart, Paul Muni, and Edward G. Robinson. As Warner Bros. thrived, Warner became a prominent social figure. Yet he was regarded as undignified and coarse when compared with the other studio heads. He became a fixture on the gossip pages, mostly for his personal life.

In 1916, Warner met and married Irma Solomon while living in San Francisco. Together they had a son, Jack Warner, Jr. Over the course of his marriage, Warner had many affairs, including one in the 1930s with a sometimes actress named Ann Paige that lasted for three years. Warner eventually divorced his wife and married Paige in 1936. Together, they had a daughter named Barbara. The Warner family, especially Harry, did not approve of Warner's second wife, which deepened the already cavernous rift. Harry Warner treated his brother badly, in a very controlling way. Warner's niece Betty Warner Sheinbaum told Stein of *The New Yorker,* "Jack was constantly rebelling, and everything he did was just shocking to my father. He treated Jack as if he were a bad little boy, and they were constantly at odds. It wasn't that their relationship deteriorated—it was just always bad." For his part, Warner lied to his brothers, except for Sam when he was alive, and cheated them on deals.

In the 1940s, Warner tried to increase his power in the studio and Hollywood, but faced increasing problems within his studios employees and its stars. Warner worked people hard, expecting much from them. His stubbornness in labor negotiations ended up costing the studio money. Such unnecessary outlays did not extend to Warner Bros. films. The studio developed a new film style called *film noir,* in part because it was cost effective to shoot everything in fog so that whole sets would not have to be built. Warner Bros. also produced star vehicles, among them 1943's *Casablanca.*

## Testified About Communism

During World War II, Warner again supported the war effort. He joined the Army Air Force and reached the rank of lieutenant colonel. The Warner Bros. studio also cooperated with the war effort. Warner was extremely patriotic, and very afraid of Communism. In the late 1940s, Warner testified before the House Un-American Activities Committee investigating Communist activity in Hollywood. Warner Bros. had made what could be read as a pro-Russian film at the request of President Roosevelt when the Russians were still American allies. After the war ended, Warner Bros. had to defend the fact that they had made the film. Warner said that he wanted to send Communists back to Russia, and would contribute to any fund that would remove them from the United States. Warner also gave the Committee several names of people he believed were Communists, but later had to retract them. Warner Bros. went on to make one of the first anti-fascist films, *Confessions of a Nazi Spy.*

In the 1950s, the fight between Warner and his brother Harry reached its peak. In 1956, Warner deceived his brother into selling off the studio. In fact, Warner had arranged a deal to sell both of their shares after the initial buyout was complete. Jack Warner put himself in charge of Warner Bros. as studio president. At the time, he was spending half the year gambling in the south of France. Warner's relationship with his wife Ann was also problematic. Though she was the only person he trusted, he treated her poorly, having many affairs. They lived separate lives. However, Warner did not divorce her because he was afraid that she might get half of the studio. Betty Warner Sheinbaum told Stein of *The New Yorker*, ''The sad thing was that Jack didn't have friends. He had yes-men. He loved people who lived like kings. But although he sought out society, he always seemed so uneasy and defensive when he was in it.''

In 1958, Harry Warner suddenly died. Within days, Warner was involved in a serious car accident in the Cap d'Antibes, France. Authorities believed Warner probably fell asleep at the wheel and lost control of his car. He was in a coma for nearly a week and full recovery took months. His family believed he was going to die. When Warner later learned Jack Warner, Jr., had said something to this effect to the press, he broke off the relationship with his son for the rest of his life. In 1966, at the age of 74, Warner sold his studio for $32 million to Seven Arts productions, a holding company. Warner retained his position as the head of the studio until 1969 when he finally retired.

Though Warner had retired from the studio, he did not retire from the entertainment industry, but instead branched out into theater and independent film production. First, he financed a Broadway musical *Jimmy* which totally failed and cost him $1.5 million. Then Warner produced two independent movies in 1972, *Dirty Little Billy* and *1776*, both of which fared poorly at the box office. In 1974, Warner took a fall on a tennis court which left him injured for the rest of his life. Warner suffered a stroke in 1977 and another the next year. He died from edema on September 9, 1978 in his Los Angeles home. As Leah Rozen wrote in *People Weekly*, ''Jack Warner wasn't the brightest, the smoothest or the best of Hollywood's founding studio moguls, but he was the one who lasted the longest.''

### Further Reading

*American National Biography,* edited by John A. Garraty and Mark C. Carnes, Oxford University Press, 1999.
Schatz, Thomas, *Genius of the System: Hollywood Filmmaking in the Studio Era,* Pantheon Books, 1988.
Sperling, Cass Warner and Cork Millner with Jack Warner, Jr., *Hollywood Be Thy Name,* Prima Publishing, 1994.
*Fortune,* February 17, 1986.
*The New Yorker,* February 23, 1998.
*People Weekly,* October 8, 1990. □

# Thomas J. Watson, Jr.

**Thomas J. Watson, Jr. (1914–1993) assumed control of International Business Machines (IBM) from his father in 1956. Under his leadership, IBM entered the computer market, focusing on sales, service, and adaptation. He also changed IBM's management style and invested in new plants and laboratories. Toward the end of his life, Watson became involved**

**in arms control and Soviet-U.S. relations, serving as the ambassador to the Soviet Union in 1979.**

Thomas J. Watson, Jr. was born on January 14, 1914 to Thomas J. Watson, Sr. and Jeannette Watson, in Short Hills, New Jersey. The Watsons later had two daughters, Jane and Helen, and another son, Arthur. Thomas Watson, Sr. began managing the Computin g-Tabulating-Recording Company (CTR) in 1914. In the 1920s, Thomas Watson, Sr. became chief executive officer and renamed the company IBM.

### Trouble at School

Thomas Watson, Jr. was a poor student and often in trouble. He embarrassed his father, a member of the school board, by putting skunk odor in the school's ventilating system, forcing the school to close for the day. Watson had trouble reading and had little self-confidence. The greatest moment of his childhood was when he flew in an airplane for the first time, at age ten, and saw his first film with sound, both on the same day. Although his father always told him he was free to choose any career, Thomas Watson, Sr. groomed his son from an early age to take over IBM, taking him to sales conventions, factories, and meetings.

Because his grades were poor, Watson needed his father's help getting into college. He attended Brown University, where he also received poor grades, but managed to graduate. In September of his freshman year, Watson learned to fly, gaining a great deal of self-confidence. Besides flying, Watson spent his time at college drinking and socializing. In his senior year, Watson decided that he wanted to work for IBM. He began as a sales trainee that fall, after spending the summer of 1937 traveling to Asia, Germany, and Russia.

## Trained at IBM School

Watson began his sales training at IBM's school in Endicott, New York. The IBM school strove to inspire enthusiasm, loyalty, and high ideals in its trainees. Over the front door the motto "THINK" was written. Students and teachers alike wore the company "uniform," dark business suits with white shirts. When Watson went to a bar for a drink after school, the bartender asked "Doesn't your father have a big policy about liquor?" Watson recalled in his autobiography, *Father, Son & Co.* The policy applied to drinking on the job or on IBM property, but Watson felt Endicott was a rather unpleasant place, where he was singled out as the boss' son.

Watson spent most of his training time learning about IBM's punch card system, an automated accounting system. Although he did poorly in school, he graduated and was given a prime sales territory, the western half of Manhattan's financial district. He did very well, but felt it was because of who he was, not what he did. His three years in sales were full of self doubt. By 1940, Watson made some sales calls in the morning and spent the rest of the day flying airplanes. His evenings were spent drinking and dancing in nightclubs. His behavior caused a stir at IBM, but his father did not say much as Watson managed to stay out of the gossip columns.

## Flew for His Country

In early 1940, war seemed inevitable. Watson knew he wanted to fly planes for his country, but wanted to avoid flight school and military discipline. He joined the National Guard and during the week "marked time" at IBM. On weekends he practiced flying with his squadron. In September 1940, the National Guard was mobilized, and Watson became a military pilot at Fort McClellan in Alabama.

After the bombing of Pearl Harbor, Watson married Olive Cawley, a model he had met in 1939. He was transferred to California, where his squadron flew along the coast, looking for Japanese submarines. He disliked his commander, and asked his father to help him. A week later Watson was transferred to the Command and General Staff School at Fort Leavenworth, Kansas. Watson became the aide-de-camp of Major General Follett Bradley. Together they traveled to Moscow where they set up the Alaska-Siberia ferry route to bring planes to the Soviets. Watson held other positions during the war, flying about 2,500 hours in five years.

In 1942, Olive gave birth to a baby boy, who died at the age of two months. In 1944, their son Tom was born. The couple also had five daughters.

## Headed IBM

After the war, Watson returned to IBM to work as the assistant to Charles Kirk, IBM's executive vice president. Watson became a vice president, one of only five, in 1946.

By 1950, Watson and Al Williams were running the company, with Thomas Watson, Sr. occasionally making a major decision. In 1952, Watson became president; his father was chairman of the board. Four year later, he became the official head of IBM. One month later, his father died.

Watson's management style differed from his father's. Watson wanted managers to use their imaginations and to make decisions without always checking in with him. Although Watson could be harsh, he tried to loosen things up at IBM. Soft collars on shirts, rather than hard ones, were now allowed. IBM employees could have an occasional drink. Watson also decentralized the company's administration, encouraged more research and development, and increased the company's debt.

Watson saw that IBM's punch cards would need to be replaced by computers. The success of IBM's 604 Electronic Calculator convinced Watson that the field of electronics would be expanding rapidly, so he enlarged the company's research department. In six years, the company increased the number of engineers and technicians from 500 to over 4,000. In the early 1950s, Watson worried about the UNIVAC computer, produced by Remington Rand. He wanted to create a computer to compete with it. In 1953, IBM unveiled the 701, a computer for scientific use. The IBM 702, an accounting computer, was up and running by 1956. In 1954, the company started delivering a small business computer, the 650, which could perform complex accounting operations.

In the early 1960s, IBM began developing a new computer, the System/360. Development took longer and cost more than expected, with hundreds of computer programmers having to write millions of lines of code. The development of this software alone cost half a billion dollars. The new computers used integrated circuits, an innovation at the time. In 1964, Watson announced the System/360, even though it was not fully developed. By 1966, the System/360 was running with the long awaited software. System/360, a compatible multiple model system, was revolutionary. The feature of compatibility did not yet exist in computers. System/360 would allow any of the computers in this "family" to use the same software, disk drivers, and printers as any other computer in the family. A business could start with a small, inexpensive model and move up to bigger, more powerful ones by mixing and matching components from IBM's catalog.

In 1974, IBM's president, Frank Cary, set up a part of IBM called General Systems, to develop minicomputers. He established major research centers in San Jose, California and Boulder, Colorado. The San Jose center became known for its informality and unusual methods of problem solving. Watson approved of the innovations because he felt IBM needed change.

## Chose Health over IBM

In 1952, the Antitrust Division of the Justice Department brought a restraint of trade case against IBM. Watson went over his father's head, allowing IBM's lawyers to settle the case by signing a consent decree in January 1956. In

1969, the Justice Department filed an antitrust complaint accusing IBM of monopolizing the computer industry. The government wanted IBM broken up. This was one of the biggest antitrust cases ever. The government felt that IBM's marketing tools were used to destroy their competition. Six months after the suit was filed, IBM gave up the marketing practice of bundling—selling everything a computer customer would need for one price. Instead, each component was sold separately. The government's case dragged on until 1981, when the Reagan administration finally dropped it.

Although Watson intended to retire from IBM in 1974, he had a heart attack in late 1970 that caused him to reconsider the decision. After he recovered, he decided that he wanted to live more than he wanted to run IBM. Thomas Learson assumed the chairmanship and Frank Cary took over as president and CEO. Watson remained as the head of the board's executive committee, where he could retain some control. During his time at IBM, Watson oversaw the remarkable growth of the company. In 1957, the company hit $1 billion in sales. When he resigned in 1971, the company had sales of $7.5 billion a year.

### An Active Retirement

While still in the hospital, Watson began making plans for a new sailboat. When he recovered, Watson and his crew sailed around Newfoundland. In 1974, he made a major voyage off the coast of Greenland, over 500 miles above the Arctic Circle.

Because he was one of the few liberal businessmen of the times, Watson became involved with government during the Kennedy years. He served on several committees and commissions, including the Advisory Committee on Labor-Management Policy, which dealt with unemployment, and the Peace Corps steering committee. Watson and his wife attended many social events at the White House. President Johnson asked Watson to be his secretary of commerce, but Watson turned him down. In 1977, President Jimmy Carter asked Watson to chair the General Advisory Committee on Arms Control and Disarmament (GAC). This commission advised the president on nuclear strategy. In 1978, GAC reported to Carter that the MX missile should not be developed because it was impractical.

In 1979, Watson became the U.S. ambassador to Moscow. He felt like a pawn in U.S.-Soviet relations, which at that time were quite bad. The Soviet Union had invaded Afghanistan. In response, the U.S. ended grain sales and boycotted the Moscow Olympics. When Carter lost the election to Ronald Reagan, Watson's stint in diplomacy ended. He then founded the Center for Foreign Policy Development at Brown University.

On his return from his ambassadorship, Watson began speaking and writing about arms control. In 1987, he flew across the Soviet Union, retracing the route he took during WW II, when he helped set up the Alaska-Siberia ferry route to bring planes to the Soviets. In 1990, he published his autobiography.

For over three decades, Watson amassed one of the best scrimshaw collections in the country, including 200 intricately carved pieces, all made of whalebone by American whalers. The collection was kept in his home in Greenwich, Connecticut, and at his summer home on North Haven Island, Maine. Watson sailed and flew planes, helicopters, and stunt planes. He had a personal fleet that included a Lear jet, a Breezy, a Twin King Air, a Taylor Cub, and a Bell jet 206 helicopter. His favorite was his stunt plane, a high-tech model, weighing only 850 pounds. Watson perfected a stunt show featuring inward loops and upside down flying. He rode a motorcycle around the island, dodging mouflon sheep. He also tinkered with antique cars, and had four Ford Model T automobiles. He kept them on the island to teach his grandchildren how to drive. Watson died of complications following a stroke on December 31, 1993 in Greenwich, Connecticut.

### Further Reading

Rodgers, William, *Think: A Biography of the Watsons and IBM,* Stein and Day, 1969.
Sobel, Robert, *IBM: Colossus in Transition,* Times Books, 1981.
Watson, Thomas J., Jr. and Peter Petre, *Father, Son & Co.: My Life at IBM and Beyond,* New York, Bantam Books, 1990.
*Business Month,* August 1990.
*Electronic News,* January 10, 1994.
*Forbes,* September 17, 1990. □

# Pat Weaver

**Sylvester "Pat" Weaver (born 1908) was responsible for some of the most innovative and entertaining programming on both radio and television. He saw radio through its infancy and then moved on to television. Weaver was the creative force behind Fred Allen's popular radio show *Town Hall Tonight* in the 1930s. As an executive with the National Broadcasting Company (NBC) in the 1950s, he created such enduring programs as the *Today* show and the *Tonight* show.**

Pat Weaver was born in Los Angeles on December 21, 1908, one of four children of Sylvester L. Weaver and Isabel Dixon Weaver. Weaver's father was a successful roofing manufacturer. As a young man, Weaver worked in his father's Los Angeles sales office and New York business office, but he did not enjoy the business.

In 1926, his father enrolled him at Dartmouth, despite Weaver's desire to attend Stanford. By the end of his freshman year, Weaver informed his father that he did not want to join the family business; he wanted to become a writer. During his time at Dartmouth, he made friends with several influential people, including Nelson Rockefeller. He also indulged his love of movies, seeing almost every show that played at the local theater during his four years as a student. In 1930, Weaver graduated magna cum laude and Phi Beta Kappa.

Weaver traveled extensively as a young man. He spent a summer during his college years with his family in Europe. His father rented a house in Oxford. Although the family ventured to Paris, Brussels, and Geneva, they spent most of their weekends in London. Weaver, who already had a love for Broadway, became enthralled with English theatre. This experience was influential in his decision not to join his father's roofing business. After graduating from Dartmouth, Weaver traveled to Europe again, this time with his friend Jerome Pearre.

### The Radio Years

Upon his return to the United States in 1931, Weaver began searching for employment. Still desiring to become a writer, Weaver was well aware that the economic situation of the early 1930s made employment opportunities limited. He finally landed a job as a writer and salesperson with a direct mail advertising agency, Young and McCallister Printing Company. He soon moved on to become editor of the Los Angeles Advertising Club's newsletter, *The Blue Pencil.* His comedic writings came to the attention of Don Lee, who owned several Columbia Broadcasting System (CBS) radio stations on the West Coast. In 1932, Weaver accepted a job at Lee's CBS radio station KHJ as a comedy writer for $150 a month.

Radio was in its infancy. Although Weaver had been hired to write comedy, he soon found himself involved in almost all aspects of the radio business. Much of the radio station's programming was done in-house, forcing Weaver and his coworkers to perform the duties of producers, writ-ers, directors, actors, announcers, and sound-effects creators as they were needed. He also became involved in selling advertising time to commercial businesses and often served as the station's newscaster. As a result, Weaver was immersed in the radio business, gaining a wealth of experience. While at KHJ, he helped create such popular radio shows as *The Merrymakers* and *Calling All Cars.*

### Radio and Advertising

After a year at a sister station in San Francisco, Weaver decided to relocate to New York. At the time, radio programming was created and owned by advertising agencies, not radio stations. Through old Dartmouth friends, Weaver became acquainted with Chester LaRoche, the president of the prestigious advertising firm Young and Rubicam. In the fall of 1935, LaRoche asked Weaver to produce a newly acquired, already popular and successful NBC show, *Town Hall Tonight,* featuring Fred Allen. Weaver, who admired Allen deeply, jumped at the chance to work with him.

For the next two years, Weaver worked closely with Allen to produce *Town Hall Tonight.* In 1937, Weaver's responsibilities expanded to include all of Young and Rubicam's shows. With this promotion, Weaver's perception of his position changed. "Until then, I had considered myself a radio man, even though I worked for an advertising agency. From now on, I would have to regard myself primarily as an advertising executive, even though I was involved in more radio production than ever." In late 1937, he was appointed manager of the radio division and named to the board of directors.

### American Tobacco Company and the War

Not yet 30 years old, Weaver was preparing to become the thirty-eighth stockholder in Young and Rubicam at the end of 1938, with the promise of a vice presidency soon to follow. However, the American Tobacco Company, a client of Young and Rubicam, managed to lure Weaver away by offering him a position as an advertising manager. Although the position paid about one half of his salary at Young and Rubicam, Weaver was enticed by the challenge of revamping one of the company's main products, Lucky Strike cigarettes. The first thing he did was change the brand of his three-pack a day smoking habit to Lucky Strikes.

In less than three years, Weaver had maneuvered Lucky Strikes back to the top, surpassing its main competition, Camel and Chesterfield, in sales. By that time, war was looming, and Weaver was anxious to do his part. He worked approximately nine months setting up Spanish-speaking radio programming to bring propaganda to Latin America. During this time, while working out of Los Angeles, he began courting Elizabeth Inglis, an actress. Soon after the bombing of Pearl Harbor on December 7, 1941, Weaver enlisted in the Navy and asked Inglis to marry him; they were married on January 23, 1942. In the spring, Weaver received his orders from the Navy and subsequently spent two years at sea on a sub chaser, but never saw any action. In November 1944, he was reassigned to the Armed Forces Radio Service in Hollywood, where he remained as a producer until the end of the war.

## NBC Television

After being discharged in early 1945, Weaver returned to New York City with his wife, who was pregnant with their first child, Trajan Victor Charles. He returned to his job at the American Tobacco Company. In June 1947, Weaver quit smoking cigarettes and returned to Young and Rubicam as vice president in charge of radio, television, and movies. He also became a member of the plans board, a stockholder, and a member of the elite five-person executive board that controlled the agency. Weaver was anxious to get involved with the new phenomenon, television. His idea was that the networks, not the advertisers, would develop television programming. When his advertising cohorts did not enthusiastically receive his thoughts, he took his plans to NBC. In his autobiography, Weaver remembered telling the NBC executives, "I won't come to NBC just to sell time to ad agencies. I'll come only if we can create our own shows and own them, and if we can sell every kind of advertising to support the program service." As a result, in June 1949, Weaver left Young and Rubicam once again, this time to become the NBC vice president in charge of television, and director of a new television network. In the same year, Weaver's wife became pregnant with their second child, Susan Alexandra (who would later become known as actress Sigourney Weaver).

When he arrived at NBC, most of the television shows were produced by sponsors, and NBC's productions usually went on without advertisers. On his first day at work, he discovered that a show called *Meet the Press* was being taken off the air because NBC could not find a sponsor to buy it. Weaver instantly called the producer and re-hired the show as an NBC production. *Meet the Press* is television's longest running show to date. Over the next several years, Weaver worked diligently to create shows that came under contract with NBC and were sponsored by numerous advertisers. His first success came with the dramatic show *Robert Montgomery Presents*.

## *Your Show of Shows* and *Today*

Weaver's next big project was to program an entire evening of television. What ultimately came to fruition was the program *Your Show of Shows* followed by *Caesar's Hour*. The Saturday evening shows featured such talented writers and performers as Sid Caesar, Carl Reiner, Mel Brooks, Neil Simon, and eventually Woody Allen. The shows became so popular that their success broke down much of the resistance to Weaver's determination to have multiple sponsors for a show. Weaver, who is seldom shy about noting his own successes, stated in his autobiography, "All jokes aside, the revolution I had envisioned in the whole system of ownership, sponsorship, and control of television programming was underway." However, he continued to be considered a traitor for promoting the network over the advertising agencies by many of his former advertising buddies.

In 1951, Weaver finally sold an idea for a show he had been developing for several years: an early morning news show that both educated and entertained. Weaver named the show *Today*. After finally convincing the network that

people would watch television that early in the morning, Weaver began the creation of *Today*. The first show aired at 7:00 a.m. in New York on January 14, 1952. Although the critics disliked it, the viewers loved it, and the audience base grew steadily, as did sponsorship. *Today* is the second-longest running television show in history, behind *Meet the Press*.

## Conflicts Led to Resignation

In late 1952, Weaver was passed over for the position of president of NBC. Threatening to quit, he was enticed to stay under the terms of his contract. He agreed to a five-year deal that stipulated that he could not be fired, nor could he quit. He was promoted to vice president of the network, but had little to do. Eight months later, in September 1953, the president of the network, Frank White, resigned due to poor health. Weaver was named the new president of NBC.

Back in power, Weaver turned his attention to his next project, a late-night comedy show that would become the *Tonight* show. After developing the concept as a show based on an ad-lib format with some rehearsal for certain segments, Weaver convinced Steve Allen to act as host. The first *Tonight* show aired on September 27, 1954, and was a huge success from the outset.

In December 1955, David Sarnoff, president of Radio Corporation of America, which owned NBC, appointed his son Bobby Sarnoff as president of NBC in place of Weaver. Not completely surprised by this, Weaver did not have a good relationship with David Sarnoff. He stayed on as chairperson of the board until September 1956 when he finally resigned.

## After NBC

Unable to find work at another network, Weaver started his own independent network, Program Service. The adventurous attempt folded two years later. Weaver also worked as a consultant on several projects, including the hit western show *Maverick*. He oversaw Nelson Rockefeller's bid for governor in 1958 and worked as his personal advisor for all his subsequent campaigns.

In 1958, Weaver accepted a position with the McCann Erickson advertising agency, which became Interpublic, where he remained until 1963. In that year, Weaver once again jumped at the innovative and unknown by becoming involved with the first pay television operation. The California pay television station offered three channels, including movies, sports, and performing arts. The project was met with strong protest by the networks and theatres, and it was plagued by lawsuits. Nonetheless, the stock climbed over 17 points. Getting back into advertising and television, Weaver started consulting on a part-time basis for a variety of enterprises including Westinghouse, Comsat, and Disney. He also continued to develop ideas for innovative television.

Weaver lives in Santa Barbara, California, and he continues to use his creative energies to envision the future of television and beyond. He ended his autobiography by writing, "I am proud of what I have accomplished in broadcasting and cable, but the future of communications is so fascinating, I wish I had another lifetime to help in realizing its potential."

## Further Reading

*Contemporary Authors*, edited by Kathleen Edgar, Gale Research, 1995.

Weaver, Pat, *The Best Seat in the House*, Alfred A. Knopf, Inc., 1994.

*Advertising Age*, November 2, 1998.

*Booklist*, January 15, 1994.

*Business Week*, April 18, 1994. □

# Jack Welch

**John F. "Jack" Welch Jr. (born 1935) rose from the ranks of General Electric (GE) to be named the company's youngest ever chief executive officer in 1981. After making difficult personnel decisions early in his tenure, which included shedding more than 100,000 employees, Welch began a period of growth and success that is unparalleled in business history. As the new millennium dawns, GE, under Welch's leadership, is the largest company in the world and a symbol of American ingenuity and power.**

B old, competitive, and controversial are all traits that describe Jack Welch, one of the world's most powerful business leaders. Although he is now worth countless millions, Welch was born on November 19, 1935 into a middle class family in Peabody, Massachusetts, the only child of a train conductor/union leader and a strong-willed mother, Grace. Welch's father worked grueling hours to support his family, often leaving the house at 5:30 a.m. and not getting home until 7:30 p.m. Grace and the boy used to wait for the elder Welch at the train station. Welch recalls that the talks he had with his mother at the station served as his early education.

Welch's competitive fires can be traced back to his teenage years playing hockey, basketball, and baseball. In high school, Welch was co-captain of the golf team, lettered in hockey, and served as treasurer of the senior class. The five foot eight inch Welch was known as a feisty competitor whose will to win was limitless. Welch's mother also instilled in him a fierce will to achieve through long discussions and games of blackjack and gin rummy. "I had a pal in my mom," Welch told John A. Byrne of *Business Week*. "We had a great relationship. It was a powerful, unique, wonderful, reinforcing experience."

Welch combined popularity and intelligence with a quick wit. He was the class jokester. With his mother encouraging him, Welch studied chemical engineering at the University of Massachusetts, becoming the first person in his family to go to college. Several professors acted as Welch's mentors and persuaded him to attend graduate school. He then went on to earn a doctorate from the University of Illinois in 1960. When he got the degree, his mother was so proud that she called the Salem newspaper to report that "Dr. Welch" received his Ph.D.

## Joined General Electric

After graduate school, Welch joined General Electric as a junior engineer in Pittsfield, Massachusetts. Frustrated by the company's bureaucracy, Welch quit a year later. He saw little room for advancement at GE. His boss, Reuben Gutoff, recognized Welch's talent, and talked him into staying. Gutoff even promised Welch that he would provide him a more entrepreneurial work environment, although supported with all the resources of a corporate giant.

As Welch climbed the corporate ladder, he was convinced that even a huge corporation like GE could remain nimble. By 1967, Welch was among the rising young stars in the GE plastics division. He kept the small company mentality close to heart and would later lead the charge to erase the big company malaise that could stifle ideas and action. In his early years, he helped GE Plastics explode from a $28 million after-thought into a billion dollar business.

## The "Neutron Jack" Years

Welch moved through several different divisions as he progressed. Eventually, at age 42, he moved to the corporate headquarters in Fairfield, Connecticut, when he was named one of three vice-chairmen. After a fierce competition for the top spot, Welch was named chairman in 1981, the youngest CEO ever appointed at GE. "I think I'm the most happy man in America today," Welch told Thomas C. Hayes of *The New York Times,* "and I'm certainly the most fortunate."

Welch attracted controversy almost immediately. He was much different than his predecessor, the British gentleman Reginald H. Jones. Welch was brash and told managers that if they did not move quickly enough, he would "kick ass." The new leader was obsessed with turning GE into a flexible, lean business that ranked first or second in every industry in which it did business.

An early spotlight was thrust on Welch when GE purchased RCA, the parent company of NBC, in late 1985 for $6.3 billion in cash. At the time, it was the largest corporate acquisition in history and brought RCA back into the family. GE had founded RCA in 1919, but had to sell the subsidiary in 1933 because of antitrust threats. After the initial euphoria surrounding the deal wore off, Welch realized that NBC was losing $150 million a year, despite dominating prime time television and news rating. Welch set high financial goals for NBC and turned the business around by cutting costs and replacing unhappy network executives. By 1997, after more than a decade of Welch's cajoling, NBC became the undisputed leader of network television. GE transformed NBC into a profitable company that still provided high quality.

Welch and GE were successful economically across the board. However, during his first seven years as CEO, Welch cast off more than 100,000 workers, nearly 25 percent of GE's workforce. The mass layoffs earned Welch the derogatory nickname "Neutron Jack." Critics equated his name with corporate greed, arrogance, and contempt for workers. GE sold off many of its traditional businesses, such as housewares and televisions, and moved into high-tech manufacturing, broadcasting, and investment banking. Welch was willing to take risks and change the company's ingrained corporate culture to fit his strategic vision.

Welch's supporters countered by noting GE's amazing return on equity. In Welch's first six years, GE's total return to shareholders reached 273 percent. Welch told Russell Mitchell of *Business Week* that he wanted GE "to become the most competitive business enterprise in the world."

### World's Greatest CEO

Despite picking up other monikers, such as "Trader Jack," based on his love of acquisitions, Welch transformed his image as GE's fortunes improved. Soon, he was becoming widely regarded as the best CEO in the world. The company had always been heavily watched by business analysts for the latest management trends, but under Welch's tenure, GE came to define successful business management.

Part of Welch's improving image was his emphasis on GE's Management Development Institute corporate training program. The center at Croton-on-Hudson (Crotonville), known within GE as "The Pit," was a showcase for Welch. The company spent $500 million a year on education and training at Crotonville. He appeared at the center more than 250 times over 17 years and worked with 15,000 GE managers and executives. "The students see all of Jack here,"

wrote Byrne of *Business Week.* "The management theorist, strategic thinker, business teacher, and corporate icon who made it to the top despite his working class background."

In recent years, Welch has turned his attention to "people" issues and has worked to create informality at the company. This push has allowed communications to open across layers and fostered a sense of entrepreneurship at the world's largest corporation. Throughout the year, Welch met with managers across several levels of leadership. As Byrne wrote, the meetings also allowed Welch "to make his formidable presence and opinions known to all."

When Welch needed information, he often slipped into factories and plants unexpectedly. A Welch trademark has been the handwritten notes he dashes off to employees. Welch wrote them out and then faxed them all over the company. Welch saw this extra effort as another way of breaking through the bureaucracy that initially hindered his progress at GE. "The idea flow from the human spirit is absolutely unlimited," Welch told Byrne, "All you have to do is tap into that well. I don't like to use the word efficiency. It's creativity. It's a belief that every person counts."

Since taking over in 1981, Welch has used the company's economic diversity as a tool to move into other industries with fast-growing profits. He has reshaped GE with more than 500 acquisitions worth $53.2 billion. Welch was also instrumental in the mid- to late 1980s movement among American companies to get leaner, tougher, and globally competitive. GE's non-U.S. sales grew to 45 percent in 1994, up from 22 percent in 1986. *Forbes* writer James R. Norman wrote, "Nearly every one of its (GE's) major products has become a growth business with the stepped-up development overseas."

### The Future of GE

Welch's newest strategy was called "Six Sigma," which was a quality program that generated fewer than 3.4 defects per million operations in a manufacturing or service process. Despite the program's huge investment in training thousands of employees, Welch believed Six Sigma will save GE billions. In 1995, Welch launched the program with 200 projects, but the next year it grew to 3,000 and then 6,000 in 1997. The productivity gains and profit of $320 million exceeded Welch's expectations.

Welch was both revered and feared within GE. While not a cult personality, Welch realized what his leadership symbolized. To many, Welch was as synonymous with GE as Thomas Edison. In 1997, Welch was named to the National Business Hall of Fame in Cincinnati.

The GE that Welch has led since 1981 is a company that employs between 240,000 and 260,000 people in more than 100 countries. Shareholders have been rewarded throughout Welch's tenure. A $100 dollar investment in GE the day Welch took over would have been worth over $2,000 in 1998. He also achieved his goal of making GE the company with the highest market value in the world. In 1997, GE's stock value eclipsed $200 billion.

It is impossible to pin down exactly how Welch has achieved all the lofty goals set year in and year out at GE.

Perhaps, it is simply the fact that Welch may be the hardest working CEO ever. While leading a company worth more than $200 billion, he also found the time to know by sight the names and responsibilities of the top one thousand people at GE. In fact, the CEO met and interacted with several thousand employees each year.

Characteristically, Welch summed up his thoughts in a few short sentences in an interview with *Fortune* magazine, "I have the greatest job in the world. We go from broadcasting, engines, plastics, the power system—anything you want, we've got a game going. So from an intellectual standpoint, you're learning every day."

Welch will retire in 2000 when he hits GE's mandatory retirement age of 65. Do not, however, think Welch will fade into the sunset or even slow down. He may play much more golf (one of his lifelong passions), but Welch will also remain an important figure in corporate America. Nearly akin to an ex-president, like Jimmy Carter, Welch's retirement will allow him to redefine the way an ex-CEO operates.

## Further Reading

Lowe, Janet, *Jack Welch Speaks: Wisdom from the World's Greatest Business Leader,* John Wiley & Sons, 1998.
O'Boyle, Thomas F., *At Any Cost: Jack Welch, General Electric, and the Pursuit of Profit,* Knopf, 1998.
Slater, Robert, *Jack Welch and the GE Way: Management Insights and Leadership Secrets of the Legendary CEO,* McGraw-Hill, 1999.
Tichy, Noel M. and Stratford Sherman, *Control Your Destiny or Someone Else Will: How Jack Welch is Making General Electric the World's Most Competitive Company,* Doubleday, 1993.
*Business Week,* December 14, 1987; June 8, 1998.
*FW,* September 8, 1987.
*Forbes,* October 10.
*Fortune,* January 11, 1999.
*Industry Week,* December 2, 1991.
*Time,* October 3, 1994.
*Wall Street Journal,* August 4, 1988.
"History of GE," http://www.ge.com (March 1, 1999). □

# Helmut Werner

**Helmut Werner (born 1936) made a name for himself as a brilliant and innovative manager during his four years as chief executive officer and chairperson of the board of Mercedes-Benz. When Werner joined Mercedes-Benz in 1993, sales were declining and production costs were soaring. Through cost-cutting measures, new car designs, and revamped marketing, Werner almost single-handedly returned Mercedes-Benz to a profitable force in the automotive industry.**

Werner was born on September 2, 1936, in Cologne, Germany, the eldest son of a prominent bank director. In 1956, he graduated from the Abiture Beethoven-gymnasium, and went on to earn a business degree from the University of Cologne in 1961. Werner intended to be an auditor, but only completed the initial stages of the seven-year training program. Following his graduation from college, Werner took a position with Englebert & Co. He found himself well suited to the challenges and rewards of sales, and he became the sales manager in 1969. A year later, Werner moved on to become the general product manager for Uniroyal Europe in Liege, Belgium. In 1978, he was hired as the company's managing director. He served on the executive board of Continental Gummi-Werke AG in Hannover, Germany, in 1979, and was the company's chairperson from 1982 to 1987.

## At Mercedes-Benz

In 1987, Werner became a member of the executive board of Daimler-Benz, the parent company of Mercedes-Benz. His time at Mercedes-Benz brought him recognition as a brilliant and crafty manager. He became chief executive officer (CEO) of Mercedes-Benz on May 27, 1993. Over the next four years, he recreated Mercedes-Benz's image and turned the company around, from losing money to once again gaining a substantial profit.

When Werner came on the scene in the early 1990s, Mercedes-Benz was the world's largest producer of luxury cars. However, for several years, sales had been falling, and production costs were rising rapidly. It was clear to Werner that Mercedes-Benz could not continue to depend on high-performance, expensive cars to sustain the company. Even before he was officially in his new position as CEO in 1993, Werner announced drastic changes and a new direction for the company. Noting the affects of worsening traffic congestion and environmental concerns, he suggested that the prestigious image of Mercedes-Benz's cars was meaningless. His plan called for a new line of vehicles aimed at a lower-priced market. Werner also began focusing on cutting production costs, reducing development time, and taking the company global. When he announced his intentions for the company, many in the auto industry were skeptical of his ability to fulfill these goals.

In a 1990 study done by the Massachusetts Institute of Technology's International Motor Vehicle Program, Mercedes-Benz was confronted with the harsh reality that a 35 percent productivity gap had developed between it and Toyota, as well as other Japanese producers. Mercedes-Benz appeared to be moving in the wrong direction, and the numbers bore that out. In 1992, Mercedes-Benz produced 530,000 cars—48,000 fewer than the year before. In 1993, the German car company experienced an $800 million loss. Its biggest seller, the E-Class model, was eight years old, and another mainstay, the C-Class model, was 10 years old. Production numbers were falling, and losses were growing. Werner needed to act quickly.

### Increased Productivity

Werner set out to train his production and managerial staff to think differently. One of the first actions he took was to reduce the number of management levels between his office and the production floor from six to four. In an exercise to make a point about every manager's expendability, Werner had every one of them draft a letter of resignation, thus sending the message: be productive or leave. He also made plant managers responsible for operating within budgetary limits. In the past, Mercedes-Benz's development and production strategy began with the engineers who would set out to design the best car possible. Cost and time were not considered. After the vehicle was designed, the sticker price was determined by adding a profit to the cost of the car. Werner turned that around, first setting a target sticker price and then building the car accordingly. In an interview with reporter Diana Kurylko of *Automotive News* in November 1993, Werner commented, "We have to combine the good old qualities with what is necessary to really deal with the future demands of customers. Cost comes very much into the discussion. People in our company have really started to understand what kind of challenge is being presented by this new formula."

Mercedes-Benz engineers had a reputation for extended design time, taking months to make simple changes such as a headlight. Werner wiped out the mentality that each new car needed to be heavier, equipped with more technology, and increasingly expensive. He also pressured his engineers to work faster. By 1996, productivity rose over 30 percent, saving an estimated $2.3 billion.

Werner's cost-cutting measures also had an immediate impact. The company saved 4 billion marks ($2.34 billion)

in 1993, and the labor force was reduced by over 11,000 to 148,500 workers. In 1994, Werner led cost-cutting measures that equaled $2.75 billion. As a result of these changes, Mercedes-Benz was able to offer models over the next for years that were priced competitively with its main rivals, such as Toyota's high-end Lexus division. The sticker price of the 1996 C-Class in the United States was $29,900, which was $700 less than Lexus's comparable ES300 model. Just five years earlier, the Baby Benz 190 cost over $9,000 more than its counterpart, the Lexus ES250. Over the course of three years, Werner turned the loss of $800 million in 1993 to a gain in 1996 of almost $1.5 billion.

### New Models, New Image

Besides creating a new environment that focused on increased productivity and reduced cost, Werner also moved to give the company a make-over in image and offer smaller, more affordable models. His goal was to introduce models into every market, not just high-priced luxury cars. He envisioned compact cars, minivans (or "people carriers" as they are referred to in Europe), and sports utility vehicles. New and redesigned models introduced during Werner's reign included the 1996 SLK, a roadster with a base price of $35,300. The car was immediately popular with affluent forty-somethings, and the first production run of 35,000 was sold out until 1998. Werner also made plans to introduce a small car, the A-Class, which would measure only 11 feet and sell for about $20,000 in Germany. In 1996, the V-Class, a van, was introduced for $35,400 base price. Mercedes-Benz included the M-class, an off-the-road vehicle, with a base price of $35,000, into its 1997 lineup. The next year held plans for the Smart micro-car, just 7.5 feet long, in a joint venture with Switzerland's SMH Swatch watchmaker, selling for $10,000 to $14,500. Although Werner refused to comment on the reports, the rumor circulated around the automotive industry that Mercedes-Benz planned for nearly 30 new models to be in the market by 2008.

Werner also worked to increase a sluggish market for Mercedes-Benz in the United States. Advertising in the United States was revamped to appeal to the baby boomers. One spot featured the phrase penned by the 1960s cultural icon Janis Joplin, "Lord, won't you buy me a Mercedes-Benz." Additionally, new models of the E-class included cup holders, not a popular feature for Germans, but considered a basic necessity by Americans. As a result, Mercedes-Benz sales increased in the United States in 1996 by over 17 percent.

### Globalization

Werner's strategy also included the globalization of Mercedes-Benz. In his interview with Diana Kurylko of *Automotive News,* Werner said, "In the automotive industry you can only survive in the long run on a global basis. This is a global market." New markets targeted by Werner and Mercedes-Benz included Latin America (specifically Brazil and Argentina), India, Thailand, Vietnam, and China. He also looked for new locations that would facilitate less costly production and cheaper parts. In 1996, only five percent of the company's automobiles were made outside of Germany. Werner's goal was to increase that number to 25 percent within 10 years, without reducing the production numbers in Germany. Mercedes-Benz already maintained a plant in Mexico, and plans were made for the minivan model to be produced in Spain and the sport utility vehicle to be produced in the United States at the company's plant in Alabama.

## Resigned from Mercedes-Benz

Werner had stunned the auto world by doing much of what he had promised when he became CEO at Mercedes-Benz. While the company was celebrating its success, its mother company, Daimler-Benz, was not doing well. Jurgen Schrempp had become chairperson of the money-losing conglomerate in May 1995. He sold or shut down one-third of Daimler-Benz's businesses, including much of its aerospace business. By 1996, the Mercedes-Benz division, which had up to then run almost independently from Daimler-Benz, accounted for 75 percent of Daimler-Benz's sales of 105 billion marks ($65 billion dollars), and almost all of its profits. With its workload diminished by the downsizing, the Daimler-Benz board had more time to turn its attention to Mercedes-Benz, and the Mercedes-Benz board, including Werner, began to be perceived as an unnecessary layer of leadership. Rumors began to fly that Schrempp was moving to push Werner out.

The rumors proved to be true, and in early 1997, the Mercedes-Benz board was dissolved and Schrempp took control of Mercedes-Benz. On January 16, 1997, Werner officially resigned from Mercedes-Benz. During his almost four years at Mercedes-Benz, Werner is credited with eliminating huge losses suffered in 1993, restoring profit growth, and increasing productivity dramatically. He also prepared the way for the merger between Daimler Benz AG and Chrysler Corporation in May 1998. The new Daimler-Chrysler company is expected to be one of the largest automakers in the world, with sales of $130 billion and 421,000 employees.

After leaving Mercedes-Benz, Werner served as the chairperson of the Supervisory Board of the Expo 2000 and as a member of the supervisory boards of Alcatel Alsthom, IBM Deutschland GmbH, Gerling-Konzern Versicherungs-Beteilgungs AG, and BASF AG. Werner was named a principal in Penske Capital Partners, L.L.C., a company that acquires businesses in the transportation industry. In 1998, he became chair of the industrial and trading group Metallgesellschaft. He also sat on the board of directors of the JP Morgan Germany Advisory Council.

## Further Reading

*Business Leader Profiles for Students,* edited by Sheila M. Dow, Gale Research, 1999.
*Automotive News,* November 27, 1993; December 13, 1993; January 20, 1997.
*Business Week,* August 26, 1996.
*Economist,* January 30, 1993; December 7, 1996. □

# Mae West

**Mae West (1893–1980) played the sultry, provocative woman in numerous popular films and plays. Her sexuality and off-color comments made her films and plays the frequent target of censors. West also wrote and produced several plays and recorded albums.**

Mae West was born Mary Jane West on August 17, 1893, in Brooklyn, New York. Her father, John, held various jobs as a livery stableman, a detective, a salesman, and a prizefighter. Her mother, Matilda, was a model and dressmaker. By the age of seven, West was singing and dancing in amateur performances and winning local talent shows. She soon left behind formal education and joined a professional stock company headed by Hal Clarendon, where she played the character of "Little Nell" in a long-running melodrama.

In her early teens, West joined a vaudeville company, where she met Frank Wallace, who soon became her song-and-dance partner. Unknown to the public for more than 30 years, she and Wallace married in 1911 when West was only 16. Both the relationship and the stage partnership soon ended, but West and Wallace did not divorce until 1942.

## Became Vaudeville and Stage Star

While still a teen-ager, West became a star on the vaudeville stage. Her first Broadway appearances were in 1911, in the revues *A la Broadway* and *Hello Paris.* The following year she appeared in *A Winsome Widow,* produced by Florenz Ziegfeld, Jr. In 1918, West took a role in the musical comedy *Sometime,* in which she introduced a dance known as the "Shining Shawabble." She soon became a hit on the New York vaudeville stage, becoming known for her flashy and tight-fitting clothing as well as her provocative comments, delivered in dialects or a throaty voice. Her costumes would typically include an assortment of rhinestones, leopard skins, and huge plumed hats, all worn on her five-foot-tall body. West was unique in being one of the few women who performed solo in vaudeville, and even at her young age, she commanded a salary of several hundred dollars per week.

## Plays Caught Censors' Attention

In 1926, West wrote a play that was co-produced on Broadway by Jim Timony, a lawyer who was reportedly also her lover. The aptly named *Sex* became both a popular success and the target of censorship groups such as the Society for the Suppression of Vice. As described in *Becoming Mae West,* the play included "prostitutes caught in arousing embraces, guns, knockout drinks, a jewelry heist, cops, an offstage suicide, bribery, and the threat of a shootout." In the 41st week of its run, police arrested the cast and West was found guilty of corrupting the morals of

youth. She was sentenced to ten days in a New York City prison but was released two days early for good behavior.

West's second play, *The Drag* in 1926, sympathetically tackled a subject that was not discussed on stage at the time—homosexuality. After a two-week run in New Jersey, West was persuaded not to bring it to Broadway. Her third play, *Adamant Lil* in 1928, was a great success. West played the title role of an 1890s saloon singer with underworld connections. In this play, she uttered her famous line to a Salvation Army captain: "Why don't you come up and see me sometime?" Two other plays, *Pleasure Man* in 1928 and *The Constant Sinner* in 1931, were also targeted by the censors; *Pleasure Man* was closed by the police after its first performance and never reopened; *The Constant Sinner* closed after two performances when the district attorney threatened to bring charges.

### Launched Hollywood Film Career

In the early 1930s, after the constant struggles with censorship of her plays, West decided to move to Hollywood and embark on a film career, hoping that she would enjoy more freedom there. Her popularity with the public was already so great that even though the Great Depression had begun, she won a $5,000-per-week contract with Paramount Pictures. In her first film, *Night After Night* in 1932, West portrayed the girlfriend of a gangster played by George Raft. When a woman comments, "Goodness, what beautiful diamonds," West gives her famous response: "Goodness had nothing to do with it."

West's next film, *She Done Him Wrong* in 1933, was a film adaptation of her play, *Adamant Lil.* It was a huge public success, and was also noteworthy for introducing a young actor, Cary Grant, who was found by West and chosen for the male lead. Later that year, Grant also co-starred with West in *I'm No Angel,* an even bigger box office smash. In this film, West (playing a circus performer) got to act out a lifelong fantasy of being a lion tamer. Refusing a double, she went into the cage herself carrying a whip.

During the mid-1930s West became one of the most popular and highly paid actors in Hollywood. She also became a shrewd real estate investor, once making a profit of almost $5 million on a $16,000 investment. Her film career reached its peak, with two more successes in *Go West, Young Man* in 1936 and *Every Day's a Holiday* in 1938, in which she played a character named Peaches O'Day who used her wiles to sell the Brooklyn Bridge to a naive man.

Then came one of her best-known films, *My Little Chickadee* in 1940, in which West and her co-star, W.C. Fields, gave one of the all-time great film comedy performances; she also wrote the screenplay. West's character, Flower Belle Lee, was a woman of dubious reputation who decided to enter into a sham marriage to become respectable. As her husband, she chose the con man and card shark Cuthbert J. Twillie, played by Fields. Perhaps as a joke on the censors, on their "wedding" night, Fields discovered that West has vanished, and in her place in their bed is a tied-up goat. They agree to go their separate ways, and his parting line to her is, "Come up and see me sometime."

### Career Declined in the 1940s

In the 1940s, West's popularity declined. She also finally acknowledged the marriage she had walked away from while a teen-ager. In the mid-1930s, her husband Frank Wallace had begun to tour the country with a nightclub act in which he called himself "Mae West's husband." Then, in 1942, Wallace filed for divorce and sought alimony from West. She eventually settled the case with an undisclosed private financial agreement.

West starred in the 1943 film musical *The Heat's On,* but reviews were not particularly favorable. She decided to return to the stage where her career had begun, and wrote and starred in *Catherine Was Great,* a risque play about the Russian empress that played on Broadway in 1944, and then went on a national tour. In 1948, West starred in *Ring Twice Tonight* (later retitled *Come On Up*), in which she played the unlikely role of an FBI agent masquerading as a nightclub singer. The play never reached Broadway after initial performances in Los Angeles. This project was followed by a stage revival of *Adamant Lil,* in which West travelled between New York and London from 1948 to 1951.

### An Elderly Siren

In the early 1950s, when West was over 60, she tried to revive her career by creating a nightclub act, "Mae West and Her Adonises," that still portrayed her as a sultry siren. A group of young, handsome bodybuilders dressed in loincloths assisted her in the act. Paul Novak, one of the bodybuilders, became her companion for the last 26 years of her life.

West's autobiography, *Goodness Had Nothing To Do With It,* was published in 1959, and contains humorous stories about her career and her love life. In the 1960s, she recorded an album of Bob Dylan and Beatles songs, *Way Out West,* plus a holiday album, *Wild Christmas.* West's film career was briefly reborn when she appeared in two films that have been ranked among the worst ever made. *Myra Breckinridge* (1970), based on the Gore Vidal novel, was notable chiefly for being the film in which future stars Farrah Fawcett and Tom Selleck were introduced to the public. In *Sextette* (1977), made when West was 84, her husband was played by the young Timothy Dalton.

Despite her "loose" professional image, West did not drink or smoke, and made her home in the same modest Los Angeles apartment for half a century. West began to decline in her later years, and was rumored to have slept in makeup in case she had to leave her home in an emergency. She became increasingly interested in paranormal events, and insisted she was in contact with a pet monkey who had died. It has also been reported that West feared being reincarnated. After suffering a stroke, she died on November 22, 1980 in Los Angeles. As she said in her autobiography, West had no regrets about her life: "I freely chose the kind of life I led because I was convinced that a woman has as much right as a man to live the way she does if she does no actual harm to society."

## Further Reading

*Benet's Reader's Encyclopedia of American Literature,* Harper-Collins, 1991.
*Dictionary of American Biography,* Scribner's, 1995.
Leider, Emily Wortis, *Becoming Mae West,* Farrar, Strauss, and Giroux, 1997.
West, Mae, *Goodness Had Nothing To Do With It,* Prentice-Hall, 1959.
*Interview,* May 1997.
"Mae West," *Biography Life File,* http://mmnewsstand.com/static/products/4002/west.html (February 10, 1999). □

# Edward Weston

**In the 1930s, Edward Weston (1886–1958) helped form the influential Group f/64 with other notable photographers such as Ansel Adams, Imogen Cunningham, and Willard van Dyke. His sharp, brilliantly printed images are some of the finest twentieth-century photographic works. Weston's work helped photography gain recognition as an art form in its own right.**

Edward Weston was born on March 24, 1886 in Highland Park, Illinois. As a child, he saved pennies to buy used photographic equipment. At the age of 16, his

father gave him a Kodak Bulls-Eye number two camera. Weston began to take pictures at his aunt's farm and in the parks of Chicago. In 1903, at the age of 17, Weston first exhibited his work at the Chicago Art Institute.

After the earthquake and fire in San Francisco on April 19, 1906, Weston traveled to California to take a job as a surveyor for San Pedro, Los Angeles, and the Salt Lake Railroad. Weston returned to Chicago to attend the Illinois College of Photography, but soon returned to California to visit a sister living in a small town near Los Angeles. Remaining in California, Weston helped found the Camera Pictorialists of Los Angeles. In 1909, he married Flora Chandler, with whom he had four sons. Edward Chandler Weston was born in 1910 and Theodore Brett Weston in 1911. The Westons' third son, Laurence Neil Weston, was born in 1916 and Cole Weston in 1919.

Weston owned a portrait studio in Glendale, California. His soft-focus, diffused images and sentimental approach was popular at that time and his business did well. He also began to publish articles in magazines, including *American Photography, Photo Era,* and *Photo-Miniature.*

## Changed His Style

Weston became unhappy with what he felt was just a mechanical imitation of painting styles. Richard Lacayo, in *Time* magazine described Weston's early career. "By the early 1920s he had already established an international reputation for mildly swoony images in gray-beige tones. He had also grown restless with pictorialism, which took its inspiration from impressionism, symbolism. . . . In time, he found a new expressive vocabulary in the angles and hard lines of constructivism and cubism, which he matched to a new photographic method. The focus was sharp. The prints were made directly from the negative, without an enlarger. The chemical manipulations that produced the soulful fogs of pictorialism were forgotten.''

Although Weston was married and a father of four, he strained against the conventions of family life. His friends were members of the West Coast counterculture, people who shared his interest in vegetarianism and his love of modern art. Shortly after the birth of his fourth son, he met Tina Modotti. This was the beginning of their long relationship and photographic collaborations. Her husband was a political radical in Mexico who died in 1922. Weston traveled to Ohio to visit his sister in 1922. While there he took photographs of the Armco Steel Plant. From Ohio he traveled to New York and met Alfred Stieglitz, Paul Strand, Charles Sheeler, and Georgia O'Keefe. At this point in his career, Weston gave up pictorialism and started a transition period of self-analysis and self-discipline.

In 1923 Weston went to Mexico with Modotti and one of his sons. For the next three years he socialized with several artists including Diego Rivera, José Clemente Orozco, Jean Charlot, and David Alfano Siqueiros. He took pictures, including many portraits. The Mexican portraits illustrate what Weston had learned from photographer Alfred Stieglitz, "maximum of detail with a maximum of simplification." Some of the photographs that Weston and Modotti made in Mexico appeared in the book *Idols Behind Altars* by Anita Brenner.

### Detailed Studies Defined Style

In 1926, Weston came back to California. There he started work on a series of highly detailed studies of cabbages, peppers, rock formations, sand dunes, trees bent by the wind, twisted kelp, water, cacti, and seashells. His most famous photographs are exquisitely detailed, richly toned shots of peppers, shells, and cypress trees. He also created studies of the human figure. His technique was uncluttered and direct. Weston used an 8 x 10 inch view camera, always in natural daylight. He used four-hour exposures to capture detail. He never enlarged, cropped, or retouched his photographs. The pictures he made at this time were crucially important in separating him from his previous style. Richard Lacayo wrote in *Time*, "The pictorialists used soft focus for atmospheric purposes but also as a way to make the particular stand for the general. With these radiant close-ups, Weston kept their goal but reversed the approach, bearing down on the details as a new way to make the mundane suggest the divine. . . . The forward-looking sectors of the American art audience were waiting for pictures like these, sensuous and sharp. . . . For all their shimmer, they had a just-the-facts quality that proposed the romantic impulse as the highest form of lucidity. (That they could also be sexually voluptuous, something Weston claimed was unintended, did not hurt.)" Weston said of his work, "The camera should be used for rendering the very

substance and quintessence of the thing itself, whether it be polished steel or palpitating flesh.''

Weston moved up the Pacific Coast to Carmel, California, in 1929. There he photographed the rocky beaches and cypress trees at Point Lobos. Near Carmel, Weston also discovered the sand dunes that inspired some of his most important images. His love of nature strengthened his friendship with Ansel Adams, the famous nature photographer, whom he had met a few years earlier.

Weston kept journals or "day books" of his activities and ideas. He first published some of these writings as *From My Day Book* in 1928. Others were published after he died. In 1930, Weston exhibited his work in New York for the first time at the Delphic Studios Gallery and later at Harvard Society of Contemporary Arts with Walker Evans, Eugene Atget, Sheeler, Stieglitz, and Modotti. Weston was a founding member of Group f/64 that formed in 1932 and included Ansel Adams, Imogen Cunningham, Consuelo Kanaga, and Willard van Dyke. This influential group was dedicated to the highly detailed prints that resulted from using a large camera with a very small aperture. They set their lenses to that aperture, f/64, to gain maximum image sharpness of both foreground and distance. Even though he had several large exhibitions, Weston still did not earn a lot of money. In 1935 he started the "Edward Weston Print of the Month Club" selling photographs at $10 each.

### Married Charis Wilson

In 1937 Weston received the first Guggenheim Foundation fellowship in photography. Using his prize money he traveled through the western United States, taking along his model and assistant Charis Wilson. Weston and Wilson married in 1938. On the trip west, Weston took pictures that later appeared in his book *California and the West,* published in 1940, with text by Charis Wilson Weston. The relationship between Weston and Wilson helped form his vision of the naked female form as a photographic subject. Critic Susan Sontag was quoted in *Time* as saying, "The peppers Weston photographed are voluptuous in a way his female nudes rarely are. In fact, he made nude photography respectable.''

In 1940 he participated in the U.S. Camera Yosemite Photographic Forum with Ansel Adams and Dorothea Lange. He was commissioned by the Limited Editions Club to illustrate a new edition of Walt Whitman's *Leaves of Grass,* published in 1941. In 1951 Weston became an honorary fellow of the Photographic Society of America.

In 1946 Weston began experiencing the symptoms of Parkinson's disease, an illness characterized by muscle tremors, slowing of movement, and weakness. Weston took his last photographs at Point Lobos in 1948. In 1952 his *Fiftieth Anniversary Portfolio* was published with his images printed by his son Brett. In 1955 Weston chose several of what he called "Project Prints" and had his sons Brett and Cole and Dody Warren print them under his supervision. Lou Stoumen released the film *The Naked Eye* in 1956 in which several of Weston's prints and footage of Weston himself appeared. Edward Weston died at his home in Carmel Highlands, California, on January 1, 1958.

## Work Remains Popular

Weston's work influenced many photographers such as Minor White, Paul Caponigro, Wynn Bullock, Cole Weston, and Brett Weston. In 1975 the Museum of Modern Art in New York City held a major retrospective of his work.

The centennial of Weston's birth in 1986 was marked by three museum shows. The J. Paul Getty Museum in Malibu, California, exhibited 45 of his pictures. Sixty were shown at the Art Institute of Chicago. The San Francisco Museum of Modern Art held a retrospective of 237 prints. The exhibition traveled for two years to a dozen other cities, including New York, Washington, Los Angeles, and Atlanta. The centennial of his birth was noted on the Monterey Peninsula by two major shows as well as by a lecture and seminar by his son, photographer Cole Weston. At the Friends of Photography Gallery in Carmel, his trademark works, close-ups of seashells, the rocks and trees of Point Lobos, nudes, and sand dunes were shown. At the Monterey Peninsula Museum of Art "The Monterey Photographic Tradition: The Weston Years" exhibited some 100 works by Edward Weston, his sons Brett and Cole, and others including Ansel Adams, Morley Baer, Al Weber, and Minor White. By juxtaposing photographs of similar subjects by different artists, the exhibition illustrated how the photographers influenced one another.

Commenting on the San Francisco exhibit, Lacayo noted "his photographs' unique confidence, force and completeness. Seen today, in a time of crayoned prints, tableaux arranged for the camera and photographs about photography, they bear the stamp of a grand and lucid purpose." *Weston's Westons: Portraits and Nudes,* an exhibition of his work at New York's International Center of Photography, was shown in 1990. An exhibit, *The Garden of Earthly Delights: The Photographs of Edward Weston and Robert Mapplethorpe,* was shown at the midtown Manhattan branch of the International Center of Photography in 1995.

Weston's goals for his work were clear yet complex: "To photograph a rock, have it look like a rock, but be more than a rock." Weston's greatest achievement was affirming photography's complete independence from painting, thus establishing it as a modern art in its own right.

## Further Reading

*The Daybooks of Edward Weston: Mexico California,* edited by Edward Weston, Beaumont Newhall, and Nancy Newhall, Aperture, 1996.
*Edward Weston: Forms of Passion,* edited by Gilles Mora, New York, Harry N. Abrams, 1995.
*Edward Weston: Photography and Modernism,* edited by Theodore Stebbins, Jr., Bulfinch Press, 1999.
Maddow, Ben, *Edward Weston: His Life,* Aperture, 1989.
*Time,* November 24, 1986.
"Biography of Edward Weston (1886–1958)," *Photocollect,* http://photocollect.com/bios/weston.html (April 9, 1999). □

# Ryan White

**Ryan White (1971–1990) contracted AIDS through a blood transfusion when he was 13 and worked to educate people about the disease until his death at age 18. As a result of his efforts, and those of his mother Jeanne, Congress passed the Ryan White Comprehensive AIDS Resources Emergency Care (CARE) Act, which provides health care resources to Americans with HIV/AIDS who have no insurance or not enough insurance to get proper care.**

R yan White was born on December 6, 1971 in Kokomo, Indiana. When he was three days old, doctors informed his parents that he had hemophilia, an inherited disease in which the blood does not clot. People who have this disease are vulnerable, since an injury as simple as a paper cut can lead to dangerous bleeding. Fortunately for White and his parents, a new treatment, called Factor VII, recently had been approved by the U.S. Food and Drug Administration. This treatment is made from blood and contains the clotting agent that allows healthy people to heal quickly from wounds.

Even with the treatment, White had to be very careful. He bled easily and the most dangerous and painful bleeds occurred when a blood vessel bled in a joint. "A bleed occurs from a broken blood vessel or vein," White explained in his testimony before the President's Commission on AIDS. "The blood then had nowhere to go so it would swell up in a joint. You could compare it to trying to pour a quart of milk into a pint-sized container of milk." He was in and out of the hospital for the first six years of his life but despite this managed to live a fairly normal childhood.

In December 1984, when he was 13, White contracted pneumonia and had surgery to remove part of his left lung. After two hours of surgery, his doctors told his parents that he had contracted the incurable disease of Acquired Immunodeficiency Syndrome, or AIDS, through his Factor VII blood transfusions. Someone with the disease had donated blood, and the virus had been in the blood that White received. (Since that time, better screening procedures have been put in place to make blood transfusions safer). "I spent Christmas and the next thirty days in the hospital," White told the President's Commission on AIDS. "A lot of my time was spent searching, thinking and planning my life. I came face to face with death at 13 years old."

White's doctors told him that he had six months to live, but White decided that he would continue to live a normal life, attend school, and spend time with his friends. "I hate the idea of anything that makes me seem sick forever. Maybe I have an incurable disease, but I don't have to be a permanent invalid," he said in his book *Ryan White: My Own Story*.

## Struggles Against Ignorance and Hatred

White had not counted on the ignorance, fear, and hatred he would encounter in his small home town of Kokomo, Indiana. At first, people there claimed that there were no health guidelines for a person with AIDS to attend a normal school. Even after the Indiana State Board of Health set guidelines saying it would be safe for the other children if White attended school, the school board, his teachers, and the principal tried to keep him out of school. They feared he would spread the disease, even though it was known by that time that AIDS cannot be spread by casual contact. White and his mother took the case to court. Eventually they agreed to meet some of their neighbors' concerns by having White use a separate restroom, not take gym class, drink out of a separate water fountain, and use disposable eating utensils and trays at lunch. Even so, 20 students were pulled out of school by their parents, who started their own school to keep their children from having any contact with White.

Ryan later told the Commission that his townspeople's ignorance and fear regarding AIDS led him to become the target of jokes and some spread lies about him biting people, spitting on vegetables and cookies (and thus supposedly spreading the disease), restaurants throwing away dishes he had eaten from and students vandalizing his locker and writing obscenities and anti-gay slurs (because at that time, AIDS was believed to be a disease primarily of gay men) on his books and folders. An even more frightening incident occurred when someone fired a bullet into White's home.

White told the Commission, "I was labeled a troublemaker, my mom an unfit mother and I was not welcome anywhere. People would get up and leave so they would not have to sit anywhere near me. Even at church, people would not shake my hand." This lack of acceptance, even in church, was a blow to the Whites, who were committed Christians. As White's mother told Phil Geoffrey Bond in *Poz*, a magazine for people with HIV and AIDS, "I worked with a Pentecostal [person] who told me, 'You know, Ryan wouldn't have AIDS if he went to my church.'"

Ryan wrote in his book, "I had plenty of time back then to think about why people were being mean. Of course it was because they were scared. Maybe it was because I wasn't that different from everybody else. I wasn't gay; I wasn't into drugs; I was just another kid from Kokomo. . . . I didn't even look sick. Maybe that made me more of a goblin to some people."

## White's Story is Publicized

White's ordeal was soon publicized and he began receiving enormous amounts of media attention. He received thousands of letters supporting his right to go to school, and met politicians, movie stars, and top athletes, all of whom supported him. He appeared on numerous television programs, including *CBS Morning News*, the *Today Show*, *Sally Jessy Raphael*, *Phil Donohue*, *Hour Magazine*, the *Home Show*, Peter Jennings' "Person of the Week," *Nightline*, *West 57th Street*, *P.M. Magazine*, *Entertainment Tonight*, and *Prime Time Live*. White was also featured on the cover of the *Saturday Evening Post*, *Picture Week*, and *People* magazines.

Meanwhile, White's family was struggling with his medical expenses. As White became more ill, his mother had to miss more days from her work at General Motors and the family couldn't pay their bills. His sister Andrea, a championship roller skater, dropped her lessons and travel to competitions because the family simply did not have the money for them, or for anything else. White's health was steadily declining and he was being tutored at home. He dreamed of his family moving into a larger house and being accepted in a community. This dream became a reality when an ABC movie, *The Ryan White Story*, was made about his life. Ryan acted in the movie, playing his best friend, Chad. "I wanted to make that movie because I was hoping that what we went through will never happen to anyone else," White wrote in his book.

In 1987, using the money from the movie, White's family moved to Cicero, Indiana, where they found acceptance. "For the first time in three years," Ryan told the Commission, "we feel we have a home, a supportive schooi, and lots of friends. . . . I am a normal, happy teenager again. I have a learner's permit. I attend sports functions and dances. My studies are important to me. I made the honor roll just recently, with two As and two Bs . . . I believe in myself as I look forward to graduating from Hamilton Heights High School in 1991."

## AIDS Activism

Before White's experience was publicized, there had been no public reports of children who had AIDS. Following his diagnosis, White and his mother Jeanne became two of the world's best-known AIDS activists and educators. Jeanne founded the Ryan White Foundation, the only national organization in the United States devoted to HIV (human immunodeficiency virus, the virus that causes AIDS) and AIDS education for young people. They realized that much of the hatred aimed at White was the result of ignorance. "It was difficult, at times, to handle, but I tried to ignore the injustice," White wrote in his book, "because I knew the people were wrong. My family and I held no hatred for those people because we realized they were victims of their own ignorance. We had great faith that, with patience, understanding, and education, my family and I could be helpful in changing their minds and attitudes around."

When White was 16, he testified before the President's Commission on AIDS, describing his experience with bigotry as well as the financial difficulties his family had experienced as a result of his illness. White was a compelling spokesman but he was not alone. By 1991, local health departments, hospital emergency rooms and other health care providers experienced a surge in the number of patients who desperately needed care but could not pay for it. As the number of cases increased, many areas in the United States reported becoming overburdened with the cost of caring for people with AIDS who had little or no health insurance.

White died on April 8, 1990 in Cicero, Indiana. During his short 18-year life he accomplished more than many people who live long, healthy lives. His activism and legacy of concern for others with AIDS remains. "I've seen how people with HIV/AIDS are treated and I don't want others to be treated like I was," he said. Shortly after his death, White's mother went to Congress to speak to politicians on behalf of people with AIDS. She spoke to 23 representatives, although Jesse Helms of North Carolina refused to speak to her even when she was alone with him in an elevator. Most representatives, however, were sympathetic to her story.

White's activism, and that of his mother Jeanne, helped AIDS patients all over the United States receive care that they otherwise could not have afforded. The public was also educated about the nature of the disease. In 1990, just a few months after White's death, Congress passed P.L. 101-381, the Ryan White Comprehensive AIDS Resources Emergency Care (CARE) Act. The Act is administered by the Health Resources and Services Administration and aims to improve the quality of care for low-income or uninsured individuals and families with HIV and AIDS who do not have access to care. The Act supports locally developed care systems and is founded on partnership between the U.S. federal government, states, and local communities. It emphasizes outpatient, primary, and preventive care in order to prevent overuse of expensive emergency room and inpatient facilities.

Between the Act's authorization in 1991, and May of 1996, nearly $2.8 billion in federal funds were appropriated to provide care to more than 500,000 low-income Americans living with HIV or AIDS. From 1993 to 1996, funding for the program increased from $348 million to $738.5 million. The Act was reauthorized in May 1996 and continues to provide care to Americans living with HIV and AIDS.

White's mother, Jeanne, has collaborated with writer Susan Dworkin to write a book about her experiences with White, *Weeding Out the Tears: Mother's Story of Love, Loss and Renewal,* published in 1997. White wrote in his book, ". . . I drifted back to a question some kid asked me once. 'Would you give up all your fame to get rid of AIDS?' he wanted to know. How dumb can you get! I snapped my fingers at him. "Like that, I'd give it up like that.'"

## Further Reading

"Fascinating Facts About Ryan," Ryan White Foundation, http://ryanwhite.org/rwfact.htm (February 26, 1999).
"Jeanne White: Ryan White's Mom," *Jeanne White Background,* http://www.ryanwhite.org/jw-1.htm (February 26, 1999).
"Life After Ryan: Jeanne White Inherits the Spotlight," *POZ,* http://www.thebody.com/poz/backissues/12_96_1_97/white.html (February 26, 1999).
"Ryan White CARE Act," *HIV INSite,* http://kali.ucsf.edu/topics/ryan_white_care_act/ (February 26, 1999).
"Ryan White Comprehensive AIDS Resources Emergency (CARE) Act," Bureau of Primary Health Care, http://www.bphc.hrsa.dhhs.gov/hiv/hiv1_4.htm (February 26, 1999).
"Ryan White: My Own Story," *Amazon.com,* http://www.amazon.com/exec/obidos/ISBN%3 . . . 3228/drjohnhollemanA/002-8804493-7871437 (February 26, 1999).
"Ryan White Foundation's Special Sections," Ryan White Foundation, http://ryanwhite.org/ (February 26, 1999).
"Ryan White's Philosophy of Life," *Ryan White's Philosophy of Life,* http://www.ryanwhite.org/rwp.htm (February 26, 1999).
"Ryan White's Testimony Before the President's Commission on AIDS," Ryan White Foundation, http://ryanwhite.org/rwtest3.htm (February 26, 1999).
"Weeding Out the Tears," *Jeanne White Book,* http://www.ryanwhite.org/jwb-1.htm (February 26, 1999).
"Welcome to Ryan's Club," Ryan White Foundation, http://ryanwhite.org/rc98.htm (February 26, 1999). □

# Ted Williams

**Ted Williams (born 1918) was one of baseball's most fearsome hitters. Despite five seasons lost to military service in World War II and the Korean War, the "Splendid Splinter" of the Boston Red Sox hit 521 home runs in his career and batted .344.**

Always pursuing perfection in his sport's most difficult task, Ted Williams was nearly unstoppable in hitting major league pitches. He perennially led baseball in the two most important aspects of hitting—getting on base and driving in runners. He was the last player to hit .400, achieving that mark in 1941. For his total absorption in the game he loved, Williams was nicknamed "Teddy Ballgame." Long after his career ended, he continued to symbolize excellence in hitting and dedication to baseball.

## Enjoyed Hitting the Ball

"The most fun in baseball is hitting the ball," Ted Williams told Dave Kindred of *Sports Illustrated.* "That's all I did . . . for 20 years of my early life." Williams was born on August 30, 1918 in San Diego, California. Growing up during the Great Depression, he played pickup baseball in a neighborhood park year-round. His mother worked tirelessly for the Salvation Army and his father ran a passport photography shop and worked late hours, allowing young Williams the freedom to play ball until dark. He even took his bat to school. He was a tall, thin teenager who pitched and played outfield in junior high school, American Legion and sandlot teams, and at Herbert Hoover High School. In his autobiography, *My Turn at Bat,* Williams said "there was nobody who had any more opportunities than I had, along with the God-given physical attributes and the intense desire."

As a teenager, Williams learned not to swing at balls that were out of the strike zone. Try as they might, pitchers could never get him to chase bad pitches. "Getting on base is how you score runs," Williams explained. "Runs win ball games. I walked a lot in high school, and in the minors I walked 100 times. . . . You start swinging at pitches a half-inch outside, the next one's an inch out and pretty soon you're getting nothing but bad balls to swing at."

Williams began his professional career with the San Diego Padres, then a minor league team, in 1936. In December 1937 the Padres sold him to the Boston Red Sox. "The Red Sox didn't mean a thing to me," Williams wrote in

his autobiography. "A fifth-, sixth-place club, the fartherest [sic] from San Diego I could go." Yet Williams would become synonymous with Red Sox baseball.

When he first came to spring training with the Red Sox in 1938, he was 19 and extremely cocky. The legend is that someone told him "Wait'll you see Jimmie Foxx hit" and Williams replied "Wait till Foxx sees me hit." In his autobiography Williams debunked the myth: "I never said that, but I suppose it wouldn't have been unlike me."

For all his bombast, Williams was a driven, obsessed young man. "I thought the weight of the damn world was always on my neck, grinding on me," he recalled. "I wanted to be the greatest hitter who ever lived. . . . Certainly nobody ever worked harder at it. It was the center of my heart, hitting a baseball."

## A Smashing Debut

In 1938, at the Red Sox's farm club in Minneapolis, Williams led the league in hitting but almost ended his career when he smashed his fist into a water cooler. "I was impetuous, I was tempestuous," he recalled. "I blew up . . . I'd get so damned mad, throw bats, kick the columns in the dugout so that sparks flew, tear out the plumbing, knock out the lights, damn near kill myself."

Williams had a smashing rookie season in 1939, hitting 31 home runs and driving in 145 runs. His fielding was indifferent, but his hitting was electrifying. He had only one apparent weakness—an inability to hit to the opposite field. Standing close to the plate but refusing to swing at outside pitches, the left-handed-batting Williams pulled almost all his hits to right field. Many opposing managers eventually defended against him with the "Williams Shift"—moving the shortstop to the right-field side of second base. But even that didn't stop him.

"Hitting is a correction thing," Williams told Kindred. "Every swing you're changing. Every thought you're correcting. Every time up, you're thinking. My whole life was hitting." If he was battling a slump, Williams might have stayed up all night thinking about what to change.

In 1941, only his third season in the majors, Williams captivated the nation by chasing a .400 season batting average. For part of the year, Williams' quest was overshadowed by New York Yankee star Joe DiMaggio's record 56-game hitting streak. In the All-Star Game in Detroit that year, Williams hit a game-winning home run. On the last day of the season, Williams was hitting exactly .400, and Red Sox manager Joe Cronin offered him the chance to sit out a doubleheader. "I told Cronin I didn't want that," Williams recalled. "If I couldn't hit .400 all the way I didn't deserve it." He got six hits and finished at .406, a mark most experts believed would never be equaled. DiMaggio was named the league's Most Valuable Player that season, as the Red Sox finished second to the Yankees.

## Hit the Top

The 1941 season was the first of six times that Williams won the American League batting championship. That year, he also won the first of four home run titles. He led the league in walks eight times and in runs scored six times. No batter other than Babe Ruth had so excelled in the three most important aspects of offense—hitting for a high batting average (.344 career mark), hitting for power (521 home runs) and getting on base.

"No hitter ever had more confidence at the plate than Ted Williams, every bit of it fully justified," observed baseball historians Lawrence Ritter and Donald Honig in *The Image of their Greatness*. "No player ever had better eyesight, better judgment of a pitched ball, a purer swing, more power, more intense concentration." Legends grew about Williams' 20/10 vision. He said he could see the rotation of baseballs pitched to him, discerning whether the pitch was a fastball or a curve.

In every at-bat, he was gathering new data. "A trip to the plate was an adventure for me, one that I could reflect on and store up information," Williams said in his autobiography. "I honestly believe I can recall everything there was to know about my first 300 home runs—who the pitcher was, the count, the pitch itself, where the ball landed. I didn't have to keep a written book on pitchers—I lived a book on pitchers."

After the 1942 season, Williams joined the Marines as a fighter pilot and flight instructor. He missed three seasons because of World War II, and the Red Sox faltered without him. In 1946, with Williams back in the lineup, Boston won the American League pennant and Williams won the Most Valuable Player award. Williams appeared in the World Series for the only time in his career, but hit a disappointing .200 with only one RBI, and the Red Sox lost to the St. Louis Cardinals.

The Red Sox just missed a pennant in 1948 by losing a one-game playoff to Cleveland. In 1949, they again came close, losing on the last day of the season to the Yankees. That year, Williams hit .343 with 43 homers and 159 runs batted in and was again Most Valuable Player. But in 1950, he crashed into an outfield fence chasing a fly ball during the All-Star Game, and suffered bone chips in his elbow which bothered him the rest of his career.

## Pursuit of Perfection

At a peak salary of $125,000, Williams was the highest-paid player of his era. He became known as the "Splendid Splinter," "The Thumper," and later in his career, "Teddy Ballgame," because of his intense concentration on the game. *Sports Illustrated* reporter S.L. Price observed that Williams "bent his life into a furious pursuit of perfection."

Gruff and prickly, Williams had an explosive temper. Price characterized his speech as a "uniquely cadenced blend of jock, fishing and military lingo, marked by constant profanity" and described him as "alternately cold and warm, bitter and sentimental, obnoxious and funny, tough and generous—but always savagely independent."

In Boston, he was loved and loathed, with critics picking on his defensive lapses and me-against-the-world attitude. Fans sometimes called him "Terrible Ted." After being booed in one game for dropping a fly ball, he spat toward the stands. He never tipped his hat to the crowd or acknowl-

edged their cheers. After hitting a home run in his last at-bat in Boston in 1960, he refused to take a curtain call.

"I should have had more fun in baseball than any player who ever lived," Williams said. "My twenty-two years in baseball were enjoyable, but many times they were unhappy too. . . . I felt a lot of people didn't like me. I did things I was ashamed of. . . . I was not treated fairly by the press." Critics said he wasn't a clutch hitter or a team player, walked too often, and didn't hustle. "They didn't think I was tryin'," he told Price. "God almighty, I was tryin'. But I was a long, skinny guy, couldn't run."

What he could do, like almost no one else who ever lived, was hit. "He lived to swing a bat, this tall, brash, fidgety youngster with the Hollywood good looks," wrote Ritter and Honig. "He seemed to be never without a bat in his hands, be it on the field, in the dugout, in the clubhouse, and even in his hotel room, where one day an errant practice swing accidentally smashed a dresser mirror to pieces."

Criticizing "gutless" politicians and "unfair" draft laws, Williams went back into the service during the Korean War. He missed most of the 1952 and 1953 seasons. Battling injuries, he announced he was retiring after the 1954 season, but changed his mind. In 1957, nearly 40 years old, Williams had an incredible season, hitting .388 and becoming the oldest player ever to win a batting championship. But he was miserable. "I spent the season being mad at the world for one reason or another," he said. "I don't think I said two words to the Boston writers all year." After the 1960 season, Williams, 42, retired, even though he had hit .316 that year. Historians would forever debate how high his career totals might have soared if he hadn't missed those seasons in the prime of his career.

## Lived with Memories

In 1966, Williams was inducted into the Baseball Hall of Fame. From 1969 through 1971, he managed the Washington Senators and stayed on as manager when they moved and became the Texas Rangers in 1972. They were a lackluster team and Williams had little success as a manager. With his baseball career over, he poured much of his energies into his love of fishing.

Williams remained active and outspoken after retiring to Florida. Despite three strokes in his 70s that left him partially blind, he led a petition campaign to get Shoeless Joe Jackson into the Hall of Fame. Williams was bilked by a scam-artist partner in the sports memorabilia craze of the late 1980s and lost nearly $2 million. His clean, readable signature was easily forged. His son, John-Henry, cruised stores nationwide to uncover forgeries, then opened a family-run memorabilia business. In 1994, Williams established the Ted Williams Museum and Hitters Hall of Fame in Hernando, Florida, and established his own annual Greatest Hitters Award. In 1995, Boston named a tunnel under Boston Harbor after him.

Fishing and fending off frequent interview seekers, Williams watched Red Sox games on television. He told one reporter: "No one pulls harder for them than I do . . . I'll always be a die-hard Red Sox fan." And he added: ". . . look at what a great game it is. . . . It's strong, and I'm like a kid sitting in front on my TV watching. . . . Baseball will always survive.''

## Further Reading

*The Baseball Encyclopedia,* Macmillan, 1990.
Ritter, Lawrence and Honig, Donald, *The Image of their Greatness,* Crown, 1979.
Williams, Ted, as told to Tom Underwood, *My Turn at Bat: The Story of My Life,* Simon & Schuster, 1969.
*Sport,* November 1998.
*Sporting News,* November 14, 1994.
*Sports Illustrated,* December 25, 1995; November 25, 1996; February 2, 1998. □

# Helen Wills

**Helen Wills (1905–1998) was one of the dominant American and international female tennis players during the late 1920s and most of the 1930s. She won 31 major international tennis championships. In her prime, she won 180 straight matches against the best women in tennis without losing a single set. In 1938, she retired from tennis and became an artist, exhibiting her paintings and drawings throughout the U.S. and Europe.**

Born in Centerville, California, on October 6, 1905 to Clarence Wills, a surgeon, and Catherine Wills, a teacher, Helen Newington Wills was raised in an environment of high expectations. She was tutored at home by her mother until she was eight years old. She later graduated from the top ranked Anna Head School in Berkeley, and attended the University of California at Berkeley where she became Phi Beta Kappa because of her academic excellence.

Wills and her mother were always the best of friends. When she was on the tennis circuit, her mother was her chaperone, friend, and support. Just the presence of her mother in the stands provided Wills with the strength she needed. As a child, the future tennis champion was not strong. In fact, her health was somewhat fragile. To counter this, her father attempted to interest her in outdoor activities. First, she started swimming. When her father bought her a horse, she began riding. Helen also accompanied her father when he was shooting duck and quail. When she was eight, her father bought her a tennis racket and played with her every day. According to Helen, she did not fall in love with tennis right away. ''I spent most of my time until thirteen outdoors running with dogs, playing cowboys and Indians, riding horses.'' Her father pushed her towards tennis, most likely because it was the unofficial state sport of California and a state-supported building program of tennis courts allowed people of varying economic backgrounds the opportunity to play. The gentle climate and the public support, both economically and spiritually, produced many national and international champions.

## Played in the Park

Tennis started Wills' physical development. She would later claim that tennis was far more strenuous than any sport, other than rowing. During World War I, her father was a U.S. Army physician in Europe. Wills and her mother spent that year in Vermont, during which time she did not play tennis. The following year, the family returned to California and settled in Berkeley, where Wills played tennis with her father and other children at Live Oak Park. There, her game improved substantially. To Wills, tennis was a fun game that mirrored real life. While playing in the park, she was spotted by William ''Pop'' Fuller of the Berkeley Tennis Club. She was invited to join so that she could get some instruction and play against better players. In 1919, before her 14th birthday, she was a member. Fuller rapidly guided Wills and arranged matches for her. She had a great ability to concentrate and shut out the world. Wills was determined to win, but did not bemoan losing. She started to beat all the club members. She was an excellent observer, developed speed and power, and was able to anticipate her opponents' moves.

## Began Competing

Wills began competing in tennis tournaments in 1919. That year, she won the Bay Region tournament and competed in the California State Tennis Championships. In 1920, she met Hazel Wightman, a tennis star, who coached her for several weeks and later played unbeaten doubles with her on the national and international circuits. After winning the California Women's Championship in 1921, Wills went to the East Coast with her mother to play in other tournaments. She won the National Girls Championship, but lost in another tournament. At this time, she was only five feet tall, but a power house. She was impressive, but still had a long way to go. That year was the first time Wills saw world tennis star, Suzanne Lenglen, play.

In 1922, Wills won the California Women's Championship for the second time, and the National Junior Tournament. She also advanced to the final round of the National Women's Singles, where she was defeated by Molla Mallory, the dominant female player in American tennis. Wills then proceeded to win the national doubles title by defeating Mallory and her partner. She came close to defeating Mallory several other times that summer, and began to get a sympathetic audience at matches. By the end of 1922, Wills was ranked third among American women.

In 1923, Wills graduated from the private Anna Head School and enrolled at Berkeley to study art. Between 1922 to 1923, she had gained 5 inches and 25 pounds. At 17, she now stood 5 feet 7 inches tall and weighed 150 pounds. Her strength and speed had improved, and she had the best serve among American female players. In 1923, 17-year-old Wills beat Molla Mallory, who had won seven national championships, in the National Women's Singles by a score of 6-1, 6-2.

In 1924, she represented the U.S. in the English-American Wightman Cup tournament, in the Olympic games, and at Wimbledon. In the latter two contests, she hoped to meet Suzanne Lenglen, who had come to England to see Wills play. Wills, however, played erratically, losing in the first and second rounds of the singles of the Wightman Cup, but took the doubles with her old tutor Hazel Wightman. At Wimbledon, Lenglen withdrew, becoming hysterical and claiming that she had jaundice, and Wills lost in the finals to a British opponent. However, she and Wightman won the doubles. A week later Lenglen also withdrew from the Olympics, which Wills proceeded to win by earning a gold medal.

Returning home, Wills won the national singles, doubles, and mixed doubles titles. In 1925 she did not go to Europe, and Lenglen won the European titles. Surprisingly, in an eastern tournament, Wills was beaten in the finals by Elizabeth Ryan, an expatriate American who was a frequent doubles partner of Lenglen. In the Wightman Cup, which was held in the U.S. that year, she won with some difficulty. In the nationals, she also won the singles with some difficulty, indicating that she was not yet a match for Lenglen.

## "The Match of the Century"

In February 1926, Wills finally met Lenglen in Cannes, France, in what has been called "The Match of the Century." Wills, accompanied by her mother, had negotiated her own way over to France, ostensibly to paint and continue her education but, in reality, to challenge the best female tennis player in the world. The newspapers began a maelstrom of publicity. Wills was portrayed as the sweet, virginal 20-year-old versus the lascivious, worldly and jaded 26-year-old Lenglen. Somewhat surprisingly, the French public also took a liking to Wills, even though she was the opponent. Wills played a number of smaller tournaments in southern France to warm up for the battle with Lenglen. After it seemed the two would never meet in singles competition, the two arranged to play at the Carlton Club in Cannes. Lenglen was considered to be the overwhelming favorite. While Wills lost the first set 6-3, she was clearly challenging Lenglen's game. In the second set, Wills started to take control 3-1, but a fault line call against Wills rattled her, and she lost her lead. Wills eventually lost the second set 8-6, but not before a series of exceptionally hard fought games. While Wills had lost the battle, she began to win the war. The world public began to realize that Lenglen was not unbeatable. After Lenglen went professional, the two never played again.

While in France to play Lenglen, Wills met a young businessman and stockbroker named Frederick Moody whom she married in 1929, and divorced in 1937. Two years later she married Irish polo player Aiden Roark. She divorced him in the 1970s.

Aside from Lenglen, there was no one who could stop Wills. From 1927 to 1933, she won every singles match she entered. During this period she played against the best female tennis players, and had a run of 180 matches in which she never lost a set. A back injury in 1935 forced Wills to stop playing for three years. After being told that she was not strong enough, and having everything to lose and nothing to gain, Wills entered her last Wimbledon competition in 1938. Having lost twice in preliminary tournaments elsewhere, she fought her way to the finals at Wimbledon, facing unseeded Helen Jacobs, who had shoulder and leg injuries. According to a tournament official, Wills was having trouble winning matches, "and anyone could see that time was catching up with her." In what appeared to be evenly matched early play, Jacobs tore her Achilles tendon, and thereafter played in great pain, and with a loss of mobility. She remained in the match, but lost almost every point thereafter. After winning her eighth Wimbledon singles championship, Wills retired permanently from tennis.

Besides being shy, there was a cool side to Wills' personality. She had a lingering feud with competitor Helen Jacobs, and she was cold to tennis star Alice Marble. She was, however, very kind and considerate to her friends. Wills' coldness on the courts was attributed to her utter concentration and ability to shut out the world.

## A Quiet Retirement

Wills wrote three books, including a tennis instruction book, a mystery novel, *Death Serves an Ace,* and her autobiography, *15-30: The Story of a Tennis Player,* published in 1937.

After her marriage to Roark, Wills moved first to the Los Angeles area and in the 1950s to Carmel Valley in central California. She continued her art work, and occasionally played tennis, but was a private person and generally stayed out of the limelight.

Wills died at the Carmel Convalescent Hospital in Carmel, California on January 1, 1998, at the age of 92. She left her estate to the University of California at Berkeley. In March 1999, a number of her books, including many inscribed to her by the authors, were auctioned. The inscribed copies were mostly from literary figures of the 1920s and 1930s, but also from Presidents Hoover and Nixon.

Wills believed that tennis was a war rather than a social engagement. *Time* magazine described Wills as an "imperturbable tennis ace.... Her trademark white eyeshade set an enduring fashion trend, but there was nothing frivolous about Little Miss Poker Face, as she was known. She stood her ground like a tank, drilling out bullet serves and powerful baseline drives."

## Further Reading

Engelmann, Larry, *The Goddess and the American Girl: The Story of Suzanne Lenglen and Helen Wills,* Oxford University Press, 1988.
*Sports Illustrated,* Fall 1991; January 12, 1998.
*Time,* January 12, 1998. □

# Stevie Wonder

**Stevie Wonder (born 1950) is one of the most cherished rhythm-and-blues singers and songwriters of his generation. The 19-time Grammy winner is known for his soulful voice and catchy tunes as well as for his commitment to political and humanitarian causes.**

I n the course of following Stevie Wonder on his relentless travels, journalists have come to realize just how beloved an entertainer he is. "It dawned on me," wrote Giles Smith in the *New Yorker,* "that a substantial part of Stevie Wonder's public life consists of the voices of complete strangers telling him they love him." *Rolling Stone*'s David Ritz had a similar opinion. "Following Stevie Wonder around New York is exhilarating work," he wrote. "I get the feeling that he loves being Stevie Wonder. He loves the attention, the adulation, the chance to perform." Ritz also remarked that Wonder's "optimism is infectious."

It is believed that Wonder, born Stevland Judkins Morris in Saginaw, Michigan on May 13, 1950, was blinded due to an overabundance of oxygen in his incubator shortly after his premature birth. "I vaguely remember light and what my mother looks like," he said in a 1986 *Life* interview, "but I could be dreaming." His father left the family early on. He and his five siblings were raised by their mother. She moved the family to Detroit, where they struggled to survive. Though he has spoken good-naturedly in adulthood about the limitations of his blindness, Wonder told Ritz that as a child he soothed his mother's tears by telling her that he "wasn't sad." He recalled, "I believed God had something for me to do." Along with his siblings, Wonder sang in the Whitestone Baptist Church choir and demonstrated a gift for playing the piano, harmonica, and drums by age eleven.

Thanks to the intercession of a friend, Wonder was introduced to Berry Gordy, president of Detroit-based Motown Records, and Gordy's producer Brian Holland. Gordy placed the exceptional youngster's career in the hands of his associate Clarence Paul, whom he designated as Wonder's mentor. Gordy told Paul, according to Ritz, that his job was to "bring out his genius. This boy can give us hits." Handed the show business moniker "Little Stevie Wonder," the prodigious adolescent—signed to the Motown offshoot label Tamla—did indeed yield hits.

## Motown Encouraged Discipline

Wonder's fourth single, "Fingertips Part 2," appeared in 1963 and became the first live performance of a song to reach the top of the U.S. pop chart. Also that year, Wonder became the first recording artist to reach the number one position on the *Billboard* Hot 100 and Rhythm & Blues singles charts simultaneously. Unable to attend a regular Detroit school because of his schedule, Wonder was sent to the Michigan School for the Blind at Motown's expense.

"Motown meant discipline to me," Wonder recalled to Ritz. "The attitude was 'Do it over. Do it differently. Do it until it can't be done any better.'" Under such demanding circumstances the young performer grew up fast and he put aside the "little" label in 1964. Over the next few years he churned out hits like "Uptight," "Nothing's Too Good for My Baby," "I Was Made to Love Her," and "For Once in My Life." By 1968, his label had amassed enough chart-toppers to fill his first greatest hits album.

In 1969, Wonder met President Richard Nixon at the White House, where he received a Distinguished Service Award from the President's Committee on Employment of Handicapped People. Meanwhile, he continued to produce hits like "My Cherie Amour," which sold over a million copies, and "Signed Sealed Delivered (I'm Yours)." In 1970, Wonder married Syreeta Wright, a Motown employee and aspiring singer; the two wrote together, and Wonder produced several successful records for her. The marriage was short-lived, however; they divorced in 1972. Wright has said that Wonder's music was her chief rival. "He would wake up and go straight to the keyboard," she recalled in a *New Yorker* interview. "I knew and understood that his passion was music. That was really his No. 1 wife." Wonder fathered children by three other women over the next couple of decades, though he did not remarry. "I was at the birth of two of my children," he confided in *Life*. "I felt them being born—it was amazing."

When Wonder turned 21, he was due the money he had earned as a minor through an arrangement stipulated in a previous agreement. But Motown only paid him $1 million of the $30 million he had earned during that time. After considerable legal wrangling he managed to attain a unique degree of artistic and financial autonomy. "At 21, Stevie was interested in being treated well and in controlling his life and in presenting his music, and all those things were extraordinary things for a young man to ask at that point," explained Johanan Vigoda, Wonder's long-time attorney, in the *New Yorker*. "It wasn't the freedom to be dissolute or undisciplined. He wanted to be free so that he could bring the best of himself to the table."

What Wonder brought to the table—with the establishment of his own music publishing company and near-total creative freedom—was an increasingly sophisticated body of work that managed to fuse the high spirits of classic soul, the syncopations of funk, exquisite melodies, and his own introspective and increasingly politicized lyrics. He demonstrated the versatility of the synthesizer when it was still something of a novelty in the rhythm & blues world.

## Accident Redoubled Commitment

Wonder's momentum was almost stopped permanently by a 1973 automobile accident that nearly claimed his life and left him with deep facial scars. If anything, however, this event caused him to become more focused. Virtually all of Wonder's work during the early to mid-1970s was essentially pop, most notably his albums *Talking Book, Innervisions, Fulfillingness' First Finale,* and the epic *Songs in the Key of Life.* His songs from that period, including "Superstition" and "Higher Ground," "Boogie on Reggae Woman," "Sir Duke," "I Wish," and "You Are the Sunshine of My Life," were unrivaled both artistically and commercially. "What artist in his right mind," mused singer-songwriter and soul icon Marvin Gaye to *Rolling Stone*'s Ritz, "wouldn't be intimidated by Stevie Wonder?"

In 1979, Wonder released *Journey through the Secret Life of Plants,* the theme of which many listeners found eccentric. "It was a consideration of the physical and spiritual relationships between human beings and plants,"

Wonder explained to Ritz, quipping that "some called it shrubbish." Though he increasingly failed to match the sales peaks of the preceding decades, Wonder was still a giant presence in the world of pop. His *Hotter Than July,* with its reggae-driven hit "Master Blaster (Jammin')," indicated his continuing creative restlessness. "That Girl," his love song "I Just Called to Say I Love You"—which won an Academy Award for best song and stands as Motown's top-selling single internationally—and his duet with ex-Beatle Paul McCartney on the anti-racism anthem "Ebony and Ivory," all achieved great success.

## Delved Into Politics and Charity Work

Over the years Wonder became progressively more involved in politics, lobbying for gun control, against drunk driving, against the apartheid system enforced by South Africa's white minority, and on behalf of a national holiday in recognition of civil rights martyr Martin Luther King, Jr. He played a number of benefits and made public service announcements, often winning honors for his advocacy. The slogan under his picture on a poster for Mothers Against Drunk Driving read: "Before I ride with a drunk, I'll drive myself." He also contributed his labor to the Charge Against Hunger campaign organized by American Express.

Wonder was less musically prolific in the 1980s, but still achieved a great amount of success. He won a Grammy for *In Square Circle* in 1986 and was inducted into the Rock and Roll Hall of Fame in 1989. He won praise for his work on the soundtrack to Spike Lee's 1991 film *Jungle Fever.* It was said that Wonder composed the material in just three weeks. "Movies are always a good challenge," he told Neil Strauss of the *New York Times*, "because it's taking what's happening visually and, even though I'm not able to see it, getting a sense of the movie and finding a new way to work with it." His work for *Jungle Fever* preempted the release of a collection of songs he had been crafting while living in the African nation of Ghana; the resulting disc did not hit stores for several years.

In 1992, Wonder signed a unique lifetime pact with Motown. "This is a guy you don't ever want to see recording for anyone else," company president Jheryl Busby told the *New Yorker* in 1995. "I worked hard to make Stevie see that we had his interests at heart. Stevie is what I call the crown jewel, the epitome. I wasn't looking at Stevie as an aging superstar but as an icon who could pull us into the future." Wonder himself seemed to share this sense of his eternal newness: "I'm going to be 45," he reflected to Ritz, "but I'm still feeling new and amazed by the world I live in. I was in the Hard Rock Cafe in Tokyo last week, and they started playing my records, and I started crying, crying like a little kid, thinking how God has blessed me with all these songs."

## *Conversation Peace* Met with Mixed Reactions

When *Conversation Peace*—the album on which Wonder had been working for nearly eight years—was released in 1995, it garnered a range of reactions. *Vibe* deemed it "a decidedly mixed bag, leapfrogging back and forth between divine inspiration and inoffensive professionalism." Reviewer Tom Sinclair took particular exception to the "cloying sentimentality" of some of the songs, as did other critics. *Entertainment Weekly* praised the album's sound, but noted that "the song selection here, while frisky, is thin, making this comeback small Wonder." *Time*'s Christopher John Farley, however, while allowing that the recording "isn't a slam dunk," called it "another winner for Wonder." In 1996, Wonder added two more Grammy Awards to his extensive collection, receiving another best male rhythm & blues vocal performance honor and one for best rhythm & blues song for the tune "For Your Love" off of *Conversation*. In addition, he was given a Lifetime Achievement Award that year.

Wonder's 1995 concert tour garnered acclaim. "Running 2 1/4 hours, it was an outstanding show—full of pure, old-fashioned R & B," declared *Los Angeles Times* writer Dennis Hunt of Wonder's performance at the Universal Amphitheatre. Pondering the performer's endurance and the disappearance of most of his contemporaries from the scene, Hunt observed, "Some may point to exquisite taste as the key to Wonder's success, but the real secret is his ability to stay current, to be fluent in the R & B style of the moment." Not surprisingly, critics were virtually unanimous about Wonder's 1995 live double CD, *Natural Wonder*, which *Rolling Stone* called "an important and revelatory statement."

Wonder remained in the limelight, performing at a White House dinner for Prime Minister Tony Blair of Britain in February of 1998, and appearing as a White House guest later that year. Also in 1998 he performed on the soundtrack of the animated Disney film *Mulan*. In January 1999, Wonder provided a dazzling halftime show during the Super Bowl. He was awarded yet another Grammy in 1999—his nineteenth—for best male rhythm & blues vocalist. In addition, he continued his humanitarian work, establishing along with German firm SAP, the SAP/Stevie Wonder Vision Awards. These awards recognized efforts to aid blind people in the workplace.

Wonder has continued his songwriting between other projects, and has expressed the desire to do a gospel album. But regardless of the genre he pursues, his music will undoubtedly reflect his spirituality. He has inspired a new generation of artists, including rock group the Red Hot Chili Peppers, who made their bid for mainstream popularity with a version of "Higher Ground," Lenny Kravitz and Michael Franti of Spearhead. However, he nonetheless expressed his determination to keep growing. "You're influenced all the time," he said in the *New York Times*, "and the day that you cannot be influenced by anything good is the day that you really have let your art die."

## Further Reading

Rees, Dafydd, and Luke Crampton, *Rock Movers & Shakers*, Billboard, 1991.
*Entertainment Weekly*, March 31, 1995.
*Jet*, May 8, 1995; May 22, 1995; March 16, 1998; February 23, 1998.
*Life*, October 1986.
*Los Angeles Times*, January 16, 1995.
*New Yorker*, March 13, 1995.
*Rolling Stone*, July 13, 1995; January 25, 1996
*Time*, September 4, 1995; April 10, 1996; June 22, 1998; June 29, 1998.
*Vibe*, March 1995. □

# Steve Wozniak

**Steve Wozniak (born 1950) invented the Apple computer and helped found the Apple Computer Company. One of the wealthiest and most famous inventors in the U.S., Wozniak left behind the world of business to spend his time teaching children about computers.**

Stephen Gary Wozniak was born on August 11, 1950 in San Jose, California, to Margaret Wozniak, a homemaker, and Jerry Wozniak, an electrical engineer. When he was eight, the family, including two other children, Leslie and Mark, moved to nearby Sunnyvale to be closer to his father's job at Lockheed Missiles and Space Company. Wozniak became interested in mathematics when he was in the fourth grade. The recognition and encouragement of a teacher helped to improve his self esteem. Wozniak loved to read; his favorite books were about Tom Swift, Jr., a young engineer who worked with his father inventing airplanes and rocket ships. In the fifth grade, after reading a book about a ham radio operator, Wozniak built his own radio transmitter and receiver from a kit. At 11, he built a machine he called a "ticktacktoe" computer. He also played on an all-star Little League team and ran in races. In junior high, Wozniak received a letter for swimming.

At Cupertino Junior High School, Wozniak won a blue ribbon for the best electronics project at the Bay Area Science Fair. He designed a binary adding and subtracting computer. At Homestead High School, Wozniak was too advanced for the electronics and math courses. His electronics teacher sent him to Sylvania, a large electronics company, to program its computers. He won an award as the best math student at Homestead in 1966, attended seminars at the University of Santa Clara, and scored an 800 on his math Scholastic Aptitude Test.

Wozniak attended the University of Colorado his freshman year of college. There he preferred skiing to studying. Because his parents could not afford the high out-of-state tuition, Wozniak returned to California to attend DeAnza Community College. For his junior year, he went to the University of California, at Berkeley. There, with the help of a high school friend named Steve Jobs, who was later to be his business partner at Apple Computer, he designed a "little blue box," a device for making illegal free telephone calls. They sold them to fellow students for $150. Wozniak, who had a talent for mimicry, said he used the box to call the Vatican, where only a sharp-eared bishop prevented him from talking to the pope by stating, "You are not Henry Kissinger."

## The Birth of Apple

At the end of his junior year, and short on money, Wozniak got a job at Hewlett-Packard (HP), an electronics company in Palo Alto, California. Within several months, he was a full engineer. At the center of the computer revolution, HP suited Wozniak because of its advanced technology and its laid-back atmosphere. The company allowed employees to work on their own projects at night. Doing so, Wozniak created some of the first graphics for computers and computer games. Steve Jobs, who worked at Atari, invited him to help design a spin-off of Pong called "Breakout." In four days, the two had designed it and split the $750 bonus offered by Atari. Wozniak learned many years later that Jobs had received substantially more money than he had. This discovery factored into the breakup of their friendship.

Wozniak and Jobs attended meetings of the Homebrew Computer Club where the Silicon Valley engineers exchanged ideas and showed off their inventions. These meetings led Wozniak to design an inexpensive personal computer. He decided that it should be easy to program, affordable, and fun. Wozniak also started a Dial-a-Joke service, where people could call for a joke of the day. One day he talked with Alice Robertson, a woman whom he married in January 1976.

Working at night at HP, Wozniak completed his computer design. When Jobs saw it, he thought it could be a commercial success and wanted to market it. While Wozniak would not leave his day job, he agreed to form a computer company with Jobs. According to Wozniak, "We never expected to make any money, but it was a chance to have a business once in our lives." Jobs came up with the name "Apple," because he had once worked in an apple orchard when he had experimented with vegetarianism in India. The Apple Computer Company was officially started on April 1, 1976. Having sold personal possessions to raise money, they decided to work in Jobs family's garage. By luck and determination, one month later they received an order for 100 computers for a total of $50,000. When he showed the computer at work, management decided that his personal computer did not match its business focus. The partners eventually sold 175 Apple I computers.

## Apple II A Great Success

While Wozniak was still working for HP, he spent his nights improving the Apple, while Jobs figured out how to market it. Through contacts, Jobs recruited Mike Markkula, a marketing genius who had retired at age 33, to help run the company. After a short time, Wozniak's night-time efforts paid off in a much improved Apple II that was aimed at the average person rather than the electronic expert. It had sound, computer animation, high resolution images, and expanded game playing ability. The experienced Markkula wrote a business plan in which he anticipated sales of $500 million within ten years, and invested $250,000 of his own money in the venture. Finally, in October of 1976, Wozniak resigned from HP.

In January of 1977, the trio incorporated Apple Computer. The company moved to larger quarters twice, recruited an ever-growing staff, and acquired an eye-catching logo—a rainbow-colored apple with a bite taken out of it. The launch of the Apple II was scheduled to coincide with the first West Coast Computer Faire. Priced at only $1,298, the computer was a great success. By the end of its first year, the company had made almost three quarters of a million dollars in sales with a profit of $42,000.

At the same time that his business was taking off, Wozniak's marriage was floundering. His lack of social skills and his obsession with computers made his wife Alice feel increasingly isolated. Although they tried counseling for a year, they divorced after four years of marriage. Alice got one-third of Wozniak's Apple stock in a divorce settlement which quickly grew into a fortune.

After the initial separation, Wozniak became a workaholic. During this time, he developed a way to connect the Apple computer to a printer, thereby making it more useful. He also developed the floppy disk, a removable plastic disk with information on it that can be put into the computer memory for storage or for accessing without being stored. These innovations greatly increased the ability of average people to use the Apple computer. By the end of 1978, Apple sales had increased ten times, making Apple one of the fastest growing companies in the United States. Apple computers were now stocked by more than 300 dealers. By 1979, Apple employed one thousand people.

At this point, both Wozniak and Jobs were being eased out of the power structure by business people such as Markkula. Because Wozniak was so well known, he was frequently asked to give lectures and interviews with the press and television. While the Apple II was now the world's best selling computer, the company decided to plan ahead by developing the Apple III, a small business computer comparable to the IBM personal computer. Although it was priced at just under $3,000, the computer did not sell well because it experienced hardware failures, leading to bad reviews. Not much software was developed for it.

## Away From Apple

Frustrated with Apple management, Wozniak took up flying, and started courting Candi Clark, a former Olympic kayaker and accountant at Apple. In December 1980, Apple stock went public and was sold out in minutes. Within a month, Wozniak was worth about $50 million. In February 1981, while flying Clark and other companions to Los Angeles, Wozniak crashed his plane, nearly killing everyone on board. He married Clark four months later and decided to take a leave of absence from Apple in order to return to college. Frustrations with Apple management and nearly losing his life made him reconsider his priorities. "The company had become big business, and I missed tinkering. I just wanted to be an engineer," Wozniak told *People* magazine.

Wozniak returned to Berkeley in 1981 to earn a computer science degree under the pseudonym of "Rocky Clark," the first name from one of his dogs, and the last from his new wife. Several credits shy of graduation, he left Berkeley, but received equivalency credits for work done at Apple. Wozniak was officially awarded a degree several years later, in 1986.

In 1982 and 1983, Wozniak produced two music concerts, called the US Festival, which combined the best music groups with the best computer stuff, a "hot tunes and high tech" event. Although he lost a lot of money on the festivals, he felt they were a success because both he and the concert goers had fun.

## Returned to Develop the Macintosh

In 1982, Wozniak returned to the Apple II section of Apple Computers. In-fighting at the company was becoming bitter. Wozniak started designing a new computer called the Lisa, a cheaper version of which was later called the Macintosh. It had a mouse, folders, and pull-down menus and displayed pictures. However, the company had lost the camaraderie Wozniak liked so much. The development of the Macintosh led to more friction between the department led by Jobs and the Apple II department. There were strained relations between Jobs and Wozniak, who was hurt that the Apple II had not received its due recognition as a computer that had a billion dollars in sales by 1982. Jobs felt that the Apple II was obsolete. In February 1985, Wozniak left Apple for good.

Wozniak helped start a new company, CL9, to develop an infrared remote control device that would control household appliances. He continued to feud with Jobs, who felt betrayed because Wozniak had left Apple. When Wozniak discovered that Jobs had not evenly split the money earned from the development of the Breakout game, their relationship was further strained.

In 1989, Wozniak sold the unsuccessful CL9. Since then, he has spent most of his time donating money to various charitable organizations in San Jose, including the Tech Museum of Innovation, the Children's Discovery Museum, and the San Jose-Cleveland Ballet.

Wozniak and Candi Clark had three children, Jesse, Sara, and Gary; they were divorced in 1987. In 1989, he met Suzanne Mulkern, a mother of three, who shared his shyness, love of children, and sense of humor. They married in 1990. Wozniak now spends his time teaching children about the wonders of computers.

## Further Reading

Gold, Rebecca, *Steve Wozniak: A Wizard Called Woz,* Lerner, 1994.

Greenberg, Keith Elliot, *Steven Jobs and Stephen Wozniak: Creating the Apple Computer,* Blackbirch, 1994.

Kendall, Martha E., *Steve Wozniak: Inventor of the Apple Computer,* Walker, 1994.

*Maclean's,* May 11, 1992.

*People,* May 30, 1983. □

# Chien-Shiung Wu

**Among the team of experimental physicists who developed the first atomic bomb for the U.S. government during World War II, Chien-Shiung Wu (1912–1997) spent 37 years as a leading researcher at Columbia University. She was noted for her meticulous experimental work in studying radioactive interactions. Her most famous experiment overturned what long had been considered a fundamental law of nature, the principle of conservation of parity.**

Throughout her life, Wu battled the gender bias which belittled the accomplishments of women in science. Despite her remarkable achievements, boundless professional energy, and brilliant problem-solving skills, Wu was often slow to be rewarded for her work, particularly in the early stages of her career. Known as a thorough and precise experimenter, Wu was always in demand because of her trusted ability to test new theories. Many thought Wu should have won the Nobel Prize for leading the experiments which disproved the principle of conservation of parity. Instead, the prize was awarded to her two male colleagues who had proposed, but not conducted, the experiments.

## Encouraged to Excel

Wu was born in Liu Ho, near Shanghai, China, on May 31, 1912. Her father, Wu Zhongyi, had been an engineer. In 1911, he abandoned that profession to take part in the revolution that overthrew the Manchu dynasty. After the revolution, he opened a school for girls in Liu Ho. His wife,

Fan Fuhua, became a tutor, and the couple became known as strong advocates for education. They encouraged their daughter to put her utmost effort into academic excellence.

Wu attended her father's elementary school until she was nine, then enrolled in a teacher training program at the Suzhou Girls' School, about fifty miles from home. She soon became frustrated at the lack of science instruction there, and taught herself physics, chemistry, and mathematics using books and notes of students enrolled in other programs at Suzhou. She was active in political causes and became a class leader. Other politically minded students realized that Wu was immune to dismissal due to her stellar academic performance. She graduated as valedictorian with the highest grades in her class.

Selected to attend the National Central University in Nanjing, Wu prepared by continuing to teach herself physics. She began at the university as a mathematics major but soon switched to physics. She earned a bachelor's degree in 1934, and for two years after that taught physics at the university level and did research in X-ray crystallography.

In 1936, encouraged by her academic advisor to continue her studies in the United States, Wu left China. Her intention was to enroll at the University of Michigan, finish her doctorate quickly, and return to China. But when she reached San Francisco, she was offered an opportunity to attend the University of California at Berkeley. Faculty members in the physics department included Robert Oppenheimer, who would later lead the Manhattan Project that developed the first atomic bomb, and Ernest Lawrence,

inventor of the atom-smashing machine known as the cyclotron. She enrolled at Berkeley and, in 1940, earned her doctorate in physics. Her studies and some post-doctoral work at Berkeley immediately established her as an expert in nuclear fission.

## Worked on the Bomb

Wu's achievements at Berkeley clearly merited a faculty appointment there. At the time, however, there were no women teaching physics at any major American universities, and she was not offered a job. In 1942, she married physicist Luke Yuan, whom she had met at Berkeley, and they moved to the East Coast. Yuan worked on radar devices at RCA laboratories and Wu took up a teaching position at Smith College in Northampton, Massachusetts.

Wu was not entirely happy at Smith and remained there only a year. She was eager to continue her research. With a shortage of physicists due to World War II, the gender bias against women relaxed, and Wu received job offers from Columbia University, Massachusetts Institute of Technology, and Princeton. Wu accepted a job at Princeton, becoming that school's first female instructor. For a few months, she taught introductory physics to naval officers.

Wu had barely settled at Princeton before she was recruited to join Columbia University's Division of War Research. There, the U.S. Army's secret effort to develop an atomic bomb (dubbed the "Manhattan Project"), was under way. Top scientists had decided that Wu's expertise was needed, and they were right. When an atomic chain reaction stopped unexpectedly during testing, the legendary scientist Enrico Fermi was puzzled. Wu was familiar with a rare gas produced by nuclear fission that had halted the reaction. Her knowledge cleared up the problem and enabled the research to proceed. Wu also helped develop a process to enrich uranium ore to produce large quantities of uranium fuel for the bomb. Her work was vital to the historic effort.

After World War II, Wu stayed on as a senior researcher at Columbia. In 1947, her son, Vincent Wei-chen Yuan, was born; he would grow up to become a nuclear scientist himself. Wu and her husband were both offered positions at National Central University in China. They decided not to return to a country that was now Communist-ruled, and became American citizens in 1954.

At Columbia, Wu was passed over several times for faculty positions before she was finally appointed to the physics faculty in 1952. She would not become a full professor until 1958. Wu was always enthusiastic about her work and spent long days in the laboratory. Her demand for hard work and excellence from her students earned her the nickname "The Dragon Lady."

## Landmark Experiment

Wu became an expert in radioactive beta decay, the process by which an atom emits electrons. Her precise and thorough experiments clarified many highly technical aspects of beta theory. Her first accomplishment was to confirm Fermi's theory that most of the electrons ejected from the nucleus in beta decay traveled at extremely high velocities. Other experimenters had not been able to prove this fact because they had used radioactive films of uneven thickness. Wu's ability to solve such problems gained her a reputation as a top experimenter.

For 30 years, physicists had remained wedded to the principle of conservation of parity, which held that nature does not distinguish between left and right in nuclear reactions. Researchers made all their observations fit this theory, even though no experiments had ever solidly confirmed it. In 1956, Tsung-Dao Lee of Columbia and Chen Ning Yang of Princeton suggested that the principle might not apply to interactions between subatomic particles involving the "weak force," one of the four basic forces of nature. They approached Wu to conduct an experiment.

Wu joined forces with a team of researchers at the National Bureau of Standards in Washington, D.C., which had one of the few laboratories in the nation that could chill materials to the very low temperatures required for the experiment. Laboring tirelessly for six months in difficult conditions, Wu and her colleagues worked with cobalt 60, a radioactive isotope, cooled to minus 459 degrees Fahrenheit, measuring precisely what happened when the cobalt nuclei broke down during atomic interactions. To the surprise of Wu, who had given the radical theory only a one-in-a-million chance of being confirmed, her research found that more particles flew off in the direction opposite the spin of the nuclei, like a left-handed screw. That proved parity did not apply to weak subatomic interactions, showing that beta decay is not always symmetrical.

In January 1957, Wu and her colleagues announced their startling result. The discovery changed thinking about the basic structure of the physical world, and it precipitated an avalanche of studies about the weak interactions of subatomic particles. According to biographer Ursula Allen, her finding "stunned the scientific world. . . . Wu's experiment was a milestone in nuclear physics." Wu later wrote of her landmark experiment: "These were moments of exhilaration and ecstacy! A glimpse of this wonder can be the reward of a lifetime. Could it be that excitement and ennobling feelings like these have kept us scientists marching forward forever?"

Yang and Lee were awarded the Nobel Prize in Physics in 1957 for their work in challenging the principle of parity. Wu did not share in the award, even though her work was essential to proving the men's theory.

## Delayed Recognition

As a result of the parity experiment, Wu began getting the recognition she deserved. In 1958, Wu was the first woman to get an honorary doctorate in science from Princeton. In 1964, Wu became the first woman to receive the National Academy of Science's prestigious Cyrus B. Comstock Award.

Her work included the first successful measurements of low-energy electrons emitted by beta decay. In 1963, in collaboration with Columbia research physicists Y.K. Lee and L.W. Mo, Wu's experiments proved the R.P. Feynman and Murray Gell-Mann theory of conservation of vector current in beta decay, supporting Fermi's basic theory of weak interactions in the nucleus. Wu's thorough work, *Beta Decay*, published in 1965, became a standard reference book for nuclear physicists.

Wu was known for the daring of her experimental ventures. One of her most creative experiments came when she tested beta decay in a 2,000-foot-deep salt mine under the city of Cleveland. She also extensively studied X-rays in the 1960s at the Brookhaven National Laboratory. Her innovative work continued for decades. In the late 1970s, though already at retirement age, Wu was doing experimental research on nuclear interactions using Columbia's cyclotron.

In 1972, Wu became a member of the American Academy of Arts and Sciences. Three years later, she became the first woman to be elected president of the American Physical Society. That same year, she received the National Medal of Science, the nation's highest award for scientific achievement.

Wu retired in 1981 and became a professor emeritus at Columbia. In her 70s, she lectured widely and taught special courses in many places, expanding her observations beyond pure science, to matters of public policy. Wu often remarked on the lack of women in sciences, maintaining that it was not the intellectual capacity or socioeconomic status of women that was the reason, but the bedrock tradition of the hard sciences that impeded their way. On February 16, 1997, she died of a stroke at a hospital near her home in Manhattan, New York.

## Further Reading

*Modern Scientists and Engineers,* McGraw-Hill, 1980.
*Notable Twentieth-Century Scientists,* edited by Emily J. McMurray, Gale Research, 1995.
*Notable Women in the Physical Sciences,* edited by Benjamin F. Shearer and Barbara S. Shearer, Greenwood Press, 1997.
*New York Times,* February 18, 1997. □

# Z

# Darryl F. Zanuck

**Darryl F. Zanuck (1902–1979) produced some of the most important and controversial films in Hollywood. He co-founded 20th Century-Fox studios and helped entertain moviegoers as a producer for over 50 years. Three of his films won Academy Awards for best motion picture and many more received nominations.**

Zanuck was born on September 5, 1902 in Wahoo, Nebraska, the son of an alcoholic hotel clerk, Frank Zanuck, and Louise Torpin. His parents quarreled often about Frank's drinking and gambling. Soon after a huge fight with his father over her promiscuity with a traveling salesman, Louise Zanuck left the family and moved to Arizona. Her son moved in with his grandparents, the Torpins. After his mother remarried and moved to California, his father left town without telling young Zanuck. Rejoining his mother and new stepfather, Joseph Norton, in California, Zanuck became part of an abusive, dysfunctional family. Norton was a violent alcoholic who beat his wife and flung Zanuck across the room when he tried to protect his mother. Norton insisted that Zanuck be enrolled at a military academy. The boy was eight years old. Zanuck was so bored and lonely there that he began running away. On the streets of Los Angeles he ran into his father, who convinced him to return to the academy and began taking him to movies twice a week. But one day his father failed to show up for their visit. Zanuck never saw or heard from him again.

Wandering the streets of Los Angeles looking for his father, Zanuck was picked up by the police and brought to his mother. She made it clear she did not want her 12-year-old son around and shipped him back to Nebraska to be raised by his Torpin grandparents. When he was 15, Zanuck lied about his age and joined the U.S. Army. There he began boxing as a flyweight, but never saw battle. Returning to Nebraska after the war, Zanuck told his grandmother that he was going to California to rejoin his mother. She bought him a bus ticket and gave him a hundred dollars for emergencies. At the age of 17, Zanuck arrived in Pasadena with no intention of seeing his mother. He had one goal in mind: to become a writer.

## A Dream Come True

Zanuck sold his first story to a pulp fiction magazine and then decided to sell the story to a film studio. His girlfriend suggested he join the Los Angeles Athletic Club to make contacts with movie people. When Zanuck attempted to join, however, he was rejected. He had been blackballed because people thought he was Jewish (he was not), and the club did not admit Jews. Zanuck later used the experience to produce the Academy Award winning, *Gentleman's Agreement,* Hollywood's first film dealing with anti-Semitism.

At the age of 19, Zanuck wrote and sold his first Hollywood screenplay. At age 20 he became a gag writer for Mack Sennet and later for Charlie Chaplin and Harold Lloyd. Working for Warner Brothers, Zanuck wrote the scripts for the highly popular Rin Tin Tin movies, which starred a German shepherd. At 23, Zanuck became head of production for Warner Brothers. Two years later he produced the movie *The Jazz Singer,* often called the first "talkie" or movie with sound. In reality it was a silent movie with several sound musical and talking sequences, but it

**435**

Goetz. The new studio made many successful films such as *The Bowery* and *Call of the Wild.*. The studio's biggest money-maker was *The House of Rothschild*, about a wealthy Jewish family from Vienna, and the anti-Semitism they experienced. The movie was controversial at the time because the Nazis had just come to power in Germany. *The House of Rothschild* cemented Zanuck's reputation as Hollywood's boldest and most enterprising producer.

### The Birth of 20th Century-Fox

Feeling frustrated with the distribution of their films, Schenck and Zanuck engineered the merger of their studio with Fox Films, which had the best distribution in the industry and a chain of movie theaters across the U.S. The new studio was called 20th Century-Fox, and Zanuck was vice president in charge of production. Through the merger Zanuck gained some big-name stars, such as Shirley Temple, Will Rogers, and Janet Gaynor. Zanuck was considered the most hands-on of the major studio moguls, exhibiting great talent in re-making movies in the cutting room. Besides making hundreds of routine pictures, Zanuck also produced several films based on liberal causes, such as *The Grapes of Wrath* and *Wilson.* He continued making films on controversial subjects, such as *Gentlemen's Agreement* and *Pinky.* Many of his movies were sentimental, content-rich dramas such as the Academy Award winning, *How Green Was My Valley* and *Twelve O'Clock High.*

After more than three decades together, Zanuck's wife threw him out of the house when she learned he was having an affair with Bella Darvi. Zanuck gave up day-to-day control of the studio and went to Paris with Darvi. There he started an independent film company. Many of his later films made in Europe were produced in part to help the careers of his mistresses—Darvi, Juliette Greco, Irina Demick and Genevieve Gilles. None of these actresses were popular with directors, critics, or audiences and most of the movies he made there failed, with the exception of *The Longest Day.* Darvi accumulated large gambling debts and eventually committed suicide. Zanuck had a stroke in Paris and was depressed and alone.

### Leadership Tensions

In 1962, Zanuck returned as president of 20th Century-Fox. He appointed his son, Richard, head of production at the Hollywood studio. Although the headquarters of the company was in New York, Zanuck continued living in France. Tensions arose between father and son over the making of the movie *Patton.* In 1969, the board of 20th Century-Fox suggested that Richard become president of the company and Darryl become chairman of the board. Zanuck agreed to the change, but later felt he had been manipulated. In December 1970, Zanuck got his revenge. He coldly and cruelly humiliated his son at a board of directors meeting and replaced Richard as president of the company with himself. Virginia Zanuck, outraged at her husband's behavior, threw her support and 100,000 shares of stock behind a group of dissident shareholders, who had grown tired of Zanuck's penchant for mingling business with pleasure.

brought about the end of the silent film era and changed the nature of the film industry forever. Leonard Mosley, author of *Zanuck: The Rise and Fall of Hollywood's Last Tycoon,* called the movie, "probably the most momentous movie in the history of the motion picture industry." Zanuck added sound to all his subsequent movies. The new talking pictures made Warner Brothers the most successful studio in Hollywood.

Zanuck made another wise choice when he cast James Cagney, a song-and-dance man, in the starring role in *The Public Enemy,* a gangster movie released in 1931. Zanuck came up with the idea for the famous "grapefruit scene" in which Cagney pushes half a grapefruit into his girlfriend's face. Although very successful, critics attacked the film as immoral.

Zanuck married an actress named Virginia Fox in 1924. The couple's new financial security led Virginia Zanuck to decide that the time was now right for starting a family. In 1931, she gave birth to Darrylin and had a second daughter, Susan, two years later. Richard was born in 1934. Although it was very unusual at the time, Darryl Zanuck was present at the birth of all his children, whom he adored. Marriage, for Zanuck, did not include fidelity. He is said to have had numerous affairs with actresses.

### A New Venture

In April 1933, after Zanuck realized he would never be more than an employee at Warner Brothers, he left to form 20th Century Films with Joseph Schenck and William

## The Bitter End

In May 1971, the board of directors of 20th Century-Fox forced Zanuck out. His health deteriorated, leading to hospitalization. Richard began visiting his father and the two reconciled. Zanuck and his girlfriend, Genevieve Gilles, went to his home in Palm Springs so that he could recover. Much to their surprise, Virginia Zanuck had left her Santa Monica home and had gone to Palm Springs to await the return of her husband. Gilles was thrown out. Virginia and Darryl celebrated their 50th wedding anniversary in January 1974 with a few friends and family members.

Zanuck's death on December 22, 1979 in Palm Springs, California, ignited a feud over his will. Gilles was outraged to learn that she would inherit nothing and tried to fight the will in court. In October 1982, Virginia Zanuck died of a lung infection complicated by emphysema. Richard was shocked to learn that she had virtually cut his two sons out of her will. Richard tried to fight the will, but he and his sister settled the matter out of court.

Milton Sperling, one of Zanuck's employees, wrote in a letter, "His vulgarity made me laugh, as it was intended to. His cruelty impressed me with its manliness. His insatiable appetites awed me. . . . He was a role model and in unconsciously emulating him, I caused myself no end of trouble. . . . He loved film, made instant decisions, encouraged talent. He'd deride today's committee-ridden, computer-oriented, agent-accountant management apparatus." Darryl Zanuck's death ended the era of the all-powerful Hollywood movie mogul.

## Further Reading

Mosley, Leonard, *Zanuck: The Rise and Fall of Hollywood's Last Tycoon*, Little Brown, 1984.
*Money*, July 1985.
"Biography for Darryl F. Zanuck," *Internet Movie Database*, http://us.imdb.com (February 24, 1999). □

# Adolph Zukor

**Adolph Zukor (1873–1976) was known as the "father of the feature film in America." From running penny arcades to creating Paramount Pictures Corporation, Zukor had a hand in the development of every aspect of the film industry. He worked at Paramount every day until his 100th birthday, and held the title of chairman emeritus until his death at the age of 103.**

Adolph Zukor was born in the rural village of Risce, Hungary on January 7, 1873. His parents ran a small store and grew crops. Zukor did not remember his father, who died when the boy was one year old and his brother Arthur was three. Their mother was the daughter of a rabbi. She remarried, but died when Zukor was eight. The two brothers went to live with an uncle. Zukor was an

unexceptional student. At the age of 12, he was apprenticed to a store owner for whom he swept, ran errands, and did chores. He attended night school twice a week. Zukor got paid nothing for his work, but received clothes and shoes from an orphans' fund. Learning of America from letters sent by immigrants, Zukor decided that he wanted to travel there. In 1888, he asked the orphans' fund for the money to travel to America. He received enough for a steamship ticket and $40, which he sewed inside his vest.

In New York, Zukor found work as an apprentice in a fur shop for $4 a week. With other immigrant boys, he boxed, played baseball, and sang Hungarian songs. He also attended night school. Over the years he saved several thousand dollars. Around age 21, he returned to Hungary for a visit and saw some of Europe. He married Lottie Kaufman, also a Hungarian immigrant, in 1897. The couple had two children, Mildred and Eugene. Zukor started a fur business with his wife's uncle, Morris Kohn. The partners, with two other men, started a penny arcade, complete with peep machines, a shooting gallery, punching bags, stationary bicycles, and candy. The business did very well, bringing in $500 to $700 a day. Zukor decided to get out of the fur business and devote all his time to the arcade. He worked closely with Marcus Loew at this time, becoming treasurer of his company.

Zukor put in a motion picture theater on the floor above the arcade. Called the Crystal Hall, it had a glass staircase with water cascading inside it over colored lights. It cost five cents to see a movie. Zukor developed his own brand of "talking" pictures. He had actors stand behind the movie screen and say their lines in synchronization with the silent action on the screen, which they could see in reverse.

## Film Finds an Audience

At this time, movies, or "flickers" as they were called, were very short, no more than about 12 minutes. People in the industry felt that American audiences would not want to see anything longer. Zukor disagreed. He felt that audiences would sit through a movie for an hour or more, if it had a good story. Zukor tested his theory by buying the rights to a three-reel European religious movie, *Passion Play.* Zukor described the audience's reaction in his autobiography: "The scene was one of the most remarkable I have ever witnessed. Many women viewed the picture with religious awe. Some fell to their knees. I was struck by the moral potentialities of the screen." The film had a good run and proved to Zukor that Americans would sit through longer pictures.

Zukor learned of a French producer, Louis Mercanton, who wanted to make a four-reel movie starring the famous French actress Sarah Bernhardt, in her successful play *Queen Elizabeth.* Mercanton's project was being delayed for lack of funds. Zukor advanced Mercanton $40,000 to secure the North American rights to the movie. He was taking a great risk, but he wanted to see how American audiences reacted to a film of this length. On July 12, 1912, the movie premiered. Zukor noted, "To begin with, the audience had not been restless despite the hour and a half running time. . . . The performance was of historical importance because it went a long way toward breaking down the prejudice of theatrical people toward the screen."

While he had waited for the French film to be made, Zukor tried producing feature films in the U.S. His idea was to make movies of "Famous Players in Famous Plays." However, he had difficulty raising money for the venture. To do so, in 1912 he sold part of his stock in Loew's company and stepped down as treasurer. His other problem was finding stage actors who would appear in films. Zukor discussed the matter with Daniel Frohman, a theatrical producer, who seemed open to the idea of bringing stage actors to the screen. Zukor wrote, "Frohman made no commitments. But I have always placed that night as one of the most important in the history of motion pictures. Thereafter Frohman was a powerful advocate of the movies in the theatrical world." Frohman joined Zukor in business and helped set up the opening of *Queen Elizabeth.*

## Famous Players Film Company

Zukor formed a partnership with Edwin S. Porter, a screen director who agreed to furnish his experience, talent, and prestige, but no money. With him, in their Manhattan studio, the Famous Players Film Company made America's first feature-length film. *The Prisoner of Zenda,* opened successfully in 1914.

Mary Pickford, a famous stage actress, began working for Zukor. She, her mother, and Zukor opened a film studio in California to take advantage of the sunny winters. "Why Hollywood? There was no particular reason. It was an undeveloped suburb of Los Angeles, mostly orange and lemon groves. The chief attraction was a rentable farmhouse suitable for dressing rooms, a small laboratory, and offices. We threw up a rude stage at what is now the corner of Sunset and Hollywood Boulevards." Many movies were still made in the New York studio to be near the stage players, but Zukor spent much time in Hollywood.

In 1916, Famous Players merged with the Jesse L. Lasky Feature Play Company to form the Famous Players-Lasky Corporation, with Samuel Goldwyn as chairman of the board, Cecil De Mille as director-general, Zukor as president, and Lasky as vice-president. In 1914, W.W. Hodkinson founded Paramount Pictures Corporation, whose purpose was to distribute films. When disagreements over policy arose, the stockholders chose Zukor to head the company, feeling that he was best equipped to guide features to success. Once in control, Zukor arranged for a loan of ten million dollars to improve and buy theaters, thus giving Paramount control over the creation, distribution, and exhibition of movies. In the 1920s, Famous Players-Lasky began releasing their films under the Paramount name.

Zukor built the modern film industry using the star system. Players with star potential were tried out in small parts. By studying audience reaction, box-office figures, and fan mail, the studio attempted to determine which player people wanted to see on the screen. If the audience liked a player, the studio would supply the right roles and publicity. Often the audience surprised the studio by favoring an actor not thought to be star material. Zukor noted that the idea of a producer "discovering" a star is "nonsense." "Stardom is a matter over which only audiences have any real control."

To keep an eye on things, Zukor made a habit of visiting movie sets every morning. This way he got to know the players and technicians. "Besides putting me closer to production, I hoped that such visits would make everybody feel that the business office was more than a place where we made contracts and counted the money. The fact was that we kept as close tabs on the human element as on box-office receipts. Also, I was secretly envious of those who had an intimate hand in production. . . . "

In 1928, the first all-talking movie was released. Paramount began using a sound system called Photophone for some of its films. Since it took a while for movie theaters to acquire and install sound systems, Paramount continued to make silent pictures, which were often made into talkies later. In the *1929 Film Daily Year Book,* Zukor stated, "The year will be memorable for the proper development of the talking picture. The year will see the balance struck between talking pictures, sound pictures, and silent pictures. By no means is the silent picture gone or even diminished in importance. Yet there is no doubt that sound pictures have entered permanently to serve as a vital screen force. . . . There have always been subjects which could not be augmented in value and strength by the addition of sound and dialogue. Such subjects will always continue to be made in their natural form: —Silence."

## Guided Paramount Through Hard Times

During the Depression, the company fell on hard times and many failed attempts were made to get rid of Zukor. In 1932, he restructured the company. Four years later, he became the chairman of the board. He retained that honorary title until his death. In 1948, Zukor received a special Academy Award for his services to the industry over a period of 40 years. He died in Los Angeles on June 10, 1976, at the age of 103.

## Further Reading

Zukor, Adolph, with Dale Kramer, *The Public is Never Wrong: The Autobiography of Adolph Zukor,* G.P. Putnam's Sons, 1953.

*Cornell Hotel & Restaurant Administration Quarterly,* April 1995.

*New York Times,* July 10, 1987.

''Successful Soundtracks to Accompany Silent Films,'' *Silent Soundtrack Success Stories,* http://www.zzapp.org/freepark/sss.htm (March 9, 1999).

''Unequalled Distribution: Adolph Zukor,'' *The Film 100,* http://www.film100.com/cgi/direct.cgi?v.zuko (March 9, 1999). □

# INDEX

# HOW TO USE THE *SUPPLEMENT* INDEX

The *Encyclopedia of World Biography Supplement* Index is designed to serve several purposes. First, it is a cumulative listing of biographies included in the entire set (volumes 1-19). Second, it locates information on thousands of specific topics mentioned in volume 19 of the encyclopedia—persons, places, events, organizations, institutions, ideas, titles of works, inventions, as well as artistic schools, styles, and movements. Third, it classifies the subjects of *Supplement* articles according to shared characteristics. Vocational categories are the most numerous—for example, Artists, Authors, Military leaders, Philosophers, Scientists, Statesmen. Other groupings bring together disparate people who share a common characteristic.

The structure of the *Supplement* Index is quite simple. The biographical entries are cumulative and often provide enough information to meet immediate reference needs. Thus, people mentioned in the *Supplement* Index are identified and their life dates, when known, are given. Because this is an index to a *biographical* encyclopedia, every reference includes the *name* of the article to which the reader is directed as well as the volume and page numbers. Below are a few points that will make the *Supplement* Index easy to use.

*Typography.* All main entries are set in boldface type. Entries that are also the titles of articles in *EWB* are set entirely in capitals; other main entries are set in initial capitals and lowercase letters. Where a main entry is followed by a great many references, these are organized by subentries in alphabetical sequence. In certain cases—for example, the names of countries for which there are many references—a special class of subentries, set in small capitals and preceded by boldface dots, is used to mark significant divisions.

*Alphabetization.* The Index is alphabetized word by word. For example, all entries beginning with *New* as a separate word *(New Jersey, New York)* come before *Newark.* Commas in inverted entries are treated as full

stops *(Berlin; Berlin, Congress of; Berlin, University of; Berlin Academy of Sciences).* Other commas are ignored in filing. When words are identical, persons come first and subsequent entries are alphabetized by their parenthetical qualifiers (such as *book, city, painting*).

Titled persons may be alphabetized by family name or by title. The more familiar form is used—for example, *Disraeli, Benjamin* rather than *Beaconsfield, Earl of.* Cross-references are provided from alternative forms and spellings of names. Identical names of the same nationality are filed chronologically.

Titles of books, plays, poems, paintings, and other works of art beginning with an article are filed on the following word *(Bard, The).* Titles beginning with a preposition are filed on the preposition *(In Autumn).* In subentries, however, prepositions are ignored; thus *influenced by* would precede the subentry *in* literature.

Literary characters are filed on the last name. Acronyms, such as UNESCO, are treated as single words. Abbreviations, such as *Mr., Mrs.,* and *St.,* are alphabetized as though they were spelled out.

Occupational categories are alphabetical by national qualifier. Thus, *Authors, Scottish* comes before *Authors, Spanish,* and the reader interested in Spanish poets will find the subentry *poets* under *Authors, Spanish.*

*Cross-references.* The term *see* is used in references throughout the *Supplement* Index. The *see* references appear both as main entries and as subentries They most often direct the reader from an alternative name spelling or form to the main entry listing.

This introduction to the *Supplement* Index is necessarily brief. The reader will soon find, however, that the *Supplement* Index provides ready reference to both highly specific subjects and broad areas of information contained in volume 19 and a cumulative listing of those included in the entire set.

# INDEX

## A

**AALTO, HUGO ALVAR HENRIK** (born 1898), Finnish architect, designer, and town planner **1** 1–2

**AARON, HENRY LOUIS** (Hank; born 1934), American baseball player **1** 2–3

**ABBA ARIKA** (circa 175–circa 247), Babylonian rabbi **1** 3–4

**ABBAS I** (1571–1629), Safavid shah of Persia 1588–1629 **1** 4–6

**ABBAS, FERHAT** (born 1899), Algerian statesman **1** 6–7

**ABBOTT, BERENICE** (1898–1991), American artist and photographer **1** 7–9

**ABBOTT, GRACE** (1878–1939), American social worker and agency administrator **1** 9–10

**ABBOTT, LYMAN** (1835–1922), American Congregationalist clergyman, author, and editor **1** 10–11

**ABBOUD, EL FERIK IBRAHIM** (1900–1983), Sudanese general, prime minister, 1958–1964 **1** 11–12

**ABC**
see American Broadcasting Company

**ABD AL-MALIK** (646–705), Umayyad caliph 685–705 **1** 12–13

**ABD AL-MUMIN** (circa 1094–1163), Almohad caliph 1133–63 **1** 13

**ABD AL-RAHMAN I** (731–788), Umayyad emir in Spain 756–88 **1** 13–14

**ABD AL-RAHMAN III** (891–961), Umayyad caliph of Spain **1** 14

**ABD EL-KADIR** (1807–1883), Algerian political and religious leader **1** 15

**ABD EL-KRIM EL-KHATABI, MOHAMED BEN** (circa 1882–1963), Moroccan Berber leader **1** 15–16

**Abdications** (politics)
Great Britain
Simpson, Wallis **19** 343–345

**ABDUH IBN HASAN KHAYR ALLAH, MUHAMMAD** (1849–1905), Egyptian nationalist and theologian **1** 16–17

**ABDUL RAHMAN, TUNKU** (1903–1990), Former prime minister of Malaysia **18** 340–341

**ABDUL-HAMID II** (1842–1918), Ottoman sultan 1876–1909 **1** 17–18

**'ABDULLAH AL-SALIM AL-SABAH, SHAYKH** (1895–1965), Amir of Kuwait (1950–1965) **1** 18–19

**ABDULLAH IBN HUSEIN** (1882–1951), king of Jordan 1949–1951, of Transjordan 1946–49 **1** 19–20

**ABDULLAH IBN YASIN** (died 1059), North African founder of the Almoravid movement **1** 20

**ABE, KOBO** (born Kimifusa Abe; also transliterated as Abe Kobo; 1924–1993), Japanese writer, theater director, photographer **1** 20–22

**ABEL, IORWITH WILBER** (1908–1987), United States labor organizer **1** 22–23

**ABELARD, PETER** (1079–1142), French philosopher and theologian **1** 23–25

**ABERDEEN, 4TH EARL OF** (George Hamilton Gordon; 1784–1860), British statesman, prime minister 1852–55 **1** 25–26

**ABERHART, WILLIAM** (1878–1943), Canadian statesman and educator **1** 26–27

**ABERNATHY, RALPH DAVID** (born 1926), United States minister and civil rights leader **1** 27–28

**ABIOLA, MOSHOOD** (1937–1998), Nigerian politician, philanthropist, and businessman **19** 1–3

**ABRAHAMS, ISRAEL** (1858–1925), British scholar **1** 29

**ABRAMOVITZ, MAX** (born 1908), American architect **18** 1–3

**ABRAMS, CREIGHTON W.** (1914–1974), United States Army commander in World War II and Vietnam **1** 29–31

**ABRAVANEL, ISAAC BEN JUDAH** (1437–1508), Jewish philosopher and statesman **1** 31

**ABU BAKR** (circa 573–634), Moslem leader, first caliph of Islam **1** 31–32

**ABU MUSA** (born Said Musa Maragha circa 1930), a leader of the Palestinian Liberation Organization **1** 32–33

**ABU NUWAS** (al-Hasan ibn-Hani; circa 756–813), Arab poet **1** 33–34

**ABU-L-ALA AL-MAARRI** (973–1058), Arab poet and philosopher **1** 32

**ABZUG, BELLA STAVISKY** (1920–1998), lawyer, politician, and congresswoman **1** 34–35

**Academy of Motion Picture Arts and Sciences** (United States, established 1927)
Fairbanks, Douglas **19** 107–108

**ACHEBE, CHINUA** (born 1930), Nigerian novelist **1** 35–37

**ACHESON, DEAN GOODERHAM** (1893–1971), American statesman **1** 37–38

**Acquired immune deficiency syndrome** (AIDS)

**445**

**ANDREWS, CHARLES McLEAN** (1863–1943), American historian **1** 231

**ANDREWS, FANNIE FERN PHILLIPS** (1867–1950), American educator, reformer, pacifist **1** 231–232

**ANDREWS, ROY CHAPMAN** (1884–1960), American naturalist and explorer **1** 232–233

**ANDROPOV, IURY VLADIMIROVICH** (1914–1984), head of the Soviet secret police and ruler of the Soviet Union (1982–1984) **1** 233–234

**ANDROS, SIR EDMUND** (1637–1714), English colonial governor in America **1** 234–235

**ANDRUS, ETHEL** (1884–1976), American educator and founder of the American Association of Retired Persons **19** 5–7

**ANGELICO, FRA** (circa 1400–1455), Italian painter **1** 235–236

**ANGELL, JAMES ROWLAND** (1869–1949), psychologist and leader in higher education **1** 236–237

**ANGELOU, MAYA** (Marguerite Johnson; born 1928), American author, poet, playwright, stage and screen performer, and director **1** 238–239

**Anheuser-Busch**
Busch, Adolphus **19** 47–49

**ANNA IVANOVNA** (1693–1740), empress of Russia 1730–1740 **1** 240–241

**ANNAN, KOFI** (born 1938), Ghanaian secretary-general of the United Nations **18** 19–21

**ANNE** (1665–1714), queen of England 1702–1714 and of Great Britain 1707–1714 **1** 241–242

**ANOKYE, OKOMFO** (Kwame Frimpon Anokye; flourished late 17th century), Ashanti priest and statesman **1** 242–243

**ANOUILH, JEAN** (1910–1987), French playwright **1** 243–244

**ANSELM OF CANTERBURY, ST.** (1033–1109), Italian archbishop and theologian **1** 244–245

**ANTHONY, ST.** (circa 250–356), Egyptian hermit and monastic founder **1** 246–248

**ANTHONY, SUSAN BROWNELL** (1820–1906), American leader of suffrage movement **1** 246–248

**ANTIGONUS I** (382–301 B.C.), king of Macedon 306–301 B.C. **1** 248–249

**ANTIOCHUS III** (241–187 B.C.), king of Syria 223–187 B.C. **1** 249–250

**ANTIOCHUS IV** (circa 215–163 B.C.), king of Syria 175–163 B.C. **1** 250

**ANTISTHENES** (circa 450–360 B.C.), Greek philosopher **1** 250–251

**ANTONELLO DA MESSINA** (circa 1430–1479), Italian painter **1** 251–252

**ANTONIONI, MICHELANGELO** (born 1912), Italian film director **1** 252–253

**ANTONY, MARK** (circa 82–30 B.C.), Roman politician and general **1** 253–254

**ANZA, JUAN BAUTISTA DE** (1735–1788), Spanish explorer **1** 254–255

**AOUN, MICHEL** (born 1935), Christian Lebanese military leader and prime minister **1** 255–257

**APELLES** (flourished after 350 B.C.), Greek painter **1** 257

**APGAR, VIRGINIA** (1909–1974), American medical educator, researcher **1** 257–259

**APITHY, SOUROU MIGAN** (1913–1989), Dahomean political leader **1** 259–260

**APOLLINAIRE, GUILLAUME** (1880–1918), French lyric poet **1** 260

**APOLLODORUS** (flourished circa 408 B.C.), Greek painter **1** 261

**APOLLONIUS OF PERGA** (flourished 210 B.C.), Greek mathematician **1** 261–262

**APPELFELD, AHARON** (born 1932), Israeli who wrote about anti-Semitism and the Holocaust **1** 262–263

**APPIA, ADOLPHE** (1862–1928), Swiss stage director **1** 263–264

**Apple Computer Company**
Rock, Arthur **19** 316–317
Wozniak, Steve **19** 430–432

**APPLEGATE, JESSE** (1811–1888), American surveyor, pioneer, and rancher **1** 264–265

**APPLETON, SIR EDWARD VICTOR** (1892–1965), British pioneer in radio physics **1** 265–266

**APPLETON, NATHAN** (1779–1861), American merchant and manufacturer **1** 266–267

**AQUINO, BENIGNO** ("Nino"; 1933–1983), Filipino activist murdered upon his return from exile **1** 267–268

**AQUINO, CORAZON COJOANGCO** (born 1933), first woman president of the Republic of the Philippines **1** 268–270

**ARAFAT, YASSER** (also spelled Yasir; born 1929), chairman of the Palestinian Liberation Organization **1** 270–271

**ARAGON, LOUIS** (1897–1982), French surrealist author **1** 271–272

**ARANHA, OSVALDO** (1894–1960), Brazilian political leader **1** 272–273

**ARATUS** (271–213 B.C.), Greek statesman and general **1** 273–274

**ARBENZ GUZMÁN, JACOBO** (1913–1971), president of Guatemala (1951–1954) **1** 274–276

**Arbitration, industrial**
see Labor unions

**ARBUS, DIANE NEMEROV** (1923–1971), American photographer **1** 276–277
Model, Lisette **19** 254–256

**ARCHIMEDES** (circa 287–212 B.C.), Greek mathematician **1** 277–280

**ARCHIPENKO, ALEXANDER** (1887–1964), Russian-American sculptor and teacher **1** 280–281

**Architecture**
Foster, Norman **19** 115–117

**ARDEN, ELIZABETH** (Florence Nightingale Graham; 1878?–1966), American businesswoman **1** 281–282

**ARENDT, HANNAH** (1906–1975), Jewish philosopher **1** 282–284

**ARENS, MOSHE** (born 1925), aeronautical engineer who became a leading Israeli statesman **1** 284–285

**ARÉVALO, JUAN JOSÉ** (1904–1951), Guatemalan statesman, president 1944–1951 **1** 285–286

**ARIAS, ARNULFO** (1901–1988), thrice elected president of Panama **1** 286–287

**ARIAS SANCHEZ, OSCAR** (born 1941), Costa Rican politician, social activist, president, and Nobel Peace Laureate (1987) **1** 287–289

**ARIOSTO, LUDOVICO** (1474–1533), Italian poet and playwright **1** 289–290

**ARISTARCHUS OF SAMOS** (circa 310–230 B.C.), Greek astronomer **1** 290–291

**ARISTIDE, JEAN-BERTRAND** (born 1953), president of Haiti (1990–91 and 1994–95); deposed by a military coup in 1991; restored to power in 1994 **1** 291–293

**ARISTOPHANES** (450/445–after 385 B.C.), Greek playwright **1** 293–294

**BLUFORD, GUION STEWART, JR.** (born 1942), African American aerospace engineer, pilot, and astronaut **2** 341–343

**BLUM, LÉON** (1872–1950), French statesman **2** 343–344

**BLUME, JUDY** (born Judy Sussman; b. 1938), American fiction author **2** 344–345

**BLUMENTHAL, WERNER MICHAEL** (born 1926), American businessman and treasury secretary **2** 345–346

**BLY, NELLIE** (born Elizabeth Cochrane Seaman; 1864–1922), American journalist and reformer **2** 346–348

**BLYDEN, EDWARD WILMOT** (1832–1912), Liberian statesman **2** 348–349

**BOAS, FRANZ** (1858–1942), German-born American anthropologist **2** 349–351

**BOCCACCIO, GIOVANNI** (1313–1375), Italian author **2** 351–353

**BOCCIONI, UMBERTO** (1882–1916), Italian artist **2** 353–354

**BÖCKLIN, ARNOLD** (1827–1901), Swiss painter **2** 354–355

**BODE, BOYD HENRY** (1873–1953), American philosopher and educator **2** 355–356

**BODIN, JEAN** (1529/30–1596), French political philosopher **2** 356–357

**BOEHME, JACOB** (1575–1624), German mystic **2** 357

**BOEING, WILLIAM EDWARD** (1881–1956), American businessman **2** 357–358

**BOERHAAVE, HERMANN** (1668–1738), Dutch physician and chemist **2** 358–359

**BOESAK, ALLAN AUBREY** (born 1945), opponent of apartheid in South Africa and founder of the United Democratic Front **2** 359–360

**BOETHIUS, ANICIUS MANLIUS SEVERINUS** (480?–524/525), Roman logician and theologian **2** 360–361

**BOFFRAND, GABRIEL GERMAIN** (1667–1754), French architect and decorator **2** 361

**BOFILL, RICARDO** (born 1939), post-modern Spanish architect **2** 362–363

**BOGART, HUMPHREY** (1899–1957), American stage and screen actor **2** 363–364

**BOHEMUND I** (of Tarantò; circa 1055–1111), Norman Crusader **2** 364

**BOHLEN, CHARLES (CHIP) EUSTIS** (1904–1973), United States ambassador to the Soviet Union, interpreter, and presidential adviser **2** 364–366

**BÖHM-BAWERK, EUGEN VON** (1851–1914), Austrian economist **2** 366

**BOHR, NIELS HENRIK DAVID** (1885–1962), Danish physicist **2** 366–368

**BOIARDO, MATTEO MARIA** (Conte di Scandiano; 1440/41–1494), Italian poet **2** 369

**BOILEAU-DESPRÉAUX, NICHOLAS** (1636?–1711), French critic and writer **2** 369–371

**BOK, DEREK CURTIS** (born 1930), dean of the Harvard Law School and president of Harvard University **2** 371–372

**BOK, SISSELA ANN** (born 1934), American moral philosopher **2** 372–374

**BOLEYN, ANNE** (1504?–1536), second wife of Henry VIII **18** 47–49

**BOLINGBROKE, VISCOUNT** (Henry St. John; 1678–1751), English statesman **2** 374–375

**BOLÍVAR, SIMÓN** (1783–1830), South American general and statesman **2** 375–377

**BOLKIAH, HASSANAL** (Muda Hassanal Bolkiah Mu'izzaddin Waddaulah; born 1946), Sultan of Brunei **18** 49–51

**BÖLL, HEINRICH** (1917–1985), German writer and translator **2** 377–378

**BOLTWOOD, BERTRAM BORDEN** (1870–1927), American radiochemist **2** 378–379

**BOLTZMANN, LUDWIG** (1844–1906), Austrian physicist **2** 379–380

**BOMBAL, MARÍA LUISA** (1910–1980), Chilean novelist and story writer **2** 380–381

**BONAPARTE, JOSEPH** (1768–1844), French statesman, king of Naples 1806–1808 and of Spain 1808–1813 **2** 381–382

**BONAPARTE, LOUIS** (1778–1846), French statesman, king of Holland 1806–1810 **2** 382–383

**BONAVENTURE, ST.** (1217–1274), Italian theologian and philosopher **2** 383–384

**BOND, HORACE MANN** (1904–1972), African American educator **2** 384–386

**BOND, JULIAN** (born 1940), civil rights leader elected to the Georgia House of Representatives **2** 386–387

**BONDFIELD, MARGARET GRACE** (1873–1953), British union official and political leader **2** 388–389

**BONDI, HERMANN** (born 1919), English mathematician and cosmologist **18** 51–52

**BONHOEFFER, DIETRICH** (1906–1945), German theologian **2** 389–391

**BONHEUR, ROSA** (Marie Rosalie Bonheur; 1822–1899), French artist **19** 29–31

**BONIFACE, ST.** (circa 672–754), English monk **2** 391

**BONIFACE VIII** (Benedetto Caetani; 1235?–1303), pope 1294–1303 **2** 392–393

**BONIFACIO, ANDRES** (1863–1897), Filipino revolutionary hero **2** 393–394

**BONINGTON, RICHARD PARKES** (1802–1828), English painter **2** 394–395

**BONNARD, PIERRE** (1867–1947), French painter **2** 395–396

**BONNIN, GERTRUDE SIMMONS** (Zitkala-Sa; Red Bird; 1876–1938), Native American author and activist **18** 52–54

**BONO, SONNY** (Salvatore Bono; 1935–1998), American entertainer and U.S. Congressman **18** 54–56

**BONVALOT, PIERRE GABRIEL ÉDOUARD** (1853–1933), French explorer and author **2** 396

**BOOLE, GEORGE** (1815–1864), English mathematician **2** 396–397

**BOONE, DANIEL** (1734–1820), American frontiersman and explorer **2** 397–398

**BOORSTIN, DANIEL J.** (born 1914), American historian **2** 398–400

**BOOTH, CHARLES** (1840–1916), English social scientist **2** 400–401

**BOOTH, EDWIN** (1833–1893), American actor **2** 401–402

**BOOTH, EVANGELINE CORY** (1865–1950), British/American humanist **2** 402–403

**BOOTH, JOHN WILKES** (1838–1865), American actor **2** 404

**BOOTH, JOSEPH** (1851–1932), English missionary in Africa **2** 404–405

**BOOTH, WILLIAM** (1829–1912), English evangelist, Salvation Army founder **2** 405–406

BRADBURY, RAY (born 1920), American fantasy and science fiction writer **2** 473–474

BRADDOCK, EDWARD (1695–1755), British commander in North America **2** 474–475

BRADFORD, WILLIAM (1590–1657), leader of Plymouth Colony **2** 475–476

BRADFORD, WILLIAM (1663–1752), American printer **2** 476–477

BRADFORD, WILLIAM (1722–1791), American journalist **2** 477

BRADLAUGH, CHARLES (1833–1891), English freethinker and political agitator **2** 478

BRADLEY, ED (born 1941), African American broadcast journalist **2** 478–481

BRADLEY, FRANCIS HERBERT (1846–1924), English philosopher **2** 481–482

BRADLEY, JAMES (1693–1762), English astronomer **2** 482–483

BRADLEY, MARION ZIMMER (born 1930), American author **18** 60–62

BRADLEY, OMAR NELSON (1893–1981), American general **2** 483–484

BRADLEY, TOM (born 1917), first African American mayor of Los Angeles **2** 484–485

BRADMAN, SIR DONALD GEORGE (born 1908), Australian cricketer **2** 485–486

BRADSTREET, ANNE DUDLEY (circa 1612–1672), English-born American poet **2** 486–487

BRADY, MATHEW B. (circa 1823–1896), American photographer **2** 487–488

BRAGG, SIR WILLIAM HENRY (1862–1942), English physicist **2** 488–489

BRAHE, TYCHO (1546–1601), Danish astronomer **2** 489–490

BRAHMS, JOHANNES (1833–1897), German composer **2** 490–492

BRAILLE, LOUIS (1809–1852), French teacher and creator of braille system **2** 492–493

BRAMANTE, DONATO (1444–1514), Italian architect and painter **2** 493–494

BRANCUSI, CONSTANTIN (1876–1957), Romanian sculptor in France **2** 494–496

BRANDEIS, LOUIS DEMBITZ (1856–1941), American jurist **2** 496–497

BRANDO, MARLON (born 1924), American actor **2** 497–499

BRANDT, WILLY (Herbert Frahm Brandt; 1913–1992), German statesman, chancellor of West Germany **2** 499–500

BRANSON, RICHARD (born 1950), British entrepreneur **19** 34–36

BRANT, JOSEPH (1742–1807), Mohawk Indian chief **2** 500–501

BRANT, MARY (1736–1796), Native American who guided the Iroquois to a British alliance **2** 501–503

BRANT, SEBASTIAN (1457–1521), German author **2** 503–504

BRAQUE, GEORGES (1882–1967), French painter **2** 504–505

BRATTAIN, WALTER H. (1902–1987), American physicist and co-inventor of the transistor **2** 505–507

BRAUDEL, FERNAND (1902–1985), leading exponent of the *Annales* school of history **2** 507–508

BRAUN, FERDINAND (1850–1918), German recipient of the Nobel Prize in Physics for work on wireless telegraphy **2** 508–509

**Brazil, Federative Republic of** (nation; South America)
rainforest preservation
Mendes, Chico **19** 243–245

BRAZZA, PIERRE PAUL FRANÇOIS CAMILLE SAVORGNAN DE (1852–1905), Italian-born French explorer **2** 509–510

BREASTED, JAMES HENRY (1865–1935), American Egyptologist and archeologist **2** 510–511

BRÉBEUF, JEAN DE (1593–1649), French Jesuit missionary **2** 511–512

BRECHT, BERTOLT (1898–1956), German playwright **2** 512–514

BRENNAN, WILLIAM J., JR. (born 1906), United States Supreme Court justice **2** 514–515

BRENTANO, CLEMENS (1778–1842), German poet and novelist **2** 515–516

BRENTANO, FRANZ CLEMENS (1838–1917), German philosopher **2** 516–517

BRESHKOVSKY, CATHERINE (1844–1934), Russian revolutionary **2** 517–519

BRETON, ANDRÉ (1896–1966), French author **2** 519–520

BREUER, MARCEL (1902–1981), Hungarian-born American architect **2** 520–521

BREUIL, HENRI EDOUARD PROSPER (1877–1961), French archeologist **2** 521–522

**Breweries**
Busch, Adolphus **19** 47–49
Coors, Adolph **19** 76–78

BREWSTER, KINGMAN, JR. (1919–1988), president of Yale University (1963–1977) **2** 522–523

BREWSTER, WILLIAM (circa 1566–1644), English-born Pilgrim leader **2** 523–524

BREYER, STEPHEN (born 1938), U.S. Supreme Court justice **2** 524–527

BREZHNEV, LEONID ILICH (1906–1982), general secretary of the Communist party of the Union of Soviet Socialist Republics (1964–1982) and president of the Union of Soviet Socialist Republics (1977–1982) **2** 527–528

BRIAN BORU (940?–1014), Irish king **18** 62–64

BRIAND, ARISTIDE (1862–1932), French statesman **2** 528–529

BRICE, FANNY (1891–1951), vaudeville, Broadway, film, and radio singer and comedienne **3** 1–2

BRIDGER, JAMES (1804–1881), American fur trader and scout **3** 2–3

BRIDGES, HARRY A.R. (1901–1990), radical American labor leader **3** 3–5

BRIDGMAN, PERCY WILLIAMS (1882–1961), American physicist **3** 5–6

BRIGHT, JOHN (1811–1889), English politician **3** 6–7

BRIGHT, RICHARD (1789–1858), English physician **3** 7–8

BRIGHTMAN, EDGAR SHEFFIELD (1884–1953), philosopher of religion and exponent of American Personalism **3** 8–9

BRISBANE, ALBERT (1809–1890), American social theorist **3** 9

BRISTOW, BENJAMIN HELM (1832–1896), American lawyer and Federal official **3** 9–10

**British India**
*see* India (British rule)

BRITTEN, BENJAMIN (1913–1976), English composer **3** 10–11

BROAD, CHARLIE DUNBAR (1887–1971), English philosopher **3** 12

**CLAPHAM, SIR JOHN HAROLD** (1873–1946), English economic historian **4** 71

**CLAPP, MARGARET ANTOINETTE** (1910–1974), American author, educator, and president of Wellesley College (1949–1966) **4** 71–72

**CLAPPERTON, HUGH** (1788–1827), Scottish explorer of Africa **4** 72–73

**CLAPTON, ERIC** (born 1945), English guitarist, singer, and songwriter **18** 90–92

**CLARENDON, 1ST EARL OF** (Edward Hyde; 1609–1674), English statesman and historian **4** 73–75

**CLARK, GEORGE ROGERS** (1752–1818), American Revolutionary War soldier **4** 75–76

**CLARK, JOHN BATES** (1847–1938), American economist **4** 76–77

**CLARK, JOHN MAURICE** (1884–1963), American economist **4** 77–78

**CLARK, KENNETH B.** (born 1914), American social psychologist **4** 78–79

**CLARK, KENNETH M.** (Lord; 1903–1983), English art historian **4** 79–80

**CLARK, MARK WAYNE** (1896–1984), American general **4** 80–81

**CLARK, TOM CAMPBELL** (1899–1977), President Harry S. Truman's attorney general and Supreme Court justice **4** 81–82

**CLARK, WILLIAM** (1770–1838), American explorer and soldier **4** 82–83

**CLARK, WILLIAM ANDREWS** (1839–1925), American copper entrepreneur and politician **4** 83–85

**CLARKE, ARTHUR CHARLES** (born 1917), English author **18** 92–94

**CLARKE, KENNETH HARRY** (born 1940), Conservative politician and Great Britain's chancellor of the exchequer (1993–) **4** 85–87

**CLARKE, MARCUS ANDREW HISLOP** (1846–1881), English-born Australian journalist and author **4** 87–88

**CLARKE, SAMUEL** (1675–1729), English theologian and philosopher **4** 88

**CLAUDE LORRAIN** (1600–1682), French painter, draftsman, and etcher **4** 89–90

**CLAUDEL, PAUL LOUIS CHARLES** (1868–1955), French author and diplomat **4** 90–91

**CLAUDIUS GERMANICUS, TIBERIUS** (Claudius I; 10 B.C.–A.D. 54), emperor of Rome 41–54 **4** 91–92

**CLAUSIUS, RUDOLF JULIUS EMANUEL** (1822–1888), German physicist **4** 92–94

**CLAVER, ST. PETER** (1580–1654), Spanish Jesuit missionary **4** 94

**CLAY, HENRY** (1777–1852), American lawyer and statesman **4** 94–96

**CLAYTON, JOHN MIDDLETON** (1796–1856), American lawyer and statesman **4** 96–97

**CLEAVER, LEROY ELDRIDGE** (1935–1998), American writer and Black Panther leader **4** 97–98

**CLEISTHENES** (flourished 6th century B.C.), Athenian statesman **4** 98–99

**CLEMENCEAU, GEORGES** (1841–1929), French statesman **4** 99–101

**CLEMENS NON PAPA, JACOBUS** (circa 1510–circa 1556), Flemish composer **4** 101

**CLEMENT V** (1264–1314), pope 1304–1314 **4** 101–102

**CLEMENT OF ALEXANDRIA** (circa 150–circa 215), Christian theologian **4** 102–103

**CLEMENTE, ROBERTO** (1934–1972), Hispanic American baseball player **19** 70–72

**CLEOMENES I** (flourished circa 520–490 B.C.), Spartan king **4** 103

**CLEOMENES III** (circa 260–219 B.C.), king of Sparta 235–219 **4** 103–104

**CLEON** (circa 475–422 B.C.), Athenian political leader **4** 104–105

**CLEOPATRA** (69–30 B.C.), queen of Egypt **4** 105–106

**CLEVELAND, JAMES** (1932–1991), African American singer, songwriter, and pianist **4** 106–108

**CLEVELAND, STEPHEN GROVER** (1837–1908), American statesman, twice president **4** 108–110

**CLINE, PATSY** (born Virginia Patterson Hensley; 1932–1963), American singer **4** 110–112

**CLINTON, DeWITT** (1769–1828), American lawyer and statesman **4** 112–113

**CLINTON, GEORGE** (1739–1812), American patriot and statesman **4** 113–114

**CLINTON, SIR HENRY** (1738?–1795), British commander in chief during the American Revolution **4** 114–115

**CLINTON, HILLARY RODHAM** (born 1947), American politician and first lady **4** 115–117

**CLINTON, WILLIAM JEFFERSON** (''Bill'' Clinton; born 1946), 42nd president of the United States **4** 117–119

**CLIVE, ROBERT** (Baron Clive of Plassey; 1725–1774), English soldier and statesman **4** 119–120

**CLODION** (1738–1814), French sculptor **4** 121

**CLODIUS PULCHER, PUBLIUS** (died 52 B.C.), Roman politician **4** 121–122

**Clothing industry**
Bauer, Eddie **19** 13–14
Hilfiger, Tommy **19** 144–146
Knight, Phil **19** 183–186

**CLOUET, FRANÇOIS** (circa 1516–circa 1572), French portrait painter **4** 122–123

**CLOUET, JEAN** (circa 1485–circa 1541), French portrait painter **4** 122–123

**CLOUGH, ARTHUR HUGH** (1819–1861), English poet **4** 123–124

**CLOVIS I** (465–511), Frankish king **4** 124

**COBB, TYRUS RAYMOND** (1886–1961), baseball player **4** 124–126

**COBBETT, WILLIAM** (1763–1835), English journalist and politician **4** 126–127

**COBDEN, RICHARD** (1804–1865), English politician **4** 127–128

**COCHISE** (circa 1825–1874), American Chiricahua Apache Indian chief **4** 128

**COCHRAN, JACQUELINE** (Jackie Cochran; 1910–1980), American aviator and businesswoman **18** 94–96

**COCHRAN, JOHNNIE** (born 1937), African American lawyer **4** 128–131

**COCKCROFT, JOHN DOUGLAS** (1897–1967), English physicist **4** 131–132

**COCTEAU, JEAN** (1889–1963), French writer **4** 132–133

**COEN, JAN PIETERSZOON** (circa 1586–1629), Dutch governor general of Batavia **4** 133

**COETZEE, J(OHN) M.** (born 1940), white South African novelist **4** 133–135

**COFFIN, LEVI** (1789–1877), American antislavery reformer **4** 135

**COFFIN, WILLIAM SLOANE, JR.** (born 1924), Yale University chaplain who spoke out against the Vietnam War **4** 135–137

# D

member of British royal family **4** 529–533

**DIAS DE NOVAIS, BARTOLOMEU** (died 1500), Portuguese explorer **4** 533–534

**DÍAZ, PORFIRIO** (José de la Cruz Porfirio Díaz; 1830–1915), Mexican general and politician **4** 534–536

**DÍAZ DEL CASTILLO, BERNAL** (circa 1496–circa 1584), Spanish soldier and historian **4** 536–537

**DÍAZ ORDAZ, GUSTAVO** (1911–1979), president of Mexico (1964–1970) **4** 537–538

**DICKENS, CHARLES JOHN HUFFAM** (1812–1870), English author **4** 538–541

**DICKEY, JAMES** (1923–1997), American poet **19** 87–89

**DICKINSON, EMILY** (1830–1886), American poet **4** 541–543

**DICKINSON, JOHN** (1732–1808), American lawyer, pamphleteer, and politician **4** 543–544

**DIDEROT, DENIS** (1713–1784), French philosopher, playwright, and encyclopedist **5** 1–2

**DIEBENKORN, RICHARD** (born 1922), American abstract expressionist painter **5** 2–4

**DIEFENBAKER, JOHN GEORGE** (1895–1979), Canadian statesman **5** 4–5

**DIELS, (OTTO PAUL) HERMANN** (1876–1954), German organic chemist **5** 5–6

**DIEM, NGO DINH** (1901–1963), South Vietnamese president 1955–1963 **5** 6–7

**DIESEL, RUDOLF** (1858–1913), German mechanical engineer **5** 7

**DIKE, KENNETH** (Kenneth Onwuka Dike; 1917–1983), African historian who set up the Nigerian National Archives **5** 7–8

**DILLINGER, JOHN** (1903–1934), American criminal **5** 9

**DILTHEY, WILHELM CHRISTIAN LUDWIG** (1833–1911), German historian and philosopher **5** 10

**DIMAGGIO, JOE** (born Giuseppe Paolo DiMaggio, Jr.; b. 1914), American baseball player **5** 10–11

**DIMITROV, GEORGI** (1882–1949), head of the Communist International (1935–1943) and prime minister of Bulgaria (1944–1949) **5** 11–13

**DINESEN BLIXEN-FINECKE, KAREN** (a.k.a. Isak Dinesen; 1885–1962), Danish author **5** 13–14

**DINGANE** (circa 1795–1840), Zulu king **5** 14–15

**DINKINS, DAVID** (born 1927), African American politician and mayor of New York City **5** 15–18

**DINWIDDIE, ROBERT** (1693–1770), Scottish merchant and colonial governor **5** 18–19

**DIOCLETIAN** (Gaius Aurelius Valerius Diocletianus; 245–circa 313), Roman emperor 284–305 **5** 19–20

**DIOGENES** (circa 400–325 B.C.), Greek philosopher **5** 20–21

**DIOP, CHEIKH ANTA** (1923–1986), African historian **5** 21–22

**DIOR, CHRISTIAN** (1905–1957), French fashion designer **5** 22

**Diplomats, American**
20th century (in England)
Kennedy, Joseph **19** 176–178
20th century (in Union of Soviet Socialist Republics)
Watson, Thomas J. Jr. **19** 408–410

**DIRAC, PAUL ADRIEN MAURICE** (1902–1984), English physicist **5** 23–24

**DIRKSEN, EVERETT McKINLEY** (1896–1969), Republican congressman and senator from Illinois **5** 24–26

**DISNEY, WALTER ELIAS** (1901–1966), American film maker and entrepreneur **5** 26–27

**DISRAELI, BENJAMIN** (1st Earl of Beaconsfield; 1804–1881), English statesman, prime minister 1868 and 1874–1880 **5** 27–29

**District of Columbia**
*see* Washington, D.C.

**DIVINE, FATHER** (born George Baker?; c. 1877–1965), African American religious leader **5** 29–32

**DIX, DOROTHEA LYNDE** (1802–1887), American reformer **5** 32–33

**DIX, OTTO** (1891–1969), German painter and graphic artist **5** 33–34

**DJILAS, MILOVAN** (1911–1995), Yugoslavian writer **5** 34

**DO MUOI** (born 1917), prime minister of the Socialist Republic of Vietnam (1988–) **5** 53–55

**DOBELL, SIR WILLIAM** (1899–1970), Australian artist **5** 34–35

**DOBZHANSKY, THEODOSIUS** (1900–1975), Russian-American biologist who studied natural selection **5** 35–37

**DOCTOROW, EDGAR LAURENCE** (born 1931), American author **19** 89–91

**DODGE, GRACE HOADLEY** (1856–1914), American feminist, philanthropist, and social worker **5** 37–38

**DODGE, JOHN FRANCIS (1864–1920), AND HORACE ELGIN** (1868–1920), American automobile manufacturers **18** 121–123

**DOE, SAMUEL KANYON** (1951–1990), Liberian statesman **5** 38–39

**DOI TAKAKO** (born 1928), chairperson of the Japan Socialist party **5** 39–41

**DOLE, ELIZABETH HANFORD** (born 1936), American lawyer, politician, and first female United States secretary of transportation **5** 41–43

**DOLE, ROBERT J.** (born 1923), Republican Senator **5** 43–46

**DOLE, SANFORD BALLARD** (1844–1926), American statesman **5** 46

**Dolittle, Doctor John** (fictional character)
Lofting, Hugh **19** 207–209

**DOLLFUSS, ENGELBERT** (1892–1934), Austrian statesman **5** 47

**DÖLLINGER, JOSEF IGNAZ VON** (1799–1890), German historian and theologian **5** 47–48

**DOMAGK, GERHARD JOHANNES PAUL** (1895–1964), German bacteriologist **5** 48–50

**DOMINGO, PLACIDO** (born 1941), Spanish-born lyric-dramatic tenor **5** 50–51

**DOMINIC, ST.** (circa 1170–1221), Spanish Dominican founder **5** 51–52

**Domino's Pizza**
Monaghan, Tom **19** 256–258

**DOMITIAN** (Titus Flavius Domitianus Augustus; 51–96), Roman emperor 81–96 **5** 52–53

**DONATELLO** (Donato di Niccolò Bardi; 1386–1466), Italian sculptor **5** 55–56

**DONATUS** (died circa 355), schismatic bishop of Carthage **5** 56–57

**DONG, PHAM VAN** (born 1906), premier first of the Democratic Republic of Vietnam (DRV) and after 1976 of the Socialist Republic of Vietnam (SRV) **5** 57–59

**DONIZETTI, GAETANA** (1797–1848), Italian opera composer **5** 59–60

**DONLEAVY, JAMES PATRICK** (born 1926), Irish author and playwright **19** 91–93

**DONNE, JOHN** (1572–1631), English metaphysical poet **5** 60–61

**DONNELLY, IGNATIUS** (1831–1901), American politician and author **5** 62

**DONNER, GEORG RAPHAEL** (1693–1741), Austrian sculptor **5** 63

**DONOSO, JOSÉ** (1924–1996), Chilean writer **5** 63–65

**DOOLITTLE, HILDA** (1886–1961), American poet and novelist **5** 65–66

**DOOLITTLE, JAMES HAROLD** (1896–1993), American transcontinental pilot **5** 66–68

**DORIA, ANDREA** (1466–1560), Italian admiral and politician **18** 123–125

**DORR, RHETA CHILDE** (1868–1948), American journalist **5** 68–69

**DORSEY, JIMMY** (James Dorsey; 1904–1957), American musician and bandleader **19** 93–95

**DOS PASSOS, RODERIGO** (1896–1970), American novelist **5** 69–71

**DOS SANTOS, JOSÉ EDUARDO** (born 1942), leader of the Popular Movement for the Liberation of Angola and president of Angola **5** 71–72

**DOS SANTOS, MARCELINO** (born 1929), Mozambican nationalist insurgent, statesman, and intellectual **5** 72–74

**DOSTOEVSKY, FYODOR** (1821–1881), Russian novelist **5** 74–77

**DOUGLAS, DONALD WILLS** (1892–1981), American aeronautical engineer **5** 77

**DOUGLAS, GAVIN** (circa 1475–1522), Scottish poet, prelate, and courtier **5** 77–78

**DOUGLAS, SIR JAMES** (1286?–1330), Scottish patriot **5** 80–82

**DOUGLAS, MARY TEW** (born 1921), British anthropologist and social thinker **5** 79–80

**DOUGLAS, STEPHEN ARNOLD** (1813–1861), American politician **5** 80–82

**DOUGLAS, THOMAS CLEMENT** (1904–1986), Canadian clergyman and politician, premier of Saskatchewan (1944–1961), and member of Parliament (1962–1979) **5** 82–83

**DOUGLAS, WILLIAM ORVILLE** (1898–1980), American jurist **5** 83–85

**DOUGLASS, FREDERICK** (circa 1817–1895), African American leader and abolitionist **5** 85–86

**DOVE, ARTHUR GARFIELD** (1880–1946), American painter **5** 86–87

**DOVE, RITA FRANCES** (born 1952), United States poet laureate **5** 87–89

**DOW, CHARLES** (1851–1902), American journalist **19** 95–97

**DOW, NEAL** (1804–1897), American temperance reformer **5** 89–90

**Dow Jones & Company** (New York City) Dow, Charles **19** 95–97

**DOWLAND, JOHN** (1562–1626), British composer and lutenist **5** 90

**DOWNING, ANDREW JACKSON** (1815–1852), American horticulturist and landscape architect **5** 90–91

**DOYLE, SIR ARTHUR CONAN** (1859–1930), British author **5** 91–92

**DRAGO, LUIS MARÍA** (1859–1921), Argentine international jurist and diplomat **5** 92–93

**DRAKE, DANIEL** (1785–1852), American physician **5** 93–94

**DRAKE, SIR FRANCIS** (circa 1541–1596), English navigator **5** 94–96

**Drama** (literature)
criticism
Beerbohm, Max **19** 16–18

**DRAPER, JOHN WILLIAM** (1811–1882), Anglo-American scientist and historian **5** 96–97

**DRAYTON, MICHAEL** (1563–1631), English poet **5** 97–98

**Dream Songs, The** (poem series) Berryman, John **19** 22–25

**DREISER, (HERMAN) THEODORE** (1871–1945), American novelist **5** 98–100

**DREW, CHARLES RICHARD** (1904–1950), African American surgeon **5** 100–101

**DREW, DANIEL** (1797–1879), American stock manipulator **5** 101–102

**DREXEL, KATHERINE** (1858–1955), founded a Catholic order, the Sisters of the Blessed Sacrament **5** 102–103

**DREYFUS, ALFRED** (1859–1935), French army officer **5** 103–105

**DRIESCH, HANS ADOLF EDUARD** (1867–1941), German biologist and philosopher **5** 105

**DRUSUS, MARCUS LIVIUS** (circa 124–91 B.C.), Roman statesman **5** 105–106

**DRYDEN, JOHN** (1631–1700), English poet, critic, and dramatist **5** 106–107

**DRYSDALE, SIR GEORGE RUSSELL** (1912–1981), Australian painter **5** 107–109

**DUANE, WILLIAM** (1760–1835), American journalist **5** 109

**DUARTE, JOSÉ NAPOLEÓN** (1926–1990), civilian reformer elected president of El Salvador in 1984 **5** 109–111

**DUBČEK, ALEXANDER** (1921–1992), Czechoslovak politician **5** 112–113

**DUBE, JOHN LANGALIBALELE** (1870–1949), South African writer and Zulu propagandist **5** 113

**DU BELLAY, JOACHIM** (circa 1522–1560), French poet **5** 113–114

**DUBINSKY, DAVID** (1892–1982), American trade union official **5** 114–115

**DUBNOV, SIMON** (1860–1941), Jewish historian, journalist, and political activist **5** 115–116

**DU BOIS, WILLIAM EDWARD BURGHARDT** (1868–1963), African American educator, pan-Africanist, and protest leader **5** 116–118

**DU BOIS-REYMOND, EMIL** (1818–1896), German physiologist **5** 118–119

**DUBOS, RENÉ JULES** (1901–1982), French-born American microbiologist **5** 119

**DUBUFFET, JEAN PHILLIPE ARTHUR** (born 1901), French painter **5** 119–120

**DUCCIO DI BUONINSEGNA** (1255/60–1318/19), Italian painter **5** 121–122

**DUCHAMP, MARCEL** (1887–1968), French painter **5** 122–123

**DUCHAMP-VILLON, RAYMOND** (1876–1918), French sculptor **5** 123

**DUDLEY, BARBARA** (born 1947), American director of Greenpeace **5** 123–124

**DUDLEY, THOMAS** (1576–1653), American colonial governor and Puritan leader **5** 124–125

**DUFAY, GUILLAUME** (circa 1400–1474), Netherlandish composer **5** 125–126

**ELIOT, GEORGE** (pen name of Mary Ann Evans; 1819–80), English novelist **5** 254–256

**ELIOT, JOHN** (1604–1690), English-born missionary to the Massachusetts Indians **5** 256–258

**ELIOT, THOMAS STEARNS** (1888–1965), American-English poet, critic, and playwright **5** 258–261

**ELIZABETH** (Elizabeth Petrovna; 1709–61), empress of Russia 1741–61 **5** 261–263

**ELIZABETH I** (1533–1603), queen of England and Ireland 1558–1603 **5** 263–266

**ELIZABETH II** (born 1926), queen of Great Britain and Ireland **5** 266–269

**ELIZABETH BAGAAYA NYABONGO OF TORO** (born 1940), Ugandan ambassador **5** 269–271

**ELIZABETH BOWES-LYON** (Elizabeth Angela Marguerite Bowes-Lyon; born 1900), queen of Great Britain and Ireland (1936–1952) and Queen Mother after 1952 **5** 261–263

**Elizabethan literature**
see English literature—Elizabethan

**ELLINGTON, "DUKE" EDWARD KENNEDY** (born 1899), American jazz composer **5** 273–274

**ELLISON, RALPH WALDO** (1914–1994), African American author and spokesperson for racial identity **5** 274–275

**ELLSBERG, DANIEL** (born 1931), U.S. government official and Vietnam peace activist **5** 275–277

**ELLSWORTH, LINCOLN** (1880–1951), American adventurer and polar explorer **5** 277

**ELSASSER, WALTER MAURICE** (1904–1991), American physicist **5** 277–278

**EMERSON, RALPH WALDO** (1803–1882), American poet, essayist, and philosopher **5** 278–280

**EMINESCU, MIHAIL** (1850–1889), Romanian poet **5** 280–281

**EMMET, ROBERT** (1778–1803), Irish nationalist and revolutionary **5** 281–282

**EMPEDOCLES** (circa 493–circa 444 B.C.), Greek philosopher, poet, and scientist **5** 282

**ENCINA, JUAN DEL** (1468–1529?), Spanish author and composer **5** 283

**ENDARA, GUILLERMO** (born 1936), installed as president of Panama by the U.S. Government in 1989 **5** 283–284

**ENDECOTT, JOHN** (1588–1655), English colonial governor of Massachusetts **5** 284–285

**ENDERS, JOHN FRANKLIN** (1897–1985), American virologist **5** 285–286

**ENGELS, FRIEDRICH** (1820–1895), German revolutionist and social theorist **5** 286–288

**ENGLAND, JOHN** (1786–1842), Irish Catholic bishop in America **5** 288

**English art and architecture**
architecture
Foster, Norman **19** 115–117
illustration
Caldecott, Randolph **19** 52–55

**English literature**
children's literature
Caldecott, Randolph **19** 52–55
Lofting, Hugh **19** 207–209
Milne, Alan Alexander **19** 253–254
drama criticism
Beerbohm, Max **19** 16–18
essays (19th–20th century)
Beerbohm, Max **19** 16–18
modern (novel)
Hughes, Richard **19** 158–160
Lowry, Malcolm **19** 209–211
Rhys, Jean **19** 310–312

**ENNIN** (794–864), Japanese Buddhist monk **5** 288–289

**ENNIUS, QUINTUS** (239–169 B.C.).Roman poet **5** 289

**ENSOR, JAMES** (1860–1949), Belgian painter and graphic artist **5** 289–290

**Environmental activists** (Brazil)
Mendes, Chico **19** 243–245

**EPAMINONDAS** (c. 425–362 B.C.), Theban general and statesman **5** 291–292

**EPHRON, NORA** (born 1941), American author, screenwriter and film director **18** 130–132

**EPICTETUS** (circa 50–circa 135), Greek philosopher **5** 292

**EPICURUS** (circa 342–270 B.C.), Greek philosopher, founder of Epicureanism **5** 292–294

**EPSTEIN, ABRAHAM** (1892–1945), Russian-born American economist **5** 294–295

**EPSTEIN, SIR JACOB** (1880–1959), American-born English sculptor **5** 295–296

**Equal Rights Amendment** (United States; proposed constitutional amendment)
Paul, Alice **19** 277–280

**Equal Rights Party** (United States)
Lockwood, Belva **19** 205–207

**EQUIANO, OLAUDAH** (1745–circa 1801), African author and former slave **5** 296–297

**ERASISTRATUS** (c. 304 B.C.–c. 250 B.C.), Greek physician and anantomist **5** 297–298

**ERASMUS, DESIDERIUS** (1466–1536), Dutch author, scholar, and humanist **5** 298–300

**ERASMUS, GEORGES HENRY** (born 1948), Canadian Indian leader **5** 300–301

**ERATOSTHENES OF CYRENE** (circa 284–circa 205 B.C.), Greek mathematician, geographer, and astronomer **5** 301–302

**ERCILLA Y ZÚÑIGA, ALONSO DE** (1533–1594), Spanish poet, soldier, and diplomat **5** 302

**ERHARD, LUDWIG** (1897–1977), German statesman, West German chancellor 1963–66 **5** 302–304

**ERIC THE RED** (Eric Thorvaldsson; flourished late 10th century), Norwegian explorer **5** 304

**ERICKSON, ARTHUR CHARLES** (born 1924), Canadian architect and landscape architect **5** 304–306

**ERICSON, LEIF** (971–circa 1015), Norse mariner and adventurer **5** 306–307

**ERICSSON, JOHN** (1803–1889), Swedish-born American engineer and inventor **5** 307–308

**ERIGENA, JOHN SCOTUS** (circa 810–circa 877), Irish scholastic philosopher **5** 308–309

**ERIKSON, ERIK HOMBURGER** (1902–1994), German-born American psychoanalyst and educator **5** 309–310

**ERLANGER, JOSEPH** (1874–1965), American physiologist **5** 310–311

**ERNST, MAX** (born 1891), German painter **5** 311–312

**ERSHAD, HUSSAIN MOHAMMAD** (born 1930), Bengali military leader and president of Bangladesh (1982–1990) **5** 312–314

**ERTÉ** (Romain de Tirtoff; 1892–1990), Russian fashion illustrator and stage set designer **5** 314–316

**ERVIN, SAM J., JR.** (1896–1985), lawyer, judge, U.S. senator, and chairman of the Senate Watergate Committee **5** 316–317

**FARLEY, JAMES A.** (1888–1976), Democratic Party organizer and political strategist **5** 381–383

**FARMER, FANNIE MERRITT** (1857–1915), American authority on cookery **5** 383

**FARMER, JAMES** (born 1920), civil rights activist who helped organize the 1960s "freedom rides" **5** 383–385

**FARMER, MOSES GERRISH** (1820–1893), American inventor and manufacturer **5** 385

**FARNSWORTH, PHILO T.** (1906–1971), American inventor of the television **5** 386–387

**FAROUK I** (1920–1965), king of Egypt 1937–1952 **5** 387–388

**FARRAGUT, DAVID GLASGOW** (1801–1870), American naval officer **5** 388–389

**FARRAKHAN, LOUIS** (Louis Eugene Walcott, born 1933), a leader of one branch of the Nation of Islam popularly known as Black Muslims and militant spokesman for Black Nationalism **5** 389–390

**FARRELL, JAMES THOMAS** (1904–1979), American novelist and social and literary critic **5** 390–391

**FARRELL, SUZANNE** (née Roberta Sue Ficker; born 1945), American classical ballerina **5** 391–393

**Fast food industry**
Sanders, Colonel **19** 323–325

**"Father of. . ."**
see Nicknames

**FAULKNER, BRIAN** (1921–1977), prime minister of Northern Ireland (1971–1972) **5** 393–395

**FAULKNER, WILLIAM** (1897–1962), American novelist **5** 395–397

**FAURÉ, GABRIEL URBAIN** (1845–1924), French composer **5** 397–398

**FAWCETT, MILLICENT GARRETT** (1847–1929), British feminist **5** 398–400

**FAYE, SAFI** (born 1943), Senegalese filmmaker and ethnologist **5** 400–401

**FECHNER, GUSTAV THEODOR** (1801–1887), German experimental psychologist **5** 401–402

**FEE, JOHN GREGG** (1816–1901), American abolitionist and clergyman **5** 402–403

**FEIFFER, JULES RALPH** (born 1929), American satirical cartoonist and playwright and novelist **5** 403–404

**FEIGENBAUM, MITCHELL JAY** (born 1944), American physicist **5** 404–405

**FEIGL, HERBERT** (born 1902), American philosopher **18** 135–137

**FEIJÓ, DIOGO ANTÔNIO** (1784–1843), Brazilian priest and statesman **5** 405–406

**FEININGER, LYONEL** (1871–1956), American painter **5** 406–407

**FEINSTEIN, DIANNE** (Goldman; born 1933), politician, public official, and San Francisco's first female mayor **5** 407–408

**FELICIANO, JOSÉ** (born 1945), Hispanic American singer and guitarist **19** 109–110

**FELLINI, FEDERICO** (1920–1993), Italian film director **5** 408–409

**FELTRE, VITTORINO DA** (1378–1446), Italian humanist and teacher **5** 409–410

**Feminist movement**
see Women's rights

**FÉNELON, FRANÇOIS DE SALIGNAC DE LA MOTHE** (1651–1715), French archbishop and theologian **5** 410–411

**FENG KUEI-FEN** (1809–1874), Chinese scholar and official **5** 411–412

**FENG YÜ-HSIANG** (1882–1948), Chinese warlord **5** 412–413

**FERBER, EDNA** (1887–1968), American author **5** 413

**FERDINAND** (1865–1927), king of Romania 1914–1927 **5** 413–414

**FERDINAND I** (1503–1564), Holy Roman emperor 1555–1564, king of Hungary and Bohemia 1526–64 and of Germany 1531–1564 **5** 414–415

**FERDINAND II** (1578–1637), Holy Roman emperor 1619–1637, king of Bohemia 1617–1637 and of Hungary 1618–1637 **5** 415

**FERDINAND II** (1810–1859), king of the Two Sicilies 1830–1859 **5** 415–416

**FERDINAND III** (1608–1657), Holy Roman emperor 1637–1657, king of Hungary 1626–1657 and of Bohemia 1627–1657 **5** 416–417

**FERDINAND V** (1452–1516), king of Castile 1474–1504, of Sicily 1468–1516, and of Aragon 1479–1516 **5** 417–418

**FERDINAND VII** (1784–1833), king of Spain 1808 and 1814–1833 **5** 418–420

**FERGUSON, ADAM** (1723–1816), Scottish philosopher, moralist, and historian **5** 420–421

**FERGUSON, HOWARD** (born 1908), Irish musician and composer **18** 137–138

**FERMAT, PIERRE DE** (1601–1665), French mathematician **5** 421–422

**FERMI, ENRICO** (1901–1954), Italian-American physicist **5** 422–424

**FERNÁNDEZ DE LIZARDI, JOSÉ JOAQUIN** (1776–1827), Mexican journalist and novelist **5** 424–425

**FERNEL, JEAN FRANÇOIS** (circa 1497–1558), French physician **5** 425–426

**FERRARO, GERALDINE** (born 1935), first woman candidate for the vice presidency of a major U.S. political party **5** 426–428

**FERRER, GABRIEL MIRÓ** (1879–1930), Spanish author **5** 428

**FERRER, JOSÉ FIGUÉRES** (born 1906), Costa Rican politician **5** 428–429

**FERRERO, GUGLIELMO** (1871–1942), Italian journalist and historian **5** 429–430

**FERRY, JULES FRANÇOIS CAMILLE** (1832–1893), French statesman **5** 430

**FEUCHTWANGER, LION** (1884–1958), post-World War I German literary figure **5** 430–432

**FEUERBACH, LUDWIG ANDREAS** (1804–1872), German philosopher **5** 432

**FEYNMAN, RICHARD PHILLIPS** (1918–1988), American physicist **5** 432–434

**FIBONACCI, LEONARDO** (circa 1180–circa 1250), Italian mathematician **5** 434–435

**FICHTE, JOHANN GOTTLIEB** (1762–1814), German philosopher **5** 435–436

**FICINO, MARSILIO** (1433–1499), Italian philosopher and humanist **5** 436–437

**FIEDLER, ARTHUR** (1894–1979), American conductor of the Boston Pops **5** 437–438

**FIELD, CYRUS WEST** (1819–1892), American merchant **5** 438–439

**FIELD, DAVID DUDLEY** (1805–1894), American jurist **5** 439–440

**FIELD, MARSHALL** (1834–1906), American merchant **5** 440–441

**FIELD, STEPHEN JOHNSON** (1816–1899), American jurist **5** 441–442

**FIELDING, HENRY** (1707–1754), English novelist **5** 442–444

**FIELDS, W. C.** (stage name of William Claude Dukenfield; 1879–1946), American comedian **5** 444

**FIGUEIREDO, JOÃO BATISTA DE OLIVEIRA** (born 1918), Brazilian army general and president (1979–1985) **5** 445–446

**FILLMORE, MILLARD** (1800–1874), American statesman, president 1850–1853 **5** 447–448

**FILMER, SIR ROBERT** (died 1653), English political theorist **5** 448

**FINKELSTEIN, RABBI LOUIS** (born 1895), American Jewish scholar and head of Conservative Judaism **5** 448–450

**FINLAY, CARLOS JUAN** (1833–1915), Cuban biologist and physician **5** 450

**FINNEY, CHARLES GRANDISON** (1792–1875), American theologian and educator **5** 450–451

**FIRDAUSI** (934–1020), Persian poet **5** 451–452

**FIRESTONE, HARVEY SAMUEL** (1868–1938), American industrialist **5** 452–453

**FIRST, RUTH** (1925–1982), South African socialist, anti-apartheid activist, and scholar **5** 453–454

**FISCHER, BOBBY** (born 1943), American chess player **5** 454–456

**FISCHER, EMIL** (1852–1919), German organic chemist **5** 456–457

**FISCHER, HANS** (1881–1945), German organic chemist **5** 457–459

**FISCHER VON ERLACH, JOHANN BERNHARD** (1656–1723), Austrian architect **5** 459–461

**FISH, HAMILTON** (1808–1893), American statesman **5** 461–462

**FISHER, ANDREW** (1862–1928), Australian statesman and labor leader **5** 462

**FISHER, IRVING** (1867–1947), American economist **5** 462–463

**FISHER, SIR RONALD AYLMER** (1890–1962), English statistician **5** 463–464

**FISK, JAMES** (1834–1872), American financial speculator **5** 464–465

**FISKE, JOHN** (1842–1901), American philosopher and historian **5** 465–466

**FISKE, MINNIE MADDERN** (Mary Augusta Davey; 1865–1932), American "realistic" actress who portrayed Ibsen heroines **5** 466–467

**FITCH, JOHN** (1743–1798), American mechanic and inventor **5** 467–468

**FITZGERALD, ELLA** (1918–1996), American jazz singer **5** 468–469

**FITZGERALD, FRANCES** (born 1940), American author **5** 469–470

**FITZGERALD, FRANCIS SCOTT KEY** (1896–1940), American author **5** 470–472

**FITZGERALD, GARRET** (born 1926), Irish prime minister (1981–1987) **5** 472–474

**FITZHUGH, GEORGE** (1806–1881), American polemicist and sociologist **5** 474

**FITZPATRICK, THOMAS** (1799–1854), American trapper, guide, and Indian agent **5** 474–475

**FIZEAU, HIPPOLYTE ARMAND LOUIS** (1819–1896), French physicist **5** 475

**FLAHERTY, ROBERT** (1884–1951), American documentary filmmaker **5** 476–477

**FLAMININUS, TITUS QUINCTIUS** (circa 228–174 B.C.), Roman general and diplomat **5** 477

**FLAMSTEED, JOHN** (1646–1719), English astronomer **5** 477–478

**FLANAGAN, HALLIE** (1890–1969), American director, playwright, and educator **5** 478–479

**FLANNAGAN, JOHN BERNARD** (1895–1942), American sculptor **5** 480

**FLAUBERT, GUSTAVE** (1821–1880), French novelist **5** 480–482

**FLEISCHMANN, GISI** (1894–1944), Czechoslovakian leader who rescued many Jews from the Nazi Holocaust **5** 482–483

**FLEMING, SIR ALEXANDER** (1881–1955), Scottish bacteriologist **5** 485–486

**FLEMING, SIR SANDFORD** (1827–1915), Scottish-born Canadian railway engineer **5** 485–486

**FLETCHER, ALICE CUNNINGHAM** (1838–1923), American anthropologist **5** 486–487

**FLETCHER, JOHN** (1579–1625), English playwright **5** 487

**FLETCHER, JOSEPH FRANCIS** (1905–1991), American philosopher who was the father of modern biomedical ethics **5** 488–489

**FLEXNER, ABRAHAM** (1866–1959), American educational reformer **5** 489–490

**FLINDERS, MATTHEW** (1774–1814), English naval captain and hydrographer **5** 490

**FLORES, CARLOS ROBERTO** (Carlos Roberto Flores Facussé;born 1950), Honduran politician **18** 138–140

**FLORES, JUAN JOSÉ** (1801–1864), South American general, president of Ecuador **5** 491

**FLOREY, HOWARD WALTER** (Baron Florey of Adelaide; 1898–1968), Australian pathologist **5** 491–492

**FLORY, PAUL** (1910–1985), American chemist and educator **5** 492–494

**FLOYD, CARLISLE** (born 1926), American composer of operas **5** 494–496

**FLYNN, ELIZABETH GURLEY** (1890–1964), American labor organizer **5** 496–497

**FLYNN, JOHN** (1880–1951), founder and superintendent of the Australian Inland Mission **5** 497–498

**FO, DARIO** (born 1926), Italian playwright and actor **18** 140–143

**FOCH, FERDINAND** (1851–1929), French marshal **5** 498–499

**FOLEY, TOM** (born 1929), Democratic representative from the state of Washington and Speaker of the U.S. House of Representatives (1989–1995) **5** 499–501

**Folklore** (literature)
Courlander, Harold **19** 78–80

**FONDA, JANE** (born 1937), actress whose career included films, television, exercise videocassettes, and writing **5** 501–502

**FONG, HIRAM LEONG** (born 1907), American politician and businessman **18** 143–144

**FONSECA, RUBEM** (born 1925), Brazilian author **5** 502–504

**FONTANE, THEODOR** (1819–1898), German author **5** 504

**FONTEYN, DAME MARGOT** (Margaret "Peggy" Hookham; 1919–1991), classical ballerina who devoted her career to the Royal Ballet in England **5** 504–505

**Food industry**
Birdseye, Clarence **19** 25–27
Heinz, Henry John **19** 136–138
Hershey, Milton **19** 142–144
Ilitch, Mike **19** 163–165

**FOOT, MICHAEL** (born 1913), left-wing journalist and British Labour Party member of Parliament **5** 505–507

psychology, and social philosophy **6** 125–127

**FRONDIZI, ARTURO** (1908–1995), leader of the Argentine Radical Party and Argentine president (1958–1962) **6** 127–128

**FRONTENAC ET PALLUAU, COMTE DE** (Louis de Buade; 1622–1698), French colonial governor **6** 128–130

**FRONTINUS, SEXTUS JULIUS** (circa 35–circa 104), Roman magistrate, soldier, and writer **6** 130

**FROST, ROBERT LEE** (1874–1963), American poet **6** 130–133

**FROUDE, JAMES ANTHONY** (1818–1894), English historian **6** 133–134

**FRUNZE, MIKHAIL VASILIEVICH** (1885–1925), Soviet military leader **6** 134

**FRY, ELIZABETH** (1780–1845), British refromer **6** 134–136

**FRY, WILLIAM HENRY** (1813–1864), American composer **6** 136–137

**FRYE, NORTHROP** (Herman Northrop Frye; born 1912), Canadian literary scholar **6** 137–139

**FUAD I** (1868–1936), king of Egypt 1922–1936 **6** 139

**FUCHS, SIR VIVIAN** (born 1908), English explorer and geologist **6** 140

**FUENTES, CARLOS** (born 1928), Mexican author and political activist **6** 141–142

**FUGARD, ATHOL** (born 1932), South African playwright **6** 142–143

**Fugitive slaves**
*see* African American history (United States)

**FUJIMORI, ALBERTO KEINYA** (born 1938), president of Peru **6** 143–145

**FUJIWARA KAMATARI** (614–669), Japanese imperial official **6** 145

**FUJIWARA MICHINAGA** (966–1027), Japanese statesman **6** 145–146

**FUKUYAMA, FRANCIS** (born 1952), American philosopher and foreign policy expert **6** 146–147

**FULBRIGHT, JAMES WILLIAM** (1905–1995), American statesman **6** 147–149

**FULLER, ALFRED** (1885–1973), American businessman and inventor **19** 117–118

**FULLER, MILLARD** (born 1935), American lawyer and social activist **18** 153–155

**FULLER, RICHARD BUCKMINISTER** (born 1895), American architect and engineer **6** 149–150

**FULLER, SARAH MARGARET** (1810–1850), American feminist **6** 150–151

**Fuller Brush Company** (United States) Fuller, Alfred **19** 117–118

**FULTON, ROBERT** (1765–1815), American inventor, engineer, and artist **6** 151–152

**FURPHY, JOSEPH** (1843–1912), Australian novelist **6** 152–153

**FUSELI, HENRY** (1741–1825), Swiss painter **6** 153–155

**FUSTEL DE COULANGES, NUMA DENIS** (1830–1889), French historian **6** 155

**FUX, JOHANN JOSEPH** (1660–1741), Austrian composer, conductor, and theoretician **6** 155–156

# G

**GABLE, WILLIAM CLARK** (1901–1960), American film actor **6** 157–158

**GABO, NAUM** (1890–1977), Russian sculptor and designer **6** 158–159

**GABOR, DENNIS** (1900–1979), Hungarian-British physicist who invented holographic photography **6** 159–160

**GABRIEL, ANGE JACQUES** (1698–1782), French architect **6** 160–161

**GABRIELI, GIOVANNI** (circa 1557–1612), Italian composer **6** 161–162

**GADAMER, HANS-GEORG** (born 1900), German philosopher, classicist, and interpretation theorist **6** 162–163

**GADDAFI, MUAMMAR AL-** (born 1942), head of the revolution that set up the Libyan Republic in 1969 **6** 163–165

**GADSDEN, JAMES** (1788–1858), American soldier and diplomat **6** 165–166

**GAGARIN, YURI ALEXEIVICH** (1934–1968), Russian cosmonaut **6** 166–167

**GAGE, MATILDA JOSLYN** (1826–1898), American reformer and suffragist **6** 167–169

**GAGE, THOMAS** (1719/20–1787), English general **6** 169–170

**GAGNÉ, ROBERT MILLS** (born 1916), American educator **6** 170

**GAINSBOROUGH, THOMAS** (1727–1788), English painter **6** 170–172

**GAISERIC** (died 477), king of the Vandals 428–477 **6** 172

**GAITÁN, JORGE ELIÉCER** (1898–1948), Colombian politician **6** 172–173

**GAITSKELL, HUGH** (1906–1963), British chancellor of the exchequer (1950–1951) and leader of the Labour Party (1955–1963) **6** 173–174

**GALBRAITH, JOHN KENNETH** (born 1908), economist and scholar of the American Institutionalist school **6** 174–177

**GALDÓS, BENITO PÉREZ** (1843–1920), Spanish novelist and dramatist **6** 177–178

**GALEN** (130–200), Greek physician **6** 178–180

**GALILEO GALILEI** (1564–1642), Italian astronomer and physicist **6** 180–183

**GALLATIN, ALBERT** (1761–1849), Swiss-born American statesman, banker, and diplomat **6** 183–184

**GALLAUDET, THOMAS HOPKINS** (1787–1851), American educator **6** 185

**GALLEGOS FREIRE, RÓMULO** (1884–1969), Venezuelan novelist, president 1948 **6** 185–186

**GALLOWAY, JOSEPH** (circa 1731–1803), American politician **6** 186–187

**GALLUP, GEORGE** (1901–1984), pioneer in the field of public opinion polling and a proponent of educational reform **6** 187–189

**GALSWORTHY, JOHN** (1867–1933), English novelist and playwright **6** 189–190

**GALT, SIR ALEXANDER TILLOCH** (1817–1893), Canadian politician **6** 190–191

**GALT, JOHN** (1779–1839), Scottish novelist **18** 156–158

**GALTIERI, LEOPOLDO FORTUNATO** (born 1926), president of Argentina (1981–1982) **6** 191–193

**GALTON, SIR FRANCIS** (1822–1911), English scientist, biometrician, and explorer **6** 193–194

**GALVANI, LUIGI** (1737–1798), Italian physiologist **6** 194–195

**GÁLVEZ, BERNARDO DE** (1746–1786), Spanish colonial administrator **6** 195–196

**GÁLVEZ, JOSÉ DE** (1720–1787), Spanish statesman in Mexico **6** 196

**GALWAY, JAMES** (born 1939), Irish flutist **18** 158–160

**GINASTERA, ALBERTO EVARISTO**
(1916–1983), Argentine composer **6**
328–329

**GINGRICH, NEWT** (born 1943),
Republican congressman from Georgia
**6** 329–332

**GINSBERG, ALLEN** (1926–1997),
American poet **6** 332–333

**GINSBURG, RUTH BADER** (born 1933),
second woman appointed to the
United States Supreme Court **6**
333–336

**GINZBERG, ASHER** (Ahad Ha-Am;
means "one of the people;" 1856–
1927), Jewish intellectual leader **6**
336–337

**GINZBERG, LOUIS** (1873–1953),
Lithuanian-American Talmudic scholar
**6** 337–338

**GINZBURG, NATALIA LEVI** (1916–
1991), Italian novelist, essayist,
playwright, and translator **6** 338–339

**GIOLITTI, GIOVANNI** (1842–1928),
Italian statesman **6** 339–340

**GIORGIONE** (1477–1510), Italian
painter **6** 340–341

**GIOTTO** (circa 1267–1337), Italian
painter, architect, and sculptor **6**
342–345

**GIOVANNI, YOLANDE CORNELIA, JR.**
(born 1943), African American poet **6**
346–347

**GIOVANNI DA BOLOGNA** (1529–
1608), Italian sculptor **6** 345–346

**GIPP, GEORGE** (1895–1920), American
football player **19** 124–126

**GIRARD, STEPHEN** (1750–1831),
American merchant and philanthropist
**6** 347–348

**GIRARDON, FRANÇOIS** (1628–1715),
French sculptor **6** 348–349

**GIRAUDOUX, JEAN** (1882–1944),
French novelist, playwright, and
diplomat **6** 349–350

**GIRTY, SIMON** (1741–1818), American
frontiersman **6** 350

**GISCARD D'ESTAING, VALÉRY** (born
1926), third president of the French
Fifth Republic **6** 350–352

**GIST, CHRISTOPHER** (circa 1706–
1759), American frontiersman **6**
352–353

**GIULIANI, RUDOLPH WILLIAM** (born
1944), mayor of New York City **6**
353–355

**GLACKENS, WILLIAM** (1870–1938),
American painter **6** 355–356

**GLADDEN, WASHINGTON** (1836–
1918), American clergyman **6**
356–357

**GLADSTONE, WILLIAM EWART** (1809–
1898), English statesman **6** 357–360

**GLASGOW, ELLEN** (1873–1945),
American novelist **6** 360–361

**GLASHOW, SHELDON LEE** (born 1932),
American Nobel Prize winner in
physics **6** 361–362

**GLASS, PHILIP** (born 1937), American
composer of minimalist music **6**
362–364

**GLENDOWER, OWEN** (1359?–1415?),
Welsh national leader **6** 364–365

**GLENN, JOHN HERSCHEL, JR.** (born
1921), military test pilot, astronaut,
businessman, and United States
senator from Ohio **6** 365–367

**GLIGOROV, KIRO** (born 1917), first
president of the Republic of
Macedonia **6** 367–369

**GLINKA, MIKHAIL IVANOVICH** (1804–
1857), Russian composer **6** 369–370

**GLOUCESTER, DUKE OF** (1391–1447),
English statesman **6** 370–371

**GLUBB, SIR JOHN BAGOT** (1897–
1986), British commander of the Arab
Legion 1939–56 **6** 371–372

**GLUCK, CHRISTOPH WILLIBALD**
(1714–1787), Austrian composer and
opera reformer **6** 372–374

**GLUCKMAN, MAX** (1911–1975), British
anthropologist **6** 374–375

**GM**
see General Motors Corporation

**GOBINEAU, COMTE DE** (Joseph Arthur
Gobineau; 1816–1882), French
diplomat **6** 375–376

**GODARD, JEAN-LUC** (born 1930),
French actor, film director, and
screenwriter **19** 126–128

**GODDARD, ROBERT HUTCHINGS**
(1882–1945), American pioneer in
rocketry **6** 376–377

**GÖDEL, KURT** (1906–1978), Austrian-
American mathematician **6** 377–379

**GODFREY OF BOUILLON** (circa 1060–
1100), French lay leader of First
Crusade **6** 379

**GODKIN, EDWIN LAWRENCE** (1831–
1902), British-born American
journalist **6** 380

**GODOLPHIN, SIDNEY** (1st Earl of
Godolphin; 1645–1712), English
statesman **6** 380–381

**GODOY Y ÁLVAREZ DE FARIA,
MANUEL DE** (1767–1851), Spanish
statesman **6** 381–382

**GODUNOV, BORIS FEODOROVICH**
(circa 1551–1605), czar of Russia
1598–1605 **6** 382–383

**GODWIN, WILLIAM** (1756–1836),
English political theorist and writer **6**
383–384

**GOEBBELS, JOSEPH PAUL** (1897–
1945), German politician and Nazi
propagandist **6** 384–385

**GOEPPERT-MAYER, MARIA** (1906–
1972), American physicist **6** 385–387

**GOETHALS, GEORGE WASHINGTON**
(1858–1928), American Army officer
and engineer **6** 387–388

**GOETHE, JOHANN WOLFGANG VON**
(1749–1832), German poet **6**
388–391

**GOGOL, NIKOLAI** (1809–1852),
Russian author **6** 391–393

**GOH CHOK TONG** (born 1941), leader
of the People's Action Party and
Singapore's prime minister **6** 393–395

**GOIZUETA, ROBERTO** (1931–1997),
Cuban American businessman and
philanthropist **18** 160–162

**GÖKALP, MEHMET ZIYA** (1875/76–
1924), Turkish publicist and
sociologist **6** 395–396

**GOKHALE, GOPAL KRISHNA** (1866–
1915), Indian nationalist leader **6** 396

**GOLD, THOMAS** (born 1920), American
astronomer and physicist **18** 162–164

**GOLDBERG, ARTHUR JOSEPH** (1908–
1990), U.S. secretary of labor,
ambassador to the United Nations,
and activist justice of the U.S.
Supreme Court **6** 397–398

**GOLDBERG, WHOOPI** (born Caryn E.
Johnson; born 1949), African
American actress **6** 398–402

**GOLDEN, HARRY** (1902–1981), Jewish-
American humorist, writer, and
publisher **6** 402–403

**GOLDIE, SIR GEORGE DASHWOOD
TAUBMAN** (1846–1925), British
trader and empire builder **6** 404

**GOLDING, WILLIAM** (1911–1993),
English novelist and essayist **6**
404–406

**GOLDMAN, EMMA** (1869–1940),
Lithuanian-born American anarchist **6**
406–407

**GOLDMARK, JOSEPHINE** (1877–1950),
advocate of government assistance in

**HEINZ, HENRY JOHN** (H.J. Heinz; 1844–1919), American businessman **19** 136–138

**HEISENBERG, WERNER KARL** (born 1901), German physicist **7** 261–263

**HELLER, JOSEPH** (born 1923), American author **7** 263–265

**HELLER, WALTER** (1915–1987), chairman of the Council of Economic Advisors (1961–1964) and chief spokesman of the "New Economics" **7** 265–266

**HELLMAN, LILLIAN FLORENCE** (born 1905), American playwright **7** 267–268

**HELMHOLTZ, HERMANN LUDWIG FERDINAND VON** (1821–1894), German physicist and physiologist **7** 268–269

**HELMONT, JAN BAPTISTA VAN** (1579–1644), Flemish chemist and physician **7** 269–271

**HELMS, JESSE** (born 1921), United States Senator from North Carolina **7** 271–272

**HELPER, HINTON ROWAN** (1829–1909), American author and railroad promoter **7** 272–273

**HELVÉTIUS, CLAUDE ADRIEN** (1715–1771), French philosopher **7** 273–274

**HEMINGWAY, ERNEST MILLER** (1898–1961), American novelist and journalist **7** 274–277

**HÉMON, LOUIS** (1880–1913), French-Canadian novelist **7** 277

**HENDERSON, ARTHUR** (1863–1935), British statesman **7** 277–278

**HENDERSON, RICHARD** (1735–1785), American jurist and land speculator **7** 278–279

**HENDRIX, JIMI** (born Johnny Allen Hendrix; 1942–1970), African american guitarist, singer, and composer **7** 279–283

**HENG SAMRIN** (born 1934), Cambodian Communist leader who became president of the People's Republic of Kampuchea (PRK) in 1979 **7** 283–285

**HENRY I** (876–936), king of Germany 919–936 **7** 285–286

**HENRY I** (1068–1135), king of England 1100–1135 **7** 286–287

**HENRY II** (1133–1189), king of England 1154–1189 **7** 287–289

**HENRY III** (1017–1056), Holy Roman emperor and king of Germany 1039–1056 **7** 290

**HENRY III** (1207–1272), king of England 1216–1272 **7** 290–292

**HENRY IV** (1050–1106), Holy Roman emperor and king of Germany 1056–1106 **7** 292

**HENRY IV** (1367–1413), king of England 1399–1413 **7** 292–293

**HENRY IV** (1553–1610), king of France 1589–1610 **7** 293–295

**HENRY V** (1081–1125), Holy Roman emperor and king of Germany 1106–1125 **7** 295–296

**HENRY V** (1387–1422), king of England 1413–1422 **7** 296–297

**HENRY VI** (1421–1471), king of England 1422–61 and 1470–1471 **7** 298–299

**HENRY VII** (1274–1313), Holy Roman emperor and king of Germany 1308–1313 **7** 299–300

**HENRY VII** (1457–1509), king of England 1485–1509 **7** 300–302

**HENRY VIII** (1491–1547), king of England 1509–1547 **7** 302–305

**HENRY, AARON** (born 1922), African American civil rights activist **7** 306–307

**HENRY, JOSEPH** (1797–1878), American physicist and electrical experimenter **7** 307–308

**HENRY, MARGUERITE** (Margurite Breithaupt; 1902–1997), American author **19** 138–140

**HENRY, O.** (pseudonym of William Sydney Porter; 1862–1910), American short-story writer **7** 308–309

**HENRY, PATRICK** (1736–1799), American orator and revolutionary **7** 309–311

**HENRY THE NAVIGATOR** (1394–1460), Portuguese prince **7** 305–306

**HENSON, JIM** (James Maury Henson, 1936–1990), American puppeteer, screenwriter, and producer **19** 140–142

**HENSON, JOSIAH** (1789–1883), African American preacher and former slave **7** 311–312

**HENSON, MATTHEW A.** (1866–1955), African American Arctic explorer **7** 312–314

**HENZE, HANS WERNER** (born 1926), German composer **7** 314

**HEPBURN, AUDREY** (born Edda Van Heemstra Hepburn-Ruston; 1929–1993), Swiss actress and humanitarian **7** 314–316

**HEPBURN, KATHARINE** (born 1907), American actress on the stage and on the screen **7** 316–317

**HEPPLEWHITE, GEORGE** (died 1786), English furniture designer **7** 317–318

**HEPWORTH, BARBARA** (1903–1975), English sculptor **7** 318–319

**HERACLIDES OF PONTUS** (circa 388–310 B.C.), Greek philosopher **7** 319–320

**HERACLITUS** (flourished 500 B.C.), Greek philosopher **7** 320

**HERACLIUS** (circa 575–641), Byzantine emperor 610–641 **7** 320–321

**HERBART, JOHANN FRIEDRICH** (1776–1841), German philosopher-psychologist and educator **7** 321–322

**HERBERG, WILL** (1906–1977), Jewish theologian, social thinker, and biblical exegete **7** 322–323

**HERBERT, EDWARD** (1st Baron Herbert of Cherbury; 1583–1648), English philosopher, poet, diplomat, and historian **7** 324

**HERBERT, GEORGE** (1593–1633), English metaphysical poet and Anglican priest **7** 324–326

**HERDER, JOHANN GOTTFRIED VON** (1744–1803), German philosopher, theologian, and critic **7** 327–328

**HERNÁNDEZ, JOSÉ** (1834–1886), Argentine poet **7** 328–329

**HERNÁNDEZ COLÓN, RAFAEL** (born 1936), Puerto Rican governor **7** 329–330

**HEROD THE GREAT** (circa 73–4 B.C.), king of Judea **7** 333–334

**HERODOTUS** (circa 484–circa 425 B.C.), Greek historian **7** 330–333

**HERON OF ALEXANDRIA** (flourished circa 60), Greek engineer, mathematician, and inventor **7** 334–335

**HERRERA, JUAN DE** (circa 1530–1597), Spanish architect **7** 335

**HERRERA LANE, FELIPE** (1922–1996), Chilean banker and economist **7** 336

**HERRICK, ROBERT** (1591–1674), English poet and Anglican parson **7** 336–339

**HERRIOT, ÉDOUARD** (1872–1957), French statesman and author **7** 339–340

**HERSCHEL, SIR JOHN FREDERICK WILLIAM** (1792–1871), English astronomer **7** 340–341

# I

**IACOCCA, LIDO (LEE) ANTHONY** (born 1924), American automobile magnate **8** 86–88

**IBÁÑEZ DEL CAMPO, CARLOS** (1877–1960), Chilean general and president **8** 88

**ÍBARRURI GÓMEZ, DOLORES** (1895–1989), voice of the Republican cause in the Spanish Civil War **8** 88–90

**IBERVILLE, SIEUR D'** (Pierre le Moyne; 1661–1706), Canadian soldier, naval captain, and adventurer **8** 90–91

**IBM**
see International Business Machines

**IBN AL-ARABI, MUHYI AL-DIN** (1165–1240), Spanish-born Moslem poet, philosopher, and mystic **8** 91

**IBN BATTUTA, MUHAMMAD** (1304–1368/69), Moslem traveler and author **8** 91–92

**IBN GABIROL, SOLOMON BEN JUDAH** (circa 1021–circa 1058), Spanish Hebrew poet and philosopher **8** 92

**IBN HAZM, ABU MUHAMMAD ALI** (994–1064), Spanish-born Arab theologian and jurist **8** 93

**IBN KHALDUN, ABD AL-RAHMAN IBN MUHAMMAD** (1332–1406), Arab historian, philosopher, and statesman **8** 93–94

**IBN SAUD, ABD AL-AZIZ** (1880–1953), Arab politician, founder of Saudi Arabia **8** 94–95

**IBN TASHUFIN, YUSUF** (died 1106), North African Almoravid ruler **8** 95–96

**IBN TUFAYL, ABU BAKR MUHAMMAD** (circa 1110–1185), Spanish Moslem philosopher and physician **8** 96

**IBN TUMART, MUHAMMAD** (circa 1080–1130), North African Islamic theologian **8** 96–97

**IBRAHIM PASHA** (1789–1848), Turkish military and administrative leader **8** 97–98

**IBSEN, HENRIK** (1828–1906), Norwegian playwright **8** 98–100

**ICKES, HAROLD LECLAIRE** (1874–1952), American statesman **8** 100–101

**ICTINUS** (flourished 2nd half of 5th century B.C.), Greek architect **8** 101

**IDRIS I** (1889–1983), king of Libya 1950–69 **8** 102

**IDRISI, MUHAMMAD IBN MUHAMMAD AL-** (1100–1165?), Arab geographer **8** 102–103

**IGLESIAS, ENRIQUE V.** (born 1930), Uruguayan economist, banker, and public official **8** 106–107

**IGNATIUS OF ANTIOCH, SAINT** (died circa 115), Early Christian bishop and theologian **8** 107–108

**IGNATIUS OF LOYOLA, SAINT** (1491–1556), Spanish soldier, founder of Jesuits **8** 108–109

**IKEDA, DAISAKU** (born 1928), Japanese Buddhist writer and religious leader **8** 109–110

**IKHNATON** (ruled 1379–1362 B.C.), pharaoh of Egypt **8** 110–111

**ILIESCU, ION** (born 1930), president of Romania (1990–) **8** 111–112

**ILITCH, MIKE** (born 1929), American businessman **19** 163–165

**ILLICH, IVAN** (born 1926), theologian, educator, and social critic **8** 112–114

**IMAM, ALHADJI ABUBAKAR** (1911–1981), Nigerian writer and teacher **8** 114–115

**IMAOKA, SHINICHIRO** (1881–1988), progressive and liberal religious leader in Japan **8** 115

**IMHOTEP** (ca. 3000 B.C.–ca. 2950 B.C.), Egyptian vizier, architect, priest, astronomer, and magician-physician **8** 116–117

**India, Republic of** (nation, southern Asia)
• SINCE 1947 (REPUBLIC)
prime ministers
Vajpayee, Atal Behari **19** 393–395

**Indiana Jones** (film series)
Lucas, George **19** 211–213

**Indians** (North American)
athletes
Mills, Billy **19** 251–253
culture
Courlander, Harold **19** 78–80

**Indonesia, Republic of** (nation, southeast Asia)
post-Suharto
Habibie, Bacharuddin Jusuf **19** 134–136

**Industrial revolution**
shoe industry
Matzeliger, Jan **19** 232–234

**INGE, WILLIAM RALPH** (1860–1954), Church of England clergyman, scholar, social critic, and writer **8** 118–119

**INGENHOUSZ, JAN** (1730–1799), Dutch physician, chemist, and engineer **8** 119–120

**INGERSOLL, ROBERT GREEN** (1833–1899), American lawyer and lecturer **8** 120–121

**INGRES, JEAN AUGUSTE DOMINIQUE** (1780–1867), French painter **8** 121–123

**INNESS, GEORGE** (1825–1894), American painter **8** 123–124

**INNIS, HAROLD ADAMS** (1894–1952), Canadian political economist **8** 124–125

**INNOCENT III** (Lothar of Segni; 1160/1161–1216), pope 1198–1216 **8** 125–127

**INÖNÜ, ISMET** (1884–1973), Turkish military man, statesman, and second president **8** 127–129

**INSULL, SAMUEL** (1859–1938), English-born American entrepreneur **8** 130

**Integration** (racial, United States)
see African American history

**Intel Corporation**
Rock, Arthur **19** 316–317

**International Business Machines** (IBM)
Gerstner, Lou **19** 121–124
Hollerith, Herman **19** 151–152
Watson, Thomas J. Jr. **19** 408–410

**International Peace Bureau** (Geneva, Switzerland)
MacBride, Sean **19** 218–220

**International Tennis Hall of Fame**
Connolly, Maureen **19** 72–74

**Internet**
Andreessen, Marc **19** 3–5
McNealy, Scott **19** 241–243
Case, Steve **19** 61–64

**INUKAI, TSUYOSHI** (1855–1932), Japanese journalist and statesman **8** 130–131

**IONESCO, EUGÈNE** (1912–1994), Franco-Romanian author **8** 131–132

**IQBAL, MUHAMMAD** (1877?–1938), Indian Moslem poet and philosopher **8** 132–133

**IRELAND, JOHN** (1838–1918), American Catholic archbishop **8** 133–134

**IRELAND, PATRICIA** (born 1945), president of the National Organization for Women (NOW) **8** 134–135

**IRENE OF ATHENS** (ca. 752–803), Byzantine empress 797–802 **8** 135–138

# L

**LEVERRIER, URBAIN JEAN JOSEPH** (1811–1877), French mathematical astronomer **9** 361–362

**LÉVESQUE, RENÉ** (1922–1987), premier of the province of Quebec, Canada (1976–1985) **9** 362–363

**LEVI BEN GERSHON** (1288–circa 1344); French Jewish scientist, philosopher, and theologian **9** 363–364

**LEVI, CARLO** (1902–1975), Italian writer and painter **9** 364

**LEVI, PRIMO** (1919–1987), Italian author and chemist **9** 365–366

**LEVI-MONTALCINI, RITA** (born 1909) Italian and American biologist who discovered the nerve growth factor **9** 366–368

**LÉVI-STRAUSS, CLAUDE GUSTAVE** (born 1908), French social anthropologist **9** 371–372

**LEVINAS, EMMANUEL** (1906–1995), Jewish philosopher **9** 368–369

**LEVINE, JAMES** (born 1943), American conductor and pianist **9** 369–371

**LEVITT, WILLIAM** (1907–1994), American real estate developer **19** 199–201

**LEVY, BERNARD-HENRI** (born 1948), French moralist and political philosopher **9** 372–373

**LEVY, DAVID** (born 1937), Israeli minister of foreign affairs and deputy prime minister **9** 373–374

**LÉVY-BRUHL, LUCIEN** (1857–1939), French philosopher and anthropologist **9** 374–375

**LEWIN, KURT** (1890–1947), German-American social psychologist **9** 375–376

**LEWIS, ANDREW** (circa 1720–1781), American general in the Revolution **9** 376–377

**LEWIS, CARL** (born Frederick Carlton Lewis; born 1961), African American track and field athlete **9** 377–380

**LEWIS, CECIL DAY** (1904–1972), British poet and essayist **9** 380

**LEWIS, CLARENCE IRVING** (1883–1964), American philosopher **9** 381

**LEWIS, CLIVE STAPLES** (C.S.; 1898–1963), British novelist and essayist **9** 381–382

**LEWIS, ESSINGTON** (1881–1961), Australian industrial leader **9** 382–384

**LEWIS, GILBERT NEWTON** (1875–1946), American physical chemist **9** 384–385

**LEWIS, HARRY SINCLAIR** (1885–1951), American novelist **9** 385–387

**LEWIS, JOHN LLEWELLYN** (1880–1969), American labor leader **9** 387–388

**LEWIS, JOHN ROBERT** (born 1940), United States civil rights activist and representative from Georgia **9** 388–390

**LEWIS, MATTHEW GREGORY** (1775–1818), English novelist and playwright **9** 390–391

**LEWIS, MERIWETHER** (1774–1809), American explorer and army officer **9** 391–392

**LEWIS, OSCAR** (1914–1970), American anthropologist **9** 392–393

**LEWITT, SOL** (born 1928), American Minimalist and Conceptualist artist **9** 393–395

**LI HUNG-CHANG** (1823–1901), Chinese soldier, statesman, and industrialist **9** 407–409

**LI PENG** (born 1928), premier of the People's Republic of China **9** 433–435

**LI PO** (701–762), Chinese poet **9** 437–439

**LI SSU** (280?–208 B.C.), Chinese statesman **9** 442–443

**LI TA-CHAO** (1889–1927), Chinese Communist revolutionist **9** 447

**LI TZU-CH'ENG** (circa 1606–1645), Chinese bandit and rebel leader **9** 452

**LIANG CH'I-CH'AO** (1873–1929), Chinese intellectual and political reformer **9** 395–396

**LIANG WU-TI** (464–549), Chinese emperor of Southern dynasties **9** 396–397

**LIAQUAT ALI KHAN** (1896–1951), Pakistani statesman **9** 397

**LIBBY, WILLARD FRANK** (1908–1980), American chemist **9** 397–398

**LICHTENSTEIN, ROY** (1923–1997), American painter, sculptor, and printmaker **9** 398–399

**LIE, TRYGVE HALVDAN** (1896–1968), Norwegian statesman and UN secretary general **9** 400–401

**LIEBER, FRANCIS** (circa 1798–1872), German American political scientist **9** 401–402

**LIEBERMANN, MAX** (1847–1935), German painter **9** 402–403

**LIEBIG, BARON JUSTUS VON** (1803–1873), German chemist **9** 403–404

**Life** (magazine)
Eisenstaedt, Alfred **19** 100–102
Parks, Gordon **19** 275–277
Smith, William Eugene **19** 348–350

**LIGACHEV, YEGOR KUZ'MICH** (born 1920), member of the Central Committee of the Communist Party of the Soviet Union (1966–1990) **9** 404–406

**LIGETI, GYÖRGY** (born 1923), Austrian composer **9** 406–407

**LIGHTNER, CANDY** (born 1946), American activist and founder of Mothers Against Drunk Driving **19** 201–203

**LILBURNE, JOHN** (1615–1657), English political activist and pamphleteer **9** 409–410

**LILIENTHAL, DAVID ELI** (1899–1981), American public administrator **9** 410–411

**LILIUOKALANI, LYDIA KAMAKAEHA** (1838–1917), queen of the Hawaiian Islands **9** 411–412

**LIMBOURG BROTHERS** (flourished circa 1399–1416), Netherlandish illuminators **9** 412–413

**LIN, MAYA YING** (born 1959), American architect **9** 413–415

**LIN PIAO** (1907–1971), Chinese Communist military and political leader **9** 429–430

**LIN TSE-HSÜ** (1785–1850), Chinese official **9** 431–432

**LINCOLN, ABRAHAM** (1809–1865), American statesman, president 1861–1865 **9** 415–418

**LINCOLN, BENJAMIN** (1733–1810), American military officer **9** 418–419

**LIND, JAKOV** (Heinz "Henry" Landwirth; born 1927), Austrian autobiographer, short-story writer, novelist, and playwright **9** 419–420

**LINDBERGH, ANNE MORROW** (born 1906), American author and aviator **9** 420–421

**LINDBERGH, CHARLES AUGUSTUS** (1902–1974), American aviator **9** 421–423

**LINDSAY, JOHN VLIET** (born 1921), U.S. congressman (1959–1965) and mayor of New York (1966–1973) **9** 423–424

# M

**MPHAHLELE, EZEKIEL** (a.k.a. Bruno Eseki; born 1919), South African author and scholar **11** 221–223

**MQHAYI, SAMUEL EDWARD KRUNE** (1875–1945), South African novelist and poet **11** 223

**MUAWIYA IBN ABU SUFYAN** (died 680), Umayyad caliph **11** 223–224

**MUBARAK, HOSNI** (born 1928), president of Egypt **11** 225–226

**MUELLER, OTTO** (1874–1930), German expressionist painter **11** 226–227

**MUGABE, ROBERT GABRIEL** (born 1924), Zimbabwe's first elected black prime minister **11** 227–229

**MUHAMMAD, ELIJAH** (Poole; 1897–1975), leader of the Nation of Islam ("Black Muslims") **11** 230–231

**MUHAMMAD BIN TUGHLUQ** (ruled 1325–1351), Moslem sultan of Delhi **11** 229

**MUHAMMAD TURE, ASKIA** (circa 1443–1538), ruler of the West African Songhay empire **11** 231–232

**MÜHLENBERG, HEINRICH MELCHIOR** (1711–1787), German-born American Lutheran clergyman **11** 232–233

**MUHLENBERG, WILLIAM AUGUSTUS** (1796–1877); American Episcopalian clergyman **11** 233–234

**MUIR, JOHN** (1838–1914), American naturalist **11** 234

**MUJIBUR RAHMAN, SHEIK** (1920–1975), Bengal leader who helped found Bangladesh **11** 234–236

**MULDOWNEY, SHIRLEY** (born ca. 1940), American race car driver **11** 236–238

**MULLER, HERMANN JOSEPH** (1890–1967), American geneticist **11** 238–239

**MÜLLER, JOHANNES PETER** (1801–1858), German physiologist and anatomist **11** 239–240

**MÜLLER, KARL ALEXANDER** (born 1927), Swiss-born solid-state physicist **11** 240–241

**MÜLLER, PAUL HERMANN** (1899–1965), Swiss chemist **11** 241–242

**MULRONEY, MARTIN BRIAN** (born 1939), prime minister of Canada **11** 242–246

**MUMFORD, LEWIS** (1895–1990), American social philosopher and architectural critic **11** 246–247

**MUNCH, EDVARD** (1863–1944), Norwegian painter and graphic artist **11** 247–248

**MUNDELEIN, GEORGE WILLIAM** (1872–1939), American Roman Catholic cardinal **11** 248–249

**MUÑOZ MARÍN, JOSÉ LUÍS ALBERTO** (1898–1980), Puerto Rican political leader **11** 249–250

**MUÑOZ RIVERA, LUÍS** (1859–1916), Puerto Rican political leader **11** 250

**MUNSEY, FRANK ANDREW** (1854–1925), American publisher **11** 251

**MÜNZER, THOMAS** (1489?–1525), German Protestant reformer **11** 251–252

**Muppet Show** (television series) Henson, Jim **19** 140–142

**MURASAKI SHIKIBU** (circa 976–circa 1031), Japanese writer **11** 252–253

**MURAT, JOACHIM** (1767–1815), French marshal, king of Naples 1808–1815 **11** 253–254

**MURATORI, LODOVICO ANTONIO** (1672–1750), Italian historian and antiquary **11** 254–255

**MURCHISON, SIR RODERICK IMPEY** (1792–1871), British geologist **11** 255–256

**Murder, Inc.** Buchalter, Lepke **19** 42–44

**Murder victims** United States Versace, Gianni **19** 399–401 Walsh, Stella **19** 404–406

**MURDOCH, JEAN IRIS** (born 1919), British novelist **11** 256–257

**MURDOCH, RUPERT** (born 1931), Australian newspaper publisher **11** 257–258

**MURILLO, BARTOLOMÉ ESTEBAN** (1617–1682), Spanish painter **11** 258–259

**Muromachi shogunate** see Japan—1338–1573 (Ashikaga shogunate)

**MURPHY, AUDIE** (1924–1971), American army officer and actor **18** 299–301

**MURPHY, CHARLES FRANCIS** (1858–1924), American politician **11** 259–260

**MURPHY, FRANK** (1890–1949), American jurist and diplomat **11** 260–261

**MURRAY, JAMES** (1721–1794), British general **11** 261–262

**MURRAY, JOSEPH** (born 1919), American physician **18** 301–303

**MURRAY, LESLIE ALLAN** (born 1938), Australian poet and literary critic **11** 262–263

**MURRAY, PHILIP** (1886–1952), American labor leader **11** 264–265

**MURROW, EDWARD ROSCOE** (1908–1965), American radio and television news broadcaster **11** 265–266

**MUSA MANSA** (died 1337), king of the Mali empire in West Africa ca. 1312–1337 **11** 266

**MUSGRAVE, THEA** (born 1928), Scottish-born composer **11** 266–268

**MUSIAL, STAN** (Stanislaus Musial, Stanley Frank Musial; born 1920), American baseball **19** 260–262

**Musicals** (United States) directors Prince, Hal **19** 295–298 librettists/lyricists Arlen, Harold **19** 7–9 producers Prince, Hal **19** 295–298

**Musicians, American** bandleaders Dorsey, Jimmy **19** 93–95 Marsalis, Wynton **19** 224–226 Miller, Glenn **19** 250–251 blues singers Rainey, Ma **19** 306–308 composers (20th century) Arlen, Harold **19** 7–9 Bowles, Paul **19** 31–34 Levant, Oscar **19** 197–199 gospel singers Jackson, Mahalia **19** 166–168 guitarists Feliciano, José **19** 109–110 lyricists Rodgers, Jimmie **19** 317–319 Silverstein, Shel **19** 341–343 Wonder, Stevie **19** 428–430 pianists Arlen, Harold **19** 7–9 Levant, Oscar **19** 197–199 saxophonists Dorsey, Jimmy **19** 93–95 singers Arlen, Harold **19** 7–9 Feliciano, José **19** 109–110 Houston, Whitney **19** 152–155 Rodgers, Jimmie **19** 317–319 Wonder, Stevie **19** 428–430 trombone players Miller, Glenn **19** 250–251 trumpeters Marsalis, Wynton **19** 224–226 violinists Stern, Isaac **19** 365–367

**MUSIL, ROBERT EDLER VON** (1880–1942), Austrian novelist, dramatist, and short story writer **11** 268–269

**OLBRICH, JOSEPH MARIA** (1867–1908), Austrian Art Nouveau architect and a founder of the Vienna Secession **11** 494–495

**OLDENBARNEVELT, JOHAN VAN** (1547–1619), Dutch statesman **11** 495–496

**OLDENBURG, CLAES** (born 1929), American artist **11** 496–498

**OLDS, RANSOM ELI** (1864–1950), American inventor and automobile manufacturer **18** 313–315

**OLIPHANT, PATRICK BRUCE** (born 1935), American newspaper editorial cartoonist **11** 498–500

**OLIVER, JAMES** (1823–1908), American inventor and manufacturer **11** 500–501

**OLIVETTI, ADRIANO** (1901–1960), Italian manufacturer of typewriters, calculators, and computers **11** 501–502

**OLIVIER, LAURENCE** (1907–1989), English actor and director **11** 502–503

**OLMSTED, FREDERICK LAW** (1822–1903), American landscape architect **11** 503–504

**OLNEY, RICHARD** (1835–1917), American statesman **11** 504–505

**OLSON, CHARLES** (1910–1970), American poet **11** 505–506

**Olympic Games**
athletes
Ederle, Gertrude **19** 98–100
Griffith Joyner, Florence **19** 130–133
Joyner-Kersee, Jackie **19** 170–173
Mills, Billy **19** 251–253
Nurmi, Paavo **19** 272–274
Stephens, Helen **19** 363–365
Walsh, Stella **19** 404–406

**OLYMPIO, SYLVANUS E.** (1902–1963), first president of the Republic of Togo **11** 506–507

**OMAR AL-MUKHTAR** (circa 1860–1931), national hero of Libya and member of the Senusy **11** 507–508

**OMAR IBN AL-KHATTAB** (died 644); second caliph of the Moslems **11** 508–509

**OMAR IBN SAID TAL, AL-HAJJ** (circa 1797–1864), West African Moslem leader **11** 509–510

**OMAR KHAYYAM** (1048–circa 1132), Persian astronomer, mathematician, and poet **11** 510–511

**ONASSIS, JACQUELINE LEE BOUVIER KENNEDY** (1929–1994), American First Lady **11** 511–513

**OÑATE, JUAN DE** (circa 1549–circa 1624), Spanish explorer **11** 513–514

**ONDAATJE, MICHAEL** (Philip Michael Ondaatji; born 1943), Canadian author and poet **18** 315–317

**O'NEILL, EUGENE** (1888–1953), American dramatist **11** 514–516

**O'NEILL, TERENCE MARNE** (1914–1990), Northern Ireland prime minister **11** 516–517

**O'NEILL, THOMAS P.** ("Tip"; 1912–1994), American politician **11** 517–519

**ONG TENG CHEONG** (born 1936), Singapore's fifth president **11** 519–520

**ONSAGER, LARS** (1903–1976), American chemist **11** 520–523

**OORT, JAN HENDRIK** (1900–1992), Dutch astronomer **11** 523–524

**OPPENHEIM, MERET** (1913–1985), Swiss Surrealist artist **11** 524–525

**OPPENHEIMER, J. ROBERT** (1904–1967), American physicist **11** 525–526

**ORCAGNA** (1308?–1368?), Italian painter, sculptor, and architect **11** 526–527

**ORELLANA, FRANCISCO DE** (circa 1511–1546), Spanish explorer **11** 527–528

**Organized Crime** (United States)
Buchalter, Lepke **19** 42–44
Luciano, Lucky **19** 214–215

**ORIGEN** (Origenes Adamantius; circa 185–circa 254), Early Christian theologian **11** 528–529

**ORLANDO, VITTORIO EMMANUELE** (1860–1952), Italian statesman **11** 529–530

**ORLÉANS, CHARLES** (1394–1465), French prince and poet **11** 530

**ORLÉANS, PHILIPPE II** (1674–1723), French statesman, regent 1715–23 **11** 530–531

**OROZCO, JOSÉ CLEMENTE** (1883–1949), Mexican painter **12** 1–2

**ORR, BOBBY** (Robert Gordon Orr; born 1948), Canadian hockey player **12** 2–4

**ORR, JOHN BOYD** (1st Baron Orr of Brechin; 1880–1971), Scottish nutritionist and UN official **12** 4–5

**ORTEGA, DANIEL** (born 1945), leader of the Sandinista National Liberation Front and president of Nicaragua **12** 5–7

**ORTEGA Y GASSET, JOSÉ** (1883–1955), Spanish philosopher and essayist **12** 7–8

**ORTELIUS, ABRAHAM** (Abraham, Ortels; 1527–1598), Flemish cartographer **12** 8–9

**ORTIZ, SIMON J.** (born 1941), Native American author and storyteller **12** 9–12

**ORTON, JOHN KINGSLEY** ("Joe;" 1933–1967), British playwright **12** 12–14

**ORWELL, GEORGE** (1903–1950), British novelist and essayist **12** 14–15

**OSBORNE, JOHN** (1929–1994), English playwright **12** 16–17

**OSBORNE, THOMAS MOTT** (1859–1926), American reformer **12** 17–18

**OSCEOLA** (circa 1800–1838), Seminole Indian war chief **12** 18

**OSGOOD, HERBERT LEVI** (1855–1918), American historian **12** 18–19

**OSLER, SIR WILLIAM** (1849–1919), Canadian physician **12** 19–20

**OSMAN I** (Othman; 1259–1326), Turkish warrior-leader who established the Ottoman state as an independent entity **12** 20–22

**OSMEÑA, SERGIO** (1878–1961), Philippine lawyer and statesman **12** 22–24

**OTIS, ELISHA GRAVES** (1811–1861), American manufacturer and inventor **12** 24

**OTIS, HARRISON GRAY** (1765–1848), American statesman **12** 25

**OTIS, JAMES, JR.** (1725–1783), American Revolutionary statesman **12** 25–27

**OTTERBEIN, PHILIP WILLIAM** (1726–1813), American clergyman **12** 27–28

**OTTO I** (912–973), Holy Roman emperor 936–973 **12** 28–29

**OTTO III** (980–1002), Holy Roman emperor 996–1002 and German king 983–1002 **12** 29–30

**OTTO, LOUIS KARL RUDOLF** (1869–1937), German interpreter of religion **12** 30–32

**OTTO OF FREISING** (circa 1114–1158), German historiographer and philosopher of history **12** 30

**OUD, JACOBUS JOHANNES PIETER** (1890–1963), Dutch architect **12** 32

**OUSMANE, SEMBENE** (born 1923), Senegalese novelist and film maker **12** 32–33

African American sculptor and teacher **13** 499–501

**SAVAGE, MICHAEL JOSEPH** (1872–1940), New Zealand labor leader, prime minister 1935–40 **13** 501–502

**SAVIGNY, FRIEDRICH KARL VON** (1779–1861), German jurist **13** 502–503

**SAVIMBI, JONAS MALHEIROS** (born 1934), founder and leader of UNITA (National Union for the Total Independence of Angola) **13** 503–505

**SAVONAROLA, GIROLAMO** (1452–1498), Italian religious reformer and dictator of Florence **13** 505–506

**SAW MAUNG** (born 1928), leader of armed forces that took power in Burma (now Myanmar) in a 1988 military coup **13** 506–507

**SAXE, COMTE DE** (1696–1750), marshal of France **13** 507–508

**Saxe-Coburg-Gotha dynasty** (Great Britain)
*see* Great Britain-since 1901 (Windsor)

**SAY, JEAN BAPTISTE** (1767–1832), French economist **13** 508–509

**SAYRE, FRANCIS BOWES** (1885–1972), American lawyer and administrator **13** 509

**SAYYID QUTB** (1906–1966), Egyptian writer, educator, and religious leader **13** 509–511

**SCALFARO, OSCAR LUIGI** (born 1918), Christian Democratic leader and president of the Italian Republic **13** 511–512

**SCALIA, ANTONIN** (born 1936), U.S. Supreme Court justice **13** 513–514

**SCARGILL, ARTHUR** (born 1938), president of the British National Union of Mineworkers **13** 514–515

**SCARLATTI, DOMENICO** (1685–1757), Italian harpsichordist and composer **13** 515–517

**SCARLATTI, PIETRO ALESSANDRO GASPARE** (1660–1725), Italian composer **13** 517–518

**SCHACHT, HJALMAR HORACE GREELEY** (1877–1970), German economist and banker **13** 518–519

**SCHAFF, PHILIP** (1819–1893), Swiss-born American religious scholar **13** 519–520

**SCHAPIRO, MIRIAM** (born 1923), Artist **13** 520–521

**SCHARNHORST, GERHARD JOHANN DAVID VON** (1755–1813), Prussian general **13** 521–522

**SCHARPING, RUDOLF** (born 1947), minister-president of Rhineland-Palatinate and chairman of the German Social Democratic Party **13** 522–524

**SCHECHTER, SOLOMON** (1849–1915), Romanian-American Jewish scholar and religious leader **13** 524

**SCHEELE, KARL WILHELM** (1742–1786), Swedish pharmacist and chemist **13** 525–526

**SCHELLING, FRIEDRICH WILHELM JOSEPH VON** (1775–1854), German philosopher **13** 526–527

**SCHIELE, EGON** (1890–1918), Austrian Expressionist painter and draftsman **14** 1–2

**SCHIESS, BETTY BONE** (born 1923), American Episcopalian priest **18** 360–362

**SCHIFF, JACOB HENRY** (1847–1920), German-American banker **14** 2–3

**SCHILLEBEECKX, EDWARD** (born 1914), Belgian Roman Catholic theologian **14** 3–4

**SCHILLER, JOHANN CHRISTOPH FRIEDRICH VON** (1759–1805), German dramatist, poet, and historian **14** 4–7

**SCHINDLER, OSKAR** (1908–1974), German businessman and humanitarian **18** 362–365

**SCHINDLER, SOLOMON** (1842–1915), German-American rabbi and social theorist **14** 7–8

**SCHINKEL, KARL FRIEDRICH** (1781–1841), German architect, painter and designer **14** 8

**SCHLAFLY, PHYLLIS** (born 1924), American political activist and author **14** 9–10

**SCHLEGEL, FRIEDRICH VON** (1772–1829), German critic and author **14** 10–11

**SCHLEIERMACHER, FRIEDRICH ERNST DANIEL** (1768–1834), German theologian and philosopher **14** 11–12

**SCHLEMMER, OSKAR** (1888–1943), German painter, sculptor, and stage designer **14** 12–13

**SCHLESINGER, ARTHUR MEIER** (1888–1965), American historian **14** 13

**SCHLESINGER, ARTHUR MEIER, JR.** (born 1917), American historian and Democratic party activist **14** 13–15

**SCHLESINGER, JAMES RODNEY** (born 1929), American government official **14** 15–16

**SCHLICK, FRIEDRICH ALBERT MORITZ** (1882–1936), German physicist and philosopher **14** 16–17

**SCHLIEMANN, HEINRICH** (1822–1890), German merchant and archeologist **14** 17–18

**SCHLÜTER, ANDREAS** (circa 1660–1714), German sculptor and architect **14** 18–19

**SCHMIDT, HELMUT** (born 1918), Social Democrat and chancellor of the Federal Republic of Germany (the former West Germany), 1974–82 **14** 19–21

**SCHMOLLER, GUSTAV FRIEDRICH VON** (1838–1917), German economist **14** 21

**SCHNEIDERMAN, ROSE** (1882–1972), labor organizer and activist for the improvement of working conditions for women **14** 22–23

**SCHNITZLER, ARTHUR** (1862–1931), Austrian dramatist and novelist **14** 23–24

**SCHOENBERG, ARNOLD** (1874–1951), Austrian composer **14** 24–26

**SCHOLEM, GERSHOM** (1897–1982), Jewish scholar **14** 26

**SCHONGAUER, MARTIN** (circa 1435–91), German engraver and painter **14** 26–28

**SCHÖNHUBER, FRANZ XAVER** (born 1923), German right-wing political leader **14** 28–29

**School of Paris** (art)
*see* French art—School of Paris

**SCHOOLCRAFT, HENRY ROWE** (1793–1864), American explorer and ethnologist **14** 29

**SCHOPENHAUER, ARTHUR** (1788–1860), German philosopher **14** 29–31

**SCHOUTEN, WILLIAM CORNELIUS** (circa 1580–1625), Dutch explorer and navigator **14** 31

**SCHRODER, GERHARD** (born 1944), German chancellor **19** 325–327

**SCHRÖDINGER, ERWIN** (1887–1961), Austrian physicist **14** 31–33

**SCHROEDER, PATRICIA SCOTT** (born 1940), first U.S. congresswoman from Colorado **14** 33–35

**SCHUBERT, FRANZ PETER** (1797–1828), Austrian composer **14** 35–37

**SCHULLER, GUNTHER** (born 1925), American musician **14** 37–38

# W

WAUNEKA, ANNIE DODGE (1910–1997), Navajo nation leader and Native American activist **18** 409–410

WAVELL, ARCHIBALD PERCIVAL (1st Earl Wavell; 1883–1950), English general, statesman, and writer **16** 147–148

WAYLAND, FRANCIS (1796–1865), American educator and clergyman **16** 148–149

WAYNE, ANTHONY (1745–1796), American soldier **16** 149–150

WAYNE, JOHN (Marion Mitchell Morrison; 1907–79), American actor **16** 150–151

WEAVER, JAMES BAIRD (1833–1912), American political leader **16** 151–152

WEAVER, PAT (Sylvester Laflin Weaver, Jr.; born 1908), American television executive **19** 410–413

WEAVER, ROBERT C. (1907–1997), first African American U.S. cabinet officer **16** 152–153

WEBB, BEATRICE POTTER (1858–1943), English social reformer **16** 153–154

WEBB, SIDNEY JAMES (Baron Passfield; 1859–1947), English social reformer, historian, and statesman **16** 154–155

WEBBER, ANDREW LLOYD (born 1948), British composer **16** 155–156

WEBER, CARL MARIA FRIEDRICH ERNST VON (1786–1826), German composer and conductor **16** 156–157

WEBER, MAX (1864–1920), German social scientist **16** 157–160

WEBER, MAX (1881–1961), American painter **16** 160

WEBERN, ANTON (1883–1945), Austrian composer **16** 160–162

WEBSTER, DANIEL (1782–1852), American lawyer, orator, and statesman **16** 162–164

WEBSTER, JOHN (circa 1580–circa 1634), English dramatist **16** 164

WEBSTER, NOAH (1758–1843), American lexicographer **16** 164–166

WEDEKIND, FRANK (Benjamin Franklin Wedekind; 1864–1918), German dramatist, cosmopolite, and libertarian **16** 166–167

WEDGWOOD, CICELY VERONICA (1910–1997), British writer and historian **16** 167–168

WEDGWOOD, JOSIAH (1730–1795), English potter **16** 168–169

WEED, THURLOW (1797–1882), American politician **16** 169–170

WEEMS, MASON LOCKE (1759–1825), American Episcopal minister and popular writer **16** 170

WEGENER, ALFRED LOTHAR (1880–1930), German meteorologist, Arctic explorer, and geophysicist **16** 170–171

WEI HSIAO-WEN-TI (467–499), Chinese emperor **8** 5

WEI JINGSHENG (born 1950), Chinese human rights activist **18** 410–412

WEI YÜAN (1794–1856), Chinese historian and geographer **16** 180–181

WEIDENREICH, FRANZ (1873–1948), German anatomist and physical anthropologist **16** 171–172

WEIL, SIMONE (1909–1943), French thinker, political activist, and religious mystic **16** 172–174

WEILL, KURT (1900–1950), German-American composer **16** 174–175

**Weimar Republic**
*see* Germany—Republic

WEINBERG, STEVEN (born 1933), Nobel Prize-winning physicist **16** 175–177

WEINBERGER, CASPER WILLARD (born 1917), U.S. public official under three presidents **16** 177–178

WEISMANN, AUGUST FREIDRICH LEOPOLD (1834–1914), German biologist **16** 178–180

WEIZMAN, EZER (born 1924), Israeli air force commander and president of Israel (1993–) **16** 181–182

WEIZMANN, CHAIM (1874–1952), Israeli statesman, president 1949–52 **16** 183–184

WELCH, JACK (John Francis Welch, Jr.; born 1935), American businessman **19** 413–415

WELCH, ROBERT (1899–1985), founder of the John Birch Society **16** 184–185

WELCH, WILLIAM HENRY (1850–1934), American pathologist, bacteriologist, and medical educator **16** 185–186

WELD, THEODORE DWIGHT (1803–1895), American reformer, preacher, and editor **16** 186

WELDON, FAY BIRKINSHAW (born 1931 or 1933), British novelist, dramatist, essayist, and feminist **16** 186–188

WELENSKY, SIR ROY (1907–1991), Rhodesian statesman **16** 188

WELLES, GIDEON (1802–1878), American statesman **16** 188–190

WELLES, ORSON (1915–1985), Broadway and Hollywood actor, radio actor, and film director **16** 190–191

WELLES, SUMNER (1892–1961), American diplomat **16** 191–192

WELLESLEY, RICHARD COLLEY (1st Marquess Wellesley; 1760–1842), British colonial administrator **16** 192–193

WELLINGTON, 1ST DUKE OF (Arthur Wellesley; 1769–1852), British soldier and statesman **16** 193–195

WELLS, HERBERT GEORGE (1866–1946), English author **16** 195–196

WELLS, HORACE (1815–1848), American dentist **16** 196

WELLS, MARY GEORGENE BERG (born 1928), American businesswoman **16** 197–198

WELLS-BARNETT, IDA B. (1862–1931), American journalist and activist **16** 198–199

WELTY, EUDORA (born 1909), American author and essayist **16** 199–201

WEN T'IEN-HSIANG (1236–1283), Chinese statesman **16** 203

WENCESLAUS (Wenceslaus IV of Bohemia; 1361–1419), Holy Roman emperor 1376–1400, and king of Bohemia 1378–1419 **16** 201–202

WEN-HSIANG (1818–1876), Manchu official and statesman **16** 202–203

WENTWORTH, WILLIAM CHARLES (1790–1872), Australian statesman, writer, and explorer **16** 203–204

WERFEL, FRANZ (1890–1945), Austrian poet, novelist, and playwright **16** 204–205

WERNER, ABRAHAM GOTTLOB (1749–1817), German naturalist **16** 205–207

WERNER, HELMUT (born 1936), German business executive **19** 415–417

WERTHEIMER, MAX (1880–1943), German psychologist **16** 207–208

WESLEY, CHARLES (1707–1788), English hymn writer and preacher **16** 208–209

WESLEY, JOHN (1703–1791), English evangelical clergyman, preacher, and writer **16** 209–210

WEST, BENJAMIN (1738–1820), English American painter **16** 210–212

WEST, CORNEL (born 1953), American philosopher **16** 212–213